# European Labour Law

2nd edition

BRIAN BERCUSSON

CAMBRIDGE
UNIVERSITY PRESS

CAMBRIDGE UNIVERSITY PRESS
Cambridge, New York, Melbourne, Madrid, Cape Town, Singapore, São Paulo, Delhi

Cambridge University Press
The Edinburgh Building, Cambridge CB2 8RU, UK

Published in the United States of America by Cambridge University Press, New York

www.cambridge.org
Information on this title: www.cambridge.org/9780521613507

First published 2009

Printed in the United Kingdom at the University Press, Cambridge

*A catalogue record for this publication is available from the British Library*

ISBN 978-0-521-61350-7 paperback

# European Labour Law

*European Labour Law* explores how individual European notional legal systems, in symbiosis with the European Union, produce a transnational labour law system that is distinct and genuinely European in character.

Professor Brian Bercusson describes the evolution of this system, its national, transnational and global contexts and its institutional and substantive structures. The collective industrial-relations dimension of employment is examined, and the labour law of the EU as manifested in, for example, European works councils is analysed. Important subjects which have traditionally received little attention in some European labour law systems are covered, for example the fragmentation of the workforce into atypical forms of employment. Attention is also given to the enforcement of European labour law through administrative or judicial mechanisms and the European social dialogue at intersectoral and sectoral levels.

This new edition has been extensively updated, as the EU's influence on this area of social policy continues to grow.

**Professor Brian Bercusson** was Professor of European Social and Labour Law at King's College London. Immediately before taking up his position at King's, he held the Chair in European Law at the University of Manchester. Previously, Professor Bercusson served as Jean Monnet Fellow and Professor of Law at the European University Institute, and was a visiting professor at the University of Siena.

# The Law in Context Series

*Editors:* William Twining (University College London)
Christopher McCrudden (Lincoln College, Oxford)
Bronwen Morgan (University of Bristol).

Since 1970 the Law in Context series has been in the forefront of the movement to broaden the study of law. It has been a vehicle for the publication of innovative scholarly books that treat law and legal phenomena critically in their social, political and economic contexts from a variety of perspectives. The series particularly aims to publish scholarly legal writing that brings fresh perspectives to bear on new and existing areas of law taught in universities. A contextual approach involves treating legal subjects broadly, using materials from other social sciences, and from any other discipline that helps to explain the operation in practice of the subject under discussion. It is hoped that this orientation is at once more stimulating and more realistic than the bare exposition of legal rules. The series includes original books that have a different emphasis from traditional legal textbooks, while maintaining the same high standards of scholarship. They are written primarily for undergraduate and graduate students of law and of other disciplines, but most also appeal to a wider readership. In the past, most books in the series have focused on English law, but recent publications include books on European law, globalisation, transnational legal processes and comparative law.

## Books in the Series

Anderson, Schum & Twining: *Analysis of Evidence*
Ashworth: *Sentencing and Criminal Justice*
Barton & Douglas: *Law and Parenthood*
Beecher-Monas: *Evaluating Scientific Evidence: An Interdisciplinary Framework for Intellectual Due Process*
Bell: *French Legal Cultures*
Bercusson: *European Labour Law*
Birkinshaw: *European Public Law*
Birkinshaw: *Freedom of Information: The Law, the Practice and the Ideal*
Cane: *Atiyah's Accidents, Compensation and the Law*
Clarke & Kohler: *Property Law: Commentary and Materials*
Collins: *The Law of Contract*
Cranston: *Legal Foundations of the Welfare State*
Davies: *Perspectives on Labour Law*
Dembour: *Who Believes in Human Rights?: The European Convention in Question*
de Sousa Santos: *Toward a New Legal Common Sense*
Diduck: *Law's Families*
Elworthy & Holder: *Environmental Protection: Text and Materials*
Fortin: *Children's Rights and the Developing Law*
Glover-Thomas: *Reconstructing Mental Health Law and Policy*

# Contents

# Preface

The first edition of this book was published in 1996, and although it was by no means the first book on the subject, it was in some way the most original, stimulating and rigorous. As well as being also the most comprehensive in terms of the issues covered, it was the first convincingly to make the case for European Labour Law as a wide-ranging discipline in its own right, with a distinct identity separate from national labour law systems, but influenced by them. Such visionary thinking was to elevate the debate about European Labour Law at a time when, imperfectly schooled in EC law, many British labour lawyers in particular encountered EC Labour Law only collaterally through matters like equal pay or the transfer of undertakings, and then sometimes only cautiously, nervously and reluctantly.

There are now many more books on European Labour Law which have been published since 1996. But few show the same learning, the same experience, or the same understanding of the subject as are revealed in the pages that follow. Indeed, this volume is only Part One (the General Part) of what had been intended as a two volume enterprise (with Part Two (the Special Part) being an examination of the substance of the law). As such, the present volume is concerned principally with the evolution, development and identity of European Labour Law; the process by which European Labour Law is made (notably by Social Dialogue as a means of setting and implementing labour standards), and the emerging constitutionalisation of labour rights, notably in the EU Charter of Fundamental Rights of 2000.

Doubtless, Brian would not have allowed the opportunity to pass without updating the text at various points, and I should take this opportunity here to indicate three developments in descending level of importance. The first is the decision of the European Court of Human Rights in *Demir and Baykara v Turkey* (12 November 2008) which succeeded in putting a smile back on the faces of labour lawyers everywhere. Decided within 12 months of the ECJ's decisions in *Viking* and *Laval* (considered in some detail on chapter 21 below), the Grand Chamber of the European Court of Human Rights consciously and deliberately overruled its earlier decisions on the matter to hold that the right to freedom of association in article 11 of the European Convention on Human Rights (ECHR) now includes the right to collective bargaining.

Moreover, according to the Court, not only does the right to freedom of association include a right to bargain collectively, but there may be a duty to have in place 'legislation to give effect to the provisions of international labour conventions' (para 157), the latter being the yardstick against which the substance of the right to collective bargaining for the purposes of article 11 is to be assessed. This recognition of the right to collective bargaining on the basis of ILO Convention 98 is not only an astonishing development, but at a time when trade unions are looking for ways to challenge the decisions of the ECJ in *Viking* and *Laval*, it is an extremely timely one, given the commitment of the ECJ to take full account of the Strasbourg jurisprudence. The decision in *Demir* thus creates the alluring possibility of complaints being made in the Strasbourg Court against an EU Member State about the latter's failure to comply with the ECHR because of obligations arising under EU law.

The second issue to which attention might be directed is the Temporary Agency Workers Directive (2008/104/EC), which came too late for inclusion in the text, and represents one of the few social rights' achievements of the Barroso Commission, of which there is a great deal of well-placed criticism in the pages that follow. The importance of the Directive – to some extent inspired by, but not a product of, the Social Dialogue process – relates to its introduction of the principle of equal treatment for temporary agency workers, in the sense that the 'basic working and employment conditions of temporary agency workers shall be, for the duration of their assignment at a user undertaking, at least those that would apply if they had been recruited directly by that undertaking to occupy the same job' (Article 5(1)). This principle is, however, subject to a number of important exceptions, including the following in Article 5(4):

Provided that an adequate level of protection is provided for temporary agency workers, Member States in which there is either no system in law for declaring collective agreements universally applicable or no such system in law or practice for extending their provisions to all similar undertakings in a certain sector or geographical area, may, after consulting the social partners at national level and on the basis of an agreement concluded by them, establish arrangements concerning the basic working and employment conditions which derogate from the principle established in paragraph 1. Such arrangements may include a qualifying period for equal treatment.

The enigmatic Article 5(4) is another concession to the United Kingdom, with the website of the Department for Business, Enterprise and Regulatory Reform (incongruously the government department responsible for workers' rights) already containing the text of an agreement between the government, TUC and CBI (negotiated some time before the Directive was even finally approved). This is an agreement on 'how fairer treatment for agency workers in the United Kingdom should be promoted, while not removing the important flexibility that agency work can offer both employers and workers'. Tilting the balance more clearly in favour of 'flexibility' rather than 'fairness' (at least for some), the parties have undertaken that the principle of equal treatment for temporary agency workers may be postponed for the first 12 weeks of the employment, which means that it will not apply to agency workers on short term placements. See www.berr.gov.uk.

The other major development which addresses issues dealt with in the text at various points is the John Major Maastricht-style opt out from the Solidarity provisions of the EU Charter of Fundamental Rights negotiated by Tony Blair and Gordon Brown as a condition of accepting the Treaty of Lisbon. That opt-out is now enshrined in domestic law – as a result of the European Union (Amendment) Act 2008 – and provides that

1. The Charter does not extend the ability of the Court of Justice of the European Union, or any court or tribunal of Poland or of the United Kingdom, to find that the laws, regulations or administrative provisions, practices or action of Poland or of the United Kingdom are inconsistent with the fundamental rights, freedoms and principles that it reaffirms.
2. In particular, and for the avoidance of doubt, nothing in Title IV of the Charter creates justiciable rights applicable to Poland or the United Kingdom except in so far as Poland or the United Kingdom has provided for such rights in its national law.

The provisions of the Charter in question are those dealing with rights to information and consultation, the right to collective bargaining, and the right to strike. Quite what significance this will have is unclear, not just because the future of the Lisbon Treaty remains uncertain (though probably now more secure in a climate of global financial crisis), but also because developments in the Strasbourg Court may mean that fundamental human rights will find themselves adopted as universal principles of EU Law (with no British or Polish opt – outs) by routes other than the EU Charter of Fundamental Rights. If this is correct, it will reinforce the predictions in the text below, that the United Kingdom will be unable to build high enough barriers to keep back the rising tide of European Labour Law, even on the right to strike.

As many readers of this book will know (and as will by now be clear), this edition is being published posthumously. The book was completed and submitted to Cambridge University Press shortly before Brian's sudden death on 17 August 2008. The manuscript is published as submitted, and no liberties have been taken with the text, by either the copy-editor, or by myself as proofreader. In other words, nothing has been done to detract from a book that reflects Brian's great ambition for European Labour Law (a theme that shines through the first parts of the book), his great optimism about the new institutions that are distinguishing features of European Labour Law (a theme that stands out in the middle sections of the book), or his growing disappointment (not to be confused with pessimism) with some national governments and the European Commission, as well as the European Court of Justice (a theme that emerges in the final sections of the book).

That disappointment would, however, have been lifted by the *Demir* case, and by the even more recent decision of the European Court of Human Rights in *Enerji Yapi-Yol Sen v Turkey*, 21 April 2009, where it appears to have been held that article 11 of the ECHR now also protects the right to strike. For Brian was never in any doubt about the purpose of Labour Law generally, or European Labour Law in particular, at a time when much of the vigour and colour have been drained from both disciplines. Nor was he ever in any doubt about the responsibility of the labour lawyer to be steadfast and imaginative in the defence of workers' rights. As will again be clear from the pages that follow, Brian combined profound scholarship with an unyielding commitment to the trade union movement, by which he was held in the highest regard. This book is an extraordinary legacy to labour lawyers everywhere, and a brilliant synthesis of scholarship and commitment by a man who stood at the forefront of his discipline.

**KD Ewing**

# Section I

# Labour law and Europe

**Part I**

# European labour law

# Chapter 1

# European labour law and the social dimension of the European Union

## Introduction: European labour law challenges the dominance of EU economic law

The European Economic Community (EEC) created by the Treaty of Rome of 1957 had as its central core the economic law of the EEC. Despite its transformation into the European Union (EU), European law remains dominated by the economic law perspective of establishment of a common market. But European integration is no longer a purely economic project. European labour law is a central part of the political and social dimension of the EU.

European labour law as a central component of the European Union poses a fundamental challenge to the economic law profile of the EC. Labour was posited in the Treaty of Rome as one of the factors guaranteed free movement, along with capital, goods and services. As such, labour was equated to a commodity. By so doing, the EEC challenged a fundamental premise of international labour law, embodied in the constitution of the ILO: that labour is not a commodity.[1]

Labour is not the same as goods, services or capital. Labour engages human beings. Living in the EU means for most people spending the greater part of their adult waking life working. The EU law which addresses that part of people's lives, EC labour law, is much more directly central to the peoples of Europe than the regulation of capital movements, financial services, take-overs and mergers, international trade or customs duties or other barriers to free movement of goods and services, which absorbs most of the attention of EC lawyers.[2]

European labour law is the core of the social conception of European integration and the social dimension of EU law. The European Court of Justice recognised the changing profile of the EU in cases concerned with the

---

[1] See P. O'Higgins, '"Labour is not a Commodity" – an Irish Contribution to International Labour Law', (1997) 26 *Industrial Law Journal* 225.

[2] The European Commission's Directorate-General V retains this early addiction to the theme of free movement. It continues to devote a disproportionate effort to promoting free movement of workers among Member States, ignoring the unchanging reality that the vast majority of people do not wish, unsurprisingly, to leave their own homeland to serve the labour market needs of other countries.

equal pay provision in the original EEC Treaty (Article 119, now Article 141). Initially, in the famous *Defrenne* decision, Article 119 was characterised as having not only an economic but also a social objective.[3] More recently the Court has declared that the equal pay provision is to be interpreted as no longer primarily concerned with the economic objective of securing fair competition in a common market between the employers of women workers, so that all would be required to observe the equal pay principle. Instead, the objective of the equal pay provision is primarily social.[4]

EC labour law is part of the substantive law of the EC. However, unlike, for example, the EC economic law governing free movement of goods or competition, an awareness of EC labour law is absent from most of the general literature on EC law. EC labour law simply fails to register on the radar screen of most EC lawyers, or, when it does, focuses almost exclusively on discrimination law. To some extent, this is the understandable legacy of the origins of the EU in the European Economic Community's Treaty of Rome which had as its primary objective the establishment of the common market. But that was half a century ago. The literature and teaching on EU law now focus more on the public/ constitutional law and institutional dimensions of the EU. However, the prism through which the public law and institutions of the EU are seen is focused on these economic origins.[5]

To comprehend the significance of this bias in EC law studies, try to imagine the concept of EC law in the literature without the EC economic law on free movement (of goods, services, capital and labour in the single market) and competition. The literature on the public law of the EC, the institutions, their competences and interactions, is permeated by the assumptions that they function so as to secure these economic objectives, which are perceived as fundamental to the whole enterprise of European integration.[6]

---

[3] Case 43/75, *Defrenne* v. *SABENA (No. 2)*, [1976] ECR 455, paras. 10, 12.

[4] Case C-50/96, *Deutsche Telekom AG* v. *Schroder*, [2000] ECR I-743, para. 57.

[5] Marginalisation of EC labour law in general EC law texts may, arguably, be justified where these texts remain within a framework limited to the public law of the EU. If such texts claim to be books on EU law in general, however, and additionally include treatment of the European single market, free movement or other substantive areas, social policy can no longer be reduced to discrimination law without gross distortion of the profile of the EU. If EC lawyers do not attend more closely to EC labour law, the question may well be put not only of whether there can be Europe without 'Social Europe', but whether there can be an understanding of EU law without the social dimension of EU social and labour law. See B. Bercusson, S. Deakin, P. Koistinen, Y. Kravaritou, U. Mückenberger, A. Supiot and B. Veneziani, *A Manifesto for Social Europe*, European Trade Union Institute (ETUI), Brussels, 1996; also in (1997) 3 *European Law Journal* 189–205.

[6] The European Commission's Directorates are informally ranked in terms of their economic status: the internal market directorate, the competition directorate and the external trade directorate are the most important. The Commission's actions in regulating economic competition attract the most attention, just as its support for agriculture takes up the largest portion of the EC's budget. The critical judgments of the European Court involve breaking down barriers to free movement. The Court's teleological interpretation of the Treaties and of EC legal measures are in terms of European integration, but this implies a specific vision of the kind of integration sought: economic, social and/or political integration.

The dominant economic profile of the EC has always been subject to challenge from other visions, both of political economy[7] and of political integration. The theoretical frameworks constructed to comprehend the EU embodied both economic and political dimensions.[8] And, thirty-five years after the founding of the EEC, the transformation of the European Community into the European Union in 1992 led to major changes.[9] But the outcome, rather than a comprehensive transformation, left EC law with its dominant traditional economic profile, the new non-economic competences in justice and home affairs and foreign and security policy being hived off into separate pillars, part supranational and part intergovernmental.

Nevertheless, despite their relative obscurity, radical institutional and constitutional changes were to be found in the new social chapter introduced by the Maastricht Treaty (the constitutionalisation of the EU social dialogue) and in the new Employment Title introduced by the Treaty of Amsterdam (the 'open method of coordination').[10]

Yet many texts on EC labour or employment law[11] begin with or include a section, often detailed and substantial, introducing general EC law concepts, presumably justified by the assumption of the relative ignorance of the labour law reader of the basic elements of Community law.[12] A comparable introduction to a text on *national* labour law would be highly unlikely, in part because

---

[7] F. Snyder, 'Ideologies of Competition in European Community Law', (1989) 52 *Modern Law Review* 149; reprinted in 'Ideologies of Competition: Two Perspectives on the Completion of the Internal Market', Chapter 3 in F. Snyder, *New Directions in European Community Law*, London: Weidenfeld & Nicolson, 1990, pp. 63–99.

[8] P. Craig and G. de Búrca, *EU Law*, 3rd edn, Oxford: Oxford University Press, 2003, Chapter 1, 'The Development of European Integration', pp. 1–48. J. Weiler, 'The Transformation of Europe', (1991) 100 *Yale Law Journal* 2403; published with a new afterword as Chapter 2 in J. Weiler, *The Constitution of Europe*, Cambridge: Cambridge University Press, 1999, pp. 10–101.

[9] In the Treaties of Maastricht (1991), Amsterdam (1997) and Nice (2000).

[10] These have attracted some attention in the general EC law literature. Their interest for EC lawyers, however, appears to lie more in their institutional innovation than in their substantive policy content. Hence, it is the engagement of private actors in the form of the social partners in EC law-making through the social dialogue which is perceived as the primary feature of the EU social dialogue. It is the institutional engagement of Commission, Council and Member States in formulation of the 'soft law' of Guidelines, National Action Plans, Reviews and Recommendations which attracts attention to the Employment Title's new processes and measures. The relation between these and their substantive policy content – social policy, working conditions, labour standards, employment and labour market measures – is neglected. It is reminiscent of the view that the substantive labour law content of many of the leading constitutional decisions of the European Court of Justice (*Defrenne* v. *Société Anonyme Belge de Navigation Aerienne (Sabena)*, Case 43/75, [1976] ECR 455; *Marshall* v. *Southampton and South-West Hampshire Area Health Authority (Teaching)*, Case 152/84, [1986] ECR 723; *Von Colson and Kamann* v. *Land Nordrhein-Westfalen*, Case 14/83, [1984] ECR 1891; *Francovich and Bonfaci* v. *Italy*, Cases C-6/90 and C-9/90, [1991] ECR I-5357) is of secondary interest or value. The argument of this book is that the character of the European Union, and of EU law, cannot be divorced from this substantive content.

[11] See Chapter 4 below.

[12] Such an account of the law and institutions of the EC is obviously otiose for those readers coming from an EC law background – an interesting assumption that EC law specialists will be less interested in the subject of EC labour law than labour law specialists.

knowledge of the basic elements of national law and institutions may be presumed. More importantly, however, the absence of such an introduction is likely to be the consequence of the recognition that labour law in many countries is not perceived as deriving solely, or even mainly, from the normal law-making institutions and procedures of civil law. Specifically, the central role of the social partners, trade unions and employers' organisations, in the formulation and implementation of labour law norms means that an introduction to national labour law by way of 'normal' law-making procedures and institutions would be seriously misleading.[13]

In sum, this book challenges assumptions as to the dominant economic character of the EU and of EU law by putting forward an analytical framework for the social dimension of the EU. The argument is that EC labour law, although only one of the many substantive dimensions of EC law, is central to a definition of the EU in social terms: Social Europe.

## EC labour law and the EU's social constitution

The early history of the EC, reflecting its origins in a project to construct a European common market, is marked by a constitutional debate concentrated on the economic dimension.[14] Developments moving away from the economic focus in the direction of a political construct for European integration, from Maastricht to the Convention on the Future of Europe, have looked to other constitutional models. These hesitate before the juridical and political choices involved in adopting the traditional state constitutional model for an evolving European polity which is not always agreed to possess the attributes of a state.[15] Debates on EU citizenship in particular have highlighted the contrast between EU citizenship and state citizenship.[16]

---

[13] The inclusion of the equivalent information on 'normal' EC law in EC labour law texts implies the assumption that EC labour law, unlike national labour law, *does* derive from the same institutional sources as other EC law, and that its nature and origins are not autonomous and different. This assumption is questionable at least. To start a text with such an account, without questioning this assumption, may be to lay the foundations for a misapprehension of EC labour law.

[14] This debate gave rise to theories about an economic constitution of the EC. M. Streit, 'The Economic Constitution of the EC', (1995) 1 *European Law Journal* 1. M. Poiares Maduro, *We, the Court: The European Court of Justice and the European Economic Constitution*, Oxford: Hart, 1998.

[15] J. Weiler, 'Does European Need a Constitution? Demos, Telos and the German Maastricht Decision', (1995) 1 *European Law Journal* 219. D. Grimm, 'Does Europe Need a Constitution?' (1995) 1 *European Law Journal* 282–302. J. Habermas, 'Remarks on Dieter Grimm's "Does Europe Need a Constitution?"' (1995) 1 *European Law Journal* 303–7. M. Jachtenfuchs, 'Theoretical Perspectives on European Governance', (1995) 1 *European Law Journal* 115–33. J. Weiler, 'Introduction: The Reformation of European Constitutionalism', Chapter 6 in *The Constitution of Europe*, pp. 221–37. P. Craig, 'Constitutions, Constitutionalism and the European Union', (2001) 7 *European Law Journal* 125–50.

[16] U. Mückenberger, 'Social Citizenship in the European Union', Chapter 6 in Bercusson *et al.*, *A Manifesto for Social Europe*, pp. 91–104; and U. Mückenberger, 'Introduction', Chapter 1 in U. Mückenberger (ed.), *Manifesto Social Europe*, ETUI, Brussels, 2001, pp. 1–16. J. Weiler,

These debates were sharpened by the adoption in December 2000 in Nice of the EU Charter of Fundamental Rights.[17] The most significant feature of the EU Charter is the inclusion of social and economic rights as fundamental rights alongside the more traditional civil and political rights. In particular, Chapter IV, entitled 'Solidarity', includes the key dimensions of the post-1945 settlements in Europe: protection of the welfare state, of individual employment and of collective labour. The EU Charter includes provisions which are at the heart of labour law and industrial relations in Europe: freedom of association (Article 12), right of collective bargaining and collective action (Article 28), workers' right to information and consultation within the undertaking (Article 27), freedom to choose an occupation and right to engage in work (Article 15), prohibition of child labour and protection of young people at work (Article 32), fair and just working conditions (Article 31), protection of personal data (Article 8), non-discrimination (Article 21), equality between men and women (Article 23) and protection in the event of unjustified dismissal (Article 30).

The inclusion in the EU Charter of such fundamental rights of labour raises a central question: is EC labour law to be considered only as part of the substantive private law of the EC, or is it now also to be conceived in public law terms? In other words, among the various constitutional frameworks being considered for the European Union, alongside the political and/or economic constitution, is there an EU social constitution protecting a European welfare state? Is there emerging a European constitutional principle analogous to the German *sozialstaat* or the French *ordre public social*? And what is the place of EC labour law within a European social constitution?

To elevate EC labour law to the constitutional level has both substantive and procedural consequences. As to procedures, for example, it highlights the constitutional/institutional innovations of the EC Treaty's attribution of law-making power to the EU social partners through the social dialogue. This raises questions, among others, of democratic legitimacy, the hierarchy of norms and judicial review. Is the EU social dialogue better understood in industrial-relations terms of collective bargaining, or as a law-making process?[18] Other procedural developments raise equally difficult questions; for example, the

---

'To Be a European Citizen: Eros and Civilization', Chapter 10 in *The Constitution of Europe*, pp. 324–57. N. Reich, 'Union Citizenship – Metaphor or Source of Rights?', (2001) 7 *European Law Journal* 4–23. B. Bercusson *et al.*, 'A Manifesto for Social Europe', (1997) 3 *European Law Journal* 189–205. Comments by A. Lo Faro, 'The Social Manifesto: Demystifying the Spectre Haunting Europe', and A. Larsson, 'A Comment on the "Manifesto for Social Europe"', (1997) 3 *European Law Journal*, 300–3, 304–7.

[17] Charter of Fundamental Rights of the European Union, proclaimed at the meeting of the European Council held in Nice from 7 to 9 December 2000, and adopted by the Commission, the Council and the Member States, OJ C364/01 of 18 December 2000. The 'adjusted' version of this Charter is proposed to be made legally binding by the Reform Treaty of Lisbon.

[18] Similar questions have been raised in national contexts where the nature of collective bargaining crosses over into public law-making from private bargaining, as when collective agreements are embodied in legislation or extended by ministerial decree. See the discussion in Chapter 18.

constitutional profile in terms of effective enforcement of the 'soft law' created by the 'open method of coordination' in the Employment Title, increasingly invoked as a model in other policy areas.

As to substantive consequences, the fundamental rights in the EU Charter reflect some, though not all, of the contents of EC labour law in EC legislation, such as labour law directives, and the legal measures transposing them into the laws of the Member States. This EC legislation, by virtue of the doctrine of supremacy of EC law, already possesses a constitutional character insofar as it overrides national legal measures. To this is now added a further EU constitutional dimension in the form of the EU Charter. The EC legislation itself is often open to much interpretation, and also leaves much to the discretion of Member States. The Charter, embodying substantive labour rights, provides another avenue to challenge both EC and national legislation which parallels those rights.

An early indication arrived barely eight weeks after the EU Charter was adopted on 7 December 2000. A British trade union, the Broadcasting, Entertainment, Cinematographic and Theatre Union (BECTU), challenged the UK government's implementation of the Working Time Directive. The UK government made the entitlement to four weeks' paid annual leave provided in Article 7 of the Directive conditional on a qualification period of thirteen weeks' employment, though there was no such qualification in the Directive. Since EC law has supremacy over national law, the UK, as a Member State, is obliged to respect the rights guaranteed by EC law. BECTU complained because many of the union's members on short-term contracts were being deprived of their right to paid annual leave under EC law by the UK government's legislation.

On 8 February 2001 Advocate General Tizzano delivered his advisory Opinion upholding BECTU's complaint. What is particularly important about the Advocate General's Opinion is that he looks at the right to paid annual leave 'in the wider context of fundamental social rights'.[19] A worker's right to a period of paid annual leave is to be given the same fundamental status as other human rights and guaranteed absolute protection. Advocate General Tizzano then pointed out that 'Even more significant, it seems to me, is the fact that that right is now solemnly upheld in the Charter of Fundamental Rights of the European Union, published on 7 December 2000 by the European Parliament, the Council and the Commission after approval by the Heads of State and Government of the Member States.'[20] He freely admits that 'formally, [the EU Charter] is not in itself binding'.[21] However, he states unequivocally:[22]

> I think therefore that, in proceedings concerned with the nature and scope of a fundamental right, the relevant statements of the Charter cannot be ignored; in

---

[19] Case C-173/99, *Broadcasting, Entertainment, Cinematographic and Theatre Union (BECTU)* v. *Secretary of State for Trade and Industry*, [2001] ECR I-4881, para. 22.
[20] *Ibid.*, para. 26.    [21] *Ibid.*, para. 27.    [22] *Ibid.*, para. 28.

particular, we cannot ignore its clear purpose of serving, where its provisions so allow, as a substantive point of reference for all those involved – Member States, institutions, natural and legal persons – in the Community context. Accordingly, I consider that the Charter provides us with the most reliable and definitive confirmation of the fact that the right to paid annual leave constitutes a fundamental right.

This approach highlights the constitutional potential of fundamental social and labour rights, including trade union rights, in the EU Charter. The rights in the EU Charter are 'a substantive point of reference', and not only for the Community institutions, but also for Member States and even for private persons, human and corporate. EC labour law embodied in the EU Charter potentially acquires a constitutional character: it is part of the EU's social constitution.

There remains the question of the relation of this social constitution to the 'economic constitution', the economic freedoms guaranteed by the Treaty. The struggle between these two constitutional frameworks reflects the conflict between markets and social protection, between free trade and trade union freedom, which has characterised the evolution of labour law from its beginnings. It remains to be played out in the EU context and will engage all the actors on the European stage: EU institutions, Member States and the social partners, trade unions and employers' associations at EU and national levels.[23]

## EC labour law: constitutionalising national labour laws

The elevation of EC labour law to the constitutional level of fundamental rights also has important implications for the labour law of the Member States. The emergence of national labour laws was often the chronicle of slow and painful separation from civil law, in particular, recognition of the employment contract as possessing a nature distinct from commercial contracts. Similarly, the emergence of collective labour regulation by the social partners raised questions of the anti-competitive ('restraint of trade') and public law nature of collective agreements and their authors.

In some Member States, fundamental rights of labour have been included in national constitutions. This has guaranteed some labour rights a degree of constitutional protection and thereby 'constitutionalised' parts of labour law. In other Member States, international labour law has had similar effects, as where a monist theory of international law means that the European Social Charter and ILO Conventions will have effect within a domestic legal system.

---

[23] Battle has been joined with the decisions of the European Court of Justice in Case C-438/05, *International Transport Workers' Federation, Finnish Seamen's Union* v. *Viking Line ABP, OÜ Viking Line Eesti*, 11 December 2007, Case C-341/05, *Laval un Partneri Ltd* v. *Svenska Byggnadsarbetareförbundet, Svenska Byggnadsarbetareförbundet, avd. 1, Svenska Elektrikerförbundet*, 18 December 2007, Case C-346/06, *Rechtsanwalt Dr. Dirk Rüffert* v. *Land Niedersachsen*, 3 April 2008 and Case C-319/06, *Commission* v. *Luxembourg*, 19 June 2008.

EC labour law, by virtue of its character as a supranational law with supremacy over national labour laws, already partakes of the character of a higher norm. The EU Charter's labour rights, becoming part of an EU social constitution, would reinforce this status. The EU social constitution may become the vehicle for the constitutionalisation of national labour laws.

Supremacy does not tolerate contradiction, but it does allow for discretion in application, in means, if not ends. National labour law must bend before it or break; but the deep roots of national labour law give it strength to resist, and its suppleness can soften and shape. Both can serve to mould the imperiousness of EU labour law supremacy.

The constitutional nature of some labour law norms is familiar to national legal orders accustomed to general constitutional provisions overriding sectional labour laws, though much less so to those legal orders where constitutional norms impinge less frequently, if at all, as in the UK. The impact of EC norms overriding domestic labour laws in the same way as national constitutional norms attributes to EC norms a constitutional quality. In itself, this creates an uneasy relationship with national constitutional norms, as domestic norms, domestic constitutions and EC law interact. It becomes even more complex if EC law itself is 'constitutionalised', including the EU Charter and its labour law provisions.[24]

The next part of this chapter explores the theme of 'regulatory competition', including between national and transnational norms. This theme can be projected as a major theme of this book: the strategic choice facing the institutional architecture of the European social model. Is EU labour law to be constitutionally embedded as the social partners become institutional actors in the EU's law making and law enforcement processes? Is the social model a central and integral element of European integration? Or is EU labour law a mere adjunct to legal regulation of an internal market in which the social partners are subordinate players in an industrial relations sub-system?[25]

In other words, regulatory competition is not only between levels (national v. transnational/EU), actors (states v. social partners) and instruments (collective agreements v. legislation) but, more fundamentally, it is over substance. Which is to prevail: competitive markets or a social model?[26]

---

[24] Even without this competing EU constitutional dimension, EU law transforms the legal character of domestic norms transposing EU law through doctrines such as indirect effect: requiring them to be interpreted consistently with EU norms.

[25] The question of legitimacy becomes central in these different visions of the EU constitution.

[26] An archetypal case is exemplified in litigation over the legality of collective industrial action by workers which confronts freedom of establishment or free movement of services where these threaten to undermine labour standards through 'social dumping'. See Case C-341/05, *Laval* and Case C-438/05 *Viking*. B. Bercusson, 'The Trade Union Movement and the European Union: Judgment Day', (2007) 13 *European Law Journal* (No. 3, May) 279–308. B. Bercusson, *Collective Action and Economic Freedoms: Assessment of the Opinions of the Advocates General in Laval and Viking and Six Alternative Solutions*, European Trade Union Institute (ETUI-REHS), Brussels, 2007, available, together with an Executive Summary in French, at www.etui-rehs.org/research/publications. And see Chapter 21 below.

The debates at EU level over the standard 'Community method' of law-making, the European social dialogue, the open method of coordination and a general deregulation agenda mirror the same issues in the labour laws of the Member States. Will trade unions and collective bargaining survive and flourish or wither and die? Will legislative authorities intervene in labour markets to balance out the inequality between employers and employees, or opt for other methods ('soft law'), or even deregulate?

The struggle at EU level is a proxy for these national struggles. Progress for one or the other tendency in individual Member States can be derailed by a different outcome at EU level. For example, deregulation and decollectivisation in the UK are confronted with EU regulation and requirements of worker representation. Trade union collective action in the Nordic countries is confronted with restrictions based on EU law. The consequence is that national actors, not least the social partners, target the EU level as a crucial forum in their national strategies.

In this way, the future of EU labour law foretells the future of national labour laws. It is not easy to predict the future of trade unions, collective bargaining and collective action at national levels if social dialogue and its concomitants decline at EU level. But if the EU's institutional architecture promotes EU social dialogue, trade unions will have a role at EU and hence at Member State level; collective bargaining will survive (even if in the new forms required by articulation with EU level labour standards); and collective industrial action will be protected.

## *European* labour law in the context of EC law and national labour laws

The analytical framework for this book requires some explication of the relationship of EC law to EC *labour* law, but also of the distinction drawn between *EC* labour law and *European* labour law.

The structures of *EC labour law* found in existing texts on the subject demonstrate the influence of prototypical models of EC law and national labour laws. An approach adopting the EC law model dictates an emphasis on individual employment and free markets in labour, with an emphasis on the internal dynamics of EC institutions. The model derived from national labour laws adopts the traditional dichotomy of individual employment protection and collective labour rights, with occasional recognition of labour market policy and the role of the social partners.

A legalistic approach to EC labour law has the merit of a clear structure. The law-making institutions of the Community: Council, Commission, Court and so on, and its legal provisions: Treaties, Regulations, Directives and other legal measures determine the structure. The account comprises the description of the institutions, and groups together the legal provisions in various combinations or categories more or less familiar from national labour law traditions. The outcome constitutes the structure of EC labour law.

A contextual approach to EC labour law offers other possibilities. One is to adopt a chronological account as a substitute for an analytical framework. Understanding the historical evolution of EC labour law is necessary. But a chronological account is not sufficient.[27] Nor can an account of EC labour law be a purely political narrative of its evolution. There is a need to put the history and politics into a legal context. An analytical structure is required which takes both features into account: the historical and political context, but also the importance of legal technique, the constraints imposed by legal provisions and processes of law-making and law-interpreting.

Hence, the evolution of *EC labour law* may be analysed in terms of a number of different legal strategies which have been adopted. These strategies are the consequence of the political context involving dynamics both internal to the Community, between the EC institutions, and external to the Community, between the Community and external actors including Member States and organisations of interest groups at national, supra- and sub-national levels.

A proposed structure for *European* labour law in context should also take into account the national labour laws of Member States and their very different labour law traditions. EC labour law is only partly an instrument of the EC institutions. It is also, even primarily, an instrument regulating employment and labour relations in Member States. As such it is an instrument of the Member State governments, and of organisations of interests, mainly employers and workers, within the Member States. The legal measures which result from EC legal strategies interact with national labour law traditions. The interaction occurs at the point of formulation, when national labour laws influence the form and content of EC labour law, and also at the point of implementation, when these national labour law systems determine the impact of EC labour law within Member States. A structure of *European* labour law has to reflect also the different traditions of national labour law systems of Member States.

The proposed structure that emerges should reflect the law and context of both the EC and of Member States' labour law traditions, both the various legal strategies adopted as a consequence of the political conjuncture of the EC at different moments of its history, and the interaction of these strategies with national labour laws.

Finally, the proposed structure poses the question of whether *European* labour law is merely the passive reflection of EC law and national labour laws. Is there discernible a specific identity which, taking account of both these sources of inspiration, begins to constitute a structure of European labour law? The specific identity of European labour law within the constitutional context of an emerging Social Europe has been noted. It is in the constitutional

---

[27] The result can resemble a list of dates and facts. EC labour law becomes a chronological recital of what are held to be significant pieces of legislation, or European Court decisions, or provisions of and amendments to the Treaties.

context of the European Union that *European* labour law achieves an identity going beyond EC law and national labour law systems.

### Regulatory competition and coordination between transnational (EU) and national laws in transnational labour regulation

The impact of European labour law on labour standards in the Single European Market has led to growing awareness of the potential of transnational labour standards at the international level.[28]

The evolution of a transnational labour law on the European continent has significance for the development of international labour standards beyond the geographical limits of Europe. The role of regional integration in the process of economic globalisation is a well-known theme: 'The basic issue is the relationship between forces of globalization and forces of regionalisation. Regionalism is one possible approach to "a new multilateralism"', and 'Europe represents the most advanced regional arrangement the world has seen'.[29] It has been said of the supranational political entity which is the European Union that it 'continues to occupy a central position as a catalyst and a precursor of global institutional developments'.[30]

The view of the EU as a catalyst and precursor in the field of global labour regulation may be viewed either as an optimistic aspiration or a fearful threat; the reality arguably still falls somewhat short of fulfilling such a role. However, the experience of European labour law highlights what scholars have identified as three 'primary and interrelated concerns ... in debates about global regulation':[31]

> First comes the question of how institutions emerge and evolve in mediating the dynamic of the global marketplace. Secondly, there is a functional policy concern – the problem of the appropriate level for public governance of economic activities. This has long been a question within federal systems, and is now posed

[28] There has been a burgeoning of the literature concerned with labour standards in international trade and the labour practices of multinational corporations. B.A. Hepple, 'New Approaches to International Labour Regulation', (1997) 26 *Industrial Law Journal* 353; B. Bercusson, 'Labour Regulation in a Transnational Economy', (1999) 6 *Maastricht Journal of European and Comparative Law* 244–70; B.A. Hepple (ed.), *Social and Labour Rights in a Global Context: International and Comparative Perspectives*, Cambridge, Cambridge University Press, 2001; B.A. Hepple, *Rights at Work: Global, European and British Perspectives*, London: Sweet & Maxwell, 2005; B.A. Hepple (ed.), *Labour Laws and Global Trade*, Oxford: Hart, 2005. B. Bercusson and C. Estlund (eds.), *Regulating Labour in the Wake of Globalisation: New Challenges, New Institutions*, vol. II, Columbia-London Law Series, Oxford: Hart, 2008.

[29] Bjorn Hettne, 'Global Market versus the New Regionalism', in David Held and Anthony McGrew (eds), *The Global Transformations Reader*, 2nd edn, Cambridge: Polity Press, 2000, pp. 359–69, at pp. 359, 362.

[30] William Bratton, Joe McCahery, Sol Picciotto and Colin Scott (eds.), *International Regulatory Competition and Coordination: Perspectives on Economic Regulation in Europe and the United States*, Oxford: Clarendon Press, 1996, p. 4.

[31] *Ibid.*, p. 2.

at the international level. Thirdly, there is a problem of democratic deficit. This stems from a perception that internalized economic activities are no longer subject to control or facilitation by national governments acting alone, while international structures are institutionally underdeveloped.

The institutional, functional and political dimensions of labour regulation in the EU have encountered many of the problems identified when international systems involve competing regulatory authorities in the sphere of labour regulation and efforts are made to coordinate them. European labour law offers many practical illustrations of the concerns in the debate over regulatory competition, in the EU context, specifically, between EU labour law and national labour laws.[32] The following provides some practical illustrations from European labour law as they affect regulatory strategies and institutions, levels of regulation and regulatory legitimacy.

## Competing regulatory strategies and institutions in the EU

Labour regulation in the European Union is best understood in the context of the evolution of the European Communities in general since their foundation with the European Coal and Steel Community (ECSC) in 1951. Throughout more than half a century, the Community has experienced a variety of often competing legal strategies for the formulation and implementation of labour law and social policy.

The earliest strategy is that which characterised the founding of the ECSC by the Treaty of Paris in 1951: an active labour market policy and labour involvement in regulation. In complete contrast, the following period was characterised by a strategy of neo-liberal laissez-faire, reflected in the almost total absence of social policy and labour law provisions in the Treaty of Rome of 1957. This strategy was contested in turn by an ambitious Social Action Programme adopted in 1974, which, through directives, sought to harmonise labour legislation in the common market. This strategy was brought to a halt by opposition of a Conservative government elected in the UK in 1979 with a domestic strategy of deregulation of labour markets. The result was the EU exploring a non-legislative strategy in the form of indirect financial instruments and the launching of the European social dialogue in 1985. The 1992 objective of the Single European Market led to pressures for a strategy to achieve a social dimension through fundamental social and economic rights of workers in a non-binding Community Charter. Then the social dialogue strategy was formally institutionalised in the Maastricht Protocol and Agreement on Social Policy of 1992, now incorporated into the EC Treaty by the Treaty of Amsterdam of 1997. The Treaty of Amsterdam also introduced a new Employment

---

[32] For a more detailed account, see B. Bercusson, 'Regulatory Competition in the EU System: Labour', in D. Esty and D. Geradin (eds.), *Regulatory Competition and Economic Integration: Comparative Perspectives*, Oxford: Oxford University Press, 2000.

Chapter into the Treaty of Rome, with a novel regulatory mechanism: the 'open method of coordination'. On 7 December 2000, an EU Charter of Fundamental Rights, including many social and labour rights, was unanimously approved by the European Parliament, Commission and Council. Although presently limited to a political declaration, it is to be given a formal legal status, despite the failure of the Constitutional Treaty for Europe, in the proposed Lisbon Treaty. In the meantime, it has been repeatedly cited before and by the European Court of Justice.

What this history shows is the extraordinary range of competing legal and institutional strategies which have characterised attempts to construct a European labour law, and the struggles that have taken place among the Member States, the Community institutions and organised interest groups, primarily organisations of employers and trade unions, in the course of developing these strategies. These institutional struggles over regulatory territory in the sphere of employment and labour relations are emblematic of international regulatory competition and coordination. The institutions involved, the legal strategies adopted, and the political tactics used offer many lessons for international labour regulation on a wider global scale.

To take just one illustration, rich in irony for the UK, the UK government's stance from 1979 in preventing the adoption at Community level of labour law directives by blocking the requisite unanimity in the Council of Ministers was dictated by its domestic policy. This stance coupled 'deregulation' at domestic level with an equally wholesale policy of exclusion of trade unions. This included both exclusion of trade unions from areas of policy where they had previously been part of tripartite policy-making machinery (such as industrial training and manpower policy), and, more crucially, the reduction and weakening wherever possible of collective bargaining.

It is, therefore, ironic that it was this UK blockage of labour legislation at EU level which provided the critical impetus to a transformation in legal strategy for social policy and labour law at EU level: the emergence of a competing regulatory strategy in the form of dialogue between the social partners at European level. The doubtless unintended consequence of the UK government policy of decollectivisation of industrial relations at domestic level was the huge advance in collectivisation of industrial relations at EU level. Deregulation of collective bargaining in the UK produced regulation through social dialogue at EU level. While the British trade unions (TUC) and employers (CBI) were ignored in London, they were engaged in the process of negotiating EU level collective agreements in Brussels![33]

---

[33] The framework agreements on parental leave (1996) and part-time work (1997) being examples. These became EU legislation in the form of legally binding directives, at a time when the UK government had excluded itself from participating in the legislative process through the 1992 Maastricht 'opt-out'.

## Competing levels of regulation in the EU

In the EU context, the issue of competing levels of labour regulation appears in various guises. Of these, perhaps the best known concerns the competition between Member States and the EU institutions where both have competence to regulate labour matters. Less well known, but equally important for labour law, is the competition between Member States and/or EC regulation and collective regulation by trade unions and employers through collective agreements at national and European levels.[34] A number of examples illustrate this competition as it takes place on different levels of regulation. The range of subjects in these examples – free movement of goods, competition policy, health and safety, multinational enterprises and working time – highlights the scope for the regulatory potential of transnational European labour law.

## Free movement of goods and transnational industrial action

Obstructions to free movement of agricultural produce from other countries caused by protesting farmers led to a complaint by the Commission against France for failing to take appropriate measures to guarantee free movement of goods.[35] At the same time, the Commission was considering a proposal emanating from D-G XV (Internal Market), headed by then Commissioner Mario Monti. This proposal sought to put pressure on Member States to take measures removing obstacles when required to by the Commission.

Both these developments aroused considerable anxiety in trade unions, particularly in the transport sector, where industrial action could have similar effects on the free movement of goods. The outcome of lengthy consultations was a Regulation which includes the following provision:[36]

> This Regulation may not be interpreted as affecting in any way the exercise of fundamental rights as recognised in Member States, including the right or freedom to strike. These rights may also include the right or freedom to take other actions covered by the specific industrial relations systems in Member States.

The EU drew back from asserting that its regulatory power over the free movement of goods prevailed over national regulation of collective industrial action, at least in so far as these took the form of the exercise of fundamental rights.[37]

---

[34] The applicable principle goes under the title of 'subsidiarity', which has both 'vertical' and 'horizontal' dimensions. See footnote 44 below.

[35] Case C-265/95, *Commission* v. *France*, [1997] ECR I-6959.

[36] Council Regulation (EC) No. 2679/98 of 7 December 1998 on the functioning of the internal market in relation to the free movement of goods among the Member States. OJ L337/8 of 12 December 1998 (the 'Monti Regulation'), Article 2. For an early reaction to the initial proposal, which did not include Article 2, see B. Bercusson, 'The Full Monti: Stripping Away Strikers' Rights', *Thompsons Labour and European Law Review*, Issue 20, March 1998, 4–5.

[37] But see now Case C-341/05, *Laval* and Case C-438/05, *Viking*.

## Member State improvements on EU minimum standards

In an Opinion of 28 April 1998 in the *Borsana* case,[38] Advocate General Mischo applied the principle of proportionality so as to annul Member State legislation imposing stricter rules than those required by health and safety directives. This Opinion aroused considerable disquiet among trade unions at EU and national levels.

In its decision in the *Borsana* case, handed down on 17 December 1998, the European Court rejected Advocate General Mischo's Opinion. The key paragraph of the judgment reads:[39]

> Since the legislation at issue is a more stringent measure for the protection of working conditions compatible with the Treaty and results from the exercise by a Member State of the powers it has retained pursuant to Article 118a(3) [now Article 137(4) EC] of the Treaty, it is not for the Court to rule on whether such legislation and the penalties imposed therein are compatible with the principle of proportionality.

Contrary to the Advocate General, the Court was unwilling to allow EC law to interfere with the discretion of the Member States to improve upon EC regulatory standards in the field of health and safety.

## Collective agreements and competition law: anti-trust immunity?

In cases referred to the European Court of Justice[40] by a court in the Netherlands under Article 177 (now Article 234) of the EC Treaty, the issue was the relationship between the EC rules on competition in Article 85(1) (now Article 81(1)) EC and collective agreements between representatives of employers and employees. Advocate General Jacobs addressed this fundamental issue by asking: 'is the "encouragement of collective bargaining under Community law" such as to exempt collective agreements from EC law's competition rules?'[41] At stake was whether the national law of the Member States regulating the legal status of collective agreements, a central element of their industrial relations systems, was to be overthrown by the application of EC competition law.

The Advocate General concluded that: 'collective agreements between management and labour on wages and working conditions should enjoy automatic immunity from antitrust scrutiny'. However, he went on to add: 'Nevertheless

---

[38] *Società italiana petrole SpA (IP)* v. *Borsana Srl*, Case C-2/97, [1998] *ECR* I-8597.

[39] *Ibid.*, paragraph 40.

[40] *Albany International BV* v. *Stichting Bedrijfspensioenfonds Textielindustrie*, Case C-67/96; with joined Cases C-115/97, C-116/97 and C-117/97, [1999] ECR I-5751.

[41] *Ibid.*, paragraphs 166–94. Or, as the Advocate General put it, is there an anti-trust immunity for collective agreements? Advocate General Jacobs also addressed the question 'is there a fundamental right to bargain collectively?' (paragraphs 132–65). If there is such a right in EC law, it would protect collective agreements. The case is dealt with in more detail later.

I consider that the proposed antitrust immunity for collective agreements between management and labour should not be without limitations.'[42] A number of conditions were posed by the Advocate General for collective agreements to achieve legality in the EU.[43] These conditions raised more questions than they answered and potentially placed EC law in direct conflict with national laws of the Member States which recognised the legality of collective agreements.

In a decision on 21 September 1999, the European Court of Justice rejected the contention that collective agreements were in conflict with the competition provisions of the EC Treaty. The Court acknowledged the inherently restrictive effects on competition of collective agreements which fixed the price of labour. But the Court was equally aware of the risks to be run by allowing national laws on collective agreements to be undermined by EC competition law.

### Implementation of EC law: legislation and/or collective agreements?

Regulation in national labour law includes not only legislation but also collective agreements between trade unions and employers and their organisations, the 'social partners'. The fundamental role of the social partners in European labour law is seen by the Commission as 'recognition of a *dual form of subsidiarity* in the social field: on the one hand, subsidiarity regarding regulation at national and Community level; on the other, subsidiarity as regards the choice, at Community level, between the legislative approach and the agreement-based approach'.[44]

Article 137(3) of the EC Treaty provides an example of the application of horizontal subsidiarity at national (Member State) level. The implementation of directives at Member State level may be entrusted to management and labour, subject to a guarantee by the Member State of the results imposed by the directive. Decisions of the European Court have upheld the competence of the social partners, as opposed to the public authorities, to implement EC measures through collective agreements, though these must satisfy certain conditions: the agreements concerned must cover all employees, and must include all the directive's requirements.[45]

---

[42] *Ibid.*, paragraphs 179, 186.

[43] *Ibid.*, paragraph 194: '[My] conclusion on antitrust immunity for collective agreements is that collective agreements between management and labour concluded in good faith on core subjects of collective bargaining such as wages and working conditions which do not directly affect third markets and third parties are not caught by Article 85(1) of the Treaty.'

[44] Communication of the Commission of 14 December 1993, COM(93) 600 final, paragraph 6(c). This is said to be 'in conformity with the fundamental principle of subsidiarity enshrined in Article 3B (now Article 5) of the Treaty'. As between horizontal and vertical subsidiarity, *vertical* subsidiarity refers to the division of competences between *different levels*: European and national; *horizontal* subsidiarity refers to the division of responsibilities between public authorities and, for example, the social partners *at the same level*.

[45] In *Commission of the European Communities* v. *the Kingdom of Denmark*, Case 143/83, [1985] ECR 427, the European Court of Justice held: 'that Member States may leave the implementation

The possibility of implementing directives through the actions of the social partners at national level was confirmed by the Commission in an exchange of letters with the Danish social partners. The Commission recognised the principle that directives relating to labour market matters may be implemented in Denmark through collective agreements without the need for legislation.[46]

## Negotiated regulation of multinational enterprises

The European Works Councils Directive 94/45/EC of 1994 requires the establishment of a European Works Council (EWC) or a procedure in Community-scale undertakings and Community-scale groups of undertakings for the purposes of informing and consulting employees in multinational enterprises.[47] The Directive is characterised by a regulatory strategy of delegation to the social partners, management and labour, of the competence to negotiate the relevant European labour law standards. Central management and the representatives of the workforce are to negotiate the EWC agreement.[48]

A comprehensive analysis of some 386 EWC agreements concluded under Article 13 of the Directive, which exempted from its requirements voluntary agreements negotiated before 22 September 1996, revealed that in September 1994, there were only 40 voluntary EWCs; two years later one-third of companies covered by the Directive had EWC agreements establishing EWCs.[49]

of the principle of equal pay in the first instance to representatives of management and labour' (paragraph 8). The Court reaffirmed this principle in a second case involving Italy, *Commission of the European Communities* v. *the Italian Republic*, Case 235/84, [1986] ECR 2291, when implementation of Council Directive 77/187 was at issue.

[46] This exchange of letters took place on 11 May 1993. A similar exchange of letters took place between the Commission and the Swedish government on 29 May 1993. The principle had been introduced earlier by the Danish Commissioner Henning Christophersen. Its standard formulation in many directives is known as the 'Christophersen clause'.

[47] Council Directive 94/45/EC of 22 September 1994 on the establishment of a European Works Council or a procedure in Community-scale undertakings and Community-scale groups of undertakings for the purposes of informing and consulting employees. OJ L254/64 of 30 September 1994. The Directive was formally extended to the UK by Council Directive 97/74/EC of 15 December 1997. OJ 1998 L10/22.

[48] The range of issues to be negotiated is impressive: national law applicable, the signatory parties, coverage, EWC composition, numbers and seat allocation, the term of office, functions and procedure, venue, frequency and duration of meetings, financial and material resources, duration of the agreement and the procedure for its renegotiation, issues for information and consultation, experts, confidentiality, select committee, employee-side meetings prior to full EWC meetings, rules on deputies to employee representatives, languages policy and interpretation provided, procedure for agreeing the agenda and joint procedure for drawing up minutes or other record. This list is derived from a review of agreements negotiated under Article 6 of the Directive one year after it came into force; *European Works Councils Bulletin* No. 11, September/October 1997, pp. 12–17.

[49] 'EWC agreements under Article 13 reviewed', *European Works Councils Bulletin* No. 15, May/June 1998, pp. 8–12. The rush to conclude agreements is indicated by the fact that more than three-quarters of agreements were concluded in the twelve months up to September 1996, and one in three were signed in September 1996 itself.

For the remaining majority of eligible companies still to negotiate agreements, the delegation to social partners of the power to make agreements is not complete. It is subjected to a subtle structuring process which shapes the strategies pursued by the social partners. The subtlety of the Directive's strategy lies in *apparently* leaving all to the unfettered negotiations of the Special Negotiating Body (SNB) representing the workers and central management. The Directive explicitly allows for the exclusion of the minimum requirements laid down in an Annex to the Directive in any agreements reached.[50]

*Formally*, the content of the agreement is not confined by the Annex. But the Annex's subsidiary requirements apply where the SNB and the central management so decide, central management refuses to commence negotiations within six months of a request, or three years elapse after a request without an agreement.[51] *In practice*, central management will have to offer incentives to persuade the SNB to make an agreement offering less than the subsidiary requirements in the Annex. On the other side, the employees' representatives on the SNB are also not bound by the Annex. Negotiations can flexibilise Annex requirements. Both sides have an incentive to treat it as the basis for negotiations. The Annex can be seen as a package which could be negotiated and varied, if enough incentives are offered.

In practice, therefore, the structure of negotiations between the SNB and central management is such that the subsidiary requirements in the Annex become the effective threshold for agreements. This happens where the SNB is not willing to settle for less than the subsidiary requirements. The regulatory strategy is that the Directive provides the framework, but it is the negotiations between the social partners which determine the final outcome.

### The role of collective bargaining in EU regulation of working time

When introducing its first proposal for a directive on working time, the Commission explained that it 'intends to propose a groundwork of basic provisions on certain aspects of the organization of working time connected with workers' health and safety at work'.[52] However, 'other issues mentioned in the action programme in the field of the adaptation of working time should be left to both sides of industry and/or national legislation'.[53] The delicate balance between legislation and collective bargaining was spelled out twice in the Explanatory Memorandum in almost identical terms; once at the beginning and again in its final provisions:[54]

---

[50] Article 6(4): 'The agreements referred to in paragraphs 2 and 3 shall not, unless provision is made otherwise therein, be subject to the subsidiary requirements of the Annex.'

[51] Article 7(1).

[52] Proposal for a Council Directive concerning certain aspects of the organisation of working time, COM(90) 317 final – SYN 295, Brussels, 20 September 1990; OJ C254 of 9 October 1990; Explanatory Memorandum, p. 2, paragraph 2.

[53] *Ibid.*, p. 3.    [54] *Ibid.*, p. 4, paragraph 3 and again in paragraph 32 on pp. 16–17.

given the differences arising from national practices, the subject of working conditions in general falls to varying degrees under the autonomy of both sides of industry who often act in the public authorities' stead and/or complement their action. To take account of these differences and in accordance with the principle of subsidiarity the Commission takes the view that negotiation between the two sides of industry should play its full part within the framework of the proposed measures, provided that it is able to guarantee adherence to the principles set out in the Commission's proposals … In other words, it is important in this field to take into consideration the fact that such agreements concluded by management and labour can in principle make a contribution to the application of Community directives, without, however, releasing the Member States concerned from the responsibility for attaining the objectives sought via these instruments.

The final text of the Directive included a large number of provisions which made collective bargaining an element in the setting of EC standards on working time. In the final text, the role of collective bargaining in determining *some* of the EU standards on working time had undergone a significant *qualitative* change. In the past, it was largely confined to allowing for derogations to prescribed standards.[55] The present Directive also allows for collective agreements themselves to fix or define relevant standards, usually only with the consent of the Member State concerned, but in one exceptional case, with *priority* over Member State legislation (daily rest periods, Article 4).

## Competition for legitimacy among institutions and levels

The Maastricht Treaty on European Union transformed EC labour law by formally 'constitutionalising' the European social dialogue in the Protocol and Agreement on Social Policy. Following the UK's opt-back-in to the Social Policy Agreement, the role of the social dialogue in the making of EC labour law was formally enshrined in Articles 138–139 of the EC Treaty by the Treaty of Amsterdam of June 1997. Almost exactly one year after the Amsterdam summit, the Court of First Instance (CFI) delivered a judgment which highlighted the constitutional nature of the integration of social dialogue into the EC Treaty.[56]

In *UEAPME*, an organisation representing artisans and small and medium undertakings challenged the legality of the Parental Leave Directive before the

---

[55] These remained in Directive 93/104/EC of 23 November 1993 concerning certain aspects of the organisation of working time, OJ L307/18 of 13 December 1993. Article 17(3) allowed for general derogations 'by means of collective agreements or agreements concluded between the two sides of industry at national or regional level or, in conformity with the rules laid down by them, by means of collective agreements or agreements concluded between the two sides of industry at a lower level'. See now as amended by Directive 2000/34 of 22 June 2000, OJ L195/41, consolidated in Directive 2003/88/EC of 4 November 2003 concerning certain aspects of the organisation of working time; OJ L299/9 of 18 November 2003.

[56] Case T-135/96, *Union Européene de l'Artisanat et des Petites et Moyennes Entreprises (UEAPME)* v. *Council of the European Union*, [1998] ECR II-2335; [1998] IRLR 602.

CFI.[57] The Parental Leave Directive was the first product of the new social dialogue procedure under the Protocol and Agreement on Social Policy. The CFI contrasted two possible outcomes. The first outcome follows from the normal EU legislative process leading to a directive approved by the Council. The CFI declared: 'the democratic legitimacy of measures adopted by the Council pursuant to Article 2 of the Agreement derives from the European Parliament's participation in that first procedure'. The second outcome results from the European social dialogue. In such a case, the directive which emerges from the Council embodies the agreement reached by labour and management. Of this, the CFI said:[58]

> In contrast, the second procedure, referred to in Articles 3(4) and 4 of the Agreement (Articles 138(4) and 139 EC), does not provide for the participation of the European Parliament. However, the principle of democracy on which the Union is founded requires – in the absence of the participation of the European Parliament in the legislative process – that the participation of the people be otherwise assured, in this instance through the parties representative of management and labour who concluded the agreement which is endowed by the Council acting on a qualified majority, on a proposal from the Commission, with a legislative foundation at Community level. In order to make sure that that requirement is complied with, the Commission and the Council are under a duty to verify that the signatories to the agreement are truly representative.

In sum, the judgment raised profound issues of the democratic legitimacy of the regulatory procedures of EC labour law-making; specifically, the representativeness and autonomy of the social partners engaged in social dialogue, compared to the 'democratic' legislative processes involving the Commission, Council and European Parliament, and the role of litigation before the European Court as a control mechanism of this legitimacy and autonomy.[59]

## Conclusion

European labour law provides a reservoir of experience of key issues facing transnational labour regulation. Although confined to the European continent, with a relatively limited variation of economic, political and social arrangements among Member States, it nonetheless has had to confront questions which are also on the agenda of efforts to achieve global transnational labour regulation. These include which regulatory strategies to adopt, which regulatory institutions to enlist, at what levels (transnational or national) and

---

[57] Council Directive 96/34/EC of 3 June 1996 on the framework agreement on parental leave concluded by UNICE, CCEP and the ETUC, OJ L145/4 of 19 June 1996.

[58] *UEAPME*, paragraph 89.

[59] The case also raises issues of general concern to EC lawyers engaged in debates over the democratic deficit of the EC, the role of private organisations in EC law-making, and *locus standi* before the European Court of Justice. For discussion of some of these issues, see B. Bercusson, 'Democratic Legitimacy and European Labour Law', (1999) 28 *Industrial Law Journal* (June) 153–70 and Chapter 18 below.

engaging which actors (states or social partners); how is the legitimacy of whichever regulatory arrangements are adopted to be assured, and how can they be tested? The experience of European labour law has much to teach about regulatory competition and coordination between national and international levels.

## A new legal order of labour law: EU labour law

The European Community was created by the Treaty of Rome of 1957. The law of the EC was famously declared by the European Court of Justice in *Van Gend en Loos* to be:[60]

> a new legal order of international law for the benefit of which the states have limited their sovereign rights, albeit within limited fields, and the subjects of which comprise not only Member States but also their nationals.

This new legal order may also be said to have a labour law.

Since its beginnings, a fundamental debate has been conducted on whether the framework of analysis of the law of the EC should be inspired by the law of international organisations (international law) or by the law of an emerging confederation of states ((supra)national constitutional law).[61] A third approach is inspired by the sociology of law and analyses EC law looking beyond the interaction of Member States and EC institutions.[62]

This debate is also of fundamental importance for understanding specifically the labour law of the EC. International labour law, national labour laws and sociology of labour law provide different frameworks for the analysis of both the content and the anticipated evolution of EC labour law. Just as the debate over EC law in general has benefited from the potential use of concepts adopted from the different analytical frameworks of international law, constitutional law and sociology of law, similarly, EC labour law may benefit from these different approaches.

## Contrasting international and EU labour law

International labour law has its most important source in the norms promulgated by the International Labour Organisation (ILO), established in 1919, which declared as one of its principles that 'labour should not be regarded merely as a commodity or article of commerce'.[63] The analytical framework for

---

[60] Case 26/62, *N. V. Algemene Transport- en Expeditie Onderneming van Gend & Loos and Nederlandse administratie der belastingen (Netherlands Inland Revenue Administration)*, [1963] ECR 1, at p. 12.

[61] Weiler, 'The Transformation of Europe'.

[62] Snyder, *New Directions in European Community Law*.

[63] Article 427 of the Treaty of Versailles, 1919, which contained the first ILO Constitution. The Constitution was revised in 1944, and Article 1 declared its aims and purposes to be those of the Declaration annexed to the Constitution, which 'reaffirms the fundamental principles on which

such norms addresses their content, the procedures of their adoption and mechanisms of their enforcement.

In terms of their content, ILO norms have slowly but surely increased in number and scope and are now numerous and cover a huge range of topics. However, the standard of the norms adopted has often been minimal: the lowest common denominator. In terms of their adoption and enforcement, the tripartite principle of participation of representatives of employers and workers alongside governments has increased the likelihood of approval of norms by ILO institutions and enhanced their legitimacy. However, the mechanisms of enforcement of norms adopted have been acknowledged as often inadequate.[64]

EC labour and social law does not strictly conform to this framework of analysis. Labour, and even more so social matters, are relatively marginal to the original objectives of the European Economic Community, founded in 1957 to establish a common market for goods, services, capital and labour. In terms of their content, the development of norms regarding labour during five decades of existence of the EC has been spasmodic, episodic and unsystematic. They have ranged unsystematically from norms in which the principle of freedom of movement in a Community-wide labour market overrides social considerations of protection of workers (as when technical standards for products are stipulated which are lower than national labour law standards,) to norms which have provided rights and protection far beyond existing Member State provisions (as in equality between men and women). In terms of their adoption, tripartism has been limited, until recently, and there has been frequent institutional blockage of approval of norms proposed. However, the mechanisms of enforcement extend far beyond the possibilities available to the ILO machinery.

These qualities of content and procedures of adoption and enforcement of norms are important to understanding the specificity of EC labour law. Its content is much less comprehensive and systematic than the ILO norms. Given the quite different objectives of the EC, the influence of ILO norms has been relatively insignificant.[65] The absence of tripartism has adversely affected both the approval and the effective enforcement of norms, despite the fact that EC enforcement procedures are formally more constricting than those of the ILO. The role of Member States and their national labour laws has been greater than that in international labour law and organisations.

the Organisation is based and, in particular, that – (a) labour is not a commodity'. O'Higgins, ''Labour is not a Commodity'''.

[64] See the essays by B. Creighton and G.S. Morris in K.D. Ewing, C.A. Gearty and B.A. Hepple (eds.), *Human Rights and Labour Law: Essays for Paul O'Higgins*, London: Mansell, 1994, at pp. 1 and 29; also P. O'Higgins, 'Britain and International Labour Standards', Chapter 20 in R. Lewis (ed.), *Labour Law in Britain*, Oxford: Blackwell, 1986; K. Ewing, *Britain and the ILO*, 2nd edn, London: Institute of Employment Rights, 1994.

[65] But see the chapter by Tonia Novitz in Philip Alston (ed.), *Labour Rights as Human Rights*, Oxford: Oxford University Press, 2005.

## National labour laws

National labour legislation emerged much earlier than international and EC labour law. But it is important to emphasise that the conceptualisation of these legislative and other norms into national labour laws with coherent intellectual frameworks was much more recent. This can be demonstrated in a number of Member States.[66]

In *Britain*, for practitioners and most scholars in universities, labour law scarcely existed before 1960. In 1959, only four of about twenty law faculties taught labour law and of these only one could go back to before the First World War, the London School of Economics. A major stimulus was the arrival in 1933 of Otto Kahn-Freund, who wrote seminal papers in 1954 and 1959. As labour relations gradually became a focus of economic and political debate, the first books on modern labour law were published in the 1960s. By 1966, thirteen of twenty-four law faculties had a modern labour law course option.

In contrast, *Germany* has one of the longest established traditions of legal education in labour and social law, with monographs developing the subject even before the First World War, though it was only in the years between 1918 and 1933 that it took shape in recognisably modern form. The tradition was revived after the Second World War, and in 1986 all thirty-one (West) German law faculties and departments of legal studies had one or more professorships in labour law. In the *Netherlands*, although a separate labour law chair was established at the University of Amsterdam in 1926, it has been asserted that those appointed before 1954 were generalists with interests in labour law, whereas specialists in the subject only came afterwards.

In *France*, though the first texts appeared during the 1930s, until the Second World War labour law was not really considered to be a separate discipline, not yet having emerged from the confines of civil law. After 1945 the subject was increasingly included in faculty syllabuses until in 1955 it became a compulsory subject: there were two student books in 1950, but eight in 1986. In *Belgium* also, labour law became a subject for teaching at the law schools only after the Second World War, though only in the late 1950s did it become mandatory.

In *Italy*, labour law was long perceived either as a branch of private or company law or ideologically linked to trade union autonomy until the subject was renewed by Gino Giugni and Federico Mancini in the 1950s, the former elaborating the theory of *ordinamento intersindacale* in 1960. The first professorial chair in labour law was only established in *Sweden* at the University of Stockholm in 1966, and the first chair of labour law in *Denmark* was only occupied decades later.

In general, therefore, the formation of the intellectual framework for national labour laws, in the case of the original six Member States, took its modern form

---

[66] For an account, see B. Bercusson, 'Law, Legal Education and Practice and Labour and Social Law', in B. De Witte and C. Forder (eds.), *The Common Law of Europe and the Future of Legal Education*, Deventer: Kluwer, 1992, p. 423.

in the years following the end of the Second World War, that is to say, almost contemporaneously with or not far from the founding of the EEC and the first developments of its labour and social law.

## European labour law: a symbiosis of EU and national labour laws

National labour laws in the original six Member States were not conceived of in terms of the EC and its labour law. But the evolution and conceptualisation of the labour and social law of the EC was inevitably influenced by the mature and maturing conceptualisations of the national labour laws of the original Member States and of later adherents. Conversely, as EC labour and social law norms developed, they began to influence the formulation and conceptualisation of national labour laws. The two processes are thus linked in a specific symbiosis.[67]

A major premise in understanding EC labour law is, therefore, the need to avoid thinking about it *exclusively* in terms of EC institutions and legal provisions. Accounts of EC labour law may require an understanding of the institutions and the basic legal framework of the EC. But equally, if not more necessary, is an appreciation of the relationship of EC labour law with *national* labour law systems.

It is easy to demonstrate that national labour law systems were subjected to mutual influences. One can cite the influences of Germany on Denmark,[68] France on Belgium,[69] various foreign influences on French labour law,[70] the revolution wrought by the German-trained Otto Kahn-Freund on British labour law,[71] and that of the Italian Workers' Statute of 1970 on Spanish labour law.

It would seem likely, therefore, that EC labour law also is not wholly autonomous and independent. It is easy to point to many developments due to the influence of highly developed and technically sophisticated national labour law systems.[72] Not surprisingly, in formulating EC labour law, the law- and

---

[67] The EC influence is most obvious in the case of the later adherents to the EC, especially those emerging from dictatorships in the 1970s, Spain, Portugal and Greece. The process of incorporation of the *acquis communautaire*, including EC labour law, was required in the twelve new Member States joining the EU in 2004 and 2007. EC labour law was an established body of norms to which the new Member States were required to conform. This also occurred in countries of the European Economic Area (Norway, Iceland, Liechtenstein).

[68] O. Hasselbach, 'Denmark', in S. Edlund (ed.), *Labour Law Research in Twelve Countries*, Stockholm: Swedish Work Environment Fund, 1986, p. 12.

[69] R. Blanpain, 'Belgium' in Edlund, *Labour Law Research*, p. 139.

[70] G. Lyon-Caen, '*Les apports du droit comparé au droit du travail*': *Livre du centenaire de la société de législation comparée*, 1969, pp. 315–28.

[71] Lord Wedderburn, R. Lewis and J. Clark (eds.), *Labour Law and Industrial Relations: Building on Kahn-Freund*, Oxford: Clarendon Press, 1983.

[72] For an illustration of this in the regulation of part-time work, see Paul Davies and Mark Freedland, 'The Role of EU Employment Law and Policy in the Demarginalisation of Part-Time Work: A Study in the Interaction between EU Regulation and Member State Regulation', in

policy-making institutions of the EC had to come to terms with these systems and were influenced by them.

A number of examples from different periods illustrate the historical continuity of this influence. The insertion of Article 119 (now Article 141) into the Treaty of Rome was due to the insistence of France, concerned to extend its own legislation on equal treatment for men and women. The Commission's proposals beginning in the 1970s on workers' participation in company structures owe their inspiration to the German labour law on co-determination. The Thatcher government's declared policy of labour law deregulation in Britain during the 1980s led to the blockage of new EC social regulations during that decade. The Danish tradition of basing labour law primarily on collective agreements between the social partners (trade unions and employers' associations) rather than legislation, and Italian emphasis on the autonomy of the social partners, led to pressures allowing for EC labour law directives to be implemented through collective agreements. The experience of the constitutionalisation of social and economic rights in the new or revised constitutions of Spain, Portugal, Greece and the Netherlands contributed to the formulation of the Community Charter of Fundamental Social Rights of Workers of December 1989. Finally, the adhesion of Sweden in 1995, with its long experience of an active labour market policy in combating unemployment, was a decisive element in the adoption of a new Employment Title in the Treaty of Amsterdam in 1997.

A different rhythm of interaction is evident in the dynamics of national labour law systems in relation to EC labour law. It is illuminating to look at developments in national labour laws *during* the evolution of EC labour law. What were the main concerns of national labour laws of the Member States during the period in question, and did the focus on certain issues in collective and individual labour law in Western Europe during this period change over time?

For example, I have argued that certain issues were the focus of attention in the national labour laws of Member States during the 1970s and 1980s which can be distinguished from other issues predominating at earlier times or during this period.[73] Certain substantive issues absorbed the attention of national labour lawyers, in legislatures, academe and practice; in the sphere of individual employment law, regulation of new forms of work and protection against termination of employment. In collective labour law, the framework of attention shifted between regulation of the outcomes of collective bargaining, of the processes of reaching agreements, and of the organisations of workers and

Silvana Sciarra, Paul Davies and Mark Freedland (eds), *Employment Policy and the Regulation of Part-Time Work in the European Union: A Comparative Analysis*, Cambridge: Cambridge University Press, 2004, pp. 63–82. For influences the other way, in terms of the impact on Member States of EU regulation of fixed-term work, see K. Ahlberg, B. Bercusson, N. Bruun, H. Kountouros, C. Vigneau and L. Zappalà, *Transnational Labour Regulation: A Case Study of Temporary Agency Work*, Brussels: Peter Lang, 2008.

[73] B. Bercusson, 'Europaisches und nationales Arbeitsrecht – Die gegenwartige Situation', (1991) *Zeitschrift für auslandisches und internationales Arbeits- und Sozialrecht* 1–40.

employers themselves. Different periods can be identified by their concentration on different substantive issues.

Whatever the mutual influences of national labour laws and EC labour law, these dynamics within national labour law systems were not necessarily synchronised with developments in EC labour law. Looking at the same period, clear divergences are apparent between labour policies pursued at national level and at EC level. A number of contrasts may be presented between developments at national level and developments at EC level during the same period. Often what emerges is not a parallel development at all, but rather something completely different.

Three examples will illustrate this. First, the Treaty of Paris in 1951 provided the ECSC authorities with powers to enable them to restructure the coal and steel industries. This included measures to deal with the social consequences for workers of this process, including retraining, relocation and housing. The policies adopted are recognisable as a form of active labour market policy which was at the time only beginning to develop in Sweden, and was relatively unknown in Member States of the then future EC. The Treaty of Rome, much closer in spirit to the labour market policies of Member States during the 1950s, did not follow the precedent of the ECSC.

Secondly, the first fifteen years of the EC, 1957–72, are usually identified as its neo-liberal phase, with the emphasis on free movement of workers and labour mobility within the common market, to the exclusion of other social policy initiatives. This was the period of economic boom in Western Europe, the consolidation of the welfare state, of managed capitalism, workers' rights and industrial democracy initiatives. This was to have its impact on EC labour law only later in the 1970s, after the Paris Summit of 1972 and the Social Action Programme of 1974.

Finally, the social dialogue at European level as an instrument of EC social policy only emerged after 1985, when periods of neo-corporatist concertation were all but finished in Member States. Its late institutionalisation in the Protocol and Agreement on Social Policy of the Maastricht Treaty on European Union negotiated in 1991 stands out in contrast to national labour law tendencies.

In sum: the symbiosis of national labour law systems and EC labour law is of major importance in understanding both EC law and national labour laws. The nature of their relationship, however, is complex, with major dissonances between them at certain periods, and variation between Member States in terms of their interaction with EC labour law.

## Sociology of labour law

The sociological approach to EC labour law looks beyond the interaction between Member States and EC institutions. It looks also at the role of sub- and supranational actors, processes and outcomes as being of equal importance to those on the state level: a shift from the dominant focus on the Member State–Community axis to other levels where non-state actors are involved. This includes how interest groups *within* Member States influence national law and politics as they interact with Community law, and how the organisation of interests at *European* level (employers, trade unions, the poor, farmers, women's groups, and so on) interacts with both Community and national law and politics. In this approach, EC labour law focuses not only on Community or national institutions, but on EC law as influenced (e.g. as regards formulation) by other supranational actors and (e.g. as regards implementation) by sub-national actors.

One illustration of the implications of this approach is the question of the legitimacy of EC law. It follows that issues of legitimacy incorporate a wider range of polities, with institutional arrangements for representation of interests going beyond state and Community structures. The interaction of legitimacy arrangements within interest groups with those of Community law-making institutions produces a wider and more complex politics than is normally admitted by constitutional or supranational architects. Legitimacy as an issue implies this wider politicisation of the process of European law-making.[74]

The sociological approach is particularly significant for EC labour law in view of the potential significance of the European social dialogue, including as major protagonists the organisations of workers and employers at European level, in the formulation and implementation of EC social and labour law.

## Chronology and context: the dynamics of EU labour law

The meaning of 'labour law' derives from a specific context. In the case of the ILO norms, for example, the historical context following the First World War dictated that the norms promoted have as their objective the protection of workers and their organisations, and that workers' and employers' organisations take part in their formulation. The EC context is quite different.[75]

### Free movement of workers in a common market

The EC was founded to create a common market in services, goods, capital and labour. Freedom of movement for labour in a common market as a founding

---

[74] The importance of the sociological approach was evident when the European Court of First Instance addressed the question of the representativeness of the parties to the first social dialogue agreement incorporated into the Directive in Parental Leave. *Union Européenne de l'Artisanat et des Petites et Moyennes Entreprises (UEAPME)* v. *Council of the European Union*, Case T-135/96, [1998] ECR II-2335.

[75] Indeed, contrast between the EC and the ECSC demonstrates just how significant the context is in determining the meaning of 'labour law'. The active labour market policy of the ECSC, with labour representation in its major organs regulating the coal and steel industries with their powerful trade unions, was in stark contrast with the neo-liberal labour market policy which prevailed in the EC between 1957 and 1972.

objective is quite different from the objectives associated with national labour laws and also those of international labour standards. This primary association of EC labour law with free movement provides the initial context of labour and social law of the Community in its earlier stages. Certain qualities emerged from this experience that are worth exploring.

Free movement of labour in a neo-liberal labour market is often perceived as *the* social dimension of the EC. *Prima facie*, then, free movement of workers is an economic, not a social concept. But free movement creates many problems said to be of a purely social nature: transfer of pensions and social benefits, entitlements of migrant workers to unemployment, social security and other benefits, family issues of education, housing, and so on. So many social issues may come to be dealt with under the rubric of economic free movement of labour.

The balance between the economic and the social perceptions of free movement as an area of EC labour law is always in question. Legislative provisions and court decisions may be concerned with economic and not social consequences – that is, restraints on free movement and not the social consequences of these restraints. 'Anti-social' restrictions and penalties *are* tolerated unless they interfere with freedom of movement. The derogations allowed for public policy, security and health reasons emphasise how 'unsocial' this part of EC law is.

The EC law prohibition on discrimination illustrates this. The ban emerges primarily from the 'equality' principle prohibiting discrimination against non-nationals. If the same 'anti-social' treatment is meted out to nationals,[76] it is lawful. The curtailment of social vision by economic ideology is clear where the Court refuses to protect nationals against their own state where EC migrants would be protected.[77]

On the other hand, this overlap of EC economic and social policy in the area of free movement has been the source of major developments in EC social policy with potentially far-reaching implications. For example, the definition of 'worker' by the European Court under the Treaty provisions dealing with free movement developed independently of national legal definitions.[78] Albeit sharing certain core elements, it has asserted its claim to override national legal definitions.[79] This has important implications for national labour laws, and not only in the regulation of free movement.[80]

---

[76] For example, the case of identity cards in *Commission* v. *Belgium*, Case 321/87, [1989] ECR 997.

[77] So-called 'reverse discrimination'; see *R.* v. *Saunders*, Case 175/78, [1979] ECR 1129. Craig and de Burca comment that this 'has given rise to some particularly invidious results in the context of the rights of workers and their families'. *EU Law*, p. 671.

[78] *Hoekstra (née Unger)* v. *Bestuur der Bedrijfsvereniging voor Detailhandel en Ambachten*, Case 75/63, [1964] ECR 177.

[79] *Levin* v. *Staatssecretaris van Justitie*, Case 53/81, [1981] ECR 1035. The Court refused to adopt this approach in other areas of EC labour law; *Mikkelsen*, Case 105/84, [1986] 1 CMLR 310. But see now as regards equal pay comparators, *Allonby* v. *Accrington & Rossendale College*, Case C-256/01, [2004] IRLR 224.

[80] For a critical view, see the discussion in A. Supiot, *Critique du Droit du Travail*, Paris: Presses Universitaires de France, 1994, preliminary chapter, 'Entre contrat et statut: une vue européenne de la relation de travail', at pp. 22–7.

## From free movement to labour and social law and policy

How did EC labour and social law develop beyond the confines of free movement of workers? This is a fundamental issue of much more than historical
interest. It concerns an explanation of the dynamics of EC social policy development. What factors operate to develop, either progressively through new initiatives, or regressively through repeal of previous initiatives, the social dimension
of the EC? There are at least two approaches to explaining the substance and
development of EC labour law and social policy.

The first takes as its starting point the Treaties and other legal measures and
EC institutions. The law contained in these instruments is the substantive basis
for social policy; its development is a function of the dynamic operation of the
EC institutions. But the law operates to limit the potential creativity of the EC
institutions within the confines of the competences allowed for by the Treaties.

One example of this approach arises from the provisions of Article 51 of the
EU Charter of Fundamental Rights adopted by the European Council at Nice in
December 2000. This purports to limit the scope of application of the Charter:[81]

1. The provisions of this Charter are addressed to the institutions and bodies of
   the Union with due regard for the principle of subsidiarity and to the
   Member States only when they are implementing Union law. They shall
   therefore respect the rights, observe the principles and promote the application thereof in accordance with their respective powers.
2. This Charter does not establish any new power or task for the Community or
   the Union, or modify powers or tasks defined by the Treaties.

The intent of those who promoted this provision was, as evident in the second
paragraph of Article 51, to preclude any expansion of the competences of the
EU beyond what already exists in the Treaties. But even the legalistic approach
does not exclude social policy development, provided it falls within the legal
prospect of the Treaty. This is still much room for creativity. Taking up the
example of Article 51 of the EU Charter, the precise scope of the powers and
tasks of the Community or the Union is much debated, and has been the subject
of disputes before, and decisions of, the European Court of Justice. It may be

---

[81] This appeared as Article II-111 of the Treaty Establishing a Constitution for Europe, where it was
amended to read (amendments in italics): '1. The provisions of this Charter are addressed to the
[*institutions, bodies, offices and agencies*] of the Union with due regard for the principle of
subsidiarity and to the Member States only when they are implementing Union law. They shall
therefore respect the rights, observe the principles and promote the application thereof in
accordance with their respective powers *and respecting the limits of the powers of the Union as
conferred on it in the other Parts of the Constitution.* 2. This Charter does not *extend the field of
application of Union law beyond the powers of the Union or* establish any new power or task for …
the Union, or modify powers and tasks defined *in the other Parts of the Constitution*'. Treaty
Establishing a Constitution for Europe adopted by the Member States in the Intergovernmental
Conference meeting in Brussels, 17–18 June 2004, OJ C310/1 of 16 December 2004. This version
(with minor changes) was adopted by the Lisbon Treaty, which proposes to make the Charter
legally binding.

that, despite the second paragraph, the Charter provides scope for the Court to interpret the powers and tasks of the Community, where these are unclear, in light of the objective of protection of the rights prescribed by the Charter.

Further, the legalistic approach has not precluded unilateral initiatives by EC institutions, again within the constraints of EC law. Examples would be the development by interpretations of the Court of Justice of principles such as that of non-discrimination, or the initiative of the Commission in the form of the European social dialogue launched by its President, Jacques Delors, in 1985.

This approach, which focuses on internal dynamics within the EC – its law and institutions – to explain social policy development may be contrasted with a second approach which incorporates and emphasises a dynamic between EC law and institutions and the external environment, comprising also non-EC law and non-Member State actors.

A major force in the development of EC labour and social law and policy is the interaction of Member States, both individually and collectively, with EC institutions. This is not simply to look to the role of the Council of Ministers, as an EC institution, and its activities in the EC law and policy-making process. It is a political perspective which looks to the policies of individual Member States, or some of them, and regards their pressures upon EC institutions, including the Council of Ministers, but also, and, in particular, the Commission and even other EC institutions, as a major determinant of EC social law and policy. These pressures as a factor in the development of EC labour law may be illustrated by the cases mentioned earlier of influences of national labour law on EC labour law.

Again, the example of Article 51 of the EU Charter may be invoked to illustrate the limits of a legalistic approach restricting the application of the Charter. The Member States are bound 'only when they are implementing Union law'. The situation may be anticipated of one of the fundamental rights enunciated in the Charter being blatantly violated by a Member State, which asserts that its action has nothing to do with implementing Union law. The EU's human rights reputation would not benefit from the exposure allowed by this provision. Such a situation may stimulate an individual or organisation to challenge the Member State's assertion that it is not implementing Union law. If such a challenge was to reach the European Court, the Court might prefer an expansive interpretation of the scope of Union law to condoning a blatant violation of the Charter.[82]

---

[82] Referring to the right to take collective action, including strike action, in Article 28 of the EU Charter, Claire Kilpatrick observes: 'The horizontal provisions of the EU Charter unequivocally close this off as a potential legal avenue (Article 51(1) EUCFR), stating that the Charter applies to the Member States "only when they are implementing Union law". Even if lawyers are inventive in constructing links with EU law to satisfy this criterion, the ECJ will be understandably reluctant to ignore the limits indicated by this provision. However, this does not mean that the EU Charter may not provide a useful source for groups to press for legal change within individual Member States'. Book Review of T. Hervey and J. Kenner (eds.), *Economic and Social Rights under the EU Charter of Fundamental Rights: A Legal Perspective*, (2004) 33 *Industrial Law Journal* 291 at pp. 296–7.

The difference between the two approaches lies in whether the emphasis is put on law or on politics as an explanation for the development of EC labour law and social policy. It is a question of emphasis because those who take the legalistic approach do not exclude political pressures, and those who emphasise politics do not exclude legal constraints and possibilities. The question is whether one starts with a view of the law as setting the limits to EC labour law and social policy, or whether one starts with the view that the political will and ability of the actors involved determines its development. As put by a former Commissioner for Social Affairs, commenting on the adoption of the pathbreaking Social Action Programme of 1974:[83]

> [it] reflected a political judgment of what was thought to be both desirable and possible, rather than a juridical judgment of what were thought to be the social policy implications of the Rome Treaty.

## An analytical framework for European labour law in context

### The first edition of *European Labour Law*

The structure adopted for the first edition of this book[84] emphasised three specific qualities of *European* labour law.

The first is the *variety of legal strategies* which have been utilised in the formulation and enforcement of EC labour law – a consequence of its search for an appropriate framework of instruments and measures in the changing political context of the general development of EC law.

The second is that *certain substantive areas* of EC law have had a significant impact on the labour law of the Member States. Detailed exposition of both its substance and the context of its implementation in different national labour law systems reveals a body of labour law of a distinctly *European* character.

The third derives from the emergence of *two structural pillars*: first, a typology of individual employment relationships regulated by European labour law and, secondly, the role of social dialogue and collective agreements as definitive features in the European regulation of labour.[85]

These were called structural pillars because they constitute the poles of attraction around which the future European labour law would crystallise. Formulation of this law involved techniques increasingly linked to collective bargaining and social dialogue. Substantive content reflected the exigencies of protection of a fragmented workforce requiring a regulatory framework appropriate to its particular circumstances.

---

[83] M. Shanks, *European Social Policy, Today and Tomorrow*, Amsterdam: Elsevier, 1977, p. 13.

[84] B. Bercusson, *European Labour Law*, London: Butterworths, Law-in-Context Series, 1996.

[85] Tendencies mooted in B. Bercusson, 'Maastricht: A Fundamental Change in European Labour Law', (1992) 23 *Industrial Relations Journal* 177–90.

In sum, the combination of a variety of legal strategies, areas of significant substantive regulation, and two structural pillars constituted the first edition's proposed structure of European labour law.

## The second edition

The first edition of this book ended its first chapter by posing a challenge for European labour law: 'to find a structure which reconciles general collective regulation with diversified categories of individual employment'.[86] The problem was how to link collective rule-making with individual protection. The first edition also ended its last chapter with the call for 'the strategic integration of the [1989 Community] Charter [of the Fundamental Social Rights of Workers] and the [Protocol and] Agreement [on Social Policy of the Maastricht Treaty] into a social constitution for the European Union'.[87]

These remain central features. The hopes for the 1989 Community Charter in the 1996 Intergovernmental Conference were not fulfilled. But the prospects are brighter for the EU Charter of Fundamental Rights adopted at Nice in December 2000. The Convention on the Future of Europe recommended its incorporation into the new Constitutional Treaty, the proposed Lisbon Treaty provides for it to have legally binding effect and the European Court of Justice has invoked it as reflecting fundamental rights protected as a general principle of EU law.[88] The EU Charter is the foundation for a constitutional perspective on European labour law.[89]

The contention that European labour law is at the heart of the EU social constitution magnifies the gulf which exists between national labour laws and EU labour law. Not only is the latter supreme, but it partakes of a constitutional quality both at EU level and at national level. This is less shocking to Member States where constitutions overlap with labour laws on, for example, freedom of association or sex equality. It is more of a shock to those Member States where labour law lacks any constitutional dimension, as in the UK.

A structure adapted to this emerging perspective on European labour law as the EU's 'social constitution' comprises two main elements: an institutional architecture and a substantive content. This second edition of *European Labour Law* retains the three specific qualities of European labour law identified in the first edition, but adapts them to this new perspective.

---

[86] Bercusson, *European Labour Law*, p. 26. See the discussion in U. Mückenberger and S. Deakin, 'From Deregulation to a European Floor of Rights: Labour Law, Flexibilisation and the European Single Market', (1989) 3 *Zeitschrift für ausländisches und internationales Arbeits- und Sozialrecht* 153.

[87] Bercusson, *European Labour Law*, p. 608.     [88] See below, Chapter 7.

[89] This was already prefigured in the first edition's Chapters 33–39; e.g. Chapter 34: 'The Constitutional Basis for Autonomous Development of European Labour Law'; and Part X (Chapters 37 and 38): 'Fundamental Social Rights and Future Strategy'.

**Section I**, *Labour law and Europe*, provides the *background* to this constitutional perspective.

**Part I**, *European labour law*, comprises three chapters. Chapter 1, this chapter, elaborates and explains the *analytical framework* adopted for the second edition of this book. It analyses and illustrates certain features which characterise European labour law as a form of *transnational labour regulation* and identifies the *qualities which distinguish European, national and international labour law*. Chapter 2 examines the particular relationship of European labour law to one EU Member State, *the UK*. Chapter 3 explores the different analytical frameworks which emerge from the ever-expanding *literature on European labour law*.

**Part II**, *History and strategies of European labour law*, examines the first specific quality of European labour law: the variety of legal strategies utilised in the formulation of EC labour law. Four chapters provide an account of the historical development of EC labour law through an analysis of the different legal strategies adopted over the past half century. The *early strategies* adopted by EC labour law, described in detail in three chapters of the first edition,[90] are condensed into Chapter 4 in order to make space for the more recent strategic innovations of the *European social dialogue* (Chapter 5), the *European Employment Strategy* (Chapter 6), the *EU Charter of Fundamental Rights* and the preparation of the *Treaty Establishing a Constitution for Europe*, now substantially embodied in the proposed Treaty of Lisbon (Chapter 7).

**Section II**, *The structure of European labour law*, elaborates the constitutional perspective on European labour law which characterises the analytical framework of the second edition of this book. This constitutional perspective is based on an institutional architecture of the European social model, expressed through the structure's focus on three elements: (i) substantive fundamental principles and rights, (ii) their enforcement through a variety of mechanisms and (iii) an overarching collective framework exemplified by the European social dialogue.

**Part III**, *Labour law and the European social model*, describes the specific form and content of labour law's contribution to the European social model (ESM) and draws on the other two specific qualities identified in the first edition: a certain significant substantive content and structural pillars of collective labour law and individual employment law.

Chapter 8 outlines the foundation of the *institutional architecture of the European social model*: fundamental rights, the role of the social partners in the EU social dialogue (at the macro-level of transnational coordination of

---

[90] 1st edn, Chapter 3: 'Two contrasting strategies: the ECSC (European Coal and Steel Community) and the EEC' (pp. 43–8), Chapter 4: 'Harmonisation strategy: the Social Action Programme 1974' (pp. 49–64), and Chapter 5: 'Strategies to outflank the UK veto: financial instruments and qualified majority voting procedures' (pp. 65–71).

collective bargaining and at the micro-level of the enterprise) and the open method of coordination.

Chapters 9 and 10 develop the first element of the structure, the *substantive content* of labour law's contribution to the European social model in the form of fundamental principles and rights. European *collective* labour law is distinguished from European *individual* employment law. Each is described in terms of fundamental *principles* constituting a collective regulatory framework, and fundamental substantive *rights* underpinning the regulatory framework. Chapter 9 outlines fundamental *principles* of European *collective* labour law, including collectively bargained labour standards, workers' collective representation and workers' participation and analyses the fundamental *collective rights* of European labour as reflected in the EU Charter of Fundamental Rights. Chapter 10 examines the collective *principles* which shape European *individual* employment law as regards equal treatment, workers' participation in the enterprise, health and safety, free movement and new forms of work and illustrates the fundamental *rights* of *individual* employees reflected in the EU Charter. The *role of the European Court of Justice* in relation to these fundamental principles and rights in examined in Chapter 11.

Section II's account of the structure of European labour law continues with the second element of the structure: **Part IV** on *Enforcement of European labour law*. This comprises an analysis of *general principles of enforcement* of European labour law (Chapter 12), followed by accounts of its *administrative enforcement* (Chapter 13), the *role of the social partners* in implementation and enforcement (Chapter 14), *judicial enforcement through individual claims* (Chapter 15) and the potential of *collective claims* (Chapter 16).

The third element constituting the structure of European labour law is developed in **Part V** on *The European social dialogue*. Three chapters analyse the *experience to date* of the European social dialogue (Chapter 17), its *democratic legitimacy*, both by way of *external review* and its *internal operation* (Chapter 18), and the threats to it by EU institutions and its future prospects (Chapter 19).

**Section III**, on *The futures of European labour law*, explores options currently before the EU. **Part VI** describes the different agendas and different visions of European labour law respectively of, first, the legislative institutions, the European Commission, the Member States in the Council and the European Parliament, and, secondly, of the European Court of Justice. Each agenda has a specific vision of the future of European labour law.

Chapter 20 explores the future as foreseen in the present European Commission's neo-liberal outlook manifest in its Green Paper on 'Modernising Labour Law to Meet the Challenges of the 21st Century'.[91]

---

[91] European Commission Green Paper, 'Modernising Labour Law to Meet the Challenges of the 21st Century'. COM(2006) 798 final, Brussels, 22 November 2006.

Chapter 22 analyses the prospects for European labour law in the European Court of Justice. The apocalyptic decisions of the *grande chambre* of the European Court of Justice in *Viking* and *Laval* in December 2007 appear to signal a decisive choice for the future of European labour law, one which harks back to the nineteenth-century clash in many EU Member States between the economic freedoms of employers and fundamental rights to collective action by trade unions. The Court's vision is subjected to a critical analysis and the chapter concludes with an alternative vision: the *ordre communautaire social*. Finally, Chapter 21 recounts the painful quest of the EU institutions and the Member States for a Constitutional Treaty, ultimately rejected by referenda in France and the Netherlands in 2005. The quasi-constitutional residue of the Lisbon Treaty of December 2007 includes the EU Charter of Fundamental Rights, but, despite commitments to social progress and social justice,[92] leaves open the choice of futures for European labour law.

## European labour law and Social Europe

European labour law no longer makes only the exceptional appearance in texts on national labour law. Time was it appeared only occasionally in textbooks on labour law, where it was a vehicle for traditional comparative law insights[93] or the manifestation of specific European Community requirements on domestic legal development.[94] British labour law is traditionally focused on the domestic context. The orthodox analysis is that of a fundamentally voluntarist-abstentionist tradition reflecting domestic historical origins, followed by corporatist legal interventions from the mid-1960s to the late 1970s, and decollectivisation and deregulation beginning with the election of the Conservative government in 1979.[95]

The election of a new Labour government in 1997 marked a watershed, at least in principle. Changes introduced in British labour law were driven, in part,

---

[92] The Lisbon Treaty proposes to replace the present Article 2 of the Treaty on European Union with a new Article 2, including in sub-paragraph 3 (italics added): 'The Union shall establish an internal market. It shall work for the sustainable development of Europe based on balanced economic growth and price stability, a highly competitive social market economy, *aiming at full employment and social progress*, and a high level of protection and improvement of the quality of the environment. It shall promote scientific and technological advance. It shall combat social exclusion and discrimination, and shall *promote social justice* and protection, equality between women and men, solidarity between generations and protection of the rights of the child'.

[93] The most dedicated comparativist in this sense was Otto Kahn-Freund in his *Labour and the Law*, 1972, 3rd edn, edited and with an introduction by P. L. Davies and M. R. Freedland, London: Stevens, 1983.

[94] It is particularly ironic that, for example, British labour law is perceived as European only in these ways. For the dominant conceptualisation of British labour law is the intellectual product of Otto Kahn-Freund, a labour lawyer who analysed the British system using the tools of the German labour law tradition founded by Sinzheimer – an intellectual legacy with a specific set of normative assumptions. See R. Lewis, 'Kahn-Freund and Labour Law: An Outline Critique', (1979) 8 *Industrial Law Journal* 202.

[95] Wedderburn, Lewis and Clark (eds.), *Labour Law and Industrial Relations*.

by a domestic agenda, a minimum wage and statutory trade union recognition, however modest their effects in practice. More important, however, the new UK government reversed the previous Conservative government's policy towards European labour law by abandoning the UK's 'opt-out' under the Protocol on Social Policy of the Maastricht Treaty.[96] The UK thereby rejoined the mainstream of European labour law.[97]

It is not only in Britain, however, that ever more frequently European legal developments are intruding upon national perspectives on labour law.[98] The labour law of the Member States of the EU, including the UK, is increasingly influenced by EC labour law. The dynamic of national labour laws is no longer determined solely or even mainly by domestic developments. It is not merely that national labour laws are required to incorporate EC norms. EC norms are themselves the reflection of the national labour laws of Member States. In this indirect way, national labour laws are influential in the development of each other and UK labour law too is becoming more European. Particularly since the adoption of the Maastricht Treaty and its Social Policy Protocol and Agreement (now in the Social Chapter of the EC Treaty), EC labour law reflects ever more the experience of the labour laws of the EU Member States.[99]

The labour law of the UK, and of other Member States, is, and will become, more truly European than appears from the formal imprint of EC labour law. It is European rather as reflecting the cumulative experience of national labour laws, filtered through the prism of the EC institutions and refined in the crucible of the developing European polity. The tendency towards convergence of UK labour law with the labour laws of other Member States of the EC is driven in the main by the institutional pressures of EC membership, and, to a lesser extent, is the consequence of the workings of an international economy and, though less significant, a single European labour market. The dynamic of this convergence process is complex and its results are far from complete. But European labour lawyers must come to terms with this new dynamic of labour law evolution and its results.

European labour law as a central element of the European social model regulates that very large part of almost everybody's life: working. Collective organisations of workers and employers, the 'social partners', are central to the

---

[96] This entailed adopting a number of EC measures which had been enacted during the period of the opt-out, including directives on European works councils, parental leave and part-time work.

[97] Though sadly, repeating history as farce, the new Labour government too sought refuge in an opt-out in the Lisbon Treaty from the EU Charter of Fundamental Rights, an attempt likely doomed to fail.

[98] In the UK, this was recognised in particular by Bob Hepple; see B.A. Hepple, 'The Crisis in EEC Labour Law', (1987) 16 *Industrial Law Journal* 129, B.A. Hepple and A. Byre, 'EEC Labour Law in the United Kingdom – A New Approach', (1989) 18 *Industrial Law Journal* 129, and B.A. Hepple, 'Social Rights in the European Economic Community: A British Perspective' (1990) 11 *Comparative Labor Law and Policy Journal* 425.

[99] Bercusson, 'Maastricht'. Also B. Bercusson, 'The Dynamic of European Labour Law after Maastricht', (1994) 23 *Industrial Law Journal* 1.

specific European social model of employment and industrial relations. This
was captured in Title VI of Part I of the now defunct Constitutional Treaty:
'The Democratic Life of the Union'. Article I-48 confirmed that the Union
recognises and promotes the social partners and autonomous social dialogue.
The presence and role of organisations of employers and trade unions, and the
institutional forms of their interaction at different levels, distinguish the
European democratic model in social life in general, and working life in
particular.

European labour law remains an arena of struggle against those with the
economic and political power to exploit workers and repress trade unions.
Proclamation of the fundamental rights of labour in the EU Charter and
its promotion by the Treaty of Lisbon does not change this. Protection of the
fundamental rights of workers will continue to have to be fought for in court
litigation, in legislative battles and in the struggles of the labour movement.

As with the first, the second edition of this book is intended as a contribution
to understanding how European labour law, through the developing labour
law of the European Union, may contribute to the progressive evolution of a
European social model: Social Europe.

# Chapter 2

# EU labour law and the UK

## Introduction: the 'British problem'

The United Kingdom occupies a singular position in EU labour law: over the last twenty-eight of its thirty-five years (80 per cent) as a Member State of the EU, British governments have provided the most consistent and effective opposition to the extension of rights for workers and trade unions in EU law. The Conservative government elected in May 1979, first under the leadership of Margaret Thatcher and then John Major, pursued a specific social and labour policy with remarkable consistency and determination throughout that period. The New Labour government elected in May 1997 was committed to a vision of labour law which, in the words of its leader, Tony Blair, 'would leave British law the most restrictive on trade unions in the western world'.[1]

The consequences of this continuous opposition to labour regulation for the UK's relationship to European labour law – both the impact of EC law on domestic labour law, and also the impact of the social and labour policies of UK governments on the development of EC labour law – have been unmistakable. The mutual impact can be described in terms of a reversal of policy flow: up to 1979, UK domestic labour law policy was influenced in important ways by EC labour law; since 1979, it is EU labour and social policy which has been heavily influenced by domestic UK social and labour policies.

## The 1970s

The accession to the EC of the UK in 1973 coincided with the beginning of a period of legislative activity in the EC. The sex equality Directives (equal pay,[2]

---

[1] Article by Tony Blair in *The Times*, 31 March 1997. That little has changed was evidenced by the bitter remark of a delegate to the Convention on the Future of Europe in 2003/2004 that the creation of a constitution for Europe was a more difficult task than that facing the authors of the Constitution of the United States more than 200 years earlier because then the Americans had already solved their 'British problem'!

[2] Directive 75/117/EEC of 10 February 1975, OJ L45/19 of 19 February 1975.

equal treatment,[3] social security[4]) and the Directives on collective dismissals,[5] acquired rights upon transfers of undertakings[6] and protection of workers in insolvency[7] were mostly approved by the Council of Ministers during the period of the Labour governments of 1974–9. Their impact on domestic labour and social law has been profound.

## The 1980s

In the period of Conservative government from 1979–97, and mainly during the 1980s, the principal EC legislative activity on labour policy was confined to the sphere of health and safety at work. Other EC legislative activity in the labour field was largely halted in the face of the UK government's rejection of almost all proposals from the Commission, and their consequent failure to achieve the necessary unanimous approval in the Council of Ministers.

This UK veto was one of the reasons which led Jacques Delors, the newly elected President of the Commission, to initiate the policy in 1985 of stimulating the European social dialogue between trade unions and employers' organisations at EU level as an alternative path to a social dimension for the EC. The development of the social dialogue, its gradual emergence as a pillar of EC social policy, formalised in the Maastricht Protocol and Agreement of 1991, was the unintended and unforeseen consequence of UK domestic policy. It is ironic that the Conservative government's policy of reducing the influence of trade unions and decollectivising industrial relations domestically should have been a prime cause of the emergence of the trade unions and of collective bargaining as a major instrument of social and labour policy at European level.

The 1980s witnessed a dramatic transformation of the attitudes, contributions and reactions of the national actors in the UK to European social integration. The reactions and adaptations of domestic labour law to the unified European market reflected the tension between, on the one side, a UK government which promoted unrestrained competition on labour standards and sought to restrict collective determination of such standards by the social partners, and, on the other side, other Member State governments which insisted on some supranational minima below which labour standards should not descend. This tension was reflected in the attitudes and behaviour of the social partners in the UK, as well as those of the various Member States and at EC level. As the Conservative government manifested its hostility to the social

---

[3] Directive 76/207/EEC of 9 February 1976, OJ L39/40 of 14 February 1976.
[4] Directive 79/7/EEC of 19 December 1978, OJ L6/24 of 10 January 1979; Directive 86/378/EEC of 24 July 1986, OJ L225/40 of 12 August 1986; Directive 86/613/EEC of 11 December 1986, OJ L359/56 of 19 December 1986.
[5] Directive 75/129, OJ L48/29 of 22 February 1975.
[6] Directive 77/187, OJ L61/26 of 5 March 1977.    [7] Directive 80/987, OJ L283/23.

dimension of the integration process, trade unions reversed their previous hostility. A pivotal moment in the change in trade union attitudes to European labour law was the warm reception given to the address by Jacques Delors, President of the European Commission, to the annual Trades Union Congress in September 1988.

The continuing tension was manifest in the Community Charter of Fundamental Social Rights of Workers of December 1989, signed by all the Member States with the exception of the UK. The contradiction between Member State policies was formally incorporated into EC law by the Maastricht Protocol and Agreement on Social Policy. The UK government opted out of this 'Social Chapter' of the Treaty on European Union, but the UK social partners remained within the organisations of labour and management at EC level, the European Trade Union Confederation (ETUC) and the European private employers' confederation (UNICE), which were empowered under the Maastricht Agreement to develop the labour and social law and policy of the European Union. The UK government's policy of the 1980s succeeded, despite itself, in projecting at European level the model of collective bargaining autonomy which was the distinguishing characteristic of UK labour law up to the 1980s.

### The 1990s

At the same time, the UK courts became more familiar with the techniques and potential of EC law. The dynamic tension between EC and UK labour law and policy was reflected in the decisions by the European Court of Justice[8] in the mid-1990s regarding failures by the UK to implement EC labour law directives, thereby reinforcing EU labour law measures of the 1970s (Directives on

---

[8] More generally, It has been observed: 'Looking at policy areas reveals interesting patterns, as the judicial discourse in some fields appear "dominated" by some governments. On social policy, for example, 50 governmental observations were British and 30 German (out of 161 observations).' Marie-Pierre F. Granger, 'When Governments Go to Luxembourg ...: The Influence of Governments on the Court of Justice', (2004) 29 *European Law Review* 3–31, at p. 15.

**Table 2.1** Observations submitted in the area of social policy

| | | | |
|---|---|---|---|
| Austria | 10 | Italy | 5 |
| Belgium | 14 | Luxembourg | 0 |
| Denmark | 0 | The Netherlands | 10 |
| Finland | 8 | Portugal | 3 |
| France | 16 | Spain | 5 |
| Germany | 30 | Sweden | 3 |
| Greece | 1 | United Kingdom | 50 |
| Ireland | 6 | Total | 161 |

Collective Dismissals and Transfers of Undertakings[9]) and of the few pieces of legislation which survived the UK veto in the aftermath of the new impetus generated by the Community Charter of Fundamental Social Rights of Workers of 1989 (notably, the Working Time Directive of 1993[10]).

These changes were reflected in the willingness of various national actors to allow for delegation upward to supranational bodies of competences and actions in the social field. Together with the momentum of the European social dialogue, generated by the UK's blockage of the institutional legislative process of the EC, progress in EC labour law might have appeared unstoppable. Indeed, one of the first acts of the newly elected Blair government of May 1997 was to fulfil its election manifesto commitment to withdraw the UK's Maastricht opt-out, which meant the acceptance of Directives (European works councils, parental leave, part-time work) adopted under it. By the Treaty of Amsterdam of June 1997, the UK rejoined the mainstream of EU labour law.

Consistently with Blair's vision of maintaining the existing strictures of British labour law, however, the UK's New Labour government found a different method of blocking new EU labour legislation, more sophisticated than the blunt Thatcher veto, but at least as effective, if not more so. Allying itself with centre-right governments in Spain (José Maria Aznar), Italy (Silvio Berlusconi) and Portugal (José Manuel Barroso), at the Lisbon Summit of 2000, the UK government successfully pushed for the adoption of a specific approach to labour and social policy. Following its domestic agenda of reducing the so-called 'burdens on business' of labour regulation, a new method of policy implementation was promoted at EU level: the 'open method of coordination', a 'soft law' mechanism replacing the traditional binding 'hard' labour law directives.

## 2000–

In the meantime, the UK government took the lead in mobilising other Member States in the Council of Ministers to block adoption of a number of proposed directives; among others, a framework directive on information and consultation of workers' representatives (after three years, the UK-led blocking minority disintegrated in 2002, but not before the UK extracted concessions considerably weakening the directive and delaying its application to the UK), a draft directive on protection of temporary agency workers (the UK has more temporary agency workers than any other Member State) and a proposal for revision of the working time directive (the UK's campaign to maintain its unique opt-out from the 48-hour maximum working week was reflected, it is said, in a diplomatic effort unrivalled since the Second World War!)

---

[9] *Commission of the European Communities* v. *United Kingdom*, Case C-382/92 and C-383/92, [1994] *ECR* 2435 and 2479.
[10] *United Kingdom* v. *Council*, Case C-84/4, [1996] ECR I-5755.

The UK's new 'deregulation' approach was confirmed when Blair vetoed other Member States' candidates for the Presidency of the European Commission following the departure of Romano Prodi, and promoted the compromise appointment of Barroso.[11] The Commission's Communication of 9 February 2005 on the Social Agenda for the period 2005–10 contains not one single proposal for *new* legislation in the labour law field.[12]

## The positive contribution of EU labour law to UK labour law

Many, if not most of the advances in UK employment protection law over the past thirty-five years since the UK joined the European Community (EC) in 1973 have been the result of EU legislation. Without European law, there would not be employment rights in the UK to:

- equal pay;
- equal treatment in employment;
- consultation over collective dismissals,
- protection in transfers of undertakings;
- protection against a two-tier workforce in privatisation;
- European works councils;
- paid annual leave and working time restrictions;
- parental leave;
- equal treatment for part-timers and workers on fixed-term contracts; or
- information and consultation of employees' representatives in enterprises with 50+ workers.

One UK source estimates that 40 per cent of UK employment law derives from EU requirements.[13]

Although looking back is sometimes painful, remembering opportunities missed, nonetheless, the catalogue of successes is such as to justify the claim that the glass is much more than half full. This is so particularly if one assesses the record of EC labour law against what has been achieved domestically in the UK. While, compared to the level of trade union rights in other EU Member States, the achievements of the EC may seem modest, it is probably British trade unions which have been the greatest beneficiaries of European labour law. Some examples over the period from 1992 illustrate the record of advances in European labour law.

---

[11] The Barroso Commission has attempted little and achieved nothing as regards labour regulation. The last significant achievement was under the Prodi Commission, in March 2002 (Council Directive No. 2002/14 establishing a framework for informing and consulting employees in the European Community. OJ 2002 L80/29). See Chapter 20.

[12] Communication from the Commission on the Social Agenda, COM(2005) 33 final, Brussels, 9 February 2005.

[13] Better Regulation Taskforce, *Employment Regulation: Striking a Balance*, May 2002, cited in C. Kilpatrick, 'Has New Labour Reconfigured Employment Legislation?', (2003) 32 *Industrial Law Journal* 135 at p. 141.

## 1992: European social dialogue

In the Social Policy Protocol of the Maastricht Treaty on European Union (TEU), the EU Member States acknowledged the central role of European trade unions (ETUC) and employers' organisations (UNICE (now BusinessEurope) and CEEP) in formulating and implementing EC labour law.[14] The position achieved by trade unions in Western European social democracies after the Second World War has come under threat from neo-liberals since the later decades of the twentieth century. European labour law has so far provided one safeguard guaranteeing their position.

## 1993: Working time regulation

The following year, 1993, saw the adoption of Council Directive 93/104/EC of 23 November 1993 concerning certain aspects of the organisation of working time.[15] The Conservative government's challenge to the legitimacy of this directive was rejected by the European Court in November 1996.[16] The Court broke new ground by declaring that regulation of working time was essential to protect health and safety.[17]

## 1994: European Works Councils

For many decades trade unions had tried to engage with the most powerful private economic actors in the global economy: multinational corporations, which were usually able to evade the economic and political pressures available to trade unions on a national basis. European labour law made a first step towards this objective in Council Directive 94/45/EC of 22 September 1994 on the establishment of a European Works Council or a procedure in Community-scale undertakings and Community-scale groups of undertakings for the purposes of informing and consulting employees.[18]

---

[14] The UK's Conservative government had 'opted-out' in 1992, but the change of government in 1997 allowed the UK to 'opt-in', and the Treaty of Amsterdam in 1997 amended the EC Treaty to incorporate this recognition of trade unions into the EC constitutional legal order.

[15] OJ L307/18 of 13 December 1993.

[16] *United Kingdom of Great Britain and Northern Ireland* v. *Council of the European Union*, Case C-84/94, [1996] ECR I-5755.

[17] The Directive led to the enactment in the UK of the Working Time Regulations 1998, amended in 1999. The then Conservative government had insisted on a ten-year opt-out from Article 6 of the Directive (the 48-hour maximum working week). This was exploited by the Blair government to evade the otherwise mandatory 48-hour maximum average working week.

[18] OJ L254/64 of 30 September 1994. This required multinational enterprises with establishments in two or more Member States to inform and consult representatives of their multinational workforce. Most of the estimated 2,000+ companies affected were based in EU Member States, but others were based in the USA, Japan and elsewhere. Some of these had recognised trade unions, but few had dealt with trade unions in all their establishments and almost none allowed for coordination among trade union representatives in their subsidiaries. Now all could be

### 1996: Posted workers

Council Directive 96/81/EC adopted on 24 September 1996 was concerned with the growing number of workers posted by undertakings to work temporarily in another Member State.[19] The concern was that foreign enterprises could undermine local labour standards by applying lower home country conditions in countries where standards were higher. The legal framework proposed by the Commission looked to the decision of the European Court of Justice in *Rush Portuguesa Lda* v. *Office national d'immigration, which authorised Member States to require posting enterprises to respect local legislation and collective agreements.*[20]

### 1995, 1997, 1999: European framework agreements

On 14 December 1995 the ETUC, UNICE and CEEP concluded the first European framework collective agreement, which, under the 'Social Chapter' of the EC Treaty, became Council Directive 96/34 on the Framework Agreement on Parental Leave.[21] This was followed by two other framework agreements, on part-time workers in 1997 and fixed-term work in 1999.[22]

### 2000: European Employment Strategy

The Lisbon European Council of 23–24 March 2000 laid down an 'overall strategy' which aimed at 'full employment … in Europe in an emerging new

---

required to deal with a body composed of employee representatives from their establishments in EU Member States. The potential is slowly emerging of regular meetings of the representatives of workers in global companies, provided with information about the companies' operations and required to be consulted about decisions affecting the workforce.

[19] Council Directive 96/81/EC [1996] OJ L18/1. Such arrangements are common in the construction industry, but also in transport, telecommunications, entertainment, repairs, maintenance and servicing. At the time, there were some 60,000 British and Irish building workers in Germany alone.

[20] Case 113/89, [1990] ECR 1417.     [21] OJ L145/4.

[22] Council Directive 97/81/EC of 15 December 1997 concerning the Framework Agreement on Part-Time Work concluded by UNICE, CEEP and the ETUC; OJ L14/9 of 20 January 1998; Council Directive 1999/70/EC of 28 June 1999 concerning the Framework Agreement on Fixed-Term Work concluded by ETUC, UNICE and CEEP (OJ L175/43 of 10 July 1999). The Framework Agreements on Fixed-Term Work and Part-Time Work confront the 'new forms of employment' which are part of employers' strategies on flexibility. The strategic response at EU level in the case of part-time work was affected by the long-established policy on sex equality, as most part-time workers are women, as well as EU policies on reconciliation of work and family life, of which the first Framework Agreement on Parental Leave was another manifestation. The combination of these policies led not to a rejection of flexibility in the form of part-time work, but to its regulation, in an effort to achieve the objectives of these and other policies. In the case of the Framework Agreement on Fixed-Term Work, the labour market strategy of flexibility was directly confronted by a counter-strategy of employment security. The Fixed-Term Work Agreement starts from the premise that the worker's quality of life is enhanced by security of employment.

society which is more adapted to the personal choices of women and men'. The objectives of the European Employment Strategy (EES) are being implemented through the institutional framework of the 'open method of coordination' in the Employment Title of the EC Treaty, introduced in 1997. This new instrument of regulating the labour market strategies of Member States offers opportunities for trade union influence.

### 2000: Fundamental social rights

An EU Charter of Fundamental Rights was adopted at the European Council at Nice in December 2000. The Charter breaks new ground by including a long list of social and economic rights, including fundamental trade union rights.[23]

### 2002: Information and consultation

Representative structures established by legislation or by generally applicable collective agreements in many EU Member States provide for bodies (e.g. 'works councils' or 'enterprise committees') to receive information and be engaged in consultation, or even codetermination, on a range of matters relating to the company's economic position having implications for the workforce, as well as on decisions affecting the day-to-day working life of employees. A Framework Directive on Information and Consultation, adopted on 18 February 2002, put the subject of works councils on the British labour law agenda at a time when only in Ireland and the UK was such a general and permanent system lacking.[24]

## The negative side: UK obstruction of EU labour law

During the long period of Conservative government between 1979 and 1997, despite the persistent and active opposition of the United Kingdom, the European Community's social agenda was transformed. A body of important legislation including directives on health and safety, working time and European works councils was enacted. The adoption of the 'social chapter' and the emergence of the EU-level social dialogue introduced EC law-making through collective bargaining. The election of a Labour government in May 1997 enabled the United Kingdom once again to join the mainstream of EU integration on issues of social policy.

---

[23] See Chapters 7 and 11.
[24] Directive 2002/14/EC of the European Parliament and of the Council of 11 March 2002 establishing a general framework for informing and consulting employees in the European Community. OJ L80/29 of 23 March 2002.

But more was expected after 1997. The Commission and the Member States, most of which were then also under Social Democratic governments, anticipated that the United Kingdom would, at least, subscribe to a dynamic social agenda long delayed by the Conservative government's obstruction, and, at best, provide leadership in formulating and advancing the EC's social agenda.

It transpired, however, that the New Labour government's conception of a European social agenda was as opposed to labour regulation as its predecessor. The dramatic economic transformation resulting from European economic and monetary union did not bring any recognition on the part of the United Kingdom of a need for intervention to secure the rights of workers or the industrial balance of power between trade unions and management in a transnational market. On the contrary, observers of the process of social policy formation in Brussels were dismayed at the continuity in the United Kingdom's agenda on EC labour legislation.

The 'European agenda' of the New Labour government may be illustrated by comparing it to that government's first flagship labour legislation: the Employment Relations Act 1999 (ERA). The ERA dealt with issues, such as family-friendly policies, which were obviously influenced by the EC agenda of social and labour legislation. Other parts of the ERA, on trade union recognition and industrial action, are perceived as part of a purely domestic United Kingdom agenda. However, they are closely related to EU concerns, including a number of initiatives on the European agenda concerned with collective workers' representation.

Unfortunately for the European agenda on collective workers' representation, British governments (and the new Labour government is no exception) have played a major role in attempting to emasculate or block EU initiatives aimed at promoting collective worker representation. The European agenda of United Kingdom governments aims at defeating or reducing to the minimum EU legislation which supports a role for collective workers' representation in the enterprise, or in economic management. This has sometimes played into the hands of other Member State governments, similarly inclined but anxious not to offend their national trade union movements and social democratic electorates, and of the EU Commission, chastened by political reaction to tone down some of its more ambitious initiatives in this direction.

While understandable in the case of a Conservative government in the United Kingdom committed to a policy of deregulation and decollectivisation, a much harsher judgement awaits the new Labour government elected in 1997. After eighteen years of Conservative negative reaction to EU social and labour initiatives, it had the political opportunity and moral capacity to renounce the previous government's stance on the European social agenda. The new government could have taken a lead in Europe to establish, what is critical, an irrevocable foundation in EC law for collective worker representation. Instead, it chose to join, even stimulate, a small minority of Member States blocking the social and labour initiatives of others in this direction. By doing so, it not only abandoned leadership, it also stifled progress and, most important, left open the possibility for a future Conservative United Kingdom government to continue its anti-trade union agenda, free of any constraints imposed by the EC law which might have provided a bulwark against such reaction.

That is the significance of a European agenda. Not only does it establish standards for collective worker representation. Once established in EC law, it becomes very difficult for a single Member State to retreat from these standards. EU law provides a legal foundation safeguarding fundamental social and labour rights against the regressive political depredations of an anti-trade union government in a Member State. Non-regression is one of the foundations of the EU social model.

The more pessimistic part of what follows describes the campaign of attrition, led by the United Kingdom government, on the European agenda of collective labour rights. First, there was the Conservative government's resistance to the establishment of labour standards to prevent the threat of 'social dumping' in the case of workers posted from one Member State to another. Secondly, there is an account of the New Labour government's contribution to weakening the Commission's attempt to extend collective workers' rights to information and consultation in the enterprise.

## UK opposition to the Council Directive on Posting of Workers

One possible method of mitigating international competition over labour standards ('social dumping') is through the stipulation of common compulsory labour standards; e.g. in the form of collective agreements. The extent to which the UK government has been willing to acknowledge this labour law tradition of a number of Member States as a potential inspiration for EC labour law proposals on common labour standards is revealing of its views on international competition and its implications for labour standards. An example will illustrate the UK government's attitude.

The introduction of Portuguese workers into France by a Portuguese construction firm led to a complaint by the French authorities concerned about lower standards of wages and employment conditions and consequent 'social dumping'. The invocation of the principle of freedom to provide services, albeit through employees, brought the case before the European Court which declared:[25]

> in response to the concern expressed in this connection by the French government, that Community law does not preclude Member States from extending their legislation, or collective labour agreements entered into by both sides

---

[25] *Rush Portuguesa Lda* v. *Office national d'immigration*, Case 113/89, [1990] ECR 1417, at p. 1445, paragraph 18.

of industry, to any person who is employed, even temporarily, within their territory, no matter in which country the employer is established; nor does Community law prohibit Member States from enforcing those rules by appropriate means.

The principle of compulsory adherence to collective agreements by all employers was familiar to the French labour law tradition, and inspired the Court. It was adopted by the Commission in the proposal for a Council Directive on the posting of workers in the framework of the provision of services.[26] Article 3(1) of the proposed Directive provided that:

> Member States *shall see to it* that, whatever the law applicable to the employment relationship, the undertaking ... does not deprive the worker of the terms and conditions of employment which apply for work of the same character at the place where the work is carried out, provided that (a) they are laid down by laws, regulations and administrative provisions or by collective agreements ...

In this way, EC legislation would establish a mandatory level of labour standards in an attempt to preclude competition over working conditions between firms engaged in transnational economic activities. However, the UK government's position on this Directive was negative:[27]

> [it] believes that the Directive should only be adopted if it is necessary to deal with real problems at Community level and is workable in practice. At present, the Government sees little evidence that legal uncertainty or differences in legislation among Member States are significant obstacles to the posting of workers.

The Posting Directive 96/71/EC was nonetheless adopted. The concerns of the European Court as regards 'social dumping' and the relevance of collective agreements were reflected in a report by the Commission on implementation of the Directive in 2003:

> The question of the applicability of collective agreements is particularly important, since wages are chiefly determined by collective bargaining. Most Member States' legislations provide for the application or extension of universally applicable collective agreements to posted workers. Some Member States do not have universally applicable collective agreements. Consequently, the only rules that these States apply to posted workers are those contained in the law or in other legislative texts.

It was a reflection of the Barroso Commission's attitude to labour regulation that it proposed a directive for the liberalisation of services in the EC which ignored the fears of 'social dumping' which had led to the Posting Directive.[28]

---

[26] COM(91) 230 final, SYN 346, Brussels, 1 August 1991.

[27] *Industrial Relations Legal Information Bulletin* No. 444, March 1992, at p. 9.

[28] Proposal for a Directive on Services in the Internal Market, COM (2004) 2/3 final, adopted 13 January 2004.

The French and German governments expressed outright opposition to the proposal. The New Labour government of the UK came out in support.

### UK opposition to the Council Directive establishing a general framework for informing and consulting employees in the European Community

A Commission proposal in 1998[29] signalled the fundamental change in EU social policy due to the expansion of the social competences of the EU with the Maastricht Agreement on Social Policy, now in Article 137 of the EC Treaty. The EC's objective in this proposal was not merely harmonisation of national law, as with the Directives on Collective Dismissals 1975 and Acquired Rights 1977, which were based on Article 95 (ex 100) of the EC Treaty. Nor was it a special case of transnational enterprises, as with the Directive on European Works Councils 1994. Rather, the objective is 'to make the essential changes to the existing legal framework ... appropriate for the new European context'.[30] As such, the proposed directive was a major step on the road to a European social model.

The United Kingdom's New Labour government was the most actively hostile opponent to the proposal, not least because approval of the proposal could be achieved by a qualified majority vote, precluding a British veto. For a long period, the United Kingdom successfully achieved a blocking minority of Member States sufficient to prevent progress.

For example, the French Presidency of the Council of Ministers beginning in July 2000 made the proposal one of their priorities. Due to the efforts of the UK in the Social Affairs Council of 27–28 November 2000, the proposal was again blocked.[31] Moreover, by then the United Kingdom government's trench warfare had been successful in gutting much of what was innovative in the proposal. The draft approved by COREPER which came before the Social Affairs Council on 27–28 November 2000 indicates in the footnotes to each provision those Member States which have reservations, partial or fundamental.[32] The United Kingdom registers far more reservations than any other Member State, and, indeed, the vast majority of reservations.

For example, in the COREPER draft, Article 2, paragraph 1.c refers to workers' representatives. The United Kingdom registered a reservation, echoing the Conservative government's objections to the Working Time Directive, regarding the legal basis. The reservation argues that the reference to workers'

---

[29] COM/98/612 of 11 November 1998.     [30] *Ibid.*, Preamble, paragraphs 15–16.

[31] 'France in Retreat on EU Social Affairs Plans', *Financial Times*, 29 November 2000, p. 11.

[32] *Transmission d'un text du groupe des Questions sociales du 13 novembre 2000 au Comité des Représentants permanents, no. prop. C'ion 13099/98 SOC 428 – COM (1998) 612 final; Objet: Propositions de directive du Parlement européen et du Conseil établissant un cadre général relatif é l'information et la consultation des travailleurs dans la Communauté européenne. Accord politique.* Council Document 13038/00, SOC 410. CODEC 843 Brussels, 14 November 2000.

representatives may affect the legal basis as 'representation and collective defence of the interests of workers and employers' requires a different legal basis. The United Kingdom was referring to then Article 137(3) EC (now Article 137(1)(f)), which requires unanimity, whereas the proposal was based on then Article 137(2) (information and consultation) (now Article 137(1)(e)), which allows for majority voting. The United Kingdom's motivation for undermining the legal basis of qualified majority voting in favour of one requiring unanimity does not require explanation.

More substantively, the COREPER draft eliminated two of the most important and innovative provisions of the original proposal of the Commission.

### Consultation prior to decision-making

Article 1(1) of the Commission's draft stated that 'The purpose of this Directive is to establish a general framework for informing and consulting employees in undertakings within the European Community.' From this statement of the obligation of information and consultation, it was not clear whether the procedure was obligatory *before*, or only *after* the employer made the decision.

In Article 2(1)(e) of the Commission's proposed draft, there was a definition of 'consultation' as meaning 'the organisation of a dialogue and exchange of views between the employer and the employees' representatives'. It went on: 'including, in the case of decisions within the scope of the employer's management powers, an attempt to seek *prior* agreement on the decisions referred to in Article 4.1.c'.

In the COREPER draft of 14 November 2000, the substance of this definition of 'consultation' has been transferred to a new Article 3, paragraph 3ter. The crucial exception is that the word 'prior' is deleted. Attached is a footnote in which the United Kingdom registers a 'fundamental reservation' on the grounds that its content goes beyond consultation and raises a question as to the legal basis of the directive. It appears that only the United Kingdom government, and no other Member State, felt compelled to object to the principle that consultation should include an attempt by employers to seek the prior agreement of the workers affected. The nature of the United Kingdom government's objection is highlighted by contrast with the only other reservation in that footnote. The Commission expressed its reservation regarding the deletion of the word 'prior'.

### Sanctions for serious breach

In the Commission's draft directive, Article 7(3) required Member States to provide for a special sanction on employers for serious breaches of the obligations to inform and consult with respect to certain decisions referred to in Article 4(1)(c):

> likely to lead to substantial changes in work organisation or in contractual relations, including those covered by … [the Collective Dismissals and Acquired Rights Directives].

The sanction was that a decision by the employer in certain circumstances:

> shall have no legal effect on the employment contracts or employment relationships of the employees affected. The non production of legal effects will continue until such time as the employer has fulfilled his obligations.

This appeared to be similar to a 'status quo' clause in a collective agreement, which precludes unilateral action by the employer to change working conditions.[33]

The Commission's draft, Article 7(3)(a), defined a case of 'serious' breach as meaning (italics added):

> the total absence of information and/or consultation of the employees' representatives *prior* to a decision being taken.

It was not clear whether the seriousness related to the *total* failure, or its timing after the decision. Arguably, it was the former, which would mean that *any* lesser failure to inform or consult *prior* to the decision would qualify at least as a breach, if not a serious breach.

None of this was to survive the onslaught on the Commission's proposal. In the COREPER draft, this provision for sanctions in the case of serious breach is deleted. The Commission, supported by Luxembourg, expressed its opposition to the suppression of this paragraph, and Belgium proposed an alternative text. An unspecified majority of the other Member States noted their preference for the deletion of the paragraph. The United Kingdom's position is not noted, but may be surmised.[34]

The reduced content of the final directive is evidence that the United Kingdom government's negative role continued as far as the rights of workers and trade unions are concerned.

---

[33] The proposed directive required employers to 'work in a spirit of co-operation' (Article 1(2)). A court might hold that some kinds of unilateral action violated the spirit of cooperation required during the information and consultation process. In particular, this provision would have reinforced the sanctions available for breaches of the Collective Dismissals and Acquired Rights Directives, and would have required the amendment of the national legislation implementing these directives.

[34] Mark Hall comments on the sanctions envisaged in the Information and Consultation of Employees Regulations 2004 (SI 2004/3426) (ICE), introduced to implement Directive 2002/14, a penalty to be imposed on the employer, up to a maximum of £75,000: 'The effectiveness of the sanctions available in cases of non-compliance may be another aspect of the ICE Regulations that receive close scrutiny at EU level'. 'Assessing the Information and Consultation of Employees Regulations', (2005) 34 *Industrial Law Journal* 103 at p. 118. The *dénouement* to the French presidency provided another illustration. In a desperate attempt to demonstrate some social progress, the French belatedly scheduled an emergency Social Affairs Council at the end of December 2000, and placed the draft directive on the agenda, confident that the UK's blocking minority could be overcome. To their fury, the UK successfully invoked a rarely used procedural rule requiring 14 days' notice of any item placed on a Council agenda, thus ruling out any discussion of the directive.

## UK government's implementation of EU labour law: minimalist incorporation, maximalist subsidiarity, unrelenting resistance to the collective dimension

### Minimalist incorporation

EC social and labour law has been incorporated into UK labour law in various ways: first, by the passing of primary legislation.[35] Secondly, EC law may be implemented through secondary legislation.[36] Thirdly, the UK courts have come to accept the EC law doctrines of vertical direct effect and, more gradually, that UK legislation is to be interpreted in accordance with the requirements of Community law (*Garland*,[37] *Duke*,[38] *Litster*[39]).[40] Where such means have not sufficed to secure the incorporation of EC labour legislation, the Commission has pursued infringement proceedings under Article 226 (ex 169) of the Treaty of Rome.[41]

The UK government has claimed a better than average record of compliance.[42] Nonetheless, there was dissatisfaction with the then Labour government's legislative implementation of EC law requirements during the 1970s. In the 1980s, the tension between the Conservative government's EC obligations and its avowed commitment to non-intervention in labour standard fixing led to an approach of minimum compliance. This in turn bred litigation strategies whereby individuals and groups (such as the Equal Opportunities Commission) pursued claims, invoking the Treaty's Article 234 (ex 177) reference procedure to the European Court of Justice.[43]

---

[35] An example is the Social Security Act 1989 which implemented the requirements of EC Directive 86/378 on equal treatment for men and women in occupational social security schemes. Directive 86/378/EEC of 24 July 1986, OJ L225/40 of 12 August 1986.

[36] Section 2(2) of the European Communities Act 1972 gives power to ministers to make regulations; for example, the Equal Pay (Amendment) Regulations 1983 which amended the Equal Pay Act 1970 to incorporate the possibility of claims based on equal value in accordance with Directive 75/117/EEC of 10 February 1975, OJ L45/19 of 19 February 1975.

[37] Case 12/81, [1982] ECR 911.    [38] [1988] AC 618.    [39] [1989] ICR 341.

[40] For details, see Chapter 15.

[41] As in the case of equality legislation, *Commission of the EC* v. *the UK*, Case 61/81, [1982] ECR 2601; Case 165/82, [1984] ECR 192.

[42] For example, the Secretary of State for Employment, G. Shepherd, claimed in a speech just prior to the UK taking up the Presidency of the Council in July 1992, that the UK was the first Member State to have implemented all eighteen Directives in the social field which were then due for implementation, a record matched only by Germany. *Industrial Relations Legal Information Bulletin* No. 450, June 1992, p. 15.

[43] In the period up to the mid-1990s, the impact of EC labour law on UK labour law was greatest in the field of equality between the sexes. The Equal Pay Act 1970 preceded the UK joining the EC, and, following infringement proceedings, had to be amended by the Equal Pay (Amendment) Regulations 1983. Similarly, the UK Sex Discrimination Act 1975 was passed before the Equal Treatment Directive, but again, following infringement proceedings, the legislation was amended, beginning with the Sex Discrimination Act 1986. Subsequent legislation was required to take account of decisions of the Court of Justice (*Johnston* v. *RUC*, Case 222/84, [1986] ECR 1651). The hours thresholds which excluded many part-timers from statutory rights were reviewed following the decision of the House of Lords in *Equal Opportunities Commission* v. *Secretary of State for Employment* [1994] 1 WLR 409 (HL). The annulment of the compensation limits for discrimination required further legislation (*Marshall* v. *Southampton and South West*

The strategy of seeking to compensate for the UK government's resistance through interpretations of the European Court has sometimes paid off spectacularly. But the tension has some overall negative effects. This can be illustrated by two directives of the 1970s.

Perhaps the clearest example of the UK government's minimalist approach to EC labour law combining with its overall market philosophy to produce inadequate implementation of EC law has been the case of the Acquired Rights Directive 77/187/EEC.[44] The UK Transfer of Undertakings (Protection of Employment) Regulations 1981 excluded non-commercial ventures. This gave a clear passage to the privatisation policies of the government during the 1980s, largely premised on the transfer to private contractors of provision of formerly public services allowing them to compete by reducing existing pay and labour standards. The guarantees of the Directive were deemed inapplicable by the implementing legislation which deemed public services to be 'non-commercial'. However, later decisions of the European Court called this into question.[45] The consequence was not only a belated amendment of the implementing legislation, but also litigation attempting to compensate those who suffered loss of pay and worsened conditions when their jobs were transferred to private contractors without the EC law guarantees.[46]

A second example of the tension between UK government policy and EC labour law was the requirement of the Collective Dismissals Directive 75/129/EEC that representatives of the workforce be consulted.[47] At the time of the Directive's passage, there had been a procedure in UK law by which workers could require employers to recognise their representatives.[48] In line with the policy of decollectivisation of industrial relations, the Conservative government repealed this legislation.[49] Hence, the UK implementing legislation did not allow for the case where the requirement of consultation is frustrated by the

---

*Area Health Authority (No. 2)*, Case 271/91, [1993] ECR I-4367. Similarly, the 1986 Directive on Equality in Social Security required enactment of section 23 and Schedule 5 of the Social Security Act 1989, which outlawed discrimination in occupational benefit schemes. Directive 92/85/EEC which sets out minimum employment rights for pregnant workers required extensive amendments introduced through legislation in 1993. Directive 92/85/EEC of 19 October 1992, OJ L348/1 of 28 November 1992. Evelyn Ellis concluded: 'The directive will require little or no change to the law in any Member State apart from the UK'; 'Protection of Pregnancy and Maternity', (1993) 22 *Industrial Law Journal* 63 at p. 67.

[44] OJ L61/26 of 5 March 1977. M. Radford and A. Kerr, 'Acquiring Rights – Losing Power: A Case Study of Ministerial Resistance to the Impact of European Community Law', (1997) 60 *Modern Law Review* 23–43.

[45] *Dr. Sophie Redmond Stichting* v. *Bartol*, Case 29/91, [1992] IRLR 367.

[46] Five public sector trade unions issued 128 writs against the UK government, on the basis of the *Francovich* principle (see Chapter 15), relating to a large number of employees affected in the past by compulsory competitive tendering as a result of which the employees lost their jobs or were re-employed by contractors at lower rates of pay or on less favourable terms and conditions. *Industrial Relations Law Bulletin* No. 488, January 1994, p. 16.

[47] OJ L48/29 of 22 Februsry 1975.    [48] Employment Protection Act 1975, section 11.

[49] Employment Act 1980.

inability of workers to require employers to recognise their representatives.[50] The infringement proceedings brought by the Commission resulted in the European Court condemning the UK government for failing adequately to implement the Directive[51] and the government was obliged to produce legislative proposals for mandatory worker representation.

Reliance on litigation strategies depends on vigilance and resources. Where these are lacking, the UK government's minimalist approach to implementing EC law can produce long periods during which EC labour law fails to operate as it should in the UK.[52]

## Maximalist subsidiarity

The UK's unwillingness to promote EC regulation of labour may be encapsulated in one word: 'subsidiarity', frequently invoked in blocking social policy proposals. Examples of the potential conflict between the ambitions of EC social and labour policy and the radically different approaches of UK governments may be found in the attitudes of Conservative and Labour governments, both of which invoke the principle of 'subsidiarity' to justify resistance to EC intervention and support of domestic policy priorities of labour regulation.

The Conservative government elected in 1979 adopted this approach to EC intervention to support domestic deregulation in the field of health and safety at work. The Commission's Third Action Programme on health and safety of 1987[53] proposed an extensive list of new health and safety directives. Framework Directive 89/391/EEC[54] included provision for a series of individual directives ('daughter' directives) to cover specific risks, of which several have so far been adopted.

---

[50] B.A. Hepple and A. Byre, 'EEC Law in the UK: A New Approach', (1989) 18 *Industrial Law Journal* 129. See the comment by L. Dolding in (1992) 21 *Industrial Law Journal* 310 at 314.

[51] *Commission of the EC* v. *UK*, Cases 382/92 and 383/92, decided 8 June 1994, [1994] ECR I-2435. Continued inconsistency between the Collective Dismissals Directive of 1975 and the UK legislation implementing its provisions has been explicitly noted, but to no avail. *MSF* v. *Refuge Assurance plc* [2002] IRLR 324 (EAT).

[52] An example is the implementation in the UK of Council Directive 1999/70/EC of 28 June 1999 concerning the Framework Agreement on Fixed-Term Work concluded by ETUC, UNICE and CEEP, OJ L175/43 of 10 July 1999. It was estimated by the Trades Union Congress in 2001 that 1.7 million workers in the UK, 7 per cent of the total workforce, were employed on fixed-term contracts or as 'casuals' or agency workers. It was pointed out at the time of enactment of the implementing measure, the Fixed-Term Employees (Prevention of Less Favourable Treatment) Regulations 2002, S.I. 2002. No. 2034, that, by the government's own admission, only 25,000–53,000 fixed-term employees (between 1 and 3 per cent of the TUC's estimated total fixed-term workers, or 2 and 5 per cent of the DTI's total) would benefit from the Regulations' prohibition on discrimination. A. McColgan, 'The Fixed-Term Employees (Prevention of Less Favourable Treatment) Regulations 2002: Fiddling While Rome Burns?' (2003) 32 *Industrial Law Journal* 194, at pp. 198–9.

[53] Inspired by the enactment of Article 118A, inserted into the Treaty of Rome by the Single European Act 1986.

[54] OJ L183/1 of 12 June 1989.

In the UK, the Workplace (Health, Safety and Welfare) Regulations 1992 implement the EC Framework Directive and six of its 'daughters', and came into force on 1 January 1993. This new legislation repealed much of the preceding industry-specific legislation.[55] In support of the new legislation, it is said that 'they simplify much of the outdated industry-specific legislation … by making many requirements universal to all worksites'.[56] However, the aim of the Health and Safety Commission in implementing the Directives was to minimise the impact of any changes in the law.[57] What emerges is that the EC attempt to achieve European standards of health and safety was seized upon as the excuse by the UK government for an effort at deregulation.[58]

The UK government's attitude towards EC health and safety legislation was not one which aimed at harmonising its standards with a view to improvement up to those of other Member States; rather it was turned to the ends of a domestic political objective of deregulation, which, with respect to existing standards in some cases, has been argued to be regressive.

For example, the provisions in paragraph 2 of Article 100A (now Article 95 EC), added to the Treaty of Rome by the Single European Act 1986, excluded from qualified majority voting proposals 'relating to the rights and interests of employed persons'. This exclusion was the result of pressures from the UK government.[59]

Another example illustrating the contrasting attitudes of UK governments, both Conservative and New Labour, and those of the other Member States towards EC intervention is that of the Council Directive on working time. On 25 July 1990, the Commission of the European Communities adopted a proposal for a Council Directive concerning certain aspects of the organisation of working time.[60] Following a lengthy legislative itinerary, at a meeting of the

---

[55] Large sections of the Factories Act 1961 and the Offices, Shops and Railway Premises Act 1963 were repealed.

[56] (1993) *Occupational Health Review*, (January/February), p. 3.

[57] In a number of areas, the wording of the Regulations is different to the wording of the Directive. Also, in some cases, previously more detailed duties in the old legislation have been replaced with more general duties in the new Regulations. It has been argued that in some respects, therefore, the Regulations fail to meet the standards required by the Directives, though this apparent lacuna may be met through judicial interpretation.

[58] The tendency was repeated with the publication on 18 January 1994 of the Deregulation and Contracting Out Bill. Clause 27 of the Bill provided the Secretary of State for Employment with potentially sweeping powers of repeal and revocation applicable to all safety legislation. It was said that, with these powers, it will be necessary to ensure that the new Bill is not used to repeal any legislation that would bring it in conflict with the Framework Directive, the preamble of which states that it 'does not justify any reduction in levels of protection already achieved in Member States'. *Health and Safety Information Bulletin*, No. 219, March 1994, pp. 8–9.

[59] This perspective was and is manifest in respect of a number of proposals. The UK government criticised the legal basis chosen for the maternity rights directive, arguing that they were concerned with employment and pay, hence requiring unanimity in the Council of Ministers. It argued that neither of the legal bases chosen for the European Company Statute proposals was appropriate. M. Hall, 'The Social Charter Action Programme: Progress and Prospects', (1991) 20 *Industrial Law Journal* 147, at pp. 148–9.

[60] COM(90) 317 final – SYN 295, Brussels, 20 September 1990; OJ C254 of 9 October 1990, p. 4.

Ministers of Social and Labour Affairs on 1 June 1993, all but one of the Member States voted in favour. The UK abstained and announced its intention to challenge the legal basis of the proposed Directive in the European Court.[61] The Directive was adopted by the Council at a meeting on 23 November 1993 and has become the law of the EU.[62]

The legal basis of the Directive was Article 118A (now Article 137(1)) of the EC Treaty which stipulates that:

> the Member States shall pay particular attention to encouraging improvements, especially of the working environment, as regards the safety and health of workers, and shall set as their objective the harmonization of conditions in this area.

The Commission emphasised the World Health Organisation's definition that health is a state of complete physical, mental and social well-being and does not merely consist of an absence or disease or infirmity.[63] The Commission took the view that it is not necessary for working time to create *serious* health hazards to fall within Article 118A. EC legislation on working time is justified as regards psychological and social aspects of the working environment, such as monotony, lack of social contacts at work or a rapid work pace.

The UK's then Conservative government insisted that the proposal related to working conditions, not health and safety. Hence, the correct legal basis required a unanimous vote. The UK government lodged an appeal with the European Court of Justice to challenge the legal basis selected and asserted that it would not introduce implementing legislation until the Court had reached its decision.[64]

The Court handed down its decision in the week before the final date for implementation of the Directive.[65] It rejected the UK government's challenge. Implementation of the Working Time Directive thus fell to the New Labour government elected in May 1997. That government too manifested unwillingness to delegate competence in the social field. For example, the Working Time Regulations 1998[66] included a provision excluding from eligibility for the Directive's provision of annual leave workers who did not reach a threshold of thirteen weeks' continuous employment. Again, it was left to a trade union, many of whose members were on short-term contracts, to successfully challenge this domestic provision before the European Court.[67]

---

[61] *EIRR* No. 233, June 1993, p. 2; *Industrial Relations Law Bulletin* No. 475, June 1993, p. 12.

[62] Council Directive 93/104/EC of 23 November 1993 concerning certain aspects of the organisation of working time. OJ L307/18 of 13 December 1993. See *Europe* No. 6113, 24 November 1993, p. 10.

[63] *United Kingdom* v. *Council*, Case C-84/94, [1996] ECR I-5755.

[64] See the accounts in *Industrial Relations Law Bulletin*, No. 475, June 1993, p. 12; *Europe* No. 5991 of 2 June 1993, p. 7.

[65] *United Kingdom* v. *Council*, Case C-84/94, [1996] ECR I-5755.

[66] Working Time Regulations 1998. SI 1998, No 1833 (as amended).

[67] *Broadcasting, Entertainment, Cinematographic and Theatre Union (BECTU)* v. *Secretary of State for Trade and Industry*, Case C-173/99, [2001] ECR I-4881, Opinion of Advocate-General, 8 February 2001; ECJ decision, 26 June 2001.

The continuity in UK government emphasis on subsidiarity, common to both Conservative and New Labour governments, is particularly evident as regards what was Article 18 of the original Directive of 1993.[68] This contained 'Final provisions' and prescribed the standard obligation of Member States to comply (as envisaged in Article 189 of the EC Treaty): three years after adoption of the Directive.[69] Exceptionally, Article 18(1)(b)(i) began: 'However, a Member State shall have the option not to apply Article 6 ...' (the 48-hour maximum working week), and ended:

> Before the expiry of a period of seven years counted from the expiry of the period of three years referred to in (a), the Council shall, on the basis of a Commission proposal accompanied by an appraisal report, re-examine the provisions of this point (i) and decide on what action to take.

The possible delay in the implementation of Article 6 of the Directive for up to ten years, and possibly longer, was much vaunted by the Conservative government as a major success in its negotiations over EC social policy. However, it was the New Labour government which implemented the Regulations exploiting the opt-out. The manner in which it did so has been severely criticised, not least by the Commission.[70] The New Labour government was also confronted with the expiration of the ten-year period in November 2003. It took up the same policy of demanding the retention of the opt-out and citing the specificities of the UK labour market and its long-hours working culture. This episode demonstrates vividly the lengths to which delegation to the EU of competence in the social field will be resisted by UK governments.

## Unrelenting resistance to the collective dimension

The Conservative governments of 1979–97 implemented a consistent policy of decollectivisation of industrial relations. The domestic policy of the New Labour government elected in 1997, while not overturning the legislation of its predecessors, did appear to reflect some elements of a collective approach to employment relations, notably in the trade union recognition provisions of the Employment Relations Act 1999 (ERA). The collective dimension of this

---

[68] Now Article 22 of the consolidated Directive 2003/88/EC of 4 November 2003 concerning certain aspects of the organisation of working time; OJ L299/9 of 18 November 2003.

[69] Article 18(1)(a) of the 1993 Directive.

[70] European Commission, 'Communication from the Commission to the Council, the European Parliament, the Economic and Social Committee and the Committee of the Regions concerning the re-exam of Directive 93/104/EC concerning certain aspects of the organization of working time', COM(2003) 843 final, Brussels, 30 December 2003. C. Barnard, S. Deakin and R. Hobbs, 'Opting Out of the 48-hour Week: Employer Necessity or Individual Choice? An Empirical Study of the Operation of Article 18(1)(b) of the Working Time Directive in the UK', (2003) 32 *Industrial Law Journal* 223–52.

modest domestic initiative,[71] however, is overshadowed by the New Labour government's ferocious resistance to similar initiatives at EU level. This is evident also as regards the EU directives which the New Labour government was unable to resist and hence bound to implement into UK law. The UK Regulations implementing both the European Works Councils Directive 1994 and the framework information and consultation Directive of 2002 reveal the nature and degree of the resistance of UK governments since 1979 to the collective dimension of the European social model evident in those directives' emphasis on workers' collective representation.[72]

The United Kingdom has not had any choice but to transpose into domestic law certain existing EU legislation on collective worker representation. However, the New Labour government's transposition of the European Works Councils Directive and the framework information and consultation Directive reveals a specific concept of collective worker representation, a concept also reflected in the ERA's provisions on collective representation. This concept may not be beyond challenge under EU law.

## UK implementation of the European agenda on collective workers' representation: the case of European works councils

Promotion of collective workers' representation is a fundamental element in EC labour law.[73]

There is a long list of provisions where EC law requires collective workers' representatives to be informed and consulted.[74] In general terms, EC law leaves it to the national laws of the EU Member States to define who the representatives of workers are to be. For example, the Directive on Collective

---

[71] G. Gall, 'The First Five Years of Britain's Third Statutory Union Recognition Procedure', (2005) 34 *Industrial Law Journal*, 345–8. S. McKay and S. Moore, 'Union Recognition Agreements in the Shadow of the Law',(2004) 34 *Industrial Law Journal*, 374–6.

[72] However, one major advantage offered by EC law is that domestic law must give way to it. For example, the former Conservative government was forced to change the law on workers' representation concerning collective redundancies and transfers of undertakings when the European Commission challenged United Kingdom law before the European Court of Justice. *Commission of the European Communities* v. *United Kingdom*, Case C-382/92, [1994] ECR 2435. Similarly, it may be possible to challenge, through litigation, the Government's concept of collective worker representation where it deviates too markedly from the model of collective workers' representation promoted by the EU. Such challenges may, eventually, allow a remedy for some of the deficiencies in the ERA's concept of collective representation.

[73] This section draws on B. Bercusson, 'A European Agenda?' in K. Ewing (ed.), *Employment Rights at Work: Reviewing the Employment Relations Act 1999*, Institute of Employment Rights, 2001, 159 at pp. 172–85.

[74] In the cases of collective redundancies and transfers of undertakings, to participate in the regulation of the working environment so as to protect the health and safety of workers, to establish standards for the organisation of working time and allow for flexible derogation from standards prescribed by legislation, to establish Special Negotiating Bodies for the purposes of negotiating European works councils and then undertake the functions of these transnational works councils, and to participate in the EU social dialogue procedure laid down in the EC Treaty itself which had led to framework agreements and directives on parental leave, part-time work and fixed-term contracts.

Redundancies[75] provides in Article 1(b) that 'workers' representatives means the workers' representatives provided for by the laws and practices of the Member States'. Similarly, the Directive on Transfers of Undertakings[76] provides in Article 2(1)(c) that:

> representatives of employees' and related expressions shall mean the representatives of the employees provided for by the laws or practices of the Member States.

To this extent, EC law does not aspire, at first glance, to create a system of collective worker representation apart from that already established in the Member States.

Yet such a conclusion does not stand easily with the decision of the European Court of Justice in *Commission* v. *United Kingdom*.[77] There the Court required the United Kingdom to create a system of worker representation where none existed. Designation of worker representatives was made mandatory by the Court due to the Directive:[78]

> which require[s] Member States to take all measures necessary to ensure that workers are informed, consulted and in a position to intervene through their representatives in the event of collective redundancies [or the transfer of an undertaking].

In order to effectively perform the tasks of information and consultation specified in the directives, worker representatives must possess the experience, independence and resources required to protect the interests of the workers they represent. Member State laws or practices for the designation of workers' representatives must ensure that the national law on workers' representation is adequate to achieve this.

The case of the transposition of the European Works Councils Directive[79] into domestic law indicates how EC law may influence the law on collective worker representation in the United Kingdom.

The establishment of new organs of worker representation at EU level, in the form of European works councils, raises the question of the criteria for

---

[75] Council Directive 98/59/EC of 20 July 1998 on the approximation of the laws of the Member States relating to collective redundancies, OJ L225/16, consolidating Council Directive 75/129, OJ L48/29, as amended by Directive 92/56/EEC, OJ L245/3.

[76] Council Directive 77/187/EEC of 14 February 1977 on the approximation of the laws of the Member States relating to the safeguarding of employees' rights in the event of transfers of undertakings, businesses or parts of undertakings or businesses, OJ L161/27, as amended by Council Directive 98/50/EC, OJ L201/88, consolidated in Directive 2001/23 of 12 March 2001, OJ L/82/16.

[77] Case C-382/92 and Case C-383/92, [1994] ECR I-2435, 2479.

[78] Case C-383/92, paragraph 23; Case C-382/92, paragraph 26.

[79] Council Directive 94/45/EC of 22 September 1994 on the establishment of a European Works Council or a procedure in Community-scale undertakings and Community-scale groups of undertakings for the purposes of informing and consulting employees. OJ L254/64 of 30 September 1994. Council Directive 97/74/EC of 15 December 1997 extending to the United Kingdom Directive 94/45/EC. OJ L10/22 of 16 January 1998.

determining who are the workers' representatives who can establish and participate in these bodies. The European Works Councils Directive was implemented in the United Kingdom through the Transnational Information and Consultation of Employees Regulations 1999 (TICE), which came into force on 15 January 2000. These Regulations raise a number of difficulties of reconciling the concept of workers' representation in the directive with that in the Regulations.

Transposing EC directives into UK legislation has led to a proliferation of employee representation structures for different purposes.[80] From a tradition of single channel employee representation, British labour law, moving in the opposite direction from the American 'trade union representational monopoly', has skipped over continental dual channel systems into multi-channel employee representation systems. Different representation systems are linked to different functions.[81]

---

[80] To these are now added the union recognition and employee representation provisions of the ERA 1999.

[81] 'Many systems have found it useful, for a variety of reasons, to use legislation to allocate particular worker representation mechanisms or functions to dedicated structures … The key point for our purposes is that creating dedicated structures (such as statutory bodies) for particular worker representation functions (such as information and consultation) does not straightforwardly imply a rejection of union representation. The creation of dedicated structures does, however, raise the important question in each specific system as to what role to give union representation within each dedicated representation structure.' Paul Davies and Claire Kilpatrick, 'UK Worker Representation After Single Channel' (2004) 33 *Industrial Law Journal* 121–51, at p. 128. The authors assert (p. 129) that 'EU law makes any union monopoly rule impossible as a blanket solution in the area of information and consultation rights'. (Cf. the nuance on p. 138, footnote 48: 'Community law does not require a recognised union monopoly role'.) This appears to look to the ECJ ruling in *Commission of the European Communities* v. *United Kingdom*, Cases C-382/92 and C383/92, [1994] ECR 2435. I suggest this is to read the decision in reverse: the ECJ banned restricting such rights to recognised unions where unions were not widely recognised; it did not exclude Member States adopting procedures leading to mandatory union recognition and then designating the union as the representative for the purposes of the information and consultation requirement of the directives. Whatever its political difficulties, there is in principle no obstacle in EU law to a union monopoly rule. The authors propose giving unions with a certain level of support (10 per cent: 'an appropriate measure of worker support') and a role (pp. 129 and 139–41). The question is whether 'recognition' looks to the employer, rather than to a legislative mechanism conferring 'recognition'. Otherwise, EU law and policy is subordinated to the vagaries of employer choice, which the ECJ condemned. There is nothing to prevent Member States prescribing 'recognition' with any level of support. The authors advocate powers affecting non-union members for 'sufficiently representative unions' (pp. 137–8). As stated in their footnote 49, the 'references [in the EC directives] seem to be to the existing structures, not to structures which the Member States are required to create'. But they add in the text 'equally there is nothing in those Directives to prevent this step being taken'. So Member States are not precluded from creating mandatory recognition structures (specifically mandating unions), arguably more consistent with the EC requirement of mandatory worker representation than no structures at all. Indeed, there may be EU law obstacles to a mandatory balloting procedure which excludes workers from representation for the purposes of information and consultation. See the authors' discussion at pp. 134–6 ('Dispensing altogether with a representative structure is never an acceptable regulatory choice'), and on p. 137: 'Because all of the EC information and consultation

The TICE Regulations compound this complexity with a multitude of representational possibilities. Different forms of representation are proposed for five different aspects of the Regulations:

1. Representatives on European Works Councils (EWCs) established under Article 6 agreements negotiated, or on Special Negotiating Bodies (SNBs) established under other Member State laws (due to the initial United Kingdom opt-out).
2. Representatives negotiating, or already on, EWCs established under Article 13 agreements.
3. Representatives on an SNB established under the United Kingdom Regulations.
4. Representatives entitled to initiate the SNB procedure under the Regulations.
5. Representatives on statutory EWCs established under the Regulations.

From the point of view of industrial relations, the obvious question is whether British industrial relations is best served by further multiplying the channels of employee representation with different functions. From a legal point of view, these five categories may be critically examined in light of the requirements of EC law. Specifically, it will be argued that the Regulations have genetically modified the concept of representation with respect to members of the SNB and EWC. These are not 'employees' representatives' as defined in the Regulations.[82]

1. *Representatives on EWCs established under Article 6 agreements negotiated, or on SNBs established, under **other** Member State laws (due to the United Kingdom opt-out)*

   The Consultative Document proposing the Regulations stated: 'As a general rule the Government does not wish to disturb agreements already in place or negotiations already underway'.[83] However, it seems this does not preclude replacing the management side 'where a UK-based company has an EWC agreement made prior to implementation here, using a representative agent in another Member State'.[84]

   Where such an EWC has no, or too few, representatives of British workers, these are to be appointed. However, where the company is still in the

---

directives require each employee to be represented for information and consultation purposes, the UK is obliged to add a third possibility for groups of workers where there is insufficient union presence: elected representatives selected by workforce ballot'. The authors do not deal with the case where the mandatory ballot fails to reach the threshold for recognition required by UK legislation. Indeed, the UK case cited by the authors of an employer blocking recognition of a representative union where the employer recognised an unrepresentative union demonstrates the converse case. The authors conclude that 'UK law needs a criterion of "representativity"' (p. 132). A new criterion of 'recognition' is as exigent.

[82] Regulation 2(1) provides a single definition of 'employees' representatives'. This definition includes both trade unions and other representatives.

[83] Chapter 2, 'Summary', paragraph 37.

[84] Consultative Document, Chapter 2, 'Summary', paragraph 5.

process of negotiating an EWC agreement with an already established SNB, two situations are covered. First:

> Where *no* UK representatives have been appointed to the SNB, or *less* than the number to which the UK employees are entitled as of 15 [January 2000], the company should, when so required by the law of the Member State in question, take the necessary steps to appoint the appropriate number of representatives, *in accordance with the procedures set out in the UK regulations (i.e. by ballot).*

This is provided for in Regulation 47(5)(a) and 47(6). Secondly:

> Where UK representatives have been appointed *before* the UK regulations entered into force, they would not have to be re-appointed, *regardless of how they were chosen.*

In the words of Regulation 46(5)(b) they

> shall be treated … as a UK Member of the SNB who has been elected or appointed in accordance with [UK Regulations].

The confirmation of UK employees' representatives in the SNB, *regardless of how they were chosen* means treating them *as if they had been elected by ballot* under the UK Regulations. Ballots are required even where there are established trade union representatives. The government is willing to disrupt established industrial relations arrangements but not a newly created SNB.[85]

2. ***Representatives** negotiating, or already on, EWCs established under **Article 13 agreements***

In the case of Article 13 agreements, the government appears to accept that almost anything goes. The Consultative Document stated:[86]

> The regulations do not specify who the employee-side parties to such an agreement must be. The Government believes that in view of the variety of employee-side signatories to existing Article 13 agreements it would be undesirable to limit the flexibility of the parties on this matter. Clearly, both sides must be satisfied that it meets the criteria to be a valid Article 13 agreement, including that it covers the entire workforce.

Hence, the Regulations are excluded (Regulations 44 and 45). It is submitted that the government should not favour flexibility over democratic legitimacy and established industrial relations arrangements involving trade union representation. If the latter are violated, the European Court of Justice is unlikely to ratify the result in the name of flexibility.[87]

---

[85] This is a cynical betrayal of the government's apparently total commitment to ballots and makes a mockery of the government's claim to pursue absolute democratic legitimacy of employee representatives.

[86] Chapter 3: 'Article 13 Agreements', paragraph 3.

[87] Davies and Kilpatrick state that 'in other instances, EC legislation leaves the door open for the Member States to dispense with representatives, sometimes clearly, in other instances, less so. The clearest example is Article 13 …', 'agreements under it can be made with any employee-side

3. **Representatives on an SNB** *established under the UK Regulations*

Regulation 13 (1) is categorical: '[T]he UK members of the SNB shall be elected by a ballot of the UK employees.' The only alternative permitted is nomination by '"a consultative committee" which consists wholly of persons who were elected by a ballot ... in which *all* the employees who, at the time, were UK employees, were entitled to vote'. The Consultative Document considered: 'two possible methods of selection, election by the employees or nomination by the existing employees' representatives'.[88] The government chose election by workforce ballot, directly or through a consultative committee so elected. Various policy justifications are offered for this choice, which may be contested.

One *legal* argument for ballots is advanced. This is the reference in paragraph 15 to: 'the directive's requirement that unrepresented parts of the workforce are given a say in the process'. It is submitted that this is a misinterpretation of Article 5(2)(a) of the directive, which reads:

> Member States shall provide that employees in undertakings and/establishments in which there are *no* employees' representatives through no fault of their own, have the right to elect or appoint members of the SNB.[89]

In fact, Article 5(2)(a) is concerned with Member State laws which exclude small undertakings from national legislation on works councils – not the case in the UK, as is acknowledged in paragraph 13. Article 5(2)(a) explicitly applies where there are *no* representatives, not where there are existing representatives.[90] The option of relying on existing representatives is clearly that stipulated by the Directive. The requirement of a mandatory ballot is based on this misinterpretation of the directive and, arguably, is in violation of its provisions.[91]

Could the European Court be persuaded to allow a challenge to distorted representation on an SNB (or Statutory EWC)? Such a challenge would need to confront the rationale behind the requirement of ballot procedures. This rationale emerges from the remarkable fact that, despite occasional references in the Consultative Document to employees' representatives on the SNB and EWC, the *Regulations* do *not* regard the SNB or EWC as

signatories'. They note that 'most other Member States including Belgium, Finland, France, Germany, Ireland, Italy, the Netherlands and Spain have imposed rules on the identity or "representativity" of the employee-side signatories of Article 13 agreements'. 'UK Worker Representation', at pp. 135, 147–8. This awaits the ECJ's interpretation

[88] Chapter 4: 'Article 6 Agreements', paragraph 14.

[89] This is referred to in paragraph 11, which cites the Directive's stipulation that: 'employees in undertakings and/or establishments without employees' representatives "through no fault of their own" must not be excluded from the election of appointment process'.

[90] Contrary to the government's assertion, the directive does not require that 'unrepresented parts of the workforce are given a say in the process'. The government's argument might apply to require a ballot where are no representatives. But where there are existing representatives, the Directive confers no right to elect or appoint; a ballot is not required.

[91] The detailed Regulations 13 and 14 needed to implement the mandatory ballot requirement include a total of sixteen paragraphs. They are complex, create the prospect of confusion and may potentially lead to conflicts where the employees already have established representatives.

constituted by 'employees' representatives'; at least, not as defined in Regulation 2(1), which does not prescribe an election by ballot of all UK employees.[92]

The Regulations' definition of 'employees' representatives' does not apply to the SNB or the Statutory EWC. Their 'members' are to be *elected* by ballot directly, or indirectly through a consultation committee. The concept of representation has thereby undergone a genetic mutation. SNBs and Statutory EWCs may have 'members' elected by the workforce, but these are not 'employees' representatives' as defined in the Regulations. The question is whether this disjunction of concepts of representation is acceptable under EC law in the UK context.

4. ***Representatives entitled to initiate the SNB*** procedure under the UK Regulations

The Consultative Document stated:[93] 'In the UK context, the employees' representatives who are able to submit a request for negotiations to be initiated are those meeting the definition of "employees' representatives" in the Regulations.'[94] The Consultative Document made it clear that these are: 'representatives who exist prior to the formation of an SNB or EWC (as distinct from the SNB/EWC members, who will not necessarily be the same)'.[95]

The government was categorical that these may *not* be the employees' representatives on the SNB/EWC. This is revealing. The directive requires that employees' representatives be allowed to call for initiation of negotiations. The government takes great pains to distinguish these representatives from members of the SNB which results (let alone the EWC). No explanation is forthcoming as to why 'employees' representatives', as defined in the Regulations, are not to be members of the SNB and Statutory EWC.

The implication is that the members of the SNB and EWC, elected by ballot, may *not* satisfy the definition of employees' representatives in the Regulations. *Representation becomes the outcome of a formal election.*

---

[92] Regulation 2(1) defines 'employees' representatives' as meaning:

'(a) if the employees are *of a description* in respect of which an independent trade union is recognised by their employer for the purpose of collective bargaining, representatives of the trade union who normally take part as negotiators in the collective bargaining process, and
(b) any other employee representatives elected or appointed by employees to positions in which they are expected to receive, on behalf of the employees, information –
(i) which is relevant to the terms and conditions of employment of the employees, or
(ii) about the activities of the undertaking which may significantly affect the interests of the employees,

but excluding representatives who are expected to receive information relevant only to a specific aspect of the terms and conditions or interests of the employees, such as health and safety or collective redundancies'.

[93] Chapter 4: 'Article 6 Agreements', of the Consultative Document, paragraph 2.
[94] See now Regulation 9(1)(a).
[95] Summary, of the Consultative Document, paragraph 7.

It ignores qualities emphasised in the definition in Regulation 2(1): independence (of trade unions), established industrial relations structures (recognised by the employer), and experience and function (normally take part in bargaining or receive information).

The confusion which results from the government's refusal to apply to SNBs and Statutory EWCs the Regulations' definition of 'employees' representatives' emerges from a close analysis of these provisions as they apply to Statutory EWCs.

5. ***Representatives on Statutory EWCs*** *established under the UK Regulations*

Regulation 2(1) defining 'employees' representatives' acknowledges as employees' representatives an independent trade union recognised as representing employees *of a description*. This followed the definition in section 188 (1B) of the Trade Union and Labour Relations (Consolidation) Act 1992 (TULRCA) (procedure for handling redundancies) and Reg. 10(2A) of the Transfer of Undertakings Regulations 1981 (TUPE).[96] Provided the union is recognised in respect of the category of employees of a description, it is deemed an employees' representative, even if not all employees are members.

The crucial contrast is with the Schedule to the Regulations. Regarding the UK members of the Statutory EWC, this requires a ballot of employees *except* 'in a case where *all* of those employees are represented by UK employees' representatives'. Otherwise, the members of the Statutory EWC 'shall be elected or appointed by such employees' representatives'.[97]

It might seem from the definition of employees' representatives in Regulation 2(1), that all employees are represented where trade unions are recognised as representing employees *of a description*. Not so. The Schedule continues:[98]

For the purposes of this paragraph all of the UK employees are represented by employees' representatives if *each* of the employees referred to in sub-paragraph (1) is a UK employee –

(a) *in respect of which* [sic] an independent trade union is recognised by his employer for the purpose of collective bargaining; or
(b) who has elected or appointed an employees' representative for the purpose of receiving, on the employee's behalf, information –
(i) which is relevant to the employee's terms and conditions of employment; or
(ii) about the activities of the undertaking which may significantly affect the employee's interests

but excluding representatives who are expected to receive information relevant only to a specific aspect of the terms and conditions or interests of the employee, such as health and safety or collective redundancies.

---

[96] See now the Transfer of Undertakings (Protection of Employment) Regulations 2006 (SI 2006 No. 246).
[97] Schedule to the Regulations: Subsidiary Requirements, paragraph 3(1)(a).
[98] Paragraph 3(2).

The Schedule transforms the concept of representation from a *collective* model – trade unions representing employees 'of a description' – to an *individual* model – representation must be of *each and every employee*.[99] The Consultative Document was unequivocal: 'The employee representatives will be deemed to represent all the workforce where each of the employees is an employee in respect of which an independent trade union is recognised for collective bargaining.'[100]

The question arises: would the European Court countenance a procedure whereby members of an EWC had to be elected by ballot, even though there were independent, established and experienced trade unions representing employees of a description of almost all employees, just because one individual employee rejected trade union representation? On practical grounds, the ballot requirement ignoring trade unions in this situation is hard to justify. It is even more open to question on legal grounds. The subsidiary requirements in the Annex to the EWCs Directive provide:[101]

> The European Works Council shall be composed of employees ... elected or appointed from their number by the employees' representatives or, in the absence thereof, by the entire body of employees.

The provision appears clearly to opt for election or appointment by employees' representatives. Ballots of the entire body of employees are only resorted to 'in the absence' of employees' representatives.[102]

The Directive's Annex does add: 'The election or appointment of members of the EWC shall be carried out in accordance with national legislation and/or

---

[99]  The clumsy transition is marked by the grammatical mishap of 'an employee – (a) *in respect of which* [*sic*: rather than "in respect of *whom*"] an independent trade union is recognised'.

[100]  Chapter 5: 'Statutory EWCs', paragraph 9. As Davies and Kilpatrick state: 'A moment's reflection will show how unlikely a situation this is – and indeed always has been'. 'UK Worker Representation', p. 144.

[101]  Paragraph 1(b).

[102]  This provision was dealt with in the Consultative Document: '[The directive] states that the statutory EWC shall be composed of employees of the undertaking elected or appointed from their number by the (existing) employee representatives or, in the absence thereof, by the entire body of employees.' Chapter 5: 'Statutory EWCs', paragraph 9. The brackets surrounding the word 'existing' are mysterious and indicate unease. They do not appear in Chapter 2: 'Summary', paragraph 31(a). The Consultative Document goes on to require a ballot unless all employees are represented since: 'Where the employees' representatives represent less than all the workforce, it would not be right for them to make nominations as they lack the necessary mandate to act.' This may be the view of the government, but it is an extremely narrow reading of the Annex paragraph 1(b), which does not prescribe that all employees be represented. It is not clear whether the requirement that all employees be represented refers to all employees in a single establishment or to all UK establishments. Is the role of representatives excluded if UK representatives cover all employees in all but one establishment, but not all in one small establishment? Or all employees but one (e.g. the managing director, also an employee) in an establishment? If the issue is one of mandate, it is not clear that a ballot is the only option. This is an extreme 'all or nothing' approach. For example, why not ballot only those not represented by existing employee representatives?

practice'.[103] However, the discretion thus conferred on Member States is limited to the process, not the method of election or appointment, which is fixed by the preceding paragraph as the task of the employee representatives, unless these are absent.[104]

The inconsistency of the government's argument is apparent in its own definition of 'employees' representatives' in Regulation 2(1), which merely requires representation of employees of a description, not of all employees. More striking is the inconsistency regarding the obligation of the EWC to inform the workforce. The Schedule, paragraph 9(2) provides:[105]

> the members of the EWC shall inform – (a) the employees' representatives of the employees in the establishments …; or (b) *to the extent that any employees are not represented by employees' representatives*, the employees themselves.

It is obviously the practical procedure envisaged by the Directive's Annex for election or appointment of EWC members to be by representatives except 'to the extent that any employees are not represented by employees' representatives'.

## Conclusion

This detailed analysis of the Regulations transposing the European Works Councils Directive highlights the contrast between the UK's model of collective workers' representation, based on the formal legitimacy of ballots, and the European model based on established workers' representatives with the competence, experience and independence to act effectively.[106] The implications of this contrast for a United Kingdom model based on ballots, as in the ERA, is clear. There is potential for future collision of the ERA with a European agenda of fundamental rights on worker representation in the EU Charter of

---

[103]  Paragraph 1(b).

[104]  Compare Article 5(2)(a) of the Directive, which says that Member States 'shall determine the *method* to be used for the election or appointment of the members of the SNB'.

[105]  In language similar to that used in the Directive's Annex regarding election or appointment of members of the EWC 'in the absence' of employee representatives, the Consultative Document stated: 'members of the statutory EWC are obliged to inform local employees' representatives in the undertaking or group's operations (or, in the absence of such representatives, the workforce as a whole) of the content and outcome of the information and consultation procedures carried out': Chapter 5, paragraph 16. It is not stated that local representatives must represent *all* the employees. Clearly, if they represented some or most, it would be burdensome to require information to be given to the workforce as a whole. This is precisely the line taken in the Regulations.

[106]  As reiterated by Davies and Kilpatrick: 'Our first criticism is that the UK has disconnected union-based structures from the representative mechanisms of information and consultation … in the way in which it has given preference to elected structures … unions are entirely bypassed, thereby giving elections not an auxiliary but a pole regulatory position in the selection of workers' representatives. Finally, all of the elected structures share the quality that they have been created with no regard for linking them to union-based structures in UK workplaces.' And later: 'In other words, it is fair to deduce that, as far as recognized unions are concerned, the Government would have preferred to give them no role at all in relation to selection of members of either the SNB or the fall-back body, but felt itself constrained to make a minor concessions to unions in the case of the fall-back body': 'UK Worker Representation', pp. 141–2 and 145.

Fundamental Rights, and rights of information and consultation in the frame-work Directive 2002/14.[107] It would be wise to be cautious in assuming the model of worker representation in the ERA will be indefinitely sustainable.

### Directive 2002/14: UK implementation of the Framework Directive on Information and Consultation in the enterprise

Both the UK and the other EU Member States agreed on the option of voluntary agreements between employers and employees' representatives on information and consultation. The concern was that, in the UK, voluntary agreements might be exploited by employers to reinforce direct information and consultation with individual employees.[108] This approach has been confirmed in the Regulations adopted by the New Labour government to implement the Framework Directive 2002/14 on Information and Consultation.

Article 5 of the Directive permits *different* voluntary agreements.[109] A valid request by employees for negotiations to conclude an agreement on information

---

[107] Council Directive No. 2002/14 establishing a framework for informing and consulting employees in the European Community. OJ 2002, L80/29. In an analysis by Mark Hall of the Information and Consultation of Employees Regulations 2004 (SI 2006 No 3426) (ICE) ('Assessing the Information and Consultation of Employees Regulations', (2005) 34 *Industrial Law Journal* 103) introduced to implement Directive 2002/14, he refers to the 'highly unlikely scenario' (p. 106) of trade unions representing all employees so as to be eligible as EWC representatives, and points out that 'significant parts of the Regulations have been modeled on the provisions of the 1999 TICE Regulations' (p. 111). He suggests similar difficulties arise in reconciling the UK ICE Regulations with Directive 2002/14. As to the threshold of 10 per cent or 15 employees required to trigger the Regulations 'there may be questions raised at EU level' (p. 113). As to reliance on direct forms of information and consultation, as opposed to through representatives, 'the TUC has questioned the compatibility of this approach with the Directive's requirements. This is an aspect of the Regulations which may come under particular scrutiny from the European Commission when it comes to review national implementing legislation' (p. 114). The requirement of a high threshold of support (40 per cent and a majority of those voting) to overturn existing arrangements 'could potentially be seen by the EU authorities as undermining the unconditional right to information and consultation, via representatives, which the Directive guarantees' (p. 115). On this point see below for further detail.

[108] The New Labour government's campaign of resistance to the proposed Framework Directive on Information and Consultation of employees' representatives invoked endlessly the mantra of subsidiarity, this time to support its domestic policy preference for workforce ballots. The previous UK government's policy as regards EC intervention in the field of worker representation had been condemned by the European Court's declaration that its implementation of directives of 1975 (collective dismissals) and 1977 (acquired rights) failed to satisfy the requirements of information and consultation. Nonetheless, the continuity of UK government attitudes to EC concepts of worker representation was evident in the New Labour government's implementation of the European Works Councils Directive. Analysis of the TICE Regulations revealed the continuity of UK government policy manifest in the preference for workforce ballots in contrast to, and often to the detriment of, trade union representation.

[109] '... while respecting the principles set out in Article 1'. The Article 1 principles constrain all practical arrangements for information and consultation, whether determined by Member States (Article 4(1)) or agreed between management and labour (Article 5). Article 1(1) provides that the Directive sets out 'minimum' requirements, a Community minimum standard to be complied with by all Member States. Article 1(1) refers to 'the right to information and consultation of employees'. Article 1(2) mandates that the 'practical arrangements for information and consultation' must be such 'as to ensure their effectiveness'. There is no

and consultation by their employer is made conditional on there being no pre-existing agreement. Voluntary agreements are thus made an instrument whereby employers can avoid a request triggering negotiations. It is worth elaborating this approach adopted by the UK government in the Regulations implementing the Directive, to assess whether the concerns expressed by other Member States at the time the directive was adopted are justified.

Reg. 7(1)(a) provides that 'the employer shall initiate negotiations to reach an agreement ... as soon as reasonably practicable and, in any case, within one month of a *valid employee request* being made'.[110] What is a 'valid employee request' (the 'trigger')? The minimum threshold is stipulated in Reg. 7(2) and (3): a 'valid employee request' requires at least 10 per cent of employees in the undertaking, with a minimum of fifteen employees.[111] However, the real threshold emerges from Reg. 8(1): if the request is by fewer than 40 per cent of employees employed in the undertaking and 'there exists between the employer and the employees one or more agreements which (a) are in writing; (b) cover all the employees of the undertaking; (c) have been approved by the employees; and (d) set out how the employer is to give information to the employees or their representatives and to seek their views on such information', Reg. 8(2) provides that the employer may, *instead* of negotiating an information

distinction between practical arrangements made 'in accordance with national law' by Member States by way of implementation under Article 4, or those made 'in accordance with ... industrial relations practices' by management and labour by way of derogation under Article 5. All practical arrangements made are subject to the EC criterion of 'effectiveness', one with particular resonance in EC law. Article 1(3) provides: 'When defining or implementing practical arrangements for information and consultation, the employer and the employees' representatives shall work in a spirit of cooperation and with due regard for their reciprocal rights and obligations, taking into account the interests both of the undertaking or establishment and of the employees.' By virtue of covering *both* 'defining *or* implementing practical arrangements for information and consultation', the obligation to 'work in a spirit of cooperation' applies not only in the definition of practical arrangements, but during their application. Similarly, where the practical arrangements are determined by the Member States under Article 4 '[i]n accordance with the principles set out in Article 1', this obligation applies to both employer and employees' representatives when implementing those practical arrangements. As such, the principle is of general application to any and all practical arrangements for information and consultation. The UK Regulations minimise the Directive's Article 1 principles by encouraging 'different' voluntary agreements.

[110] Reg. 11(1)(a) states that no employee request is allowed if made within three years of a 'negotiated agreement' (Reg. 14), unless that agreement is terminated earlier; or within three years of when standard information and consultation provisions applied (Reg. 11(1)(b)); and if an employer's ballot produced a result of less than 40 per cent endorsement, within three years of the request which led to that ballot (Reg. 11(1)(a)). Reg. 7(1)(b) provides: 'The reference to entering into negotiations in sub-paragraph (a) is to taking the steps set out in Reg. 13(1)': 'make arrangements ... for the employees of the undertaking to appoint or elect negotiating representatives', inform employees of their identity and invite the representatives to 'enter into negotiations'. These negotiations (Reg. 13(3)) shall last for a period not exceeding six months and may be extended (Reg. 13(4)).

[111] Since the threshold for application of the directive is an undertaking employing fifty employees, the Regulation's minimum requirement of fifteen employees amounts to an effective threshold of 30 per cent of employees in such an undertaking before their rights to information and consultation can be engaged. Is this consistent with the Directive?

and consultation agreement, hold a ballot to seek endorsement of the request. Reg. 8(5) then stipulates a requirement of 40 per cent of employees employed in the undertaking to endorse the request in order for employer to be obliged to enter into negotiations (non-voters count as not endorsing). If the 40 per cent threshold is not reached, 'the employer is no longer under the obligation in Reg. 7(1) to enter into negotiations'.

In other words, where there is a pre-existing agreement, the threshold is not 10 per cent, nor even 30 per cent, but 40 per cent. Unless the request is endorsed by 40 per cent of those employed in the undertaking, there is no requirement for the employer to enter into negotiations. Reg. 11(1)(a) goes on to provide that if the employer's ballot produces a result of less than 40 per cent endorsement, no new employee request is allowed within three years of the request which led to that ballot.[112]

It is not surprising that other Member States were sceptical of the UK's constant invocation of subsidiarity as a justification for allowing it to maintain its existing industrial relations system of information and consultation.

## The UK and the future of European social integration

The dramatic transformation in the attitudes of the national actors in the UK to European social integration occurred in the 1980s. The change of government in 1979 transformed the official attitude to one of fundamental hostility to the social dimension of the integration process. On the other hand, the trade union and labour movement reversed their previous hostility. In the face of UK governments' hostility to social integration at the national level, UK trade unions began to espouse the cause of social and labour policy at EC level.

---

[112] In sum: apart from the difficulty of the actual negotiations required to reach an information and consultation agreement, the following obstacles must be overcome in order to even initiate the negotiations: information about numbers of employees to reach 10 per cent (minimum fifteen employees) threshold (Regs. 4–6), including possible complaint to the Central Arbitration Committee for failure to provide information about number of employees; 10 per cent to make a valid request (Reg. 7); possible delay if employer claims request is not valid as not 10 per cent or below thresholds (Reg. 12(1)); possible delay if employer claims less than 40 per cent of employees made the request *and* there is a pre-existing agreement; employer to organise a ballot (Reg. 8); possible complaint by employees or representatives that (i) no pre-existing agreement exists; (ii) ballot not properly held (Reg. 9); possible new ballot (Reg. 9(3)(b)(i)); 40 per cent threshold needed in order to endorse original request (Reg. 8(5)(b)).

If the ballot fails to reach 40 per cent, then, (i) the employer is not obliged to initiate negotiations; (ii) no request can be made for three years from date of failed request. Only if 40 per cent of employees endorse the request does it finally reach the stage of the employer initiating negotiations (Reg. 10). And this does not mean actual negotiations; rather, the process begins (Reg. 13) with the election or appointment of negotiation representatives. Here we go balloting again … Contrast Reg. 10: employer notification of a decision to initiate negotiations. The Regulations could have been reduced to this: to make it mandatory for all employers over a certain threshold to initiate the negotiation process and conclude an agreement as required by the Directive, or, if no agreement can be reached, the standard conditions apply.

The Maastricht Protocol and Agreement represented the formal recognition of the fundamental divide between the then UK government and those of the other Member States regarding the social dimension of the European Union. The formal opt-out ended with the change of government in 1997, but did not signal a change in governmental attitude. Domestic policy in the form of resistance to labour regulation as a 'burden on business', and reluctance to support collective employee representation through trade unions remains reflected in governmental attitudes to EU regulation of labour standards and 'social partnership'.

However, the institutional arrangements for the production of European labour law were changed dramatically by the Protocol and Agreement on Social Policy attached to the Maastricht Treaty on European Union. Collective bargaining agreements reached through the social dialogue at EC level were given the potential to be transposed into the sphere of EC labour law. The social dialogue was prescribed as a mandatory step in the formulation of EC labour and social law and policy. The Commission, when envisaging and actually proposing labour and social policy initiatives, is obliged to consult the social partners at EC level.[113] When the social partners are consulted, they may assume the responsibility for making an agreement at EC level which shall be implemented in a number of prescribed ways in the Member States.[114] The attitudes of UK governments will not preclude the participation of the social partners from the UK – the TUC and the CBI – in the European social dialogue.

Developments in EC law on worker representation reflect the changing nature of European economic and political integration. The post-1945 settlements in the EU Member States include regulation of labour markets by political authorities and the social partners, organisations of employers and trade unions, to varying degrees in different Member States. The transnational political and economic integration of Europe is unlikely to overturn this settlement. The EC economic model is embedded in what has been called the 'European social model', which includes information and consultation of employees in undertakings. The meaning of the Directive 2002/14, its enforcement by the Commission and interpretation by the European Court of Justice will be shaped by their understanding of the EU's social model.

The emerging European social model is embracing 'citizenship' rights going beyond the traditional civil and political sphere to include 'social' rights. EU social citizenship is about that very large part of almost everybody's life: working. The European Council of Nice, in the EU Charter, confirmed that social and economic rights related to working life are fundamental to the EU social model, what it means to be an EU citizen. A defining feature of the European social model is engagement of organisations of workers and employers. They are an integral element of the institutional architecture of the European social model.

---

[113] Articles 138–9 EC.    [114] *Ibid.*

Organisations of employers and trade unions play a major role in most Member States. Rather than decisions being taken unilaterally by management, there has developed in the Member States of the EU a mandatory system of participation by workers in such decisions through representative structures of 'works councils', 'enterprise committees', trade union bodies and similar forms. These exist in almost all Member States. The representative structures established by legislation or by generally applicable collective agreements in these countries provide for bodies to receive information and be engaged in consultation, or even co-determination, on a range of matters relating to the company's economic position having implications for the workforce, as well as on decisions affecting the day-to-day working life of employees. Only in Ireland and the UK is such a general and permanent system lacking.

The EC Directive of 2002 establishes the practice of information and consultation of employee representatives as part of the European social model. Promotion of collective workers' representation is a fundamental element in EC labour law. In order to effectively perform the tasks of information and consultation specified in the directives, employees' representatives must possess the experience, independence and resources required to protect the interests of the workers they represent. Member State laws or practices must ensure that the national law on employees' representation achieves the objective of the EC directives.

Transposing EC directives into UK legislation has led to a proliferation of employee representation structures for different purposes. From a tradition of single channel employee representation, British labour law, moving in the opposite direction from the American 'trade union representational monopoly', has skipped over continental dual channel systems into multi-channel employee representation systems. Different representation systems are linked to different functions. The new directive will require the establishment of new organs of worker representation. It raises the question of the criteria for determining who are the workers' representatives who can establish and participate in these bodies. Unfortunately, the Blair government in the UK played a major role in weakening the directive, with the result that there could emerge a form of 'British industrial relations exceptionalism' in the European Union. The final text of the framework directive reflects the Blair government's campaign of resistance. The question is whether continuing resistance could lead to implementation of the Directive in British labour law which makes UK industrial relations an 'exception' to the European social model.

Despite the rearguard battles of British governments since 1979, the EU has developed a 'social model'. The proposed Treaty Establishing a Constitution for Europe attempted to fix near enough in stone the social values, objectives and policies of the EU. Ratification of the proposed EU Constitution would have committed the Member States to a 'social model' which was the achievement of generations of struggle. The EU Constitution would have locked the UK (and other) governments into a European social model.

Despite the failure to ratify the proposed Constitution, a central element of this model is rights in the EU Charter of Fundamental Rights, retained in the proposed Lisbon Treaty. The Charter will have an impact on the social policy of Member States bound by the doctrine of supremacy of EU law.[115] Few doubt that the impact on the UK, and other Member States where the gap between the social rights in the Charter and national law is greatest, is likely to be substantial.[116]

It may be that the British people need the Charter most. But other Member States will also benefit. The UK, under the governments of Mrs Thatcher and her successors, not excluding the New Labour government, was the most recalcitrant opponent in the struggle to achieve an EU social model.[117] The EU Charter will be one means of dragging the UK, kicking and screaming no doubt, away from its neo-liberal labour market policies and into an embrace with the European social model of protection of workers. In this way, the Charter offers some hope of removing a major obstacle to social progress at EU level.

---

[115] The *Financial Times* reporting the different views of the Trades Union Congress and the British government Foreign Office concluded: 'legal experts say the impact of the charter can only finally be assessed when test cases challenging UK employment practices are brought before the European Court of Justice'. 4 January 2005, p. 4. The opt-out from the EU Charter negotiated by the UK and Polish governments in the Lisbon Treaty is unlikely to affect the European Court of Justice when determining compliance with fundamental rights enumerated in the Charter. See Chapter 21.

[116] Contrast the UK's willingness to ignore repeated condemnations of its compliance with provisions of the European Social Charter and ILO Convention No. 87. See Keith Ewing, 'The Council of Europe's Social Charter of 18 October 1961: Britain and the 15th Cycle of Supervision', (2001) 30 *Industrial Law Journal* 409–13, which cites the case of the right to strike.

[117] 'Britain is the only European country where there has been radical social model policy retrenchment, resulting not from monetary integration but a breakdown in the postwar social model in a context where political institutions concentrated political authority. Elsewhere, radical change has proved politically impossible and changes have typically been the adaptation or recalibration of elements of national social models.' A. Martin and G. Ross, 'Introduction: EMU and the European Social Model', in A. Ross and G. Martin (eds.), *Euros and Europeans: Monetary Integration and the European Model of Society*, Cambridge: Cambridge University Press, 2004, pp. 1–19 at p. 18.

# Chapter 3

# The conceptualisation of European labour law

European labour law is an intellectual discipline in the process of being developed by academics (and practitioners and judges) from all over Europe. The intellectual challenge of competing conceptualisations is a hallmark of EC law in general, and EC labour law is no exception. Students of the subject are confronted with very different perspectives on the same legal material – a highly stimulating prospect allowing for debate over the merits of different analytical frameworks. The shape of EC labour law is not determined by those steeped in the British or any other national labour law tradition. Among others, Belgian, Danish, French, German, Italian and Spanish, as well as British labour lawyers are engaged in proposing conceptual frameworks for the EC labour law that applies in their jurisdictions.

The conceptualisation of European labour law is influenced by the symbiosis of national labour law systems and EC labour law, and the interaction of law and context. This can be illustrated by looking at a number of books which have appeared proposing frameworks for EC labour law.[1] Different structures of EC labour and social law emerged depending on the approach adopted. Since all seek to expound the law on the basis of the same legal measures, it is all the more remarkable that the picture of EC labour law emerging from them is so very different. The following examination of competing conceptualisations aims to stimulate thinking about the conceptualisation of European labour law.

This chapter is in three parts. First, a number of textbooks on European labour law which have emerged are analysed. The product of one or two authors' attempts to comprehend the new subject, these are classified into a number of models according to the extent to which they reflect an EU-specific

---

[1] Given the proliferation of texts, this review does not purport to be exhaustive of the monograph literature. Some of the texts mentioned were given more detailed treatment in Chapter 1 of the first edition of this book. Some of those texts have since appeared in new editions. Above all, I am confined, due to my own linguistic limitations, to books written in English, French or Italian. I can only apologise to the reader for this major constraint. One of the texts reviewed is co-authored by a Dane, and another authored by the same Dane. One of the two collections of essays reviewed is edited by a Spanish professor and includes a number of contributions from that jurisdiction; the other collection's editors include a German professor and has contributions by three German professors of labour law.

orientation or a national labour law tradition. Secondly, a number of other texts, two of which are collections of essays from labour lawyers in more than one country, are critically scrutinised in terms of the concepts they use to elucidate a perspective on European labour law. Thirdly, a more ambitious question is addressed: what do these books tell us, or fail to tell us, about European labour law in context, and about EC law in general? The answer to this question, it is suggested, lies in other books which deal with the subjects explored in texts on European labour law, but written by experts in disciplines such as industrial relations and social policy.

## Models of EC labour law

In texts on EC labour law which have appeared in different Member States so far, at least five models may be identified:

1. EC labour law as equal treatment and health and safety at work;
2. EC labour law in the traditional model of national labour law: individual employment and collective labour law;
3. EC labour law as a 'modernised' model of national labour law: employment and labour markets;
4. EC labour law as common market law focusing on the labour market; and
5. EC labour law as a miscellany of substantive topics affecting labour addressed by the EC law-making institutions.

### 1. EC labour law as equal treatment and health and safety at work

The first model pre-dates the great expansion of EC labour law competences by the Treaty of Maastricht of 1991. It is exemplified by two complementary volumes in which Angela Byre, who is British, collected laws, cases and materials on the social policy of the EC: *Leading Cases and Materials on the Social Policy of the EEC*, and *EC Social Policy and 1992: Law, Cases and Materials.*[2] As their titles indicate, the two volumes (a total of 925 pages) are a collection of primary materials on EC labour law and social policy. The outstanding feature of this text is, first, the division into only three main elements: equality, safety and employment protection; and secondly, that more than half of EC labour law and social policy is concerned with equality between the sexes, and almost a quarter with health and safety, leaving less than a quarter to other matters.

What is noteworthy about this vision of EC labour law and its focus on these specific topics is how completely at variance it is with the structure and proportions of national labour law texts. While national labour law texts often deal with equality and safety, these matters are relegated to a much inferior position both in terms of their place in the overall structure of national labour

---

[2] Both published by Kluwer in 1989 and 1992 respectively.

law, and in the amount of space allocated to them. EC labour law as it emerges from this text is primarily about equal treatment of men and women and protection of health and safety in the working environment.[3]

A concept of EC labour law concentrating on the legal material of these two subjects proved inadequate for labour lawyers in the Member States seeking a general framework for European labour law. In contrast, the pervasive effect of this conceptualisation is evident in most textbooks on EC law in general: these include substantial treatment of the EC law on sex equality when they say little or nothing about labour law: a triumph of formal content over disciplinary context.

## 2. The traditional model of national labour law: individual employment and collective labour law

In the text entitled *Droit du Travail Communautaire*,[4] by Roger Blanpain and Jean-Claude Javillier, respectively Belgian and French professors of labour law, EC labour law is structured using the traditional categories of individual and collective labour law. However, there are a number of unusual features which render these categories suspect. Individual labour law is dominated by the free movement of workers. It also includes instruments with a strong collective dimension (collective dismissals, transfer of undertakings). There is relatively little space for collective labour law, and what there is almost exclusively concerns workers' participation, not collective bargaining. Finally, despite the relatively large amount of EC legislation and case law on equality between men and women and on health and safety, neither of these is given a proportionate amount of attention and nothing like that accorded to these topics in the first model.

EC labour law as it emerges from this text is premised on the traditional dichotomy between individual and collective labour law. But, in contrast with traditional texts on national labour law, EC individual labour law is dominated by rights to free movement of workers, with less attention to sex equality and

---

[3] Undoubtedly, sex equality in employment has been a central feature of EC labour law, indeed of EC law in general. Angela Byre was the first coordinator of the Community's network of experts on equality law. Similarly, the first great expansion of EC labour law came with the insertion of Article 118A of the EC Treaty by the Single European Act 1986. This provided: 'the Member States shall pay particular attention to encouraging improvements, especially of the working environment, as regards the safety and health of workers, and shall set as their objective the harmonization of conditions in this area'. Now in Article 137(1) of the present EC Treaty. When the UK challenged the Working Time Directive 89/391/EEC, the Court confirmed the concept of the 'working environment'; 'safety and health' embraces 'all factors, physical or otherwise, capable of affecting the health and safety of the worker in his working environment', and appear to create a potentially enormous scope of application for EC law on health and safety. *United Kingdom of Great Britain and Northern Ireland* v. *Council of the European Union*, Case C-84/94, [1996] ECR I-5755, paragraph 15.

[4] Paris: Litec, 1991; 2nd edn, Paris: L.G.D.J., 1995.

workers' rights in a context of enterprise restructuring. EC collective labour law is about workers' participation in the enterprise.[5]

## 3. A 'modernised' model of national labour law: employment and labour markets

The early and established text on *Droit Social International et Européen*[6] by the late Gérard Lyon-Caen and Antoine Lyon-Caen, respectively Emeritus Professor at the University of Paris-I and Professor at the University of Paris-X, is only half concerned with EC labour law: Part One deals with international labour law. Part Two (pages 159–352), after a preliminary chapter on the history and principles from the Treaty of Rome onwards, contains only two titles. But the first of these is on the single labour market and employment policy, and includes a section on free movement, including social security and a second section on employment policy.

Only then does title two, on social policy, go on to deal, first, with individual employment (the familiar list of topics: sex equality, restructuring directives, health and safety, also including an odd chapter on the Maastricht Social Policy Agreement and social security harmonisation) and then turns to industrial relations, where the treatment of the social dialogue, and information, consultation and participation initiatives is to be found.

The text on *Diritto del Lavoro della Comunità Europea*[7] by Massimo Roccella and Tiziano Treu, both Italian labour law professors, distinguishes EC labour law as different from national labour law by virtue of the element of regulation of freedom of movement of workers through the common market. The book's emphasis on employment and labour market policy is consistent with a 'modernising' trend in academic treatment of national labour law systems. The large quantity of legal material (regulations and case-law) on free movement of workers in EC labour law is a further influence in this direction. The question remains whether free movement is a social policy objective or an economic policy objective. It sits uneasily with traditional formulations of labour law in terms of rights and protection of individual workers and collective labour relations.

A conceptualisation of the subject in terms of labour market regulation is evident in the insertion of a substantial Part II on 'Employment Policy', separated from individual employment rights or protection of employees. It is

---

[5] Another text by Roger Blanpain, with the collaboration of Chris Engels, both Belgian professors of labour law, *European Labour Law* (2nd edn, Deventer: Kluwer, 1993), adds to Part I on Individual Labour Law and Part II on Collective Labour Law also a Part III on 'European Labour Law after Maastricht', which discusses the Protocol and Agreement on Social Policy (later incorporated into the EC Treaty by the Treaty of Amsterdam 1997), and includes a short chapter on 'European Collective Agreements: A General Framework'. A third and revised edition of 1995 includes only Parts I and II, with an Epilogue. This was repeated in the 5th and revised edition of 1998.

[6] 8th edn, Paris: Dalloz, 1993.     [7] Padova: Cedam, 1992; 2nd edn, 1998.

also reflected in the treatment of 'Atypical Work', the longest chapter in the part on 'Individual Relations'. The chapter on social security, part of the 'Employment Policy' section, begins by explaining that social security under the Treaty is functionally associated with free movement and hence focuses on migrant workers only. The book is on EC *labour* law, not social security law, and the importance of social security entitlements and their mobility to the free movement of workers in the EC is undeniable. But social security has an autonomous set of objectives and doctrines which goes far beyond assisting free movement. The impression given is that social security is subordinated in EC labour law to the exigencies of assisting free movement. This distorts both the broader scope of social security, and also those potential links between labour and social security law which go beyond labour mobility.

In contrast, traditional topics, equality between men and women and health and safety, despite substantial EC regulation, are allocated much less space. On the collective side, however, in contrast with Blanpain–Javillier, the authors choose to emphasise collective bargaining at European level, rather than workers' participation within enterprises or within Community institutions.

## 4. EC labour law as the law of the common labour market

The authors of the text entitled *Droit Social Européen* are Nicole Catala, a French professor of labour law, and Réné Bonnet, editor of a French legal journal on social security.[8] EC labour law is regarded as only one part of European social law, which includes the Council of Europe, the ILO and bilateral and multilateral Treaties. European social security law is autonomous and granted almost equal status to EC labour law.

Book II on 'Community Labour Law' adopts a structure which follows neither the traditional national labour law framework of individual and collective labour law of Blanpain–Javillier, nor the more recent trend in national labour law studies towards conceptualising the subject as labour market regulation, a tendency evident in Roccella–Treu. Rather, it adopts a framework familiar from texts on EC law in other fields: the emphasis is on free movement, as with goods, services and capital, in this case of labour, and harmonisation of different national regulations within a common market – together constituting 90 per cent of the text. Such a perspective, however, finds it difficult to accommodate the concept of an EC social policy independent of the creation of a common market.

European labour law is perceived more as part of EC law than as labour law. Emerging issues in labour law – atypical work, employment and labour market policy – are not as evident as the traditional EC themes of freedom of movement and harmonisation within a common market. There is scant treatment of health and safety, and little more on equality issues. European

[8]  Paris: Litec, 1991.

labour law is EC law of the common labour market with a marginal social policy dimension.

## 5. Substantive topics affecting labour addressed by the EC law-making institutions

The striking characteristic of the book entitled *The Social Dimension of the European Community*[9] by Ruth Nielsen and Erika Szyszczak, respectively labour law professors in Denmark and the UK, recalls that of the Byre volumes of materials on EC labour law and social policy: the prominent place being attributed to two aspects of EC labour law: sex equality and the working environment (health and safety).

Nielsen and Szyszczak use substantive fields to structure EC labour law. Within those substantive fields, the traditional framework of employee protection and employee rights prevails. Their text may be compared with another book in which a group of Scandinavian labour law academics argue that the labour law systems of Sweden, Norway, Denmark and Finland constitute *The Nordic Labour Relations Model*.[10] This text also is divided into six sections, five of which are on different substantive areas. Interestingly, four of the five substantive areas which form the framework of the Nordic model parallel chapters in the Nielsen and Szyszczak text on the social dimension of the EC: equality, protection of employment rights, worker participation and the working environment.

Where they differ is that the Nordic model does not have a section on free movement of workers. This is effectively the case also among the Nordic countries. More importantly, the book on the social dimension of the EC does not have a chapter on trade union activity – a crucial difference between the Nordic model and the EC model. The role of trade unions in labour law cannot be overestimated. This difference is visible in the levels of union membership in the Nordic countries and the EC, and its implications for labour law are fundamental. The role of unions and their activities in the Nordic countries, and in the Member States of the EC, transforms the labour law applicable in virtually all substantive areas.

The text on *EC Employment Law*[11] by Catherine Barnard of Cambridge University follows where the substance of EC legal measures leads her. European labour law is represented as an area within the broad field of European social policy, if not indeed outside its central core. It is not clear why labour law should assume this position, given its relative prominence, despite

---

[9] 3rd edn, Copenhagen: Handelshojskolens Forlag, 1997.
[10] London: Dartmouth, 1992. The authors are a group of Scandinavian labour law professors: Niklas Bruun, Boal Flodgren, Marit Halvorsen, Hakan Hyden and Ruth Nielsen.
[11] London: Wiley, 1995; revised edn, 1996; 2nd edn, Oxford: Oxford University Press, 2000; 3rd edn, Oxford: Oxford University Press, 2006.

the rubric of 'Social Policy', in the Treaty.[12] This relative marginalisation of EU labour law within social policy, itself relatively marginalised in EU law in general, is reflected in the third edition, the 'Introduction' to which on the first page speaks exclusively of social policy, with no mention of employment. Labour law appears as follows, replicating an opening passage of the second edition: 'It will also be seen that while there is an identifiable body of EC law which can loosely be described as "labour" or "social" policy, its coverage is far from comprehensive, and it certainly does not represent a replication of national social policy on the EC stage' (p. 3). This tells us more about what European labour law is not, than what it is.

In the first and revised editions, the opening chapters were on the 'Community Legal System and Remedies', and 'EC Law and the Development of a Social Policy'. In the second revised edition, the emphasis on social policy is evident when the titles are changed and the order reversed, as they became 'The Evolution of EC "Social" Policy' and 'Law-Making in the Field of Social Policy'. The third edition indicates a further significant shift. Part I, the 'Introduction' (pp. 3–168) begins as before with the chapter on 'The Evolution of EC "Social" Policy' (pp. 3–61). However, the former edition's chapter on 'Law-Making in the Field of Social Policy' is divided into two chapters: Chapter 2: '(Hard) Law-Making in the Field of Social Policy' (pp. 62–104) and Chapter 3: 'The Employment Title and the Lisbon Strategy: (Soft) Law-Making in the Field of Social Policy' (pp. 105–68).

This reflects the view that the Lisbon Strategy is more than just another strategy among the many chronicled in the history of the EC labour law, but rather a paradigmatic shift[13] to a new form of law-making in the field of labour and social policy and thus merits even more attention that the preceding period of hard law-making.[14] Since 'the core of the approach lies with the idea of encouraging active economic participation in the labour market ... [g]iven

---

[12] The author's Preface states: 'Traditionally, "social" policy refers to measures which come under the broad umbrella of the welfare state, such as housing, health care, education, social security and social assistance. However, in the EU context, social policy has often been considered as broadly synonymous with employment law: the relevant Title in the Treaty (Title XI) is headed social policy and the relevant chapter (Chapter 1) "Social provisions" even though their content, especially in early days, was broadly employment related. It is with the area of social policy concerned with employment law, both individual and collective, that this book is concerned, and not with social law and policy as more broadly understood' (p. vii). The use of the term 'social policy' in the Treaty conveys the difficulty of translating into English the ambiguities of the original Treaty of Rome, and of the French language, where *droit social* embraces labour law and social security law, but not the wider ambit of social policy. See also footnote 58 below.

[13] The author's Preface acknowledges that the structure of the third edition of the book changed substantially due to the Lisbon Strategy: 'This strategy marked a sea change in the Community's approach, shifting attention away from a concentration on hard law Directives to softer forms of policy co-ordination' (p. vii).

[14] In the chapter on 'hard' law-making (pp. 62–104), the legislative process engaging the social partners in social dialogue is covered in twenty-one pages (pp. 84–104), of which ten pages are devoted to the negotiation of the Framework Agreement on Parental Leave and its implementing Directive and the challenge to it in the European Court in *Union Européenne de l'Artisanat et des*

the importance of this "third way" to the success of the EU economy, it is considered in more detail in Chapter 3'.[15] The relatively reduced significance of 'hard' law is presumably justified by the earlier conclusion that: 'If, however, the goal of European social policy is, in fact, about active labour market policies then a traditional legislative approach cannot provide the answer.'[16]

The third edition, following the substantive law trail, retains the framework of earlier editions, save that former chapters are now Parts II, 'Migrant Workers', III, 'Equality Law', IV, 'Health and Safety and Working Conditions', and V, 'Employee Rights on Restructuring Enterprises'. In this third edition, the last Part V is now separated from the final Part VI, 'Collective Labour Law'.[17]

An important point emerges from the conclusion to the final chapter of Part VI on 'Collective Labour Law', repeated in the third edition. This duly reports on EU developments, but strikes a note of scepticism about this dimension of EC labour law, by quoting Kahn-Freund's warning as a comparative lawyer concerning the difficulties of transplantation of collective labour law. The implied question is critical: is the lesson of transplantation applicable to European labour law, or, with wider implications, is European labour law a suitable case for orthodox comparative law treatment? The answers to these questions are revelatory of the (English?) perspective on EU labour law, as they are of EU law in general. Is EU labour law a partial, incomplete and haphazard construct, with all the weaknesses of artificial transplants, or is it qualitatively different: a robust creation of a new transnational legal order of labour law?

Put another way, it is undeniable that comparative research has been an invaluable tool in the EU project of harmonisation of national labour laws. However, it may be questioned whether harmonisation remains the primary inspiration for a European Union with specific social objectives and competences. In other words, the use of comparative law as a means of developing European labour law does not preclude the emergence of a system of European labour law. In her book on *European Labour Law*, Ruth Nielsen cites the same source of Kahn-Freund's warning as to the impediments to legal

---

*Petites et Moyennes Entreprises (UEAPME)* v. *Council of the European Union*, Case T-135/96, [1998] ECR II-2335 (pp. 93–102); there are two pages on sectoral social dialogue (pp. 102–4).

[15] *Ibid.*, pp. 58–9.

[16] For an analysis and critique of this view as expressed by the European Commission in its latest Green Paper, 'Modernising Labour Law to Meet the Challenges of the 21st Century' (COM (2006) 798 final, Brussels, 22 November 2006), see Chapter 20 below.

[17] The final three chapters of the first edition traced a cautious line between the individual and collective dichotomy. In the first edition, between the chapter on 'Working Conditions and Other Individual Labour Law Measures' (including the Working Time Directive) and the final chapter on 'Collective Labour Law' (including the European Works Councils Directive), a chapter was sandwiched on 'Employment Rights on the Restructuring of Enterprises', covering three Directives of 1975, 1977 and 1980. In the second edition, the last two chapters were retained, but the first disappeared, as working time is dealt with as part of health and safety, expanded to include working conditions. This is retained in the third edition. The emphasis on individual employment law is evidenced by the separation in the third edition from Part V, 'Collective Labour Law', of a new Part V, 'Employee Rights on Restructuring Enterprises', despite this latter including a substantial collective dimension.

'transplantations'. But in her view 'the present development of EU labour law seems to suggest that Kahn-Freund's thesis is only valid in respect of transmissions of national labour law and does not apply similarly to EU labour law which seems to be able to overcome the institutional and procedural barriers'.[18]

## Summary

A number of conclusions can be drawn from the review so far of books on EC labour law.

First, the early focus on the topics of sex equality and health and safety has largely disappeared as EC labour law is perceived to encompass a wider scope of labour regulation approximating more closely national labour laws. This contrasts with texts on general EC law, which continue to see equality law as the principal concern of EU social and labour policy.

Secondly, there are different approaches to the collective dimension of EC labour law. In Roccella–Treu, the emphasis is on collective bargaining and the autonomous organisations of workers and employers at European level. In Blanpain–Javillier, Nielsen–Szyszczak, Barnard and, even more so, in Catala–Bonnet, the emphasis is on worker participation, information and consultation, mainly through integration into company structures or at enterprise level. This uncertainty about the collective dimension is manifest also in the classification of the directives on collective dismissals and transfers of undertakings. In Blanpain–Javillier and Roccella–Treu, these are dealt with under the general rubric of individual employment relations. The sub-heading is that of restructuring enterprises, which allows for recognition of the collective dimension, but the framework is that of protection of individual rights. This is made explicit in the Catala–Bonnet text, and is also indicated in Nielsen–Szyszczak. Barnard separates the chapter on restructuring from that on collective labour law and reflects the comparativist's unease about European collective labour law.

Thirdly, the texts vary greatly in their treatment of social security in the framework of EC labour law. The traditional distinction between labour law and social security law is maintained even where European social security law receives the most extensive treatment, in Catala–Bonnet. In Roccella–Treu, social security is treated in the chapter following free movement, within the general section on employment policies. In Barnard too it is associated with free movement, but also with sex equality. In Blanpain–Javillier it receives only marginal attention, and in Nielsen–Szyszczak, only a mention.

In sum, the structures of EC labour law adopted by these texts reflect different points along a spectrum ranging from pure EC law to traditional labour law. At one end of the spectrum, the Catala-Bonnet text classifies the subject along strictly EC law lines: freedom of movement and harmonization are the organising categories. At the other end, Blanpain–Javillier classify the subject along

---

[18] *European Labour Law*, Copenhagen: DJOF, 2000, p. 24. Ruth Nielsen's book is discussed below.

the traditional labour law lines of individual employment protection and rights and collective labour law, albeit the latter is given relatively scant treatment and collective bargaining is marginalised.

Between these, Roccella–Treu opt broadly for the individual/collective dichotomy of traditional national labour laws, but add a substantial new section on employment policies. It is not clear whether this reflects EC law imperatives, since much of it is concerned with freedom of movement, or whether it reflects a new trend in conceptualising labour law as labour market regulation. However, their treatment of the collective dimension of EC labour law places the emphasis firmly on the traditional sphere of collective bargaining.

Nielsen–Szyszczak and Barnard do not explicitly opt for the individual/ collective division of national labour laws. Their chapters appear to be framed more in terms of substantive issues which contain a mixture of collective and individual dimensions. Most substantive issues are, however, conceptualised in the traditional terms of employment protection and collective rights, and not the new trend of labour market regulation. The focus on substantive issues leads to some of these being given treatment which is highly specific to the EU context. For example, social security is related to free movement of workers or equality between men and women; individual or collective rights are specific to the case of restructuring of enterprises.

The two ends of the spectrum: EC law–national labour law interact. On the one hand, the emphasis on free movement of workers within a common labour market in EC law finds an echo in the trend in national labour laws towards conceptualisation of the subject in terms of labour market regulation. On the other hand, the traditional national labour law objectives of individual employment protection and collective labour rights are increasingly reflected in many EC labour law provisions. The result is a significant dynamic: the older conceptions of EC labour law in terms of free movement find vindication in new developments in national labour law in the form of labour market regulation. The older national labour law conceptions of employment protection and collective labour rights find an echo in the new developments in EC labour law.

## Concepts of European labour law

A number of recent texts have attempted a variety of different approaches to European labour law. Some of these, like the above, are textbooks. Others take the form of essays. Each has something distinct to offer in conceptualising the subject.

The text by Professor Pierre Rodière of the University if Paris-I (Panthéon-Sorbonne), *Droit Social de l'Union Européenne*,[19] offers an original overview which draws a subtle and nuanced picture of EU labour law. It is not the traditional or modernised dichotomy of individual/collective labour law, nor

[19] Paris: L.G.D.J., 1998; 2nd edn, 2002. References here are to the first edition.

the application of pure common market law to labour markets, nor a list of substantive topics. Rather, while reflecting the concerns of the other models, it highlights the delicate relationship between the *general EC law* of the common market on the one hand, and two sets of rules – *national labour law* and specifically *EC labour law* – on the other hand. The text is divided into four parts, each of which, as explained in the general introduction, aims to provide a specific insight into the nature of EC labour law.

Part One, 'Institutions and Sources', aims to highlight a specific quality of EC labour law with respect to EC law in general. The first two chapters are on the *specific labour law competences* of the EC, and the way these competences affect the *institutional mechanisms for exercising EC competences*. The third chapter focuses on the specificity arising from the role of the social partners and the agreements they negotiate at EU level.

Part Two identifies the 'Foundations and Principles' of EC labour law which are held to be of a *superior order of value* or to have *particular importance*. Miscellaneous references to charters and fundamental rights are reviewed in Chapter 1, and the remaining two chapters detail the law on the free movement of persons, one of the declared foundations of the common market, and sex equality, which, though not intended, became a dominant principle.

In Part Three, Rodière brings together a number of substantive fields said to reflect areas of EC social policy foreseen by the Treaty of Rome, which give the EC institutions the task of taking measures of *approximating national laws*. There is some coherence in the bits and pieces lumped together respectively in separate chapters on employment policy (access to the labour market, employment subsidies and vocational training) and on the enterprise (European works councils and the 1975 and 1977 restructuring Directives). Less coherence is evident in the chapter on the individual employment relationship (the 1991 Directive, health and safety and working time, and the 1980 insolvency Directive).

Part Four, concerning the *coordination of national laws*, is an original section which emphasises the continuing strength of diverse national labour laws and, in particular, social security laws. Free movement requires that these be coordinated, and two chapters analyse EC law and other international conventions to determine the applicable national law and jurisdiction in labour law and social security law respectively.

This focus on the role of *private international law* in determining labour law rules reflects a particular perspective on a European Union of sovereign Member States maintaining their national labour law traditions, just as this book's *constitutional vision* of a Social Europe reflects a different perspective. Whether a European labour law can result from the relatively minimal transnational movement of workers, despite their freedom to do so, and whether this suffices for a European labour law worthy of the name may be doubted. Nonetheless, this is an original attempt to shape the subject in a coherent fashion emphasising central features including the specific nature of EC law and the continuing importance of national labour laws.

Ruth Nielsen's text, entitled *European Labour Law*,[20] begins with an assessment of the distinct character of EU labour law and its interplay with national and international labour law. The book opens with an exploration of sources, again invoking comparisons with sources of national labour laws and international labour law. Thereafter, this interplay is a constant theme through the book, with developments in EU law, such as collective agreements, or information and consultation being continuously compared and contrasted with equivalent phenomena in national labour laws and international labour law.

A number of central elements shape the structure of the subject. The distinct character of EU labour law is said to be 'best understood in a *main-streaming perspective*, i.e. a perspective where labour law is seen as an integral part of main-stream legal culture; and the development towards integration between labour law and other areas of law is highlighted'.[21] At least two sources may have inspired this approach. Article 3(2) of the EC Treaty embodies the 'mainstreaming' approach to Community activities when it enjoins: 'In all the activities referred to in this Article, the Community shall aim to eliminate inequalities, and to promote equality, between men and women.' At a theoretical level, one inspiration may have been the feminist law approach of the late Tove Stang Dahl who advocated changing categories classifying different fields of law to reflect women's reality.[22] Similarly here, the call is for categories to change to reflect the reality of labour.[23] For example, the general perspective on mainstreaming is reflected in the third chapter on collective bargaining which indicates how it infiltrates myriad areas of law, from corporate structures to the working environment to the EU social dialogue.

A second element is the 'dynamic perspective' of EU labour law which is said to support a paradigm shift in national labour law which is adapting to the knowledge-based economy. The dynamic is identified in *new sources of law and new actors*, a truism with respect to EC law, but also including soft law, and changes in the relative significance of traditional sources of law (as between judge-made law, doctrine, general principles and legislation). The introductory chapter is followed by a lengthy chapter with an extensive treatment of sources of labour law. Nielsen highlights the relatively late historical arrival of EU labour law, at a time when the economy was changing from industrial society to knowledge-based information society, and the character of the EU as a polity was emerging. EU labour law also differs as regards the decisive role of collective agreements as a source in national labour law. There is said to be a paradigm shift of labour law as developed at national level, with specific reference to sources of labour law.

---

[20] See footnote 18 above.     [21] Nielsen, *European Labour Law*, p. 15.

[22] *Women's Law: An Introduction to Feminist Jurisprudence*, Oslo: Norwegian University Press, 1987. Nielsen is a leading authority on sex equality law.

[23] This is a potentially stimulating perspective, apparent also in the brief reference to a central role for EU labour law in developing European social citizenship. Nielsen, *European Labour Law*, p. 16.

Finally, EU law is said to be *multi-layered*, but not in the political science understanding of a multi-level system of governance. This perhaps less convincing element classifies EU labour law in terms of a three-level structure of surface law, legal culture and deep structure. EU labour law exists primarily at the surface level, whereas national labour law has infiltrated into legal culture. In terms of depth and stability, compared to relatively deep-rooted legal cultures and structures, EU labour law exists on the surface level, as 'young, dynamic and immature … inchoate, fragmentary and incoherent', compared with relatively old and settled national labour law. EU labour law's youth facilitates its adaptation to modern developments such as the information society.[24]

In sum, a number of qualities of EC labour law are postulated: it aims to mainstream labour law, engaging dynamic new sources and actors, but is relatively immature and incoherent compared to national labour laws.[25] These are thoughtful pointers to the structure and evolution of European labour law.

*European Community Labour Law: Principles and Perspectives (Liber Amicorum Lord Wedderburn)*[26] is edited by Professors Paul Davies (Oxford), Antoine Lyon-Caen (Paris), Silvana Sciarra (Florence) and Spiros Simitis (Frankfurt), and includes contributors from these four countries and from Spain. The thirteen contributions are not organised under headings and no structure or order is indicated. But there is one attempt to map general structural qualities of EC labour law: the opening chapter by Antoine Lyon-Caen and Spiros Simitis, 'Community Labour Law: A Critical Introduction to its History'.

The authors argue that EC labour law 'initially consisted of a *model* [which] led to *impasses* [which] can probably be resolved only through a *revision* of the initial model'.[27] This 'initial model' had three elements. First, the principle of upward *harmonisation*, set forth in Article 117 (now Article 136) of the EC Treaty. Secondly, justifications for regulatory activity in terms of a driving dynamic of *competition*.[28] The third element, 'a kind of *statist or public syndrome*', means 'the conferment on the Community authorities, and on

---

[24] Some of these qualities are evident in the chapter on 'Employment Contracts' and 'Restructuring of Enterprises'. The characterisation is less convincing in the chapters detailing the EU law on 'Gender Equality', 'Discrimination in General' and 'Working Environment'. The structure of the book is not determined by the haphazard development of EU labour law. After dealing with sources, it begins rather with two chapters reflecting the two classical pillars of labour law: 'Collective Bargaining' and 'Employment Contracts'. There follows detailed treatment of specific fields of EU labour law: 'Gender Equality', 'Free Movement', 'Discrimination in General', 'Restructuring of Enterprises' and 'Working Environment'. The final chapter on 'Enforcement' focuses on specific developments in EU law: principles of equivalence and effectiveness, procedural aspects and remedies.

[25] These are not always flattering to EU labour law, and some chapters illustrate the obstacles they pose to a coherent framework.

[26] Oxford: Clarendon Press, 1996.    [27] *Ibid.*, p. 3 (italics in original).

[28] 'Article 117 of the Treaty presented the functioning of the common market itself as the principle [*sic?*] vehicle of harmony in the sense of "upward harmonisation" that was attributed to it'. *Ibid.*, p. 5.

them alone, of the capacities or powers to construct a form of Community labour law'.[29]

As an initial model of EC labour law, the period 1957–74 may be described in terms of an expectation of harmonisation upwards driven by the inherent dynamic of competition in the common market. The burst of legislative activity following the Social Action Programme of 1974 similarly may be characterised in terms of harmonising measures adopted by Community authorities and justified in terms of fair competition in the common market. This initial model portrays EC labour law as a mere vacuum in the period up to 1974, due to social policy inertia. Yet, in the period after 1974, identifiable social forces other than the competition dynamic justified the dramatic change in Community social policy, even though competition remained its formal rationale.[30] This conflict of formal rationale and material social forces is itself significant, and no stranger to history.

Their argument continues: 'The history of Community labour law is the history of the *impasses* to which each of the elements of the original model has led.'[31] The authors assert a growing quandary in the Community during the 1970s, as harmonisation failed to materialise, culminating, it is said, when 'the Single European Act [1986, Article 118A] introduced a new conception of the rules to be adopted'.[32] The introduction of qualified majority voting under Article 118A (now Article 137(1) and (2)) was the significant factor resolving the Council's inability unanimously to approve social policy measures in the sphere of the working environment.[33] Moreover, henceforth Community action aimed not only at harmonising conditions to achieve fair competition, but also at 'encouraging improvements, especially of the working environment, as regards the safety and health of workers', though Article 118A did reiterate that the Member States 'shall set as their objective the harmonisation of

---

[29] *Ibid.*, p. 6.   [30] See Chapter 6 below.

[31] Davies *et al.*, *European Community Labour Law*, p. 7.   [32] *Ibid.*, p. 8.

[33] Less convincingly, the authors identify the significant change in Article 118A as being that 'the rules are to consist of *minimum requirements*. In fact, the text retained the pre-existing reference to the notion of "upward harmonisation" while at the same time introducing a view of the associated action as conceived in terms of minimum requirements. Such a combination would appear, at the very least, to defy all logic. Upward harmonisation and minimum requirements do not belong to the same philosophy.' It is not clear why the authors consider the rationale of 'minimum requirements' (establishing European minimum labour standards binding all Member States) to contradict upward harmonisation. The mystery is compounded when they add: 'As it turned out, the incomprehension and tensions inevitably entailed by the reference to upward harmonisation were removed when it was omitted from the [Maastricht Treaty's] Agreement on Social Policy. Its omission, however, signified the disappearance of one of the elements of the initial Community plan.' *Ibid.*, pp. 8–9. The significance of the argument based on this deletion is somewhat belied by the reinsertion of this provision, which the authors, writing in 1996, could not have anticipated, in the subsequent Treaty of Amsterdam 1997. The new Article 117 incorporates the 'non-regression' clause into the Maastricht Treaty version. The objectives are specified 'so as to make possible their harmonisation while the improvement is being maintained'. The new Article 117 (Article 136 after the Treaty of Amsterdam) also retains the second paragraph of the previous Article 117.

conditions in this area'. The authors identify the decisive change in rationale with the Agreement on Social Policy of 1992 (now Articles 136ff. of the EC Treaty), which altered the second element of the model, the *justifications* for EC social policy, so as to expand EC social policy beyond the precedent of health and safety allowed in the Single European Act. The third element of the *statist or public syndrome* certainly changed with the Agreement on Social Policy: 'The important thing to note is the official entry of the social partners onto the Community scene.'[34]

The authors' focus on changes in objectives and justifications for regulatory activity in the field of labour at EU level illuminates the evolution of European labour law: harmonisation is outdated as an objective, competition has been superseded as the driving force and the emergence of the European social partners was a fundamental change. History is an essential tool to understanding, but history does not suffice as an analytical framework for European labour law.

Thus, Jeff Kenner, in *EU Employment Law: From Rome to Amsterdam and Beyond*, traces the evolution of EU labour law, placing it in historical context beginning with the oft-neglected European Coal and Steel Community (ECSC) Treaty, of which it is said that it arguably 'remains the most far reaching Community constitutional document, containing both specific social goals, to expand production and raise living standards, and clearly defined roles of "producers" and "workers"'.[35] In contrast, the considerable attention devoted to the Community Charter of the Fundamental Social Rights of Workers of 1989 is accompanied by the author's scepticism.[36] Arguably, Maastricht as a turning point had greater significance, belied by a one-page account of the evolution of the Maastricht Treaty's provisions on social policy, where there is only one sentence for the social partners' agreement of 31 October 1991.[37]

This treatment of the social partners' agreement highlights a significant issue in conceptualising European labour law. As this book exemplifies, one tendency among some British authors is to opt for the title of 'EU employment law' rather than the conventional domestic usage: 'labour' law. EU texts in other jurisdictions do not hesitate to emulate their domestic equivalents of *droit du travail* or *droit social*, *diritto del lavoro* and *arbeitsrecht*. The appearance of the social partners on the EU stage was belated, but given the role played by trade unions and employers' organisations in all the national labour law systems of the EU Member States, it is reasonable to expect that EU labour law would reflect this experience.[38] The choice of title has implications for the overall conceptualisation. It may that for some British lawyers still reeling under the Thatcherite

---

[34] *Ibid.*, p. 11.    [35] Oxford: Hart, 2003, p. 61.

[36] This raises the question of why the author considers the Charter a 'catalyst', let alone as defining an 'era'. The conclusion (*ibid.*, pp. 212–13) is damning.

[37] *Ibid.*, pp. 219–20. See Chapter 5 below.

[38] Similarly, the flight from the terminology of collective labour relations to that of individual employment may reflect the time-dishonoured premise that the rest of the EU will follow the

onslaught on collective solidarity and/or reconciled to the Blairite continuity of (benign) neglect, collective labour solidarity is anachronistic, an outdated vision of labour law, and the EU social dialogue just a passing phase.

Thus Kenner concludes that 'in the relatively brief period from Maastricht to Amsterdam, the Union's strategy for combating unemployment through promoting active labour market measures and surveillance of national policies had become the *raison d'être* for the Union's social policy, first pervading and then eclipsing all other priorities in both ex-Articles 117–122 EC and the Agreement on Social Policy'.[39] The subsequent emphasis on the latest labour law fashions of (fifty-seven varieties thereof) discrimination, social exclusion and soft law posits an EU mutation from the classic labour law tradition of collective solidarity, generalised employment protection and enforceable trade union rights.[40]

*Dizionario di Diritto del Lavoro Comunitario*,[41] edited by Professors Antonio Baylos Grau (Madrid), Bruno Caruso (Catania), the late Massimo D'Antona (Naples) and Silvana Sciarra (Florence), is an Italian/Spanish enterprise. It includes, besides an introductory section, thirty-one contributions grouped under nine headings, which cover the full range of topics encountered in other texts.[42]

The range of topics is explained in the editors' *'presentazione'* of the volume,[43] which elaborates a number of features which cast light on their conceptualisation of the nature and structure of EC labour law. Their choice of the form of 'dictionary' is deliberate. Firstly, to avoid the impression of a structure analogous to national labour law: EC labour law is characterised as different in

---

UK's lead. Note also the change in the English language title of a leading monthly periodical in January 2007 from *European Industrial Relations Review* to *European Employment Review*. The valuable bi-monthly periodical, *European Works Councils Bulletin*, ceased to appear altogether after December 2006.

[39] Kenner, *EU Employment Law*, p. 309.

[40] This may be to fall victim to the flood of legislation prohibiting various forms of discrimination, and the outpouring of official documentation concerned with the European Employment Strategy (annual Guidelines, National Action Plans from each Member State, Commission reviews, Council recommendations, etc.). This flood of paper may create the illusion that something of significance is actually affecting employees, employers and their organisations in the sphere of employment and industrial relations. On the one hand, Kenner is obviously aware of the danger of overemphasising the significance of discrimination, and he is not uncritical of this trend. There is an equivalent danger of overestimating the significance of the mass of material on 'soft law' and elevating it to potential constitutional importance, rather than as a manifestation of the 'gesture politics' reflected in the oft-quoted, but now less self-assured Lisbon European Council's strategic goal for the EU: 'to become the most competitive and dynamic knowledge-based economy in the world capable of sustainable economic growth with more and better jobs and greater social cohesion', which highlighted the 'open method of coordination' as a principal process through which this goal was to be achieved. The EU's 'third-way' slogans are no substitute for the vast experience of enforcement of national labour laws, which EU labour law, sooner or later, will have to confront.

[41] Bologna: Monduzzi, 1996.

[42] Attempts to detect an underlying structure are happily obviated by the editors' decision, as befits its title of a dictionary, to arrange the chapters in the alphabetical order of the topics dealt with. So, in this book, the structure of EC labour law is, at first sight, dictated by the Italian language!

[43] *Dizionario*, pp. vii–xi.

its references to multiple jurisdictions, and interacts with them in various ways in space and over time. Secondly, to avoid a bias due to a choice of topics in EC law linked to orthodox concepts of labour law, which would threaten to lose sight of how the process of EC integration in general has influenced labour law in the Member States.

The choice of title is also deliberate: *'diritto del lavoro comunitario'*, not the more common usage, *'diritto comunitario del lavoro'*.[44] This is said to allow for the inclusion of comparative material. Labour law of the EC, for the editors, is not limited to 'vertical' exchanges with the EC legal order, but also includes 'horizontal' relations between national legal orders influenced by EC law. Both are said to be sources of *'diritto del lavoro comunitario'*. This clearly opens up the scope of the subject considerably, and a number of the contributions include comparative and international, as well as EC, legal references.[45]

The selection of topics is said to have been determined by reference to a criterion of development of a 'significant nucleus' of legal material. Since this material can include comparative and even international legal references, the boundaries of the subject are not easily perceived. The chapters on substantive topics in labour law are preceded by a lengthy introductory section of six chapters said to reflect the elements which provide the dynamic development of the labour law of the EC. Following the book's insistence that European labour law includes both EC and national labour laws, these include factors purely integral to the EC system,[46] but also dynamic elements rooted in the Member States.[47] This highlights one dilemma of European labour law: weighing the advantages of providing a context of national labour law against the extension of the subject to include all the national labour law of the Member States which is influenced by EC law.

## European labour law in context

The question asked of the texts reviewed has been: *what* is European or EC labour law? But seekers after the truth of European labour law want to know not just what. Indeed, the perception of 'what' often depends on the explanation of 'why' it is and 'how' it came about. A book on European labour law in context should address the questions of *why* and *how*. As a starting point, such a context

---

[44] This could be rendered as 'labour law of the EC', rather than 'EC labour law'.

[45] See, for example, in the section on 'Collective Autonomy', the chapter on the 'Right to Strike', by Franca Borgogelli; in the section on the 'Community Labour Market', the chapter on 'Access of Employees to the Public Service', by Paolo Pascucci; in the section on 'Employees' Representation in the Enterprise', the chapters on 'Organs of Representation' and 'Bargaining and Representation' by Riccardo Del Punta, and on 'Financial Participation' by Anna Alaimo.

[46] Hence, chapters on the 'Community Legal System' by Massimo D'Antona, on 'European Integration' by Antonio Lo Faro, on 'Fundamental Social Rights' by Silvana Sciarra and on the 'Court of Justice' by Ignacio Garcia-Perrote Escartin.

[47] Hence, chapters on 'National Labour Court Systems' by Bruno Caruso, and a specific study of the 'Communitarisation of Italian Labour Law' by Fulvio Corso.

is provided by two disciplines central to understanding the why and how of EC labour law: social policy and industrial relations.

On the social policy side, one such book is *European Social Policy: Between Fragmentation and Integration*, edited by Stephan Leibfried and Paul Pierson, respectively German and American academics.[48] The editors' Preface mirrors the frustration of EC labour lawyers (and perhaps EC lawyers in general) with the techniques of either comparative law or international law in dealing with their subject:[49]

> the remarkable process of European integration was making it increasingly difficult to comprehend the dynamics of public policy without considering actions taken at both the national and the supranational levels. The traditional framework of comparative public policy seemed ill equipped for this investigation. So, too, did most discussions among international relations scholars, which cast European integration as a process of carefully constrained diplomatic bargains among essentially sovereign nation-states.

The book is not wholly concerned with Europe. A substantial second part looks at social policy integration in the United States and Canada. This is justified by the authors because:[50]

> Comparative analyses have usually subordinated institutional and territorial aspects of social policy to issues of class conflict and compromise, because the former have been less pressing in the centralised political systems that provided the prototypical models of policy evolution (Sweden and Great Britain, for example) ... Yet, there are good reasons to think that if policy designs and systems of decision-making are multitiered, this institutional fact and its territorial dimension will be important ... territorially based institutional fragmentation transforms disputes over social policy ...[51] The implications of multiple jurisdictions are equally important for social actors.

A relevant example throws light on the role of the courts in EC labour law:[52]

> joint-decision traps in the United States helped push national initiatives for social reform in a rights-based, court-led direction, with disappointing results ... the relatively activist role of the European Court of Justice in social policy stems in part from a similar desire of European federalists to avoid the daunting problems associated with joint decision-making through the European Council.

The significance of multi-tiered systems is highlighted:[53]

---

[48] Washington: Brookings Institution, 1995. In particular, the three chapters (1, 2 and 13) by the editors.

[49] *Ibid.*, p. v.     [50] *Ibid.*, pp. 19–20.

[51] 'Alongside the familiar cleavage between capital and labour may emerge a less common, territorially grounded one between high and low social-wage areas – which may also encourage territorially grounded conflict among constituent units. Such territorially based coalitions have often been prominent in social policy debates in the United States.' *Ibid.*, p. 28.

[52] *Ibid.*, p. 26. See also pp. 51, 76 and 461–2.     [53] *Ibid.*, pp. 36–7.

the dilemmas of shared decision-making in the EU lead to strategies of circumvention ... the efforts of actors to escape the gridlock in social policy-making is a central theme. For advocates of social integration, institutional constraints within the Union have made court-led policy development an important path of social reform ...

[However] multi-tiered systems make centralised policy-making difficult for a reason – to protect local interests – and circumvention of these protections is likely to generate resentment ... one aspect of the current disquiet over the Union's 'democratic deficit'.

In their concluding chapter, Leibfried and Pierson highlight factors which, they argue, explain the development of EU social policy beyond the lowest common denominator predicted by some 'pessimists', though they concede these outcomes 'remain sporadic. At EU level, it remains far easier to block policies than to enact them.'[54] They point, then:[55]

to an additional outcome characteristic of multi-tiered polities: the tendency to seek escape mechanisms from a highly restricted system of decision-making. The standard route for social policy activity within the EU – through legislation enacted under unanimity rules in the European Council – has proved highly problematic. The British veto, in particular, has promoted an extensive search for alternative institutional channels. Two such channels require particular attention: the emergence of Court-led decision-making and the adoption of the Social Protocol.

As will be demonstrated later in this book, this unfolding dynamic continues with every prospect of clashes between the rival escape channels. Trade unions and employers' organisations (the social partners) complement their escape route from the blockage in the Council with attempts to constrain the role of the European Court of Justice.[56] The European Court of First Instance attacks the democratic legitimacy of the social partners.[57]

Lawyers are well equipped to understand the role of courts, including the European Court of Justice, both in general and in the context of labour law and social policy. But the transformation in European labour law prefigured by the Maastricht Protocol and the Agreement on Social Policy underlines the need for EC labour lawyers also to understand the emergence of social partner actors at EU level. Experts in national labour law would hardly need reminding

---

[54] *Ibid.*, p. 461.    [55] *Ibid.*

[56] For example, in Council Directive 96/34/EC of 3 June 1996 on the Framework Agreement on Parental Leave concluded by UNICE, CEEP and the ETUC, OJ L145/4 of 19 June 1996, the annexed social partners' collective agreement includes in Clause 4(6) the following provision: 'Without prejudice to the respective role of the Commission, national courts and the Court of Justice, any matter relating to the interpretation of this agreement at European level should, in the first instance, be referred by the Commission to the signatory parties who will give an opinion'.

[57] Case T-135/96, *Union Européene de l'Artisanat et des Petites et Moyennes Entreprises (UEAPME)* v. *Council of the European Union* [1998] ECR II–2335; B. Bercusson, 'Democratic Legitimacy and European Labour Law', (1999) 28 *Industrial Law Journal* 157.

of the importance of trade unions and employers and their organisations. Understanding European labour law in context requires reference to a literature separate from those in law and social policy.[58]

There is a burgeoning literature on the development of a European industrial relations system.[59] One major contribution is the exhaustive study by Jon Erik Dolvik, *Redrawing Boundaries of Solidarity? ETUC, Social Dialogue and the Europeanisation of Trade Unions in the 1990s.*[60] In the spirit of open-mindedness which characterises the book, Dolvik explicitly invokes the distinction of 'Euro-optimistic' and 'Euro-pessimistic' 'views on the evolving EC/EU regime of social and labour market regulation':[61]

> in view of the realist ethos of social science, most scholars would probably refuse to be labeled as (naïve) 'optimists' or (destructive) 'pessimists'. Nonetheless, I use this distinction as a helping device to identify the different lines of thought that tend to reflect different emphases as regards theoretical orientation, empirical interpretation and normative assessments of desirable/required forms of Europeanisation of social policy and trade unions.[62]

Dolvik emphasises, however, that:[63]

> a genuine European level of industrial relations and trade unionism ... cannot be delimited to a discussion of whether autonomous collective bargaining of the kind familiar to the peak era of the post-war national welfare states is established.

On this, he notes that 'Euro-pessimistic' contributions seem to converge with 'Euro-optimistic' analysis, quoting Wolfgang Streeck:[64]

> Once it is recognised that the political and economic regime that is developing in Western Europe, whatever it may be, is a new kind of animal that is altogether different from the national state, especially in its relation to the economy, the

---

[58] Leibfried and Pierson state: 'The welfare state remains the most popular component of the postwar social contract. As Peter Flora notes, in many countries the "welfare state constituency" of producers and beneficiaries easily approaches 50 percent of the electorate.' However, 'This source of political strength, extending far beyond the traditional working class, fundamentally distinguishes the politics of social policy from that of industrial relations. Broad popular resistance to market-oriented reform is likely to be much greater in the case of social policy'. *European Social Policy*, p. 445 and footnote 29. Nonetheless, one strength of the Leibfried–Pierson volume is that it recognises that social policy, while distinct from industrial relations, is related to them – hence their volume includes illuminating contributions on both. They argue that Giandomenico Majone's 'radical disjuncture between "social policy" and "social regulation", is overstated'; *ibid.*, p. 456, note 58; also p. 33, note 61.

[59] ETUI, *A Legal Framework for a European Industrial Relations System*, Brussels, 1999; ETUI, *European Industrial Relations: A Review of the Literature*, Dublin Foundation, 2002.

[60] ARENA Report No 5/97, Fafo Report No. 238, Oslo, December 1997.

[61] *Ibid.*, pp. 15–16.

[62] Dolvik includes the author of this book among the optimists (footnote 15); consistently, however, I accept his invitation to decline the adjective.

[63] Dolvik, *Redrawing Boundaries of Solidarity?*, p. 23.

[64] *Ibid.*, p. 23. Wolfgang Streeck, 'Neo-Voluntarism: A New European Social Policy Regime?' (1995) 1 *European Law Journal* 31 at p. 32.

problem in analysing European social policy changes from how empty or full the glass is, to what kind of glass we are dealing with and what purposes it may serve.

Dolvik's book has much to offer, at many levels, to the understanding of EC labour law, particularly the norm-producing processes of EU social dialogue. For example, he provides the most detailed account yet published[65] of the negotiations which led up to the agreement of 31 October 1991 between the European social partners, ETUC, UNICE and CEEP, which was the foundation for the Protocol and Agreement on Social Policy of the Treaty on European Union.[66] At another level, he states that one concern of the study is:[67]

> to analyse the ability of union leaderships, embedded in deep-rooted national habits and belief systems, to develop shared concepts, ideas, and strategies of trade union institution-building at the European level.

Dolvik provides a detailed account and analysis of the development of the strategy debate over European collective bargaining in the European Trade Union Confederation in the aftermath of the Maastricht Agreement, including the different perspectives of trade union organisations from Italy, France, the Netherlands and Britain.[68]

These texts provide a rich resource for analysis and understanding of European labour law. They demonstrate how studies in social policy and industrial relations contribute to understanding EC labour law. The essential point is that texts on EC labour law have to be read in context.

---

[65] There are other accounts not yet published in English. One is Kare F. V. Petersen, 'Step-by-Step into the Future: Three Decades of Social Dialogue', Research Report for the Swedish Centre for Working Life (mimeo), Stockholm, 1995, pp. 89–96.

[66] Dolvik, *Redrawing Boundaries of Solidarity?*, Chapter 8, pp. 189–239.

[67] *Ibid.*, p. 31.

[68] *Ibid.*, Chapter 9, pp. 243–310, and pp. 292–301 for national interpretations.

# Part II

# History and strategies of European labour law

# Chapter 4

# Shifting strategies 1951–1986: ECSC, EEC, harmonisation, financial instruments, qualified majority voting

## Introduction: Shifting strategies 1951–2008

The history of labour law in the European Union is best understood in the context of the evolution of the European Communities in general since their foundation with the European Coal and Steel Community in 1951. Throughout more than half a century, the Community has experimented with a variety of different legal strategies for the formulation and implementation of labour law and social policy. These strategies responded to different economic and political conjunctures. Whatever may have been the original vision of a particular cohort of national and Community leaders when the Communities were founded, this long period has witnessed dramatic changes in the economic and political context. It is not surprising, therefore, that the labour law and social policy of the Community have reflected these changes.

The striking feature of this history is precisely the great variety of legal strategies which have characterised attempts by the European Communities to achieve a coherent social policy and labour law. To some extent this reflects the dialectic between the common problems facing the labour markets of the Member States and the variety of national contexts and traditions in which these problems are confronted.

One key moment was the period following the oil and energy crises beginning in 1973. Various national labour law systems were confronted with common problems of high unemployment and recession in industry. These combined inadequate and unsatisfactory participative structures and processes at enterprise level between workers' organisations and employers, and the negative consequences for both individual workers, who lost jobs or skills without satisfactory compensation, and for employers who were subject to delay, prevented from achieving desired flexibility, or exposed to additional labour costs at times of crisis.

Since the crisis of the mid-1970s signalled the end of the thirty-year post-war boom ('les trente glorieuses'), there have been elements of the crisis of labour in the enterprise which are common to all the Member States': the inexorable rise in unemployment to heights unheard of in almost half a century, the increasing economic concentration of capital and diversification of the legal forms of capital, and the changes in the international division of labour affecting in similar ways the industrial economies of Western Europe.

The underlying question is whether the *differences* among national labour laws are more important than the *common* elements of a 'European' labour law, looked at over a longer historical period in different countries.[1] The answer suggested is that the 'European labour law' which evolved over more than half a century since the foundation of the European Communities is characterised by a variety of common strategies adopted at different moments. The evolution of European labour law is explored through an account of these different legal strategies.

The earliest strategy is that which characterised the founding of the European Coal and Steel Community in 1951: an active labour market policy and labour involvement in regulation. In complete contrast, the following period was characterised by a strategy of neo-liberal laissez-faire, reflected in the almost total absence of social policy and labour law provisions in the Treaty of Rome of 1957. This strategy was in turn replaced by an ambitious Social Action Programme adopted in 1974 which sought to harmonise labour legislation in the common market. The abrupt halt to this strategy caused by the election of a Conservative government in the UK in 1979 led to a search for a non-legislative strategy in the form of indirect financial instruments and the launching of the European social dialogue in 1985.

The launching in the mid-1980s of the 1992 objective of the European Single Market led to pressures for a strategy to achieve a social dimension through the Community Charter of the Fundamental Social Rights of Workers in 1989. The social dialogue strategy was formally institutionalised in the Protocol and Agreement on Social Policy of the Maastricht Treaty on European Union of 1991, and incorporated into the EC Treaty by the Treaty of Amsterdam in 1997. The Amsterdam Treaty introduced a new Title on Employment aimed at coordinating Member State policies through an 'open method of coordination'. A forum for macro-economic dialogue among the Member States, the European Central Bank and the 'social partners' was established following a decision at the 1999 Cologne European Council.

At the end of the twentieth century, the fundamental rights strategy was revisited and, at Nice in December 2000, economic and social rights were given the same fundamental status as the more familiar civil and political rights in a 'Charter of the Fundamental Rights of the European Union'.

An attempt was made to elevate certain of these European labour law strategies to the level of constitutional status in the Treaty Establishing a Constitution for Europe adopted by the then twenty-five Member States in

---

[1] See B. Bercusson, 'Workers' Rights in the Recession', in N. Bruun (ed.), *New Technology: A New Labour Law*, Congress papers presented at a symposium in Helsinki, November 1984, Helsinki: SAK (Finnish Trades Union Confederation), 1985, pp. 110–43.

2004.[2] The constitutional status of the fundamental rights of workers and their organisations was recognised in the incorporation of the EU Charter of Fundamental Rights in Part II of the Constitutional Treaty.[3] The rejection of the proposed Constitution by referenda in France and the Netherlands, despite its ratification by eighteen Member States, led to the proposal of a more modest Reform Treaty of Lisbon in December 2007. The Lisbon Treaty contains a provision according to the Charter the same legal status as the Treaties.[4]

What this history shows is the extraordinary range of legal strategies which have characterised attempts to construct a European labour law, and the struggles that have taken place among the Member States, the Community institutions and organised interest groups, primarily the social partners, in the course of developing these strategies. This chapter outlines the shifting strategies adopted in the years from 1951 to 1986. The following chapters examine the more recent developments of the past twenty years in more detail.

## The European Coal and Steel Community: active labour market strategy

The predecessor of the Treaty of Rome was the Treaty of Paris setting up the European Coal and Steel Community (ECSC) with the six Member State founder-members in 1951. This was designed to create a common market in coal and steel, essentially an economic, not a social policy objective. However, Article 2 of the Treaty of Paris made it one objective to contribute to the development of employment and improvement of the standard of living of the Member States. Article 3 stated that the purposes of the institutions of the new Community were 'to promote improved working conditions and an improved standard of living for the workers in each of the industries for which it is responsible'.[5]

The 'employment policy' of the ECSC was based *not* on stability of employment, but on the contrary, the *adaptation* of workers to economic change. The creation of a common market in coal and steel meant closure of some plants and reconversion of others. The ECSC provided help to support the

---

[2]  Treaty Establishing a Constitution for Europe adopted by the Member States in the Intergovernmental Conference meeting in Brussels, 17–18 June 2004, OJ C310/1 of 16 December 2004.

[3]  Part I explicitly affirmed the constitutional status of the role of the social partners in making European labour law through the social dialogue, and their participation in the macro-economic dialogue through an annual Tripartite Summit. Article I-48: The social partners and autonomous social dialogue. 'The Union recognises and promotes the role of the social partners at its level, taking into account the diversity of national systems. It shall facilitate dialogue between the social partners, respecting their autonomy. The Tripartite Social Summit for Growth and Employment shall contribute to social dialogue'. Reproduced as new Article 136a EC by the proposed Treaty of Lisbon. OJ C306/1 of 17 December 2007.

[4]  Replacing Article 6 TEU. *Ibid.*, Article 1(8).

[5]  Comparison may be made with Article 117 of the Treaty of Rome: 'Member States agree upon the need to promote improved working conditions and an improved standard of living for workers'.

reconversion of enterprises and the redeployment of workers who lost their jobs. The idea was that workers ought not to have to bear the consequences of economic change which technical progress makes inevitable. Enterprises which are being transformed can be given temporary assistance to avoid the need to lay off their employees. And if they close down, wholly or partly, assistance can be given directly to the workers, to enable them to search for work elsewhere, or to retrain for other jobs.

The policy was not to protect jobs in the sense of a stable employment. Rather, to accept technological change with all the implications for restructuring labour in the enterprise, including loss of employment, but without the workers suffering *financial* detriment. They must be helped to find other work or a different occupation: 'For stability of employment there was substituted a necessary *continuity* of employment, along with changes in work.'[6] The Paris Treaty gave the ECSC High Authority powers to finance substantial resettlement schemes, including free occupational training.

The 'labour law' elements of the ECSC are to be found not only in the financial provisions relating to labour mobility, but also in two other aspects.

First, the attempt by France to insert into the Treaty of Paris a commitment to harmonise wages and social charges, arguing that higher wages and conditions and better social provision in France placed French industry in a disadvantageous competitive position. This was rejected by the other Member States, but Article 68 did authorise the High Authority to intervene if wage levels and social provisions led to a distortion of competition within the market. This power was never used.

Secondly, there was labour representation on the High Authority, the ECSC executive composed of nine members, which included a trade union representative. In addition, the High Authority was flanked by a Consultative Committee composed of employer and workers' representatives, chosen from lists put forward by representative organisations. The High Authority was later dissolved into the EC Commission and Council, and the Consultative Committee into the Economic and Social Committee.

The remarkable quality of this European labour law and policy, combining an active labour market policy with labour involvement in the mechanisms of adjustment, is highlighted by the contrast with what succeeded it in the Treaty of Rome.

## The European Economic Community: a strategy of non-intervention in the common market

The foundation of the European Economic Community by the same six Member States signing the Treaty of Rome in 1957 did not appear to represent

---

[6] Gérard Lyon-Caen and Antoine Lyon-Caen, *Droit Social International et Européen*, 7th edn, Paris: Dalloz, 1991, p. 153.

an immediate and total break with the experience of the ECSC. The ECSC High Authority in the 1950s had set up two sector committees in coal and steel, involving the social partners, to do groundwork for harmonising working conditions. Their work was considered a success, so that during the 1960s the Commission of the European Economic Community established similar committees for other economic sectors.[7] Their purpose was to 'keep watch on economic and social developments in their sectors, seek to conclude model collective agreements and submit programmes for Community action to institutions'.[8] This legacy was not to bear fruit for a considerable time.

In 1958, the Commission had begun to plan the implementation of Article 118 of the Treaty of Rome, which provided:

> Without prejudice to the other provisions of this Treaty and in conformity with its general objectives, the Commission shall have the task of promoting close cooperation between Member States in the social field, particularly in matters relating to:
>
> employment;
> labour law and working conditions;
> basic and advanced vocational training;
> social security;
> prevention of occupational accidents and diseases;
> occupational hygiene;
> the right of association, and collective bargaining between employers and workers.
>
> To this end, the Commission shall act in close contact with Member States by making studies, delivering opinions and arranging consultations both on problems arising at national level and on those of concern to international organizations.
>
> Before delivering the opinions provided for in this Article, the Commission shall consult the Economic and Social Committee.

The Commission sought the opinions of representatives of the social partners in the six Member States and agreement was reached on a series of issues which would be the subject of detailed investigation by the Commission, to be followed by the social partners who would discuss the action to be taken. It is claimed that although consultations were time-consuming, 'they took place in an excellent atmosphere'. What happened next was described as follows:[9]

> Suddenly, several governments questioned the consultations with employers' and employees' organizations. This was the beginning of the most difficult period

---

[7] Between 1955 and 1982 eight had been set up, in coal, steel, agriculture, road transport, footwear, railways, sea fishing and inland navigation. C. Brewster and P. Teague, *European Community Social Policy: Its Impact on the UK*, Institute of Personnel Management, 1989, pp. 40–2.

[8] *Ibid.*, p. 42. Only the Agricultural Workers Committee succeeded in concluding a 'Community Agreement'. This agreement stipulated that the hours worked by agricultural workers across the Community should be set at 44 hours. As agreements at the national level went much further than this stipulation, the general verdict is that it was not that important.

[9] L.H.J. Crijns, 'The Social Policy of the European Community', *Social Europe* 1/88, p. 51 at p. 53.

for the Commission in relation to social policy, a period which lasted for some years ... A solution was found on 18 December 1966, when, at a meeting in Brussels, the Council opted for a very modest form of *ad hoc* cooperation based on studies.

What had happened was simply that the founding Member State governments had taken a clear position on social policy and were not going to allow the Commission to gainsay it.

Title III of the Treaty of Rome, 'Social Policy', contained only two Chapters with only 12 Articles. In the first Chapter on Social Provisions, the Member States' position was expressed in the first of the six Articles comprising the Chapter, Article 117, as follows:

> Member States agree upon the need to promote improved working conditions and an improved standard of living for workers, so as to make possible their harmonization while the improvement is being maintained.
>
> They believe that such a development will ensue not only from the functioning of the common market, which will favour the harmonization of social systems, but also from the procedures provided for in this Treaty and from the approximation of provisions laid down by law, regulation or administrative action.

The Member States' decision, embodied in the Rome Treaty, was taken following two reports in 1956, one of a Committee set up by the Member States (the Spaak Report) and another by a committee of experts from the International Labour Organisation (the Ohlin Report). Both reports recommended that there was no need for an interventionist social dimension for the proposed common market, save for certain measures against 'unfair competition'. The Member States' decision was:[10]

> not because the drafters did not expect the Common Market to produce social benefits for the workers and citizens of the Member States. On the contrary. But these benefits were to be delivered through market mechanisms, not legislation. Legislation could be justified only where necessary to remove obstacles to the proper functioning of the market, and it was anticipated that such occasions for legislating would be few.

The Community institutions were not to be permitted by the Member States in the Council of Ministers to use their initiative to counter this strategy. As put laconically by another author:[11]

> As early as 1959, the EEC Commission stressed that it could not conceive of a Community without social objectives and that it did not intend to place a narrow interpretation on the social provisions of the Treaty (in particular Article 117).
>
> Moreover, by means of this declaration the Commission closes ranks with the European Parliament which, at its January 1959 part-session, invited the

---

[10] P. L. Davies, 'The Emergence of European Labour Law', in W. McCarthy (ed.), *Legal Intervention in Industrial Relations: Gains and Losses*, Oxford: Blackwell, 1992, p. 313 at pp. 324–5.

[11] L. Wallyn *Social Europe*, 1/87, pp. 13–14.

Governments of the Member States and the Commission to ensure the greatest possible improvement of social provisions and in particular of working conditions, whilst maintaining improvements already made.

However, it was not until 1971 that proposals began to emerge for a more systematic approach to European social policy.

What was left of social policy was that consistent with the common market: the free movement of labour. The first EC Regulation on free movement was Regulation 15 in 1961.[12] To oversee its implementation and advise the EC a Consultative Committee was established comprising two government officials from each Member State and two representatives from each of the social partners.

The other Chapter of the Social Policy Title III of the Treaty of Rome was Chapter 2 on 'The European Social Fund', the main function of which was 'to improve employment opportunities for workers in the common market'.[13] The Social Fund was regarded as a weaker version of the training and retraining schemes established by the ECSC.[14] But, up to 1968, many interventions of the Social Fund were used to reskill redundant workers and encourage emigration to other parts of the EC. By the end of 1968, 543,000 Italian workers had been retrained, and 340,000 resettled in France and Germany. One evaluation concludes that the Social Fund had 'played a positive role in reducing the labour surplus problem inside one part of the Community'. But this was action always in the perspective of easing free movement within a common market, an economic, not a social policy.[15]

## Harmonisation strategy: the Social Action Programme 1974

The policy of non-intervention adopted by the founding Member States in 1957 was gradually being worn down by developments during the 1960s. The Commission was laying the foundations for a resurgent social policy by the accumulation of statistical information and comparative studies. It systematically maintained the link with social policy in forums dealing with other areas of policy.

New structures of the social partners emerged at European level; in particular, a European liaison body was established between the two strongest union federations in France and Italy, the CGT and the CGIL, which had not been active in the Community until then. This development was actively assisted by the Commission insisting on the involvement of the social partners as much as possible in the integration process in general and in social and economic policy in particular:[16]

---

[12] 15 August 1961, OJ p. 1073/61.
[13] Article 123; this Chapter also had six articles, Articles 123–8.
[14] Brewster and Teague, *European Community Social Policy*, p. 51.
[15] *Ibid.*, pp. 59–60.     [16] *Social Europe* 1/88, p. 54.

They were not only involved in the policy informally; formal structures were also created providing them with opportunities such as tripartite committees for the European Social Fund, for the free movement of employees, for vocational training, for the social security of migrant workers, the Standing Committee on Employment (established 14 December 1970) and a number of joint consultative committees on which the two sides were equally represented, to deal with social problems in specific sectors.

The breakthrough came at the summit of the Heads of the Member States in Paris in October 1972, which concluded with the final communiqué that the Member States:

> attached as much importance to vigorous action in the social field as to the achievement of economic union ... (and considered) it essential to ensure the increasing involvement of labour and management in the economic and social decisions of the Community.

Accordingly, the Commission was instructed to draw up a Social Action Programme. By a Resolution adopted on 21 January 1974, the Council of Ministers approved the Social Action Programme involving over thirty measures over an initial period of three to four years.

The explanation often put forward for the reversal of the policy of non-intervention is that presented by Michael Shanks, who became the Commissioner for Social Affairs responsible for the implementation of the Social Action Programme:[17]

> the major threat ... was a political backlash ... The Community has to be seen to be more than a device to enable capitalists to exploit the common market; otherwise it might not be possible to persuade the peoples of the Community to continue to accept the disciplines of the market.

Another account stresses a variety of factors, worth quoting at length to illustrate the complexities of the evolution of social policy in the Community. The highlighting of the role of interest groups, particularly trade unions and employers' associations, and internal political changes *within* Member States, as well as the relations *between* the EC and Member State governments can shed light on the prospects for future shifts of policy:[18]

> First, there was a growing sense of urgency over the severe social strains in the Community. The Italians and French were particularly concerned about the growing social divide. The wave of student protests and worker strikes that swept through the industrialized West in 1968 and 1969 were especially acute in Italy and France. Germany and the Benelux countries were similarly, if less urgently, concerned with solving the underlying social problems ...

---

[17] M. Shanks, 'The Social Policy of the European Communities', (1977) 14 *Common Market Law Review* 373, at p. 377; quoted in Davies, 'Emergence', p. 326; also Brewster and Teague, *European Community Social Policy*, p. 68.

[18] A.L. Sandler, 'Players and Process: The Evolution of Employment Law in the EEC', (1985) 7 *Comparative Labor Law* 1 at pp. 3–4.

A second major factor … was the planned expansion of the Community. The decisions to include Norway, Denmark, the United Kingdom and Ireland meant that the EEC would henceforth include a more diverse set of social systems with a broad range of commercial and employment practices. Thus, future efforts to harmonize competition would need to increasingly focus on social aspects of the production process.

A third incentive … evolved out of the political campaigns over EEC membership in the prospective Member States. The British public voted to join the Community by a very narrow margin, and the opposition Labour Party was committed to reversing this decision if elected. The Norwegian public voted in a referendum not to enter the EEC … It was therefore apparent that (the EEC) needed to put a human face on its role in European affairs.

Finally, the shift in the EEC's agenda reflected political change within the Community's most influential nations. In Germany, Chancellor Willy Brandt was determined to reverse post-war German reluctance to exercise political power commensurate with its economic strength. Brandt had several reasons for making the development of an EEC social agenda an early goal of the new German political philosophy. He and his party, the Social Democrats, were committed to social progress, particularly in the employment field. In addition, the introduction of Community worker protection and worker rights' legislation compatible with German legislation would undercut the argument of German employers that the proposed domestic legislation would reduce the competitiveness of German industry. Community employment legislation would also eliminate the incentive for employers to shift investment from Germany to other European countries. The retirement of French President Charles De Gaulle changed that country's whole attitude toward the Community. De Gaulle's successors proved to be less preoccupied with French autonomy and more committed to European integration.

The three main objectives of the Social Action Programme 1974 were, first, attainment of full and better employment in the Community, secondly, improvement of living and working conditions, and, thirdly, increased involvement of management and labour in the economic and social decisions of the Community and of workers in those of undertakings.

Whatever the disputed origins, inspiration and objectives of the Social Action Programme 1974,[19] implementing it through Community legislation undoubtedly faced a legal difficulty. The Treaty of Rome did not provide any legal basis for legislation explicitly aimed at achieving social and labour policy objectives. What the Treaty did allow, however, were 'directives for the approximation of such laws, regulations or administrative provisions of the Member States as directly affect the establishment or functioning of the common market' (Article 100, now Article 94 EC). The adoption of the directives implementing the Social Action Programme 1974 proceeded on this legal basis. Consistent

---

[19] Ruth Nielsen and Erika Szyszczak concede that 'there is some academic debate as to the motivation for the changes in social policy emphasis in the early 1970s'; *The Social Dimension of the European Community*, 3rd edn, Copenhagen: Handelshojskolens Forlag, 1997, p. 41.

with the Treaty, their formal justification was, and had to be, not social policy, but as contributing to the common market. The legal ingenuity of this solution, masking political exigencies, was to reappear on subsequent occasions when the irresistible force of politics encountered the immovable object of the Treaty. To repeat the earlier judgment of the political inspiration of the Social Action Programme adopted by the Council of Ministers in 1974, the Commissioner charged with its implementation asserted that it:[20]

> reflected a political judgment of what was thought to be both desirable and possible, rather than a juridical judgment of what were thought to be the social policy implications of the Rome Treaty.

The link between European labour *law* and social *policy* was unavoidable. Given the Treaty's constraints, social policy had to be expressed through the law governing the common market, including a common market in labour. 'Harmonisation' was the magic word to achieve the desired synthesis.

The strategy of harmonisation brought into sharp focus a number of central issues of EC law and social and labour policy. Not least, the relation between them. But also, and perhaps most important, the inevitability of incorporating the industrial relations, and, in particular, the collective bargaining context into a policy of harmonisation. To illustrate this, the harmonisation of labour law in different industrial relations contexts will focus on the problem of restructuring the labour force in the enterprise, through a case study of a major plank of the 1974 Social Action Programme: the Collective Dismissals' Directive of 1975.

## Harmonisation of labour law

The starting point of a policy of harmonisation is the identification of a problem *common* to various European countries and the attempt to harmonise the law and practice relating to the problem. It emerges, however, that the identification of *common* problems, when related to the *varying* labour laws of selected national systems, does not produce a harmonised view of law and practice. This is the result of a combination of two factors which are basic to the study of law in context.

First, where similar labour laws are invoked, their effects on different industrial relations systems give rise to variable results. This is mirrored in the *formal* successes of harmonisation policy (e.g. directives), but in the variable consequences in practice of this formal success. Secondly, different industrial relations systems mean that the national labour laws invoked to deal with the problem are different.[21] This has been a major obstacle at which progress towards harmonisation as a legal policy of the EC has been halted.

---

[20]  M. Shanks, *European Social Policy Today and Tomorrow*, Amsterdam: Elsevier, 1977, at p. 13.
[21]  The impact on national labour laws of not only differing industrial relations systems, but also of other differences in the environment affecting labour problems, leads to difficulties for

Each of the two problem areas for harmonisation policy will now be examined: that arising from differing industrial relations contexts, and that arising from differing formal labour laws. The issue to illustrate these two problems will be that which was at the centre of attention in the European Community during the 1970s strategy of harmonisation: restructuring the labour force in the enterprise. The context existing during that period will be described to illustrate the challenges facing the European Community's attempts to harmonise labour law on this issue.

## Harmonisation and industrial relations context: the case of restructuring labour in the enterprise

The general problem of restructuring the labour force in the enterprise in practice is composed of a multitude of component problems: redundancy/redeployment, selection and alternatives to dismissal, and job and income security (deskilling and downgrading). Different industrial relations systems have radically different effects on a national approach to these problems through labour law.

### Redundancy and alternatives to dismissal

The ability of employers to declare redundancies will be affected by the nature and level of *trade union organisation and collective bargaining* in different industries or different countries. A policy on plant closures will vary in its form and impact depending on the strength and unity of trade union organisation, or the coverage of collective bargaining – industry-wide, regional or enterprise level – regardless of legal provisions.

Similarly, *state policy in the manpower and industrial field* (particularly the politically acceptable level of unemployment) will affect redundancy policy, apart from labour law: for example, a policy of public subsidies to employers who lay off employees during times of recession as an alternative to redundancies and in order to enable employers to retain trained labour.

Not least, if among the most difficult to establish, there is the difference between *managerial styles* which determines responses to similar labour restructuring problems: for example, whether management's response to the introduction of new technology is retraining and flexibility or reduction of personnel.[22]

---

harmonisation. For example, the comparative analysis by the Commission of the laws of the Member States relating to employees' claims in the event of the employers' insolvency distinguished three main systems of *commercial* practice relevant to the problem. See *EIRR*, No. 47 (November 1977), p. 21.

[22] See F. Bohl and K. Dull, *Changes in Organisation, Employment and Worker Representation*, Commission Doc. V/507–83-EN, Brussels, July 1982, p. 1. In the FRG, the authors found that: 'Although comprehensive technical and organisational changes by all means take place, they hardly become evident as the cause for a reduction of the workforce. Rather, such reductions in the number of employees are generally justified by economic factors (decrease in the number of orders received, etc.) and the termination of employees for personal and behavioural reasons and "voluntary" fluctuation). In principle, this situation is the result of company strategies intended to divorce a company's personnel policy from its technical and organisational changes' (p. 3).

The *composition of the labour force* may affect selection, along the lines identified by dual labour market theory: secondary workers go first. This gives rise to legal problems with respect to the selection of part-timers (mostly women) for redundancy, and the restrictions imposed by rules on equal treatment. Again, the *structure of trade unions or workers' organisations at plant level*, whether divided along craft, political, or manual/non-manual lines can affect selection procedures.

### Redeployment

The *structure of employing organisations* will be critical in policies of redeployment. The Commission made an early attempt to tackle these issues in the proposals for the Directive on Protection of Workers in the event of their employers' insolvency.[23]

The controversy over the identification of a 'decision-making centre' for the purpose of imposing obligations on employers to disclose information and consult with employee representatives illustrates the problems presented by complex employer legal structures.[24] Restructuring of labour, in light of the (average) *size of enterprises* might be so concentrated in its impact that the focus of policy ought not, perhaps, to be the enterprise, but the community.

### Deskilling and downgrading

The *structure of the union movement* and particularly the divisions between skilled and unskilled, manual and non-manual workers has attracted much comment with respect to the problems of restructuring which affect the skills of workers. This will be more difficult when unions are organised on craft lines with strict demarcation than where general or industrial unions predominate.

### Conclusion

National labour laws may all address a common set of problems, but when refracted through different industrial relations systems, two alternatives tend to result. One is that *formally similar* laws emerge as very different in their practical operation (*formal harmonisation*).[25] Alternatively, the different

---

[23] See *EIRR*, No. 53 (May 1978), p. 21.

[24] See the definition in the original draft Vredeling Directive, *EIRR*, No. 82 (November 1980), p. 22: 'The place where the management of an undertaking actually performs its functions' (Article 2 (c)). A policy-oriented definition is indicated, e.g. in the area of accident prevention, Directive 82/501/EEC on major accident hazards from certain industrial activities focuses on the 'manufacturer', defined as 'any person in charge of an industrial activity' (Article 1(2) (b)); *EIRR*, No. 96 (January 1982), p. 23.

[25] This should not be exaggerated, of course. For instance, consider the discussion of the problems arising from the various definitions of the phrase 'pressing business reasons' justifying dismissal under a draft of the Acquired Rights Directive. The Commission recognised the 'elastic definition of this concept' and refused to define it, leaving it to the courts of the Member States, an approach criticised by the European Parliament (see *EIRR*, No. 5 (May 1974), p. 9 at p. 13 and No. 13 (January 1975), p. 6). In contrast, in a report to the Council on legislation

industrial relations systems dictate *different labour law* approaches to the common problem (*substantive harmonisation*).[26]

The fragmentation of the general problem of restructuring labour into a multitude of component problems exacerbates the difficulties of an EC strategy of harmonisation. Different countries may choose to focus on different sub-sets of problems, and a single country may change the focus of its attention over time.[27]

Efforts at harmonisation might well balk at the daunting task of choosing, from among the multiplicity of problems (redundancy, redeployment and so on) and the different legal responses to them in various national industrial relations contexts, a single strand of labour law which could be uniformly drafted. The attempts – via Directives on Collective Redundancies, etc. – appear daring to so boldly select at least one major issue, while catering only inciden-tally, or not at all, for important associated issues.[28]

concerning individual dismissals, the Commission concluded that 'all Member States would appear to accept that a reduction in the volume of business or the introduction of rationalisation measures, that is, economic grounds, are sufficient justification for dismissal' (see *EIRR* No. 30 (June 1976), p. 21).

[26] For example, an Anglo-German comparative study which highlighted the contrast between the 'voluntaristic' (yet 'adversarial') industrial relations system of the UK with the 'legalistic' (yet 'cooperative') system of the FRG. See the report on *New Technology and Changes in Industrial Relations* by the Jim Conway Memorial Foundation, Cleveland, for the EC Commission, Doc. V/509–83-EN, pp. 7–10.

[27] For example, a review in January 1979 of rationalisation agreements in Germany highlighted a shift from the 'classical' approach (which emphasised consultation, transfers to similar jobs, retraining and income protection) to a new approach which focused on protection from downgrading and a fear of technological deskilling. See *EIRR* No. 60 (January 1979), p. 14. Whereas 'social plans' in the 1960s dealt primarily with severance payments, by the end of the 1970s the emphasis had shifted to transfer provisions, wage guarantees and early retirement options as well. See *EIRR* No. 83 (December 1980), p. 6.

[28] For example, the amended proposal for a Directive 'on the harmonisation of the legislation of the Member States relating to collective redundancies' presented to the Council by the Commission on 1 November 1973 provided that consultation of workers' representatives: 'should cover in particular: the possibilities of avoiding or reducing the proposed dismissals, what criteria to apply when deciding which workers to dismiss, the possibility of giving other jobs in the same enterprise to workers threatened with dismissals, whether by retraining, by transfer to another part of the enterprise or by amending their conditions of employment, possibly, compensation for reductions in salary and other benefits, measures to be taken in favour of workers to be dismissed, in particular with regard to the possibility of severance grants and priority for re-employment, procedural details, in particular the staggering of dismissals' (Article 4(2)). This list was later dropped. See *EIRR* No. 2 (February 1974), p. 2 at p. 3; No. 7 (July 1974), p. 2 at p. 3. The great gaps left in workers' protection despite this initiative on redundancy dismissals were adverted to in a report by the Commission to the Council in 1976 which stated: 'the Commission considers it necessary to work towards an improvement of Member States' legislation in favour of the workers affected by individual dismissals and towards the approximation of such legislation while the improvement is being maintained within the meaning of Article 117 of the Treaty in order to provide a logical and meaningful supplement to the measures for the protection of workers contained in the Council Directive of 17 February 1975 on the approximation of the laws of the Member States relating to collective redundancies'. See *EIRR* No. 30 (June 1976), p. 21 at p. 25.

## Harmonisation and formal labour law provisions: a case study of the Collective Redundancies Directive 1975

As a case study of attempts at harmonisation of labour law and their consequences in different industrial relations contexts, this section examines the Directive on Collective Redundancies.[29] The questions addressed include: does experience of this Directive point to successful harmonisation only of the *form* of law, or also of its *substance*, as manifested in industrial relations practice? To what extent was the Directive implemented in different forms, reflecting different industrial relations systems, in order to achieve *substantive* harmonisation, and to what extent was this successful?

At an early stage of its formulation, an Explanatory Statement accompanying the amended proposal for a Council Directive on the harmonisation of the legislation of the Member States relating to mass dismissals stated that comparison of national provision on dismissals showed notable *differences* as regards conditions and procedures and the measures taken to lessen the negative consequences of dismissal for workers. Reflecting the imperatives of the Rome Treaty, this was said to have:[30]

> a direct effect on the functioning of the Common Market in so far as they create disparities in conditions of competition which are likely to influence the decisions by enterprises, whether national or multinational, on the distribution of the posts they have to be filled. It must for example be expected that any firm intending to reorganise itself by a plan including the partial or total closedown of certain departments, will decide which departments to close down on the basis, at least in part, of the level of protection offered to the workers.

The statement went on to maintain the necessity of eliminating known disparities by harmonising the relevant national provisions.

It is interesting to note that the statement was careful to insist that the initiative to harmonise legislation did not imply that the autonomy of management and labour would be called in question. Harmonisation was not the only consideration. Social policy considerations applied also. Hence:[31]

> systematic joint action by management, the authorities and workers' representatives is the best method of obtaining Community regulations of mass dismissals which will best serve their dual purpose of providing social protection and acting as an economic regulator.

---

[29] Directive No. 75/129 of 17 February 1975, OJ L48/29 of 22 February 1975, as amended by Directive 92/56 of 24 June 1992, OJ L245/92. Now consolidated in Council Directive 98/59/EC of 20 July 1998 on the approximation of the laws of the Member States relating to collective redundancies, OJ L225/16.

[30] See text in *EIRR*, No. 1 (January 1974), p. 18.     [31] *Ibid.*, at p. 19.

### The legal position before the 1975 Directive

National legal provision *prior* to the 1975 Directive was extremely varied. This can be shown by a brief review of the legal position prior to the Directive in five Member States: Italy, France, the UK, Germany and Belgium.

In *Italy* it was said that the main procedures were much in line with the Directive's provisions, albeit taking a very different legal form.[32] At that stage, employees' position with regard to collective dismissals was safeguarded by criteria established in a General Agreement of 1966 between the main union and employers' confederations. Under the 1966 Agreement, companies with ten or more employees were required to inform district unions of decisions to reduce the workforce and provide certain other information. On receipt of such information, union officials could, within seven days, invite management to a meeting for discussions, limited to twenty-five days' duration (15 for firms of under 100 employees), during which period no dismissals could be put into effect. If dismissals were to take place, selection operated in accordance with certain criteria.

In practice, companies either used this procedure or simply notified the factory council. In the latter case, the union representatives would usually seek a legal ruling under the Workers' Statute 1970 to the effect that the individual dismissals would be without 'just cause'. If successful, the workers would be reinstated and management would then follow the correct procedure under the 1966 Agreement. The position in practice as it then stood was summarised as follows:[33]

> one of the most notable and recurring problems for workers and their representatives in these redundancy situations, is the difficulty of counteracting a management decision that staff reductions are necessary. The company is able to demonstrate that a critical situation has arisen on the basis of its own knowledge of the situation, whereas the unions may be unaware of all the facts.

In *Germany* at the time of the enactment of the Directive, it was said that the protection afforded to employees in a redundancy situation was even stronger than that provided by the Directive.[34] The relevant German legislation was the Protection Against Dismissals Act of 1969 and the Works Council Act of 1972 (amending the 1951 Act). The 1969 Act protected individual workers against 'socially unjustified dismissals' and specified methods of objecting to such dismissals. The law obliged the employer to inform the Regional Department of Labour in the event of mass redundancies, providing reasons for the dismissals and including the opinion of the Works Council. The Department could delay the dismissals up to two months. The actual decision to defer particular dismissals is taken by a tripartite committee of the Labour Department.

The 1972 Act, while very much in line with the Directive in providing for pre-redundancy consultation procedures, went one stage further by providing

---

[32] See the account in *EIRR*, No. 16 (April 1975), p. 14.     [33] *Ibid.*, at p. 16.
[34] See *EIRR*, No. 18 (June 1975), p. 12.

for the formulation of redundancy schemes or 'social plans', to be drawn up in negotiations between the Works Council and the employer. The social plan (covering who is to be made redundant, when the dismissals are to take effect, the level of redundancy payments, etc.) has the status of a plant agreement. If no agreement is reached, provisions exist for mediation and eventually a social plan can be imposed by a Conciliation Board.

In practice, however, it was said at the time that many employers chose to avoid the extensive consultations with the Works Council by offering instead large lump sum payments to workers who voluntarily accepted redundancies:[35]

> although a programme of voluntary redundancies may still be costly to the employers, it has generally been found to be a speedier and less hazardous alternative to notified collective redundancies ... With higher levels of unemployment, however, the financial burden which is incurred with collective dismissals has made it necessary for firms to rethink their policies and introduce voluntary redundancy, or reduce their work-force at a slower pace by means of natural wastage.

In *France*, it was only a new law of 3 January 1975 which brought French legislation into line with the Directive.[36] Since 1945 there had been a requirement on employers in the commercial and industrial sectors to obtain prior authorisation for redundancies from the Regional Department of Labour. It was acknowledged, however, that the requirement had rarely been observed in practice. The new legislation strengthened the provisions and provided penal sanctions for non-compliance.

In addition, a law of 13 July 1973 imposed on firms employing more than ten people obligations with respect to individual redundancies, including a meeting with the employee and the labour inspector. Moreover, the French Employers' Confederation (CNPF) agreed with the trade unions in November 1974 that the Works Council should be informed of proposed individual redundancies. Where more than ten redundancies within thirty days are proposed, the 1974 agreement provided for information to be disclosed for the purposes of consultation with the Works Council, which can then delay the final decision. The 1975 legislation implemented many of the collectively agreed requirements, though at the time it was stated: 'It is too early to say whether the penal sanctions introduced by the 1975 Act will be effective.'[37]

In the *UK* the only legislation on redundancy prior to 1975 was the Redundancy Payments Act 1965, which provided some compensation to workers losing their jobs in a redundancy situation. The gap was not filled by collective bargaining. A 1968 survey found that only a quarter of establishments with 500 or more employees had a formal written agreement with trade unions over redundancy; a further quarter had a more informal understanding.[38] A

---

[35] *Ibid.*, at pp. 12–13.    [36] *EIRR*, No. 19 (July 1975), p. 10.    [37] *Ibid.*, at p. 9.

[38] S.R. Parker *et al.*, *Effects of the Redundancy Payments Act*, Office of Population Censuses and Surveys (OPCS), London: HMSO, 1971.

Code of Practice accompanying the Industrial Relations Act 1971 laid down certain points of guidance including: 'Responsibility for deciding the size of the work force rests with management. But before taking the final decision to make any substantial reduction, management should consult employees or their representatives, unless exceptional circumstances make this impossible'; it also recommended notification of the Department of Employment about impending redundancies.[39]

The non-legally binding provisions of the Code of Practice were given statutory backing by the Employment Protection Act 1975, s. 99, which, in compliance with the Directive, made consultation and notification mandatory when redundancies are proposed. In 1977, a survey found that half of all establishments having 50–5,000 employees had a formal agreement with trade unions over redundancy, and a further quarter had a less formal understanding. There appeared to have been a very substantial increase in the extent of redundancy agreements over the ten-year period between 1968 and 1977.[40] How much of this preceded, or is attributable to the Directive is unclear.

In *Belgium* the legal position prior to the Directive was governed by two principal sets of legal provisions. First, an Act of 28 June 1966[41] included the requirement that those responsible for undertakings disclose information to the public authorities, to the chairmen of joint industrial committees of union and employer representatives, as well as to the workers affected by any closure decision. The joint industry committees under the Act had the responsibility, *inter alia*, for 'determining the methods whereby prior notice is to be given to the authorities and bodies concerned and to the workers affected, in the event of the closure of an undertaking' (Article 3). Secondly, on 8 May 1973, Belgium's major union and employers' confederations reached a national agreement on collective redundancies within the framework of the National Labour Council. This agreement was subsequently extended to non-signatories and given legal force by its conversion into a Royal Decree on 6 August 1973. The Decree provided, *inter alia*, that Works Councils (or in their absence, union shop stewards) must be informed in advance of any collective redundancy. This information must 'give rise to an exchange of views during which the workers' representatives will make known their observations and suggestions'.

Shortly following the Directive, on 2 October 1975, two new national agreements were reached within the framework of the National Labour Council. The second of these replaced and extended the provisions relating to disclosure

---

[39] The Industrial Relations Code of Practice 1972, paragraphs 44 and 46(i).

[40] W.W. Daniel and E. Stilgoe, *The Impact of Employment Protection Laws*, London: Policy Studies Institute, 1978, pp. 21–3. See generally, B. Bercusson, 'Employment Protection', Chapter 2 in C.D. Drake and B. Bercusson (eds.), *The Employment Acts 1974–1980*, London: Sweet & Maxwell, 1981, pp. 22–7.

[41] This Act was extended and modified by Acts of 30 June 1967 and 28 July 1971. See *EIRR*, No. 23 (November 1975), p. 8, from which the following account is derived.

of information in the Agreement of 8 May 1973 by requiring that where an employer decides to carry out a collective redundancy, he has to inform the workers' representatives of his decision and follow this up with consultations: 'the consultations shall deal with the possibility of avoiding and reducing the collective redundancy as well as alleviating its consequences' (Article 6). To this end, the employer is obliged to provide any useful information.

The interesting fact about these changes in Belgian law following the Directive is that the review which set out the information above concluded by commenting:[42]

> Despite the variety of these changes they are not, in general, expected to have a great impact on those involved with collective redundancies in Belgium …
>
> Belgian unions … do not foresee any great change in the procedures governing collective redundancies as a consequence of bringing the country into line with EC rules. For example, Mr. Grynberg, an official of the FGTB – the country's major socialist-orientated union federation – [said] that as far as disclosure of information was concerned, only smaller firms where there was a low level of unionisation (and consequently little pressure of improving provisions beyond nationally agreed or statutory minima) are likely to be affected.

### The legal position after the 1975 Directive

The legal position in the various Member States in the period *after* the date when they were required to implement the Directive through national legislation (10 February 1977) does not indicate complete harmony. The results of a review in March 1978 of redundancy provisions in the textile industry in the five countries reviewed above are shown in Table 4.1.[43]

The differences evident here with respect to consultation and selection procedures are found also in the provisions on financial compensation for those selected for dismissal in a redundancy situation.[44]

The results of another survey of provisions on collective dismissals in 1980, three years after the compliance date, revealed various differences at the level of *formal* law, let alone at the level of practice (Table 4.2).[45]

A similar survey three years later indicated that only France had instituted changes in the procedures applicable, and that in Italy there was a legally enforceable collective agreement for the industrial sector defining the circumstances of a collective dismissal.[46] As to compliance with the

---

[42] *Ibid.*, at p. 10. This despite the official's pointing out that the number of collective redundancies had increased dramatically during the previous few months.

[43] Extracted from the survey in *EIRR*, No. 51 (March 1978), p. 7.

[44] A ten-country survey in 1980 found that, in most countries, special redundancy payments only become available in a 'collective redundancy' situation, where significant numbers of workers are to be made redundant. However, in France and the UK (as well as Ireland) workers are entitled to special payments in an individual redundancy situation; *EIRR*, No. 75 (April 1980), p. 14.

[45] Extracted from the survey in *EIRR*, No. 76 (May 1980), p. 19.

[46] *EIRR*, No. 109 (February 1983), p. 12.

**Table 4.1** Redundancy consultation and selection procedures in the textile industry, 1978

| Belgium | France | Germany | Italy | UK |
|---|---|---|---|---|
| There will generally be prior consultations with the Works Council, but no set procedures as regards the order of redundancies. | There will generally be prior discussions with the workers concerned; no set procedures as regards the order of redundancies. | No set procedures are followed as regards the order of redundancies. | Established selection procedures as regards factors. | No set procedures as regards redundancies but LIFO* is the usual order. |

*LIFO = last-in-first-out

**Table 4.2** Redundancy dismissal procedures and compensation provisions in the textile industry, 1978

| Belgium | France | Germany | Italy | UK |
|---|---|---|---|---|
| *1. Definition of 'collective dismissal'* | | | | |
| Dismissal for 'economic and technical' reasons. | Dismissal on 'one or more grounds not attributable to the workers' themselves. | Dismissal for 'urgent requirements'. | No statutory definition; 'governed by collective agreement of unions'. | Where employers' need for employees has ceased or diminished. |
| *2. Procedures prior to dismissal* | | | | |
| Consultation and discussions; representatives to be given information; notify regional labour office. Note: special provisions on closures. | (10 or more workers): consulted and given useful information; inform Labour Inspectorate; wait for a 'reflection period'; request Labour Inspectorate authorisation. | Consult works council; notify local labour office. | Unions can call meeting for discussions; regional office to be given information. Note: regional labour office may intervene. | Must consult employer after union and notify Department of Employment. |
| *3. Payments* | | | | |
| Special payment as of right in collective dismissals. | No special statutory payments but individual dismissal payments. | Special negotiable payments for collective dismissal. | No statutory special payments, but recourse to *cassa integrazione* for collective *guadagni*. | No statutory payments for collective dismissals but individual redundancy payments. |

requirements of the Directive, Italy had been subject to a finding by the European Court of Justice (in June 1982) that it failed to comply with the Directive's requirements.[47]

---

[47] *Commission of the EC* v. *Italian Republic*, Case 91/81, [1982] ECR 2133. See the account in *EIRR*, No. 104 (September 1982), p. 19.

### Conclusion

*Prior* to the Directive, there was some law concerning collective dismissals, and there was considerable established industrial practice, depending on union strength and circumstances. But there was considerable variation, both among the laws of different countries, and within countries, between law and practice.

*After* the Directive had been promulgated, there was considerably more law on collective dismissals, but again there were considerable divergences between the laws in terms of their detailed requirements and wording. Similarly, whatever the legal changes that may have occurred consequent upon the Directive, there is some doubt as to its effect upon established industrial custom and practice concerning collective redundancies. Where this was less well established (as in the UK), there may have been changes. Where the law and practice were already well established (as in Germany), there was little. In conclusion, it is difficult to describe this process as, or ascribe it to, a wholly effective policy of harmonisation of labour law in the European Community.

The experience of harmonisation raised general questions for the future of European labour law. It was a strategy dictated by the constraints on Community action stipulated in 1957 by the Treaty of Rome. As its limitations became more apparent, the question arose: was the primary objective to be the approximation of laws of the Member States as conducive to the functioning of a common market, or were the social policy objectives to be primary, with harmonisation only one, and perhaps not the most effective, means of attaining these objectives? The former accepted the primacy of the common market; the latter, the autonomy of social objectives and labour law. If the latter was to prevail, new strategies of achieving the social policy and labour law objectives of the Community would be required.

### The UK veto and strategies to outflank it: financial instruments and qualified majority voting procedures

The Commission's strategy of harmonising legislation was premised on the assumption that the Member States would unanimously approve the measures proposed. This was a prerequisite of the legal basis proposed for these measures: Articles 100[48] and/or Article 235[49] of the Treaty of Rome. The election of a Conservative government in the UK in 1979 put an end to the Commission's

---

[48] Article 100 (first paragraph) (as revised, presently Article 94 EC): 'The Council shall, acting unanimously on a proposal from the Commission, issue directives for the approximation of such provisions laid down by law, regulation or administrative action in Member States as directly affect the establishment or functioning of the common market'.

[49] Article 235 (first paragraph) (presently Article 308 EC): 'If action by the Community should prove necessary to attain, in the course of the operation of the common market, one of the objectives of the Community and this Treaty has not provided the necessary powers, the Council shall, acting unanimously on a proposal from the Commission and after consulting the European Parliament, take the appropriate measures'.

strategy. In line with its domestic policy on labour law, ostensibly deregulation, the UK would not agree to further initiatives on labour law at Community level.

Two strategies were developed to maintain and continue Community social policy and labour law. The first was the use of indirect financial instruments to promote social policy initiatives and to further labour law objectives. The principal instrument was the European Social Fund, which took on a new dynamism in the 1980s. The second strategy involved amending the Treaty of Rome to allow for qualified majority voting on social policy issues. This culminated in the Single European Act 1986.

### Indirect financial instruments: the European Social Fund

A principal instrument of the new social policy strategy was the European Social Fund (ESF). The Fund goes back to the very origins of the Community.[50] The 1951 Treaty setting up the ECSC envisaged cash aids to workers whose firms were closed or restructured. The Treaty of Rome copied and extended the activities of the ECSC in this area. The Treaty provided for the creation of a Social Fund 'to improve employment opportunities for workers in the common market and to contribute thereby to raising the standard of living'.[51] The aim was to compensate certain groups of people for the difficulties caused by the economic changes resulting from the creation of a common market.

Significantly, major change in the Social Fund came with the massive increase in its budget in the early 1980s. In 1983, the Social Fund budget was 1.76 billion ECU. In 1982 it had already reached 1.58 billion ECU, or 5.8 per cent of the total Community budget. This represented a 42.4 per cent increase on 1981 and a 270 per cent increase on 1978. Nevertheless, because of the recession, the gap between demand and available funds remained large. In 1982 only 55 per cent of eligible requests were met.

On 17 October 1983, employment and social affairs ministers of the ten Member States adopted new regulations to guide Social Fund policy from 1984 onwards. The Social Fund concentrated on eight areas: problem regions, the young, the handicapped, migrants, women, adaptation of industry to technical progress, textiles and agriculture. For example, in expanding sectors, such as information technology, the Fund pays for the training of workers for genuinely new jobs.[52] From 1984, all the eight categories were to be rearranged under two principal types of Social Fund aid. The first, and largest, was to be reserved for young people under the age of 25. Projects to promote the employment of young people were in future to take up 75 per cent of the cash available.

The Social Fund was reformed again after the Single European Act 1986. The number of people covered by its activities was more that 2.7 million per annum.

---

[50] European File 2/84, January 1984.     [51] Article 123 (as revised, presently Article 146 EC).
[52] In 1982, the Fund gave 58.5m. ECU to programmes of this kind, assisting 35,400 people.

Aid for vocational training accounts for about 90 per cent of its annual budget.[53] It constitutes an important resource in this limited area of social policy.[54] However, it could not substitute for a general EU social policy let alone as a mechanism for European labour regulation. Indeed, it may be seen as providing a financial cover masking the vacuum of Community labour law and social policy in the early 1980s.[55]

### Qualified majority voting: the Single European Act 1986

### Article 100A(2)[56]

The Commission's proposal of the Single European Market Programme in 1985 implied the approval of a large number of directives aimed at eliminating the many obstacles to free movement identified. To achieve the approval of these directives, the Single European Act 1986 derogated from the requirement of unanimity laid down in Article 100 by adding to the Treaty of Rome a new Article 100A allowing for qualified majority voting:[57]

> 1. ... The Council shall, acting by a qualified majority on a proposal from the Commission in cooperation with the European Parliament and after consulting the Economic and Social Committee, adopt the measures for the approximation of the provisions laid down by law, regulation or administrative action in Member States which have as their object the establishment and functioning of the internal market.

[53] *Social Europe*, 2/91, p. 10.

[54] New Regulations of 1999 cover the period 2000–6 and focus on three main objectives: less developed regions, regions with serious structural problems and 'supporting the adaptation and modernization of policies and systems of education, training and employment'. ESF intervention is aiming to support the European Employment Strategy, specifically, the four pillars established in the annual Employment Guidelines: adaptability, entrepreneurship, equal opportunities and employability. Article 2 of the ESF Regulations (1262/1999) explains the aims and objectives as: to develop policies to combat unemployment; to promote social inclusion and equality; to develop education and training; to promote a skilled, highly trained and adaptable workforce; and to improve women's access to the labour market. A key area of ESF expenditure is training. A new DG XXII was established after the Treaty of Maastricht inserted a new Treaty Chapter for Education, Vocational Training and Youth (Articles 149–50 EC). The ESF is therefore also used to guarantee access to education for all young people under the age of 18 across the EU.

[55] In the 1980s, the Commission appeared to have no alternative but to accede to the UK's veto. The present Barroso Commission appears content to abandon an active Community social and labour policy. The Commission advocates use of the ESF instead of more dynamic intervention, including regulatory initiatives. In the Commission's Communication of 9 February 2005 on the Social Agenda 2006–10 (COM(2005) 33 final), in section 3.2.1, 'Synergies with the national level', 'Capacities': 'The Commission urges the social partners and the Member States to work together to assist the social partners in reinforcing the administrative capacities of national social partner organisations, for example through the possibilities provided by the structural funds – in particular the European Social Fund (ESF).' On this latest evolutionary stage of EU social and labour policy, see below, Chapter 14.

[56] Presently Article 95(2) EC.

[57] Added by Article 18 of the Single European Act 1986, which came into force on 1 July 1987. Now, as revised, in Article 95 EC.

However, at the insistence of the British government, fearful of its opposition to social policy initiatives being diluted, there was inserted into the new Article 100A paragraph 2:[58]

> 2. Paragraph 1 shall not apply to fiscal provisions, to those relating to the free movement of persons nor to those relating to the rights and interests of employed persons.

It has been argued that, as a consequence of this addition, Article 100A is 'of little significance in the employment field, for Article 100A(2) provides that it shall not apply, *inter alia*, to provisions relating to the rights and interests of employed persons'.[59] However, there is an argument to the contrary. Three possible interpretations can be offered of the restriction imposed by Article 100A(2).

A first interpretation would argue that any proposal which touches, *however indirectly and partially*, the rights and interests of employees, is excluded from majority voting.[60] A second interpretation points out that most proposals put forward by the Commission will have multiple concerns, the weight of each varying with the perspective of those affected by it.[61] A third interpretation highlights the fact, though rare, that certain proposals may be *solely* concerned with the rights and interests of employees, and be concerned with nothing else. In sum, *unanimity* in the Council of Ministers may be required for *any* proposal, however partially and indirectly concerned with employees' rights and interests; or only those proposals concerning *solely* the rights and interests of employees alone; or those proposals which *predominantly* (though not exclusively) are concerned with employees' rights and interests.

---

[58] Presently Article 95(2) EC.

[59] D. Wyatt, 'Enforcing EEC Social Rights in the United Kingdom', (1989) 18 *Industrial Law Journal* 197, 199.

[60] For example, the proposal for a European company statute, though primarily aimed at the commercial field, will undoubtedly affect the interests of employees, and certain provisions in the proposal explicitly give employees rights to participation. In July 1989, when the Commission presented the final draft of the European Company Statute, including a choice among three systems of worker involvement, it argued that only a majority vote was required in Council as the statute was part of the programme to remove the remaining internal barriers to the Single European Market. The United Kingdom, however, argued that the measure was a tax and social law, and thus needed a unanimous vote in the Council.

[61] Past initiatives of the Commission may be perceived in this light. Equal pay for women was notoriously included in the Treaty of Rome for reasons of competition over labour costs, though it undoubtedly affected the rights and interests of employees. The Directive regarding collective dismissals combats the harmful effects of sudden disequilibria in the labour market caused by mass dismissals as much as they affect employees. The provisions of the Directive on Transfers of Undertakings weaken potential union opposition to such transfers as much as they benefit employees. Does Article 100A(2) exclude from majority voting only those proposals the *predominant* aim or effect of which concerns the rights and interests of employees? Is a proposal on a minimum wage concerned with unfair competition in labour costs or employee rights and interests? Do proposals on health and safety require enterprises to bear equal burdens in reducing the costs of accidents, or do they concern the rights and interests of employees?

To the extent that labour is a factor of production in the establishment of a unified market, *most* proposals affecting that market will relate to the rights and interests of employees in some way or other. Which of these interpretations of Article 100A(2) is adopted depends upon the vision of the Community held by its author.[62]

In practice, Article 100A (now Article 95 EC) has not been invoked as a basis for social policy initiatives, and its usefulness was largely overtaken by the provisions of the EC Treaty inserted by the Protocol and Agreement on Social Policy of the Maastricht Treaty on European Union.[63] The Treaty now allocates a broad spectrum of social competences to the EC and allows for qualified majority voting on most labour law matters, thus obviating the need for resort to Article 100A.

## Article 118A

A second avenue outflanking the UK veto on social policy initiatives was the new Article 118A of the Treaty of Rome, also inserted by the Single European Act:[64]

1. Member States shall pay particular attention to encouraging improvements, especially in the working environment, as regards the health and safety of workers, and shall set as their objective the harmonization of conditions in this area, while maintaining the improvements made.

2. In order to achieve the objective laid down in the first paragraph, the Council, acting by a qualified majority on a proposal from the Commission, in cooperation with the European Parliament and after consulting the Economic and Social Committee, shall adopt, by means of directives, minimum requirements for gradual implementation, having regard to the conditions and technical rules obtaining in each of the Member States.

---

[62] This issue is as old as labour and social law itself, and is a well-known problem in many Member States. Judges are frequently called upon to adjudicate when the rights and interests of employees concerned outweigh other considerations. Does a requirement of consultation on matters of employees' health and safety include the introduction of new technology? A judgment of the Federal Labour Court in Germany held that works councils have no general right of co-determination on how visual display units (VDUs) are to be designed or installed. Under the Works Constitution Act 1972 s. 87(1) (vii), works councils have co-determination rights on 'arrangements for the prevention of industrial accidents and occupational diseases, and for the protection of health on the basis of legislation or safety regulations'. The Court concluded, however, that if the works council's demand went beyond underpinning existing legislation or safety regulations, there was no right to co-determination. *EIRR*, No. 124, May 1984, p. 9 at p. 10. Is certain industrial action by employees 'wholly or mainly' related to their terms and conditions of employment (in the UK, TULRCA, section 244(1), formerly the Trade Union and Labour Relations Act 1974, s. 29(1), as amended by the Employment Act 1982, s. 18. See R. Benedictus and B. Bercusson, *Labour Law: Cases and Materials*, London: Sweet & Maxwell, 1987, pp. 560–1)? Is the exclusion of enterprises employing fewer than fifteen employees concerned with employees' interests or those of small employers (an issue decided by the Italian Constitutional Court in 1989)? The European Court of Justice could be confronted with similar questions.

[63] Now Article 137 EC.

[64] Single European Act 1986, Article 21. Now in Article 137(1)(a) EC, as amended by the Treaty of Nice.

Once again, this provision can be interpreted in at least three ways. First, as limited to the protection of working activity in the strictest sense; secondly, as including all conditions of work which have or could have effects on the safety and health of workers, including duration of work, its organisation and its content (so as to cover, for example, night work and various forms of 'atypical' work); and finally, as including the working environment in the widest sense of the term, workers' welfare and wellbeing, as well as occupational accidents and illness and protection of health at the workplace.

Then there are also the clauses restricting the Article to minimum provisions, gradual implementation and protection of small and medium enterprises, each of which is itself open to interpretation. To illustrate the problem, the Commission's 1989 Social Action Programme referred to the significance for competitiveness of flexibility of working time. It was argued that this implies a need for harmonisation of standards regulating such flexibility across the Community to avoid distortions in the labour market that would affect competition between firms. This is to raise the well-known issue of 'social dumping', where regulatory controls on working time in one country could be undermined by competition from countries where absence of such regulatory controls gives a competitive advantage to firms.

The legal basis of a proposal on working time could have looked to its effects on competition in the internal market (the 'social dumping' argument), and invoked Article 100A. This would have allowed for approval by qualified majority voting, outflanking a UK veto. The question would then have been raised as to whether the proposed Directive was excluded from the qualified majority voting regime by virtue of paragraph 2 of Article 100A – raising the issues of interpretation discussed earlier.

In the event, the Commission opted to argue that the diversity of regulatory practices regarding flexibility of working time posed a potential threat to the wellbeing and health of workers. This hazard allowed for potential recourse to Article 118A, which also allows for qualified majority voting in the Council in matters concerning the 'working environment, as regards the health and safety of workers'. The UK unsuccessfully challenged before the Court of Justice this legal basis for the Working Time Directive subsequently adopted by the Council.[65]

In the aftermath of the Single European Act 1986, the prospects for the social policy of the EC were to depend on how the institutions of the European Community exercised their discretion in interpreting the provisions of these new articles and how they acted on their interpretations.[66]

---

[65] *United Kingdom* v. *Council*, Case C-84/94, [1996] ECR I-5755.

[66] Constitutional history demonstrates that, as Kahn-Freund commented on the Australian federal experience in unifying labour law: 'The courts may yield to the vital needs of society, whatever intellectual processes they use in order to satisfy them'. O. Kahn-Freund, 'The Impact of Constitutions on Labour Law', (1976) 35 *Cambridge Law Journal* 240, at p. 255.

# Chapter 5

# The strategy of European social dialogue

## Introduction

The UK government's stance from 1979 in preventing the adoption at Community level of legislation on labour policy was dictated by its domestic policy. This stance coupled similar 'deregulation' at domestic level with an equally wholesale policy of exclusion of trade unions and weakening wherever possible of collective bargaining.

It is, therefore, ironic that it was this UK blockage of EC labour legislation which provided the critical impetus to a transformation in legal strategy for social policy and labour law at EU level: the emergence of dialogue between the social partners at European level. The doubtless unintended consequence of the UK government policy of decollectivisation of industrial relations at domestic level was the huge advance in collectivisation of industrial relations at EU level.

Since the ECSC, there had been a long-standing range of formal machinery incorporating representatives of the trade union movements and employer organisations in EC policy-making. The explanation for their involvement is part of a general theory which perceives the Community as not just a bilateral arrangement between Community institutions and Member States, but a complex polity which engages a wide range of other actors in social (and other) policy formation and implementation.

At a general level, the dependence of the Community on Member State cooperation in pursuing its policies means it is important to engage powerful national interest groups, such as trade union confederations and employers' organisations, in the policy process. At the stage of policy formation also, the need for consensus in achieving passage of legislative proposals means that if trade unions and employers' organisations can be mobilised to support the Community proposals, national opposition may be at least neutralised. The resources of the social partner organisations can also be a useful supplement to the strained information gathering capacity of the EC institutions.

The involvement of the social partners reflected, in part, the internal dynamics of the Community institutional machinery. The Commission is most involved and was most active in establishing consultation bodies at EC level. Writing in the mid-1980s, one observer stated:[1]

> The Commission has adopted a unique approach to further its employment law agenda. It has not only maintained regular contact with the representatives of workers and employers, but has actively encouraged the development of Community level worker and employer organizations. It has done so by offering such groups the opportunity to engage in extensive negotiations on all Community employment proposals.

The European Parliament too was very open to relations with the social partners, partly because these organised interests were important to the electability of the Members of Parliament, who could also benefit from their resources for collecting information needed by MEPs, but also because the social partners could be mobilised in support of the Parliament's campaign for a greater role in EC policy-making.

This Commission–social partners–Parliament coalition emerged as a powerful force for social policy development during the 1980s. It served to offset the power of national veto in the Council of Ministers, which had a less active relationship with the social partners and did not encourage interest group involvement.

The development of the European social dialogue was supported by experience, but also by principle and pragmatic expediency. The democratic principle favours the maximum involvement of employers and workers in the formulation of the rules governing their relationship. The concept of social dialogue incorporates a principle critical in the EC context. It stipulates a relationship between collective bargaining and law which assumes a multiplicity of forms within Member States and is extremely flexible in its application within the context of Community social policy.

Social dialogue does not simply equate with collective bargaining. It implies a flexible relationship between social dialogue at all levels and Community and national institutions. Writing in 1989, I argued that 'it could take the form of a dialogue between the social partners at European level leading to proposals in the form of Directives, and/or lead directly to collective bargaining and agreements within Member States'.[2] The relationship is contingent upon national traditions of social dialogue within Member States. Collective bargaining in the UK is not the same as that in France, Italy or Germany. Besides bilateral bargaining, the social dialogue may adopt the form of tripartite structures, assume roles for public authorities and/or establish mechanisms for representation of the unorganised.

---

[1] A.L. Sandler, 'Players and Process: The Evolution of Employment Law in the EEC', (1985) 7 *Comparative Labor Law* 1, at p. 16.

[2] B. Bercusson, 'Fundamental Social and Economic Rights in the European Community', in *Human Rights in the European Community: Methods of Protection*, ed. A. Cassese, S. Clapham and J. Weiler, Baden-Baden, Nomos Verlag, 1991, pp. 195–294, at p. 208.

The emergence of the European social dialogue in the mid-1980s was dictated by the conjuncture of the 1985 Single European Market programme being threatened by the UK veto on the development of a parallel social dimension. The crucial initiative was taken by Jacques Delors, the incoming President of the Commission in January 1985. Presenting the Commission's programme to Parliament, he:[3]

> stressed that the creation of a large market had to go hand in hand with the creation and organization of a European social area; one of its cornerstones should be the social dialogue, the negotiations between employers' and workers' organizations at Community level.
>
> With a view to relaunching the Community social dialogue, the Commission President urged the various economic and social groups to mobilize and play their part in this new stage in the building of Europe, inviting to a meeting at Val Duchesse the chairmen and general secretaries of all the national organizations affiliated to UNICE, CEEP and ETUC.[4]

## The 'social partners' at EU level: ETUC, BusinessEurope (formerly UNICE), CEEP

### The European Trade Union Confederation (ETUC)

The European Trade Union Confederation (ETUC), founded in 1973, is recognised by the European Union, by the Council of Europe and by EFTA as the only representative cross-sectoral trade union organisation at European level. The ETUC presently has in its membership seventy-eight National Trade Union Confederations from a total of thirty-four European countries, as well as eleven European Industry Federations, making a total of 60 million members.[5]

The ETUC's Official Guide to its 10th Quadrennial Congress in May 2003 stated:

> The process of European integration, including recent developments such as the Economic and Monetary Union, is fundamentally changing the setting in which

---

[3] *Joint Opinions*, European Social Dialogue Documentary Series, Commission of the European Communities, p. 19, n.d.

[4] ETUC: European Trade Union Confederation; UNICE: Union des Confédérations de l'Industrie et des Employeurs d'Europe/ Union of Industrial and Employers' Confederations of Europe, renamed 'BusinessEurope' in 2007; CEEP: Centre Européen des Entreprises à Participation Publique et des entreprises d'intérêt économique general/ European Centre of Enterprises with Public Participation and of Enterprises of General Economic Interest.

[5] Other trade union structures operate under the auspices of the ETUC: Eurocadres (the Council of European Professional and Managerial Staff, representing 78 organisations in 19 countries and more than 5 million members) and FERPA (the European Federation of Retired and Elderly Persons, including 43 national pensioners trade union organisations with more than 8 million members). In addition, the ETUC coordinates the activities of the 39 ITUCs (Inter-regional Trade Union Councils), which organise trade union cooperation at cross-border level. In 1999, a Balkans Forum was created bring together all the unions of that region.

European trade unions operate. As the EU plays a growing role in areas of relevant interest for the working people, the trade unions can no longer confine their work to national level. To retain their collective bargaining power and their influence in the economy and in society at large, they need also to speak with a single voice and act collectively at European level. This is why the European Trade Union Confederation exists.

The ETUC seeks to influence the EU's legislation and policies by making direct representations to the various institutions and engaging in extensive consultation with European authorities. The ETUC also seeks to establish industrial relations with employers at EU level through the 'European social dialogue', including the sectoral social dialogue. To support its claims, the ETUC can call upon its affiliates to take action.

The ETUC determines its policies through the deliberations of its Congress and its Executive Committee. The Congress meets once every four years.[6] The Executive Committee, which meets four times a year, consists of representatives of the affiliated national confederations, the affiliated European Industry Federations and the ETUC Women's Committee.[7] The Steering Committee, a smaller body, is responsible for following up the decisions of the Executive Committee between its sessions.[8]

The Executive Committee decides on the mandate and the composition of the delegations which negotiate with the European employers' associations in the European social dialogue, and assesses the results. The ETUC's negotiating mandate is prepared in consultation with the national trade union confederations and the European industry federations. ETUC member organisations must receive all information and details of proposals concerning the potential negotiations at least four weeks before the decision in the Executive Committee,

---

[6] It elects the President (from 2003, Càndido Méndez from UGT (Spain), since 2007, Wanda Lundby-Wedin from LO-Sweden), the General Secretary (from 2003, John Monks) and the two Deputy General Secretaries (from 2003, Reiner Hoffmann and Maria Helena André). The President's role is to chair the ETUC's governing bodies. The General Secretary is the head and the spokesperson of the Confederation.

[7] The President, the General Secretary and the two Deputy General Secretaries are *ex officio* members. Decisions can be taken by a qualified two-thirds majority vote. There are also observers without a right to vote.

[8] In the areas of social research, trade union training and health and safety at the workplace, the ETUC has set up special institutions which benefit from the financial support of the EU. The European Trade Union Institute (ETUI) is the study and research centre of the ETUC in the socio-economic field and for industrial relations. The Trade Union Technical Bureau (TUTB) undertakes support and expert appraisal missions for the ETUC in the fields of health and safety, of the working environment as well as in the context of European standardisation work. The European Trade Union College (ETUCO) is the ETUC's training body, with the tasks of providing support for the trade union training activities undertaken by the member organisations and to hold training courses at European level. These bodies have now been combined to become a single organisation: ETUI-REHS (European Trade Union Institute for Research, Education, Health and Safety).

so as to enable adequate consultations at national and federal level. On the basis of the responses to this information, the ETUC secretariat submits a draft decision to the Executive Committee. The mandate for negotiations with European employers' organisations and the adoption of a draft agreement must have the support of at least two-thirds of the organisations directly concerned.

## BusinessEurope

BusinessEurope (formerly UNICE) is the European private sector employers' organisation.[9] The six founding Member States of the EC were all represented in the eight founder-member federations of UNICE: the BDI and BDA (Germany), the CNPF (France), Confindustria (Italy), the FEDIL (Luxembourg), the FIB (Belgium) and the VNO and FKPCWV (the Netherlands).[10]

BusinessEurope's mission includes fostering solidarity between its member organisations, encouraging a Europe-wide competitive industrial policy, and acting as a spokesperson body to the European institutions. Unlike the ETUC, its trade union analogue, BusinessEurope does not include sectoral employer organisations.

In 2003 there were thirty-five members and four observers from twenty-eight countries, including the European Union countries, the European Economic Area countries, and some Central and Eastern European countries. BusinessEurope has a two-tier structure. One tier is of elected representatives of the member associations. The supreme authority of BusinessEurope is the Council of Presidents (meeting at least twice a year) which is composed of the Presidents of each national member federation, electing among themselves the BusinessEurope President and Vice-Presidents. The second tier of salaried officials comprises the Executive Committee, composed of the Director-Generals of each member association but chaired by the President, meeting at least twice a year, the Secretariat, supplemented by a Committee of Permanent Delegates of national affiliates, and a Finance Committee. Besides these core structures, BusinessEurope has set up five main specialised Policy Committees and about sixty Working Groups, with a staff of forty-five under the direction of the Secretary-General.

BusinessEurope is the leading employers' organisation acting in the European social dialogue. It is BusinessEurope's Social Affairs Committee which prepares BusinessEurope's mandate for social dialogue, which is then adopted by a consensus decision of the Council of Presidents. The Social Affairs

---

[9] UNICE emerged in March 1958, changing its title from the Union des Industries des pays de la Communauté européenne in the wake of the European Economic Community created by the Treaty of Rome. However, its origins go back to 1949, when the Conseil des Fédérations Industrielles d'Europe (CIFE) was created after the Second World War.

[10] The Federation of Greek Industries was accepted as an associate member.

Committee is a consultative body consisting of persons nominated by BusinessEurope's member organisations.

The Council of Presidents, the supreme decision-making body of BusinessEurope, adopts as its primary rule decision by consensus. This does not mean that all decisions have to be unanimous, but that voting may be resorted to only if all attempts to reach common agreement have failed. The voting rules provide that affiliates representing three Member States affected by the decision can block a proposal to start negotiations. The approval of a draft European agreement, however, requires unanimity among the affected members. 'Affected' in this sense are not only affiliates from the EU Member States but also members from the rest of the European Economic Area.

## CEEP

CEEP (Centre Européen des Entreprises à Participation Publique et des enterprises d'intérêt économique general/ European Centre of Enterprises with Public Participation and of Enterprises of General Economic Interest) is the EU-level organisation of employers in the public sector, established in 1961. It is the public sector counterpart to BusinessEurope.[11] CEEP was established as an international association consisting of enterprises and organisations with public participation or carrying out activities of general interest, whatever their legal or ownership status.[12] Under its articles of association, CEEP's main objective as a social partner is to represent enterprises and other employers with public participation and of general economic interest vis-à-vis the EU institutions.

CEEP's General Assembly exercises all the powers needed to achieve the organisation's objectives.[13] The CEEP Social Affairs Committee prepares the

---

[11] CEEP is currently recognised by the European Commission as one of the social partners referred to as 'management' in Articles 138–9 of the EC Treaty. In *Union Européenne de l'Artisanat et des Petites et Moyennes Entreprises (UEAPME)* v. *Council of the European Union*, Case T-135/96, [1998] ECR II-2335, the Court of First Instance declared that CEEP was representative of employers in the public sector. Though normally acting jointly with BusinessEurope, CEEP may engage in social dialogue independently. A first framework agreement was signed by CEEP and the ETUC on 6 September 1990 covering two sectors: rail transport and energy distribution. The framework agreement provided for initial vocational training, training in new technologies and for better health and safety at work and mobility of workers with guaranteed continuity and transferability of various aspects of social protection.

[12] The statutes of CEEP are very open and do not impose any exclusive clauses on recruitment. Its members operate at every level – European, national, regional or local – and may also be affiliated to national professional federations, and thus indirectly be members of other associations. CEEP's territorial area is not limited: while full members must be based in EU countries, enterprises from non-EU countries can join as associate members.

[13] Election of the President, appointment and dismissal of the Secretary-General and administration, approval of the budget, etc. Prior to enlargement, it had forty-seven members from the fifteen Member States. The President of CEEP is elected by the General Assembly every three years, and is assisted by a first Vice-President and other Vice-Presidents who lead the National Sections. The President's main task is to represent CEEP in its external relations. The

mandate for social dialogue which must be approved by the General Assembly. It is a preparatory and consultative body whose members are appointed by the national sections, but its meetings are open to participants from associated members in countries outside the EU. There are no voting rules and the number of participants is not restricted.

## The 'Val Duchesse' social dialogue

'Val Duchesse' is the term used to describe the emergence of the European social dialogue in the mid-1980s. The social partners met at the castle of Val Duchesse outside Brussels on 31 January 1985 and agreed to engage in furthering the social dialogue. At a second meeting on 12 November 1985, they set up two joint working parties: one to examine macro-economic problems and the other to study problems raised by the introduction of new technologies. The Macro-Economic Working Group adopted two 'joint opinions' on 6 November 1986 and 26 November 1987. The Working Party on New Technologies and the Social Dialogue adopted a joint opinion on training and motivation, and information and consultation on 6 March 1987.

The social dialogue received crucial formal recognition through the insertion into the Treaty of Rome, by the Single European Act 1986, of a new Article 118B:[14]

> The Commission shall endeavour to develop the dialogue between management and labour at European level which could, if the two sides consider it desirable, lead to relations based on agreement.

The social dialogue moved to a second phase with a meeting held at the Palais d'Egmont on 12 January 1989, which set up a political steering group. Further working parties were set up and further joint opinions were produced in the years that followed.[15]

---

Council of Administration is responsible for the general management and administration of CEEP. A Delegates' Committee, with the same membership as the General Assembly, is the guidance body for policy and scientific matters. A Congress of CEEP, held every three years, determines strategy and lays down guidelines for future action.

[14] Single European Act, Article 22. Now to be found, as revised, in Articles 138(1) and 139(1) EC.

[15] By way of illustration, the following were the first fifteen Joint Opinions: 1. Fundamental principles behind the cooperative growth strategy for more employment; 2. Training, motivation, information and consultation of workers; 3. Basic principles of the cooperative growth strategy for unemployment; 4. Creation of a European occupational and geographical mobility; 5. Basic education, initial training and vocational training for adults; 6. Transition from school to adult and working life; 7. New technologies, work organisation, adaptability of the labour market; 8. Ways of providing the broadest possible effective access to training; 9. Transparency and transferability of vocational qualifications and diplomas throughout Europe; 10. New cooperative strategy in order to increase employment; 11. Equal access for men and women to education and vocational training; 12. Economic policy guidelines; 13. Community's future role and measures in the fields of education and training; 14. Guidelines for turning recovery into a sustained and job-creating growth process; 15. Contribution of vocational training to combating unemployment.

As the term 'joint opinions' may indicate, the social partners engaged in the dialogue, and in particular the employers' organisations, were ambivalent about the formal outcomes of the process they were involved in. The employers' organisations could hardly resist the pressures coming from the Commission to participate, and they supported the Single European Market programme on the whole, but that did not imply a commitment to what Article 118B characterised as 'relations based on agreement'.[16]

## 'Social dumping' and 'social regime competition'

The attitudes of the social partners towards the European social dialogue initiated in 1985 have to be seen in the context of the common market in general and the renewed impetus also launched by Delors in 1985 as the '1992 Single European Market Programme'. The creation of the single European market allows for enterprises heretofore operating in the context of a national market to be exposed to competition with others in other Member States. One element in this competition is labour costs.[17] This means that pressure will be exerted on enterprises with high *direct* wage costs to secure the productivity that will enable them to compete with enterprises elsewhere in the Community with lower wage costs.[18] This aspect of competition, aimed at rewarding productivity, was one of the objectives of the Single European Market programme.[19]

However, the cost of labour includes both direct and *indirect* labour costs. National systems of labour law and social protection impose *indirect* labour costs on enterprises, such as employer contributions to social security funds and social protection schemes, sick pay, other social payments, vocational training costs and, not least, the costs of compliance with labour standards.

[16] Almost two decades later, the process of formulating 'joint opinions' was considered in the Commission's Communication of 26 June 2002: 'The European social dialogue, a force for innovation and change' (COM(2002) 341 final, section 2.3.3, p. 17): 'It enabled [the social partners] to explore and discuss together the key themes of the European venture: setting in place a cooperation strategy on economic policy, completion of the internal market, application of the Social Charter of the Fundamental Rights of Workers [1989] and preparation of economic and monetary union'.

[17] Labour costs – the total expenditure borne by employers in order to employ workers – are summarised by Eurostat ('EU labour costs 1999', Statistics in focus, Population and social conditions, Theme 3, 3/2001): 'Labour costs considerably influence the choices of political, economic and social decision-makers, as they account for some two-thirds of the production costs of goods and services. Moreover, knowledge of labour cost levels is an essential tool in the strategic planning of investment, production, employment policy or wage levels in collective bargaining'.

[18] Hourly direct labour costs may be defined as direct hourly pay: basic pay plus overtime, shift and other regularly paid premiums. In addition, there may be additional elements of direct labour costs such as holiday pay, Christmas bonus payments and irregular cash payments and bonuses.

[19] The European Commission, while suggesting that harmonisation of indirect wage costs (such as dismissal protection, social security contributions and other forms of taxation) should take place, considered that harmonisation of direct costs (rules governing wages and salaries) was unnecessary because 'differences in productivity levels attenuate these differences in unit labour costs to a considerable degree' (COM (90) 228).

Lower labour and social standards in some Member States may entail lower indirect labour costs for enterprises in those Member States. The result is to give enterprises in those countries with lower indirect labour costs a competitive advantage compared with enterprises in Member States with higher labour and social standards. This advantage may be offset by other factors which favour enterprises in countries with higher labour and social standards, such as better transport infrastructures or a more highly trained and skilled workforce. Nonetheless, differences in direct and indirect labour costs may constitute a significant competitive edge.

One consequence of such differences has been argued to raise the threat of 'social dumping'. As a result of what has been called 'social policy regime competition'[20] between Member States, Member States will be under pressure to reduce their labour and social standards in order to ease the burden of high indirect wage costs on enterprises. Enterprises, particularly multinational enterprises, will be tempted to locate new investments or even relocate existing establishments to countries where lower labour and social standards entail lower indirect labour costs. Tables 5.1 and 5.2 graphically illustrate the position as it stood in 1990, early in the history of the European social dialogue. Table 5.3 provides a contemporary comparison.[21]

Social dumping posited two alternative scenarios for the institutional arrangements of formulation and implementation of EU labour law and social policy. One scenario envisaged the *transfer* of social policy jurisdiction to the EU level. Harmonised or uniform social and labour standards throughout the Community, established through EU legal measures, would secure the objective of greater equalisation of indirect labour costs for all enterprises, and reduce, if not eliminate, the threat of unequal standards distorting competition in favour of Member States with lower standards. The second scenario favoured the opposite: *retention* of national competence over social and labour standards, accepting the consequence of direct competition between different Member State social regimes.

---

[20] W. Streeck, 'La dimensione sociale del mercato unico europeo: verso un'economia non regolato?', (1990) 28 *Stato e Mercato* 29 at p. 48.

[21] In 1999, the average hourly labour costs in western Germany were DM 49.23, which is calculated to be around 39 per cent higher than average hourly labour costs in Germany's competitor countries. However, this gap is said to be steadily declining (by some 15 per cent since 1996). The countries with the lowest average hourly labour costs in manufacturing are Portugal (DM 12.03) and Greece (DM 16.29), significantly below the next lowest, Spain (DM 26.20). Average hourly labour costs in eastern Germany have risen by 55 per cent since 1992, though still one-third below those in western Germany. Additional labour costs rose faster than direct wage costs between 1980 and 1999, increasing the share of additional costs as a proportion of overall labour costs. The rate of increase is greater in some countries than in others. The country with the highest proportion of additional costs is Italy (97 per cent, up from 85 per cent in 1989), followed by Belgium (95 per cent, up from 80 per cent), France (93 per cent, up from 80 per cent) and Austria (93 per cent, up from 82 per cent). The country with the lowest proportion of additional costs is Denmark (25 per cent, up from 22 per cent in 1980). The country with the most rapid increase in the proportion of additional costs is Finland, up from 55 per cent in 1980 to 78 per cent in 1999.

**Table 5.1** Hourly labour costs in industry in the EC, 1990 in ECUs

| | |
|---|---|
| Germany | 20.08 |
| Belgium | 19.30 |
| Netherlands | 17.47 |
| Denmark | 17.19 |
| France[*] | 15.27 |
| Luxembourg[+] | 14.48 |
| Italy[*] | 14.24 |
| UK | 12.20 |
| Ireland | 11.64 |
| Spain | 11.30 |
| Greece[*] | 5.24 |
| Portugal | 3.57 |

*1988 figures
+ 1989 figures
*Source:* Eurostat (1992) 'Labour costs: updating 1989–90', Luxembourg.

**Table 5.2** The structure of labour cost in industry in the EC, 1990

| Country | Direct cost (%) | Of which remuneration (%) | Indirect cost (%) | Of which social security (%) |
|---|---|---|---|---|
| Denmark | 96.2 | 83.1 | 3.8 | 3.0 |
| UK | 86.8 | 84.2 | 13.2 | 11.5 |
| Luxembourg[*] | 82.8 | 67.4 | 17.4 | 16.3 |
| Ireland | 82.2 | 70.5 | 17.8 | 14.9 |
| Greece[+] | 80.0 | 61.0 | 19.0 | 19.0 |
| Germany[+] | 76.3 | 56.0 | 23.7 | 21.5 |
| Spain | 74.9 | 53.3 | 25.1 | 24.5 |
| Portugal | 74.2 | 56.0 | 25.8 | 21.7 |
| Netherland | 73.3 | 54.3 | 26.7 | 23.2 |
| Italy[+] | 70.0 | 50.3 | 30.0 | 26.7 |
| Belgium | 69.5 | 49.1 | 30.5 | 28.9 |
| France[+] | 68.0 | 51.4 | 32.0 | 28.6 |

*1988 figures
+ 1989 figures
*Source:* Eurostat (1992): 'Labour costs up-detial 1989–1990'.

These two scenarios were obviously linked with wider political strategies concerned with the pace and direction of European integration in general. In that general context of European integration, however, the interesting feature of the two apparently opposing scenarios regarding EU social policy and labour law is that *both* lead to a *loss* of Member State autonomy in these fields of policy.

**Table 5.3** Direct and additional hourly labour costs (HLC) in manufacturing industry in 2003 (euros)

| Country* | Direct hourly labour costs | Total hourly labour costs | Total hourly labour costs | Additional labour costs as % of direct labour costs | |
|---|---|---|---|---|---|
| | | | | 1980 | 2003 |
| Norway | 18.96 | 9.19 | 28.15 | 48 | 49 |
| Denmark | 20.63 | 6.70 | 27.33 | 22 | 33 |
| West Germany | 15.13 | 11.96 | 27.09 | 75 | 79 |
| Switzerland | 16.79 | 8.81 | 25.60 | 47 | 53 |
| Finland | 13.58 | 10.45 | 24.03 | 55 | 77 |
| Belgium | 12.46 | 11.34 | 23.80 | 80 | 91 |
| Netherlands | 12.90 | 10.30 | 23.20 | 76 | 80 |
| Sweden | 13.30 | 9.47 | 22.77 | 64 | 71 |
| Austria | 11.47 | 9.86 | 21.32 | 82 | 86 |
| Luxembourg | 14.01 | 7.14 | 21.15 | 41 | 51 |
| France | 10.48 | 9.67 | 20.15 | 80 | 92 |
| US | 13.91 | 5.99 | 19.91 | 37 | 43 |
| United Kingdom | 12.84 | 5.88 | 18.72 | 39 | 46 |
| Japan | 10.93 | 7.35 | 18.28 | 64 | 67 |
| Ireland | 12.96 | 5.15 | 18.11 | 34 | 40 |
| East Germany | 10.17 | 6.68 | 16.86 | – | 66 |
| Canada | 12.13 | 4.70 | 16.83 | 32 | 39 |
| Italy | 8.58 | 8.11 | 16.69 | 85 | 95 |
| Spain | 8.69 | 7.28 | 15.97 | – | 84 |
| Greece | 6.07 | 4.12 | 10.18 | 56 | 68 |
| Portugal | 3.98 | 3.02 | 7.00 | – | 76 |
| Czech Republic | 2.35 | 1.95 | 4.30 | – | 83 |
| Hungary | 2.28 | 1.76 | 4.04 | – | 77 |
| Poland | 2.06 | 1.20 | 3.26 | – | 58 |
| Slovakia | 1.88 | 1.34 | 3.22 | – | 71 |

*Source:* 'Comparative Manufacturing Industry Labour Costs in 2003', *European Industrial Relations Review* No. 378, July 2005, Table 2, p. 35.

The first scenario is explicit about this result: Member States relinquish their competence over social policy and labour law in favour of regulation of these areas by harmonised and uniform EU standards. Future developments in these policy areas are thereby left to EU initiatives.

But the second scenario also, though not so explicitly, entails the reduction or elimination of national autonomy in social policy and labour law-making. This is because Member States considering initiatives in the field of social policy or labour law will be highly conscious of the implications of undertaking such initiatives for enterprises on their national territory. Any initiative which involves compliance costs with labour regulations or social protection measures will impose higher indirect labour costs compared with enterprises in the other Member States. This is bound to make it more difficult to obtain internal political consensus for such social legislation. Moreover, the pressure will continue on Member States to reduce their social and labour standards to the levels prevailing in countries with competing enterprises.

What both scenarios have in common, therefore, is a policy of 'deregulation' at national level; either because this is the result of social policy regime competition, or because regulation at national level is replaced by exercise of regulatory competence in social and labour matters at EU level.

The dangers posed by 'social dumping' and 'social regime competition' as a result of the 1992 Single European Market programme led to a fierce and protracted political battle between the social partners – a kind of class struggle at European level.

The strategy of the trade unions at European level has been characterised as dictated by a 'political-distributive' logic.[22] This recognised the dangers posed by social dumping in the single market, but also acknowledged the advantages to be reaped by enterprises free to compete without national hindrance. The aim was to achieve a balance between the costs of the social protection necessary to offset the risk of social dumping, and the losses to enterprises entailed by this necessary degree of regulation. The strategy, therefore, was one of political *regulation* at European level to secure the fair distribution of the benefits of the single market, requiring attention to questions of labour and social standards and implementation mechanisms.

The strategy of employers' organisations has been characterised as dictated by an 'economic-productive' logic.[23] The social dimension of the single market was to aim at achieving the maximum productive and competitive efficiency. For firms in the European Community, the principal competitive challenge came from outside the EC – mainly from the USA and Japan. Enterprises in those countries benefited from significantly lower social and labour standards, a competitive advantage which hindered enterprises in Europe. The social policy of the EC in the new single European market should, therefore, aim at reducing this competitive advantage by eliminating that social and labour regulation which was such a burden on European enterprises. Freed of such a burden, the productive and competitive efficiency of European enterprise would achieve the requisite growth generating the economic benefits for living and working standards. European employers, therefore, had a positive social policy: that of *deregulation* to allow for the necessary flexibility and competitiveness.

Each of these social policy strategies for the single European market had an accompanying *legal* strategy. The deregulation strategy put forward by the employers' organisations was based on the assumption that there were to be no common social and labour standards imposed through EC measures. This had the advantage that it would reduce the need for a central regulatory bureaucracy, not required, given the non-interventionist policy. It had the corollary benefits of operating to inhibit social regulation initiatives at national level, for fear of burdening Member State enterprises. Finally, it allowed for

---

[22] Streeck, 'La dimensione sociale'.      [23] *Ibid.*

regulatory social regime competition, in which Member States would compete against each other to lower indirect social and labour costs.

The consequences for labour of such a strategy would have been negative. The benefits of the single European market were, at that stage, purely speculative and highly uncertain. The exclusion of any attempt at social regulation meant the widely anticipated restructuring of enterprises would be unrestrained. There would be no EC political regulatory regime capable of supporting social protection or labour rights, collective or individual. And the prospect of social dumping would become a reality, with particular threats to social security regimes imposing employer contributions.

The struggle that ensued between these protagonists and their strategies involved not only the social partners but also the Community institutions which also had a stake in the outcome. Its outcome was marked by two major developments: the Community Charter of Fundamental Social Rights of Workers of December 1989, and the Protocol and Agreement on Social Policy of the Treaty on European Union agreed at Maastricht in December 1991, which came into effect in November 1993. The Protocol and Agreement of 1991 pushed into prominence the consensus between the two sides of industry – employers and trade unions at EU level – that the social dialogue should become a, if not the, primary instrument for social and labour regulation in the EU.[24] The Community Charter of 1989 was evidence that the Member States were determined to embark on such a legislative programme.

---

[24] In the first edition of this book (1996, pp. 78–94), the prospects of a strategy of European social dialogue for European labour law were assessed in the light of a more detailed analysis of the potential of social dialogue at *sectoral* level, both in the Member States and at EU level. The question of whether European labour law will develop towards recognition of labour law standards established through the European social dialogue was examined, in particular, in light of whether the level of the sector is adapted to assume the role proposed by the Maastricht Agreement for the formulation of EC social policy, and the embodiment of EC labour standards. The importance of the sectoral level of bargaining was increasing in Europe, with the exception of the UK. This was one of three trends in collective bargaining identified by a study carried out for the Commission by Vaughan-Whitehead. The three trends were decentralisation to company level, diversification of remuneration and extension of sectoral bargaining (D. Vaughan-Whitehead, 'Wage Bargaining in Europe: Continuity and Change', *Social Europe*, Supplement 2/90). His analysis suggests that within the majority of Member States sectoral bargaining has moved into the position once occupied by multi-sector national level bargaining, while at the same time company bargaining has taken up some of the issues which might previously have been resolved at sectoral level. Issues such as flexibility, early retirement and training, previously the subject of national bargaining, are moving down to the sectoral bargaining level, whilst wage bargaining, previously an area determined by sectoral bargaining, is moving down to enterprise bargaining. This shift was particularly important when considering an EC-wide framework for social dialogue. For although it has been well recognised that wage bargaining is unlikely to be the subject of Europe-wide agreement, it is precisely those areas which are now identified within Member States as being within the competence of sectoral bargaining that could most easily be translated into European agreements. For reasons of space, this analysis and discussion of trends in sectoral bargaining at national and EU levels (in the latter, with particular reference to the construction and metalworking sectors) could not be included in the second edition. However, the argument remains valid and will be taken up in subsequent discussion of the European sectoral social dialogue. See Chapter 18 below.

## The Community Charter of the Fundamental Social Rights of Workers 1989

On 9 December 1989, the Member States of the European Community, gathered together in the European Council at Strasbourg, solemnly declared, with the sole dissent of the United Kingdom, a Charter of the Fundamental Social Rights of Workers.[25] The development of the 1992 programme carried with it increasing concern with the social consequences of the creation of the Single European Market. The social policy of the EC, as developed over its first thirty years, did not seem adequate to the task.[26] An attempt to overcome the stalemate preventing the Council approving many Commission proposals on social policy was made by the launching in 1985 of the Val Duchesse 'social dialogue' between the European level trade union and employers' organisations (ETUC, UNICE and CEEP), reinforced by the provision in Article 118B of the Treaty inserted by the Single European Act.[27] But this effort did not fulfil the perceived need for the formulation and implementation of a comprehensive social dimension for the 1992 programme.

Building upon the Belgian Presidency (the Labour and Social Affairs Council of May 1987) and an opinion of the Economic and Social Committee (the Beretta Report of November 1987),[28] a working party of the Commission in 1988 proposed a body of minimum social provisions.[29] Thereafter, the development was very rapid: following an Opinion of the Economic and Social Committee in February 1989[30] and a Resolution on Fundamental Rights of the European Parliament in March 1989,[31] a first draft of a Community Charter of Fundamental Social Rights was published by the Commission in May 1989, a second draft was produced in October 1989 and the December summit approved the final Charter. Shortly before, the Commission had produced a Communication concerning its Action Programme relating to the implementation of the Community Charter.[32]

Due to the opposition of the UK government, the Charter could not be integrated into the Treaty of Rome in 1989. Its legal status remains that of a political declaration. As such it has had important legal consequences through

---

[25] *Social Europe* 1/90, p. 45.

[26] For a summary of the social policy of the Community during this period, see *Social Europe*, 1/87, pp. 51–62; 1/88, pp. 19–20.

[27] For an outline of the development of the social dialogue in the Community, see Annex 10 to The Social Dimension of the Internal Market, Interim Report of the Interdepartmental Working Party of the Commission, *Social Europe*, Special Edition, Brussels, 1988.

[28] *Opinion of the Economic and Social Committee on the Social Aspects of the Internal Market (European Social Area)*, Brussels, 19 November 1987, CES(87) 1069.

[29] See Report of the Interdepartmental Working Party.

[30] *Opinion of the Economic and Social Committee on Basic Community Social Rights*, Brussels, 22 February 1989; CES 270/89 F/OUP/CH/ht.

[31] Resolution of 15 March 1989, OJ C96, 17 April 1989, p. 61.

[32] COM(89) 568 final, Brussels, 19 November 1989.

its inspiration of a Social Action Programme which resulted in various legally binding measures.[33]

The precise nature of the political commitment of eleven Member States which approved the Charter took concrete shape over the following months and years in the actions of the Commission, which elaborated various Community instruments, drawing upon the Community Charter as an indication of the direction of developments in this area. In this sense the Charter was similar in intent, though much more precise in form, to the 1974 declaration of the Social Action Programme by the Council in Paris which launched a dynamic phase of social policy in the Community. The results of the impetus given to social policy by that declaration were manifest in the many instruments adopted during the 1970s.

However, even the most sympathetic observer would admit that the achievements under the 1989 Programme were not up to the expectations expressed by the Community Charter. The commitments undertaken by eleven Member States in 1989 remain unfulfilled.

The Community Charter of Fundamental Social Rights of Workers of 1989 represented a commitment by the Member States of the European Union to a set of social policy and labour law objectives. But it was not a *final* document embodying the ultimate aspirations of social and economic rights or the definitively highest ideals regarding social and economic rights.[34] It has to be put in its historical context. The 1989 Charter was a phase in the evolution of the European Community in the context of the completion of the 1992 Single European Market programme.

---

[33] In the longer term, the Court of Justice may be called upon to adjudicate upon the meaning, and perhaps challenges to the validity, of these measures proposed by the Commission and adopted by the Council (some by qualified majority). It may be expected that the decision of the Court will be influenced by the wording of the Charter. Analysis of the content of the Charter in the first edition of this book (Chapter 37, pp. 575–98) aimed to clarify the meaning of the Charter approved by the Member States. The analysis identified the possible scope of the initiatives which could be taken by the Commission in fulfilment of the desire of these Member States to develop Community policy in the form of fundamental social rights, and elaborated the background against which decisions of the Court of Justice on these initiatives may be taken. The detailed analysis focused upon some (though not all) important elements of social policy manifest in the Charter, particularly in light of changes which occurred in arriving at the final draft approved in December 1989.

[34] The changing nature of economic and social rights was noted in the debates over whether the European Convention of Human Rights should be extended to include such rights, in light of the Council's European Social Charter. The need to take account of this changing nature was emphasised in the formulation of such rights: 'there are no "ideal" standards, as standards may be, and are, adjusted by law to take account of a variety of factors such as social changes, higher productivity, health and hygiene requirements resulting from advancing industrialization, etc. It is therefore impossible, in a text designed to be permanently valid, to lay down precise rules applicable to all European countries for a long period, if not for ever.' A. Berenstein, 'Economic and Social Rights: Their Inclusion in the European Convention on Human Rights, Problems of Formulation and Interpretation', (1981) 2 *Human Rights Law Journal* (no. 3–4) 257, at pp. 272–3. A Report prepared for the European Parliament and the Commission during 1989, prior to the approval of the Community Charter, stated: 'The challenge for the EC is to formulate and define social and economic rights in such a way and in such an instrument as will allow for their flexible and dynamic character.' Bercusson, 'Fundamental Social and Economic Rights', p. 201.

In practice, the 1989 Charter served as the political legitimation for the Commission in formulating its legislative programme. It was cited in the Preambles to measures proposed by the Commission and approved by the Council since then, as well as in the Preamble to the Maastricht Protocol and Agreement on Social Policy.[35] This demonstrates the Charter's function as the inspiration for an as yet unrealised social programme.

The adoption of the Charter was a powerful signal that the Community was potentially poised to embark on a programme of social legislation. The impact of this on the European social dialogue was soon to be evident. First, it served to stimulate the move towards expanding the social and labour competences of the EC. Secondly, formulation, implementation and enforcement of the rights of workers in most Member States were commonly achieved through the social partners at national level. Similarly, the Charter's rights at Community level were to be implemented through the mechanism produced two years later in the Protocol and Agreement on Social Policy of the Maastricht Treaty on European Union.

## The Protocol and Agreement on Social Policy of the Maastricht Treaty on European Union 1991

The conclusion of a Protocol to the Treaty on European Union (TEU) and an Agreement on Social Policy at the Maastricht Summit of December 1991 put in place a fundamental change in European labour and social law and policy, both in substance and in the procedures of formulation and implementation. The substance of the Protocol and Agreement on Social Policy to the TEU is important, but equally important was the procedure of their formulation and adoption.

The key documents proposing the changes were drafted by the Member State holding the Presidency of the Council of Ministers – the Netherlands. But their final form, and most of the substance of the provisions which eventually became the Agreement between the eleven Member States were the result of negotiations between the peak organisations of employers (UNICE and CEEP) and of workers (ETUC) at European level which led up to the agreement of 31 October 1991 between the ETUC, UNICE and CEEP, which was the foundation for the Protocol and Agreement on Social Policy of the Treaty on European Union.[36]

---

[35] The Protocol begins by 'Noting that 11 Member States … wish to continue along the path laid down in the 1989 Social Charter'. The Agreement begins: 'The undersigned 11 High Contracting Parties … Wishing to implement the 1989 Social Charter on the basis of the *acquis communautaire* …'. The Declaration by the Governments of the EFTA States on the Charter provides that they 'endorse the principles and basic rights laid down in the Charter'.

[36] An exhaustive study by Jon Erik Dolvik provides the most detailed account yet published of the negotiations. *Redrawing Boundaries of Solidarity? ETUC, Social Dialogue and the Europeanisation of Trade Unions in the 1990s*, ARENA Report No. 5/97, Fafo Report No. 238, Oslo, December 1997, Chapter 8, pp. 189–239. Dolvik provides an incisive analysis of what appears to have been the Commission's strategy in February–March 1991 in setting the social policy agenda for the Maastricht Summit, at pp. 194–7.

On the one hand, the social partners, in particular the employers, were threatened with extended use of qualified majority voting (QMV), but simultaneously tempted with the prospect of avoiding legislation by substituting negotiated agreements. On the other hand, Member States were to be 'faced with an input from the [European level] social partners that would be difficult to reject':[37]

> By designing its proposal in this way the Commission might mobilise a source of legitimacy which could bolster its case in two ways, through an advanced, double-edged operation. By simultaneously using the risk of QMV being adopted by the IGC [the Member States in the Intergovernmental Conference] to convince employers to agree on the 'negotiate or we will legislate' formula, the latter was, on the other hand, used as a means of convincing Member States to accept extended QMV. In other words, by using 'supranational' resources built up within the social dialogue as a card in intergovernmental bargaining *and* using intergovernmental bargaining as a card in the social dialogue, the Commission (as the only political actor present in both settings) was trying to exploit tensions between intergovernmentalism and supranationalism to construct a new institutional framework of Community social policy.

This early strategy was only successful following further dynamic developments, a process Dolvik characterises as 'Social dialogue negotiations in the shadow of IGC' and, eventually, 'Stumbling into the 31 October agreement'.[38]

The negotiations culminating in the Agreement dated 31 October 1991 between the ETUC and UNICE/CEEP produced a new draft of Articles 118(4), 118A and 118B of the Treaty of Rome.[39] With few modifications, this Agreement was adopted by the eleven Member States as the basis for the future labour and social law of the European Union. This remarkable success of the social dialogue at EC level provides a striking example of the fundamental change in European labour law.

The negotiations at Maastricht produced the Treaty on European Union signed by the Member States of the European Community on 7 February 1992, a Protocol on Social Policy and an Agreement, annexed to the Protocol, between eleven Member States, with the exception of the UK, also on Social

---

[37] *Ibid.*, p. 197.

[38] In addition to analysis, Dolvik provides fascinating details on, for example, the position of the British employers (CBI) and the Swedish and German trade unions. See *ibid.*, pp. 202–3, and footnote 125.

[39] *Agence Europe*, No. 5603, 6 November 1991, 12. This account focuses on five documentary sources: 1. the first draft of the Dutch Presidency (*Europe Documents*, No. 1733/1734, 3 October 1991); 2. the accord between the ETUC/UNICE/CEEP concerning a new draft of Articles 118, 118A and 118B of the Rome Treaty (*Agence Europe*, No. 5603, 6 November 1991, 12); 3. the second draft of the Dutch Presidency (*Europe Documents*, No. 1746/1747, 20 November 1991); 4. the Protocol on Social Policy of the 12 Member States and the Agreement between the eleven Member States concluded at Maastricht on 9–10 December 1991, (*Europe Documents*, No. 1750/1751, 13 December 1991); 5. the Protocol on Social Policy of the twelve Member States and the Agreement between the eleven Member States signed at Maastricht on 7 February 1992 (*Europe Documents*, No. 1759/1760, February 1992).

Policy.[40] The Protocol notes that eleven Member States 'wish to continue along the path laid down in the 1989 Social Charter [and] have adopted among themselves an Agreement to this end'; accordingly, all twelve Member States:

1. Agree to authorise those 11 Member States [excluding the UK] to have recourse to the institutions, procedures and mechanisms of the Treaty for the purposes of taking among themselves and applying as far as they are concerned the acts and decisions required for giving effect to the above-mentioned Agreement.
2. The [UK] shall not take part in the deliberations and the adoption by the Council of Commission proposals made on the basis of this Protocol and the abovementioned Agreement ... Acts adopted by the Council ... shall not be applicable to the [UK].

Article 1 of the Agreement, the redrafted Article 117 of the Treaty of Rome,[41] greatly expanded the legal competences of the Community in the field of social policy:

> The Community and the Member States shall have as their objectives the promotion of employment, improved living and working conditions, proper social protection, dialogue between management and labour, the development of human resources with a view to lasting high employment and the combating of exclusion.

Within this new sphere of Community social policy, the Council is authorised[42] to proceed by qualified majority voting to 'adopt, by means of directives, minimum requirements for gradual implementation' in the following five 'fields':[43]

> improvement in particular of the working environment to protect workers' health and safety;
> working conditions;
> the information and consultation of workers;

---

[40] The Agreement comprised a new formulation of some of the Articles on social policy of the Treaty of Rome. The opt-out of the UK raised a question of whether the Agreement and its consequences were to be regarded as part of EC law. The issue was expected to have been resolved by the anticipated victory of the Labour Party in the British general election of April 1992, which was predicted to result in the UK becoming party to the Agreement. Its provisions would then have substituted for the provisions in the Treaty. As the Conservative Party won the election, this did not happen, and there continued in existence two parallel sets of provisions: one applicable to all the Member States in the Treaty, and one applicable to the Member States party to the Agreement. This continued until, following the victory of the Labour Party in the UK general election of May 1997, by the Treaty of Amsterdam of June 1997, the UK relinquished the opt-out. For further analysis of the legal nature of the Protocol and the Agreement on Social Policy, and the legal position for the duration of the UK opt-out between 1993 and 1997, see the first edition of this book, pp. 525–32.
[41] As revised, now in Article 136 EC.
[42] By Article 2, paragraphs 1 and 2 of the Agreement, the redrafted Article 118 of the Treaty of Rome. As revised, now in Article 137 EC.
[43] The Protocol, Article 2, deemed the new qualified majority in the Council, given the absence of the UK, to be forty-four votes among the eleven Member States.

equality between men and women with regard to labour market opportunities and treatment at work;

the integration of persons excluded from the labour market.

This was an expansion of the competence of the Community to act in the social policy area even where one or more Member States are opposed. Unanimity was required in the following five 'areas':[44]

social security and social protection of workers;

protection of workers where their employment is terminated;

representation and collective defence of the interests of workers and employers, including co-determination, subject to paragraph 6;

conditions of employment for third-country nationals legally residing in Community territory;

financial contributions for promotion of employment and job-creation, without prejudice to the provisions relating to the Social Fund.

Paragraph 6 of Article 2, however, provided that:

The provisions of this Article shall not apply to pay, the right of association, the right to strike or the right to impose lock-outs.[45]

These provisions expanded both the legal scope and the ability of the EC to develop social policy and labour law at European level. In the past, there had been many disputes over whether there was any legal basis for social policy measures, and, if so, whether the legal basis allowed for qualified majority voting or required unanimity in the Council. The new and more complex formulations of competence, and the apparent overlap between those fields allowing for qualified majority voting,[46] those areas subjected to unanimity[47] and those excluded altogether[48] were to give rise to much debate when measures were proposed by the Commission.[49]

What was the relation of the new competences in the Agreement to the old competences in Articles 117–118B of the Treaty?[50] The Protocol and Agreement

---

[44] Article 2, paragraph 3.

[45] This exclusion contradicted the expressed intention in the Protocol that fourteen Member States 'wish to continue along the path laid down in the 1989 Social Charter; that they have adopted among themselves an Agreement to this end …'. The Social Charter contained explicit guarantees related to pay (Article 5), the right of association (Article 11) and the right to strike (Article 13). The implication must be that the exclusions in this paragraph are to be interpreted narrowly. In contrast, there is doubt as to whether paragraph 6 operates similarly to limit the scope of 'agreements concluded at Community level' under Article 4 of the Agreement. Paragraph 6 is now Article 137(5) EC.

[46] Article 2(1).    [47] Article 2(3).    [48] Article 2(6).

[49] A notorious example was the Commission's Social Charter Action Programme proposal on 'atypical workers', ultimately divided into three separate proposals, each with its own legal basis and voting procedure.

[50] The recital to the Protocol stipulated: 'that this Protocol and the said Agreement are without prejudice to the provisions of this Treaty, particularly those relating to social policy which constitute an integral part of the *acquis communautaire*'. 'This Treaty' refers to the Treaty on

aimed, in the words of the latter's Preamble: 'to implement the 1989 Social Charter on the basis of the *acquis communautaire*'. The 1989 Social Charter's objectives were ambiguous as regards consolidation or development of social rights. In particular, in the final draft of the Charter's Preamble a new clause was added: 'whereas the implementation of the Charter must not entail an extension of the Community's powers as defined by the Treaties'.[51] The Protocol and Agreement comprised a major extension of the Community's powers in the social field as regards the Member States party to the Agreement. This implied the proposal of measures going *beyond* (hence 'without prejudice to') the present *acquis communautaire*, based on the powers in the EC Treaty to which that *acquis* was restricted, and henceforth engaging the new legal powers.[52]

Like the Community Charter of 1989, the Agreement may be regarded not only as a legal, but also as a political document.[53] It not only defined the new scope of Community social policy, *more important*, it directed the Commission to produce proposals to implement the new competences. It was not only a legal question of what the competences of the Member States were in social policy. In practice, the crucial issue was the *Commission's* role. Social policy proposals could be conceived in either the old or the new framework of competences. The question was whether the Commission was *able* to continue in the old pattern, or was *obliged* to operate a new social policy within the framework of the new competences.

A determining role was to be played by the social partners. As will be elaborated below, under the Maastricht Agreement, they had the right to be consulted and, if they wished, to request that agreement be sought on the issue by way of social dialogue.[54] These rights only operated in the case of social policy proposals under the new competences. Since the Commission had the duty to promote social dialogue,[55] there was an implication that the new competences – allowing for social dialogue – should be used.[56]

Analysis of the implications of the Maastricht Treaty on European Union for the labour and social law and policy of the EC requires a detailed interpretation of the texts. But it must also address the dynamics of the Protocol and Agreement on Social Policy – how they were to work in practice. This involves an analysis of the scope of potential social policy proposals emanating from the

European Union, which made only one change to the relevant parts of the EC Treaty (Articles 117–21): Article G(33) replacing the first subparagraph of Article 118a(2).

[51] B. Bercusson, 'The European Community's Charter of Fundamental Social Rights of Workers', (1990) 53 *Modern Law Review* 624 at p. 625.

[52] As put in the Maastricht Treaty's Article B on the objectives of the Union: 'to maintain in full the *acquis communautaire* and build on it'. Article C again refers to 'respecting and building upon the *acquis communautaire*'. Barry Fitzpatrick notes the potential problem of reconciling existing directives with amendments to them approved under the Agreement. 'Community Social Law after Maastricht', (1992) 21 *Industrial Law Journal* 199, at p. 204.

[53] Bercusson, 'The European Community's Charter'.

[54] Articles 3(4) and 4.      [55] Article 3(1).

[56] Indeed, the question was whether the social partners could challenge proposals under the old legal basis (the former EC Treaty provisions) as excluding them unnecessarily.

Commission and the way in which the actors involved – EC institutions, Member States and the social partners – plan their strategies accordingly.

It is the interaction between Commission proposals and the social dialogue which constitutes the defining quality of the process of social policy formation in the EC: what I have called 'bargaining in the shadow of the law'.[57] The social dialogue takes place on many levels. Agreements at EC level and the process of their articulation with Member State labour laws may encompass many different actors. This multiplicity of actors poses a complex problem of choice of levels for social policy formation and implementation. It can be summed up in the word 'subsidiarity'. The conclusion to this chapter seeks to provide some clarification of this principle as it may be applied in the area of EC labour and social law and policy.

## The role of the European social dialogue in formulating European labour law

At EC level, collective bargaining derived two major impulses – linked to each other – from the Maastricht Agreement. The first was Article 3's alteration of Article 118B regarding the Commission's role in promoting the social dialogue at EC level. The second concerned the role of EC level collective bargaining in the formulation of Community labour law.

### Promotion of social dialogue

The first reinforcement of social partner action at EC level emerged, not from the Dutch Presidency's first draft, but from the ETUC/UNICE/CEEP Accord. This proposed to replace the existing Article 118B:

> The Commission shall endeavour to develop the dialogue between management and labour at European level …

Instead, the new Article 118B proposed by the social partners at EC level was approved at the Maastricht Summit and became Article 3(1) of the Agreement appended to the Union Treaty:[58]

> The Commission shall have the task of promoting the consultation of management and labour at Community level and shall take any relevant measure to facilitate their dialogue by ensuring balanced support for the parties …

---

[57] B. Bercusson, 'Maastricht: A Fundamental Change in European Labour Law', (1992) *Industrial Relations Journal* 177. As described by G. Lyon-Caen: 'Si la Commission veut soutenir le processus de négotiation, il faut qu'elle "terrorise" les interlocuteurs sociaux par les projets de textes que les uns et (ou) les autres jugeront excessifs ou dangereux.' In *Le droit social et la Communauté européenne après le Traité de Maastricht*, Paris: Recueil Dalloz Sirey, 1993, p. 152, quoted in F. Dorssemont, 'Contractual Governance by Management and Labour in EC Labour Law', in A. Van Hoek, A. Hol and O Janssen (eds.), *Multilevel Governance in Enforcement and Adjudication*, Antwerp and Oxford: Intersentia, 2006, 285 at p. 295.

[58] Now Article 138(1) EC.

This seems to reinforce the obligation of the Commission regarding the social dialogue at EC level beyond the former 'endeavour to develop'. But it also implicitly reflects the subsidiarity principle. The most 'relevant measure' which the Commission can take 'to facilitate their dialogue' is to devolve to them the task of formulating and implementing agreements on EC labour law.

### Participation of the social partners in the formulation of EC labour law: 'bargaining in the shadow of the law'

#### Consultation

The second impulse to action by the social partners at EC level surfaced in the Dutch Presidency's first draft. This provided, first, formal recognition for what was already the practice at EC level. The proposed new Article 118A provided:

> Before submitting proposals in the social policy field, the Commission shall consult management and labour on the advisability of Community action.

This also reflects the subsidiarity principle, requiring consideration not only of the advisability of the *substance* of Community action, but also of the appropriate *level* of implementation.

More significant was the proposal which was in not the Dutch Presidency's first draft, but in the second draft, which adopted an amended text of Article 118A agreed by the ETUC/UNICE/CEEP. The substance (and virtually the identical wording) of the text formulated by the social partners became Article 3, paragraphs 2–4 of the Agreement. The final text of the Agreement was as follows:[59]

2. To this end, before submitting proposals in the social policy field, the Commission shall consult management and labour on the possible direction of Community action.
3. If, after such consultation, the Commission considers Community action advisable, it shall consult management and labour on the content of the envisaged proposal. Management and labour shall forward to the Commission an opinion or, where appropriate, a recommendation.
4. On the occasion of such consultation, management and labour may inform the Commission of their wish to initiate the process provided for in Article 4. The duration of the procedure shall not exceed nine months, unless the management and labour concerned and the Commission decide jointly to extend it.

One change appeared in the Agreement from the text produced by the social partners. This was introduced by the Dutch Presidency and required Commission consent to a prolongation beyond nine months of the independent procedure of the social partners.

---

[59] Now Article 138(2), (3) and (4) EC.

However, it should be noted that a second change emerged in the Dutch Presidency's second draft, which did *not* appear in the text of the Union Treaty signed in Maastricht on 7 February 1992. The Treaty, following the wording in the social partners' Accord, provided that the second consultation of the Commission with the social partners was to be 'on the *content* of the envisaged proposal'. However, the Dutch Presidency's second draft *and*, astonishingly, the Agreement made at Maastricht in December 1991, both provided for this second consultation to be simply 'on the envisaged proposal'.

Comparison of the texts casts some light on their meaning. Consultations limited to 'the content of the envisaged proposal' might be interpreted as excluding, for example, issues to do with the appropriate legal basis, or even implementation procedures as opposed to 'substantive' content. Consultations 'on the envisaged proposal' might have been limited to whether a proposal should be made, and not its substantive content. The original wording of the social partners requiring consultation 'on the content of the envisaged proposal' was restored in the final Treaty. However, it is unlikely that this change will affect the practice of the Commission's consultation procedure.

### Social dialogue: 'bargaining in the shadow of the law'

The process referred to in Article 138(4) EC[60] is the subject of Article 139(1):[61]

> Should management and labour so desire, the dialogue between them at Community level may lead to contractual relations, including agreements.

Since 1985, the Commission had stressed that negotiations between employers' and workers' organisations at EC level were a cornerstone of the European social area which goes hand in hand with the creation of the Single European Market.[62] These negotiations came to be known as the 'European social dialogue'.

Collective bargaining/social dialogue *within* Member States is regarded as reflecting a balance of power between labour and capital, exercised traditionally through the weapons of industrial conflict. The Maastricht Agreement did not address even the possibility of industrial conflict at European level. Indeed, Article 139(5)[63] seemed explicitly to withhold regulatory competences which would be most relevant.

The logic to this auto-exclusion was, perhaps, that the EC level social dialogue is qualitatively different in that the normal means of pressure – strikes – are not (yet) operational at Community level. The prospect of the

---

[60] Article 3(4) of the Agreement; the redrafted Article 118A(4).
[61] Article 4(1) of the Agreement; the redrafted Article 118B.
[62] It was thus stated by Jacques Delors in presenting the Commission's programme to Parliament in January 1985. Commission of the EC, *Joint Opinions*, European Social Dialogue Documentary Series, 'Introduction', p. 19.
[63] Article 2(6) of the Agreement.

EC social dialogue implies rather a tripartite process – involving the social partners and the Commission/Community as a dynamic factor. This is the scenario described as 'bargaining in the shadow of the law'.[64]

This prospect arises out of a major ambiguity as to the timing of the initiation of the process of social dialogue during the Commission's consultations. Article 138(4) EC[65] simply states that the process may be initiated by the social partners 'on the occasion of such consultation'. The question is: *which* consultation of the two envisaged by Article 138[66] – before, and/or after the Commission produces its envisaged proposal?

Each possibility has implications for the bargaining tactics of the social partners at EC level. In both cases there occurs a familiar situation of 'bargaining in the shadow of the law'. If the procedure may be initiated at the stage of consultations when only 'the possible direction of Community action' is being considered, but *before* the Commission presents its envisaged proposal, the parties have to assess whether the result of their bargaining will be more advantageous than the unknown content of the EC action. There will be pressures on the social partners to negotiate and agree to avoid an imposed standard which pre-empts their autonomy, and which may be also a less desirable result.

This incentive is lost if the procedure may be initiated only at the stage of consultations *after* the Commission presents its envisaged proposal. The parties may be more or less content with the proposal. They may still judge that the result of further bargaining would be more advantageous than the known content of the proposed EC action, taking into account the possible amendment of the Commission proposal as it goes through the EC institutions. The side *less* satisfied with the envisaged proposal will have an incentive to negotiate and agree to a different standard. The side *more* contented may still see advantages in a different agreed standard. The social partners are often able and willing to negotiate derogations from specified standards which allow for flexibility and offer advantages to both sides.

Indeed, the negotiation of the Accord which led to the insertion of these provisions into the Maastricht Treaty Protocol can be invoked as a concrete example of the process in action. The combination of expansion of competences and extension of qualified majority voting proposed in the Dutch Presidency's first draft was sufficient to induce UNICE/CEEP to agree to a procedure allowing for pre-emption of what threatened to be Community regulatory standards in a wide range of social policy areas; this despite the potentially obligatory effects of agreements between the social partners proposed by the Dutch Presidency.

---

[64] Bercusson, 'Maastricht', from which the next four paragraphs are taken.
[65] Article 3(4) of the Agreement.    [66] Article 3 of the Agreement.

## A hypothetical case of 'bargaining in the shadow of the law'

The possibility is not excluded that the procedure may be initiated at *either* occasion of consultation – before and/or after the proposal. This would allow for negotiations aimed at pre-empting a proposal; or, if these do not take place, or fail, negotiations allowing for agreed derogations and flexibility.

The tactics involved may be illustrated by a hypothetical case. The Commission, in accordance with Article 138(2) EC[67] consults the social partners on the possible direction of Community action regarding a specific aspect of working conditions. The assumption of the case is that such action is desired by the ETUC – which is willing to negotiate an agreement – and less so by BusinessEurope.[68]

BusinessEurope may judge that the Commission proposal is likely to set a standard too high and/or too rigid. In this case it will have an incentive to pre-empt this result by agreeing to initiate the procedure under Article 138(4) EC.[69] Alternatively, BusinessEurope may judge that the Commission proposal is likely to set a standard tolerably low and/or flexible. There will be less incentive to agree to initiate the procedure at this stage. But BusinessEurope might still prefer to avoid any risk by initiating the procedure and trying to avoid the Commission proposing a standard.

If BusinessEurope waits until the Commission produces its envisaged proposal, two scenarios emerge. First, the proposal is too high and/or too rigid. In this case BusinessEurope will have an incentive to avoid this result by agreeing to initiate the procedure under Article 138(4) EC.[70] However, it does so from a weakened position, since the Commission proposal becomes a probable minimum standard. In the second scenario, the proposal is tolerably low and/or flexible. There will be less incentive for BusinessEurope to agree to initiate the procedure, but negotiations may still be desirable to increase flexibility or allow for derogations.

Given the current positions of the social partners at Community level, the prospects of and incentives for negotiation and agreement are greater the *higher* the social policy standard espoused by the Commission. It is for the Commission to give a clear signal that the factor breaking any deadlock in bargaining will not be the classic weapons of class struggle as evident in national contexts, but the stimulus of Commission activity in the form of proposals for social legislation. This imposes a heavy burden of responsibility on the Commission. But this has been so ever since it launched the European social dialogue through the Val Duchesse initiative in 1985. The Commission's initiative was crucial to the achievement of the Accord reached by the social

---

[67] Article 3(2) of the Agreement; formerly Article 118A(2).

[68] Though here, as elsewhere, the agglomeration of national interests in each of the social partners at Community level is assumed to be capable of generating a single view.

[69] Article 3(4) of the Agreement; formerly Article 118A(4).

[70] *Ibid*

partners on 31 October 1991 and incorporated into the Maastricht Agreement. It is by further such initiatives that the European social dialogue will continue to develop.

## A 'twin-track' procedure?

The procedure of social dialogue has aspects which are clearly voluntary. First, it cannot be initiated without the consent of both the social partners.[71] Secondly, Article 139(1) EC[72] makes it clear that neither party is obliged to agree. Thirdly, the Commission seems free to produce proposals even when the social partners initiate the procedure, or during it. Finally, extension of the procedure beyond the nine-month period proposed is subject not only to the joint decision of the social partners, but also to the decision of the Commission.

The obligatory pre-emption, if any, by the social partners of EC labour law does not take effect at the point of initiation or for the duration of the procedure. It is not clear whether the Commission is precluded from pursuing its original social policy proposal even when informed by management and labour of their wish to initiate the process under Article 139 which may culminate in an agreement. The nine-month duration (which may be extended) does not explicitly preclude a parallel process of social policy formulation by the Commission. It might even be that such a 'twin-track' process would impart a certain dynamism to both Commission and social partners. However, while it is not clear that the Commission is thus pre-empted in the formulation of social policy, it is as regards the successful outcome of the procedure – 'agreements concluded at Community level' – that the potentially obligatory nature of the procedure emerges.

## 'Agreements concluded at Community level'

The debate over the potential of European social dialogue which has taken place since the first meetings between the social partners at Val Duchesse in 1985 has posited four types of 'European agreement':

(i) an inter-confederal/inter-sectoral agreement between the social partners organised at European level (ETUC/Business-Europe/CEEP);
(ii) a European industry/sectoral/branch agreement between social partners organised on an industry/sectoral/branch basis at European level;
(iii) an agreement with a multinational enterprise having affiliates in more than one Member State;
(iv) an agreement covering more than one Member State.

---

[71] Now Article 138(4) EC, Article 3(4) of the Agreement, formerly Article 118A(4).
[72] Article 4(1) of the Agreement; the redrafted Article 118B(1).

To define the phrase 'agreements concluded at Community level' in Article 139 (2) EC in restrictive terms of geography or of actors seems counter-productive.[73] If the phrase 'agreements concluded at Community level' were taken to require that agreements must engage all and only Member State organisations of workers and employers, this could eliminate all the four types of agreements mentioned above as possibly emerging from the European social dialogue. The first two because the social partners at European level are not organised so as to include exclusively organisations of workers and employers of EC Member States. Non-Member State organisations are included, and some organisations within Member States are not included. The last two because the enterprises and regions concerned do not include all Member States.

The 'Community' dimension of 'agreements concluded at Community level' is considerably diluted by the potentially paradoxical fact that, in contrast to the limitations imposed by restricted competences and voting procedures on organs of the EC, such agreements are *not* subject to any explicit restriction either as to content or to majority or unanimous voting. Nor do the procedures of reaching agreements entail the direct involvement of EC institutions.[74] The European social dialogue is not formally dependent on EC law, whatever benefits it may derive from use of the Community legal framework.

The conclusion proposed is that the phrase 'agreements concluded at Community level' can be understood in terms of the European social dialogue as carried on since 1985. Therefore, at the least, agreements emerging from the European social dialogue should be deemed to fall within the meaning of the phrase. But, in addition, other agreements with a European Community element (geographical, actors) may also be eligible for inclusion within the framework of Article 139(2).[75]

## Implementation of 'agreements concluded at Community level'[76]

The *obligatory* implementation of agreements reached through the social dialogue at Community level was declared ('*shall* be implemented') in the first Draft presented by the Dutch Presidency. The ETUC/UNICE/CEEP Accord of 31 October 1991 (paragraph 1) repeated the Dutch first draft proposal

---

[73] For example, for the duration of the UK's opt-out from the Agreement, 'Community level' agreements could engage the organisations of British employers and trade unions members of the ETUC and BusinessEurope, but not the Member State in which these agreements were to be applied.

[74] At a time when assertions are frequent as to the democratic deficit of measures adopted by Community institutions, this raises important questions as to the legitimacy of such agreements. Issues of the legitimacy of European social dialogue agreements are discussed below in Chapter 18.

[75] Now Article 139(2) EC.

[76] See A. Jacobs and A. Ojeda-Aviles, 'The European Social Dialogue: Some Legal Issues', in *A Legal Framework for European Industrial Relations*, June 1999, ETUI, Brussels, pp. 57–75. Olaf Deinert, 'Modes of Implementing European Collective Agreements and Their Impact on Collective Autonomy', (2003) 32 *Industrial Law Journal*, 317–25. D. Schiek, 'Autonomous Collective Agreements as a Regulatory Device in European Labour Law: How to Read Article 139 EC', (2005) 34 *Industrial Law Journal*, 23–56.

regarding the voluntary nature of the dialogue which may lead to agreements. However, unlike the Dutch first draft, the second paragraph of the proposed Article 118B stated that: 'Agreements concluded at the Community level *may* be implemented ...'.[77]

The intention was clearly to make implementation of such agreements *voluntary also* as regards Member States or social partners within them, as well as in the case of action by the Community organs – which under the first Dutch draft was already voluntary in the sense that it was subject to the request of the social partners.

The second Dutch draft which followed the ETUC/UNICE/CEEP Accord raised problems because of the differences between the English and French versions. The English version *reinstated* the wording rendering implementation *obligatory* via national procedures and practices. The French version, however, *did not change* the wording relating to the obligatory or voluntary nature. The outcome is not helpful in understanding this key point.

The situation was further confused by a change which occurred in the French version between the agreement in Maastricht in December and the signing of the Treaty in February. The English version remained the same: a high level of obligation: 'Agreements concluded at Community level *shall* be implemented ...'.[78] The French version changed one key word: instead of the December version: 'La mise en oeuvre des accords conclus au niveau communautaire *interviendra* ...', there appears in the Union Treaty Accord: 'La mise en oeuvre des accords conclus au niveau communautaire *intervient* ...'.

The key issue remains the degree of obligation regarding implementation of EC level agreements. Once an agreement has been concluded at Community level, there are two methods of implementing the agreement reached:[79]

> Agreements concluded at Community level shall be implemented either in accordance with the procedures and practices specific to management and labour and the Member States or, in matters covered by Article 137,[80] at the joint request of the signatory parties, by a Council decision on a proposal from the Commission.
>
> The Council shall act by qualified majority, except where the agreement in question contains one or more provisions relating to one of the areas for which unanimity is required pursuant to Article 137(2). In that case, it shall act unanimously.[81]

---

[77] The French version is not so clearly permissive: 'La mise en oeuvre des accords conclus au niveau communautaire *interviendra* ...'.

[78] Article 4(2). Now Article 139(2) EC. The article by Schiek, 'Autonomous Collective Agreements', helpfully reproduces this text in German, Spanish, French, Dutch, Italian and Danish (footnote 84 on p. 45).

[79] Article 139(2) EC, formerly Article 4(2) of the Agreement; the redrafted Article 118B.

[80] Formerly Article 2 of the Agreement.

[81] The revision of Article 137 by the Treaty of Nice led to the present wording of this second paragraph of Article 139(2) (Treaty of Nice, Article 10). The substance, however, was not changed.

## National practices and procedures

The first of the two methods of implementation is that 'Agreements concluded at Community level shall be implemented ... in accordance with the procedures and practices specific to management and labour and the Member States.'[82] It should be noted that the reference to management and labour is supplemented by '*and* the Member States'. It seems from this formulation that some degree of obligation is imposed directly on Member States by the word 'shall'. One question is: if such implementation is obligatory, how does such an obligation operate? Several possibilities exist.

One possibility is that the Member States are obliged to develop procedures and practices (which may be peculiar to themselves) to implement the agreements reached at EC level. This would seem to require some formal machinery of articulation of national standards with those laid down in the agreements. The experience of implementation of EC legal measures, such as directives, through collective bargaining provides a basis for assessing whether Member States have complied with this obligation.

A second possibility is that the Member States are not obliged to develop new procedures and practices to implement the agreements. But where there exists machinery of articulation of national standards with those laid down in the agreements, this is to be used.[83]

A third possibility is that, given the nature of the authors of the standards (EC level organisations of employers and workers), the procedures and practices peculiar to each Member State may consist of mechanisms of articulation of Community agreements with collective bargaining in the Member State concerned. Member States are not obliged to create such mechanisms, but national law may not interfere with such mechanisms which already exist, or which may be created by the social partners within the Member State to deal with the new development at EC level.

A fourth possibility is that the European social partners themselves determine the methods of implementation of their agreements in the Member States. Such an autonomous model of implementation is characteristic of the Nordic Member States, initially with the 'Basic Agreement' of 1899 in Denmark.[84]

---

[82] Article 139(2) EC, formerly Article 4(2) of the Agreement.

[83] An interpretation advanced by Olaf Deinert proposes that European social dialogue agreements would have the same legal effects in Member States as any other national collective agreement. Deinert, 'Modes of Implementing European Collective Agreements'.

[84] For a proposal to this effect published on the 100th anniversary of the Danish September Agreement, B. Bercusson, 'Prospects for a European "September Agreement"', in M. Andreasen, J. Kristiansen and R. Nielsen (eds.), *Septemberforliget 100 Ar*, Copenhagen: DJOF Publishing, 1999 pp. 21–54. As put by Dagmar Schiek, 'where there is a strong European tradition of autonomous regulation, the Treaty grants the European social partners the opportunity to autonomously define the effect of their social partner agreements ... as has been proposed by the Danish Trade Union Congress'. She further argues that such a 'basic agreement' 'would have to be considered Community law. In principle, a European social partner basic agreement would

This possibility of a process of articulation of 'agreements concluded at Community level' with 'procedures and practices specific to management and labour' does not detract from the significance of the following words: '*and* the Member States'. This may be a reflection of the jurisprudence of the European Court of Justice concerned with implementation of EC legal measures through collective bargaining, encapsulated in Article 137(3) EC.

The extent of Member State obligations was the subject of a Declaration, on Article 4(2), attached to the Maastricht Treaty Agreement:

> The Conference declares that the first of the arrangements for application of the agreements between management and labour Community-wide – referred to in Article 118B(2)[85] – will consist in developing by collective bargaining according to the rules of each Member State, the content of the agreements, and that consequently this arrangement implies no obligation on the Member States to apply the agreements directly or to work out rules for their transposition,[86] nor any obligation to amend national legislation in force to facilitate their implementation.

This Declaration raises a series of difficulties. What is the legal effect of a declaration on an Agreement attached to a Treaty? Such declarations on Community legal instruments are not granted any status before the Court of Justice. How, if at all, does it change and/or reduce the obligation of the Member States regarding implementation? The obligation is *transformed* from implementation to *developing* the content of the agreement by domestic bargaining. This is not necessarily implicit in the implementation process; indeed, it goes beyond it. Finally, if there is no obligation to apply agreements directly, or to transpose them, or even to facilitate implementation, what is left of the obligation to implement?

The fragile legal quality of such declarations may be emphasised. The denial of obligations to take legislative action in support of implementation does not exclude the obligation to avoid legislation having a negative impact on the implementation of EC-level agreements. This is an unusual twist to the doctrine of 'inderogability' to be found in some Member States. That doctrine precludes individual employment contracts derogating from collective agreements, or, exceptionally, authorises collective agreements to derogate from legislative standards. Here, the doctrine would be invoked to preclude Member State legislation inhibiting articulation of agreements within Member States with EC-level agreements.

share the supremacy of EC law. There is a certain qualification, as Article 139(2) stipulates for the case of autonomous implementation that this must be in line with practices and usages of the Member States ... However, the principle of supremacy of EU law would also apply to the European basic Social Partner Agreement. Accordingly, Member States would be barred from disabling the legal effects of the European social partner agreements.' Schiek, 'Autonomous Collective Agreements', pp. 54, 55.

[85]   Now Article 139(2) EC.

[86]   This is interpreted by Schiek as meaning that 'implementation through national legislation is excluded in principle'. 'Autonomous Collective Agreements', p. 53. *Contra*, below.

### The scope of 'agreements concluded at Community level': different competences for the social dialogue and the EC institutions

Implementation is particularly affected by the possibility that agreements may be reached without the direct involvement of EC institutions, and are not subject to any explicit restriction either as to content or to majority or unanimous voting. One question is whether there is an obligation to implement agreements reached outside EC competence. The answer requires clarification of the meaning of Community competence.

For example, what is the position of agreements reached which are opposed by sufficient Member States to block approval had they been presented to the Council under either majority or unanimous voting requirements? It may be argued that voting requirements do not affect the agreement, as it has been reached in another forum authorised by the Member States. If so, the Member States have authorised agreements outside the formal scope of EC competence in the sense that the agreement is at odds with the procedural requirements requiring unanimity or a specific majority for the exercise of the competence in question.

A double set of EC competences emerges: first, the competences applicable to the measures adopted by EC institutions; but also, second, a different set of competences allotted to the social partners, and carrying with it the obligation to implement 'agreements concluded at Community level'. These latter would thus fall within the scope of EC law, with all the enforcement implications canvassed above.

This proposition is argued on the basis of the adoption of extraordinary new procedures for the development of EC law, restricting the direct participation of Community institutions, and, in particular, rendering inapplicable the consequent restrictive voting requirements closely tied to specific areas of competence. This new approach to formulating EC labour law may imply that the detailed limits on competences carefully attached to the old institutions and procedures are not necessarily to be carried over to the new institutions and procedures.

For example, Article 137(2)(b) EC provides that the Council may adopt Directives by qualified majority vote as regards the fields specified in Article 137(1)(a)–(i) EC,[87] but must act unanimously as regards the areas specified in Article 2(3).[88] But:[89] (italics added)

> The provisions of *this Article* shall not apply to pay, the right of association, the right to strike or the right to impose lock-outs.

---

[87] As revised by the Treaty of Nice, Article 137(1) (a)–(i) EC, 'except for the fields referred to in paragraph 1(c), (d), (f) and (g)'.

[88] As revised by the Treaty of Nice, 'the fields referred to in [Article 137(1)] (c), (d), (f) and (g)'.

[89] Article 137(5) EC, formerly Article 2(6) of the Agreement.

The question is whether this exclusion of competences as regards the procedures in *Article 137* applies to the radically different procedures laid down in *Articles 138 and 139*. If not, by implication, under *Article 138*, the Commission *may* make a proposal in a social policy field specified in Article 137(5) which, under Article 138(4), is then taken up by management and labour, with the possible result of an agreement on the subject at Community level,[90] which 'shall be implemented' in one of the ways specified in Article 139(2). This difference in potential competences may be understood because of the particular delicacy of the matters listed in Article 137(5) touching, as they do, upon the area of the autonomy of the social partners (right of association, the rights to strike or impose lock-outs) and the most central of collective bargaining subjects (pay).

If it is possible to justify and understand this difference between Community competences for procedures involving the Commission, Council and Parliament on the one hand, and competences for procedures involving the Commission, management and labour on the other, then it may be that the competences listed generally in Article 137 are *not* to limit the potential of the social dialogue procedure prescribed in Articles 138 and 139.[91]

To summarise: the starting point is Article 136, which specifies the social policy objectives, and hence competences, of the Community and the Member

---

[90]  Article 139(1) EC; formerly Article 4(1) of the Agreement.

[91]  It may be argued that the reference in Article 138(1) EC to 'the Community' implies that the competences referred in Article 137 EC exhaust those which the EC can exercise in the field of social policy. The question remains whether the scope of EC competences can be separated from the mechanisms for the implementation of those competences, and whether Article 137(5) EC refers to the scope of the competences defined in Article 137 EC, or only to the institutional mechanisms outlined in Article 137(2) EC. One indication is that Article 137(3) EC refers explicitly to Article 137(2) EC (mechanisms only), whereas Article 137(5) EC refers to (the whole of) '[T]he provisions of this Article …'. Another is to compare Article 137(4) (2nd indent) EC ('The provisions adopted pursuant to this Article …') and Article 137(5) EC ('The provisions of this Article …'). The additional words 'adopted pursuant to' indicate a distinction of mechanisms from competences, and limited to those adopted by the institutional mechanism described in Article 137(2) EC. It could be argued that Article 137(5) EC, while using slightly different language, implies the same. A counter-argument is that Article 137(4) (2nd indent) EC could be interpreted as meaning either (a) the provisions adopted *only* by the institutional legislative mechanism (with the Article 137(5) EC exclusion), or (b) *all* provisions adopted within the new competences, including those resulting from the social dialogue mechanism. It would seem that (b) is the more likely since it could hardly have been intended to allow Member States to adopt or introduce more stringent protective measures *only* when they take the form of Directives adopted under Article 137(2) EC. If so, Article 137(5) EC which follows could be regarded either as also covering both mechanisms, or, by reason of the different language, differing in (impliedly) distinguishing the institutional from the social dialogue mechanism. These arguments show how the language of the Article is not precise. Therefore, it is open to argue that Article 137(5) EC (which follows Article 137(4) (2nd indent) EC, but does not use the language 'adopted pursuant to') might nonetheless be read as referring only to the competences of the institutional mechanism. Hence, it does not exclude the social policy competence of labour and management to negotiate agreements on pay, etc. within the framework of the social policy provisions of the Treaty. I am grateful to Marcus Geiss, an LL.M. student at the University of Manchester, 1994–5, with whom I had fruitful discussions on this issue.

States in very general terms. Article 137 then lays down certain processes for achieving such objectives by the usual procedure of Council Directives – specifying some of the competences for qualified majority voting, unanimity for others, and excluding still others.

Article 138(2) simply provides for Commission proposals 'in the social policy field' which may be taken up by management and labour in the new procedure of social dialogue. These proposals may go beyond those specified in Article 137, though still within the EC competences specified in Article 136.

Member State obligations to implement agreements at EC level within those competences flow from Article 139(2).[92] Finally, it is interesting to note that Article 139(2) provides for the second method of implementing agreements concluded at Community level – by a Council decision on a proposal from the Commission *'in matters covered by Article 137'*, with a further paragraph specifying the voting requirements. This reinforces the argument that the range of competences in social policy reserved to the social partners is distinct from that of the EC institutions.

## Council decision

A second method is envisaged to implement Community level agreements at Member State level. The second paragraph of a revised Article 118B proposed in the first Draft of the Dutch Presidency provided:

> In matters falling within Article 118, where management and labour so desire, the Commission may submit proposals to transpose the agreements referred to in paragraph 1 into Community legislation. The Council shall act under the conditions laid down in Article 118.

Unlike paragraph 1, this makes implementation of agreements conditional on a Commission proposal. Moreover, unlike the obligation under the first paragraph to implement agreements, such a proposal of the Commission is made explicitly subject to the conditions of Article 118 as to competences and voting procedures.

The Commission's proposals are 'to transpose the agreements'. This seems expressly to limit the discretion of the Commission to change the content of the agreements reached. However, the nature of the Community legal instrument proposed is left to the Commission's discretion and the Council's action.

The ETUC/UNICE/CEEP Accord altered this provision to implementation of:[93]

---

[92] Also Article 10 of the Treaty: 'Member States shall take all appropriate measures, whether general or particular, to ensure fulfilment of the obligations arising out of this Treaty or resulting from action taken by the institutions of the Community.'

[93] Proposed revision of Article 118B(2).

> Agreements concluded at Community level … in matters covered by Article 118 (Article 2), at the joint request of the signatory parties, by a Council decision on a proposal from the Commission concerning the agreements as they have been concluded.

As with the Dutch Presidency's proposal, this makes implementation of agreements conditional on a Commission proposal. Again, such a proposal of the Commission is subject to conditions as to competences and voting procedures. Finally, while the word 'transpose' is deleted, its substance is retained by the requirement that agreements be implemented 'as they have been concluded'.

The final version adopted as Article 4(2) of the Agreement[94] annexed to the Protocol on Social Policy incorporated the text agreed by the social partners with the exception of the provision agreed by the ETUC/UNICE/CEEP that the Commission proposal and Council decision must adopt the agreements reached by the social partners 'as they have been concluded'. This seems to open the way for the Commission possibly to change the content of the agreements. It is contested whether this is so. After all, the wording still is: 'Agreements … shall be implemented … on a proposal from the Commission'. The ambiguity remains a crucial one: how much are the Member States and the Commission entitled to vary the agreements reached at EC level?

Another critical issue is the nature of the instrument to be used to implement the agreement. The first draft of the Dutch Presidency left it to the discretion of the Commission and Council to determine the appropriate instrument. The ETUC/UNICE/CEEP Accord and the final text refer to a 'proposal from the Commission' and 'a Council decision'. A Council Decision is one of the specific instruments of Community legislation listed in Article 249. It is not clear whether the reference in Article 139(2) is to such an instrument, or rather reflects the Dutch Presidency's preference for the Commission and Council to have a choice of instruments.

In six of the then nine EC languages, the *same* word for 'decision' is used in Article 249 of the Treaty and Article 139(2) of the Agreement. The French and Italian versions, like the English, use the ambiguous term: 'prennent des décisions'; 'prendono decisioni'; 'une décision'; 'una decisione'. In the German, Danish and Dutch versions of the Agreement, a different word is used in Article 139(2). Thus, in its Danish version, the Agreement uses the term for 'arriving at a decision' (*ved en afgorelse*), not the technical term to 'take decisions' (*ved besltninger*) used in Article 249.[95]

---

[94] Now Article 139(2) EC.

[95] I am grateful to Mr Tore Hakonsson, a researcher at the European University Institute, for providing this translation. The same point is made with reference to the German version by the European Trade Union Institute's Working Paper prepared for a conference in Luxembourg, 1–2 June 1992, *The European Dimensions of Collective Bargaining after Maastricht*, Working Documents, Brussels, 1992, at p. 104, paragraph 19.

A possible choice of instruments to be decided upon by the Commission and Council is a much more flexible approach. It also avoids some of the technical problems of utilising a Decision which 'shall be binding in its entirety upon those to whom it is addressed' (Article 249 EC), 'shall state the reasons on which they are based and shall refer to any proposals or opinions which were required to be obtained pursuant to this Treaty' (Article 253 EC) and 'shall be notified to those to whom they are addressed and shall take effect upon such notification' (Article 254(3) EC). Further, on the terms of Article 137(3), implementation may be entrusted to management and labour only of *directives*. Use of other instruments might preclude such articulation.[96]

On the other hand, leaving it to Commission discretion and Council action to determine the instrument of implementation does leave open the possibility of their choosing non-legally binding instruments. This might be inconsistent with the intention of the social partners that their agreements should have legal effect. It would also contribute to an unequal application of agreements across Member States in some of which these agreements are or are not legally enforceable. Whatever the technical problems, a Decision would, given a sufficiently broad definition of a class of addressees, resolve some of the problems of general application and enforcement of agreements.

A further change occurred in the wording in the December agreement. As proposed by the Dutch Presidency, the Council decision was to be taken 'under the conditions laid down in Article 118'. The Maastricht Agreement changed this:[97]

> The Council shall act by qualified majority, except where the agreement in question contains one or more provisions relating to one of the areas referred to in Article 2(3) [Article 137(3) EC], in which case it shall act unanimously.[98]

Article 137(1) EC[99] listed certain fields, proposals in which were, by virtue of Article 137(2),[100] subject to majority voting. The agreements might:

(i) cover only such areas;
(ii) cover areas neither within majority nor unanimous voting procedures i.e. not within the competence of EC institutions;[101]
(iii) cover only areas within the unanimous voting procedure;
(iv) cover areas which fell partly within more than one of the above ('one or more provisions ...' (mixed agreements)).

---

[96] This issue became of extreme importance when the Convention on the Future of Europe proposed to alter the taxonomy of legal instruments, including those available to implement European social dialogue agreements.

[97] Article 4(2), paragraph 2.

[98] The revision of Article 137 by the Treaty of Nice led to a revision of the wording of this second paragraph of Article 139(2) (Treaty of Nice, Article 10), which now reads: 'The Council shall act by qualified majority, except where the agreement in question contains one or more provisions relating to one of the areas for which unanimity is required pursuant to Article 137(3). In that case it shall act unanimously.' The substance, however, is not changed.

[99] Article 2(1) of the Agreement.     [100] Article 2(2) of the Agreement.

[101] Though within that of the social partners, see discussion above.

Cases (i) and (iii) seem clear. Case (ii) is problematic as to whether a Council decision can be taken at all. Case (iv) seems, under the final text agreed at Maastricht, to subject 'mixed agreements' to unanimity.[102]

Finally, the introduction of the social dialogue as an alternative channel to the formulation of European labour law raises the question of the role of the principle of subsidiarity.

## Subsidiarity

The subsidiarity principle was the subject of explicit elaboration in the Union Treaty agreed at Maastricht, though this does not mean it has necessarily been clarified:[103]

> The Community shall act within the limits of the powers conferred upon it by this Treaty and of the objectives assigned to it therein.
>
> In areas which do not fall within its exclusive competence, the Community shall take action, in accordance with the principle of subsidiarity, only if and insofar as the objectives of the proposed action cannot be sufficiently achieved by the Member States and can therefore, by reason of the scale or effects of the proposed action, be better achieved by the Community.
>
> Any action by the Community shall not go beyond what is necessary to achieve the objectives of this Treaty.

### The choice among multiple levels of action

The issue has been made rather more complex by the injection of EC level action involving not EC institutions, but the social partners at EC level. The problem is that *EC level* action can now be undertaken *by the social partners* as well as by the Commission. Similarly action at national level can include that by the social partners as well as by Member States.

The question is: how does the principle of subsidiarity apply in the resulting complex of interactions? Formerly it could be said to apply to EC action v. Member State action. But is the same standard applicable as between:

- EC level action by the social partners v. Member State action; or
- EC action v. action by the social partners within the Member State; or
- EC level action by the social partners v. action by the social partners within the Member States?

---

[102] A similar argument arose concerning the interpretation of Article 100A(2) (now Article 95(2) EC) of the Treaty of Rome (as amended by the Single European Act 1986). This subjects to unanimity proposals relating to the rights and interests of employed persons. It was argued that if the proposal related solely to such rights and interests, it was subject to unanimity. If it related only marginally to such rights and interests, it was eligible for majority voting, even though it also related to them. The problems arose when the proposal related to such rights and interests, but also to other matters. Bercusson, 'The European Community's Charter', pp. 633–34. See Chapter 4 above.

[103] Article 3B, as revised and now in Article 5 EC.

Are any or all of these subject to the same principle of subsidiarity? Or are they subject to a principle of subsidiarity formulated differently?

Finally, there is the question of whether EC action or action by the social partners at EC level is preferable; similarly, at Member State level, whether action by the state or the social partners is preferable. Neither of these choices seems directly governed by the subsidiarity principle, but the choice between them is subject to the same logic as the subsidiarity principle.

The result of the application of the subsidiarity principle to the classic choice between Member State or EC action (but now also between EC social partner action v. Member State action/social partner action at Member State level) will also be determined by the choices made as between Commission/EC–social partner level action and Member State/social partner-within-Member-State action.

## Application of the subsidiarity principle in Community social policy

The principle of subsidiarity only applies when the EC and Member States *both* have competence. The question is *which* of the two (EC or Member States) is to exercise the competence. As defined in Article 5 EC, there are *two* conditions for EC action: first, *insufficient* achievement by Member States of the objectives of the proposed action; *and*, secondly, *better* achievement by the Community by reason of the scale or effects of the proposed action.

The issue is to be posed in *relative* terms: which level is *better* (as in '… cannot be sufficiently achieved by the Member States and can … be better achieved by the Community'). The EC could argue Member State insufficiency, and the Member States could argue that the EC is no better (or worse). This raises the difficult question of which *criteria and standards* to adopt to assess sufficiency. The allocation of competences depends on a reliable assessment of relative sufficiency. The terms of the assessment are critical; in particular, what is the role of economic or other criteria and standards?

The debate over subsidiarity may be influenced by the European Economic Community logic of economic rather than political (let alone social) union. Exclusivity/competences are the language of legal/political union. Efficiency (sufficiently achieved) and 'scale or effects' are the language of economic union. The ambiguity is apparent in the (slippery) terms in which the debate has been conducted: (political-social) objections to centralisation are dressed up in (economic) terminology of efficiency. But economic theory includes political and social considerations to varying extents. The neo-classical school of economics, which underlies the old conception of the European Economic Community, is unlikely to be sustainable in the context of the Treaty on European Union.

On the other hand, efficiency may have to be weighed against fundamental constitutional principles of Member States which include other values. For example, in the specific context of the application of the principle of subsidiarity to the question of whether the social partners at the EC or at Member State level should take action, or whether it should be the EC or the Member States themselves, the principle of the *autonomy of the social partners*, at EC level as well as at Member State level, should be brought into the equation. 'Efficiency' might dictate EC or Member State action, but long-standing hegemony of the social partners, at one or other levels of bargaining, over certain policy areas may dictate leaving it to management and labour to settle the substance of EC labour policy in that area.[104]

Subsidiarity being a relative test as between levels, if, for example, the social partners are unable to adopt measures as a result of the intransigence of one side, this will be a sign that the competence may be exercised at a different level. Similarly if the EC is unable to adopt measures due to majority or unanimous voting requirements, competence should be exercised by the social partners at the 'better' level.

There is a further point. The subsidiarity principle has been misconceived as implying an allocation of powers to *either* a higher or lower level. The test of relative sufficiency indicates that it is not a question of exclusive allocation. Instead, deciding which level is *better* implies that *both* have something to contribute. Though one may be better *overall*, the other may be more advantageous *in some respects*. The solution might be to use the subsidiarity principle to delineate the respective advantages of *each* level and promote *cooperation* between them, rather than assign exclusive jurisdiction to one or the other. *Within* the relevant field of competence, different levels can coordinate their action. This is a familiar problem in labour law and industrial relations: the relative roles of legislation and collective bargaining in regulating different policy areas.

This ties up with the problems of criteria and standards for efficiency. The allocation of competences, particularly if cooperation/interdependence rather than exclusivity is the objective, depends on a reliable assessment of relative sufficiency, a concept which should be expanded beyond its narrow economic confines. More than ever it becomes clear that a court of law is ill-equipped to deal with the issue.

The problem of subsidiarity becomes, therefore, one of practical application. What are the procedures and institutional structures appropriate for resolving conflicts over which level or levels take action? What may be required is a body

---

[104] A practical illustration of this principle may underlie the exclusion of competence exercised under Article 137 on the right of association and the right to strike in Article 137(5) EC. However, the argument has been made above as to the social partners retaining competence on this issue to make 'agreements ... at EC level (which) shall be implemented' (Article 139(2) EC). Article 137(1)(f) EC still grants some competence for the EC institutions on matters of 'representation and collective defence of the interests of workers and employers'.

which could adjudicate, mediate, arbitrate, report or whatever in an effort to unfreeze any stalemate, and, more importantly, give guidance aimed at coordination of cooperative action at different levels. Labour law and industrial relations dispute resolution machinery in Member States provide a reservoir of experience.

The Maastricht Treaty invited the exploitation of this experience precisely because it made explicit the use of collective bargaining/social dialogue – at EC level and within Member States – in the formulation and implementation of Community labour law.

## Summary and conclusion

The outcome of the Maastricht Summit was of outstanding importance for the future of Community labour law. The implementation of EC labour law through collective bargaining within Member States is explicitly recognised. A role for the social partners at EC level in formulating EC labour law is introduced. The procedure is that of 'bargaining in the shadow of the law'. The social dialogue is delicately timed to take place during the Commission's procedure of consulting the social partners about social policy proposals. This raises complex issues of subsidiarity. If the social partners at EC level reach agreements, it appears that Member States are obliged to implement these agreements within their national legal orders; it is not clear how this is to be accomplished.

This chapter explored various issues which arise from the attempt to understand the problems of interpretation and implementation of the social dialogue process in Articles 138–9 EC. As to the legal nature of the likely outcomes of these provisions (directives, decisions, Community level agreements), the conclusion was that these are part of Community law and the methods of enforcing EC law should be available to them.

Regarding the scope of the new competences and majority voting, the new competences replaced those in the Treaty of Rome. The Commission was able to produce proposals based on these new competences.

In conclusion, the social dialogue at EC level is characterised by its tripartite nature, and the Commission plays a key role. The role of different levels in developing social policy is likely to be influenced by the principle of subsidiarity – understood as a measure of the relative sufficiency of actions by the Community or the social partners. The decision as to relative sufficiency is a highly political one, and requires the development of appropriate procedures and institutional structures.

After 1991, the future of European labour law appeared to lie with the instruments agreed by the Member States at Maastricht: directives and Community level collective agreements, to be implemented within Member States, and enforced, *inter alia*, using the techniques developed to enforce EC law.

The European social dialogue thus emerges as a critical feature of EC labour and social law and policy.[105] It is important to appreciate the novel features of this process and avoid the temptation to chart the future path of European social dialogue following national models, either in detail or even in some of their basic principles. These are the product of much reflection and experience which must be respected. But at the same time their application in a transnational context is quite new, and hence requires new thinking.

For example, the fundamental principle of the autonomy of the social partners is granted almost, if not literally, constitutional status in the legal orders of Member States. This is reflected in the Treaty's respect for the requirement that the social partners' consent be obtained before their agreements can be transmuted into EC legal measures (Article 137(2) EC). But once so transmuted, the need arises for enforcement of these measures, a process which national experience has shown to present dangers to the autonomy of the social partners which challenge even the most experienced labour tribunals. EC institutions have to respond to these challenges.

Again, the legitimacy of the agreements adopted raises questions of the legitimacy of the social partners who through them develop fundamental social and economic rights. Decline in membership and proliferation of organisational forms have been among the dominant characteristics of Western European labour for some time.[106] The implications for the role of the social partners in the European social dialogue are not hard to perceive. They can be summarised by asking two questions: first, what bodies or organisations claiming representativeness are to benefit from the rights granted by the Treaty; and secondly, what legal obligations and liabilities are to be imposed upon them?[107]

Traditionally, labour law has been much concerned with the external relations of the actors involved in industrial relations, specifically with their relations to each other through collective bargaining. Increasingly, however, labour law has been forced to grapple with the issue of internal constitutional structures, particularly of the new and changing actors emerging.[108] These questions become of the first importance if the process creating EC social policy and labour law by-passes existing institutions, such as the European Parliament and the Economic and Social Committee, and is based instead upon trade union and employer confederations organised at Community level. All the

---

[105] My Report for the Commission of October 1989 on 'Fundamental Social and Economic Rights in the European Community' proposed that collective bargaining/the social dialogue in Member States and transnationally should be the primary instrument for developing and implementing fundamental social and economic rights in the EC. Bercusson, in Cassese, Clapham and Weiler (eds.), *Human Rights in the European Community*, pp. 287–9.

[106] B. Bercusson, 'Europaisches und nationales Artbeitsrecht: Die gegenwartige Situation', (1991) 5 *Zeitschrift fur auslandisches und internationales Arbeits- und Sozialrecht* 1, 20–9.

[107] See below Chapter 18.

[108] It is worth recalling the prediction of Simitis that the 'third generation' of labour law would be concerned with this issue. S. Simitis, 'Juridification of Labor Relations', in G. Teubner (ed.), *Juridification of Social Spheres*, Berlin and New York: De Gruyter, 1987, 113 at pp. 142–3.

more so if the legal consequences of their activities extend beyond the existing membership of trade unions and employers' associations.

## The outlook after Maastricht

The 1989 Charter emphasised labour and workers' rights. Labour and workers' rights were also reflected in the role given to the social dialogue in the Maastricht Protocol and Agreement. The Charter and the Protocol and Agreement had an obvious synergy. A post-Maastricht strategy at the Intergovernmental Conference of 1996 could have aimed to integrate the Charter and the Maastricht Protocol and Agreement into one constitutional document for incorporation into the Treaty.

The logic of this strategy was that the two documents complement each other. The Charter is a set of substantive provisions which, by virtue of their nature as fundamental social rights, possess a high degree of political legitimacy; but the Charter lacks legal status and an implementing mechanism. The Maastricht Protocol and Agreement were a dynamic mechanism for formulating, implementing and enforcing social rights, but only potentially: they provided a set of competences, but no driving substantive content that will set it in motion.

A new role for the Charter required new mechanisms, then absent, of formulation, implementation and enforcement of fundamental social rights. The obvious step was to link the Charter with the Maastricht Protocol and Agreement on Social Policy.

The Protocol and Agreement only provided for passive competences. The Charter provided the social policy objectives to be achieved through the mechanisms of the Protocol and Agreement. These fundamental social objectives would confer a further legitimacy on the mechanisms of the Protocol and Agreement.

In exchange, the legal status of the Protocol and Agreement, as part of the Treaty on European Union, would provide the engine for the implementation of the Charter. This could be furthered in various ways; for example:

(a) qualified majority voting would suffice for measures implementing fundamental social rights;
(b) periodic revision would mean a time limit on Member States' implementation of fundamental social rights;
(c) failure to implement the fundamental social rights specified could allow for them to become directly effective; or for the European Parliament to complain to the European Court about the failure to act.

Combining the Charter and the Protocol and Agreement would provide the Charter with a mechanism for implementation, and incorporate into the Protocol and Agreement a set of fundamental social rights granting them greater legitimacy. The objective would be a social constitution for the EU which mandates the implementation of specified fundamental social objectives, and provides an instrument, a timetable and a set of fall-back mechanisms to stimulate their achievement.

However, the cautious stance of the Commission, the trend towards conservatism in social policy on the part of some Member States, and the fragility of the Charter and Protocol and Agreement, meant that this opportunity for the strategic integration of the Charter and the Protocol and Agreement into a social constitution for the European Union was not taken up. Instead, the EU's social and labour policy took yet another direction. A constitutional strategy was to return to the agenda only ten years later, when the Convention on the Future of Europe in 2003 confirmed the European social dialogue as a constitutional foundation of the EU and proposed a new Constitutional Treaty incorporating an EU Charter of Fundamental Rights. In the meantime, European labour law adopted yet another strategy at EU level: the 'open method of coordination'.

## Chapter 6

# The European Employment Strategy, the open method of coordination and the 'Lisbon Strategy'

## Introduction: employment policy priority

By the end of the 1980s, the political and economic integration of Europe on a transnational basis was being driven by political decisions creating a Single European Market for goods, services and capital. Labour, however, was the exception. Despite the guarantees of free movement, the economic and political framework for labour markets continued to be national, not European.

The foundations of the post-1945 labour market settlements in the Member States included the overlapping elements of basic labour standards, full employment and a welfare state. The regulation of labour markets in the context of these settlements was undertaken by political authorities and the social partners, organisations of employers and trade unions, to varying degrees in different Member States. Confronted with the emergence of the Single European Market, these foundations of the post-1945 settlements were threatened, and national political authorities and social partners appeared inadequate. The European Union belatedly began to address the question of the legal and institutional architecture required to re-establish these foundations on a European basis: the European 'social model'.

The emerging legal and institutional architecture included the European social dialogue, embodied in the historic Agreement on Social Policy annexed to the Protocol on Social Policy of the Maastricht Treaty on European Union (TEU), now incorporated into Articles 136–9 of the EC Treaty by the Treaty of Amsterdam. A second major strategy was the adoption of a new Title in the EC Treaty, the Employment Title (Articles 125–30), inserted by the Amsterdam Treaty of 1997. The resulting 'social dialogue' of the social partners, and the 'open method of coordination' (OMC) of the European Employment Strategy (EES) aimed to produce basic labour standards and reduce unemployment, policies often overlapping with welfare state provision.

The Commission's (Delors) White Paper of 1993, *Growth, Competitiveness, Employment: The Challenges and Ways Forward into the 21st Century* declared that employment was one of the most important areas of concern of the EC and proposed:[1]

---

[1] COM 93/700, *Bulletin of the European Communities Supplement* 6/93, p. 124.

a thorough-going reform of the labour market, with the introduction of greater flexibility in the organization of work and the distribution of working time, reduced labour costs, a higher level of skills, and pro-active labour market policies.

The European Council of 9–10 December 1994 in Essen confirmed the EU's commitment to the promotion of employment and agreed what became known as the 'Essen Strategy', a strategy of coordination of national employment policies aimed at achieving the specified objectives. The contrast with previous strategies was clear:[2]

> This pressure, however, is not being exerted along the lines of the single market program. That initiative involved the adoption of legally binding directives adopted by QMV [qualified majority voting] if necessary, numerous ECJ [European Court of Justice] cases, and very explicit monitoring of the single market's implementation. By contrast, labor market reforms are being promoted by the 'open method of coordination', which explicitly eschews binding EU legislation. Policy convergence must be driven by national rather than EU legislation and political choices. Unlike the single market program, employment policy is being steered by the Commission, ECOFIN [Economic and Financial Affairs Council], and the ECB [European Central Bank] in such a way that it is individual national politicians who must take the lead in carrying out the very painful reforms desired by the Commission and the ECB. The 'open method of coordination' fundamentally puts the burden on national politicians working within their own national contexts to legislate while the Community method which created the single market put the burden on the Council of Ministers to pass appropriate legislation.

Once again, there should be noted the influence of national experience on the evolution of this new legal and policy strategy at EU level. The accession in 1995 of Sweden, Finland and Austria as new Member States brought into the EU countries with impressive credentials in the field of active labour market policies, national policies they were anxious to preserve, and powerful trade union movements. The new Director of the Commission's Directorate-General V on Employment and Social Affairs was a Swede, Allan Larsson. The introduction in 1997 of a new Title on Employment in the EC Treaty to implement the new European Employment Strategy through a new legal method, the 'open method of coordination' is largely due to these developments.

## Unemployment and labour force participation

Labour force participation measures the proportion of a specific population (e.g. women, older workers) considered to be capable of working which is

---

[2] Alberta M. Sbragia, 'Shaping a Polity in an Economic and Monetary Union: The EU in Comparative Perspective', in A. Martin and G. Ross (eds.), *Euros and Europeans: Monetary Integration and the European Model of Society*, Cambridge: Cambridge University Press, 2004, p. 51 at pp. 64–5.

participating in the labour market. The declining number of persons active in the labour market makes labour force participation an issue of growing significance in the EU and has been a primary concern of the European Employment Strategy. The Essen European Council of 9–10 December 1994 first identified priorities for job creation which have become increasingly elaborated in the annual Employment Guidelines beginning in 1997.[3] In 1997, the labour force participation rate in the EU overall was 60.5 per cent, compared to rates of well over 70 per cent in the USA and Japan. The labour force participation rate varied significantly among Member States; Denmark, the Netherlands, Sweden and the UK had achieved rates of labour force participation of 70 per cent or more whereas Italy had the lowest participation rate at 53.5 per cent.

The June 1997 Amsterdam Presidency Conclusions referred, without further definition, to 'full employment' as an objective. The Council was reluctant to commit itself to quantitative targets, but the Commission's draft 1998 Employment Guidelines specified a long-term target of 70 per cent labour force participation. In the shorter term, a target of 65 per cent would require an additional 12 million jobs over five years.

The Luxembourg European Council of 20–21 November 1997, also known as the 'Jobs Summit', was intended to address what was perceived as an employment crisis in the EU, reflected in the adoption of the Employment Title by the Treaty of Amsterdam concluded in June 1997. It launched the process envisaged in the Employment Title before the Treaty of Amsterdam had been ratified. The 'open method of coordination' envisaged by Article 128 EC of the Treaty's Employment Title became known as the 'Luxembourg process'.

The process involves annual employment guidelines, national employment action plans and a joint employment report (Article 128 EC):

1. The European Council shall each year consider the employment situation in the Community and adopt conclusions thereon, on the basis of a joint annual report by the Council and the Commission.
2. On the basis of the conclusions of the European Council, the Council acting by a qualified majority .... shall each year draw up guidelines which the Member States shall take into account in their employment policies ...
3. Each Member State shall provide the Council and the Commission with an annual report on the principal measures taken to implement its employment policy in the light of the guidelines for employment ...
4. The Council, on the basis of the reports ... shall each year carry out an examination of the implementation of the employment policies of the Member States in the light of the guidelines for employment. The Council, acting by a qualified majority on a recommendation of the Commission, may ... make recommendations to Member States.

---

[3] COM(97) 497.

5. On the basis of the results of that examination, the Council and the Commission shall make a joint annual report to the European Council on the employment situation in the Community and on the implementation of the guidelines for employment.

The 'Luxembourg process' undertakes the coordination of Member States' employment policies in the form of employment guidelines and National Action Plans. The Luxembourg Summit of November 1997 adopted an initial set of guidelines for 1998.[4] The guidelines were to be translated into national employment policies by National Action Plans (NAPs) prepared by the Member States and submitted to the Commission and Council for examination. The results of the analysis of the National Action Plans were published in the 1998 Joint Employment Report with an initial evaluation of the implementation of the national plans. The Commission then presented amended guidelines for adoption by the Council. The Luxembourg process continued on an annual basis.

## Employment rates and EES targets

The impulse towards combating unemployment was again subject to changing political currents. Already by the time of the Lisbon Council of 2000 the position was much different from that of the mid- and late 1990s:[5]

> The Lisbon Summit of 2000 saw the presentation of the Anglo-Spanish Strategy for Sustainable Development. It represented the Aznar government's emphasis on market deregulation and his ideological predisposition to agree with Tony Blair's views on the requirements for a competitive economy. With the commitment of the Aznar government to a variety of changes which began to move the labor market and the system of benefits toward a more neo-liberal model, Tony Blair had found an ally ... But it was with the election of Italy's Berlusconi government in May 2001 that the issue of labor flexibility began to find real traction on the continent ... In 2002, a coalition between the UK, Spain, and Italy began to form which attempted to strengthen the EU's support for the kinds of initiatives they were undertaking. In February 2002, the British and Italian governments signed a joint declaration calling for more flexible labor markets.

The Presidency Conclusions of the Lisbon European Council of 23–24 March 2000 began with the heading: 'Employment, Economic Reform and Social Cohesion'. The focus was employment. The first Employment Guidelines of 1998 (Council Resolution of 15 December 1997 on the 1998 Employment Guidelines) began the Preamble with the statement: 'Whereas the issue of employment is central to the concerns of Europe's citizens ...'. In the second set of Guidelines of 1999 (Council Resolution on the 1999 Employment

---

[4] Council Resolution 128/198 of 15 December 1997 on the 1998 Employment Guidelines, [1998] OJ C30/1.
[5] Sbragia, 'Shaping a Polity', pp. 66–8.

Guidelines) this was amended to read: 'Whereas employment is the top priority of the European Union …'.

The Commission's Social Policy Agenda 2000–5 confirmed that unemployment remained high (around 9 per cent of the European workforce is unemployed) and the average employment rate was only 62 per cent in 1999.[6] The problems with the employment rate in the EU were specifically identified as follows:[7]

- a services gap: the EU has a much lower level of employment in the services sector than the USA;
- a gender gap: only half of the women in the EU are in work compared to two-thirds in the USA;
- an age gap: the rate of employment in the 55–65 age group is too low (36 per cent in the EU compared to 57 per cent in the USA);
- a skills gap: skill requirements in the EU are not matched by existing supplies, particularly in information technology; long-term structural unemployment: half of those out of work have been unemployed for more than a year;
- marked regional imbalances both in Europe and within Member States: EU unemployment is concentrated in Eastern Germany, France, Southern Italy, Spain and Greece; it is highest in certain less developed regions, outlying regions and declining industrial areas.

The strategy in the draft employment guidelines of 2003 specified three overarching objectives of which the first is 'Full Employment'. National targets are set to achieve an overall employment rate of 67 per cent in 2005 and 70 per cent in 2010, an employment rate for women of 57 per cent in 2005 and 60 per cent in 2010, and an employment rate of 50 per cent for older workers in 2010.

## Formulating the European Employment Strategy: Guidelines

The 'European Employment Strategy' (EES) is implemented through a process which begins with the formulation of policy 'Guidelines'. As explained in Article 128(2) EC:

> On the basis of the conclusions of the European Council, the Council, acting by a qualified majority on a proposal from the Commission and after consulting the European Parliament, the Economic and Social Committee, the Committee of the Regions and the Employment Committee referred to in Article 130, shall each year draw up guidelines which the Member States shall take into account in their employment policies. These guidelines shall be consistent with the broad guidelines adopted pursuant to Article 99(2).

[6] COM(2000) 379 final, Brussels, 28 June 2000, Section 2.1, pp. 9–10.
[7] See 'The European Employment Strategy: A New Field for Research', speech by Allan Larsson, Director-General, Employment and Social Affairs, European Commission, to the European Society of the London School of Economics, 17 January 2000.

Thereafter (Article 128(3)):

> Each Member State shall provide the Council and the Commission with an annual report on the principal measures taken to implement its employment policy in the light of the guidelines for employment [the National Action Plan].

The Council and Commission prepare a joint report to the European Council of that year, which, on the basis of proposals by the Commission, may make (non-binding) recommendations to Member States concerning their employment policies.

The Guidelines draw on what are considered the more successful labour market policies of Member States and their knowledge and experience in combating unemployment. Solutions proposed to tackle the problem of unemployment have varied considerably among EU Member States. Between 1977 and 1997, countries such as Denmark, Ireland, the Netherlands, Portugal and the United Kingdom were relatively successful in reducing high levels of unemployment. In other Member States, such as France, Germany, Spain, Italy, Belgium and Greece, high levels of unemployment persisted while others such as Austria and Luxembourg maintained low levels of unemployment. The Guidelines of the EES seek to draw lessons from the evaluation of different measures of employment policy adopted by Member States. Guidelines seek to accumulate the experience of employment policy developed at national level and extend the lessons to be learned through a process of policy coordination.

The Employment Guidelines adopted at the Special Luxembourg European Council Summit (the 'Jobs Summit' of November 1997) were arranged around four 'pillars': employability (targeting the age gap of older workers), entrepreneurship (targeting the services gap to encourage growth in this sector), adaptability (targeting the skills gap) and equal opportunities (targeting the gender gap).

## Employability

The first of the four pillars established in 1997 by the European Employment Strategy is 'employability', which aims to prevent long-term unemployment and facilitate access to the labour market, including Guidelines aimed at developing training and skills, combating age barriers and reviewing tax and benefit systems. Thus, the first Guideline of 1998 set a target that every unemployed person is offered a new start before reaching one year of unemployment (or in the case of young persons, six months). This new start could take the form of training, retraining, work practice, a job or other employability measure.[8] Other 1998 Guidelines under the employability pillar included training for at least 20 per cent of the unemployed, more apprenticeships and the promotion of life-long learning. The 1999 Guidelines included a review of the tax and benefit

---

[8] Council Doc. 13200/97, adopted in a Council Resolution of 15 December 1997.

system to provide incentives for the unemployed and inactive to enhance their employability.[9]

As we have seen the strategy in the employment Guidelines of 2003 specifies three overarching objectives of which the first is 'Full Employment', with national targets of various kinds. However, the Commission's assessment of the implementation of the 2001 Employment Guidelines revealed major differences.[10] One group of Member States had already reached (Denmark, the Netherlands, Sweden and the UK) or were very close to the 2010 employment target. Another group had relatively low employment rates, in some cases below 60 per cent (Italy had the lowest participation rate of 53.5 per cent, and 39.6 per cent among women). The Recommendation of 2002 on the implementation of Member States' employment policies highlighted the difficulties in achieving the target employment rates.[11]

In evaluating the employability pillar, the Commission has observed that more needs to be done for disadvantaged groups such as the disabled, ethnic minorities and immigrants. It pointed to increasing gaps between beneficiaries of education and training measures, with a widening gap in access to training between those with low skills and those with higher education. The emphasis on active ageing was not reflected in lifelong learning being less developed among the elderly, as well as in small and medium-sized enterprises (SEEs) and among those on flexible work contracts. Finally, school drop out rates remained high at nearly 20 per cent.[12]

## Entrepreneurship

The second of the four pillars of the European Employment Strategy is 'entrepreneurship'. This aims at promoting the development of new businesses in general and the growth of small and medium-sized enterprises in particular. This is to be achieved by the creation of a new culture of entrepreneurship in Europe, apparently inspired by a North American model characterised by deregulatory measures.

Frequently recurring points for action are: liberalisation and simplification of regulations of relevance to entrepreneurship and SMEs, improvement of the access of start-up enterprises and SMEs to financial markets, reduction of the (start-up) costs, in particular the costs of personnel, for new enterprises and SMEs, improvement of access to innovations, cooperation with and strengthening of networks between innovative enterprises and research and knowledge institutions, promotion of the implementation of innovations and information and communications technology (ICT) applications by start-up enterprises and

---

[9] Guideline 4, Council Resolution of 22 February 1999, OJ 1999, C69/2.
[10] SEC(2001) 1398.    [11] Decision 2002/178/EC, OJ 2002, L60/70.
[12] *Taking Stock of Five Years of the European Employment Strategy*, COM(2002) 416, 17 July 2002.

SMEs, and improvement of the services provided by the authorities to start-up enterprises and SMEs.

The 1998 Employment Guidelines Nos. 8–12 under this heading included cutting burdens for businesses, reducing tax and social security obstacles to self-employment and setting up small businesses, and reversing the long-term trend towards higher taxes and charges on labour. The Commission's Social Policy Agenda 2000–5 cites 'promoting entrepreneurship and job creation, which will be helped by creating a friendly environment for starting up and developing innovative businesses, particularly SMEs'.[13] The Employment Guidelines Nos. 8–12 for 2001–2 looked to mobilisation of local activities, reforming taxes to promote employment and training, and stimulating provision of services through review of administrative and tax barriers. The second 'priority for action' of the recast European Employment Strategy for 2003 is to 'foster entrepreneurship and promote job creation'.

An evaluation after five years of operation of the European Employment Strategy, as regards entrepreneurship, indicated that, despite attempts at simplifying administration, administrative charges were still a major constraint for business performance.[14] However, reliable indicators were not available to assess the impact of their reduction on job creation. The overall tax burden on labour had been reduced by 2 per cent between 1997 and 2001, but the mix between tax measures and benefit measures for the unemployed required improvement especially to prevent early withdrawal from the labour market.

## Adaptability

Adaptability is the third of the four pillars of the European Employment Strategy (EES). The adaptability pillar is entitled 'Encouraging adaptability of businesses and their employees':[15]

> [It] covers adaptability in terms of the organisation of work, working patterns and contracts, as well as adaptability in terms of regulatory and training systems. It recognises explicitly that a balance must be struck between the need of businesses for flexibility, and the needs of employees for security and employability, and that striking this balance will not always be an easy task.

For example, in terms of more flexible types of contract, there is acknowledged the need to ensure that those working under flexible contracts enjoy adequate security, which must nonetheless be compatible with the needs of the business.[16]

---

[13]  COM(2000) 379 final, Brussels, 28 June 2000, under heading 4.1.1 (p. 16): 'Towards more and better jobs'.
[14]  *Taking Stock of Five Years of the European Employment Strategy*, COM(2002) 416, 17 July 2002.
[15]  Commission Green Paper, *Partnership for a New Organisation of Work*, COM(97) 128 final.
[16]  Guideline 15, 2001, 2002.

However, an evaluation after five years of operation of the European Employment Strategy as regards the adaptability pillar was critical.[17] It had failed to introduce a balance between flexibility, security and job quality; flexibility had increased to the detriment of employment security. New jobs were due to the increase in flexible work contracts, though these latter are more likely to lead to unemployment, often long-term unemployment. Increased working time flexibility was more concerned with long-term employment and less with job creation in the short term.

Finally, as to quality in work, unlike new Guidelines,[18] the former Guidelines under the adaptability pillar emphasised promoting 'the modernisation of work organisation and forms of work which *inter alia* contribute to improvements in quality of work'.[19]

The role of the social partners is particularly stressed in the implementation of the adaptability pillar of the European Employment Strategy. The 1998 Employment Guidelines under Pillar III, 'Encouraging adaptability in business and their employees', included

> *Modernizing work organization.* In order to promote the modernization of work organization and forms of work, *a strong partnership should be developed at all appropriate levels (European, national, sectoral, local and enterprise levels).*[20]

Guideline 13[21] continues:

> the social partners are invited to negotiate at the appropriate levels, in particular at sectoral and enterprise levels, agreements …

Guideline No. 16 in the 1999 Guidelines changed this to:

> The social partners are invited to negotiate at all appropriate levels agreements … to modernize the organization of work, including flexibility in working arrangements, with the aim of making undertakings productive and competitive and achieving the required balance between flexibility and security [and, beginning with Guidelines for 2001, 'increasing the quality of jobs']). Such agreements may, for example, cover the expression of working time as an annual figure, the reduction of working hours, the reduction of overtime, the development of part-time working, lifelong training and career breaks.

Despite this, the regular annual reports on adaptability and quality in work have repeatedly emphasised the inadequacy of the response of the social partners. The mid-term review assessment in the Joint Employment Report 2000 stated (p. 90): 'the translation of the objectives within the adaptability pillar into action is lagging behind'. The Report insisted that action under this pillar is to a large extent the responsibility of the social partners. It is their involvement in

---

[17] *Taking Stock of Five Years of the European Employment Strategy*, COM(2002) 416, 17 July 2002.
[18] COM(2003) 176 final, Part C, p. 14.    [19] Council Decision 2002/177/EC, Annex III.
[20] Words in italics added in the 1999 Guidelines.    [21] No. 16 in the 1999 Guidelines.

implementing adaptation in the workplace and in companies which is needed. However: 'Member States implement social partnership to a varying degree, and many [National Action Plans], through inadequate reporting, fail to reflect activity and initiatives actually taking place.' The Report repeated the emphasis on the need for active engagement of the social partners and that this should be transparent.

The Guidelines persist in emphasising the roles of the social partners, as expressed most clearly in the 2001 and 2002 Employment Guidelines. The 2002 Guidelines state under objective D:

> Member States shall develop a comprehensive partnership with the social partners for the implementation, monitoring and follow-up of the Employment Strategy. The social partners at all levels are invited to step up their action in support of the Luxembourg process. Within the overall framework and objectives set by these guidelines, the social partners are invited to develop, in accordance with their national traditions and practices, their own process of implementing the guidelines for which they have the key responsibility, identify the issues upon which they will negotiate and report regularly on progress, in the context of the national Action Plans if desired, as well as the impact of their actions on employment and labour market functioning. The social partners at European level are invited to define their own contribution and to monitor, encourage and support efforts undertaken at national level.

Evaluation after five years of operation of the European Employment Strategy[22] led to new draft Employment Guidelines announced by the Commission in April 2003. They appeared under a different rubric. The Employment Strategy now comprised three overarching objectives: (i) Full Employment, (ii) Improving Quality and Productivity at Work and (iii) Strengthening Social Cohesion and Inclusion.

Following these are ten 'priorities for action' to be implemented by the Member States in pursuit of the three overarching objectives. The third priority for action is 'Address Change and Promote Adaptability in Work'. One sub-heading is:

> Strong involvement of the social partners: national social partners to ensure effective implementation of [Employment Guidelines] in all areas under their responsibility, in particular concerning the management of change and adaptability, synergy between flexibility and security, human capital development, gender equality, making work pay and health and safety at work. European social partners invited to contribute to the implementation of the [Employment Guidelines] and to support efforts undertaken by national social partners.

While the role of the social partners is emphasised in relation to adaptability, it is also applicable to the achievement of all the overarching objectives and priorities for action.

---

[22] *Taking Stock of Five Years of the European Employment Strategy*, COM(2002) 416, 17 July 2002.

However, the *European* social partners appear to be relatively sidelined to a support role for *national* social partners. The new Guidelines provide:[23]

> Partnership with social partners should be promoted at national, sectoral, regional local and enterprise levels to ensure the implementation, monitoring and follow-up of the Employment Strategy.

The former Guidelines under the Adaptability Pillar stated:[24]

> In order to promote the modernisation of work organisation and forms of work which *inter alia* contribute to improvements in quality of work, a strong partnership should be developed at all appropriate levels (European, national, sectoral, local and enterprise levels.

### Equal opportunities

The fourth of the four pillars of the EES is equal opportunities. It followed on from the extensive experience of the EU in promoting equal opportunities for men and women, embodied in the 'mainstreaming' policy commitment in Article 3(2) EC introduced by the Treaty of Amsterdam:

> In all the activities [of the Community] referred to in this Article, the Community shall aim to eliminate inequalities, and to promote equality, between men and women.

The 1998 Employment Guidelines Nos. 16–18 focused on tackling gender gaps in employment, both generally and in particular sectors, reconciling work and family life, including adequate childcare provision and facilitating return to work after absence.

The Commission's evaluation of the first NAPs on employment for 1998 identified a serious lack of national policy actions under the fourth pillar. In its Guidelines for the 1999 NAPs, the Commission introduced the concept of 'gender mainstreaming': equality between the sexes must be a component of every employment policy conducted under all four pillars of the strategy. The 2002 Employment Guidelines instruct Member States to address equal pay, the gender impact of tax and benefit systems, consultation with gender equality bodies, gender impact assessments under each guideline and separate indicators to measure progress in general equality in relation to each guideline.

Another evaluation of the equal opportunities pillar after five years of operation of the European Employment Strategy emphasised the impetus given to policies on the equal opportunity pillar, particularly by the introduction of gender mainstreaming across all the pillars.[25] Over the five years women

---

[23] COM(2003) 176 final, Part C, p. 14.     [24] Council Decision 2002/17/EC, Annex III.
[25] *Taking Stock of Five Years of the European Employment Strategy*, COM(2002) 416, 17 July 2002.

had benefited from the majority of new jobs created; the gender gap in employment rate was reduced from 20 per cent to 18 per cent and the unemployment gap declined from 12 per cent to 9 per cent. However, the relative lack of engagement of the social partners was criticised, for example, in the area of pay differentials (still 16 per cent in the private sector in 1998) and parental leave, when governments are expected to meet targets as to childcare facilities by 2010.

Though the gender dimension was primary, equal opportunities was also applicable to other groups excluded from the labour market. This was reflected in the Amsterdam Treaty's insertion of a new Article 13 EC granting competence to 'take appropriate action to combat discrimination based on sex, racial or ethnic origin, religion or belief, disability, age or sexual orientation'. Following on from earlier initiatives, the 1998 Employment Guideline No. 19 was concerned to promote the integration of people with disabilities into working life. The 1999 Guidelines requested Member States to give:[26]

> special attention to the needs of the disabled, ethnic minorities and other groups and individuals who may be disadvantaged, and develop appropriate forms of preventive and active policies to promote their integration into the labour market.

The 2002 Guidelines included, for example, developing policies for 'active aging' (Guideline 3) and promoting social inclusion by access to employment (Guideline 7).

## Critique of the EES: economic policy and legal strategy

A critical test for the EES concerns the respective importance in combating unemployment of the Guidelines' proposals for structural labour market reforms as compared to macro-economic reforms. In this respect, the last sentence of Article 128(3) EC is important: 'These guidelines shall be consistent with the broad guidelines adopted pursuant to Article 99(2)'. The Broad Economic Policy Guidelines (BEPGs) adopted pursuant to Article 99(2) EC aim to implement the undertaking in Article 99(1) EC that 'Member States shall regard their economic policies as a matter of common concern and shall coordinate them within the Council.'

The approach to economic policy using Guidelines mirrors the approach later adopted in the EES, with two major differences. First, the coordination of employment policy and economic policy was the subject of Council Resolutions at Amsterdam in 1997 on the 'Stability and Growth Pact'[27] and 'Growth and Employment'.[28] However, while the former allows for sanctions available under the Economic Policy chapter of the EC Treaty (Articles 98–104), there are no

---

[26] Council Resolution on the 1999 Employment Guidelines, [1999] OJ L69/2.
[27] OJ 1997, C236/1.     [28] OJ 1997, C236/3.

such enforcement provisions available under the Employment Title of the EC Treaty (Articles 125–30).

Secondly, while Article 128(3) EC requires consistency of the EES Guidelines with the BEPGs drawn up under Article 99(2) EC, the Treaty does not require the Council, in drawing up the BEPGs, to ensure they are consistent with the EES Guidelines. Although the Resolution on Growth and Employment 'called upon' the Council to take the EES Guidelines into account when formulating the BEPGs, this is not equivalent to the Treaty obligation in Article 128(3) EC.

The strategy of the EES is thus open to criticism on at least two fronts: from the point of view of economic policy and as a legal strategy.

## Economic policy

Economic and monetary union (EMU) is the process by which the economic and monetary policies of the EU Member States are harmonised, culminating in the introduction of a single currency, the euro. The convergence required for economic and monetary union was prescribed by the EC Treaty setting criteria to be met by a Member State before it can take part.[29] Compliance with the criteria is to be examined by the Commission and the European Central Bank.

Eleven Member States met these criteria by the deadline of the third stage of EMU (1 January 1999) and Greece also did so two years later, before the euro was introduced on 1 January 2003 replacing the national currencies for more than 300 million EU citizens. Three of the pre-enlargement fifteen Member States remain outside the euro: Denmark, Sweden and the United Kingdom. One post-enlargement Member State, Slovenia, has qualified.

With the objective of maintaining monetary stability, the convergence criteria relating to government deficit and government debt were to continue after the introduction of the euro. To that end, the Member States adopted a Stability and Growth Pact embodied in a European Council resolution adopted at Amsterdam on 17 June 1997 and two Council Regulations of 7 July 1997. This allowed for the Council to impose financial penalties on participating Member States which failed to comply. It remains unclear whether failure by some Member States to comply will in practice trigger the sanctions envisaged.

The implications of Europeanisation of economic policy-making following EMU for employment and industrial relations in the EU are potentially vast.

---

[29] The criteria are: the ratio of government deficit to gross domestic product must not exceed 3 per cent; the ratio of government debt to gross domestic product must not exceed 60 per cent; there must be a sustainable degree of price stability and an average inflation rate, observed over a period of one year before the examination, which does not exceed by more than 1.5 per cent that of the three best performing Member States in terms of price stability; there must be a long-term nominal interest rate which does not exceed by more than 2 per cent that of the three best performing Member States in terms of price stability; the normal fluctuation margins provided for by the exchange-rate mechanism on the European monetary system must have been respected without severe tensions for at least the last two years before the examination. Article 121 EC, Articles 1–4 of the Protocol on Convergence Criteria.

The focus on monetary stability presents challenges for policies aimed at growth, with consequences for employment levels. In particular, the rigid convergence criteria for public debts and deficits pose difficulties for public finances at a time of economic downturns and retrenchment, again with implications for employment and social policy in general. The elimination of national currencies means devaluation will no longer be available to enable national adjustment to competitive pressures. One consequence will be that labour costs will become a focus of competitive pressure, with consequences for collective bargaining and industrial relations.

On the other hand, the Commission argues that the macro-economic policies of the EMU enhance the EU's social agenda. For instance, a stable EU labour market should reduce the opportunities for social dumping. But from the start there has been confusion over the relationship of employment policy to macro-economic policy. The consensus over economic policy which led to EMU was not achieved in the case of employment policy and this ambivalence was reflected in the arguments over the stability and employment pact. The compromise reached in the Employment Title requires employment policy to be consistent with economic policy while reaffirming the objective of a high level of employment. The lack of consensus over political objectives leads to institutional confusion and reduces the effectiveness of the process of policy coordination.

The critical issue remains the respective importance in combating unemployment of the Guidelines' proposals for structural labour market reforms as compared to macro-economic reforms. The argument is put as follows:[30]

> Based on the orthodox view that monetary policy has no long-run effects on growth and employment, that rationale permits the European Central Bank to abdicate from any responsibility for unemployment, which it ascribes entirely to structural factors, especially 'rigidities' in the labor market, which it is up to other actors to remedy. Pending such a remedy, the ECB insists, the best it can do to promote growth and employment – also part of its Treaty mandate – is to maintain price stability, defined as very low inflation.

Martin posits an alternative position: 'that a period of growth above its trend rate – a growth spurt – is needed to reduce unemployment … differences in monetary policy largely explain the unemployment variations, without denying that labor market institutions can have some effect on monetary policy's impact'.[31] His conclusion is grim:[32]

> If the ECB's policy orientation is indeed wrong and the alternative view more nearly correct, then, there will be no progress to the renewed goal of full

---

[30] Andrew Martin, 'The EMU Macroeconomic Policy Regime and the European Social Model', in A. Martin and G. Ross (eds.), *Euros and Europeans: Monetary Integration and the European Model of Society*, Cambridge: Cambridge University Press, 2004, p. 20 at p. 48.
[31] *Ibid.*     [32] *Ibid.*, p. 50.

employment. Unless there is a shift in the EMU policy regime towards one in which monetary policy takes responsibility for growth and employment as well as price stability, Europe is therefore likely to experience continued high unemployment, posing what is probably the most serious threat to the European social model.

This conclusion has implications also for the European Employment Strategy:[33]

> The EES, on its own, is unlikely to produce far-reaching changes, however. Its central objective is to increase the EU employment rate, but it has few ways of actually doing so. Its mandate excludes issues about the demand for labor, a factor at least as important for employment levels as the supply-side matters to which the EES is largely confined. All of the activation, training, energetic job prospecting and efforts to engage women and older workers in the workforce are unlikely to make much difference without many more jobs.

## Legal strategy

The economic policy function of the EES may, however, be linked with the particular legal strategy adopted: exposure to the repeated annual ritual of guidelines, national action plans, reviews and recommendations. This is what Martin and Ross assert may be:[34]

> an additional underlying agenda. If it cannot deliver on its employment creation promises, it could nonetheless be a useful tool to give key national actors lessons

---

[33] Andrew Martin and George Ross, 'Conclusions', in Martin and Ross (eds.), *Euros and Europeans*, p. 309 at p. 324.

[34] *Ibid.* For other underlying agendas, Janine Goetschy: 'a fundamental criticism which can be made of the content of the EES ... concerns the quality of jobs created ... precarious employment tends to become "banalized", normalized, officially recognized. The development of precarious forms of employment, a more fragmented (because more "flexible") workforce, the growth of private services and of SMEs (where employment protections and conditions are normally inferior to those in the rest of the economy) is integral to the EU strategy of job creation. These dimensions are no longer questioned in EU employment policy or in the guidelines. The demand for a disposable workforce and flexible labour markets is taken for granted; its ideological content is no longer perceived. Hence, the EU employment guidelines are not an innocent vehicle; they imply a new productive and working order within the EU, which should be open to serious political debate.' 'The European Employment Strategy: Genesis and Development', (1999) 5 *European Journal of Industrial Relations* 117 at pp. 135–6. Diamond Ashiagbor: 'a re-orientation from an approach to labour market regulation which had as its core a strong concept of employment protection and high labour standards, to an approach which prioritises employment creation, and minimises the role of social policy, since social policy is seen as potentially increasing the regulatory burden'. 'EMU and the Shift in the European Labour Law Agenda: From "Social Policy" to "Employment Policy"', (2001) 7 *European Law Journal*, p. 311. Sally Ball: 'The strategy is laced with notions of employee self-reliance, self-improvement and adaptability, as well as one of its pillars being dedicated to a deregulatory agenda. It does not, either within its annual guidelines to date, or within its surveillance procedure, place sufficient emphasis upon employee protection, social rights or social dialogue to merit an assessment that it promotes 'decent' employment as well as full employment'. 'The European Employment Strategy: The Will But Not the Way?', (2001) 30 *Industrial Law Journal* 353 at p. 374.

in 'EMU-speak' through iterative exercises that communicate the idea, however, illusory, that monetary policy is job-creation neutral and that only supply-side changes can create jobs.

The legal strategy of the EES has not escaped criticism. Guidelines have been criticised on a number of grounds. First, they are a 'soft law' instrument. Non-binding EU guidelines may not lead Member States to change their national employment policies. There is a fear, moreover, that non-binding guidelines are a tempting alternative model of EU social and labour regulation, allowing for more Member State autonomy compared to the binding 'hard law' legislative method.[35] The dominant method of regulation shifts from the 'Community method', which engages the role of the Commission and the European Parliament and instead increases 'intergovernmentalism' and the role of the Council.[36]

The question of the impact of the EES Guidelines on *national* employment policies is difficult to answer. Even when national policies are in line with Guidelines, it is difficult to prove that they are so as a result of the Guidelines, as opposed to autonomous policy choices. Again, positive results in terms of employment outcomes are not easy to trace back to policies in the Guidelines, as opposed to changes in the overall economic climate. The Commission's evaluation after five years of operation of the European Employment Strategy asserted that national employment policies appeared to have become more convergent under the EES on a number of subjects, and especially to have fostered political agreement on adoption of prevention and activation policies.[37] The evaluation pointed to reduction of structural unemployment levels, a

[35] An example is the Commission's initial proposal of a Directive on temporary agency work. Commission of the European Communities, *Proposal for a Directive of the European Parliament and the Council on Working Conditions for Temporary Workers*, COM(2002) 149 final, Brussels, 20 March 2002; *Amended Proposal*, COM(2002) 701 final, Brussels, 28 November 2002. One commentator noted 'that the employment promoting objectives of the EES have the potential to impair and weaken the aim of providing minimum standards of protection for temporary workers, which is becoming increasingly soft and adaptable, depending on different national contexts and dynamics'. L. Zappala, 'The Temporary Agency Workers' Directive: An Impossible Political Agreement?' (2003) 32 *Industrial Law Journal* 310 at p. 317.

[36] It is becoming clear that the Employment Guidelines have had an important impact and steering effect on *EC* labour legislation. For example, Directive 2000/43/EC on race and ethnic discrimination is an element in the overall EES aiming to create a labour market that promotes inclusion of minority groups. Council Directive 2000/43 implementing the principle of equal treatment between persons irrespective of racial or ethnic origin, OJ 2000, L/180/22. The Preamble to the Directive refers both to the Employment Guidelines for the year 2000, approved at the Helsinki Council meeting in December 1999, and to Article 2 EC.

[37] *Taking Stock of Five Years of the European Employment Strategy*, COM(2002) 416, 17 July 2002. Cf. the following assessment of the four pillars agreed in December 1997: 'The four pillars, which were agreed upon in a top-down manner, became the core features of the EES for the five years to come and imply for some countries important structural reforms, which are not necessarily in tune with their dominant national policy objectives or traditions. These four pillars are not "neutral decisions" but imply important policy choices. The employment policy model behind the EES is a compromise between the liberal and the Nordic models. On the labour demand side the EES, with its attention for entrepreneurship and adaptability, is inspired by the liberal model emphasising labour market deregulation and tax reductions; whereas on the labour supply side

more employment-intensive pattern of economic growth and more rapid labour market adjustments and responsiveness of employment to economic changes. However, this was accompanied by the expansion of temporary contracts and part-time work and, after five years of the EES Guidelines, almost 13 million were still unemployed (of whom 42 per cent are long-term unemployed).

Finally, the coexistence in the Treaty of the EES with the broader macro-economic policy regime has a two-edged effect on economic policy disputes. It may expose actors to the orthodoxy promulgated by the ECB and others, but also, as stated by Martin and Ross:[38]

> The EES gives actors a new arena to voice their own conceptions of the kind of changes needed in labor market institutions ... In this sense the employment strategy is also a venue for articulating the positions of those who disagree with a macroeconomic policy regime that abdicates responsibility for employment and places it entirely on supply-side measures. For such reasons the EES – and, more broadly, OMC – as a new way of promoting social Europeanization out of national diversity, has elicited enthusiasm among progressive social policy experts, who see it as a useful tool for positive reform and a forum that provides new legitimacy for national 'social partners,' particularly unions and civil society groups.

## Tripartite concertation

In their Contribution to the Laeken European Council on 7 December 2001, the European social partners (ETUC, UNICE and CEEP) 'believe it necessary to reaffirm ... the distinction between bipartite social dialogue and tripartite concertation [and] the need better to articulate tripartite concertation around the different aspects of the Lisbon strategy' (Section 1). Accordingly, the European social partners proposed to articulate concertation on the Lisbon strategy in a single forum (Section 4). This tripartite concertation committee for growth and employment 'would examine the Community's overall economic and social strategy ahead of the spring European Council'.[39]

---

the EES is inspired by the Nordic model focusing on employability via training and active labour market policies. As a consequence, the "adjustment costs" are much higher for the central continental and the Southern countries. This is illustrated by the number of Recommendations addressed to the member states; the continental and Southern countries are (roughly) twice as much the subject of Recommendations compared to the Nordic countries, the UK and Ireland. The OMC seems in fact to pay little consideration to the fact that countries whose employment policy is particularly distant from the one put forward by the EU will most likely face enormous political problems in implementing the guidelines and recommendations.' Stijn Smismans, *EU Employment Policy: Decentralisation or Centralisation through the Open Method of Coordination?* European University Institute, EUI Working Paper Law No. 2004/1, at p. 15. For the still greater challenges anticipated to face the ten new Member States as of May 2004, see Mike Ingham and Hilary Ingham, 'Enlargement and the European Employment Strategy: Turbulent Times Ahead?' (2003) 34 *Industrial Relations Journal* 379.

[38] Martin and Ross, 'Conclusions', pp. 324–5.

[39] This is apart from the 'macro-economic dialogue' established after the Cologne European Council of June 1999 in which there is a regular exchange of views between the representatives of

In accordance with a Council Decision of 6 March 2003,[40] the Tripartite Social Summit for Growth and Employment was established (Article 1) to support reinforcement of the concertation between social partners and European institutions on economic and social policies. This institutionalises meetings just before the spring European Council, bringing together the Heads of States or Governments of the present and two subsequent Presidencies of the Council, the Commission and representatives of the social partners (Article 3). The meetings take place at least once a year (Article 4(1)) with the task 'to ensure … that there is continuous concertation between the Council, the Commission and the social partners in order to enable the social partners to contribute, on the basis of their social dialogue, to the various components of the integrated economic and social strategy launched at the Lisbon European Council in March 2000 and supplemented by the Gothenburg European Council in June 2001' (Article 2).[41]

In Section 2.1 on 'Organising tripartite concertation', the Commission's Communication of 26 June 2002 stated that 'Fruit of the political desire closely to associate the social partners in the advances made in European integration, concertation is firmly rooted in Community practice' (p. 12). It stated that the proposed new Tripartite Social Summit for Growth and Employment 'will provide for an informal discussion on the social partners' contribution to the Lisbon strategy'. It added, however, that 'Economic and monetary matters are dealt with in the context of the macroeconomic dialogue which should be pursued in accordance with its own procedures. The macroeconomic dialogue is thus not affected by this decision' (p. 13).

## How 'soft' can law become?

Soft law is the term applied to EU measures, such as guidelines, declarations and opinions, which, in contrast to regulations, directives and decisions, are not binding on those to whom they are addressed. It is important to distinguish soft law's lack of legally binding effect from its potential impact in practice. It is

the Commission, the Council, the European Central Bank and the social partners. In relation to the open method of coordination, applicable 'to fields of interest to the social partners: employment, social inclusion, pensions, and soon, vocational training', the Commission 'suggests that each area under the method of open coordination should form the subject of organised dialogue with the social partners along the lines of the arrangements for the macroeconomic dialogue, more precisely, its dual setup at technical and political levels'.

[40] Initially proposed in the Commission's Communication, 'The European social dialogue, a force for innovation and change' (COM(2002) 341 final, Brussels, 16 June 2002).

[41] The first formal Tripartite Social Summit for Growth and Employment took place on 20 March 2003, co-chaired by the Greek Prime Minister, then current President of the EU Council of Ministers, and the President of the European Commission and attended by high-level representatives of the social partners, the Social Affairs Commissioner and the Ministers of Labour from Greece and those of the Member States holding the next two Presidencies (Italy and Ireland). A second – extraordinary – Tripartite Social Summit for Growth and Employment took place on 11 December 2003 in Brussels, the eve of the European Council, with the current and future Presidencies of the Council, the social partners and the Commission (President Prodi and Commissioner Diamantopoulou).

claimed that soft law may impact on policy development and practice precisely by reason of its lack of legal effect. Rather, because of its informal 'soft' influence, for example, in demonstration effects through pilot projects, illustration of possibilities and persuasive character, Member States and other actors may undertake voluntarily to do what they are unwilling to contemplate if legally obligated. Soft law, therefore, is sometimes presented as a more flexible instrument in achieving policy objectives.[42]

In reality, however, soft law tends to be used in the EU context where Member States are unable to agree on the use of a 'hard law' measure which is legally binding, or where the EU lacks competence to enact hard law measures. The Member States and EU institutions are thus able to adopt EU policy proposals, while leaving their implementation optional for those Member States who do not wish to be bound. They are thus a standing temptation for the Commission when faced with resistance from some Member States which threatens to block policy proposals.

The resort to the 'soft law' mechanism of coordination through the Employment Guidelines requires the Commission to invest considerable effort in an attempt to formulate targets and measures capable of assessing Member State compliance with the EES. It may be that weaknesses can be compensated for by improved statistical measures (benchmarks) and compliance procedures (e.g. peer review). Ultimately, however, the utility of measures or procedures will depend on the quality (nature and precision) of the targets established in the Guidelines, and their impact.[43]

In this last respect, much store is being set on the iterative pattern of annual guidelines, National Action Plans, reviews and recommendations. In itself, the process may produce discernible effects. But the lack of independent powers of scrutiny or enforcement, by the Commission or others, means placing a great burden on this iterative pattern alone to achieve the desired results.

More fundamentally, even if the Commission does manage to control the development and implementation of the EES, the question is whether this is a Community policy which is being implemented, or whether the EES, as the Employment Title states, remains only a 'co-ordinated strategy for employment' (Article 125) accommodating national policies.

---

[42] Often advocated in terms of 'mutual learning processes' between the EU and Member States, or presented in metaphorical terms of 'reflexiveness'. For an illustration in the sphere of regulation of part-time work, see Silvana Sciarra, Paul Davies and Mark Freedland (eds.), *Employment Policy and the Regulation of Part-Time Work in the European Union: A Comparative Analysis*, Cambridge: Cambridge University Press, 2004.

[43] A review of the empirical research on the impact of the OMC concludes 'that the OMC has only restricted, if not negligible, direct effects in the short term, while it may have some indirect effects in the medium to long term. On the basis of this assumption, a series of arguments against the current "spread" of the OMC will be put forward. Some proposals on how to neutralise some of the shortfalls of the OMC will follow.' V. Hatzopoulos, 'Why the Open Method of Coordination is Bad for You: A Letter to the EU', (2007) 13 *European Law Journal* (No. 3, May) 309–42 at p. 310.

EC social and labour regulation traditionally classifies regulatory measures as either harmonisation or coordination, and as either 'hard law' or 'soft law'. The Employment Title is usually characterised as a typical soft law coordination measure. The Member States cooperate in the field of employment policy, but the Employment Title does not confer any competences on the Community to regulate national labour markets.

This may give a misleading picture of the relationship and mutual influence between the Employment Title and labour regulation in general, and the *acquis communautaire* of EC labour law in particular.

The Employment Guidelines have a certain impact and steering effect on EC labour legislation.[44] EC labour law, traditionally perceived as minimum labour standards in the form of harmonisation directives, has been under considerable constraint due to a combination of ideological hostility and a static view of subsidiarity militating in favour of deregulation. The EES may provide a new lease of life by legitimating and justifying EC labour regulation.

As recent EC labour regulations are closely linked to the EES, labour regulation is perceived as a tool for the realisation of the EES. Employment policy, social inclusion and the promotion of socially sustainable development become important elements in the social objectives of labour law. In this way, the EES becomes the accepted framework not only for the employment and social policies of the Member States but also for the harmonisation of national legislation in the field of EU social policy and labour law.[45]

The relationship between the *acquis* and the EES is a two-way street. The *acquis* is a legally binding framework of labour regulation which constrains the scope and nature of the policies adopted under the EES. At the same time, the EES expands the scope of the *acquis* by inspiring new regulations aimed at achieving the objectives of the EES, but based on the social chapter provisions of the Treaty, among others.[46]

---

[44] The new Directive 2000/43/EC on race and ethnic discrimination (OJ 2000, L180/22) is an element in the overall EES aiming to create a labour market that promotes inclusion of minority groups. The Preamble to the Directive refers both to the Employment Guidelines for the year 2000, approved at the Helsinki Council meeting in December 1999, and to Article 2 EC. Similarly, a relationship between equal opportunities as a pillar of the EES and EC labour law is being established. For example, the Directive on Parental Leave 96/34/EC, with its explicit ambition to be a 'means of reconciling work and family life and promoting equal opportunities and treatment between women and men' (Preamble) can easily be regarded as within the equal opportunities pillar of the EES.

[45] The potential contribution of the EES to development of the law on social protection in the EC is also significant. At one level, the financial constraints on social security systems means that the EES exerts pressure to make social protection law more 'employment-friendly'. This presents a danger in the form of the 'working poor'. The original convergence strategy for social protection law among the Member States has given way to coordination, which is in line with the EES method of implementation.

[46] This potential can be illustrated by observing the relationship between the pillars on entrepreneurship and adaptability and labour law. The promotion of adaptability may be promoted by the Framework Directive 2002/14 on Information and Consultation, and the entrepreneurship pillar may be linked with proposals on self-employed workers.

## The Lisbon Strategy

The Lisbon European Council of 23–24 March 2000 articulated a new strategic goal for the EU: 'to become the most competitive and dynamic knowledge-based economy in the world capable of sustainable economic growth with more and better jobs and greater social cohesion'. In particular, this included modernising the 'European social model, investing in people and combating social exclusion'. The strategy was designed 'to enable the Union to regain the conditions for full employment'.[47]

As well as a new strategic goal, the Lisbon Council highlighted the 'open method of coordination' as a principal process through which this goal was to be achieved. The specific application of this method to the European Employment Strategy was confirmed and was to be strengthened through an additional annual meeting of the European Council in the spring of each year, for which an annual synthesis report would be prepared, devoted to considering economic and social questions.[48]

In its Social Policy Agenda 2000–5, the Commission confirmed the Lisbon Strategy and stated, under the rubric 'Achieving the new strategic goal', that 'a guiding principle of the new Social Policy Agenda will be to strengthen the role of social policy as a productive factor'. Reflecting the approach favoured by the Lisbon Council, the Commission stated: 'This new Social Policy Agenda does not seek to harmonise social policies. It seems to work towards common European objectives and increase co-ordination of social policies in the context of the internal market and the single currency.'[49] It continued: 'To achieve these priorities, an adequate combination of all existing means will be required.'[50] However, although a variety of means were listed, the scope of application allocated to each was significant.

The first was 'The open method of co-ordination, inspired by the Luxembourg Employment Process and developed by the Lisbon and Feira Councils'. There was no limit specified to the scope of matters suitable for the application of this method. In contrast, the second means listed was: 'Legislation: Standards should be developed or adapted, where appropriate, to ensure the respect of fundamental social rights and to respond to new challenges. Such standards can also result from agreements between the social partners at European level.' The scope of legislation required to achieve the European social model is here limited to fundamental social rights and new challenges. Thirdly: 'The Social Dialogue as the most effective way of modernising contractual relations, adapting work organisation and developing adequate balance between flexibility and security'. The role of social dialogue is even more limited to work relationships within the enterprise.

[47] Lisbon Presidency Conclusions, paragraphs 5 and 6.     [48] *Ibid.*, paragraph 36.
[49] COM(2000) 379 final, Brussels, 28 June 2000, Section 1.2, pp. 5, 7.     [50] *Ibid.*, p. 14.

Other means are specified: structural funds, programmes and policy and research to underpin policy initiatives, and mainstreaming to be strengthened and further developed. Nonetheless, the unlimited scope of the open method of coordination as an instrument for achieving the Lisbon Strategy is in clear contrast with the restricted scope of legislation and social dialogue. The elaboration of 'fundamental social rights' and 'adapting work organisation' leaves room for extensive intervention of both legislation and social dialogue. But the emphasis is on the open method of coordination as the instrument for achieving the Lisbon Strategy.

## The Lisbon Strategy and the changes to the EC Social Chapter by the Treaty of Nice

The Lisbon Strategy's approach emphasising coordination is reflected in the changes to the Social Chapter of the EC Treaty adopted by the Treaty of Nice in December 2000. At first sight, Article 137(2)(a) EC appeared to reflect the previous provision in Article 137(2) insofar as it provides that:

> The Council ... may adopt measures designed to encourage cooperation between Member States through initiatives aimed at improving knowledge, developing exchanges of information and best practices, promoting innovative approaches and evaluating experiences ...

However, the new Article 137(2)(a) appears rather to transpose into the Social Policy Chapter the approach of employment policy coordination adopted in the Employment Title's Article 129 EC.[51]

This is because Article 137(2)(a) EC was amended by the Treaty of Nice in two apparently minor ways. First, it added to the provision encouraging cooperation between Member States the phrase 'excluding any harmonisation of the laws and regulations of the Member States'. Secondly, this phrase replaced the former Article 137(2)'s provision limiting cooperation measures solely 'in order to combat social exclusion'. This former limitation has now been eliminated by the incorporation of the reference to combating social exclusion to the new Article 138(1)(j) EC.

Its replacement by the insertion of the new phrase, however, has two very significant implications. The first outcome of the amendments made by the Treaty of Nice is that coordination/cooperation is an approach which may henceforth be applied to *all* social policy areas listed in the revised Article 137(1) EC (not just 'in order to combat social exclusion'). Secondly, in social policy

---

[51] 'The Council ... may adopt incentive measures designed to encourage cooperation between Member States and to support their action in the field of employment through initiatives aimed at developing exchanges of information and best practices, providing comparative analysis and advice as well as promoting innovative approaches and evaluating experiences, in particular by recourse to pilot projects. Those measures shall not include harmonisation of the laws and regulations of the Member States'.

generally, as in the case of employment policy, 'any harmonisation of the laws and regulations of the Member States' through the process of cooperation/coordination is excluded. These Treaty amendments appear to confirm the Commission's approach as stated in its Social Policy Agenda 2000–5: 'This new Social Policy Agenda does not seek to harmonise social policies. It seems to work towards common European objectives and increase co-ordination of social policies …' (p. 7).

These amendments to Article 137 EC by the Treaty of Nice mark the new departure in EU social policy signalled by the Lisbon Strategy. EU social policy is not primarily to be implemented through the adoption by means of directives of minimum requirements[52] in the fields listed in Article 137(1)(a–i) EC. Rather, in all these fields there is the *alternative* of measures designed to encourage cooperation between Member States (Article 137(2)(a)), formerly restricted to combating social exclusion (ex Article 137(2) EC), and explicitly 'excluding any harmonisation of the laws and regulations of the Member States'.[53]

A contrasting view is that of Working Group XI on Social Europe of the Convention on the Future of Europe. The Final Report of Working Group XI specifies (paragraph 41):[54]

> that the [OMC] can be applied *only* where no Union legislative competence is enshrined in the Treaty and in areas *other than* those where the coordination of national policies is governed by a special provision in the Treaty defining such coordination (in economic matters (Article 99) and in the area of employment (Article 128) in particular).

The result is that the scope for the OMC in labour policy, under these conditions, is extremely limited. The Working Group states unequivocally that the OMC has *no* application in the sphere of employment and labour relations where legislative measures are applicable, or in employment policy where the Treaty specifies procedures.

These limitations on the operation of the OMC are repeated again in paragraph 43 of the Final Report of Working Group XI. But there is one slight, and very important difference: after excluding areas where the Union has legislative competence or specific provision is made, the Working Group adds: '*or* where the Union *has competence* only for defining *minimum* rules, in order to go

---

[52] Article 137(2)(b) EC, formerly 137(2) EC.

[53] A third amendment by the Treaty of Nice highlights the significance of the exclusion of harmonisation of laws and regulations. This was the deletion from Article 137(1) EC, the list of areas in which the Council could adopt directives, of the provision concerning 'financial contributions for promotion of employment and job creation' (formerly allowed by Article 137(3) EC). These were equivalent to the 'incentive measures' authorised by Article 129 EC, but, unlike Article 129, Article 137(3) EC did not exclude harmonisation of laws and regulations. The deletion of this provision means harmonising directives in relation to 'financial contributions for promotion of employment and job creation' are now excluded.

[54] CONV 516/1/03 – Rev 1, Brussels, 4 February 2003.

*beyond* these rules'. This is significant both in expanding the scope and defining the standards which can be established through the OMC.

As to *scope*: Article 137(2)(b) EC (post-Nice) specifies that the Council: 'may adopt, in the fields referred to in paragraph 1(a) to (i), by means of directives, *minimum* requirements …'. Working Group XI *seems* to open the door for the OMC to operate in the fields of employment and labour relations referred in Article 137(1)(a)–(i). However, the OMC can *only* be used to 'go *beyond* these minimum rules'. This means that the OMC *cannot* operate where there are *no* rules. Where EU legislative competence has not been exercised, there are no rules beyond which the OMC can go.

As to *standards*: where legislative competence exists, and *has* been exercised to establish minimum rules, the OMC *cannot* establish inferior, or even equal standards. It must operate to promote *higher* standards.[55] The practical consequence is that the OMC *cannot* become a substitute for legislation on social, employment and labour standards. It cannot replace legislation, including that resulting from social dialogue framework agreements. The Member States are precluded from using the OMC in those fields.

## The Lisbon Strategy in trouble

The European Employment Strategy (EES) became institutionalised with the insertion into the EC Treaty by the Treaty of Amsterdam of a new 'Employment Title' (Articles 125–30 EC). This enshrined in the Treaty the 'Luxembourg process'.[56]

The Commission, particularly DG-V (Employment, Social Affairs and Equal Opportunities) invested huge efforts in the development of the EES. The follow-up process to its formal recognition in the new Employment Title of the EC Treaty was evident in the ability of the Commission to present Guidelines in the immediate aftermath of the adoption of the Amsterdam Treaty in 1997, long before it came into effect. The EES has produced annual sets of Employment

---

[55] The final paragraph 47 of Section IV voices a view 'mentioned in the Group' which might seem to contradict what came before. This is that: 'Some areas to which the [OMC] method could be applied [include] the establishment of minimum social standards'. This seems to contradict the Working Group's earlier very clear exclusion of the OMC where there *were* legislative social standards. The exception was where the legislation established minimum standards, but then the OMC could operate *not* to establish minimum social standards, but only to go *beyond* these minimum standards. In fact, there is no contradiction, as clarified by the next sentence: 'Members of the Group thought social protection and inclusion was particularly well suited to this approach'. In precisely those fields *there is no provision for legislative minimum standards*. Article 137(2) states that EU measures are to take the form of directives establishing minimum requirements as regards Article 137(1)(a)–(i), *but not as regards Article 137(1)(j)* ('the combating of social exclusion') and 137(1)(k) ('the modernisation of social protection systems*, without prejudice to point (c))'. (Article 137(1)(c) does refer to 'social security and social protection of workers'.) Since in those fields there is no provision for legislative minimum standards, the OMC may operate.

[56] Called after the Luxembourg 'Jobs Summit' of 1997 (COM(99)442).

Guidelines, the Member States have undertaken annual cycles of National Action Plans, annual Joint Employment Reports have been produced, and Recommendations have emerged following the coming into force of the Amsterdam Treaty on 1 May 1999.

The implementation of the EES through the Luxembourg process of 'the open method of coordination' has strengths: it is an iterative process, carried out in a pluri-annual perspective, with a set of guidelines including targets and deadlines and a review and evaluation procedure which impacts on national administrations.

But the process has weaknesses: lack of sanctions, uncertain relation to macro-economic policy, scarcity of financial support for innovative developments, instrumentalisation by national administrations using formulas of the EES to inauthentically bolster domestic policies, lack of definition of key concepts, questionable quality of jobs created, a focus on national administrations which ignores devolution of employment policy to sub-national units, replacement of social justice values with needs of the labour market, failure to address wages as an essential element in labour markets and inadequate response of the social partners.[57]

Nonetheless, by the time of the Lisbon European Council of 23–24 March 2000, the Council was prepared to commit itself to precise targets to increase the average employment rate from 61 per cent to 70 per cent by 2010 and increase women's labour force participation from 51 per cent to 60 per cent over the same period.[58] The problem was perceived as exacerbated by the demographic changes entailed in the ageing population and declining birth rate, leading to a decline in the working-age population. The Stockholm European Council of 23–24 March 2001 set interim targets for labour force participation in general of 67 per cent (57 per cent for women) by 2005 and a new long-term target of 50 per cent for 'older persons' aged 55–64 by 2010.[59] The Commission's report on the progress of its five-year Social Policy Agenda 2000–5, issued on 13 February 2003, estimated that the 2010 targets of 70 per cent employment rate for the working-age population as a whole, 60 per cent for women and 50 per cent for older workers means that some 15 million additional jobs need to be created. There were conflicting views as to whether this could be delivered by the policy and its legal strategy.[60]

---

[57] Goetschy, 'The European Employment Strategy', pp. 281–301.
[58] Lisbon Presidency Conclusions, paragraph 30; see also the Commission's Social Policy Agenda 2000–5, COM(2000) 379 final, Brussels, 28 June 2000, Section 4.1.1.1, p. 15.
[59] Stockholm Presidency Conclusions, paragraph 9.
[60] 'Positive Assessment of European Employment Strategy', *European Industrial Relations Review* No. 344 (September 2002), pp. 27–30. 'Commission Reviews Member States' Employment Progress', *European Industrial Relations Review* No. 347 (December 2002), pp. 19–25. 'EU in Danger of Missing Key Employment Targets', *European Industrial Relations Review* No. 363 (2004), pp. 37–40.

In 2005, half way to the deadline of 2010, the Commission acknowledged that the Lisbon Strategy was in trouble. In a Communication dated 2 February 2005 to the Spring European Council, the President of the Commission, José Manuel Barroso, acknowledged:[61]

> Today, we see that combination of economic conditions, international uncertainty, slow progress in the Member States and a gradual loss of focus has allowed Lisbon to be blown off course.

This was not exactly news to many observers outside the Commission. In November 2004, Wim Kok, former Prime Minister of the Netherlands, presented the report of a High Level Group on the Lisbon Strategy which had been requested by the Commission. The Report stated that:[62]

> At Lisbon and at subsequent Spring Economic Councils, a series of ambitious targets were established to support the development of a world-beating European economy. But halfway to 2010 the overall picture is very mixed and much needs to be done in order to prevent Lisbon from becoming a synonym for missed objectives and failed promises.

The Kok Report concluded that the disappointing delivery of the Lisbon Strategy was due to an overloaded agenda, poor coordination, conflicting priorities and, not least, a lack of political action. It had harsh things to say about the process of its implementation (p. 42):

> The open method of coordination has fallen far short of expectations. If Member States do not enter the spirit of mutual benchmarking, little or nothing happens.

Despite the negative assessment of the Lisbon agenda ('Too many targets will be seriously missed' (p. 11)), the Kok Report endorsed both the objectives and the process: (pp. 11–12):

> Does that mean the ambition is wrong? The answer is no. The ambition is needed more than ever, whether to meet the challenges of enlargement, an aging population or the intensified global competition – let alone the need to lower current levels of unemployment … Should the 2010 deadline be lifted? Again no. The 2010 deadline is important for signalling and reinforcing the urgent need for action.

Despite the negative assessment of the OMC, the Kok Report concluded (pp. 42–3):

> The central elements of the open method of coordination – peer pressure and benchmarking – are clear incentives for the Member States to deliver on their

---

[61] Communication to the Spring European Council, *Working Together for Growth and Jobs. A New Start for the Lisbon Strategy*, Communication from President Barroso in agreement with Vice-President Verheugen, Brussels, 2 February 2005, COM(2005) 24, p. 12.

[62] Report from the High Level Group chaired by Wim Kok, *Facing the Challenge. The Lisbon Strategy for Growth and Employment*, Office for Official Publications of the European Communities, November 2004, p. 10.

commitments by measuring and comparing their respective performance and facilitating exchange of best practice. The High Level Group proposes a radical improvement of the process, making better use of the 14 indicators and then better communicating the results in order to ratchet up the political consequences of non-delivery.[63]

The Communication from Barroso of 2 February 2005 accepted this assessment, focusing, however, on the need to maintain the ambition (p. 12) (bold in original):

> The most important conclusion of the Kok report is that 'the promotion of growth and employment in Europe is the next great European project'. The Commission proposes to refocus the Lisbon agenda on actions that promote **growth and jobs** in a manner that is fully **consistent with the objective of sustainable development**. The actions falling under this strategy should reinforce the Union potential to meet and further develop our environmental and social objectives.

Following the European Council of March 2005, the Commission declared: 'The European Council of March 2005 has just relaunched the Lisbon strategy by refocusing on growth and employment in Europe, in accordance with the Commission's proposals ... Particular attention needs to be paid to the delivery of the Lisbon agenda.'[64] On the implementation side, the Commission proclaimed that, instead of separate Broad Economic Policy Guidelines based on Article 99 EC and separate Employment Guidelines based on Article 128 EC, these were henceforth to be incorporated into one and the same document, albeit in two parts: Part I: the BEFGs and Part II: the EGs.

However, the challenge was evident in the Commission's sombre assessment of the position in April 2005:[65]

> Unemployment rates are projected to decrease, albeit slowly, to 8.7% in 2006. The estimated overall employment rate is 62.9% for EU-25 in 2003, which is

---

[63] The Report noted (p. 43): 'More than a hundred indicators have been associated with the Lisbon process, which makes it likely that every country will be ranked as best at one indicator or another. This makes this instrument ineffective. Member States are not challenged to improve their record. Simplification is vital. The establishment by the European Council of a more limited framework of 14 targets and indicators offers the opportunity to improve the working of the instrument of peer pressure ... These 14 indicators offer the opportunity for Member States to further emphasise the growth and employment dimension of Lisbon *if they choose*' (italics added). Perhaps 'choice' is the issue. Research was undertaken interviewing seventy chief executive officers active in social security administration across fifteen European states as to the extent to which the OMC was having an impact upon national policy. The result: 'their answer was strikingly unanimous: very little, if not to say none. It is mainly the playing field of some experts who are assigned to report for this governance technique to the EU, but it never reaches the core of the policy debate in the decision-making instances.' Paul Schoukens, Review Article: 'Europe at Struggle with Social Welfare', (2007) 13 *European Law Journal* 424–33 at p. 433.

[64] Commission of the European Communities, *Integrated Guidelines for Growth and Jobs (2005–2008)*, Brussels, 12 April; 2005, COM(2005) 141 final; Explanatory Memorandum, p. 6.

[65] *Ibid.*, p. 3.

significantly below the agreed target level of 70%. Progress towards the female employment rate target of 60% has been slow, with the rate now standing at 56.1% for EU-25, but is expected to pick up again. The employment rate for older workers, which continued to climb to just over 40.2% has the largest gap to bridge towards the 50% target for 2010. At the same time, progress in improving quality in work has been mixed and the economic slowdown has raised the profile of social inclusion problems. Long-term unemployment increased again after several years of decline and seems unlikely to fall in the near future.

## Lisbon's change priorities: substance and process

The Commission's Communication of 2 February 2005 had signalled what appeared to be a specific invitation:[66]

> This strategy must be taken forward through a renewed partnership between the Member States and the Union – with the full involvement of the social partners.

It may be this promise which led the European social partners (UNICE/ UEAPME, CEEP and ETUC), on 15 March 2005, to issue a 'Joint declaration on the mid-term review of the Lisbon strategy' and to 'urge the Spring European Council to grasp the opportunity of the mid-term review to restore confidence in the Lisbon strategy'. Specifically:

> ETUC, UNICE/UEAPME and CEEP support the proposal to prepare national Lisbon programmes to bridge the delivery gap.
>
>     They stress the importance of involving social partners at national level, when developing these programmes, and at the European level, when assessing the implementation and results of the Lisbon strategy.

As a result, in a later Communication of 20 July 2005, the Commission seemed at least to pay lip service to this strategy:[67]

> On 2 February 2005, the Commission proposed a new start for the Lisbon Strategy focusing the European Union's efforts on two principal tasks – delivering stronger, lasting growth and more and better jobs … The European Council of March, as well as the European Parliament and the European social partners, gave full support to the Commission's proposal to relaunch and refocus the Lisbon Strategy.

However, this Communication of 20 July 2005 reveals a radically different set of priorities in the Commission's view of the revised Lisbon Strategy (p. 7) (bold in original):

---

[66] Communication to the Spring European Council, *Working Together for Growth and Jobs. A New Start for the Lisbon Strategy*, Communication from President Barroso in agreement with Vice-President Verheugen, Brussels, 2 February 2005, COM(2005) 24.

[67] Communication from the Commission to the Council and the European Parliament, *Common Actions for Growth and Employment. The Community Lisbon Programme*. SEC(2005) 981, Brussels, 20 July 2005, COM(2005) 330 final, p. 2.

In order to attract more investment, generate employment and accelerate growth, it is important to facilitate market-entry within sectors and between member states. The Community will therefore give **top priority to the completion of the internal market and to improving the regulatory environment** as the two most important policy levers to create jobs and improve Europe's growth performance.

Indeed, apart from acknowledging the support of the social partners at the beginning, the ten-page Communication of 20 July 2005 includes only one further reference to the social partners (p. 9):

These objectives and priorities are also at the core of the recently launched **Social Agenda** and are reflected in the integrated guidelines for growth and jobs. While the main responsibility for employment, social protection, education and training policies lies with national public authorities, the Community will complement their efforts. European social partners will be invited to play a major role.

Contrast the Kok Report's statement in its section 4 on 'Building an inclusive labour market for stronger social cohesion' (p. 31):

The call for more reform is too frequently seen as no more than code for more flexibility which in turn is seen as code for weakening worker rights and protections; this is wrong ... Nor should reform mean that the social dialogue is taken out of the heart of Europe's labour market. It is essential to its productivity and ability to adopt to change.

The Kok Report's conclusion stated (p. 44):

The promotion of growth and employment in Europe is the next great European project. Its execution will require political leadership and commitment of the highest order, along with that of the social partners whose role the High Level Group wishes to sustain.

At a meeting of the Tripartite Social Summit on 4 November 2004, at which Wim Kok presented his conclusions, the then holder of the Presidency of the Council (Prime Minister Balkenende) together with the then President of the Commission, Romano Prodi, had stated that:

the social dialogue is crucial as concertation and consensus are at the heart of the European Social model. They confirmed that the contribution of the social partners is essential in unleashing the potential for economic and employment growth.[68]

In contrast, the Communication of 20 July 2005 retreats from a wholehearted commitment to a role for the social partners to a mere invitation. In appearing to marginalise the social partners, and stating as its '**top priority ... the**

---

[68] Joint Presidency/Commission Press Release, Directorate-General for Employment, Social Affairs and Equal Opportunities, Brussels, 4 November 2004.

**completion of the internal market and ... improving the regulatory environment**', the Communication reflects what many fear is the ideological agenda of this particular Commission.[69] This agenda contrasts with the political priorities of many Member States, not to mention the social partners and, not least, the European trade union movement.

[69] One early critical assessment of the EES (Ball, 'The European Employment Strategy) included the heading: 'Is the European Employment Strategy Good for Employees?', with further sub-headings 'Too Much Flexibility?' and 'Quality of Jobs as well as Quantity?' (pp. 366ff.). It was argued that the EES 'does not, either within its annual guidelines to date, or within its surveillance procedure, place sufficient emphasis upon employee protection, social rights or social dialogue to merit an assessment that it promotes "decent" employment as well as full employment'. The author still felt able to conclude that the (previous) Commission 'currently considers its rights-based agenda to be just as important as the EES, which in itself may serve to allay some of the concerns about the agenda promoted by that strategy' (p. 373). Not any more.

# Chapter 7

# The strategy of fundamental rights: the EU Charter of Nice 2000 and a 'constitutional' strategy

## Origins and context of the EU Charter

The European Council meeting in Cologne in June 1999 appointed a working group, self-denominated the 'Convention', comprising representatives of three groups: the Member State Governments (15), the European Parliament (16), national parliaments (30) and the Commission (1), to formulate an EU Charter of Fundamental Rights and Freedoms, to be presented to the European Council in Nice in December 2000.[1] On the basis of this draft document, it was intended that the European Parliament, Commission and Council would proclaim a European Charter of Fundamental Rights. It was left to the Nice European Council to decide whether and, if so, how the Charter should be integrated into the Treaties.

The story of fundamental rights in the EU did not begin with the Cologne Summit of June 1999 and the work of the Convention in 1999–2000. There is a long history of attempts in the EC to promote fundamental rights. Fundamental rights in the EU legal order have been developed by the European Court of Justice as a result of the sensitivity of national constitutional courts to respect for fundamental rights protected by national legal orders of the EU Member States. The need for general principles of *EU* law to include protection for fundamental rights is driven by the implications for *national* constitutional protection of such rights of the doctrine of supremacy of EU law.[2] The evidence of these past struggles is to be found in Treaty provisions, decisions of the European Court of Justice and many resolutions and other declarations from the EU institutions. Perhaps the most important for labour law was the Community Charter of the Fundamental Social Rights of Workers proclaimed at Strasbourg in December 1989.

Each of these manifestations of fundamental rights has to be seen in its historical, political, institutional, economic and legal context, linked with a

---

Parts of this chapter are drawn from my contributions to B. Bercusson (ed.), *European Labour Law and the EU Charter of Fundamental Rights*, Baden-Baden: Nomos, 2006.

[1] Cologne European Council, 3–4 June 1999, Presidency Conclusions, pp. 44–5 and Annex IV.

[2] P. Craig and G. de Búrca, *EU Law: Text, Cases and Materials*, 3rd edn, Oxford: Oxford University Press, 2003, Chapter 8, 'General Principles I: Fundamental Rights', pp. 317–70.

specific phase of development in the EC, now EU. The evolution of social and labour policy in the EU described in preceding chapters illustrates this. For example, the first surge of social policy-making in the EC followed the political shock of the late 1960s, with enormous labour unrest across Western Europe, and the economic shocks of the 1970s, following the oil crisis arising out of the 1973 Middle East war. The result was a Social Action Programme enacted during the 1970s, with important directives on sex equality and restructuring of enterprises, and many supportive decisions of the European Court of Justice. Again, the political pressure for a social dimension to complement the economic focus of the 1992 Single European Market Programme led to the Community Charter of 1989 and, eventually, to the Maastricht Protocol on Social Policy, which became part of the Social Chapter of the EC Treaty.[3]

The EU Charter of Fundamental Rights was formally adopted as a political declaration by the Member States of the European Union meeting under the French presidency in the European Council at Nice in December 2000.[4] It is important to analyse the political, economic, institutional and legal context in which the EU Charter emerged.[5]

## Political context

The political context was one in which an Intergovernmental Conference (IGC) was charged with preparing an agenda for the Nice European Council of December 2000, which was eventually to produce the Treaty of Nice. The priorities of the IGC, endlessly debated in the Member States, included enlargement (the procedures for application and admission of new Member States), institutional reform (to reform voting in the Council, the number and distribution of members of the Commission, the case load of the European Court and the composition of the European Parliament) and common security and defence policy (the management of military and non-military crises).

What was striking about the work of the IGC was the absence of a social agenda or priorities. Arguably, the failure to incorporate a social policy dimension into the IGC agenda endangered the enlargement of the EU, undermined

---

[3] Social rights at EU level develop in the context of other policies taken up in the process of promoting European integration. For example, fundamental rights linked to working time are linked with a variety of such policies: qualified majority voting on health and safety allows for the Working Time Directive; the Employment Title promotes adaptability of working time, one of the pillars of the EES Guidelines; a fundamental right to sex equality involves reconciliation of work and family life, with consequences in the form of directives on parental leave and part-time work. As stated in another context: 'The regulation of working time at EU level engages the EU institutions [when] it finds a place on the Community's integration agenda'. B. Bercusson, 'Les temps communautaires', (2000) *Droit Social* (March) 248–56, at pp. 252–3: para. III.A.

[4] Charter of Fundamental Rights of the European Union, proclaimed at the meeting of the European Council held in Nice from 7 to 9 December 2000, and adopted by the Commission, the Council and the Member States, OJ C364/01 of 18 December 2000.

[5] The following section draws on the Introduction, which the author helped draft, to Ulrich Mückenberger (ed.), *Manifesto Social Europe*, Brussels: European Trade Union Institute, 2001.

institutional reforms and threatened the security of Europe. Institutional reform was undoubtedly important. But the IGC 2000's institutional reform agenda simply ignored the specific institutional arrangements for social policy.

The Maastricht Protocol and Agreement on Social Policy, now Articles 136–9 of the EC Treaty, installed labour and management as central actors in the formulation of EU social policy through the European social dialogue. The institutional reforms needed were not only to Council voting procedures or numbers of Commissioners. A major problem was the increasing reluctance of European employers' organisations to engage in social dialogue or to develop sectoral organisations capable of engaging in social dialogue. Similarly, the Commission had failed to adopt a general legislative programme, which would promote and stimulate the social dialogue. Social Europe required mechanisms to stimulate action by the social partners and EU institutions to achieve the necessary social policies. The question was how EU institutions and the actors in the social dialogue can become more actively, and cooperatively, engaged in the process of creating Social Europe.

The initiative to formulate an EU Charter of Fundamental Rights, therefore, was one part of the political response to an awareness that the IGC agenda, and the Member States, had failed to address social policy issues.

### Economic context

The economic context of the EU Charter can be appreciated by recalling the Presidency Conclusions of the Lisbon European Council of 23–24 March 2000, which began with the heading: 'Employment, Economic Reform and Social Cohesion'. The Council laid down an 'overall strategy' which aimed at 'modernising the European social model, investing in people and combating social exclusion' (paragraph 5). In particular (paragraph 6):

> This strategy is designed to enable the Union to regain the conditions for full employment and to strengthen regional cohesion in the European Union. The European Council needs to set a goal for full employment in Europe in an emerging new society which is more adapted to the personal choices of women and men.

One question was whether and how the fundamental rights embodied in the EU Charter could affect the future economic and social policy agenda of the EU in general, and, in light of the emphasis on employment policy, the substantive content of the European Employment Strategy (EES) in particular.

It seems clear that the emphasis in 2000 was on employment policy. Analysis of the positions adopted by the Member States in the course of the negotiations which led to the Employment Title of the Treaty (inserted by the Treaty of Amsterdam) revealed two broad labour market concerns which appeared to dominate the EU's determination to intervene by way of a European Employment Strategy: changing demography and unemployment. These concerns both overlap and may conflict.

First, demographic changes in the workforce in the EU mean there is a steadily ageing population, with more older and retiring workers, and a decline in the birth rate, with fewer young entrants into the workforce. This is combined with a relatively low employment rate averaging about 60 per cent, when labour force participation in the USA and Japan is about 70 per cent. Secondly, the EU average unemployment level of about 10 per cent reflects wide variation among Member States, but compares badly with unemployment levels in the USA and Japan. Women comprise the most important segment of the workforce which is increasing: entry of women workers into the labour market accounts for almost all the growth in employment.

Understanding the EU Charter's provisions on social and labour rights requires attention to be paid to these labour market concerns, and the extent to which the Charter reflects the EU's economic policy objectives focusing on employment. For example, does the policy aim at redressing the demographic changes with a view to increasing the employment rate; or does it aim to reduce the level of unemployment? In so far as they overlap, measures may be adopted which appear to address both concerns. However, there may also be conflict, as a high employment rate may be achieved without necessarily achieving a reduction in unemployment (e.g. by drawing in previously inactive parts of the population), and the impact of certain measures aimed at reducing unemployment may do little for the employment rate (e.g. early retirement schemes).

Clarification of these objectives is necessary in order to understand the wider social agenda of the EU. For example, issues of equal opportunities (facilitating women's labour force participation) and social protection (tackling social exclusion and its consequences for employment) reveal the overlaps between established items of the EU's social agenda and the measures adopted under the EES. Regulation of working time, of new ('atypical') forms of work, of work organisation, of vocational training – all dealt with in the EU Charter – are among a host of issues which overlap with the concerns of the EES.

Clarity of the EU's political economy objectives may help in understanding the institutional structure for their implementation and effectiveness, including the role of the EU Charter. Not least, the EU Charter may play a role in establishing both the formal legitimacy of economic policy, in the form of the institutional involvement of the European Court and other EU institutions, the social partners and others, and also its social legitimacy, as the primary economic problem of unemployment is tackled, but with the safeguards of the social and labour standards in the EU Charter.

## Institutional context

The institutional context of the EU Charter includes the institutional structure specific to the European Employment Strategy – the open method of coordination (sometimes called the 'Luxembourg' process) – which is encapsulated in Article 128 of the Employment Title of EC Treaty: annual Guidelines, National

Action Plans, reviews, reports and recommendations. Specifically, the social partners are called upon to play a major role in the 'Luxembourg process' of the EES: 'The social partners need to be more closely involved in drawing up, implementing and following up the appropriate guidelines.'[6] This was reinforced at the Feira Council, which invited the social partners 'to play a more prominent role in implementing and monitoring the Guidelines which depend on them'.[7]

One critical issue is how the institutional mechanism of the Luxembourg process, and, specifically, the role of the social partners, is to be coordinated with the institutional mechanism of labour regulation through the social dialogue in Articles 138–9 of the EC Treaty. The fundamental rights of the social partners guaranteed by the EU Charter approved at Nice could influence the institutions and actors involved, the processes of social dialogue and employment policy coordination and the legal and policy measures which result.

## Legal context

Finally, the EU Charter emerged in a specific legal context which highlighted sharp divisions of opinion regarding its legal status and its political and legal consequences. The specific concern was whether social and economic rights, as contrasted with civil and political rights, should be included, and, if so, should be justiciable, or considered 'only' programmatic rights.

As regards civil and political rights, there was little dispute as to their justiciability. It was recognised that such rights had long been included in justiciable form in the European Convention on Human Rights (ECHR) of the Council of Europe. However, there were debates over whether their inclusion in an EU Charter should have a content and meaning different from, and enforcement machinery separate or independent from that of the Council of Europe institutions in Strasbourg.

The UK government's representative in the Convention, Lord Goldsmith, was particularly active in this debate. In an early contribution to the Convention of 7 February 2000,[8] he emphasised that the Cologne European Council's Conclusions were 'a clear steer towards a political statement limited to existing rights'. He proposed a structure comprising two interrelated parts:

> Part A would contain a succinct and user-friendly statement of rights and responsibilities, while Part B would complement and build on Part A by explaining the nature and scope of those rights and pointing to the appropriate source instrument and how they are justiciable.

---

[6] Lisbon Presidency Conclusions, paragraph 28.
[7] Commission Proposal for a Council Decision on guidelines for Member States' employment policies for the year 2001, Explanatory Memorandum, p. 3.
[8] CONTRIB 18.

The implication was that the EU Charter would do no more than point out to EU citizens what rights they had under *other* legal instruments, without adding anything, except as an information source.[9] In contrast, the French position, as advanced by their government's representative, M. Guy Braibant, was that there should be an extensive list of rights going beyond what was currently provided, but programmatic rights, not necessarily justiciable.

As regards social and economic rights, one division in the Convention was between those who favoured including them, and those who wished to exclude them altogether. The latter considered that such rights were not part of the existing *acquis communautaire*, or fell outside the competences of the EU. Their objective was to ensure that the EU Charter should not in any way become an instrument for the future expansion of EU competences in the social sphere.

Those who wished to include social and economic rights were further divided among those who separated some rights as 'subjective' or 'justiciable' (e.g. protection of children and adolescents, dignity at work, protection against dismissal, vocational training, maternity protection and parental leave) from other rights which were 'programmatic' (e.g. health protection, social protection, elderly persons, disabled persons, migrant workers, housing). The strategy would be for such programmatic rights to be placed in a separate chapter and introduced by a clause declaring that the EU recognised as a political objective to create proper conditions for the implementation of that category of rights. Some social rights would be incorporated into the first section of the Charter, alongside justiciable civil and political rights. But there would be a separate, more extensive list of social rights which are not guaranteed by the EU itself (though they may be by some Member States).

Another tactic in this debate was the argument for inclusion of a 'horizontal' clause in the EU Charter which would make it clear that no extension of EU competences was to be allowed through the Charter's provisions. This could be made either generally applicable to the whole of the Charter, or specifically aimed at the clauses on social and economic rights.

## The outcome at Nice, December 2000

The political initiative for an EU Charter of Fundamental Rights was designed to balance the social policy vacuum in the agenda of the Intergovernmental Conference 2000. The debate over fundamental social rights brought two legal perspectives into conflict. On one side were those who wanted to exclude social rights entirely, or minimise their content, or marginalise them into a separate 'programmatic' section, or make them purely declaratory, or subject them to special 'horizontal' conditions to prevent the EU acquiring any further social competences. On the other side were those who wanted to include social

---

[9] Lord Goldsmith's approach can be seen in his one example of an economic and social right: 'Every citizen has the right as an EU national to set up a business anywhere in the EU.'

rights, maximise their content, grant them the same status as civil and political rights, make them justiciable or otherwise enforceable, and not limit them by reference to existing EU competences.[10]

The choice facing the European Council of Nice was a difficult one. On the one hand, to reject the Charter would be regarded as a setback for 'Social Europe', confirmation of the primacy of the EU's economic profile in general and of deregulated markets in particular. It would send a negative message about social rights to candidate states in the context of enlargement. On the other hand, some Member States were unequivocal in their refusal to accept a legally binding Charter, let alone incorporating it into the Treaty.

The outcome gave something to each side. One the one hand, the Charter breaks new ground by including in a single list of fundamental rights not only traditional civil and political rights, but also a long list of social and economic rights. On the other hand, although the EU Charter was approved by the European Council, it was limited to a political declaration. It was not given a formal legal status.

The incorporation of the EU Charter into the law of the EU would have an impact on the Member States, bound by the Charter through the doctrine of supremacy of EU law. The EU Charter includes provisions which are at the heart of labour law and industrial relations in Europe:

- protection of personal data (Article 8)
- freedom of assembly and of association (Article 12)
- right to education (including access to vocational and continuing training)
- freedom to choose an occupation and right to engage in work (Article 15)
- non-discrimination (Article 21)
- equality between men and women (Article 23)
- workers' right to information and consultation within the undertaking (Article 27)
- right of collective bargaining and action (Article 28)
- right of access to placement services (Article 29)
- protection in the event of unjustified dismissal (Article 30)
- fair and just working conditions (Article 31)
- prohibition of child labour and protection of young people at work (Article 32)

It remains to be seen whether and how declaring social and economic rights will affect the EU's economic policy, in particular, the EU's strategy on employment, and whether the enshrining of fundamental rights of association, information and consultation, and collective bargaining and action will influence the institutional operation of the EU where the social partners have major roles to play in

---

[10] For a fascinating account of the workings of the Convention, see Florence Deloche-Gaudez, *The Convention on a Charter of Fundamental Rights: A Method for the Future? Notre Europe*, Research and Policy Paper No. 15, November 2001.

the spheres of social policy and the open method of coordination implementing the EES.

The outstanding questions were two-fold. First, in the short term, what were the legal prospects of the political declaration by the European Council of an EU Charter of Fundamental Rights? Secondly, in the longer term, what would be the legal effects of an EU Charter if given formal legal status by being incorporated into the Treaties? This was to become a subject of intense debate in the Convention on the Future of Europe which eventually proposed that the Charter be incorporated as Part II of the Treaty Establishing a Constitution for Europe. It remains a central issue with the proposed Lisbon Treaty's provision stating that the Charter is to have the same legal status as the Treaties.

## Legal prospects and legal effects of the EU Charter

### Legal prospects of the political declaration of the EU Charter

The EU Charter was proclaimed as a political declaration. It is not part of Community 'hard' law. The European Community Charter of the Fundamental Rights of Workers of 1989 was also only granted declaratory status. But it had three effects which could also emerge for the EU Charter.

### Reference in the Treaties

The 1989 Charter is referred to in the Preamble to the Treaty on European Union (TEU):

> [Member States] confirming their attachment to fundamental social rights as defined in the European Social Charter signed at Turin on 19 October 1961 and in the 1989 Community Charter of the Fundamental Social Rights of Workers.

It is also referred to in Article 136 of the EC Treaty:

> The Community and the Member States, having in mind fundamental social rights such as those set out in the European Social Charter signed at Turin on 19 October 1961 and the 1989 Community Charter of the Fundamental Social Rights of Workers.

On the one hand, it would seem anomalous if the new EU Charter, unanimously proclaimed by all the Member States as enshrining fundamental rights, was not accorded the same status and was treated differently from the 1989 Charter. On the other hand, difficulties could arise where there appear to be conflicts between them. In particular, there might be resistance if the EU Charter was regarded as regressive in relation to the Charters of 1961 and 1989, at least so far as social rights are concerned.

### Action Programme

Following the declaration of the Community Charter in 1989, the Commission produced a Social Action Programme with legislative proposals based on the

Charter. These proposals (covering, for example, European works councils, working time, burden of proof in sex discrimination, etc.) referred to their inspiration by relevant provisions on fundamental social rights of workers in the 1989 Charter. The Commission might come under similar pressure to make proposals implementing social rights guaranteed by the new EU Charter.

This is particularly so where it is clear that the EU has the competence to take action in that area of policy. It would be anomalous if some fundamental social rights in the EU Charter (e.g. Article 31(2): working time) were already implemented through directives, while other equally fundamental social rights (e.g. Article 14: 'Right to education', including vocational and continuing training; or Article 30: 'Protection in the event of unjustified dismissal') were proclaimed, but there was no EU legislation supporting that fundamental right, despite clear competence in the Treaty to enact directives in this area (e.g. Article 137(1)(d): 'protection of workers where their employment contract is terminated').

## Litigation

As a form of 'soft' law, the EU Charter could be used by the European Court of Justice as an interpretive guide in litigation concerned with social rights. Such litigation could take the form of legal action by way of preliminary references (Article 234 EC) challenging Member States' implementation of Union law when such national legislation arguably violates fundamental social rights in the Charter. The interpretation of EC directives, or national implementing legislation, could be influenced by the social rights guaranteed in the EU Charter.

An early and encouraging indication arrived barely eight weeks after the EU Charter was approved in Nice in a case in which the broadcasting union, BECTU challenged the UK government's implementation of the Working Time Directive.[11] Advocate General Tizzano's Opinion upholding BECTU's complaint stated (paragraph 28):

> I think therefore that, in proceedings concerned with the nature and scope of a fundamental right, the relevant statements of the Charter cannot be ignored; in particular, we cannot ignore its clear purpose of serving, where its provisions so allow, as a substantive point of reference for all those involved – Member States, institutions, natural and legal persons – in the Community context.

This was the worst nightmare of those who fought against the inclusion of fundamental social rights, including trade union rights, in the EU Charter. The trade union rights in the EU Charter are 'a substantive point of reference', and not only for the Community institutions, but also for Member States (for example, as in *BECTU*, where a Member State is responsible for transposing an EC directive including the fundamental social right to paid annual leave), and even for private persons, human and corporate.

---

[11] *Broadcasting, Entertainment, Cinematographic and Theatre Union (BECTU)* v. *Secretary of State for Trade and Industry*, Case C-173/99, [2001] ECR I-4881. Opinion of the Advocate-General, 8 February 2001; ECJ decision, 26 June 2001. See Chapter 1 for details.

The potential of the fundamental rights in the EU Charter will be apparent when they are compared with Member State laws which restrict or inhibit the rights of workers and their representatives, for example, to information and consultation, to join trade unions and have their unions recognised for the purposes of collective bargaining, and to take strike action. What if an employer refuses to enter into collective agreements, or dismisses strikers exercising their fundamental right to take strike action, or closes down the undertaking without advance information and consultation? Will EU law become available to challenge violations of what are declared in the EU Charter to be the fundamental human rights of trade unionists?

Of course, the EU Charter can be used only where the issue is governed by EU law (as in *BECTU*, where paid annual leave was regulated by the Working Time Directive). There are EU laws on information and consultation, where the EU Charter may become very relevant, but other areas, such as strikes and collective bargaining, may not be covered by any EU law or only peripherally so. Nonetheless, as EU law continuously expands, the actions of Member States and private individuals and corporations may come to be challenged where they fail to respect what are now recognised as the fundamental human rights of workers and their representatives. Direct actions against the Member States by the Commission, or by individuals under the *Francovich* principle, may also become possible.[12]

### Legal effects of the EU Charter if equated to the EC Treaty

If the EU Charter was equated to the Treaty, as proposed by the Lisbon Treaty, the legal consequences of such incorporation could be significant.

### Direct effect

As with equal pay for men and women (Article 141 EC), the Court could attribute binding direct effect to provisions of the Charter which were considered sufficiently clear, precise and unconditional. This effect would apply both vertically (against Member States and their 'emanations'), and horizontally (against private persons or bodies). Examples might include:

> Article 8(2): 'Everyone has the right of access to data which has been collected concerning him or her, and the right to have it rectified.'
>
> Article 30: 'Every worker has the right to protection against unjustified dismissal, in accordance with Community law and national laws and practices.'
>
> Article 29(2): 'Every worker has the right to limitation of maximum working hours, to daily and weekly rest periods and to an annual period of paid leave.'

---

[12] *Francovich and Bonfaci* v. *Italy*, Cases C-6/90 and C-9/90, [1991] ECR I-5357.

Provisions of the Charter which are not considered to satisfy the conditions for direct effect may be invoked to challenge EU law, including Commission proposals for legislation, or Member State laws which are said to violate the fundamental rights guaranteed. Such challenges could be mounted in national courts and referred to the Luxembourg Court under Article 234 EC. Examples might include:

> national legislation transposing the Parental Leave Directive which included derogations denying rights guaranteed by the EU Charter, Article 33: 'the right ... to parental leave following the birth or adoption of a child'; an example would have been the exclusion of parents with children under 5 years of age at the date of transposition;
>
> EU competition law invoked to challenge collective agreements protected by the Charter, Article 28: 'the right to negotiate and conclude collective agreements'.

### Indirect effect

The doctrine of 'indirect effect' established by the European Court of Justice with respect to directives requires national courts to interpret national laws consistently with EC law. It would apply with even greater force to the rights guaranteed in a Charter equated to the Treaty than in the case of a Charter with merely declaratory status.

### State liability

The violation by the EU or a Member State of a fundamental right guaranteed by the Charter in the Treaty would very likely constitute a breach of EU law giving rise to liability under the *Francovich* principle.[13]

### Expansion of competences

The EU Charter states in Article 51(2): 'This Charter does not establish any new power or task for the Community or the Union, or modify powers and tasks defined by the Treaties.'[14] However, the competences of the Community and the Union are frequently a subject of litigation between those seeking to extend, or to limit them.

Where there is doubt as to whether a measure adopted by the Community or the Union falls within their respective competences, the European Court will be more likely to uphold the measure where it can be linked with a Charter provision, rather than to interpret the Treaty to restrict the powers of the Community to protect the fundamental rights guaranteed by the Charter. In this way the powers and tasks of the Community and Union provided for in the Treaties are impliedly expanded where these are necessary in order to safeguard

---

[13] *Francovich and Bonfaci* v. *Italy*, Cases C-6/90 and C-9/90, [1991] ECR I-5357.

[14] This appears as Article II-111 of the Treaty Establishing a Constitution for Europe, where it was amended. See footnote 17 below.

the EU Charter rights. All the more so if the Community action in question aims explicitly to implement a fundamental right guaranteed by the EU Charter.

### Action Programme

Finally, social rights guaranteed by the Treaty would put pressure on the Commission to make proposals for their implementation. The threat of the European Court invoking the doctrine of 'direct effect' in the absence of such implementing measures would be an incentive to Community legislative action.

## The relation of the EU Charter to national law and practice

The relation of the EU Charter to the national laws of the Member States highlights one of the themes of this book: the symbiosis between EU labour law and national labour laws. The problem is raised because in various Articles of the Charter, rights are stated to be, for example, 'in accordance with', or 'under the conditions provided by' national laws and practices. The Charter's references to national laws and practices affect the trade union and labour rights in Articles 27 (Workers' right to information and consultation within the undertaking), 28 (Right of collective bargaining and action) and 30 (Protection in the event of unjustified dismissal). In contrast, *no* restrictions of this character are expressed in other Articles of the Charter, including Article 12 (Freedom of assembly and of association), Article 15 (Freedom to choose an occupation and right to engage in work), Article 21 (Non-discrimination), Article 23 (Equality between men and women), and Article 30 (Fair and just working conditions).

The Charter's references to 'national laws and practices' purport to *limit* the EU Charter rights by reference to these national laws (and practices) and, by so doing, raise a number of problems, which may be resolved by certain principles basic to EU law.

First, the fundamental principle of the supremacy of Community law would be undermined if Charter rights were limited by national laws and practices. This would be even more obvious, and more unacceptable, if and when the Charter is equated to the Treaties. Member State courts adjudicating a dispute over violation of a Charter right could override the Charter if it conflicted with national laws and practices. The European Court of Justice would also have to give priority over EU fundamental rights to national laws and practices. The ECJ is unlikely to agree to this. More likely, where national laws and practices restrict the rights granted, the supremacy of Community law requires that the *objectives* of the Community in granting these rights should allow for an interpretation *overriding* the limitations in national laws and practices.

Second, these 'national' standards appear to be less national than international standards. Article 52(3) of the Charter states that corresponding Charter rights, including those referring to national laws and practices, are to be the same as those in the European Convention on Human Rights (ECHR).

National laws and practices must not, and cannot, conflict with the ECHR, since all Member States have ratified the ECHR. Article 53 similarly binds the Charter to a level of protection not less favourable than various international standards. Again, national laws and practices should comply with these international standards. The EU Charter's reference to national law means no more than compliance with these international standards. National laws and practices may not prescribe standards less favourable than international standards.

Third, if Charter rights are limited to national laws and practices, the national standard becomes not the minimum, but the maximum standard. This eliminates any added value of the Charter. The added value of the Charter will only be realised if the references to national standards in the Charter are treated as fixing the minimum standards on which Charter rights may improve.

Fourth, the most important justification for the Charter is that it establishes a common set of fundamental rights guaranteed to all citizens of the EU. This is lost if fundamental rights are subject to national laws and practices. The danger of national laws providing different minimum fundamental rights will only be avoided if the Charter is interpreted as establishing a common set of fundamental rights which may go beyond national laws and practices.

Finally, the references to national laws and practices are in some twelve different Articles of the Charter and include six different formulations. This diversity should be ignored as much as possible in favour of a common interpretation.

Interpretation of the Charter is complex enough without having to ascertain the precise meaning of the different references to national laws and practices. For reasons of supremacy, uniformity, EC objectives and maximum standards of human rights, the differences in the formulations should be interpreted to produce a *minimum* of diversity among and deference to national standards.

The references to national laws and practices are concentrated in the chapter on 'Solidarity' rights. Formulations confining rights in *general* 'in accordance with Community and national laws and practices' refer to some collective (collective bargaining/action) and individual (dismissal) rights in the chapter on Solidarity. But Article 12 (Freedom of association including in trade unions) is not so confined. As limitations on rights by reference in general to national laws and practices are concentrated in the rights in the chapter on Solidarity, this contradicts the ethos of the Charter. The Charter aims to create solidarity by assuring a common floor of fundamental rights throughout the EU. The references to national laws and practices should be interpreted narrowly, in particular, so as not to contradict the objectives of solidarity.

## Political dynamics of the EU Charter

The EU Charter includes a large number of fundamental trade union rights and social and labour standards. Much effort in previous years aimed to encourage discussion of these rights and standards in the EU context. It is the EU Charter which has put fundamental trade union rights and social and labour standards on the political agenda of the EU. The result may be political struggles over interpretation of the text of the relevant articles of EU Charter, and the means of their implementation.

One stated objective of the EU Charter was to make fundamental rights more visible, relevant and important to EU citizens. The agreement of the EU institutions to formally proclaim the Charter at Nice in December 2000 gave the Charter great visibility.

Those who supported the EU Charter saw one of its objectives as potentially increasing the value of the EU for citizens, and attracting greater loyalty to the European integration process. This sets up a specific political dynamic. Though subject to debate, the content of these proposed rights and standards are, to some extent, the prisoners of enhanced visibility of the Charter. The EU, having made fundamental rights so visible on the EU agenda, needs to ensure that they are enforceable in law and effective in practice. If not, the result would be great disillusionment. The prospect of such a failure to make the promised fundamental rights effective creating bitter disappointment among citizens in general, and especially those who are promised specific trade union, social and labour rights, in turn will exert pressure to make the Charter effective.

## The Charter and the EU institutions and Member States

There is a further political dynamic at work in the EU Charter. The debates in the Convention which created the Charter, and elsewhere, demonstrate that there were many divisions among the Member States regarding the content and scope of trade union, social and labour rights. Many of these divisions are reflected in the final text. Having reached an agreed text, however ambivalent, the EU Charter achieves a status in the EU which can become the launch pad for further developments. In the Charter, the Member States have unanimously agreed on principles of trade union rights and social and labour policy. On the basis of this unanimous approval, EU institutions may now propose policies for the effective application and implementation of these principles.

This was the case with the Social Action Programme implementing the Community Charter of 1989. The Member States cannot now withdraw from their commitment to principles in the EU Charter, though there may be disputes over their precise meaning and the content of eventual policy proposals. Much depends on the political initiatives taken to implement the Charter. Compared with the Treaty position when the 1989 Charter and subsequent Action Programme were proclaimed, the competences of the Community are much greater in the trade union, social and labour fields. If the Charter is given Treaty status, it will become politically imperative for the EU institutions, including the European Court of Justice, to secure its effective implementation.

## EU competences and inter-institutional relations

Comparing the EU Charter's provisions with both international instruments ratified by some or all Member States, and with the domestic constitutions of many Member States, it is evident that the EU Charter corresponds to much that is already within the powers, objectives and competences of Member States. However, the trade union and social and labour rights contained in the EU Charter, particularly if given some of the interpretations proposed,[15] certainly stretch, if not go beyond, a narrow view of the present competences of the EU.

This difference between the potential impact of the EU Charter on Member States and the EU creates tension in the inter-institutional relations among the EU institutions in at least four ways.

First, and most obviously, tension will be created between the Member States and the EU institutions. The EU Charter's commitment to a number of trade union, social and labour rights will challenge narrow interpretations of EU competences in these fields. This will be so particularly if EU institutions, relying on the political legitimacy attached to Member States' proclamation of fundamental rights in the EU Charter, bring forward proposals for the effective application and implementation of these rights. Some Member States may argue that such proposals fall outside EU competences, narrowly interpreted. This indicates two further sources of tension.

Secondly, the EU Charter may create tensions among different Member States. Although some such proposals seeking to implement rights in the EU Charter will arouse the opposition of Member States concerned with expansion of EU competences, many of the proposals to implement trade union, social and labour rights will be perfectly consistent with the constitutional traditions and practices of many of the Member States. These proposals will, therefore, be of much less concern to them, and may even be welcomed as a development of EU policy consistent with their own constitutional traditions.

Thirdly, experience also demonstrates that there are disputes among the EU institutions themselves as to the scope of EU competences. Broadly speaking, on the one hand, the supranational Commission takes an expansive view of the EU's competences; on the other hand, the Council takes a more conservative view in line with Member States concern with national sovereignty; the European Court of Justice delicately holds the balance in promoting European integration somewhere in between. The EU Charter offers opportunities to the Commission and the Court for a potentially expansive

---

[15] See the commentary in Bercusson (ed.), *European Labour Law*.

interpretation of present EU competences, which is likely to encounter opposition from the Council.[16]

Finally, there are the tensions resulting from pressures of sub-national and supranational actors on Member States and EU institutions. Policy-making is not the exclusive preserve of EU institutions. The commitments in the EU Charter to trade union, social and labour rights will be seen as vital to the interests of many powerful non-EU actors within the Member States and also those organised at EU supranational level. These will seek to achieve fulfilment of the commitments in the EU Charter, and will increase pressure on those Member States and EU institutions whose action is necessary to implement the rights promised in the EU Charter.

While it is impossible to predict with any certainty, it seems likely that these tensions will give rise to a combination of pressures: from Member States attuned to the trade union, social and labour rights promised in the Charter, from EU institutions with an interest in expanding the supranational dimension of the EU and perceiving in trade union, social and labour rights one possible avenue to promote European integration, and from social and political actors who see the EU Charter as commitments vital to the achievement of their objectives. There will certainly be counter-pressures, but the resulting tension is likely to lead to some expansion of EU competences, and, possibly, a degree of convergence among Member States as regards trade union, social and labour rights.

## Legal dynamics of the EU Charter

The legal expression of this political dynamic leading to potential expansion of EU competences in response to the declaration of rights in the EU Charter may take many forms. There are now a variety of different potential actors, processes and outcomes in the field of social and labour policy in the EU: legislation, litigation, social dialogue, the European Employment Strategy's 'open-method of coordination', and so on. Each offers different options for the legal implementation of the rights promised in the EU Charter.

---

[16] '… the court, instead of stating that no specific provision of EU law applied in the facts of the cases under examination, reasoned by reference to (disputable) general principles, which are aimed at the protection of fundamental human and social rights. It may be that the court will increasingly make reference to fundamental rights and general principles in order to make up for the effects of "new governance" instruments, such as the OMCs, which produce only "soft" outcomes. Since EC hard legislation will be rare in fields in which some EU coordination takes place, the court will be obliged to control national measures by reference to general principles and fundamental rights, in order to protect effectively the latter.' V. Hatzopoulos, 'Why the Open Method of Coordination is Bad for You: A Letter to the EU', (2007) 13 *European Law Journal* (No. 3, May) 309–42, at p. 337.

The potential impact of the Charter can be illustrated by Article 51, 'Scope':[17]

1. The provisions of this Charter are addressed to the institutions and bodies of the Union with due regard for the principle of subsidiarity and to the Member States only when they are implementing Union law. They shall therefore respect the rights, observe the principles and promote the application thereof in accordance with their respective powers.
2. This Charter does not establish any new power or task for the Community or the Union, or modify powers or tasks defined by the Treaty.

This Article was inserted in order to limit the potential application of the Charter. However, the attempts in Article 51 to limit the application of the EU Charter are ambiguous and open to interpretations which may imply a wider application than anticipated. If equated to the Treaties, the Charter would have the powerful legal effects of fundamental rights (direct effect and supremacy). The EC Treaty fundamental rights would be a basic norm with which all action, at EU and national level, would have to comply.[18]

## Conclusion

On balance, it is suggested that the EU Charter is a positive contribution to labour law in the EU for a number of reasons.

[17] This appears as Article II-111 of the Treaty Establishing a Constitution for Europe, where it is amended to read (amendments in italics): '1. The provisions of this Charter are addressed to the *[institutions, bodies, offices and agencies]* of the Union with due regard for the principle of subsidiarity and to the Member States only when they are implementing Union law. They shall therefore respect the rights, observe the principles and promote the application thereof in accordance with their respective powers *and respecting the limits of the powers of the Union as conferred on it in the other Parts of the Constitution*. 2. This Charter does not *extend the field of application of Union law beyond the powers of the Union or* establish any new power or task for … the Union, or modify powers and tasks defined *in the other Parts of the Constitution*.' Treaty Establishing a Constitution for Europe adopted by the Member States in the Intergovernmental Conference meeting in Brussels 17–18 June 2004, OJ C310/1 of 16 December 2004. This is the text referred to by the Lisbon Treaty (without the references to the now defunct Constitution).

[18] An article in the *Financial Times* of 4 January 2005 (p. 4) concerning 'employers' view on support for the [EU] constitution' states: 'A sticking point for business remains the Charter of Fundamental Rights, which lays out a range of civil, political, economic and social rights to all people living in the EU. Some employers fear new rights for trade unions on the back of article II-88 of the charter which says that "workers and employers have the right to negotiate and conclude collective agreements and, in cases of conflicts of interest, to take collective action to defend their interest, including strike action". Research for the Trades Union Congress by Professor Brian Bercusson of King's College London concluded that "the EU constitution locks the UK and other governments into a European social model" that would boost worker rights. But the Foreign Office denied this: "The charter doesn't create any new rights. We spent a very long time looking at this, in particular the disputed article. It does not create the right to strike". It had been on the insistence of the UK government that clauses were inserted into the treaty making it clear that the charter applied only to member states when they were implementing EU law and did not create any new powers for the Union. However, legal experts say the impact of the charter can only finally be assessed when test cases challenging UK employment practices are brought before the European Court of Justice'.

It is an *independent source of rights*. The EU Charter has a substantive content going beyond, and is not limited to national practice in individual Member States. As illustrated above, in Case 173/99, *BECTU*, the Advocate General's Opinion of 8 February 2001 invoked the EU Charter in condemning the UK's limited implementation of rights to paid annual leave, a fundamental right under the Charter.

National provisions which reflect Charter rights may achieve *higher legal ranking* in the national system; perhaps even constitutional status. At a minimum, there can be no regression from national provisions reflecting Charter rights. National laws providing rights which go beyond the Charter are useful in promoting an expansive interpretation of the Charter.

While it is necessary to specify more clearly the relation of the EU Charter to international sources, it may go *beyond* these. For example, where the EU Charter provisions do not include the limitations stipulated in the European Convention on Human Rights, the EU Charter may afford greater or more extensive protection.

The 1989 Community Charter of Fundamental Social Rights was not regarded seriously because of the established prejudice against recognition of social and economic rights, seen as different from classical civil and political rights. In the EU Charter, *social and economic rights* are recognised as having the same status as civil and political rights. The consequence is that fundamental rights, declared by the European Court to be protected as part of the EU legal order, will have a greater chance to include social and economic rights.

The inclusion of many social rights in a single Charter means it is not possible to interpret one single Article in isolation without considering others. This can be used to *expand* many rights which may be limited in isolation. For example, the scope of Article 27, 'information and consultation' can be expanded when linked to Article 31, 'fair and just working conditions', which in turn implies respect for dignity, protected by Article 1, 'human dignity'.

The Charter is an important milestone in the development of Social Europe. It can be of value in developing the social dimension by putting *pressure on EU institutions* to promote a European social model. The EU Charter can be used to support a concept of European social citizenship which overcomes the division between classical human rights and social and economic rights.

This positive assessment should not overlook the potential risks. The EU Charter might be exploited to further a very different agenda. The very wide scope of the EU Charter offers the possibility to reopen many fundamental principles established in national systems: e.g. forms of worker representation, justifications for dismissal, penalties for discrimination, scope of information and consultation. For example, the right to conclude collective agreements could be used to impose obligations on unions; e.g. a peace obligation, or a duty to negotiate 'in good faith'. Or there is a risk of undermining national protection; e.g. dismissal might be held to be justifiable on some grounds not allowed in Member State laws.

Nonetheless, the history of EC law is that of the emergence of a new legal order. This new legal order developed new concepts of implementation and enforcement of EC law. When directives stipulated policy results, but left to Member States the choice of form and method (Article 249 EC), the European Court of Justice developed doctrines testing the adequacy of Member State implementation, looking especially to effectiveness (*effet utile*), for example, of sanctions and remedies.

The social and economic rights in the EU Charter include those of a programmatic nature. Implementation of the Charter aims to build a bridge between *programmatic* (social and economic rights) and *justiciable* (civil and political) rights. Justiciable rights equate to effective and enforceable rights. The challenge is to *establish* clearly *justiciable rights*: e.g. trade union freedom of association, information and consultation, collective bargaining and collective action, and, further, to *develop* implementation of *programmatic* social and economic rights: e.g. health, education, etc.

The tasks of an implementation strategy are three-fold. First, with respect to *justiciable* rights, to develop effective implementation, looking to effective sanctions, preventing regressions, removing qualifications, thresholds, exclusions, modifications. Secondly, *moving more social and economic rights towards justiciability*; formulating them as positive and enforceable rights; including effective sanctions. Thirdly, with respect to *programmatic* rights, implementation through effective monitoring of government policy and actions, with possible judicial review of consistency and powers of nullification.

It is important that the EU Charter acquires the character of a *dynamic* instrument, that Member States have to actively accommodate any new fundamental social rights: a form of dynamic subsidiarity.[19] There are lessons to be learned from other international experience in implementing fundamental social rights, including the procedures of the ILO's Freedom of Association Committee, and the supervision and the collective complaints procedure of the European Social Charter.

Still other methods of monitoring social and economic rights are on the EU agenda: a role for the social partners in monitoring EU Charter rights at the appropriate levels; the monitoring of Member States action in the social and employment policy field through the 'open method of coordination' embodied in the Employment Title of the EC Treaty; monitoring compliance through regulation of contracts allocated in the sphere of public procurement, and others. The EU Charter opens a new chapter in the legal enforcement of the rights of employees and trade unions, both at transnational and national levels.

---

[19] B. Bercusson, 'Subsidiarity and Solidarity', Chapter 4, pp. 63–74, in B. Bercusson, S. Deakin, P. Koistinen, Y. Kravaritou, U. Mückenberger, A. Supiot and B. Veneziani, *A Manifesto for Social Europe*, Brussels: European Trade Union Institute, 1996 (also translated into Finnish, French and German).

The proclamation of the Charter in December 2000 was shortly to be followed by the proposal of the Convention on the Future of Europe, established following the Laeken Summit of December 2001, to integrate the Charter into a 'Treaty Establishing a Constitution for Europe'.

## A 'constitutional strategy' for the economic, political and social integration of Europe

The proposed Treaty Establishing a Constitution for Europe was the latest in a long line of Treaties defining the legal framework for the integration of Europe.[20]

The legal form of this integration began with the European Economic Community (EEC) Treaty in 1957. As its title indicates, the legal framework of the EEC Treaty aimed primarily, if not exclusively, at European economic integration. For workers, this was closely limited to free movement among the Member States making up the common market.

This focus on a particularly narrow view of economic integration in terms of a common market was always contested. The legal framework of the EEC Treaty was first changed by the Single European Act (SEA) of 1986, in which the '1992 Programme' sought to make the 'Single European Market' more effective, but also extended the social content of the market to include, importantly, health and safety of workers. The attempt to adopt a more comprehensive framework for labour and social protection in the EC was reflected in the Community Charter of the Fundamental Social Rights of Workers of 1989, which was adopted by all Member States except for the UK.

It was the Maastricht Treaty on European Union (TEU) of 1992 which transformed the common market conception of the EC into a political and social entity: the EU. The TEU enormously expanded the social competences of the EU to include individual employment protection (e.g. regulation of working conditions), and collective labour rights (e.g. information and consultation). It also specified a formal procedure guaranteeing a role for the social dialogue between the EU social partners in making these regulations. The Amsterdam Treaty of 1997 took up the growing concern with the high levels of unemployment during the 1980s and 1990s and inserted a new Employment Title into the Treaty, expanding the role of the EU in the employment policies of the Member States. At the European Council summit at Nice in December 2000, the EU Charter of Fundamental Rights drafted by a unique 'Convention', and including fundamental rights of labour, was proclaimed.

The proposed Treaty Establishing a Constitution for Europe adopted on 18 June 2004 was the culmination of this historical process of European

---

[20] Unless otherwise indicated, citations and quotations are from the Treaty Establishing a Constitution for Europe adopted by the Member States in the Intergovernmental Conference meeting in Brussels 17–18 June 2004, published in OJ C310/1 of 16 December 2004.

integration. It was produced by a second 'Convention', the Convention on the Future of Europe.

## The Convention on the Future of Europe

A Convention comprising representatives of the European Parliament, the parliaments of the Member States of the EU, the Member State governments and the European Commission, as well as with the participation of representatives of the accession countries and others, and chaired by Valéry Giscard d'Estaing, a former President of France, together with a Praesidium, was formally inaugurated on 28 February 2002. It was established in order to address a series of questions facing the EU which had not been satisfactorily addressed by the normal method of an Intergovernmental Conference (IGC).

The perceived failures of the IGC preceding the European Council meeting at Nice in December 2000 contrasted with the perceived success of the body established by the Cologne Council of June 1999 with the mandate to produce an EU Charter of Fundamental Rights for consideration by the European Council at Nice. That EU Charter was duly produced, and unanimously approved as a political declaration at Nice in December 2000. The success of the body which drafted the EU Charter (self-denominated the 'Convention') impressed the Member States sufficiently for another 'Convention' with a similar composition to be established for the purpose of proposing solutions to the problems formulated at the Laeken Summit in December 2001, many of which the Nice Summit was perceived not to have resolved, including the final legal status of the EU Charter of Fundamental Rights itself. There was some debate about whether the working methods of the first Convention were appropriate for or could be adapted to fulfil the tasks facing the second Convention, with a much broader mandate, working on more contested terrain, and with fewer formal reference instruments than those of the first Convention. The political, economic, institutional and legal context of the Convention which produced the EU Charter continued to influence the second Convention.[21] Nonetheless, on 18 July 2003, this 'Convention on the Future of Europe' produced a draft Treaty Establishing a Constitution for Europe.[22]

The working methods of the Convention included the establishment at the beginning of its deliberations of ten Working Groups to report to the plenary Convention on a number of specific topics.

Working Group II was concerned with the EU Charter of Fundamental Rights. Although the EU Charter was approved by the European Council at Nice, it was limited to a political declaration. The 'Convention on the Future of Europe' was to consider whether and, if so, how the Charter should be

---

[21] See Chapter 9.
[22] Draft Treaty Establishing a Constitution for Europe, CONV 850/03, Brussels, 18 July 2003.

integrated into the Treaties. The Final Report of Working Group II was presented to the Plenary of the Convention on 29 October 2002. It recommended that the EU Charter be integrated into the Treaty. The Convention accepted this recommendation and incorporated the whole of the EU Charter as Part II of the proposed Constitutional Treaty.[23]

The EU Charter broke new ground in recognising social and labour rights on a par with classic civil and political human rights. Despite this, conspicuous by its absence from the agenda of the Convention on the Future of Europe was any apparent consideration of the future social dimension of the European Union. The Praesidium of the Convention appears to have regarded social issues as peripheral to the concerns of the Future of Europe, and to have assumed that such issues would be dealt with in the margins of the reports of the other Working Groups.

However, a number of organisations at national and European level, including the European Trade Union Confederation, considered that commitments to full employment, improved labour standards and trade union rights were central to their vision of the future of Europe. Together with members of the Convention, they worked towards building pressure to establish a specific Working Group XI on Social Europe. Their efforts finally succeeded when the Convention decided on 22 November 2002 to establish such a Working Group. This late decision meant work had to proceed very rapidly. The first constitutive meeting of the Working Group was held on 10 December 2002, the second meeting on 10 January 2003. Working Group XI produced draft reports and presented its Final Report to the Plenary of the Convention on 6 February 2003, to be considered by the Plenary during its final deliberations in the following months.

As with the proposals of Working Group II on the Charter, the debates and conclusions of Working Group XI throw light on prospective developments in the social and labour dimension of the EU.

The Final Reports of Working Group II on the EU Charter and of Working Group XI on Social Europe, and the final amendments made by the Member States at the Brussels Summit of 17–18 June 2004 which approved the proposed Constitutional Treaty, provide important insights into the conflicting perspectives on the role of constitutional provisions including fundamental rights in the EU and Member State legal orders, and in particular, their potential for the

---

[23] However, a number of 'adjustments' were made to the Charter as it appears in the proposed Constitution. These derive mainly from the amendments to the Charter by the Convention on the Future of Europe, as proposed by its Working Group II, but also from further amendments introduced by the Member States at the Brussels Summit of 17–18 June 2004 which approved the Constitutional Treaty proposed by the Convention on the Future of Europe. These amendments will assume importance if and when the Lisbon Treaty, which refers to this text, is ratified by the Member States. They will become extraneous to the text of the Charter if the Lisbon Treaty including the 'adjustments' is not ratified and there remains only the original Charter text. In either event, analysis of these 'adjustments' is important for the light they cast on the future development of fundamental social and labour rights in the EU.

renewal of European labour law. The following sections analyse the proposals made by Working Groups II and XI of the Convention on the future of Europe, as amended by the IGC meeting in Brussels on 17–18 June 2004, as they appear in the proposed Treaty Establishing a Constitution for Europe.

Although the Constitutional Treaty is now defunct, perhaps its most important component as regards labour law was the EU Charter. This Charter is retained in the proposed Lisbon Treaty. It is therefore important to focus on the constitutional implications for the EU of the Charter as it emerged from the process of elaborating the Constitutional Treaty.

## 'Adjusting' the Constitution: EU fundamental rights v. limited EU competences[24]

The EU Charter, by including fundamental social and labour standards, sets up a specific political dynamic. Failure to make the promised fundamental rights effective will create bitter disillusionment, especially among those who are promised specific social and labour rights, and will undermine their loyalty to the European integration project. The values of the Charter are a declared part of the construction of Social Europe. Its objectives are to be secured through the exercise of the competences allocated under the Treaties.

Perhaps the most sensitive issue arising from the Charter's social and labour rights is their potential impact on EU competences. Giving the Charter the same legal value as the Treaties would entail a review of the respective competences of Member States and the EU.[25] The allocation of competences is critical for the success, or even the possibility of developing a system of industrial relations at EU level.[26]

In the Convention on the Future of Europe, Working Group II was given the task of formulating proposals regarding the EU Charter. The most notable aspect of the Working Group's report was its unanimous recommendation that the EU Charter be incorporated into the Constitutional Treaty. Less noted, however, was the heated debate in Working Group II on the potential impact of incorporation of the Charter on the division of competences between the EU and the Member States, particularly as this would affect social and labour competences.

---

[24] This section draws on B. Bercusson, 'The Role of the EU Charter of Fundamental Rights in Building a System of Industrial Relations at EU Level', (2003) 9 *Transfer: European Review of Labour and Research* (No. 2) (Summer), pp. 209–28, and 'Episodes on the Path Towards the European Social Model: The EU Charter of Fundamental Rights and the Convention on the Future of Europe', in C. Barnard, S. Deakin and G. Morris (eds.), *The Future of Labour Law, Liber Amicorum Sir Bob Hepple*, Oxford: Hart, 2004, pp. 179–99.

[25] The new Article 6 EC TEU proposed by the Treaty of Lisbon reads: 'The Union recognises the rights, freedoms and principles set out in the Charter of Fundamental Rights of the European Union of 7 December 2000, as adapted at Strasbourg, on 12 December 2007, which shall have the same legal value as the Treaties'.

[26] Arguably, whatever the division of competences, effective implementation of the Charter must be guaranteed, whether by the EU or the Member States.

The proposal in the Final Report of Working Group II[27] that the EU Charter be integrated into the Constitutional Treaty of the European Union was endorsed in the Draft of Articles 1–16 of the Constitutional Treaty produced by the Convention's Praesidium on 6 February 2003.[28] Draft Article 5(1) provided:

> The Charter of Fundamental Rights shall be an integral part of the Constitution. The Charter is set out [in the second part of/in a Protocol annexed to] this Constitution.

A footnote added: 'The full text of the Charter, *with all the drafting adjustments given in Working Group II's final report* (CONV 354/02) will be set out either in a second part of the Constitution or in a Protocol annexed thereto, as the Convention decides.' Annex II of the Praesidium's draft, the 'Explanatory Note', repeated that the Charter was to be incorporated 'with all the drafting adjustments mentioned in the Working Group's final report'.[29]

This endorsement was reinforced by the Final Report of Working Group XI on Social Europe.[30] A footnote in the Final Report of Working Group XI stated:[31]

> Regarding the ways and means to integrate the Charter itself in the Constitutional treaty, the Group referred to and confirmed the conclusions of the Final Report of Working Group II.

This unfortunate endorsement in a footnote raises the question of how closely Working Group XI considered the Final Report of Working Group II, in particular, the contentious 'adjustments' proposed by Working Group II.[32]

---

[27] CONV 354/02, 22 October 2002.     [28] CONV 528/03.

[29] The final draft Constitution produced by the Convention reaffirms this position: Draft Treaty Establishing a Constitution for Europe, CONV 850/03, Brussels, 18 July 2003.

[30] The Praesidium produced its draft of Articles 1–16 on 6 February 2003, the same day that the Final Report of Working Group XI was presented by its Chair to the Plenary of the Convention. The Praesidium's draft texts were introduced by acknowledging that they 'reflect the reports of the Working Groups on Legal Personality, the Charter, Economic Governance, Complementary Competencies, the Principle of Subsidiarity and External Action, as well as the guidelines that emerged on the basis of their recommendations during the plenary debate'. The draft could not take account either of the Final Report of Working Group XI, or, manifestly, of any debate on the Report in the Plenary. This failure compounded the Praesidium's inability to recognise the importance of Social Europe by failing to establish a Working Group early in its proceedings. In a conversation with the author, Jean-Luc Dehaene, Vice-Chair of the Convention, claimed that earlier drafts of Working Group XI's final report had been taken into account.

[31] Paragraph 11, page 8.

[32] In the discussion in the Plenary, a number of Members of the Convention from the European Parliament criticised Working Group II's proposed 'adjustments' to the horizontal clauses. Sylvia-Yvonne Kaufmann referred to the dangers of the proposed 'adjustments' introducing new elements by the back door. Elena Paccioti warned that 'adjustments' to the horizontal clauses evinced an attempt to water down the Charter. However, the Member of the Convention representing the German Parliament, Jürgen Meyer, argued that the new clauses were mere clarifications which did not change the substance of the Charter.

Some of the conclusions reached by Working Group II, such as the extent to which Member States are bound by the Charter, were ambiguous, and render ambivalent the apparent endorsement by Working Group XI. It is vital, therefore, that these proposed 'adjustments' be critically scrutinised.

The 'adjustments' to the EU Charter proposed by Working Group II on the Charter were described as follows in its Final Report:[33]

> It is important to note that these adjustments proposed by the Group do not reflect modifications of substance. On the contrary, they would serve to confirm, and render absolutely clear and legally watertight, certain key elements of the overall consensus on the Charter on which the previous Convention had already agreed … all drafting adjustments proposed herein fully respect the basic premise of the Group's work, i.e. to leave intact the substance agreed by consensus within the previous Convention.

On the contrary, the proposed 'adjustments' may be characterised as, first, an attack on fundamental rights in general; and secondly, an attack on social rights in particular.

Specifically, on the issue of a potential conflict between Charter rights and the Treaty's allocation of competences, the Working Group upsets the consensus reached in the Convention which drafted the Charter, and confirmed by the EU institutions which unanimously proclaimed it at Nice in December 2000. Despite its statement to the contrary, Working Group II reopened questions resolved by the earlier Convention, relying in one case on 'understandings' reported by a few members of that Convention who happened to be in this Working Group, or the important guidance provided by the 'Praesidium's explanations',[34] though the Praesidium itself explicitly denied that it represented the Convention's authority and the Working Group conceded 'they have no legal value'.[35]

Instead of reinforcing the status of fundamental rights in the Charter, the Working Group's recommendations abandon them or allow for their violation where they are said to fall outside EU competence, all in order to protect the Treaty's delimitation of competences as between the EU and the Member States.

The Working Group had no authority to reopen this question, let alone propose 'adjustments' which change the consensus reached in the earlier Convention.[36] Some of their proposed 'adjustments' illustrate the danger to fundamental rights in general, and highlight the restrictions on social and labour rights in particular. In so doing, they threaten to undermine the EU

---

[33] Section A.II.1.    [34] Section A.II.6.    [35] Section A.III.3.

[36] Professor Grainne de Búrca has written one of 'Ten Reflections on the Constitutional Treaty for Europe' prepared by the European University Institute, a contribution submitted to the Convention by Giuliano Amato, one of two Vice-Presidents of the Convention and a member of its Praesidium (CONV 703/03 of 28 April 2003). Professor de Búrca analysed Working Group II's proposed 'adjustments' and recommended that, with one minor exception, they should be rejected. Amato states that he does 'not endorse every single word of this study'.

Charter's potential role in establishing a system of industrial relations at EU level.

The relevant proposals of additions and amendments ('adjustments') to the Charter made by Working Group II, now in the final text of the EU Charter as reproduced in Part II of the EU Constitutional Treaty and referred to by the Lisbon Treaty, are analysed below. But first, the contribution of the IGC to this further 'adjustment' of the EU Charter as it was to appear in the EU Constitution needs to be described and assessed. In particular, the attempt to invoke 'explanations' as interpretive aids to understanding the meaning of the Charter's provisions.

## The Intergovernmental Conference summit of 17–18 June 2004 and the 'explanations' to the Charter

The EU Charter was one element in the negotiations in the Convention on the Future of Europe over the future constitution of the EU. The social and labour rights of the Charter were the source of most of the disputes with and objections from some Member States in the previous Convention which had drafted the Charter. These disputes and objections surfaced again in the deliberations of Working Groups II and XI of the Convention on the Future of Europe as it struggled to elaborate a Constitutional Treaty.

The EU Charter continued to influence the negotiations in the Intergovernmental Conference (IGC) beginning in October 2003, concluding at the Brussels summit of 17–18 June 2004 with the adoption of the EU Constitutional Treaty incorporating the EU Charter.

The European Council summit meeting on 17–18 June 2004 to decide on the draft EU Constitution saw a last attempt by the UK's New Labour government to water down the labour standards and trade union rights in the EU Charter. The account of the negotiations left no doubt as to the inspiration for these amendments: 'France and Germany also objected to a UK proposal that the Charter of Fundamental Rights could not be allowed to overturn national legislation in areas such as labour market policy.'[37] The report continued: 'Mr Blair and Gordon Brown, the chancellor, made clear this week that the UK could not sign up to the constitution if it gave the European Court of Justice the right to change UK industrial relations law.' Specifically:

> The charter contains a series of supplementary explanations which ensure none of its provisions can be allowed to alter national laws. British government lawyers say this must be written into the body of the treaty text rather than into its preamble – but France and Germany are resisting the move.

This was not the first time that these mysterious supplementary 'explanations' were invoked in disputes over the Charter.

[37] *Financial Times*, 18 June 2004, p. 6.

## The origins of the 'explanations' of the EU Charter

The Praesidium of the Convention which had drafted the EU Charter submitted a final text of 28 September 2000,[38] accompanied by another explanatory text of 11 October 2000,[39] to the European Council at Biarritz on 13–14 October 2000. This latter document comprised 'explanations' to accompany the text of the Charter. These explanations were unambiguously not drafted or approved by the Convention which prepared the Charter, a fact repeatedly emphasised by the Praesidium itself. The EU's website reproduces the Charter alongside these explanations of the Praesidium. There it is stated categorically twice in footnotes to the text of the Charter:

> These explanations have been prepared at the instigation of the Praesidium. They have no legal value and are simply intended to clarify the provisions of the Charter.

## The 'adjustment' by the Praesidium of the Convention on the Future of Europe

Nonetheless, the Praesidium of the Convention on the Future of Europe made an 'adjustment' to the EU Charter which was not proposed by its Working Group II on the EU Charter in the Annex to its Final Report. In that Report, Working Group II had restricted itself to stating:[40]

> Upon possible incorporation of the Charter, attention should then be drawn in an appropriate manner to the Explanations which, though they state that they have no legal value, are intended to clarify the provisions of the Charter. In particular, it would be important to publicise them more widely.

The additional 'adjustment' made by the Praesidium of the Convention was to the Preamble to the EU Charter. This was the only substantive alteration made to the Charter's Preamble. It reads ('adjustment' in italics):[41]

> The Charter reaffirms, with due regard for the powers and tasks of the Union and the principle of subsidiarity, the rights as they result, in particular, from the constitutional traditions and international obligations common to the Member States, the European Convention for the Protection of Human Rights and Fundamental Freedoms, the Social Charters adopted by the Union and by the Council of Europe and the case law of the Court of Justice of the European Union and of the European Court of Human Rights. *In this context, the Charter will be interpreted by the Courts of the Union and the Member States*[42] *with due regard for*

---

[38]  CONVENT 50, CHARTE 4487/00, Brussels, 28 September 2000 (OR. French).
[39]  CONVENT 49, CHARTE 4473/00, Bruxelles, le 11 octobre 2000 (in French).
[40]  Final Report of Working Group II, CONV 354/02, Section III, para. 3, p. 10.
[41]  CONV 802/03, 12 June 2003. Draft Constitution, Volume II, Draft revised text of Parts Two, Three and Four. Reproduced in the draft Constitutional Treaty of 18 July 2003.
[42]  It is worth noting here that the reference to courts of the Member States is further evidence of the expectation that the Charter will be accorded legal status in disputes before national courts as well as the ECJ.

*the explanations prepared at the instigation of the Praesidium of the Convention which drafted the Charter.*

The Praesidium of the Convention drafting the Constitutional Treaty went far beyond its remit in this proposed 'adjustment' to the Preamble to the EU Charter. Far from being aimed at drawing attention to and publicising the explanations, the 'adjustment' appears intended to attribute a legal value to the explanations disclaimed by their authors, and repeated by Working Group II's acknowledgement that 'they have no legal value'.

The inspiration and source of this 'adjustment' is questionable. It is suggested that it was yet another concession to those Member States seeking to dilute the potential content of fundamental rights guaranteed by the EU legal order.[43] Again, this contrasts with the careful disclaimer, reproduced twice in footnotes to the text of the Charter on the EU's website, that 'These explanations have been prepared at the instigation of the Praesidium. They have no legal value and are simply intended to clarify the provisions of the Charter.'

Only the first sentence of that disclaimer is reproduced in the Praesidium's 'adjustment' to the Preamble. The second sentence, which is not reproduced, states precisely the opposite to the positive assertion of the 'adjustment' to the Preamble that '... the Charter *will* be interpreted by the Courts of the Union and the Member States with due regard for the explanations'. This purports to attribute to the Explanations the status of mandatory interpretive rules which the Praesidium of the Charter Convention was careful not to claim. Their caution was fully justified, among other reasons, because of the changing composition of the Praesidium[44] and differing extent of its members' involvement during its activities.[45]

---

[43] It is notable, for example, that the Praesidium of the Convention drafting the Constitutional Treaty did not include in the Preamble Working Group II's emphasis on a 'rule of interpretation' whereby 'rather than following a rigid approach of a "lowest common denominator", the Charter rights concerned should be interpreted in a way offering a high standard of protection which is adequate for the law of the Union ...'. Final Report of Working Group II, CONV 354/02, Section II, para. 5, p. 7. Instead, this is relegated to the explanations to Article 52(4). See below, text to footnote 72.

[44] See the Preface to the Charter on the EU's website.

[45] Perhaps the Praesidium of the Convention on the Future of Europe, responsible for this 'adjustment', was hoping to set a precedent, anticipating that a similar reference to its own 'explanations' to the Constitutional Treaty might be similarly immortalised! In this it was anticipated by Working Group II, which said of its own proposed 'adjustments': 'To the extent that the Convention takes on board the drafting adjustments proposed by this Group, the corresponding explanations given in this report should be fully integrated with the original explanations.' But Working Group II at least retained some modesty by following this immediately with the affirmation that those original explanations 'have no legal value'. Final Report of Working Group II, CONV 354/02, Section III, para. 3, p. 10.

### The contribution of the Chairman of the Working Party of Legal Experts reviewing the text of the draft Treaty

The Intergovernmental Conference of the EU Member States established a Working Party of IGC Legal Experts to undertake editorial and legal adjustments to the draft Treaty establishing a Constitution for Europe. In its Report of 25 November 2003[46] the Working Party refers to 'five footnotes drafted on the responsibility of the Chairman of the Working Party, on particular legal points'. One of these is attached to the Preamble to the EU Charter following the sentence added by the Praesidium of the Convention on the Future of Europe which stipulates:

> In this context the Charter will be interpreted by the courts of the Union and the Member States with due regard to the explanations prepared at the instigation of the Praesidium of the Convention which drafted the Charter.

The footnote reads as follows:[47]

> The Legal Adviser to the IGC [is of the opinion that] suggests adding at the end of this sentence, for reasons of legal certainty and transparency, a phrase to point out that the explanations mentioned here have been updated on the responsibility of the Praesidium of the European Convention; if this were not done, the existing text would be inaccurate. The following addition is supported by the great majority of delegations (with the German, Austrian, Belgian, Luxembourg and French delegations opposing it, because they feel that it raises issues of political desirability): '(…) the explanations prepared at the instigation of the Praesidium of the Convention which drafted the Charter **and updated on the responsibility of the Praesidium of the European Convention'**.
>
> Also, since the text explicitly states that the Charter will be interpreted by the courts of the Union and of the Member States '*with due regard to*' those explanations, it would be legally inconceivable that the text of the explanations should not be available to those courts and to the Union's citizens. The Legal Adviser therefore suggests that they be made universally accessible, by ensuring that they are published in the 'C' series of the Official Journal of the European Union.

The reference to explanations 'updated on the responsibility of the Praesidium of the European Convention' adds to concerns about the legal status of these explanations, since that Praesidium had no authority to undertake such updating and did not even refer to it in the sentence it added to the Preamble. The opposition expressed by five Member States to this 'technical' amendment highlights these concerns.

---

[46] CIG 50/03.

[47] See also the report of the Chairman of the Working Party, Mr Jean-Claude Piris, Director-General of the Council Legal Service, CIG 51/03 of 25 November 2003, which replicates the substance of this text. Differences include that the objections of the five delegations are put down to 'political expediency' and the amendment suggested reads '… and updated *under* the responsibility of the Praesidium of the European Convention …'

## The European Council's amendments of 18 June 2004

The European Council summit met on 17–18 June 2004 to decide on the draft EU Constitution. At a ministerial meeting of 14 June 2004 the Irish Presidency of the Council had put forward three options concerning the legal effect of the EU Charter.[48] The first was to retain the Preamble as it stood. The second addressed the legal value of the 'explanations' by specifying that they were 'a way of providing guidance'. The third prescribed that the Charter 'shall be interpreted with due regard to the explanations'.

The final outcome of the summit reflected the dispute manifested in the Working Party of Legal Experts. The Preamble to the EU Charter was amended adding the phrase suggested by the Chair of the Working Party referring to the explanations of the Praesidium which drafted the Charter: 'and updated under the responsibility of the Praesidium of the European Convention'.[49]

In addition, there was also added another paragraph 7 to Article 52 of the EU Charter (Scope and interpretation of rights and principles):

> The explanations drawn up as a way of providing guidance in the interpretation of the Charter of Fundamental Rights shall be given due regard by the courts of the Union and of the Member States.

As regards the legal status of the explanations, this outcome seems, if anything, to have diluted their legal force. The authority seemingly attributed to the explanations by the Preamble's apparent mandatory requirement that that Charter '*will* be interpreted by the courts of the Union and the Member States *with due regard* to the explanations' is reduced in new Article 52(7) of the Charter. Instead, the explanations are merely '*a way of providing guidance in the interpretation of the Charter*' and 'shall be given *due regard* by the courts of the Union and of the Member States'.

So 'will be interpreted' becomes 'shall be given due regard'. Article 52(7) takes precedence over the Preamble. Moreover, perhaps reflecting the reservations of the five Member States expressed in the footnote attached by the Chairman of the Working Party to the amendments to the Preamble suggested by the Legal Adviser to the IGC, the text of new Article 52(7) of the Charter makes *no reference* to the updated explanations.

To these constitutional amendments, the European Council added a 'Declaration for incorporation in the Final Act concerning the explanations relating to the Charter of Fundamental Rights':[50]

> The Conference takes note of the explanations relating to the Charter of Fundamental Rights prepared under the authority of the Praesidium of the

---

[48]  Document CIG 80/04, Brussels, 12 June 2004, Annex 13.

[49]  CIG 85/04. Brussels, 18 June 2004. PRESID 27, Annex 10. See the Provisional consolidated version of the draft Treaty Establishing a Constitution for Europe, CIG 86/04, Brussels, 25 June 2004.

[50]  *Ibid.*

Convention which drafted the Charter and updated under the responsibility of the Praesidium of the European Convention, as set out below.

This Declaration, to be incorporated in the Final Act, emphatically merely 'takes note' both of the original explanations and the update. The explanations are not incorporated into the Charter, which is Part II of the EU Constitution. Rather the explanations are to be attached to this Declaration. The Declaration includes the following paragraph:[51]

> These explanations were originally prepared under the authority of the Praesidium of the Convention which drafted the Charter of Fundamental Rights of the European Union. They have been updated under the responsibility of the Praesidium of the European Convention, in the light of the drafting adjustments made to the text of the Charter by that Convention (notably to Articles 51 and 52) and of further developments of Union law. Although they do not as such have the status of law, they are a valuable tool of interpretation intended to clarify the provisions of the Charter.

The reference to updating 'in light of ... further developments of Union law' is reflected in a number references in the 'updated' explanations to legislation adopted after December 2000. For example, the 'updated' explanation to Article 8, 'Protection of personal data', refers to Regulation No. 45/2001 on the protection of individuals with regard to the processing of personal data. The 'updated' Explanation to Article 27, 'Workers' right to information and consultation within the undertaking', now includes a reference to Directive 2002/14/EC (general framework for informing and consulting employees in the European Community). There are citations of post-2000 decisions of the ECJ in the explanations to Articles 1 and 3 (the same case).

However, the updating itself highlights one obvious and outstanding problem of the explanations. Both the original explanations and those added by the Convention on the Future of Europe will rapidly become outdated as new legislation is adopted and new decisions of the ECJ are added to the corpus of EU law. The inadequacy of the explanations as an interpretive instrument will soon be apparent.[52]

There are also serious questions about the quality of the updating exercise. An example is selectivity: the 'updated' explanation to Article 30 of the Charter refers to the consolidated Directive 2001/23/EC on the safeguarding of employees rights in the event of transfers of undertakings, and Directive 80/987 on the protection of employees in the event of the insolvency of their employer, as amended by Directive 2002/84/EC. However, Article 23 refers to Directive 76/207/EC on the implementation of the principle of equal treatment for men and women as regards access to employment, vocational training and

---

[51] *Ibid.*, page 15.
[52] An interesting prospect would be a procedure for regular updating. However, the potential overlap with the interpretive jurisdiction of the ECJ, and possible conflict, cannot be avoided.

**Table 7.1** Court decisions cited in explanations

| Article | No. of decisions |
| --- | --- |
| 11 | 1 |
| 15 | 3 |
| 16 | 4 |
| 19 | 1 (Eur. Ct. of HR) |
| 20 | 3 |
| 41 | 7 (1 cited twice) |
| 47 | 4 (plus 1 Eur. Ct. of HR) |
| 50 | 2 |
| 51 | 4 |
| 52 | 1 |

promotion, and working conditions, but does not mention that this Directive was revised by Council Directive 2002/73/EC.[53]

Selectivity is likely to be even more of a pitfall with respect to citation of decisions of the European courts. The original explanations contained references to thirty-one court decisions scattered very unevenly among the Articles of the Charter. Only ten Articles cited decisions (see Table 7.1).

The 'updated' explanations added four decisions which were decided post-December 2000: one to each of Articles 1, 45, 50 and 52 (the last of these referring to the new Article 52(4) inserted by the Convention). Additional 'updated' explanations to the new Article 52(4) also included references to three pre-December 2000 decisions.[54]

## The aftermath: the political effect of the 'explanations' and the role of the European Court of Justice

In the aftermath of the European Council summit of 17–18 June 2004, at a press conference of 18 June 2004 at the end of the meeting, the British Prime Minister Tony Blair announced:

> the Charter of Rights is expressed specifically in such a way that it means that the industrial relations law of our country cannot be altered by the European Court of Justice through the Charter of Fundamental Rights.

In his statement to the UK Parliament on 21 June 2004 on the EU Constitutional Treaty he was even more explicit:

[53] OJ 2002 No. L269/15.

[54] The 'updated' explanations provide some evidence of the political controversy which surrounded the amendments made by the Convention on the Future of Europe and reflected in the selective use of case law. See below the analysis of the amendments to Articles 51(2) and 52(5).

The EU Treaty includes, in the Charter of Fundamental Rights, the rights of the citizen under EU law. The Charter expressly rules out establishing any new power or task for the European Union or any change in the powers of the European Union. In each area the rights are expressly limited to those available under existing national law and practices and under existing Union law. So, for example, Article 28 of the Charter says that workers and employers have the right to negotiate and conclude collective agreements at the appropriate levels, but only 'in accordance with Union law and national laws and practices'. In addition, the Charter contains explanations for each Article making it clear, for example, that 'the ... limits for the exercise of collective action, including strike action, come under national laws and practices, including the question of whether it may be carried out in parallel in several member states'. The Treaty requires those explanations to be given due regard by the Courts.

On the contrary, the Charter does not contain the explanations. And while they 'shall be given due regard by the courts', the Charter text specifies that they were 'drawn up as a way of providing guidance in the interpretation'. They are clearly not of equal status to the text of the Charter.

Whatever the impact of the British Prime Minister's statement in the domestic context of public opinion in the UK, it is unlikely to influence opinion outside UK political circles, even less so in the courts of the UK when the Charter is invoked, and least of all in the most important forum deciding the legal effect of the Charter: the European Court of Justice.

On the last day of the European Council summit the *Financial Times* included the report of an interview with the President of the European Court of Justice, Vassilios Skouris.[55] The article begins by stating that:

> The European Union's new constitution should allow court rulings ... making the EU's controversial charter of fundamental rights legally binding, according to the EU's top judge. Vassilios Skouris, president of the European Court of Justice, was unable to promise that the charter would not directly affect individual jurisdictions such as the UK.

Noting that 'the UK has always been wary of giving it legal force, because it enshrines the right to strike', the report quoted the judge as saying that the draft Constitution 'will bring new areas and new subjects under the court's jurisdiction', such as the Charter. The report continued:

> Mr Skouris also called for the charter on fundamental rights to be made legally binding within the constitution – a move EU leaders are likely to make today.
> 'A complete catalogue of fundamental rights will simplify things in the interest of legal certainty', he said. The UK has been considering a compromise to the constitution text that could give the charter legal force over EU institutions but not over national laws.

---

[55]  18 June 2004, p. 6.

However, many lawyers doubt if the legal impact of the charter can be ring-fenced in this way. Mr Skouris could not give assurances that the charter would not have an impact on UK law.[56]

A leading commentator, John Palmer, Political Director of the European Policy Centre, analysing the results of the European Council wrote:[57]

> The treaty also makes clear that the provisions of the Charter of Citizens' Fundamental Rights will be judiciable in the European Court of Justice – in spite of fierce opposition initially from the British government. These include some highly sensitive issues such as workers' rights to strike. The text does stipulate that the ECJ must take 'due consideration' of national laws in these areas when reaching judgments. However the final decision on how to balance the contents of the Charter and the 'explanations' of national circumstances will be left to the judges in Luxembourg. Case law seems certain to evolve over the years ahead and it would be surprising if it did not evolve in ways which supported the values of the Charter.

The attempt by the British New Labour government to 'protect' the UK's restrictive labour laws from the fundamental rights proclaimed in the European Constitution failed.[58] The fallback of reliance on the 'explanations' to mitigate the consequences of the Charter is similarly unlikely to have the effect desired. There would be no 'protecting' UK labour laws, frequently condemned by the supervisory bodies of the ILO and the Council of Europe for violations of international labour standards, from the impact of the fundamental trade union rights guaranteed by the EU Charter.[59]

---

[56] The report states that the judge 'added that he did not expect a large influx of cases due to the charter and tried to minimise British fears that essential professions, such as policemen, could go on strike: "The right of workers to take strike action doesn't mean that everybody has the right to strike all the time and under any circumstances", he said.'

[57] Communication to Members S56/04, 'The Constitutional Treaty – Opening the Way to a "Core Europe?"', 20 June 2004, p. 4.

[58] On 16 June 2004, the front page of the *Financial Times* proclaimed that in the forthcoming negotiations over the EU Constitution 'Blair "will protect" UK labour laws'. The New Labour government asserts that the small print of amendments it promoted, not least at the Intergovernmental Conference of 17–18 June 2004, will 'protect' the UK's low labour standards. By proclaiming hostility to EU employment rights for workers, the New Labour government has gone out of its way to make it difficult for the British trade union movement to support the proposed EU Constitution. Outraged reaction by trade union leaders was the understandable response (Derek Simpson and Tony Woodley in the *Guardian*, 30 June 2004; Brendan Barber and John Monks in *Tribune*, 25 June 2004).

[59] However, the UK government refused to accept this defeat. After the Constitution was rejected, its replacement, the Lisbon Treaty, proposed to give the EU Charter the same legal value as the Treaties. Together with Poland, the UK negotiated an 'opt-out' from the Charter in the form of a Protocol to the Lisbon Treaty. It is not clear this Protocol will achieve the UK's stated objective. See Chapter 22.

## The substance of the Praesidium's 'explanations'

The Preamble states that the EU Charter reaffirms:

> '... rights as they result, in particular, from the ... international obligations common to the Member States, the European Convention for the Protection of Human Rights and Fundamental freedoms, the Social Charters adopted by the Union and by the Council of Europe[60] and the case law of the Court of Justice of the European Union and of the European Court of Human Rights. In this context, the Charter will be interpreted by the Courts of the Union and the Member States with due regard for the explanations ...'.

This provision makes use by the courts of the Praesidium's explanations more difficult because the Praesidium's explanations are not always comprehensive or consistent in referring to, for example, those 'international obligations common to the Member States' which are explicitly the interpretative context, the inspiration and source of the EU Charter's provisions. In particular, in the case of those provisions referring to individual employment and collective labour rights, the absence in the Praesidium's explanations of references to the core ILO Conventions which bind all Member States is noticeable, and regrettable. A couple of examples illustrate this point.

## Article 12: Freedom of assembly and of association

The Praesidium's explanations to Article 12 (Freedom of assembly and of association) state that 'Paragraph 1 of this Article corresponds to Article 11 of the ECHR [European Convention on Human Rights]' and further asserts that 'The meaning of the provisions of paragraph 1 is the same as that of the ECHR, but their scope is wider since they apply at all levels, including European level.' This wider scope, which applies to all levels from the workplace up to the EU level, could have immense implications for the exercise of freedom of association going beyond the ECHR provisions.

The Praesidium's explanations go on to add 'This right is also based on Article 11 of the Community Charter of the Fundamental Social Rights of Workers.' The precise scope of Article 11 of the Community Charter (Freedom of association and collective bargaining) has been the subject of scrutiny and could extend beyond the confines of the provision in the ECHR.[61]

---

[60] The 'updated' explanations include twenty-two references to the European Social Charter and Revised European Social Charter and fifteen references to the Community Charter of the Fundamental Social Rights of Workers. See the Provisional consolidated version of the Declarations to be annexed to the Final Act of the Intergovernmental Conference, CIG 86/04, ADD 2, Brussels, 25 June 2004.

[61] B. Bercusson, *European Labour Law*, Chapter 37, pp. 585–9.

## Article 28: Right of collective bargaining and action

The Praesidium's explanations to Article 28 (Right of collective bargaining and action) state:[62]

> This Article is based on Article 6 of the European Social Charter and on the Community Charter of the Fundamental Social Rights of Workers (points 12 to 14). The right of collective action was recognised by the European Court of Human Rights as one of the elements of trade union rights laid down by Article 11 of the ECHR ... *The modalities and limits for the exercise of* collective action, including strike action, come under national laws and practices, including the question of whether it may be carried out in parallel in several Member States.

First, there is an obvious contradiction between requiring respect for the ECHR and the assertion that collective action 'comes under national laws and practices'. The contradiction is evident when the European Court of Human Rights finds a Member State's law to be in violation of the ECHR, as was recently the case with the UK in respect of Article 11.[63]

Secondly, collective action 'carried out in parallel in several Member States' engages precisely the transnational dimension of collective action in the European single market. Confining it to national laws and practices contradicts a fundamental right of European collective action. It is inevitably addressed at EU level,[64] not least by the European Court of Justice.[65]

---

[62] The eight words in italics were not in the explanations provided by the Praesidium of the Convention which drafted the Charter. They were added by the Praesidium of the Convention on the Future of Europe. They cannot be characterised as 'updating', the ostensible justification for changes in the explanations adverted to in the additional phrase attached to the Preamble by the IGC on 18 June 2004 (though not mentioned in the new Article 52(7) of the Charter). This additional phrase rather confirms the view as to the political calculations which underlie the attempt to foist the 'explanations' as an interpretive framework on the courts. It is tantamount to a suggestion that Member State laws which restrict strike action do not violate the right to strike, but merely limit the modalities of its exercise.

[63] *Wilson and the National Union of Journalists; Palmer, Wyeth and the National Union of Rail, Maritime and Transport Workers; Doolan and others* v. *United Kingdom* [2002] IRLR 128, decided 2 July 2002. For a detailed discussion of the potential impact on British labour law of what has been called 'probably the most important labour law decision for at least a generation', see K. Ewing, 'The Implications of *Wilson and Palmer*', (2003) 32 *Industrial Law Journal* 1–22.

[64] See Council Regulation (EC) No. 2679/98 of 7 December 1998 on the functioning of the internal market in relation to the free movement of goods among the Member States. OJ L337/8 of 12 December 1998 (the 'Monti Regulation'), Article 2.

[65] See *Eugen Schmidburger, Internationale Transporte Planzuge* v. *Republic of Austria*, Case C-112/00, 12 June 2003. See now the decisions in Case C-341/05, *Laval un Partneri Ltd* v. *Svenska Byggnadsarbetareforbundet, Svenska Byggnadsarbetareforbundet, Avdelning 1, Svenska Elektrikerforbundet*, Case C-438/05, 18 December 2007; *Viking Line Abp OU Viking Line Eesti* v. *The International Transport Workers' Federation, The Finnish Seamen's Union*, 11 December 2007.

### Other international labour standards

Apart from references to specific European and international instruments, there are other international obligations binding EU Member States. These are not always mentioned by the Praesidium's explanations, though the Preamble emphatically states that the Charter reaffirms these obligations. This indicates the incompleteness of the Praesidium's explanations, which no doubt explains the admirable caution expressed by that Praesidium which drafted the Charter with respect to the use to be made of its explanations.

It would seem that, under pressure from some Member States anxious to restrict the ambit of the EU Charter's rights, the amendment to the Preamble was attempting to elevate the explanations to a status never intended by its authors, the Convention which drafted the Charter, or even the Convention's own Working Group II, which did not include any such recommendation its own list of 'adjustments'.

The Preamble's reference to international obligations must have important consequences for the interpretation of the EU Charter. For example, trade union collective action has often been restricted, allegedly to protect public and/or essential services. The ILO's Freedom of Association Committee has established international standards on collective action in public/essential services. Relying on Article 28 of the EU Charter (right to collective action), trade unions could promote challenges to more restrictive national laws.

Again, Article 12(1) of the Charter on freedom of association could be interpreted as guaranteeing rights which go beyond what is provided in some national laws, for example, regarding interference in a union's internal affairs, rights to representation, recognition by an employer, access to union members at the workplace, or to take part in union activities.

In conclusion, this last amendment to the EU Charter's Preamble begins, after the reaffirmation 'in particular [of] international obligations common to the Member States', with the phrase '[i]n this context'. The explanations should be read, and the EU Charter interpreted, with full weight attached to this context of the international obligations of the EU and its Member States.

## The legal effect of the 'explanations'

The amendments made to the EU Charter by the IGC of 17–18 June 2004 at the behest of the UK government focused on the 'explanations' and were a last-ditch attempt to achieve the UK's objective pursued throughout the two Conventions: the elimination or reduction so far as possible of fundamental rights in the sphere of employment and industrial relations.

A number of arguments, using textual, systematic and historical approaches to interpretation, are summarised below regarding the potential legal effect of the IGC's amendments to the EU Charter. These arguments reflect awareness of the intentions of the UK government which promoted the amendments, but also of those governments which resisted and watered down those amendments.

First, the additional sentence added to the Preamble by the Praesidium of the Convention on the Future of Europe was quite strong: '... the Charter will be interpreted ... with due regard for the explanations ...'. In comparison, the new Article 52(7) added by the IGC seems weaker: 'The explanations ... providing guidance in the interpretation ... shall be given due regard ...'. So 'will be interpreted' becomes 'shall be given due regard'. Article 52(7) takes precedence over the Preamble. The Preamble refers to 'updated' explanations, but Article 52(7) does not.

Secondly, the IGC's Working Party of Legal Experts recommended the explanations be published only in the 'C' section of the Official Journal.[66] This proposal reflects the suggestion 'drafted on the responsibility of the Chairman of the Working Party' (the Legal Adviser to the IGC, Mr Jean-Claude Piris, Director-General of the Council Legal Service), referred to in the text of the Draft Treaty published 'following editorial and legal adjustments by the Working Party of IGC Legal Experts'.[67] The 'C' series, of course, includes non-binding documents.

Third, the IGC's 'Declaration for incorporation in the Final Act concerning the explanations relating to the Charter of Fundamental Rights' says only that the IGC 'takes note of the explanations'. The explanations are to be 'set out below' this Declaration, not as part of the EU Charter incorporated as Part II of the EU Constitutional Treaty. There it is stated: 'Although they do not as such have the status of law, they are a valuable tool of interpretation intended to clarify the provisions of the Charter.'

Fourth, there are no amendments looking to the explanations in the substantive text of the Charter rights, only to the Preamble, to the title of the 'horizontal' Article 52, and a new Article 52(7). The amended Preamble and new Article 52(7) referring to 'explanations' do not change the rights in the Charter.[68] These amendments address interpretation

---

[66] '... since the text explicitly states that *"the Charter will be interpreted by the courts of the Union and the Member States with due regard to the explanations prepared at the instigation of the Praesidium of the Convention which drafted the Charter"*, it would be legally inconceivable for the text of such explanations not to be available to those courts and to Union citizens; it is therefore suggested that the explanations be made universally accessible by ensuring that they are published in the "C" series of the Official Journal of the European Union'. CIG 51/03, 25 November 2003, paragraph 7.

[67] CIG 50/03, 25 November 2003, page 1. It should be recalled that in the Working Party this amendment was 'supported by the great majority of delegations (with the German, Austrian, Belgian, Luxembourg and French delegations opposing it, because they feel it raises issues of political desirability) ...'. Page 68, footnote 1.

[68] For example, the often quoted 'explanation' to Article 28 (as cited by Tony Blair in his statement to the House of Commons of the UK Parliament on 21 June 2004) states, not as an interpretation but as a prescription, that 'national laws and practices' impose substantive limits to the rights declared in the Charter. It is submitted that there is an 'interpretation' of the words 'national laws and practices' in Article 28 which does not limit the rights in that Article.

questions only. They cannot change the substance of the rights in, or text of, the Charter.[69]

Fifth, it will be necessary to review the 'updated' explanations, but, for example, the original 'explanation' to Article 52 (on the EU's website) does not reflect its new title. It begins: 'The purpose of Article 52 is to set the scope of the rights guaranteed'. It says nothing about interpretation.

Sixth, and finally, the 'explanations' have been repeatedly characterised, not least by those who drafted them, and as stated on the EU's website, as of 'no legal value'. They were not published in the Official Journal alongside the Charter,[70] only on the EU's website. Their legal value has been upgraded at most to the level of 'due regard' and 'providing guidance'.

At this point, there are important questions about the transparency and legitimacy of the process which produced the 'explanations'. They were produced by the Praesidium of the Convention which drafted the Charter, but without the participation or approval of that Convention. They were given prominence in the Preamble of the Charter by the Praesidium of the Convention on the Future of Europe, again without the participation or approval of that Convention.

## Working Group II's 'adjustments' to the text of the EU Charter

### Article 51(1): Limits of the powers of the Union

An amendment to Article 51(1) proposed by Working Group II and adopted by the Convention on the Future of Europe added 20 words (in italics):

Article 51: Scope
1. The provisions of this Charter are addressed to the institutions and bodies of the Union with due regard for the principle of subsidiarity and to the Member States only when they are implementing Union law. They shall therefore respect the rights, observe the principles and promote the application thereof in accordance with their respective powers *and respecting the limits of the powers of the Union as conferred on it by other parts of the Constitution.*[71]

---

[69] For example, the change (already in the draft of the Constitutional Treaty of 18 July 2003) in the heading of Title VII (the section of the Charter on 'horizontal' provisions), from 'Scope' to 'General provisions governing the interpretation and application of the Charter', and, more specifically after 18 June 2004, also to 'horizontal' Article 52 (from 'Scope of guaranteed rights' to 'Scope and interpretation of rights and principles') cannot transform 'rights' into 'principles'.

[70] OJ C364/21 of 18 December 2000.

[71] The additional language inserted by Working Group II is in italics. The text which appears in the draft Treaty Establishing a Constitution for Europe, produced by the Convention on the Future of Europe, CONV 850/03, Brussels, 18 July 2003 is identical, with a small addition in the first lines which read: 'The provisions of this Charter are addressed to the Institutions, bodies *and agencies* of the Union …', and the last line of the amendment now reads: '… as conferred on it *in the* other Parts of the Constitution'. The Charter is Part II of the EU Constitution.

This limitation aims to prevent any reliance on fundamental rights which the European Court has used, for example, to interpret Article 18 of the EC Treaty.[72] The proposal aims to obstruct any attempt by the European Court to develop interpretations of EU citizenship to include a concept of 'social citizenship' based on the EU Charter's fundamental social and labour rights.[73] It aims to block using the Charter to enhance the status of 'EU social citizenship' in order, for example, to promote a system of industrial relations at EU level.[74] That this is the target is also indicated by a new paragraph inserted in the 'updated' explanations to Article 52(2):[75]

> Paragraph 2 refers to rights which were already expressly guaranteed in the Treaty establishing the European Community and have been recognised in the Charter, and which are now found in other Parts of the Constitution (notably the rights derived from Union citizenship). It clarifies that such rights remain subject to the conditions and limits applicable to the Union law on which they are based, and for which provision is now made in Parts I and III of the Constitution. The Charter does not alter the system of rights conferred by the EC Treaty and now taken over by Parts I and III of the Constitution.

Whether the amendment succeeds in these aims is far from certain. The 'scope of the powers of the Union' conferred by/in the other parts Constitution is a matter of interpretation for the European Court of Justice, including an

---

[72] See on Article 18's rights to free movement and residence of EU citizens, Case C-184/99 *Rudy Grzelczyk* v. *Centre public d'aide sociale d'Ottignies-Louvain-la-Neuve* [2001] ECR I-6193; Case C-413/99, *Baumbast, R* v. *Secretary of State for the Home Department*, judgment of 17 September 2002; Case C-200/02, *Kunqian Catherine Zhu*, judgment of 19 October 2004, Case C-209/03, *Dany Bidar*, judgment of 15 March 2005.

[73] Some evidence of this intent specifically referring to the impact of the Charter on the Member States is to be found in the 'updated' explanations. The Convention which drafted the Charter specified that 'the requirement to respect fundamental rights defined in a Union context is only binding on the Member States when they act in the *context* of Union law …'. The updated explanations changed 'context' to '*scope*'. See the Provisional consolidated version of the Declarations to be annexed to the Final Act of the Intergovernmental Conference, CIG 86/04, ADD 2, Brussels, 25 June 2004, page 59. See also below, analysis of Article 51(2).

[74] Needless to say, it was not part of the Working Group's task to add new limitations not agreed in the earlier Convention. The proposed 'adjustment', aimed at limiting the rights of EU citizens, does not enhance the EU's political legitimacy. The vast majority of the earlier cases (twenty-six cases up to 20 August 2002) in which the Charter was referred to by the Advocates General (every one of the eight Advocates General had referred to the Charter at least once) or the Court of First Instance are concerned with the rights of EU citizens to good administration and impartial justice. It was questionable for the Convention to follow Working Group II and go on record as denying these rights to EU citizens.

[75] Article 52(2) reads: 'Rights recognised by this Charter for which provision is made in other Parts of the Constitution shall be exercised under the conditions and within the limits defined by these relevant parts'. The paragraph from the 'updated' explanations is in the Provisional consolidated version of the Declarations to be annexed to the Final Act of the Intergovernmental Conference, CIG 86/04, ADD 2, Brussels, 25 June 2004, page 62. It may be noted that this explanation was not considered necessary by the Praesidium of the Convention which drafted the Charter. Its inclusion cannot be explained by any amendment to Article 52(2) of the Charter. It merely reiterates the position of some Member States hoping to limit the impact of the Charter.

enhanced profile of EU citizenship informed, not least, by the Charter of Fundamental Rights itself.

### Article 51(2): Attack on fundamental rights in general

Working Group II proposed the following additions (in italics) to Article 51(2) of the EU Charter:[76]

> This Charter does not *extend the scope of application of Union law beyond the powers of the Union or* establish any new power or task for [the Community or] the Union or modify powers and tasks defined *by the other [chapters/parts] of* [this Treaty/the Constitutional Treaty].

In making this proposal in its Final Report to 'adjust' Article 51(2):[77]

> the Group considers it useful to confirm expressly, in Article 51(2), in light of established case law, that the protection of fundamental rights by Union law cannot have the effect of extending the scope of the Treaty provisions beyond the competences of the Union.

A footnote referred to the judgment of the ECJ in Case C-249/96, *Grant* v. *South-West Trains*.[78] Surprisingly, this claim and footnote have now appeared in the 'updated' explanations to Article 51(2):[79]

> Paragraph 2 also confirms that the Charter may not have the effect of extending the field of application of Union law beyond the powers of the Union as established in the other Parts of the Constitution. The Court of Justice has already established this rule with respect to the fundamental rights recognised as part of Union law (judgment of 17 February 1998, C-249/96 *Grant*, 1998 ECR I-621, paragraph 45 of the grounds). In accordance with this rule, it goes without saying that the incorporation of the Charter into the Constitution cannot be understood as extending by itself the range of Member State action considered to be 'implementation of Union law' (within the meaning of paragraph 1 and the above-mentioned case law).[80]

This claim of support by the ECJ of the Working Group's view, replicated in the 'updated' explanations, is suspect.

---

[76] The draft Treaty Establishing a Constitution for the Union, CONV 850/03, Brussels, 18 July 2003, reproduces this as follows: 'This Charter does not extend the *field* of application of Union law beyond the powers of the Union or establish any new power or task for the Union, or modify powers and tasks defined in the other Parts of the Constitution'.

[77] Final Report, Section II.2.    [78] [1998] ECR I-621 at paragraph 45.

[79] See the Provisional consolidated version of the Declarations to be annexed to the Final Act of the Intergovernmental Conference, CIG 86/04, ADD 2, Brussels, 25 June 2004, page 60.

[80] But see the discussion in the following section on Article 21 of the Charter.

First, the decision in *Grant* has been widely criticised as retreating from the principle of the prohibition of discrimination on grounds of sex established in the earlier ECJ decision in *P* v. *S and Cornwall County Council*.[81]

Secondly, the ECJ's refusal in *Grant* to prohibit discrimination on the grounds of sexual orientation as outside EU competence was reversed by the insertion by the Treaty of Amsterdam of Article 13 EC. This was pointed out by the Court itself in its judgment,[82] implying that the fundamental right at issue in *Grant* could have been protected in the event of Article 13 conferring EU competence. Arguably similar to Article 13 EC in the case of discrimination, the EU Charter confers competence as regards a wide range of human rights, including labour rights.

Finally, Working Group II and the 'updated' explanations specifically cite paragraph 45 of the judgment in *Grant*:

> However, although respect for fundamental rights which form an integral part of those general principles is a condition of the legality of Community acts, those rights cannot in themselves have the effect of extending the scope of the Treaty provisions beyond the competences of the Community (see, *inter alia*, on the scope of Article 235 of the EC Treaty as regards respect for human rights, Opinion 2/94 [1996] ECR I-1759, paragraphs 34 and 35).[83]

The ECJ was responding to the argument that the scope of the Community's respect for fundamental rights was to be interpreted in light of national law and international conventions. The reference in brackets is to one of those: Opinion 2/94 concerned the European Convention on Human Rights.

However, the position is arguably very different with respect to an EU Charter of Fundamental Rights. This is not an *external* human rights standard laid down in national or international law by which to measure EU competences as regards fundamental rights. It is the *internal* EU standard establishing the competence of the EU in the areas covered by the EU Charter.

In sum, the 'adjustment' is phrased in wholly negative terms ('... *does not extend the scope* ...'). Its objective is to limit the fundamental rights proclaimed

---

[81] Case C-13/94 [1996] ECR I-2143. See C. Barnard, 'The Principle of Equality in the Community Context: *P, Grant, Kalanke* and *Marschall*: Four Uneasy Bedfellows' [1998] 57 *Cambridge Law Journal* 352. Kenner comments: 'the judgement in *P*. v. *S* (Case C-13/94, [1996] ECR I-2143) may have appeared superficially "courageous" but, rather than being a decision of potential constitutional importance, it represents an example of what de Búrca has aptly described as the Court's selective application of the equality principle, a form of judicial "gesture politics"'. Jeff Kenner, *EU Employment Law: From Rome to Amsterdam and beyond*, Oxford: Hart, 2003, at pp. 439–40.

[82] Paragraph 48.

[83] The argument as to limitation of competences as the basis of the decision in *Grant* is also undermined by the later decision of *D*. v. *Council*, Case C-125/99P, [2001] ECR I-4319, where the issue was clearly within EU competence as it involved the EU's treatment of its own employees. The claim for a household allowance for the same-sex partner was rejected, but there was no hint in the judgment that the EU lacked competence to deal with it. Only that the EU legislature had not adopted legislation to allow same-sex partners that allowance as 'married' persons (paragraph 38). See Craig and de Búrca, *EU Law*, p. 388.

in the Charter and confine them within the scope of EU competences. For example, this 'adjustment' might be used to argue for a restrictive interpretation of the Treaty Articles on the EU social dialogue (Articles 138 and 139 EC), countering a broad interpretation of those Treaty provisions to reinforce the social partners and the social dialogue, supported by the fundamental trade union rights in the Charter.

If there is a potential conflict between Treaty competences and Charter rights, the Working Group's solution was not to reinforce the status of fundamental rights, but to protect the allocation of competences in the Treaty, even at the price of violations of the Charter. Interpreted as such, this 'adjustment' will scarcely reinforce the social legitimacy of the EU. Again, the earlier Convention did not think it necessary or desirable to add these phrases, and, as repeatedly emphasised by both Working Group II and the Convention on the Future of Europe which made the amendments, no substantive change is intended.

### Illustration (i): Article 21 of the Charter

The 'adjustments' to Article 51 reflect a major concern of those who sought to limit the impact of the fundamental rights in the EU Charter by reference to the limited competences of the Union. The issue is particularly well illustrated by Article 21(1) of the Charter:

> Any discrimination based on any ground such as sex, race, colour, ethnic or social origin, genetic features, language, religion or belief, political or any other opinion, membership of a national minority, property, birth, disability, age or sexual orientation shall be prohibited.

The Praesidium of the Convention which drafted the Charter did not deem it necessary in its explanation to Article 21(1) to do more than point out that:

> Paragraph 1 draws on Article 13 of the EC Treaty, Article 14 of the ECHR and Article 11 of the Convention on Human Rights and Biomedicine as regards genetic heritage. Insofar as this corresponds to Article 14 of the ECHR, it applies in compliance with it.

Yet the reference to Article 13 does raise questions. Article 13 states:

> Without prejudice to the other provisions of this Treaty and within the limits of the powers conferred by it upon the Community, the Council, acting unanimously on a proposal from the Commission and after consulting the European Parliament, may take appropriate action to combat discrimination based on sex, racial or ethnic origin, religion or belief, disability, age or sexual orientation.

There is clearly some discrepancy between Article 13 EC and Article 21 of the Charter. Unlike the former, the latter includes a prohibition of discrimination based on, among others, colour, social origin, genetic features, language, membership of a national minority, property or birth. The Convention which drafted the Charter was not apparently deterred by this discrepancy from declaring a fundamental right not to be discriminated against on the extra grounds listed in Article 21. The Praesidium of that Convention was content to reflect this by noting that Article 21 only 'draws on Article 13 of the EC Treaty'.

Yet the discrepancy highlights the prospect of a complaint based on one of the 'extra' grounds of discrimination in Article 21, protected by the EU Constitution, but not referred to in the Treaty, or at least not in Article 13. Although the Convention on the Future of Europe made no attempt to amend Article 21 of the Charter, this prospect obviously galvanised certain parties to the extent that the Praesidium felt constrained to add a long paragraph to the heretofore brief, now 'updated' explanation attached to Article 21:[84]

> There is no contradiction or incompatibility between paragraph 1 and Article [III-8] [the successor to Article 13 EC] of the Constitution which has a different scope and purpose: Article [III-8] confers power on the Union to adopt legislative acts, including harmonisation of the Member States' laws and regulations, to combat certain forms of discrimination, listed exhaustively in that Article. Such legislation may cover action of Member State authorities (as well as relations between private individuals) in any area within the limits of the Union's powers. In contrast, the provision in paragraph 1 does not create any power to enact anti-discrimination laws in these areas of Member State or private action, nor does it lay down a sweeping ban of discrimination in such wide-ranging areas. Instead, it only addresses discriminations by the institutions and bodies of the Union themselves, when exercising powers conferred under other articles of Parts I and III of the Constitution, and by Member States only when they are implementing Union law. Paragraph 1 does not alter the extent of powers granted under Article [III-8] nor the interpretation given to that Article.

The explanation appears to concede that discrimination based on the 'extra' grounds in Article 21 will allow for complaints against the EU institutions or the Member States when implementing Union law. That is already some indication that the Charter has expanded the scope of EU law.

Not yet answered is the question of discrimination based on the 'extra' grounds in Article 21 which is attributable to the EU, or to Member States implementing EU law, or occurs between private individuals *outside* 'the limits of the Union's powers'. The explanation asserts that that Article 21(1) 'does not create any power to enact anti-discrimination laws in these areas of Member State or private action, nor does it lay down a sweeping ban of discrimination in such wide-ranging areas'. The extent of the power to enact laws under Article III-8 (Article 13 EC) is not in question. But Article 21(1)'s ban on discrimination based on these 'extra' grounds is unequivocal. The claim that it bans such discrimination only in an 'area within the limits of the Union's powers' is

---

[84] See the Provisional consolidated version of the Declarations to be annexed to the Final Act of the Intergovernmental Conference, CIG 86/04, ADD 2, Brussels, 25 June 2004, page 37.

precisely the issue which will confront the ECJ hearing such a complaint. The ECJ will either uphold the complaint on the basis of the Charter's prohibition extending the powers of the EU to cover such forms of discrimination; or reject the complaint as falling outside the limits of the EU's powers. The choice appears clear and stark: which is to prevail: fundamental rights or EU competences? The solution already indicated by the Court's case law is to interpret EU competences as including fundamental rights, in this case, as manifest in the EU Charter. The implications for EU competences in the field covered by the social and labour rights in the EU Charter are potentially profound.

The competences of the Community and the Union are frequently a subject of litigation between those seeking to extend, or to limit them. If there is a potential conflict between the scope of Treaty competences and some Charter rights, the solution should be to reinforce the status of fundamental rights, not abandon them or allow their violation in order to protect the Treaty. It is likely that in such cases, the European Court of Justice will prefer to give an expanded interpretation of the powers and tasks of the Community and Union where these are necessary in order to safeguard the EU Charter rights.

At least, it should be left to the ECJ to resolve this conflict. The ECJ has played a cautious but essential role in protecting fundamental rights. It has done this, contrary to the line proposed in the 'adjustments', in the interests of protecting the Treaty from national constitutional courts which would reject it precisely because the Treaty appeared to contradict fundamental rights in national constitutions. By recognising fundamental rights as not conflicting with the Treaty, thus giving way to the objections of these national constitutional courts, the ECJ has preserved the Treaty.

Working Group II's 'adjustments', by seeking to stifle this development, threaten a confrontation with national constitutional courts which the ECJ, and the earlier Convention, wisely sought to avoid. The proposed effect of the 'adjustment' is to require the Court to interpret the Treaty as not allowing the Community to protect the fundamental rights guaranteed by the Charter.[85]

If Community measures promoting an EU industrial relations system were challenged as outside EU competences they could nevertheless find support in the Charter. This is essential in so far as these rights support an EU system of industrial relations. If the competences of the EU do not cover all the fundamental rights guaranteed by the Charter, this means that the EU could not protect these rights.

---

[85] For example, a measure adopted by the Community or the Union (on collective bargaining, the right to strike, collective agreements, freedom of association or any other aspect of an EU industrial relations system) could be challenged as outside EU competences. The European Court will be likely to uphold the measure where it can be linked with a Charter provision. This will be very clear if the Community action before the Court has the explicit objective of implementing a fundamental right guaranteed by the EU Charter.

### Illustration (ii): Articles 12 and 28 of the Charter

Freedom of association and the right to take collective action are explicitly guaranteed in Articles 12 and 28 of the Charter.[86] But Article 137(5) of the EC Treaty[87] appears explicitly to exclude the right of association and the right to strike.[88] A potential conflict with Article 137(5) therefore emerges with the EU Charter.

One argument is that there is no contradiction between the Charter and Article 137(5), since the Charter in Article 51(1) states:

> The provisions of this Charter are addressed to the institutions and bodies of the Union[89] with due regard to the principle of subsidiarity and to the Member States only when they are implementing Union law.

It is argued that by virtue of Article 137(5), freedom of association and the right to strike fall *exclusively within Member State competence*. The EU Charter affects 'Member States *only when they are implementing Union law*'. As there can be no Union law on these matters, there is no contradiction between the EU Charter and Article 137(5).[90]

However, this argument is based on the questionable assumption that there is *no* EU competence over the matters listed in Article 137(5). Article 137(5) begins:

> The provisions *of this Article* shall not apply to pay, the right of association, the right to strike or the right to impose lock-outs.

There is nothing which excludes Community competence as regards these matters being exercised under *any other Article* of the Treaty.[91] The equation of the *EU Charter* to the same legal value the Treaties, as proposed by the Treaty

---

[86] Article 12 of the EU Charter provides for 'freedom of association at all levels, in particular in … trade union … matters … which implies the right of everyone to form and to join trade unions for the protection of his or her interests'. Article 28 of the Charter provides for 'the right … in cases of conflicts of interest, to take collective action to defend their interests, including strike action'.

[87] Before the Treaty of Nice, Article 137(6).

[88] 'The provisions *of this Article* shall not apply to pay, the right of association, the right to strike or the right to impose lock-outs'.

[89] 'The provisions of this Charter are addressed to the Institutions, bodies, offices and agencies of the Union …'. As amended in the Provisional consolidated version of the draft Treaty establishing a Constitution for Europe, CIG 86/04, Brussels, 25 June 2004. See discussion above.

[90] In other words, *if* Article 137(5) provides that such action falls outside Community competence, the EU Charter does not affect the position as Article 51(2) (as 'adjusted') states: 'This Charter does not extend the field of application of Union law beyond the powers of the Union or establish any new power or task for the Union, or modify powers or tasks defined in other Parts of the Constitution'.

[91] Indeed, the Final Report of Working Group XI on Social Europe states (paragraph 28): 'Although Article 137(5) EC rules out the adoption of uniform minimum requirements on pay, it does not rule out the possibility of adopting measures under other provisions of the Treaty, even if these measures have an impact on pay. The result is that a number of Community instruments contain provisions on pay.' Examples are the EC directives on equal pay and equal treatment, which were adopted on the legal basis of Article 308 (ex 235) of the EC Treaty.

of Lisbon, would provide *another possible legal basis* for Community action. It can be argued that the Community *could* take action to achieve the rights of association and collective action in the EU Charter if these rights were not being sufficiently achieved by the Member States.[92]

In sum: *it may not be necessary to delete Article 137(5)*, as *Community action is already possible* under Treaty provisions *other* than Article 137. This possibility is reinforced by equation of the EU Charter to the Treaties.

Admittedly, this argument that the Union has the competence to act to protect fundamental rights is technically legalistic. Otherwise, however, the proclamation of fundamental values confronts an Article 137(5) which appears to deny the Union competence to implement those values. This contradiction undermines both these values and the Union. It would have been more consistent with the Convention's endorsement of the EU Charter to delete Article 137(5).[93]

The Lisbon Treaty's granting the Charter the same legal value as the Treaties is inextricably linked to the question of EU competences. The Treaties should reflect the values of the Charter. If fundamental rights are subordinated to EU competences, they are only protected to the limit of EU competences. Instead, the Treaty can be interpreted, and should be amended, to accommodate the Charter, not the Charter to fit the Treaty.[94]

### Article 52(4): The standard of 'constitutional traditions common to the Member States'

Working Group II proposed a new Article 52(4) of the Charter, which has been inserted:

> Insofar as this Charter recognises fundamental rights as they result from the constitutional traditions common to the Member States, those rights shall be interpreted in harmony with those traditions.

This 'adjustment' is said to be 'based on the wording of the current Article 6(2) TEU'. This states: 'The Union shall respect fundamental rights, as guaranteed

---

[92] According to the principle of subsidiarity defined in Article 5 EC: 'In areas which do not fall within its exclusive competence, the Community shall take action ... only if and insofar as the objectives of the proposed action cannot be sufficiently achieved by the Member States and can therefore ... be better achieved by the Community'.

[93] Alternatively, Article 137(5) should be amended. There are at least two alternative proposals: (i) add to Article 137(5): 'subject to the provision that the Community may take measures to protect rights guaranteed by Articles 12 and 28 of the EU Charter of Fundamental Rights'; (ii) a new article modelled on Article 308 (ex 235) of the Treaty: 'If action by the Community should prove necessary to [guarantee the rights provided in the EU Charter], and this Treaty has not provided the necessary powers, the [EU institutions] shall take the appropriate measures.' Member States concerned by this proposal could retain the requirement of unanimous voting on any measures proposed on matters listed in Article 137(5).

[94] But see now the decisions of the European Court of Justice in *Viking* and *Laval*, critically assessed in Chapter 21.

by the European Convention for the Protection of Human Rights and Fundamental Freedoms [ECHR] signed in Rome on 4 November 1950 and as they result from the constitutional traditions common to the Member States, as general principles of Community law.'

The 'adjustment' does not clarify, it obscures. This is because Article 52(3) of the Charter (immediately preceding the proposed amendment) refers to the ECHR (as does Article 6(2) TEU) and says 'In so far as this Charter contains rights which correspond to rights guaranteed by the [ECHR], the meaning and scope of those rights shall be *the same* as those laid down by the said Convention.' The proposed 'adjustment' does not follow this language, but says 'shall be *interpreted in harmony*' with national constitutional traditions. This change of language is potentially significant and not helpful.

It also complicates, and is unnecessary, since Article 53 of the Charter already includes a reference protecting Member States' constitutions. Again, the Working Group, and the Convention on the Future of Europe drafting the Constitutional Treaty, appeared to think they could improve on the careful compromises reached in the earlier Convention.

Prior to this amendment, the Preamble stated that the Charter 'reaffirms … the rights as they result, in particular from the constitutional traditions and international obligations common to the Member States'. Article 53 stipulated: 'Nothing in this Charter shall be interpreted as restricting or adversely affecting human rights and fundamental freedoms as recognised, in their respective fields of application, by … the Member States' constitutions.'

In addition to the reaffirmation of common constitutional traditions and protection of national constitutions from any restriction or adverse effect, what does this new paragraph contribute to interpretation of the fundamental rights in the Charter? To say they 'shall be interpreted in harmony with those traditions' is a musical metaphor presumably excluding only dissonance.

Working Group II had also emphasised a 'rule of interpretation' whereby 'rather than following a rigid approach of a "lowest common denominator", the Charter rights concerned should be interpreted in a way offering a high standard of protection which is adequate for the law of the Union …'.[95] This is now found in the 'updated' explanations:[96]

> The rule of interpretation contained in paragraph 4 has been based on the wording of Article 6(2) of the Treaty on European Union (cf. now the wording of Article 7(3) of the Constitution) and takes due account of the approach to common constitutional traditions followed by the Court of Justice …[97] Under that rule, rather than following a rigid approach of 'a lowest common denominator', the Charter rights concerned should be interpreted in a way offering a high

---

[95] Final Report of Working Group II, CONV 354/02, Section II, para. 5, p. 7.

[96] See the Provisional consolidated version of the Declarations to be annexed to the Final Act of the Intergovernmental Conference, CIG 86/04, ADD 2, Brussels, 25 June 2004, page 64.

[97] Two cases are cited: Case C44/79 and Case 155/79.

standard of protection which is adequate for the law of the Union and in harmony with the common constitutional traditions.

So the Charter's rights are not a minimum standard. Harmony does not mean accepting the lowest standards of protection. Rather it means a 'high standard of protection'.

In this connection, it is important that the 'common constitutional traditions' emphasised in the Preamble and in Article 53 are bracketed with, in the case of the Preamble, 'the European Convention for the Protection of Human Rights and Fundamental Freedoms, the Social Charters adopted by the Union and by the Council of Europe' and, in the case of Article 53, 'international law and … international agreements to which the Union or all the Member States are party, including the ECHR'. The assumption must be that those common constitutional traditions reflect, if not incorporate, the fundamental rights' standards of those international law measures. Indeed the 'updated' explanation to Article 53 states 'This provision is intended to maintain the level of protection currently afforded within their respective scope by Union law, national law and international law. Owing to its importance, mention is made of the ECHR.'[98]

## Article 52(5): Attack on social rights in particular

Another additional paragraph was added to Article 52 (Article 52(5)):

> The provisions of this Charter which contain principles may be implemented by legislative and executive acts taken by the institutions and bodies of the Union, and by acts of Member States when they are implementing Union law, in the exercise of their respective powers. They shall be judicially cognisable only in the interpretation of such acts and in the ruling on their legality.

This new limitation aims to prevent 'principles' being interpreted in future as containing elements of positive rights for individuals. This proposal was vainly resisted by some members of Working Group II, who complained that it resurrected the distinction between rights and principles which had been rejected by the drafting Convention.[99]

This is an attempt to reverse what was a central compromise in the earlier Convention which drafted the Charter: that social and economic rights should

---

[98] It may be noted here that the former explanation to Article 53 included the statement that the level of protection was not to be lower than the ECHR. This has now been transferred to the 'updated' explanation to Article 52(3).

[99] In criticising the Working Group's amendments during the Convention Plenary's debate on the Final Report of Working Group II, Olivier Duhamel, a Member of the Convention from the European Parliament, stated they were 'unnecessary and retrograde' and singled out the alleged distinction between 'rights and principles', as did Anne Van Lancker, who specifically identified the distinction between rights and principles as attempting to limit the Charter. The French government representative, Pierre Moscovici, warned that the distinction between rights and principles could limit the interpretation of those principles.

not be separated from traditional 'rights' by characterising them as 'principles' which are not justiciable positive rights.[100] That Convention decided that all rights should have the same status.[101] This was a compromise in exchange for that Convention not seeking to assert that the Charter should have legal constitutional status. Instead, that final legal status would be determined by the Member States. However, the Convention which drafted the Charter rejected the view, advocated by a number of its members, that there should be differences in the legal status of different parts of the Charter.

The language of the Charter uses the word 'rights'. The Title of Article 52 in the Charter as presented by the Convention which drafted it was 'Scope of guaranteed rights'. As amended, it reads: 'Scope and interpretation of rights and principles'. The explanation to Article 52 by the Praesidium of the Convention which drafted the Charter begins: 'The purpose of Article 52 is to set the scope of the rights …'. To this, the 'updated' explanations prepared by the Praesidium of the Convention on the Future of Europe have added: '… and principles of the Charter, and to lay down rules for their interpretation'.[102]

By reasserting the distinction between 'rights and 'principles', with the implication that the latter have lesser legal effects, Working Group II was trying to open the door to transforming some 'rights' into mere 'principles'.[103] The Working Group even admitted that it was aiming at social rights when it stated:[104]

> This is consistent both with case law of the Court of Justice and with the approach of the Member States' constitutional systems to 'principles' *particularly in the field of social law.*[105]

---

[100] The distinction between hard (justiciable) rights and soft (programmatic) rights arose in discussions over whether social and economic rights, as contrasted with civil and political rights, were appropriate for inclusion in the EU Charter. As stated above in Chapter 7, on one side were those who wanted to exclude social rights entirely, or minimise their content, or marginalise them into a separate 'programmatic' section, or make them purely declaratory, or subject them to special 'horizontal' conditions to prevent the EU acquiring any further social competences. On the other side were those who wanted to include social rights, maximise their content, grant them the same status as civil and political rights, make them justiciable or otherwise enforceable, and not limit them by reference to existing EU competences. The latter prevailed.

[101] As affirmed in a dissent in the Working Group by Elena Paccioti, a Member of the Convention from the European Parliament.

[102] See the Provisional consolidated version of the Declarations to be annexed to the Final Act of the Intergovernmental Conference, CIG 86/04, ADD 2, Brussels, 25 June 2004, page 61.

[103] Some Members of the Convention, including M. Giuliano Amato, Vice-President, and Peter Hain, representative of the UK government, put forward the argument that some parts of the Charter (again 'principles', as contrasted with 'rights) are not 'justiciable'.

[104] Section A.II.6, page 8.

[105] Cf. the statement of the representative of the French government in the Convention which drafted the Charter, M. Guy Braibant: 'en ce qui concerne les droits sociaux, nous avons retenu un compromis qui consiste a parler des droits et de principes avec un sous-compromis pour ne pas parler de principes uniquement en matière sociale et ce compromis global sur les droits et les principes a été une des conditions de l'acceptation du projet de Charte par les Britanniques'. 'La Charte des droits fondamentaux', (2001) *Droit Social*, January, 69 at p. 70.

Again, this interpretation of the amendment in Article 52(5) is presented in the 'updated' explanations to 'clarify' the Charter:[106]

> Paragraph 5 clarifies the distinction between 'rights' and 'principles' set out in the Charter. According to that distinction, subjective rights shall be respected, whereas principles shall be observed (Article 51(1)). Principles may be implemented through legislative or executive acts (adopted by the Union in accordance with its powers, and by the Member States only when they implement Union law); accordingly, they become significant for the Courts only when such acts are interpreted or reviewed. They do not however give rise to direct claims for positive action by the Union's institutions or Member States authorities. This is consistent both with case law of the Court of Justice … [107] and with the approach of the Member States' constitutional systems to 'principles' particularly in the field of social law. For illustration, examples of principles recognised in the Charter include e.g. Articles 25, 26 and 37. In some cases, an Article of the Charter may contain both elements of a right and of a principle, e.g. Articles 23, 33 and 34.

To single out social rights as principles eligible for weaker protection is not acceptable. It characterises social and labour rights as 'second class' rights. It threatens many social and labour rights which would be at the heart of a system of industrial relations at EU level and thereby inhibits developments promoting such an EU system.

However, the 'adjustment' may not have the effect claimed for it. First, it does not apply to most of the provisions regarding employment and industrial relations in Chapter IV: 'Solidarity', of the Charter.[108] Secondly, it seems that the field of social law as understood by the 'updated' explanations is far from coherent. The illustrations given as 'examples for principles recognised in the Charter' include Article 25 entitled 'The rights of the elderly', and Article 26, which begins: 'The Union recognises and respects the right of persons with disabilities …'. In many factual situations, both are easily capable of being translated into positive and justiciable rights. The other example given is clearly remote from established rights in labour law: Article 37: 'Environmental protection', which refers to 'the principle of sustainable development'.

Illustrations said to contain 'both elements of a right and of a principle' were Article 23: 'Equality between men and women', perhaps the field with the most extensive and established positive rights in EU social and labour law; Article 33: 'Family and professional life', which includes the 'right to protection from

---

[106] See Provisional consolidated version of the Declarations to be annexed to the Final Act of the Intergovernmental Conference, CIG 86/04, ADD 2, Brussels, 25 June 2004, pages 64–65.

[107] Two cases are cited: Case T-13/99, Case C-265/85.

[108] Article 27: 'Workers' right to information and consultation within the undertaking', Article 28: 'Right of collective bargaining and action', Article 29: 'Right of access to placement services', Article 30: 'Right to protection against unjustified dismissal', Article 31: 'Right to working conditions which respect his or her health, safety and dignity'.

dismissal for a reason connected with maternity'; and Article 34: 'Social security and social assistance', which refers to 'entitlements' and 'rights'.

The alleged distinction between rights and principles is far from clear. The 'updated' explanations do nothing to clarify it. They only add to the confusion surrounding the distinction. This distinction was rejected by the Convention which drafted the Charter. The attempt by the Praesidium of the Convention on the Future of Europe in its 'updated' explanations to revive the distinction between rights and principles, to be used against rights 'particularly in the field of social law', is unlikely to recommend itself to the European Court of Justice, least of all in the field of labour law.

### Article 52(6): National laws and practices

Lastly, another additional paragraph was added to Article 52 (Article 52(6)):[109]

> Full account shall be taken of national laws and practices as specified in the Charter.

There is little doubt that social rights were the target of this amendment. The references in the Charter to 'national laws and practices' are concentrated in Chapter IV, 'Solidarity', including most fundamental social rights. Working Group II's Final Report merely observes that 'it seems appropriate to the Group to include a clause in the Charter recalling [the references to national laws and practices]'.

The exact legal consequences of the references to national laws and practices are far from clear. The 'updated' explanations shed little light by commenting: 'Paragraph 6 refers to the various Articles in the Charter which, in the spirit of subsidiarity, make reference to national laws and practices.' The Convention which drafted the Charter did not regard this added paragraph as an appropriate horizontal clause and the repeated mantra of the Convention and its Working Group II was that no substantive changes were to be made to the Charter; the 'adjustments' are only 'clarifications'.

## The Final Report of Working Group XI on Social Europe

The mandate of the Convention's Working Group XI on Social Europe included a number of questions. The first three listed in the mandate concerned the European Union's social values, objectives and competences. Three others were concerned with processes of social policy-making: the open method of coordination, legislation and the role of the social partners. Finally, the question was raised of the relationship between coordination of economic and social

---

[109] Now in Part II (Article II-112(6)) of the proposed Treaty Establishing a Constitution for the Union, which reproduces Article 52(6) as follows: 'Full account shall be taken of national laws and practices as specified in this Charter'.

policies. Analysis of the Final Report of Working Group XI on Social Europe[110] reveals a number of indicators of the path towards the European social model.

### Basic values

Working Group XI explicitly noted the consensus on integration of the EU Charter into the Treaty and 'that the Charter should not be reopened'.[111] But it also 'noted that the Charter and Article 2 [of the draft Constitutional Treaty of 28 October 2002[112]] have *different* scopes'. This raises the question of the legal effect of the Charter if it is acknowledged that its values *differ* (in scope) from those in Article 2 of the future Constitutional Treaty.[113]

Nonetheless, the Draft of Articles 1 to 16 of the Constitutional Treaty produced by the Convention's Praesidium on 6 February 2003[114] did not include the EU Charter among 'The Union's values' in its draft Article 2.[115] There is thereby opened a dangerous distinction between the Constitution's 'Fundamental rights' in proposed Article I-7[116] and in the Lisbon Treaty's equivalent provision,[117] and proposed Article I-2's 'respect for human rights', on which '[t]he Union is founded'.[118]

---

[110] CONV 516/1/03 – Rev 1, Brussels, 4 February 2003.     [111] Paragraph 8.

[112] CONV 369/02, 28 October 2002, Article 2: 'This article sets out the values of the Union: human dignity, fundamental rights, democracy, the rule of law, tolerance, respect for obligations and for international law.' Article 2 was destined for the EU Charter, depending on the proceedings of Working Group II. See Part II of the draft Treaty Establishing a Constitution for the Union, CONV 850/03, Brussels, 18 July 2003, Article 2.

[113] In Part II of the draft Treaty Establishing a Constitution for the Union, CONV 850/03, Brussels, 18 July 2003, Article 2 reads: 'The Union is founded on the values of respect for human dignity, liberty, democracy, equality, the rule of law and respect for human rights. These values are common to the Member States in a society of pluralism, tolerance, solidarity and non-discrimination.' In the final text of the Constitutional Treaty, Part I, Article I-2 reads: 'The Union is founded on the values of respect for human dignity, freedom, democracy, equality, the rule of law and respect for human rights, including the rights of persons belonging to minorities. These values are common to the Member States in a society in which pluralism, non-discrimination, tolerance, justice, solidarity and equality between women and men prevail'. This text is proposed to be added as new Article 1a EC by the Treaty of Lisbon.

[114] CONV 528/03.

[115] Nor is the Charter mentioned among the Union's values in Article I-2 of the final text of the proposed Constitutional Treaty.

[116] Article I-7 ('Fundamental rights') of the proposed Constitutional Treaty begins: 'The Union shall recognise the rights, freedoms and principles set out in the Charter of Fundamental Rights which constitutes Part II of the Constitution'.

[117] Article I-9(1) of the proposed Constitutional Treaty: 'The Union shall recognise the rights, freedoms and principles set out in the Charter of Fundamental Rights which constitutes Part II.' The new Article 6 EC TEU proposed by the Treaty of Lisbon reads: 'The Union recognises the rights, freedoms and principles set out in the Charter of Fundamental Rights of the European Union of 7 December 2000, as adapted at Strasbourg, on 12 December 2007, which shall have the same legal value as the Treaties'.

[118] Perhaps more alarming still was the apparent precedence of the guarantee accorded in Article I-4: 'Fundamental freedoms and non-discrimination' (on grounds of nationality only) to '[f]ree movement of persons, goods, services and capital, and freedom of establishment'.

## Competences: application to Member States

Some Member States, including the UK, have attempted to deny that Member States have any obligation to comply with the EU Charter.[119] The EU Charter was proclaimed by the EU institutions, and its Preamble ends by saying: 'The Union therefore recognises the rights, freedoms and principles set out hereafter.' But this is not the same as being addressed exclusively to the EU. On the contrary, there is the explicit reference in Article 51(1) of the Charter, which states:

> The provisions of this Charter are addressed to the Institutions, bodies and agencies of the Union with due regard for the principle of subsidiarity and to the Member States only when they are implementing Union law.

The word 'implementing' could be interpreted as confining the Charter's impact to specific implementing measures of national law. The European Court takes a wider view, that EU law applies to all national laws falling within the scope of EU competence, whether or not there are specific implementing measures.[120]

With respect to some Charter rights, there is a question as to whether they fall within EU competences. But this argument allows for at least two interpretations. First, if the Charter is only addressed to the EU institutions, and the EU has no competence, then these Charter rights are completely meaningless. Can this have been intended? Alternatively, these rights (and the others) in the Charter are within EU competence and also affect Member States.[121]

---

[119] For the continuing resistance of some Member States to the inclusion of the EU Charter in the Constitutional Treaty, see the letter dated 12 May 2003 from Peter Hain, a Member of the Convention representing the UK government, replying to a letter from the President, Giscard d'Estaing, concerning the Charter: 'Your letter suggests that it is now settled that the Charter should form Part II of the Constitution. As you know, our Government has always held the view that we could make no commitment to the incorporation of the Charter until we had sight of the whole package outlined in the recommendations of the Working Group … The challenge is to find ways to give our citizens legal certainty and clarity in relation to the Charter's ambiguous or conflicting texts.' CONV 736/03 of 13 May 2003. The UK resistance has culminated in the Protocol attached to the Lisbon Treaty which purposes to exclude the application of the Charter to the UK and Poland.

[120] In its Final Report, the Convention's Working Group II on the EU Charter confirmed that 'it is in line with the principle of subsidiarity that the scope of application of the Charter is limited, in accordance with its Article 51(1), to the institutions and bodies of the Union, and to Member States *only* when they are implementing Union law'. To this is attached a footnote which states: 'It should be noted that, upon possible incorporation of the Charter into the Treaty, the current wording of Article 46(d) TEU would *have to be brought in line with* existing case law and Article 51 of the Charter on the (limited) application of fundamental rights to acts of Member States.' Article 46(d) TEU asserts that the powers of the European Court as regards provisions of the EC Treaty (and other Treaties) shall apply, as regards Article 6(2) TEU (fundamental rights) *only* 'with regard to action of the institutions'. Whatever the debate over exactly how limited it is, it appears that the Charter is intended to apply to the Member States. Section II.2, page 5. But see now the Lisbon Treaty's revision of Article 6 TEU.

[121] Indeed, some Charter rights seem to be specifically targeted on Member States. For example, Chapter VI, Justice: Article 47 refers to remedies and fair trial as regards 'rights and freedoms guaranteed by the law of the Union'. But this must include claims based on Union law before

Of particular interest are the explicit guarantees of freedom of association and the right to take collective action in Articles 12 and 28 of the Charter. Though Article 137(5) of the EC Treaty appears explicitly to exclude the right of association and the right to strike, it was argued that this does not mean there is no EU competence over the matters listed in Article 137(5).[122]

The Final Report of the Convention's Working Group II went further in a statement which implied that the Charter *does* bind Member States:[123]

> The fact that certain Charter rights concern areas in which the Union has little or no competence to act is not in contradiction to it, given that, although the Union's *competences* are limited, it must *respect* all fundamental rights wherever it acts and therefore avoid indirect interference also with such fundamental rights on which it would have the competence to legislate.

When Member States act *within* the sphere of EU competence, they must comply with, or at least respect, the fundamental rights in the Charter. The implication that even where there may be *no* EU competence, the EU must *still* respect fundamental rights also arguably affects Member States. Even when Member States act outside EU competence, they too must respect fundamental rights.[124]

Social Europe, as manifest in the values of the EU Charter, potentially stretches, if not goes beyond, a narrow view of the present competences of the EU. The paradox is clear: fundamental/universal rights are confronted with limited EC/EU competences. The central problem is the clash between limited EU competences and the EU Charter's fundamental rights. If fundamental rights are subject to competences, it undermines the concept of fundamental rights. Values elevated by the EU to the status of fundamental rights are only protected to the limit of EU competences. The EU would have to ignore fundamental rights where they come up against the limitations of its competences. However, a potential tension exists between EU competences to achieve Social Europe and the alleged democratic deficit of the EU. Some, if not most Member States are reluctant to grant to the EC institutions the new powers and tasks of implementing Social Europe.

Sadly, the record of the United Kingdom in holding back progress towards Social Europe is second to none, and was amply manifested in the Convention on the Future of Europe. The earnest appeal of the UK government's

---

national courts. Article 48: the presumption of innocence and right of defence does not limit itself to rights and freedoms of the EU. Article 49 excludes liability where there is no criminal offence under national law. Article 50 prohibits 'double jeopardy'. If a Member State repealed this last rule, arguably this could be challenged as a violation of the Charter.

[122] Article 137(5) begins: 'The provisions *of this Article* shall not apply to pay, the right of association, the right to strike or the right to impose lock-outs.' There is nothing which excludes Community competence as regards these matters being exercised under *any other Article* of the Treaty. Hence, the Community *could* take action to achieve the rights of association and collective action in the EU Charter if these rights were not being sufficiently achieved by the Member States.

[123] Section II.2, page 5.

[124] This appears to be the view taken by the European Court in *Viking*, see Chapter 21.

representative, Peter Hain, to the Convention for fairness at work and social justice[125] might carry more conviction were the Blair government's record in obstructing and then failing to adequately implement EC labour legislation were not so abysmal. His claim of wanting 'to strengthen social dialogue and improve partnership between employer and employee representatives' is breathtaking when, carrying on where the previous Conservative government left off, the Blair government played a central role in obstructing the information and consultation directive. This record belies the claimed support for a 'new social agenda' and the disingenuous 'yes to employment rights' of the UK government's representative.[126]

In the Convention, the UK government evidently hoped, once again, to delay, obstruct, and claw back any ambitions the EU has to progress towards a European social model of improved working conditions and dialogue between management and labour, which are declared to be its objectives in Article 136 of the Treaty of Rome. The UK, having lost the battle to exclude from the list of fundamental human rights those of workers to information and consultation, to collective bargaining and collective action, including strike action,[127] there was little surprise at the Blair government's next shameless attempt to downgrade these rights as mere 'principles' unworthy of judicial protection.[128] Not everybody in the Convention on the Future of Europe was seduced by Mr Hain's siren song of a Social Europe with lofty values and objectives, but, crucially, without basic and enforceable labour standards.[129]

---

[125] Peter Hain, 'The Way to Get Europe to Work', *Financial Times*, 29 January 2003.

[126] Once again belied by the UK government's successful mobilisation of a minority of Member States sufficient to block the draft directive granting rights to equal treatment of agency workers. See again, the letter dated 12 May 2003 from Peter Hain challenging the legal status of the EU Charter (footnote 119 above; CONV 736/03 of 13 May 2003). In that letter, he appears to indicate support from other members of the Convention by referring to an earlier contribution (CONV 659/03 of 14 April 2003). This is misleading because that contribution merely raised the question of the method of incorporating the Charter into the Treaty, not the principle of incorporation. The UK's fall-back position was doubtless already being prepared: a specific provision limiting the application of the Charter to the EU institutions.

[127] Now in Articles 27 and 28 of the EU Charter of Fundamental Rights.

[128] Similarly, the cynicism of Mr Hain's appeal in his article in the *Financial Times* for 'diversity and flexibility', 'with 10 countries joining the EU next year' is not lost on the workers of those countries, for whom it means lower wages, poorer working conditions, weakened trade unions and disregard for health and safety standards. Characterising efforts to establish basic minimum labour standards across Europe as a 'crude policy of harmonisation', or 'intrusive, detailed rules' rings hollow against the UK's domestic record in legislating watered-down employment rights.

[129] The UK government's objective of full employment in a high-skill economy is admirable, and shared by other Member States. Its espousal is undermined by the government's continuing opposition to European labour standards, which other Member States do not see as incompatible with this economic and employment policy objective. Getting Europe to work is only half the story and rendered less plausible when accompanied by active opposition to basic employment rights. Far from suffering 'enormous damage', working people in Britain have benefited greatly from European employment rights.

## The Treaty Establishing a Constitution for Europe

A Draft Treaty Establishing a Constitution for Europe was presented by the Convention on the Future of Europe on 18 July 2003.[130] The Intergovernmental Conference of the EU Member States approved an amended draft on 18 June 2004.[131] Up to now, the main emphasis has been on Part II, which 'constitutionalised' the EU Charter of Fundamental Rights. This remains central following the demise of the Constitutional Treaty. The Treaty of Lisbon retains the Charter. The UKI's opt-out is of doubtful effect. It is important, therefore, to understand the significance of the Charter.

Since 1979, for the past thirty years, British governments have provided the most consistent and effective opposition to the extension of rights for workers and trade unions in the EU's legal framework. Despite this, it is important to realise that UK governments have not completely succeeded in preventing the EU from extending rights to workers and trade unions.

Despite the rearguard battles of UK governments since 1979, the EU has developed a 'social model'. One fundamental quality underpins the value of the EU Charter as far as the EU, and the UK in particular, is concerned. It fixes near enough in stone fundamental social rights of labour.

This has been an overlooked quality of EU labour regulation. However much the UK (but also other Member States) fought to resist EU labour standards, once these were adopted it was almost impossible to repeal them or regress from them. Now the EU Charter makes these and other gains as near permanent as can be.

Once (and if) the Treaty of Lisbon is ratified, the UK and the other Member States will be committed to a 'social model' which was the achievement of generations of struggle.[132] Just as in the UK no future Conservative (or New Labour government) can take away labour rights in directives, the EU Charter

---

[130] Draft Treaty Establishing a Constitution for Europe, CONV 850/03, Brussels, 18 July 2003.

[131] Provisional consolidated version of the draft Treaty Establishing a Constitution for Europe, CIG 86/04, Brussels, 25 June 2004. See final text of the Treaty Establishing a Constitution for Europe adopted by the Member States in the Intergovernmental Conference meeting in Brussels 17–18 June 2004, OJ C310/1 of 16 December 2004.

[132] In a contribution to a special supplement of the newspaper, *Libération*, just prior to the French referendum of 29 May 2005, I wrote: 'few doubt that the impact on the UK, and other Member States where the gap between the social rights in the Charter and national law is greatest, is likely to be most substantial. So it may be that the British people need the Charter most. But other Member States, including France, will also benefit. The UK, under the governments of Mrs Thatcher and her successors, not excluding the New Labour government, was the most recalcitrant opponent in the struggle to achieve an EU social model. The EU Charter will be one means of dragging the UK, kicking and screaming no doubt, away from its neo-liberal labour market policies and into an embrace with the European social model of protection of workers. In this way, the Constitution offers some hope of removing a major obstacle to social progress at EU level.'

locks the UK and other Member State governments into a European social model. It makes it less easy to give in to the pressures of globalisation and some politicians' inclinations towards liberalisation of markets at the expense of workers and others. The EU Charter formally binds EU Member States to fundamental social rights and trade union freedoms.

# Section II

# The structure of European labour law

**Part III**

# Labour law and the European Social Model

# Chapter 8

# The institutional architecture of the European social model

The theme of the institutional architecture of the European social model[1] brings together a number of issues of central importance to the twenty-seven Member States of the European Union and the three associated states of the European Economic Area, of immediate concern to the candidate countries seeking membership of the EU, but also potentially of interest to the rest of the world.[2] The interest for others, not least the USA, arises because of the clear contrast the American experience presents when compared with the European social model, and in particular, its institutional architecture. Its importance for the rest of the world arises precisely because, while there may be no or little military competition in a uni-polar world dominated by the USA, the economic[3] and political stature of the EU makes the European economic and social model the subject of considerable attention elsewhere. It is not suggested that the institutional architecture of the European social model can or should be exported, but certain of its features provide a basis for reflection, if not emulation in other parts of the world.

This chapter begins with some reflections on the 'constitutional moment' in the EU and its implications for the European social model, explores certain structural qualities of the European social model, in contrast with American experience and outlines the principal features of the emerging institutional architecture of the European social model.

---

[1] This chapter is based on the Phleger Lecture delivered on 8 May 2002 while I was Phleger Visiting Professor at Stanford Law School, California. A shortened and revised version of the lecture was presented at the W.G. Hart workshop at the Institute of Advanced Legal Studies in London, 25–27 June 2003, published as 'The Institutional Architecture of the European Social Model' in T. Tridimas and P. Nebbia (eds.), *European Union Law for the Twenty-First Century: Rethinking the New Legal Order*. Vol. II, Oxford: Hart, 2004, pp. 311–31.

[2] For example, the Japanese interest in the European social model. See the three-page headlined dossier in *Le Monde Economie* of 28 May 2002, entitled 'Le Japon en crise s'intéresse au modèle social européen'.

[3] The largest single unit in the world economy, the EU-15 in 1997, before the enlargement of May 2004, had a nominal GNP of about $6 trillion, compared with $5 trillion for the USA and $3 trillion for Japan and a population approaching that of the USA and Japan combined.

## The 'constitutional' context of the European social model

### The EU social model and fundamental rights of employment and industrial relations

The Commission's 1994 White Paper on Social Policy described a 'European Social Model' in terms of values which 'include democracy and individual rights, free collective bargaining, the market economy, equality of opportunity for all and social welfare and solidarity'.[4] The model is based on the conviction that economic and social progress are inseparable: 'Competitiveness and solidarity have both been taken into account in building a successful Europe for the future.'

The EU social model of employment and industrial relations is exemplified by the EU Charter of Fundamental Rights. The Charter breaks new ground by including in a single list of fundamental rights not only traditional civil and political rights, but also a long list of social and economic rights.[5] The inclusion of social and economic rights in the EU Charter took on greater significance due to the proposal of the Convention on the Future of Europe to incorporate the EU Charter as Part II of the Constitutional Treaty of the European Union. It survived the demise of the Constitutional Treaty and is proposed to have the same legal status as the Treaties in the Reform Treaty of Lisbon. Its current actual legal effects, and the potential future effects of attributing to it a formal legal status will have consequences in a constitutional context; specifically, its implications for the concept of EU citizenship.

### The debate over (and meaning of) EU 'social' citizenship

#### 'EU citizenship'

Article 8 of the Maastricht Treaty on European Union, as amended by the Amsterdam Treaty, now in Article 17 of the EC Treaty, created a new status of EU citizenship.[6] As currently stated in the EC Treaty, the rights of EU citizens

---

[4] COM(94) 333, paragraph 3.

[5] Of particular interest to employment and industrial relations are provisions on protection of personal data (Article 8), freedom of association (Article 12), freedom to choose an occupation and right to engage in work (Article 15), non-discrimination (Article 21), equality between men and women (Article 23), workers' right to information and consultation within the undertaking (Article 27), right of collective bargaining and collective action (Article 28), protection in the event of unjustified dismissal (Article 30), fair and just working conditions (Article 31), prohibition of child labour and protection of young people at work (Article 32) and reconciliation of family and professional life (Article 33). See B. Bercusson (ed.), *European Labour Law and the EU Charter*, Baden-Baden: Nomos, 2006. Summary version in English, 102 pp., Brussels: European Trade Union Institute, 2002; also available in Dutch, French, German, Greek, Italian, Spanish and Swedish.

[6] '1. Citizenship of the Union is hereby established. Every person holding the nationality of a Member State shall be a citizen of the Union. Citizenship of the Union shall complement and not replace national citizenship. 2. Citizens of the Union shall enjoy the rights conferred by this Treaty and shall be subject to the duties imposed thereby'.

are meagre.[7] The current poverty of EU citizenship is highlighted by contrast with citizenship of Member States. This raises the delicate question of the relationship of EU citizenship to Member State nationality, inextricably entwined by virtue of Article 17. This is both a technical legal question (who determines nationality) and a substantive issue: whether, and if so how, does EU citizenship add to the content of national citizenship?[8]

## 'Social' citizenship

The second question raises sensitive and problematic issues. Does citizenship have meaning in EU law going beyond nationality of a Member State, a substantive content separate from nationality? The issue has been explored by Norbert Reich, who puts forward two respects in which EU citizenship could go beyond nationality.[9] First, the EU confers rights on Member State nationals under EC law which go beyond what nationals obtain under Member State law. With reference to this chapter's concern with a European social model, much depends on whether these extra rights may be characterised as 'citizenship' rights, in particular, when they go beyond the traditional civil and political content to embrace a wider set of 'social' rights.

Secondly, the EU confers rights on individuals irrespective of Member State nationality. Individuals possess specifically EU rights when they are EU residents, workers, consumers and so on. National citizenship is not the criterion for entitlement to 'EU citizenship' rights of a worker to equal pay (Article 141), to rights as a consumer to information, education and organisation (Article 153(1)), to a resident's rights to petition the European Parliament (Article 194), of any person's right of access to EU documents (Article 255), or to protection of personal data (Article 286). Taken together, EU citizenship thereby includes (social) rights wider than rights attached to Member State nationality; the EU grants these rights not only to Member State citizens, but also to third country nationals; and, therefore, EU 'citizenship' means something different from Member State nationality.

In his discussion of the concept of EU citizenship, Reich addresses an issue which has aroused considerable debate: the difficulties the EU encounters in attributing 'citizenship' to individuals which contrasts with traditional 'nationality' based concepts of citizenship. In brief, the problem stems from the lack of

---

[7] Free movement (Article 18), the right to vote and stand as a candidate in municipal elections and for the European Parliament (Article 19), to diplomatic and consular protection (Article 20) and to petition and protection by the Ombudsman of the European Parliament (Article 21).

[8] The technical question is the easier, and can be answered unequivocally: Article 17 and its history imply that EU citizenship is understood as a mere corollary of Member State nationality. Citizenship is not the subject of autonomous definition by EU law. The EU cannot define, establish, revoke or refuse to recognise nationality established by a Member State.

[9] N. Reich, 'Union Citizenship – Metaphor or Source of Rights?' (2001) 7 *European Law Journal* 4–23.

perception of the EU as a nation, in the alleged absence of a commonality of history, polity, language or law.

Joseph Weiler has argued that a nationality-based concept of citizenship contradicts the supranational essence of the EU: the *telos* of European integration as an ever closer union of 'peoples', not the creating of one 'people' (*demos*). This entails a decoupling of nationality and citizenship.[10] For Reich, national citizenship becomes a residual category, a matter of historical contingency. A preferable understanding of EU citizenship would look to residence as a central criterion for EU citizenship rights.

As with much else, the question of 'what' can best, or only be answered by asking why and how. Why is there a search for 'EU citizenship'? Weiler suggests the reasons for the striving to create a concept of EU citizenship lie in the exhaustion of the original EU project: peace and prosperity produce the paradox of success. An anxiety related to manifestations of modernity similar to the *fin-de-siècle* atmosphere conducive to the rise of fascism as the early twentieth-century response, currently aggravated by the post-modern attack on truth, reality and coherence, leads to a search for meaning. The nation provides the comfort of belonging, a shield against existential aloneness. To this is contrasted the banal offer of bread and circuses by the EU as a market culture, as if the EU is a brand, an image, a product to whom the individual is a consumer, not a citizen.

Weiler argues for decoupling nationality and citizenship, but then recoupling them so that the state becomes merely an instrument, the organisational framework for the nation. The EU is to control state excesses but preserve nations: the essence of the supranational vision. By separating nation and state, differences expressed in other than state forms, national cultures, will be protected, not national states. This allows for maintaining the European *telos* without looking for a European *demos*, the decoupling of nationality and citizenship allows for co-citizenship of individuals who do not share same nationality. Or, another way of putting it, multiple *demoi*: Member State nationals and EU citizens.[11] He hints at an EU specificity rooted in mutual social responsibility embodied in the welfare state and human rights. There is a complex commitment to diversity, coupled with acceptance that a larger (European) *demos* has the right to make decisions binding all, but conditional on a commitment to maintaining diversity. In a phrase, substantive values of multicultural diversity, a welfare state and human rights are coupled with decisional procedures in a European political framework.

Reich also hints at developments which could legitimise EU institutions through a political and social concept of citizenship, contingent on evolution

[10] J.H.H. Weiler, 'To Be A European Citizen: Eros and Civilization', Chapter 10 in *The Constitution of Europe*, Cambridge: Cambridge University Press, 1999, pp. 324–57.

[11] See D. Grimm, 'Does Europe Need a Constitution?' (1995) 1 *European Law Journal* 282–302; J. Habermas, 'Remarks on Dieter Grimm's "Does Europe Need a Constitution?"' (1995) 1 *European Law Journal* 303–7.

of the EU. The question posed by Reich is that, if not 'nationality'-based, how would one characterise EU citizenship: as 'economic' (*bourgeois*), participatory (*citoyen*), or some other? What would it mean for EU citizenship to change from the 'market citizen' (*bourgeois*) to citizenship without an exclusively economic role?[12]

The concept of 'European social citizenship' was the basis of a project organised by a group of academics from a number of Member States who in 1996, and again in 2000, put forward a Manifesto which aimed to construct EU citizenship on the basis of the concept of 'social citizenship'.[13] As developed by T.H. Marshall, the levels of citizenship rights begin with civil rights (legal equality), political rights (to participate in the exercise of national sovereignty) and evolve towards social rights (manifested in welfare state solidarity).[14] The Manifesto of 1996 elaborated a concept of European 'social' citizenship as the defining *telos* of the European project, and the meaning of EU citizenship.[15]

Citizenship is not just about voting a few times a year, worshipping if you happen to believe, marrying and founding a family if you so choose. A central aspect of EU social citizenship is about that very large part of almost everybody's life: working. The inclusion in the EU Charter of social and economic rights related to working life confirmed that these are to be considered fundamental to the EU social model, what it means to be an EU citizen.

## Enlargement, citizenship and the institutional architecture

The theme of this chapter is the institutional architecture of the European social model. The analysis is premised on the dominance of the model prevailing in

---

[12] See M. Everson, 'The Legacy of the Market Citizen', in J. Shaw and G. More (eds.), *New Legal Dynamics of European Union*, Oxford: Clarendon Press, 1995, pp. 73–90.

[13] B. Bercusson, S. Deakin, P. Koistinen, Y. Kravaritou, U. Mückenberger, A. Supiot and B. Veneziani, *A Manifesto for Social Europe*, Brussels: European Trade Union Institute, 1996; U. Mückenberger (ed.), *Manifesto Social Europe*, Brussels: ETUI, 2001. See also B. Bercusson *et al.*, 'A Manifesto for Social Europe', (1997) 3 *European Law Journal* 189–205.

[14] T.H. Marshall, *Citizenship, Social Class and Other Essays*, Cambridge: Cambridge University Press, 1950.

[15] The search for such a European *telos* has been formulated in analogous terms of a challenge to the legitimacy of the EU due to a 'redistributional deficit'. Miguel Poiares Maduro highlights the redistributive consequences of EU policies of economic integration based on efficiency enhancing and wealth maximisation. Miguel Poiares Maduro, 'Where to Look for Legitimacy', unpublished paper delivered to an ARENA conference on Democracy and European Governance, Oslo, 4–5 March 2002. The distribution is not equal; the richer and more competitive gain more. Cf. the USA, 'Between 1982 and 2004, median earnings of fully employed men grew by only 2.7 percent, which is about as close to stagnation as one can get for a twenty-two year period.' A. Hacker, 'The Rich and Everyone Else', *New York Review of Books*, 53, No. 9, 25 May 2006, pp. 16–19. The assumptions regarding redistribution at the time of adhesion to the EU may be relied upon so long as decision-making based on unanimity legitimises the results: all would have to agree to the decision. Increasing economic integration, coupled with expansion of the EU, both in terms of members and competences, and changes in institutional decision-making, may result in redistributional effects which are no longer acceptable. The EU is endangered unless mechanisms can be developed to legitimise the redistributional impact.

the fifteen EU Member States prior to the latest enlargements of 2004 and 2007 to include twelve new Member States.

The widening of membership to the EU has often had an impact on employment and industrial relations in the EU. The six founding nations (Belgium, France, Germany, Italy, Luxembourg and the Netherlands) which established the EEC under the Treaty of Rome in 1957 shared a common West European continental tradition of employment and industrial relations. The UK, Ireland and Denmark, which joined in 1973, had different experiences marked by Anglo-Saxon and Nordic traditions. Their accession coincided with a decisive change in the EU's social policy with the adoption of the Social Action Programme in 1974.

The enlargement to include Greece (1981) and Portugal and Spain (1986) brought into the EU three countries which had only recently emerged from regimes of dictatorship, and brought with them new constitutional experiences evincing a sensitivity to fundamental social rights, evident in the 1989 Community Charter of the Fundamental Social Rights of Workers.

The accession of Austria, Finland and Sweden in 1995 brought into the Union three countries with relatively high levels of trade union membership, traditions of social partnership and active labour market policies, and the Treaty of Amsterdam of 1997 included a new Title on Employment.

The accession of ten new Member States in 2004, and a further two in 2007, as with previous enlargements, will have an impact on labour markets, employment and industrial relations in the EU. A number of Member States have limited the free movement of workers from the new acceding countries for a transitional period.[16] There has been a trend towards relocation of investment, with accompanying jobs, towards accession countries with relatively low labour costs and a skilled labour force. The development of industrial relations systems based on collective bargaining and social dialogue has followed a slow and painful path with the emergence of functioning market economies.[17]

The evolution of a concept of 'social citizenship' will apply to the nationals of the new Member States as to nationals of all the preceding fifteen Member States. However, the theme of this chapter is less to elaborate the concept of EU social citizenship as a fundamental element of the European social model. Rather it is intended to explore the institutional architecture of such a model.

---

[16] For details on how these restrictions have worked in practice during their first phase from 1 May 2004 to 30 April 2006, see 'Commission Issues First Report on Worker Mobility', *European Industrial Relations Review* No. 386, March 2006, pp. 34–6.

[17] The industrial relations systems of the accession countries will need to acclimatise to emerging patterns of industrial relations in the EU, in particular, such general characteristics in accession countries as heterogeneous and fragmented trade unions and employers' organisation, limited scope of collective bargaining, with collective bargaining systems more decentralised and operating mainly at company level, underdeveloped sectoral level bargaining, low levels of collective bargaining coverage and meagre content of collective agreements, the widespread absence of works councils, the absence of social dialogue in the public sector, and an asymmetrical tripartitism, with strong governments confronting weaker social partners.

What are the implications of this latest enlargement for the institutional architecture? One reflection was as follows:[18]

> The European social model is a Western European phenomenon. The Central and Eastern European countries (CEECs) have very different histories ... The new order, which varies from country to country, is characterised by social policy improvisation, weak and divided employer and union organizations, and an absence of the kinds of social forces that built the European social model in the West. The CEECs live in a different era from the one that fostered the building of the European model of society ... It is not surprising that social policy has been much less important than market, monetary, legal and administrative matters in the accession dealings around the *acquis communautaire* ... [However] the CEECs are by and large small economic places that will be held to high standards of EU behaviour in the near future. There are larger concerns about population migration and CEEC political futures than about social policies.

While the new accession states may influence specific social and labour policy choices in the EU, they are unlikely to undermine the structural foundations of the European social model presented here.

The focus of this enquiry is what I regard as a, if not the defining feature of the institutional architecture of the European social model: the roles of trade unions and employers' organisations.

## Defining features of the European social model

### Trade union density

The starting point is the disconcertingly variable fact of trade union density: union membership as a proportion of the working population in the EU Member States. The author of one study has pointed out:[19]

> It is not difficult to be impressed by the differences in unionization levels across countries. **The range of variation in unionization levels among advanced industrial societies is larger than in any other social-economic or political indicator**.

Visser's analysis of patterns of development in unionisation in ten Western European countries, eight of them EU Member States,[20] demonstrated certain similarities: a general surge in unionisation around and during the First World War, membership losses following the peak in 1919–20 and even more in the course of the economic depression after 1929, another increase during and after

[18] A. Martin and G. Ross, 'Conclusions', in A. Martin and G. Ross (eds.), *Euros and Europeans: Monetary Integration and the European Model of Society*, Cambridge: Cambridge University Press, 2004, p. 309 at pp. 327–8.

[19] Jelle Visser, *In Search of Inclusive Unionism*, Bulletin of Comparative Labour Relations, No. 18, Deventer: Kluwer, 1990, at p. 36 (the author's emphasis).

[20] Austria, Denmark, France, Germany, Italy, the Netherlands, Sweden, the United Kingdom, and also Norway and Switzerland.

**Table 8.1** Gross trade union density rates (including retired workers)

| Year | AU | DE | FR | GE | IT | NE | SW | UK |
|------|------|-------|-------|------|------|------|------|------|
| 1913 | ... | 23.1 | ... | 21.5 | ... | 16.9 | 9.4 | 23.1 |
| 1920 | 51.0 | 48.2 | 7.2 | 52.5 | ... | 35.8 | 27.7 | 45.2 |
| 1930 | 37.6 | 36.9 | 7.2 | 32.7 | ... | 30.1 | 36.1 | 25.4 |
| 1939 | ... | 46.6 | 23.6a | ... | ... | 32.5 | 53.7 | 31.6 |
| 1950 | 62.3 | 58.1 | 20.5b | 34.7 | 50.3 | 43.0 | 67.7 | 44.1 |
| 1960 | 63.4 | 63.1 | 19.3c | 38.3 | 35.2 | 41.8 | 73.0 | 44.2 |
| 1970 | 62.1 | 64.4 | 21.3 | 37.6 | 38.3 | 39.7 | 73.2 | 48.5 |
| 1980 | 58.4 | 79.8 | 17.2 | 41.0 | 54.4 | 35.3 | 88.0 | 52.9 |
| 1985 | 57.9 | 82.2d | 14.5 | 39.3 | 51.0 | 28.6 | 91.5 | 44.2 |

a = 1936; b = 1954; c = 1962; d = 1984

the Second World War which this time, for most countries, is not followed by massive decline, with density rates remaining fairly level for the 1950s and 1960s, another upward trend at the end of the 1960s lasting until the latter 1970s and a decline beginning in the early 1980s. Table 8.1 illustrates this pattern.[21]

The downward trend noted by Visser in the 1980s continued towards the end of the century. Even where membership losses slowed or were reversed, density was still falling due to increasing employment levels. Table 8.2 sets out union density in the EU Member States in 2000.[22]

The general downward trend produces a pattern: a group of four countries with a high union membership density (ranging from 69.2 per cent in Belgium up through the Nordic countries to 87.5 per cent in Denmark. A second larger group of countries has a medium union density hovering around the 29–40 per cent level, and including the three big economies of Italy (35.4 per cent), Germany (29.7 per cent) and the UK (29 per cent). In between these are two small countries: Luxembourg with 50 per cent and Ireland with 44.5 per cent. Finally, two big countries with low levels of union density: Spain with 13.5 per cent and France, the lowest with only 9.1 per cent union density. The

[21] Visser, *In Search of Inclusive Unionism*, Table 5 on p. 34.

[22] Source: European Foundation for the Improvement of Living and Working Conditions, Dublin; European Industrial Relations Observatory (EIRO) on-line; comparative overview of 'Industrial relations in the EU, Japan and USA, 2000', Table 2. Much of the information which follows is derived from this survey. For the density ratio of the principal employer peak organisations in thirteen EU Member States, see F. Traxler, 'Employers and Employer Organisations in Europe: Membership Strength, Density and Representativeness', (2000) 31 *Industrial Relations Journal*, pp. 308–16, Table 1 on p. 310. The percentage ranges from 100 per cent in Austria to the 70s (Netherlands (79 per cent), France (75 per cent), Spain (74 per cent), Germany (West) (73 per cent), Belgium (72 per cent)), to the mid-50s (Sweden and the UK (54 per cent)) to the low 40s (Denmark and Finland (42 per cent)), to the 30s (Ireland and Italy (38 per cent), Portugal (34 per cent)).

**Table 8.2** Union density in the EU Member States, 2000

| Country | Union density (%) |
|---|---|
| Denmark | 87.5 |
| Finland | 79.0 |
| Sweden | 79.0 |
| Belgium | 69.2 |
| Luxembourg** | 50.0 |
| Ireland | 44.5 |
| Unweighted EU average | 43.8 |
| Austria | 39.8 |
| Italy** | 35.4 |
| Greece | 32.5 |
| Weighted EU average | 30.4 |
| Portugal* | 30.0 |
| Germany** | 29.7 |
| UK | 39.0 |
| Netherlands | 27.0 |
| Spain | 15.0 |
| USA | 13.5 |
| France | 9.1 |

\* 1999 figure
\*\* 1998 figure

combination of size and density means that though the unweighted average union density of the fifteen countries is 43.5 per cent, the largest countries have considerably lower density so that the weighted EU average is only 30.4 per cent. The median figure was Italy at 35.4 per cent. In contrast, trade union density in the USA in 2000 was 13.5 per cent, lower than any EU country except France.

## Actors and levels

Union membership and density, though fundamental, is only part of the picture, and, from the institutional point of view, arguably the less important part. The trade union membership figures have to be translated into institutional or organisational forms, trade unions, and the importance of these organisational forms depends on their regulatory functions, which in turn depend on their relations with employers, their organisations and the state, and the outcomes of these relationships in terms of regulatory instruments, such as collective agreements.

### Trade unions

Although a common starting point is the definition of a 'trade union' given by the Webbs in 1894 – 'a continuous association of wage-earners for the purpose of maintaining or improving the conditions of their employment'[23] – a comparative perspective is required on trade unions in Europe. Three elements frame a comparative perspective on European trade unions: their *purposes*, *autonomy* and *membership*. Just as the purposes of trade unions, their degrees of autonomy and even their concept of membership have to be understood in a specific national context, similarly, trade unions in the European context also acquire a specific character.

The attribution of specific *purposes* to unions is a fundamental element distinguishing trade union movements. For example, the Webbs included in their definition a specific purpose of the union: 'the purpose of maintaining or improving the conditions of their *employment*'. The second edition of their book changed this to read 'maintaining or improving the conditions of their *working lives*', a change explained as being because the phrase 'employment' implied that unions 'have always contemplated a perpetual continuance of the capitalist or wage system'.[24] Trade unions in Europe, to a greater or less extent and more or less willingly, accommodate themselves to the EU's economic system, and their purposes are shaped accordingly.

*Autonomy* implies an external environment in relation to which trade unions are more or less autonomous. Comparative studies have located two major systems determining trade union autonomy: the political system, including parties and states, and the economic system. One six-country study argued that it was collective bargaining which accounts for various aspects of trade unions, including membership, union government and workplace organisation.[25] *Autonomous* union movements are concentrated in those countries where collective bargaining is the principal method of union action (and include five of Clegg's six countries). Where collective bargaining is the principal method of union action, the relation of regulation of internal union affairs to the collective bargaining system is critical.[26] Union movements designated as *autonomous* by Martin include seven from the EU Member States, all of which fall into the category of industrial market economies with liberal democratic political systems: Austria, Denmark, Finland, Germany, Ireland, Sweden and the UK.[27] In contrast, the category of trade union movements which are ancillary to or dominated by political parties in the EU includes Belgium, France, Italy, Luxembourg, the Netherlands, Portugal and Spain.

Trade unions at EU level aspire to collective bargaining in the form of the European social dialogue, but also channel much of their efforts towards influencing the political and administrative processes at EU level.

---

[23]  Sidney and Beatrice Webb, *The History of Trade Unionism*, London: Longmans, 1894, p. 1.

[24]  Ibid., 2nd edn, London: Longmans, 1920, p. 1, note.

[25]  H. A. Clegg, *Trade Unionism under Collective Bargaining: A Theory Based on Comparisons of Six Countries*, Oxford: Blackwell, 1976.

[26]  P. Lange, 'Politiche dei redditi e democrazia sindacale in Europa occidentale', (1983) 3 *Stato e Mercato* 425–74 at p. 425.

[27]  Ross M. Martin, *Trade Unionism: Purposes and Forms*, Oxford: Clarendon Press, 1989.

As to the specific categories of persons eligible for trade union *membership*, traditionally this included employees, as defined in different national systems of labour law. Other groups of potential members were sometimes excluded, perhaps by reason of the law not protecting, or even proscribing the right of these groups to unionise: the self-employed, professionals, retired persons, the unemployed, the armed forces, management employees, domestic servants, clergymen, agricultural workers, part-timers, civil servants and so on. In Europe, the changing nature of the workforce is interacting with the member-ship basis of unions to produce severe difficulties for unions.[28]

Thus trade unions in Europe are characterised by a specific range of pur-poses, qualities of autonomy and categories of membership. The European Trade Union Confederation (ETUC), which brings these trade unions together, encapsulates some of these in the Preamble to its Constitution:

> The ETUC, consisting as it does of free, independent and democratic trade union confederations and European industry federations, aspires to be a unified and pluralistic organization representing all working people at European level.

There is a marked contrast between the *unity* of organisation at *EU* level and the *diversity* at *national* level. The ETUC, established in 1973, combines two important features. First, centralisation: the ETUC includes almost all major confederations in the EU Member States (and elsewhere in Europe, 78 in total from 34 European countries; a total affiliated union membership of 60 million). Secondly, sectoral structures: also affiliated to the ETUC are eleven European Industry Federations, which group together most national trade union organ-isations along industrial lines.

Trade union organisation in the EU Member States is marked by a diversity reflecting these same two features: relative centralisation and sectoral struc-ture.[29] Relative centralisation is evident in four countries: in Austria, Germany, the UK and Ireland, there is a dominant or single national central organisation. However, in Austria and Germany the central organisations comprise a rela-tively small number of unions organised primarily on industrial lines, whereas in the UK and Ireland they comprise a larger number of unions which cross industrial, general and occupational lines.

In contrast, in seven continental European countries – Belgium, France, Italy, Luxembourg, the Netherlands, Portugal and Spain – there are multiple and competitive trade union centres, divided on political and confessional lines with the number of main confederations ranging from five in France down to two in Portugal and Spain, in many cases, organised in sectoral federations.

In the three Nordic countries, decentralisation, but without competition, takes the form of separate confederations organised in different occupational

---

[28] B. Bercusson, 'Europaisches und nationales Arbeitsrecht – die gegenwartige Situation', (1991) *Zeitschrift fur auslandisches und internationales Arbeits- und Sozialrecht* 1–40.

[29] The following analysis focuses on the EU-15, prior to the enlargements of 2004 and 2007.

groups: blue-collar, white-collar and professional/academic, again comprising industrial and occupational unions. Finally, in Greece, the confederations are divided along public and private sector lines, and comprise different types of member organisations.

In sum: the strongly marked features of centralisation and sectoral organisation at EU level are reflected in different combinations at national level: more or less centralisation and more or less sectoral organisation.[30]

### Employers' organisations

Organisations of employers at national level, in the aftermath of the Second World War, undertook to establish European organisations of employers' federations. This began in 1949 with the establishment of the Conseil des Fédérations Industrielles d'Europe (CIFE), and, within this organisational framework the Union des Industries des pays de la Communauté européenne. This last was composed of the national industrial federations from the six member states of the European Coal and Steel Community. This body became the Union des Industries de la Communauté européenne (UNICE) in March 1958. By 2003 this had grown to thirty-four members and five observers from twenty-seven countries, including the EU countries, the EEA countries and some Central and Eastern European countries.

Presently, at EU level, employers' organisations reflect one of the dimensions which marks trade union organisation: they are highly centralised in the Union of Industrial and Employer Confederations of Europe (UNICE, renamed BusinessEurope in 2007), which brings together almost all the main national intersectoral confederations of private sector employers and business in the EU Member States. Since many services and indeed industries in Europe are publicly owned or controlled, a similar central organisation, the European Centre of Enterprises with Public Participation (CEEP) brings together enterprises and organisations with public participation or carrying out activities of general economic interest. These are the organisations which engage with the ETUC in social dialogue and negotiations at EU level.

However, the second dimension, sectoral organisation, is severely lacking on the employers' side. While there are many organisations representing business at EU level, their primary function is trade promotion or lobbying for business interests. They do not engage with their equivalent organisations, the European industry federations affiliated to the ETUC.

---

[30] By way of comparison, and in contrast with the national level in most EU Member States, but not at EU level, in the USA trade unions were grouped until recently into a single main national centre, the AFL-CIO comprising a relatively large number of industrial and occupational unions. The similarity (centralised, few, industrial) may be noted between the EU level structures and those in Austria and Germany, on the one hand, and those of Ireland and the UK (centralised, many, mixed) with the USA on the other. Most continental EU Member States have multiple centres organised on sectoral lines. Nordic countries and Greece have multiple centres with less marked sectoral structures.

Again, at national level, the contrast with the EU level is marked. On the one hand, there is, as at EU level, also in most Member States a single organisation usually representing private sector employers, and although there are exceptions (as in Germany), the tendency is towards representation both of the private sector's business and trade interests and of their interests as employers. But in contrast to EU level, at national level it is sectoral employers' organisations which play a key role in collective bargaining with trade unions in most EU-15 Member States: Austria, Belgium, Denmark, Finland, France, Germany, Greece, Italy, the Netherlands, Portugal, Spain and Sweden. Again, the UK, and also Ireland (where there is, however, intersectoral bargaining) and Luxembourg are the exceptions, where bargaining is concentrated at company level.[31]

In sum, in configuring an institutional architecture for the EU social model, I suggest it will be impossible to ignore the predominance of certain actors and levels in most Member States. Organisations of employers and trade unions, at intersectoral and sectoral levels, play a major role. This role can be further traced through the interaction of these actors at different levels and the institutional forms of this interaction. By tracing this interaction and its institutional forms, there will emerge an awareness of the extent to which these organisations influence social life in general, and working life in particular.

## Interactions and institutional forms: processes and levels

The EU economic model of employment and industrial relations is determined by the organisational forms of workers and employers at EU and national levels; specifically, their interactions in a variety of ways and at different levels, often characterised as 'social partnership'. Perhaps the most familiar is collective bargaining between an employer and a union at sectoral level in most countries, though also at company or enterprise level. But in the EU, this is only one of three institutional forms of interaction. The other two are processes at national

---

[31] Again, the comparison with the USA is instructive. Unlike the EU, and even compared with many Member States, intersectoral industrial relations on a national level is not possible in the absence of an employers' body. The National Association of Manufacturers and the US Chamber of Commerce do not deal with trade unions. Indeed, there are employers' organisations established for the sole purpose of excluding trade unions. Similarly, in clear contrast with most EU Member States, sectoral employers' organisations do not operate on a national scale in the USA. Rather, where it exists, bargaining takes place at enterprise or local level. Once again, it is striking how the EU level interaction of employers' and trade union organisations at intersectoral level, and, though to a much lesser extent, at sectoral level, reflects a pattern at the national level evident in most Member States. The exception again is the UK at intersectoral level and the UK, Ireland and Luxembourg at the sectoral level. These latter Member States are more similar to the American formula of little or no bargaining with trade unions at national-intersectoral or sectoral levels, but focus on the company or enterprise level. The first edition of this book explored the importance of sectoral bargaining for the European social dialogue, looking in particular at the construction and metalworking industries, and its relation to European labour law, Chapter 6, pp. 78–94.

level (macro-level) and at the workplace (micro-level). It is the existence of all three levels and their interrelationship which define the specific character of the European social model.

## Consultation and dialogue at the macro-level

At EU level, the creation of a European social dialogue beginning in 1985, culminating in its 'constitutionalisation' in the Maastricht Treaty on European Union is a riveting story. Bipartite negotiations between the 'social partners' at the intersectoral level have led to agreements translated into legally binding directives on parental leave, part-time workers and fixed-term work. Even where negotiations have failed to start or be completed, the social dialogue has had consequences, examples being the European Works Councils Directive, the directive on information and consultation at national level, and the proposed directive regulating temporary agency work. At sectoral level, with the encouragement of the European Commission, sectoral social dialogue committees have been established on the initiative of the sectoral social partners.[32]

The 'social partners' are also involved in institutional frameworks engaging both EU institutions and the Member States, including the 'macro-economic dialogue' where the peak organisations meet at regular intervals with the Member States, the Commission and the European Central Bank. These macro-level arrangements are a reflection of practices in most Member States, in a variety of forms of tripartite or bipartite 'Economic and Social Councils' in countries such as Belgium, France, Greece, Italy, the Netherlands, Portugal and Spain. These advisory and consultative bodies deal with a variety of social and economic matters of concern to the members of the social partner organisations. The outcome is often tripartite agreements between the social partners and governments on general economic policy, including incomes policy (Ireland, Italy, Portugal) or specific issues such as social security or employment (Portugal and Spain). Such agreements may be bipartite at intersectoral level, laying down guidelines for pay and conditions (Belgium, Finland, Greece) or other specific issues such as working time (Belgium, France).

Again, the UK stands out as having few such institutional arrangements. In this, as in other features, it shares the absence of a tradition of bipartite or tripartite dialogue at national level with the USA.

## Collective bargaining

This is the most familiar process by which organisations of workers and employers settle the central issues of pay, hours of work, and other elements of the terms on which work is to be performed. At EU level, however, collective

---

[32] As reported in the Commission's Communication, 'The European Social Dialogue, a Force for Innovation and Change' (COM(2002) 341 final, Brussels, 26 June 2002), twenty-seven sectoral social dialogue committees had been set up at the joint request of the social partners in the sectors concerned.

bargaining on these central terms has not yet developed. The exceptions to this rule only serve to highlight its present immobility: European sectoral agreements on working time in, for example, the transport sectors. But two phenomena are emerging which demonstrate that the terrain is moving: first, the emergence of processes akin to bargaining in some European works councils; and, secondly, the beginnings of a process of European coordination of collective bargaining at national level.

It is in the Member States where collective bargaining is evident as the most important process regulating working life, and much besides. On the key issue of pay determination, the most important, dominant level of bargaining is at the intersectoral level in three countries (Belgium, Finland and Ireland) and at the sectoral level in eight others (Austria, Germany, Greece, Italy, the Netherlands, Portugal, Spain and Sweden). In two countries the dominant level of bargaining is not evident (Denmark, Luxembourg) and in two others the dominant level is the company (UK and France).[33]

Even the clear predominance of centralised bargaining on pay does not adequately convey the importance of collective bargaining. An even more powerful indicator of its role is its coverage: the proportion of workers whose pay is determined by collective agreements. Centralisation, intersectoral and sectoral, means that collective agreements will cover all employers in the sector or the country, even where workers are not members of trade unions and employers are not members of employers' organisations and not parties to the collective agreement. Table 8.3 illustrates this.

The significance of this collectivised system of pay determination is not only economic. It highlights the third dimension of the process whereby working life is determined through collective processes. These engage organisations of workers not only at the macro-level and the sectoral level, but also at workplace level, supplementing and reinforcing the levels above.

### Information, consultation and participation

Macro-level consultation and dialogue influence major decisions on social and economic policy, and collective bargaining determines pay and other terms and conditions of employment. But the day-to-day working life of most people in the office, shop or factory is subject to myriad decisions concerning, for example, working practices (performance), conduct at work (disciplinary matters), health and safety, and many others. Rather than these decisions being taken unilaterally by management, there has developed in the Member States of the EU a mandatory system of participation by workers in such decisions through representative structures of 'works councils', 'enterprise committees',

---

[33] The degree of centralisation of collective bargaining in most Member States is, therefore, in striking contrast to the USA, where, like the UK and France, the individual company level is predominant, and other levels of bargaining are unknown, the only appearance of centralisation being the phenomenon of 'pattern bargaining' in some industries.

**Table 8.3** Collective bargaining coverage, Europe, Japan and USA

| Country | Coverage (%) |
| --- | --- |
| Austria | 98 |
| France | 90–95 |
| Belgium | 90+ |
| Sweden | 90+ |
| Finland | 90 |
| Italy | 90 |
| Netherlands | 88 |
| Portugal | 87 |
| Denmark | 83 |
| Spain | 81 |
| Average of 13 EU Member States | c. 80 |
| Germany | 67 |
| Luxembourg | 58 |
| Average of 9 (then) candidate countries | c. 40 |
| UK | 36 |
| Japan | 21 |
| USA | 15 |

*Sources:* EIRO. Figures for EU Member States and candidate countries – referring to various years from 1999 to 2002, and in some cases estimates – are in most cases as calculated by EIRO for TN0301102S and TN0207104F; figure for Japan (2001) is from JIL; figure for USA (2001) from BLS (cf.: www.eiro.eurofound.eu.int/2002/12/feature/TN0212101F.html).

trade union bodies and similar forms. These exist in almost all the old Member States (thirteeen: Austria, Belgium, Denmark, Finland, France, Germany, Greece, Italy, Luxembourg, the Netherlands, Portugal, Spain and Sweden).

The representative structures established by legislation or by generally applicable collective agreements in these countries provide for bodies to receive information and be engaged in consultation, or even co-determination, on a range of matters relating to the company's economic position having implications for the workforce, as well as on decisions affecting the day-to-day working life of employees. Only in Ireland and the UK was, until very recently, such a general and permanent system lacking.[34]

EC law has now taken a decisive step towards establishing the practice of information and consultation of employee representatives as part of the

---

[34] As is the case, again, also in the USA. The American prohibition rests on the National Labor Relations Act's concern that workplace 'labor organisations' in the form of non-union representative bodies would be an instrument used by employers to undermine independent trade unions.

European social model. The decision by the French car manufacturer Renault in February 1997 to close its factory at Vilvoorde in Belgium was announced without warning to the 3,000 workers employed there, and without any prior information or consultation of their trade union representatives. This brutal act of mass dismissals triggered a political storm which revived long-standing demands for EU legislation.

Despite the strong encouragement of the European Commission, the European organisation of employers (UNICE, now BusinessEurope) twice explicitly refused to enter into negotiations (social dialogue) with the European Trade Union Confederation with a view to reaching a framework agreement to regulate this type of situation. Consequently, on 11 November 1998, the European Commission published a Proposal for a Council Directive establishing a general framework for informing and consulting employees in the European Community. The objective was 'to make the essential changes to the existing legal framework ... appropriate for the new European context'.[35]

However, the UK's New Labour government actively opposed the proposal and, although it could be approved by a qualified majority vote, for over three years the UK successfully mobilised a blocking minority of Member States. Only on 18 February 2002 did the Council of Ministers finally adopt Directive 2002/14 establishing a general framework for improving information and consultation rights of employees in the European Community.[36]

Contrasting the presence and role of trade unions and workers' representative organisations in the USA with European experience illustrates the singularity of the European social model. Its manifestation, in all its diversity, at both EU and Member State levels, in the form of macro-level dialogue, collective bargaining at intersectoral and sectoral levels, and collective participation in decision-making at the workplace is the most salient quality distinguishing the European social model. These institutional forms determine the social model of working life, a central component of social citizenship.

## The emerging institutional architecture of the European social model

The current constitutional moment offers the prospect of developing an institutional design for a European social model reflecting these elements of macro-level dialogue, collective bargaining at intersectoral and sectoral levels, and

---

[35] Proposal for a Council Directive establishing a general framework for informing and consulting employees in the European Community, COM/98/612, 11 November 1998; Preamble, Recitals 15–16.

[36] See now the Preamble to the final Directive, particularly Recital 17: '... the object is to establish a framework for employee information and consultation appropriate for the new European context described above [in Recitals 6–16] ...'. Council Directive No. 2002/14 establishing a framework for informing and consulting employees in the European Community. OJ 2002, L80/29.

collective participation in decision-making at the workplace. Some of the elements are already in place, others are missing or compromised, and the whole requires coordination.

## Fundamental rights: in place

The political initiative for an EU Charter of Fundamental Rights aimed to balance the social policy vacuum in the agenda of the IGC which preceded the European Council of Nice in December 2000. The Charter breaks new ground by incorporating social and economic rights, including collective labour rights. It remains to be seen whether and how social and economic rights will affect the EU's economic policy, in particular, the EU's strategy on employment, and whether the enshrining of fundamental rights of association, information and consultation, and collective bargaining and action[37] will influence the institutional operation of the EU where the social partners have major roles to play in the spheres of social policy and employment policy.

## Macro-economic dialogue and collective bargaining: the need for imaginative coordination

There are two well-known frameworks for collective bargaining at EU level: the European social dialogue and EU level coordination of collective bargaining.

### The European social dialogue

A particularly dominant feature of European collective industrial relations is the social dialogue, as stated by the Commission:[38]

> The social dialogue is rooted in the history of the European continent, and this distinguishes the Union from most other regions of the world. Accordingly, in its various forms in the different Member States, the social dialogue is a component of democratic government and also of economic and social modernisation.

The Commission's Communication of 26 June 2002 begins its Executive Summary by stating: 'The social dialogue and the quality of industrial relations are at the centre of the European social model.' The Commission states that 'Social dialogue is the driving force behind successful economic and social reforms … Negotiations between the social partners are the most suitable way forward on questions related to modernisation and management of

---

[37] Article 12: Freedom of assembly and of association. Article 27: Workers' right to information and consultation within the undertaking. Article 28: Right of collective bargaining and action. For further analysis, see Chapter 9.

[38] The introduction to the Commission's Communication on 'The European Social Dialogue, a Force for Innovation and Change', COM(2002) 341 final, Brussels, 26 June 2002, p. 6.

change.' Accordingly, the Commission makes proposals for strengthening the role of the social partners at European, national, local and company level.[39]

The EC Treaty contains the legal framework for the EU social dialogue in the Social Chapter, Articles 138–9. The social dialogue legislative process begins with the obligatory consultation of the social partners by the Commission in two stages: first, when the social policy is first being developed, and, secondly, at the stage of an actual proposal. There follows the possibility of the EU social partners undertaking a social dialogue. This EU social dialogue may produce an agreement. This agreement may be proposed by the Commission to the Council for a decision, usually transforming the framework agreement into a directive.[40]

Problems with the EU social dialogue include, first, that employers will only negotiate if there is a credible prospect that failure to reach agreement will result in Community legislation ('bargaining in the shadow of the law'). However, the political conditions are not currently present for the Commission and Member States to embrace a legislative agenda. Secondly, employers are reluctant to negotiate agreements which are transformed into the generally binding form of EC directives. They want a more flexible result of the social dialogue process. This presents risks in terms of the effective implementation of such 'non-binding' agreements.[41]

## Coordinated collective bargaining

Coordination of European collective bargaining is the consequence of a political rationale resulting from European Monetary Union and aims to counter downwards pressure on wage costs. It parallels the coordinated national bargaining which has been practised in some Member States where centralised national bargaining has been replaced by more decentralised systems of bargaining, but there is still a role for the national level. The process is sometimes

---

[39] *Ibid.*, pp. 10–12. With a view to the acceding countries, the Commission's Communication of 26 June 2002 begins the section on enlargement by affirming that (Section 3, p. 19) 'social dialogue is enshrined in the Treaty and forms an integral part of the *acquis communautaire*'. In its Conclusions to the Communication, the Commission confirms that 'Strong social dialogue structures [are] an integral part of the Community *acquis*' (p. 22).

[40] At EU inter-sectoral level, the results so far include: three framework agreements concluded and transformed into EC directives: on parental leave (1996), part-time work (1997) and fixed-term work (1999); a Framework Agreement on the Regulation of Telework on 23 May 2002, formally signed on 16 July 2002, to be implemented by the members of the signatory parties 'in accordance with the national procedures and practices specific to management and labour' (Article 139(2) EC); a second such agreement, on work-related stress, was reached in 2004; a third on harassment and violence at work in 2007; two negotiations have failed to produce an agreement: that on European works councils led to a directive in 1994; when that on temporary agency work ended, a draft directive was introduced and is still under consideration; on at least one issue, UNICE refused to negotiate: information and consultation at national level. Political agreement on a proposed directive was reached at the Social Affairs Council of June 2001 and the Directive was adopted in February 2002.

[41] These problems will be discussed in detail in Chapters 17–19.

called centrally coordinated decentralisation, or organised decentralisation. The coordination of European collective bargaining reflects this Member State experience by attempting at EU level to coordinate national and sub-national levels of collective bargaining.

At its 9th Congress in Helsinki in June–July 1999, the ETUC set up a 'committee for the coordination of collective bargaining' to develop strategies. The committee formulated guidelines on the coordination of collective bargaining, endorsed at an ETUC Executive Committee meeting on 14–15 December 2000. The guidelines' three main objectives are:

- to allow trade unions at European level to provide a general indication of wage bargaining developments in response to the European Commission's Broad Economic Policy Guidelines and the European Central Bank (ECB) guidelines, and generally to influence the macroeconomic dialogue at European level;
- to avoid situations which may lead to social and wage 'dumping' and wage divergence in Europe; and
- to coordinate wage claims in Europe, and especially in those countries which are part of the euro single currency area, and to encourage an 'upward convergence' of living standards in Europe.

The guidelines contain a formula for pay claims:

- nominal wage increases should at least exceed inflation, while maximising the proportion of productivity allocated to the rise in gross wages in order to secure a better balance between profits and wages; and
- any remaining part of productivity should be used to fund other aspects in collective agreements, such as 'qualitative aspects of work where these are quantifiable and calculable in terms of cost'.

As part of the implementation procedures of this guideline, the ETUC Executive Committee proposed to review wage developments each year, and progress on qualitative aspects of work every two years through a common analysis of the situation in the EU Member States and Member States of the European Economic Area (EEA). The annual report at the end of 2002 showed that wage increases were consistently below the level indicated by the guideline's formula, though closer to it than in previous years.

Another example on the sectoral level is the coordination rule of the European Metalworkers' Federation (EMF), proposed by the EMF's 3rd Collective Bargaining Conference in 1998 and confirmed by the EMF Executive Committee and EMF Congress in 1999. The rule states: 'that the main reference point for the EMF affiliates must be to maintain purchasing power and achieve a balanced participation in productivity increases'. The rule has had effects not so much on individual bargaining situations, but mainly in the sharing of information and growing cooperation which can provide support in cases of conflicts. Nonetheless, a number of significant developments are worth emphasising.[42] Most interesting is the conclusion that wage increases in 2000 were in line with the European Central Bank's definition of price stability, with implications for the ECB's policy on interest rates. This opens up the prospect of a dialogue with the institutions responsible for EU macro-economic policy, including the ECB, promoting an agenda of job-creation and growth. The EMF's role is particularly important in the European context since the metalworking sector often sets the pattern for collective bargaining in Member States.

The problem is that, so far, this is a wholly unilateral initiative. There is no evidence of an employer response to engage with such an exercise in wage, or any other form of coordination. As with the social dialogue, the question is how to stimulate an employer response with a view to developing an operational EU industrial relations system of coordinated bargaining.

A final example concerns cross-border coordination of collective bargaining. Cross-border trade union cooperation refers to unilateral forms of cooperation among trade unions across more than one Member State. It is a pre-condition for bilateral cross-border social dialogue with employers and their organisations.[43]

For example, the 'Doorn Group' takes its name from the Dutch town where, on 4–5 September 1998, trade union confederations from Belgium (FGTB/ABVV and CSC/ACV), Germany (DGB and DAG), Luxembourg (CGT-L and LCGB) and the Netherlands (CNV, FNV and MHP), as well as major sectoral unions representing metalworking, chemicals, construction and private and public services, met to discuss recent trends in collective bargaining and the possible impact of EU Economic and Monetary Union. The result of the Doorn Summit was a joint policy statement which expressed a strong need for close cross-border coordination of collective bargaining within the EU Economic and Monetary Union.

The Doorn declaration represented the first time that unions from different European countries had determined a set of joint bargaining guidelines. In order to prevent possible downward competition in wages and working conditions, the unions involved agreed 'to achieve collective bargaining settlements that correspond to the sum total of the evolution of prices and the increase in labour productivity', 'to achieve both the strengthening of mass purchasing power and employment-creating measures (e.g. shorter work times)', and

---

[42] *Report on the European Coordination Rule* to the 4th EMF Collective Bargaining Conference, Oslo, 20–21 June 2001.

[43] The Commission's Communication of 18 September 1996 concerning the development of the social dialogue at Community level emphasised the growing need to assist the development of new levels of dialogue and referred specifically to the social dialogue in transnational enterprises and at regional level, particularly in cross-border regions.

regularly to 'inform and consult each other on developments in bargaining policy'.[44]

The search is for institutional frameworks for these forms of coordination.

### Adapting institutional frameworks: the European Employment Strategy and the EU social dialogue

The EU is a new supranational political formation. Its social model will include features which are unique to it. It is part of the task of building an EU social model to creatively exploit some of the unusual, even unique features of the EU system.

Employment and labour market policy are a major concern of the EU, the Member States and the social partners at EU and national levels. The development of the European Employment Strategy emerged in the late 1990s as one of the more dynamic areas of EU policy in the economic and social field.

Employment policy is the paradigm case of the open method of coordination. The OMC is encapsulated in Article 128 EC. The Council and Commission formulate an annual joint report put to the European Council, which adopts conclusions and draws up guidelines which the Member States 'shall take into account in their employment policies'. Each Member State is to make an annual report on 'the principal measures taken to implement its employment policy in the light of the guidelines for employment' (the National Action Plan (NAP)). These are prepared with varying degrees of social partner. The NAPs go to the Council and Commission which prepare a joint report to the European Council of that year, which, on the basis of proposals by the Commission, may make (non-binding) recommendations to Member States concerning their employment policies. Other follow-up procedures may take the form of peer review, launched in 1999 with the aim of promoting the transferability of good practice in active labour market policy.

At present, however, the social dialogue is not institutionally integrated into the open method of coordination implementing the European Employment

---

[44] 'The participating trade unions aim to achieve collective bargaining settlements that correspond to the sum total of the evolution of prices and the increase in labour productivity ... The trade unions of the four countries intend to examine how they can back up their demands beyond national frontiers when necessary ... By attuning their wage policies, the participating organisations aim principally to prevent a bidding down of collectively bargained incomes between the participating countries, as sought by the employers. The trade unions see this neighbourly initiative as a step towards European cooperation on collective bargaining.' The participants expressed the hope that unions in other Member States would join their initiative, particularly in the countries using the euro. A coordinating working group of experts was established to meet regularly to exchange information and experience. The Doorn declaration also called for 'employment creation agreements at the sectoral and enterprise levels, including redistribution of work and shorter working hours'. The text is on the World Wide Web at the site of the International Federation of Chemical, Energy, Mine and General Workers' Unions (ICEM), www.icem.org.

Strategy through Article 128 EC.[45] The consequence is that the OMC suffers from a serious problem. The social dialogue and the social partners feature regularly in the political rhetoric of the EU institutions and the Member States when promoting the EES. An active role of the social partners is accepted as an essential political condition for its success. However, the social dialogue is not institutionally integrated or even mentioned in the Employment Title of the EC Treaty. The social partners are only marginally situated in the institutional structure of the EES.

In sum, social policy and employment policy in the EU are presently managed through separate institutional frameworks: the social dialogue and the EES. Can they be combined in an institutional design integrating the best features of the EU social dialogue and the OMC for their mutual reinforcement?

The EU social dialogue, both intersectoral and sectoral, could make a major contribution to the EES. The EU intersectoral framework agreements on part-time and fixed-term work, and sectoral agreements on working time in the sectors excluded from the Working Time Directive, demonstrate the potential of the social partners to regulate the labour market consistently with the Community's employment policy objectives.[46]

The open method of coordination of the EES offers an institutional framework that could reinforce EU social dialogue. It avoids Member States' reluctance to adopt legislative solutions, and substitutes Guidelines. But these are mandatory. They must be adopted every year. It removes employers' resistance

---

[45] Despite its close relation to social policy, when the EES was incorporated into the EC Treaty by the Treaty of Amsterdam, it was placed in a separate Employment Title (Articles 125–30) quite removed from the Social Chapter (Articles 136ff.).

[46] Council Directive 93/104/EC of 23 November 1993 concerning certain aspects of the organisation of working time (OJ L307/18 of 13 December 1993) adopted in 1993 excluded most transport sectors ('air, rail, road, sea, inland waterway and lake transport'). The intention was never that this should be a permanent exclusion, but that these sectors should reach social dialogue agreements at EU level adopting working time arrangements tailored to their exigencies. For example, this was accomplished by an agreement in the maritime sector on 30 September 1998, given legal effect by Directive 1999/63/EC concerning the Agreement on the organisation of working time of seafarers concluded by the European Community Shipowners' Association (ECSA) and the Federation of Transport Workers' Unions in the European Union (FST) (OJ 1999, L167/33), and for the civil aviation sector by an agreement in March 2000, given legal effect by Directive 2000/79/EC concerning the European Agreement on the Organisation of Working Time of Mobile Workers in Civil Aviation concluded by the Association of European Airlines (AEA), the European Transport Workers' Federation (ETF), the European Cockpit Association (ECA), the European Regions Airline Association (ERA) and the International Air Carrier Association (IACA) (OJ 2000, L302/57). In the rail sector, an agreement to apply the directive was reached also on 30 September 1998. However, its translation into a directive was delayed because the EU social partners in the rail sector were unwilling to proceed unless and until a similar arrangement was made in the road transport sector. However, the EU social dialogue in the road transport sector remained deadlocked, mainly over the issue of whether it should cover self-employed drivers. The deadlock was broken in the road transport sector only in February 2002 and took the form of Directive 2002/15/EC of 11 March 2002 (OJ 2002, L80 of 23 March 2002).

to negotiating agreements which lead to binding directives and substitutes framework agreements which may be implemented in the form of Guidelines.

An institutional design could integrate the best features of the EU social dialogue and of the OMC:

1. Mandatory annual guidelines take the form of framework agreements which emerge from an EU-level social dialogue between EU social partners. These framework agreements/guidelines are supported by affiliated social partners. They draw on the experience of national employment pacts, and/or reflect proposals by the Commission.
2. Affiliated social partners at Member State level produce mandatory annual National Action Plans to implement the EU framework agreements/ guidelines.
3. The Commission and Council review and report on implementation of the framework agreements/guidelines. Where necessary, they issue recommendations where implementation is inadequate. If recommendations are ignored, the Commission and Council take measures in the form of specific decisions or general directives.

## Adding coordination of collective bargaining: towards 'cooperative corporatism'

The development of a coordinated collective bargaining system at EU level faces the same problem as the EU social dialogue: employers are not engaged. In the case of the EU social dialogue, it is suggested that the EES might be used to stimulate an employer response. It aims to replicate the institutional pressures on employers of the Commission and Council formulating annual guidelines and recommendations and national administrations formulating annual National Action Plans.

Similarly, the trade unions' development of a coordinated bargaining policy at EU level could become of interest to EU institutions and Member States. There is growing awareness of the advantages of tripartite 'employment pacts' at national level, bolstered by various institutional constellations involving the social partners. On the one hand, there is a thesis of 'competitive corporatism'.[47] This argues that such corporatist national pacts are concerned with seeking a national competitive advantage. On the other hand, coordinated collective bargaining at EU level raises the prospect that a form of regulatory cooperation at EU level, 'cooperative corporatism', could emerge.

The objective would be for the protagonists of coordinated collective bargaining to achieve a response from institutions responsible for macro-economic policy: Member State governments and the European Central Bank. This is a

---

[47] M. Rhodes, 'Globalization, Labour Markets and Welfare States: A Future of "Competitive" Corporatism?', in M. Rhodes and Y. Mény, *The Future of European Welfare: A New Social Contract?*. Basingstoke: Palgrave Macmillan, 1998, pp. 178–203.

form of reinforced macroeconomic dialogue. If the ECB, Member State governments and trade unions at EU level could agree on a coordinated wage policy, this would remove a major threat of inflation and promote monetary stability. In return, trade unions could demand commitments on a range of policies involving employment and related social policy areas.

The institutional price demanded by trade unions would require governments to pressure employers – at Member State and EU level – to enter into social dialogue. However, the institutional response of governments and the ECB could, by itself, act as a pressure on employers to engage, so as not to be left out of the policy exchanges between EU trade unions and national and EU public authorities. This is exactly the kind of pressure which has been lacking to stimulate the social dialogue.

The social dialogue dynamic of 'bargaining in the shadow of the law' becomes more sophisticated; not just law, but a combination of coordinated bargaining and macro-economic dialogue. Even the employment policy of the EES becomes a means of pressuring employers to come to the bargaining table.

The concept is of an EU social model combining coordinated collective bargaining and elements of the EES and the EU social dialogue: exchanges of employment policy and social policy with wages policy. The architecture of the European social model is a form of regulatory cooperation at EU level. 'Cooperative corporatism' builds on coordinated collective bargaining and the institutional machinery of the EES and the EU social dialogue.[48]

## The micro-level: industrial democracy and social citizenship

A Council meeting of Ministers of Agriculture (including fisheries) held in Brussels on 18 February 2002 finally adopted the long-awaited Directive establishing a general framework for improving information and consultation rights

---

[48] In accordance with a Council Decision of 6 March 2003, the Tripartite Social Summit for Growth and Employment was established (Article 1), bringing together the Council Presidency and the two subsequent Presidencies, the Commission and representatives of the social partners (Article 3) at least once a year (Article 4(1)) with the task 'to ensure … that there is continuous concertation between the Council, the Commission and the social partners in order to enable the social partners to contribute, on the basis of their social dialogue, to the various components of the integrated economic and social strategy launched at the Lisbon European Council in March 2000 and supplemented by the Gothenburg European Council in June 2001' (Article 2). This Council Decision was in line with the contribution by the social partners to the Laeken European Council of 7 December 2001. That contribution stated that the ETUC, UNICE and CEEP 'believe it necessary to reaffirm … the distinction between bipartite social dialogue and tripartite concertation [and] the need better to articulate tripartite concertation around the different aspects of the Lisbon strategy' (Section 1). Accordingly, in Section 4 of their contribution, the European social partners proposed to 'articulate concertation on the Lisbon strategy in a single forum'. This tripartite concertation committee for growth and employment 'would examine the Community's overall economic and social strategy ahead of the spring European Council'.

of employees in the European Community.[49] The stated purpose in Article 1(1) is: 'to establish a general framework setting out minimum requirements for the right to information and consultation of employees in undertakings or establishments within the Community'. The Commission, almost all the other Member States where there is already a statutory right to employee representation in all companies above a certain workforce size, and the European Parliament actively promote the role of employee representatives in general and trade unions in particular.[50]

## Conclusion: the European social model – from institutional structure to substantive content

The task of designing the institutional architecture of the European social model presents an enormous opportunity in the present constitutional moment. It has potential implications reaching beyond the twenty-seven EU Member States: to future accession countries, to those benefiting from the world's largest source of foreign aid, and to the trading partners of the world's largest trade bloc. But the future institutional architecture of the European social model leaves open many questions to be answered and challenges to be addressed. Many of these will be the subject of the following chapters.

This chapter outlined an institutional architecture of the European Social Model, however incomplete and imperfect. This is due not least to the fact that since the founding of the EC the development of social policy and labour legislation has been hampered by 'subservience to the process of market integration'.[51] Not surprisingly, much of the attention devoted to the labour law of the EU has focused on those relatively highly developed areas pertinent

---

[49] A fishy result in more than one sense. Since the original proposal of the Commission in November 1998, the United Kingdom government had been actively blocking adoption of the Directive in the Council. When the blocking minority of Member States finally collapsed under pressure from the Swedish Presidency of the Council in June 2001, the UK government persisted in its objective of weakening the Directive.

[50] The UK Labour government's resistance to the bitter end is recognised in the highly unusual joint declaration of the European Parliament, the Council and the Commission attached to the Minutes of the Council which adopted the directive on 18 February 2002. This declaration recalled the judgments of the European Court of Justice of 8 June 1994 with regard to employee representation (*Commission of the European Communities* v. *United Kingdom*, Cases C-382/92 and C-383/92, [1994] ECR 2435, 2479). Those judgments had condemned the then UK Conservative government for its failure to provide for information and consultation of employee representatives in the cases of collective dismissals or transfers of undertakings, as required by EC Directives of 1975 and 1977.

[51] '[S]ubservience to the process of market integration fatally hinders the development of a rationale for Community action in the social policy field … So long as a piece of Community labour legislation can be promoted only on the basis that it contributes to the integration of markets, Community law in this area will remain hobbled.' P.L. Davies, 'The Emergence of European Labour Law', in W. McCarthy (ed.), *Legal Intervention in Industrial Relations: Gains and Losses*, Oxford: Blackwell, 1992, p. 313 at pp. 346–7.

to the functioning of the common market.[52] However, in the aftermath of the fundamental changes introduced by the Protocol and Agreement on Social Policy of Treaty on European Union adopted at Maastricht in December 1991,[53] now Articles 136–9 of the EC Treaty and the commitment of the EU institutions and the Member States to the EU Charter of Fundamental Rights adopted at Nice in December 2000,[54] what has been called the European social model requires a more comprehensive and systematic approach to European labour law.

The following chapters address the substantive content of the European Social Model. This comprises two pillars:

1. a framework of principles and fundamental rights for European collective labour law (Chapter 9), and
2. a framework of principles and fundamental rights for European individual employment protection (Chapter 10).

A final chapter explores the role of the European Court of Justice in the European Social Model.

However, substantive content is only as good as its effective implementation and enforcement. Following the description in Part III of the substantive content of the European Social Model, Part IV elaborates a framework for the effective collective and individual enforcement of European labour law (Chapters 12–16).

---

[52] Analysis of a number of recent textbooks on European labour law revealed an emphasis on free movement of labour, or directives having the objective of harmonising labour standards throughout the Single European Market. See Chapter 3.

[53] B. Bercusson, 'Maastricht: A Fundamental Change in European Labour Law', (1992) 23 *Industrial Relations Journal* 177. And generally, the first edition of this book (1996).

[54] B. Bercusson, 'Social and Labour Rights under the EU Constitution', in G. De Burca and B. De Witte (eds.), *Social Rights in Europe*, OUP, 2005, pp. 169–197.

# Chapter 9

# A framework of principles and fundamental rights for European collective labour law

## Introduction

Freedom of association was not one of the founding principles and collective bargaining was not one of the operating mechanisms of the common market. It has not been easy to perceive in the emerging law of a European common market a role for collective organisations of labour and capital. Accompanying this conceptual disarray about the nature of the law governing collective labour relations at EU level has been scepticism as to the feasibility of development of a system of industrial relations at the level of the EU.[1] The result has been a general pessimism about the prospects for collective labour law in the EU. Much of the confusion and some of the scepticism are due to the absence at EU level of legal measures and institutional and organisational structures recognisable in terms of traditional and familiar collective labour laws and national industrial relations systems.[2]

Instead, up to, and to some extent, even after the adoption of the Protocol and Agreement on Social Policy attached to the Maastricht Treaty on European Union, the collective labour law of the EU was to be found embedded in a variety of legal measures which did *not* have the regulation of collective labour relations as their primary objective. These measures include those aimed at harmonising national labour laws, or regulating the implications for labour of transnational economic activities. However, these measures did embody fundamental principles of collective labour law and, more important than their regulation of discrete areas and issues, they had a *spill-over* effect.

The spill-over effect arises, in part, from the interpretation of these measures by the European Court, particularly in its review of national legislation

---

[1] W. Streeck and P. Schmitter, 'From National Corporatism to Transnational Pluralism: Organised Interests in the Single European Market' (1991) 19 *Politics and Society* 133; W. Streeck, 'Neo-voluntarism: A New European Social Policy Regime', (1995) 1 *European Law Journal* 31.

[2] A similar situation has prevailed in much of the legal and political debate over the process of European integration and the development of the European polity in general.

implementing EU law.[3] But in addition, spill-over occurs because these EU measures incorporate in their substantive provisions *principles* of European collective labour law reflecting *national* experience. *Both* their reflection and recognition in European Court judgments *and* their incorporation in EU legal measures transform these principles from having purely national effect into EU law. By way of EU law, principles derived from *some* national experiences are imported into *other* Member States where their full implications can have unexpectedly spectacular effects.[4]

The substantive content of European collective labour law reflects principles manifest in some of these EU law measures. The *dynamic* of its development has been the spill-over effect of these principles, through their translation into the status of EU law, and their development by decisions of the European Court.[5] The expansion of the substantive social competences of the EU opened the way for development of the collective labour law of the EU without the considerable constraints of strict adherence to the objectives of market integration. The adoption of the Protocol and Agreement on Social Policy attached to the Maastricht Treaty on European Union created the potential for autonomous development of European collective labour law. The principle of collective negotiation of social policy embodied in the new institutional arrangements for the production of EU labour law now in Articles 138–9 EC may be seen as the founding constitutional basis for the collective labour law of the EU.[6]

The first edition of this book outlined a framework of principles which, it was argued, were by 1996 already embodied in the collective labour law of the EU, and which would be further developed in the future.[7] The present framework of principles comprises:

---

[3] A role as engine of institutional change already played in the constitutional development of the EU. J.H.H. Weiler, 'The Transformation of Europe', (1991) 100 *Yale Law Journal* 2403.

[4] For an example to be explored below *Commission of the EC* v. *UK*. Cases 382/92 and 383/92, [1994] ECR I-2435.

[5] The spill-over effect is not specific to collective labour law, but applies also to individual labour law. For example, the Working Time Directive 94/104/EC of 23 November 1993, Article 18(1)(b)(i), allows overtime working above the 48-hour weekly limit by individual agreement of the worker; but the worker is to be subject to no detriment for refusal to work more than 48 hours. Discipline or dismissal of a worker for refusing to work more than 48 hours is a starting point for the development of principles in this area of the individual labour law of the EU.

[6] It was argued even at that early stage that these principles constituted a future framework of the collective labour law of the EU. B. Bercusson, 'The Collective Labour Law of the European Union', (1995) 1 *European Law Journal* 157–79. See also Chapters 34 and 35 of the first edition of this book, and B. Bercusson, 'The Dynamic of European Labour Law after Maastricht', (1994) 23 *Industrial Law Journal* 1.

[7] They included collectively bargained labour standards, workers' collective representation, workers' participation and protection of strikers against dismissal. Chapter 33 of Bercusson, *European Labour Law*, 1996.

### Collectively bargained labour standards

Collective agreements as protected by (and from) EC law
Collective agreements as 'essential' standards
Collective agreements as universal standards
Collective agreements as EU standards: working time
Negotiating EU standards: the Framework Directive 2002/14 on information and consultation

### Workers' collective representation

Mandatory representation
Health and safety representatives
European Works Councils
Representation for purposes of information and consultation in the enterprise

### Workers' participation

Participation in health and safety: beyond consultation?
European works councils: the end of management prerogative?
Information and consultation: a general framework
Participation and timing
Participation: from consultation to negotiation

### Protection of collective action

Protection of strikers against dismissal

These principles are now reflected in the fundamental collective rights in the EU Charter of December 2000.

## Collectively bargained labour standards

EU labour law has been inspired by recourse to collective agreements as labour standards in the labour laws of a number of Member States.

### Collective agreements as protected by (and from) EC law

In cases referred to the European Court of Justice by the Netherlands courts under Article 173 (now Article 234) of the Treaty,[8] the issue was the relationship between the EC rules on competition in Article 85(1) (now Article 81(1))

---

[8] *Albany International BV* v. *Stichting Bedrijfspensioenfonds Textielindustrie*, Case C-67/96; with joined cases C-115/97, C-116/97 and C-117/97; [1999] ECR I-5751; Opinion of Advocate-General Jacobs, 28 January 1999; decision of the European Court of Justice, 21 September 1999.

of the Treaty,[9] and collective agreements.[10] Advocate-General Jacobs declared that the cases:[11]

> raise the fundamental issue of the relationship between the prohibition contained in Article 85(1) (Article 81(1)) of the Treaty and collective agreements concluded between representatives of employers and employees, an issue which the Court has not yet had occasion to consider.

In his Opinion, Advocate-General Jacobs denied the existence of a fundamental trade union right to collective bargaining in EU law and stated that collective agreements have only limited protection from EU competition rules. The Opinion includes important statements on three questions: does Community law protect rights of association[12] and to take collective action?[13] and 'is there a fundamental right to bargain collectively'?[14]

---

[9] This reads: 'The following shall be prohibited as incompatible with the common market: all agreements between undertakings, decisions by associations of undertakings and concerted practices which may affect trade between Member States and which have as their object or effect the prevention, restriction or distortion of competition within the common market, and in particular those which: (a) directly or indirectly fix purchase or selling prices or any other trading conditions; (b) limit or control production, markets, technical development, or investment; (c) share markets or sources of supply; (d) apply dissimilar conditions to equivalent transactions with other trading parties, thereby placing them at a competitive disadvantage; (e) make the conclusion of contracts subject to acceptance by other parties of supplementary obligations which, by their nature or according to commercial usage, have no connection with the subject of such contracts'.

[10] The specific question was (paragraph 68): 'is Article 85(1) (Article 81(1)) of the Treaty infringed where representatives of employers and employees within a particular sector of the economy agree collectively to set up a single sectoral pension fund with an exclusive right to administer the collected contributions and apply jointly to the authorities to make affiliation to the fund compulsory for all persons belonging to that sector?'

[11] Paragraph 79.

[12] As regards rights of association and to take collective action, the Advocate-General stated: (paragraphs 158–9) 'The Community legal order protects the right to form and join trade unions and employers' associations which is at the heart of freedom of association. In my view, the right to take collective action in order to protect occupational interests in so far as it is indispensable for the enjoyment of freedom of association is also protected by Community law'. This conclusion, while welcome, contains important limitations. The implication is that *only* the right to form and join, the heart of the freedom of association, is protected. Other aspects of freedom of association may not be protected.

[13] The right to take collective action is subjected to two conditions. First, it must be 'in order to protect occupational interests'. A conflict could go beyond narrow 'occupational interests'. Secondly, the right to strike is protected *only* to the extent of its link to freedom of association. So most industrial action after the employer had recognised a trade union might not be protected.

[14] As regards a fundamental right to bargain collectively, the Advocate-General concluded in the negative: (*ibid.*, paragraph 160) '… it cannot be said that there is sufficient convergence of national legal orders and international legal instruments on the recognition of a specific fundamental right to bargain collectively'. There is no analysis of national legal orders in the Opinion. His conclusion is surprising because the Opinion, at another point, refers to the German law: 'The [Bundesarbeitsgericht (Federal Labour Court)] stated … that collective bargaining was one of the activities protected by the fundamental rights granted by Article 9(3) of the Grundgesetz (German Basic Law)' (paragraph 91). The Advocate-General dismissed the ILO Conventions (he did not mention that all Member States have ratified ILO Convention Nos. 87 and 98). Convention No. 98 is dismissed in two sentences (paragraph 147) and he rejected the

Finally, on the specific question before him as to whether collective agreements are exempt from EU competition rules, the Advocate-General's view was that there are justified limitations on the alleged right to bargain collectively, including the restrictions imposed by the EU's competition rules, notably, Article 85(1) (now Article 81(1)).[15] He was not deterred when the Commission pointed out that this meant most collective agreements would be prohibited and void.[16] In his view:[17]

> The authors of the Treaty either were not aware of the problem or could not agree on a solution. The Treaty does not give clear guidance. In those circumstances one has to draw a line according to established principles of interpretation.

The line drawn by the Advocate-General was as follows:[18]

> Since the Treaty rules encouraging collective bargaining presuppose that collective agreements are in principle lawful, Article 85(1) cannot have been intended to apply to collective agreements between management and labour on core subjects such as wages and other working conditions. Accordingly, collective agreements between management and labour on wages and working conditions should enjoy automatic immunity from antitrust scrutiny ...
>
> Nevertheless I consider that the proposed antitrust immunity for collective agreements between management and labour should not be without limitations.

Three conditions were posed for collective agreements to achieve legality in the EU:[19]

Community Charter of Fundamental Social Rights of 1989 (paragraph 37: 'very limited legal effects'), the Council of Europe's Social Charter of 1961 (paragraph 146. The Treaty of Amsterdam 1997 amended Article 117 (now 136) EC and the Preamble to the Treaty on European Union to make the 1989 and 1961 Charters obligatory reference points), and the European Convention on Human Rights. (Oddly, this conclusion is not consistent with Professor Jacobs writing before he became Advocate-General: '... now that all the Member States of the European Communities have ratified the Human Rights Convention, the material provisions of the Convention can reasonably be considered as part of the law common to the Member States of the Communities, even though not all of them recognize the Convention as part of their domestic law' (F. Jacobs, *The European Convention on Human Rights*, Oxford: Clarendon Press, 1975, p. 279) as supporting a fundamental right to collective bargaining.)

[15] Paragraph 161.   [16] Paragraph 175.   [17] Paragraph 179.   [18] Paragraphs 179, 186.

[19] Paragraph 194 (italics added). These italicised conditions raise more questions that they answer. For example, Article 85(1) (now Article 81(1)) also applies to the implied agreement between the *employers* making the collective agreement. The criterion of good faith applies to this implied agreement (paragraph 245): 'The issue is whether the implied agreements between employers – as far as they are not covered by antitrust immunity – "have as their object or effect the prevention, restriction, or distortion of competition" within the meaning of Article 85(1).' It appears that the implications for employees or trade unions have no bearing on the legality of the collective agreement. Similar problems arise with regard to questions of what constitute 'core subjects of collective bargaining' and which agreements 'do not directly affect third markets and third parties'. Of particular interest to British labour lawyers is that Advocate-General Jacobs perceived the issue in terms of an 'immunity' of collective agreements from competition law ('an antitrust immunity'), an approach derived from the history of trade union law in Britain (the Trade Union Act 1871) and the USA (the Clayton Antitrust Act 1914). In contrast, the continental European approach of fundamental and positive trade union legal rights would have formulated the issue in terms of a 'right' of trade unions to enter into collective agreements.

[My] conclusion on antitrust immunity for collective agreements is that collective agreements between management and labour concluded in *good faith* on *core subjects* of collective bargaining such as wages and working conditions which *do not directly affect third markets and third parties* are not caught by Article 85(1) of the Treaty.

Advocate-General Jacobs' Opinion meant that the legal protection of many, if not most collective agreements, painfully achieved over decades of struggle by trade unions in the Member States[20] was now potentially threatened by the supremacy of EC competition law. The Opinion seemed to offer to employers a weapon to challenge collective agreements, and competition lawyers soon began to raise questions in the professional legal literature about what trade unions could and could not demand in collective agreements.[21]

On 21 September 1999, the European Court of Justice handed down one of its most important labour law decisions. The Court rejected the Advocate-General's contention that collective agreements were in conflict with the competition provisions of the EC Treaty.[22] The Court emphasised the social policy objectives found in Articles 2 and 3 of the EC Treaty. These are to be given at least equal weight to competition policy objectives. More significant in the long term was the Court's decisive pronouncement on the provisions of the EC Treaty (Articles 118 and 118B, now Articles 140 and 138–9 EC) and, in addition and in particular, the provisions in the Agreement on Social Policy (Articles 1 and 4, now Articles 136 and 138 EC), which explicitly stipulate the objective of social dialogue and collective bargaining between employers and workers, including at EU level.[23] The Court's conclusion is:[24]

59. It is beyond question that certain restrictions of competition are inherent in collective agreements between organisations representing employers and workers. However, the social policy objectives pursued by such agreements would be seriously undermined if management and labour were subject to Article 85(1) [now Article 81(1)] of the Treaty when seeking jointly to adopt measures to improve conditions of work and employment.

60. It therefore follows from an interpretation of the provisions of the Treaty as a whole which is both effective and consistent that agreements concluded in the context of collective negotiations between management and labour in pursuit of such objectives must, by virtue of their nature and their purpose, be regarded as falling outside the scope of Article 85(1) of the Treaty.

---

[20] In the UK, by granting immunity from judicial doctrines on restraint of trade, beginning with the Trade Union Act 1871.

[21] Kiran Desai, 'EC Competition Law and Trade Unions', *European Competition Law Review* (March) 1999.

[22] The Court did not refer to the Advocate-General's Opinion, either on this issue, or on the issue of fundamental trade union rights.

[23] Paragraphs 55–8.    [24] Paragraphs 59–60.

While there are still questions as to the precise scope of the rights protected by the Court, its decision has at least two potentially fundamental implications for the future of labour law, both in the EU and in the UK.

First, EU labour law is not following the much criticised path of UK labour law, which has traditionally regarded trade unions and their collective agreements as merely enjoying special 'immunities' or 'privileges'. Instead, EU social policy acknowledges that there are trade union rights with equal or greater status than competition law.[25] These trade union rights derive support from the EC Treaty Articles 2 and 3.[26]

Particularly important is the Court's reliance in the *Albany* judgment on the provisions of the Social Chapter (including Articles 138 and 139), reinforced by their insertion into the EC Treaty by the Treaty of Amsterdam. The EC Treaty itself now not only encourages and recognises social dialogue and collective agreements at EU level, but also authorises their mandatory extension in the form of Council directives.

Secondly, the success of the European Trade Union Confederation in achieving the agreement of 31 October 1991, which became the Social Chapter and is now in the EC Treaty, may now be seen to have been even more important than previously realised. It enabled the Court in *Albany* to assert that the EC Treaty protected collective agreements.

It highlights how the struggle by the European trade union movement, through the ETUC, to obtain trade union rights *at EU level* is of vital importance for the protection of trade union rights *in the Member States*, in the face of unforeseeable challenges from the EU law emerging from the economic and monetary union of the EU. The initiatives to enshrine fundamental rights in the EC Treaty, culminating in the EU Charter of Fundamental Rights of December 2000, aimed to ensure not only that trade union rights are safeguarded, but that the existing rights recognised by the Court in *Albany* are not diminished by any new formulation.

## Collective agreements as 'essential' standards

The Commission's proposal for a Directive on proof of an employment relationship[27] was clearly inspired by the experience of the UK requirement that employers provide employees a written statement of particulars of terms and

---

[25] This has implications for labour laws in the Member States, including in the UK, which attempt to restrict trade union rights guaranteed by the EC Treaty. For example, if Member States try to constrain collective agreements by invoking competition law, these will encounter the EU law's protection of trade unions against competition law.

[26] However, the future significance of the Court citing these provisions may be affected because, although they applied in the *Albany* case, they were later redrafted and restructured by the Treaty of Amsterdam.

[27] Commission Proposal for a Council Directive on a form of proof of an employment relationship, COM(90) 563 final, Brussels, 8 January 1991.

conditions of employment.[28] UK law reflected the role of collective bargaining in determining terms and conditions of employment by offering employers an *alternative* to individual detailed written statements specifying all or any of the prescribed terms and conditions. The alternative was to refer the employee to 'some document which the employee has reasonable opportunities of reading in the course of his employment or which is made reasonably accessible to him in some other way', which in practice usually meant reference to the collective agreement.

The EC Directive[29] modified the UK law slightly but significantly, by making such reference to collective agreements *explicit and direct*. Among the '*essential aspects* of the contract or employment relationship' to be included in the written document provided by the employer under the Directive are 'the *collective agreements* governing the employee's conditions of work'.[30] There is much that requires clarification in these provisions of the Directive and the UK law:

- Which collective agreements, and at which levels, must be covered?
- What information about the agreement needs be provided: parties, date, establishments and/or categories of employees covered, etc.?
- Is coverage required of substantive terms of employment and/or also procedural provisions affecting the worker's representatives? E.g. representational rights, or others not so easily incorporated into individual contracts.
- Does 'governing' mean:
  legally binding on the employer as party to collective agreement; apparently not, since both the EC and UK provisions envisage the employer not being a party to the agreement;
  legally binding in that they are incorporated into individual contracts of employment;
  effectively governed, in that the employer observes in practice the same (or similar) terms?

---

[28] Then the Employment Protection (Consolidation) Act 1978, sections 1–6, replaced by the provisions of the Trade Union Reform and Employment Rights Act 1993, Schedule 4, now in the Employment Rights Act 1996, section 1. The Explanatory Memorandum accompanying the Commission's proposal included a table (p. 6) which indicated that only in the UK and Ireland was such a requirement imposed on employers. One explanation for the successful passage of this element of EC social legislation may be the less than principled willingness of the UK in the Council of Ministers to approve the extension at EC level of requirements already imposed on British employers, while vetoing similar such attempts by other Member States.

[29] Council Directive 91/533 of 14 October 1991 on an employer's obligation to inform employees of the conditions applicable to the contract or employment relationship. OJ 1991 L288/32.

[30] Directive 91/533, Article 2(2)(j)(i). Collective agreements were *not* among the items of information required to be provided by the UK law. On the other hand, the Directive allowed for cross-reference to collective agreements, but only as regards a few key heads of the information required to be provided (Article 2(3): holidays, length of notice, remuneration, working hours). The transmutation of the UK law entailed by the passage of the Directive has meant that the UK law has had to be amended to bring it into line with the new requirements.

- If a mere reference is made to an agreement in the employee's contract, does this imply that all provisions of the agreement apply, not only those specified in the Directive?

These issues remain unresolved. For example, UK law requires provision of 'particulars ... of ... any collective agreements which directly affect the terms and conditions of the employment including, where the employer is not a party, the persons by whom they were made'.[31] It is not clear what precisely is the information required to be conveyed in these particulars. Is the UK law's requirement that the agreement '*directly* affect the terms and conditions of the employment' an inaccurate transposition of the Directive?

There is scope for litigation where employers fail to include information on collective agreements; or include information contradicting collectively agreed provisions. If there is no reference to agreements which arguably govern conditions of work, this is a violation of the EU law which requires an adequate and effective remedy. Complaints to national tribunals could require a reference to the European Court to clarify the many ambiguities.

EU law has clearly linked the determination of individual workers' terms of employment to the provisions of collective agreements; this will now be a requirement in the labour law of every Member State.

## Collective agreements as universal standards

The Commission's Proposal for a Council Directive concerning the posting of workers in the framework of the provision of services[32] aimed to prescribe the 'working conditions applicable to workers from another State performing work in the host country in the framework of the freedom to provide services, especially on behalf of a subcontracting undertaking'.[33] The Commission relied upon the decision of the European Court in *Rush Portuguesa Lda* v. *Office National d'Immigration*.[34]

In that case, the Court was confronted with a building and public works undertaking governed by Portuguese law, which had entered into a subcontract with a French company for works in France and, to carry out these works, brought its Portuguese workforce from Portugal. In response to the question put to the Court as to whether: '... the right of a Portuguese company to provide services throughout the Community [could] be made subject to conditions ...',[35] the Court had made the following statement:[36]

> Finally, it should be stated, in response to the concern expressed in this connection by the French Government, that Community law, does not preclude

---

[31] The Trade Union Reform and Employment Rights Act 1993, Schedule 4, paragraph 1(3)(j), following the language of the Employment Protection (Consolidation) Act 1978.

[32] COM(91) 230 final-SYN 346, Brussels, 1 August 1991.

[33] Action Programme, Part II, Section 4B.    [34] Case 113/89, [1990] ECR 1417.

[35] *Ibid.*, at 1420.    [36] *Ibid.*, p. 1445, paragraph 12.

Member States from extending their legislation, or collective agreements entered into by both sides of industry, to any person who is employed, even temporarily, within their territory, no matter in which country the employer is established; nor does Community law prohibit Member States from enforcing those rules by appropriate means.

The rule of EU law was that Member State regulation of terms and conditions of employment, by law or *collective agreement*, was permissible.

The Commission in its later proposal confirmed that 'Member States may decide to set and apply minimum pay levels applicable on their territory in order to ensure a minimum standard of living appropriate to the country concerned.'[37] The Commission was fully aware of the implications of competition in labour standards for Community social policy:[38]

National differences as to the material content of working conditions and the criteria inspiring the conflict of law rules may lead to situations where posted workers are applied lower wages and other working conditions than those in force in the place where the work is temporarily carried out. This situation would certainly affect fair competition between undertakings and equality of treatment between foreign and national undertakings; it would from the social point of view be completely unacceptable.

In this context, the proposed Directive made a clear policy choice going beyond what had been stated by the Court to be the legal principle in EC law:[39]

the need to eradicate discrimination between national and non-national undertakings and workers with respect to the application of certain working conditions, justify a Community proposal which … intends to create a hard core of mandatory rules laid down by statutes or by *erga omnes* collective agreements, without disrupting the labour law systems of the Member States and particularly their legislative or voluntaristic approach and their collective bargaining systems.

Hence Article 3(1) of the subsequently proposed Directive provided:

Member States shall see to it that, whatever the law applicable to the employment relationship, the undertaking does not deprive the worker of the terms and conditions of employment which apply for work of the same character at the place where the work is temporarily carried out, provided that:

(a) they are laid down by laws, regulations and administrative provisions, collective agreements or arbitration awards covering the whole of the occupation and industry concerned having an 'erga omnes' effect and/or being made legally binding in the occupation and industry concerned.

As with much of EC labour law, this relatively minor proposal aimed to create potentially important consequences. The Directive, by providing an entitlement of posted workers to collectively agreed standards, raises a legitimate expectation that posted workers should not be better off in this respect than host country workers. To maintain the difference would be to discriminate

---

[37] Explanatory Memorandum, paragraph 12.     [38] *Ibid.*     [39] *Ibid.*, paragraph 18.

against host country workers. Countries which extend generally applicable agreements to *posted* workers will be under pressure to extend them to *all* undertakings. Hence the Directive is a step towards the objective that *all* workers, *whether posted or not*, should not to be deprived of the terms and conditions of employment laid down by law or collective agreements. This would give a great new potential to collective agreements. Those countries where there are generally applicable agreements would have to extend them to cover first posted workers, and then all workers not so covered.

In the event, the Directive which eventually emerged was a considerable dilution of the ambitions of the Commission's initial proposal. The Posting of Workers Directive 96/71/EC came into effect on 16 December 1999. Employers who post workers temporarily to work in other EU Member States must observe certain terms and conditions of employment. Mandatory terms and conditions are those laid down 'by law, regulation or administrative provision'. Terms laid down 'by collective agreements or arbitration awards which have been declared universally applicable' also apply.[40] But such collective agreements apply *only* insofar as they concern the activities referred to in the Annex: 'all building work' (Article 3(1)). However, Article 3(10), 2nd indent, allows Member States the option to extend such collective agreements to apply to 'activities other than those referred to in the Annex'.

A survey in 2003 of the implementation of the Directive by the Commission concluded:[41]

> The question of the applicability of collective agreements is particularly important, since wages are chiefly determined by collective bargaining. Most Member States' legislations provide for the application or extension of universally applicable collective agreements to posted workers. Some Member States do not have universally applicable collective agreements. Consequently, the only rules that these States apply to posted workers are those contained in the law or in other legislative texts.[42]

A later Communication from the Commission on Guidance on the Posting of Workers in the framework of the provision of services states:[43]

> Terms and conditions in collective agreements that are generally applicable must be applied to posted workers in the construction sector. However, Member States may choose to apply these collective agreements to posted workers in other sectors. In fact, most Member States have chosen to do so in all sectors.

---

[40] Article 3(8).

[41] Commission of the EC, Communication from the Commission, *The Implementation of Directive 96/71/EC in the Member States*, COM(2003) 458 final, Brussels, 15 July 2003, section 3.1, p. 9.

[42] In the UK, although the Directive *required* Member States in some cases to apply collective agreements in certain sectors (building work), the government rejected using collective agreements to set mandatory standards. However, if in future litigation the European Court was to interpret the Directive to make collective agreements mandatory labour standards, this could have a major impact on the UK law on collective bargaining. See B. Bercusson, 'Protection for Workers Sent to Work in EU', *Thompsons Labour and European Law Review*, Issue 7, January 1997, pp. 6–7.

[43] MEMO/06/151 of 4 April 2006.

## Collective agreements as EU standards: working time

The Commission's first proposal for a Directive on Working Time stated the intention 'to propose a groundwork of basic provisions on certain aspects of the organization of working time'.[44] However, 'other issues mentioned in the action programme in the field of the adaptation of working time should be left to both sides of industry and/or national legislation'.[45] The role of the social partners in negotiating flexibility of capacity utilization through agreements on working time was acknowledged, with reference to experience in Germany, the Netherlands, Belgium, Greece, France, Italy and Portugal.[46] The Explanatory Memorandum carefully outlined the division of competences between legislation and collective bargaining:[47]

> given the differences arising from national practices, the subject of working conditions in general falls to varying degrees under the autonomy of both sides of industry who often act in the public authorities' stead and/or complement their action. To take account of these differences and in accordance with the principle of subsidiarity the Commission takes the view that negotiation between the two sides of industry should play its full part within the framework of the proposed measures, provided that it is able to guarantee adherence to the principles set out in the Commission's proposals.

The first two drafts of the Working Time Directive reflected this explicit recognition of the role of collective bargaining in the form of an important, if cautious, initiative by providing for the possibility of general derogation in Article 12(3), and also allowing for the possibility of implementation of the Directive through collective agreements.[48]

This traditional approach was transformed into a radical advance in the final draft, which gave collective bargaining a central role in the setting of some EC standards on working time.[49] This was a significant *qualitative* change from being confined to the role of derogating from established standards to itself independently prescribing standards. The present Directive allows for collective agreements to *fix* or *define* relevant standards. In one exceptional case, collective agreements are even given *priority* over Member State legislation. As regards *rest breaks* during working hours, the Directive gives *priority* to collective agreements over legislation in *determining* the EC standard:[50]

---

[44] COM(90) 317 final – SYN 295, Brussels, 20 September 1990; OJ C254 of 9 October 1990, p. 4; Explanatory Memorandum, page 2, paragraph 2.

[45] *Ibid.*, p. 3.     [46] *Ibid.*, p. 13, paragraph 25.

[47] *Ibid.*, p. 4, paragraph 3 and again in paragraph 32 on pp. 16–17.     [48] Article 14.

[49] Council Directive 93/104/EC of 23 November 1993 concerning certain aspects of the organisation of working time. OJ L307/18 of 13 December 1993.

[50] Council Directive 93/104/EC of 23 November 1993 concerning certain aspects of the organisation of working time; OJ L307/18 of 13 December 1993, as amended by Directive 2000/34 of 22 June 2000, OJ L195/41. Consolidated in Directive 2003/88/EC of 4 November 2003 concerning certain aspects of the organisation of working time; OJ L299/9 of 18 November 2003, Article 4. This is a step further down the road taken by the European Court of Justice that collective bargaining was an adequate means of implementing Community labour law

Breaks

Member States shall take the measures necessary to ensure that, where the working day is longer than six hours, every worker is entitled to a rest break, the details of which, including duration and the terms on which it is granted, shall be laid down in collective agreements or agreements between the two sides of industry or, *failing* that, by national legislation.

Collective bargaining determines the EU standard.[51] Only in its absence is the standard to be prescribed by legislation.

In addition, according to the Directive's provisions, collective bargaining is engaged in *setting* substantive EU standards in relation to night work, daily rest breaks and maximum weekly working hours, including overtime and annual holidays. Member States are to consult the social partners before legislating standards on night work, and it is arguable that Article 13 requires employers to consult workers and their representatives when s/he 'intends to organize work according to a certain pattern'. Any derogations at enterprise level are explicitly subject to framework agreements negotiated at national or regional levels.

It becomes evident that the Directive is likely to engage national courts, and eventually the European Court, in questions of collective labour law not previously encountered. The Directive will bring before these courts issues of proper consultation of trade unions, by Member States or employers, the relations between collective agreements and law, different levels of collective agreements, and individual contracts and collective agreements. In this sense the Working Time Directive broke new ground in the development of a European collective labour law.[52]

## Negotiating EU standards: the Framework Directive 2002/14 on Information and Consultation

The Framework Directive on Information and Consultation[53] reflected a Community policy to accommodate the desire of the social partners for flexibility in adapting the directive through collective agreements.

The Proposal for a Council Directive establishing a general framework for informing and consulting employees in the European Community[54] permitted Member States to authorise voluntary agreements, including different

---

obligations. *Commission of the European Communities* v. *the Kingdom of Denmark*, Case 165/82, [1983] ECR 427, at pp. 434–5, paragraph 8.

[51]　Though without specifying the appropriate level.

[52]　See, for example, *Sindicato de Médicos de Asistencia Pública (Simap)* v. *Conselleria de Sanidad y Consumo de la Generalidad Valenciana*, Case C-303/98, [2000] ECR I-7963; *Bernhard Pfeiffer et al. c. Deutsches Rotes Kreuz Kreisverband Waldshut eV*, joined cases C-397/01 to C-403/01. Opinion of Advocate-General M. D. Ruiz-Jarabo Colomer, 6 May 2003; Second Opinion, 27 April 2004; ECJ decision, 5 October 2004.

[53]　Directive 2002/14/EC of the European Parliament and of the Council of 11 March 2002 establishing a general framework for informing and consulting employees in the European Community. OJ L80/29 of 23 March 2002.

[54]　COM/98/612 of 11 November 1998, Article 3.

arrangements. These agreements may be different, but there are limitations: 'respecting the general objectives laid down by the Directive'; 'subject to conditions and limitations laid down by the Member States'. Further, Article 4(1) provided: 'Member States shall ensure that information and consultation are effective and useful.'

The UK government's attitude to the proposed directive was one of root and branch opposition. However, being in a minority in the Council of Ministers, in the course of its rear-guard battle against the proposal, the UK government was determined to instrumentalise the policy of social partner flexibility to alleviate domestic political pressure from employers unfamiliar with and anxious about the imposition of the new system. The majority of Member States, with such systems already in place, and, in particular, the European Parliament, were highly suspicious, and rightly so, that the UK would seek to exploit any such Member State discretion and social partner flexibility to minimise, if not evade the obligations prescribed by the directive.[55]

On 30 May 2001, the Commission produced its revised draft directive on information and consultation, incorporating some of the amendments proposed by the European Parliament. On 11 June 2001, the Social Affairs Council reached political agreement on a draft directive. The Council draft granted enormous discretion to Member States by allowing practically unlimited scope for different provisions for the practical arrangements for information and consultation to be provided for by agreement (Article 4). In contrast, the Commission/Parliament draft provided much less scope for different arrangements by agreement.

The final Directive reflects these tensions in provisions that are more or less ambivalent.[56] Article 5 of the Directive authorises Member States to entrust management and labour (the social partners) to make voluntary agreements, including different arrangements, 'while respecting the principles set out in Article 1'. Apart from the requirement of 'effectiveness', Article 1 imposes procedural, as well as other substantive constraints specific to those negotiated agreements.

Another point concerns the relation between practical arrangements for information and consultation determined by the Member States and, where Member States choose to allow them, those negotiated in agreements between management and labour. Article 4 refers to the Member States determining practical arrangements 'without prejudice to any provisions and/or practices in force more favourable to employees'. This seems to mean that social partner agreements are to take precedence over Member State provisions where they

---

[55]  See the Preamble, Recital 16.

[56]  The European Parliament attempted to prescribe trade unions as the employees' representatives. A declaration was attached to the decision of the Council adopting the directive, recalling the European Court's judgment in *Commission of the European Communities* v. *United Kingdom*, Cases C-382/92 and C-383/92, [1994] ECR 2435, 2479, which illustrates the continuing scepticism about the UK's commitment to the directive.

are in force and are more favourable to employees.[57] Both, however, are subject to respect for the principles set out in Article 1 of the directive. The extent of permissible derogations from the provisions of the Directive by agreements between management and labour remains one of the most sensitive issues.

In the earlier European Works Council Directive of 1994, in the event of failure to reach agreement on a European Works Council, that directive prescribed a set of minimum standards (the 'subsidiary requirements') as necessary to avoid ineffective and sub-standard arrangements being negotiated. None of this is provided for in the 2002 Directive. Instead, the autonomous agreements may explicitly differ from the detailed requirements laid down in Article 4, and are subject only to the principles set out in Article 1. This leaves any 'different' provisions wide open to challenge, a result nobody wants.

In the final Directive, Article 5 allows management and labour to negotiate 'provisions which are different' from the Directive. The resulting collective agreements establish what is accepted as an EU standard. Problems have arisen regarding the adequacy of voluntary EWC agreements negotiated under Article 13 (and, in time, under Article 6) of the EWC Directive. This provision is also likely to require assessment of voluntary agreements negotiated under this directive.

## Workers' collective representation

The collective representation of workers has been a principle manifested in numerous policy initiatives of the Commission. They owe their origin to national labour law provisions for representation of workers in enterprises, in the form of organs based on the workplace[58] or based on corporate structures.[59]

Although many of these proposals did not succeed in gaining the approval of the legislative organs of the Community, in a number of areas the EU has provided for workers' collective representation: regarding health and safety, in the form of European works' councils in multinational enterprises, in domestic enterprises above a specified size and in the structures of the European company. Further, on the basis of two other Directives, the European Court has declared that workers' collective representation is mandatory.

### Mandatory representation

Mandatory recognition of employee representatives has been declared in Cases 382/92 and 383/92, *Commission of the EC* v. *UK*, decided by the Court

---

[57] Cf. Article 4 of the Working Time Directive, quoted above, as regards daily rest breaks.

[58] Draft Directive on procedures for informing and consulting employees, OJ C297 of 15.11.80 and OJ C217 of 12 August 1983.

[59] Draft Fifth Directive concerning the structure of public limited companies and the powers and obligations of their organs, OJ C240 of 19 August 1983; draft Directive concerning the European Company Statute, OJ C263 of 16 October 1989.

on 8 June 1994.[60] The cases concerned complaints by the Commission about defective implementation by the UK of the EC Directives on 'acquired rights'[61] and 'collective dismissals'[62] with respect to the duty to designate worker representatives.

Both Directives require workers' representatives to be informed and consulted. The UK legislation implementing the Directives provided for information and consultation only where there are 'recognised' trade unions.[63] The Commission complained that the UK had not provided rules for the designation of workers' representatives where this did not take place on a voluntary basis.

The Commission argued that the Directives impose an obligation on employers to inform and consult in every instance. The UK argued that the obligation arises only if national law and practice provide for representatives. In both cases the Court held that 'The United Kingdom's point of view cannot be accepted'. The Court took identical views with respect to both Directives:[64]

26. ... as United Kingdom law now stands, workers affected by (collective redundancies/the transfer of an undertaking) do not enjoy protection under ... the directive(s) in cases where an employer objects to worker representation in his undertaking.

27. In those circumstances, United Kingdom law, which allows an employer to frustrate the protection provided for workers by ... the directive(s), must be regarded as contrary to those (directives) ...'

In this, the Court subscribed to the views of Advocate-General Van Gerven, in an opinion delivered on 2 March 1994:[65]

to make the activity of workers' representatives totally dependent on voluntary recognition by employers is incompatible with the protection of workers as apparent from the directives in the light of their objective, structure and wording.

The nature of workers' collective representation is likely to become further regulated by EU law. Designation of worker representatives was made mandatory by the Court due to the consequences for the rights of workers under the Directive:[66]

which require(s) Member States to take all measures necessary to ensure that workers are informed, consulted and in a position to intervene through their representatives in the event of collective redundancies (or the transfer of an undertaking).

In order to effectively perform the tasks of information and consultation specified in the Directives, worker representatives must possess the experience, independence and resources required to protect the interests of the workers

---

[60] [1994] ECR I-2435.   [61] Directive 77/187, OJ L51/26.   [62] Directive 75/129, OJ L48/29.

[63] Trade Union and Labour Relations (Consolidation) Act 1992, section 188(1); the Transfer of Undertakings (Protection of Employment) Regulations 1991, Regulation 10(2)).

[64] Case 383/92, paragraphs 26-7, in terms identical to those of Case 382/92, paragraphs 29–30.

[65] *Ibid.*, paragraph 9.   [66] Case C-383/92, paragraph 23; Case C-382/92, paragraph 26.

they represent. In order to achieve the objective of the EC Directive, Member State laws or practices for the designation of workers' representatives must ensure that the national law on workers' representation is adequate to attain this.

## Health and safety representatives

The relevant law is the Framework Directive 89/391/EEC of 12 June 1989.[67] The objective, structure and wording of the Framework Directive require that safety be the concern of *multiple* categories of workers and their representatives. Close analysis of the provisions reveals that the Directive appears to support a distinction between *representatives* (general representatives, who fulfil certain functions in health and safety, and specialist representatives in health and safety) and *workers* (some with specific responsibilities, and 'designated' workers). Different methods of *appointment* are indicated for each category of worker and workers' representative:

> general workers' representatives[68] – in accordance with the laws and/or practices of the Member States;
> workers' representatives with specific responsibility for the safety and health of workers – in accordance with national laws and/or practices;[69]
> designated workers – by the employer;[70]
> workers with specific responsibilities for safety and health[71] – no method of appointment indicated.

This may seem an excessive enumeration of different categories. However, the Directive was formulated in a *European* context, where there is a variety of experience. There is no need to emphasise the social and human aspects of safety and health, or its economic significance. Safety and health warrants more than the one set of representatives. Specialisation and diversification of responsibilities may be needed to secure the objective of safe and healthy workplaces. The Directive's multiple categories are an indication of this.

Specifically, the Directive prescribes a role in health and safety for *general* workers' representatives. They have rights to be consulted over the planning and introduction of new technologies,[72] to submit observations during inspection visits,[73] and generally to be consulted and take part in discussions on all questions relating to safety and health at work.[74]

The Directive requires the appointment of workers' representatives. This requirement is *not* conditional on employer recognition of trade unions. Nor can it be substituted by information and consultation of *individual* employees.

---

[67] Council Directive 89/391/EEC of 12 June 1989 on the introduction of measures to encourage improvements in the safety and health of workers at work. OJ L183/1.

[68] Articles 6(3)(c), 11(1), 11(6).     [69] Articles 3(c), 11(2), 11(3).     [70] Articles 7(1), 8(2).

[71] Articles 11(2), 11(4), 14(2)(d–f).     [72] Article 6(3)(c).     [73] Article 11(6).

[74] Article 11(1). UK law, which fails to make any provision obliging employers to respect these rights of general workers' representatives, is not in compliance with EU law.

EU law prescribes the system of appointing representatives as being in accordance with national laws and/or practices.[75] The Directive does not permit the functions of safety representatives appointed by trade union to be limited to employees represented by those trade union representatives. The representatives act on behalf of *all* employees.[76]

## European works councils

Directive 94/45/EC of 22 September 1994 requires the establishment of a European Works Council (EWC) or a procedure in Community-scale undertakings and Community-scale groups of undertakings for the purposes of informing and consulting employees.[77] The Directive was to be implemented by the Member States no later than 22 September 1996.[78] In the short term, the priority is the *establishment* of the Special Negotiating Bodies (SNBs) which negotiate the creation of the EWCs. Once the SNB is established, the next phase is the *negotiation* of an agreement creating an EWC and defining its composition, functions, and so on.

The method of election or appointment of SNB members appears to be by delegation to Member State rules:[79]

> a SNB shall be established in accordance with the following guidelines:
>
> (a) The Member States shall determine the method to be used for the election or appointment of the members of the SNB who are to be elected or appointed in their territories ...

The members of the SNB arguably must be employees' representatives. The SNB members representatives from each Member State will reflect national criteria of election or appointment of employees' representatives.[80] A government, such as that of the UK, might try to legislate rules for the election or appointment of members of the SNB which ignore or exclude trade union representatives. This is challenged by various provisions of the Directive.[81]

Sub-paragraph (2) of Article 5(2)(a) provides:

> Member States shall provide that employees in undertakings and/or establishments in which there are no employees' representatives *through no fault of their own*, have the right to elect or appoint members of the SNB.

---

[75] Article 3(c). This means, in the light of UK practice, appointment by trade unions. It is arguable that EU law supports the appointment of safety representatives by trade unions even where they are *not* recognised. See *Griffin* v. *South West Water Services Ltd.*, [1995] IRLR 15.

[76] UK law which restricts their functions to the employees they represent is not in compliance with EU law.

[77] OJ L254/64 of 30 September 1994.     [78] Article 14(1).     [79] Article 5(2).

[80] For example, in the UK context, this would seem to imply trade union representatives. However, see the critique of the UK's implementation of the EWC Directive in Chapter 2.

[81] For a detailed analysis of the UK's implementation of the EWC Directive's provisions on worker representation, see Chapter 2.

It is arguable that this creates a presumption that employees *only* elect or appoint where 'there are *no* employees' representatives *through no fault of their own*'. Otherwise, it is employees' representatives who are, or elect or appoint, the SNB.[82]

The function of the SNB is to establish the EWC by agreement with the central management. The structure and objective of the Directive, and in particular the subsidiary requirements of the Annex, support the view that the SNB should reflect the eventual composition of the EWC. The Annex to the Directive prescribes:[83]

> The *EWC* shall be composed of employees ... elected or appointed from their number by the employees' representatives, or, in absence thereof, by the entire body of employees.
>
> The election or appointment of the EWC shall be carried out in accordance with national legislation and/or practice.

The Annex envisages an EWC composed of, or elected or appointed by, the employees' representatives. An SNB which agrees to an EWC *not* so elected or appointed is arguably *not* achieving the objective of the Directive.

The Annex's subsidiary requirements apply where[84] the SNB and the central management so decide; central management refuses to commence negotiations within six months of a request; or three years elapse after a request without an agreement. The negotiating strategy inherent in the structure of the Directive is based on an SNB composed of employees' representatives. The SNB is in a strong negotiating position. If central management refuses to negotiate within six months, or refuses to agree to employees' representatives nominated by the SNB within three years, the EWC will be set up comprising those elected or appointed by the employees' representatives alone.

## Information and consultation in the enterprise

In the Framework Directive on Information and Consultation[85] the prospect is offered by Article 5 of management and labour negotiating 'provisions which are different' from those laid down by the Directive. This Directive's provisions may be compared with those in the EWC Directive. That Directive allowed for autonomous negotiation of European works councils. But such agreements could only be negotiated by the special negotiating body, which crucially was

---

[82] The meaning of 'through no fault of their own' becomes clear in light of the following sub-paragraph 3 of Article 5(2)(a): 'This second subparagraph shall be without prejudice to national legislation and/or practice laying down thresholds for the establishment of employee representation bodies.' Such thresholds are *not* the fault of employees; hence, they then have the right to elect or appoint the SNB.

[83] Paragraph 1(b).    [84] Article 7(1).

[85] Directive 2002/14/EC of the European Parliament and of the Council of 11 March 2002 establishing a general framework for informing and consulting employees in the European Community. OJ L80/29 of 23 March 2002.

subject to specific representation and voting requirements. In the case of Directive 2002/14, the European Parliament attempted in Amendment 3 on second reading to specify that the 'social partners' eligible to negotiate different agreements on behalf of employees were 'the competent representative organisation of the trade unions, the employee representatives of the undertaking, as provided by law'. Though supported by the Commission, this proposal failed.

The level at which there may be negotiated 'provisions which are different from those referred to in Article 4' is left to the choice of Member States. In most Member States, the relevant provisions are established in national legislation or in national intersectoral agreements.[86] Article 5 appears to allow for the maximum flexibility in terms of the level of negotiation of different provisions, subject to the level being 'appropriate'. It may be that a UK government would look to agreements at undertaking or even establishment level, allowed by Article 5. This means that the 'management and labour' authors of the agreement will be the employer and the employees' representatives. If so, there is a specific condition to be applied as a consequence of Article 5's reference to 'respecting the principles set out in Article 1'. The 'social partners' entrusted with 'defining freely and at any time through negotiated agreement the practical arrangements' must 'work in a spirit of cooperation'.[87]

In stipulating this condition, the Member States presumably aimed at ensuring that the balance of forces, in particular at undertaking or establishment level, does not unduly influence the negotiations and any resulting agreement, which may include provisions different from those referred to in Article 4.[88] Failure to comply with the obligation to work in a spirit of cooperation in the particular case of negotiations undertaken in the context of Article 5 could lead to the resulting agreement being deemed invalid as not satisfying the requirement of Article 5, as not 'respecting the principles set out in Article 1', in which case the fall-back provisions of Article 4 will apply.

---

[86] Hence, perhaps, the reference to 'management and labour' (the social partners), in contrast to 'employer and employees' representatives'. The German language version of Article 5, however, uses the term 'Vereinbarungen', which refers to works councils' agreements. The French 'accords' has a similar connotation.

[87] Article 1(3):'When defining ... practical arrangements for information and consultation, the employer and the employees' representatives shall work in a spirit of cooperation and with due regard for their reciprocal rights and obligations, taking into account the interests both of the undertaking or establishment and of the employees'.

[88] This would be a particular concern in the absence, again invoking the phrase in Article 10, of a 'general, permanent and statutory system of information and consultation of employees, nor a general, permanent and statutory system of employee representation at the workplace'. Hence, *ad hoc* arrangements for employee representation adopted in order to allow for 'workforce agreements' under the Working Time Regulations 1998, or for the purposes of information and consultation under provisions in the Regulations implementing the CRD and ARD (the Collective Redundancies and Transfer of Undertakings (Protection of Employment) (Amendment) Regulations 1999 (SI 1999 No 1925)) may not suffice to satisfy the requirements of the new Framework Directive.

## Workers' participation

The Directives on Acquired Rights and Collective Dismissals have long provided for obligatory information and consultation of workers' representatives. To these have now been added further elaborations of collective participation by Directives on health and safety, on European works councils, and in the Framework Directive on Information and Consultation.

### Participation in health and safety: beyond consultation?

The 1989 Framework Directive[89] draws a distinction between consultation of workers' *general* representatives and consultation of workers' representatives *with specific responsibility for safety and health.*

With respect to workers' *general* representatives, Article 11(1) provides that employers:

> shall consult workers and/or their representatives <u>and</u> allow them to take part in discussions on all questions relating to safety and health at work. This presupposes:
>
> > the consultation of workers,
> > the right of workers and/or their representatives to make proposals,
> > balanced participation in accordance with national laws and/or practices.

A statement was entered in the record by the Council and Commission at the conclusion of the Council discussions on the common position on the Directive. It sought to give a very broad 'formal' latitude to the meaning of 'balanced participation':[90]

> The notion of balanced participation embraces a range of multiple forms of worker participation which vary considerably between Member States. The present directive places no obligation on the Member States to provide a specific form of balanced participation.

Whatever else it may mean, and however it may be formally defined, it seems clear that 'balanced participation' is *not* the same as consultation. Arguably, it must include some different and additional element of involvement of workers' representatives.

Similarly, with respect to workers' representatives *with specific responsibility for safety and health*, the Directive appears to highlight the difference in the two concepts by providing for alternatives:[91]

---

[89]  Council Directive 89/391/EEC of 12 June 1989 on the introduction of measures to encourage improvements in the safety and health of workers at work. OJ L183/1.

[90]  Council Document 9869/88 RESTRICTED SOC 82 of 12 December 1988, p. 22, quoted in Laurent Vogel, *Prevention at the Workplace: an initial review of how the 1989 Community Framework Directive is being implemented.* European Trade Union Technical Bureau for Health and Safety (TUTB), Brussels, 1994, p. 83.

[91]  Article 11(2).

workers' representatives with specific responsibility for the safety and health of workers shall take part in a balanced way, *or* shall be consulted in advance and in good time by the employer, with regard to (the items listed).

The scope of 'balanced participation' is thus beyond the concept of 'consultation' – perhaps even as is defined in the European Works Council Directive 94/45/EC of 22 September 1994.

## European works councils: The end of management prerogative?

The purpose of the Directive 'is to improve the right to information and to consultation of employees'.[92] The consultation prescribed by the Directive is defined as:[93]

> the exchange of views and establishment of dialogue between employees' representatives and central management or any more appropriate level of management.

The *establishment of dialogue* required by the Directive implies an active and continuous process of communication and interaction between the European works council and management.

The Directive requires the creation of a EWC for the purposes of information and consultation. Equipped with information, the EWC is, through consultation, to influence the decision-making of central management. Consultation takes time, and the EWC can use the threat of delay to influence management decisions.

In an apparently paradoxical provision, the Annex stipulates that a meeting 'shall not affect the prerogatives of the central management'.[94] But the whole purpose of the Directive is to subject management decision-making to a procedure of information and consultation. Breach of the procedure must lead to an EU law *remedy* capable of restraining unilateral management action – hence, the special Article on 'Compliance with this Directive'.[95] Management prerogatives are to be subject to procedures of information and consultation of the EWC, procedures which are to be enforced by effective EU law remedies.

## Information and consultation: a general framework

In the Framework Directive on Information and Consultation, the substance of the definition of 'consultation' is Article 4(4):[96]

---

[92] Council Directive 94/45/EC of 22 September 1994 on the establishment of a European Works Council or a procedure in Community-scale undertakings and Community-scale groups of undertakings for the purposes of informing and consulting employees. OJ L254/64 of 30 September 1994, Article 1(1).

[93] Article 2(1)(f).      [94] Paragraph 3, sub-paragraph 4.      [95] Article 111 and (3).

[96] Directive 2002/14/EC of the European Parliament and of the Council of 11 March 2002 establishing a general framework for informing and consulting employees in the European Community. OJ L80/29 of 23 March 2002.

Consultation shall take place:

(a) while ensuring that the timing, method and content thereof are appropriate;
(b) at the relevant level of management and representation, depending on the subject under discussion;
(c) on the basis of information supplied by the employer in accordance with Article 2(f) and of the opinion which the employees' representatives are entitled to formulate;
(d) in such a way as to enable employees' representatives to meet the employer and obtain a response, and the reasons for that response, to any opinion they might formulate;
(e) with a view to reaching an agreement on decisions within the scope of the employer's powers referred to in paragraph 2(c).

This is the definitive description of the process of participation by employees' representatives in management decision-making, which is established by this Directive as a cornerstone of the European social model.

The quality of the consultation required is measured against a criterion of what is 'appropriate'. 'Appropriateness' and 'effectiveness' are the overriding criteria in EC law to assess the practical arrangements determined by Member States. Article 4(4)(d) fleshes out the element of 'establishment of dialogue' in the definition of 'consultation' in Article 2(g) by specifying the employer's 'response, and the reasons for that response'. This 'reasoned response' is not an explanation for management's decision; this has not yet been taken. Rather, it is the employer's response to the opinion of the employees' representatives on the employer's proposals. If that opinion puts forward options, the employer needs to respond to them and justify any rejection of these options.

The method of consultation envisages a pro-active approach by employees' representatives; not only to react to the employer's proposals, but to formulate their own. Article 4(3) describes their activity in terms of conducting an adequate study in preparation for consultation. The ensuing 'opinion' is not the end of the process, but only its beginning; it requires a reasoned response by the employer, which is only another element in the process of consultation 'with a view to reaching an agreement'.

As will be elaborated later, the practical arrangements which Member States are required to determine for information and consultation in accordance with Articles 2 and 4 incorporate the following process comprising nine sequential stages:

1. transmission of information/data (Article 2(f))
2. acquaintance with and examination of data (Article 2(f))
3. conduct of an adequate study (Article 4(3))
4. preparation for consultation (Article 4(3))
5. formulation of an opinion (Article 4(4)(c))
6. meeting (Article 4(4)(d))
7. employer's reasoned response to opinion (Article 4(4)(d))

8. 'exchange of views and establishment of dialogue' (Article 2(g)), 'discussion' (Article 4(4)(b)) 'with a view to reaching an agreement on decisions' (Article 4(4)(e))
9. 'the employer and the employees' representatives shall work in a spirit of cooperation and with due regard for their reciprocal rights and obligations, taking into account the interests both of the undertaking or establishment and of the employees (Article 1(3)).

The practical arrangements to be determined by Member States for the exercise of the right to information and consultation must reflect this process. Information and consultation becomes a legally structured process.

### Timing of consultation: from consultation to negotiation

Consultation is a stage in the process of management of the enterprise in which those consulted can influence decision-making. The process of influencing management decision-making is complex. The timing of consultation in the enterprise is critical, as studies have confirmed the need for early access to the decision-making process, and a predetermined decision-making procedure. Council Directive No. 2002/14 establishing a framework for informing and consulting employees in the European Community stipulates (Article 4(4)(a)): 'Consultation shall take place ... while ensuring that the timing ... thereof [is] appropriate.' Previous directives required the consultation to be 'in good time'.[97] Others have specified 'as soon as possible'.[98]

What is 'appropriate' timing under Directive 2002/14 may vary according to circumstances: the nature of the decision and its impact, the organisation of employees' representation, and so on. A crucial ambiguity remains: whether or not the process of information and consultation is to take place *prior* to a decision being made by the employer. Article 1(1) states that the purpose of the directive is 'to establish a general framework [for] information and consultation of employees'. This statement, however, does not make it clear whether the information and consultation process is obligatory *before*, or only *after* the employer makes the decision.

---

[97] Article 2 of Council Directive 75/129 of 17 February 1975 on the approximation of the laws of the Member States relating to collective dismissals, consolidated in Council Directive 98/59/EC of 20 July 1998, OJ L225/16; Article 7 of Council Directive 77/187 of 14 February 1977 on the approximation of the laws of the Member States relating to the safeguarding of employees' rights in the event of transfers of undertakings, businesses or parts of businesses, consolidated in Directive 2001/23 of 12 March 2001, OJ L/82/16.

[98] Council Directive 94/45/EC of 22 September 1994 on the establishment of a European Works Council or a procedure in Community-scale undertakings and Community-scale groups of undertakings for the purposes of informing and consulting employees; OJ L254/64 of 30 September 1994; Annex, paragraph 3: 'This information and consultation meeting shall take place as soon as possible ...'.

However, in 'decisions likely to lead to substantial changes in work organisation or in contractual relations', the Commission's initial draft proposals did make it clear that the mandatory information and consultation must include 'an attempt to seek *prior* agreement on the decisions'. A further indication of the Commission's position was in Article 7(3)(a) of the initial draft proposals, which defined a case of 'serious' breach as meaning 'the total absence of information and/or consultation of the employees' representatives *prior* to a decision being taken'. In the final version of the Directive, the word 'prior' is deleted, specifying only that 'consultation shall take place … with a view to reaching an agreement on decisions' (Article 4(4)(e). This might appear to indicate a shift towards the view that information and consultation only concerns decisions *already* taken, rather than employee representatives being engaged *prior* to management making a decision.

The final Directive remains ambivalent. The Preamble, which provides an interpretive framework for the Directive, contains a number of indications that information and consultation precludes decisions without consultation 'beforehand' (Recital 6), and criticises '*a posteriori*' approaches to the process of change (Recital 13). The ambiguity caused by the absence of the word 'prior' may be interpreted to promote the objectives of the directive: that information and consultation take place before the decision is made, avoiding an *a posteriori* approach to decision-making in the enterprise.

Council Directive 75/129 of 17 February 1975 was the first EU intervention interrupting discretionary managerial decision-making by requiring consultation of workers' representatives in cases of collective dismissals. The scope of the Collective Dismissals Directive has general implications going far beyond the narrow vision of it as confined to specific economic circumstances. It imports a policy of collectivisation of decision-making on dismissals in general, requiring involvement of workers' representatives on this key issue in industrial relations. Over time, obligatory consultation of workers' representatives has been extended beyond the specific case of collective dismissals to become a general and permanent feature of EU industrial relations.

There is some justice, therefore, that a decision concerned with information and consultation in the event of collective dismissals appears to have potentially transformed the obligation of information and consultation applicable to a wide range of management decision-making under the new Directive 2002/14.

A case decided on 27 January 2005, following an Opinion of Advocate-General Tizzano, *Irmtraub Junk c. WolfangKuhnel als Insolvenzverwalter uber das Vermogen der Firma AWO*,[99] concerned interpretation of the Collective Dismissals Directive and specifically the timing of the process of information and consultation. Article 2(1) provides: 'Where an employer is contemplating

---

[99] Case C-188/03, Opinion of Advocate-General Tizzano, 30 September 2004, ECJ decision, 27 January 2005.

collective redundancies, he shall begin consultations with the workers' representatives in good time with a view to reaching an agreement.'

The ECJ upholds the Opinion of the Advocate-General that the Directive obliges the employer to *complete* consultations *before* the decision is made. By decision is meant the date of the *notice* of termination of employment, not the date when the dismissals take effect:

42. With regard to the consultation procedure, this is provided for, within the terms of Article 2(1) of the directive, 'with a view to reaching an agreement'. According to Article 2(2), this procedure must, 'at least, cover ways and means of avoiding collective redundancies or reducing the number of workers affected, and of mitigating the consequences by recourse to accompanying social measures'.

43. It thus appears that Article 2 of the directive imposes an obligation to negotiate.

44. The effectiveness of such an obligation would be compromised if an employer was entitled to terminate contracts of employment during the course of the procedure or even at the beginning thereof. It would be significantly more difficult for workers' representatives to achieve the withdrawal of a decision that has been taken than to secure the abandonment of a decision that is being contemplated.

45. A contract of employment may therefore be terminated only after the conclusion of the consultation procedure, that is to say, after the employer has complied with the obligations set out in Article 2 of the directive.

The ECJ's judgment has general implications for the position under Directive 2002/14. One of the most contentious issues in the adoption of that Directive was determining the timing of the process of information and consultation: was it to take place prior to management's decision or afterwards? *Junk* provides powerful support for the view that the language of Directive 2002/14 should be interpreted consistently with that of the 1975 Directive so as to preclude management taking decisions until the process of information and consultation is completed.

## Protection of strikers against dismissal

A right to strike is largely a right to protection against dismissal of strikers. Does EU law provide some legal support or protection for strikers?

In the UK, when workers strike, the employer may or may not terminate their contracts. If he or she does, there is little or no protection under UK law. This contrasts with many other Member States of the EU, where a constitutional right to strike does not allow the employer to dismiss. A strike means suspension of the contract of employment; strikers normally have a right to return to work.

EU law does have rules on collective dismissals. Council Directive 75/129 of 17 February 1975 on the approximation of the laws of the Member States relating to collective redundancies[100] contains the potential for legal tactics defending strikers against dismissal. The Directive requires the employer to inform and consult workers' representatives when he contemplates redundancy dismissals. The Directive defines 'collective redundancies' as meaning:[101]

> dismissals effected by an employer for one or more reasons not related to the individual workers concerned.

The amendment of the Directive in 1992 reinforced this by adding a new paragraph, which current reads: 'terminations of an employment contract which occur on the employer's initiative for one or more reasons not related to the individual workers concerned shall be assimilated to redundancies'.[102]

Where workers go on strike, the employer may contemplate dismissing strikers. These dismissals related to a strike would arguably be 'for one or more reasons not related to the individual workers concerned'. Hence, the Directive applies. If the employer tries to dismiss strikers before carrying out the procedures of information and consultation of the workers' representatives, a litigation strategy would be to persuade a national tribunal to make a reference to the European Court for an interpretation of the Directive under Article 234 of the Treaty. An interim injunction to stop dismissals of strikers should be granted; alternatively, an undertaking in damages to compensate all workers affected if the claim is subsequently upheld.

The strategy may be particularly effective in the case of employers refusing to recognise, or withdrawing recognition from a trade union (de-recognition). An employer refusing union recognition, or attempting de-recognition may contemplate dismissals of employees (trade union members) refusing to accept this decision. Dismissals of trade union members for refusal to accept de-recognition are dismissals by reason of 'one or more reasons not related to the individual workers concerned'. The Directive applies.

The employer who contemplates that dismissals may result from his decision to de-recognise 'shall begin consultations with workers' representatives in good time with a view to reaching an agreement'.[103] The employer must examine 'ways and means of avoiding collective redundancies or reducing the number of workers affected'.[104] An employer genuinely concerned to avoid dismissals could easily continue recognition to avoid the dismissals. Continuing union recognition is even implicit in the provision that these consultations 'shall

---

[100] Council Directive 75/129 of 17 February 1975 on the approximation of the laws of the Member States relating to collective dismissals, OJ L48/29, as amended by Directive 92/56 of 24 June 1992, OJ L245/92. Now consolidated in Council Directive 98/59/EC of 20 July 1998 on the approximation of the laws of the Member States relating to collective redundancies, OJ L225/16.

[101] Article 1(1)(a).    [102] Directive 98/59/EC, Article 1(1)(a), last sub-paragraph.

[103] 1992 amending Directive, inserting new Article 2(1).    [104] Article 2(2).

begin ... with a view to reaching an agreement'. They are premised on there being an agreement with (union) representatives.

It should, if belatedly, be recognised that the Collective Dismissals Directive embodies an EU policy that striking workers may be defending *collective* interests. As such they are covered by EU law against dismissals effected for such collective 'reasons not related to the individual workers concerned'.

## The spill-over effect of the European social dialogue

The spill-over effect of EU legislation into general principles of collective labour law, described in this chapter, was compounded by the operation of the new constitutional basis of collective labour law contained in the Protocol and Agreement on Social Policy attached to the Maastricht Treaty on European Union. The emergence and evolution of this new set of norms of collective negotiation of social policy and labour law through social dialogue may aspire, but cannot hope to achieve, *neutrality* of impact on national systems.[105] Awareness of the role of judicial interpretation in the formation of national systems of collective labour law is likely to have an impact on the new framework of collective social dialogue at EU level. But judicial interpretations by the European Court or national courts are unlikely simply to replicate existing national norms.

The congruence of different national systems with an emerging EU system of industrial relations and collective bargaining is variable. The compatibility of collective labour law at Member State level is under scrutiny to assess the extent to which national collective labour law requires modification to accommodate the EU dimension. The formulation of a collective labour law at EU level requires, at a minimum, that certain Member State rules of collective labour law, deemed essential to the desired development of EU-level industrial relations, would have to be guaranteed in EU law, regardless of the legal position at Member State level.

This is not to underestimate the difficulty. For example, a precondition of national trade union participation in the EU social dialogue might be that the representativeness of the national trade union be somehow assessed.[106] This might be contested either on the ground that national, not EU criteria, were

---

[105] For example, in October 2006, the former President of France, Jacques Chirac, in a speech before the Economic and Social Council of France, announced his intention to ensure that, *following the European model*, his government would not undertake any legislative initiative without prior consultation of the social partners. This was promptly followed in the case of the introduction of new provisions of the Code de travail with the new proposals transmitted to the social partners on 26 October, with consultation scheduled for 6 November, before continuing the legislative procdure. Nicolas Sarkozy has indicated his intention to follow this procedure.

[106] For a recent survey of trade union representativeness and collective bargaining in a number of Member States, see *Revue de Droit du Travail*, November 2006 (pp. 336–43, UK, Italy), December 2006 (pp. 408–18, Germany), January 2007 (pp. 54–61, Sweden, the Netherlands, Spain).

appropriate, or, more fundamentally, on the basis of the principle of trade union autonomy.

Again, the equilibrium reached between trade unions and workers' representatives at *enterprise* level is complex and variable among Member States. Collective labour law at EU level is bound to impact upon this equilibrium. The question is how, and whether, the impact should be oriented in a specific policy direction. For example, systems which were wholly oriented towards decentralisation of collective bargaining, and denied trade unions rights at any level above that of the enterprise would be incompatible with the evolution of an EU system of industrial relations.

Given the *existing* links with Member State trade unions, it would strengthen the legitimacy of EU-level trade union organisations if collective labour law formulated at EU level reinforced *trade union* representation over enterprise or workplace-based representation. The strengthening of *sector* or *multi-sector* trade union organisations in Member States is another choice to be made. On the other hand, the creation of European works' councils, for the first time, promotes a *transnational* system of worker representation *based on the enterprise*. It poses the possibility, for the first time, of a direct legitimising link being forged between enterprise representatives and EU-level organisations. The emerging role of *sector* trade union representation on EWCs would argue for the reinforcement of EU-level sector trade union rights.

The formulation of a collective labour law of the EU will aim to infuse the national systems with the spirit of an emerging EU industrial relations system. The content of the resulting legal framework is normatively driven by a vision of EU industrial relations. The development of a harmonious framework of collective labour law integrating Member State systems into an emerging EU system of industrial relations and social dialogue is a delicate task. It entails respect for the principles of national systems, while undertaking their adaptation to a transnational system, which as yet does not possess the accumulated legitimacy of traditional systems, and achieving this adaptation without disturbing national equilibria.

Differences in collective labour law among the twenty-seven Member States are attributed to different national traditions and histories. Basic trade union rights common to the Member States are now to be found in the EU Charter of Fundamental Rights, analysed in the following Chapter 13, and are reflected in the EU legislation and decisions of the European Court of Justice analysed in this chapter.

There is wide variation among the formal legislative provisions at Member State level. This is further highlighted by the *absence* of any formal provision in some Member States, for example, on trade union rights which, in others, are guaranteed constitutional status. This *formal* diversity does not mean that there is no common recognition of collective labour law principles. In *substantive* terms, Member States do guarantee certain principles through a variety of formal provisions and effective practices.

For example, beyond the elementary, though fundamental, right of association, difficulties of formulation of common trade union rights emerge. Trade union rights in the Member States have developed into a wide variety of rights to trade union recognition, worker representation, collective bargaining and information and consultation. The search for categories of uniform regulation must begin with the reality of diversity, but, as will be shown later in this volume, need not be defeated by it.

To move from this reality to a formulation of collective labour rights at EU level means addressing a deeper issue – how to act at EU level and, first, not unduly disturb national *equilibria*; secondly, *support* the emerging system of EU-level industrial relations and social dialogue.

*National* collective labour laws were *not* developed with *transnational* industrial relations or collective bargaining in mind. The law of the Member States needs to accommodate the European dimension, particularly in light of the Treaty provisions on EU social dialogue.

Questions arise as to how far transnational trade union rights are consistent with purely national-level trade union rights, and if, and how, they can be integrated into a harmonious whole. But, like it or not, a dynamic is at work whereby a framework of collective labour law at EU level is being formulated. EU legal interventions in areas of social policy and labour law lead inevitably to EU rules being established regarding collective labour relations – the 'spill-over' effect.

The only question is what will be the relative contribution of the different actors involved – social partners, EU legislative institutions, or the European Court – to the process of formulation of this framework of collective labour law. The dynamic operation of an increasingly integrated single European market means abstention is not an option.

Nor is this a mere *desideratum* of European integration. The Member State systems of industrial relations are threatened by decline unless there is an EU-level framework of collective labour law. National systems are inadequate to protect against the operations of multinational enterprises. The development of an international European economy dictates an EU-level legal framework. Internationalisation of the economy beyond Europe, the global economy, also challenges national systems. But the absence of machinery to create a global framework of rules does not mean action at EU level should be postponed. Ultimately, to defend Member State systems in the faced of internationalisation of the economy, a framework of European collective labour law is needed.[107]

---

[107] See B. Bercusson and C. Estlund (eds.), *Regulating Labour in the Wake of Globalization: New Challenges, New Institutions*, Oxford: Hart, vol. II of the Columbia-London Series, 2008. K. Ahlberg, B. Bercusson, N. Bruun, H. Kountouros, C. Vigneau and L. Zappalà, *Transnational Labour Regulation: A Case Study of Temporary Agency Work*, Brussels: Peter Lang, Brussels, 2008.

## Fundamental collective rights in European labour law

The principles of the collective labour law of the European Union outlined above include collectively bargained labour standards, workers' collective representation, workers' participation and protection of workers' collective industrial action. However, these fundamental collective principles were developed, like EU labour law in general, in piecemeal fashion, in response to specific economic and political conjunctures, and are scattered in an incoherent structure throughout provisions in the Treaty and various directives, as well as in the case-law of the European Court. The collective principles which underpin the European social model were not developed on the basis of a clear legal foundation.

The EU Charter of Fundamental Rights adopted at Nice in December 2000 provides such a legal foundation. As such, it is of primary legal significance for European labour law. The fundamental rights to freedom of association (Article 12), workers' right to information and consultation within the undertaking (Article 27) and rights of collective bargaining and action (Article 28) provide the starting point for the future coherent and systematic evolution of collective labour law of the EU. This collective labour law is the framework within which the European labour law of individual employment protection will emerge. This is all the more so if, as proposed and probable, the Charter becomes legally binding on a par with the Treaties.

The purpose of the next part of this chapter is to analyse the evolution of these foundational provisions, their sources in national and international labour laws on the fundamental rights of labour, their potential scope, the problems posed in their interpretation, and their application to labour regulation in the EU and the Member States.

The potential of fundamental collective rights of labour in the EU legal order will be apparent when they are compared with Member State laws which restrict or inhibit the rights of workers and their representatives to information and consultation, to join trade unions and have their unions recognised for the purposes of collective bargaining, and to take strike action. If an employer refuses to enter into collective agreements, or dismisses strikers exercising their fundamental right to take collective action, or closes down the undertaking without advance information and consultation, EU law may become available to challenge violations of what are declared to be the fundamental collective rights of workers.

Fundamental rights is an area where the EU legal order has heretofore been developed by the European Court of Justice with great care, given the sensitivity of national constitutional courts to intrusions upon national legal orders of EU legal measures asserting the doctrine of supremacy of EU law.[108] Of course, the

---

[108]  P. Craig and G. de Búrca, *EU Law: Text, Cases and Materials*, 3rd edn, Oxford: Oxford University Press, 2003, Chapter 8, 'General Principles I: Fundamental Rights', pp. 317–70.

EU Charter can be used only where the issue is governed by EU law. There are EU laws on information and consultation, where the EU Charter may become very relevant, but other areas, such as strikes and collective bargaining, are much less familiar to the Court. Nonetheless, as EU law continuously expands, the actions of Member States and private individuals and corporations may come to be challenged where they fail to respect what are now recognised as the fundamental human rights of workers and their representatives. Conversely, the European Court will be confronted with the challenge of defining more precisely the content of these new fundamental rights when exercised by organisations of workers.[109]

## The Court's fundamental rights jurisprudence

How may the European Court of Justice go about identifying fundamental collective rights of labour, including fundamental trade union rights? This can best be understood in light of the Court's past record of assertion of the protection of fundamental rights in the EU's legal order. Two of the earliest seminal decisions illustrate the Court's approach.

In *Stauder*, the Court referred to 'the fundamental human rights enshrined in the general principles of Community law and protected by the Court'. Advocate-General Roemer referred to 'general legal principles of Community law in force' which were to be 'guided by reference to the fundamental principles of national law'. They were 'an unwritten constituent part of Community law'.[110] In the decision in *Internationale Handelsgesellschaft*, the Court held that the validity of an EC measure cannot be affected by a claim that it is counter to fundamental rights or principles of national law. However, on the question of whether there were analogous fundamental rights in EC law, the Court stated:[111]

> respect for fundamental rights forms an integral part of the general principles of Community law protected by the European Court of Justice … inspired by the constitutional traditions common to the Member States.

The explicit endorsement of fundamental rights in the EU legal order, backed by this reference to the common constitutional traditions of the Member States, is now reinforced by Article 6(2) of the Treaty on European Union:

> The Union shall respect fundamental rights, as guaranteed by the European Convention for the Protection of Human Rights and Fundamental Freedoms

---

[109] The EU Charter has been cited in the Opinions of every Advocate-General and in judgments of the Court of First Instance. For an account of forty-four cases up to August 2003 where the Charter was cited by Advocates-General and the Court of First Instance, see the Appendix in B. Bercusson (ed.), *European Labour Law and the EU Charter of Fundamental Rights*, Baden-Baden: Nomos, 2006. The Charter was first cited also by the European Court of Justice in Case C-540/03, *Parliament* v. *Council*, decided 27 June 2006.

[110] *Stauder* v. *City of Ulm*, [1969] ECR 419; ECJ, paragraph 7; A–G, p. 428.

[111] *Internationale Handelsgesellschaft* v. *Einfuhr- und Vorratstelle fur Getreide und Futtermittel*, Case 11/70, [1970] ECR 1125, paragraph 4.

signed in Rome on 4 November 1950 and as they result from the constitutional traditions common to the Member States, as general principles of Community law.

Both the jurisprudence and the Treaties now point to the need to identify within Member States the common traditions regarding fundamental trade union rights. In other words, the future interpretations of the fundamental trade union rights in the EU Charter will look to the legal and constitutional practices protecting these rights in the laws of the Member States.[112]

## A preliminary point regarding minimum standards

The European Court's formulation of fundamental trade union rights need not necessarily seek the lowest common denominator or minimum standard. An indication of this is the Court's interpretation of what was then a new Article 118A (now in Article 137 EC) inserted into the Treaty of Rome by the Single European Act of 1986. Article 118A aimed at 'encouraging improvements, especially in the working environment, as regards the health and safety of workers', and specified that:

> 2. In order to help achieve the objective laid down in the first paragraph, the Council ... shall adopt by means of directives, minimum requirements for gradual implementation, having regard to the conditions and technical rules obtaining in each of the Member States.

On the basis of then Article 118A, the Ministers of Social and Labour Affairs at a meeting on 1 June 1993, approved a Commission proposal for a Council Directive concerning certain aspects of the organisation of working time. The UK, however, abstained and announced its intention to challenge the legal basis of the proposed Directive in the European Court. Nonetheless, the Directive was adopted by the Council at a meeting on 23 November 1993 and has become the law of the EU.[113] The UK government took the view that the working time proposal should have been adopted on a legal basis which required unanimous voting, and lodged an appeal with the European Court of Justice to challenge the legal basis selected.

---

[112] Confirmation of this was forthcoming in the first case in which the EU Charter was cited by the Court of First Instance (CFI). In a decision of 30 January 2002 in *max.mobil Telekommunikation Service GmbH* v. *Commission*, the CFI twice referred to provisions of the EU Charter, first Article 41(1) (Right to good administration), and then Article 47 (Right to an effective remedy and to a fair trial) in the following terms (Case T-54/99, paragraphs 48 and 57): 'Such judicial review is also one of the general principles that are observed in a State governed by the rule of law and are common to the constitutional traditions of the Member States, as is confirmed by Article 47 of the Charter of Fundamental Rights, under which any person whose rights guaranteed by the law of the Union are violated has the right to an effective remedy before a tribunal.'

[113] Council Directive 93/104/EC of 23 November 1993 concerning certain aspects of the organisation of working time; OJ L307/18 of 13 December 1993. See *Europe* No. 6113, 24 November 1993, p. 10.

Among other grounds for dismissing the UK's challenge, the Court rejected the UK government's argument that the provision allowed only for 'minimum requirements' in the sense of constituting a minimum benchmark. The Court declared that the provision:[114]

> does not limit Community action to the lowest common denominator, or even to the lowest level of protection established by the various Member States, but means that Member States are free to provide a level of protection more stringent than that resulting from Community law, high as it may be.

There is reason to expect, therefore, that the Court would similarly not interpret the fundamental trade union rights in the EU Charter as reflecting 'the lowest common denominator, or even to the lowest level of protection established by the various Member States'.

## European law, international law and national laws

Problems and ambiguities in interpreting the fundamental collective rights in the EU Charter raise two prospects. First, international labour standards, national constitutions and other national legal measures could be used to interpret ambiguities in the formulations of the Charter. Secondly, the emerging interpretation of fundamental rights in the Charter could influence the fundamental collective rights of labour as they have been applied in the Member States, and also at international level. This is yet another illustration of the dynamic interaction of EC law and national labour laws.

Fundamental collective labour rights in the European Union are not identical in all the twenty-seven Member States. The historical, legal and industrial relations traditions of the Member States have produced differences in national laws which highlight the problem of producing a set of uniform collective labour rights derived from a single EU Charter.

For example, what is included in the scope of 'freedom of association'? There is no exact legal equivalence in the meaning of 'freedom of association' in British or Irish law, 'liberté syndicale' in French or Belgian law, 'Koalitionsfreiheit' in German or Austrian law, or 'libertà sindacale' in Italian law. In Sweden, freedom of association includes the right to take advantage of union membership and to work for the organisation; in the Netherlands, the right to participation through works councils (an institutional issue) is not included in freedom of association (self-organisation), which is tied to trade unions; in Germany, it took twenty-five years of doctrinal debate before the right of association guaranteed in the constitution was generally held to imply the right to strike.

This ambivalence is reflected in the EU Charter itself. The right to freedom of association is provided in Article 12 of the EU Charter, 'Freedom of assembly

---

[114] *UK* v. *Council*, Case C-84/94, [1996] ECR I-5755, paragraph 56.

and of association'. But the Charter also includes other rights: to collective bargaining and to collective action (Article 28). However, in some Member States, these are assumed to be part of a right to 'freedom of association'. The uncertainty was evident in the evolution of Article 12. The references to freedom of association of trade unions were initially included in a group of articles all concerned with the collective rights of labour. However, at a late stage, the trade union rights of association were isolated into Article 12 and included in a different Chapter, entitled 'Freedoms'. Subsequent attempts to unite trade union rights of association with the other collective rights of labour failed, and, in the final draft, Article 12 was kept separate from the other collective rights, which were placed in the chapter entitled 'Solidarity'.

Despite national differences, it is possible to analyse collective labour rights in the Member States and provide a comprehensive list of such rights. The extent to which Member States' laws include some, many, or even all of the rights on this list will differ. Often, Member States will acknowledge the same fundamental rights, though they may, in defining the scope of such rights, not always include the same elements.

One approach to identifying the rights which the European Court of Justice might be prepared to recognise as protected by the EU Charter could be to identify those fundamental rights which are protected in all, or a majority of Member States. These rights form the beginnings of an effort to construct a common tradition of protection of collective labour rights.[115]

## EU Charter, Article 12: Freedom of assembly and of association

1. Everyone has the right to freedom of peaceful assembly and to freedom of association at all levels, in particular in political, trade union and civic matters, which implies the right of everyone to form and to join trade unions for the protection of his or her interests.[116]

---

[115] The remainder of this chapter is a revised and edited version of parts of an extended commentary on the labour law implications of the EU Charter; Bercusson (ed.), *European Labour Law and the EU Charter*. A summary version in English (102 pp.) and translated into Dutch, French, German, Greek, Italian, Spanish and Swedish, was published by the European Trade Union Institute, Brussels, 2002–3. The summary versions are available on-line on the website of the European Trade Union Institute, the research arm of the European Trade Union Confederation. The commentary was the work of the Research Group on Transnational Trade Union Rights (Thomas Blanke, Niklas Bruun, Stefan Clauwaert, Antoine Jacobs, Yota Kravaritou, Isabelle Schoeman, Bruno Veneziani and Christophe Vigneau), coordinated by the author, with the steady and constructive support of Reiner Hoffmann, then Director of the European Trade Union Institute. Initial drafts of the full text commentary on Articles 12, 27 and 28, then edited by the author, were produced respectively by the author, Thomas Blanke, University of Oldenburg, Germany, and Bruno Veneziani, University of Bari, Italy.

[116] The EU Charter's Article 12 was Article II-72 of the proposed Constitutional Treaty of the European Union.

Does a trade union 'right to freedom of association' include other collective trade union rights, such as the right to collective bargaining and collective agreements, the right to strike or take other industrial action?[117] Different Member State concepts of 'freedom of association' include some, many or even all of these elements. Concepts of freedom of association often overlap; that does not mean they are the same. Different Member States will include some elements and exclude others. But there are elements of trade union rights which all or most Member States agree are protected. These elements, on which there is consensus, can be assembled into a principle of 'freedom of association' at EU level.

A narrow formulation of 'freedom of association' might include a large number of Member States where such a formulation is acceptable. The *wider the range of rights*, the *fewer the number of Member States* which accept that those rights are within the scope of the fundamental trade union right of freedom of association. The aim is a formulation which includes fundamental trade union rights recognised in all (or most) Member States: a *common core* of elements of a right of 'freedom of association' which is shared by all, or a majority of the Member States.

A Research Study by the author for the European Parliament[118] found there was a unanimous consensus among the then fifteen EU Member States in favour of five trade union rights: of association/to join trade unions, not to join trade unions, to autonomous organisation, to trade union activity (including in works councils) and to a legal status for collective agreements. These would seem to comprise the elements of a right to 'freedom of association' in all those Member States.

Beyond this common core, there is a *substantial majority* (10–11 Member States) in favour of trade union rights regarding legal definition (11), information and consultation (including works councils) (10) and extension of agreements (11). There is also a substantial majority (11 Member States) in favour of trade union rights regarding financial autonomy (11) and elections/decision-making autonomy (11). There is a *substantial majority* (11 Member States) against the closed shop. Finally, there is a *clear majority* (9 Member States) in favour of trade union rights regarding the right to strike and to legal personality.

Two other trade union rights, the legal rights to recognition as trade unions and to collective bargaining of trade unions, are not clearly established. This is, perhaps, due to the overlap with legal requirements for the establishment of workers' representative bodies (works councils) in dual channel systems.

[117] The following commentary on Article 12 of the Charter is a much shortened version of a text initially drafted by the author, based on detailed discussions in the ETUI Research Group on Transnational Trade Union Rights, and finally edited by the author.

[118] B. Bercusson, *Trade Union Rights in the 15 Member States of the European Union*, Research Study for the Committee on Social Affairs and Employment, European Parliament, 1998; Summary (c. 45 pp.) translated and published in all EU languages.

In conclusion, trade union freedom of association includes the rights listed above which are recognised in all (or most) Member States. In a Member State, a claim to the right of association in the EU Charter, as a question of EU law, could be referred by a national court to the European Court of Justice under Article 234 of the EC Treaty. The Court could choose among a number of interpretations. In interpreting any formulation of the right at EU level, the European Court of Justice would be able to draw upon a range of sources, including international law, in particular, ILO Conventions, Council of Europe measures and existing EC law.

Another illustration of the potential of the fundamental collective rights in the EU Charter is Article 27.[119]

## EU Charter, Article 27: Workers' right to information and consultation within the undertaking

> Workers or their representatives must, at the appropriate levels, be guaranteed information and consultation in good time in the cases and under the conditions provided for by Community [Union] law and national laws and practices.[120]

Article 27's formulation of the right to information and consultation should be regarded as an illustration of the ongoing *process of generalisation* of specific-issue rights (reflected in earlier directives) to a fundamental social right. Perceived this way, the reference to 'in the cases and under the conditions provided for by Community law and national laws and practices' represents *added value*, and *should not be read as a limitation* on the general fundamental social right. Rather, the new general fundamental right is to infuse all national (and Community) laws on the subject. Article 27 of the EU Charter *transforms* all national laws and practices into the expression of a more *general fundamental European social right*, on which they are henceforth based, and in light of which they are henceforth to be interpreted.

Article 27's reference to national laws and practices implies that the Member States are obliged to maintain *at least* the mandatory standards of information and consultation provided by legislation or by collective agreements. In combination with Article 136 of the EC Treaty, it prescribes the direction in which future regulation is to develop: towards the 'promotion of … working conditions, so as to make possible their harmonisation while the improvement is being maintained'.

---

[119] This was Article II-87 of the proposed Constitutional Treaty of the European Union.

[120] The following commentary on Article 27 of the Charter is a revised and edited version of a text initially drafted by Thomas Blanke, University of Oldenburg, Germany, based on detailed discussions in the ETUI Research Group on Transnational Trade Union Rights, and finally edited by the author.

### Article 27: a weak version of co-determination or a new fundamental social right?

German labour law provides a particularly valuable insight into the nature of the right to information and consultation of workers within the undertaking. This is now declared a fundamental social right in the EU Charter, and placed first in the chapter entitled 'Solidarity'. Yet, in German legal doctrine, the constitutional status of this right is not unanimously accepted. It may seem curious that Germany, the Member State with probably the oldest and strongest tradition of workers' participation through works councils at establishment level, does not recognise this right as a fundamental social right, whereas the Community, dominated by countries with trade union representation systems, establishes this right as a fundamental social right.

This insight leads to two potentially important conclusions. First, the right to information and consultation is *a new fundamental social right*. Secondly, this right is *not a weak version* of the German co-determination tradition. In short, it is a genuinely new right with its own foundation.

The foundation of the German co-determination tradition was an early socialist ideology of democratic management of the entire economy and, in particular, of companies. In that tradition, workers' right to information and consultation is only a limited version of control of management. At best, it belongs to a culture of rational argumentation within undertakings. This German tradition would not be affected by such an interpretation of Article 27, a weaker version of co-determination. At most, the system of co-determination in Germany could claim a new status as a fundamental social right. But for the rest, it remains within its specific tradition which aims towards the democratisation of all social spheres, including the economy.

However, if the *new* fundamental social right in Article 27 is not based on this co-determination tradition, it is pointless to criticise it as too weak, as might be done when comparing it with established co-determination rights regarded from a (especially German) trade union point of view. Such a critique overlooks the possibility that the objective of Article 27 of the EU Charter is not co-determination and participation, which, for a majority of Member States up to the present, is the right and the duty of the trade unions.

Instead, the foundation of Article 27 of the EU Charter is the *protection of the interests of the individual worker against the dominant position of the employer in situations in which those interests could be substantially affected*. As a fundamental social right this has different sources.

Initially, it derives from the need to protect workers in *extraordinary situations*, such as collective redundancies and transfers of undertakings. It emerges further from the objective to protect in an effective way the *health and safety* of workers. It reacts also to the new problems created by *globalisation of the economy*, with the rise of transnational companies and mergers of undertakings which make workers dependent on decisions taken in other

Member States and may have the effect of weakening national traditions of workers' involvement in the decision-making process.

However, apart from these sources, Article 27 has as much or more to do with the *protection of human dignity* (Article 1 of the EU Charter) than with traditional social rights and the objective of democratisation of the economy. As such it promises greatly to expand the scope both of traditional social rights and of practices of democratisation, to encompass threats to workers' dignity in the many new forms these threats assume in a globalised economy, society and environment. As stated in the Preamble to the general Framework Directive 2002/14, workers' right to information and consultation is a consequence of creating a Europe-wide internal market founded on 'the essential values on which our societies are based'. These values include the concept of a socially responsible economy which ensures 'that *all* citizens benefit from economic development'.

Finally, there is Article 28.[121]

## EU Charter, Article 28: Right of collective bargaining and action

> Workers and employers, or their respective organisations, have, in accordance with Community law and national laws and practices, the right to negotiate and conclude collective agreements at the appropriate levels and, in cases of conflicts of interests, to take collective action to defend their interests, including strike action.[122]

The rights of collective bargaining and action are placed in the EU Charter following Article 27 (workers' right to information and consultation within the undertaking). Together with Article 12 (freedom of assembly and of association), these Articles create a small but dense network of collective labour rights protecting the dignity of workers.

### The right of collective bargaining

Explicit rights to collective labour negotiation are to be found in the constitutions of some Member States (e.g. Belgium, Italy Portugal), but otherwise rights of collective bargaining are said to derive from the broad right of association (Germany, Spain, France).

In providing for a right of collective bargaining, the EU Charter may have at least a *formal-semantic* influence on the wording used in different constitutional texts. It may have also a *substantive* impact on national legal systems

---

[121] This was Article II-88 of the proposed Constitutional Treaty of the European Union.

[122] The following commentary on Article 28 of the Charter is a revised and edited version of a text initially drafted by Bruno Veneziani, University of Bari, Italy, based on detailed discussions in the ETUI Research Group on Transnational Trade Union Rights, and finally edited by the author.

without such rights at constitutional level, as in Austria, Luxembourg, the United Kingdom, Ireland, Denmark, Finland and Sweden.

From the beginning, the intention of the Convention was evident to strengthen the widespread practice of collective bargaining in the majority of European countries through a fundamental right. However, the issues at stake include bargaining levels, coverage, scope, different degrees of engagement of various actors, union security arrangements, mandatory effects and form or type of bargaining structure. Article 28 appears to deal with only some of these – the process: collective bargaining; the outcome: the collective agreement; the actors: workers, employers, their organisations; and the levels: 'appropriate' levels. Each of these requires detailed analysis and interpretation.

National laws on rights to collective bargaining and collective agreements highlight that the most delicate and crucial problem is posed by Article 28's 'right to … conclude collective agreements'. National constitutions generally appear to emphasise the right to collective bargaining, to start and conduct negotiations. There is also some national legislation providing an obligation to negotiate on certain issues at certain intervals. The obligation to negotiate may be reciprocal, balanced by an obligation on both sides to enter into negotiations. On the other hand, some Member States reject the idea of legal regulation of the right of participation in collective bargaining, which can be obtained only through the power of the social partners. Given this spectrum of provisions, the express declaration in Article 28 of a right to collective bargaining may become the instrument for overcoming what are perceived as weaknesses in national laws on the collective bargaining process.

A right to conclude collective agreements could foreshadow an obligation to conclude such agreements, which could conflict with the fundamental right of trade union freedom in national laws. The policy not to include a right or duty to conclude an agreement is confirmed in international sources. The European Social Charter refers to 'voluntary negotiations' in Article 6 and the Council of Europe's Committee on Social Rights has expressly affirmed this point to the extent of holding that compulsory arbitration without the prior consent of the parties is not in conformity with the principle of voluntary procedures. The ILO Committee of Experts has underlined the same rationale.

In this general context of national and international norms tending to exclude the obligation to conclude collective agreements, Article 28 may be interpreted as inextricably linked to freedom of association. This prevents any interference by public authorities with respect to the content, procedure, structure and levels of collective bargaining, and with respect to collective agreements (at least in the private sector). The right of free collective bargaining includes the freedom to initiate or not to initiate negotiations, and to conclude or not to conclude any agreement. Collective agreements must be concluded without any interference by third parties (e.g. compulsory arbitration or conciliation).

However, Article 28 may nonetheless be interpreted so as to reinforce the right to conclude collective agreements. Article 28 imposes on both contracting parties the duty of mutual cooperation and to act in good faith in reaching the agreement. The right to conclude collective agreements means that both sides, 'workers and employers, or their respective organisations', must abstain, after negotiations have begun, from any harmful conduct, such as delaying tactics or wholesale and repeated rejection of positions, which limit the effective enjoyment of the right. Finally, the right to conclude collective agreements confers rights on workers, employers or their organisations, even if not affiliated to the signatory organisations, to gain access to collective agreements concluded by other parties.

## The right to take collective action

Despite earlier doubts in the Convention drafting the Charter as to EU competence, the final text of the Charter provides that the same actors who enjoy the rights to negotiate and conclude collective agreements have 'the right ... to take collective action ... including strike action'. This formulation may be read also as recognising the right to strike. If collective action includes strike action, and the former is qualified as a right, then the latter must also be a right. Again despite earlier doubts regarding Community competence, the rights to collective action and collective bargaining are to be enjoyed 'in accordance' not only with 'national laws and practices' but also with 'Community law'.[123]

The constitutions of some EU-15 Member States have explicitly recognised the right to strike: Italy, Portugal, Spain, Sweden, Greece and France. In others, it is not explicit but implied (Luxembourg, Belgium). In Austria, the UK and Denmark, it is not possible to speak of a right but only of a freedom to strike. In particular, there are severe restrictions on strikes in the UK, where there is only limited protection against dismissal of strikers and secondary action is banned.

The provision in Article 28 of the EU Charter of the right 'to take collective action ... including strike action' may lead to a fundamental change in those national legal orders where this right is not given constitutional value or is not expressed at a constitutional level. It provides a strong basis for courts to uphold the right to strike in those national legal orders where the law on strikes and lock-outs is derived from general trade union rights (Germany, the Netherlands) and is almost completely 'judge-made'.

---

[123] The ILO does not include the right to strike explicitly in the text of its Constitution and numerous Conventions. However, it has been affirmed in the case law developed by the ILO's Freedom of Association Committee, interpreting Convention No. 87. In contrast, the European Court of Human Rights has rejected the argument that a right to strike is included in the trade union right laid down in Article 11 of the ECHR. On the other hand, an express right to strike is contained in the European Social Charter 1961 and as revised in 1996. The Community Charter of 1989 proclaims that the 'right to resort to collective action .... shall include the right to strike' (Point 13). Finally, 'a right to strike' is included in the International Covenant on Economic, Social and Cultural Rights of 1966 (Article 8). See generally, T. Novitz, *International and European Protection of the Right to Strike*, Oxford: Oxford University Press, 2003.

Article 52 of the EU Charter allows for limitations, but these 'must be provided for by law and respect the essence' of the right to collective action. Further, they are 'subject to the principle of proportionality' and must be 'necessary and genuinely meet objectives of general interest recognised by the Union or the need to protect the rights and freedoms of others'.[124]

The question has arisen of potential conflict between the right to collective action and other freedoms under Community law, such as the freedom of establishment or free movement of goods. In partial response to potential conflicts between the EC law on free movement of goods and colllective industrial action, Council Regulation No. 2679/98 already provides protection for fundamental rights in national law to take collective action 'including the right or freedom to strike'.[125] The Regulation reflects a policy choice: the EU must respect the exercise of fundamental rights and freedoms of collective action at the national level. The decisions of the European Court of Justice in *Viking*[126] and *Laval*,[127] demonstrate that a potentially dangerous conflict looms between the legislative and judicial interpretations of the right to collective action.[128]

## Conclusion: *ordre communautaire social collective*

The purpose of this chapter has been to describe and analyse the *acquis communautaire social* of collective labour law in the form of fundamental principles and rights. It is submitted that, taken together, these comprise an *ordre communautaire social collective* of European labour law to which Member States and the EU institutions are bound. Both EU and national labour regulation will henceforth be scrutinised as to compliance with the collective principles and rights established in EU law, most notably, in the EU Charter of Fundamental Rights.

All concerned with labour regulation, workers, employers and their organisations, administrators and legislators at national and EU level will need to look to the *acquis communautaire social* for the guiding principles governing labour regulation. Failure to do so will expose them to judicial scrutiny as litigants before national courts challenge regulations violating these rights and

---

[124] In some constitutions, specific provisions on collective action require that essential services be guaranteed. Some constitutions require explicit derogation by law from the right to take collective action.

[125] Council Regulation (EC) No. 2679/98 of 7 December 1998 on the functioning of the internal market in relation to the free movement of goods among the Member States. OJ L337/8 of 12 December 1998, Article 2.

[126] Case C-438/05, *International Transport Workers' Federation, Finnish Seamen's Union* v. *Viking Line ABP, OÜ Viking Line Eesti*, decided 11 December 2007.

[127] Case C-341/05, *Laval un Partneri Ltd* v. *Svenska Byggnadsarbetareförbundet, Svenska Byggnadsarbetareförbundet, avd. 1, Svenska Elektrikerförbundet*, decided 18 December 2007.

[128] See the detailed analysis in Chapter 21.

principles, and, as this involves interpretation of EU law, in the EU Charter and elsewhere, the European Court will have the last word.

The scope and interpretation of these collective principles and rights are in the process of evolution. The implications for European labour law of the EU Charter's provisions on fundamental collective labour rights are only at the beginning of their exploration. As this chapter has shown, there is much room for debate as to their precise meaning and application, in both the transnational context of the EU and the national industrial relations context of the EU Member States.

This chapter aimed to describe and analyse the collective framework of European labour law, the *ordre communautaire social collective*. Within this collective framework, European labour law is developing principles and rights of individual employment protection. These latter principles and rights are the subject of the following chapter.

# Chapter 10

# A framework of principles and fundamental rights for European individual employment law

## Collective frameworks and fundamental rights of individual employment

The labour law governing the labour markets of the capitalist economies of Western Europe was shaped by collective organisations of labour and capital. More or less legal support, obstruction or repression was the lot of the collective actors, the processes of collective bargaining and the outcomes in the form of collective agreements, depending on the different political and economic trajectories of the nation states of Europe.[1] The extent to which and the methods by which individual employment in the states of Europe was shaped by these collective actors differed as well. The labour law which articulated regulation of individual employment by collective organisations of labour and capital reflected these differences.

Similarly, the labour law of the EU has developed its own specific trajectory and consequent approach to collective principles and rights in the capitalist economy of the single European market. The labour law of the EU evolved following its own trajectory, and it too has produced its own singular approach to regulation of individual employment in a collective framework.

This collective framework reflects the general quality of European labour law, combining the variety of national experience in the EU Member States with the unique qualities of the new legal order of Community law.

## A collective framework with a variety of models

European labour law has developed a collective framework for regulation of individual employment, but this appears in a variety of models. It is not clear as yet which, if any, of these models is or will become pre-eminent.

It may be that the variety of collective frameworks for regulation of individual employment provides different models which can be adapted more or less easily to the national circumstances of Member States, depending on their

---

[1] B. A. Hepple (ed.), *The Making of Labour Law in Europe: A Comparative Study of Nine Countries Up to 1945*, London: Mansell, 1987. C. Crouch, *Industrial Relations and European State Traditions*, Oxford: Clarendon Press, 1993.

congruence with national labour laws embodying more specific collective frameworks for individual employment. Again, it may be that specific collective frameworks are adapted to the exigencies of different substantive areas of regulation of individual employment (equality, employment in the enterprise, free movement of workers, health and safety, fragmentation of the workforce).

The existence of a variety of collective frameworks may be explained in more banal fashion as the result of the historical conjunctures and contingencies of the political and economic evolution of the EU. As these collective frameworks emerged at different times to shape EU interventions in specific substantive areas of individual employment, the EU regulation of these areas may remain path-dependent on earlier established collective frameworks, even where alternative collective frameworks emerge. Again, it is not yet clear which collective framework, if any, reflects the definitive collective framework for the future regulation of individual employment in the EU.

Underpinning whichever collective framework applies to regulate labour in general or specific areas of individual employment, however, are fundamental rights of the individual employee – as a human being, not a commodity or an article of commerce.

What needs to be emphasised is the risk that fundamental rights may be perceived as an alternative to a framework of collective regulation. Rather, they are complementary.[2] The function of fundamental rights of individual employment is twofold. First, to provide standards by which to assess those emerging from the collective framework.[3] Secondly, to secure that those workers falling, for whatever reason, outside the protection of collective standards are guaranteed protection. There is a mutual feedback process in both functions: the substantive content of fundamental rights of individual employment looks to evolving collective standards, and collective standards are inspired by developments in fundamental individual rights. Fundamental rights and collective standards of individual employment protection reinforce each other.

Fundamental rights of individual employment will be explored later in this chapter. The chapter begins with what is considered to be the dominant collective model: the macro-level European social dialogue and the model of its articulation with Member State systems of industrial relations, replicating a principle prevailing in many national industrial relations systems. It continues with the micro-level model of democratic participation in regulation of individual employment in the enterprise. EU regulation of specific substantive areas of individual employment has produced other models of collective regulation.

Thereafter, the chapter outlines in more detail the different models of collective regulation in European labour law governing specific areas of substantive

---

[2] Cf. the discussion of the nature and function of the 1989 Charter of the Fundamental Social Rights of Workers in the first edition of this book, Chapter 38, pp. 599–601.

[3] For example, as fundamental rights to equality may be used to assess collective agreements on equal treatment.

law: (i) equality, (ii) health and safety, (iii) free movement and (iv) fragmentation of forms of work.

## Macro-level collective regulation through the European social dialogue: extending the classic model of articulation

The European social dialogue, the emergence of which is described in Chapter 5, is the dominant model in European labour law for collective regulation of individual employment. It replicates at EU level the model of collective regulation of employment which prevails in national labour laws.

The model articulates EU level collective regulation with national systems.[4] The role played by the EU social dialogue in regulation of individual employment is most sharply visible in the directives which implement social dialogue framework agreements on parental leave, part-time work and fixed-term work and those on telework, work-related stress and harassment and violence at work. To these commonly known intersectoral agreements in the social dialogue may be added a much larger number of outcomes of the social dialogue.[5]

Serious problems of the adequacy of the collective framework model of the social dialogue are evident,[6] and it is by no means certain that these inadequacies will be addressed by the use of the 'open method of coordination' as suggested by the Commission.[7] But as regards the fundamental principle of collective regulation of individual employment, *the European social dialogue*

---

[4] The precise modalities of this articulation are the subject of much uncertainty due to the still unclear legal effects of EU social dialogue agreements, their relation to collective bargaining in the Member States, the role of articulation explicitly confirmed in Article 137(3) EC, the resort to the open method of coordination as a means of articulation, and so on.

[5] In its Communication of 26 June 2002 on the role of social dialogue in European labour law, entitled 'The European social dialogue, a force for innovation and change', the Commission noted that 'The European social partners have adopted joint opinions, statements and declarations on numerous occasions. More than 230 such joint sectoral texts have been issued and some 40 cross-industry texts …'. A detailed list may be found in the Annex to the Communication. COM(2002) 341 final, 26 June 2002. See also the Commission's website on the social dialogue, which demonstrates the range of individual employment concerns covered.

[6] While the output of the European social dialogue appears substantial, the Communication of 26 June 2002 expressed concern as to its implementation. Under the heading 'Improving monitoring and implementation', the Commission commented: 'However, in most cases, these texts did not include any provision for implementation and monitoring: they were responses to short-term concerns. They are not well known and their dissemination at national level has been limited. Their effectiveness can thus be called into question'. On the question of the perceived lack of effectiveness, the Commission noted that: 'Special consideration must be given to the question of how to implement the texts adopted by the European social partners. The recommendations of the High-Level Group on Industrial Relations and Change see the use of machinery based on the open method of coordination as an extremely promising way forward. The social partners could apply some of their agreements (where not regulatory) by establishing goals or guidelines at European level, through regular national implementation reports and regular, systematic assessment of progress achieved'. COM(2002) 341 final, 26 June 2002, Section 2.4.1, p. 18.

[7] See Chapter 6.

*model remains the most prominent and promising.*[8] Its comprehensive and effective articulation with national regulation of individual employment is hostage to political and economic changes, but its legal basis is securely enshrined in the EC Treaty Articles 138–9.[9]

That is not to say that the standards established by this method are beyond criticism. On the one hand, the social dialogue framework agreements do cover large segments of the workforce (part-time workers, fixed-term workers, workers who are parents), and deal with issues crucial to the workforce as a whole (e.g. work-related stress). On the other hand, apart from the problems of effective enforcement, the substantive standards established by these agreements have been attacked as impoverished and compromised. To that extent, substantive fundamental rights of individual employment may be invoked to complement the standards established by the collective framework. That itself creates the prospect of a dynamic (or clash) between fundamental rights and the principle of collective autonomy which is at the basis of the collective framework of regulation.

## Micro-level collective regulation of individual employment in the enterprise

Labour in the enterprise began in EU law as a factor of production. The four freedoms classed labour along with goods, services and capital as one of the factors guaranteed free circulation in the common market. For the rest, there was the undertaking regarding equal pay in Article 119 of the Treaty of Rome, and a gesture in the direction of labour market intervention in the form of vocational training. Beyond this, the commitment to labour took the form of a principle of improvement of living and working conditions, to be achieved through the operation of the common market, but without any concrete mechanisms engaging the workers in the enterprise themselves.

The provisions on free movement of labour did not address issues of collective concern to workers in the enterprise. Indirectly, however, the common market logic, though confined to harmonisation of working conditions, could be extended to embrace these matters. Given this oblique perspective, it was perhaps not surprising that the first major initiative proposed by the Commission only emerged in 1972, and took the form of the draft Fifth Directive on harmonisation of company structure and administration.[10]

The position was transformed under the impetus of the Social Action Programme following the Paris Summit of 1972, finally adopted in 1974. It came to be applied in the context of the economic dislocation in Western

---

[8] Hence, it will be dealt with at length in Part V, Chapters 17–19.

[9] This was confirmed by its retention in the proposed Constitutional Treaty, Articles III-211–12.

[10] This proposal sought to require companies with over 500 employees to include employee representatives on an obligatory supervisory board. It was unsuccessful in obtaining the approval of the Council of Ministers.

Europe consequent on the rise in oil prices following the 1973 Middle East war. Within the constraints of the logic of harmonisation in a common market, this led to two Directives: on collective dismissals and protection of individual employees in transfers of undertakings. Both these Directives included provisions requiring employers to inform and consult workers' representatives.[11]

These Directives might have been the beginning of a sustained development towards a role for labour in the enterprise.[12] However, all initiatives came to naught. The requirement of unanimity in the Council of Ministers congealed any movement they might have represented.[13] The inability of the EU to expand the scope of issues of concern to individual employees to be regulated through collective representation in the enterprise led to a familiar development of 'spill-over' from those Directives which had been adopted.[14] The legislative log-jam was finally broken under the impact of the Member States' desire for a social dimension to accompany the 1992 Single Market Programme, which led to the adoption of the Protocol and Agreement on Social Policy of the TEU. The initial result was the Directive on European Works Councils, which manifested a general strategy towards collective labour regulation in the enterprise through an information and consultation mechanism, following eight years later by the general Framework Directive on Information and Consultation.[15]

These Directives should be seen not as individual and isolated cases of special situations or circumstances where EU policy was exceptionally supportive of

---

[11] Council Directive 75/129/EEC of 17 February 1975 on the approximation of the laws of the Member States relating to collective redundancies, OJ L48/29 of 22 February 1975, as amended by Directive 92/56/EEC of 24 June 1992. OJ J245/3 of 26 August 1992, Article 1(2). Council Directive 77/187/EEC of 14 February 1997 on the approximation of the laws of the Member States relating to the safeguarding of employees' rights in the event of transfers of undertakings, businesses or parts of businesses, OJ L61/26 of 5 April 1977, Article 6.

[12] The following years saw a number of initiatives by the Commission which attempted to expand their scope: two drafts of a Directive on procedures for informing and consulting employees in large national and multinational firms in 1980 and 1983 (the so-called 'Vredling' Directive, named after the then Commissioner for Social Affairs); a revised draft Fifth Directive on company structure and administration in 1983; and a revised draft Regulation and Directive on the Statute for a European Company, in 1979 (amending earlier drafts of 1970 and 1975).

[13] Progress was only made in the sphere of health and safety at work, where a number of directives were adopted regarding information and consultation over hazards at work: lead and ionic compounds in 1982 (Council Directive 82/605/EEC of 28 July 1982, Article 11(2)(b); OJ L247/82); asbestos in 1983 (the Asbestos Directive 83/477/EEC, OJ L263/83, Articles 11(2), 14(2)(b) as amended by Council Directive 91/382/EEC of 25 June 1991); noise in 1986 (Council Directive 86/188/EEC of 12 May 1986, Articles 3(4); OJ L137/86), culminating in the Framework Directive in 1989 (Council Directive 89/391/EEC of 12 June 1989; OJ L183/1).

[14] So as to require information and consultation in an increasingly wide range of circumstances not initially anticipated: transnational issues, privatisation, outsourcing.

[15] Council Directive 94/45/EC of 22 September 1994 on the establishment of a European Works Council or a procedure in Community-scale undertakings and Community-scale groups of undertakings for the purposes of informing and consulting employees. OJ L254/64 of 30 September 1994. Council Directive No. 2002/14 establishing a framework for informing and consulting employees in the European Community. OJ 2002, L80/29.

labour in the enterprise. Rather, they reflect the general evolution of policy in the EU towards a collective framework governing individual employment in the enterprise. The specific measures embodying this policy have been shaped by the contingent difficulties of social policy formation at particular conjunctures in the development of the EU. But they should be seen in this general context.

Directives apparently covering only narrowly defined situations involving collective dismissals, transfers of undertakings and transnational enterprises have become part of a general model of collective regulation of matters affecting individual employment. In Chapter 9, the EU Charter's inclusion of workers' right to information and consultation in the enterprise (Article 27) was described in terms of 'the protection of the interests of the individual worker against the dominant position of the employer in situations in which those interests could be substantially affected'. As such, it is concerned with the protection of individual human dignity (Article 1 of the EU Charter). EU law's support for employee representatives, and their institutional interaction with employers at various levels of decision-making in the enterprise, embodies the model of collective regulation of individual employment in the enterprise, a central component of the European social model of citizenship. The collective framework of individual employment will now be elaborated in its different models applied to substantive areas of labour law: equality, health and safety, free movement and fragmentation of the workforce.

## Equality: a collective model of mutual reinforcement

The collective model of equality in individual employment contrasts with the standard account of European equality law by insisting on the collective rather the individual nature of the problem of discrimination. This has consequences for the legal mechanisms by which the problem is to be addressed. The collective approach to equality law also aims to avoid using the law on discrimination to address more general problems of inequality based on the fundamental imbalance of power in the individual employment relationship.

EU labour law concerned with equality initially posed problems for collective regulation, as equality principles challenged discriminatory collective agreements and collective bargaining structures. However, the collective model of equality law aimed to reconcile these conflicts, as the mutual benefits of extending collective regulation to groups subject to discrimination in the labour market became apparent. Equality between men and women was the first and foremost protagonist in forging this collective model.

Trade unions became aware that a feminised workforce offered prospects for reversing an otherwise declining membership, especially in the public sector, where both union density and female employment are high. Equality demands allowed for collective regulation of hiring practices, pay structures and managerial prerogatives otherwise resistant to challenge. Employers were conscious that the exigencies of changing demography increased the need to widen the recruitment pool by attracting women into employment. This might require greater flexibility in working arrangements, but in turn could offer advantages by adapting production and service provision to market demands. Workforce resistance to such changes might be more easily accommodated through collective regulation. For women, given the reality of the imbalance of power in individual employment relations, a collective model appeared a desirable alternative to legislative regulation, administrative implementation or judicial enforcement based on individual complaints and litigation.

The evolution of a collective model in sex equality law was stimulated by the early and dynamic provision in EU law for sex equality. Sex equality law challenged established discriminatory structures (male-dominated industrial relations institutions) and employment patterns (occupational sex segregation). Collective regulation had to develop a model to accommodate EU equality law. As one of the earliest and most developed fields of European labour law, it was only a matter of time before sex equality law came into conflict with traditional collective regulation, stimulating a collective model of regulating equality in individual employment.

## Evolution of the model

### The Treaty of Rome and its aftermath

There is an interesting paradox at the origins of the EU labour law on sex equality. The quantitative and qualitative significance of the EU law on equality between men and women is undisputed. The amount of legislation and the number and importance of decisions by the European Court exceed any other area of social policy. The fundamental principles created in the context of this evolution have had an impact on EU law going far beyond the area of policy concerned. It has probably had greater influence on the domestic law of the Member States than any other area of social law and policy.

Equal opportunities between women and men have been in the forefront of the social policy of the European Community since its beginnings. Article 119 (now 141) of the Rome Treaty, Directives on equal pay,[16] equal treatment[17] and social security,[18] the extensive case-law of the European Court of Justice

---

[16] Council Directive 75/117/EEC of 10 February 1975 on the approximation of the laws of the Member States relating to the application of the principle of equal pay for men and women, OJ L 45/19 of 19 February 1975.

[17] Council Directive 76/207/EEC of 9 February 1976, on the implementation of the principle of equal treatment for men and women as regards access to employment, vocational training and promotion and working conditions, OJ L39/40 of 14 February 1976.

[18] Council Directive 79/7/EEC of 19 December 1978, on the progressive implementation of the principle of equal treatment for men and women in matters of social security, OJ L6/24 of 10 January 1979; Council Directive 86/378/EEC of 24 July 1986, on the implementation of the principle of equal treatment for men and women in occupational social security schemes, OJ L225/40 of 12 August 1986; Council Directive 86/613/EEC of 11 December 1986, on the application of the principle of equal treatment between men and women engaged in an activity, including agriculture, in a self-employed capacity, and on the protection of self-employed women during pregnancy and motherhood, OJ L359/56 of 19 December 1986.

(beginning with *Defrenne* v. *Belgium*[19]), and a quantity of 'soft law' (such as the Recommendation on the Promotion of Positive Action[20]) have contributed to the prominence of this social policy. Equal treatment of men and women has achieved the status of a 'fundamental right.'[21]

The concept of equal opportunities in the EC has undergone an impressive theoretical development following debates in the women's movement. The original concept of direct and intentional discrimination in the form of less favourable treatment of women by reason of their sex expanded to include, among others, indirect discrimination, positive action, critical review of protective legislation, pregnancy, maternity and childcare and sexual harassment. The scope of the concept expanded beyond pay to include discrimination in access to work, conditions of work, vocational training, pensions, both public and private, and social welfare.

Yet these major EU initiatives towards the achievement of equality between men and women were undertaken despite the fact that women as a pressure group were relatively unorganised. During the period when these legal foundations were being laid, it was argued that the women's movement had little impact on political institutions and on the political arena in general. Hoskyns concludes that:[22]

> the scope and form of the European policy is such that it does not connect easily with either the thinking or the practice of the women's movement as this has developed since the early 1970s. Nor is the European Community set up in such a way that makes it easy for grassroots movements to become involved in its activities.

The impressive expansion of the EU law on equality was decidedly top-down in its origins. The French government negotiating the Treaty of Rome of 1957 was sufficiently anxious about competition with its domestic textile industry from Belgian employers to insist on the inclusion of Article 119 on equal pay, to preclude undercutting by lower-paid Belgian women workers. The Council of Ministers, in its path-breaking Resolution concerning a social action programme of 21 January 1974, famously reaffirmed specifically their aim:[23]

> to undertake action for the purpose of achieving equality between men and
> women as regards access to employment and vocational training and
> advancement and as regards working conditions, including pay, taking
> into account the important role of management and labour in this field,
> to ensure that the family responsibilities of all concerned may be reconciled
> with their job aspirations.

---

[19] *Gabrielle Defrenne* v. *Belgian State*, Case 80/70, [1971] ECR 445.

[20] Council Recommendation 84/635/EEC of 13 December 1984, on the promotion of positive action for women, OJ 331/84.

[21] C. Docksey, 'The Principle of Equality between Men and Women as a Fundamental Right under Community Law', (1991) 20 *Industrial Law Journal* 258.

[22] C. Hoskyns, 'Women, European Law and Transnational Politics', (1986) 14 *International Journal of the Sociology of Law* 299, at p. 300.

[23] (1974) OJ C13/01.

The inspiration of Article 119 and the initiatives that followed received the benediction of the Court of Justice in its judgment in *Defrenne* v. *SABENA*:[24]

8. Article 119 pursues a double aim.
9. First, in the light of the different stages of the development of social legislation in the various Member States, the aim of Article 119 is to avoid a situation in which undertakings established in States which have actually implemented the principle of equal pay suffer a competitive disadvantage in intra-Community competition as compared with undertakings established in States which have not yet eliminated discrimination against women workers as regards pay.
10. Secondly, this provision forms part of the social objectives of the Community, which is not merely an economic union, but is at the same time intended, by common action, to ensure social progress and seek the constant improvement of the living and working conditions of their peoples, as is emphasized by the Preamble to the Treaty.
11. This aim is accentuated by the insertion of Article 119 into the body of a chapter devoted to social policy whose preliminary provision, Article 117, marks 'the need to promote improved working conditions and an improved standard of living for workers, so as to make possible their harmonization while the improvement is being maintained'.
12. This double aim, which is at once economic and social, shows that the principle of equal pay forms part of the foundations of the Community.

Some twenty-five years later, the Court went further:[25]

the economic aim pursued by Article 119 of the Treaty, namely the elimination of distortions of competition between undertakings established in different Member States, is secondary to the social aim pursued by the same provision, which constitutes the expression of a fundamental human right.

All these legal measures have contributed to the prominence of EU policy on equality between men and women to the extent that equal treatment of men and women has achieved the status of a 'fundamental right.' This is recognised in the first sentence of Article 23 of the EU Charter of Fundamental Rights: 'Equality between men and women must be ensured in all areas, including employment, work and pay.'

It is important to appreciate that the specific nature of the EU law on equality may be explicable in terms of its development *apart* from the women's movement.[26] In contrast, the labour and trade union movement in the Member States

---

[24] *Gabrielle Defrenne* v. *Société Anonyme Belge de Navigation Arienne Sabena*, Case 43/75, 8 April 1976, [1976] ECR 455, paragraphs 8–12.

[25] *Deutsche Telekom AG* v. *Lili Schroder*, Case C-50/96, [2000] ECR I-743, paragraph 57.

[26] However, the feminist critique which has gathered apace with the evolution of the body of European law on equality continues to have a major formative influence on its future development.

and at EU level has long been formidably organised. Yet, measured in terms of the development of EU labour law, it has to be conceded that, during the period when equality law was in the forefront of developments of EU social and labour law, the successes of the European trade union movement were few and far between.

This situation has now changed. EU social and labour law has received a powerful impulse from organised labour. The institutionalisation of the European social dialogue and the competences acquired by the Community under the Maastricht Treaty's Protocol and Agreement on Social Policy are the concrete evidence of organised labour's influence. On the other hand, the original inspiration for the EU law on sex equality is changing. This is in part due to the critique of the legal concept of equality embedded in the legislation and case law, which has led to efforts being directed differently and elsewhere.

## The Amsterdam Treaty: reinforcing the focus on discrimination

### New task

The Amsterdam Treaty of 1997 introduced new provisions into the EC Treaty, including a number of changes to the 'social chapter' provisions which referred to equality and discrimination. Specifically regarding sex discrimination, there is introduced a supplement in Article 2 of the Treaty:

> The Community shall have as its task … to promote … a high level of employment and of social protection, *equality between men and women* … the raising of the standard of living and quality of life, and economic and social cohesion and solidarity among Member States.

All these were already present in Article 2 (as amended by the Maastricht Treaty), save for the reference to equality between men and women. This addition may be significant, when coupled with the expanded new Article 141 (ex Article 119) allowing for positive action.

### Mainstreaming

Further, there is a supplement to Article 3 of the EC Treaty in the form of a new paragraph:

> In all the activities referred to in this Article, the Community shall aim to eliminate inequalities, and to promote equality, between men and women.

This is again a reinforcement of positive action, but specifically recognising the policy of 'mainstreaming', whereby sex equality is not seen as a separate issue, but integrated into all policy dimensions of the EC.

### Equal value

A new Article 141 (ex Article 119) changes the EC Treaty provision on equal pay to include 'equal value':

> Each Member State shall ensure that the principle of equal pay for male and female workers for equal work *or work of equal value* is applied.

This confirms the present position, since the European Court of Justice, by holding that the Equal Pay Directive 75/117 'in no way alters the content or scope' of Article 119, effectively extended it to include equal value.[27]

### Mandate for new equality measures

The Amsterdam Treaty inserted a wholly new paragraph into Article 141 (ex Article 119):

> 3. The Council, acting in accordance with the procedure referred to in Article 251 (ex Article 189b), and after consulting the Economic and Social Committee, shall adopt measures to ensure the application of the principle of equal opportunities and equal treatment of men and women in matters of employment and occupation, including the principle of equal pay for equal work or work of equal value.

Previously, such measures as the Equal Pay Directive[28] had to be adopted under Article 94 (ex Article 100) of the Treaty, which authorised 'directives for the approximation of such laws, regulations or administrative provisions of the Member States as directly affect the establishment or functioning of the common market'. This requirement of 'market legitimacy' is no longer necessary. It is replaced by a provision allowing for the proposal of directives with the explicit mandate of ensuring the application the EC law on sex equality.[29]

### Positive action

A second new paragraph is inserted by the Amsterdam Treaty into Article 141 (ex Article 119):[30]

> 4. *With a view to ensuring full equality in practice between men and women in working life, the principle of equal treatment* shall not prevent any Member State from maintaining or adopting measures providing for specific advantages in order to make it easier for *the underrepresented sex* [formerly: women] to pursue a vocational activity or to prevent or compensate for disadvantages in professional careers.

This new provision seems to go beyond its predecessor authorising positive action.[31] More important, it is now a Treaty provision, not merely a Directive. It

---

[27] Case 96/80: *Jenkins* v. *Kingsgate* [1981] ECR 911.

[28] Council Directive 75/117/EEC of 10 February 1975 on the approximation of the laws of the Member States relating to the application of the principle of equal pay for men and women, OJ 1975 L45/19.

[29] The procedure is that of co-decision (Article 251, ex Article 189b), giving the European Parliament a greater voice in determining sex equality policies.

[30] A revised and expanded version of Article 6(3) of the Maastricht Agreement (new wording in italics).

[31] The Equal Treatment Directive 76/207, Article 2(4): 'This Directive shall be without prejudice to measures to promote equal opportunity for men and women, in particular by removing existing inequalities which affect women's opportunities in the areas referred to in Article 1(1).' Council Directive 76/207/EEC of 9 February 1976 on the implementation of the principle of equal treatment for men and women as regards access to employment, vocational training and promotion, and working conditions. OJ L39/40 of 14 February 1976.

was particularly timely in light of the decision of the European Court of Justice in *Kalanke*, widely interpreted as hostile to positive action measures.[32]

### First fruits: a new directive

The election of the new Labour government in the UK in May 1997 finally allowed for the adoption of the proposed directive on the reversal of the burden of proof in sex discrimination cases. This aims to ensure that measures taken by Member States under the principle of equal treatment are made more effective; particularly, to enable victims of discrimination to assert their rights by judicial process.[33] It states:

> Member States shall take such measures as are necessary, in accordance with their national judicial systems, to ensure that, when persons who consider themselves wronged by failure to apply to them the principle of equal treatment establish, before a court or other competent body, facts from which it can be presumed that there has been direct or indirect discrimination, it shall be for the respondent to prove that there has been no contravention of the principle of equal treatment.

The Directive applies to the situations envisaged by Article 141 (ex Article 119) (equal pay) and those under the Directives on equal treatment, access to employment, health and safety of pregnant workers and parental leave.

### Extending equality law: prohibited grounds of discrimination

The Treaty of Amsterdam inserted a new provision into the EC Treaty allowing for further EU legislative intervention in the field of discrimination. The new Article 13 EC states:

> Without prejudice to the other provisions of this Treaty and within the limits of the powers conferred by it upon the Community, the Council, acting unanimously on a proposal from the Commission and after consulting the European Parliament, may take appropriate action to combat discrimination based on sex, racial or ethnic origin, religion or belief, disability, age or sexual orientation.

This has led to new directives aimed at 'combating discrimination on the ground of religion or belief, disability, age or sexual orientation as regards employment and occupation'[34] and 'combating discrimination on the grounds of racial or ethnic origin' with a much wider scope beyond employment and occupation.[35]

---

[32] Case C-450/93: *Eckhard Kalanke* v. *Freie Hansestadt Bremen* [1995] ECR I-3051. But see now Case C-409/95, *Helmut Marschall* v. *Land Nordrhein-Westfalen* [1997] ECR I-6363; Case C-407/98 *Abrahamsson* v. *Fogelqvist* [2000] ECR I-5539.

[33] On 27 June 1997 the Council of Social Affairs Ministers reached political agreement on the Directive; it was formally adopted at the Luxembourg Summit of December 1997 and entered into force on 1 January 2001. OJ 1998 L14/6.

[34] Article 1 of Directive 2000/78 of 27 November 2000; OJ 2000 L303/16.

[35] Articles 1 and 3 of Directive 2000/43 of 29 June 2000; OJ 2000 L180/22.

To this the EU Charter of Fundamental Rights includes in Article 21(1) a general prohibition of 'any discrimination based on any ground such as sex, race, colour, ethnic or social origin, genetic features, language, religion or belief, political or any other opinion, membership of a national minority, property, birth, disability, age or sexual orientation'.

In other words, apart from sex discrimination there are at least thirteen other grounds on which discrimination is prohibited (Directives (5): racial or ethnic origin, religion or belief, disability, age, sexual orientation; EU Charter (8): colour, social origin, genetic features, language, political or any other opinion, membership of a national minority, property and birth).

## Discrimination and collective regulation

The inspirational impulse of sex equality law has expanded with the adoption of these new directives on other forms of discrimination. The EC's equal opportunities policy has looked primarily to formal legal means of implementation: legislation and enforcement through the courts or administrative agencies. However, doubts have been expressed as to whether reliance on these legal mechanisms is sufficient to achieve the EU's policy objectives.[36] National approaches may encompass social regulation through collective bargaining as well as the enactment of legislation or other means.[37] In some countries, social regulation is prioritised over legal regulation.[38] The increased importance of collective bargaining in equal opportunities policy has long been emphasised by the European Commission: 'The social partners will also be encouraged to make equal opportunities an issue in the collective bargaining process.'[39]

The growing awareness of the role of collective bargaining in implementing equal opportunities policy coincided with developments which recognised and promoted the role of social dialogue in EU social policy. The evolution of the

[36] See the Report on the 1992 Louvain-la-Neuve Conference on procedures and remedies: access to equality between women and men in the EC, C. McCrudden (1993) 22 *Industrial Law Journal* 77. Also 'The Effectiveness of European Equality Law: National Mechanisms for Enforcing Gender Equality Law in the Light of European Requirements', (1993) 13 *Oxford Journal of Legal Studies* 320.

[37] See the national reports, vol. II of M. Verwilghen (ed.), *Equality in Law between Men and Women in the European Community*, Louvain-La-Neuve: Presses Universitaires de Louvain, 1986.

[38] In the case of equal pay, for example, the Danish government argued, and the European Court accepted, that the main implementation mechanism was collective agreements (*Commission* v. *Denmark*, Case 143/83, [1985] ECR 427). In Italy, the Positive Action Act 1991 empowers various agents to promote positive action and considers collective agreements as the ideal means to control and promote positive action. Priority for reimbursement of expenses is given to positive action programmes agreed upon by employers and representative unions. M. V. Ballestrero, 'New Legislation in Italian Equality Law', (1992) 21 *Industrial Law Journal* 152. See generally, L. Gaeta and L. Zoppoli (eds.), *Il Diritto Diseguale: La legge sulle Azioni Positive*, Torino: Giappichelli, 1992.

[39] European Commission, Third Action Programme on Equal Opportunities, 1991. In response, in a meeting of the Social Dialogue Committee on 11 February 1994, the social partners at EC level (ETUC, UNICE, CEEP) proposed to undertake a joint project on equal opportunities. *ETUC Report* – Press Department 5–94.

EU social and labour law on sex equality provided valuable lessons to the trade union and labour movement in its attempts to assume a greater role in determining EU labour law through social dialogue. The critique of equality law by the women's movement contributed to radical rethinking of the shape of the future EU social and labour law. Women's influx into the labour force has produced many of the new ideas on the gender implications of the labour law on organisation of working time, the regulation of new forms of employment, in particular, part-time workers, and reconciliation of work and private/ family life. It is hardly surprising, therefore, that the first two European intersectoral social dialogue agreements were on parental leave (1994) and part-time work (1996).

The substantive law on equality – equal pay, equal treatment and social security – has been the subject of many monographs.[40] The first edition of this book focused on the contribution that the feminist critique emerging from the women's movement had in shaping the debates over EU labour law on equality, and, beyond, the emerging alternative means of implementation: specifically, the critique of equality law as it has developed, and the impact of the critique of equality law on the developing EU social law and policy on reconciliation of work and family life.[41] Here the focus is on the collective model of equality law: the implications of using social dialogue and collective bargaining as the instrument for equality law.

Changes in the composition of the labour force, demography and cultural attitudes have all worked to transform EU equality law. When allied with EU equality law, collective bargaining proves a potentially efficacious mechanism of redressing discrimination.[42] The existing pattern of labour law, dominated by individual litigation and legislative activism (as in the plethora of case-law and directives on discrimination) has obscured the development of a dynamic collective bargaining culture. Issues of direct and indirect discrimination and traditional methods of judicial and administrative enforcement have dominated. But individualisation of enforcement is always a risk given the imbalance of power in the individual employment relationship. Wider issues, such as the

---

[40] B. Creighton, *Working Women and the Law*, London: Mansell, 1979; S. Prechal and N. Burrows, *Gender Discrimination Law of the European Community*, Aldershot: Dartmouth, 1990; T. Hervey, *Justifications for Indirect Discrimination*, London: Sweet & Maxwell, 1993; E. Ellis, *European Community Sex Equality Law*, 2nd edn, Oxford: Oxford University Press, 1998; M. Bell, *European Equality Law*, Oxford: Oxford University Press, 2004.

[41] B. Bercusson, *European Labour Law*, London: Butterworths, 1996, Chapters 13, 'The Critique of the EC Labour Law on Sex Equality', 4, 'EC Equality Law in Context: Collective Bargaining', and 15, 'Equality and (Re)conciliation of Work and Family Life' (pp. 174–216). The writing of those chapters benefited considerably from my participation in the International Research Group on Equal Opportunities and Collective Bargaining, supported by the European Foundation for the Improvement of Living and Working Conditions, Dublin. Parts of the chapters were inspired by drafts of the Concept Report prepared for this Group, which was written by Professor Linda Dickens of Warwick University and myself.

[42] The first edition of this book provided a detailed illustration of this in the case of local government employment in the UK. *Ibid.*, pp. 199–203.

relation of family and work (parental leave) and working time generally (part-time work) provide more scope for collective regulation.

Collective bargaining seeks to build on the presence of women in the trade union and labour movement to further the interests of women workers by making equal opportunities for women in collective bargaining a priority. The development and analysis of the law on equal pay and equal treatment in employment, not surprisingly, has focused on legislation and case-law. Yet it is acknowledged that, in most Member States of the EU, pay and conditions of employment of men and women workers are largely determined by collective agreements. It is through collective bargaining, conducted by trade unions and employers and their associations, that the payment systems and structures, and other terms and conditions of employment, are fixed. Litigation through national courts, basing claims on EU legislation and decisions of the Court of Justice, directly affects only a tiny number of litigants. Any legal rules so established have to be mediated through the collective bargaining system.

It is that system which interprets and applies, for better or worse, the legal rules in the practical determination of pay and conditions of employment of men and women workers. If most workers in the EU experience the EU law on sex equality only through the collective bargaining activity of employers and trade unions, it is that context which really determines the application of EU law.

The two concepts of collective bargaining and equal treatment combine at the national level due to the growth in women's labour force participation and their presence within the trade unions. The sophisticated concepts of the EU's equal opportunities policy contrast with the relatively restricted agendas of trade unions' bargaining platforms and employers' personnel practices. This has already led to legal clashes before the European Court of Justice.

For example, as regards the main actors in collective bargaining, the separation of bargaining units into categories producing agreements more favourable to men has been declared discriminatory.[43] As regards collective bargaining processes, pay bargaining practices which lack transparency as regards lower paid women[44] or include criteria which discriminate against women[45] are declared unlawful. As regards the outcomes, collective agreements which contain clauses which directly or indirectly discriminate against women are unlawful[46] or must be capable of being so declared.[47]

As regulatory *legal* strategies of implementation of equal opportunities policy have been criticised, and collective bargaining has been proposed as a possibly more effective strategy, the emergence of the European social dialogue as a

[43]  *Enderby* v. *Frenchay Area Health Authority*, Case 127/92, [1993] ECR 5535.
[44]  *Handels-og Kontorfunktionaerernes Forbund i Danmark* v. *Dansk Arbejdsgiverforening*, Case 109/88 [1989] ECR 3199.
[45]  *Rummler* v. *Dato Druck GmbH*, Case 235/84 [1986] ECR 2101.
[46]  *Kowalska* v. *Hamburg*, Case 33/89 [1990] ECR I-2591.
[47]  *Commission of the EC* v. *UK*, Case 165/82, [1983] ECR 3431.

primary form of EC regulation highlights the potential of collective bargaining as a regulatory strategy for equal opportunities policy.

Council Directive 2000/78 establishing a general framework for equal treatment in employment and occupation includes explicit reference to the role of social dialogue and collective bargaining in achieving equal treatment (Article 13):[48]

> 1. Member States shall, in accordance with their national traditions and practice, take adequate measures to promote dialogue between the social partners with a view to fostering equal treatment, including through the monitoring of workplace practices, collective agreements, codes of conduct and through research or exchange of experiences and good practices.
>
> 2. Where consistent with their national traditions and practices, Member States shall encourage the social partners, without prejudice to their autonomy, to conclude at the appropriate level agreements laying down anti-discrimination rules in the fields [of work, employment and industrial relations] which fall within the scope of collective bargaining …

This is formal recognition of the collective framework for EU equality law.

## Health and safety: reviving established models of collective regulations

The collective framework for safeguarding the health and safety of individual employees was well established in the Member States before EU labour law intervened. The EU labour law on health and safety reflects the evolution of a European labour law which draws upon the national traditions of Member States and proposes a model both recognisable in its inspiration by national experience and yet different in its synthesis of the elements of different traditions. It reflects the traditional model of stipulating labour standards through precise legislative formulations. It also recognises the trend, more marked in some countries than others, towards attributing to the social partners an active role in the formulation of labour standards. In the result, the EU labour standards prescribed are relatively general; the necessary precision is obtained through the activities of those most closely involved in the field: labour and management.

### The role of workers' representatives

The provisions of the Framework Directive 89/391/EEC on health and safety of 12 June 1989[49] demonstrate how health and safety law has been 'Europeanised' by EU law. EU law provides for a *variety* of persons, with different, sometimes overlapping, functions, entitlement to facilities and assistance, protection

---

[48]  OJ 2000, L303/16.
[49]  Council Directive 89/391/EEC of 12 June 1989 on the introduction of measures to encourage improvements in the safety and health of workers at work. OJ L183/1.

against employer sanctions and methods of enforcement.[50] The logic of the EU law appears to be that functional differentiation and specialisation requires appointment of, at least, *workers* with specific responsibilities for safety and health, *designated* workers, *general* workers' representatives, and workers' *representatives* with specific responsibility for the safety and health of workers. The objective, structure and wording of the Framework Directive imply a variety of representatives.

The Directive appears to support a distinction between *representatives* (*general* representatives, who fulfil certain functions in health and safety, and *specialist* representatives in health and safety) and *individual workers* (both workers with specific responsibilities, and designated workers).[51] General representatives have other representative functions which *complement* their health and safety functions. For example, the issue of new technology has too many general implications to be left to specialist safety representatives.[52] Hence, the general formulation:[53]

> Employers shall consult workers and/or their representatives and allow them to take part in discussions on all questions relating to safety and health at work.
>     This presupposes …
>
> the right of workers and/or their representatives to make proposals,
> balanced participation in accordance with national laws and/or practices.

There must be a remit to general negotiating machinery of safety and health questions, as, again, specialists may not have a broad enough overview.[54] The overall perspective of general representatives must be recognised.[55]

---

[50] Contrast the limited provision in UK law, which can only stand if safety representatives incorporate *all* the functions, entitlements to facilities and assistance, protection against employer sanctions and methods of enforcement prescribed for workers and workers' representatives with safety responsibilities in EU law. Even if UK safety representatives were so comprehensively endowed, it is questionable whether the objective of the Directive can be achieved in a system which concentrates in one set of representatives all the separate categories which can be identified in the Directive. See the first edition of this book, Chapter 24, pp. 356–80.

[51] The implication is that appointment of the different workers and workers' representatives is not identical. A survey of national practice indicates that this is commonly to be found. See European Trade Union Technical Bureau for Health and Safety (TUTB), *A User's Guide to European Community Directives on Health and Safety at Work*, Brussels, 1993, Annex on Workers' Representation in Western Europe with particular emphasis on workplace health and safety, pp. 29–36.

[52] Hence 'the employer shall … ensure that the planning and introduction of new technologies are the subject of consultation with the workers and/or their representatives, as regards the consequences of the choice of equipment, the working conditions and the working environment for the safety and health of workers'. Framework Directive, Article 6(3)(c).

[53] Article 11(1).

[54] Also 'Workers' representatives must be given the opportunity to submit their observations during inspection visits by the competent authority.' Article 11(6).

[55] A reflection of the Directive's distinction between general workers' representatives and workers' representatives with specific responsibility for the safety and health of workers is evident in the Directive's explicit protection of the activities of the latter (Article 11(4)), but not those of the former.

EU law prescribes different methods of *appointment* for each category of worker and workers' representative.[56] Do the repeated references to 'workers *and/or* their representatives' in the Framework Directive imply an *option* for employers to inform or consult *either* workers *or* their representatives? Is an individual consultation system consistent with EU law? The argument that a system of information and consultation of individual employees satisfies the requirements of the Directive is based on the interpretation of the repeated references to 'workers and/or their representatives' (or variations thereon) in the Directive[57] as implying *choice*. *Either* workers *or* their representatives are entitled to the rights conferred of information, consultation and participation. But there are at least two arguments that an individual consultation system is inconsistent with EU law. First, the objective, structure and wording of the Directive imply a logic of involvement of *both* employees *and* their representatives.[58] Secondly, the choice offered by the word *or* is applicable only where there are *no* workers' representatives. There may be no representatives as national rules may lay down thresholds for the establishment of employee representation bodies.[59]

[56] Designated *workers* – by the employer; general workers' *representatives* – in accordance with the laws or practices of the Member States; workers' *representatives* with specific responsibility for the safety and health of workers – in accordance with national laws and/or practices; *workers* with specific responsibilities for safety and health – no method of appointment indicated.

[57] Article 6(3)(c): 'planning and introduction of new technologies are the subject of consultation with the workers and/or their representatives …'. Article 6(4): '… inform … workers and/or workers' representatives'. Article 10(1): information for 'workers and/or their representatives …'. Article 10(3): '… workers with specific functions in protecting the safety and health of workers or workers' representatives with specific responsibility …'. Article 11(1): 'Employers shall consult workers and/or their representatives …'. Article 11(2): 'Workers or workers' representatives with specific responsibility … shall take part in a balanced way, in accordance with national laws and/or practices, or shall be consulted …'. Article 11(6): 'Workers and/or their representatives are entitled to appeal …'.

[58] Hence, the multiple categories of persons engaged in health and safety activities envisaged by the Directive. The language is not otherwise explicable in those provisions where one (Article 11(5): 'Employers must allow workers' representatives …'; Article 11(6): 'Workers' representatives must be given the opportunity to submit their observations during inspection visits …'; Article 12(3): 'Workers' representatives with a specific role … shall be entitled to appropriate training') or the other (Article 13(2)(d, e, f): workers (in general) are to inform/cooperate with the employer and/or the workers with specific responsibility in certain situations), or *both* (Article 11 (4): 'workers referred to in paragraph 2 *and* the workers' representatives referred to …') have rights. This language is only explicable in terms of these multiple categories. Sometimes one, sometimes others must be informed and consulted. They are not alternatives. Which is engaged depends on which has the functions envisaged and the rights conferred by a particular provision.

[59] This is foreseen under the Acquired Rights Directive of 1977, Article 6(5), and under the European Works Councils Directive of 1994, Article 5(2)(a). See *Commission of the EC* v. *UK*, Cases C-382/92 and 383/92, [1994] ECR I-2435, at paragraphs 22–4. The Framework Directive of 1989 envisages three situations: (i) there are *no* representatives (due to thresholds); only *workers* are engaged; (ii) there *are* representatives: the employer may engage representatives only; (iii) there *are* representatives: the employer may engage representatives *and* workers. The definition of representatives is persons 'elected, chosen or designated in accordance with national laws and/or practices to represent workers' (Article 3(c)). There is now authority from the European Court's decision in *Commission of the EC* v. *UK*, Cases C-382/92 and 383/92, [1994]

In sum, the requisite functions stipulated under EU law imply a multiplicity of persons with a variety of functions for general workers' representatives, designated workers and workers with specific responsibilities for safety and health – as well as for safety representatives. That multiple persons on the workers' side are necessary, as recognised in the Framework Directive, is simply the reflection at EU level of the national experience of the Member States.[60]

### An illustration: collective regulation of working time

The role of collective bargaining in determining the EU standards of health and safety is particularly striking in the Working Time Directive.[61] The origins of the Working Time Directive illuminate the development of the specific European labour law approach to health and safety. Its origins were decidedly mixed. The impetus to health and safety initiatives was provided by the enactment of a new Article 118A by the Single European Act 1986. But the issue of working time had been the subject of attention by the Commission in the form of a draft Recommendation on the reduction and reorganisation of working time in 1983. This was followed by specific provision in the Community Charter of Fundamental Social Rights of Workers of December 1989.[62] When the Commission put forward its Action Programme to implement the Charter, it included a proposal for a Directive on the adaptation of working time. Significantly, the Commission noted:[63]

ECR I-2435, that this *obliges* Member States to provide for a system of worker representation. Such a mandatory system of representatives would be negated if employers, by confining the Framework Directive's rights to individual employees, were free to ignore workers' representatives upon whom the Directive had conferred rights to be informed and consulted.

[60] See the TUTB *User's Guide*, which reports on the division of general and safety representatives, and the multiplicity of forms of safety representatives and committees.

[61] Council Directive 93/104/EC of 23 November 1993 concerning certain aspects of the organisation of working time; OJ L307/18 of 13 December 1993, as amended by Directive 2000/34 of 22 June 2000, OJ L195/41. Consolidated in Directive 2003/88/EC of 4 November 2003 concerning certain aspects of the organisation of working time; OJ L299/9 of 18 November 2003. The significance of this Directive in the evolution of European law on health and safety cannot be overestimated. Its origins were disputed as being not in health and safety, but rather the regulation of working conditions. As such, the character of its regulation sharply divided the UK, with its tradition of collective bargaining, from continental systems of legislative regulation of working time, though neither system was undiluted. The political constraints of qualified majority voting contributed to its, perhaps opportunistic, characterisation as a health and safety measure, but this was also consistent with a wider concept of health, safety and welfare being promoted by the Commission. The outcome was a health and safety measure inspired by the differing traditions of regulation of working conditions, which also challenged the traditional dividing line between health and safety and working conditions. The potential consequences for the future development of health and safety law in Europe were profound.

[62] Article 8: 'Every worker of the European Community shall have a right to a weekly rest period and to annual paid leave, the duration of which must be progressively harmonized in accordance with national practices'.

[63] Italics added. Communication concerning the Commission's Action Programme relating to the implementation of the Community Charter, COM(89) 568 final, Brussels, 29 November 1989,

Moreover, *collective agreements* on this matter are increasing in number in many industrial sectors throughout the Community.

In order to avoid excessive differences in approach from one sector or country to another, *the basic conditions which these agreements should comply* with ought therefore to be clearly defined.

The most daring aspect of the Commission's proposal was the focus on collective agreements as the source setting the standards to be harmonised. The Commission acknowledges the role of collective agreements in regulating flexibility of working time.[64] The existence of collective agreements and the inevitable diversity in their approaches is sufficient to introduce the considerations of harmonisation and health and safety which justify the Commission defining 'the basic conditions which these agreements should comply with'.[65]

Article 8 of the Charter of 1989 thus led to an Action Programme proposal on working time with potentially far-reaching implications for the relation of collective bargaining agreements to Community standards. These can be summarised under two headings following the Action Programme's own words. What are 'the basic conditions which these agreements should comply with'? How are the 'minimum reference rules' to be formulated?

## Basic conditions with which collective agreements should comply

The aim of defining the basic conditions with which collective agreements should comply is 'to avoid excessive differences in approach from one sector or country to another'. The equal weight attached to *sectoral* differences contrasts with the frequent focus in the comparative literature on *national* differences in approach. 'Basic conditions' could refer to a number of different features which characterise national practice of collective agreements on working time.[66]

pp. 18–19. The Explanatory Memorandum to the first draft of the Working Time Directive included quotations from the Charter and Action Programme; p. 2, paragraph 1.

[64] It does not explicitly refer to the hotly contested issue in many Member States as to whether flexibility of working time *ought to be* subject to collectively agreed regulation. Nor is any comment made on the extent to which flexibility is *in practice* subjected to collectively agreed regulation.

[65] This approach was bound to come into conflict with governments opposed to collectively agreed regulation of working time flexibility, and would have a substantial impact in Member States and on industrial sectors where such regulation is relatively uncommon. The Commission further proposed 'minimum reference rules without entering into details as regards their implementation.' This implied that the proposed Directive would stipulate standards, but not implementation mechanisms.

[66] Two features of industrial relations were said to be of primary importance: the *relationship* between statutory law (or action by the State) and collective bargaining (action by the social partners); and the degree and type of *centralisation* of industrial relations institutions, particularly collective bargaining and trade unions. T. Treu, 'Introduction' to Chapter II, 'New Trends in Working Time Arrangements', in A. Gladstone (ed.), *Current Issues in Labour Relations: An International Perspective*, Berlin and New York: Walter de Gruyter, 1989, pp. 149–60, at pp. 155–6.

The Commission's *Comparative Study on Rules Governing Working Conditions in the Member States* reported that in most countries legislation had set a general standard of normal weekly working time.[67] Recently, however, measures had been introduced to allow for the possibility of regulating working hours other than on a weekly basis. The main instrument for this 'flexibilisation' was collective bargaining. The formulas included daily and weekly ceilings, normal average working hours over a specified period and reductions in working time in return for flexibility. Following this flexibility model, night work was in some countries generally forbidden, but derogation was allowed, whereas in other countries it was generally allowed, unless explicitly forbidden. While there are problems in defining 'overtime working' nine Member States (apart from Denmark, Italy and the UK) had laid down ceilings per day, week or year. The ceilings were often replaced through collective bargaining.[68]

The proposed Directive on working time flexibility aimed to outline basic procedural conditions for the *regulation of working time by collective agreements*. Introducing its first proposal for a Directive on Working Time, the Commission explained that:[69]

> Accordingly, pursuant to the Charter and as announced in its action programme, the Commission intends to propose a groundwork of basic provisions on certain aspects of the organization of working time connected with workers' health and safety at work which relate to:
>
> minimum daily and weekly rest periods;
> minimum annual paid holidays;
> minimum conditions determining the recourse to shift and especially night work;
> protection of workers' health and safety in the event of changes in working patterns resulting from adjustments in working time.

[67] Synopsis, Commission Staff Working Paper, SEC(89) 1137, Brussels, 30 June 1989.

[68] Flexibilisation through collective bargaining took a variety of forms, some of which were described in the following extract: '... a minimum core of protection, of substantive regulation ... may become smaller but it may also be different ... most legislations are not moving towards a short simple list of basic protective provisions, but may move to greater complexity in the regulation. For instance, flexibility has been realised by adding exceptions to the existing legislation, by establishing new complicated rules for calculating "averages" etc. The core is not one in the classic sense, but one of great diffusion and this may even be the case with collective bargaining. In discussing the core, different methodological possibilities come to mind. The first is the more classical one, a statutory legal core, reduced but more complex, with many exceptions; another is a derogatory possibility given either to the collective or to the individual parties. A further possibility might be that the law or (national) bargaining sets only a border limit (40-hour-week) over a certain period of time and leaves parties free to do what they like inside the boundaries ... The role, however, of public powers (as legislators and employer) remains important ... on the one hand "controlled" deregulation; on the other, and more important, financial support of the most significant forms of work reorganisation.' R. Blanpain, 'General Report', in R. Blanpain and E. Kohler (eds.), *Legal and Contractual Limitations on Working-Time in the European Community Member States*, European Foundation for the Improvement of Living and Working Conditions, Office for Official Publications of the EC, Dordrecht: Kluwer, 1988, at pp. 83–4.

[69] Explanatory Memorandum, p. 2, paragraph 2.

## Method of formulation of standards

However:[70]

> other issues mentioned in the action programme in the field of the adaptation of working time should be *left to both sides of industry* and/or national legislation. In addition these matters should be dealt with in depth within the framework of the *dialogue between both sides of industry* at Community level without prejudice to the Commission's prerogative to submit proposals should it see fit to do so.

In particular, the Commission emphasised that 'the question of *systematic overtime* is a subject best dealt with by the two sides of industry and by national provisions'.[71]

The delicate balance between legislation and collective bargaining was spelled out twice in the Explanatory Memorandum in almost identical terms; once at the beginning and again in its final provisions:[72]

> given the differences arising from national practices, the subject of working conditions in general falls to varying degrees under the autonomy of both sides of industry who often act in the public authorities' stead and/or complement their action. To take account of these differences and in accordance with the principle of subsidiarity the Commission takes the view that negotiation between the two sides of industry should play its full part within the framework of the proposed measures, provided that it is able to guarantee adherence to the principles set out in the Commission's proposals ... In other words, it is important in this field to take into consideration the fact that such agreements concluded by management and labour can in principle make a contribution to the application of Community directives, without, however, releasing the Member States concerned from the responsibility for attaining the objectives sought via these instruments.

In light of this explicit, even enthusiastic, recognition of the role of collective bargaining in the Community Charter's Action Programme and Explanatory Memorandum, the first two drafts of the Working Time Directive took an important, if cautious, initiative. There was no mention of collective bargaining

---

[70]  *Ibid.*, p. 3. Italics added.

[71]  The role of working time in achieving flexibility of capacity utilization was seen to be due to the social partners: 'In many cases legislation, but above all the conclusion of a large number of collective agreements have supported the trend towards more flexible use of productive equipment ...'. *Ibid.*, p. 4, paragraph 4. Explicit reference was made to recent draft laws on the regulation of working time in Germany, to collective agreements (or even enterprise agreements) in the Netherlands which made it possible to amend or adjust statutory maxima, and to experience in Belgium where very high numbers of hours can be worked in a week provided the average weekly working time over a thirteen-week period does not exceed thirty-eight hours (p. 8, paragraphs 12, 14). Even with night work, collective agreements may derogate from a general ban, as is often the case in Germany, Greece, France, Italy and Portugal (p. 13, paragraph 25).

[72]  *Ibid.*, p. 4, paragraph 3 and again in paragraph 32 on pp. 16–17. The former added at the beginning of the extract quoted: 'While acknowledging the need for certain basic rules with regard to working time at Community level it should be emphasized that ...'. The latter began: 'Finally, it should be emphasised that ...'.

in the Preambles, but both drafts provided for the possibility of general derogation in Article 12(3):

> In case of collective agreements made between employers and representatives of the workers at the appropriate levels, aiming at setting up a comprehensive set of provisions regarding the adjustment of working time corresponding to the specific conditions of the enterprise, including daily and weekly rest periods as well as night- and shift-work, subject to the condition that on these specific points equivalent periods of compensatory rest are granted to the workers within a reference period that must not exceed six months.

Both drafts also allowed for the possibility of implementation of the Directive through collective agreements:[73]

> Member States shall comply with this Directive ... by bringing into force the laws, regulations or administrative provisions necessary or by ensuring that the two sides of industry establish the necessary provisions through agreement, without prejudice to the obligation on the Member States to achieve the results to be obtained by this Directive.

In addition, the second draft added an Article 9:

> Consultation and participation of workers and/or their representatives shall take place in accordance with Article 11 of Directive 89/391/EEC on the matters covered by this Directive.

This initial caution was overcome in the final draft. The Preamble of the Directive incorporated a new penultimate paragraph:

> Whereas it is necessary to provide that certain provisions may be subject to derogations implemented, according to the case, by Member States or the two sides of industry ...

The final text of the Directive also included a large number of new provisions which made collective bargaining an element in the setting of EC standards on working time. In the final text, the role of collective bargaining in determining *some* of the EU standards on working time underwent a significant *qualitative* change. In the past, it had been largely confined to allowing for derogations to prescribed standards. The present Directive also allows for collective agreements themselves to fix or define relevant standards, usually only with the consent of the Member State concerned, but in one exceptional case, with *priority* over Member State legislation.[74]

   In conclusion, as evident in the Framework Directive of 1989 and illustrated by the Working Time Directive, European labour law has developed a collective model for regulating health and safety in individual employment. That framework was initially inspired by the collective frameworks in place in the Member States. This European collective model is being complemented by another model looking to new challenges to health and safety of individual employees.

---

[73] Article 14.    [74] Daily rest periods, Article 4.

This complementary model is that of the framework agreements concluded at EU level in the European social dialogue, which has produced agreements on work-related stress and harassment and violence at work.

## Free movement and social dumping: a European model of collective standards, collective organisation and collective action

The free movement of workers usually takes pride of place in general treatments of the labour law and social policy of the European Community.[75] Implicit in neo-liberal conceptions of a European common market, free movement of labour takes its place alongside the other fundamental freedoms established in the Treaty of Rome: freedom of movement of capital, goods and services. Free movement of workers was perceived as a keystone of the social dimension of the Rome Treaty.[76] However, the perception of free movement of workers as a social issue is questionable. Embedded in its labour market context, it is an economic, not a social concept. Social policy issues arose in the context of whether Member States' restrictions on entitlement to various social provisions infringed the EC law guarantee of free movement of workers.[77]

The EC law on free movement of workers, which dominated the field for potential development of EC social policy during its first decade and a half, had the potential to make major contributions to the development of European labour law.[78] But the main focus of attention in the labour law on free

---

[75] See lengthy chapters in the texts reviewed in Chapter 3. Outside the labour law context, though still considered to be within the social policy dimension, free movement of workers is now often considered alongside the EU law on the free movement of *persons* in the context of the rights of EU citizens.

[76] As applied in the context of the European labour market, free movement of workers led to many problems which could be characterised as being of a social nature. The movement of workers from one Member State to another led to questions of entitlement to social security benefits of various kinds, the transfer of acquired entitlements to such benefits, including pensions, issues concerning the families of such workers and their entitlements to education, housing and so on. As it developed, the labour market issue of free movement acquired a social baggage in the form of EC law on these myriad social issues.

[77] The ambivalence resulting from this was evident in a number of contexts. A social measure might be adopted by a Member State which denied access to a benefit to non-nationals, and thus arguably had the effect of inhibiting free movement of foreign workers. But could an EC social policy be invoked to contest such a discriminatory measure even when no effect could be demonstrated as regards the free movement of workers? When the Commission proposed social policy measures, did it have to demonstrate their relevance to free movement of workers in order to be anchored in the Treaty provisions regarding free movement? The Treaty provisions on free movement were subject to limitations justified on grounds of public policy, public security or public health – social policy grounds excluded from EC competence and reserved to national authorities (Article 48(3)). Should provisions on free movement be dealt with as part of Community labour law even when they had no social policy but only purely labour market implications?

[78] For example, the law on free movement of workers proceeded from the principle of non-discrimination on the basis of nationality. The principle of non-discrimination fed into the later development by the European Court of EC law on sex equality. The legal definition of 'worker' for the purposes of free movement was developed independently of national law definitions, and

movement remained the social protection of migrant workers. Social policy was again driven by the free movement imperative.[79] The Member States have refused to endorse a policy of harmonisation of domestic social security systems rooted in national traditions and the Commission has sought at most to move to a policy of convergence of basic social security objectives and policies. The body of law which emerged implementing these principles is technically formidable and the policy issues seemingly intractable.[80]

The underlying problem of the EC law on free movement of workers is that the context in which it was formulated changes.[81] Though much of the literature still focuses on social security issues, high unemployment threatens as much, if not more, the labour standards of workers. Migration of workers from areas of the Community with lower labour standards can undermine higher labour standards established elsewhere. For European labour law, the critical issue has become whether the policy of free movement threatens workers' conditions of employment through movement of workers from areas with low labour standards to those with higher labour standards: 'social dumping.'

expanded beyond the limitations imposed by those national labour laws, in the interests of eliminating constraints on free movement of all workers within the European labour market.

[79] The social security policies of the Member States are to be subjected to Community law intervention with this objective in mind. EC law dictates the principle of equal treatment of all nationals of the Member States, and their families, in relation to the social security law of the Member States. Further, the free movement of workers is to be facilitated by principles allowing for the aggregation of periods of insurance and employment within the whole of the Community regarding entitlement to social security rights, and the export of benefits to workers who take up residence in another Member State.

[80] The Community social security rules have been: 'criticized as being complicated to a point where their basic function, namely to guarantee the fundamental Community right of free movement of persons, has been obliterated'. C. Laske, 'The Impact of the Single European Market on Social Protection for Migrant Workers', (1993) 30 *Common Market Law Review* 515, at p. 517. For new developments, which recall parallels in the field of labour law for legislative, judicial and executive ('the open method of coordination') activism, but accompanied by a pessimistic assessment of the potential for collective solidarity in the sphere of social security provision at EU level, Stefano Giubboni, 'Free Movement of Persons and European Solidarity', (2007) 13 *European Law Journal* 360–79, at pp. 375–6: 'Overcoming these limitations would necessitate a degree of positive integration of the various national systems far greater than that which can be achieved "via the judicial route" or with the normative technique of coordination of national social security systems ... It would, in fact, be necessary to arrive at the *political* construction of a specifically European sphere of redistributive solidarity, and hence at some supranational form of welfare'; but 'it is difficult to imagine, at least at the present stage in the Community integration process, a specifically European area of redistribution linked to the constitutionalisation of fundamental social rights to [social security] benefits guaranteed directly at Community governance level'. It is to be hoped that European labour law is different.

[81] Writing in the early 1990s, Laske explained: 'it was conceived at a time of full employment, when most of the social protection was assumed by state schemes and when the typical migrant was a male blue-collar worker, employed full-time and usually moving from south to north. Today's situation (and that of post-1992 Europe) is very different: the whole of the Community is struggling with high unemployment, Member States increasingly opt-out of social security responsibilities by shifting the burden of insuring against certain risks onto the individual, and an increasingly genuine Internal Market has seen a steep migration of white-collar workers in particular from the middle management'. 'The Impact of the Single European Market', p. 521.

The decline in the traditional sources of labour mobility in the EU from areas of high unemployment, mainly in the south, brought about a change in the nature of labour mobility away from permanent migrant workers. Towards the completion of the Single European Market Programme in 1992, the Commission noted that this would bring about a considerable number of employment relationships which would be only temporarily performed in a Member State other than the State in the territory of which they are habitually performed. The Commission anticipated that:[82]

> Thus, a new intra-Community mobility of workers within their jobs, different from the traditional mobility in search for new employment, is increasingly growing within the European Community in the framework of the economic freedoms, in particular, of the freedom to provide services.

The Commission highlighted the potential of the services industry, which then accounted for half the Community's production and 40 per cent of jobs, in a wide range of activities. In particular, transnational sub-contracting was developing in the construction sector and public works:[83]

> There are more and more instances of firms based in one Member State and moving with their staff to another State to provide a service, or of firms sending their workers from their country of origin to another Member State to work for a legally distinct undertaking.

Free movement of workers in the Community had focused on the right to seek and take up permanent employment. *Conditions* of employment for migrant workers had not heretofore been regulated – subject to the overriding requirement of non-discrimination on grounds of nationality. The principle of equal treatment of migrant workers received a further impulse, however, as result of a further initiative of the Commission which was identified as part of its plan of 'encouraging high labour standards as part of a competitive Europe': the Directive concerning the posting of workers in the framework of the provision of services.[84]

As will be seen, the Directive raises fundamental issues to do with a collective model of regulation of free movement of workers in the EU. It demonstrates the complexity of European labour law's attempts to accommodate very different systems of collective bargaining and collective agreements. For example, to posit as EU labour standards those of collective agreements, a formulation has

---

[82] Explanatory Memorandum to the Proposal for a Council Directive concerning the posting of workers in the framework of the provision of services, COM(91) 230 final – SYN 346, Brussels, 1 August 1991, paragraph 1.

[83] *Ibid.*, paragraph 5. The increase in the number of transnational acquisitions by top European industrial enterprises was noted as liable to stimulate the temporary expatriation of workers within groups of companies or within companies with multiple operations throughout Europe. Paragraph 8.

[84] Directive 96/71/EC concerning the posting of workers in the framework of the provision of services. OJ 1996, L18/1.

to be found for the EU instrument which will encompass this range of different systems and their outcomes. The principle of free movement of workers across national borders is one of the four fundamental freedoms in the EU internal market. A crucial issue is how to balance the economic dimension of the internal market (free movement of workers) with the social dimension (protection of employees, but also of national industrial relations models).

The issue came to the fore once again when, on 13 January 2004, the Commission published a proposal for a draft directive liberalising the market in services.[85] The proposed Directive aimed to enhance and guarantee the freedom to provide services in the internal market in accordance with the EC Treaty. At the heart of the proposed Services Directive was the so-called 'country of origin' principle: that service providers were to be subject to the law of their country of origin (the home country), not that of the country where the services were provided (the host country).[86] This principle has wider implications, but became the subject of fierce debate as to its merits in principle and its proposed application in practice specifically regarding the labour standards of workers engaged in transnational provision of services and the consequences for 'social dumping'.[87]

In contrast to the proposed Services Directive, Directive 96/71/EC had applied a specific social policy to workers posted within the framework of free movement of services. It specified minimum terms and conditions of employment which must apply to workers posted to the host country.[88] Directive 96/71/EC arose from the same context of debates regarding working conditions of the employees of service providers. The decision of policy and principle in that Directive was clear: the employees of enterprises, including service providers,

---

[85] Proposal for a Directive on Services in the Internal Market, COM (2004) 2/3 final, adopted 13 January 2004. Services account for over two-thirds of employment in the EU Explanatory Memorandum to the proposed Services Directive, Section 1: 'Necessity and objective', p. 5: 'Services are omnipresent in today's economy, generating almost 70% of GNP and jobs ...'.

[86] *Ibid.*, Article 16.

[87] Competition between firms providing services would not occur, of course, if national labour laws were harmonised. The fact is, however, that the disparities among Member States regarding labour standards are considerable. This can be graphically demonstrated by comparing labour costs across the EU. Hourly labour costs in 2003 ranged from (in euros) 28.15 in Denmark and 27.09 in West Germany decreasing through Finland, Belgium, the Netherlands, Sweden, Austria, Luxembourg and France to 18.72 in the UK, decreasing again down through Ireland, East Germany, Italy and Spain to 10.18 in Greece and 7.00 in Portugal, down to 4.30 in the Czech Republic, 4.04 in Hungary, 3.26 in Poland and 3.22 in Slovakia.
'Comparative Manufacturing Industry Labour Costs in 2003', *European Industrial Relations Review* No. 378, July 2005, Table 2, p. 35.

[88] Further, the employer is obliged in general to observe the host country's labour law provisions having a public policy character (Article 3(10)) and that Member State's public law regulations. The limit to application of the labour law of the host Member State is that it cannot require service providers to pay 'double': 'National rules which require a service provider ... to pay employers' contributions to the host Member State's fund, in addition to those he has already paid to the fund of the Member State where he is established, constitute a restriction on freedom to provide services.' *Arblade* v. *Leloup and Sofrage SARL*, Cases C-369/96 and C-276/96, [1999] ECR I-8453.

are not to be subject to the law of the country of origin. Instead, they are entitled to equal protection of the mandatory rules of the host Member State, including collective agreements. Working conditions are to be taken out of competition, whatever the consequences for free movement.[89]

A primary principle governing free movement of workers in the EU is equal treatment and non-discrimination on grounds of nationality.[90] This traditional EU law on free movement of workers has now to be applied in the context of greater diversity in wage levels and income within a European Union comprising twenty-seven Member States. One function of collective agreements is precisely to avoid the damaging effects of competition among individual workers in the labour market producing unequal treatment. Through collective organisation and action, individual workers are able to compensate for their weaker bargaining position with employers and negotiate collective agreements to ensure equality of treatment among the collectivity of workers.

This was the path first recognised by the European Court in its decision in *Rush Portuguesa*:[91]

Community law does not preclude Member States from extending their legislation, or collective agreements entered into by both sides of industry, to any person who is employed, even temporarily, within their territory, no matter in which country the employer is established; nor does Community law prohibit Member States from enforcing those rules by appropriate means.

It was again indicated by the Posting of Workers Directive. Building on this would entail a more expansive definition of applicable collective agreements to

---

[89] For that reason, the proposed Services Directive included a derogation allowing for application of Directive 96/71/EC. This derogation is thereby limited to the scope and the minimum labour standards specified in that Directive. Workers falling outside its scope and other labour standards would fall under the proposed Services Directive.

[90] Article 39 EC: 1. Freedom of movement for workers shall be secured within the Community. 2. Such freedom of movement shall entail the abolition of any discrimination based on nationality between workers of the Member States as regards employment, remuneration and other conditions of work and employment. 3. It shall entail the right, subject to limitations justified on grounds of public policy, public security or public health: ... (c) to stay in a Member State for the purpose of employment in accordance with the provisions governing the employment of nationals of that State laid down by law, regulation or administrative action .... This is elaborated in Regulation 1612/68, Title II, 'Employment and Equality of Treatment'. Regulation (EEC) No. 1612/68 of the Council of 15 October 1968 on freedom of movement for workers within the Community [O] Sp. Ed. 1968, No. L257/2, p. 475, as amended, Article 7: 'A worker who is a national of a Member State may not, in the territory of another Member State, be treated differently from national workers by reason of his nationality in respect of any conditions of employment and work, in particular as regards remuneration, dismissal, and should he become unemployed, reinstatement or reemployment.' The principle of equal treatment is extended to nationals of third countries by the EU Charter of Fundamental Rights 2000, Article 15(3): 'Nationals of third countries who are authorised to work in the territories of the Member States are entitled to working conditions equivalent to those of citizens of the Union.' See the detailed commentary on Article 15 by Chistophe Vigneau in B. Bercusson (ed.), *European Labour Law and the EU Charter of Fundamental Rights*, Baden-Baden: Nomos, 2006.

[91] *Rush Portuguesa Lda* v. *Office national d'immigration*, Case 113/89, [1990] ECR 1417 at p. 1445, paragraph 18.

determine working conditions for the providers of services. Protection is to be secured by national collective agreements.

The challenge to collective regulation is acute in the case of transnational free movement.[92] The problem is that the original concept of free movement of workers in the Treaty of Rome did not, and the continuing project of a common European market, including a labour market, does not easily embrace transnational collective regulation. The proselytisers of the original common market ideal did not address the prospect, and their descendants have even less sympathy with such regulation. Over the last decade, the battle has been well and truly joined as the protagonists of unencumbered free movement have identified in collective regulation a major obstacle.

The model of collective regulation of free movement of workers in the EU embraces three dimensions: collective standards, collective organisation and collective action. Each has been the subject of sharp conflict.

In the case of collective standards, this initially took the form of challenges to collective agreements in principle as violating principles of competition law. The ECJ intervened to protect collective regulation, based largely on the Treaty provisions on social dialogue drafted by the social partners themselves.[93] Challenges to national law extending collective agreements to cover employers and workers from other countries working on national territory were confronted, though with occasional ambivalence.[94] The legislative response in the form of the Posting Directive was partial and unsatisfactory. Another major challenge to collective regulation was the Commission's initiative on liberalisation of the European market in services, though that attempt to exclude collective standards was successfully resisted by opposition of the European Parliament.

---

[92] There is no model in national labour laws. Free movement within one country has not been an issue for labour regulation since the times of Jean Valjean. In theory, transnational collective agreements could achieve the same protection, specifically as regards transnational services provision, as national collective agreements provide in the national context. The ECJ has upheld such agreements as exempt from competition rules. *Albany International BV* v. *Stichting Bedrijfspensioenfonds Textielindustrie*, Case C-67/96; with joined Cases C-115/97, C-116/97 and C-117/97; [1999] ECR I-5751. Might not collective agreements also be immune to the constraints (e.g. of the country of origin principle) of the law on free movement of services? Following the recent decisions in *Laval* and *Viking*, collective action appears not to be immune (Case C-341/05, *Laval un Partneri Ltd* v. *Svenska Byggnadsarbetareforbundet, Svenska Byggnadsarbetareforbundet, Avdelning 1, Svenska Elektrikerforbundet.* decided 18 December 2007; Case C-438/05, *Viking Line Abp OU Viking Line Eesti* v. *The International Transport Workers' Federation, The Finnish Seamen's Union,* decided 11 December 2007). The intersectoral and sectoral social dialogues are potential forums for the negotiation of such transnational labour standards. But the need for transnational collective regulation presupposes transnational collective organisation.

[93] Case C-67/96, *Albany, ibid.*

[94] *Arblade* v. *Leloup and Sofrage SARL*, Cases C-369/96 and C-276/96, [1999] ECR I-8453. *Finalarte Sociedad de Construcao Civil Lda and others* v. *Urlaubs- und Lohnausgleichskasse der Bauwirtschaft*, Cases C-49–50/98, C-52/98, C-54/98, C-68/98 and C-71/98, [2001] ECR I-7831.

A second important response took the form of EU law promoting transnational collective organisation and social dialogue agreements. This, though important in principle, also had limitations: in scope, coverage and operation.

The third major approach has been through autonomous collective action by workers and trade unions to challenge free movement allegedly producing 'social dumping', the subject of recent decisions of the ECJ on the legality of such collective action.[95]

Legislative and judicial battles in coming years will determine in large part whether a collective framework of EU regulation through collective standards, organisation and action succeeds in overcoming the challenges to labour standards posed by the free movement of workers.

## Fragmentation of the workforce: confronting competing models of regulation – legislation, social dialogue, open method of coordination

### Ideological foundations

The modern legal concept of work and workers is shaped by the ideology of classical liberalism.[96] As put by Alan Fox:[97]

> To insist that a man's labour is his own is not only to say that it is his to alienate in a wage contract; it is also to say that his labour and its productivity is something for which he owes no debt to civil society – a further perspective on the separation of economics and ethics. The traditional view that property and labour were *social* functions with *social* obligations was thereby undermined.

The failure to appreciate the social function of labour[98] and the focus solely on its quality as a market commodity has implications for relations at work: 'as with all market relationships, the interests of buyers and sellers are antagonistic ... Issues of control inevitably pervade this relationship.'[99] While, therefore, different *legal* formulations of the concept of the worker are possible, the labour law of the states of Western Europe starts with the relationship of employment being characterised as a contract of service, with a clear ideological foundation:[100]

> (As regards the definition of the 'employee' and the 'contract of employment') There is ... a convergence in modern legal doctrine towards the recognition of

---

[95]  Case C-341/05, *Laval*; Case C-438/05, *Viking*.

[96]  The following section is derived from R. Benedictus and B. Bercusson, *Labour Law: Cases and Materials*, London: Sweet & Maxwell, 1987, pp. 6–9.

[97]  A. Fox, *Beyond Contract: Work, Power and Trust Relations*, 1974, pp. 164–7 (italics added).

[98]  For example, housewives' domestic labour. O. Clarke and A.I. Ogus, 'What is a Wife Worth?' (1978) 5 *British Journal of Law and Society* 1.

[99]  R. Hyman, 'Trade Unions, Control and Resistance', in G. Esland and G. Salaman (eds.), *The Politics of Work and Occupations*, Milton Keynes: Open University Press, 1980, pp. 303–7.

[100]  H. Barbagelata, 'Different Categories of Workers', in R. Blanpain (ed.), *Comparative Labour Law and Industrial Relations*, Deventer: Kluwer, 1980, p. 320 (italics added).

*submission* of the employee to the employer's command or control as to the time, place and manner in which the work is to be done as a necessary criterion.[101]

Laws affecting workers, despite the very different contexts in which they function, and the diverse policies pursued, frequently adopt the contract of employment and subordination as the criteria defining the objects of their attention. Increasingly, however, the incongruence of the contract of employment with the objectives of the law in question requires reconsideration of the ideological element of subordination.[102]

### Fragmentation of the workforce

The use of labour law tools to analyse the concept of the 'worker' has been challenged as never before by the disintegration of the standard employment relationship and the emergence of new forms of work.[103] Fragmentation of the

---

[101] The emphasis on subordination in *labour* law may be contrasted with different approaches in other legal contexts. The worker as such may be an object of taxation, a subject of social security, protected by legislation on health and safety, a member of a trade union – as well as being related to the employer through a contract of service. The legal concept of the worker may vary according to the policy pursued by the legal rules affecting the workers. For example, the concept of the worker in the law of vicarious responsibility (liability for the acts of third parties) has been characterised as follows: 'the classification of a particular factual situation must always be considered in the light of the purpose for which the classification is being made. Thus in a case of vicarious liability the enquiry is always whether one person is legally responsible for the acts of another. The relationship between the parties may therefore be classified as a master-servant relationship *for this purpose* even though the relationship might not be so classified for other purposes ... [This] approach has the merit of emphasising that legal concepts are tools to be used intelligently for the purpose in hand and not to be applied blindly to a variety of uses.' P.S. Atiyah, *Vicarious Liability in the Law of Torts*, London: Butterworths, 1967, pp. 31–3. For example, in the British law on unemployment benefit, income is a more important criterion than subordination. A.I. Ogus and E. Barendt, *The Law of Social Security*, London: Butterworths, 1978, pp. 82–3.

[102] R.W. Rideout, *Principles of Labour Law*, 3rd edn, London: Sweet & Maxwell, 1979, p. 11: 'It may be that the next stage should be to say that certain elements pointing to or from service should be weighted according to the purpose for which the distinction is required. So, if vicarious liability is the issue, control should be of primary importance, whilst if qualification to receive industrial injury benefits is to be decided the main consideration should be the worker's lack of capital and his economic dependence on the payment he receives from a regular employer for his work.'

[103] U. Mückenberger and S. Deakin, 'From Deregulation to a European Floor of Rights: Labour Law, Flexibilisation and the European Single Market', (1989) 3 *Zeitschrift für ausländisches und internationales Arbeits- und Sozialrect* 153. See also U. Mückenberger, 'Non-Standard Forms of Work and the Role of Changes in Labour and Social Security Regulation', (1989) *International Journal of the Sociology of Law* 381. Yota Kravaritou elaborates two basic legal models of employment: (1) the classic job with its traditional employment contract, and (2) work under new forms of great variety, among which she distinguishes (a) those jobs which may be termed employment without an employer – the status of fake self-employed, sub-contracting, possibly homeworking and teleworking, clandestine work in the grey or black economy – and (b) new forms under a non-permanent employment contract, notably the fixed-term contract, the temporary employment contract and the employment-training contract: 'it is in this type of contract that one finds the greatest lack of traditional guarantees, and this is the place where "new" rights and minimum standards are beginning to be defined – although this has not yet happened in all countries.. Y. Kravaritou, *New Forms of Work: Labour Law and Social Security*

labour force in Europe reflects what is said to be a change in recent years in the direction of an increase in forms of work and employment which differ from the 'standard employment relationship' of 'typical work' (permanent, full-time, socially secure employment). Atypical work is defined in terms of its divergence from the model of a standard employment relationship of 'typical work'. The latter is defined as a socially secure full-time job of unlimited duration with standard working hours guaranteeing a regular income and, via social security systems geared towards wage earners, securing pension payments and protection against ill-health and unemployment. In terms of legal regulation, the debate focuses on the distinction between typical and atypical employment, which is the result of the disintegration of the standard employment relationship and the emergence of new forms of work involving part-time, casual, fixed-term, self-employed, independent or homeworkers, to name but a few. A central issue is gender specificity: that men are disproportionately in standard employment relationships and increasing numbers of women in the labour force work under 'atypical' conditions.

The standard form of employment is complemented by the growth of part-time work, fixed-term contracts, temporary agency work, homeworkers, self-employment, casual, seasonal and other 'non-standard' forms of employment. An EIRO study found that in most EU Member States (with the exception of Denmark, Greece and Portugal), there had been a decline in standard employment over the ten-year period from 1988 to 98 and an increase in particular of part-time work (except for Spain, where temporary/fixed-term full-time employment was more important than part-time work). In 1998, a majority of employees in twelve of the fifteen EU Member States still had a typical employment relationship, but this varied between 56 per cent in Portugal and 81 per cent in Luxembourg, and in three countries, the Netherlands, Greece and Spain, the share of permanent, full-time employees was only around 50 per cent or just below.[104]

It has become necessary to determine which elements of the contract of employment should be emphasised for different social purposes. This debate has been influenced less by labour lawyers than by economists and industrial relations experts. In the labour law literature, the issue of 'new forms of employment' is situated in the context of a debate in which the focus of attention tends to be on the distinction between *typical* and *atypical* employment. The literature focuses on the implications for labour and social security law of legal relations which deviate from the standard model.

The industrial relations literature places the issue of new forms of employment in the context of the debate over *labour market flexibility*.[105] In the

---

*Aspects in the European Community*, European Foundation for the Improvement of Living and Working Conditions, Luxembourg: Office for Official Publications of the EC, 1988.

[104] EIRO on-line: TN 0202101S.

[105] Specifically, 'new forms of employment' is included in that part of employers' strategies on flexibility concerned with external or numerical flexibility. The employer changes the numbers and types of employees' relationships to the enterprise in order to achieve the desired flexibility

economic literature, 'new forms of employment' is part of the more general debate on *segmentation of the labour market*.[106]

Each of these formulations by different disciplines includes the issue of 'new forms of employment' as a component of a broader problematic. The question as to strategies of the actors on new forms of employment will be answered differently depending on whether the legislator addresses the problem as one of typical/atypical employment, labour market flexibility or labour market segmentation.[107]

## National strategies

Law offers a number of specific mechanisms and strategies on new forms of employment. For example legislation providing protection based on continuity or duration of employment, or the number of employees in the establishment, operates to exclude from legal protection (or rather, did so until recently in the UK) part-timers or temporary workers, or those in small establishments. Other workers are excluded through legal doctrine distinguishing employees from the self-employed. Other legal mechanisms are more general.[108]

of response to changing market conditions. Another part of the same strategy is internal or functional or task flexibility, where existing employees are required to change their jobs at the workplace where necessary to meet market demands. Strategies on new forms of employment cannot be considered without also considering strategies on task flexibility.

[106] This examines broad cleavages in the workforce: between large employers and small employers, unionised and non-unionised workers, firms using advanced technology and firms using low technology, low-paying and high-paying sectors, and so on. These cleavages do not correspond to the 'typical/atypical' employment distinction, nor to the contours of the flexibility debate. As with the other disciplines, economists see new forms of employment as only one component of the changing labour force.

[107] For further argumentation on this point, see B. Bercusson, 'Legal, Political and Industrial Relations Strategies Regarding New Forms of Employment', in *L'Evolution des Formes d'Emploi*, Actes du colloque de la révue 'Travail et Emploi', 3–4 November 1988.

[108] For example, France and Italy share the legacy of a *system* of law, in the form of legal codes, which provide a legal context into which labour law protection of new forms of employment has to be inserted. New forms adapt differently to systems which require the logic and symmetry of *principles*, unlike other systems which are less comprehensive and systematic (the British common law). Certain types of new forms of employment in France and Italy – for example, solidarity contracts and training contracts – are easier to protect, through application of established principles of the labour law framework. In contrast, the British Youth Training Scheme was brought into existence without considering its relation to the wider labour law system. This led to great difficulties in defining the rights of young workers under these training schemes as compared with similar workers outside the schemes. In German labour law too there are legal principles of equality and generality to which certain actors' strategies for dealing with new forms of employment will be attracted. There has developed an important role for statutory law which cannot be derogated from by the contracting parties. On the other hand, the contract of employment as the starting point of much labour law in a market economy provides a pole of attraction for other actors' strategies. These opposing poles of attraction can be seen in different strategies adopted by the same actor: judges, for instance. Broadly speaking the strategy of a minority is to favour statutory rights, to 'normalise' the status of employment in the sense of integrating all workers into the standards of the labour law system. This has clear implications for new forms of employment. In contrast, the majority of judges are keenly aware of the tension

Collective agreements may protect only union members. Trade union movements organised on industrial, occupational, geographical or political lines may lead to different levels of protection for different groups depending on the strength and policy of the union organisations to which they are affiliated. The Scandinavian experience demonstrates the use of industrial relations strategies towards new forms of employment to avoid fragmentation.[109]

Scandinavia presents us with a situation where one can easily identify the 'new forms of employment', because there are so many of them. But from the point of view of labour law they are not the subjects of a special strategy. They are covered by collective agreements as part of the unionised workforce. They are just workers who have particular hours or certain kinds of contracts. But

between contract and statute. They resolve this tension by distinguishing issues concerned with hiring and dismissal – where freedom of contract is more important than equal treatment – from issues arising within an existing employment relationship – where equality is more important. This strategy sometimes comes into conflict with government strategies of deregulation. The significance of this can be seen by comparing the British case, where there is no such general principle of equality. In Germany, unequal treatment of even two male workers in terms of wages, fringe benefits, promotion, etc. is prohibited as discrimination. This affects the issue of fragmentation, or new forms of employment, because in almost every form of atypical work one finds less favourable treatment of this kind. The principle of equality becomes an element in a strategy for dealing with new forms of employment. However, in Britain there is no such principle. Employers are free to treat workers differently (save on grounds of sex, race, etc.). The strategy for dealing with new forms of employment cannot avail itself of a general equality principle. Another legal strategy is evident in the debate in Italy, and to a lesser extent in France, over flexibility of sources of labour law. The debate is concerned with the articulation between different levels of collective agreements, and between such agreements and legislation. However, the elements of normalisation, standardisation and equality are still the essence of the debate. The more devolution of terms and conditions of employment is permitted, from legislation down through levels of collective bargaining, the less standardisation results, down to the point where new forms of employment may (or may not) be permitted under workplace agreements. Yet another legal strategy looks at the social security system, which may exclude these new forms of employment. In Britain, one of the reasons for employers using new forms of employment is to avoid the burden of social security contributions payable for typical employees. In Scandinavia, however, the social security system is not generally based on the labour market, but is financed out of general taxation. Everybody is covered whether or not they are in the labour market. Similarly, most employment protection covers virtually everybody, through collective agreements covering the vast majority of the workforce which is unionised. In this way new forms of employment are in less danger of exploitation – and actors' strategies consequently change.

[109] Nearly half the total workforce is employed on a typical contract, if by typical is meant full-time indeterminate contracts. More than half the female workforce is on part-time and about 10 per cent of the male workforce is on part-time; so about 25–30 per cent of the total are on part-time contracts and another 10 per cent is on fixed-term contracts. However, the rate of unionisation is very high both for typical and so-called atypical workers. Traditionally, nearly everybody – almost 90 per cent of workers – is in a union. This means that almost all workers are covered by collective agreements: the traditional source of labour law. Indeed, some studies indicate that generally it is well-qualified women, not the low-paid unskilled workers, who are part-time. Unskilled low-paid workers are in typical work – full time – because they need to be in order to earn enough money. The 'atypical' forms of employment are not a pathological condition of the labour market. Paradoxically, one finds rather a correlation between low pay and 'typical' employment. And not only from the point of view of low pay: the increase in employment opportunities also comes in the 'atypical' labour market, whereas the 'typical' labour market is shrinking.

the whole rest of the framework of labour law does not distinguish them in any way.[110]

In France, state/political regulation of the forms of employment is very strong. Each time in France there appears in large numbers a new form of employment, historically legislation appears to regulate it.[111] In Britain, the current state/political strategy towards new forms of employment may be said to have gone toward the provision of incentives towards fragmentation of the workforce, making it disadvantageous for the employer to employ workers in typical rather than atypical forms.[112]

## European strategies: legislation, social dialogue, open method of coordination

Fragmentation of the workforce has become a central concern of European labour law. The exigencies of protection of a fragmented workforce require a

---

[110]  It is interesting that, for example, in Denmark during the 1950s there was a debate in the unions whether or not to open up to these new forms of employment, particularly part-time work. The initial attitude, particularly from the male-dominated unions, was that they would not accept it. This is still the attitude of some unions. But during the 1960s and 1970s the women-dominated unions started allowing it in their collective agreements. The trade union confederation stopped opposing it. The reason was that the unions had to choose between getting the part-time women as members, or watching an entire labour market develop outside the unions' control. If unions and collective agreements excluded part-time workers, and by law employers are bound by collective agreements, employers would be tempted to try to operate through a non-unionised part-time labour market. The unions would not take the risk of thus losing control.

[111]  This regulatory intervention of the state has the function of rendering these new forms of employment socially acceptable. The intervention makes possible and legitimate the use of this form by employers, while affording at the same time a minimum protection. There is a search for an equilibrium. In the twentieth century, this was the case with domestic labour, then fixed-term contracts, part-time work and casual labour. There is a strong tradition of state intervention in the labour market, a stronger role than is found in other areas of labour regulation, for example, wages, where collective agreements are primary.

[112]  A significant aspect of the British state/political strategy is that, on the face of it, the amount of formal legal intervention is very small. The strategy towards new forms of employment is not through traditional labour law, but through political intervention in the labour market, using measures which do not necessarily assume the form of traditional labour legislation. This occurs in a variety of ways. For example, when the government decides to use public resources to fund the training of workers, or to help young people come into the labour market. Another example is when public sector work is put out to private tender, in the knowledge that certain forms of sub-contracted labour will be used (with pay and conditions below public sector standards). Similarly, when government contracts are made without the safeguards as to pay and conditions and union membership protection which had originated in the Fair Wages policy dating back to 1891. It is at the opposite end of the spectrum from France. At some point the question becomes: is the focus of state policy 'new forms of employment'? Or is it rather a policy concerned with employment promotion, labour market flexibility or enterprise assistance? In each of these, 'new forms of employment' is but one element of a grander strategy. Employers and unions are likely to be aware, and often are involved in the development of these macro-economic strategies. The problem for labour lawyers is that their perspectives may not encompass these wider political visions. Constrained by their limited views of 'forms of employment', they adopt strategies which focus on the narrower issues of 'new forms of employment', using only the instruments of labour law and labour legislation. The result is contradictory when applied in the context of the wider state/political strategy.

regulatory framework appropriate to its particular circumstances. The EU has explored different paths towards such a regulatory framework: legislation, social dialogue and the open method of coordination.

Early initiatives took the form of proposals for legislation: Council directives on certain employment relationships in the aftermath of the approval of the Charter of Fundamental Social Rights in December 1989.[113] The proposals were accompanied by a lengthy Explanatory Memorandum which pointed out differences between Member States in the numbers and proportion of the workforce employed in such relationships. It was estimated that the workers concerned by the directives accounted for some 20 per cent of total employment.[114]

Eight main issues were considered to call for particular attention.[115] Instead of being incorporated into one directive, however, these issues were divided among three different draft Directives, each ostensibly concerned with a different theme: (1) working conditions, (2) distortions of competition and (3) health and safety, and each with a different legal basis.[116]

---

[113] Proposal for a Council Directive on certain employment relationships with regard to working conditions; Proposal for a Council Directive on certain employment relationships with regard to distortions of competition. COM(90) 228 final – SYN 280, Brussels, 13 August 1990. Another proposal introduced at the same time (Proposal for a Council Directive supplementing the measures to encourage improvements in the safety and health at work of temporary workers, COM(90) 228 final – SYN 281, Brussels, 13 August 1990) was eventually approved and became Council Directive 91/533 of 25 June 1991 supplementing the measures to encourage improvement in the safety and health at work of workers with a fixed-duration employment relationship or a temporary employment relationship. OJ 1991 L206/19.

[114] Explanatory Memorandum, paragraph 20. As regards *part-timers*, in 1988 these were over 30 per cent of the working population in the Netherlands, and more than 20 per cent in Denmark (23.7 per cent) and the UK (21.9 per cent), some 13.2 per cent in the Germany, but around 5 per cent in Spain (5.4 per cent), Italy (5.6 per cent), Greece (5.5 per cent) and Portugal (6.5 per cent) (8 per cent in Ireland) (*A Social Portrait of Europe*, Statistical Office of the European Communities (Eurostat), Luxembourg, 1991, p. 62, Table 5.6; and Explanatory Memorandum, paragraph 15). The Community average was 13.6 per cent, more than 14 million part-time employees. As regards *temporary employment*, in 1988, employees with a temporary contract were 22.4 per cent in Spain, 18.5 per cent in Portugal and 17.6 per cent in Greece, but fell from just over 11 per cent in Germany and Denmark, to 8.7 per cent in the Netherlands, 7.8 per cent in France and 5.9 per cent in the UK (*A Social Portrait of Europe*, p. 64, Table 5.13). A 1989 survey showed that 30 per cent of employment relationships in Spain were limited in time, but the figure was around 10 per cent in Italy, Greece, Ireland and Portugal and below 10 per cent in all other Member States (Explanatory Memorandum, paragraph 16).

[115] Access to training; taking into account such employees in calculating numbers or persons employment with a view to the setting-up of representative bodies for workers; information for workers' representative bodies in the event of recourse to the workers concerned; grounds for recourse to temporary employment; information for the temporary workers employed where the employer intended to recruit full-time employees for an indefinite period; rules concerning access to social assistance; access to the social services of undertakings; and the specific situations of workers employed through temporary employment businesses. Explanatory Memorandum, paragraph 48.

[116] The significance of the legal basis lies in the capacity of the Council of Ministers to approve proposed Directives either by qualified majority voting or by unanimity. The working conditions draft Directive was based on Article 100 of the Treaty of Rome, requiring unanimity.

Only the third proposal, relating to the health and safety of temporary workers, was approved by the Council of Ministers.[117] The proposals regarding these specific categories of employment can be better understood less through detailed analysis of their substantive provisions than through the context in which they emerged and in which they were considered in the early 1990s. Two of the three proposals, the two that were not approved, related to *both* part-timers *and* non-permanent workers. The third applied *only* to non-permanent workers, and it was this proposal only which was approved.

The implications of the approval of a Directive affecting only temporary workers by qualified majority voting in the Council are particularly interesting, given the composition and distribution of the labour force within the EC. Unlike part-timers, there is no general preponderance of women workers in

The working conditions draft Directive (Article 100) applied to temporary and part-time workers and covered access to training, services and social assistance/social security schemes (Articles 2.1, 3 and 4); calculation of employee numbers relating to employee representative bodies (Article 2.2); information and consultation of employee representatives (Article 2.3); informing about full-time open-ended vacancies (Article 5); contents of temporary employment contracts (Article 2.4); temporary work agencies and user companies (Article 6); and obligations of temporary employment agencies (Article 7). The draft Directive on distortions of competition was based on Article 100A. The distortions of competition draft Directive (Article 100A) also applied to temporary and part-time workers and dealt with entitlement to social protection under statutory and occupational social security schemes (Article 2); holidays, dismissal payments and seniority allowances (Article 3); and termination of a temporary contract before term (Article 4(b)). That on health and safety, on Article 118A. The health and safety draft Directive (Article 118A) applied only to temporary workers and concerned contents of the contract between the user company and the temporary work agency (Article 3); user company's responsibilities (Article 4); information and training of temporary workers (Article 5); and work requiring special medical supervision (Article 6). Both required only qualified majority voting. Prior to their presentation, there was an intense debate on which Articles of the Treaty of Rome should constitute their legal basis. The two proposed Directives on certain employment relationships were based respectively on Article 100 and Article 100A of the Treaty. Article 100 required unanimous approval in the Council of Ministers. This was not forthcoming. Article 100A allowed for qualified majority voting, but not, according to Article 100A(2), if it related to 'the rights and interests of employed persons'. The interpretation of this phrase would have been stringently tested by an attempt to extend qualified majority voting to the second proposal. The third proposal, however, was based on Article 118A of the Treaty, inserted by the Single European Act 1986, which allowed for qualified majority voting on proposals concerning 'the working environment, as regards the health and safety of workers'. The draft Directives were accompanied by considerable dispute as they progressed through the legislative procedure. Within the Commission, the Legal Service and Directorate-General V (Social Affairs) had differences over the appropriate legal bases for the draft Directives. Parliament and the Economic and Social Committee objected to the division of issues among different drafts with different legal bases. In the case of ECOSOC, a tripartite body, the employer members approved the substantive content of the draft Directives on atypical work, but objected to the legal basis allowing for qualified majority voting. In contrast, Parliament objected to the draft Directives where approval required unanimity in the Council of Ministers. Parliament put forward amendments inserting the content of the working conditions draft Directive (based on Article 100) into the other two.

[117] Council Directive 91/383 of 25 June 1991 supplementing the measures to encourage improvements in the safety and health of workers with a fixed-duration employment relationship or a temporary employment relationship, OJ 1991 L206/19.

the non-permanent workforce.[118] However, with respect to both part-timers and non-permanent workers, there is a clear North–South cleavage within the Community.

The northern European Member States have a disproportionately high number of part-timers compared to the southern European Member States.[119] The implications of a specific category of employment regulated by EC labour law are that the *costs* of such regulation are borne by the employers of that category of employees, and appear as a form of competitive disadvantage vis-à-vis employers not subject to such regulation. In so far as part-time employment is predominantly concentrated in northern Europe, employers in those countries have to bear a disproportionate cost of the equality law of the EC. Conversely, the enactment of EC regulations specifically aimed at non-permanent employment imposes costs disproportionately on southern European employers, where such employment is concentrated. The early adoption by the Council of such regulation has significance for the general debate over 'social dumping', given the generally lower labour costs of southern European employers.

Fragmentation of the workforce has not become any less dramatic over the years since the failure to adopt the Commission's proposed directives in the early 1990s. The EU's attempts to come to terms with the fragmentation of the workforce and the development of new forms of work looked to other strategies.[120] The legislative method had not succeeded. However, the failure of the Commission's proposals coincided with the coming into effect of the new Treaty provisions on social dialogue. This proved more successful in providing a framework of collective regulation for the different fragments of the workforce.

[118] See *A Social Portrait of Europe*, p. 64, Table 5.13.

[119] In 1988, part-timers were over 30 per cent of the working population in the Netherlands, and more than 20 per cent in Denmark (23.7 per cent) and the UK (21.9 per cent), some 13.2 per cent in Germany, but around 5 per cent in Spain (5.4 per cent), Italy (5.6 per cent), Greece (5.5 per cent) and Portugal (6.5 per cent) (8 per cent in Ireland). *Ibid.*, p. 62, Table 5.6. The opposite is true for non-permanent workers, who are concentrated more densely in the South. In 1988, employees with a temporary contract were 22.4 per cent in Spain, 18.5 per cent in Portugal and 17.6 per cent in Greece, but fell from just over 11 per cent in Germany and Denmark, to 8.7 per cent in the Netherlands, 7.8 per cent in France and 5.9 per cent in the UK. *Ibid.*, p. 62, Table 5.13.

[120] Legislative regulation of atypical work continued in two directions. One was to expand the scope of regulation to include not only contracts but also other 'relationships of employment'. The Council Directive on an employer's obligation to inform employees of the conditions applicable to the contract or employment relationship was an attempt to extend the boundaries of labour law beyond the conventional contract of employment. Council Directive 91/533/EEC of 14 October 1991; OJ L288/32 of 18 October 1991. A second, again exploiting the qualified majority voting regime for health and safety, was to focus attention on the issue of working time. Council Directive 93/104/EC of 23 November 1993 concerning certain aspects of the organisation of working time; OJ L307/18 of 13 December 1993, as amended by Directive 2000/34 of 22 June 2000, OJ L195/41. Consolidated in Directive 2003/88/EC of 4 November 2003 concerning certain aspects of the organisation of working time; OJ L299/9 of 18 November 2003.

The European intersectoral social dialogue produced two framework agreements which became directives, on part-time work[121] and on fixed-term work,[122] and a third framework agreement on telework, which did not become a directive. Negotiations were begun, though the social partners eventually failed to reach agreement, on temporary agency workers. Building on the social dialogue, the Commission produced a proposal for a directive on agency workers which, at the time of writing, has so far failed to be adopted by the Council of Ministers.[123]

On the one hand, this record of success in reaching European framework agreements on the regulation of the fragmented labour market is at least partial vindication of the European social dialogue model of collective regulation. On the other hand, however, this model of collective regulation is challenged by the emergence of the European Employment Strategy where pillars such as entrepreneurship, employability and even equal opportunities appear resolutely individualistic. The EES reliance on the 'open method of coordination' does invite participation of the social partners, encouraged to focus particularly on the adaptability pillar. The EU's model of a collective framework of regulation of a fragmented workforce remains divided among these different strategies.

## Conclusion

This chapter has outlined the different models of collective frameworks developed by European labour law for individual employment. The EU social dialogue is the primary collective framework at macro-level, while institutionalised structures of worker representation at enterprise level operate at the micro-level.

In the field of equality and discrimination, collective bargaining is perceived as potentially more desirable than individual mechanisms. In the field of health and safety, the long-standing engagement of collective organisations of workers in regulation is reflected in EU policy as regard both enforcement and standard setting (working time). In the field of free movement of workers, EU regulation is in the process of coming to terms with the problem of 'social dumping' and the role of collective agreements in combating this phenomenon. Finally, fragmentation of the workforce has led to legislative intervention, but also social dialogue agreements.

The next section looks at fundamental rights of individual employment which underpin and augment this collective framework.

---

[121] Council Directive 97/81/EC of 15 December 1997 concerning the framework agreement on part-time work concluded by UNICE, CEEP and the ETUC, OJ L14/9 of 20 January 1998.

[122] Council Directive 1999/70/EC of 28 June 1999 concerning the framework agreement on fixed-term work concluded by ETUC, UNICE and CEEP, OJ L175/43 of 10 July 1999.

[123] Commission of the European Communities, *Proposal for a Directive of the European Parliament and the Council on working conditions for temporary workers*, COM(2002) 149 final, Brussels, 20 March 2002; *Amended Proposal*, COM(2002) 701 final, Brussels, 28 November 2002.

## Fundamental individual employment rights in European labour law

Rights of individual employees, as regards access to employment, conditions of work and job security, are basic elements of labour law. That such individual employment rights may have a fundamental character, however, is a concept which has become increasingly accepted as a cornerstone of European labour law.

The Community Charter of the Fundamental Social Rights of Workers of 1989 included a large number of specific rights of individual employment under headings including 'employment and remuneration' (Articles 4–6), 'improvement of living and working conditions' (Articles 7–9), 'social protection' (Article 10), 'vocational training' (Article 15), 'equal treatment for men and women' (Article 16), 'health protection and safety at the workplace' (Article 19), 'protection of children and adolescents' (Articles 20–3), 'elderly persons' (Articles 24–5) and 'disabled persons' (Article 26).

The EU Charter of Fundamental Rights of 2000 refers explicitly to fundamental individual employment rights: Article 5, prohibition of slavery and forced labour; Article 14: access to vocational training; Article 15: right to engage in work; Article 23: equality between men and women; Article 26: occupational integration of persons with disabilities; Article 29: right of access to free placement services; Article 30: right to protection against unjustified dismissal; Article 31: fair and just working conditions; Article 32: prohibition of child labour and protection of young people at work; Article 33: right to protection from dismissal for maternity reasons and to paid maternity and parental leave; and Article 34: social security and social assistance, including in cases of industrial accidents and loss of employment.

The operationalisation of fundamental individual employment rights requires a reconceptualisation of the worker who bears these rights conferred by European labour law.

## The worker-citizen

The legal concept of the worker has for many years been the subject of analysis. Contention over the precise legal nature of the employment relationship is not new to European labour law. Frequently, it was the issue which, in some countries, enabled labour law to break free of civil law and become an autonomous discipline. The civil law rules of contract were perceived as inadequate to govern the contract of employment. Even in those countries which did not make such a break, it was widely acknowledged that the employment relationship could not be captured within the rules governing ordinary contracts, and that its nature required different regulation, usually by bringing in legislation, but also through collective agreements.

The dynamic of labour law development in the EU is inspired by and draws upon these preoccupations at national level, but, as always, filters them through a specific perspective, and produces a result which is still in the process of evolution. More recently, the failure of the legal concept of the employment relationship to accommodate changes arising from fragmentation of the workforce into new forms of work has subjected it to new stresses. Again, this evolution has had a reciprocal effect on Member State labour laws.[124]

Responses to the fragmentation of the workforce have produced in some Member States the application with respect to new categories of workers of employment protection provisions previously available only to 'typical' workers. To some extent, this has produced a rather unreflective replication of employment protection provisions, merely extended to include categories previously excluded. But it has also occasionally meant that such extension has been accompanied by distinct provisions recognising the *specific* qualities of the new categories being protected. A sufficiently widespread diversification of employment protection laws could lead to a *qualitative* change in labour law, by way of recognition that different categories of workers have different requirements for employment protection.

But these profound changes in the composition of the workforce could also lead to a transformation in labour law's concept of the employment relationship. This would go beyond a recognition of the specificity of the employment 'contract', beyond supplementing contractual rules with legislative regulation or collective agreement, and even beyond the multiplication of employment protection laws for specific and new categories of workers.

To some extent, the signs of change are already evident in national labour laws. One striking manifestation is in the form of constitutional provisions of social and economic rights of workers.[125] The literature in many countries has increasingly come to speak of the worker as a *citizen* in the enterprise.[126]

At EU level, the inspiration for change derived impetus from the happenstance that the concept of 'worker' first emerged in a 'non-contractual' context. For the first decades of its existence, the EC was concerned primarily with workers as a factor within the common market. It was their freedom of movement which was to be protected by EU law. Hence, it was not the relationship of the worker to the employer which was of initial concern, but the relationship of the worker to the state. As such, the preoccupation of EC law was to extend the concept of worker very widely to ensure that all those performing work were able to circulate freely among Member States.[127] It was the worker's rights

---

[124] Examples include Member State recognition of the specific needs of certain categories of workers, which has produced EC law directed specifically at temporary workers' health and safety. Conversely, the dynamics of EU equality law have had a considerable impact on the law governing part-time workers in Member States.

[125] For details, B. Bercusson, 'Fundamental Social and Economic Rights in the European Community', in A. Cassese, A. Clapham and J. Weiler (eds.), *Human Rights in the European Community: Methods of Protection*, Baden-Baden: Nomos Verlag, 1991, pp. 195–294.

[126] For example, legislation on rights of expression in France; or protection of dignity and privacy in Germany. The enormous literature on worker participation is a reflection of this.

[127] *Deborah Lawrie-Blum* v. *Land Baden-Wurttemberg*, Case 66/85, [1986] ECR 2121.

against Member States' restrictions on free movement which were the prime subject of scrutiny by EC institutions in the formative years. The Court's willingness to adopt an autonomous and extensive legal definition of worker, however, was confined to the policy area of free movement. The Court deferred to national law definitions of 'worker' when applying EC directives in other policy areas of labour law.[128]

It was perhaps this initial vision of the worker as a citizen entitled to free movement which contributed towards what is now emerging as a concept of the employment relationship at EU level. Again, the debate is not characterised by maximum clarity and linearity of development. But the signs are there to be read: the concept of the employment relationship is being subsumed in the wider debate over EU citizenship.[129]

It is not surprising that this should occur, given the conjunctural evolution of a European polity at a time when there is a palpable political exigency for the support of the EU by labour movements, and, simultaneously, the legal conceptualisation of employment is under strain in the specific context of a common market. The first of these two factors produced the impulse towards creation of the 'social dimension' of the 1992 Single European Market programme in the general form of a Community Charter of Fundamental Social Rights proclaimed by eleven Member States at Strasbourg in December 1989. The second contributed towards the specific form it took. The 1989 Charter was transformed late in the day from a Charter of the Rights of Citizens to a Charter for Workers.[130]

The implications of the subsumption of worker into citizen are many. Specifically, its impact on the legal definition of the employment relationship is that it expands this to include the worker's relationship with the state and the trade union, as well as the employer.[131] The worker is no longer legally defined separately in terms of different legal concepts/ties: contractual with the employer, as citizen with the state, and as member (contract/status) of the union.[132]

---

[128]   *Mikkelsen*, Case 105/84, [1986] 1 CMLR 310.

[129]   For example, the extrapolation of ECJ case law on the free movement of workers to embrace the free movement rights of persons in their capacity as EU citizens. *Bickel and Franz*, Case C-274/96 [1998] ECR I-7637; *Rudy Grzelczyk* v. *Centre public d'aide sociale d'Ottignies-Louvain-la-Neuve*, Case C-184/99 [2001] ECR I-6193; *Baumbast, R* v. *Secretary of State for the Home Department*, Case C-413/99 [2002] ECR I-7091; *Kunqian Catherine Zhu*, Case C-200/02, judgment of 19 October 2004; *Dany Bidar*, Case C-209/03, judgment of 15 March 2005. See also the ECJ's insistence on a Community definition of worker for the purpose of the fundamental Community law principle of equal pay between men and women in *Allonby* v. *Accrington & Rosendale College*, Case C-256/01, [2004] IRLR 224.

[130]   This both broadens and narrows its scope: workers include non-citizens; citizens include non-workers. B. Bercusson, 'The European Community's Charter of Fundamental Social Rights for Workers', (1990) 53 *Modern Law Review* 624.

[131]   For an analysis of UK labour law using this approach, see Benedictus and Bercusson, *Labour Law*, Chapter 1, pp. 9–25.

[132]   Up to now, each of these relationships was separate and, to some extent, there was a hierarchical ordering. For example, employment was subject to statute, but only if parties opted for contractual employee status. Union membership was separate, but employment could be related

The question facing the EU law on individual employment is whether the elements of citizenship, union membership/affiliation and employer–worker relationship can be creatively combined into a new legal concept of 'worker-citizen'. This would involve the worker being defined as somebody who has relations with employer, state and union (fellow-workers) – perhaps *without* a specific hierarchical ordering, and using (non-contractual) concepts to determine the rights and duties owed by each to the others. This could include rights not only as between employer–union–state and workers, but also as between employer and union and state, as well as with the worker.[133]

The concept of worker-citizen presupposes a fragmentation of the roles of worker and citizen, involving *shared responsibilities* of employer and state,[134] and corresponding *shared loyalties* of the worker to employer and state. The sphere of shared *loyalties* is less developed. The concept that the worker has *social* duties (and rights) as a citizen to which employment duties can be subordinated is only partially recognised; examples include public duties, trade union duties and time off for family responsibilities. This involves developing a careful symmetry between social responsibilities and the allocation of costs of these between employer and state/society.[135]

by contractual terms to collective agreements. What is striking is the pre-eminence of *contract* doctrines in determining the employment relationship. It was contract which determined the nature of the employment relationship, and hence whether statute applied (e.g. to whether there was a dismissal). It was contract which provided the rules determining whether a collective agreement applied. It was contract which usually determined the worker's entitlement to legislative benefits, and governed the worker's relationship to the union.

[133] What concepts operate in these different contexts, and can they be combined? In employment, as Alan Fox shows, free agreement through contract was subordinated to the almost inevitable mandatory implication of obedience. Fox, *Beyond Contract*, pp. 188–90. State citizenship status was also hierarchical – but subject to, if not Rousseau's social contract, at least a formal tenet of democratic consent to be ruled. Unions came closer to democratic practice, though also hierarchical. Employment and union membership were both also conditioned by the possibility of resignation: the 'exit' option in Hirschman's categories; A. O. Hirschman, *Exit, Voice and Loyalty: Responses to Decline in Firms, Organizations, and States*, Cambridge, MA: Harvard University Press, 1970. Unions also allowed for participation ('voice'), while employment demanded fidelity ('loyalty'), or, as Fox put it, 'trust'. Can these concepts – agreement (market), democracy (polity), trust (family) (or exit, voice and loyalty, to use Hirschman's categories) – provide an alternative to contract as the defining quality of the employment relationship? In the past, they combined in various ways: agreement (loyalty/exit – no voice) for the relationship to the employer; membership (voice/exit/loyalty) for the relationship to the union; citizenship (voice/loyalty – no exit) for relationship to the state. Can these elements be combined into a concept of worker-citizenship?

[134] For example, in the UK, the two are already frequently combined in the sphere of *responsibilities*, with the growth of the welfare state in the form of employer contributions to social security, statutory sick pay, statutory maternity pay, vocational training, and so on.

[135] The position of the trade union in this context/complex of duties and responsibilities is difficult. Unions are perceived primarily as counterparts to employers – though this is a conception of trade unionism to be found mainly in some western European states and in English-speaking countries. Elsewhere, they are seen mainly as political actors. See Ross M. Martin, *Trade Unionism: Purposes and Forms*, Oxford: Clarendon Press, 1989. This may require a rethinking of trade unions' roles in the EU. Is it surprising that the transformation of employment relationships should now require transformation of unions – beyond merely increasing membership in previously unrecruited areas? This was already evident in neo-corporatist

Turning to the conceptual apparatus needed to define the worker-citizen, at present, the worker is in a contractual relation to the employer, in a status relation to the state, and in a contract/status relation to the trade union. The worker's relationship is with *all three* simultaneously. Each must interrelate rights and duties in a coherent package. This is not, cannot be, static (status); there must be flexibility; nor is it contractual (individualistic) – it must be social to incorporate the collective union/state dimension (democratic).[136]

Kahn-Freund's solution was 'regulated contract'.[137] Its merits were extolled: freedom of choice plus protection. Contract gave choice to enter; thereafter, terms were dictated by the state or by collective agreements.[138] Kahn-Freund's solution still sees the relationship with the *employer* as of primary importance, even where this relationship is *less* central to the worker than, for example, the relationship with the state (or even with the union), as might be the case with 'atypical' workers, where family, training, social service, etc. activities might be paramount. Can European labour law take those on board? It depends on whether labour law is to remain confined to 'typical' workers, or altered to encompass other employment relationships.

In the EU context, one serious candidate is the *citizenship* concept engaging the state at the centre instead of the employer, a mixture of citizen/worker roles as an alternative solution to Kahn-Freund's regulated contract.[139] This would aim to achieve recognition of the social identities of workers' working lives, to

tendencies in Member States earlier in the post-war period. If unions are to enter into the nexus of employment/citizenship, then they will have to assume a new role – perhaps as intermediary organisations; as coordinating mechanisms between workers and their other social roles; as mediators of the duties/responsibilities of state and employer. Already, trade unions in the UK are the most frequent representatives of claimants before social security tribunals. In other countries, unions occupy parts of the administration of the welfare state: pensions, vocational training, and so on. They have other capacities to be developed. This may require a more diverse conception of trade unionism (already diverse), distinguishing the union at the workplace (relationships with other workers there) and the union outside (mediating relationships among workers in different workplaces).

[136] B. Bercusson, 'Law and the Socialist Enterprise', pp. 90–112, in R. Cotterrell and B. Bercusson (eds.), *Law, Democracy and Social Justice*, Special Issue of the *Journal of Law and Society*, Spring 1988, Oxford: Blackwell; see also (with R. Cotterrell) 'Introduction', pp. 1–4.

[137] O. Kahn-Freund, 'A Note on Status and Contract in British Labour Law', (1967) 30 *MLR* 635, at pp. 640–2.

[138] This solution has its problems. First, it is premised on one type of employment contract. What if the state or collective agreements did not reach other types of employment relationships? One solution is to secure regulation by the state and collective agreements of other types of employment relationships. Secondly, it implies that choice of entry also means choice of exit – certainly by the employee, but also by the employer (dismissal). The solution, again, is regulation by the state or collective agreements of dismissal.

[139] The question is whether, in the EU context, unions can play a more engaged role in relation to the state than they could in relation to employer. Unions share with the state the *democracy* element. They share with the employer the *exit/market* factor. Which of these liaisons is the more promising? The Maastricht Protocol showed how unions could be integrated at macro-level. Bargaining in the shadow of the law, negotiated legislation, raises the prospects for an integration of unions, state and employers into a neo-corporatist model. But there is a need for articulation of the macro-level with lower levels. This would at least require internal constitutional reforms of the ETUC and of national union structures. Legislation on worker participation is another reflection of these issues. P.C.

include entitlements which protect and encourage their societal roles.[140] The concept of 'worker-citizen' is not captured by the contract of employment, which fails to include the citizenship quality, that employment may be one only of many relationships of the worker, and not necessarily the most important.[141] It is desirable to have one overriding concept rather than, as at present, a multiplicity: employment, citizen's rights, etc. with the disadvantage of hierarchy among them, as relationships between their formal manifestations as legal instruments are needed.

The emerging European social model incorporates a strong negotiable content of, and negotiable derogations from, labour standards. There is a strong trade union role. This has implications for the law on the internal structures of unions: issues of democracy and members' rights, not yet broached, but implicit in the emerging EU debate over representativeness.[142]

The element of choice remains in that the worker-citizen chooses roles and activities, one of which is employment in various forms. But employment becomes *relational* not *only* to the employer, but also to other roles and activities.[143] The conceptual construct which emerges highlights that older models of contract are too bilateral while concepts of multilateral contract involve too much formal negotiating among parties. On the other hand, traditional concepts of (state) citizenship are too unmediated by other relationships such as employment and union membership.

An illustration would be the concept of reconciliation (or combination) of working and family life.[144] The task is one of reconciling different social

Schmitter, 'Still the Century of Corporatism?', in P.C. Schmitter and G. Lehmbruch (eds.), *Trends Towards Corporatist Intermediation*, Beverly Hills: Sage, 1979; for an application in the sphere of low pay and incomes policies, see B. Bercusson, 'Wage Determination: Instrumentalist and Neo-Corporatist Approaches', paper presented at a Colloquium on 'Law and Economic Policy – Alternatives to De-Legalisation', the European University Institute, Florence, 1985 (mimeo); for doubts in the EC context, see W. Streeck and P.C. Schmitter, 'From National Corporatism to Transnational Pluralism: Organised Interests in the Single European Market', (1991) 19 *Politics and Society* 133.

[140] Examples include caring, public, community and social service. An example which shows the way is in the Working Time Directive, Article 13: the principle of adapting patterns of working time to the worker.

[141] Conceptually, this has to be more than additional legislative constraints on contract. It 'proceduralises' contract out of existence. It becomes 'relation(al)(ship) contract', evolving and permanently negotiable. Does it mean anything to continue to call this contract when, substantively, it is something else? It would be important to come up with new terminology to exclude (in UK common law) the old conceptual baggage.

[142] In the European social dialogue, in European Works Councils, and for the purposes of negotiation and consultation as required by various directives, and the role of the Commission in shaping it.

[143] As in Article 13 of the Working Time Directive, the employer must take account of adapting work to the worker's other roles. To do this, presumably, as in the Directive, he must consult the union. The employer must also take account of/consult others: such as the family for family roles, training authorities, community, social services, etc.

[144] The Commission Consultative Document of April 1995. For details, see Chapter 15 of the first edition of this book. See now also the somewhat misleading Article 23 ('Family and professional life') of the EU Charter of Fundamental Rights of 2000.

roles.[145] This is still labour law, in so far as labour itself has changed to encompass a wider spectrum of activities. The problem was the heretofore exclusive market orientation of labour law. Labour law has come back to being a socialised instrument of society, not solely of the market.

In the EU context, the concept would have to be adapted to various national contexts. But the key shift would be that the employment relationship is opened out to embrace other relationships; and is turned into a relationship which must take account of others (both employer and worker must do so).[146] The worker-citizen concept is no longer a contract in any recognisable (common law or other) sense.[147]

European labour law is moving towards the concept of the worker-citizen as the cornerstone of the European law on individual employment. The Community Charter of the Fundamental Social Rights of Workers of 1989 represented a commitment by the Member States of the European Union to a set of social policy and labour law objectives. But it was only a first step document. By the adoption in 2000 of the EU Charter's fundamental rights of individual employment, the next step has been taken in the direction of a European social model with fundamental individual employment rights of the worker-citizen as a cornerstone.

Like the 1989 Community Charter, the EU Charter of 2000 is far from perfect. It was the product of complex, intense and highly politicised bargaining among and within the different groups within the Convention which drafted it during 1999–2000. It was further amended in Working Group II and the plenary of the Convention on the Future of Europe which included it in the draft Constitutional Treaty proposed in July 2003, and finally by the Member

---

[145] Building on this proposal, one approach would be for a concept which left the choice to enter the relationship initially to the parties. Then, if there are disputes or complaints, these are to be resolved by reconciliation tribunals: judges who are experts in family, social and community affairs, etc. They are to resolve conflicts by determining rights and obligations (towards family, community, work, etc.), just as, for example, family courts consider the interests of the children in divorce disputes. Employment tribunals are replaced, or supplemented, by other tribunals when disputes occur over reconciliation of work and other roles and responsibilities. The individual chooses, but *others* affected by the decision – employer, family, community, state, trade union – can complain to the reconciliation tribunal if they feel, for example, they are suffering a disproportionate burden; for example, too much work, too little family, too little work. It would, of course, be necessary also to promote the work identities of citizens. Those citizens whose attachment to working life is relatively marginal should be not only protected (by rights) but encouraged to develop this (by incentives). For the tribunals, careful attention would have to be paid to problems of *locus standi*, procedures, remedies (including incentives), and so on.

[146] And also allows others legal standing to challenge it when it interferes with these other relationships.

[147] It is certainly not bilateral, as others can challenge it. But it is not a multilateral contract either, as others do not participate in its formation. As a legal instrument it is *bilateral* (contractual) in formation (allowing for choice); *relational* in its implementation/application; other interests must be taken into account for its duration; and *multilateral* in its enforcement (complaints can be made about its operation (and termination?) by others than the parties).

States at the IGC which approved the Constitutional Treaty in June 2004. The outcome was a set of fundamental rights which are not ideal in their structure or drafting.[148]

At least three rights of individual employment may be considered fundamental, and formulations of them, however deficient, are to be found in the EU Charter. They concern:

- the individual worker's access to employment (Article 15: Right to engage in work);
- the conditions under which the individual employee works (Article 31: Fair and just working conditions); and
- termination of the individual worker's employment (Article 30: Right to protection against unjustified dismissal).[149]

## Article 15: Freedom to choose an occupation and right to engage in work

1. Everyone has the right to engage in work and to pursue a freely chosen or accepted occupation.[150]

Earlier versions of the Charter adopted different wording for this paragraph.[151] The final formula, 'the right to engage in work', appears to be a compromise between the right to work and the freedom to work. An enforceable right to work is considered contrary to a liberal society governed by a private market economy. This approach fails to take into account the specific nature of constitutional rights, now prominent in the EU context. This category of rights may grant subjective rights to individuals against the state, but as much or even more

---

[148] To the extent that it can be said that, like sausages, one is best advised to look at the final product of fundamental rights rather than observe them being produced.

[149] The remainder of this chapter is a revised and edited version of parts of an extended commentary on the labour law implications of the EU Charter, Bercusson (ed.), *European Labour Law and the EU Charter*. A summary version in English (102 pp.) and translated into Dutch, French, German, Greek, Italian, Spanish and Swedish, was published by the European Trade Union Institute, Brussels, 2002–3. The summary versions are available on-line on the website of the European Trade Union Institute, the research arm of the European Trade Union Confederation. The commentary was the work of the Research Group on Transnational Trade Union Rights (Thomas Blanke, Niklas Bruun, Stefan Clauwaert, Antoine Jacobs, Yota Kravaritou, Isabelle Schömann, Bruno Veneziani and Christophe Vigneau), coordinated by the author, with the steady and constructive support of Reiner Hoffmann, then Director of the European Trade Union Institute. Initial drafts of the full text commentary on Articles 15, 31 and 30, then edited by the author, were produced respectively by Christophe Vigneau, University of Paris-I (Panthéon-Sorbonne), France, Thomas Blanke, University of Oldenburg, Germany, and Niklas Bruun, Hanken School of Economics, and the University of Helsinki, Finland.

[150] This was Article II-75 of the proposed Constitutional Treaty of the European Union.

[151] The following commentary on Article 15 of the Charter is a revised and edited version of a text initially drafted by Christophe Vigneau, University of Paris-I (Panthéon-Sorbonne), France, based on detailed discussions in the ETUI Research Group on Transnational Trade Union Rights, and finally edited by the author.

they express shared values and political commitments. In this sense, the constitutional right to work is to be interpreted as a political commitment by the state to develop an active employment policy.[152]

In France, the Constitutional Court has often referred to the right to work in order to uphold the constitutional character of certain legislation.[153] More generally, the Constitutional Court has taken the view that the right to work obliges the legislature to develop the conditions for reaching full employment.[154] The French experience demonstrates that the right to work may be legally relevant in defining the constitutional or unconstitutional character of legislation affecting employment. In sum, as a constitutional right, the right to work operates so as to instruct the state to enact legislation to realise this objective.

The right to work may also have horizontal effect as between individuals. In countries where such a right is recognised by the constitution, the right to work may be invoked by courts in giving judgment in various situations. For example, cases of discrimination, or unreasonable restrictions on entering into a work relationship, or provisions that oblige a person to accept a job could be challenged by invoking the right to work.[155] Even in countries where no general right to work is recognised (UK, Ireland), such a right has been invoked to override professional restrictions on access to jobs.[156] More generally, legislation promoting access (as in quotas) to jobs of disabled persons, or supporting positive discrimination at work, in education and training could be considered as embodying the principle of the right to work. The concept of a right to work appears behind much modern legislation on training, dismissals, transfers of undertakings, and so on.[157]

---

[152] In some national constitutions, this duty imposed upon the state is clearly related to the right to work. An example is the Constitution of Luxembourg, which states that 'the law shall guarantee the right to work and assure to every citizen the exercise of this right'. However, an obligation to develop public policies to promote full employment is not only and always based on an explicit right to work. It may also be derived from the constitutional proclamation of the social character of the state (*Etat de droit social, Sozialstaatsprinzip*). This social character of the state obliges governments to improve the social life of citizens and, therefore, to reduce unemployment. In this sense, the Dutch Constitution, which does not contain the right to work, obliges the state to 'promote sufficient employment' (Article 19).

[153] Case 83–156, 28 May 1983; Case 84–2000, 16 January 1986. In a judgment of 1982, the Constitutional Court considered that the right to obtain a job gave constitutional backing for legislation limiting the possibility both to have a job and to receive a retirement pension. *Décision* 81–134, 5 January 1982, *Loi d'orientation sociale, Revue de jurisprudence constitutionnelle*, 1982, I, p. 213.

[154] For example, the Constitutional Court held in 1998 that the right to work provided support for upholding as constitutional the legislative reform of working time of the 35-hour week. Case 98–401, 10 June 1998.

[155] B. A. Hepple, 'A Right to Work', (1981) 10 *Industrial Law Journal*, pp. 71–3; A. Jacobs, 'The Right to Work and the Freedom to Work', in R. Blainpain (ed.), *The Council of Europe and the Social Challenges of the XXIst Century*, Deventer: Kluwer, 2001, pp. 59–69.

[156] Especially by trade unions: the case of the closed shop, or restrictions on access to work of non-strikers.

[157] See Benedictus and Bercusson, *Labour Law*, chapters on 'Access to Work'.

Article 15(1) does not adopt the formulation of some national legal traditions, the 'right to work'.[158] This may appear to avoid the ideological debates surrounding this right.[159] The concept of the right to work appears to be closely linked in Western European countries to the utopian liberal philosophy that emerged during the seventeenth and eighteenth centuries.[160] During this period, the right to work was closely linked to the right to life. The concept, directly inspired by the Protestant ethic, conceives of the right to work as a direct consequence and, indeed, the purpose of the right to life. Work is a value considered as inherent in any human being. Depriving a person of such a right is to deny that person's right to life.[161]

Two different interpretations are found of its legal significance and scope. In a distinction used by French scholars, the right to work embodies a fundamental ambiguity as it is considered either a 'droit créance' or 'un droit-liberté'. During the French revolution, as in other national revolutions, the widespread political claim of a right to work led to major uncertainty concerning its legal scope. For liberal philosophers, the right to work was a freedom to work, a 'droit de travailler'. This considered the removal of all obstacles preventing individuals from freely entering into employment relationships as sufficient to implement the right to work: freedom to contract is seen as the key to achieving the right to work.[162] However, as experience demonstrated that the freedom to work was not sufficient to provide work for all members of society, the socialist movement inspired by Louis Blanc argued that the concept of the right to work encompasses a subjective right for individuals to claim the right to work from the state.

The only constitutional recognition of this latter conception of the right to work may be found in the French Constitution of 1793.[163] In sum, it appears that the right to work is inspired by a philosophy of life deriving from the Protestant ethic.[164] It expressed first a liberal and individualistic concept of the

---

[158] In this respect, it is noteworthy that the French language version of the Charter speaks of *droit de travailler* rather than *droit au travail*.

[159] However, scrutiny of the debates shows that several amendments expressly proposed the formula of 'the right to work' for the Charter. The French, German and Scandinavian members of the Convention were the most favourable towards using the expression 'the right to work'. G. Braibant, *La Charte des droits sociaux fondamentaux*, Coll. inédit, Paris: Seuil, p. 135.

[160] F. Tanghe, *Le droit au travail entre histoire et utopie*, Brussels: Institut Universitaire Européen, Publications des Facultés universitaires Saint Louis, 1989.

[161] The vital importance given to work by the Protestant ethic led some countries to establish an obligation to work. The Poor Law system in England during the sixteenth century provides an example of forced labour.

[162] This right to work constitutes the principle behind the abolition of guilds in France by Turgot, already in 1776 and later during the French revolution.

[163] Article 21: '*la société doit la subsistance aux citoyens malheureux, soit* en leur procurant du travail, soit en assurant les moyens d'exister à ceux qui sont hors d'état de travailler'. The Ateliers Nationaux ('National Workshops') established by the 1848 revolution were an attempt to give a binding character to the right to work as against the state.

[164] G. Aubin and J. Bouveresse, *Introduction historique au droit du travail*, Paris: PUF, 1995, pp. 148–9.

organisation of the labour market. Later, the right to work was interpreted by socialists as the founding principle for solidaristic social organisation. However, even though the interpretation of the legal scope of the right to work differed as between liberals and socialists, both agreed on the importance of work as consequential to life and to personal fulfilment. The right to work constitutes, therefore, the cornerstone of the modern conception of both the liberal and the welfare state. The formula adopted in Article 15(1), the 'right to engage in work', might seem a subtle compromise between different views held by members of the Convention.

## Article 31: Fair and just working conditions

1. Every worker has the right to working conditions which respect his or her health, safety and dignity.
2. Every worker has the right to limitation of maximum working hours, to daily and weekly rest and to an annual period of paid leave.[165]

### Health, safety and dignity

The right to fair and just working conditions[166] in Article 31 of the EU Charter transforms the general objective of labour law as a whole into a subjective right of all workers, and elevates this subjective right (and the general objective) to the status of a fundamental social right. The right to working conditions which respect health and safety of workers dates back to the beginnings of industrialisation when the demand for limitations on working time, for daily and weekly rest periods and to an annual period of paid leave were central to workers' struggle for fair working conditions.

The right to respect for the worker's dignity at work adds a new component to these older rights. It highlights that the inviolability of human dignity is a crucial concern in labour relations and is not automatically guaranteed. It characterises the development of growing sensibility in employment relations towards the need to protect not only physical safety and psychological well-being, but the whole personality of the worker. The EU Charter's recognition of a fundamental individual employment right to just and fair working conditions with respect to human dignity is a remarkable step towards acknowledging a central problem in labour relations: the inequality of power as between the individual employee and employer in determining the conditions of employment.

---

[165] This was Article II-91 of the proposed Constitutional Treaty of the European Union.
[166] The following commentary on Article 31 of the Charter is a revised and edited version of a text initially drafted by Thomas Blanke, University of Oldenburg, Germany, based on detailed discussions in the ETUI Research Group on Transnational Trade Union Rights, and finally edited by the author.

A constitutional right to dignity, guaranteed by the state, has been the foundation on which the legal systems of some Member States[167] have developed legal obligations limiting employers' behaviour.[168] Central aspects of the employment contract, such as wages, intensity of work and working time were traditionally, and until recently, not regarded as crucial to the concept of human dignity. But the growing relevance and increasing generalisation of the concept of human dignity is opening up such a perspective.[169] The basic premise behind the law's quality control of employment contracts is the inequality existing between workers and employers in defining working conditions, which can lead to violation of fundamental rights of the workers.[170]

The right to fair and just working conditions with respect to dignity at work goes beyond traditional individual employment rights. The title of Article 31 of the Charter is very broad: it provides in general for 'fair and just working conditions' as a fundamental individual employment right of workers.[171] It is submitted that Article 31's guarantee of fair and just working conditions covers all working conditions in so far as they can affect human dignity, always under threat due to employment relations characterised by the inequality between the individual worker and the employer. EU Member States are obliged by Article 31 to provide effective regulation within their national legal systems to protect the human dignity of workers across the whole field of conditions at work.

## Article 30: Protection in the event of unjustified dismissal

Every worker has the right to protection against unjustified dismissal, in accordance with Community law and national laws and practices.[172]

---

[167]   In the Greek Constitution, this is found in Article 2, paragraph 1 (human dignity) and Article 5, paragraph 1 (the development of the personality). The right to fair working conditions includes a guarantee that working conditions respect human dignity.

[168]   Examples are controls on assessments and supervision of employees, e.g. psychological tests, collecting personal data, monitoring phone calls, e-mail contacts and use of the Internet, analysis of genetic dispositions.

[169]   For example, there is in the German legal system a development towards increasingly rigorous legal control of the equity of working conditions, including the amount of wages. The starting point was Article 10, paragraph 1 of the law on vocational training (*Berufsausbildungsgesetz*: right to an equitable wage for trainees). Then followed the control of usury exercised by the Federal Civil Court (BGH NZA 1997, 1167 = NJW 1997, 2689), up until the control of the adequacy of standard employment contracts stated by the reform of the German civil code of 2 January 2002 (*Schuldrechtsreform* BGBl I S.41).

[170]   The criteria for assessing quality are the rules laid down in collective agreements. The limit determining what is an unlawful level of remuneration, as developed by legal doctrine and court decisions, is an amount below 70–80 per cent of the collectively agreed rate. See Wolfgang Däubler, 'Die Auswirkungen der Schuldrechtsmodernisierung auf das Arbeitsrecht', *Neue Zeitschrift für Arbeitsrecht* 2001, 1329, 1335.

[171]   It is notable that paragraph 2 of Article 31 prescribes limitations on maximum working hours, rest periods and paid leave with no allowance for derogations, or qualifications such as 'in accordance with Community law and national laws and practices', which are found in other provisions of the Charter.

[172]   This was Article II-90 of the proposed Constitutional Treaty of the European Union.

Recognition of the right to protection against unjustified dismissal[173] as a fundamental right in the EU Charter confirms that a central element in the 'European social model' is continuity in employment, and that termination of employment relationships or contracts of employment must be justified.[174]

---

[173] The following commentary on Article 31 of the Charter is a revised and edited version of a text initially drafted by Niklas Bruun, Hanken School of Economics, and the University of Helsinki, Finland, based on detailed discussions in the ETUI Research Group on Transnational Trade Union Rights, and finally edited by the author.

[174] The International Labour Organisation played a major role in the development of legal protection against dismissal in many of the Member States of the European Union. The ILO adopted the Recommendation on Termination of Employment (Recommendation No. 119) as early as 1963, and a full set of instruments on the subject in 1982. Recommendation No. 166 and Convention No. 158. These instruments have been accepted by the following Member States: Finland, France, Luxembourg, Portugal, Spain and Sweden. Convention No. 158 of 1982 applies to all branches of economic activity and to all employed persons. A Member State may exclude certain categories of workers from the application of the Convention: workers hired on a fixed-term contract, or for a probationary period, or engaged on a casual basis for a short period of time. The Convention lays down fundamental principles for protection against termination of employment. Termination of employment means termination at the initiative of the employer. Termination requires a valid reason connected to the capacity or conduct of the worker, or based on the operational requirements of the undertaking, establishment or service. The Convention specifies reasons that do not qualify as valid reasons for termination. Furthermore, there are procedural requirements that must be respected when employment is terminated. A worker whose employment is to be terminated is entitled to a reasonable period of notice or compensation in lieu thereof, unless guilty of serious misconduct. According to the Convention, a worker who considers that his or her employment has been unjustifiably terminated is entitled to appeal against that termination to an impartial body, such as a court, labour tribunal, arbitration committee or arbitrator. If such a body finds the termination unjustified they shall either declare the termination invalid and/or propose reinstatement of the worker or order payment of adequate compensation or other relief. The Convention also regulates the worker's entitlement to any severance allowance, and other forms of income protection when employment has been terminated. Recommendation No. 166 of 1982 deals in particular with fixed-term contracts, and also with some procedural matters. Other specific ILO instruments also include provisions on the subject of dismissal. See the ILO Convention No. 135 concerning protection and facilities to be afforded to workers' representatives in the undertaking, ILO Convention No. 145 on the continuity of employment of seafarers and ILO Convention No. 151 concerning protection of the right to organise and procedures for determining conditions of employment in the public service. The Council of Europe drafted the Revised European Social Charter with the ILO Convention as a background model. Article 24 is headed: 'The right to protection in cases of termination of employment'. Article 24 provides: 'With a view to ensuring the effective exercise of the right of workers to protection in cases of termination of employment, the Parties undertake to recognise: (a) the right of all workers not to have their employment terminated without valid reasons for such termination connected with their capacity or conduct or based on the operational requirements of the undertaking, establishment or service; (b) the right of workers whose employment is terminated without a valid reason to adequate compensation or other appropriate relief. To this end the Parties undertake to ensure that a worker who considers that his employment has been terminated without a valid reason shall have the right to appeal to an impartial body.' This Article must be interpreted in light of existing ILO Conventions and Recommendations on protection against unjustified dismissal, which in turn have significantly influenced several Member States' national laws on protection against dismissal. It forms in turn the explicit background and inspiration for Article 30 of the EU Charter. Article 24 of the Revised European Social Charter is silent on the right of the worker to a reasonable period of notice. The reason for this is that Article 4 ('The right to a fair

Article 30 of the EU Charter protects *every worker*. This is the basic philosophy behind the notion of protection against dismissal as a fundamental right. It follows that all categories of worker, both private and public sector workers, are entitled to protection, as are employees working in atypical employment relationships.

Protection is granted in cases of *unjustified* dismissal.[175] The justification for the dismissal must be substantive, not formal. It is not enough to state that a national law contains a provision that dismissal may take place when there is a 'fair' reason for the termination of the employment. Dismissal in such a case is not justified unless it can be proved that the reason in that special case fulfilled specific substantive requirements for a termination. In addition there might be procedural requirements.[176]

Article 30 may contribute to the harmonisation of European law on dismissals. Two arguments support this role.

Harmonisation of the law of dismissal on economic grounds could contribute to cost neutrality. In a number of Member States there is regular debate as to whether it is cheaper for multinational companies to lay off and close down in one country rather than another. Harmonisation would preclude multinationals facing restructuring dismissing workers where the law on dismissal makes this economically advantageous.

As to dismissal for individual reasons, harmonising the minimum content of the fundamental right to protection against unjustified dismissal in Article 30 the Charter, including procedural requirements, would suit a well-functioning European labour market where free movement for workers is a real option.

---

remuneration') in the Revised European Social Charter contains a clause stating that 'With a view to ensuring the effective exercise of the right to a fair remuneration, the Parties undertake: ... 4. to recognise the right of all workers to a reasonable period of notice for termination of employment ...'. This raises the question whether a reasonable period of notice can be included in 'the right to protection again unjustified dismissal' in Article 30 of the EU Charter. The explicit reference in the explanations to Article 30 in Convent 49 only to Article 24 of the Revised European Social Charter might seem to indicate a negative answer. On the other hand, the choice of the term 'unjustified dismissal', in contrast with the concept 'termination of employment' found in the ILO instruments and Revised European Social Charter, seems to favour a broad notion which could cover all aspects of 'unjustified dismissal'.

[175] The Charter does not use the word 'unlawful' dismissal, nor 'unfair' dismissal.

[176] There is good reason to argue that ILO Convention No. 158 and the European Social Charter, and the interpretation of these instruments, may be used as a common international source defining cases where dismissals may be justified. This although there are several Member States which have not ratified the ILO Convention.

# Chapter 11

# The European Court of Justice, the EU Charter of Fundamental Rights and the European social model

## Introduction

The European Union's Charter of Fundamental Rights proclaimed at the summit held at Nice on 7 December 2000 became Part II of the proposed Treaty Establishing a Constitution for Europe. Under the proposed Reform Treaty of Lisbon, it is to have the same legal status as the Treaties.

The EU Charter includes provisions which are at the heart of labour law and industrial relations in Europe.[1] The EU Charter will have an impact not only on the EU's institutions, but perhaps even more, on the Member States, also bound by the Charter through the doctrine of supremacy of EU law. The inclusion of fundamental rights concerning individual employment and collective industrial relations in an EU Charter may well confer on them a constitutional status within national legal orders. In some cases, the EU Charter's labour standards and industrial relations requirements may exceed those of some Member State laws. The European Court of Justice may adopt interpretations consistent with international labour standards, where again national labour laws may fall short. In sum, the EU Charter promises a renewal of labour law, both at European transnational level and within the Member States of the EU.

## The role of the ECJ in enforcement of the EU Charter

The European Court of Justice becomes a central player in the enforcement of the EU Charter. The Court will decide disputes where Member States are charged with failing to implement, or allegedly violating rights in the EU Charter. The Court has played this role in the past, relying on other fundamental rights, such as free movement of goods, services, capital and labour, which are guaranteed in the EC Treaty. The EU Charter provides a further

---

[1] Freedom of association (Article 12), right of collective bargaining and collective action (Article 28), workers' right to information and consultation within the undertaking (Article 27), freedom to choose an occupation and right to engage in work (Article 15), prohibition of child labour and protection of young people at work (Article 32), fair and just working conditions (Article 31), protection of personal data (Article 8), non-discrimination (Article 21), equality between men and women (Article 23), protection in the event of unjustified dismissal (Article 30).

means whereby the Court can promote European integration, this time in the social and labour field.

To illustrate this potential role of the European Court, consider the action of a Member State which appears to violate the fundamental rights guaranteed by the EU Charter. National and/or supranational actors may mobilise opposition. Under this pressure, or independently, the Commission may seek to negotiate a solution to the apparent conflict. However, pressure may lead to proceedings before the Court, shifting a political conflict to a judicial forum. The prospect of litigation itself is a political lever, as those anticipating legal action may change their behaviour.

Similarly, the initiative of an EU institution apparently contravening fundamental rights guaranteed by the EU Charter may mobilise opposition, leading to challenges before the Court. Again, experience shows that the threat of a legal challenge can influence the Commission's preparing initiatives, and enhance bargaining power in negotiations over adoption of a measure in Council.

Litigation based on the EU Charter could become an important means of securing social and labour rights, and could influence the political agendas of both EU institutions and the Member States. For example, the European Court of Justice may be willing to recognise as protected by the EU Charter those fundamental trade union rights which all, or most, or even a critical number of Member States insist should be protected. The Court may interpret the articles of the EU Charter on fundamental trade union rights consistently with other international labour standards and will be sensitive to where national laws have protected trade union rights. For this reason, it is important that the social partners should have direct access to the Court to intervene, or initiate complaints before the European Court to protect fundamental rights. A litigation strategy could enable the social partners to use the rights guaranteed by the EU Charter to shape a system of industrial relations at EU level.

## Explaining the European Court of Justice's response, or lack of it, to the EU Charter

Since its proclamation on 7 December 2000, every Advocate-General has cited the Charter in one or more Opinions, as has the Court of First Instance in a number of judgments.[2] However, the European Court of Justice remained

---

[2] In the first thirty months of its existence, up to July 2003, there were forty-four citations of the Charter before the European courts. For details of these forty-four cases, see the Appendix, prepared by Stefan Clauwaert and Isabelle Schömann, in B. Bercusson (ed.), *European Labour Law and the EU Charter of Fundamental Rights*, Baden-Baden: Nomos, 2006. The Charter has also been invoked in EU legislation. By early 2001 there were already forty-three references to the EU Charter of December 2000 in EU legislation: J. Kenner, *EU Employment Law: From Rome to Amsterdam and Beyond*, Oxford: Hart, 2003, p. 512, note 11.

extremely prudent in its response to the Charter as regards integration of the EU Charter into the Community legal order, preferring to rely on the existing range of international human rights instruments. The legal advice and policy orientations encouraging references to the Charter, to be found in the Opinions of all the Advocates-General, were for long ignored or cautiously circumvented by the Court.

For example, an ECJ decision involving the EU Charter was the *Omega* case.[3] This concerned an alleged restriction on free movement of services and goods as a consequence of a German regulation banning a video game including play at killing people. The defence invoked the German consti-tutional principle of protection of human dignity as falling within the permissible public policy derogation to free movement. The ECJ concluded (paragraph 41):

> Community law does not preclude an economic activity consisting of the commercial exploitation of games simulating acts of homicide from being made subject to a national prohibition measure adopted on grounds of protect-ing public policy by reason of the fact that the activity is an affront to human dignity.

In its reasoning, the Court recalled that fundamental rights form an integral part of the EU legal order and, in paragraph 34 of the judgment, specifically cited paragraphs 82 to 91 of the Opinion of Advocate-General Stix-Hackl in the case. Paragraph 91 of the Advocate General's Opinion stated:

> The Court of Justice therefore appears to base the concept of human dignity on a comparatively wide understanding, as expressed in Article 1 of the Charter of Fundamental Rights of the European Union. This Article reads as follows: 'Human dignity is inviolable. It must be respected and protected.'

The Court itself would not directly cite the EU Charter. Rather, the first judicial reference to the EU Charter was made by the Court of First Instance in a decision of 30 January 2002. In *max.mobil Telekommunikation Service GmbH* v. *Commission*, the CFI twice referred to provisions of the EU Charter, first Article 41(1) (Right to good administration), and then Article 47 (Right to an effective remedy and to a fair trial) in the following terms:[4]

> Such judicial review is also one of the general principles that are observed in a State governed by the rule of law and are common to the constitutional traditions of the Member States, as is confirmed by Article 47 of the Charter of Fundamental Rights, under which any person whose rights guaranteed by the law of the Union are violated has the right to an effective remedy before a tribunal.

---

[3] *Omega Spielhallen- und Automatenaufstellungs-GmbH* v. *Oberbrgermeisterin der Bundesstadt Bonn*, Case C-36/02, decided 14 October 2004.
[4] Case T-54/99, paragraphs 48 and 57.

Even as a mere political declaration, the EU Charter appeared to be accepted by some as reflecting fundamental rights which are an integral part of the EU legal order.[5]

## The ECJ finally cites the Charter: 27 June 2006

The question was whether, and how long this could last. The answer arrived with the first citation of the EU Charter, five and half years after its proclamation, by the European Court in *European Parliament* v. *Council*, decided 27 June 2006.[6] Parliament sought the annulment of a sub-paragraph in a Council Directive on the right to family reunification. In doing so, the Court states:[7]

> The Parliament invokes, first, the right to respect for family life … This principle has been repeated in Article 7 of the Charter which, the Parliament observes, is relevant to interpretation of the ECHR in so far as it draws up a list of existing fundamental rights even though it does not have binding legal effect. The Parliament also cites Article 24 of the Charter …
>
> The Parliament invokes, second, the principle of non-discrimination on grounds of age which, it submits … is expressly covered by Article 21(1) of the Charter.

In contrast, the Court refers to the Council's position, which is hostile to the Charter:[8]

> Nor should the application be examined in light of the Charter given that the Charter does not constitute a source of Community law.

As to the Court's own view of the precise legal effects of the Charter, the key text in the judgment is under the rubric 'Findings of the Court'[9] with regard to the issue 'The rules of law in whose light the Directive's legality may be reviewed'.[10] The Court states:[11]

> The Charter was solemnly proclaimed by the Parliament, the Council and the Commission in Nice on 7 December 2000. While the Charter is not a legally

---

[5] At least four arguments may be put forward to explain the reticence on the part of the European Court of Justice to cite the EU Charter. First, the uncertain legal status of the Charter, not integrated into the Treaties. A second argument is that, although purporting to provide a codified catalogue of rights, many provisions of the Charter cannot easily be used on their own as the basis for litigation or even judicial review. A third argument is that for the Court to enforce fundamental rights based on the EU Charter, even if only by way of judicial review, would inevitably be regarded as the Court's assuming a seemingly constitutional role. Finally, a more prosaic reason why the Court has not yet referred to the Charter may be its decisional procedures, which require unanimity, and some judges may be resisting a reference to the Charter. See the chapter on 'Legal Prospects and Legal Effects of the EU Charter' by the author, Stefan Clauwaert and Isabelle Schömann, in Bercusson (ed.), *European Labour Law and the EU Charter of Fundamental Rights*.

[6] Case C-540/03.　　[7] *Ibid.*, paragraphs 31–2.　　[8] *Ibid.*, paragraph 34.

[9] *Ibid.*, beginning paragraph 35.　　[10] *Ibid.*, beginning paragraph 30.　　[11] *Ibid.*, paragraph 38.

binding instrument, the Community legislature did, however, acknowledge its importance by stating, in the second recital in the preamble to the Directive, that the Directive observes the principles recognised not only by Article 8 of the ECHR but also in the Charter. Furthermore, the principal aim of the Charter, as is apparent from its preamble is to reaffirm 'rights as they result, in particular, from the constitutional traditions and international obligations common to the Member States, the Treaty on European Union, the Community Treaties, the [ECHR], the Social Charters adopted by the Community and by the Council of Europe and the case-law of the Court … and of the European Court of Human Rights'.

In other words, while not legally binding itself, the Charter reaffirms rights which are legally binding due to their provenance from other sources which are recognised by Community law as legally binding sources. The Court elides this subtle distinction (reaffirming other binding instruments v. declaring rights) when, in another section under the rubric 'Findings of the Court', it uses the word 'recognises':[12]

> The Charter recognises, in Article 7, the same right to respect for private or family life. This provision must be read in conjunction with the obligation to have regard to the child's best interests, which are recognised in Article 24(2) of the Charter, and taking account of the need, expressed in Article 24(3), for a child to maintain on a regular basis a personal relationship with both his or her parents.

The recognition was made easy for the Court, as noted by Advocate-General Kokott in her Opinion of 8 September 2005:[13]

> In so far as it is relevant here, Article 7 of the Charter of Fundamental Rights of the European Union … is identical to Article 8 of the ECHR. Moreover, the first sentence of Article 52(3) of the Charter (Article II-112 of the Treaty establishing a Constitution for Europe) provides that its meaning and scope are to be the same.

As interesting as her reference to the proposed Constitutional Treaty is the following statement of Advocate General Kokott:[14]

> Article 21 of the Charter of Fundamental Rights of the European Union expressly prohibits certain forms of discrimination, including that based on age. While the Charter still does not produce binding legal effects comparable to primary law, (73) it does, as a material legal source, shed light on the fundamental rights which are protected by the Community legal order. (74)[15]

---

[12] *Ibid.*, paragraph 58.    [13] *Ibid.*, paragraph 60.    [14] *Ibid.*, paragraph 108.

[15] Footnote 74 cites a number of Opinions of other Advocates-General, including that of Advocate-General Tizzano in *Broadcasting, Entertainment, Cinematographic and Theatre Union (BECTU)* v. *Secretary of State for Trade and Industry*, Case C-173/99, [2001] ECR I-4881, Opinion of Advocate-General, 8 February 2001, the second citation of the Charter before the ECJ some two months after its proclamation, and other Opinions by Advocate-General Kokott herself.

## The Charter and the Member States

It is perhaps significant that the Court should have first cited the Charter in a legal action by one EU (supranational) institution, the Parliament, against another, the Council (representing the Member States). In this context, the statements of the Court concerning the Member States are important. The Court repeats the mantra that fundamental rights 'are also binding on Member States when they apply Community rules'.[16]

The Court continues: 'consequently, they are bound, as far as possible, to apply the rules in accordance with those requirements …'. This could be read two ways. First, Member States are obliged to apply Community rules in accordance with fundamental rights. If this is not possible, their application (indeed, the Community rule itself) is challengeable as violating fundamental rights. Alternatively, Member states are obliged to apply Community rules in accordance with fundamental rights only as far as possible. If this is not possible, their application (and the Community rule) is still valid. It would seem that the first interpretation is preferable, and supported by the Court's immediately preceding statement which appears to emphasise Member States' margin of appreciation, but again only 'in a manner consistent with the requirements flowing from the protection of fundamental rights'.[17]

The tension between the law of the EU and that of the Member States is particularly evident in disputes over EU competences. The ECJ may rely on the Charter to support EU legislative initiatives based on the EU Charter against challenges from Member States or other EU institutions. The Charter may also be used by EU institutions challenging Member State failures to implement, or even violations of, rights in the EU Charter. In this way, the ECJ plays a political role in overcoming political opposition to European integration, a role it has frequently fulfilled in the past, relying on fundamental freedoms (of movement of goods, services, capital and labour) guaranteed in the EC Treaty. The EU Charter now provides another legal basis on which the ECJ may choose to rely in overcoming challenges to European integration in the social and labour field.

Two examples can illustrate this potential role of the ECJ. First, a decision, legal measure or action of a Member State may appear to contravene the fundamental rights guaranteed by the EU Charter. A number of national and supranational actors may mobilise opposition to this decision or action. Under the pressure of these actors, or independently, the Commission itself may undertake negotiations with a view to resolving the apparent conflict. Ultimately, however, lack of success, or other political pressures, may lead the Commission, or the European Parliament, to take legal action in the ECJ, challenging the decision or action on the grounds of violation of the EU

---

[16] Case C-540/03, paragraph 105. This leaves open the question of when it can be said that the Member State's law is implementing Community rules; see, for example, *Werner Mangold* v. *Rudiger Helm*, Case C-144/04, decided 22 November 2005.

[17] *Ibid.*, paragraph 104.

Charter. Resolution of the dispute thereby shifts what is a political conflict to a judicial forum. The terrain shifts from political negotiation to litigation. The ECJ's willingness to entertain such challenges will depend on many factors, not least the legal status of the EU Charter, the extent to which upholding the challenge will promote European integration, or, on the contrary, pose political risks to the integration project, or even to the ECJ itself. Litigation thus becomes a political lever: those challenged in this way may anticipate such legal action, so that, even without the intervention of the ECJ, their behaviour may change.

A second example presents the converse, where a decision, legal measure or action of the EU institutions appears to contravene fundamental rights guaranteed by the EU Charter.[18] Once again, national and supranational actors may mobilise to oppose this, perhaps particularly effectively in one or other Member State where their political leverage is significant. The Member State government under such pressure, or also independently, may challenge the EU measure in litigation before the ECJ, arguing on the basis of violation of the EU Charter. Again, this offers diverse options to the ECJ. Experience on many occasions prior to the Charter's adoption has illustrated the utility of such litigation tactics, formerly based on Treaty arguments. The threat of a legal challenge gives Member States additional bargaining power both in the negotiations leading to adoption of the measure in Council, and also to influence the Commission preparing drafts of the measure beforehand.

## An example: collective industrial action in the Single European Market

The EU Charter represents values which are integral to Social Europe. In the sphere of employment and industrial relations, these values include those reflected in the fundamental rights to collective bargaining and collective action. Recent litigation before the European Court confronted the Charter with freedom of movement in the Single European Market.

Free movement in the Single European Market has transformed the balance of economic power in the EU. The social partners at EU level have not achieved a balance of economic power in the transnational EU market, where the freedom of enterprises to move throughout the Single European Market has shifted the balance of economic power towards employers.

A crucial element in maintaining a balance of economic power in Member States is the legal right to take collective action. Transnational collective action is one defensive response to the change in the transnational balance of

[18]  For an illustration of an individual challenge, the EU Charter, Article 30 ('Protection in the event of unjustified dismissal') and the decision of the ECJ of 27 June 2006 declaring it to reflect fundamental rights protected by Community law were cited by the Civil Service Court of the EU in a decision upholding the appeal against dismissal of a temporary employee of the EU, Case F-1/05, *Pia Landgren* v. *European Training Foundation*, 26 October 2006, paragraphs 70–1.

economic power. But national rules on collective action are inadequate to regulate transnational collective action. A legal problem has arisen where *national* laws on *collective action* encounter *EU law* on *free movement* of goods, services, capital or workers.

Employers are seeking to override national and international guarantees of the right to collective action, invoking their freedom of movement in EU law. Two references to the ECJ posed the question of whether collective action at EU level contravenes the Treaty provisions on free movement, or whether EU law, and specifically, the fundamental right to collective action in the EU Charter will enable the ECJ to adapt the EU law on free movement to redress the balance of economic power on a European scale.

EC Treaty provisions on free movement are not absolute. Free movement is limited by public policy considerations, both in the Treaty[19] and as developed by the European Court of Justice through its extensive case-law. The reference to the ECJ by the English Court of Appeal in *Viking*[20] highlighted this issue of the limits to free movement: whether EC Treaty provisions on free movement may be limited by collective action which is lawful under national law. The specific issue raised was the potential of Article 28 of the EU Charter, which provides for the fundamental right to take collective action, including strike action.[21]

The *Viking* case involved industrial action by the Finnish Seamen's Union (FSU). Due to the ITF being based in London, the employer in dispute was able to initiate proceedings before the British High Court. The employer's claim was based on EU law: that the industrial action had violated the employer's freedom of establishment and to provide services, as provided in the EC Treaty, Articles 43 and 49. The FSU invoked the Finnish Constitution which protects the fundamental right to strike. At first instance in the English High Court, the judge upheld the employer's complaint: EU law overrode any national law, even the national constitution of a Member State. The English Court of Appeal reversed this decision. Instead, it referred to the ECJ a number of questions.[22] Three of the questions put to the

---

[19]   Articles 30 (goods), 39(3) (workers), 46(1) (establishment), 55 (services), 58(1) (capital).

[20]   Case C-438/05, *Viking Line Abp OU Viking Line Eesti* v. *The International Transport Workers' Federation, The Finnish Seamen's Union.*

[21]   See also the reference by the Swedish Labour Court in *Lava* , where Swedish trade unions boycotted a building site employing Latvian workers where the employer refused to sign a Swedish collective agreement. Case C-341/05, *Laval un Partneri Ltd* v. *Svenska Byggnadsarbetareforbundet, Svenska Byggnadsarbetareforbundet, Avdelning 1, Svenska Elektrikerforbundet.* Both cases are extensively analysed in Chapter 21 below.

[22]   The first of these raised the analogy with the *Albany* case (*Albany International BV* v. *Stichting Bedrijfspensioenfonds Textielindustrie*, Case C-67/96; with joined Cases C-115/97, C-116/97 and C-117/97, [1999] ECR I-5751). The *Albany* case was concerned with whether EU competition law is compatible with collective agreements fixing the price of labour (wages). Advocate-General Jacobs said the Treaty did not give clear guidance but concluded that, as the Treaty encourages collective bargaining and social dialogue, these are in principle lawful. Consequently, EU competition law cannot have been intended to apply to collective agreements. The European

European Court raised the issue of whether EU law includes a fundamental right to strike.[23]

Analogous issues have arisen in the past. Case C-265/95, *Commission v. France*[24] concerned French farmers committing criminal acts aimed at free movement of agricultural products from Spain. The Court upheld the Commission's complaint, declaring that:

> by failing to adopt all necessary and proportionate measures in order to prevent the free movement of fruit and vegetables from being obstructed by actions by private individuals, the French Republic has failed to fulfil its obligations under Article 30 of the EC Treaty, in conjunction with Article 5 of that Treaty.

There followed a Commission proposal for a Regulation on the functioning of the internal market in relation to the free movement of goods among the Member States in terms close to those used by the Court. An intensive lobbying

---

Court's judgment did not address issues of fundamental rights. But the Court cited the Maastricht Treaty's recognition of social dialogue agreements at EU level (Articles 138–9 EC) as grounds for holding collective agreements lawful regardless of Treaty provisions on competition law. The question is whether the Court would come to the same conclusion as regards transnational collective action and the Treaty's provisions on free movement. The short answer was: no.

[23] *Question 7*: If collective action by a trade union or association of trade unions is a directly discriminatory restriction under Article 43 of the EC Treaty or Regulation 4055/86, can it, in principle, be justified on the basis of the public policy exception set out in Article 46 of the EC Treaty on the basis that (a) *the taking of collective action (including strike action) is a fundamental right protected by Community law*; and/or (b) the protection of workers? *Question 8*: Does the application of a policy of an association of trade unions which provides that vessels should be flagged in the registry of the country in which the beneficial ownership and control of the vessel is situated so that the trade unions in the country of beneficial ownership of a vessel have the right to conclude collective bargaining agreements in respect of that vessel, strike a fair balance between *the fundamental social right to take collective action* and the freedom to establish and provide services, and is it objectively justified, appropriate, proportionate and in conformity with the principle of mutual recognition? *Question 9*: Where: – a parent company in Member State A owns a vessel flagged in Member State A and provides ferry services between Member State A and Member State B using that vessel; – the parent company wishes to re-flag the vessel to Member State B to apply terms and conditions of employment which are lower than in Member State A; – the parent company in Member State A wholly owns a subsidiary in Member State B and that subsidiary is subject to its direction and control; – it is intended that the subsidiary will operate the vessel once it has been re-flagged in Member State B with a crew recruited in Member State B covered by a collective bargaining agreement negotiated with an ITF affiliated trade union in Member State B; – the vessel will remain beneficially owned by the parent company and be bareboat chartered to the subsidiary; – the vessel will continue to provide ferry services between Member State A and Member State B on a daily basis; a trade union established in Member State A takes collective action so as to require the parent and/or subsidiary to enter into a collective bargaining agreement with it which will apply terms and conditions acceptable to the union in Member State A to the crew of the vessel even after re-flagging and which has the effect of making it pointless for the parent to re-flag the vessel to Member State B, does that collective action strike a fair balance between *the fundamental social right to take collective action* and the freedom to establish and provide services and is it objectively justified, appropriate, proportionate and in conformity with the principle of mutual recognition?

[24] Case C-265/95, *Commission* v. *France*, [1997] ECR I-6959.

effort by the European trade union movement led to the insertion of a new Article 2 in the eventual Council Regulation No. 2679/98:[25]

> This Regulation may not be interpreted as affecting in any way the exercise of fundamental rights as recognised in Member States, including the right or freedom to strike. These rights may also include the right or freedom to take other actions covered by the specific industrial relations systems in Member States.

Case C-112/00, *Schmidberger*,[26] involved an international transport undertaking which brought an action against the Republic of Austria on the basis that its lorries were unable to use the Brenner motorway between Germany and Italy, due to the failure on the part of the Austrian authorities to ban a demonstration by environmentalists which led to the closure of the motorway and consequent restriction of the free movement of goods. This failure was said to give rise to liability of the Member State to pay compensation for the losses suffered by Schmidberger. The Court held that the failure to ban the demonstration was a violation of Article 30 by the Member State.

On the question of whether it could be justified, the Court held that the aims of the environmentalists were irrelevant. Rather, the question was whether the ban was justified on grounds of respect of the fundamental rights of the demonstrators to freedom of assembly guaranteed by the European Convention for the Protection of Human Rights (ECHR) and the Austrian Constitution. The Court held (paragraph 74):

> since both the Community and its Member States are required to respect fundamental rights, the protection of those rights is a legitimate interest which, in principle, justifies a restriction of the obligations imposed by Community law, even under a fundamental freedom guaranteed by the Treaty such as the free movement of goods.

However, the Court seemed willing to contemplate restrictions on freedom of expression or assembly, as allowed by the ECHR. The Court also emphasised that 'the competent authorities enjoy a wide margin of discretion'.

The question is whether and how far the Court will accept restrictions on transnational collective action, or will intervene to curb Member States which permit such action where there is a clash between free movement in the EU and fundamental rights in the Community legal order. Enforcement by the ECJ of fundamental rights in the EU Charter may provide the key to the future of the law on industrial action, shaped in different ways over past centuries in the Member States. Many other aspects of European labour law may be determined by the European Court's enforcement of the EU Charter of Fundamental Rights.

---

[25] Council Regulation (EC) No. 2679/98 of 7 December 1998 on the functioning of the internal market in relation to the free movement of goods among the Member States. OJ L337/8 of 12 December 1998 (the 'Monti Regulation').

[26] Case C-112/00, *Eugen Schmidberger, Internationale Transporte und Planzuge* v. *Republic of Austria*, [2003] ECR I-5659.

The Court's decisions in the cases of *Laval* (Case C-341/05) and *Viking* (Case C-438/05) have sent ambivalent signals at best. On the one hand, the Court cites Article 28 of the Charter in confirming that the right to take collective action 'must therefore be recognised as a fundamental right which forms an integral part of the general principles of Community law the observance of which the Court ensures'.[27]

Yet the impact of the Charter may dilute the legal status of fundamental rights as general principles of EC law. For the fundamental rights in the Charter are heavily qualified by 'horizontal' provisions (Articles 51–4).[28] For example, Article 51 provides that the Charter is addressed 'to the Member States only when they are implementing Union law'. This could be interpreted as confining the Charter's impact to specific implementing measures of national law. The European Court has taken a wider view: that EC law applies to all national laws falling within the scope of EU competence, whether or not they are specific implementing measures. This was illustrated in the decisions in *Viking* and *Laval*. The argument made to the Court was that Article 137 EC, which provides for harmonising directives, explicitly excludes the regulation of the right to strike from Community competence (Article 137(5)). Rejecting the argument, the Court held that even in the areas in which the Community does not have competence, as regards the rights at issue, Member States must nevertheless exercise their competence consistently with Community law.[29] The Court proceeded immediately to declare that the right to take collective action is a fundamental right protected by Community law.[30] The conclusion is that restrictive national laws are subject to the Treaty's protection of the right to strike.

Another example is that the Lisbon Treaty provides that the Charter is to have the same legal status, but no more, than the Treaty. The proclamation of the Charter in December 2000 was followed by cases in which the Court did not appear to provide unqualified endorsement of such fundamental rights as protection of freedom of expression (*Schmidberger*, Case C-112/00) or of human dignity (*Omega*, Case C-36/01). Rather, the Court engaged in balancing fundamental rights with economic freedoms protected by Treaty provisions. The Court appeared at times to be requiring those claiming fundamental rights to justify their exercise where the rights claimed interfered with the economic freedoms prescribed by the Treaty. It is not clear that the Court starts from the premise that fundamental social rights are not mere derogations from

---

[27] *Viking*, paragraph 44; *Laval*, paragraph 91.

[28] These provisions in the Charter of December 2000 were repeatedly 'adjusted', first by the Convention on the Future of Europe, and again at the summit in June 2004 which accepted the Charter as Part II of the Constitutional Treaty. The Charter of the Treaty of Lisbon is that last version in which considerable 'adjustments' were made to the 'horizontal' provisions with the intention of limiting the scope and legal effects of the Charter.

[29] *Laval*, paragraph 87; *Viking*, paragraph 40.

[30] *Viking*, paragraphs 43–4; *Laval*, paragraphs 90–1.

economic freedoms but are protected by EU law. Accordingly, in balancing the rights, the question is not whether fundamental rights justify restrictions on free movement; rather economic freedoms must be interpreted to respect fundamental rights.

Explicit equivalence in the Lisbon Treaty of fundamental rights in the Charter with economic freedoms in the Treaty can only exacerbate the problem of balance. This was particularly evident in the *Viking* and *Laval* cases. Both the Advocates-General and the Court engaged in tortuous attempts to define criteria by which fundamental rights to collective action protected by the Charter could be reconciled with economic freedoms protected by the Treaty. The solutions adopted are open to criticism, and reveal both the limits of fundamental rights in the Charter, but also their power to at least offset some of the effects of unbridled economic freedoms in the form of unconstrained social dumping.[31]

Finally, it is necessary to refer to what has become notorious in EU labour law as British 'exceptionalism'. In the Lisbon Treaty, the UK government has insisted upon an opt-out from a legally binding EU Charter of Fundamental Rights, and specifically from its social and economic rights, although the UK had solemnly proclaimed these rights together with the other EU Member States in December 2000. The other Member States acceded to this demand which is embodied in a legally binding Protocol to the Lisbon Treaty. Yet the likely consequences are far from predictable.

One scenario can be summarised as follows. The UK has opted out of the Charter. This is supposed to mean that the European Court cannot use the Charter to override UK laws. However, this will not prevent a litigant asking a UK court to override a particular UK law which arguably brutally violates the Charter's guaranteed right. Nor will it prevent a UK court deciding that there is enough uncertainty to refer the matter to the European Court in Luxembourg. The European Court will likely follow its established jurisprudence, that protection of fundamental rights is a general principle of Community law which the Court is pledged to uphold. Further, that the EU Charter merely reflects these fundamental rights protected by EC law. Hence, the opt-out does not matter: UK laws which violate the rights guaranteed by this general principle of EC law (as reflected in the Charter) cannot stand. One awaits the UK labour law case which follows this trajectory.

The *Viking* case is an illuminating illustration. The decision of the European Court was referred back to the English Court of Appeal. The European Court has declared that Community law protects the fundamental right to collective action, referring to the Charter. The *Viking* case concerns, first, collective action

---

[31] B. Bercusson, *Collective Action and Economic Freedoms: Assessment of the Opinions of the Advocates-General in Laval and Viking and Six Alternative Solutions*, Brussels: European Trade Union Institute (ETUI-REHS), 2007, available, together with an Executive Summary in French, at www.etui-rehs.org/research/publications.

by the FSU in Helsinki, where Finnish law protects the right to strike, and, secondly, collective action by the International Transport Workers' Federation (ITF) in London, subject to English law which condemns secondary action. In deciding on the lawfulness of the FSU's action under Finnish law, may the English Court take the Charter into account, as Finland has clearly accepted the Charter, or will the Court refuse to take any account of the Charter, as instructed by the opt-out? In deciding on the lawfulness of the ITF's action under English law, will the UK's opt-out be taken into consideration? The *Viking* case was due to come before the Court of Appeal before the Lisbon Treaty is ratified and comes into effect (if it ever does).[32]

The impact of the Charter is likely to be greatest on the UK and other Member States where the gap between the social rights in the Charter and national law is greatest. I have argued[33] that the British people need the Charter most, but that other Member States would also benefit. The UK, under the governments of Mrs Thatcher and her successors, including the New Labour government, was the most recalcitrant opponent in the struggle to achieve an EU social model. Fundamental rights proclaimed in the EU Charter would be one means of dragging the UK, unwillingly no doubt, into an embrace with the European social model of protection of workers. As and when the UK opt-out is revealed to be inoperable, the Charter now offers some hope of removing a major obstacle to social progress in the EU.

The history of protection of fundamental rights is one of constant struggle against those with the economic and political power to violate them. Proclamation of the EU Charter and its promotion by the Treaty of Lisbon does not change this. Protection of the fundamental rights of workers will continue to have to be fought for in court litigation, in legislative battles and in the struggles of the labour movement.

## Access to the ECJ to enforce the Charter

An important factor regarding the potential role of the ECJ concerns the prospects of a litigation strategy, based on the EU Charter, being utilised by other actors, apart from the EU institutions and Member States. One problem is access to the ECJ. Access to the ECJ in order to complain of violations of

---

[32] There is a further point of British constitutional law involved. The European Communities Act 1972 requires UK courts to give effect to EC law. There is a continuing debate as to whether the constitutional doctrine of Parliamentary sovereignty requires the courts to uphold subsequent legislation which appears to conflict with EC law as having been impliedly repealed. One view is that the normal doctrine of 'implied repeal' does not apply. However, express repeal is another matter. The question arises whether the UK's explicit opt-out from the EU Charter in the Lisbon Treaty, prior to ratification, constitutes such an express repeal.

[33] In a special edition of the French newspaper, *Libération*, prior to the French referendum on the proposed Constitutional Treaty in May 2005.

fundamental rights in the EU Charter could influence the political agendas both of EU institutions and of the Member States.[34]

For example, enabling the European Trades Union Confederation to initiate legal action before the ECJ could be especially important in enabling trade unions to challenge measures affecting fundamental trade union rights, or to use the threat of litigation to influence negotiations. This acts as a powerful signal of political conflicts and channels them into modes of resolution, either political or judicial. One problem with such a procedure is that it is essentially defensive; it is used to block action which contravenes fundamental rights rather than to stimulate action to implement them. This might be avoided through use of the preliminary ruling reference procedure under Article 234 of the Treaty, which would enable claims based on the Charter to be lodged before national courts, and, eventually, referred to the ECJ.

Such use could create a problem for the ECJ in terms of its case load, as it would come under additional pressure from claims for or actions based on violation of fundamental rights in the EU Charter. In so far as the ECJ in the past frequently aimed to break institutional deadlocks and support European integration, using the Charter as grounds for challenge to EU law could put the ECJ in the position of blocking measures, not promoting integration, a fundamental change in its role.[35]

## Juridification and legitimising governance arrangements in social and labour policy

To control its case load, the Court would need a procedure of admissibility.[36] If the ECJ used narrow grounds to deny access in claims for or complaints of breach of fundamental rights, it would lose some of its legitimacy. Wider consideration is required of which type of EU judicial structure is appropriate for enforcement of the EU Charter, as fundamental rights have the potential to translate political conflicts into legal channels: a juridification of European politics.[37]

The positive side of judicial discourse on political questions is that court cases upholding fundamental rights can provide public legitimation of the outcomes in an EU where legitimacy is a valuable commodity. The question is: whether, and which, rights would be better legitimated through litigation before the

---

[34] See Chapter 16.

[35] Looking to the role played by fundamental rights in the past, these were not much used by the Court, except when conflicts arose with national constitutional courts. An EU Charter with constitutional status could change this case load. The experience of national constitutional courts, e.g. German and Italian, indicates the size of the case load which could develop.

[36] For example, Article 230 of the EC Treaty has been interpreted by the ECJ as setting a very high standard for admissibility of claims by individuals.

[37] For a comparison of this potential role of the ECJ with American experience, see the quotations from Stephan Leibfried and Paul Pierson (eds.), *European Social Policy: Between Fragmentation and Integration*, Washington: The Brookings Institution, 1995, Chapter 3.

ECJ.[38] In general, the so-called 'democratic deficit' of the EU has important implications for the Charter. The effect of the Charter differs from similar catalogues in national constitutions because the EU is much less democratically legitimised. The Charter is a much sharper instrument where, as in the EU, the legislature can claim only marginally stronger democratic legitimation than the Court. The ECJ can permit itself to disagree much more easily when judging legislation in relation to fundamental rights.[39]

EU competences in the field of social and labour policy require legitimising governance arrangements. The Charter can play a major role in building the legitimacy of these governance arrangements. Fundamental rights may be used to ascribe legitimacy to collective bargaining and collective action, and information and consultation on a wide range of issues at the level of the enterprise.[40] The Charter can be used to legitimise the actors, processes and outcomes of the EU industrial relations system and thereby supply the necessary legitimacy to the governance arrangement of European industrial relations.

However, there are limits to the ECJ's 'general principles' case-law as it applies to fundamental rights, and some parts of the Charter may be regarded as beyond this case-law; not least, some of the social rights in the Charter's chapters entitled 'Solidarity' and 'Equality'. In the case of some of these rights, it is possible that the Charter could orient the ECJ towards the need to protect some trade union, social and labour rights. But this is more difficult where social rights require positive action to achieve them. Article 51 of the Charter provides that the EU and Member States shall 'promote the application' of the Charter rights. This points to positive measures. But would the ECJ review whether the EC legislator or Member States were sufficiently promoting the application of the Charter rights and strike down measures which violated them? This would be a major innovation. Such a 'positive dimension' is almost entirely absent from the ECJ's fundamental rights case-law. Its introduction would require major judicial activism.

A central problem is posed by the EU Charter itself in Article 51(2): 'This Charter does not establish any new power or task for the Community or the

---

[38] And, of course, there will be circumstances where judicial proceedings are the last recourse before a recalcitrant government. A recent case before the European Court of Human Rights was the first successful complaint by a trade union invoking Article 11 of the ECHR, which resulted from a decade-long futile struggle against employers and governments denying fundamental trade union rights. *Wilson and the National Union of Journalists, Palmer and the National Union of Rail, Maritime and Transport Workers*, Application No. 30668/96 and others, 2 July 2002.

[39] Compare Germany, with a democratically elected legislature, where the Bundesverfassungsgericht takes this into account in exercising its power of judicial review; so that it is willing to allow much more room for discretion. The legislature is allowed freedom as to the purposes for which it may intervene in areas of fundamental rights. There is less impact of fundamental rights.

[40] Similarly, the rights to engage in work, vocational training and equal opportunities, all provide support for arrangements in the European Employment Strategy.

Union, or modify powers and tasks defined by the Treaties.' The problem is that there are no explicit EU powers to promote many Charter rights. To that extent, EU and related Member State activities may fall outside the scope of the Charter.[41]

The paradox is clear: fundamental rights are confronted with limited EU competences. The central problem is the clash between limited EU competences and the EU Charter's fundamental human rights. If fundamental human rights are subject to competences, it undermines the concept of fundamental human rights. Values elevated by the EU to the status of fundamental human rights are only protected to the limit of EU competences. The solution is for the powers and tasks of the Community and Union provided for in the Treaties to be expanded by the ECJ where these are necessary in order to safeguard and enforce Charter rights.

---

[41] One example illustrates the potential conflict: Article 137(5) EC appears explicitly to exclude the right of association and the right to strike from labour law directives adopted under that Article. Yet freedom of association and the right to take collective action are explicitly guaranteed in Articles 12 and 28 of the Charter.

**Part IV**

# Enforcement of European labour law

# Chapter 12

# General principles of enforcement of European labour law

## Introduction

*European* labour law, as the law of the EU, has specific qualities of enforceability which distinguish it from *domestic* labour laws. However, European *labour* law also has specific qualities which distinguish it from *other branches* of EC law.

In domestic law, it is recognised that different branches of law have adapted specialised enforcement mechanisms to their specific exigencies. As the various branches of EU law develop, it becomes apparent that to talk in general terms of enforcement of EU law risks overlooking the specific enforcement mechanisms adopted in different branches.

Comparative analysis of national systems of labour law reveals differences between the enforcement mechanisms used in labour laws of different countries. The enforcement of EU law will have its own characteristics, but it will bear the imprint of the national system in which it operates.[1]

The specific quality of EU labour law, in terms of the combination of different enforcement mechanisms to be adopted, is still open to debate. Everything that has been said about the nature of European labour law, its synthesis of national experience in the form of EU level regulation, applies also to the issue of enforcement of EU labour law. Enforcement mechanisms of European labour law cannot be a wholly autonomous product. National traditions of labour law enforcement will not easily give way to purely EU legal technique. Rather, the EU has experimented with a number of traditional techniques, some of which have had more success than others.

The enforcement of EU labour law is relatively straightforward where it grants clear rights to individuals and national law has correctly implemented these rights through legal measures capable of effective enforcement through the domestic courts. Enforcement is not so straightforward where EU law confers rights on individuals, but the adequacy of their implementation in national law is subject to dispute. In such cases, enforcement may proceed

---

[1] For a comparative exercise outlining the different roles for social partners, the administration and the judiciary in the application of labour law in France, Germany, Italy, Spain and the UK, see A. Supiot *et al.*, *L'Application de droit du travail dans les pays membres de la CE*, Documentation de Ministère de Travail, 1989.

through the domestic courts invoking innovative EU legal doctrines of direct and indirect effect, or invoking other remedies (e.g. *Francovich*[2]). Such situations make it necessary to rethink the way in which domestic legal frameworks of enforcement are conceptualised for the purposes of European labour law.

## Public/private sector employees

For example, in many continental jurisdictions, the special position of public sector employees, in particular, civil servants, has been recognised by the specific legal status attributed to them, their exclusion from the normal judicial procedures and enforcement of labour law, and the availability of alternative, often public law, administrative procedures for the vindication of their rights.

EU labour law cuts across these differences. The supranational nature of EU law has placed states under special obligations. This has required domestic courts to interpret national law in light of EU law, and also to allow for claims against the state even by private sector employees (the *Francovich* remedy).

In particular, however, the doctrine of direct effect has potentially dramatic consequences for the enforcement of EU labour law in the public sector. The scope of the potential defendants – emanations of the state – and the extensive use of directives as the form of EU labour law, means that employees of these emanations may be able to claim rights before domestic courts which are not available to private sector employees. On the other hand, the specificity of the public/private employee distinction may be eroded through the development of remedies of private employees against the state for failures adequately to implement Directives guaranteeing employment rights (*Francovich* claims).

The outcome may be the emergence of a code of public sector employment rights which can be derived from already determined directly effective provisions of directives and Treaty Articles, supplemented by close scrutiny of other directives not yet declared directly effective, but having that potential and promoting litigation to secure direct effect.[3]

The recognition of public sector/service employees as a distinct category of employment in European labour law is an unintended consequence of the doctrine of vertical direct effect of directives. Such employees may accumulate an arsenal of labour law rights enforceable before domestic tribunals based on directly effective provisions of directives. The growth of a distinctive set of directly enforceable rights may have long-term consequences for the special treatment of this category of employees.

A similar trawl among EU labour law measures might produce a list of potential *Francovich* actions based on inadequate implementation by the

---

[2] *Francovich and Bonfaci* v. *Italy*, Cases C-6/90 and C-9/90, [1991] ECR I-5357.
[3] Examples would be both later directives on working time, provision of information to and consultation of employees, health and safety measures and earlier directives on collective dismissals and acquired rights.

state. This could allow for claims against a widely defined range of employers constituting emanations of the state, in particular, as the concept of the state in EC law develops away from ownership criteria or legal form and focuses on public service, public control and/or special powers. These are some of the potential consequences for enforcement of national labour law which arise from the interaction of domestic and supranational jurisdictions.[4]

## Adequacy of remedies and sanctions

The domestic provision of remedies in the enforcement of labour law is subject to scrutiny where it is EU labour law which is being enforced. A number of cases have already found domestic procedures and sanctions wanting, particularly, but not exclusively, in sex discrimination cases. The limitations on awards of compensation and the rules on the burden of proof have had to be revised

More generally, national enforcement of labour law has been criticised in a number of areas: from the adequacy of tribunal procedures to the sanctions available for breaches, including the compensation awarded for damage suffered. In a number of cases, the compensation awarded has been reduced by complex provisions for set-off. Such provisions have been condemned by the European Court of Justice already in the case of 'protective awards' for failure to consult workers' representatives as required by EU law.[5]

Set-off provisions exist in other parts of domestic labour law, some of which have been criticised in terms similar to the arguments advanced in *Commission of the EC* v. *UK*. To bring the battery of EU labour law to bear on such provisions, it is necessary to have a basis in EU law for the right being claimed. Once this is available, the domestic provisions for compensation may be attacked as falling below the EU standard.

By far the most important area of workers' compensation is for personal injury at work. Coincidentally, it is also the area where a great deal of EU legislation is to be found. Compensation for injury at work is subject to a highly sophisticated set of rules, some of which provide for set-off. These range from doctrines of employees' contributory negligence to claw-back provisions whereby the state seeks to recoup social security benefits paid to workers off work due to injury. It may be that such provisions are vulnerable to the charge that they infringe the principle that violations of EU law be effectively compensated and deterred.

---

[4] There are wider constitutional implications going beyond labour law. It changes the terms of the debate away from the issue of public ownership and towards more general issues of what constitutes public service, state responsibility towards its own employees and for implementation of social policy in general. It even has implications for the convergence criteria for economic and monetary union and its consequences for threatened public services and public sector employment – said to be one of the reasons Norway rejected EU membership.

[5] *Commission of the EC* v. *UK*, Cases 382/92 and 383/92, [1994] ECR I-2435.

EU labour law on health and safety has been regarded mainly in terms of its impact on substantive law. But the implications for the domestic remedies available for violations of EU health and safety law – from the role of inspectorates, such as the Health and Safety Executive in the UK, to the availability of monetary compensation – could be substantial.

## Structure of the European labour law on enforcement

The success of enforcement of EU labour law has perhaps been greatest where EU legal technique meshes with the national tradition. One account of the application of labour law in *national* jurisdictions identified three principal mechanisms: through the administration, through the courts and through the social partners (*administrative*, *judicial* and *industrial relations* mechanisms of enforcement).[6] There are differences in the effectiveness and in the importance attached to each of these mechanisms of enforcement among the labour law systems of the Member States. Various mechanisms interact and overlap in different ways within each national jurisdiction.

Within each Member State, an equilibrium among the different mechanisms has been established. This is not to say that all such national equilibria are functionally equivalent. That in some Member States the administrative, judicial or industrial relations mechanism is predominant does not imply that the overall equilibrium in each Member State assures equally effective enforcement. Specifically, the presence or absence of strong mechanisms of judicial enforcement is not determining.

Although there is controversy about the particular efficacy of one or other mechanism in a specific national context, one axiom of labour law should be remembered. The effectiveness of labour law rules is in inverse proportion to the distance between those who make the rules and those who are subjected to them: the greater the distance, the less their effectiveness; the lesser the distance, the greater their effectiveness.

The presumption is that rules originating from social partners engaged in collective bargaining, being closest to those subject to these rules, achieve a higher level of effectiveness. Conversely, those emerging from legislative or administrative processes, distant from employers and workers, will have relatively less efficacy. Whatever the national equilibrium among the various mechanisms of enforcement, the argument is that those systems in which the social partners are more prominent in rule-making will be those in which the effectiveness of enforcement is greater.

---

[6] A. Supiot, 'L'application du droit du travail en Europe', *Travail et Emploi*, 1991, No. 47. A similar framework was adapted to enforcement of EU labour law in the first edition of this book: B. Bercusson, *European Labour Law*, London: Butterworths, 1996, Part III, Chapters 7–11, 'Enforcement of European Labour Law'. It is further adapted in this edition.

In EU law, the principle of effective enforcement (*effet utile*) has been the driving force of doctrinal developments ever since the pathbreaking decision in *Van Gend en Loos*,[7] in which the European Court of Justice pointed out the need for decentralised enforcement of EC Treaty obligations through national courts by individuals, alongside the established mechanism of administrative enforcement by the European Commission through complaints to the ECJ. Since then, numerous doctrinal developments, indeed revolutions, such as the extension of direct effect to directives, indirect effect (consistent interpretation), state liability, and so on have continued to reinforce the importance of effectiveness.

The increasing prominence of EU labour law in national systems raises, first, complex issues of the *interaction* of *national enforcement* mechanisms and *enforcement of EU* labour laws in the EU Member States. Secondly, the *evolution* of EU social and labour policy means the boundaries between different sources and methods of enforcement of EU labour law are becoming increasingly fluid.

The chapters in Part IV explore a number of examples in which national experience of enforcement of labour law will be placed in the European context. The examples are those of administrative enforcement, implementation through the social partners, the potential of judicial liability mechanisms, and a strategy of 'Euro-litigation'.

The problems of *administrative* enforcement at EU level are evident. The question is how to co-opt national administrative enforcement mechanisms. One important illustration is in the form of a national enforcement mechanism which has been taken up in part at EU level: contract compliance. Further, the proposal to set up a specialised agency at EU level for the enforcement of fundamental rights raises the prospect of this agency acting to enforce the fundamental rights of workers.

Where the *social partners* are the instruments of implementation and enforcement of national labour law, the use of this mechanism as a channel for EU labour law implementation is promising. The evolution of the EU law allowing for the social partners to take upon themselves the role of implementing and enforcing EU labour law will be analysed.

The development of *judicial liability* for breaches of EU law is particularly important in systems where litigation plays a major role in labour law enforcement. The European Court has made a sustained effort to scrutinize the remedies, sanctions and procedures available at national level for the enforcement of EU law. The many illustrations of this effort in the field of labour law will be examined.

Finally, EU law offers new possibilities in the form of strategies aimed at countering national law perceived as contrary to EU policy. A classic example of this in the UK was the use of EU law to undermine attempts by large retail

---

[7] *NV Algemene Transporten Expeditie Onderneming van Gend en Loos* v. *Nederlandse Administratie der Belastingen*, Case 26/62, [1963] ECR 1.

outlets to open on Sundays – the so-called 'Sunday trading' cases. The potential of such '*Euro-litigation*' strategies in the labour law context will be explored through, first, the use of fundamental rights as the basis for challenging national law perceived as contrary to EU law and, secondly, the possibility of trade unions at EU level, the European Trade Union Confederation (ETUC), acting as litigators before the ECJ to challenge acts of the EU institutions, including legislative acts.

The remainder of this chapter reports the results of a recent comparative study which provided important insights into the relationship between enforcement of labour law in the Member States and effective enforcement of EC labour law.

## Interaction of principles of enforcement of national labour law with EU labour law

Effective enforcement of labour law is an area where studies of both EC labour law and comparative labour law can make significant and complementary contributions. An important book resulting from a project undertaken by scholars from different countries offers a series of rich and stimulating insights from a comparative perspective on problems of enforcement of EC labour law.[8]

The specific value of using the methodology of comparative law to investigate enforcement of EC law arises because the evolution of EC principles of effective enforcement depends on different Member State rules and practices. Broadly speaking, EC law determines substantive rules, but domestic law determines remedies and procedures. The account of the differing strategies in various EU Member States to enforce the same EC regulations on working time, sex equality and restructuring of enterprises justifies the conclusion of the book's editor, Jonas Malmberg, that:

> For analysis of the enforcement of EC labour law, the national level must be put into the picture. The traditional strategies of national actors for the making and enforcement of labour law can be used as a starting-point to set up a frame of reference for such analysis.

### Effective enforcement and formal remedies in EC labour law

However, the study of EC labour law through the comparative method must be complemented by analysis of EC law materials. For example, as explained by

---

[8] J. Malmberg (ed.), *Effective Enforcement of EC Labour Law*, Uppsala: Iustus Forlag, 2003; see Foreword by B. Bercusson, pp. 17–25, on which the remainder of this chapter is based. Also B. Bercusson, 'Application du droit du travail: les interactions entre droits nationaux et communautaire', *Travail et Emploi*, 2004 (October), No. 100; Ministère de l'emploi, du travail et de la cohesion sociale, France, pp. 27–38. This latter article also explores the evolution at EU level of hybrid methods of enforcement and application of labour law, merging administrative, judicial and industrial relations processes.

Jonas Malmberg in the introduction to the book, there is an important distinction between the full *effectiveness* of rights deriving from EC law and the *formal* remedies for breach of EC law. The latter is much narrower and, despite the undoubted overlap, the distinction is important. Nonetheless, although the book is first and foremost a study of EC labour law in comparative context, it also aims to extract from the case-law of the European Court of Justice a set of formal principles of effective enforcement of EC labour law.

## The 'principle of effective enforcement' of EC labour law

The book succeeded in elucidating subtle and important qualities distinguishing the enforcement of EC labour law. The outcome of the cumulation of three principles – equivalence, effectiveness and proportionality – is the emergence of the 'principle of effective enforcement' and is applied to cover not only judicial, but also administrative and industrial relations processes of enforcement of EC labour law. In his contribution to the introduction to the book, Barry Fitzpatrick provides a closely argued analysis of the ebb and flow of the ECJ's doctrine on effective judicial protection based on principles of equivalence, effectiveness and proportionality.[9]

## Industrial relations processes in relation to administrative or judicial enforcement

A chapter on industrial relations processes investigates the extent to which the combination of EC labour law and the respective systems of national labour law contribute to the use of negotiations as a means of enforcement in the fields of restructuring, working time and equal treatment. The incorporation of rules of EC labour law into collective agreements implies the commitment of the negotiating parties to enforcement, and may both promote compliance and lessen the need for administrative or judicial enforcement.[10]

Linking these insights on industrial relations processes with judicial processes, the obvious fact, sometimes overlooked by lawyers, is that when a worker or a workers' representative is confronted with an employer's violation of his or her rights, the first step is not to go to court but to seek to resolve the conflict through discussion. Judicial processes are thus preceded by negotiations engaged in the similar exercise of assessing facts and interpreting rules, including formal legal rules. Collective bargaining, including information and consultation, is an integral process of enforcement of rules in conflicts also over EC labour law.

---

[9] This formulation of principle and, in particular, the extension of its application beyond the traditional judicial (see S. Sciarra (ed.), *Labour Law in the Courts: National Judges and the European Court of Justice*, Oxford: Hart, 2001) to administrative and industrial relations processes of enforcement of EC labour law is original and holds lessons for other areas of EC law.

[10] Taco van Piejpe, in Malmberg (ed.), *Effective Enforcement of EC Labour Law*, pp. 77–108.

## Overlaps: *locus standi* of collective actors in administrative and judicial processes

Hence, for EC labour lawyers, the rules on industrial relations processes may be of equal significance to the question of the requirements which Member States must meet with respect to access to a court and *locus standi* in order correctly to implement EU labour law directives. The complementary areas of enforcement overlap in the major problem of the *locus standi* of workers' representatives in labour law litigation, and the issue of securing the interests of the individual worker where they diverge from those of the collective representative. The use of collective actors in judicial enforcement procedures of EC labour law is underdeveloped compared with its relatively widespread use in the Member States, at least until recent EC initiatives attributing *locus standi* to interest groups.[11]

## Enforcement of fundamental labour law rights: the EU Charter

The adoption of the EU Charter of Fundamental Rights, including many labour law rights and principles means that questions of the enforcement, and not only the justiciability, of rights and principles of labour law will become a focus of attention. Alternatives to judicial processes of effective enforcement of the social and labour rights in the EU Charter may become a central element in this debate.

Jonas Malmberg points out that it 'might it be argued that the more fundamental the Community right which is infringed, the more intrusive should be the remedial structure.' He contrasts 'ordinary' labour rights, with 'fundamental social rights': equality, health and safety and even information and consultation of workers, and asks:

> Should it be a factor in Community law enforcement that the level of scrutiny of national remedies, and wider judicial process, should be stricter where fundamental social rights are at issue?

This argument is particularly timely in the aftermath of the struggle over the issue of sanctions in the directive on information and consultation at national level.[12] The incorporation in the final Directive of the traditional formula regarding judicial sanctions was a retreat from the Commission's approach in

---

[11] As in Article 9(2) of the Framework Employment Equality Directive 2000/78, Council Directive 2000/78 establishing a general framework for equal treatment in employment and occupation. OJ 2000 L303/16, and Article 6(3) in the amended Equal Treatment Directive 2002/73/EC), Council Directive 76/207/EEC of 9 February 1976 on the implementation of the principle of equal treatment for men and women as regards access to employment, vocational training and promotion, and working conditions, OJ 1976 L39/40, as revised by Council Directive 2002/73/EC, OJ 2002 L269/15.

[12] Council Directive No. 2002/14 establishing a framework for informing and consulting employees in the European Community. OJ 2002 L80/29.

its initial draft proposal seeking more targeted remedies for specific and serious breaches.[13] However, as Article 27 of the EU Charter makes workers' right to information and consultation a fundamental right, the question of what sanctions are required for its effective enforcement may now perhaps be revived.

### The role of administrative intervention in enforcement of EC labour law

As regards administrative processes of enforcement, it is argued that, historically, these were established in national labour laws because workers were unable in practice to enforce their rights through judicial processes.[14] There is an apparent paradox that EC labour law has failed to recognise this feature of labour law and failed to develop specific instruments of administrative enforcement. Sylvaine Laulom points to some indicators in the form of requirements of administrative intervention in EC laws on collective redundancies (informing public authorities) and the new Race Directive (designation of special bodies to promote equal treatment). It is not so much that the pendulum has to switch to the other direction, for administrative processes may not be sufficient for effective enforcement of the directives concerned. Rather, it is that effective enforcement of the directives may require some administrative intervention to reinforce individual or collective action.

### Administrative intervention depends on the context of the rights enforced

Comparative analysis makes possible suggestions for how Member States could or would respond to a requirement of administrative enforcement of EC labour law. But Sylvaine Laulom points out the need to look at the functions of administrative organs in three areas analysed, of working time regulation, sex equality and restructuring. Most importantly, she demonstrates that the nature of administrative intervention is dependent on the area concerned:

> The administrative processes and the industrial relations processes or judicial processes are strongly interrelated in all the three fields of labour law under study and in all the Member States investigated. But these interrelations are slightly different in the three areas. The task of administrative authorities in the field of working time has a traditional foundation due to the established link between working time and health and safety. Nevertheless, the rising importance of collective bargaining in the regulation of working time can imply some modifications to the functions of administrative bodies … [C]oncerning equality, the Member States, where a labour inspectorate has specialized powers, have provided for independent authorities to ensure observance of equality principles. This shows the need for some form of control auxiliary to the collective and judicial enforcement of equality rights.

---

[13] For a detailed account, see B. Bercusson, 'The European Social Model Comes to Britain', (2002) 31 *Industrial Law Journal* 209–44.

[14] Sylvaine Laulom, in Malmberg (ed.), *Effective Enforcement of EC Labour Law*, pp. 109–35.

## The neglected but essential role of interim remedies

An example of exceptional practical significance, though often ignored in labour law, concerns the issue of interim decision-making powers in questions of enforcement of EC labour law.[15] Jonas Malmberg points out that though labour disputes may be resolved through legal proceedings, these normally take considerable time and, given the practical continuity of employment relationships: 'it is of great importance to establish which of the parties' interpretation of their duties applies until the dispute is finally solved'. In particular: 'The first question is to what extent one of the parties has the power to enforce his interpretation without awaiting a decision of a court', or in the Swedish terminology, which party has the 'priority of interpretation'.[16] Comparative analysis provides a number of important indicators. For example:

> the rules on priority of interpretation and burden of litigation differ largely depend on whom the enforcing party is ... an administrative authority ... the workers' representatives ... or individual employees ... there are examples where the workers' representatives are given a priority of interpretation, with the rules in the Swedish Co-determination Act as the most striking example.

Jonas Malmberg shows that in none of the Member States may an employee be dismissed for a refusal to follow an order which he correctly thinks is contrary to the Working Time Directive. In most of the countries, a dismissal will not be considered lawful if the employee's opinion is later found wrong, but he or she had good reason for it. In particular, one situation where the employee normally will have good reason for his or her opinion is when she or he relies on the opinion or the advice of the labour inspector or workers' representatives.

Interim measures largely depend on the ultimate sanctions available. Where the sanction is pecuniary compensation, a claim for an interim decision on payment will normally be turned down, since such a claim can usually be subsequently satisfied.

As mentioned above, the significance of this is particularly poignant in light of the Commission's initial proposal for a specific penalty, that of retaining the status quo of employment for employees affected, for serious breach of an employer's duty in Article 7(3) of the then proposed draft Directive on Information and Consultation. Sadly, this provision for a special sanction was eventually deleted following pressure from certain Member State governments when the final Directive was adopted in 2002. The consequences for interim remedies may be significant, for as Jonas Malmberg points out:

---

[15] This is a particularly Swedish concern, manifested in the Co-determination Act of 1976. This legislation raised a set of issues to be addressed by Swedish labour lawyers, yet only rarely dealt with in the labour law literature of other countries. They remain of great interest, however, not least to EC labour lawyers. Jonas Malmberg, *ibid.*, pp. 159–90.

[16] There are also other related questions, such as which of the parties has the consequent burden of bringing the dispute to court to enforce his or her interpretation, and, subsequently, in what circumstances the court may make an interim decision.

> The availability of interim measures seems to be most important in dismissal cases ... Such an interim measure will be granted if the employee makes it sufficiently clear that the dismissal is not valid (*fumus boni iuris*). It seems to me to be generally held that there is a case of urgency (*periculum in mora*) in these situations.

## European Court interventions in national judicial enforcement procedures and national judicial responses

Antonio Lo Faro provides a meticulous and subtle analysis of the ECJ decisions relating to judicial processes of enforcement as regards timeliness, burden of proof[17] and the issue of national courts examining whether national legislation complies with EC law (*ex officio* application of EC law).[18] Examples are three time-related questions: (i) how much time is allowed to claim a right before a court?; (ii) when does time begin to run?; and (iii) what are the possible retroactive effects of a claim? A close analysis of the ECJ's case-law produces an understated conclusion which scarcely disguises a critical note:

> Whereas the lack of *external* uniformity *among* national procedures and remedies is an understandable result of a Community policy that has never been keen on procedural harmonisation, or at least always aware of its difficulties, the lack of *internal* uniformity *within* the Court of Justice jurisprudence seems much less comprehensible or justifiable. It is not only national procedural limitations as such that may render the exercise of Community rights 'excessively difficult'. An ever-changing understanding of their compatibility with Community law may also render effective judicial protection less than easy.

This critical assessment of the ECJ's contribution contrasts with important developments in some Member States of great potential interest. For example:

> in some cases national time limits to challenge before a court the validity of a dismissal have somehow been 'communitarised' by national judges. In Germany and the Netherlands, for example, the *Bundesarbeitsgericht* and the *Hoge Raad* have been ready to extend the time limits laid down in ordinary dismissal cases, when the contested dismissal is allegedly grounded on a transfer of undertaking, contrary to what Community law prescribes.

Antonio Lo Faro characterises this as a sort of '"procedural added value" which can sometimes be found when a Community right is claimed before a national court'. Indeed: 'In a burst of Europeanism probably unparalleled in any other Member State, the German legislation excludes whatsoever limitations on the retroactivity of claims brought for the application of Community legislation on equal treatment.'

---

[17] Not only in sex discrimination but also in the less noted but important cases involving the employer's provision of written information regarding terms of employment under Directive 91/533.

[18] In Malmberg (ed.), *Effective Enforcement of EC Labour Law*, pp. 190–214.

### Judicial remedies are context-specific, but there are general principles: the holder of a right is entitled to a remedy and the implications for collective rights

Michael Gotthardt focuses on questions of specific remedies rather than general enforcement processes, and asks: 'Has European law and the jurisprudence of the ECJ had the consequence that national sanctions in the fields under consideration are becoming more similar? Are specific sanctions preferred in special fields?'[19] He concludes that different remedies are appropriate in different fields:

> Whether a sanction is effective can only be assessed for a concrete right in a field of law. For example, a damages claim for economic loss usually has no value in the field of working time, because economic loss for the employee tends not to occur. Even though, for example, in Germany, the Netherlands and the UK such a claim is possible, this is only a theoretical sanction. In such cases, the legal system may provide for other sanctions, such as nullity of agreement, claims for performance, or even punitive damages solely for infringement of the norm (as in Sweden). The legal situation is the same concerning the right to information and consultation of employees' representatives. The representatives do not usually suffer an economic loss due to violation of these rights.

But there are nonetheless principles to be respected in determining the specific sanctions available, for example, that the holder of a right is entitled to the corresponding judicial remedy. Article 47 of the EU Charter of Fundamental Rights provides that everyone whose rights are guaranteed by the law of the Union, and then infringed, has the right to an effective remedy. The principle is particularly germane to the debate over the sanctions available for breach of the EU directive on information and consultation of workers' representatives. Comparative law confirms that it is generally the holder who is entitled to assert the sanction. In this respect, Michael Gotthardt notes the exception, for example, in Germany concerning the rights to information and consultation following from the Collective Redundancies Directive. But even in the national debate, it is argued that the works council must be entitled to an effective sanction so as to enforce its own rights. This debate takes on new significance with the EC Directive on Information and Consultation.

### Enforcing EC labour law in new Member States

Andrzej Marian Swiatkowski provides a case study of some of the lessons developed in earlier chapters as applied to Poland:[20] for example, whether

---

[19]  Michael Gotthardt, *ibid.*, pp. 223–61.
[20]  Andrzej Marian Swiatkowski in *ibid.*, pp. 263–90.

industrial relations process can be regarded as an effective means of enforcing EC labour law in Poland. Specifically, do collective agreements represent a normative alternative to state legislation in the process of implementation of European labour law, and are collective agreements regarded as a legal source of labour law in Poland?

His conclusion, following the established case-law of the European Court, is that collective agreements may be used to effectively implement European labour law on certain conditions: that they enjoy the status of being a constitutionally supported source of labour law, that they have general coverage and that their scope is not limited. Though it is necessary for some changes to be made to national labour law, he argues that, with minor adjustments, collective agreements can serve as important legal tools for the introduction of European labour law into Poland. If so, this conclusion would serve to alleviate anxieties about the potential of social dialogue in this largest of the new Member States. It has important implications for public administration as both alternative and complementary to the collective and individual rights approach to enforcement.

## Four lessons for the effective enforcement of EC labour law

The final chapter of the book summarises succinct lessons.[21] Jonas Malmberg highlights again the complementary functions of different enforcement processes: administrative, industrial relations and judicial, and emphasises their different impacts at micro- (individual) and macro- (collective) levels.

It may be that the operation of these different processes can be mutually beneficial. For example, it may be argued that macro- (collective) methods of enforcement of labour law are stronger and micro- (individual) methods relatively weaker at national level, but the reverse is true at EU level. If so, does this offer a positive prospect of the European Court of Justice reinforcing the micro-level of national judicial procedures of enforcing EU labour law? Conversely, could national industrial relations systems contribute to supporting an EU industrial relations system capable of

---

[21] Contributed by different authors. First, Sylvaine Laulom postulates that comparative and European labour law are inseparable. Unquestionably, these essays demonstrate that their relationship is rich, but the challenge remains of unravelling their complex relationship. Secondly, Antonio Lo Faro asserts that judicial protection and the principle of state liability in EC law are connected and coexist. The question remains, however, of what precisely is the nature of their coexistence. Can they be functional equivalents in EC labour law, or does state liability merely serve to stimulate Member States towards more effective enforcement of EC labour law? Thirdly, Michael Gotthardt describes a hierarchy of basic and specified principles and sanctions in EC labour law directives, and proposes a method for selecting appropriate remedies. The question is whether the proposed subsidiarity principle is adequate, or merely disguises an empty cupboard.

undertaking effective enforcement of EC labour law at macro- (collective) level?[22] The objective is mutual reinforcement of EU and national systems of labour law.

---

[22] Research at the now sadly disbanded Swedish National Institute for Working Life aims to contribute to answering the latter question by examining the role of European social dialogue agreements in EC labour law See K. Ahlberg, B. Bercusson, N. Bruun and C. Vigneau, *Fixed-term Work in the EU: A European Agreement against Discrimination and Abuse*, Stockholm: National Institute for Working Life, 1999. Also K. Ahlberg, B. Bercusson, N. Bruun, H. Kountouros, C. Vigneau and L. Zappalà, *Transnational Labour Regulation: A Case Study of Temporary Agency Work*, Brussels: Peter Lang, 2008.

# Chapter 13

# Administrative enforcement of European labour law

## Introduction

The EU institutions do not possess the resources which can even begin to equate to the resources of national Ministries of Labour or labour inspectorates. The original vision might have been that the EU itself should police observance by the Member States of their obligations.[1] To this end, complaints by the Commission of non-compliance by Member States have sometimes had important consequences.[2] However, the procedure of administrative enforcement through Commission complaint is extremely slow: failure to comply with EU legislation is condemned often more than a decade later. An illustration of the inefficacy of the procedure is the case of Italy, using an example of administrative enforcement of labour law which culminated in the European Court condemning Italy in 1989. First, the context of the judgment.

By the end of 1988, the number of EC directives in effect were 622, and Italy had up to then failed to implement 278, for 196 of which the date for implementation had already passed, and for 48 of these last the expiry date for implementation was over five years previously. Italy was one of the countries most frequently condemned by the European Court for violating its EU obligations. Up to the end of 1988 there were 34 judgments condemning Italy which had not been complied with, and another 28 proceedings pending; moreover, there were five cases where Italy had been condemned twice for

---

[1] Article 226 of the EC Treaty provides: 'If the Commission considers that a Member State has failed to fulfil an obligation under this Treaty, it shall deliver a reasoned opinion on the matter after giving the State concerned the opportunity to submit its observations. If the State concerned does not comply with the opinion within the period laid down by the Commission the latter may bring the matter before the Court of Justice.'

[2] A number of cases involving the UK demonstrate the impact: from the complaint leading to the decision in 1982 which forced the UK to introduce the Equal Value Regulations 1983 to implement Article 119 of the Treaty of Rome allowing women to claim their work was of equal value to that of a man (*Commission of the European Communities* v. *United Kingdom of Great Britain and Northern Ireland*, Case 61/81 [1982] ECR 2601; similarly Case 165/82 [1983] ECR 3431), to the complaint leading to the decision on 8 June 1994 which required the UK to introduce legislation on worker representation in order to comply with the Directives on Information and Consultation of worker representatives of 1975 and 1977 (*Commission of the EC* v. *UK*, Cases 382/92 and 383/92, [1994] ECR I-2435).

the same failure to comply, including failure to implement Directive 75/129 of 17 February 1975 on collective dismissals.[3]

In this context, a case of administrative enforcement of EU labour law is that of the condemnation of Italy on 2 February 1989 for failure to implement Council Directive 80/987 of 20 September 1980 on the protection of workers in the event of the insolvency of their employer.[4] The transposition of Council Directive 80/987 of 20 September 1980 was to be completed by 23 October 1983 and the Member States were to have notified to the Commission the text of the provisions adopted.

On 3 November 1983 the Commission sent to the Italian government a request to this effect and the Italian government sent a list of provisions which it considered should be taken into account regarding transposition. Over seventeen months later, on 24 April 1985, the Commission, having examined these provisions, conveyed to the Italian government its view that these provisions were not sufficient to constitute adequate transposition, and requested the Italian government to reply within two months.

The Italian government did not reply. Almost eleven months later, on 19 March 1986, the Commission gave a formal reasoned opinion under Article 169 of the Treaty (now Article 226 EC) to the effect that Italian law did not conform to the requirements of the Directive and formally invited the Italian government to adopt the requisite provisions within one month. In reply to this opinion, the Italian permanent representative to the Community sent a note on 25 April 1986 pointing out the problems confronting Italy in the current situation which precluded complete transposition, and, to show its good will, established a special committee to prepare the necessary proposals, asking in the meanwhile for an extension of time to find the most appropriate solution.

The Commission refused to grant the extension and, nine months later, on 28 January 1987 commenced proceedings before the European Court of Justice for non-fulfilment by Italy of its Treaty obligations. Over two years later, the Court gave judgment against Italy on 2 February 1989, some nine years and four months after the Directive had been adopted unanimously by all the Member States, including Italy.

---

[3] Cases 91/81 [1982] ECR 2133 and 131/84 [1985] ECR 3531. To complete the picture, Italy had also been condemned by the Court for failing to implement Directive 77/187 of 14 February 1977 on transfers of undertakings and protection of employees; Case 235/84 (1986] ECR 2291; A. Zambelli commented on the judgment of the European Court in *Commission of the European Communities* v. *Italian Republic*, Case 22/87 of 2 February 1989, [1989] ECR 143; 'Diritto comunitario e tutela contro l'insolvenza dell'imprenditore: l'ennesima inadempienze dell'Italia', (1991) *Rivista Italiana di Diritto del Lavoro* 269, at pp. 275–89.

[4] *Ibid*. Of particular importance as it was this failure which was held subsequently to justify a pathbreaking claim against the Italian state to compensate for damage caused to workers who were thus unable to benefit from this EC Directive: *Francovich and Bonfaci* v. *Italian Republic*, Cases C-6/90 and 9/90 [1991] ECR I-5357.

A more recent, but equally egregious example involving the UK concerns the Working Time Directive of 1993, due to be implemented by 23 November 1996.[5] The UK had challenged the legality of the Directive before the European Court, which rejected the challenge on 12 November 1996.[6] As the UK had by then taken no steps to implement the Directive, the requisite Regulations implementing the Directive were only adopted in 1998.[7] These Regulations, purporting to implement Articles 3 and 5 of the Directive, provided that an adult worker is entitled to daily and weekly rest periods. However, the UK's Department of Trade and Industry published a set of guidelines which included the following statement: 'employers must make sure that workers can take their rest, but are not required to make sure that they do take their rest'.

On 21 March 2002 the Commission sent a letter of formal notice to the UK under Article 226 EC alleging that, among others, Articles 3 and 5 were not correctly implemented.[8] The UK replied by letter of 31 May 2002, and, not satisfied, the Commission sent a reasoned opinion to the UK on 2 May 2003 requesting the UK to take measures necessary to comply within two months. By letter of 30 June 2003, the UK replied insisting that the national measures implementing Articles 3 and 5 were consistent with the Directive. The Commission decided to bring an action before the ECJ.[9] The Court stated that Articles 3 and 5 meant:[10]

> that workers must actually benefit from the daily and weekly periods of rest provided for by the directive ... Member States are under an obligation to guarantee that each of the minimum requirements laid down by the directive is observed, including the right to benefit from effective rest.

The Court condemned the UK's implementation of the Directive:[11]

> by restricting the obligations on employers as regards the workers' right to actually benefit from the minimum rest periods provided for in Articles 3 and 5 of Directive 93/104 and, inter alia, letting it be understood that, while they cannot prevent those rest periods from being taken by the workers, they are under no

---

[5] Council Directive 93/104/EC of 23 November 1993 concerning certain aspects of the organisation of working time; OJ L307/18 of 13 December 1993, as amended by Directive 2000/34 of 22 June 2000, OJ L195/41. Consolidated in Directive 2003/88/EC of 4 November 2003 concerning certain aspects of the organisation of working time; OJ L299/9 of 18 November 2003.

[6] *United Kingdom* v. *Council*, Case C-84/4, [1996] ECR I-5755.

[7] The Working Time Regulations 1998. SI 1998, No 1833.

[8] The Commission's action stemmed from a complaint made by the British trade union, Amicus. *European Industrial Relations Review* No. 393, October 2006, p. 2.

[9] Based on the third paragraph of Article 249 EC: 'A directive shall be binding, as to the result to be achieved, upon each Member State to which it is addressed, but shall leave to the national authorities the choice of form and methods.' Rejecting the UK's challenge on the admissibility of a complaint based on Article 249, rather than a complaint of non-implementation of the Directive's specific Articles, the Court stated that the Commission's objection: 'does not refer to the incorrect implementation of Articles 3 and 5 of that directive per se but rather to the existence, in the form of the guidelines, of national measures likely to encourage a practice of non-compliance with its provisions relating to the daily and weekly rest rights of workers'. *Commission of the European Communities* v. *United Kingdom*, Case C-484/04, decided 7 September 2006, paragraph 29.

[10] *Ibid.*, paragraphs 39–40.     [11] *Ibid.*, paragraph 44.

obligation to ensure that the latter are actually able to exercise such a right, the guidelines are clearly liable to render the rights enshrined in Articles 3 and 5 of that directive meaningless and are incompatible with the objective of that directive, in which minimum rest periods are considered to be essential for the protection of workers' health and safety.

There had long been dissatisfaction with the UK's implementation of these provisions in the form of mere 'entitlements', with no effective means of securing that workers could avail themselves of the mandatory rest periods deemed minimum requirements for their health and safety. Yet it was not until 7 September 2006, almost ten years after the date by which these rights were to be guaranteed, that the UK's implementation of the Directive was condemned.

In sum, the effective enforcement of EU labour law by a central Brussels administration is not presently on the cards. However, administrative enforcement of EU labour law may be improved if national authorities undertake this task. The co-option of national administrative authorities by the EU administration is a complex process.[12]

Two more recent developments in administrative enforcement of EC labour law are worth reviewing briefly. The first, the 'open method of coordination', has been operating for some years, while the second is only at the initial stage of its operations: the Fundamental Rights Agency. Each offers a perspective on how the administrative enforcement of European labour law could proceed.

Finally, more detailed treatment is provided of a potentially powerful mechanism for the administrative enforcement of labour law: public procurement policies requiring compliance by public contractors with labour standards. The first edition of this book explored this potential in the Directives of 1993 then regulating public procurement in the EU.[13] Since then, in the process of revising those Directives, which finally bore fruit in 2004, a ferocious battle was fought over the question of whether the revised Directives could or should explicitly become an instrument for the enforcement of labour standards in the form of so-called 'social clauses' in public contracts. The positions adopted by the EU institutions, including the European Court of Justice, Member States and other actors in the course of this dispute reveal ideological divisions beneath the surface of European labour law and cast a strong light on conflicting visions of the EU's role in enforcement of European labour law.

## Administrative enforcement of European labour law through the 'open method of coordination'

The 'open method of coordination' (OMC) is a form of EU 'soft law', a process of policy-making which does not lead to binding EU legislative measures nor require Member States to change their law. The OMC aims to spread best

---

[12] F. Snyder, 'The Effectiveness of European Community Law: Institutions, Processes, Tools and Techniques', (1993) 56 *MLR* 19, at pp. 27–40.

[13] B. Bercusson, *European Labour Law*, London: Butterworths, 1996, Chapter 8, pp. 103–20.

practices and achieve greater convergence towards the main EU goals. The method involves fixing guidelines for the Union, combined with specific time-tables for achieving the goals in the short, medium and long term; translating these European guidelines into national and regional policies, by setting specific targets and adopting measures, taking into account national and regional differences; establishing, where appropriate, quantitative and qualitative indicators and benchmarks, tailored to the needs of different Member States and sectors, as a means of comparing best practices; and periodic monitoring, evaluation and peer review, organised as mutual learning processes.

The Employment Title of the EC Treaty, introduced by the Treaty of Amsterdam, is perceived as the original model of the 'open method of coordination', encapsulated in Article 128 EC. However, the OMC is not restricted to the sphere of employment. The Commission's Social Policy Agenda 2000–5[14] envisaged the OMC being applied to all areas of social policy.[15]

This Social Policy Agenda approved by the European Council meeting at Nice in December 2000 was the successor to the Social Action Programme 1998–2000. Like its predecessors, it contained a lengthy list of initiatives. As to the mechanisms for achieving its objectives, however, there appeared to be change of emphasis:[16]

> The Social Policy Agenda does not seek to harmonise social policies. It seeks to work towards common European objectives and increase co-ordination of social policies in the context of the internal market and the single currency.

The European Council at Nice, in adopting the Social Agenda, declared that in its implementation:[17]

> all existing Community instruments bar none must be used; the open method of co-ordination, legislation, the social dialogue, the Structural Funds, the support programmes, the integrated policy approach, analysis and research.

The Commission's Social Policy Agenda 2000–5 confirmed that to achieve its priorities 'an adequate combination of all existing means will be required'.[18] Although a variety of means were listed, the scope of application allocated to each was significant. The first was '[T]he open method of co-ordination, inspired by the Luxembourg Employment Process and developed by the Lisbon and Feira Councils'. There was no limit specified to the scope of matters suitable for the application of this method of administrative enforcement of EU social and labour policy.

---

[14] Adopted in June 2000 (COM(2000) 379).
[15] A specific example is the Community Action Programme to combat discrimination, adopted in November 2000 which operated in the period 2001–5. Decision 2000/750/EC, OJ 2000, L303/23. The OMC is also being applied to other policy areas such as research and development, social protection, enterprise policy and immigration.
[16] COM(2000) 379, p. 7.
[17] Nice European Council, 7–9 December 2000, Annex 1, paragraph 28.
[18] COM(2000) 379, p. 14.

Employment policy is the paradigm case of the open method of coordination. It is clear that the OMC is a wholly different institutional framework from that for social policy envisaged in the Social Chapter, Articles 136–9 EC. The shift of terrain to employment rather than social and labour policy is accompanied by a shift of administrative framework, from legislation and social dialogue to 'open method of coordination'.

It is to be expected that problems arise when the actors in one regulatory framework (legislation, social dialogue) are excluded or marginalised in the new structure, but do not vacate the policy territory, especially where there are substantive policy overlaps (as in the regulation of forms of employment; e.g. part-time, fixed-term, agency work). Similarly, problems may arise as the regulatory terrain shifts from the EU to the Member States. Norms formulated at EU level (EES Guidelines) may be so vague as to leave effective policy-making to actors at Member State level. Institutional machinery for monitoring at EU level may be ineffective, leaving Member States free to implement norms as they please (National Action Plans).

The resort to the 'soft law' mechanism of coordination through the Employment Guidelines means the Commission is investing considerable effort in an attempt to formulate targets and measures capable of assessing Member State compliance with the EES. Improved statistical measures (benchmarks) and compliance procedures (e.g. peer review), the quality (nature and precision) of the targets established in the Guidelines, and their impact, are factors determining the success of the OMC in the employment field. Much store is set on the iterative pattern of annual guidelines, National Action Plans, reviews and recommendations. In itself, the process may produce discernible effects. But the lack of independent powers of scrutiny or enforcement, by the Commission or others, means placing a great burden on this iterative pattern alone to achieve the desired results.[19]

## Administrative enforcement of European labour law through a specialised agency: the case of the Fundamental Rights Agency

The proposed creation of a Fundamental Rights Agency (FRA)[20] at EU level[21] was driven by the adoption of the EU Charter of Fundamental Rights at Nice in December 2000 and its incorporation into the proposed Constitutional Treaty

---

[19]  More fundamentally, even if the Commission does manage to control the development and implementation of the OMC, the question is whether this is a Community policy which is being implemented, or whether the OMC, as the Employment Title states, remains only a 'co-ordinated strategy for employment' (Article 125 EC) accommodating national policies.

[20]  For more detail, see B. Bercusson, 'The contribution of the EU Fundamental Rights Agency to the Realization of Workers' Rights', in O. De Schutter and P. Alston (eds.), *Monitoring Fundamental Rights in the EU: The Contribution of the Fundamental Rights Agency*, Oxford: Hart, 2005, pp. 189–226, on which this section draws.

[21]  *The Fundamental Rights Agency, Public Consultation Document* (SEC(2004) 1281), Communication from the Commission, COM(2004) 693 final, Brussels, 25 October 2004.

for Europe.[22] Much depends on what emerges by way of mechanisms for the enforcement of the fundamental rights of labour proposed by the EU Charter.

This section outlines a potential role envisaged for the Fundamental Rights Agency in the administrative enforcement of European labour law.[23] Such a role acknowledges the central position of labour in the European social model, and aims to engage with the OMC and social dialogue to promote a process for realisation of fundamental labour rights. The process outlined is 'mainstreaming' fundamental rights of workers by specifying (i) minimum procedural standards, (ii) an obligation on the social partners to engage in a 'spirit of cooperation', and (iii) detailed requirements regarding the process of information and consultation in concluding agreements elaborating the fundamental rights of workers.

## The Fundamental Rights Agency, social dialogue and the OMC

The defining feature of the European social model is engagement of organisations of workers and employers.[24] Information and consultation of workers or their representatives in the enterprise is a fundamental right under the EU Charter (Article 27). The current trend in EU labour regulation is to focus on the 'soft law' administrative mechanism of the OMC and the autonomous industrial relations mechanism of the social dialogue. In this current context, how can the FRA contribute to the realisation of the fundamental rights of workers?

*As regards the social dialogue*, the problem is that there is no prescribed outcome, so failure to reach agreement is acceptable and increasingly a consequence. Yet fundamental rights are not negotiable; agreement must be reached. When an outcome is mandatory, negotiations tend to succeed as parties will be forced to compromise for fear of imposition of a solution by others.[25]

The FRA could contribute as follows. First, the bare outline of procedures required of the Commission under Article 138 EC consultation needs to be

---

[22] *Ibid.*, footnote 6: 'The Charter of Fundamental Rights ... has been included in part II of the Treaty establishing a Constitution for Europe, with binding legal force. It constitutes an authentic expression of the fundamental rights protected by the Community legal framework.'

[23] Its potential role in the general context of EU labour regulation depends on the wider context of mechanisms of implementation, application and enforcement of the rights of workers and their organisations through judicial, administrative and industrial relations mechanisms. This context includes substantive obstacles to realisation of the fundamental rights of workers, not least (i) the potential conflict of EU fundamental rights with limited EU competences, (ii) the distinction between 'rights' and 'principles' and the implications for justiciability, (iii) the relation of EU fundamental rights to national laws and practices, (iv) the significance of the 'Explanations' to the Charter, and (v) the role of international labour standards. These substantive obstacles are analysed in Chapter 7.

[24] See Chapter 8.

[25] The Maastricht Agreement on Social Policy reflected this logic of 'bargaining in the shadow of the law'.

extensively elaborated. Secondly, given the paucity of results in the form of social dialogue agreements, a requirement to 'work in a spirit of cooperation' could be imposed to put pressure on the social partners to engage in social dialogue in a constructive manner. Thirdly, the FRA could play a role where failure to reach 'agreements' produces other 'texts', for which the Commission recommends an implementation and enforcement procedure analogous to the OMC.

*As regards the OMC,* the problem is the process whereby administrative guidelines are formulated at EU level by the Commission and Council, and implemented through the OMC process prescribed in Article 128 EC. The problem is not failure to reach policy conclusions, but ineffective implementation of them. This reflects a lack of engagement of key players: notably the social partners. The problem of enforcement of 'non-binding' texts is resolved by increasing the engagement of the social partners at all levels, not only at EU level, so that their commitment to the outcome will guarantee effective implementation.

What these processes of OMC and social dialogue have in common is the engagement of various institutional actors at EU level: EU institutions and the EU social partners. They are to produce outcomes in the form of agreements, guidelines or other 'process-oriented' texts. Here the axiom of effective labour law enforcement formulated earlier, effectiveness as a function of the proximity of norm creators to those subject to the norms, should be recalled.[26]

The Fundamental Rights Agency could provide crucial assistance to the processes of OMC and social dialogue.[27] The main task envisaged for the Agency is to flesh out these processes of OMC and social dialogue by playing

---

[26] This axiom is reflected in the Commission's most recent Communication on the role of the social partners: 'The evolution of the social dialogue is consistent with the Commission's more general efforts to improve European governance. The social dialogue is indeed a pioneering example of improved consultation and the application of subsidiarity in practice and is widely recognised as making an essential contribution to better governance, as a result of the proximity of the social partners to the realities of the workplace. Indeed, the social partners are different in nature from other organisations, like pressure or interest groups, because of their ability to take part in collective bargaining.' *Partnership for Change in an Enlarged Europe – Enhancing the Contribution of European Social Dialogue,* Communication from the Commission, COM(2004) 557 final, Brussels, 12 August 2004, Section 3.1, page 6.

[27] It is worth noting the functional equivalence between various aspects of the OMC procedure and the so-called 'mainstreaming' policy being promoted in various contexts, including those for other fundamental rights. See the chapters by O. De Schutter and C. McCrudden in De Schutter and Alston (eds.), *Monitoring Fundamental Rights in the EU.* The aspect which both the OMC and mainstreaming have in common is procedural in nature: the procedure whereby specified objectives (e.g. a high level of employment, fundamental rights of workers) are to be achieved in both cases involves a specific process of decision-making. In mainstreaming, the authorities responsible are to take into account the fundamental rights through a variety of mechanisms (e.g. information, impact assessments, action plans, etc.). In OMC, the process is minimally outlined in Article 128 EC. In what follows the procedure proposed for the realisation of the fundamental rights of workers expands this to incorporate a role for the social partners, and to elaborate a more detailed process of decision-making.

an active role. The Communication outlines 'Tasks to be entrusted to the Agency'.[28]

## Promoting a process for realisation of fundamental labour rights

As applied to realisation of the fundamental rights of workers, the starting point is the EU Charter's fundamental rights of collective bargaining (Article 28) and information and consultation in the enterprise (Article 27), supported by EC Treaty Articles 138–9. Given the very wide scope of the fundamental rights of workers prescribed in the EU Charter,[29] the Agency has a legitimate interest in securing their effectiveness. It cannot usurp the European Court's role in ultimately interpreting the Charter. Nor should it attempt by itself to flesh out the substantive standards. Its role should be to promote agreement between the social partners on the content of these rights, such a process being that best suited to effective enforcement.[30]

One problem is that the process of decision-making by way of social dialogue which could produce such agreements or texts is scarcely known outside a narrow circle of practitioners,[31] and little exists by way of guidance, with the Barroso Commission not going beyond exhortation. Yet there is a body of EU law which could be drawn upon: EU Directives on information and consultation are concerned with fundamental rights of workers in specific situations such as collective dismissals, acquired rights in the event of transfers of undertakings and European Works Councils; more generally, the procedure has been elaborated in a framework Directive 2002/14 of 2002.[32] And, of course, the process itself is declared a fundamental right in Article 27 of the EU Charter.

[28] COM(2004) 693 final, Brussels, 25 October 2004. Sections 5: 1. Data collection and analysis, 2. Opinions and views intended for the EU institutions and the Member States, 3. A communications and dialogue strategy with various members of civil society.

[29] E.g. fair and just working conditions (Article 31), protection against unjustified dismissal (Article 30), etc.

[30] For an essay along these lines, directed towards the earlier Community Charter of the Fundamental Rights of Workers of 1989, see B. Bercusson, 'Fundamental Social and Economic Rights in the European Community', in A. Cassese, A. Clapham and J. Weiler (eds.), *Human Rights and the European Community: Methods of Protection*, Volume II of *European Union: The Human Rights Challenge*, Baden-Baden: Nomos, 1991, pp. 195–294, and especially at pp. 206–11, 217–18, 226–30, 284–5.

[31] But see now the account in Chapter 5 and in Part V, Chapters 17–19.

[32] Council Directive 75/129 of February 17, 1975 on the approximation of the laws of the Member States relating to collective dismissals, OJ L48/29, as amended by Directive 92/56 of 24 June 1992, OJ L245/92; consolidated in Council Directive 98/59/EC of 20 July 1998, OJ L225/16. Council Directive 77/187 of 14 February 1977 on the approximation of the laws of the Member States relating to the safeguarding of employees' rights in the event of transfers of undertakings, businesses or parts of businesses, OJ L61/26, as amended by Directive 98/50/EC of 29 June 1998, OJ L201/88 of 17 July 1998; consolidated in Directive 2001/23 of 12 March 2001, OJ L/82/16. Council Directive 94/45/EC of 22 September 1994 on the establishment of a European Works Council or a procedure in Community-scale undertakings and Community-scale groups of undertakings for the purposes of informing and consulting employees; OJ L254/64 of 30

These Directives indicate procedures to be followed in the field of fundamental rights of workers analogous to the 'mainstreaming' procedure advocated in other fields: procedures to encourage agreement, and ultimately promote outcomes to realise the EU Charter's fundamental rights of workers.

### 'Mainstreaming' fundamental labour rights

The Fundamental Rights Agency should be responsible for securing the operationalisation of this process at EU level in the context of the OMC and the EU social dialogue.[33] A model draws on the elements outlined in detail in Directive 2002/14 which specifies the objectives and principles underlying the process of decision-making and what is required, substantively and procedurally, by way of information and consultation.[34] The process aims to ensure outcomes which secure the fundamental rights of workers. In this way, the process is akin to 'mainstreaming'. The key difference is that mainstreaming in the area of fundamental rights of workers requires a process engaging not only, or even primarily, the public authorities. Rather, the objective is to ensure that the process engages to the fullest extent the social partners at relevant levels.

### Minimum requirements

The Fundamental Rights Agency would need to set out the 'minimum' requirements for the process whereby the social partners engage in the OMC and the EU social dialogue. At the moment, there is less than a minimal skeleton of requirements in Article 128 EC (OMC) and Articles 138–9 EC (EU social dialogue). It is essential that this process be elaborated.

Article 1(1) of Directive 2002/14 provides that it sets out 'minimum' requirements. Article 1(1) refers to 'the right to information and consultation of employees', the same right declared in Article 27 of the EU Charter of Fundamental Rights. Article 1(2) mandates that the 'practical arrangements

---

September 1994. Council Directive No. 2002/14 establishing a framework for informing and consulting employees in the European Community; OJ 2002 L80/29.

[33] The processes of mainstreaming, information and consultation and social dialogue aim to structure decision-making in such a way as to secure outcomes that take account of specified policy objectives affected by fundamental rights. In the sphere of the *OMC*, the decision-makers are government administrations or EU institutions. The question is how to integrate the social partners into that decision-making process. In the sphere of the *social dialogue*, the challenge is to secure outcomes which take account of and are consistent with the fundamental rights of workers. Social dialogue by definition engages the social partners; the problem is failure to engage and agree. Given the delicacy of its tasks, a major issue concerns the composition of the FRA, or that part of it responsible for dealing with fundamental labour rights. For example, as in many Member State bodies, its composition as regards rights in the field of labour policy should be tripartite, including representatives of the social partners as well as experts.

[34] Council Directive No. 2002/14 establishing a framework for informing and consulting employees in the European Community. OJ 2002 L80/29.

for information and consultation', must be such 'as to ensure their effectiveness', a criterion with particular resonance in EC law (*effet utile*).[35]

### 'Spirit of cooperation'

The failure to agree, in the case of the EU social dialogue, is attributable to the social partners' acting in their sectional interests alone. This is not the only model available. Article 1(3) of Directive 2002/14 provides:

> When defining or implementing practical arrangements for information and consultation,[36] the employer and the employees' representatives shall *work in a spirit of cooperation* and with due regard for their *reciprocal* rights and obligations, taking into account the interests *both* of the undertaking or establishment and of the employees.

The FRA could elaborate such an obligation for the EU social partners in the social dialogue, providing detailed guidance regarding procedures.[37]

### Conclusion

The procedure envisaged for mainstreaming fundamental rights of workers incorporates a series of stages derived from the information and consultation process established in EU labour law and proclaimed as a fundamental right in Article 27 of the EU Charter. They characterise, in a pragmatic way, the process required for the effective implementation of the fundamental rights of workers. It goes beyond exhortation and becomes a legally structured process. It is the

---

[35] As regards the *OMC*, the minimum requirements for procedures engaging the social partners would apply to the EU institutions (Commission and Council) responsible for formulating the Guidelines. They would apply to procedures whereby the Member State authorities responsible for formulating the national action plans engaged with the social partners. In the *social dialogue*, the minimum requirements would apply to the behaviour of the social partners negotiating agreements through the social dialogue.

[36] By virtue of covering *both* 'defining *or* implementing practical arrangements for information and consultation', the obligation to 'work in a spirit of cooperation' applies not only in the definition of practical arrangements, but during their application. The principle is of general application to any and all practical arrangements for information and consultation.

[37] For example, an essential basis for decision-making is information. 'Information' is defined in Article 2(f) of Directive 2002/14 by reference to process ('transmission'), nature ('data') and purpose ('to acquaint ... and to examine'). Other provisions supplement both the substantive content of the information to be disclosed and the process by which it is to be disclosed. Article 4(3) prescribes the practical arrangements for information which are to be determined by the Member States. The FRA could prescribe more detailed provisions regarding the substantive content and the process of information needed for the OMC or the social dialogue process. Similarly with regard to 'consultation'. Although the Collective Dismissals and Acquired Rights Directives did not define 'consultation', both Directives specify the obligation to 'consult ... with a view to reaching an agreement' (Acquired Rights Directive 1977, Article 7(2); Collective Dismissals Directive 1975, Article 2(1)). This phrase is found in Article 4 of Directive 2002/14; specifically, Article 4(4)(e). Article 4 of Directive 2002/14 prescribes that 'Member States shall determine the practical arrangements for exercising the right to information and consultation'. The task of elaborating standards could fall also to the Fundamental Rights Agency.

definitive description of the process of participation by the social partners in decision-making, here the elaboration of the fundamental rights of workers. The implementation and enforcement of the fundamental rights of workers are to be secured through this process.[38]

The importance of the administrative enforcement of this process cannot be overstated. The pressure exerted by engagement in these mandatory processes is crucial to both achieving agreement through the social dialogue, and effective enforcement of OMC policies. The task of the FRA is to exert the administrative pressures necessary to secure the effective engagement of the social partners, so that these processes reflect the labour law axiom highlighted above.

The effective enforcement of non-binding texts reached through the social dialogue (e.g. the agreements on telework, work-related stress and harassment and violence at work) is a function of the degree of engagement of the social partners at national level. The more dense the process of engagement in concluding the agreements, the more effectively they will be enforced. The answer to complaints regarding the lack of effect of agreements implemented through the 'practices and procedures of labour and management' (Article 139(2) EC) is for the Fundamental Rights Agency to secure the requisite engagement of the social partners at all relevant levels. This can be done by formulating the procedures and processes securing participation by all those affected ('mainstreaming'). Similarly, the Commission's concerns at the ineffectiveness of 'process-oriented' texts can be met by increasing the intensity of engagement of the social partners.

One objection is that fundamental rights are *a priori* not open to negotiation. However, given vagueness of definition and infinite variety of contexts, they need further specification. The procedures of specification are all important. Judicial and administrative specification is the traditional method. However, as regards fundamental rights of workers, the labour law axiom looks rather to the social partners. The task of the Fundamental Rights Agency is to operationalise this axiom and secure its effectiveness.[39] Labour law experience indicates that these processes offer the best chance for realisation of the fundamental rights of workers. The Fundamental Rights Agency can provide important

---

[38] For *social dialogue*, where agreement is the central criterion of success, everything is bent on enforcing procedures, in the expectation that they will produce agreement. The task of the Fundamental Rights Agency is to promote active engagement in the procedures to the maximum. It is different for the *OMC*: it is not so much agreement reached as some other process-oriented text (e.g. a guideline), engaging EU and Member State authorities. The key then becomes enforcing the outcome (usually non-binding). To this end, the maximum engagement of the parties in the process may enhance the effectiveness of the ultimate text reached, since they will have committed themselves actively to achieving it.

[39] Again, the parallel with 'mainstreaming' may be drawn. But instead of specifying a policy objective to be taken into account by a procedure realigned to facilitate that outcome (e.g. obligatory impact assessments, action plans, etc.), the emphasis in the labour law field is to administer procedures engaging the social partners.

administrative support for these processes of autonomous engagement of the social partners.[40]

## Administrative enforcement of labour law through EU regulation of public procurement: 'social clauses'

The administrative enforcement of labour law may be greatly facilitated through the imposition of prescribed conditions on contractors with public authorities.[41] At EU level, this mechanism emerged in the context of the regulation of public procurement to ensure the proper functioning of a single European market. When public authorities at national and sub-national levels inserted labour clauses in public contracts, the question arose whether such clauses conflicted with EU law.

### The position in 1989

At an early stage, the legal position was stated in a Commission Communication of 22 September 1989 on regional and social aspects of public procurement:[42]

> (in) a broad range of social matters including, for example, professional training, health and safety, labour relations and the suppression of racial, religious discrimination or discrimination on the grounds of sex ... the procurement Directives neither forbid nor expressly authorize Member States to regulate the matter. Accordingly, they and procuring entities are free under Community law to pursue such objectives, provided they respect the Directives' provisions and the constraints of the Treaty. It also follows that Member States are free under

---

[40] Despite the experience in many Member States of active engagement by social partners in processes of information and consultation and social dialogue, the Fundamental Rights Agency cannot alone create the necessary culture of engagement in elaborating fundamental rights of workers. One should not be deluded into thinking that institutional design is the answer; without political will, such proposals are sand castles. But fundamental rights are not a luxury. Not least, information and consultation is not only a fundamental right of workers, it is also critical to the successful management of economic and social change. The successful economic integration of Europe is dependent on management of necessary change. Respect for the fundamental right of information and consultation and the commitment to social dialogue are essential conditions for this success.

[41] This is a long-established mechanism of enforcement of domestic labour law in the labour laws of Member States of the EU. The use by public authorities of the procurement process to achieve social and labour policy objectives has been the subject of controversy in the United Kingdom for well over a century since the adoption of Fair Wages Resolutions by the House of Commons in 1891 and 1946 which inspired the provisions of the ILO Labour Clauses (Public Contracts) Convention No. 94 of 1949 and Recommendation No. 84 of the same name and date. For an exhaustive account, see B. Bercusson, *Fair Wages Resolutions*, London: Mansell, 1978. The years since then have seen the UK's denunciation (deratification) of ILO Convention No. 94 in 1982, followed by revocation of the Fair Wages Resolution in 1983.

[42] OJ C311/7 of 12 December 1989, p. 12, paragraph 46. This relied on the decision of the European Court of Justice in *Gebroeders Beentjes B.V.* v. *the Netherlands*, Case 31/87, [1988] ECR 4365.

Community law to restrict the capacity of procuring entities to pursue objectives of this kind.

It appeared at that stage that the issue was whether the EU should pursue a policy of enforcing labour law by authorising or even requiring the insertion of 'social clauses' in public contracts. The Action Programme of 1989 relating to the implementation of the Community Charter of Fundamental Social Rights for Workers declared that 'the Commission could formulate a proposal aiming at the introduction of a "social clause" into public contracts'.[43]

### Post-1989 disputes

However, opposing the inclusion of social clauses were powerful advocates in some parts of the Commission, notably the Internal Market Directorate XV, in some Member States and among some interest groups. These groups argued for contracts to be awarded purely on the basis of lowest tender price and economic advantage, to the exclusion of labour standards. Over the following years, the issue of social clauses and public procurement was the subject of endless documents and innumerable private meetings and public hearings involving the Commission, the European Parliament, national authorities, trade unions at national and EU level, in particular, the European Public Services Union, and many other activists and lobbyists. There were proposals and Communications by the Commission, by the European Parliament and its various committees, as well as briefing papers from many of those engaged.[44] One important player has been the European Court of Justice. The ECJ made crucial decisions concerning the use of labour, social and environmental standards in public procurement. The meaning of these decisions was the subject of dispute between the various players, often claiming support by the Court for different and sometimes opposing positions.

---

[43] COM(89) 568 final, Brussels, 29 November 1989, p. 24.

[44] For example, proposals from the European Parliament's Social and Employment Affairs Committee aimed to ensure that current legal provisions in the social and employment field are complied with by all candidates submitting tenders for public contracts, so as to prevent unfair competition; what matters is to create a level playing field for all candidates. The process was to include four steps: (i) potential tenderers must be given access to appropriate information about employment protection and working conditions, which must be defined; (ii) compliance with these standards must be checked by the contracting authority during the preselection, and candidates who have breached social legislation may be excluded; official lists of approved economic operators will be used to assess suitability of candidates; (iii) selection of candidates and award of contracts will be conditional on compliance with the legal provisions relating to employment protection and working conditions; (iv) there are to be review and enforcement procedures after award of the contract. To promote its agenda, the MEPs organised hearings of experts to consider these and other proposals. The author testified before and gave evidence to these hearings.

## The Commission in 2001

An example is to be found in a Working Document of 3 April 2001 prepared by the Internal Market Directorate General on 'Interpretation of Community public procurement law and the possibilities for incorporating social considerations in public procurement'.[45] The Introduction to the document refers to the 'principal purpose of the directives', and cites, in footnote 6, the judgments of the European Court in Case C-380/98: *Cambridge University* of 3 October 2000, points 16 and 17 and Case C-237/99, *Commission* v. *the French Republic* of 1 February 2001, points 41–2. In virtually identical language in these two cases, the Court confirms, first (italics added):

> the *purpose* of coordinating at Community level the procedures for the award of public contracts is to eliminate barriers to the freedom to provide services and goods and therefore to protect the interests of traders established in a Member State who wish to offer goods or services to contracting authorities established in another Member State ...'

The Court continues:

> *Consequently*, the aim of the directives is to avoid both the risk of preference being given to national tenderers or applicants whenever a contract is awarded by the contracting authorities and the possibility that a body financed or controlled by the State, regional or local authorities or other bodies governed by public law may choose to be guided by considerations other than economic ones.

The Court's position is that the only constraint in EC law on non-economic (or social) considerations is where they lead to barriers to free movement. Barriers may be created by blatant national preference or non-economic considerations. Equally, economic considerations (availability of skilled workers, size and capacity of firms) may lead to national preference.

The *danger* is to read the Court as saying that *economic considerations* are *incorporated* into the purpose of EC procurement policy (via best price or best value) as the objective of the policy, so as to constrain non-economic considerations. This is incorrect. Economic considerations are *not* the EC policy on public procurement. Non-economic considerations are problematic only, but *only*, if they lead to barriers to free movement.

In this sense, economic considerations and social considerations are be adjudged against the same policy: do they create barriers to free movement? This is the essence of the European Court's position.

The task of D-G XV's interpretation document should be[46] to 'identify ... the possibilities under the current directives to take account of social considerations in public procurement'. Instead, the interpretation assumes that economic considerations of best price/best value are the primary objectives, and

---

[45] Document CC/01/10 EN, Brussels, 3 April 2001, MARKT/B2/NSK.
[46] As stated in the box on page 4 of the Document.

everything else is subordinate. Most of the interpretation document is concerned to explain why social considerations are inconsistent with economic considerations, and, hence, can only be accommodated at the margins and with great difficulty.

The aims of EC law are free movement and non-discrimination. D-G XV is therefore correct to state that:[47]

> Generally, any contracting authority can, when defining the goods or services it intends to buy, choose to buy goods, services or works which correspond to its concerns as regards social policy, provided that it respects the rules and principles of the EC Treaty, including the principle of non-discrimination.

Unfortunately, D-G XV appears to confuse the purpose of EC *law* with that of the *procurement contract*. Having repeated that '"[S]ocial considerations" can be incorporated into the definition of the subject-matter of the contract', the document continues:[48]

> Social considerations do not alter the primary purpose of the contract, which is to buy goods or services at the best price or for the best value for money.

This is fundamentally to misconstrue the legal position. Best price/best value may be the purpose of a *procurement contract*, but it is not that of *EC law* or the public procurement directives. It is a fundamental error to confuse the purpose of EC law with that of public procurement.

## The revised Directives of 2004

After many years, and much controversy, the EC Directives on public procurement were finally revised in 2004. A revised Directive now regulates how public authorities acquire through contract the supplies, services and works they need.[49]

Formally, the principal concern of the EC in regulating public procurement is only to secure the proper functioning of the single European market. This means ensuring that public authorities to do not abuse their contracting power to favour their own national economic operators in obtaining these valuable contracts by direct or indirect discrimination against economic operators from other Member States. Obviously, blatant exclusion of other nationals from access to the public procurement market would violate EC law. But experience

---

[47] In the first box on page 5 of the document.    [48] In the second box on page 5.

[49] Directive 2004/18/EC of the European Parliament and of the Council of 31 March 2004 on the coordination of procedures for the award of public works contracts, public supply contracts and public service contracts, OJ L134/114 of 30 April 2004. A parallel Directive applies to the procurement contracts of undertakings in a number of sectors (energy, water, transport, postal services). Directive 2004/17/EC of the European Parliament and of the Council of 31 March 2004 coordinating the procurement procedures of entities operating in the water, energy, transport and postal services sectors, OJ L134/1 of 30 April 2004.

shows that many indirect means of exclusion are available, and have been used to keep these valuable contracts within the Member State concerned.

One aspect of the revision process concerned the issue whether social clauses prescribing labour standards, as well as social and environmental criteria, should be included in the revised directives. On one side were those who argued that such clauses should be excluded in principle, or because they were said to lead to discrimination and unfair competition, or because they believed that such policies are simply not the business of the European Union. On the other side were those who regarded such social clauses as not only desirable, but even necessary in the case of those EU Member States which had ratified ILO Convention No. 94 of 1949 on Labour Clauses (Public Contracts).

The struggle was not only about the sectional interests of those who support labour, social or environmental standards. More fundamentally, it was about the nature of the European Union itself: whether it is to be solely concerned with promoting a competitive European market, or is also engaged in promoting social policies. Public procurement is a potentially powerful administrative mechanism for enforcing labour standards.

### The Council's proposed Directive of 2002

On 28 May 2002, the Council of Ministers adopted a proposal as the Member States' formal position.[50] The text of the proposal revealed some of the tensions which had emerged in the debate. It reflected the conflicting positions, appearing to make concessions to one side, while qualifying these concessions in order to please others. During and after the summer of 2002, this text was the subject of tough negotiations with the European Parliament and Commission. Three examples illustrate how that text reflected conflicting, and sometimes contradictory positions.

### 'Contract performance conditions' and labour standards

The Preamble to the Council's proposal, Recital 22, and Article 26A, appeared to allow 'contract performance conditions' related to labour standards. However, it had been argued that 'contract performance conditions' were not the same as 'contract conditions' or 'award criteria.' For example, the Commission interpreted the European Court's decision in the *Pas de Calais* case[51] as permitting contract performance conditions relating to labour, but denied that these were conditions in the contract or criteria for the award of the contract. This argument was been criticised as both not consistent with the Court's judgment, and absurd in practice. If contracting authorities can control labour standards by imposing contract performance conditions, then

---

[50] Council Proposal for a Directive on the Coordination of Procedures for the award of Public Supply Contracts, Public Services Contracts and Public Workers Contracts, DOC. 9270/02 OF 28 May 2002.

[51] Case 225/98, *Commission of the European Communities* v. *French Republic*, 26 September 2000.

these seem no different from other contractual conditions. Again, on the one hand, the proposal accepted that 'contract performance conditions' include 'basic ILO Conventions', but did not specify which Conventions. So the scope of the labour standards that could be specified as contract performance conditions was not clear.

### Mandatory labour standards?

The Preamble to the Council's proposal, in Recital 22a, specified that collective agreements apply during performance of a public contract. But, again, it was not clear which collective agreements, and what was their permitted scope. Reference was made to the Posting Directive 96/71/EC, which applies in cross-border public contracts, and also allows for collectively agreed standards to apply, but with important limitations.

Moreover, the Preamble's promise of mandatory labour standards was not kept in the text of the Articles of the Directive. Instead, the closest thing was the option allowed for contracting authorities or Member States to provide information on mandatory labour standards (Article 27). On the other hand, the Council's proposal did provide that non-compliance with collective agreements may constitute grave misconduct allowing for exclusion of a contractor (Article 46(2)(d)).

### Award criteria

Again, on the one hand, the proposal in Recital 31 of the Preamble asserted that 'it is appropriate to allow the application of two award criteria only', and offered protection of labour standards as one possible relevant criterion where the contract is awarded on the basis of 'the most economically advantageous tender'. But despite the Preamble's qualified reference to labour standards as a possible criterion for award of a contract, again, Article 53 did not refer at all to labour or social requirements. This despite the European Court's holding in the *Pas de Calais* case that such additional criteria are not excluded. Yet, on the other hand, the legitimacy of labour standards as award criteria for public contracts could be inferred from Article 54, which allowed for rejection of abnormally low tenders after checking 'compliance with the provisions relating to employment protection and working conditions in force at the place where the work or service is to be performed'.

In sum, the Council's proposal was a recipe for future conflict. A commitment to labour standards on public contracts was just about visible. But it was hidden away in options which Member States and contracting authorities could choose,[52] and all were couched in ambiguous language, whereas it would have

---

[52] They included observance of labour standards as contract performance conditions, information on labour standards for tenderers, exclusion of tenderers for violations of labour standards (grave misconduct), and labour standards as secondary award criteria.

been simple to formulate a commitment in unambiguous language to mandatory labour standards.[53]

On 30 September 2002, the Council of Ministers adopted a second proposal covering procurement contracts by entities in the fields of energy and transport. The debate continued as the European Parliament gave their views and proposed amendments on the proposals. This process highlighted major differences between the European Parliament and the Council, which had eventually to be resolved in a Conciliation Committee.

One example will illustrate the kind of detailed debate which took place over the wording of the final directives. Different wordings were disputed concerning one of the criteria for award of a contract: whether it was 'economically advantageous'. The alternatives were whether the contract had to be economically advantageous 'for the contracting authority' or 'from the point of view of the public interest of the contracting authorities'.

The second formula aimed to increase the power of the contracting authority to use its *subjective* judgment as to what is 'economically advantageous'. It allowed the contracting authority to decide to include award criteria reflecting the public interest, including social and environmental requirements, which from its point of view are economically advantageous to it. In contrast, the first formula, 'for the contracting authority', supports a more *objective* standard of what is 'economically advantageous' for the contracting authority. The contracting authority could still argue that award criteria imposing social and environmental requirements are economically advantageous. But it could face opposition, and possible legal challenges, arguing that it is not the contracting authority's subjective point of view which decides what is economically advantageous, but an objective assessment of what is economically advantageous *for* the contracting authority. The formula finally adopted in Article 53 of Directive 2004/18/EC was a compromise:

> the criteria on which the contracting authorities shall base the award of public contracts shall be ... when the award is made to the tender most economically advantageous from the point of view of the contracting authority.

Final agreement on the text of the revised Directives was only reached on a result which leaves much to be desired. The Directives could easily have been adapted to include or exclude labour standards. Instead, contracting authorities, tenderers and contractors are left in doubt. The result is that the European Court will have to tidy up the mess on a case-by-case basis. Yet the case-law of

---

[53] It was interesting that there were a number of provisions in the Council proposal which much more clearly accepted environmental standards (Preamble Recital 2a, Recital 17 and Articles 24(3)(b) and (5a) and Annex VI, paragraph 1, Recital 30b and Articles 49(2)(5A) and 50a)). Perhaps most frustrating was the explicit inclusion of 'environmental characteristics' among possible contract award criteria in Article 53(1)(a), while labour standards and social criteria were not mentioned, although both environmental and social requirements were specified in Recital 31 of the proposal.

the Court itself was the subject of many disputes as interpretations of the Court's decisions differed widely.

## The role of the European Court of Justice

Attempts at administrative enforcement of labour policy through social clauses in public procurement have come before the European Court, but different interpretations of the Court's decisions made uncertain the view that European labour law allows use of the procurement process to enforce labour standards. Certain decisions of the European Court of Justice were invoked by the Commission pursuing a policy objective: to exclude or limit the use of social and labour policy factors in the procurement process.[54] The arguments and counter-arguments for the different propositions advanced are presented below.

## Social criteria may be included as the EC directive does not stipulate mandatory and exhaustive criteria

Until recently, the leading case on whether social objectives can be stipulated in public procurement was *Beentjes*.[55] In an Interpretative Communication of the Commission on the Community law applicable to public procurement and the possibilities for integrating social considerations into public procurement,[56] the Commission repeated in this text of October 2001, in slightly different words, the misreading of EC law in an earlier draft of the Communication of April 2001:[57]

> The directive set out *exhaustive and mandatory*, qualitative selection criteria, which can be used to justify the choice of candidates or tenderers. Selection criteria different from those set out in the directives would thus not comply with the current directives.

However, the European Court's judgment in *Beentjes*[58] specifically contradicts the Commission's view, but is not mentioned in the Communication:

---

[54] *Beentjes* (Case C-31/87, [1988] ECR 4635), *Commission v. France (Pas de Calais)* (Case C-225/98, decided 26 September 2000), and '*Helsinki Bus*' (Case C-513/99, decided 17 September 2002).

[55] *Gebroeders Beentjes BV* v. *The Netherlands*, Case C-31/87, [1988] ECR 4635.

[56] COM(2001) 566 final, Brussels, 15 October 2001. Comparisons will be made with an earlier draft of this Communication. Working Document of 3 April 2001 prepared by the Internal Market Directorate General on 'Interpretation of Community public procurement law and the possibilities for incorporating social considerations in public procurement'. Document CC/01/ 10 EN, Brussels, 3 April 2001, MARKT/B2/NSK. The author's experience in numerous meetings with officials in the UK's Office of Government Commerce (OGC) and the Department of Trade and Industry, the authorities responsible for implementation of the revised procurement directives, is that this Communication has been repeatedly cited in support of the UK government's position seeking to limit the scope of social clauses in public contracts. This is one reason for the detailed analysis which follows.

[57] Page 9 (italics added), citing *Beentjes*, paragraph 17 as authority.

[58] Paragraph 20 (italics added).

Furthermore, the directive does *not* lay down a uniform and exhaustive body of Community rules; within the framework of the common rules which it contains, the Member States remain free to maintain or adopt substantive and procedural rules in regard to public works contracts on condition that they comply with all the relevant provisions of Community law, in particular the prohibitions flowing from the principles laid down in the Treaty in regard to the right of establishment and the freedom to provide services.

In other words, it is the general principles of EC law that determine Member State and EC competence, not the specific rules of the Directive.

### Social criteria may be compatible with EC law, and need not be related to economic or financial criteria

It is correct, therefore, but grossly misleading to state in the Communication that:[59]

> In the *Beentjes* case cited above, the Court found that a condition regarding the employing of long-term unemployed persons had no relation to the checking of tenderers' suitability on the basis of their economic and financial standing and their technical knowledge and ability (ground 28 of the judgment).

This is coupled with the footnote 30 attached:[60]

> *Similarly*, a criterion regarding the good standing of executives of an undertaking was rejected by the Court of Justice, on the basis that it 'constituted a means of proof which does not come within the closed category authorised by directive 71/305/EEC on economic and financial standing of undertakings, in its judgment of 10.2.82 in Case 76/81, *Transporoute* (points 9 and 10)'.

The extremely misleading implication is that the Court '*similarly ... rejected*' the criterion of employment of long-term unemployed. This is incorrect. The statement of the Court is clear: the condition regarding employment of long-term unemployed *is* irrelevant to the specified criteria of economic and financial standards and technical knowledge. That does *not* mean that it cannot be used as a *separate and independent criterion*. This is clearly the sense of the following paragraphs 29 and 30 of the Court's judgment:

> 29. ... in order to be compatible with the directive such a condition must comply with all the relevant provisions of Community law, in particular the prohibitions flowing from the principles laid down in the Treaty in regard to the right of establishment and the freedom to provide services.
>
> 30. The obligation to employ long-term unemployed persons could *inter alia* infringe the prohibition of discrimination on the grounds of nationality ... if it became apparent that such a condition could be satisfied only by tenderers from the State concerned or indeed that tenderers from other Member States would have difficulty in complying with it. It is for the national court to determine, in the

---

[59] Page 9, again following closely the language of the earlier draft.
[60] Identical to footnote 40 in the earlier draft (italics added).

light of all the circumstances of the case, whether the imposition of such a condition is directly or indirectly discriminatory.

Obviously, the Court anticipates the possibility that a criterion of employment of long-term unemployed persons could infringe EC law, but equally, *it could be perfectly compatible with EC law*. Indeed, there would be nothing for the national court to determine if the criterion in question had been rejected by the European Court.

In sum, the Commission's interpretation provides an extremely misleading view of EC law based on its selective quotation from the *Beentjes* case.

### Social criteria are permitted provided they do not contravene EC law on free movement and nationality discrimination

This misreading of *Beentjes* leads to the misleading statement which concludes the following paragraph of the Commission's Communication of October 2001:[61]

> In view of the references which may currently be required in order to assess the economic and financial standing of tenderers, it is not possible for social considerations to be included in such references.

The context of the paragraph clearly demonstrates that this is so *only* in so far as these references relate to proving economic or financial standing, *but not otherwise*. Again, the Court explicitly acknowledged that social criteria *could* be used, provided they did not contravene the prohibition of discrimination on grounds of nationality.[62]

The Commission's view that social criteria are excluded by EC law from the scope of public procurement is not a correct account of EC law as interpreted by the European Court of Justice. This is conclusively indicated by the subsequent decision in *Commission* v. *France*, Case C-225/98.[63]

### Social criteria are acceptable as additional criteria for award of the contract regardless of their economic relevance, but may indeed be relevant to the economic advantage of the contracting authority

It was shocking, if not surprising, that the Communication of October 2001 did not pay more attention to the European Court's decision in *Commission* v. *France*, Case C-225/98. The ECJ rejected a Commission challenge to a French public works contract which included social criteria. The Commission complained of failure of a Member State to fulfil its obligations regarding public works contracts under the procurement Directive 71/305/EEC, as amended by

---

[61] Page 9.

[62] Further misleading use is made of the *Beentjes* decision when the Communication addresses the question of criteria of award of the contract (see below).

[63] *Commission of the European Communities* v. *French Republic (Pas de Calais)*, Case C-225/98, decided 26 September 2000.

Directive 89/440/EEC and 93/37/EEC. The complaint related to the additional criterion linked to the campaign against unemployment.

That case explicitly rejected the Commission's reliance on *Beentjes* that the use of social criteria did not apply to award of contracts:[64]

> As regards the Commission's argument that *Beentjes* concerned a condition of performance of the contract and not a criterion for the award of the contract, it need merely be observed that, as is clear from paragraph 14 of *Beentjes*, the condition relating to the employment of long-term unemployed persons, which was at issue in that case, had been used as the basis for rejecting a tender and therefore necessarily constituted a criterion for the award of the contract.

In light of this, the Commission's Communication has to concede that:[65]

> The public procurement directives list, by way of example, a number of criteria that the contracting authorities can use as a basis to identify which tender would be the most advantageous from an economic point of view. [But] Other criteria may also be applied.

The use of the criterion of 'most economically advantageous tender' in awarding public procurement contracts raises a number of questions as to whose economic advantage is required to be promoted. But most important is whether this criterion allows for the use of social considerations as a criterion for the award of contracts. Contrary to the Commission's view in *Commission* v. *France*, it is submitted that the inclusion of social considerations as award criteria is permissible for two reasons. First, and more important, the European Court of Justice upheld the validity of such other criteria in Case C-225/98: *Commission* v. *France*. Secondly, economically advantageous criteria include specifying the manner in which the contract/work is carried out, which includes social considerations.

### Social criteria may be economically advantageous when concerned with the manner in which the contract/work is carried out; an example: equal opportunities for women

Factors including employment conditions, industrial relations and dispute resolution are related to the manner in which the contract is carried out, can be economically advantageous, and could be formulated as award criteria reflecting social considerations.[66] In its concern to exclude any criteria regarding employment, the earlier draft of the Communication included a remarkable display of anachronistic qualities. It unashamedly stated:[67]

---

[64] Paragraph 52.   [65] Page 12, italics added.

[66] Technical specifications regarding the performance of the contractor can include expertise in managing personnel working on the contract. For example, such expertise could be reflected in specifications as to management performance relating to records of violations of mandatory labour standards, on health and safety, wage entitlements, or of dismissal, or of disputes between management and employees or their representatives, including unions, leading to industrial conflict.

[67] Page 13.

A criterion requiring, for example, that the enterprise employs a given percentage of women cannot, however, constitute evidence of the technical capacity of a supplier.

This flies in the face of the literature on personnel management and public service provision which highlights the need for diversity in the workforce and the benefits this provides in terms of efficiency of performance and quality of service.[68]

The final Communication repeated the draft text's view that it is:[69]

> incompatible with the current public procurement directives [to take into account] criteria relating to whether tenderers ... have set up a programme for the promotion of equal opportunities, as they would be considered criteria which are unrelated to the subject-matter of a given contract or to the manner in which the contract is executed.

This view may be contested: equal opportunity policies may well be related to the manner in which a contract is executed.

### Social criteria may, but need not, concern the nature of the work which is the subject-matter of the contract or the manner in which it is carried out, provided they do not contravene EC law on free movement and nationality discrimination

This was the view adopted by the European Court in Case C-225/98, *Commission* v. *France*. However, the Commission's Communication went far beyond the Court in stipulating restrictions on these other criteria:[70]

> As a general rule, the public procurement directives impose two conditions with regard to criteria used for determining the most economically advantageous tender. First, the principle of non-discrimination has to be observed. Second, the criteria used should generate an economic advantage for the contracting authority ...

---

[68] But even worse, it sent an extremely negative signal to the rest of the Community. D-G XV was refusing to support the use of criteria which would reflect the Amsterdam Treaty's amendments explicitly requiring that 'In all [its] activities ... the Community shall aim to eliminate inequalities and to promote equality, between men and women' (Article 3(2): mainstreaming sex equality) and endorsing positive action to this end (Article 141(4)). Footnote 44 was simply insulting. Following the rejection of positive action measures for women, a box acknowledged cases where 'specific experience is necessary having regard to the subject-matter of the contract'. The attached footnote 44 gave as examples 'construction of a hospital or creche' – classic examples of occupational sex segregation. Nor was this an isolated example. Equal opportunities policy in the form of positive action was again unashamedly rejected as '"social preference" criteria which are unrelated to the subject-matter of a given contract. Such a criterion is not permitted under the public procurement directives, having regard to their objectives' (page 16). Again, the final paragraph in section 5.2 on page 17 includes an extremely cautious reference to possible 'positive actions', a further indication of how little D-G XV values the commitment to sex equality in Article 3(2) EC.

[69] Page 13.    [70] *Ibid.*

> The common factor shared by all criteria used for evaluation of offers is that they must ... all concern the nature of the work which is the subject-matter of the contract or the manner in which it is carried out.

Only the reference to the principle of non-discrimination accurately reflects the Court's judgment. The subsequent criteria and conditions are nowhere to be found in the judgment and were precisely the submissions rejected by the Court in Case C-225/98, *Commission* v. *France*:

> 48. The first point to be noted here is that, by this complaint, the Commission alleges that the French Republic has infringed Article 30(1) of Directive 93/37 purely and simply by referring to the criterion linked to the campaign against unemployment as an award criterion in some of the disputed contract notices.
>
> 49. Under Article 30(1) of Directive 93/37, the criteria on which the contracting authorities are to base the award of contracts are either the lowest price only or, when the award is made to the most economically advantageous tender, various criteria according to the contract, such as price, period for completion, running costs, profitability, technical merit.
>
> 50. None the less, that provision does not preclude all possibility for the contracting authorities to use as a criterion a condition linked to the campaign against unemployment provided that that condition is consistent with all the fundamental principles of Community law, in particular the principle of non-discrimination flowing from the provisions of the Treaty on the right of establishment and the freedom to provide services (see, to that effect, *Beentjes*, paragraph 29).

As stated earlier, it is *not* the case that the criteria used in determining the most economically advantageous tender are the exclusive and exhaustive criteria for award of the contract.[71]

A short section 1.4.2 of the Commission's Communication, '*Additional criterion*', finally acknowledges, for the first time, the existence of 'additional' criteria to those stated heretofore to be exhaustive and exclusive and declares, without apparent irony:[72]

> The concept was first mentioned in the *Beentjes* case cited above, where the Court held that a criterion relating to the employment of long-term unemployed persons was *not* relevant either to the checking of a candidate's economic and financial suitability *or* of the candidate's technical knowledge and ability, *or* to the award criteria listed in the relevant directive. The Court also held that this criterion was *nevertheless compatible* with the public procurement directives if it complied with all relevant principles of Community law.

---

[71] Paragraph 20 of *Beentjes*, quoted above but not cited by the Commission, makes this clear. Paragraph 27 of the *Beentjes* judgment confirms that awards *may* be made on the basis of comparison so as to choose the most economically advantageous, but does not exclude *other* criteria. The position as regards criteria appears to be the same with respect to *both* selection of suitable tenderers and award of the contract. The Commission seems unable to accept this proposition. It does not even have the courtesy to cite the Court's decision in its argumentation in the Communication's section on the criteria for award.

[72] Pages 14–15; italics added.

The Communication does not appear to recognise that this pronouncement of the Court is in direct conflict with the Commission's position as stated in the preceding section of the Communication.

### Social criteria are not confined to where there are two or more economically equivalent tenders

This may be because the Commission goes on to distort the Court's position:[73]

> In Case C-225/98, the Court of Justice held that contracting authorities can base the award of a condition on a condition related to the combating of unemployment, provided that this condition was in line with all the fundamental principles of Community law.

To this, the Commission adds the following condition:[74]

> *but only where the said authorities had to consider two or more economically equivalent tenders.*

This proviso added by the Communication has no basis in the decision of the Court.[75] Nowhere in the judgment of the Court is there any statement that social criteria may be applied only to select as between two or more economically equivalent tenders. It is clear that the Commission is seeking to re-establish its premise that only economic factors may enter into the award of a contract through this misrepresentation of the Court's decision.[76]

---

[73] Page 15.    [74] Italics added.

[75] A mysterious footnote 59 refers to the Annual Report on the Activities of the European Union, point 1119, page 407 – but this is no legal authority.

[76] The only basis for the Commission's interpretation is the reference made to the position of the French authorities on the social criterion concerned: 'This condition was regarded by the Member State in question [France] as an additional, non-determining criterion and was considered only after tenders were compared from a purely economic point of view.' Again, there is no support cited for the Commission's assertion as to this use of social criterion. In the Court's judgment, the French authorities' position on this point is reflected in paragraph 47: 'Relying on paragraphs 28 and 37 of *Beentjes*, the French Government contends that an additional award criterion of that kind has been permitted by the Court of Justice. It states, furthermore, that the award criterion in question in this case does not constitute a primary criterion, such as those referred to in Article 29 of Directive 71/305, the purpose of which is to make it possible to determine which is the most advantageous tender, but a secondary criterion which is not decisive'. The Court follows this summary of the French government's position with its own view in paragraphs 48–50 quoted above. It is not even clear from paragraph 47 that the French government regarded the social criterion as secondary in the sense that it was to be applied only after economically equivalent tenders. There is certainly no suggestion in the judgment that the *Court* intended to postulate a second proviso to that of fundamental principles, or, specifically, that social criteria were a secondary factor in any sense, let alone one to be used only in selecting between economically equivalent tenders. There is, therefore, no basis for the Commission's interpretation of the case. The European Court accepts that social considerations are permissible as criteria for public procurement, without the conditions attached by the Commission.

### Social criteria need not be economically advantageous for the contracting authority, but from the point of view of the contracting authority

The Communication of 2001 categorically affirmed that 'the criteria used should generate an economic advantage for the contracting authority'.[77] Again, social considerations are deemed acceptable 'where they provide an economic advantage for the contracting authority which is linked to the product or service which is the subject-matter of the contract'.[78] The Communication poses the question whether:[79]

> each individual award criterion has to provide an economic advantage which directly benefits the contracting authority, or if it is sufficient that each individual criterion has to be measurable in economic terms, without the requirement that it directly provides an economic advantage for the contracting authority in the given contract.

In the latter case, would the public authority be able to use the criterion of a more general economic advantage for society, even if not reflected in an economic advantage for the public authority deriving from the specific purchase?

By way of illustration, in the earlier draft of the Communication, an example of economic advantage deriving from a criterion of employment of unemployed persons was said to:[80]

> relate to the reduction of expenditure associated with social security benefits or to the increase in the volume of expenditure of the employed persons. They do not, therefore, present any advantage for the individual contract in question.

The requirement that criteria provide an economic advantage for the contracting public authority, which may not be responsible for social security or macro-economic policy, highlights the narrowness of the Communication's vision of social criteria. On such a view of particular economic advantage, a requirement of minimum or fair wages and working conditions would be ruled out as an advantage which concerned only third parties, whatever the advantages for the Community as a whole. An interpretation of EC law which promotes the Commission's ideology of naked economic advantage may be questioned where it purports to override democratically elected public authorities choosing to pursue social policies through public procurement.[81]

The criteria relating to economic advantage are, therefore, interpreted by the Commission extremely narrowly. The Communication tries to limit to a very narrow spectrum the social criteria which may bear on economic advantage for the contracting authority. The narrowness of the Commission's concept of what constitutes economic advantage is evident from its citation of a case then

---

[77] Page 13.     [78] Box on page 14.     [79] Page 14.     [80] Pages 15–16.

[81] Footnote 54 referred to a case handled by the Commission where the contracting authority stipulated social criteria which explicitly favoured local contractors. Somewhat disingenuously, the Commission condemns these criteria as not relevant to economic advantage and, 'Moreover', discriminatory against non-local tenderers. The latter condemnation is clearly supported by the Court's case law, but not the former.

pending before the European Court, Case C-513/99, *Stagecoach Finland Oy Ab* ('*Helsinki Bus*'),[82] where award of a contract to provide bus services includes the criteria of noise and polluting emissions. The Commission declares that it favours a position limiting environmental criteria to those which:[83]

> provide an economic advantage which directly benefits the contracting authority [in contrast to criteria] measurable in economic terms, without the requirement that it directly provides an economic advantage for the contracting authority in the given contract.

The Commission's approach is that environmental considerations which may massively affect others are secondary to a narrow economic advantage to the public authority. The Court declined to follow this path.[84] One point in particular reinforces the argument that the case rejects the Commission's position. The addition in Article 53 of the revised Directive 2004/18/EC of the words 'from the point of view of the contracting authority' appears to reflect the Court's approval that 'factors which are not purely economic may

---

[82] *Concordia Bus Finland Oy Ab* v. *Helsingin Kaupunki, HKL-Bussiliikenne (Helsinki Bus),* Case C-513/99, decided 17 September 2002; cited in footnote 55 of the Communication.

[83] Page 14.

[84] Of the Court's decision in Case C-513/99 on 17 September 2002, the '*Helsinki Bus*' case, the Commission claimed that it was consistent with its position on revision of the Directives, while environmental groups claimed it required an important change in the direction of EU policy. The relevant paragraphs of the Court's judgment provide support for the latter. Paragraphs 54–5, 57, 69: '54. In order to determine whether and under what conditions the contracting authority may, in accordance with Article 36(1)(a), take into consideration criteria of an ecological nature, it must be noted, first, that, as is clear from the wording of that provision, in particular the use of the expression for example, the criteria which may be used as criteria for the award of a public contract to the economically most advantageous tender are not listed exhaustively … 55. Second, Article 36(1)(a) cannot be interpreted as meaning that each of the award criteria used by the contracting authority to identify the economically most advantageous tender must necessarily be of a purely economic nature. It cannot be excluded that factors which are not purely economic may influence the value of a tender from the point of view of the contracting authority. That conclusion is also supported by the wording of the provision, which expressly refers to the criterion of the aesthetic characteristics of a tender … 57. In light of … the wording [in the Treaty of Amsterdam] … which lays down that environmental protection requirements must be integrated into the definition and implementation of Community policies and activities, it must be concluded that Article 36(1)(a) of Directive 92/050 does not exclude the possibility for the contracting authority of using criteria relating to the preservation of the environment when assessing the economically most advantageous tender …. 69 … Article 36(1)(a) of Directive 92/50 is to be interpreted as meaning that where, in the context of a public contract for the provision of urban bus transport services, the contracting authority decides to award a contract to the tenderer who submits the economically most advantageous tender, it may take into consideration ecological criteria such as the level of nitrogen oxide emissions or the noise level of the buses, provided that they are linked to the subject-matter of the contract, do not confer an unrestricted freedom of choice on the authority, are expressly mentioned in the contract documents or the tender notice, and comply with all the fundamental principles of Community law, in particular the principle of non-discrimination'. This last phrase has been invoked by the Commission and, in the UK, by the OGC in order to constrain the use by contracting authorities of social criteria.

influence the value of a tender from the point of view of the contracting authority'.

## The position before and after *Rüffert*[85]

This detailed analysis of the debates leading up to the formulation of the EU legislation on public procurement and the potential use of social clauses as a means of administrative enforcement of European labour law is vitally important for a full understanding of the intentions behind and meaning of many of the Articles in the revised Directive. Much of the debate concerned interpretation of decisions of the European Court of Justice. These debates are important because the new Directives do not make the earlier case law of the European Court of Justice obsolete. On the contrary, the first Recital of the Preamble of Directive 2004/18/EC confirms:

> This Directive is based on Court of Justice case-law, in particular case-law on award criteria, which clarifies the possibilities for the contracting authorities to meet the needs of the public concerned, including in the environmental and/or social area, provided that such criteria are linked to the subject-matter of the contract, do not confer an unrestricted freedom of choice on the contracting authority, are expressly mentioned and comply with the fundamental principles mentioned in recital 2.

The references to the earlier case-law are clear where the Preamble also confirms that:[86]

> Contract performance conditions are compatible with this Directive provided that they are not directly or indirectly discriminatory and are indicated in the contract notice or in the contract documents.[87] They may, in particular, be intended to favour on-site vocational training, the employment of people experiencing particular difficulty in achieving integration, the fight against unemployment or the protection of the environment. For instance, mention may be made, amongst other things, of the requirements – applicable during performance of the contract – to recruit long-term job-seekers or to implement training measures for the unemployed or young persons, to comply in substance with the provisions of the basic International Labour Organisation (ILO) Conventions, assuming that such provisions have not been implemented in national law, and to recruit more handicapped persons than are required under national legislation.

However, the position appears to have been utterly transformed by the astonishing ECJ decision in *Rüffert* on 3 April 2008. The issue in *Rüffert* was whether a public authority in Germany could require a contractor from Poland to

---

[85] ECJ decision of 3 April 2008 in Case C-346/06, *Rechtsanwalt Dr. Dirk Rüffert* v. *Land Niedersachsen*.

[86] Recital 33.

[87] 'Contract performance conditions' were the subject of further contention in Case C-346/06, *Rüffert*. See the Opinion of Advocate-General Bot, 20 September 2007, discussed below.

observe collective agreements. Failure to comply led to heavy financial penalties and ultimately cancellation of the contract. The contractor complained that this was incompatible with Article 49 EC, as compliance meant they lost their competitive advantage and consequently it constituted an impediment to market access.[88]

In his Opinion of 20 September 2007, Advocate-General Bot stated:[89]

> The question raised by the court making the reference once again calls on the Court to strike a balance between the freedom to provide services, on the one hand, and the overriding requirements of the protection of workers and the prevention of social dumping, on the other.

The large majority of Member States making submissions considered this restriction justified by the objective of worker protection and proportionate to achievement of that objective.[90] The Polish government disagreed.[91] The Commission took the view that only universally applicable collective agreements qualified under the Posting Directive. The public authority was seeking to apply specifically local collective agreements.[92]

Advocate-General Bot cited the EC Directives on procurement which allow public authorities to make compliance with collective agreements a contract performance condition – another indication of the Community legislator's reconciliation of market freedoms with social regulation.[93] The Advocate-General concluded that there was little doubt that a restriction on the freedom to provide service exists.[94] But the public authority was not violating Article 49 because it sought to ensure the protection of posted workers.[95] This was an appropriate means of preventing social dumping as it ensures that local workers and posted workers on the same site will be treated equally.[96]

It therefore came as a considerable shock when the fifth chamber of the ECJ, in a brief decision, took an entirely different view from the Advocate-General. The ECJ subordinated the policy of allowing social clauses in public contracts to

---

[88] *Ibid.*, Opinion of Advocate-General Bot, paragraph 41.    [89] *Ibid.*, paragraph 2.

[90] *Ibid.*, paragraph 47.    [91] *Ibid.*, paragraph 51.    [92] *Ibid.*, paragraphs 52–5.

[93] *Ibid.*, paragraphs 58–60.    [94] *Ibid.*, paragraph 102.

[95] *Ibid.*, paragraph 118. It follows (also from the Services Directive) that if public authorities imposing severe sanctions on contracted service providers from other Member States for failure to comply with collective agreements are not violating Article 49, workers and trade unions taking lawful collective action to achieve the same result should not be considered to be violating Article 49.

[96] *Ibid.*, paragraph 119. Although it could facilitate free movement if employers could obtain a competitive advantage by treating migrant workers less favourably, this is clearly prohibited by Community law. To claim that applying collective agreements to employees of service providers from other countries operates to restrict free movement faces the same principled objection. It is sometimes argued that this prejudices the jobs of migrant workers. This argument tends to come not from workers but from service providers/employers. Trade unions representing the workers concerned, both in the host country and the migrant workers, oppose undermining collective standards. Migrant workers, who are subject to the same cost of living in the host country, are not prominent in litigating to demand they should be paid less than provided in collective agreements.

protect collective agreements to the priority of eliminating obstacles to free movement. Seemingly oblivious to the exhaustive debates over this issue in the formulation of the directives on public procurement, the ECJ looked elsewhere for inspiration and found it, surprisingly, in the Posting Directive.[97] Relying instead on the recent ECJ decision in *Laval*,[98] neither acknowledging the powerful reasoning the Advocate-General nor providing any convincing reasoning of its own, and contradicting an established view as to the objectives of the Posting Directive, the ECJ invoked the Posting Directive as the standard applicable also in public procurement to fix the maximum limit to which public authorities may prescribe adherence to collective agreement.

The ECJ thus upset the carefully negotiated compromise negotiated among the EU legislative institutions allowing scope for Member States' social policy to stipulate award conditions in public procurement: as stated in Article 53 of the revised Directive 2004/18/EC 'from the point of view of the contracting authority'. In the *Helsinki Bus* case, the Court had appeared to agree that 'factors which are not purely economic may influence the value of a tender from the point of view of the contracting authority'.[99] The Court in *Rüffert* ruled that out as potentially conflicting with the freedom to provide services guaranteed by Article 49 EC. If the ECJ persists in taking this line, it risks not only inconsistency in its case-law and precipitating a clash with the EU legislative policy, but also conflict with international labour law.

## European labour law and international labour law on public procurement

The Preamble to Directive 2004/18/EC cites specifically as possible contract performance conditions those: 'to comply in substance with the provisions of the basic International Labour Organisation (ILO) Conventions, assuming that such provisions have not been implemented in national law'.[100]

ILO Convention No. 94 of 1949 concerning Labour Clauses in Public Contracts requires public contracts in ratifying states to include clauses ensuring working conditions, including those in collective agreements. The ILO Convention has been ratified by eight Member States.[101] The ECJ in *Rüffert*

---

[97] Directive 96/71/EC concerning the posting of workers in the framework of the provision of services. OJ 1996 L18/1.

[98] Case C-341/05, *Laval un Partneri Ltd* v. *Svenska Byggnadsarbetareförbundet, Svenska Byggnadsarbetareförbundet, avd. 1, Svenska Elektrikerförbundet*, decided 18 December 2007.

[99] *Concordia Bus Finland Oy Ab* v. *Helsingin Kaupunki, HKL-Bussiliikenne (Helsinki Bus)*, Case C-513/99, paragraph 55.

[100] Recital 33.

[101] Of the EU-15. Of nine Member States which have ratified the Convention, only the UK has denounced ILO Convention No. 94, in 1982, and that was for domestic policy reasons associated with the Thatcher government's privatisation programme. The ratifying Member States are: Austria, Finland, France (1951), Belgium, Italy, Netherlands (1952), Denmark (1955) and Spain (1971).

paid no heed to the requirements of international labour law in the form of ILO Convention No. 94. Yet Article 307 EC provides:

> The rights and obligations arising from agreements concluded before 1 January 1958 or, for acceding States, before the date of their accession, between one or more Member States on the one hand, and one or more third countries on the other, shall not be affected by the provisions of this Treaty.[102]

So at least eight Member States present potential problems regarding their ILO obligations under Article 307.[103] Should the ILO Conventions remain in force as earlier international agreements, there would result a division among Member States as regards their power to impose social clauses making collective agreements mandatory labour standards.

In its Communication, D-G XV accepted that:[104]

> A contracting authority may impose on the party to whom a contract is awarded labour clauses such as those mentioned in ILO Convention No. 94, provided that they respect the relevant provisions of Community law.

---

[102] It continues: 'To the extent that such agreements are not compatible with this Treaty, the Member State or States concerned shall take all appropriate steps to eliminate the incompatibilities established. Member States shall, where necessary, assist each other to this end and shall, where appropriate, adopt a common attitude. In applying the agreements referred to in the first paragraph, Member States shall take into account the fact that the advantages accorded under this Treaty by each Member State form an integral part of the establishment of the Community and are thereby inseparably linked with the creation of common institutions, the conferring of powers upon them and the granting of the same advantages by all the other Member States'.

[103] In Case C-158/91, *Levy* [1993] ECR I-4287, the Court recognised the binding nature of ILO Convention 89 prohibiting night work for women. Piet Eeckhout, *External Relations of the European Union*, Oxford: Oxford University Press, 2004, pp. 338–9, takes the view that to deviate from this would mean allowing EC law to impose a breach of international law. Eeckhout notes, however, that in contrast with *Levy*, an Opinion of Advocate- General Lenz in joined Cases 209–213/84, *Ministere public* v. *Asjes* [1986] ECR 1425, 1453, conditions the effect of the first paragraph of Article 307 by compliance with the second paragraph. I. Macleod, I.D. Hendry and S. Hyett, *The External Relations of the European Communities*, Oxford: Clarendon Press, 1996, p. 230, take the view that Article 307's requirement of respect for pre-existing agreements 'extends to permitting the Member State to fulfil its obligations, if necessary by allowing it to maintain in place legislation which would otherwise be contrary to its Community obligations'.

[104] The last paragraph on page 8 says that to require public procurement contractors to comply with ILO Conventions (footnote 22: child labour, freedom of association, etc.), these 'must previously have been ratified by a given country and, where necessary, have been incorporated into their national law'. No authority is provided for this statement. The document continues: 'Most of these Conventions concern the respect of fundamental economic and social rights which have already been implemented in social and other legislation, and are therefore applicable in any event'. It is not clear that EC law on public procurement requires that ILO Conventions must have been ratified or incorporated. So long as the fundamental economic and social rights in these Conventions are applied on a transparent and non-discriminatory basis by the contracting authority, it does not matter if the Member State has ratified or incorporated them.

This has two consequences. The very wide scope of the clauses covered in the ILO Convention No. 94 is acknowledged.[105] D-G XV's acquiescence that such clauses, including provisions of collective agreements, can be made obligatory in public procurement raises questions about the extreme caution regarding the compatibility of social clauses with EC law which is manifest in the rest of the interpretation document.[106]

Hence, despite *Rüffert*, it does not seem that EC law poses any threat to the full application of ILO Convention No. 94. Rather, a valid interpretation is that ILO Convention No. 94 is consistent with EC law, including the procurement Directives. This ILO Convention requires social clauses going far beyond anything envisaged by current directives. If the Convention is consistent with EC law, there can be no objection in EC law to incorporating similar clauses in public contracts. Many Member States clearly support such a policy by continuing their ratification of the Convention. They thereby confirm the importance of this mechanism of administrative enforcement of labour standards. In the absence of more effective mechanisms of administrative enforcement, the enforcement of European labour law has much to gain from the use of social clauses in public procurement.[107]

---

[105]  Footnote 25.

[106]  Unless the caveat: 'provided that they respect the relevant provisions of Community law', is regarded as withdrawing much of D-G XV's apparent acceptance of this Convention.

[107]  See generally, Christopher McCrudden, *Buying Social Justice: Equality, Government Procurement, & Legal Change*, Oxford: Oxford University Press, 2007.

# Chapter 14

# Implementation and enforcement of European labour law and employment policy through the social partners at national and EU levels

## The evolution of the case law on implementation and enforcement of EU labour law through the social partners

Compared to administrative officials or judges, the social partners are much less remote from the site of enforcement of labour law. Their proximity means that they have the potential to be effective guarantors of the application of the rules. This function is reinforced by EU law's recognition of the role of collective agreements in implementing directives – a recognition that emerged slowly from the case law of the European Court of Justice.

Article 249 of the Treaty of Rome stipulates that:

> A directive shall be binding, as to the result to be achieved, upon each Member State to which it is addressed, but shall leave to the national authorities the choice of form and methods.

Non-compliance with this obligation allows the Commission eventually to make a complaint to the European Court. Directives habitually referred to the obligation of Member States to implement their provisions through 'laws, regulations and administrative provisions'.[1]

In *Commission of the European Communities* v. *Italian Republic*,[2] the Italian government argued 'in substance' that legislation, regulatory provisions and *collective agreements* combined to achieve adequate implementation of Directive 75/129 on collective dismissals. The Italian government argued that to take the contrary view was formalist:[3]

> In its opinion, the Commission set out from the formalistic stand-point that the directive can be complied with only by the adoption of implementing measures, irrespective of where the provision of directives are already complied with in the

---

[1] For example, Council Directive 77/187 of 14 February 1977 on the approximation of the laws of Member States relating to the safeguarding of employees' rights in the event of transfers of undertakings, businesses or parts of businesses (OJ 1977 L61/26), Article 8: '1. Member States shall bring into force the laws, regulations and administrative provisions needed to comply with this Directive.'

[2] Case 91/81, [1982] ECR 2133.    [3] *Ibid.*, p. 2142.

legal order of a Member State. It contends that the Commission inferred purely from the fact that the implementing measures were not put into effect that the Italian Government had not complied with the obligations arising out of the directive, without ascertaining whether the aims of the directive were already ensured in the Italian legal order.

Responding to this argument, Advocate-General Verloren Van Themaat came to a specific conclusion regarding the role of collective agreements in implementing Directives:[4]

> with regard to Article 100 of the EEC Treaty and Article 6 of the directive, they cannot be regarded as 'methods' within the meaning of Article 189 of the Treaty or as 'laws, regulations or administrative provision' within the meaning of Article 6 of the directive.

To the contrary, the Court seemed to respond in some degree to the substantive argument of the Italian government. Upholding the Commission's complaint, the European Court pointed out that certain sectors were not covered by agreements, and that the agreements did not include all the provision required by Community law.[5] The conclusions of Advocate-General Verloren Van Themaat had also pointed out the defects of the Italian agreements regarding their coverage and scope. But, significantly, there was no reference in the Court's judgment to his conclusion regarding the formal role of collective agreements. It appeared that the Court was unwilling to hold collective agreements formally inadequate when there was no need to, as they were, on the facts of the case, in any event substantively inadequate.

This preference for substantive over formal logic was again manifested in *Commission of the European Communities* v. *United Kingdom of Great Britain and Northern Ireland*.[6] The European Court held that the failure of the UK government to enact legislation providing for the nullification of collective agreements violating the provisions of Directive 76/207 on equal treatment of men and women constituted non-fulfilment of its obligations under Article 189. Although collective agreements in the UK lacked legal effect, the European Court stated:[7]

> The directive thus covers all collective agreements without distinction as to the nature of the legal effects which they do or do not produce. The reason for that generality lies in the fact that, even if they are not legally binding as between the parties who sign them or with regard to the employment relationships which they govern, collective agreements nevertheless have important *de facto* consequences for the employment relationships to which they refer, particularly in so far as they determine the rights of the workers and, in the interests of industrial harmony, give undertakings satisfy or need not satisfy [*sic*]. The need to ensure that the directive is completely effective therefore requires that any clauses in such agreements which are incompatible with the obligations imposed by the directive upon

---

[4] *Ibid.*, p. 2145.   [5] *Ibid.*, p. 2140, paragraphs 8–9.
[6] Case 165/82, [1983] ECR 3431.   [7] *Ibid.*, p. 3447, paragraph 11.

the Member States may be rendered inoperative, eliminated or amended by appropriate means.

In this the Court reflected the realist view of Advocate-General Rozès, who stated:[8]

> a situation in which possibly discriminatory provisions continue to exist in documents such as collective agreements … is just as ambiguous – above all for workers who in most cases have no legal training … workers have easier access to collective agreements … than to Directive 76/207 or to the United Kingdom laws depriving those documents, in general, of legally binding force. Thus, workers may believe that because their contracts of employment reproduce possibly discriminatory provisions from the types of document referred to they are legal and may not be challenged at law and the workers may therefore be deprived of the advantages of a directive which was in fact adopted for their benefit. In order to avoid such risks of confusion, the best course is to make it possible for such discriminatory provision to be removed from those documents, as required by the directive.

A definitive step towards formal recognition of collective agreements was taken in *Commission of the European Communities* v. *Kingdom of Denmark*.[9] In that case, the Danish government's position was explicitly that collective agreements were its choice of form and method for implementation of the obligations of Council Directive 75/117 on equal pay. It was argued that the Danish legislation was but a secondary guarantee of the equality principle in the event that this principle was not guaranteed by collective agreements. An agreement of 1971 made such provision and covered most employment relations in Denmark.[10]

Significantly, in this case Advocate-General Verloren Van Themaat did not refer to his earlier conclusion excluding collective agreements as measures implementing Council Directives. He merely noted that:[11]

> From the point of view of legal certainty it would undoubtedly have been preferable had Denmark simply incorporated in its legislation the interpretation of the principle of equal pay laid down in Article 1 of the directive, in accordance with the view of the Commission.

The Court held:[12]

> that Member States may leave the implementation of the principle of equal pay in the first instance to representatives of management and labour. That possibility does not, however, discharge them from the obligation of ensuring, by appropriate legislative and administrative provisions, that all workers in the Community are afforded the full protection provided for in the directive. That State guarantee must cover all cases where effective protection is not ensured by other means, for whatever reason, and in particular cases where the workers in question are not union members, where the sector in question is not covered by a

---

[8] *Ibid.*, p. 3454.   [9] Case 143/83, [1985] ECR 427.   [10] *Ibid.*, p. 434, paragraph 7.
[11] *Ibid.*, p. 430.   [12] *Ibid.*, pp. 434–5, paragraph 8.

collective agreement or where such an agreement does not fully guarantee the principle of equal pay.

However, in a second case involving Italy, *Commission of the European Communities* v. *Italian Republic*,[13] Advocate-General Sir Gordon Slynn returned to the attack. He invoked the conclusion of Advocate-General Verloren Van Themaat in the earlier case involving Italy: 'a collective bargaining agreement is not a "method" for implementing a directive under Article 189 of the Treaty'.[14] He also cited the text of the Directive in question (Directive 77/187), which, following the language normally used in Directives, specified implementation through laws, regulations or administrative provision – not mentioning collective agreements.[15] Despite this, the Court cited its own judgment in *Commission of the European Communities* v. *Kingdom of Denmark* and reiterated that:[16]

> it must be remembered that, as the Court held in its judgment of 30 January 1985 in Case 143/83 (*Commission* v. *Denmark* [1985] ECR 427), it is true that the Member States may leave the implementation of the social policy objectives pursued by a directive in this area in the first instance to management and labour. That possibility does not, however, discharge them from the obligation of ensuring that all workers in the Community are afforded the full protection provided for in the directive. The State guarantee must cover all cases where effective protection is not ensured by other means.

The substantive logic received a further impulse in *Commission of the European Communities* v. *French Republic*.[17] The Commission challenged the French government's delegation to the social partners of the task of amending agreements violating the provisions of Directive 76/207 on equal treatment. This time Advocate-General Sir Gordon Slynn argued that 'it was not sufficient to leave it to labour and management without specific requirements as to the time or methods of enforcement'.[18] Moreover, he pointed out, 'There is no State guarantee of effective enforcement of the principle of equality should the negotiation process between the two sides of industry fail.'[19] To support this he added:[20]

> The results of the legislation in practice demonstrate the absence of any effective State guarantee of compliance, notwithstanding the existence of a procedure for government approval of collective agreements. It appears that in 1983 in France 1,050 collective agreements were concluded in branches of working activity and 2,400 in individual undertakings. In 1984 the figures were 927 and 6,000 respectively. By contrast, only 16 collective agreements were renegotiated on a non-discriminatory basis.

Citing these figures, the Court concluded:[21]

> Such figures are extremely modest when compared with the number of collective agreements entered into each year in France ... The requirement that collective

---

[13] Case 235/84, [1986] ECR 2291.    [14] *Ibid.*, p. 2295.    [15] *Ibid.*
[16] *Ibid.*, p. 2302, paragraph 20.    [17] Case 312/86, [1988] ECR 6315.    [18] *Ibid.*, p. 6329.
[19] *Ibid.*    [20] *Ibid.*    [21] *Ibid.*, pp. 6637–8, paragraphs 20–3.

agreements must be approved and the possibility that they may be extended by the public authorities have therefore not led to a rapid process of renegotiation.

The French Government's argument that collective negotiation is the only appropriate method of abolishing the special rights in question must be considered in the light of that conclusion.

In that regard, it is enough to observe that, even if that argument were to be accepted, it could not be used to justify national legislation which, several years after the expiry of the period prescribed for the implementation of the directive, makes the two sides of industry responsible for removing certain instances of inequality without laying down any time-limit for compliance with that obligation.

It follows from those considerations that the French Government's argument that the task of removing special rights for women should be left to the two sides of industry working through collective negotiation cannot be accepted.

This case also illustrates the limitations of the litigation procedure. The figures cited do not indicate what proportion of agreements contained discriminatory clauses. The figure of sixteen agreements amended has to be assessed not against the total number of agreements, but against those containing clauses requiring amendment. Research by the French Commission Nationale de la Négociation Collective had produced reports on the number of agreements containing such clauses.[22] These indicated that relatively few contain clauses pertaining to equality. This puts the evaluation by the Court and the Advocate-General in a different light.

Subsequently, there has been a series of other decisions of the European Court reinforcing the substantive approach to collective agreements in the area of equal pay and equal treatment. Collective agreements are condemned if they make unequal provision for men and women,[23] provide for discriminatory criteria for pay calculations and lack transparency as regards pay determination.[24] Each case involved the Court making a close examination of the practical workings of a collective agreement. In each case it was the substance of the agreement that was condemned. But it was already clear by 1989 that collective agreements were formally acceptable as instruments for the implementation of Community law obligations.

## The acknowledgment by Council and Commission

This was evident in the Preamble to the Community Charter of Fundamental Social Rights of Workers of 1989:[25]

---

[22] Commission Nationale de la Négociation Collective, *Bilan Annuel de la Négociation Collective 1984, L'Egalité professionnelle entre les femmes et les hommes* (Ministère des Affaires Sociales et de l'Emploi, June 1985, mimeo), and similar reports published in following years.

[23] Case 170/84, *Bilka-Kaufhaus GmbH* v. *Karin Weber von Hartz* [1986] ECR 1607. Case 33/89, *Maria Kowalska* v. *Freie und Hansestadt Hamburg* [1990] ECR 3199.

[24] Case 109/88, *Handels og Kontorfunkionaerenes Forbund i Danmark* v. *Dansk Arbejdsgiverforening* [1989] ECR 3199.

[25] The text of the Charter is published in *Social Europe*, 1/90.

Whereas such implementation may take the form of laws, collective agreements or existing practices at the various appropriate levels and whereas it requires in many spheres the active involvement of the two sides of industry.

The Charter further declared in Article 27:

It is more particularly the responsibility of the Member States, in accordance with national practices, notably through legislative measures or collective agreements, to guarantee the fundamental social rights in this Charter.

The Commission followed suit. In proposals under the Action Programme to give effect to the Charter, it began to insert an implementation provision, which accords a role to collective bargaining.[26] Such proposals began to be approved by the Council of Ministers. For example:[27]

Member States shall adopt the laws, regulations and administrative provision necessary to comply with this Directive no later than 30 June 1993, or shall ensure by that date that the employers' and workers' representatives introduce the required provisions by way of agreement, the Member States being obliged to take the necessary steps at all times to guarantee the results imposed by this Directive.

Article 2(4) of the Agreement annexed to the Protocol on Social Policy of the Treaty on European Union, signed at Maastricht on 7 February 1992, stipulated:[28]

A Member State may entrust management and labour, at their joint request, with the implementation of directives ... In that case, it shall ensure that, no later than the date on which a directive must be transposed in accordance with Article 189, management and labour have introduced the necessary measures by agreements, the Member State concerned being required to take any necessary measure enabling it at any time to be in a position to guarantee the results imposed by that directive.

The Commission's Medium Term Social Action Programme 1995–7 provided:[29]

11.1.9 – implementation of Directives by collective agreements: in light of the European Court of Justice case law and the Agreement on Social Policy, and taking into account diverse national practices, the Commission will present a

---

[26] Proposal for a Council Directive on certain employment relationships with regard to distortions of competition, Article 6; COM(90) 228 final-SYN 280, Brussels, 13 August 1990. Proposal for a Council Directive concerning certain aspects of the organization of working time, Article 14; COM(90) 317 final-SYN 295, Brussels, 20 September 1990.

[27] Council Directive 91/533 of 14 October 1991 on an employer's obligation to inform employees of the conditions applicable to the contract or employment relationship. OJ 1991 L288/32, Article 9(1).

[28] This version was derived from the ETUC/UNICE/CEEP accord of 31 October 1991, and differs from that initially proposed by the Dutch Presidency: 'A Member State may entrust management and labour with the implementation of all or part of the measures which it has laid down in order to implement the directives adopted in accordance with paragraphs 2 and 3.' *Europe Documents* No. 1734, 3 October 1991, proposal for new Article 118(4). The present Article 137(3) EC is virtually identical to that agreed by the EU social partners.

[29] COM(95) 134 final, Brussels, 12 April 1995, paragraphs 11.1.9–11.1.10.

Communication addressing the entire area of implementation of Community directives by collective agreements. The Communication will also consider and reflect on ways and procedures to involve the social partners in the process of control of transposition and enforcement of Community law (1996).

11.1.10 A clause concerning implementation by collective agreements will be inserted in all future directives, where the issues may fall under the bargaining power of the social partners.

Article 137(3) EC provides the latest point of a long process whereby first individual Member States, then the European Court, then eleven Member States in Article 27 of the Community Charter, and finally the Council have formally recognised the role of collective bargaining in the implementation of EC labour law.

## Employment policy: post-1945 settlements and the Single European Market

The political and economic integration of Europe proceeds on a transnational basis. Political decisions have created a Single European Market for goods, services and capital. Labour, however, is the exception. Despite the guarantees of free movement, the economic and political framework for labour markets continues to be national, not European. The consequences of this are many; not least, some economists argue that it prejudices the theoretical underpinnings of a successful single currency.

The foundations of the post-1945 settlements in the Member States included the overlapping elements of basic labour standards, full employment and a welfare state. The regulation of labour markets in the context of these settlements was undertaken by political authorities and the social partners, organisations of employers and trade unions, to varying degrees in different Member States.

Confronted with the emergence of the Single European Market, these foundations of the post-1945 settlements are threatened, and national political authorities and social partners appear inadequate. The European Union has belatedly begun to address the question of the legal and institutional architecture required to re-establish these foundations on a European basis: the European 'social model'.

At EU level, the emerging legal and institutional architecture includes the historic Agreement on Social Policy annexed to the Protocol on Social Policy of the Maastricht Treaty on European Union (TEU), now incorporated into Articles 136–9 of the EC Treaty by the Treaty of Amsterdam, and a new Employment Title, also inserted into the EC Treaty (Articles 125–30) by the Amsterdam Treaty. The resulting 'social dialogue' of the social partners, and the 'European Employment Strategy' (EES) aim to produce basic labour standards and reduce unemployment, policies often overlapping with welfare state provision.

## A belated policy response: employment is the priority

The Presidency Conclusions of the Lisbon European Council of 23–24 March 2000 began with the heading: 'Employment, Economic Reform and Social Cohesion'. The Council laid down an 'overall strategy' which aimed at 'modernising the European social model, investing in people and combating social exclusion' (paragraph 5). In particular (paragraphs 6–7):

> This strategy is designed to enable the Union to regain the conditions for full employment and to strengthen regional cohesion in the European Union. The European Council needs to set a goal for full employment in Europe in an emerging new society which is more adapted to the personal choices of women and men ... Implementing this strategy will be achieved by improving the existing processes, introducing a new open method of coordination at all levels, coupled with a stronger guiding and coordinating role for the European Council to ensure more coherent strategic direction and effective monitoring of progress. A meeting of the Council to be held every Spring will define the relevant mandates and ensure that they are followed up.

In the Joint Employment Report (JER) 2000, Part I: The European Union, the Commission concluded (p. 13):

> In order to implement the Lisbon strategy, no new processes in addition to those already in force – the Broad Economic Policy Guidelines, Luxembourg, Cardiff, Cologne – will be required. Instead, policy-making at the EU level in a number of areas – innovation, economic reform, education and training, social protection – will be strengthened by the adoption of an open method of co-ordination, based on guidelines, benchmarks and systematic monitoring. This method is now consolidated within the European Employment Strategy.

In accordance with the conclusions of the Lisbon Council, under the heading 'Employment, Economic Reform and Social Cohesion', the Swedish Presidency hosted the first European Council in spring 2001, the task of which was to define relevant mandates on employment policy. This was to seek to formulate a consensus on the objectives of the EES with respect to economic policy at national and Community levels; in the words of the conclusions of the Lisbon Summit, 'to ensure more coherent strategic direction and effective monitoring of progress'.

## The institutional implications of employment policy

As was manifest at the Lisbon European Council, employment is one of the most important areas of concern of the EC, unemployment being perceived as one of the most serious problems facing the European economy. The EES is the policy response. Critical discussion often focuses on the substantive content of the EES, and the economic theory or theories behind it. At least as important are the institutional implications of the EES.

The institutional structure of the EES is encapsulated in Article 128 EC. The Council and Commission formulate an annual joint report put to the European

Council, which adopts conclusions and draws up guidelines which the Member States 'shall take into account in their employment policies'. Each Member State is to make an annual report on 'the principal measures taken to implement its employment policy in the light of the guidelines for employment' (the National Action Plan). This goes to the Council and Commission which prepare a joint report to the European Council of that year, which, on the basis of proposals by the Commission, may make (non-binding) recommendations to Member States concerning their employment policies.

The social partners were from the beginning also called upon to play a major role in the process of the EES:[30]

> The social partners need to be more closely involved in drawing up, implementing and following up the appropriate guidelines.

This was reinforced at the following Feira Council which invited the social partners 'to play a more prominent role in implementing and monitoring the Guidelines which depend on them'.[31]

The institutional process of employment and labour market policy was dynamic in the sense not only of its operation, but in terms of its structure, as macro-economic policy-making joined with employment policy-making in annual joint summits beginning in spring 2001 under the Swedish Presidency.

In light of this, it was a matter of concern that the Intergovernmental Conference (IGC) which was to convene at Nice in December 2000 reflected on the reform of the institutional structures of the EC – numbers of Commissioners, decision-making in the Council – particularly in light of the prospect of enlargement and expansion of the number of Member States, but did not address the unique institutional architecture of EU social policy. That architecture was also in need of analysis, assessment and reform. Its legal and institutional architecture was quite different from that applicable to the regulation of goods, services and capital in the Single European Market. The institutions and actors and their roles, the nature of the processes of social dialogue and employment policy coordination, and the legal quality of the measures that emerge are singular.

A striking failure of the IGC of 2000, and subsequent institutional reviews, was that it ignored the established machinery of EC decision and policy-making in the sphere of social and labour law. There appears to be – in the case of certain Member States, understandable in terms of their political complexion and ideology, but less understandable in others – an unwillingness, at different levels and by different Member States, to recognise, embrace or promote the revolutionary institutional mechanism of social and labour policy-making created by the Maastricht Treaty's Protocol and Agreement on Social Policy,

---

[30] Lisbon Presidency Conclusions, paragraph 28.

[31] Commission Proposal for a Council Decision on guidelines for Member States' employment policies for the year 2001, Explanatory Memorandum, p. 3.

incorporated into the EC Treaty (Articles 136–9) by the Treaty of Amsterdam (the 'Social Chapter').

The social policy legislative process begins with the obligatory consultation of the social partners by the Commission in two stages, when the social policy is first being developed and at the stage of an actual proposal. There is then envisaged the possibility of the social partners undertaking a social dialogue which may produce an agreement to be put by the Commission to the Council for a decision (usually transforming the framework agreement into a directive).

The results of the social dialogue demonstrate the inescapable link between the activity of the social partners producing these framework agreements and the EES. The substantive content of agreements on parental leave, part-time and fixed-term work, and, until its failure, the social dialogue on agency workers, is closely related to the EES, with its concern, in particular, with job creation and the development of new forms of work. One example: the framework agreements encourage part-time work and discourage fixed-term work, a clear policy promoting specific forms of employment and not others.

The central question is: what are the actual and potential relationships between the legal and institutional structures of the European Employment Strategy, on the one hand, and EU social and labour policy on the other?

## Regulatory competition and cooperation

Competition between regulatory frameworks may arise not only between levels (subsidiarity), but also between wholly different institutional frameworks (as within the Social Chapter itself, Articles 136–9 EC, between legislation and social dialogue). The EES constitutes an additional institutional framework in the competition. The shift of terrain to another area of substantive policy, employment rather than social and labour policy, is accompanied by a shift of institutional framework, from legislation and social dialogue to 'open method of coordination.'

Problems arise when the actors in the other regulatory frameworks are excluded or marginalised in the new structure, but do not vacate the policy territory, especially where there are substantive policy overlaps (as in the regulation of forms of employment; e.g. part-time, fixed-term, agency work).

Competition between levels of regulation may also arise, as when the regulatory terrain shifts from the EU to the Member States. Norms formulated at EU level may be so vague as to leave effective policy-making to actors at Member State level. Social partners may be mobilised, but primarily or only at Member State level. Institutional machinery for monitoring at EU level may be ineffective, leaving Member States free to implement norms as they please.

The adoption of legal instruments and measures at EU level to address labour market issues occurred against the backdrop of experience in the Member States of national strategies on the economic problems of the labour market and unemployment. In particular, this experience took the form of 'social' or 'employment' pacts involving the social partners. The legal and institutional qualities of national experiences are important both for their contribution to the development of instruments and measures at EU level, and also because the EES interacts with national institutional structures directed at the achieving the same objectives.

These national employment strategies, often involving tripartite social or employment pacts between the social partners and public authorities, present a number of features of potential relevance to the EES. For example, such pacts at national level are not aimed solely at the labour market but include aspects of the social security system, fiscal reforms, education and training policies and broader macro-economic policy. Transposed to EU level, this would greatly enrich the agenda of the EU social dialogue.

Again, tripartite social pacts highlighted the importance of industrial relations systems being integrated, with articulation between levels of collective bargaining, so that agreements reached at centralised level (national, sectoral) would be easily implemented and monitored. Integrated systems such as those in Belgium and Ireland are favourably compared with the extreme decentralisation prevailing in the United Kingdom.

The legal and institutional qualities of national experience, in terms of formal, but also informal structures and processes, and the use of legal, but also quasi-legal instruments and measures, indicate possibilities for similar structures, processes, instruments and measures at EU level. Formal legal measures such as directives may be appropriate for certain aspects of the EES, but not for others, such as certain aspects of work organisation. The open coordination procedure of the EES could draw on national experience, just as, in some Member States, public authorities and the social partners were drawing on the EES Guidelines in formulating their ideas and vocabulary.[32]

The social partners within the Member States, called upon to play an important part in the EES, are, in many cases, also the protagonists of analogous strategies adopted on a tripartite basis at national level. The social partners could attempt, where possible, to link up and coordinate aspects of the EES which are complementary with national social or employment pacts. The European Council and the Commission, in formulating the Guidelines under the EES, could seek to coordinate the Guidelines with national experience and ensure that review of the application of specific Guidelines takes into account the development of social pacts in a particular national context.[33]

---

[32] For example, the German 'Alliance for Jobs' included a steering committee, a group of experts for benchmarking, working groups on specific issues such as tax and pension reform, and expert groups on specialist issues such as biotechnology. It resembled a form of modern programme management as much as legal implementation of an employment strategy.

[33] For example, the absence of representatives of interest groups apart from the traditional social partners is often felt to be a deficiency. Employment policy requires consideration of societal

Regulatory competition features in the literature on tripartite 'employment pacts' at national level, bolstered by various institutional constellations involving the social partners. On the one hand, the thesis of 'competitive corporatism' implies the seeking of national competitive advantage through corporatist national pacts. On the other hand, a role for the social partners in the process of the EES raises the prospect that a form of regulatory cooperation at EU level, 'cooperative corporatism', could emerge.

The institutional structures and operational mechanics of the EES and the EU social dialogue can be examined with a view to the potential for their integration or, at least reconciliation. However, the novelty of the processes concerned needs to be borne in mind. They commenced relatively recently: 1997 in the case of the EES, 1993, when the EU social dialogue under the Maastricht Protocol and Agreement on Social Policy came into effect. There is considerable uncertainty as to their evolution, which renders the prospect of integration or reconciliation contingent at best, and vulnerable to developments.[34] Nonetheless, an effort may be made to envisage how the EES fits with the institutional structure of EC social and labour law.

## The institutional role of the social partners in labour law and employment policy

The feature which both have in common, and which is the most striking, is the role of the social partners. Social dialogue is a prominent feature of the rhetoric of the EES. But, in contrast with the Maastricht legislative procedure for social and labour law, *the social dialogue is not mentioned and the social partners are only marginally situated in the institutional structure of the EES*. The social partners are only referred to indirectly in the Treaty's Employment Title (Articles 125–30).[35]

structures of service provision, especially public services, often territorially based. NGOs may also be important providers of services in local, regional and national economies.

[34] For a critical view, see Michel Gold, Peter Cressey and Evelyne Léonard, 'Whatever Happened to Social Dialogue? From Partnership to Managerialism in the EU Employment Agenda', (2007) 13 *European Journal of Industrial Relations* 7–25.

[35] Thus, Article 126(2) EC: 'Member States, having regard to national practices related to the responsibilities of management and labour, shall regard promoting employment as a matter of common concern and shall coordinate their action in this respect within the Council, in accordance with the provisions of Article 128'. The phrase 'having regard' seems to refer only to social partners at national, not EU level; and it is unclear how this regard relates to promoting employment; in some Member States, the social partners enjoy some prerogatives in this field. More important is Article 127(2), whereby the Council draws up annual guidelines 'On the basis of the conclusions of the European Council … on a proposal from the Commission and after consulting the European Parliament, the Economic and Social Committee, the Committee of the Regions and the Employment Committee'. *There is no mention of the social partners*. Article 130 concerns the newly established Employment Committee: 'with advisory status to promote coordination between Member States on employment and labour market policies. The tasks of the Committee shall be: – to monitor the employment situation and employment policies in the Member States and the Community; – without prejudice to Article 207 [COREPER], to formulate opinions at the request of either the Council or the Commission or on its own

In contrast to their invisibility in the *institutional* structure of the EES, the social dialogue and the social partners feature regularly in the *political* rhetoric accompanying the EES. The documents and declarations are full of exhortations to the social partners. What is not clear is how the demand for their active role is consistent with their lack of an institutional basis in the EES.

The assertion of an active labour market policy was a major Community achievement. However, it requires closer scrutiny as regards its institutional implications.[36] The rhetoric of the Member States and EU institutions appears to reflect awareness of the risk that the associated institutional structures of social partnership are a prerequisite for success of the EES. Yet the evidence in the practice of the EES does not appear to bear this out. The emphasis in the Guidelines on employability and entrepreneurship contains only marginal references to the social partners. That on adaptability, most closely associated with social dialogue, is characterised by the Joint Employment Reports as the most disappointing. Apart from rhetorical appeals to voluntary action by enterprises and other social actors, the primary mechanisms for achievement of the Guidelines appear to be incentives linked to tax and social security – both firmly in the grip of the Member States.

The disparity between the institutional position of the social partners in the Employment Title and the Social Chapter is fundamental. Although the evolution of the EES has to some extent accommodated the social partners in its operational workings, the question remains whether this can compensate for their absence in the Employment Title.

## Comparing institutional dynamism in the EES and the EU social dialogue

The disparity between the strong institutional position of the social partners in the Social Chapter and their relative weakness in the Employment Title is highlighted by the contrast between the relative dynamism of the two processes, which is far stronger as regards the EES.

The Commission plays a key role in the EU social dialogue. In the absence of the conventional pressures available in the balance of forces which characterise collective bargaining or social dialogue in the Member States, the EU social dialogue is highly contingent on the dynamic of 'bargaining in the shadow of

initiative, and to contribute to the preparation of the Council proceedings referred to in Article 128. In fulfilling its mandate, the Committee shall consult *management and labour*.' But the social partners are not members of the Committee: 'Each Member State and the Commission shall appoint two members of the Committee.'

[36] For example, it is reminiscent of the active labour market policy adopted for the coal and steel sector in the European Coal and Steel Treaty. However, that Treaty integrated the social partners closely in the institutions engaged in the active labour market policy, albeit on a sectoral basis. They were even represented in the High Authority! Again, the significant Swedish contribution to the achievement of the Employment Title is linked with that country's reputation for successful active labour market policy – but cannot be disconnected from that country's equally well-earned reputation for highly developed social partnership.

the law'. The institutional structure of the process laid down in the Social Chapter presupposes two main dynamic elements: first, Commission initiatives, which may be taken up by the social partners; secondly, the social partners, and, in particular, the EU employers' organisations, will be induced to enter into a social dialogue only if they anticipate the alternative being EU legislation.

Neither of these dynamic elements is notable at the present time. The original dynamic of 'bargaining in the shadow of the law' has faded with the decline of the Commission as an initiating force in social policy. There is, and has been for some time, an absence of Commission legislative initiatives which could serve to stimulate the EU social dialogue. This is reflected in the unwillingness of employer organisations to enter into dialogue, manifested in the twice-repeated refusal to enter into dialogue on the Information and Consultation Directive, or to actively respond to, let alone propose alternatives to the ETUC's agenda for EU social dialogue.

The contrast between the Commission's role in the EU social dialogue and in the EES is sharp. The Commission (particularly D-G V under its former Director-General Alan Larsson) invested huge efforts in the development of the EES and the achievement of the new Employment Title was a spectacular success. The follow-up process was impressive, evident in the ability of the Commission to present Guidelines in the immediate aftermath of the adoption of the Amsterdam Treaty in 1997, long before it came into effect. The results are that the EES has produced repeated annual sets of Employment Guidelines and there have been regular cycles of National Action Plans, Joint Employment Reports and Recommendations following the coming into force of the Amsterdam Treaty on 1 May 1999.

These achievements appear impressive. However, parallel to its paralysis in social dialogue, the EES also reflects a decline in Commission status even in the EES. The seizure by the Member States in the European Council of the political initiative is, in part, reflected in the institutional structure of the EES, where the Commission is jointly tied to the Council in the preparation of a joint report, on which basis the Council decides on Guidelines, albeit proposed by the Commission. Based on scrutiny of the National Action Plans, the Commission may propose recommendations, but again these are based on the joint Commission/Council report.

## Mutual reinforcement of the EES and EU social and labour law?

The EU's most significant institutional contribution to social policy – the creation and development of EU social dialogue – is marginalised *in* the EES. Similarly, the EU social dialogue risks becoming marginalised *by* the EES. The emphasis so far has been on the (disappointing) role of the social dialogue in the EES. If the social partners are marginalised in the EES, the scenario of a withering away of the EU social dialogue becomes more likely. On the other hand, a revival of the EU social dialogue could serve not only to assist the success of the EES, but also assist the evolution of EU social and labour law, a vital component of the EU social dimension.

It might have been assumed that the EU social dialogue (intersectoral or sectoral) would be *a*, if not *the* primary contribution of the social partners to the EES. After all, the EU intersectoral framework agreements on part-time and fixed-term work (and sectoral agreements on working time in the sectors excluded from the Working Time Directive) demonstrated the potential of the social partners to regulate the labour market, with the Community's objectives on employment explicitly in mind.

However, it appears that the primary, if any, social partner engagement in the EES (whatever the rhetoric) is at national or sub-national levels. This is evident in the way implementation of the Guidelines is perceived as being primarily at national, local or enterprise level. Employers' organisations (UNICE/ BusinessEurope) emphasise the impact of what is being done voluntarily, usually at enterprise level. This outcome reduces the EU-level social dimension by emphasising action at national, local or enterprise level.

It is suggested that the EES offers an institutional framework that could reinforce EU social dialogue, which, in turn, would assist the success of the EES. The challenge is to develop an institutional design which would graft on to the 'open method of coordination' process of the EES the social partners' involvement in various forms (EU-level intersectoral and sectoral dialogue). Four suggestions will be put forward by way of illustration.

First, the institutional structure could easily accommodate the EU social partners' involvement in the elaboration and implementation of Guidelines. Article 128(2) currently gives them no role whatsoever in the elaboration of the Guidelines formulated at EU level. Yet the Social Chapter, in Article 138(2), requires the Commission 'before submitting proposals in the social policy field [to] consult management and labour on the possible direction of Community action'. Such consultation would be mandatory if this was a proposal related, for example, to 'the integration of persons excluded from the labour market' (Article 137(1)(h)). It is not at all clear that proposals concerning Employment Guidelines are exempt from this requirement. If this vital procedural requirement has been ignored, the whole process could be at risk of judicial nullification.

Secondly, Member States' elaboration and implementation of the National Action Plans envisaged by Article 128(3) do not refer at all to the social partners. Yet this would seem to be an obvious requirement, evident in the numerous tripartite social or employment pacts negotiated in Member States. The interaction of these national experiences with the EES is obvious: their success (in Denmark, the Netherlands, Ireland) was one of the inspirations for the EES. By institutionally engaging the social partners in the formulation of National Action Plans, the EES could inspire social pacts on employment. The existing articulation between the social partners at national level with their EU-level organisations would greatly benefit the process of implementation of Guidelines formulated with the participation of the EU-level organisations and implemented with the participation of their affiliates in the Member States.

Thirdly, the Employment Guidelines could go well beyond their existing modest remit in encouraging social partners' involvement. Yet there appears to be, at first, some hesitancy and even some regression.[37] Guidelines could indicate procedural as well as substantive targets; for example, along the lines of requirements of information and consultation at enterprise level already in the *acquis communautaire*. The role of incentive measures envisaged by Article 129 could be influential.[38]

Finally, there should be noted the developments in the coordination of collective bargaining across national borders. Does coordination through the OMC process have anything to teach us regarding the prospects of coordination of national bargaining? Could there be an equivalent to Guidelines, National Action Plans, Review and Recommendations applied to collective bargaining in the Member States, perhaps at sectoral level? Could the EES process interact with coordinated bargaining to their mutual benefit? Social partners (if employers were willing) would thus assume their much touted role in the EES in the form of coordinated collective bargaining and agreements on EES issues (adaptability, but also employability, linking dialogue on vocational training and equal opportunities), but also other issues, such as wage demands. It is precisely the linkage of such qualitative demands with wage demands which provided the key to success of employment pacts in some Member States.

---

[37] For example, the first Guidelines of 1998, under Pillar I ('Improving Employability'), included Guideline 4 under the rubric of 'Encouraging a partnership approach': 'the social partners are *urged*, at their various levels of responsibility and action, to *conclude* as soon as possible *agreements* with a view to increasing the possibilities for training, work experience, traineeships or other measures likely to promote employability'. In contrast, under Pillar III ('Encouraging Adaptability in Business and their Employees'), under the rubric 'Modernizing work organization', Guideline 13 merely stated 'the social partners are *invited to negotiate*, at appropriate levels, in particular at sectoral and enterprise levels, agreements to modernize the organization of work'. The same formulation was repeated in the 1999 Guidelines. However, the Guidelines for 2000, while keeping the formula under Pillar I (now Guideline 5), proposed to change the formula under Pillar III so that Guideline 16 read: 'The social partners are *urged to agree and implement a process* in order to modernise the organisation of work.' In contrast, the Guidelines for 2001 altered the emphasis under Pillar I to highlight the role of benefits, taxes and training systems. The reference to the social partners in Guideline 7 is much reduced: 'Member States will, as appropriate with the social partners, step up their efforts to identify and prevent emerging bottlenecks.' Guideline 14 under Pillar III, though preceded by a paragraph claiming that 'a strong partnership should be developed at all appropriate levels (European, national, sectoral, local and enterprise levels)', continues: 'The social partners are *invited to negotiate* and implement at all appropriate levels agreements to modernise the organisation of work'.

[38] On 25 July 2000, the Commission adopted a cooperation incentive package to boost the employment strategy. This aimed to provide financial incentives by creating the legal basis for funding in the area of mainstreaming equal opportunities across the employment field. The role of Commission funding in developing and spreading the organisation of European works councils is a reminder of the potential of such funding.

In sum: the EES could be institutionally accommodated to the EU social dialogue with a view to their mutual reinforcement. To posit one scenario: Guidelines could emerge from an EU-level social dialogue between EU social partners with mandates from affiliated social partners drawing on experience of national employment pacts, or following on from proposals by the Commission. Affiliated social partners at Member State level could produce National Action Plans to implement the Guidelines embodied in EU framework agreements. The Commission and Council could review and report on implementation and supplement this with recommendations in the form of EU legislative proposals where implementation was inadequate.

## Conclusion

The role of the social partners in the EES has been strongly and continuously advocated by the Member States and the EU institutions.[39] However, greater responsibilities of the social partners can only be achieved with considerably greater support, both financial and political, on the part of both Member States and the EU institutions. Financial support is necessary to equip the social partners with the capacity to undertake the tasks specified. Political support is required to encourage the social partners to cooperate in the achievement of the tasks, but also to secure that national administrations fully and wholeheartedly embrace the participation of the social partners at all stages of the Luxembourg process, from the formulation of Guidelines, to their implementation through National Action Plans, through to the evaluation of the National Action Plans by the EU institutions.

The European Council should formally require both Member States and EU institutions to respect their obligations to support the social partners. Failure to provide this support renders calls for action by the social partners mere rhetoric, and is mirrored in the failures of the EES.

---

[39] For example, the Guidelines for 2001 reiterated these appeals, beginning with a statement of 'horizontal objectives' which includes, in paragraph C, an invitation 'to identify the issues upon which they will negotiate and report regularly on progress'. Under the Adaptability pillar, in Guideline 14, this is made even more explicit: 'Within the context of the Luxembourg Process, the social partners are invited to report annually on which aspects of the modernisation of the organisation of work have been covered by the negotiations as well as the status of their implementation and impact on employment and labour market functioning'. In paragraph E of the horizontal objectives, it is stated: 'The Social Partners should develop appropriate indicators and benchmarks and supporting statistical databases to measure progress in the actions for which they are responsible.'

# Chapter 15

# Individual judicial enforcement of European labour law

## Introduction

The development of a model whereby EC labour law could be enforced by individuals seeking redress before national tribunals and courts – a judicial liability model – could have followed one of at least two tracks. Enforcement of EC law could have been left entirely to *national* law. The national system of remedies, procedures and sanctions could have been exploited to maximise the enforcement of substantive EU labour law rights. Building on the foundation of these purely national remedies, procedures and sanctions, an effort might be made to develop certain minimum standards of enforcement.

Alternatively, the attempt might be made to create an entirely original form of judicial liability system, developing a new *EU* law on remedies, procedures and sanctions, to which national law must conform. This solution would require the EU institutions to prescribe a system of harmonised rules on enforcement covering remedies, procedures and sanctions. The legislative organs of the EU have refused to do so; there is lacking a consensus among Member States that this is either necessary or desirable.

The consequence of the failure to develop a harmonised system of enforcement of EU labour law is, however, that there may be considerable diversity among Member States with regard to the efficacy of enforcement of generally applicable EU labour law norms. Those Member States with less efficacious remedies, more procedural restrictions, and weaker sanctions may better be able to avoid compliance with EU labour law by effectively reducing the likelihood of judicial redress for those benefiting from it, or the likelihood of liability of those subject to it.

The failure of the legislative organs of the EU to develop a judicial liability model has in some measure been compensated for by the efforts of the European Court of Justice to develop a role for the national judiciaries in securing enforcement of EC law, including labour law. Member State obligations regarding compliance with EC law are set out in Article 10 of the EC Treaty:

> Member States shall take all appropriate measures, whether general or particular, to ensure fulfilment of the obligations arising out of this Treaty or resulting from

action taken by the institutions of the Community. They shall facilitate the achievement of the Community's tasks.

They shall abstain from any measure which could jeopardize the attainment of the objectives of this Treaty.

One avenue for the enforcement of this obligation was through measures adopted by national governments in the Council of Ministers. Another could be through the EU's administration, the Commission, creating links with national administrations responsible for law enforcement. However, national judiciaries are also organs of the Member States, and, as such, incur responsibility for ensuring fulfilment of the Article 10 obligation. A third possibility, therefore, was the chain linking the European Court with national judiciaries through the Article 234 preliminary reference procedure. This could be used as a separate channel for developing rules concerning the enforcement of EU law.

The constitutional novelty of recasting national courts as part of a supranational judicial hierarchy, with the European Court at its apex, was a major enterprise. Article 234 contained the seeds of such an enterprise by providing that, on questions of EU law, *any* court or tribunal may:

> if it considers that a decision on the question is necessary to enable it to give judgment, require the Court of Justice to give a ruling thereon.

The undermining of national hierarchies by allowing lower courts to leapfrog higher levels was thus encouraged. The European Court was also situated within national hierarchies by virtue of the last paragraph of Article 234:

> Where any such question is raised in a case pending before a court or tribunal of a Member State, against whose decisions there is no judicial remedy under national law, that court or tribunal shall bring the matter before the Court of Justice.

These provisions were the constitutional basis allowing the European Court to adapt and develop remedies for EU labour law violations. The supremacy of EU law would allow for rules so developed to prevail over national rules which might restrict the enforcement of EU labour law, even where this meant that national legislation was to be ignored or supplemented, or new remedies created.

The disintegrative effects of such doctrines on national state structures – disrupting judicial hierarchies and constitutional linkages between the judicial, executive and legislative branches of Member States – may be seen as part of the catalytic effect of the emergence of a supranational entity.

The multiplier effect is evident in so far as EU law infiltrates domestic law through various doctrines: for example, the doctrine requiring domestic law to be interpreted consistently with EU law. So where such domestic law, permeated by EU law, is not adequately enforced, EU law on remedies, procedures and sanctions may be invoked to achieve the effectiveness required by EU law. The issue may be perceived as the engagement by the European Court of domestic courts in the enforcement of EU law; a subtle strategy of cooperation or co-optation or even seduction.

Naturally, this process has not been uncontroversial; in particular, where the judicial liability model for enforcing EU law has impinged directly on Member States. The prospect of empowering national courts to uphold liability of Member States for violations of EU law, perhaps in conditions where national law explicitly prohibits such liability under domestic law, has created anxiety among Member States.

There are many other dimensions which require closer attention. The technique adopted by the European Court of laying down EU law principles, but leaving the application of these principles to national courts is fraught with difficulty. EU labour law is no exception. For example, the European Court has laid down the principle that indirect discrimination is justifiable on objective grounds, which must, however, comply with the general principle of proportionality – but both objective grounds and proportionality are to be left for national courts to decide. Or that the doctrine of the direct effect of Directives is limited to emanations of the state, as defined by certain criteria, but that it is for national courts to apply these criteria in deciding whether a particular entity is an emanation of the state.

Nor has the ECJ always been consistent. For example, in the sensitive area of determining whether a transfer of economic activities constitutes an 'undertaking' so as to fall under the provisions of the Acquired Rights Directive, the ECJ's many twists and turns seemed finally to have resolved themselves in an approach which left to national courts the decision whether, using a number of criteria laid down in *Spijkers*,[1] the transfer in question was covered by EC law. However, in the *Helsinki Bus* case,[2] the ECJ seemed to ignore its earlier approach and arrogate to itself the decision on whether a particular set of economic facts (transfer of physical assets) was definitively an undertaking.

This chapter is concerned with the European Court's principles regarding the effective enforcement of EU labour law, where it has prescribed such principles regarding remedies, procedures and sanctions.

## A supranational judicial liability system

The starting point for enforcement of European labour law is the recognition of the supranational quality of EU labour law. This is a labour law which is not determined or confined by national jurisdictions. National rules on law enforcement continue to play *a*, perhaps, *the* major role. But the nature and quality of these national rules have been transformed by the infusion of rules having supranational origin: EU law.[3]

---

[1] *Jozef Maria Antonius Spijkers* v. *Gebroeders Benedik Abbatoir C.V. & Alfred Benedik en Zonen B.V.*, Case 24/85, [1986] ECR 1119.

[2] *Oy Liikeenne Ab* v. *Liskojarvi and Juntunnen*, Case 172/99, [2001] IRLR 171.

[3] A preliminary point to be emphasised is that the effort to develop a judicial liability model for enforcement of EU labour law is contingent on the existence of substantive labour law rights. Liability only arises where there are substantive EU law rights to be violated. There has to be an

This is something both fundamental and difficult to grasp. It requires a mental shift: from seeing domestic labour law as a *national* and autonomous system of rules and institutions, to seeing domestic labour law as *part* of a *transnational* system of rule-making and enforcement machinery comprising the institutions of the EU established by the Member States, including the UK.

The distinctive quality of the EC Treaty was defined by the European Court of Justice in *Van Gend en Loos*:[4]

> The objective of the EEC Treaty, which is to establish a Common Market, the functioning of which is of direct concern to interested parties in the Community, implies that this Treaty is *more* than an agreement which merely creates mutual obligations between the contracting States. This view is confirmed by the preamble to the Treaty which refers not only to government but to peoples. It is also confirmed more specifically by the establishment of institutions endowed with sovereign rights, the exercise of which affects Member States and also their citizens. Furthermore, it must be noted that that nationals of the States brought together in the Community are called upon to cooperate in the functioning of this Community through the intermediary of the European Parliament and the Economic and Social Committee.
>
> In addition the task assigned to the Court of Justice under Article 177[5], the object of which is to secure uniform interpretation of the Treaty by national courts and tribunals, confirms that the States have acknowledged that *Community law has an authority which can be invoked by their nationals before those courts and tribunals.*
>
> The conclusion to be drawn from this is that *the Community constitutes a new legal order of international law for the benefit of which the States have limited their sovereign rights*, albeit within limited fields, *and the subjects of which comprise not only Member States but also their nationals.* Independently of the legislation of Member States, *Community law therefore not only imposes obligations on individuals but is also intended to confer upon them rights* which become part of their legal heritage. These rights arise not only where they are expressly granted by the Treaty, but also by reason of obligations which the Treaty imposes in a clearly defined way upon individuals as well as upon the Member States and upon the institutions of the Community.

EU law right before there can be an attempt to exploit EU law to expand domestic remedies, procedures and sanctions to protect that right.

[4] *N.V. Algemene Transport- en Expeditie Onderneming van Gend & Loos and Nederlandse administratie der belastingen (Netherlands Inland Revenue Administration)* Case 26/62, [1963] ECR 1 (italics added).

[5] Now Article 234: 'The Court of Justice shall have jurisdiction to give preliminary rulings concerning: (a) the interpretation of this Treaty; (b) the validity and interpretation of acts of the institutions of the Community and of the ECB; (c) the interpretation of the statutes of bodies established by an act of the Council, where those statutes so provide. Where such a question is raised before any court or tribunal of a Member State, that court or tribunal may, if it considers that a decision on the question is necessary to enable it to give judgment, request the Court of Justice to give a ruling thereon. Where any such question is raised in a case pending before a court or tribunal of a Member State against whose decisions there is no judicial remedy under national law, that court or tribunal shall bring the matter before the Court of Justice.'

This principle of supranational law was reaffirmed by the European Court in *Costa* v. *ENEL*:[6]

> By contrast with ordinary international treaties, the Treaty has created its own legal system which, on the entry into force of the Treaty, became an integral part of the legal systems of the Member States and which their courts are bound to apply.

But the significance of the ruling that EU law could create enforceable legal rights for individuals in national courts was greatly magnified by the European Court ruling that precedence was to be accorded to EU law over domestic law. The Court not only characterised EU law as part of domestic law, it declared the *supremacy* of EU law over other domestic law:[7]

> The precedence of Community law is confirmed by Article 189[8], whereby a regulation 'shall be binding' and 'directly applicable in all Member States'. This provision, which is subject to no reservation, would be quite meaningless if a State could unilaterally nullify by means of a legislative measure which could prevail over Community law.

This goes beyond the incorporation into domestic law of certain rules. It means that rules may be created by EU institutions even where a Member State opposes such rules in those EU institutions. These rules must be enforced in domestic courts even where this involves overriding rules produced by domestic law-making institutions.

EU labour law rules take precedence over domestic labour law rules. This is well known in certain areas of substantive law, such as the law on sex discrimination, where domestic law has been shaped, and, in cases of conflict, has been repeatedly overridden, by EU law. Probably the best-known example of the impact of these rulings in labour law is the *Defrenne* case, where the European Court decided that:[9]

> The principle that men and women should receive equal pay, which is laid down by Article 119 [now 141], may be relied on before the national courts. These courts have a duty to ensure the protection of the rights which that provision vests in individuals, in particular in the case of those forms of discrimination which have their origin in legislative provisions.

The wider the range of competences of the EU institutions, the more the EU law they create will come to replace increasingly wide areas of domestic labour law.

---

[6] *Costa* v. *Ente Nazionale per l'Energia Elettrica (ENEL)*, Case 6/64, [1964] ECR 585.     [7] *Ibid.*

[8] Now Article 249: 'In order to carry out their task and in accordance with the provisions of this Treaty, the European Parliament acting jointly with the Council, the Council and the Commission shall make regulations and issue directives, take decisions, make recommendations or deliver opinions. A regulation shall have general application. It shall be binding in its entirety and directly applicable in all Member States. A directive shall be binding, as to the result to be achieved, upon each Member State to which it is addressed, but shall leave to the national authorities the choice of form and methods. A decision shall be binding in its entirety upon those to whom it is addressed. Recommendations and opinions shall have no binding force'.

[9] *G. Defrenne* v. *Sabena*, Case 43/75, [1976] ECR 455.

Indeed, the 'spill-over' effect makes it difficult to insulate most areas of domestic labour law from the influence of EU labour law.

Given that it may be applied in national courts, the doctrine of supremacy also applies to rules on enforcement of labour law, including remedies and procedures. EU law has developed special techniques and principles by which EU labour law may be enforced in national courts. Where EU enforcement requirements come into conflict with national procedures and remedies, again, they take precedence and must be applied by national courts overriding domestic rules.[10]

The techniques of enforcement of EC labour law in national courts include doctrines of 'direct' and 'indirect' effect and state liability. EC law has also developed principles concerning procedures and remedies available for violations of EC labour law which must be applied by national courts.

## Direct effect

Decisions of the European Court have attributed to Treaty Articles and regulations the legal quality of 'direct effect', their provisions being enforceable by individuals in national courts and taking precedence over domestic law. However, there was little labour law to be found in the Treaty, and that in Regulations was primarily concerned with free movement of workers. Most EC labour legislation takes the form of Directives. The decision of the European Court to extend the principle of direct effect to Directives was of crucial importance:[11]

> If, however, by virtue of the provisions of Article 189[12] regulations are directly applicable and, consequently, may by their very nature have direct effects, it does not follow from this that other categories of acts mentioned in that article can never have similar effects. It would be incompatible with the binding effect attributed to a directive by Article 189 to exclude, in principle, the possibility that the obligation which it imposes may be invoked by those concerned. In particular, where the Community authorities have, by directive, imposed on Member States the obligation to pursue a particular course of conduct, the *useful effect* of such an act would be weakened if individuals were prevented from

---

[10] Some spectacular instances have included the *Factortame* decision allowing interim remedies against the Crown contrary to domestic rules, the decision in *Marshall (No. 2)* abolishing the limits on compensation for sex discrimination in the UK legislation, and *BECTU*, where national legislation limiting the applicability of paid annual leave provisions of the EC's Working Time Directive were overridden. *R. v. Secretary of State for Transport, ex parte Factortame Ltd. and others*, Case C-213/89, [1990] ECR I-2433; *Marshall v. Southampton and South West Area Health Authority (No. 2)*, Case C-271/91, [1993] ECR I-4367; *Broadcasting, Entertainment, Cinematographic and Theatre Union (BECTU) v. Secretary of State for Trade and Industry*, Case C-173/99, [2001] ECR I-4881.

[11] *Yvonne van Duyn v. Home Office*, Case 41/74, [1974] ECR 1337 (italics added).

[12] Now Article 249 EC.

relying on it before their national courts and if the latter were prevented from taking it into consideration as an element of Community law …

Accordingly … (the provision in the Directive in question) confers on individuals rights which are enforceable by them in the courts of a Member State and which the national courts must protect.

The rationale for attributing direct effect to Directives was to secure the 'useful effect' (*effet utile*) of EC legislation. The preceding doctrines, that EC law was a new transnational legal order capable of conferring rights on individuals, produced an interpretation of Article 249 which emphasised the binding result to be achieved by the Directive, rather than leaving 'to the national authorities the choice of forms and methods'.

However, given that Directives were drafted with a view to prescribing 'the result to be achieved' rather than individual rights, the Court was cautious in treating them as always straightforwardly applicable law to be implemented by national courts:[13]

It is necessary to examine, in every case, whether the nature, general scheme and wording of the provision in question are capable of having direct effects on the relations between Member States and individuals.

In the case of the Directive in question the Court emphasised that:[14]

the provision lays down an obligation which is not subject to any exception or condition and which, by its very nature, does not require the intervention of any act on the part either of the institutions of the Community or of Member States.

The impulse to secure the effectiveness of EC law was the initial rationale for direct effect. But a different rationale soon emerged which, while upholding the applicability of the doctrine to Directives, had implications for its potential scope. The Court emphasised again, as regards a Directive as an act of EC law, that:[15]

the effectiveness of such an act would be weakened if persons were prevented from relying on it in legal proceedings and national courts prevented from taking it into consideration as an element of Community law.

Consequently a Member State which has not adopted the implementing measures required by the directive in the prescribed periods *may not rely*, as against individuals, *on its own failure* to perform the obligations which the directive entails.

It follows that a national court requested by a person who has complied with the provisions of a directive not to apply a national provision incompatible with the directive not incorporated into the internal legal order of a defaulting Member State, must uphold that request if the obligation in question is unconditional and sufficiently precise.

In terms of justifying direct effect of Directives, the 'effectiveness' (*effet utile*) rationale implied a general prospect of enforcement in national courts by

[13] *Ibid.*    [14] *Ibid.*
[15] *Pubblico Ministero* v. *Tullio Ratti*, Case 148/78, [1979] ECR 1629 (italics added).

individuals of rights granted by Directives. In contrast, the 'estoppel' (reliance on own failure) rationale appeared to imply a number of restrictions on this general prospect. It presupposes that the defendant in the action is the state,[16] that this defendant is a part of the state responsible for implementation of the Directive, and that the defendant has failed to perform its obligations in such a manner as to preclude it from denying the plaintiff's action.

These restrictions on the doctrine of direct effect as applied to Directives would confine its application to legal actions by citizens against the state – so-called 'vertical' direct effect. Enforcement of rights contained in Directives would not be allowed against private individuals ('horizontal' direct effect). This was finally made explicit in *Marshall (No. 1)*:[17]

> With regard to the argument that a directive may not be relied upon against an individual, it must be emphasized that according to Article 189 [now 249] of the EEC Treaty the binding nature of a directive, which constitutes the basis for the possiblity of relying on the directive before a national court, exists only in relation to 'each Member State to which it is addressed'. It follows that a directive may not of itself impose obligations on an individual and that a provision of a directive nay not be relied upon as such against such a person.

On the other hand, the state as respondent could appear in a number of guises:[18]

> it must be pointed out that where a person involved in legal proceedings is able to rely on a directive as against the State he may do so regardless of the capacity in which the latter is acting, whether employer or public authority. In either case it is necessary to prevent the State from taking advantage of its own failure to comply with Community law.

The scope of the different guises of the state depends on the criteria developed by the Court to define the state. These were laid down in *Foster* v. *British Gas*:[19]

> It follows from the foregoing that a body, whatever its legal form, which has been made responsible, pursuant to a measure adopted by the State, for providing a public service under the control of the State and has for that purpose special powers beyond those which result from the normal rules applicable in relations between individuals is included in any event among the bodies against which the provision of a directive capable of having direct effect may be relied upon.

Directives may confer directly enforceable rights on employees of the state. Such employees in EC labour law have the considerable advantage of being able to rely directly on provisions in EC directives as well as on national legislation. The scope of the definition of the state has the result that a considerable proportion of the national workforce is in this fortunate position.

---

[16] For the potential liability of national courts, as organs of the state, for failing to correctly apply EU law, see *Köbler* v. *Republik Österreich*, Case C-224/01, [2003] ECR I-1023.

[17] *M. H. Marshall* v. *Southampton and South West Hampshire Area Health Authority (Teaching)*, Case 152/84, [1986] ECR 723, paragraph 48.

[18] *Ibid.*, paragraph 49.    [19] Case C-188/89, [1990] ECR I-3313.

The potential scope of the definition of the state in EU law might not exclude privatised industries or services; for example, a private company in the now privatised water industry.[20] The legal form of the body is irrelevant, so long as it is responsible for providing a public service under the control of the state and has for that purpose special powers.

## Indirect effect

The discrepancy between employees of the state and employees of private employers in terms of their ability to claim rights under directives under the doctrine of direct effect has been partly remedied by the doctrine of 'indirect effect'. This achieves indirectly, through the technique of judicial interpretation of domestic law, the result obtainable through the doctrine of direct effect:[21]

> the Member States' obligation arising from a directive to achieve the result envisaged by the directive and their duty under Article 5 of the Treaty to take all appropriate measures, whether general or particular, to ensure the fulfilment of that obligation, is binding on all the authorities of Member States including, for matters within their jurisdiction, the courts. It follows that, in applying the national law and in particular the provisions of a national law specifically introduced in order to implement Directive No 76/207, national courts are required to interpret their national law in the light of the wording and the purpose of the directive in order to achieve the result referred to in the third paragraph of Article 189 [now 249].

The logic which dictated this result has been taken beyond the case of interpreting domestic legislation introduced to implement EU law:[22]

> It follows that, in applying national law, where the provisions in question were adopted *before or after* the directive, the national court called upon to interpret it is required to do so, *as far as possible*, in the light of the wording and the purpose of the directive in order to achieve the result pursued by the latter and thereby comply with the third paragraph of Article 189 [now 249] of the Treaty.

The UK courts have demonstrated varying degrees of willingness to follow this injunction where this would challenge traditional canons of statutory interpretation, such as the strict literal meaning of statutory language.[23] Seizing upon the discretion apparently granted to them, the House of Lords declared:[24]

> a national court must construe a domestic law to accord with the terms of a directive in the same field only if it is possible to do so. That means that the

---

[20] *Griffin & Ors.* v. *South West Water Services Limited* (1995) IRLR 15 (Ch.D.).

[21] *Von Colson and Kamann* v. *Land Nordhein-Westfalen*, Case 14/83, [1984] ECR 1891.

[22] *Marleasing* v. *Commercial Internacional de Alimentacion* Case C-106/89, [1990] ECR I-4135 (italics added).

[23] Contrast *Pickstone* v. *Freemans plc* [1991] AC 66 (HL) and *Litster* v. *Forth Dry Dock and Engineering Co. Ltd.* [1990] 1 AC 546 (HL) with *Duke* v. *GEC Reliances Ltd.* [1988] ICR 339 (HL).

[24] *Webb* v. *EMO Air Cargo Ltd.* [1993] ICR 165, per Lord Keith.

domestic law must be open to an interpretation consistent with the Directive whether or not it is also open to an interpretation inconsistent with it.

It seems that the European Court means the doctrine of indirect effect to go beyond a mere interpretive aid to domestic legislation. This emerged in *Coloroll Pension Trustees Ltd.* v. *Russell*:[25]

> national courts are bound to provide the legal protection which individuals derive from the direct effect of provisions of the Treaty … They are therefore bound, particularly in the context of Article 119 [now 141], to the full extent of their discretion under national law, to interpret and apply the relevant domestic provisions in conformity with the requirements of Community law and, where this is not possible, to disapply any incompatible domestic provisions.

Indirect effect can thus be seen both as an addition to and as the corollary of the doctrine of direct effect. In the case of EU laws having direct effect, as in the case of Article 141, but presumably also where provisions of directives have direct effect, and even where they do not the doctrine of indirect effect allows for national courts to disregard domestic law where interpretation cannot resolve a conflict between the directive and domestic law. This will be of vital importance to the enforcement of EU rights against private persons (horizontal direct effect), where domestic law is the only legal basis. In the case of provisions lacking direct effect, the interpretive effort must be made, but it is not certain how far the UK courts will go, nor how energetically the European Court will encourage them, in disregarding national legislation inconsistent with EU law.

## 'Horizontal' indirect effect

The doctrine of 'indirect effect' established by the European Court of Justice with respect to directives requires national courts to interpret national laws consistently with EC law. Recent developments in the doctrine illustrate its potential.[26]

The *Pfeiffer* case concerned the German legislation (Arbeitszeitgesetz) implementing the Working Time Directive 93/104/EC.[27] Article 3 of the Arbeitszeitgesetz specifies a working day of eight hours which may be prolonged to ten hours provided the average of eight hours' daily work is maintained. Article 7.1.1 allows for derogation from Article 3 by a collective agreement prolonging daily hours of work beyond ten hours. A collective agreement with the German Red Cross provided for such a prolongation so

---

[25] Case C-200/91, [1994] ECR I-4389.

[26] *Bernhard Pfeiffer et al. c. Deutsches Rotes Kreuz Kreisverband Waldshut eV*, joined Cases C-397/01 to C-403/01. Opinion of Advocate-General M. D. Ruiz-Jarabo Colomer, 6 May 2003. Second Opinion of 6 May 2004. ECJ decision, 5 October 2005.

[27] Council Directive 93/104/EC of 23 November 1993 concerning certain aspects of the organisation of working time; OJ L307/18 of 13 December 1993, as amended by Directive 2000/34 of 22 June 2000, OJ L195/41. Consolidated in Directive 2003/88/EC of 4 November 2003 concerning certain aspects of the organisation of working time; OJ L299/9 of 18 November 2003.

as to allow a working week exceeding forty-eight hours (Article 14.2 of the agreement). The questions referred to the ECJ under Article 234 EC included whether Article 6[28] of Directive 93/104 had direct effect so as to allow an individual to complain to a national court where the Member State has not correctly implemented the Directive.

In *Pfeiffer*, the Opinion of Advocate-General M. D. Ruiz-Jarabo Colomer of 6 May 2003 concluded that Article 6(2) of the Directive was sufficiently clear, precise and unconditional to have direct effect. However, the Advocate-General acknowledged that the ECJ has refused to allow an individual to rely on the direct effect of directives to make claims in national courts against other private individuals. Directives do not have so-called 'horizontal' direct effect.[29]

The Advocate-General then referred to the ECJ's doctrine of 'indirect' effect of directives, which requires a national court to interpret national law consistently with the objectives of the directive.[30] The Advocate-General argued that it follows that Article 6(2) of Directive 93/104 overrides Article 7.1.1 of the Arbeitszeitgesetz which allows a collective agreement to prolong the working day beyond ten hours, and Article 14 of the collective agreement must be interpreted so that the workers concerned are not required to work more than forty-eight hours on average.[31]

The new elements in the Advocate-General's reasoning appeared to be, first, that provisions of directives having direct effect must be taken into account by national courts, but *not only* when they are invoked in claims against Member States ('vertical' direct effect). Secondly, there is no 'horizontal' direct effect of directives, but the direct effect of directives means that *not only legislation*,[32] but *also other legal measures* (including *private law measures* such as collective agreements) based on a national law which contravenes directly effective provisions of a directive must be interpreted consistently with the directive. Finally, in contrast with the ECJ's view that national courts are *not* obliged to disapply national *legislation* where it is impossible to interpret it consistently with EC law,[33] the Advocate-General's view is that national courts *are* obliged to interpret *other legal measures* (here, collective agreements) consistently with the directive, where these other legal measures are based on national law which is inconsistent with directly effective provisions of a directive.

This appeared to be a new *Pfeiffer* doctrine of 'horizontal' (private law) indirect effect. National courts are obliged to interpret private law measures consistently with directly effective provisions of a directive, where these private law measures are based on national law which is inconsistent with the directly effective provisions of a directive.

---

[28] A maximum 48-hour working week.    [29] *Pfeiffer*, paragraphs 56–7.
[30] *Pfeiffer*, paragraph 58.    [31] *Pfeiffer*, paragraph 59.
[32] *Von Colson and Kamann* v. *Land Nordrhein-Westfalen*, Case 14/83, [1984] ECR 1891.
[33] *Marleasing SA* v. *La Comercial Internacionale de Alimentacion SA*, Case C-106/89, [1990] ECR I-4135.

This latter doctrine does not equate to horizontal direct effect. The effect of the directive is achieved through *interpretation* of the (intermediary) private law measure, which itself relies on the national legislation. The link between the directive and national legislation remains the central element, but it is achieved through indirect effect of the directive on the private law measure.

This doctrine has significant implications for European labour law. Contracts of employment are the most important private law measures in labour law. The *Pfeiffer* doctrine seems to state that contracts of employment, based on national law, must be interpreted consistently with the directly effective provisions of directives.

The Advocate-General presented his Opinion on 6 May 2003. In an unusual move, the Court issued an Order on 13 January 2004 reopening the procedure and transferring the case from the sixth Chamber to the Grand Chamber of the Court. An oral hearing for arguments was scheduled for 9 March 2004.

The ECJ's Order of 13 January 2003 provides some indications of why this unusual procedural step was taken. In particular, paragraph 9 emphasises the purpose of Directive 93/104, to protect workers as the weaker party to the employment contract, and adds that effective protection (*effet utile*) must be assured by both EU and national courts. In paragraph 10, the ECJ emphasises that the complaints based on Directive 93/104 are concerned with limiting daily working hours, not monetary compensation, making it difficult to launch a claim against the Member State for the harm caused by the violation of EC law.[34]

These factors indicate doctrinal concerns quite different from those of the Advocate-General. The ECJ's order highlights issues only of direct effect of directives (paragraphs 6–8). There is no reference to doctrinal questions concerned with indirect effect of directives. However, the implications of direct effect are placed in a general context of disputes between private parties (paragraphs 6–7), and specifically, in the employment context where one party, the worker, is in a weaker position.[35] In this context of directly effective provisions of a directive as regards a weaker private party, the ECJ focuses on the contrast between the remedy sought for the Member State's failure to implement the directive (limitation of working hours) and the remedy available under EU law.[36]

For the ECJ, the direct effect of the directive on national legislation continues to be essential. However, the collective agreement disappears from view, and the doctrine of indirect effect is not invoked. Instead, rather than resorting to the doctrine of indirect effect to resolve the problem, the ECJ looks to the alternative doctrinal source/inspiration of the *Francovich* case.

---

[34] *Francovich and Bonfaci* v. *Italy*, Cases C-6/90 and C-9/90, [1991] ECR I-5357.

[35] Paragraph 9: 'Ensuite, la directive 93/104 vise à protéger spécifiquement les travailleurs en tant qu'ils sont la partie faible au contrat de travail, protection dont l'effet utile doit être assuré par les jurisdictions tant communautaires que nationales.'

[36] Paragraph 10: compensation under *Francovich*.

The ECJ's order states:[37]

> the point at issue is whether, *having regard to the particular circumstances of these cases*, it is for the ECJ to define the consequences which national courts should apply when, in a dispute between private individuals, a provision of domestic law, adopted to transpose the rules laid down in a directive, is deemed incompatible with a provision of the latter in order for that provision to fulfil the requirements of producing direct effect.

The reference to '*the particular circumstances of these cases*' could refer to a number of factors, with important implications for the enforcement of rights and obligations in EU labour law. Individual employment protection through European labour law has the requisite qualities of weaker parties and a need for effective remedies which are of salience to the particular circumstances highlighted by the ECJ as requiring intervention by EU law.

The Grand Chamber (eleven judges) of the European Court of Justice handed down its decision in *Pfeiffer* on 5 October 2005. The Court reached the same conclusion as the Advocate-General, and appears to support the reasoning in the Advocate-General's Opinion.

## No horizontal direct effect of directives

Like the Advocate-General, the Court concludes that Article 6(2) of the Working Time Directive satisfies the criteria for direct effect (paragraph 104). As to the legal consequences of this, the Court affirms that it:[38]

> has consistently held that a directive cannot of itself impose obligations on an individual and cannot therefore be relied upon as such against an individual.

Hence:[39]

> It follows that even a clear, precise and unconditional provision of a directive seeking to confer rights or impose obligations on individuals cannot of itself apply in proceedings exclusively between private parties.

## Indirect effect of directives

However, the Court, referring to *Von Colson and Kamann* and Article 10 EC, adds:[40]

> It is the responsibility of the national courts in particular to provide the legal protection which individuals derive from the rules of Community law and to ensure that those rules are fully effective.

---

[37] My translation from the French: paragraph 3: '... telles que celles des affaires au principal, il y a lieu pour la Cour de préciser les conséquences que doivent tirer les jurisdictions nationales lorsque, dans le cadre d'un litige entre particuliers, une disposition du droit interne, adoptée aux fins de le point de savoir si, au regard de circonstances particulières transposer les règles édictées par une directive, s'avère incompatible avec une disposition de cette dernière pour autant que cette disposition remplit les conditions pour produire un effet direct.'

[38] *Pfeiffer*, paragraph 108.      [39] *Pfeiffer*, paragraph 110.      [40] *Pfeiffer*, paragraph 111.

This applies, *a fortiori*, to the case of:[41]

> domestic provisions which, as here, have been specifically enacted for the purpose of transposing a directive intended to confer rights on individuals.

It follows:[42]

> Thus, when it applies domestic law, and in particular legislative provisions specifically adopted for the purpose of implementing the requirements of a directive, the national court is bound to interpret national law, so far as possible, in the light of the wording and the purpose of the directive concerned in order to achieve the result sought by the directive.

This doctrine 'permits the national court ... to ensure the full effectiveness of Community law'.[43]

### Applying indirect effect beyond implementing legislation

Moreover[44] (italics added):

> Although the principle that national law must be interpreted in conformity with Community law concerns chiefly domestic provisions enacted in order to implement the directive in question, it does not entail an interpretation merely of those provisions but requires the national court to consider *national law as a whole* in order to assess to what extent it may be applied so as not to produce a result contrary to that sought by the directive.

### Applying interpretive methods recognised by national law

Crucially[45] (italics added):

> In that context, if the application of *interpretative methods recognised by national law* enables, in certain circumstances, a provision of domestic law to be construed in such a way as to avoid conflict with another rule of domestic law or the scope of that provision to be restricted to that end by applying it only in so far as it is compatible with the rule concerned, the national court is *bound* to use those methods in order to achieve the result sought by the directive.

The 'interpretative methods recognised by national law' must be applied equally to safeguard EU law. If a rule of national law would prohibit contracts of employment derogating from legislative minimum standards, that interpretive method must accord the same status to EU law, to prohibit contracts of employment derogating from EU legislation[46] (italics added):

> In this instance, the principle of interpretation in conformity with Community law requires the referring court to do *whatever lies within its jurisdiction*, having regard to the *whole body of rules of national law*, to ensure that Directive 93/104 is

---

[41] *Pfeiffer*, paragraph 112.   [42] *Pfeiffer*, paragraph 113.   [43] *Pfeiffer*, paragraph 114.
[44] *Pfeiffer*, paragraph 115.   [45] *Pfeiffer*, paragraph 116.   [46] *Pfeiffer*, paragraphs 118–119.

fully effective, in order to prevent the maximum weekly working time laid down in Article 6(2) of the directive from being exceeded …

   Accordingly, it must be concluded that, when hearing a case between individuals, a national court is required, when applying the provisions of domestic law adopted for the purpose of transposing obligations laid down by a directive, to consider the *whole body of rules of national law* and to interpret them, *so far as possible*, in the light of the wording and purpose of the directive in order to achieve an outcome consistent with the objective pursued by the directive … the national court must thus do whatever lies within its jurisdiction to ensure that the maximum period of weekly working time, which is set at 48 hours by Article 6(2) of Directive 93/104, is not exceeded (para. 119).

This seems to adopt at EU level a principle common to many continental labour law systems whereby standards laid down in legislation or collective agreements cannot be derogated from by individual contracts of employment. The principle is now extended to EU directives: provisions in contracts of employment cannot derogate from the standards laid down by directives.[47]

### The ECJ v. the Advocate-General

It may be that there is a subtle difference between the doctrine enunciated in the Court's judgment and the Opinion of the Advocate-General. *Both* are clear that national legislation, specifically that implementing a directive, must be interpreted consistently with the directive, 'so far as possible'. The Advocate-General may be read as importing an *EU rule of interpretation* requiring that courts interpret other (private law) measures consistently with a directive, without qualification. The Court appears to say that EU law requires courts to use interpretive methods *recognised by national law*, and 'to use those methods in order to achieve the result sought by the directive'.[48]

   As a general rule, national laws of the Member States accept the principle that private law contracts cannot derogate from legislative minimum guarantees. This is the norm in labour law. There is no qualification that this rule applies in the interpretation of private law contracts only 'so far as possible'.

   EU law requires national *legislation* to be interpreted consistently with directives, but *only* so far as possible. Where this *is* possible, private law

---

[47] In contrast to other European labour laws, UK law only partially acknowledges this principle. The parties to a contract of employment cannot derogate from legislation, unless the legislation expressly so provides; the Working Time Regulations implementing the Directive being an example. However, this is not so for collective agreements, legally binding or otherwise. Individual contracts may alter the terms of collective agreements incorporated into individual contracts of employment.

[48] Paragraph 116: 'if the application of *interpretative methods recognised by national law* enables, in certain circumstances, a provision of domestic law to be construed in such a way as to avoid conflict with another rule of domestic law or the scope of that provision to be restricted to that end by applying it only in so far as it is compatible with the rule concerned, the national court is *bound* to use those methods in order to achieve the result sought by the directive'.

measures, including contracts, *must* be interpreted consistently with the directive/legislation, even where private law measures *cannot* be interpreted consistently with the directive. This is because of the domestic law rule that private law measures cannot derogate from/violate domestic legislation.

The protection offered by the directive is to the *weaker party* to the employment contract. Should 'horizontal direct effect' apply where directly effective provisions of directives aim to protect the weaker party in the employment context? This would be a doctrine of *effet utile* specific to EC labour law. Directives affording protection to workers can be invoked before national courts to override contracts of employment which are inconsistent with directives. They are an exception to the general rule precluding horizontal direct effect.

The lack of an *effective remedy* is of special concern in the case of violation of EC labour law directives. *Francovich*[49] only allows financial compensation against the state. *Factortame*[50] allowed for other (interim) remedies.[51] Another remedy would be to require national law to allow directly effective provisions of directives to override inconsistent contracts of employment.[52]

The *outcome* reached by the Court equates to that of the Advocate-General, even if the doctrinal route is somewhat different. Private law contracts of employment must be interpreted consistently with national legislation and directly effective provisions of directives – *even where such an interpretation of the contract is not possible*, providing interpretive methods recognised by national law support such an approach to contracts conflicting with legislation, as they do in labour legislation.

## The idiosyncratic position of the UK

The UK will be covered by this rule. But, not for the first time, the UK has its own idiosyncratic approach. While legislation prevails over individual contracts of employment, collective agreements do not automatically prevail. In so far as the

---

[49] *Francovich and Bonfaci v. Italy*, Cases C-6/90 and C-9/90, [1991] ECR I-5357.

[50] *R. v. Secretary of State for Transport, ex parte Factortame Ltd. and Others*, Case C-213/89, [1990] ECR I-2433.

[51] See Chapter 12 on the specific need for interim remedies in labour disputes, particularly those involving dismissals, where reinstatement or reengagement in employment, not compensation is the desired remedy.

[52] There is a final '*particular circumstance*' to this case: the presence of the *collective agreement*. It would be dangerous if the ECJ's conclusions were somehow confined to the case where national provisions allowed for derogations by collective agreement. This could take the form of requiring national courts to interpret *only* collective agreements (somehow analogous to legislation) consistently with directives. Even worse, following the *Francovich* line of reasoning, the ECJ might be tempted to allow claims for compensation against the authors of collective agreements (as with the Member State, the author of the legislation) which violate directly effective rights in a directive. Similarly, the violation by the EU or a Member State of a fundamental right guaranteed by EU Law (in the Treaty or, for example, in the EU Charter of Fundamental Rights) would very likely constitute a breach of EU law giving rise to liability under the *Francovich* principle.

EU measure is a directive, treated as equivalent to legislation, the UK position is the same as that in other Member States with a general principle of *'favor'* precluding derogation from the more favourable provision in legislation.[53]

This highlights a specific issue: the implications for EU social dialogue agreements, specifically, those not transformed into directives. As so-called 'voluntary' agreements, their ambiguous legal status in EU law could raise questions regarding the legal effects of individual contracts of employment which deviate from the standards laid down in such agreements.[54]

### An example: the UK's opt-out from the Working Time Directive

This new doctrine may be applied to a specific issue of considerable current interest: the derogation clause from Article 6(b) of the Working Time Directive whereby a Member State may choose not to apply Article 6, on condition, *inter alia*, that an individual worker must agree to work more than forty-eight hours.[55] The Court emphasised:[56]

> Any derogation from those minimum requirements must therefore be accompanied by all the safeguards necessary to ensure that, if the worker concerned is encouraged to relinquish a social right which has been directly conferred on him by the directive, he must do so freely and with full knowledge of all the facts. Those requirements are all the more important given that the worker must be regarded as the weaker party to the employment contract and it is therefore necessary to prevent the employer being in a position to disregard the intentions of the other party to the contract.

It may be that the current *cause célèbre* regarding Article 22(1)(a) of the Working Time Directive was in the mind of the Court. This concerns the UK's use of the opt-out, which has come under considerable criticism by the Commission.[57] The Court acknowledged that: (paragraph 105)

---

[53] Arguably, it would apply with even greater force to the rights guaranteed in the EU Charter of Fundamental Rights.

[54] An example is the 'telework agreement' of July 2002. This has been the subject of controversy concerning the mechanisms required to implement the agreement in order to comply with Article 139(2) EC. The telework agreement has been implemented in the UK by guidelines on the DTI (now BERR) website. The legal implications for contracts of employment of teleworkers which do not comply with these guidelines would depend on which of two arguments prevailed regarding the *'interpretative methods recognised by national law'*. One would be that EU social dialogue agreements, bolstered by Article 139(2) EC, acquired a status equivalent to directives so as to fall under the UK law granting legislative standards a legal effect overriding contrary provisions in a contract of employment. The alternative would be to regard EU social dialogue agreements as analogous to domestic non-binding collective agreements, from which individual contracts of employment are free to deviate.

[55] Article 22(1)(a) of the Directive.

[56] *Bernhard Pfeiffer et al. c. Deutsches Rotes Kreuz Kreisverband Waldshut eV*, joined Cases C-397/01 to C-403/01, paragraph 82.

[57] 'Communication from the Commission to the Council, the European Parliament, the Economic and Social Committee and the Committee of the Regions concerning the re-exam of Directive

Directive 93/104 leaves the Member States a degree of latitude when they adopt rules in order to implement it … [but] even though it also permits them to derogate from Article 6, those factors do not alter the precise and unconditional nature of Article 6(2) [now 6(b)] … the Member States' right not to apply Article 6 is subject to compliance with all the conditions set out in Article 18(1)(b)(i) [now 22(1)(a)] of the directive.

The conclusion could take the form of the following sequence of propositions:

1. Member States' failure to comply with all the conditions set out in Article 22(1)(a) means that the derogation has not been properly complied with.[58]
2. An invalid derogation means that Article 6 applies, and Article 6(b) has direct effect. It can be invoked against the state or emanations of the state. There is potential *Francovich* liability.
3. National legislation must be interpreted consistently with Article 6, so far as possible.
4. Where this is possible, *interpretive methods recognised by national law* must be used by the courts to achieve an outcome consistent with the objective pursued by the directive.[59]

In the UK context, this means courts must interpret individual contracts of employment so as to eliminate any (invalid) contractual provision whereby an employee agrees to work more than forty-eight hours weekly as conflicting with the 48-hour maximum prescribed by the legislation.

## State liability

Enforcement of rights granted by EU law is constantly under the pressure to reflect a logic which looks to the Treaty of Rome as an international law instrument, and hence engaging exclusively mutual responsibility among the Member States, or of them vis-à-vis the institutions of the EU. However, the supranational jurisdiction of the European Court has had a disaggregating effect upon concepts of state liability. The nation state as the traditional subject of international law is not treated as a monolithic entity, but broken up into elements which can be separately subjected to different pressures of EU law enforcement.

93/104/EC concerning certain aspects of the organization of working time' (COM(2003) 843 final, Brussels, 30 December 2003).

[58] In one sense, this is a question of *interpreting* UK legislation to ascertain its compatibility with the directive. The *Von Colson and Kamann* doctrine means indirect effect does *not* apply if it is *not* possible to reconcile the national law and the directive so as to require the national court to uphold the UK legislation. On the other hand, if the UK legislation fails to comply with the conditions for derogation, there is no valid derogation.

[59] The UK conditions of derogation are in Article 4(2) of the Working Time Regulations 1998 (as amended). Arguably, as the Commission's Communication of 2003 appears to confirm, they are inadequate to satisfy the conditions laid down in Article 22(1) of the directive. As invalid derogating provisions, Regulation 4(1), which prescribes the 48-hour maximum working week, applies.

Above all, the European Court singled out national courts as independent organs of the state responsible for enforcement of EU law rights through doctrines of direct and indirect effect. This has forced national courts to confront the other organs of the state, the legislature and executive, in case of the latter's failure to implement or apply EU law. Further disaggregation is manifest in the European Court's holding different emanations of the Member States responsible under the doctrine of direct effect.

The doctrine of direct effect itself, however, can be seen still as hamstrung by the insistence of the European Court on the exclusively *vertical* responsibility of the state for implementation of EU directives, even where EU law imposes responsibilities on private individuals. The *effet utile* rationale for direct effect would incline towards holding even private individuals responsible for directly enforceable provisions of EU law which should be effective. The 'estoppel' rationale for direct effect is an uneasy compromise: emanations of the state are liable even where the responsibility for the non-implementation of the EU Directive lies with *other* organs of the state.

The European Court made a succinct statement of the existence of state liability as a matter of principle in the *Francovich* case.[60] Workers who suffer damage when their employer becomes insolvent were the subject of an EC Directive which required Member States to secure their protection.[61] Italy failed to implement the Directive. The individual workers brought a claim before their national courts for compensation for the damage they had suffered due to this failure. In a preliminary reference under Article 177 (now 234), the European Court appears to have greatly reinforced the rights of individuals to claim a remedy which results from breaches of Community law for which the state can be held responsible:[62]

> The full effectiveness of Community rules would be impaired and the protection of the rights which they grant would be weakened if individuals were unable to obtain redress when their rights are infringed by a breach of Community law for which a Member State can be held responsible.
>
> The possibility of obtaining redress from the Member State is particularly indispensable where, as in this case, the full effectiveness of Community rules is subject to prior action on the part of the State and where, consequently, in the absence of such action, individuals cannot enforce before the national courts the rights conferred upon them by Community law.
>
> It follows that the principle whereby a State must be liable for loss and damage caused to individuals as a result of breaches of Community law for which the State can be held responsible is inherent in the system of the Treaty ...
>
> It follows from all the foregoing that it is a principle of Community law that the Member States are obliged to make good loss and damage caused to individuals by breaches of Community law for which they can be held responsible.

[60] *Andrea Francovich and Others* v. *Italian Republic*, joined Cases C-6//90 and C-9/90, [1991] ECR I-5357.
[61] Directive 80/987/EEC, OJ L283/23.    [62] *Francovich*, paragraphs 33–7.

The principle of state liability was said also to be explicit in Article 10 of the Treaty. It relies on a basic principle of the new legal order: that national courts must protect the rights conferred by EC law on individuals, including enforcement of these rights where the state is responsible. The principle of state liability thus established was not unconditional:[63]

> Although State liability is thus required by Community law, the conditions under which that liability gives rise to a right to reparation depend on the nature of the breach of Community law giving rise to the loss and damage.
>
> Where, as in this case, a Member State fails to fulfil its obligation under the third paragraph of Article 189 [now 249] of the Treaty to take all the measures necessary to achieve the result prescribed by a directive, the full effectiveness of that rule of Community law requires that there should be a right to reparation provided that three conditions are fulfilled.
>
> The first of those conditions is that the result prescribed by the directive should entail the grant of rights to individuals. The second condition is that is should be possible to identify the content of those rights on the basis of the provisions of the directive. Finally, the third condition is the existence of a causal link between the breach of the State's obligation and the loss and damage suffered by the injured parties.
>
> Those conditions are sufficient to give rise to a right on the part of individuals to obtain reparation, a right founded directly on Community law.

The elements of liability which emerge from the *Francovich* decision include (i) a breach of EC law; (ii) attributable to the Member State; (iii) which causes damage to an individual. The breach of EU law in the *Francovich* case itself was a violation of the EU Directive by reason of the national legislator failing to act to implement it. But total failure to implement a directive is only one type of violation of EU law. Implementation of a directive by a Member State may be partial or incorrect or inadequate. There are numerous decisions of the European Court upholding complaints against Member States, including the UK government, for faulty implementation of a directive. Breaches may also occur of EU laws other than directives, as when a Member State fails to adapt its national law to the requirements of other EU laws.

Advocate-General Léger in *Hedley Lomas* took the view that the principle of state responsibility was not limited to claims for a remedy against EC measures lacking 'direct effect', as was the position in the *Francovich* case. It is a principle of judicial protection of the individual's EC rights:[64]

> My conclusion from this is that an action for damages against a State is not only a remedy for imperfect direct effect. It is not limited to the situation in *Francovich*. It is a vital component of the judicial protection of individuals relying on Community law, from the moment when the provision or decision occasioning the damage is capable of giving rise to rights on the part of individuals.

---

[63] *Ibid.*, paragraphs 38–41.

[64] *The Queen* v. *Ministry of Agriculture, Fisheries and Food, ex parte Hedley Lomas (Ireland) Ltd.*, Case C-5/94, [1996] ECR I-2553, paragraph 94.

Hence while a decision of the European Court condemning a Member State for violation of Community law (as was the case in *Francovich*) may be sufficient, it was not necessary.[65]

The breach in the *Francovich* case was attributable to the national legislature, for failure to implement the Directive. It is evident that violations of EC law may also be committed by other emanations of the state, as established in the doctrine of the direct effect of directives. It has since been held that the principle applies regardless of which organ of the state is responsible for the violation of EC law – even the legislature or the courts.[66]

In *Brasserie du Pecheur* and *Factortame III* the argument was advanced that state responsibility should parallel that of the non-contractual liability of the Community institutions under Article 288 EC. As developed by the Court in its case-law on Article 288, this imposes a heavy burden on the plaintiff to prove fault by the defendant institutions. Advocate-General Léger in *Hedley Lomas* had rejected this parallel; instead, he asserted that the degree of fault required for state responsibility was variable depending on the nature of the Community obligation violated and the nature of the violation committed:[67]

> the nature of the wrongful act or omission required in order for the State to incur liability depends on the nature of the Community obligation incumbent on it and on the nature of the breach committed.

On the question whether the entitlement to compensation is conditional on fault (intent or negligence) on the part of the state officials responsible for the failure to adapt national law, the Court's response in *Brasserie du Pecheur* was to characterise the condition in terms of 'sufficiently serious' breach:[68]

> the concept of fault does not have the same content in the various legal systems ...
> ... where a breach of Community law is attributable to a Member State acting in a field in which it has a wide discretion to make legislative choices, a finding of

---

[65]  *Ibid.*, para. 117.

[66]  *Firma Brasserie du Pecheur SA v. Federal Republic of Germany, The Queen v. Secretary of State for Transport, ex parte Factortame Ltd and others (Factortame III)*, joined Cases C-46/93 and C-48/93, [1996] ECR I-1029. In *Hedley-Lomas*, Advocate-General Léger had argued that 'The State as a whole incurs liability for a breach of Community law, irrespective of whether the damage is attributable to the legislature or to administrative action – or even to a court judgment incompatible with the Treaty.' *Ibid.*, paragraph 114. It took some time before this was tested, but the European Court eventually upheld a claim for damages against a national court violating Community law. *Köbler v. Republik Österreich*, Case C-224/01, [2003] ECR I-1023. The irony is thus created of a lower court hearing a complaint that a higher court violated Community law, with the prospect of appeal.

[67]  *Ibid.*, para. 169.

[68]  *Brasserie du Pecheur* [1996] ECR I-1029, paragraphs 76–9. In *R v. HM Treasury, ex parte British Telecommunications plc*, Case C-392/93, [1996] ECR I-1631, and *Denkavit International v. Bundesamt fur Finanzen*, Cases C-283, 291 and 292/94, [1996] ECR I-5063, the Court held breaches not to be sufficiently serious. In *Dillenkofer and others v. Federal Republic of Germany*, Cases C-178–9/94, 188–190/94, [1996] ECR I-4845, it was held that failure to transpose a directive within the prescribed time limit amounted to a sufficiently serious breach.

a right to reparation on the basis of Community law will be conditional, inter alia, upon the breach having been sufficiently serious.

So, certain objective and subjective factors connected with the concept of fault under a national legal system may well be relevant for the purpose of determining whether or not a given breach of Community law is serious.

The obligation to make reparation for loss or damage caused to individuals cannot, however, depend upon a condition based on any concept of fault going beyond that of a sufficiently serious breach of Community law. Imposition of such a supplementary conditions would be tantamount to calling in question the right to reparation founded on the Community legal order.

A number of questions arise from comparing state responsibility under *Francovich* and the doctrine of direct effect. Both require the claimant to demonstrate that the directive confers rights. But, for the purposes of *Francovich* liability, the right granted by the directive need not be so clearly and precisely defined as is required for it to have direct effect. The European Court held that the rights in the 1980 Insolvency Directive at issue in *Francovich* were insufficiently defined for the purposes of direct effect, but *were* adequately defined for the purposes of state liability.

The principle of state responsibility has potentially enormous implications for the enforcement of EU labour law. If an individual has a definable interest protected by the directive, failure by the state to act to protect that interest may lead to state liability where the individual suffers damage, provided causation can be demonstrated. The directives on health and safety at work, on equal treatment of men and women, and an increasing number of directives regulating individual and collective interests of workers are a fertile field for exploration of the scope of state liability.

## Remedies in national courts

The European Court cannot itself adjudicate on complaints by individuals that rights under EC law, deriving from the doctrines of direct effect and *Francovich* liability, have been violated. These doctrines have been developed through the requests by national courts for preliminary rulings under Article 234 of the EC Treaty. The substantive claim based on EU law will be initiated before a national court. The role of national courts in the enforcement of EU law was described as follows by the European Court:[69]

in the absence of any relevant Community rules, it is for the national legal order of each Member State to designate the competent courts and to lay down the procedural rules for proceedings designed to ensure the protection of the rights which individuals acquire through the direct effect of Community law, provided that such rules are not less favourable than those governing the same right of action on an internal matter ... The position would be different only if those rules

---

[69] *Comet v. Produktschap*, Case 45/76, [1976] ECR 2043.

and time-limits made it impossible in practice to exercise rights which the national courts have a duty to protect.

Given the variety of national court structures, procedures and sanctions available in different national systems, it is likely that the efficacy of enforcement of EU law will reflect this variety. The European Court has recognised the necessity for enforcement of EU law in national courts, insisting that national courts exert themselves to enforce EU law:[70]

> although the Treaty has made it possible in a number of instances for private persons to bring a direct action, where appropriate, before the Court of Justice, it was not intended to create new remedies in national courts to ensure the observance of Community law other than those already laid down by national law. On the other hand the system of legal protection established by the Treaty, as set out in Article 177 [now 234] in particular, implies that it must be possible for every type of action provided for by national law to be available for the purpose of ensuring observance of Community provision having direct effect, on the same conditions concerning the admissibility and procedure as would apply were it a question of ensuring observance of national law.

The European Court has attempted to maintain an equilibrium between the autonomy of national systems to enforce EU law and the imperative of effective and uniform enforcement of EU law across all Member States. Referring to the third paragraph of Article 249 of the Rome Treaty, the Court held:[71]

> Although that provision leaves Member States to choose the ways and means of ensuring that the directive is implemented, that freedom does not affect the obligation imposed on all the Member States to which the directive is addressed, to adopt, in their national legal systems, all the measures necessary to ensure that the directive is fully effective, in accordance with the objective which it pursues.

The European Court has moved in the direction of scrutinising national systems of judicial protection of EU law rights by laying down some general principles regarding the adequacy of national laws on remedies. In the context of an EU Directive on sex discrimination, it stated:[72]

> full implementation of the directive does not require any specific form of sanction for unlawful discrimination, it does entail that that sanction be such as to guarantee real and effective judicial protection. Moreover it must also have a real deterrent effect on the employer. It follows that where a Member State chooses to penalise the breach of the prohibition of discrimination by the award of compensation, that compensation must in any event be adequate in relation to the damage sustained.

The principle of equivalence of EU law remedies to national remedies applies, but that remedies for breach of EU law must be effective means that national autonomy as regards enforcement of EU law is subject to this requirement.

---

[70] *Rewe* v. *Hauptzollamt Kiel*, Case 158/80, [1981] ECR 1805.
[71] *Von Colson and Kamann* v. *Land Nordrhein-Westfalen*, Case 14/83, [1984] ECR 1891.
[72] *Ibid.*, paragraph 23.

## Sanctions

The *Von Colson* case illustrates the approach by the Court of critical scrutiny of the remedies for sex discrimination provided under German law by way of compensation:[73]

> national provision limiting the right to compensation of persons who have been discriminated against as regards access to employment to a purely nominal amount, such as, for example, the reimbursement of expenses incurred by them in submitting their application, would not satisfy the requirements of an effective transposition of the directive.

However, the European Court has put limits on its intervention:[74]

> Article 6 [of the Equal Treatment Directive] requires Member States to introduce into their national legal systems such measures as are necessary to enable all persons who consider themselves wronged by discrimination 'to pursue their claims by judicial process'.

The Court regarded this as requiring Member States:[75]

> to adopt measures which are sufficiently effective to achieve the objective of the directive and to ensure that those measures may in fact be relied on before the national courts by the persons concerned.

As regards specific sanctions, however, the Court was cautious:[76]

> Such measures may include, for example, provisions requiring the employer to offer a post to the candidate discriminated against or giving the candidate adequate financial compensation, backed up where necessary by a system of fines. However the directive does not prescribe a specific sanction; it leaves Member States free to choose between the different solutions suitable for achieving its objective.[77]

The adequacy of sanctions provided by national law for the enforcement of individual rights in EU law has been challenged in other labour law contexts. The Directives on Collective Dismissals of 1975[78] and Acquired Rights of

---

[73] *Ibid.*    [74] *Ibid.*    [75] *Ibid.*    [76] *Ibid.*

[77] The equilibrium is nicely illustrated by the Court's decision regarding UK law remedies for sex discrimination in *Marshall No. 2: M.H. Marshall* v. *Southampton and South West Hampshire Area Health Authority (Teaching) (No. 2)*, Case C-271/91, [1993] ECR I-4367, paragraphs 24–6. '... the objective is to arrive at real equality of opportunity and (this) cannot therefore be attained in the absence of measures appropriate to restore such equality when it has not been observed ... Such requirements necessarily entail that the particular circumstances of each breach of the principle of equal treatment should be taken into account. In the event of discriminatory dismissal contrary to Article 5(1) of the Directive, a situation of equality could not be restored without either reinstating the victim of discrimination or, in the alternative, granting financial compensation for the loss and damage sustained. Where financial compensation is the measure adopted in order to achieve the objective indicated above, it must be adequate, in that it must enable the loss and damage actually sustained as a result of the discriminatory dismissal to be made good in full in accordance with the applicable national rules'.

[78] Council Directive 75/129 of 17 February 1975 on the approximation of the laws of the Member States relating to collective dismissals, OJ L48/29, as amended by Directive 92/56 of 24 June 1992,

1977[79] both require employers to inform and consult employee representatives. The 1981 Regulations which implemented the latter Directive in UK law[80] provided that an employer who fails to consult employee representatives may be ordered to pay appropriate compensation to employees affected by the transfer. The compensation payable (called a 'protective award') was subject to a maximum of two weeks' pay.[81] In addition, the Regulations allowed for compensation awarded to be set off against other compensation which might be awarded to the employee. On the Commission's complaint that these sanctions were inadequate, the European Court agreed that:[82]

> The financial penalty is accordingly weakened; if not entirely removed ... It follows that if an employer is also found to be at fault on the basis of the [Employment Protection Act], the penalty is not truly deterrent. Accordingly, the United Kingdom legislation does not comply on this point with the requirements of Article 5 of the Treaty.[83]

The adequacy of financial *compensation* as a remedy in labour law may be questioned. Particularly in the case of the exercise of collective rights, such as information and consultation, it is arguable that the award of compensation to employees affected by the employer's failure to inform or consult employee representatives is insufficient to achieve 'real and effective judicial protection and have a real deterrent effect on the employer'.[84]

The question whether national rules restricting remedies available for violations of EU law could be ignored was answered in the affirmative in *Factortame*. The plaintiff had asked for interim relief against the Crown. The request was initially denied by the UK courts on the grounds that UK law did not allow for such a remedy against the Crown. On a reference for a preliminary ruling under Article 234:[85]

OJ L245/92. Now consolidated in Council Directive 98/59/EC of 20 July 1998 on the approximation of the laws of the Member States relating to collective redundancies, OJ L225/16.

[79] Council Directive 77/187 of February 14, 1977 on the approximation of the laws of the Member States relating to the safeguarding of employees' rights in the event of transfers of undertakings, businesses or parts of businesses, OJ L61/26, as amended by Directive 98/50/EC of 29 June 1998, OJ L201/88. Consolidated in Directive 2001/23 of 12 March 2001, OJ L82/16.

[80] The Transfer of Undertakings (Protection of Employment) Regulations 1981, SI 1981 No. 1794. See now the Transfer of Undertakings (Protection of Employment) Regulations 2006, SI 2006 No. 246.

[81] Increased to four weeks' pay by the Trade Union Reform and Employment Rights Act 1993.

[82] *Commission of the European Communities* v. *United Kingdom*, Case C-382/92, [1994] ECR 2435.

[83] On the complaint regarding the Collective Dismissals Directive, the ECJ held similarly: 'By providing that a "protective award" may be set off in full or in part against any amounts otherwise payable by an employer to an employee under the latter's contract of employment or in respect of breach of that contract, the United Kingdom legislation largely deprives that sanction of its practical effect and its deterrent value. Moreover, an employer will not be penalized even moderately or lightly by the sanction except and only to the extent to which the amount of the "protective award" which he is ordered to make exceeds the sums which he is otherwise required to pay to the person concerned.' *Commission of the European Communities* v. *United Kingdom*, Case C-383/92, [1994] ECR 2435.

[84] *M.H. Marshall* v. *Southampton and South West Hampshire Area Health Authority (Teaching) (No. 2)*, Case C-271/91, [1993] ECR I-4367.

[85] *R* v. *Secretary of State for Transport, ex parte Factortame*, Case C-213/89, [1990] ECR I-2433.

The Court has also held that any provision of a national legal system and any legislative, administrative or judicial practice which might impair the effectiveness of Community law by withholding from the national court having jurisdiction to apply such law the power to do everything necessary at the moment of its application to set aside national legislative provisions which might prevent, even temporarily, Community rules from having full force and effect are incompatible with those requirements, which are the very essence of Community law.

It must be added that the full effectiveness of Community law would be just as much impaired if a rule of national law could prevent a court seised of a dispute governed by Community law from granting interim relief in order to ensure the full effectiveness of the judgment to be given on the existence of the rights claimed under Community law. It follows that a court which in those circumstances would grant interim relief, if it were not for a rule of national law, is obliged to set aside that rule.

An illustration from labour law of the application of these EU law rules would be to challenge the adequacy of compensation and claim the alternative remedy of injunctive relief on a complaint alleging failure to inform and consult employee representatives. The response of one UK court illustrates the difficulties of persuading UK judges to exploit the potential of EU law to scrutinise the adequacy of remedies under UK law.[86]

---

[86]  *Griffin & Ors.* v. *South West Water Services Limited* [1995] IRLR 15 (Ch.D), Blackburne J. '… where, as here, the Directive leaves to the Member State the choice of remedy for breach of the Directive, the Directive cannot be interpreted so as to require the Member States to select one mode of sanction for breach of the Directive in preference to another, at any rate where the sanction selected is capable of guaranteeing real and effective judicial protection and real deterrent effect … the sanction selected by Parliament for breach of s.188 is … a protective award … Whilst, therefore, there may be a question, as there was in case C-383/92, as to the adequacy of the award which the industrial tribunal is empowered to make having regard to some feature of the legislation which provides for the sanction, I do not consider that it is open to me to disregard the exclusive sanction which Parliament has selected for giving effect to the duty to consult, where it arises, and to grant to the plaintiffs a form of relief for which the 1992 Act makes no provision. Even if it were open to me in appropriate circumstances to disregard the exclusive sanction which Parliament has provided and grant injunctive relief of the kind sought, I am not persuaded that I would have any sufficient grounds for doing so. It seems to me that an order restraining an employer from effecting any redundancies unless he has "consulted with" his employees' representatives "with a view to reaching an agreement", which is what the plaintiffs seek, is one which is fraught with practical difficulties, not the least of which would be the difficulty faced by the employer in knowing just what he would be obliged to do and over what period in order to achieve compliance with the order and avoid proceedings for contempt. The vagueness and uncertainty inherent in an order of the kind sought was, as it seems to me, well illustrated by Mr Hendy's description of the process which an injunction would require …: "All that is required is for representatives of SWW (the employer) to sit down with representatives of Unison (the trade union) having given them the chance to absorb the material disclosed in this case, and say, 'This is what we propose: what do you say, can we reach an agreement?' They must listen, take on board what is said, see what can be the subject of agreement and what not, and then carry out what they, SWW, have decided in the light of those consultations to do." I can well see, therefore why Parliament has chosen to provide for breaches of the duty to consult and inform under s.188 by leaving it to an industrial tribunal which is particularly well equipped to consider such matters and, where a breach is established, by providing for the breach to be penalised by an award of compensation'.

The choice of remedy for breach of the Directive may be left to national law, but EU law requires this choice to be scrutinised closely. That the UK Parliament does not allow a remedy by way of injunctive relief does not preclude consideration of this remedy if it is capable of guaranteeing real and effective judicial protection and a real deterrent effect.

## Procedures

The adequacy of sanctions is only one aspect of the enforcement of EU law. National procedures for obtaining redress can also obstruct the real and effective judicial protection guaranteed by EU law. *Access* to the judicial process has been held to be a general principle of law which must be taken into consideration in Community law. 'The right to an effective judicial remedy' was elaborated in *Johnston* v. *RUC*, where the European Court was asked:[87]

> whether Community law, and more particularly Directive No. 76/207, requires the Member States to ensure that their national courts and tribunals exercise effective control over compliance with the provisions of the directive and with the national legislation intended to put it into effect ...
>
> As far as this issue is concerned, it must be borne in mind first of all that Article 6 of the directive requires Member States to introduce into their internal legal systems such measures as are needed to enable all persons who consider themselves wronged by discrimination 'to pursue their claims by judicial process'. It follows from that provision that the Member States must take measures which are sufficiently effective to achieve the aim of the directive and that they must ensure that the rights thus conferred may be effectively relied upon before the national courts by the persons concerned.

*Johnston* v. *RUC* concerned the provision in UK law which allowed a government Minister, by issuing a certificate on grounds of national security or public safety or order, to exclude from the courts a complaint based on a Directive. The European Court condemned the issuing of such a certificate on the grounds that it:[88]

> allows the competent authority to deprive an individual of the possibility of asserting by judicial process the rights conferred by the directive. Such a provision is therefore contrary to the principle of effective judicial control laid down in Article 6 of the directive.

This provision of the Directive guaranteeing access to justice was held to be directly effective:[89]

> As regards Article 6 of the directive ... in so far as it follows from that article, construed in the light of a general principle which it expresses, that all persons who consider themselves wronged by sex discrimination must have an effective

---

[87] Case 222/84, [1986] ECR 1651, paragraphs 13, 17.
[88] *Ibid.*, paragraph 20.     [89] *Ibid.*, paragraph 58.

judicial remedy, that provision is sufficiently precise and unconditional to be capable of being relied upon as against a Member State which has not ensured that it is fully implemented in its internal legal order.

The EU law right to an effective judicial remedy raises a number of questions about access to justice for complainants. Particular procedures for obtaining access to employment tribunals might be demonstrated to have a deterrent effect on claimants wishing to invoke EU labour law rights. Failure to provide adequate avenues of redress is a breach by the Member State of its obligations.

An example of the extent to which national procedures providing redress for breaches of EC law can be questioned is where a Member State applies its normal procedure of establishing liability to labour law. In European civil law procedure, the burden of proving the claim is normally imposed on the applicant. In Dutch law, a legal action in damages based on breach of the principle of equal treatment embodied in a directive could succeed only if the applicant proved the employer to be at fault. This was challenged as violating the directive on the basis that infringement of the equal treatment principle, once established, is sufficient to make the employer liable without proof of fault. The European Court held:[90]

> It must be observed that, if the employer's liability for infringement of the principle of equal treatment were made subject to proof of a fault attributable to him and also to there being no ground of exemption recognized by the applicable national law, the practical effect of those principles would be weakened considerably.
>
> It follows that when the sanction chosen by the Member State is contained within the rules governing an employer's civil liability, a breach of the prohibition of discrimination must, in itself, be sufficient to make the employer liable, without there being any possibility of invoking the grounds of exemption provided by national law.

Similarly, the Court was prepared to shift the burden of proof in an equal pay claim concerned with a system of individual pay supplements completely lacking in transparency. The Court held that female employees seeking to prove their claim:[91]

> would be deprived of any effective means of enforcing the principle of equal pay before the national courts if the effect of adducing such evidence was not to impose upon the employer the burden of proving that his practice in the matter of wages is not in fact discriminatory ...
>
> ... under Article 6 of the Equal Pay Directive Member States must, in accordance with their national circumstances and legal systems, take the measures necessary to ensure that the principle of equal pay is applied and that effective

---

[90] *Dekker* v. *Stichting Vormingscentrum voor Jong Volwassenen (VJV Centrum) Plus*, Case 177/88, [1990] ECR I-3941, paragraphs 24–5.

[91] *Handels- og Kontorfunktionaerernes Forbund i Danmark* v. *Dansk Arbejdsgiverforening (Danfoss)*, Case 109/88, [1989] ECR 3199, paragraphs 13–14.

means are available to ensure that it is observed. The concern for effectiveness which thus underlies the directive means that it must be interpreted as implying adjustments to national rules on the burden of proof in special cases where such adjustments are necessary for the effective implementation of the principle of equality.

These cases demonstrate that the remedies available under national law are open to challenge. The effectiveness of EC law is too important to be left only to national enforcement procedures.

# Chapter 16

# Euro-litigation: collective judicial enforcement of European labour law

## Introduction

The use of judicial procedures by collective actors in order to obtain redress for grievances is a form of citizen involvement. Public interest litigation is one of a wide range of mechanisms whereby interest groups may seek to become involved as a means of promoting their interests. The use of EU law in a litigation strategy by particular collective interest groups is a means of enforcement of EU law going beyond the tactics of identifying new categories of plaintiff or defendant, or criticising the adequacy of domestic remedies. It has strategic potential in the form of what has come to be known as 'Euro-litigation'.

Judicial enforcement of European labour law through legal actions brought by collective organisations of workers and employers is a form of public interest litigation.[1] However, public interest litigation in the field of employment and industrial relations may be expected to differ from that involving agricultural policy, public procurement, trade practices, anti-dumping, state aids and competition law.[2] Similarly, it is important to distinguish among the very different substantive areas often subsumed under the heading of 'social policy', which can include, *inter alia*, various aspects ranging from citizenship rights, the

---

[1] The following is adapted in part from B. Bercusson, 'Public Interest Litigation in Social Policy', in H.-W. Micklitz and N. Reich (eds.), *Public Interest Litigation before European Courts*, Baden-Baden: Nomos, 1996, pp. 261–95. See also a short piece analysing the prospects for the ETUC's obtaining the status of a 'privileged applicant' under Article 230 EC: 'The ETUC and the European Court of Justice', (2000) 6 *Transfer: European Review of Labour and Research* (Winter) 720–5. 'Les syndicats européennes devant la Cour de Justice de Luxembourg', *Liaisons Sociales Europe* No. 14, (26 July–12 September 2000), pp. 2–3.

[2] As remarked in the conclusion of a lengthy analysis of the European Court's discretion to review: legality under Article 173 EC: '... the nature of the subject-matter under scrutiny will, not surprisingly, play an important part both in determining whether to accord standing and in determining the standard or intensity of review which is adopted ... The breadth of subject matter covered by Community law renders this diversity of judicial approach highly likely. Any assessment of Community law must always be evaluated against the backdrop of the substantive issues involved before the Court. In this way a richer understanding can be gained of the Court's decisions concerning review of legality, whether these relate to procedural or substantive aspects of the topic.' P. P. Craig and G. de Búrca, *EU Law: Text, Cases and Materials*, Oxford: Clarendon, 1995, 'Conclusion' to Chapter 11 'Review of Legality', pp. 446–510 at p. 509.

environment, consumer protection, social security and social protection, as well as employment and labour relations.

EU law is mostly used in two ways. First, as a source of substantive rules.[3] Secondly, to provide remedies against the state[4] or just better remedies.[5] But EU law can also be used in a litigation strategy by powerful collective actors.

An illustration was the strategic use of EU law against UK legislation prohibiting Sunday trading. The strategy of the big stores that wanted to stay open on Sunday was two-fold. In the short term, they sought to attack in pre-emptive fashion local authority attempts to enforce UK legislation prohibiting Sunday trading. They claimed that the UK legislation violated Article 30 of the Treaty of Rome on free movement of goods, as it precluded the stores from selling imports. The stores' use of EU law demonstrated to the local authorities that attempts to stop Sunday trading would be costly, as the local authorities would be liable to compensate the stores for any losses suffered by closure unlawful as contrary to EU law. Moreover, in the interim, the local authorities could be required to give financial undertakings to provide such compensation if the stores' claim was ultimately successful.[6] In the long term, by inhibiting enforcement of the UK law against Sunday trading, the stores wanted to legitimise the practice of Sunday trading in public opinion, with the aim of preparing the way for UK legislation. The strategy was vindicated when, even though their claim based on EU law was ultimately rejected by the European Court of Justice.[7] the government introduced legislation permitting trading on Sunday.

The question is whether EC law has potential use in a litigation strategy in the sphere of employment or labour relations law by collective interest groups involved, in particular, workers and trade unions.[8] This prospect is immediately confronted by a number of different considerations which

---

[3] For example, to override restrictive national law which fails to implement EC law adequately – as when the UK's Transfer of Undertakings (Protection of Employment) Regulations 1981 were both interpreted in light of the Acquired Rights Directive of 1977 (*Litster* v. *Forth Dry Dock and Engineering Co. Ltd.* [1990] AC 546 (HL) and condemned as not complying with the Directive (*Commission of the EC* v. *UK*, Case 382/92 [1994] ECR I-2435). Or when the UK's Working Time Regulations were condemned for failing to implement the rights to paid holidays or rest periods in the Working Time Directive, *Broadcasting, Entertainment, Cinematographic and Theatre Union (BECTU)* v. *Secretary of State for Trade and Industry*, Case C-173/99, [2001] ECR I-4881; *Commission* v. *UK*, Case 484/04, decided 7 September 2006.

[4] *Francovich and Bonfaci* v. *Italian Republic*, Cases C-6/90 and 9/90 [1991] ECR I-5357: state responsibility to compensate workers suffering damage by reason of failure to implement Directive granting employment rights.

[5] *Marshall* v. *Southampton and South West Area Health Authority (No. 2)*, Case 271/91, [1993] ECR I-4367: statutory limitation on compensation for sex discrimination overruled.

[6] R. Rawlings, 'The Eurolaw Game: Some Deductions from a Saga', (1993) 20 *Journal of Law and Society* 309.

[7] *Torfaen BC* v. *B & Q plc*, Case 145/88, [1989] ECR 3851.

[8] For the proposed use of this strategy against employer attempts to derecognise trade unions, see the first edition of this book, 1996, Chapter 11, pp. 145–63. The objective in the short term would be to make derecognition costly for employers; in the long term, to delegitimise derecognition and prepare the way for a legal right to recognition.

moderate expectations. First, there is the diversity of trade union and labour movements among the Member States.[9] Secondly, public interest litigation, using EU law or other law, in the sphere of employment and labour relations may be affected by the general attitude towards litigation of the major interest groups involved, in this case, the trade unions.[10] Enforcement of labour law by complaints through tribunals and courts is only one option. In other countries it operates alongside more (or less) dynamic labour inspectorates and other forms of dispute resolution (internal grievance procedures and arbitration).

Thirdly, litigation by collective actors as a form of citizen involvement in decision-making processes in the EU has two outlets: Article 230[11] and

[9] Trade union movements may be unitary, but are frequently divided on religious, ideological and occupational lines. They have different purposes, degrees of autonomy and types of membership. There are unions linked with political parties, with low levels of competition among them, as in Belgium and the Netherlands, and with higher levels of competition, as in France and Italy. There are movements with relative autonomy from political parties, as in Great Britain, the Nordic countries, Germany and Austria. There are different degrees of centralisation and democracy, with different functions and relationships of unions in single-channel representative systems and, alongside works councils or elected enterprise committees, in dual- or plural-channel representative systems. At the most basic level, the percentage of workers organised in a trade union in the EU Member States varies considerably.

[10] The most common ground for labour litigation tends to be connected with dismissals from employment. In this area, the role of unions is complicated due to the existence of other forms of worker representation. For example, there is a reluctance of works councils in France and Germany to become involved in labour court proceedings involving dismissal, as they prefer to seek resolution of individual disputes through collective negotiations inside the plant. The case load of different labour courts/tribunals revealed a fluctuating ratio of cases in countries of comparable size (UK:France:Germany) in the 1980s of roughly 1:4:10. The numbers of courts, of cases heard per court and of labour court judges are also remarkably diverse. See Ralf Rogowski, 'The Resolution of Labour Conflicts: An International Comparison', dissertation submitted for the Ph.D. at the European University Institute, Florence, 1991, Table IV-3 on p. 248, Table IV-4 on p. 251 and Table IV-5 on p. 254. In unfair dismissal cases, union officials represent 22 per cent of plaintiffs in UK tribunals, 29 per cent in German labour courts. But one quarter of plaintiffs are not represented in Germany; 45 per cent in the UK. German plaintiff-employees use legal representation twice as often as British applicants. The rate of success may or may not be a function of this representation profile; many other factors may operate. Nonetheless, the figures indicate a significantly higher success rate for employees claiming unfair dismissal in German labour courts than in British tribunals. *Ibid.*, at pp. 258–60, 266–7 and 273.

[11] Article 230 EC: 'The Court of Justice shall review the legality of acts adopted jointly by the European Parliament and the Council, of acts of the Council, of the Commission and of the ECB, other than recommendations and opinions, and of acts of the European Parliament intended to produce legal effects vis-à-vis third parties. It shall for this purpose have jurisdiction in actions brought by a Member State, the European Parliament, the Council or the Commission on grounds of lack of competence, infringement of an essential procedural requirement, infringement of this Treaty or of any rule of law relating to its application, or misuse of powers'. 'The Court of Justice shall have jurisdiction under the same conditions in actions brought by the Court of Auditors or by the ECB for the purpose of protecting their prerogatives'. 'Any natural or legal person may, under the same conditions, institute proceedings against a decision addressed to that person or against a decision which, although in the form of a regulation or a decision addressed to another person, is of direct and individual concern to the former'. 'The proceedings provided for in this Article shall be instituted within two months of the publication of the measure, or of its notification to the plaintiff, or, in the absence thereof, of the day on which it came to the knowledge of the latter, as the case may be'.

Article 234[12] EC. Article 230 allows for judicial review by the ECJ, but Article 234 preliminary reference proceedings are more commonly the basis for litigation strategies by collective interest groups seeking review by the European Court.

Article 230 raises the fundamental question of the relationship between participation in decision-making and *locus standi* to challenge decisions before the European Court. Participation implies that the interests of the participants *were* taken into account, at least formally, to varying extents. Arguably, if *locus standi* itself is *a* form of participation, the *higher* the degree of *other* forms of participation, the *narrower* the access should be allowed to attempts to reverse the decision. On the other hand, *if* interest groups are affected who were *not* able to participate, then *a fortiori*, they should have *easier* access and *wider* grounds to challenge. It is more likely they will be wronged than those who were at least able to participate.

However, if certain collective interest groups *were* explicitly excluded from participation, it may be for good reasons; for example, their interests are secondary or illegitimate, or are taken into account in ways other than direct participation, or the groups in question were disqualified for certain reasons, such as lack of representativeness. Hence, they should not be considered as having standing save in exceptional cases. Indeed, to allow them *locus standi* might disrupt policy-making processes which have been structured to accommodate only some interests deemed representative and legitimate. It might lead to interference by the European Court with political processes deliberately shaped to include some interests and not others.

So the argument that participation is equivalent to access to the ECJ under Article 230 depends on the structure of political decision-making and how much participation there is of collective interest groups in the substantive area concerned. If, in the sphere of employment and labour relations law, there is already a high degree of engagement of collective interest groups, the correlation may not be that more participation should lead to greater access to the Court through Article 230.

Moreover, there is a fundamental problem in regarding participation as an undifferentiated value separated from the specific institutional framework of a particular policy area. Participation via litigation is not the same as participation by influencing the administration of policy or via structured dialogue

---

[12] Article 234 EC: 'The Court of Justice shall have jurisdiction to give preliminary rulings concerning: the interpretation of this Treaty; the validity and interpretation of acts of the institutions of the Community and of the ECB; the interpretation of the statutes of bodies established by an act of the Council, where those statutes so provide. Where such a question is raised before any court or tribunal of a Member State, that court or tribunal may, if it considered that a decision on the question is necessary to enable it to give judgment, request the Court of Justice to give a ruling thereon. Where any such question is raised in a case pending before a court or tribunal of a Member State against whose decisions there is no judicial remedy under national law, that court or tribunal shall bring the matter before the Court of Justice'.

between the collective interests concerned. It is not at all evident that participation through litigation or judicial review strategies is the most desirable form.[13]

Finally, research has led some to the conclusion that the *cultural context* of national systems tends to favour specific structures and mechanisms of collective interest group representation and participation in the law of employment and labour relations.[14] This research emphasised the central role in national labour law systems of key groups: labour court judges in Germany, labour law administrators in France, and the social partners in the UK. The perception of labour law, its formulation and implementation, differs among these groups and, it was argued, this explains many differences in the substantive labour law of these countries.

The references made above to the *differing* extent and nature of litigation in the field of employment in the Member States is an indication that, in different national systems of labour law, the attraction of litigation will vary. The role of litigation procedures will differ in each country depending on the prominence attached to litigation as a method of participation in the formulation and implementation of EU labour law. As a form of citizen involvement in decision-making, other and/or better functional equivalents may exist. The nature and intensity of review, the standards applicable and the expertise available may indicate a body other than the courts as the desirable forum. The preferred form of participation may look to administrative accommodation or social dialogue rather than litigation procedure.

In sum: the use of litigation by collective interest groups as a form of participation and citizen involvement depends, first, on the structures of interest representation and participation in the specific substantive area of policy concerned; and secondly, on the national cultural context, which may perceive litigation before the European Court as a more or less familiar, useful and congenial mechanism of participation.

## Litigation before the ECJ

The European Court of Justice ever more frequently is making decisions with important consequences for the vital interests of trade unions. Four examples follow.

---

[13] The sociology of litigation strategies, not least those involving EU law, such as the series of cases using Article 234 in the Sunday trading litigation, tells us a great deal about the nature of this form of participation and the barriers posed by the need for substantial legal and financial resources, the presence of 'repeat players', the tactics of multiple claims and so on – enough to make one suspicious of appeals to the straightforward democratic quality of litigation as an avenue of participation. See Rawlings, 'The Eurolaw Game'.

[14] B. Bercusson, U. Mückenberger and A. Supiot, *Application du Droit du Travail et Diversité Culturelle en Europe* (mimeo), work presented to the Conference on 'Convergence des Modèles Sociaux Européens?', Paris, 8–9 October 1992 (399 pp. + 14 pp. summary in French).

In Case T-135/96, *UEAPME*,[15] an organisation representing artisans and small and medium undertakings (UEAPME) challenged the legality of the Parental Leave Directive before the European Court of First Instance. The Parental Leave Directive was the first product of the Maastricht Protocol and Agreement on Social Policy (now Articles 136–9 of the EC Treaty).[16] The Court's judgment raised profound issues of the democratic legitimacy of EU labour legislation and of the autonomy of the social partners engaged in social dialogue. It was significant that the Court was willing to allow a number of national employer associations to intervene in support of UEAPME's application.[17] But the ETUC did not intervene.

Case C-2/97, *Borsana*,[18] was a challenge to Italian legislation on health and safety. In an Opinion of 28 April 1998, Advocate-General Mischo applied the principle of proportionality to nullify legislation imposing higher standards than the minimum requirements of EC health and safety directives. This Opinion aroused considerable disquiet among trade unions at EU and national levels. The European Court's decision handed down on 17 December 1998 rejected the Opinion and upheld the powers of Member States to introduce more stringent protection of working conditions. But trade unions did not intervene to make representations to the Court.

In November 1997, D-G V of the Commission proposed a Council Regulation creating a mechanism whereby the Commission could intervene to remove obstacles to trade. The next month saw a Court decision on 9 December 1997 which condemned the French government for failing to act to prevent interference with the free movement of goods by French farmers.[19] The Commission's proposal had concerned European trade unions because of its potential implications for strikes or other industrial action disrupting trade. The Court's decision made these fears very realistic. It was only following intensive ETUC lobbying that the final Regulation included a pathbreaking provision asserting the fundamental quality of 'the right or freedom to strike'.[20]

---

[15] *Union Européenne de l'Artisanat et des Petites et Moyennes Entreprises (UEAPME)* v. *Council of the European Union*, Case T-135/96, [1998] ECR II-2335.

[16] Council Directive 96/34/EC of 3 June 1996 on the Framework Agreement on parental leave concluded by UNICE, CEEP and the ETUC. OJ L145/4 of 19 June 1996.

[17] [1997] ECR II-383.

[18] *Società italiana petroli SpA (IP)* v. *Borsana Srl*, Case C-2/97 [1998] ECR I-8597.

[19] Case C-265/95, *Commission* v. *France*, [1997] ECR I-6959.

[20] Regulation 2679/98/EC of 7 December 1998; OJ L337/8 of 12 December 1998, Article 2: 'This Regulation may not be interpreted as affecting in any way the exercise of fundamental rights as recognised in Member States, including the right or freedom to strike. These rights may also include the right or freedom to take other actions covered by the specific industrial relations systems in Member States'. Even this did not prevent the then Commissioner for Internal Market Affairs (F. Bolkestein) from asserting, in an answer of 16 October 2000 to a Parliamentary Question from Jonas Sjostedt, that the Commission would intervene where there was obstacle to free movement of goods, whether or not it arose in the context of a trade union dispute.

Finally, cases referred to the European Court by courts in the Netherlands under Article 234 of the EC Treaty challenged collective agreements between representatives of employers and employees. The collective agreements were said to conflict with EC rules on competition in Article 81(1) (ex 85(1)) of the EC Treaty. In Case C-67/96 and others, *Albany*, without any intervention from trade unions, an Opinion of 28 January 1999 by Advocate-General Jacobs denied the existence of a fundamental trade union right to collective bargaining in the EU legal order. He also stated that collective agreements had only limited protection from the rules on competition in EU law. On 21 September 1999, the European Court did not follow this Opinion and upheld the legality of collective agreements relying, in part, on the recognition of the EU social dialogue in the EC Treaty.[21]

These cases are a powerful signal that trade union rights and interests in EU law are increasingly on the agenda of the European courts. Cases may arrive before these courts without trade unions being party to them or being forewarned that they raise issues of concern to them. It is vital for the social partners to have access to the European Court to ensure that the Court takes into account the implications of any decisions it may make for trade unions and employers at European and national levels. For example, European trade unions need to take steps to develop a defensive litigation strategy so that the ETUC or its affiliated organisations can intervene in judicial proceedings when the case raises important issues concerning the rights and interests of workers and trade unions.

Of particular interest is the possibility of direct action before the European Court by the social partners using Article 230 of the EC Treaty. The special position of the social partners before the European Court is a consequence of their institutional role following from the social policy provisions in the EC Treaty (Articles 136–9). These provisions formalise the legislative role of the EU social partners in social policy and labour law. This has particular significance as regards the interpretation and application of the EU framework agreements concluded between the social partners and the directives which include these agreements.

## Direct access to the ECJ by the social partners under Article 230 EC

The question is whether the social partners' institutional legislative role in EU labour law gives rise to a right to take direct legal action before the ECJ under Article 230.

---

[21] *Albany International BV* v. *Stichting Bedrijfspensioenfonds Textielindustrie*, Case C-67/96; with joined Cases C-115/97, C-116/97 and C-117/97; [1999] ECR I-5751; Opinion of Advocate-General Jacobs, 28 January 1999; decision of the European Court of Justice, 21 September 1999.

## Social partners as 'privileged' applicants

In the Treaty of Rome, Article 173(2), the predecessor of Article 230 EC, distinguished privileged and non-privileged applicants. Privileged applicants specified were 'a Member State, the Council or the Commission'. In the *Comitology* case, the European Parliament's claim to be a privileged applicant to the same extent as the other institutions named had been rejected by the Court.[22] However, in the *Chernobyl* case, the Court had reconsidered its position.[23] It acknowledged that the earlier rejection of Parliament's claim had been justified by pointing out:[24]

> that various legal remedies were available to ensure that the Parliament's prerogatives were defended. As was observed in that judgment, not only does the Parliament have the right to bring an action for failure to act, but the Treaties provide means for submitting for review by the Court actions of the Council of the Commission adopted in disregard of the Parliament's prerogatives.

However, the Court now concluded that:[25]

> 20. ... The existence of those various legal remedies is not sufficient to guarantee, with certainty and in all circumstances, that a measure adopted by the Council or the Commission in disregard of Parliament's prerogatives will be reviewed ...
>
> 23. Those prerogatives are one of the elements of the institutional balance created by the Treaties. The Treaties set up a system for distributing powers among the different Community institutions, assigning to each institution its own role in the institutional structure of the Community and the accomplishment of the tasks entrusted to the Community ...
>
> 25. ... it is the Court's duty to ensure that the provisions of the Treaties concerning the institutional balance are fully applied and to see to it that Parliament's prerogatives, like those of the other institutions, cannot be breached without it having available a legal remedy, among those laid down in the Treaties, which may be exercised in a certain and effective manner ...
>
> 28. In accordance with the Treaties, the Parliament's prerogatives include participation in the drafting of legislative measures, in particular participation in the cooperation procedure laid down in the EEC Treaty.

Accordingly, a complaint by Parliament that the procedure for cooperation had not been respected was held to be admissible under Article 173 (now 230). This ruling was subsequently adopted by the Member States who, by the Treaty on European Union, amended Article 173 to include the provision that:

> The Court shall have jurisdiction under the same conditions in actions brought by the European Parliament and by the ECB for the purpose of protecting their prerogatives.[26]

---

[22] Case 302/87. *European Parliament* v. *Council* [1988] ECR 5615.
[23] Case C-70/88, *European Parliament* v. *Council* [1990] ECR I-2041.
[24] *Ibid.*, paragraph 15.     [25] *Ibid.*, paragraphs 20, 23, 25 and 28.
[26] The Treaty of Nice further amended Article 230 to include the European Parliament among the other 'privileged' applicants (Member States, the Council and the Commission) entitled to bring actions without qualification.

The precise scope of the prerogatives in question was left unclear. In a number of cases, the rights of Parliament to participate in the legislative process had been the subject of litigation, with Article 173 (now 230) being used to promote the Parliament's rights to be consulted. Thus, in a case brought by the Commission, the Court held that the participation of the Parliament was:[27]

> the reflection at Community level of a fundamental democratic principle, according to which people were to take part in the exercise of power through the intermediary of a representative assembly.[28]

Further, in *European Parliament* v. *Council*,[29] it was held to cover the right to be consulted in accordance with a provision of the Treaty, so that adoption of an act on a legal basis not providing for such mandatory consultation infringed Parliament's prerogatives. Optional consultation was not sufficient to meet the prerogatives of Parliament.

The Court, and then the Member States in the Treaty on European Union, clearly regarded the institutional balance in the EC as requiring that the prerogatives of the European Parliament be respected. This had two outcomes. First, the European Parliament was recognised as entitled to challenge acts of the institutions under Article 173 (now 230) where these threatened its prerogatives. Secondly, these prerogatives included the right to participate in the legislative process.

The case-law on Article 173 developed before the Social Policy Agreement engaged the EU social partners in the process of negotiating agreements which could become directives. On the basis of principles which emerged from the case-law on Article 173 (in particular, the *Chernobyl* case[30]), a number of parallel developments could potentially occur. First, there is the question of whether the 'prerogatives' of the EU social partners under the Protocol are 'one of the elements of the institutional balance created by the Treaties'.[31] Secondly, the question of whether the Court will insist on its:[32]

> duty to ensure that the provisions of the Treaties concerning the institutional balance are fully applied and to see to it that [the social partners'] prerogatives, like those of the other institutions, cannot be breached without [them] having available a legal remedy, among those laid down in the Treaties, which may be exercised in a certain and effective manner.

---

[27] *Commission* v. *Council* (Titanium Oxide), Case C-300/89, [1991] ECR I-2867.

[28] These words were virtually repeated by the Court of First Instance (CFI) in Case T-135/96, *UEAPME*, which cited the titanium oxide case, *UEAPME*, paragraph 88. The CFI did not, however, cite two other cases where Parliament's claim to more substantial participation was rejected by the Court. Case C-155/91, *Commission* v. *Council* (Waste Directive) [1993] ECR I-939, brought by the Commission, and Case C-187/93, *European Parliament* v. *Council* (Transfer of Waste) [1994] ECR I-2857, brought by the Parliament itself. See Craig and de Búrca, *EU Law*, pp. 73–8, at p. 77.

[29] Case C-316/91, [1994] ECR I-625.

[30] *European Parliament* v. *Council*, Case C-70/88, [1990] ECR I-2041.

[31] *Ibid.*, paragraph 23.　　[32] *Ibid.*, paragraph 25.

UEAPME,[33] not then recognised as one of the EU social partners, invoked paragraph 20 of the *Chernobyl* case (quoted above), and claimed that a remedy under Article 173 was necessary to:[34]

> secure judicial condemnation of a process in which its prerogatives as a representative of one of the sides of European industry have been disregarded.

The Council disputed this:[35]

> since [UEAPME] as such has no right to take part in the collective negotiation, it cannot rely on the case law to which it refers [*Chernobyl*].

Thirdly, in particular, again in the *Chernobyl* case:[36]

> in accordance with the Treaties, the [social partners'] prerogatives include participation in the drafting of legislative measures, in particular participation in the [consultation] procedure laid down in the EEC Treaty.

Does this cover the right of the social partners to be consulted in accordance with a provision of the Treaty? For example, does adoption of an act on a legal basis not providing for such mandatory consultation infringe the EU social partners' prerogatives? It was held that optional consultation was not sufficient to meet the prerogatives of the Parliament.[37]

The Social Policy Agreement places the EU social partners in an analogous position to the European Parliament with regard to the legislative process. The question is whether the Court, through litigation, would recognise this.[38]

The European Parliament's litigation strategy is a model for a similar campaign by the EU social partners to achieve a re-interpretation or revision of Article 230. Articles 138–9 EC require the Commission to consult management and labour, who may initiate the social dialogue, which may lead to agreements which shall be implemented. The case-law on Parliament's rights under Article 230 developed before the Maastricht Social Policy Agreement provided for the EU social partners to participate in the making of EC social and labour legislation. The Court regarded the institutional balance in the EU as requiring that the prerogatives of the European Parliament be respected, first, allowing Parliament to challenge acts which threaten its prerogatives, and secondly,

---

[33] Union Européenne de l'Artisanat et des Petites et Moyennes Entreprises.
[34] *UEAPME*, paragraph 61.     [35] *Ibid.*, paragraph 40.
[36] *European Parliament* v. *Council*, Case C-70/88, [1990] ECR I-2041, paragraph 28.
[37] *European Parliament* v. *Council*, Case C-316/9, [1994] ECR I-625.
[38] Silvana Sciarra cites an article by a former Advocate-General, G. Tesauro, on the Commission's obligation to consult the social partners under the Social Policy Agreement to the effect that: 'Failure to comply with this new obligation may result in infringement of Community law, in line with what the Court has stated in regard to the duty to consult the European Parliament in the law-making process.' However, she also states categorically: 'The social partners, although integrated into the law-making process, are in no way comparable to institutions of the Community'. 'Collective Agreements in the Hierarchy of European Community Sources', in P. Davies, A. Lyon-Caen, S. Sciarra and S. Simitis (eds.), *European Community Labour Law: Principles and Perspectives*, Oxford: Oxford University Press, 1996, p. 189 at pp. 202 and 204.

acknowledging that these prerogatives included the right to participate in the legislative process.

Later statements by the European Court of First Instance in *UEAPME* show an awareness of the parallel between the position of the European Parliament and that of the social partners. The EU social partners are in an analogous position to the European Parliament with regard to the legislative process.[39] In the legislative process on social policy, the social partners assume the responsibilities of the European Parliament. They should also have the same rights as privileged applicants under Article 230.[40]

## Social partners as 'non-privileged' applicants

Non-privileged applicants, as specified under Article 230, sub-paragraph 4, are of two types. First, those to whom a decision is addressed may institute proceedings against it. Secondly, others may institute proceedings 'against a decision which, although in the form of a regulation or a decision addressed to another person, is of direct and individual concern to the former'.[41] The key question is to identify those *other* persons who are *directly and individually concerned*, and may thus bring an action under Article 230. The leading decision laying down the test for who are the persons covered by Article 230, sub-paragraph 4, is *Plaumann*:[42]

> Persons other than those to whom a decision is addressed may only claim to be individually concerned if that decision affects them by reason of certain attributes which are peculiar to them or by reason of circumstances in which they are differentiated from all other persons and by virtue of these factors distinguishes them individually just as in the case of the person addressed.

The *Plaumann* formula has been interpreted in a restrictive manner in cases of commercial activity. The European Court's decision in the *Fruit and Vegetables* case[43] did not accept that an association representing a class of businessmen

---

[39] Though one problem is to decide who are the social partners with direct access to the ECJ. See Chapter 17 on selection of social partners engaged in the EU social dialogue.

[40] The social partners might want to use litigation under Article 230 in a number of specific disputes arising under the social dialogue procedure. For example, they may complain that the consultation by the Commission either did not take place or was inadequate (procedurally or substantively); or if the Commission submits to the Council a proposal, or the Council makes a decision, which amends the agreement reached by the social partners.

[41] In the case of this second group, the Court has liberalised access to Article 230 in the case of decisions in the form of a regulation, where the regulation can be characterised as a decision; for example, because it applies to a closed and definable group. *International Fruit Company BV* v. *Commission*, Cases 41–44/70 [1971] ECR 411, *Calpak SpA and Societa Emiliana Lavorazione Frutta SpA* v. *Commission*, Cases 789 and 790/79, [1980] ECR 1949.

[42] *Plaumann & Co.* v. *Commission* , Case 25/61, [1963] ECR 95.

[43] Cases 16,17/62, *Confédération Nationale des Fruits et Producteurs des Fruits et Légumes v. Council* [1962] ECR 471.

importing fruits and vegetables had the standing of a person individually concerned.[44]

Two cases are of particular interest in this context. *Parti Ecologiste 'Les Verts'* v. *Parliament* was a case which the Court conceded concerned 'a situation which has never before come before the Court'.[45] The case concerned the European Parliament allocating funds to subsidise political parties in the Parliament in the run-up to elections, which resulted in most of the funds going to parties already represented in Parliament. The Court allowed as admissible a complaint where:[46]

> Because they had representatives in the institution, certain political groupings took part in the adoption of a decision which deals both with their own treatment and with that accorded to rival groupings which were not represented. In view of this, and in view of the fact that the contested measure concerns the allocation of public funds for the purpose of preparing for elections and it is alleged that those funds were allocated unequally, it cannot be considered that only groupings which were represented and which were therefore identifiable at the date of the adoption of the contested measure are individually concerned by it.

The decision in *Les Verts* is characterised as one concerning the institutional structure of the Community. The question is whether, by analogy, other groups affected by agreements/decisions under the Social Policy Agreement embodied in Articles 138–9 EC are considered to be individually concerned in the new institutional structure of decision-making on social policy.

The second decision is that of the Court of First Instance in *Stichting Greenpeace Council (Greenpeace International)* v. *Commission*:[47]

> It has consistently been held that an association formed for the protection of the collective interests of a category of persons cannot be considered to be directly and individually concerned ... by a measure affecting the general interests of that category, and is therefore not entitled to bring an action for annulment where its members may not do so individually ...
>
> Furthermore, *special circumstances such as the role played by an association in a procedure which led to the adoption of an act within the meaning of Article 173 ... may justify holding admissible an action brought by an association whose members are not directly and individually concerned by the contested measures.*[48]

---

[44] Up to recently, the relative willingness of the Court to admit claims by non-privileged applicants has been confined to cases in specific substantive areas of EC law: anti-dumping, competition and state aid. But other cases seem to show some relaxation of the strict criteria and willingness of the European Court to expand the scope for non-privileged applicants. *Codorniu SA* v. *Council,*. Case C-309/89, [1994] ECR I-1853. See Craig and de Búrca, *EU Law*, 3rd edn, 2003, pp. 487ff.

[45] Case 294/83, [1986] ECR 1339, paragraph 35.       [46] *Ibid.*

[47] Case T-585/93, [1995] ECR II-2205, paragraph 59 (italics added).

[48] The CFI examined whether the associations (Greenpeace) could come within the exception mentioned in the second part of the above paragraph 59, but decided on the facts that they could not.

It is not clear how the *Plaumann* formula will be applied in determining access to the Court in the employment and labour relations field. In cases involving Articles 138–9 EC, the decision engages organisations with extensive affiliates, or regulates entire sectors or occupations. The question is whether complaints concerned with employment and labour relations will receive liberal treatment regarding admissibility by non-privileged applicants.

The decisions in *Les Verts* and *Greenpeace* support the view that the legislative process leading to a directive incorporating a social dialogue agreement might present specific features (a constitutional process involving representatives taking part in a decision; associations playing a role in the legislative process) which allow for a liberal interpretation of the *locus standi* conditions for use of Article 230 by non-privileged applicants. Who might these non-privileged applicants be under Articles 138–9 EC?

The approach taken by the ECJ appears to contemplate that a number of specific disputes which may be anticipated in the implementation of the social dialogue procedure could possibly lead to litigation under Article 230. This was confirmed when disappointed candidates for inclusion in the social dialogue procedure ended up before the European Court in the *UEAPME* case.[49]

Additionally, labour and management may complain that the consultation required of the Commission was not adequate, procedurally and/or substantively. If so, is the institutional balance being respected? Again, some 'representative' organisations may complain that they were not consulted, or are in various ways prejudiced by an agreement reached through the social dialogue, and, perhaps, enshrined in a Council decision. As in *Parti Ecologiste 'Les Verts'* v. *Parliament*, will the Court allow as admissible a complaint where:[50]

> Because they had representatives in the institution, certain [labour and management organisations] took part in the adoption of a decision which deals both with their own treatment and with that accorded to rival groupings which were not represented … it cannot be considered that only groupings which were represented and which were therefore identifiable at the date of the adoption of the contested measure are individually concerned by it.

Again, do other social partner organisations qualify under the exception in the *Greenpeace* case:[51]

> special circumstances such as the role played by an association in a procedure which led to the adoption of an act within the meaning of Article [230] … may justify holding admissible an action brought by an association whose members are not directly and individually concerned by the contested measures.

---

[49] *Union Européenne de l'Artisanat et des Petites et Moyennes Entreprises (UEAPME)* v. *Council of the European Union*, Case T-135/96, [1998] ECR II-2335. See below, Chapter 24.
[50] Case 294/83, [1986] ECR 1339, paragraph 35.
[51] Case T-585/93, [1995] ECR II-2205, paragraph 59.

Finally, the EU social partners may object if the Commission submits to the Council a proposal, or the Council makes a decision implementing such a proposal, which deviates from the agreement reached by the social partners.

As will be explored in more detail later, the *UEAPME* case is the first to address the salience of Article 230 to Articles 138–9 EC. The analysis of the CFI's decision so far leads to conclusions about future litigation, which may be of concern to the EU social partners, the EU institutions and others.

The first conclusion is that Directives implementing agreements reached through the social dialogue are potentially open to challenge. The application by UEAPME to annul the Parental Leave Directive may have failed, but the case has exposed the vulnerability of measures adopted under Articles 138–9 EC to applications under Article 230.

The second conclusion is that, building on the case law of the European Court in *Chernobyl*, it may be possible for the EU social partners, ETUC, UNICE and CEEP, to claim that, as participants in the legislative process, they too should be recognised as 'privileged' applicants within the meaning of Article 230. Such recognition is necessary to maintain the institutional balance within a legislative process in which the EU social partners have undoubted prerogatives. These prerogatives include, as provided in Articles 138 and 139 EC, mandatory consultation by the Commission over proposals in the social policy field, and social dialogue which may lead to agreements which 'shall be implemented'.

On the face of it, there seems little reason for the social partners to challenge a directive embodying their own agreement. However, a number of pessimistic scenarios cannot be excluded.

One scenario is that an agreement reached by the social partners is incorporated in amended form in a directive. Although the Commission has affirmed that it will only propose the agreement as reached to the Council, and 'would give the Council no opportunity to amend the agreement',[52] such a possibility cannot be excluded for ever. If labour law and social policy, including employment policy, come increasingly to the forefront of EU politics, the Commission may come under pressure to undertake close scrutiny of the content of the agreement, the Council may decline to be a passive rubber-stamp, and other EU institutions may make pronouncements on the substance of any agreement reached, leading to pressure for its amendment.[53]

A second scenario anticipates internal dissidence within the social partners leading to second thoughts by one of their affiliates about an agreement reached. The internal constitutional equilibrium of the social partners may play a role in a more active litigation strategy using Article 230. A change in the

---

[52] Commission Communication of 1993, paragraph 39.

[53] See the discussion in Chapter 19 of the Inter-Institutional Agreement on Better Law-Making of 1993.

majority view about an agreement, or even a powerful dissent, may trigger pressures for challenges to be launched.

The third conclusion is that Article 230 could allow for challenges by 'non-privileged' applicants. If the EU social partners are unable to achieve recognition as privileged applicants, they would be well placed to claim the status of a non-privileged applicant, that a legal measure incorporating an agreement to which they were parties was 'of direct and individual concern' to them. Their affiliates, not excluding dissenters, might be able, and may be tempted, to make similar claims. Then there are those organisations, such as UEAPME,[54] who could try.

A fourth conclusion is perhaps the most politically sensitive. It is well known that the European Parliament was unhappy at being sidelined from the legislative process created by the Social Policy Agreement, which provided no formal role for the European Parliament.[55] Discontent was manifest during the process of Parliament's review of the proposal to enact the directive incorporating the second framework agreement on part-time work.

In its Communication of 1998, the Commission merely stated:[56]

> The Commission will continue to inform the European Parliament of the initiation of consultations and the opening and conclusion of negotiations under Article 3 ASP [Agreement on Social Policy] [Article 138 EC]. Furthermore, it will inform the Parliament as soon as the social partners ask the Commission to draw up a legislative proposal for the implementation of an agreement under Article 4(2) ASP [Article 139(2)] to enable it to give its opinion in good time on the proposal before the Council reaches its formal decision.
>
> Issues related to the role of the European institutions in the decision-making process under the Agreement on Social Policy – and in particular the provision of information concerning negotiations between the social partners – will be the subject of further discussions between the Commission, the Council and the European Parliament in the context of the Inter-Institutional Trilogue.

It is hard to imagine the Parliament remaining content with mere information, at a time when the Treaty of Amsterdam replicated Article 2 of the Social Policy

---

[54] The CFI's judgment in *UEAPME* was, superficially, favourable in so far as a challenge to the legality of the first product of the Social Policy Agreement was rejected. However, the case opened up the Pandora's box of Article 230 as it may apply to Articles 138–9 EC. The result may be litigation by applicants seeking to challenge directives emerging from the processes of social dialogue, and perhaps even other legislation on social and labour policy.

[55] Daniela Obradovic observes that 'irrespective of the fact that the European Parliament is completely excluded from the legislative procedure laid down in Article 3 and 4 of the Agreement [Articles 138–9 EC], the Parliament has not developed a hostile attitude … Rather, its position regarding the role of the social partners in Union lawmaking can be described as an ambiguous one.' 'Accountability of Interest Groups in the Union Lawmaking Process', Chapter 18 in P. Craig and C. Harlow (eds.), *Lawmaking in the European Union*, London: Kluwer, 1998, p. 354, at p. 363; and see generally the section on 'Interest Representation in the Union and the European Parliament', pp. 362–6.

[56] COM(98) 322 of 20 May 1998, Section 5: Key Action, page 16.

Agreement (Article 137), except that the Council was now to 'act in accordance with the procedure referred to in Article 189*b* [Article 251]'. This replaced the previous reference to Article 189*c* (Article 252) of the Treaty, the 'cooperation' procedure. Instead, the new 'co-decision' procedure, introduced by the Treaty on European Union, is to apply to legislative proposals on social policy under Article 2(2) of the Agreement (Article 137(2)). If the Council does not agree to Parliament's amendments, conciliation is attempted to agree a joint text. If agreed, Parliament must approve, and then the Council can approve it by qualified majority. But if no text is agreed, Parliament can block the measure. This change means that the European Parliament will have a much more important role in determining the content of EC labour legislation in the future. Commission proposals and Council decisions will have to take into account the wishes of Parliament, on pain of a possible veto.

It seems, therefore, that the European Parliament is unlikely to sit passively by while, on the one hand, its legislative role is augmented, but, on the other hand, potentially circumvented by the social dialogue process leading to directives. In these circumstances, Parliament's undisputed recognition as a 'privileged' applicant under Article 230 may persuade it to take legal action 'for the purpose of protecting [its] prerogatives'. A challenge by the European Parliament to a Directive incorporating an agreement of which it had merely been informed, and given an opportunity to present an opinion, even in good time, raises delicate questions of constitutional prerogatives.[57]

A last conclusion again contributes to this potential litigation spiral. If it were to be the case that the EU social partners, ETUC, UNICE and CEEP, on the analogy of the European Parliament in *Chernobyl*, were to be recognised as 'privileged' applicants under Article 230 – even if only 'for the purpose of protecting their prerogatives' – there seems no reason why they should be limited to challenging directives incorporating social dialogue agreements.

The problem is highlighted by the scope of the social partners' prerogatives reflected in the obligation of the Commission to consult them 'before submitting proposals in the social policy field' and 'on the content of the envisaged proposal' (Article 138(2) and (3)). Could the social partners challenge directives on social policy which had been channelled through other legislative processes than that engaging the social dialogue procedure under the Social Policy Agreement?[58] It is not difficult to come up with examples of EC

---

[57] One commentator's view is that, despite *Chernobyl*, Parliament could not institute proceedings for annulment: 'Since Parliament is not mentioned in Article 4(2) [Article 139(2)] it is not affected.' G. Brinkman, 'Lawmaking under the Social Chapter of Maastricht', Chapter 12 in Craig and Harlow (eds.), *Lawmaking in the European Union*, p. 239 at p. 258, footnote 87.

[58] A similar possibility of legal action was anticipated in the first edition of this book in relation to Commission proposals made under the EC Treaty, rather than under the Protocol and Agreement on Social Policy, in order to include the UK, which had opted out from the latter. *European Labour Law*, 1996, p. 532.

legislation which could be tempting for one or other of the social partners to challenge as arguably possessing a social policy dimension.[59]

## Access to the ECJ by the social partners through the preliminary rulings procedure

Even if the social partners' institutional legislative role in EU labour law did not suffice to give them the right to take direct legal action before the European Court, two other avenues may be explored: (1) a general right of intervention in proceedings before the European Court; (2) a special right of intervention in proceedings concerned with European framework agreements. This last right could lay the foundation for a general system of autonomous resolution of labour disputes at EU level.

### A general right of intervention in proceedings before the European Court

Modern courts recognise that willingness to open proceedings to interventions from public interest groups with legitimate concerns improves the quality of their decision-making. It also enhances the democratic legitimacy of the court's decision. Article 40 of the Statute of the Court of Justice, appears to allow for the possibility of intervention in its first two paragraphs:[60]

> Member States and institutions of the Communities may intervene in cases before the Court.
> The same right shall be open to any other person establishing an interest on the result of any case submitted to the Court, save in cases between Member States, between institutions of the Communities or between Member States and institutions of the Communities.[61]

The conventional wisdom is that applications for intervention must be channelled through the national court making the preliminary reference.[62]

---

[59] The amendment to the Acquired Rights Directive provides one example (Directive 98/50/EC of 29 June 1998, OJ L201/88 of 17 July 1998); Article 2 of the so-called 'Monti' Council Regulation on the functioning of the internal market in relation to the free movement of goods among the Member States, perhaps another. See B. Bercusson, 'The Full Monti: Stripping Away Strikers' Rights', in *Thompsons Labour and European Law Review*, Issue 20, March 1998, pp. 4–5.

[60] The Statute of the Court (as of November 2004), and its Rules of Procedure, may be found on the EU's website: www.europa.eu.int under the link with the EU's institutions.

[61] The third paragraph of Article 40 deals with interventions involving EEA/EFTA states.

[62] David W.K. Anderson and Marie Demetriou, *References to the European Court*, 2nd edn, London: Sweet & Maxwell Litigation Library, 2002, pp. 237–9. '"The parties" who are entitled to submit written observations (by Article 20 of the EC Statute) or to appear at the oral hearing (by Article 104(4) of the Rules of Procedure) are the parties to the action pending before the national court. Whether or not a person is a "party" is a matter for the law of that national court. The European Court has so far invariably respected the discretion of the national court as regards whether a person should be regarded as a party. Written and/or oral observations have been accepted from parties who have been given leave to intervene by the national court, including non-governmental organisations submitting observations in the public interest … There is no

However, the rules governing procedure before the ECJ do not appear to address this question clearly.

On the one hand, the Rules of Procedure of the Court of Justice provide for intervention in terms which do not indicate any limitation, prescribing simply 'a statement of the circumstances establishing the right to intervene'.[63] However, 'Notes for the guidance of Counsel' published by the ECJ, include Section 13: 'Intervention', which begins with the unequivocal statement: 'Intervention is allowed only in direct actions and appeals.'[64] The exclusion by the 'Notes for the guidance of Counsel' of intervention in cases other than direct actions and appeals appears to be inconsistent both with the Court's practice, whereby interventions are permitted in references under Article 234 EC (at least with the permission of the national court making the reference), and with the provisions in the Statute of the Court and the Rules of Procedure which do not specify exclusion of interventions in preliminary references.

### Should national courts determine intervention rights before the ECJ?

Intervention before the ECJ in the case of preliminary references does appear to be allowed with the permission of the national court making the reference. Admittedly, Article 234 cases are references by national courts, and national courts determine the substance of the case. The question remains: why should national courts determine procedures before the ECJ?

difficulty from the point of view of Community law in a third party making representations to the European Court …Those eligible to intervene are more tightly defined in preliminary references than in direct actions. They are restricted to the Member States and the Commission, which may intervene as of right; the Council, Parliament and the European Central Bank, which have the right to intervene where one of their own acts is at issue; and the Member States party to the European Economic Area Agreement … where the reference concerns one of the fields of application of that Agreement [EC Statute, Article 23, Rules of Procedure, Article 104(4)]'. At page 248: 'Article 40 … of the EC Statute, which allows interventions on the part of any person establishing an interest in the result of a case, concerns contentious proceedings only. [K.P.E. Lasok, *The European Court of Justice: Practice and Procedure*, 2nd edn, London: LexisNexis, 1994, p. 153, footnote 2: 'The English text [Article 40 of the ECJ Statute] refers to intervention in a "case", but other texts use a word which has the more specific meaning of a dispute or litigation.'] It does not therefore apply to references for preliminary rulings which are deemed to be uncontentious proceedings. There are therefore no grounds for allowing the intervention of a party which is not already involved in the action before the national court. It is open to a non-party other than a Member State or Community institution to secure a hearing in the European Court by persuading the referring court to join it as a party to the main action … The limits of the Court's willingness to hear all those joined to proceedings before the referring court have yet to be explored.' At page 251: 'Parties have also been represented by trade union officials'.

[63] Rules of Procedure, Title III, Chapter 3, Article 93(1)(f).

[64] The Introduction to these 'Notes for the guidance of Counsel' states: 'This guide should therefore be seen as a working tool intended to enable Counsel to present their written and oral pleadings in the form which the Court of Justice considers most fitting. At the same time, attention will be drawn to the Court's procedural practice. However, this guide is intended neither to lay down legal rules in itself nor to override the relevant provisions in force'.

There are problems in allowing national courts to decide on intervention. National court control of interventions in Article 234 cases leads to different practice depending on national court procedural rules. This could produce discrimination between Member States; for example, where trade unions, or even the ETUC, are allowed to intervene in references in some Member States, but not in other Member States.

National court discretion to refer is carefully protected by the ECJ, for example, from limitations imposed by higher national courts. What if a national court allowed intervention, but appeal to a higher national court overruled this decision? Does this conflict with national court discretion? Would a national court in one Member State laying down a rule that no interveners are allowed in any Article 234 case be acceptable? National procedural rules on intervention reflect the practice of intervention in *national* court proceedings, not *European Court* proceedings. The context of intervention before national courts is very different. There is a need for rules specifically addressing intervention in the ECJ in Article 234 references, and these are best determined by the ECJ itself.

Applications to the ECJ to intervene are permitted in Article 230 cases. Why not in Article 234 cases? National courts do not control intervention by Member States and EU institutions in both Article 234 and Article 230 cases. Why should they control *other* interveners in Article 234 cases when they do not control other interveners in Article 230 cases?

Article 230 allows direct access to the ECJ by 'privileged' applicants (a Member State, the European Parliament, the Council or the Commission). The ECJ acknowledged that the institutional position of the European Parliament justified allowing it direct access to the ECJ (a 'privileged' applicant for the purposes of Article 230). *A fortiori*, the institutional position of the European social partners justifies indirect access through intervention in Article 234 proceedings.

Direct access to the ECJ under Article 230 is permitted to 'non-privileged' applicants on condition that the decision challenged 'is of direct and individual concern' to them. The criteria for access by 'non-privileged applicants' are interpreted by the ECJ. Interveners are similarly allowed by direct request to the ECJ. Yet Article 234 allows access to the ECJ only through national courts, and the ECJ does not determine access through the national courts. The question is: how should interveners in Article 234 references be treated? One argument is that interveners in Article 234 proceedings are the functional equivalent of 'non-privileged' applicants (and interveners) in Article 230 proceedings. In sum: the parallel is between interveners in Article 234 cases and *locus standi* as non-privileged applicants in Article 230 cases. As interveners, not initiators of direct actions, the criteria for access should be interpreted by the ECJ, and more generously.[65]

---

[65] Article III-365(4) of the proposed Treaty Establishing a Constitution for Europe relaxed the conditions for access of 'non-privileged' applicants in the case of 'a regulatory act which is of direct concern to him or her and does not entail implementing measures'.

### Intervention rights by European social partners

Intervention by the European social partners is desirable where requests for preliminary rulings raise issues of general principle crucial to European labour law. The social partners bring expertise to the ECJ that the parties do not. They represent employers and workers and their organisations in all Member States. They bring expertise on the national industrial relations systems of all the Member States. Social partner intervention would highlight the European and transnational dimensions of the questions referred, and avoid the risk that the issue might otherwise be portrayed as a narrow dispute between specific parties in the Member State concerned.

The requirement that the European social partners be treated like all other applicants, that they must establish an interest in each case in order to intervene, would force the European Court to make decisions which are highly political and consequently both difficult and dangerous for the Court.[66] It would be clearer and more consistent with the institutional position of the social partners in EC social and labour law for the ETUC to be given the same right to intervene in cases before the Court as the Member States and institutions of the Community.[67]

It would be most appropriate for the European social partners to apply directly to the ECJ to intervene. A direct request to the ECJ for *locus standi* as an intervener reflects the social partners' role as an institutional actor in the EU context, with a claim to legitimacy resting on their status as organisations representing employers and trade unions in the EU.

---

[66] Thus, even if trade unions established an interest, the exclusion of cases involving the Member States and institutions would have prevented the ETUC from intervening in important cases such as that of *Commission* v. *France*, Case C-265/95, [1997] ECR I-6959, or in others, such as the UK's challenge to the Council over the Working Time Directive (*United Kingdom* v. *Council*, Case C-84/4, [1996] ECR I-5755). Similarly, it might have been the Commission, not a company, which challenged the Italian regulation in *Borsana*, Case C-2/97, [1998] ECR I-8597, or a Member State which challenged the Parental Leave Directive, instead of UEAPME (*Union Européenne de l'Artisanat et des Petites et Moyennes Entreprises (UEAPME)* v. *Council of the European Union*, Case T-135/96, [1998] ECR II-2335). In such cases, where there are vital trade union interests at stake, the ETUC would not be allowed to intervene under the current provision. The first time a right of intervention was granted to employee representatives before the European Court concerned the enterprise committee of a French company, Legrande, which objected to the Commission's decision in the proposed merger of their company with another. Case T-77/02, of 6 June 2002. See 'Le juge européen écoute son premier comité d'entreprise', *Liaisons Sociales Europe*, No. 61, 25 July–4 September 2003, pp. 1–2. A previous attempt to intervene in such proceedings by the enterprise committee of Perrier-Vittel had been rejected.

[67] Alternative, less desirable, channels of intervention by the European social partners include the following. Article 25 of the Statute of the Court: 'The Court may at any time entrust any individual, body, authority, committee or other organisation it chooses with the task of giving an expert opinion'. Article 26 of the Statute of the Court: 'Witnesses may be heard under conditions laid down in the Rules of Procedure'. Article 28 of the Statute of the Court: 'Witnesses and experts may be heard on oath taken in the form laid down in the Rules of Procedure or in the manner laud down by the law of the country of the witness or expert'. Finally, the parties, as part of their written representations, could include submissions from the social partners.

### Special intervention rights in cases involving framework agreements

When a case comes before the European Court which involves a framework agreement concluded in the context of the EU social dialogue and embodied in a Council directive, there is a particularly strong argument for a right of intervention by the social partners. General rules on labour standards, such as those laid down in framework agreements reached through the social dialogue, lead inevitably to disputes over their interpretation. There is no current provision in the EC Treaty giving the social partners a specific and special status to institute direct proceedings before the ECJ aimed at *interpreting* an agreement. This can only be done by seeking a preliminary reference through a national court.[68]

Such a special intervention right is, in fact, anticipated in a provision to be found in each of three framework agreements reached to date. The interpretation of EU social dialogue agreements was dealt with in the framework agreements on parental leave, part-time work and fixed-term work through a specific provision (as formulated in the first agreement, Clause 4(6) of the Parental Leave Agreement):[69]

> Without prejudice to the respective role of the Commission, national courts and the Court of Justice, any matter relating to the interpretation of this agreement at European level should, in the first instance, be referred by the Commission to the signatory parties who will give an opinion.

The procedure to be followed by the Commission to obtain the opinion of the EU social partners is far from clear.[70] Even less clear is what the Commission is to do once it obtains the opinion of the signatory parties, in particular where these parties do not succeed in reaching a common opinion. If they do reach a common opinion, it would appear that the Commission is obliged to present it to the Court (the Commission has intervention rights in every case before the Court). If the parties fail to reach a common opinion, arguably the Commission should present to the Court the different opinions of the parties. In this way, the arguments of the social partners as parties to the framework agreement would

---

[68] Attempts failed in the Convention on the Future of Europe to propose amendments in the proposed Constitution with the intention of giving the social partners the right to institute proceedings directly before the ECJ on the *interpretation* of an agreement. Such amendments could be separate from challenges to validity (legality), or the two issues combined in a single provision. Either way, the intention was to allow for a direct action by the social partners before the ECJ.

[69] Council Directive 96/34/EC of 3 June 1996 on the Framework Agreement on parental leave concluded by UNICE, CEEP and the ETUC. OJ L145/4 of 19 June 1996. A similar provision is in the Preambles to the agreements on part-time and fixed-term work (Directives 97/81/EC and 1999/70/EC).

[70] This was demonstrated by experience of a dispute over the interpretation by Ireland of the Parental Leave Agreement, where the procedure appeared to consist of a hasty series of telephone calls.

reach the Court through the Commission, a form of indirect intervention in the proceedings.

However, the procedure would be much more simple, logical and effective if the social partners were permitted to have direct access to the Court to present their views, both in writing and orally, as regards the interpretation of the framework agreement reached by them.

## Conclusion

In her analysis of Article 230 in the context of a general enquiry into access to the European Court and general citizen participation, Carol Harlow ruled out opening up direct individual access to the Court through Article 230 as this 'would merely add to the Court's already over-burdened docket'.[71] Her conclusions included two options. First:

> the unpalatable truth may have to be faced that extended access to the Court of Justice is feasible only in conjunction with a move to appellate status. A series of specialist Chambers and/or tribunals, each with particular rules of standing, might be more efficient.

In a 1989 Report for the Commission and Parliament, I proposed a specialist Community tribunal on fundamental social and economic rights parallel to national labour court systems:[72]

> The jurisdiction, powers and procedures of this tribunal should reflect the special nature of the rights adjudicated upon, and their close connection with the social dialogue.

A Protocol annexed to the Treaty of Nice revised the Statute of the European Court of Justice and the Court of First Instance and introduced a number of reforms. The redistribution of responsibilities between the Court and the CFI meant that the CFI becomes the ordinary court for all direct actions. The Treaty of Nice envisaged major changes in the judicial structure of the European courts, including the creation of specialised judicial panels to hear cases in specific areas. The creation of specialised tribunals will relieve the burden on the CFI. Significantly for European labour law, the first of these specialised courts to be established was the special tribunal for employment and industrial relations disputes concerning the employees of the EU institutions. The creation of specialised tribunals allows the EU to follow a practice in the Member States of establishment of a specialised EU tribunal to deal more generally with questions of European law in the field of employment and industrial relations.

---

[71] C. Harlow, 'Towards a Theory of Access for the European Court of Justice', (1992) 12 *Yearbook of European Law* 213 at p. 246.

[72] B. Bercusson, 'Fundamental Social and Economic Rights in the European Community', in A. Cassese, A. Clapham and J. Weiler (eds.), *Human Rights in the European Community: Methods of Protection*, Baden-Baden: Nomos Verlag, 1991, p. 195, at p. 286. See also pp. 231–3 and 285–6.

Harlow's view was that the most economical way to increase interest representation without overloading the Court is not by changing the *locus standi* rules but through intervention procedure:[73]

> Modern courts increasingly show a democratic willingness to hear as many citizens as possible ... For the Court of Justice of the European Communities of its own accord to open its doors to public interest representation would at the same time enhance its standing and help to redress the general 'democracy deficit' in the Community.

Litigation strategy by collective actors has advantages and disadvantages. As regards trade unions, at a minimum, a defensive intervention strategy is necessary where cases affecting the interests of workers are brought by others to the European Court. A pro-active strategy would bring the ETUC before the Court challenging acts of the institutions where these violated the rights and interests of trade unions and workers. Increased litigation raises questions as to the composition of the European Court; specifically, whether there is a need for a chamber specialised in social and labour matters: a European Labour Court.

An alternative would build on the existing foundations of EU social dialogue agreements. The EU structure of social dialogue requires an institutional structure which can interpret and apply the emerging system of European labour regulation. Such a structure could include an autonomous system of dispute resolution governed by the social partners which provides an alternative to high profile litigation based on the Treaty. The existing provisions for interpretation of the framework agreements provide a foundation for such an autonomous system of dispute resolution.

An institutional structure for dispute resolution which enables the social partners to resolve any disputes over interpretation of their own agreements could be developed to deal with issues involving interpretation of other EU labour legislation. An autonomous system of dispute resolution, created and governed by the social partners, provides an alternative to unpredictable and uncontrollable litigation before the European Court.

---

[73] Harlow, 'Towards a Theory of Access', at p. 248.

**Part V**

# The European social dialogue

# Chapter 17

# The European social dialogue: from dynamism to benign neglect 1993–2008

The dominant feature of European collective industrial relations is the social dialogue:[1]

> The social dialogue is rooted in the history of the European continent, and this distinguishes the Union from most other regions of the world.[2]

The European social dialogue is a process which stipulates a relationship between collective bargaining and law specific to the EU. Social dialogue does not simply equate with collective bargaining. Collective bargaining takes many forms in different Member States. Besides bilateral bargaining, the social dialogue may adopt the form of tripartite structures, assume roles for public authorities and/or establish mechanisms for representation of the unorganised. Similarly, social dialogue at EU level implies a flexible relationship between social dialogue at all levels and Community and national institutions. The relationship is contingent upon national traditions of social dialogue within Member States. European social dialogue must be extremely flexible in its application within the context of Community social policy.

Collective bargaining and social dialogue within Member States is regarded as reflecting a balance of power between labour and capital, exercised traditionally through industrial conflict. The Treaty does not address even the possibility of industrial conflict at EU level. Indeed, Article 137(5) EC seems explicitly to aim to exclude regulatory competences on the right to strike. The logic to this auto-exclusion is, perhaps, that the current state of EU-level social dialogue is qualitatively different in that the normal means of pressure – strikes – are not (yet) operational at Community level.

The prospect of the EC social dialogue implies rather a tripartite process – involving the social partners and the Commission/Community as a dynamic factor. It arises due to the timing of the process of social dialogue during the Commission's mandatory consultation of the social partners in accordance with Article 138(2)–(4) EC. In the absence of industrial conflict at EU level,

---

[1] The introduction to the Commission's Communication of 2002 on 'The European social dialogue, a force for innovation and change'.
[2] COM(2002) 341 final, Brussels, 26 June 2002, p. 6.

the consultation of the social partners as part of the legislative process creates a dynamic of 'bargaining in the shadow of the law'.

An illustration is the process which led to the Parental Leave Directive.[3] This first product of the EU social dialogue illustrates the practice of mandatory consultation of the European social partners and subsequent EU social dialogue.[4] The first stage in the procedure (Article 138(2) EC) was initiated on 21 January 1995, when the Commission decided 'to consult management and labour on the possible direction of Community action with regard to reconciling working and family life'.[5] In June 1996 the Commission initiated the second stage of consultations under Article 138(3) EC, and '[On 5 July 1995], UNICE, CEEP and the ETUC informed the Commission, in accordance with Article [138(4) EC], of their desire to exercise the option available under Article [139(1)] of opening negotiations on parental leave.'[6]

The social partners' negotiations were successful: on 6 November 1995 they agreed a proposal for a framework agreement which was finally concluded on 14 December 1995 and 'submitted to the Commission with the request that it be implemented by a Council decision on a proposal from the Commission, in accordance with Article [139(2) EC]'.[7] The agreement was incorporated into Council Directive 96/34/EC on the Framework Agreement on parental leave concluded by UNICE, CEEP and the ETUC adopted by the Council on 3 June 1996.

The legal framework for the European social dialogue is in Articles 138 and 139 of the EC Treaty, first appearing in the Protocol and Agreement on Social Policy attached to the Maastricht Treaty on European Union agreed in December 1991. The interpretation and application of these provisions has developed over the period since they came into effect in November 1993. To date, two phases may be identified.

The first phase is that which led to the first social dialogue agreement on parental leave of 1996, followed by two other agreements, on part-time work in 1997 and on fixed-term work in 1999. These agreements were translated into directives. This process was elaborated in a Commission Communication of 1993. Attempts to expand this social dialogue process at European sectoral level are evidenced in Commission Communications of 1996 and 1998.

The second phase is characterised by social dialogue in which negotiations may take place, but there is either failure to reach agreement, or agreements are reached but on condition they were not transformed into legally binding

---

[3] Council Directive 96/34 on the Framework Agreement on parental leave concluded by UNICE, CEEP and the ETUC, OJ L145/4 of 19 June 1996.

[4] The process was described in the judgment of the European Court of First Instance (CFI) in *Union Européenne de l'Artisanat et des Petites et Moyennes Entreprises (UEAPME)* v. *Council of the European Union*, when an organisation representing artisans and small and medium enterprises (UEAPME) challenged the legality of the Parental Leave Directive. Case T-135/96, [1998] ECR II-2335.

[5] *Ibid.*, paragraph 5.    [6] *Ibid.*, paragraph 8.    [7] *Ibid.*, paragraph 9.

directives. The changing nature of the European social dialogue is evident, among other sources, in Commission Communications of 2002 and 2004.

## The first phase: 1993–1999

Soon after the ratification of the Maastricht Treaty the Commission presented to the Council and the European Parliament a Communication concerning the application of the Agreement on social policy.[8] The Commission acknowledged that, at least until the Intergovernmental Conference (IGC) scheduled for December 1996, the social policy of the European Union would be governed both by the EC Treaty and by the Agreement annexed to the Protocol, what it called 'two free standing but complementary legal frames of reference'.[9] It observed that: 'This situation has never occurred in the Community before.'[10]

The provisions of the Agreement concerned with the involvement of the social partners in the formulation of the social policy of the Union are contained in Articles 138–9 EC (formerly Articles 3 and 4 of the Agreement). These provisions are, in large part, concerned with the procedures to be followed by the Commission and the social partners in creating and implementing the future social policy of the Union. Since much of these procedures is to be initiated and carried through by the Commission, its interpretation of these provisions is authoritative, though not definitive.[11] It is above all of great importance to the practical operation of the procedures.

### The procedure of social policy formation as seen by the Commission

In the Communication, the Commission gave its point of view on the application of the provisions laying down these procedures, and hence it limited itself to Articles 3 and 4 (now Articles 138–9 EC), in which the involvement of the social partners is laid down. The procedure which the Commission proposes to follow falls into two distinct phases, indicated from headings in the Communication to be, first, 'Consultation of the Social Partners', and, secondly, 'From Consultation to Negotiation'.

The first phase incorporates two separate stages, reflecting in the Commission's view, the two separate consultations envisaged by Article 3(2) (Article 138(2) EC) and 3(3) (Article 138(3) EC). The first consultation begins

---

[8] COM(93) 600 final, Brussels, 14 December 1993.

[9] *Ibid.*, paragraph 8.    [10] *Ibid.*, Summary, paragraph 3.

[11] For example, the Communication, in paragraph 6(b), appears to state that there are excluded from the Agreement 'any matters relating to pay, the right of association, the right to strike and the right to impose lock-outs'. This quotation seems to reflect Article 2(6) of the Agreement (now Article 137(5) EC), which, however, only excludes these matters from: 'the provisions of this Article' – impliedly allowing for such matters to be dealt with under Articles 3 and 4 of the Agreement (now Articles 138–9 EC). Despite Article 2(6), Article 6 of the Agreement (now Article 141 EC) is explicitly concerned with EC competence on pay (equality between men and women).

on receipt of a letter sent by the Commission to the social partners. This consultation is required by Article 3(2) (Article 138(2) EC) before the Commission submits proposals in the social policy field. Its purpose is to ascertain the possible direction of Community action. At this stage, the Commission will be explaining the problem in social policy for which it may seek to find a solution in the form of measures taken at European level. This consultation period, as specified by the Commission. 'should not exceed six weeks', and it 'may be by letter or, if the social partners so desire, by the convening of an ad hoc meeting'.[12]

The first stage completed, the Commission, 'in the light of comments received … will decide whether to proceed to the second phase'. The Commission thus maintains its discretion to proceed or not, whatever the view of the social partners consulted. If so, the second consultation stage too 'will be initiated with the receipt of the second letter sent by the Commission, setting out the content of the planned proposal together with indication of the possible legal basis'.[13] The Commission proposes that the social partners should deliver a written opinion, where they wish through an ad hoc meeting, and: 'Where appropriate, they should deliver a recommendation setting out their joint positions on the draft text.'[14] Again, the duration of this second phase is restricted by the Commission to a period not exceeding six weeks.

In the course of these stages of consultation, the social partners do not only consider the substantive questions prefigured in the provisions of Article 3(2) and (3) (Article 138(2) and (3) EC): whether the Community should act; if so, the possible direction of Community action; and the content of the Commission's envisaged proposal. They must also address the question posed by Article 3(4) (Article 138(4) EC): whether they wish to initiate the process provided for in Article 4 (Article 139 EC) – the social dialogue which may lead to contractual relations, including agreements. The possibilities open to the social partners in expressing the opinion or recommendation include:

1. The Commission should not undertake any form of EC action;
2. The Commission should undertake one or other forms of EC action, possibly including various legal measures;
3. The Commission's envisaged proposal is acceptable, and should take the form of various EC actions, possibly including legal measures;
4. The Commission's envisaged proposal is not acceptable, but, if persisted with, should take the form of various Community actions, possibly including legal measures;
5. The social partners wish to initiate the social dialogue process provided for in Article 4.

The forms and contents of the responses of the social partners in this consultation phase may be very different. The Commission suggests that, even

---

[12] COM(93) 600 final, Brussels, 14 December 1993, paragraph 19.    [13] *Ibid.*    [14] *Ibid.*

before the social partners undertake to initiate the social dialogue process provided for in Article 4 (Article 139 EC):[15]

> The formal consultation of the social partners provided for in Article 3 of the Agreement [Article 138 EC] may lead to the adoption of opinions, recommendations or agreement-based relations (including agreements) within the social partners' sphere of competence.

The second phase described by the Commission is initiated when the social partners opt for the social dialogue process under Article 4 (Article 139 EC): 'From Consultation to Negotiation'. Article 3(4) (Article 138(4) EC) provides that: 'The duration of the procedure shall not exceed nine months, unless the management and labour concerned and the Commission decide jointly to extend it.' As envisaged by Article 4(1) (Article 139(1) EC), this dialogue 'may lead to contractual relations, including agreements', and these 'shall be implemented' according to procedures laid down in Article 4(2) (Article 139(2) EC).

### The Opinion of ECOSOC

The Economic and Social Committee of the EC (ECOSOC) decided to prepare an Opinion on the Commission's Communication.[16] What follows are a number of issues concerning the application of the Protocol and Agreement raised by the Commission's Communication and taken up in the ECOSOC Opinion.

---

[15] *Ibid.*, paragraph 28.

[16] Opinion 94/C 397/17, OJ 397/40 of 31 December 1994. The procedures of ECOSOC provide for the establishment of a Study Group for any Commission document which is relevant for ECOSOC. One of the members of the Study Group is designated the Rapporteur of the Opinion. Together with a designated Expert to the Rapporteur, a draft Opinion is prepared which reflects the deliberations of the Study Group. If the majority of the Study Group is in favour of the text of the draft Opinion, it will be submitted to the relevant Section of ECOSOC. ECOSOC consists of nine Sections, organised around certain subjects, such as industry, economic and financial matters, agriculture, external relations and social policy. At the end of deliberations in the Section, there is a vote. If all the members of the Section are in favour of the draft Opinion, it will be treated in the Plenary Session of ECOSOC as an item without discussion, on which there is simply a vote. If one or more members of the Section opposes the draft Opinion, a discussion is required in the Plenary Session. Amendments can be submitted by members. At the end of the discussion in the Plenary Session, the final vote on the draft Opinion is taken. If favourable, it becomes the Opinion of ECOSOC. In March 1994 ECOSOC began its deliberations with a view to drafting an Opinion. The ECOSOC Study Group on the Commission's Communication met four times, after which the draft Opinion was submitted to the Social Policy Section in November 1994. The Plenary Session of ECOSOC approved the draft Opinion by a large majority on 24 November 1994. The Rapporteur of the ECOSOC Opinion was J. J. Van Dijk; the Expert to the Rapporteur was B. Bercusson. This section of this chapter is based on our joint article: 'The Implementation of the Protocol and Agreement on Social Policy of the Treaty on European Union', (1995) 11 *International Journal of Comparative Labour Law and Industrial Relations* 3–30.

## Subsidiarity

The Agreement's confirmation of the fundamental role of the social partners in the implementation of the social dimension at EC level is seen by the Commission's Communication as:[17]

> recognition of a *dual form of subsidiarity* in the social field: on the one hand, subsidiarity regarding regulation at national and Community level; on the other, subsidiarity as regards the choice, at Community level, between the legislative approach and the agreement-based approach.

This is said to be 'in conformity with the fundamental principle of subsidiarity enshrined in Article 3B [now Article 5 EC] of the Treaty on European Union'.

The concept of subsidiarity was originally invoked in the context of the difficult issue of allocation and exercise of competences as between Member States and the Community. If this concept is also to be invoked in the context of allocation and exercise of competences as between the EC and the social partners, it has to be carefully scrutinised.

The European Parliament has emphasised the distinction between horizontal and vertical subsidiarity. *Vertical* subsidiarity refers to the division of competences between *different* levels: European and national. *Horizontal* subsidiary refers to the division of responsibilities between public authorities and, for example, the social partners at the *same* level.

The ECOSOC Opinion was alert to the implied subsumption of both horizontal and vertical subsidiarity under Article 3B (now Article 5 EC). The Opinion emphasised that the criteria specified in Article 3B of the TEU (subsidiarity) refer only to vertical, not horizontal subsidiarity. In its Opinion, ECOSOC tried to operationalise the two concepts.

As regards *vertical* subsidiarity, the Opinion indicated a choice of action at European level in a number of situations. First, there is a risk of downward pressure on social standards arising from competition between Member States on the basis of their social or labour costs. Member States seek to attract inward investment from foreign capital sources, as a way of increasing employment for its nationals. In so far as high social and labour costs are a factor in investment decisions, there is pressure on Member States to reduce social and labour standards to increase their attraction. Vertical subsidiarity supports action at European level. European level measures establishing minimum social and labour standards for all Member States can resist such negative competitive pressures. Different national labour and social standards can lead to enterprises in some Member States deriving competitive advantages from standards set below those required of enterprises in other Member States with higher labour and social standards. Again, European level measures can eliminate this competitive advantage by providing for harmonized standards of social and labour protection applicable to all employers. It was on this basis that Article 100 (now

[17] COM(93) 600 final, Brussels, 14 December 1993, paragraph 6(c).

Article 94 EC) justified the approval of Directives on collective dismissals[18] and transfers of undertakings.[19]

Secondly, some problems have a distinctive European dimension. For example, environmental issues are not divided by national political demarcations. Pollution does not halt at the frontiers of Member States. To establish an effective environmental policy will require a European approach, with implications for regulation of the standards of enterprises. An example in the social field is the Directive on European Works Councils.[20]

Finally, European Community legislation may have negative consequences for some group, which make compensatory measures at EC level necessary, For example, as a result of the completion of the internal market, the amount of work of customs officials was reduced.[21]

There is no indication that Article 3B (now Article 5 EC) has any relevance to the application of the principle of *horizontal* subsidiarity – the choice between action by the social partners *or* public authorities, at EC level (ETUC/UNICE/CEEP or EC institutions) or at Member State level (social partners or the Member States). The criteria for choosing *which* set of actors at the *same* level is appropriate are not necessarily those of Article 3B (now Article 5 EC). This has important implications for applying the principle of horizontal subsidiarity evident in Articles 3 and 4 of the Agreement (Articles 138–9 EC): in deciding whether the EC or the social partners should act.

Careful reading of the Protocol and Agreement on Social Policy and the attached Declarations enabled the ECOSOC to provide examples of *horizontal* subsidiarity.

The Member States' Declaration on Article 4(2) of the Agreement (Article 139(2) EC) provides an indication of the application of horizontal subsidiarity at national (Member State) level. The Member States expressly delegate to collective bargaining the development of the content of EC level agreements and acknowledge no obligation to undertake legislation.[22]

Article 2(4) of the Agreement (now Article 137(3) EC) provides another example of the application of horizontal subsidiarity at national (Member State) level. The implementation of directives at Member State level may be

---

[18]  Directive 75/129, OJ L48/29.    [19]  Directive 77/187, OJ L61/26.

[20]  Council Directive 94/45/EC of 22 September 1994 on the establishment of a European Works Council or a procedure in Community-scale undertakings and Community-scale groups of undertakings for the purposes of informing and consulting employees. OJ L254/64 of 30 September 1994.

[21]  The MATTHEUS programme was set up to give these customs officers the opportunities of retraining.

[22]  'The Conference declares that the first of the arrangements for application of the agreements between management and labour Community-wide – referred to in Article 118B(2) – will consist in developing by collective bargaining according to the rules of each Member State, the content of the agreements, and that consequently this arrangement implies no obligation on the member states to apply the agreements directly or to work out rules for their transposition, nor any obligation to amend national legislation in force to facilitate their implementation'.

entrusted to management and labour, subject to a guarantee by the Member State of the results imposed by the directive.

Similarly, support for different criteria for the application of the principle of horizontal subsidiarity follows from decisions of the European Court. This jurisprudence emphasised that the competence of the social partners, as opposed to the public authorities, to implement EC measures through collective agreements must satisfy certain conditions. The agreements concerned must cover all employees, and must include all the Directive's requirements.[23]

The possibility of implementing Directives through the actions of the social partners at national level was confirmed by the Commission in an exchange of letters with the Danish social partners. The Commission recognised the principle that Directives relating to labour market matters may be implemented in Denmark through collective agreements without the need for legislation.[24] This principle had been introduced earlier by the Danish Commissioner Henning Christophersen.

The ECOSOC referred to the generally recognised constitutional principle of the autonomy of the social partners.[25] This should influence any choice as to the responsibilities of the social partners and of the authorities.

The conclusion to be drawn from these examples might be that the principle of horizontal subsidiarity is confirmed by a wide range of institutions at European level: the Council, the Court of Justice and the Commission. However, the criteria set out in Article 3B (now Article 5 EC) do not apply to the concept of horizontal subsidiarity, only vertical subsidiarity. The criteria for the application of horizontal subsidiarity remain to be elaborated.

### Representativeness

The Commission must promote the consultation of management and labour[26] and shall consult management and labour.[27] Management and labour may initiate the social dialogue[28] which may lead to contractual relations including agreements between them.[29] Such agreements shall be implemented in accordance with practices specific to management and labour, or at their joint request, by a Council decision.[30]

Who are 'management and labour'? Which organisations can claim the rights to consultation, to initiate social dialogue and reach and implement agreements? The identification of organisations claiming to fall within the meaning of the 'management and labour' given entitlements under the Agreement

---

[23] See Chapter 14.

[24] This exchange of letters took place on 11 May 1993. A similar exchange of letters took place between the Commission and the Swedish government on 29 May 1993.

[25] As in ILO Convention No. 98.     [26] Article 3(1) (now Article 138(1) EC).

[27] Article 3(2) and 3(3) (now Article 138(2) and 138(3) EC).

[28] Article 3(4) (now Article 138(4) EC).     [29] Article 4(1) (now Article 139(1) EC).

[30] Article 4(2) (now Article 139(2) EC).

raises numerous potential difficulties. Organisations making claims are very different. Some organisations present themselves as European when they have affiliates in only some Member States. Different organisations claim to comprise the same categories of labour or management. The claims of some organisations are disputed by other organisations. An example would be employers in small and medium enterprises. Both UNICE (now BusinessEurope) and UEAPME claims to represent such employers, but UEAPME claims to be more representative.

The Agreement (now in Articles 138–9 EC) never uses the word 'representativeness'. But the Commission was clearly drawn to this criterion for identifying the relevant organisations of management and labour. The Commission's Communication refers to the fact that:[31]

> Since the adoption of the Maastricht Treaty, the Protocol on Social Policy and the Agreement, a number of the organisations which do not participate in the existing social dialogue have submitted formal requests to the Commission to take part directly in the social dialogue. To take a position on this question in full knowledge of the facts, the Commission carried out a study of European employers' and workers' organisations so as to enable the Commission to understand more clearly the different mechanisms by which representative social dialogues are established at national level, and to assist in assessing how this process might best operate at Community level.

Annex 3 to the Communication is entitled: 'Main Findings of the "Social Partners Study (Representativeness)"'. The concept of representativeness plays a key role in the Communication's discussion of the application of the Agreement. But its role is not that of selecting organisations eligible for consultation under the Agreement.

On the one hand, the Commission's study was undertaken to assist in identifying 'labour and management'. This study, as its title indicates, used 'representativeness' as a key criterion. The conclusions of the study are summarised in Annex 3 in the form of answers to specific questions. As regards systems of recognition of social partners, the conclusion is:

> For collective bargaining, in most countries mutual recognition is the basic mechanism, but additional formal or legal requirements may have to be fulfilled.

As regards criteria for representativeness, the conclusion is that the systems for recognition:

> make use (sometimes implicitly) of quantitative criteria of various types in about half of the Member States. Generally speaking, qualitative criteria appear to be at least as important. The study confirms the great diversity in approaches used.

---

[31] Communication, paragraph 23.

From these conclusions, the Commission drew two main messages:[32]

(a) the diversity of practice in the different Member States is such that there is no single model which could be replicated at European level, and
(b) the different Member States' systems having all taken many years to grow and develop, it is difficult to see how a European system can be created by administrative decision in the short term.

Despite these negative messages regarding the feasibility of developing criteria for identifying labour and management at European level, the Commission's Communication without more ado immediately sets out the criteria it proposes for organisations to be consulted. They should:[33]

> be cross industry or relate to specific sectors or categories and be organised at European level;
> consist of organisations which are themselves an integral and recognised part of Member State social partner structures and with the capacity to negotiate agreements, and which are representative of all Member States, as far as possible;
> have adequate structures to ensure their effective participation in the consultation process.

Annex 2 to the Communication gives an overview of the organisations which, in the Commission's view, 'currently comply broadly with these criteria'. In addition, the Commission inevitably acknowledged the special status of certain organisations:[34]

> the Commission recognises that there is a substantial body of experience behind the social dialogue established between the UNICE [now BusinessEurope], CEEP and ETUC.

Other organisations are more problematic. The Commission rejected the option of creating itself 'some form of consultation body or umbrella liaison committee'.[35] At most it expressed the desire 'to promote the development of new linking structures between all the social partners so as to help rationalise and improve the process'.[36]

The Commission's criteria ignore the problems that bedevil the use of 'representativeness' as a criterion. The conclusions of the study highlighted these problems. Representativeness as a criterion is not necessarily the most straightforward method of identifying labour and management entitled under the Agreement. Rather than facing the difficult option of explicitly renouncing the criterion of representativeness, the Commission put forward criteria which refer only to representativeness of Member States, and then only as far as possible. The Commission has effectively opted for administrative decision as

---

[32] *Ibid.*, paragraph 23.   [33] *Ibid.*, paragraph 24.   [34] *Ibid.*, paragraph 25.
[35] *Ibid.*, paragraph 27.   [36] *Ibid.*, paragraph 26.

the short-term solution to the problem of selecting which organisations fall within the scope of labour and management in the Agreement.

The question is whether the Commission's use of the study on representativeness demonstrates its implicit commitment to this criterion in the long term, or, on the contrary, confirms its belief that it is impracticable. The Commission's final word, that its selection:

> will be reviewed in the light of experience acquired in applying the new procedures instituted by the Agreement, and of the way the social dialogue develops

contains no commitment to representativeness as a criterion to be used in the future. However, the issue is unlikely to disappear. Disappointed candidates for inclusion in the procedures may seek to claim directly effective rights based on the provisions of the Agreement, as part of the Treaty.[37] The issue ended up before the European Court of First Instance in the *UEAPME* case.[38]

The ECOSOC Opinion stated bluntly the tautology that 'To render the EC social dialogue representative, it is essential that the management and labour be represented.'[39] However, it followed this up with two problematic questions:

(a)  what criteria are to be used to identify these representatives, and
(b)  how crucial is 'representativeness' as one of the criteria?

The Opinion stated that the criteria selected as indicating the representativeness of an organisation should reflect the specific context of the EC level social dialogue, a conclusion consistent with the variety of practices at Member State level which themselves reflected the specificity of national circumstances. It concluded that the definition of 'representativeness' could be shaped in two ways:[40]

(a)  designate as representative EC level social partners those organizations recognized by *national* social partners *deemed* representative by *national* law and practice;
(b)  the social partners at EC level are to be selected having regard to the nature of the *process* and of the *outcome* of EC social dialogue. These would indicate transnational criteria linked to national social partners and organizational capacity.[41]

The Commission's summary of its 'new approach to consultation' reflected a subtle and studied ambiguity.[42] It began with a generous invitation in the

---

[37]  The Confédération Européenne des Syndicats Indépendants (CESI), for example, is not given the same recognition in Annex 2 as the ETUC.

[38]  *Union Européenne de l'Artisanat et des Petites et Moyennes Entreprises (UEAPME)* v. *Council of the European Union*, Case T-135/96, [1998] ECR II-2335.

[39]  Opinion, paragraph 2.1.7.       [40]  Opinion, paragraph 2.1.9.

[41]  The ECOSOC Opinion's second criterion is also indicated in the Commission's Communication, paragraph 24, quoted above. Whether it was merely formally indicated, or carried much weight in the Commission's selection depends on the assessment of the organisations designated by the Commission in Annex 2.

[42]  Communication, paragraph 28.

form of a 'policy of wide-ranging consultation (covering) all European, or, where appropriate, national, organisations which might be affected by the Community's social policy'. This was rapidly tempered by the following paragraph's restriction that:

> Within the framework of Article 3 of the Agreement [Article 138 EC] it will undertake formal consultations with the European social partners' organisations which are listed in Annex 2 and which meet the criteria set out in para. 24.

Implicit here is a criterion of selection which distinguishes the processes of *informal* consultation of *everybody* from *formal* consultation of a more *select* group. The qualities of the latter group are also indirectly indicated by the acknowledgment that:

> The formal consultation of the social partners … may lead to the adoption of opinions, recommendations or agreement-based relations (including agreements) within the social partners' sphere of competence.

The ECOSOC Opinion focused on this issue:[43]

> 2.1.12. The criteria proposed by the Commission in paragraph 24 are ambiguous as to the need for a *negotiating* capacity of the EC social partners. Article 3(4) of the Agreement links consultation with *dialogue* and agreements (Article 4). Criteria should also include capacity to *negotiate* for and bind national structures.
>
> Agreements negotiated by the social partners at EC level should be capable of binding national social partners concerned, and affect directly, or by extension, all workers and employers in the Member States.
>
> 2.1.13. The Commission's view is that (paragraph 26): 'Only the organizations themselves are in a position to develop their own dialogue and negotiating structures.' A criterion requiring negotiating competence and ability to make agreements could assist EC level partners to achieve this.
>
> 2.1.14. Member State social partners comprising the EC level organizations should be encouraged to grant bargaining mandates to the EC level social partner organizations. Member States should be encouraged to provide the procedures and guarantees securing the general effect of EC level agreements reached. Both these are implicit in the means of implementing agreements provided in Article 4(2).

In ECOSOC's more explicit view, criteria of selection were linked to the functions of the organisations concerned as envisaged by the Agreement. Article 3(4) of the Agreement (Article 138(4) EC) links consultation with dialogue and agreements. During the consultation phase envisaged by Article 3 (Article 138 EC), the participating organisations have to be potentially capable of negotiating agreements which can bind national structures. Only European organisations which can meet the criterion of capacity to negotiate for and bind national structures can satisfy the requirements for participation in

---

[43] Opinion, paragraph 2.1.12–2.1.14.

the consultation phase. This clearly has implications for limiting the number of organisations which may be involved.[44]

## The consultation process

Article 3(2) and 3(3) of the Agreement (Article 138(2) and 138(3) EC) set out the two stages of the process of consultation of labour and management: first, consultation 'on the possible direction of Community action', and, secondly, 'on the content of the envisaged proposal'.[45]

---

[44] The debates within ECOSOC were perhaps most intense on this point, which reflects its composition. ECOSOC consists of representatives of a wide range of different groups. The members of the Workers' Group are mainly representatives from the ETUC. The ETUC was concerned to maintain its monopolistic position in the social dialogue process. At the same time, other European organisations, such as the Confédération Européenne des Syndicats Indépendants (CESI) and the Confédération Européenne des Cadres (CEC) also wished to be involved. In addition, some national trade union confederations, which are not affiliated to European organisations, wanted to have the possibility of taking part in negotiations. In particular, the CGT in France and the CGTP-Intersindical in Portugal, neither of which was then in the ETUC, claimed a position at the bargaining table. On the employers' side the situation was even more complicated. Although there are already two European employers' organisations participating in the social dialogue (UNICE, now BusinessEurope, and CEEP), a large number of employers are not represented. UNICE claims to represent small and medium enterprises, but this was denied by UEAPME (Union Européenne de l'Artisanat et des Petits et Moyennes Entreprises/European Union of Handicraft and Small and Medium Enterprises (SMEs)), which claims to be the most representative organisation for small and medium enterprises, or at least more representative of this group of employers than UNICE. UEAPME was excluded from the social dialogue negotiations which concluded the Parental Leave Agreement. As a result, on 5 September 1996, it invoked Article 230 EC before the European Court of First Instance (CFI) to challenge the validity of the Directive implementing the Agreement (Council Directive 96/34/EC of 3 June 1996 on the Framework Agreement on parental leave concluded by UNICE, CEEP and the ETUC. OJ L145/4 of 19 June 1996). The complaint was dismissed by the CFI on 17 June 1998, among other reasons, on the grounds that the social partner representing employers which negotiated the Parental Leave Agreement, UNICE, was sufficiently representative of SMEs (*Union Européenne de l'Artisanat et des Petites et Moyennes Entreprises (UEAPME)* v. *Council of the European Union*, Case T-135/96, [1998] ECR II-2335, analysed in Chapter 18). The indications were that UEAPME would appeal from the decision of the CFI to the European Court of Justice. Instead, a 'Proposal for a Cooperation Agreement between UNICE and UEAPME', dated 12 November 1998 described 'the modalities of cooperation between UNICE and UEAPME in social dialogue meetings, including negotiations' (Clause 1.2). This includes provisions whereby 'UNICE undertakes to consult UEAPME prior to taking public positions on behalf of the employers group in social dialogue and negotiating meetings' (Clause 3.1) and 'UEAPME representatives fully participate in preparatory meetings of the employers' group and in plenary meetings with ETUC' (Clause 3.2). UEAPME has thereby become a participant in the European social dialogue alongside UNICE (COM(99) 203).

[45] The Communication specified with precision how the Commission proposed to implement this process (paragraph 19): 'the first consultation of the social partners should take place on receipt of the letter from the Commission. The requested consultation may be by letter or, if the social partners so desire, by the convening of an ad hoc meeting. The consultation should not exceed six weeks … the second consultation phase will be initiated with the receipt of the second letter sent by the Commission, setting out the content of the planned proposal together with indication of the possible legal basis. On the occasion of this second consultation, the social partners should deliver to the Commission in writing and, where the social partners so wish

Article 3(4) of the Agreement (Article 138(4) EC) provides an alternative outcome of the consultation process – the social dialogue process. This was acknowledged by the Communication, but it seemed that the Commission took a strict and rigid view of when this development could arise out the consultation process. The Communication saw it following on the *second* phase of consultation[46]

The Commission's Communication presents a particular view of the consultation process which can be questioned by comparing it with the Commission's consultation practice on social policy proposals arising *before* the Maastricht Agreement. This earlier practice was outlined by the Commission itself in the Communication:[47]

> The social partners are consulted jointly on each proposal in two stages – a first consultation taking place on the basis of a Commission discussion paper, followed by a second one held within the following three months on the basis of a fresh Commission working paper, more detailed and closer to the preliminary draft which the responsible departments envisage presenting to the Commission. After these consultations, the departments of the Commission draw up an inventory of the points of agreement and disagreement, as expressed by the social partners, and pass it on to the Commission for its final deliberations on the proposal.

Compared with this earlier practice, the Commission's proposed implementation of the Agreement's consultation process seems less elaborate.

Under the first stage of the previous procedure, the Commission's discussion paper, containing its initial ideas, allowed for the social partners to exert their influence. The Commission would organise a meeting of the social partners, which gave them the opportunity to reach a compromise joint response to the Commission's proposal. This first stage would be undertaken over a period of three months, during which the social partners at EC level had to coordinate the internal consultation procedures with their national affiliates, as well as their bilateral dealings. In contrast, the first stage of the new procedure begins with a letter; it may be that the social partners never meet and only respond separately, which makes the possible coordination of a joint response less likely; and the duration of the first stage is not to exceed six weeks.

The second stage of the previous procedure would follow up with a fresh and detailed Commission working paper, not yet, though close to, a preliminary

---

through an ad hoc meeting, an opinion setting out the points of agreement and disagreement in their respective positions on the draft text. Where appropriate, they should deliver a recommendation setting out their joint positions on the draft text. The duration of this second phase shall also not exceed 6 weeks.'

[46] 'The social partners consulted by the Commission on the content of a proposal for Community action may deliver an opinion or, where appropriate, a recommendation to the Commission. Alternatively, they may also, as stated in Article 3(4) [Article 138(4) EC], 'inform the Commission of their wish to initiate the process provided for in Article 4 [Article 139 EC]'. This vision of the social dialogue as arising only after *both* stages of consultation is evident in the Operational Chart showing the implementation of the Agreement on Social Policy in Annex 4 to the Communication. *Ibid.*, paragraph 29.

[47] *Ibid.*, paragraph 16.

draft, as the basis for further joint consultations. The effort to achieve consensus during these joint consultations was evident in the practice of drawing up an inventory of the points of agreement and disagreement before the Commission begins its final deliberations on the proposal. In contrast, the second stage of the *new* procedure is again initiated on the basis of a letter setting out the content of the planned proposal; the social partners may meet, but may confine themselves to a written response in the form of an opinion or recommendation – the whole second stage also not to exceed six weeks.

The ECOSOC Opinion was critical of the new procedure envisaged by the Commission on three points in particular. First, during the initial stage, the social partners are supposed to be consulted over 'the possible direction of Community action'. This implies a consideration of various alternative directions, which have to be proposed, researched and analysed before a final selection is made. The short time period of six weeks for this stage makes it unlikely that the social partners could effectively determine a new possible direction during the first consultation round. It is a golden rule that the earlier there is involvement, the greater the possibility of exercising influence. A period of only six weeks from start to finish implies that the social partners would be involved relatively late in the policy formulation process, when much of the reflection had already been undertaken, and decisions made, by the Commission on the possible direction of Community action.

Secondly, the new procedure appears to entail less dynamic involvement by the Commission. There is less pressure on the social partners to hold meetings even with the Commission, or joint meetings. Communications between the Commission and the social partners may only be in writing. The Commission does not operate to promote compromises, indicated by the last stage of consultations being the relevant departments undertaking the drafting of points of agreement and disagreement.

Finally, the social partners at EC level are complex organisations comprising a multitude of very different national organisations, often confederations of national trade unions or employers' organisations. Proper consultation of these national organisations, which in turn have complex internal procedures requiring consultation of their affiliates, can be time-consuming. It is necessary, however, if the EC level social partners are to be able to undertake to engage themselves and their affiliates to support a social policy initiative at European level. A period of six weeks seems unlikely to suffice.[48]

---

[48] In addition to these three points, the ECOSOC challenged directly the Commission's view that the initiation of the social dialogue could only commence at the end of the second stage of consultations. ECOSOC's view was that Article 3(4) (Article 138(4) EC) does not clearly require this, and that (Opinion, paragraph 4.1.2): 'There are advantages in allowing the social partners to initiate the Article 4 [Article 139 EC] procedure also after the first consultation, *before* the Commission proposal is tendered.' The advantages listed were clearly linked to the ECOSOC's criticisms of the Commission's new procedure as far as the social partners involvement was

To remedy the defects it perceived in the Commission's proposed implementation of the new consultation process, ECOSOC made two proposals to improve the involvement of the social partners. First, it proposed to incorporate the best of the old procedures of consultation. This would mean discussion and working papers instead of letters, meetings instead of written consultation, and a longer period for each stage of the consultation: eight weeks instead of six weeks.[49]

Secondly, to enable the social partners to participate fully in social policy at European level, they should be given adequate resources to enable them to respond properly to the challenges in this field. To that end, it was proposed to create an Independent Secretariat.

The Commission's influence on the social dialogue process is conditioned by a number of factors. On the one hand, there is the new status of the social dialogue following the Protocol and Agreement on Social Policy. The European Union has provided for the mandatory participation of the social partners in the formulation of policy in the social policy field, and even delegated to them some of these competences for independent action. On the other hand, the Commission is the initiator of the legislative process of social policy. But it has been heavily involved in the social dialogue process. The current position is, therefore, that the Commission is involved in *both* processes of creating the social policy of the European Union.

As a result of the Social Protocol, the role of the Commission in the social dialogue process differs from that in the past. It does not appear to envisage the pro-active stance of the past: automatically stimulating the process by arranging, preparing and often chairing meetings of social partners. All these have involved considerable outlay of resources by the Commission in support of the social dialogue – as provided by Article 118B of the Treaty (Article 138(1) EC), introduced by the Single European Act.

The changes foreseen include a more independent role for the social partners, acting autonomously of the Commission through the social dialogue to formulate social policy. There is an inherent element of competition between the Commission, as the initiator of legislation, and the Commission as an intervener in the social dialogue process.

The law-making process in which the Commission is a key player enjoys one major advantage. The Commission has at its disposal considerable financial resources and an extensive organisation. With these, it can do research, organise meetings and conferences, draft proposals, and undertake the many tasks necessary to prepare and formulate social policy. The social partners at European level do not have such resources at their disposal.

---

concerned: 'it allows for initiation more quickly; it leaves more space for negotiation, rather than being bound by a proposal which becomes the basis for negotiation; it does not pre-empt the Commission continuing work on its proposal, perhaps in dynamic interaction with negotiations'.

[49] Specifying a time period for the two phases also helps to push the Commission to take action.

Given that the law-making role of the Commission to initiate legislation on social policy is now paralleled by the new competences of the social dialogue, the independent action of the latter, already reflected in the Commission's Communication, needs to be accompanied by the means to undertake such independent action.

To support the commitment of the social partners to social dialogue, they require a Secretariat in which they have confidence, and which is completely independent of the Commission. The proposal of ECOSOC was that the social partners should receive adequate resources to establish such an Independent Secretariat. The Commission was not eager to establish such an Independent Secretariat. The Commission preferred to build up its own experience and know-how, through a special department for the social dialogue within the Commission.

## The social dialogue process

During the consultation process:[50]

> management and labour may inform the Commission of their wish to initiate the process provided for in Article 4 [Article 139 EC]. The duration of the procedure shall not exceed nine months, unless the management and labour concerned and the Commission decide jointly to extend it.

This process is a:[51]

> dialogue between them at Community level (which) may lead to contractual relations, including agreements ... (which) shall be implemented either in accordance with the procedures and practices specific to management and labour and the Member States or, in matters covered by Article 2 [Article 137 EC], at the joint request of the signatory parties, by a Council decision on a proposal from the Commission.

The nine months' duration of the social dialogue process contrasts with the $2 \times 6$ weeks allowed for the consultation process. The duration may even exceed nine months. The Commission stipulates that the social partners may then 'request the Commission to decide with them upon a new deadline'.[52]

The ECOSOC discussions paid close attention to the question of the autonomy of the social partners in the social dialogue process envisaged by the Agreement and, in particular, what was the role of the Commission. A number of critical questions were raised concerning the autonomy of the social dialogue and the autonomy of the agreement reached.

First, did the social dialogue process depend on an initiative from the Commission, or could the social partners undertake the process of social dialogue without any initiative or involvement of the Commission? It was

[50] Article 3(4), now Article 138(4) EC.    [51] Article 4, now Article 139 EC.
[52] Communication, paragraph 33(c).

acknowledged that the social partners had been, prior to the Agreement, and were afterwards always perfectly free to engage independently in negotiations and reach agreements. Such independent action was not conditional on any Commission social policy initiative. Otherwise, the autonomy of the social partners would be compromised.

Connected with this was the question whether, once the social partners had negotiated an agreement, the Commission was obliged to submit the agreement to the Council 'at the joint request of the signatory parties', or whether the Commission had discretion and could refuse to propose the agreement to the Council.

ECOSOC had already taken the view that, once the Commission had begun the consultation process, the social partners were free to engage in social dialogue at any point, and were not bound to await the second stage of consultation under Article 3(3) (Article 138(3) EC). An agreement negotiated by the social partners, having begun the social dialogue at any point during the consultation process, fell to be implemented under Article 4 (Article 139 EC).

The further argument that followed was that if the social partners reached an agreement *entirely* independently of the consultation process, that too fell to be implemented under Article 4 (Article 139 EC). The autonomy of the social partners meant that agreements reached through the social dialogue, undertaken completely independently of any Commission involvement, fell within Article 4 (Article 139 EC).

These propositions appear to be consistent with the view of the Commission, which emphasised in the Communication 'the principle of the autonomy of the social partners … which underlies Articles 3 and 4 of the Agreement [Articles 138 and 139 EC]'.[53] The Commission seemed happy to confirm the autonomy of the social dialogue process.

A sharp division emerged between ECOSOC and the Commission, however, over what happened to agreements reached as a result of the social dialogue. The Commission's view was that:[54]

> By virtue of its role as guardian of the Treaties, the Commission will prepare proposals for decisions to the Council following consideration of the representative status of the contracting parties, their mandate and the 'legality' of each clause in the collective agreement in relation to Community law, and the provisions regarding small and medium-sized undertakings set out in Article 2(2) … [Article 137(2)(b) EC]
>
> Where it considers that it should not present a proposal for a decision to implement an agreement to the Council, the Commission will immediately inform the signatory parties of the reasons for its decision.

ECOSOC took the view that it is up to the social partners to decide whether their collective agreement should be put to the Council. The Commission has

---

[53] Communication, paragraph 35.    [54] *Ibid.*, paragraph 39.

no discretion; if there is a joint request by the signatory parties, the Commission must propose it. Of course, the *Council* may reject the proposal. But the right to reject it is not given to the Commission. There is nothing which hints that the Commission can assess the agreement in terms of the criteria listed in the Communication: representativeness and mandate. These go to the heart of the autonomy of the social partners.[55]

The only restriction is that the proposal be concerned with matters covered by Article 2 (Article 137 EC). There is no indication that only agreements which *began* with the Commission's consultation process are eligible for implementation under Article 4 (Article 139 EC). Every agreement reached under the social dialogue process should be put to the Council if the parties so request. Both process and outcome are autonomous of the Commission.

An interesting contrast with the Commission's claim that it could sit in judgment on the agreement before proposing it to the Council is its position on whether the Council can alter the agreement. In the paragraph preceding its claim, the Commission sternly warns that its proposal:[56]

> would give the Council no opportunity to amend the agreement ... the Commission will merely propose ... the adoption of a decision on the agreement as concluded.[57]

Presumably, this is in line with the principle of autonomy of the social partners and their agreements.

The obligation to present the agreement to the Council does not prevent the Commission from having an important role. The Commission is very sensitive to the Council's decision-making process, and could exercise influence over the final content of any agreement. For example, on the basis of its understanding of the Council's views, the Commission could explain to the social partners how the agreement might be shaped to achieve a positive Council decision.

Alternatively, if the proposal of the agreement to the Council was rejected, the Commission might on its own initiative present a proposal for a legislative measure embodying elements of the agreement.[58]

---

[55] But see now the judgment of the CFI in the *UEAPME* case, discussed in Chapter 18.

[56] Communication, paragraph 38.

[57] Again, *ibid.*, in paragraph 41: 'The Council decision must be limited to making binding the provisions of the agreement concluded between the social partners, so the text of the agreement would not form part of the decision, but would be annexed thereto'.

[58] It was clear that: 'without prejudicing the principle of the autonomy of the social partners ... the Commission feels that the European Parliament must be fully informed at all stages of any consultation or negotiation procedure involving the social partners'. *Ibid.*, paragraph 35. According to ECOSOC, it too should be informed. It would avoid wasting time and energy if the members of ECOSOC and the Parliament were aware of the circumstances of any failures. Such failure might lead to legislative measures being undertaken in the event of negotiations not producing an agreement on a social policy regarded as necessary or desirable.

## Implementation of agreements: procedures and practices

If the outcome of the social dialogue process is successful in producing an agreement between the social partners, Article 4(2) (Article 139(2) EC) provides that:

> Agreements concluded at Community level shall be implemented ... in accordance with the procedures and practices specific to management and labour and the Member States.

The Commission's Communication characterises this method as 'the voluntary route'.[59] The Commission has little to say about this method, and what it does say appears to be very negative.

It starts by quoting the Declaration on Article 4(2) (Article 139(2) EC) attached to the Agreement by the eleven Member States:

> The 11 High Contracting Parties declare that the first of the arrangements for application of the agreements between management and labour at Community level – referred to in Article 4(2) [Article 139(2)] – will consist in developing, by collective bargaining according to the rules of each Member State, the content of the agreements, and that consequently this arrangement implies no obligation on the Member States to apply the agreements directly or to work out rules for their transposition, nor any obligation to amend national legislation in force to facilitate their implementation.

The peremptory tone of the Declaration may explain why the Commission simply states that Article 4(2) [Article 139(2)] 'is subject to' this Declaration. However, the Declaration does raise considerable difficulty hinted at in the ECOSOC Opinion.

The Declaration, unlike Article 4(2) (Article 139(2)) which refers to straightforward implementation of EC level agreements, characterises this implementation as consisting in the *development of the content* of the EC level agreements. This is a much more dynamic articulation of the two levels of collective bargaining. It may explain why the Member States 'consequently' hastened to renounce any obligation. But such a renunciation cannot override the clear wording of Article 4(2) (Article 139(2)) which provides that agreements '*shall be implemented*'.[60]

Avoiding confrontation with the Member States, the Commission appears to regard the obligatory implementation of agreements required by Article 4(2) [Article 139(2)] as consisting of the fact only that:[61]

---

[59] Communication, paragraph 37. Writing at the same time, Gérard Lyon-Caen characterised this in French terms as a typical British 'gentleman's agreement'. G. Lyon-Caen, *Le droit social de la Communauté européenne après le Traité de Maastricht*, Paris: Dalloz, 1993, p. 152, cited in E. Mazuyer, 'Les instruments juridiques du dialogue social européen: état des lieux et tentative de clarification', *Droit Social*, April 2007, p. 486, footnote 6.

[60] The ETUC/UNICE/CEEP agreement of 31 October 1991 had provided that the agreements '*may be implemented*'.

[61] Communication, paragraph 37.

the terms of this agreement will bind their members and will affect only them and only in accordance with the practices and procedures specific to them in their respective Member States.

This recognition by the Commission of the legally binding articulation of 'agreements concluded at Community level' with 'procedures and practices specific to management and labour' is important. But it is not clear why the same legally binding quality does not extend to the following words: '*and* the Member States'. A similar legally binding quality of EC level instruments is to be found in the jurisprudence of the European Court of Justice concerned with implementation of Community Directives through collective agreements, now encapsulated in Article 2(4) of the Agreement (now Article 137(3) EC). The Commission's Communication is quite explicit in the case of implementing Directives by articulation with collective bargaining that:[62]

> the Member State concerned must provide for procedures to deal, where appropriate, with any shortcomings in the agreement implementing the directive, the purpose being to ensure that the workers concerned are in practice afforded their rights.

The jurisprudence on which this statement is based emphasised that the collective agreements must cover all employees, and must include all the Directive's requirements. Otherwise, there must be a back-up in the form of a state guarantee (usually legislation). In line with this principle, and contrary to the Commission's view, implementation of sectoral or multi-sectoral agreements may imply extension of their coverage to all employees.

The Communication states categorically that the first mode of implementation of agreements in Article 4(2) (Article 139(2)) 'is subject to the ... declaration'. But normally a Declaration is not a part of the Treaty, and the Declaration does appear to contradict the clear meaning of Article 4(2) (Article 139(2)), that 'Agreements ... shall be implemented'.[63] It is hard to escape the conclusion that the Member States are under some obligation to implement the agreements concluded by the social partners.

---

[62] *Ibid.*, paragraph 47.

[63] E. A. Whiteford argues that the Agreement annexed to the Protocol is part of EC law, but also that the Declarations to the Agreement are of a different nature to normal Declarations. Unlike normal Declarations, as analysed in academic doctrine, the Agreement's Declarations may be part of EC law. If so, she concedes, they strip Article 4(2) of much of its potential. However, if the legal effect of these declarations is unclear, and previous doctrine on the legal status of declarations would deny them the status of EC law, then an interpretation which (i) conflicts with earlier doctrine; and (ii) has the effect of denying legal effect to a provision of EC law (Article 4(2) of the Agreement), should be avoided. 'Social Policy after Maastricht', (1993) 18 *European Law Review* 202–22.

## Conclusion

The implementation of the Protocol and Agreement on Social Policy is of fundamental importance to the social policy of the European Union. In its Resolution of 6 December 1994 on certain aspects for a European Union social policy: a contribution to economic and social convergence in the Union, the Council:[64]

> NOTES that, as a means of further defining and following up its communication on implementation of the Agreement on social policy, the Commission intends to submit a working paper on the development of social dialogue.

The dynamic of the social dialogue began to operate. The social partners began gearing up to assume their responsibilities. One indication was the new Article 11b of the Constitution of the ETUC, adopted at its 8th Statutory Congress in May 1995:

> The Executive Committee shall determine the composition and mandate of the delegation for negotiations with European employers' organisations in each individual case, in accordance with the voting procedures set out in Article 16. The decision shall have the support of at least two thirds of the member organisations directly concerned by the negotiations.[65]

At its meeting at the end of June 1995, the ETUC Executive Committee adopted Rules of Procedure for implementing Article 11b of the Constitution. These included the following:[66]

> 14.  If the negotiations do not achieve a result before the 9-month deadline, the Secretariat shall inform the Executive Committee to that effect and make a recommendation either to prolong the deadline provided by the Social Agreement or else to stop the negotiations and ask the Commission to restart the legislative process.

---

[64]  OJ C368/6 of 23 December 1994, paragraph 23.

[65]  In case of urgency, decisions concerning the mandate for composition of the delegation may be made in writing. The Executive Committee shall establish the internal rules of procedure to be followed in the event of negotiations. The Secretariat shall supervise the bargaining delegation. The Executive Committee shall be given regular progress reports on bargaining in process. Decisions on the outcomes of negotiations shall be taken by the Executive Committee in accordance with the voting procedures set out in Article 16. The decision shall have the support of at least two-thirds of the organisations directly concerned by the negotiations, which shall have had the opportunity to hold internal consultations. Regular reports on European sectoral bargaining, carried out by European industry committees, shall be made to the Executive Committee. Its consistency with ETUC policy shall thus be ensured'.

[66]  '3. The "organisations concerned" shall be confederations from EU Member States, including the TUC, regardless of the UK opt-out, confederations from EEA countries, European industry committees and the Women's Committee ... 6. ... Once the agreement has been transmitted to the Council by the Commission, the latter may adopt a Decision on the agreement which makes it legally applicable by the 14 Member States under the scope of the Protocol. In the UK and EEA countries, however, the union and employers' organisations may decide to implement the agreement on a voluntary basis.'

These and other developments led to the early successes of the social dialogue: three intersectoral agreements transformed into Directives: on parental leave (1996), on part-time work (1997) and on fixed-term work (1999).[67] The seven fat years of 1993–9, however, were followed by seven lean years of 2000–6 in a political context which produced a different process and outcome of the European social dialogue.

## The second phase: 2000–2008

### The Commission moves towards soft law

The Commission's Social Policy Agenda (2001–5), adopted on 28 June 2000[68] was approved by the European Council meeting at Nice in December 2000. It was the successor to the Social Action Programme 1998–2000 and, like its predecessors, contained a lengthy list of initiatives.

It is regarding the mechanisms for achieving its objectives that there appears to be a change of emphasis:[69]

> The Social Policy Agenda does not seek to harmonise social policies. It seeks to work towards common European objectives and increase co-ordination of social policies in the context of the internal market and the single currency.

In contrast with earlier commitments to legislate minimum standards, the Social Policy Agenda aims 'to ensure the respect of fundamental social rights and to respond to new challenges'.[70] On the other hand, the Social Policy Agenda continues to support an active role for the social partners.

The European Council at Nice, in adopting the Social Agenda, declared that in its implementation:[71]

> all existing Community instruments bar none must be used; the open method of co-ordination, legislation, the social dialogue, the Structural Funds, the support programmes, the integrated policy approach, analysis and research.

This reiterated the new approach of the Lisbon Strategy, reflected also in the Commission's Social Policy Agenda of 28 June 2000, which stated that 'To achieve these priorities, an adequate combination of all existing means will be required.'[72] However, the scope of application allocated to each method of achieving objectives differed. The open method of coordination was not limited as to the scope of matters to be implemented by this method. In contrast, the

---

[67] Council Directive 96/34/EC of 3 June 1996 on the Framework Agreement on parental leave concluded by UNICE, CEEP and the ETUC. OJ L145/4 of 19 June 1996. Council Directive 97/81/EC of 15 December 1997 concerning the Framework Agreement on part-time work concluded by UNICE, CEEP and the ETUC. OJ L14/9 of 20 January 1998. Council Directive 1999/70/EC of 28 June 1999 concerning the Framework Agreement on fixed-term work concluded by ETUC, UNICE and CEEP. OJ L175/43 of 10 July 1999.

[68] COM(2000) 379.    [69] Social Policy Agenda, page 7.    [70] *Ibid.*, page 14.

[71] Nice European Council, 7–9 December 2000, Annex 1, paragraph 28.

[72] Social Policy Agenda, page 14.

legislative method was limited.[73] The anticipated role of the social dialogue was different and limited to work relationships within the enterprise.[74]

The central point of departure was the *unlimited scope of the open method of coordination* as an instrument for achieving the Lisbon Strategy, in clear contrast with the restricted scope of legislation and social dialogue. The Commission's new approach to social policy in the EU in the years after 2000, focusing on the soft law mechanism of the open method of coordination, was to have a major impact on the development of the European social dialogue.

The Commission's Communication of 26 June 2002 on 'The European social dialogue, a force for innovation and change' reiterated its general commitment to the social dialogue. The Communication begins the section on enlargement by affirming that 'social dialogue is enshrined in the Treaty and forms an integral part of the *acquis communautaire*'.[75] The Communication's Executive Summary begins by stating: 'The social dialogue and the quality of industrial relations are at the centre of the European social model.' In its Conclusions to the Communication, the Commission confirms that 'Strong social dialogue structures [are] an integral part of the *Community acquis*.[76]

However, a specific emphasis soon emerges. On the one hand, a preference for the *open method of coordination*, and, complementing this, stress on the *autonomous activity of the social partners*.[77] In relation to the open method of coordination, applicable 'to fields of interest to the social partners: employment,

---

[73] To be used 'where appropriate, to ensure the respect of fundamental social rights and to respond to new challenges. Such standards can also result from agreements between the social partners at European level.'

[74] 'The Social Dialogue as the most effective way of modernising contractual relations, adapting work organisation and developing adequate balance between flexibility and security.'

[75] COM(2002) 341 final, 26 June 2002, Section 3, p. 19.   [76] *Ibid.*, p. 22.

[77] The Commission's proposals are said to be 'based on the social partners' contribution to the Laeken European Council and the reflections of the High Level Group on Industrial Relations'. The Commission states that: (emphasis in original) 'Social dialogue is the **driving force** behind successful **economic and social reforms** … Negotiations between the social partners are the most suitable way forward on questions related to modernisation and management of change.' The Commission makes proposals for strengthening the role of the social partners at European, national, local and company level (pp. 10–12). For example, at sectoral level, following the Decision of May 1998 on the establishment of the sectoral social dialogue committees, the Commission reports that twenty-seven committees have been set up at the joint request of the social partners in the sector concerned. See the list in Annex 2 of the Communication. Among other actions, a Council Decision of 6 March 2003 formally established a new 'Tripartite Social Summit for Growth and Employment' to support reinforcement of the concertation between social partners and European institutions on economic and social policies. This institutionalises meetings at least once a year, just before the spring European Council, between the social partners and the Heads of State or Government of the present and two subsequent Presidencies of the Council and the Commission. The first formal tripartite social summit took place under the Greek Presidency on 20 March 2003. This is apart from the 'macro-economic dialogue' established after the Cologne European Council of June 1999 in which there is a regular exchange of views between the representatives of the Commission, the Council, the European Central Bank and the social partners.

social inclusion, pensions, and soon, vocational training', the Commission 'suggests that each area under the method of open coordination should form the subject of organised dialogue with the social partners along the lines of the arrangements for the macroeconomic dialogue, more precisely, its dual setup at technical and political levels'.[78]

### The Commission delegates to autonomous social dialogue

In their Contribution to the Laeken European Council on 7 December 2001, the European social partners (ETUC, UNICE and CEEP) reaffirmed 'their wish to develop a work programme for a more autonomous social dialogue' (Section 1).[79] The social partners announced that they were 'reflecting on the best way of developing a more autonomous social dialogue' with a view to 'better organise the work of the social dialogue in a work programme ... decided and implemented in complete autonomy' (Section 5).

In their Laeken Declaration of 7 December 2001, the social partners had stated that:

> This work programme would be built on a spectrum of diversified instruments (various types of European framework agreement, opinions, recommendations, statements, exchanges of experience, awareness-raising campaigns, open debates, etc.).

In its Communication of 26 June 2002, the Commission states that:[80]

> The Treaty also recognises the social partners' ability to undertake *independent social dialogue*, that is to negotiate independently agreements which become law. It is that ability to negotiate agreements which sets the social dialogue apart.

The Commission 'calls on the European social partners further to develop their autonomous dialogue and to establish joint work programmes'.[81]

On the occasion of the social dialogue summit in Brussels on 28 November 2002,[82] the social partners presented a Work Programme for 2003–5. The Work Programme comprises actions including reports, orientations, declarations, studies and reflections. However, 'agreements' appear only in proposals for a 'seminar in view to negotiate a voluntary agreement' on stress at work (2003) and a 'seminar to explore possibility of negotiating a voluntary agreement' on harassment (2004–5).

---

[78] Communication, 26 June 2002, page 14.

[79] They distinguished '"tripartite" concertation between the social partners and European public authorities and consultation of the social partners under Article 137 EC from "bipartite" work by the social partners, whether or not prompted by the Commission's official consultations based on Article 137 and 138 of the Treaty' (Section 3).

[80] Communication, 26 June 2002, Introduction, p. 7, italics in the original.

[81] *Ibid.*, Executive Summary, p. 4.

[82] Bringing together the social partners of thirty European countries (the fifteen Member States of the EU, the two countries which constitute with them the European Economic Area and the thirteen candidate countries).

### The outcome: autonomous dialogue produces ineffective soft law

In its Communication of 26 June 2002, the Commission had noted, under the heading 'Improving monitoring and implementation' (italics added):

> The European social partners have adopted joint opinions, statements and declarations on numerous occasions. More than 230 such joint sectoral texts have been issued and some 40 cross-industry texts … However, *in most cases, these texts did not include any provision for implementation and monitoring: they were responses to short-term concerns. They are not well known and their dissemination at national level has been limited. Their effectiveness can thus be called into question.* Moreover, in recent years the social partners have increasingly frequently discussed and adopted so-called 'new generation texts (charters, codes of conduct, agreements) containing commitments to implementation in the longer term'.

The Commission concludes that:[83]

> **The social partners** should endeavour to **clarify** the terms used to describe their contributions and reserve the term '**agreement**' for texts implemented in accordance with the procedures laid down in Article 139(2) of the Treaty.

That leaves the question of the perceived lack of effectiveness of other instruments, such as joint opinions. On this point, the Commission noted that:[84]

> Special consideration must be given to the question of how to implement the texts adopted by the European social partners. The recommendations of the High-Level Group on Industrial Relations and Change see the use of **machinery based on the open method of coordination** as an extremely promising way forward.
>
> The social partners could apply some of their agreements (where not regulatory) by establishing goals or guidelines at European level, through regular national implementation reports and regular, systematic assessment of progress achieved.

To that end, the Commission recommended:
> The social partners are requested to:

> adapt the open method of coordination to their relations in all appropriate areas;
> prepare monitoring reports on implementation in the Member States of these frameworks for action;
> introduce peer review machinery appropriate to the social dialogue.

The significance of this recommendation is highlighted by the Work Programme of the European Social Partners 2003–5.[85] Nine items in the

---

[83] Section 2.4, pp. 17–18, emphasis in the original.    [84] Section 2.4.1, p. 18.

[85] As indicated by the Commission, that Programme provides for the follow-up of the 'framework of actions' on life-long learning plus an evaluation report in 2003, 2004 and 2005. Moreover, most of the proposals in the Work programme are of this nature. For example, of the twelve actions under the heading 'Employment', in addition to the follow-up of the 'framework of actions' on life-long learning, eight items appear to be eligible for the Commission's recommendation on application of the open method of coordination (OMC).

Social Partners Work Programme under the employment heading look to such instruments, whereas only three refer to 'agreements'.[86]

This last refers to the framework agreement on telework signed on 16 July 2002. This was the first time the European social partners stated their intention not to seek a Council Directive to implement their agreement. The Delphic wording of the Work Programme's reference reflects some uncertainty as to whether this agreement is voluntary in the sense of requiring to be implemented in accordance with the procedures and parties specific to the social partners and the Member States, or voluntary as not allowing for legal enforcement.[87] In this context, the Commission's view in its Communication of 26 June 2002

[86] OMC:

| Theme | Actions | Calendar |
|---|---|---|
| Employment guidelines | Reports on social partner actions in Member States to implement employment guidelines (taking into account the cycle of 3 years) | 2003–5 |
| Gender equality | Seminar on equal opportunities and gender discrimination aiming at a framework of actions | 2003 |
| Restructuring | Identify orientations that could serve as a reference to assist in managing change and its social consequences on the basis of concrete cases | 2003 |
| Disability update of | Joint declaration of 1999 as a contribution for the European year on disability | 2003 |
| Young people | Promoting young people's interest in science and technology to help address the skills gap through joint declaration and/or awareness-raising campaign | 2003–5 |
| Racism | Updating joint declaration of 1995 (with participation of candidate countries) | 2004 |
| Ageing workforce | Seminar to discuss case studies and explore possible joint actions | 2004 |
| Undeclared work | Seminar aiming at a joint opinion | 2005 |
| Stress at work | Seminar in view to negotiate a voluntary agreement | 2003 |
| Harassment | Seminar to explore possibility of negotiating a voluntary agreement | 2004–5 |
| Telework | Monitoring of follow-up to Framework agreement | 2003–5 |

[87] The telework agreement provides that teleworkers should benefit from the same protection as other employees, and lays down guarantees in areas such as access, costs, health and safety, working time, privacy and collective rights. It was due to be implemented by July 2005. A joint report in October 2006 of the EU social partners stated that the agreement had been implemented in all EU Member Ststes except Cyprus, Estonia, Lithuania and the Slovak Republic. The means of implementation included national and sectoral collective agreements (Denmark, France, Greece, Italy and Luxembourg), codes of conduct (Ireland and the UK) and legislation (Czech Republic and Hungary). The ETUC General Secretary, John Monks, stated: 'The different experiences throughout Europe also underline that there is a need to clarify certain questions, given the fact that this is the first autonomous framework agreement to be implemented by the social partners themselves. These issues will be taken up in the framework of the European social partners' work programme 2006–08.' 'Implementing the Telework Agreement', *European Industrial Relations Review* No. 394, November 2006, pp. 2–3. The intersectoral telework agreement had precedents. On 7 February 2001, the Sectoral Social Dialogue Committee for Telecommunications adopted Guidelines for Telework in Europe.

questioning the effectiveness in implementation and monitoring of texts other than agreements may be noted.[88]

Given the overall nature of the Work Programme, therefore, the Commission's approach is of some significance. The Commission questions the ineffectiveness in implementation and monitoring of texts other than agreements. Its solution is, first, clearly to identify those areas where 'regulatory agreements' are the chosen instrument. Secondly, where other instruments are proposed (frameworks of actions, declarations, orientations, joint opinions) the OMC method may be adapted as appropriate; in particular, 'monitoring reports on implementation' and 'peer review machinery appropriate to the social dialogue'.

It remains to be seen where, or indeed whether, the OMC, hitherto not without criticism as to its effectiveness when applied to the Member States in the EES, is appropriate for the Work Programme of the Social Partners on Employment. The OMC implementing the EES through the Employment Title, Article 128 EC, suffers from a serious problem: the social dialogue is not institutionally integrated or even mentioned in the Employment Title of the EC Treaty and the social partners are only marginally situated in the institutional structure of the EES.

## Alternative options

At present, social policy and employment policy in the EU are managed through separate institutional frameworks: the social dialogue and the EES. An institutional design could integrate the best features of the EU social dialogue and of the OMC.

The precise nature of the appropriate adaptation of the OMC recommended by the Commission is vague. Proposals to adapt the OMC to the social dialogue have been made; for example, a social dialogue process which replicates the processes and measures of the OMC in the form of framework agreements at EU level, implemented at Member State level through the social partners. If such agreements were implemented, not in the form of legislative standards as directives, but 'in accordance with the practices and procedures specific to management and labour and the Member States' (Article 139(2)), they would be *functionally equivalent* to the OMC process of guidelines and national plans.

The OMC could be institutionally accommodated to the EU social dialogue with a view to their mutual reinforcement. Guidelines could emerge from an EU-level social dialogue between EU social partners with mandates from

---

[88] Its solution was to clearly identify those areas where 'regulatory agreements' are the chosen instrument. On the other hand, the Commission had suggested that: 'The social partners could apply some of their agreements (where not regulatory) by establishing goals or guidelines at European level, through regular national implementation reports and regular, systematic assessment of progress achieved.' It is not clear whether voluntary agreements fall into the category of 'agreements (where not regulatory)'.

affiliated social partners drawing on experience of national employment pacts, or following on from proposals by the Commission. Affiliated social partners at Member State level could produce National Action Plans to implement the Guidelines embodied in EU framework agreements. The Commission and Council could review and report on implementation and supplement this with recommendations in the form of EU legislative proposals where implementation was inadequate.

Another proposal may be found in the Final Report of Working Group XI on Social Europe of the Convention on the Future of Europe. On the one hand, the Working Group stated unequivocally that the OMC has *no* application in the sphere of employment and labour relations where legislative measures are applicable, or in employment policy where the Treaty specifies procedures (paragraph 41). However, the Working Group adds: '*or* where the Union *has competence* only for defining *minimum* rules, in order to go *beyond* these rules' (paragraph 43). In other words, where legislative competence exists, and *has* been exercised to establish minimum rules, the OMC may operate to promote *higher* standards. The OMC *cannot* become a substitute for legislation, including that resulting from social dialogue framework agreements. However, it may play an important role in supplementing the minimum standards established by such legislation or agreements.

The Commission's request in its Communication of 26 June 2002 for adaptation of the OMC to implementation of texts resulting from the social dialogue opens the door to proposals such as that of Working Group XI. Ultimately, if joint opinions and other non-regulatory instruments continue to be ineffective, their failure may imply other, more rigorous steps towards effectiveness, including regulatory agreements and/or legislation.

### Conclusions

In its Communication of 26 June 2002, the Commission takes the view that (i) 'The Treaty also recognises the social partners' ability to undertake *independent social dialogue*, that is to negotiate independently agreements which become law'; (ii) 'It is that ability to negotiate agreements which sets the social dialogue apart';[89] and (iii) '... social dialogue is enshrined in the Treaty and forms an integral part of the *acquis communautaire* ...'.[90]

To be part of an autonomous, independent social dialogue, part of the *acquis*, the social partners should produce agreements, and these agreements must be effectively implemented.

This raises the question of the relation of the European social dialogue to most of the actions, not involving agreements, in the social partners' Work Programme 2003–5; in particular, the effective implementation of these actions. The Commission's Communication states: 'Special consideration must be given

---

[89] Introduction, p. 7.     [90] Section 3, p. 19.

to the question of how to implement the texts adopted by the European social partners' and refers to adapting the open method of coordination, preparing monitoring reports and introducing 'peer review machinery appropriate to the social dialogue'.[91]

The various actions proposed in the Work Programme 2003–5 render ambivalent the precise nature of actions within the scope of the autonomous social dialogue. An autonomous, independent social dialogue requires the social partners to produce agreements, and these agreements must be effectively implemented. Other actions and instruments are not part of such an autonomous, independent social dialogue.

The following Work Programme of the European Social Partners 2006–8, agreed on 23 March 2006, committed them to 'negotiate an autonomous framework agreement on either the integration of disadvantaged groups on the labour market or life long learning'. Further, the social partners also declared that they 'will negotiate a voluntary framework agreement on harassment and violence in 2006'. This latter was duly concluded in 2007. The Work Programme also specified that the social partners undertake 'based on the implementation of the telework and stress agreements … [to] further develop their common understanding of these instruments and how they can have a positive impact at the various levels of social dialogue'. Despite this, the precise role and legal status of voluntary autonomous agreements in the EU legal order remain unclear.

## Another level: European sectoral social dialogue

The social partners organised on a sectoral basis at European level may also engage in social dialogue. In its Communication of 26 June 2002, the Commission expressed the view that the sectoral level 'is the proper level for discussion on many issues linked to employment, working conditions, vocational training, industrial change, the knowledge society, demographic patterns, enlargement and globalisation'.[92]

On the workers' side, European Industry Federations are constituent members of the European Trade Union Confederation.

According to Article 1 of the Constitution of the ETUC: 'The European Trade Union Confederation shall consist of National Trade Union Confederations and European Industry Federations.' Article 5 provides:

The European Industry Federations are organisations of trade unions within one or more public or private economic sectors. They represent the interests of workers in their sectors at the European level, principally in negotiation. The

---

[91] Section 2.4.1, p. 18.
[92] 'The European social dialogue, a force for innovation and change', COM(2002) 341 final, Brussels, 16 June 2002, Section 2.3.2, p. 16.

European Industry Federations shall be open to all national trade union organ-isations which are affiliated to the ETUC's National Trade Union Confederations. They shall be created on their own initiative and shall determine their own independent standing orders, in accordance with this Constitution. The European Trade Union Confederation favours the creation and development of European Industry Federations within all spheres of economic and social activity.

The European Industry Federations are represented in the ETUC's Congress (Article 8(b)), Executive Committee (Article 14) and Steering Committee (Article 21).[93]

Two examples: first, at European level, labour in the construction sector is represented by the European Federation of Building and Woodworkers (EFBWW), established in 1958.[94] Secondly, the European Metalworkers' Federation (EMF) was created as a separate body in the International Metal-workers' Federation (IMF), founded in 1893.[95] Sectoral organisation of employers at EU level is much less developed than on the trade union side. While industry federations are constitutionally integrated into the European Trade Union Confederation, in contrast, employers' organisations are highly centralised in the Union of Industrial and Employer Confederations of Europe (UNICE: now BusinessEurope) and the European Centre of Enterprises with Public Participation and of Enterprises of General Economic Interest (CEEP), which engage with the ETUC in intersectoral social dialogue and negotiations at EU level.

Although intersectoral organisations of employers dominate, nevertheless there are sectoral employers' federations at EU level. Two examples: first, the European Construction Industry Federation (FIEC), founded in 1905 as the International Federation of Building and Public Works, is the organisation of employers involved in the social dialogue with the European Federation of Building and Woodworkers.[96] Second: the Western European Metal Trades

---

[93] Affiliated European Industry Federations include: EMF (European Metalworkers' Federation), ETUF-TCL (European Federation of Textile, Clothing and Leather), EFBWW (European Federation of Building and Woodworkers), EMCEF (European Mining, Chemical and Energy Federation), ECF (European Federation of Food Workers), EFA (European Federation of Agriculture), EPSU (European Federation of Public Service Unions), FST (Federation of Transport Workers), ETUCE (European Committee for Education), UNI-Europa (Union Network International), EEA (European Alliance of Media and Entertainment), EFJ (European Federation of Journalists).

[94] The EFBWW has some fifty affiliated member unions, as in some Member States more than one union is affiliated. However, the level of union membership within the industry varies greatly between countries.

[95] It held its first European conference in 1969. The EMF has affiliates from unions based in EU Member States and others and represents about half of the EU Member State workforce in engineering.

[96] It is recognised as representative by the Commission though it does not represent small and medium firms in every Member State.

Employers' Organisation (WEM) was founded on an ad hoc basis in 1962 and formalised in 1970.[97]

Sectoral organisations at EU level on the employers' side mainly engage in trade promotion or lobbying for business interests. There is much less in the way of social dialogue with their equivalent organisations, the European Industry Federations affiliated to the ETUC.

The European Commission has sought to promote such engagement by establishing sectoral social dialogue committees. Sectoral social dialogue committees are forums established by the Commission to promote the sectoral social dialogue at EU level. Their creation was the result of a proposal in a Commission Communication of 20 May 1998.[98] Annex II to that Communication included a Commission decision setting up sectoral dialogue committees promoting the dialogue between the social partners at European level.[99]

As reported in the Commission's Communication of 26 June 2002, sectoral social dialogue committees have been set up at the joint request of the social partners in the sectors concerned.[100] The Commission stated that it wishes to continue its support and to promote the establishment of further committees so that all main sectors are covered. The Commission's intention is to 'pursue its policy of setting up new committees whenever the conditions are met: structured, *representative* players at European level having ability to negotiate agreements and willingness to undertake structured *social dialogue*' (italics added).

In its Communication of 26 June 2002, the Commission declared that it intends to 'orientate the activities of the sectoral social dialogue committees to dialogue and negotiation only, excluding information and consultation activities which can be carried out in multisectoral forums, with the exception of specific sectoral consultations'. The future of sectoral social dialogue committees depends on whether the social dialogue in these committees will succeed in conducting negotiations leading to regulatory agreements, or only a variety of less regulatory texts.[101]

---

[97] It represents metalworking employers' organisations in nine of the Member States and others outside the EC. Its federated members are recognised as being responsible for the conclusion of the collective agreements in the metal industry of the countries concerned

[98] 'Adapting and promoting the Social Dialogue at Community level'. COM(98) 322, of 20 May 1998.

[99] Commission Decision 98/500/EC of 20 May 1998, OJ L225/27 of 12 August 1998.

[100] Annex 2 of the Communication contains a list. European sectoral social dialogue committees have been established in agriculture, air transport, banking, cleaning, commerce, construction, culture, electricity, footwear, furniture, hotels and catering/tourism, inland waterways, insurance, mining, personal services, postal services, private security, railways, road transport, sea fishing, sea transport, sugar, tanning, telecommunications, temporary work, textiles/clothing, and wood.

[101] The most striking development of European sectoral social dialogue agreements emerged in a number of transport sectors as a result of negotiations following their initial exclusion from the Working Time Directive.

Many different kinds of measures are emerging from the social dialogue at the EU sectoral level. Examples include a European Agreement of 26 April 2001 on Guidelines on Telework in Commerce between EuroCommerce and UNI-Europa; a Code of Conduct signed on 26 June 2001 by the European-level social partners in the personal services (hairdressing) sector;[102] and a joint declaration on lifelong learning concluded on 3 December 2002 between the EU-level social partners in the banking sector.[103]

A list of the main sectoral social dialogue texts concluded in 2000 and 2001 included also 'safety manuals', 'joint statements' and 'joint declarations', 'resolutions', 'round-table conclusions', 'social action programmes' and 'contributions', as well as 'common declarations' and 'common opinions'. As with their homologues at intersectoral level, however, there are questions as to both their legal status and effectiveness.

## European social dialogue: benign neglect 2004–?

The Commission's latest Communication of 12 August 2004 on the social dialogue was produced after ten new Member States had joined the EU in May 2004 and is entitled 'Partnership for change in an enlarged Europe – Enhancing the contribution of European social dialogue'.[104] In its Social Agenda 2006–10, the Commission asserts:[105]

> The Commission will continue to encourage the social partners to contribute fully to the Lisbon mid-term review including by the conclusion of agreements, at all levels.
>
> While respecting the autonomy of the social partners, the Commission will continue to promote the European social dialogue at cross-industry and sectoral levels, especially by strengthening its logistic and technical support and by conducting consultations on the basis of Article 138 of the EC Treaty.

A critical evaluation of the Commission's Communication of 2004 does not augur well for the prospects of the social dialogue under the Commission's new Social Agenda.

---

[102] The Confédération Européenne des Organisations Patronales de la Coiffure (CIC Europe) for the employers and the UNI-Europa Hair and Beauty (the relevant European section of Union Network International) for the trade unions.

[103] For the employers, the banking committee for European social affairs of the European Banking Federation (FBE), the European Savings Bank group (ESBG) and the European Association of Cooperative Banks (GEBC), and for the employees, UNI-Europa Finance (Banks), the banking trade union section of the European regional organisation of Union Network International.

[104] COM(2004) 557 final, Brussels, 12 August 2004.

[105] Communication from the Commission on the Social Agenda, COM(2005) 33 final, Brussels, 9 February 2005, Section 2: 'The Two Priority Areas', in the first sub-section 2.1 under the heading 'A New Dynamic for Industrial Relations', page 8.

## Enlargement

Despite its title, in fact, there is relatively little in the Communication of 2004 concerned with adapting to enlargement. The brief (three paragraphs) second section of the 'Introduction', entitled 'Enlargement: challenges and opportunities' asserts that:

> the enlargement of the EU also presents a challenge for the European social dialogue. Social dialogue in the new Member States is characterised by the predominance of tripartism, relatively new social partner organisations, and under-developed bipartite social dialogue at national and sector levels.

One might expect the Communication to develop an active strategy to deal with this challenge. Instead, there are only two other references to enlargement towards the end of the Communication.[106] Section 4.2, entitled 'Stepping up support to the European social dialogue structures in the context of enlargement', states the Commission's position as follows:

> The Commission will continue to encourage the development of bipartite social dialogue within the new Member States and will increase its support to the European social partners in order to deal with the consequences of enlargement.
>
> It is important to note that as the social partners are autonomous and social dialogue in the EU is based on the freedom of the right to association, capacity-building is essentially a bottom-up process depending on the efforts of the social partners themselves.

The second paragraph is significant. *Laissez-faire* is the Commission's position on social dialogue. Under the guise of respect for freedom of association, the market in social dialogue must be left to operate without intervention. This is reflected in the only proposal of concrete support for social dialogue in the new Member States. In the next section 4.3, entitled 'Improving the impact and follow-up of the European social dialogue', the last indent refers to:

> Organising national seminars in each Member State – beginning in the new Member States – to raise awareness of the importance of the European social dialogue for national industrial relations.

Consciousness-raising is the Commission's elaborate and sophisticated new tool for promoting social dialogue in the new Member States.

The outcome is acknowledged at present to be, and is likely to continue to be, an underdeveloped bipartite social dialogue. It is difficult to be less than critical about this abandonment by the Commission of the social dialogue in the new Member States.

---

[106] Apart from one word on page 7.

## Laissez-faire?

The Commission's hands-off attitude to social dialogue is not much different when applied to the old Member States. Section 1, the 'Introduction' to the Communication, concludes:

> the purpose of this Communication is to promote awareness and understanding of the results of the European social dialogue, to improve their impact and to promote further developments based on effective interaction between different levels of industrial relations.

Section 2, 'The agenda for reform: competitiveness and more and better jobs', lists a number of themes ('improving adaptability', 'investing in human capital and job quality', 'attracting more people to the labour market') and under the rubric 'delivering reforms' concludes by calling on:

> the European and national social partners to take part in a genuine partnership for change by stepping up their efforts to address the themes identified above and ensuring that their contributions are as concrete and effective as possible.

It seems only fair to demand the same of the Commission.

## New generation synergies ...

Section 3, 'The role of the social partners: the need for a reinforced partnership', gives an update on progress: quantitatively, more than 300 joint texts. Qualitatively: a shift towards greater autonomy, which manifests itself in:

> 'new generation' texts, in which they undertake certain commitments or make recommendations to their national members, and seek to actively follow-up the text at the national level.

In an understatement, the Commission adds that 'the impact of their initiatives could be improved, especially the new generation texts'.

The solution is (section 2.1) 'The need for good synergies', by which is meant 'interaction between the different levels of industrial relations', and, in particular, 'interaction between the European and national levels of industrial relations is crucial'.

How can the Commission promote this? There follow a number of headings. Section 3.2.1 is headed 'Capacities': Synergies with the national level':

> The Commission urges the social partners and the Member States to work together to assist the social partners in reinforcing the administrative capacities of national social partner organisations, for example through the possibilities provided by the structural funds – in particular the European Social Fund (ESF).

In encouraging the Member States the Commission (finally) takes notice of the Treaty:

> National public authorities could potentially play a facilitating role with regard to the implementation of European texts in some Member States. Indeed, this

potential role is reflected in Article 139(2) of the EC Treaty, which states that agreements shall be implemented in accordance with the procedures and practices 'specific to management and labour *and* the Member States'. (emphasis added)

This is a remarkably lenient interpretation of the obligation in Article 139(2): that the role of Member States is only 'potential', that it is merely 'facilitating'. Would the Commission take a similarly lenient approach to the obligation of Member States to implement directives: the Member States are only 'potentially' obliged, and then only to 'facilitate' their implementation by others? Instead, the remedy is 'Awareness raising' – the social partners are encouraged to organise promotional activities.[107]

Section 3.2.2 is headed: 'Synergies between sectors'. The Commission encourages learning from experience in various sectors and as between cross-industry and sectoral levels and urges greater publicity (the Commission offers assistance) of the results of dialogue. More exhortation is to be accompanied by public relations.

Finally, Section 3.2.3: 'Synergies between the European social dialogue and the company level'. The Commission urges the social partners to explore these:

> one example is the link between the sectoral social dialogue and European works councils (EWCs).

While this is a creative idea, it has been around for quite some time, and was attempted by the European Metalworkers' Federation in the steel and vehicle manufacturing sectors. But to no avail. How does the Commission propose to put this proposal into action?

> The European social partners could use the opportunity provided by the Commission's consultation on the revision of the EWC Directive to improve the link between EWCs and the social dialogue.

The European employers' declined to engage in social dialogue on this matter and took the position that the EWCs Directive requires no revision at present. The Commission did nothing further (except to combine the consultation process on EWCs revision with the consultation on restructuring – itself an incomprehensible combination) until 2007, almost three years later, when it indicated its intention to proceed with a revision.

---

[107] The next promotional measure is transparency through taxonomy: 'The Commission has identified two main categories of texts which could qualify as "new generation" texts: autonomous agreements, and process-oriented texts which make recommendations of various kinds (frameworks of action, guidelines, codes of conduct, and policy orientations). The essential difference is that agreements are to be implemented and monitored by a given date, whereas the second kind entail a more process-oriented approach, involving regular reporting on progress made in following-up the objectives of the texts.' This hardly qualifies as an original discovery. The Commission continues: 'The Commission encourages the social partners to improve the clarity of their texts and to include detailed follow-up provisions in their new generation texts. With this end in view, the Commission invites them to draw on the typology and drafting checklists included as annexes, and to invest in joint follow-up actions.'

The Commission offers ideas for others to explore.[108] But what is the Commission itself doing? The answer lies in the last section of the Communication: Section 4: 'The Commission's role in supporting social dialogue'.

Section 4.1 entitled 'Strengthening and enlarging partnership' contains the Commission's by now familiar welcome and encouragement to the social partners, but, as regards the Commission's own action, it merely concludes:

> the Commission will monitor the follow-up given by the social partners to their contribution and assessment of the achievement of the Lisbon objectives.

How does 'monitoring' constitute 'strengthening and enlarging partnership'?

Section 4.2 is headed 'Stepping up support to the European social dialogue structures in the context of enlargement'. Again, there is merely more encouragement: of sectoral social dialogue, or bipartite social dialogue within the new Member States. But again, as noted above, this does not mean actually doing anything:

> capacity-building is essentially a bottom-up process depending on the efforts of the social partners themselves.

What the Commission does intend to do is to *'extend and update the studies on representativeness'* – outsourced to the European Foundation in Dublin.

Section 4.3 is entitled 'Improving the impact and follow-up of the European social dialogue'. It will be recalled that in section 3 the Communication identified the problems of impact and follow-up as a defect in the dialogue of the social partners: 'the impact of their initiatives could be improved, especially the new generation texts'.

Ominously, section 4.3 starts with more welcomes and encouragement to the social partners. But, finally, the Communication asserts: 'The Commission will … assist the social partners in following up their texts.' Yet the promised assistance consists merely of:

> exploring ways of promoting the sharing of experience …
> providing support for the social partners which will be accessible on the social dialogue website … a typology … a lexicon … a drafting checklist … good examples … information…
> organising national seminars … to raise awareness …

The only concrete, though unquantified, commitment is 'reinforcing financial support for joint follow-up actions by the European social partners'. The tenor is distinctly underwhelming. Only in the penultimate section of the Communication does the Commission finally engage with reality.

Section 4.4, 'Autonomous agreements', finally confronts the Communication's admission of a fatal lack of impact of the results of the social dialogue. This is

---

[108] 'Another avenue which could be explored further when seeking to promote synergies between the European and company level is the link between social dialogue and company policies to promote Corporate Social Responsibility (CSR)'.

obviously attributable to failures in the process of their implementation. As previously noted, in section 3.2.1 the Commission appeared reluctant to confront the Member States with their responsibilities under Article 139(2) EC with regard to implementing social dialogue agreements. There is less hesitation with regard to the social partners:

> The Commission fully recognises the negotiating autonomy of the social partners on the topics falling within their competence.
>
> However in the specific case of autonomous agreements implemented in accordance with Article 139(2), the Commission has a particular role to play if the agreement was the result of an Article 138 consultation, inter alia because the social partners' decision to negotiate an agreement temporarily suspends the legislative process at Community level initiated by the Commission in this domain ...[109]
>
> Upon the expiry of the implementation and monitoring period, while giving precedence to the monitoring undertaken by the social partners themselves, the Commission will undertake its own monitoring of the agreement, to assess the extent to which the agreement has contributed to the achievement of the Community's objectives.
>
> Should the Commission decide that the agreement does not succeed in meeting the Community's objectives, it will consider the possibility of putting forward, if necessary, a proposal for a legislative act. The Commission may also exercise its rights of initiative at any point, including during the implementation period, should it conclude that either management or labour are delaying the pursuit of Community objectives.

What is needed, of course, is precisely this sort of approach to be applied not to the *aftermath* of a social dialogue, when its results are to be implemented, but *much earlier*: when the social partners are engaging in dialogue. It is then that the Commission's commitment to take action in the event of failure to agree, action in the form of a proposed legislative measure, can provide the crucial stimulus to concluding an agreement: the dynamic of 'bargaining in the shadow of the law'.

If anything, the Commission's veiled threat as regards implementation may have the opposite effect: of deterring employers from concluding even 'autonomous' agreements. The primary motivation for such agreements has been precisely their non-binding character – the fact that implementation is left to the voluntary action of the social partners – with the well-known consequence of lack of impact. If this is threatened by Commission monitoring and possible follow-up implementation, then employers will see disappear what little incentive they have to make any agreements at all.

The logic of the Commission's position in the case of a refusal by employers to engage in a social dialogue producing a binding agreement would be to adapt

---

[109] This is the practice. However, as explained earlier, the Treaty does not appear to require suspension of the legislative process when the social partners decide to engage in social dialogue. Indeed, in certain circumstance, continuation of the legislative process may stimulate the social dialogue.

its proposed *post*-agreement intervention to the *pre*-agreement stage: to propose legislative action not to stimulate implementation of an agreement, but to stimulate the agreement itself. The formulation of the dynamic in terms of 'bargaining in the shadow of the law' is well known.

It is not clear whether the Commission understands this dynamic, or deliberately misunderstands it. The last paragraph of section 4.4 states:

> While recognising the broad scope of the social partners' competences, in line with the previous concerns of the Commission, where fundamental rights or important political options are at stake, or in situations where the rules must be applied in uniform fashion in all Member States and coverage must be complete, preference should be given to implementation by Council decision. Autonomous agreements are also not appropriate for the revision of previously existing directives adopted by the Council and European Parliament through the normal legislative procedure.

At least three important issues are raised by this passage.

First, it represents a further elaboration of the Commission's Social Policy Agenda (2001–4).[110] Of the ambitions of that Agenda, it was stated that 'To achieve these priorities, an adequate combination of all existing means will be required' (p. 14). The second means listed was:

> Legislation: Standards should be developed or adapted, where appropriate, to ensure the respect of fundamental social rights and to respond to new challenges. Such standards can also result from agreements between the social partners at European level.

It was not clear that agreements in this policy area between the social partners would necessarily be implemented through a Council decision. The Communication of 2004 now clarifies that this is to be the case, and further extends the range of agreements which must be implemented through a Council decision. As this brings with it the need for Commission, Council and possibly even judicial review by the European Court of Justice of such agreements, it is not clear how this is consistent with the repeated affirmations by the Commission of social partner autonomy.

A second important issue is that the range of agreements to be implemented through Council decision is now extended to 'situations where the rules must be applied in uniform fashion in all Member States and coverage must be complete'. This formulation reflects very closely the case law of the European Court of Justice regarding implementation of directives through collective agreements (now in Article 137(3) EC). One implication, therefore, is that agreements implemented through a Council decision will take the form of directives.

But another, more disturbing, implication is that the *other* method of implementation envisaged by Article 139(2): 'in accordance with the procedures and

---

[110] Adopted in June 2000, COM(2000) 379, approved by the European Council meeting at Nice in December 2000.

practices specific to management and labour and the Member States', need *not* necessarily be applied in uniform fashion, *nor* need coverage be complete. Yet this would undermine precisely the Commission's complaint about lack of impact of agreements reached. It would also raise grave questions as to the equal application of Community law in the form of social dialogue agreements.

A third important issue results from the fact that, to date, the Commission has (albeit belatedly and arguably following an incorrect procedure) consulted the social partners in two cases of revision of existing directives: the Working Time Directive and the European Works Councils Directive. One is entitled to presume that this was intended, as provided in Article 138(4) EC, to allow for the possibility of social dialogue. Yet in this last paragraph of section 4.4 of the Communication, the Commission declares that implementation of any resulting social dialogue agreement must be through a Council decision.

The current consensus is that neither the Commission, nor anybody else, has the expectation that any social dialogue agreement will be concluded on revision of either Directive. But the Commission's statement in this Communication that any such agreement would be made legally binding through a Council decision is probably the one certain way of removing any incentive by employers to reach agreement. The Commission proposes to do the one thing that will destroy any prospect of reaching an agreement.

### Transnational collective bargaining

There is one daring last fling at an initiative in the final section 4.5 of the Communication: 'Preparing further developments':

> Interest in and the importance of transnational collective bargaining has been increasing in recent years, particularly in response to globalisation and economic and monetary union. EWCs are adopting a growing number of agreements within multinational companies which cover employees in several Member States. There is also a growing interest in cross-border agreements between social partners from geographically contiguous Member States, as well as agreements between the social partners in particular sectors covering more than one Member State.
>
> In view of this trend, the Commission is conducting a study of transnational collective bargaining and will make its results available to the social partners. At a later stage the Commission will consult the social partners on their outcome regarding the development of a Community framework for transnational collective bargaining.

The Communication thus links the outcomes of the EU social dialogue with a new formulation – 'transnational collective bargaining' – and raises the prospect of a Community framework for transnational collective bargaining.[111]

---

[111] This transmutation of social partner consultation leading to social dialogue and thence into collective bargaining is curiously echoed in a later decision of the European Court of Justice, which determined that the obligation to consult in a number of directives is tantamount to an

There has long been a demand for a more detailed framework of procedural rules for the European social dialogue.[112] Of course, the autonomy of the social partners requires that, in the first place, they must be responsible for drafting such rules.[113] But where the social dialogue is manifestly falling into desuetude, or producing only ineffective results with little impact, the responsibility of the EU institutions is to propose a procedural solution.

The Commission concludes its Communication on this tantalisingly abrupt high note of ambition. It was mildly encouraging, therefore, that the new Social Agenda of 9 February 2005 appeared to take this further:[114]

> The Commission plans to adopt a proposal designed to make it possible for the social partners to formalise the nature and results of transnational collective bargaining. The existence of this resource is essential but its use will remain optional and will depend entirely on the will of the social partners.

The Communication of 9 February 2005 on the Social Agenda 2005–10 included only this one specific proposal which the Barroso Commission explicitly committed itself to adopting: on transnational collective bargaining. Yet even this has been abandoned: in a conference organised by the Commission on 27 November 2006, the survey of transnational collective agreements conducted by D-G V was marginalised and the expert study proposing a directive was brusquely buried. Instead it was announced that no regulatory initiative was in prospect and the Commission planned at most another Communication in 2007.

## Conclusion

This 2004 Communication reveals the Commission, the engine of European integration, as largely failing in what the Treaty, in Article 138(1), describes as its:

> task of promoting the consultation of management and labour at Community level and shall take any relevant measure to facilitate their dialogue by ensuring balanced support for the parties.

---

obligation to negotiate. *Irmtraud Junk c. Wolfgang Kuhnel als Insolvenzverwalter uber das Vermogen der Firma AWO,*Case C-188/03, 27 January 2005.

[112] See the Opinion of the European Economic and Social Committee, Opinion 94/C 397/17, OJ 397/40 of 31 December 1994, and the analysis above, which appeared in the first edition of this book in 1996, at pp. 553–70.

[113] For an essay describing how such a European level agreement might be drafted on the model of the Danish (and other Nordic) Basic Agreements, B. Bercusson, 'Prospects for a European "September Agreement"', in M. Andreasen, J. Kristiansen and R. Nielsen (eds.), *Septemberforliget 100 Ar,* Copenhagen: DJOF Publishing, 1999, pp. 21–54. For a proposal along similar lines, D. Schiek, 'Autonomous Collective Agreements as a Regulatory Device in European Labour Law: How to Read Article 139 EC' (2005) 34 *Industrial Law Journal* 23–56.

[114] Communication from the Commission on the Social Agenda, COM(2005) 33 final, Brussels, 9 February 2005, Section 2: 'The Two Priority Areas'. Oddly, this proposal appears not in the first section 2.1, under the heading 'A New Dynamic for Industrial Relations', but rather under a different heading: 'Towards a European Labour Market'.

This was the provision inserted by the Single European Act 1986, and under which the then President of the Commission, Jacques Delors, and the then Director-General of D-G V, Jean Degimbe, and their staff initiated and then promoted the EU social dialogue which culminated in the Maastricht Treaty Protocol on Social Policy and the social dialogue agreements and Directives on Parental Leave, Part-Time Work and Fixed-Term Work.

Since this last agreement of 1999, however, the decline has been precipitous, and the Commission is not the least responsible. This latest Communication is evidence of the poverty of its ambition. With the greatest optimism, perhaps the phrase which describes best the current state of the European social dialogue is 'benign neglect'. The future of the European social dialogue requires a Commission that takes its responsibilities more seriously.

The fundamental strategic issue is the role of the EU social partners and the EU social dialogue in the EU constitutional and legal order. Is the role of the social partners confined to an industrial relations sub-system subordinate to the internal market regulated by the EU institutions? Or is it a role of autonomous regulation of social policy, and in particular, of the sphere of employment and industrial relations, by constitutionally recognised social partners?

# Chapter 18

# External and internal scrutiny of the democratic legitimacy of the European social dialogue

## External review of the democratic legitimacy of the European social dialogue

The Maastricht Treaty on European Union transformed EC labour law by formally 'constitutionalising' the social dialogue in the Protocol and Agreement on Social Policy. Following the Treaty of Amsterdam of June 1997, and the UK's opt-in to the Social Policy Agreement, the role of the social dialogue in the making of EC labour law is formally enshrined in the EC Treaty.

At the very moment when the Amsterdam Treaty was incorporating the social dialogue process into the EC Treaty, there was litigation pending before the Court of First Instance (CFI) which challenged the first product of that process: the Parental Leave Directive and annexed Agreement.[1] In a decision almost exactly one year after the Amsterdam Summit, the CFI delivered a judgment which highlights the constitutional nature of the integration of social dialogue into the EC Treaty.[2] The judgment raises profound issues of the democratic legitimacy of EC labour law and legislation, the autonomy of the social partners engaged in social dialogue, and the role of litigation as a control mechanism of this legitimacy and autonomy.[3]

The *UEAPME* case is a potential landmark in the history of European labour law. It concerns a choice between competing legal conceptualisations of the EU social dialogue. Put simply, *EC* labour law can be defined, described and developed in concepts derived from the *constitutional law* of the EC, or in concepts drawn from *labour law* traditions of the Member States. However, it is

---

[1] Council Directive 96/34/EC of 3 June 1996 on the Framework Agreement on parental leave concluded by UNICE, CCEP and the ETUC, OJ L145/4 of 19 June 1996.

[2] *Union Européenne de l'Artisanat et des Petites et Moyennes Entreprises (UEAPME)* v. *Council of the European Union*, Case T-135/96, [1998] ECR II-2335. Hereinafter referred to as *UEAPME*.

[3] See B. Bercusson, 'Democratic Legitimacy and European Labour Law', (1999) 28 *Industrial Law Journal* 153–70, on which this chapter is based. Also E. Franssen and A. Jacobs, 'The Question of Representativity in the European Social Dialogue', (1998) 35 *Common Market Law Review* 1295; G. Britz and M. Schmidt, 'The Institutionalised Participation of Management and Labour in the Legislative Activities of the European Community: A Challenge to the Principle of Democracy under Community Law', (2000) 6 *European Law Journal* 45–71; N. Bernard, 'Legitimising EU Law: Is the Social Dialogue the Way Forward? Some Reflections around the *UEAPME* Case', in J. Shaw (ed.), *Social Law and Policy in an Evolving European Union*, Oxford: Hart, 2000.

suggested that, in terms of *European* labour law, the future is likely to be conceptualised as an amalgam of the two.

This chapter begins by analysing the structure of the CFI's judgment. The main interest of the judgment lies in the CFI's propositions regarding the parties, the process and the outcome of the EU social dialogue. These propositions use constitutional law concepts which challenge fundamental premises of the legislative procedure through social dialogue established by the Maastricht Social Policy Agreement, now in Articles 138–9 EC. This section critically assesses these propositions. The final conclusions contrast the CFI's EU constitutional law model of democratic legitimacy of the social dialogue with the industrial relations model rooted in national labour law systems and argues for a 'European labour law' which combines the two models.

## The background to the *UEAPME* case

In *UEAPME*, an organisation representing artisans and small and medium undertakings (SMUs) challenged the legality of the Parental Leave Directive before the CFI. The Parental Leave Directive was the first product of the Protocol and Agreement on Social Policy. The process which led to the Directive's adoption by the Council of Ministers was the test-bed for the EU institutions' understanding of how that Agreement was to be implemented; in particular, the Commission's Communication on the Implementation of the Agreement.[4]

The first stage in the new procedure prescribed in Article 3(2) of the Maastricht Social Policy Agreement (Article 138(2) EC) was initiated on 21 January 1995, when the Commission decided 'to consult management and labour on the possible direction of Community action with regard to reconciling working and family life'.[5] The first stage of the consultation process engaged UEAPME. The CFI judgment recounts that:[6]

> On 6 April 1995, the applicant [UEAPME] and some of the other representative associations consulted addressed to the Commission a document stating a common position. The signatories to that document urged the Commission to do everything in its power to ensure that certain important issues and certain representatives of management and labour were not excluded from the negotiations.

In June 1995 the Commission initiated the second stage of consultations under Article 3(3) of the Social Policy Agreement (Article 138(3)) and, again, on 5 July

---

[4] COM(93) 600 final, Brussels, 14 December 1993.
[5] *UEAPME*, paragraph 5. This followed a gap of almost twelve years since 1983, when the Commission had first drafted a proposal for a Directive on parental leave and leave for family reasons, which was never adopted by the Council. For the early history, see Commission Consultative Document, *Reconciliation of Professional and Family Life*, February 1995, para. 2.
[6] *UEAPME*, paragraph 6.

1995, UEAPME and the other associations submitted a statement of a common position. The CFI decision states:[7]

> On the same date, UNICE, CEEP and the ETUC informed the Commission, in accordance with Article 3(4) of the Agreement (Article 138(4)), of their desire to exercise the option available under Article 4(1) (Article 139(1)) of opening negotiations on parental leave.

The EU social partners' negotiations were successful: on 6 November 1995 they agreed a proposal for a framework agreement which was finally concluded on 14 December 1995 and 'submitted to the Commission with the request that it be implemented by a Council decision on a proposal from the Commission, in accordance with Article 4(2) (Article 139(2)) of the Agreement'.[8]

The EU social partners did not involve others in their negotiations. After they had made their proposed agreement, UEAPME formally communicated to the Commission 'its regret at having been unable to take part in the dialogue between management and labour, and submitted its criticisms of the proposed framework agreement'.[9] UEAPME, together with other organisations consulted and informed, but not signatories to the agreement, were sent copies of the framework agreement on 20 December 1995, and attended a meeting for information and discussion on 5 January 1996.[10] The agreement was incorporated into Directive 96/34, adopted by the Council on 3 June 1996.

On 5 September 1996, UEAPME brought an action under Article 173 (now Article 230) of the EC Treaty for annulment of the Directive.[11] However, EC law placed constraints on UEAPME's ability to mount a challenge to the Directive, and, consequently, forced the arguments on legal issues of the social dialogue into unexpected channels, which led to unanticipated results and conclusions.

The significance of UEAPME's use of Article 173 (Article 230) was considerable. It required the CFI to formulate its decision in the terms used by this Article, in light of its interpretation and application in earlier cases. Article 173 has had an important role in the constitutional development of the EU, and, more particularly, for the role of the European Parliament. The use of Article 173 to determine the standing of UEAPME to seek annulment highlighted the constitutional profile of the social dialogue, and explains, in part, the approach of the CFI.

---

[7] *UEAPME*, paragraph 8.     [8] *UEAPME*, paragraph 9.

[9] *Ibid.*; UEAPME's communications were on 30 November and 13 December 1995.

[10] *UEAPME*, paragraph 10.

[11] The relevant parts of Article 173 (now Article 230 EC) are as follows: 'The Court of Justice shall review the legality of acts adopted jointly by the European Parliament and the Council, of acts of the Council, of the Commission ... Any natural or legal person may ... institute proceedings against a decision addressed to that person or against a decision which, although in the form of a regulation or a decision addressed to another person, is of direct and individual concern to the former'.

## The CFI's challenges to the Social Policy Agreement

### The structure of the CFI's judgment

The arguments put to the Court by the Council, the Commission and the applicant, UEAPME, were infused with two basic lines of reasoning. One focused on the issue of the strict technical requirements of Article 173. A second demonstrated awareness that the Social Policy Agreement reflected a tradition of social dialogue between social partners, a tradition based not only on the experience of social dialogue at EU level (brief as it then was), but one with highly sophisticated concepts (*erga omnes*, etc.) evolved over decades of experience in a variety of national contexts of the Member States.

In contrast to this argumentation, the CFI, instead, chose to use the technical questions posed by Article 173 to develop a different line of reasoning based on the emerging constitutional law of the EU. This reasoning, addressing fundamental issues of the constitutional nature of the EU, contrasted with argumentation recognising the social dialogue traditions of the social partners. This contrast highlights different approaches which are fundamental to the future of European labour law and will be addressed in the final section of this chapter.

Given a complaint under the rubric of Article 173, the starting point was, of necessity, the Directive itself, and the first question to be addressed was whether UEAPME had *locus standi* to challenge the directive incorporating the Parental Leave Agreement. The perception that Article 173 dictated the starting point was obvious from the arguments of the Council: that as a directive, not a decision, it cannot be challenged;[12] that the measure is neither of direct nor individual concern to UEAPME;[13] that the issue of representativeness is germane only to the question of whether the measure is of direct and individual concern;[14] that UEAPME's role in the procedure leading to the Directive (consultation by the Commission being strictly separate from negotiation between the social partners) does not, again, entail that the measure is of direct and individual concern to it.[15]

Similarly, the Commission's arguments again focus on the assertion that UEAPME is neither individually nor directly concerned.[16] UEAPME's counter-arguments followed the same logic: that being left out of the negotiations places it in a special position;[17] that even as a legislative measure it is of individual concern;[18] and that UEAPME in particular was individually concerned by the Directive;[19] and also directly affected.[20]

However, instead of referring to these arguments, the CFI used the technical question of *locus standi* under Article 173 to raise, and focus on, a much more general and politically delicate constitutional law issue. The route followed by the CFI in addressing this central issue shaped the structure of its decision, and

---

[12] Paragraph 25.    [13] Paragraphs 26–30.    [14] Paragraph 31.    [15] Paragraphs 32–9.
[16] Paragraphs 41–2.    [17] Paragraph 46.    [18] Paragraphs 48–9 and 59.    [19] Paragraph 51.
[20] Paragraphs 53–5 and 60.

needs to be carefully plotted. The following is a summary of three essential elements: the legitimacy of social dialogue agreements, the representativity of the parties to them, and the control by EU institutions of the social dialogue process.

The opening question posed by the CFI was whether *agreements* reached through the social dialogue, which are, following the provisions of Article 4(2) of the Social Policy Agreement (Article 139(2) EC), incorporated into directives, may be challenged on grounds of their *legitimacy*.

In answering this question of the political, legal and constitutional legitimacy of the social dialogue, however, the CFI shifted the focus of attention from the obvious targets in the case before it: the complainant (UEAPME, an outsider to the social dialogue), and the object of the complaint (the Directive proposed by the Commission and approved by the Council, which incorporated the Parental Leave Agreement, the outcome of the social dialogue).

Instead, the focus of the CFI's attention in answering the question became the *parties* to the social dialogue, in this case, the parties to the social dialogue leading to the Parental Leave Agreement: UNICE, CEEP and the ETUC. The technical question of the *locus standi* of UEAPME, transformed into the general issue of legitimacy, was used by the CFI to raise the question of whether the parties to the Parental Leave Agreement are *representative* and, if not, whether this allowed for a challenge to the Directive/Agreement.

Finally, in addressing the question of the representativity of the social partners, the CFI put forward propositions regarding the constitutional responsibilities of the EU institutions. In doing so, the CFI raised questions with respect to the *process* of social dialogue, and of the *autonomy* of the parties to it.

In this way, through the prism of a challenge under Article 173, the CFI laid down a number of propositions regarding the parties, the process and the outcome of the EU social dialogue as constitutionalised in the Social Policy Agreement (now in the EC Treaty). The next section describes the propositions of the CFI. The final section critically analyses these propositions, and addresses the alternative framework of traditional social dialogue recognised in the argumentation of the parties to the case.

### Challenging social dialogue agreements: democratic legitimacy of social dialogue

The object of the complaint was a Directive not addressed to UEAPME. As a complainant, UEAPME had to overcome two obstacles. The first was that Article 173 refers to decisions and Regulations, not directives.[21] The CFI nonetheless disposed of this issue quickly:[22]

---

[21] The CFI was categorical: 'Directive 96/34 is a legislative measure and does not constitute a decision within the meaning of Article 189 of the Treaty'. Paragraph 67.

[22] Paragraph 69.

It should be borne in mind that, in certain circumstances, even a legislative measure which applies to the economic operators concerned in general may, according to the case law … be of individual concern to some of them.

The key question, which enabled the CFI to launch itself into fundamental legal questions concerning the EU social dialogue, was an apparently narrow technical issue:[23]

it is necessary to determine whether, nothwithstanding the legislative character of Directive 96/34, the applicant may be regarded as directly and individually concerned by it.

The CFI rejected UEAPME's claim to 'special rights in the context of the procedural mechanisms established by the [Social Policy] Agreement'.[24] Reviewing the wording of Articles 3 and 4 of the Agreement (now Articles 138–9 EC) in light of the Commission's Communication of 1993, it concluded that these:[25]

do not confer on any representative of management and labour, whatever the interests purportedly represented, a general right to take part in any negotiations entered into in accordance with Article 3(4) of the Agreement, even though it is open to any representative of management and labour which has been consulted pursuant to Article 3(2) and (3) of the Agreement to initiate such negotiations.

Nor, in the specific circumstances of UEAPME's representing small and medium-sized undertakings, did the reference to SMUs in Article 2(2) of the Agreement confer an individual right to participate.[26]

The CFI was careful, therefore, at this stage, to exclude anything regarding the *social dialogue* procedure from distinguishing UEAPME as singularly affected by the resulting agreement, so as to confer on it the standing to invoke Article 173.

The issue might have rested there, with the complaint rejected. Instead, the CFI chose to develop the question of *locus standi* under Article 173 as raising issues of constitutional importance. It therefore continued:[27]

However, that is not sufficient in itself to render the present action inadmissible. In view of the particular features of the procedure which led to the adoption of Directive 93/34 on the basis of Article 4(2) of the Agreement [now Article 139(2) EC], it is also necessary to determine whether any right of the applicant has been infringed as the result of any failure on the part of either the Council or the Commission to fulfil their obligations under that procedure.

Technically, it is not the *social dialogue* procedure which is to be scrutinised under Article 173, but the *legislative* procedure involving the *Council* and the *Commission*. However, it proved impossible to segregate the two procedures:[28]

It is proper to stress the importance of the obligation incumbent on the Commission and the Council to verify the representativity of the signatories to

---

[23] Paragraph 68.    [24] Paragraph 70.    [25] Paragraph 78.
[26] Paragraph 80.    [27] Paragraph 83.    [28] Paragraph 88.

an agreement concluded pursuant to Articles 3(4) and 4 of the Agreement [now Articles 138(4) and 139 EC], which the Council has been asked to implement at Community level. The participation of the two institutions in question has the effect ... of endowing an agreement concluded between management and labour with a Community foundation of a legislative character, without recourse to the classic procedures provided for under the Treaty for the preparation of legislation, which entail the participation of the European Parliament. As the case law makes clear, the participation of that institution in the Community legislative process reflects at Community level the fundamental democratic principle that the people must share in the exercise of power through a representative assembly ... In that regard ... the democratic legitimacy of measures adopted by the Council pursuant to Article 2 of the Agreement [now Article 139 EC] derives from the European Parliament's participation in that first procedure.

In fact, despite this emphasis on *procedure*, the basis of the CFI's approach lies in its characterisation of the *outcome* of the social dialogue. The CFI declares that the outcome of the social dialogue, when embodied in a legislative measure such as a directive, must be *democratically legitimate*.

The CFI contrasted the two possible outcomes under the Maastricht Social Policy Agreement. The first outcome follows from the normal legislative process and, as quoted above, the CFI declared:

the democratic legitimacy of measures adopted by the Council pursuant to Article 2 of the Agreement [now Article 137 EC] derives from the European Parliament's participation in that first procedure.

The second outcome results from the social dialogue; the directive which emerges from the Council embodies the agreement reached by labour and management. Of this, the CFI says:[29]

In contrast, the second procedure, referred to in Articles 3(4) and 4 of the Agreement [now Articles 138(4) and 139 EC], does not provide for the participation of the European Parliament. However, the principle of democracy on which the Union is founded requires – in the absence of the participation of the European Parliament in the legislative process – that the participation of the people be otherwise assured, in this instance through the parties representative of management and labour who concluded the agreement which is endowed by the Council acting on a qualified majority, on a proposal from the Commission, with a legislative foundation at Community level. In order to make sure that that requirement is complied with, the Commission and the Council are under a duty to verify that the signatories to the agreement are truly representative.

Whatever the CFI's views on the nature of the social dialogue and legislative *procedures*, and their respective *outcomes*, there is nothing as yet in the judgment regarding the technical issue central to the complaint, the requisite criteria for *locus standi* under Article 173: that the outcome to be challenged is 'of direct and individual concern to [UEAPME]'. That technical issue was

---

[29] Paragraph 89.

addressed through the CFI's scrutiny, not of procedures or outcomes, but of the *parties* to the social dialogue: the social partners.

## Challenging the social partners: representativity

The most important part of the CFI's decision for the social partners concerns the *parties* to any social dialogue agreement. For an agreement to be democratically legitimate, the CFI stipulates that it must be ascertained:[30]

> whether, having regard to the content of the agreement in question, the signatories, taken together, are sufficiently representative.

It is here that the need to shape the judgment within the technical confines of the challenge under Article 173 was most evident:[31]

> it is necessary to determine whether, nothwithstanding the legislative character of Directive 96/34, the applicant may be regarded as directly and individually concerned by it.

This was a challenge to a specific measure by a specific party. The nature of the specific measure challenged and the specific quality of the challenger are conditions to success under Article 173. These conditions were invoked to contest the challenge; but, unfortunately, as formulated to deal with the specific challenge, they also shape the CFI's vision of the social dialogue in general.

## The specific agreement

The challenge was to a specific Directive incorporating a social dialogue agreement on Parental Leave. The CFI insisted that the representativity of the parties is measured 'in relation to the content of the agreement',[32] or 'with respect to the substantive scope of the framework agreement'.[33] It looked, for example, at who exactly were the workers covered by the agreement.[34]

The implication for the social partners is that, for the future, agreements may be democratically legitimate when signed by organisations which are *only* representative as regards the narrow scope of the agreement concerned.

This offers the social partners an opportunity, in that agreements negotiated at EU level need not be all-encompassing. On the other hand, it presents them with a challenge in that, taken individually, organisations signing these agreements may be far from representative in general.

## 'Sufficient collective representativity'[35]

This is the key phrase repeatedly used by the CFI to describe the parties to a valid agreement. It arose because of the need for the CFI to decide whether

---

[30] Paragraph 90.    [31] Paragraph 68.    [32] Paragraph 90.    [33] Paragraph 91.    [34] Paragraph 94.
[35] The official language of the case was French. This phrase first appears in paragraph 90 (and thereafter is repeated in the same formulation) as 'partenaires sociaux signataires … ont une représentativité cumulée suffisante'. This is translated relatively accurately into English as

UEAPME qualified as a complainant under Article 173 as 'directly and individually concerned' by the Directive. The CFI interpreted those words of Article 173 in the context of social dialogue agreements as follows:[36]

> representatives of management and labour … which were not parties to the agreement, and whose particular representation – again in relation to the content of the agreement – is necessary in order to raise the collective representativity of the signatories to the required level, have the right to prevent the Commission and the Council from implementing the agreement at Community level by means of a legislative instrument … they must be regarded as directly and individually concerned by that measure.

The implication for the social partners is that, even after the difficult process of social dialogue has resulted in an agreement, EC law allows non-signatories to challenge the validity of directives implementing social dialogue agreements.

The 'right to prevent the Commission and the Council from implementing the agreement at Community level by means of a legislative instrument' offers the social partners an opportunity. Agreements negotiated at EU level by social partners who do not have sufficient cumulative representativity may be challenged by legitimate representatives of labour and management. It presents a danger, however, in that organisations excluded from the social dialogue negotiations may seek to undermine these agreements.

The specific formula adopted by the CFI to legitimise EU level agreements explicitly encapsulates two elements of central importance.

### 'Sufficient'

The requisite degree of representativity is not absolute. It must merely be sufficient. This relaxation of the standard may be in recognition of the extremely varied level of trade union representation in different Member States. As with the definition of subsidiarity in Article 5 EC, however, it is not clear when the requisite degree has been 'sufficiently' achieved. An EU-level agreement may stand or fall on whether or not the parties to it have sufficient representativity to confer on the agreement the democratic legitimacy demanded by the CFI.

The relativity of the element of 'sufficiency' was evident in the CFI's finding that, even having regard to the Social Policy Agreement's emphasis on SMUs in Article 2(2) (now Article 137(2) EC), UEAPME could not argue that:[37]

> its level of representativity is so great that its non-participation in the conclusion of an agreement between general cross-industry organisations automatically means that the requirement of sufficient collective representativity was not satisfied.

'signatories, *taken together*, are sufficiently representative'. In subsequent paragraphs, however, the phrase is formulated as 'sufficient *collective* representativity' (paragraph 94). This translation of 'cumulée' as 'collective' is questionable in failing to highlight a key dimension. Representativity is *cumulative* in that the signatories (on one side) may, taken separately, not be representative, but taken together may achieve the requisite degree of representativity. A better translation of this key concept, it is suggested, would be 'sufficient cumulative representativity'.

[36] Paragraph 90.     [37] Paragraph 104.

## 'Collective'

One problem confronted by social partner organisations which may seek a role in EU-level social dialogue is that they may be exclusively national, or their transnational character, in contrast to the social partners ETUC, UNICE (now BusinessEurope) and CEEP, may be uneven: concentrated in or confined to only a number of Member States. Taken individually, such organisations could not aspire to 'sufficient collective representativity' at the EU level so long as the EU social dialogue was confined to organisations which in themselves had European scope.

One implication of the CFI's use of the word 'collective (*cumulée*), however, is that a number of such social partner organisations could sign an agreement which could, cumulatively, achieve the requisite degree of representativity. This may conflict with the Commission's understanding of 'representativeness', one of the criteria of which is and remains that the organisations 'be organised at European level'.[38]

## Representativity: criteria

While emphasising the importance of representativity, the CFI was less than clear on the question of criteria. The CFI referred to the criteria set out by the Commission in its Communication of 1993. Representativeness meant European scope (cross-industry or sectoral), comprising recognised bargaining organisations in Member States, and adequate to the task at EU level. But the CFI did not express a clear opinion about them.[39]

Reflecting the Commission's choice of criteria, the CFI seemed to look for evidence of representativity in parties 'having regard to their cross-industry character and the general nature of their mandate'.[40] Thus, as regards UNICE: 'that body represented undertakings of all sizes in the private sector, which qualified it to represent the SMUs'.[41]

The CFI acknowledged that the criterion of numbers represented may be taken into consideration; however, 'the number of SMUs represented respectively by the applicant [UEAPME] and UNICE … cannot be regarded as

---

[38] See the discussion of 'representativeness' in Chapter 17.

[39] *UEAPME*, paragraph 72: 'The Commission accordingly set out in its Communication a number of criteria, which make it possible to identify those representatives of management and labour whose representativity in its view entitles them to be consulted …'. The CFI went on to say that (paragraph 77): 'It is also clear from the wording of the Communication that the list set out in Annex 2 (management and labour organisations considered by the Commission to be representative) is drawn up to meet the organisational requirements only of the consultation stage provided for by Article 3(2) and (3) of the Agreement … it does not refer to it anywhere in the section dealing with the negotiations stage …'. The CFI emphasised the duty of the Commission and the Council to examine the representativity of the social partners parties to any agreement (paragraphs 85ff.). The CFI reviewed their examination and referred to tables and studies which 'show at the very least that both institutions kept themselves informed as to the representativity of the management and labour concerned in the present case' (paragraph 92).

[40] Paragraph 96.    [41] Paragraph 98.

decisive in relation to the content of that agreement'.[42] The statistics produced by the parties, and quoted by the CFI, demonstrated a degree of uncertainty likely to undermine any reliance on numbers.[43]

The CFI seemed rather to be satisfied if the *interests* of the category of SMUs were taken into acccount. The CFI emphasised 'the argument that UNICE does have a general mandate – to defend the interests of undertakings of whatever kind – by contrast with the more specific mandate of other cross-industry organisations, such as the applicant'.[44] It cited the text of the agreement, 'which makes it clear that the SMUs were not left out of the negotiations leading to its conclusion'.[45]

A concept of an organisation's 'representativity' based on its claim to represent interests, rather than actual numbers of members, poses problems. Even more so, if the evidence for representation of those interests is based on the text of agreements concluded. The question of interest representation in the constitutional context of the EU raises issues going far beyond the summary considerations in the CFI's judgment.

### Challenging the social dialogue: autonomy

The Social Policy Agreement established a delicate equilibrium between autonomy of the EU social partners and the role of the Commission, an equilibrium characterised as 'bargaining in the shadow of the law'.

The autonomy of the social partners was confirmed by the CFI in rejecting UEAPME's claim to participate in the negotiations leading to the Parental Leave Agreement. The CFI strongly asserted the voluntary nature of the social dialogue under the Maastricht Agreement:[46]

> the Agreement [does] not confer on any representative of management and labour, whatever the interests purportedly represented, a general right to take part in any negotiations ... even though it is open to any representative ... to initiate such negotiations ... it is the representatives of management and labour concerned, and not the Commission, which have charge of the negotiation stage properly so called.

However, the CFI took the view that this autonomy ceases when the parties wish their agreement to be transformed into an EC legal measure by a decision of the Council and turn to the Commission 'which thereupon resumes control of the procedure and determines whether it is appropriate to submit a proposal to that effect to the Council'.[47]

---

[42] Paragraph 102.
[43] Paragraph 103 cited three sets of figures for the number of SMUs represented by UEAPME, ranging from 4,835,568 to 6,600,000. The CFI itself said that the evidence showed that 'a third ... perhaps as many as two-thirds ... of those SMUs are also affiliated to one of the organisations represented by UNICE'.
[44] Paragraph 99.     [45] Paragraph 105.     [46] Paragraphs 78–9.     [47] Paragraph 84.

It would appear from this that the social partners retain their autonomy throughout the social dialogue process. However, as indicated above, the shadow of the Commission weighs on the process in so far as the prospect of the Commission's proposing legislation will influence the negotiations. The CFI has lengthened this shadow by reinforcing the Commission's power to assess the representativeness of the parties to the agreement:[48]

> on regaining the right to take part in the conduct of the procedure, the Commission must, in particular, examine the representativity of the signatories to the agreement in question.

Although apparently post-agreement, this examination in effect reaches back to the conduct of negotiations, since the social partners' exclusion of other parties from the negotiations may lead the Commission and Council to reject their agreement as insufficiently representative. The Commission can effectively force the participation of certain parties required for the 'sufficient collective representativity' needed to achieve democratic legitimacy. If these are excluded, the agreement may be successfully challenged by the excluded party.

The impact on the autonomy of the social partners of the CFI's decision is evident in its aftermath. The indications were that UEAPME would appeal from the decision of the CFI to the European Court of Justice. In the event, no appeal was made. Instead, a 'Proposal for a Cooperation Agreement between UNICE and UEAPME', dated 12 November 1998, outlines 'the modalities of cooperation between UNICE and UEAPME in social dialogue meetings, including negotiations' (Clause 1.2). This includes provisions whereby 'UNICE undertakes to consult UEAPME prior to taking public positions on behalf of the employers' group in social dialogue and negotiating meetings' (Clause 3.1) and 'UEAPME representatives fully participate in preparatory meetings of the employers' group and in plenary meetings with ETUC' (Clause 3.2).

The shadow of the Commission was further lengthened by the CFI seeming to approve the view expressed in the Commission's Communication that it would consider:[49]

> the representative status of the contracting parties, their mandate and the 'legality' of each clause in the collective agreement in relation to Community law, and the provisions regarding small and medium-sized undertakings set out in Article 2(2) [now Article 137(2) EC].

This opens up new avenues for the Commission to exert influence on the social dialogue process, as the parties negotiate under this scrutiny.

For example, the internal constitutional structure of the EU social partners is the outcome of delicate political adjustment. In the case of the ETUC, decisions to approve agreements may be taken by majority vote. If a particular agreement

---

[48] Paragraph 85.
[49] Paragraph 86, quoting paragraph 39 of the Commission's Communication of 1993.

was approved by such a majority, but the largest national trade union confederation voted against the agreement, would the Commission entertain a complaint by that confederation on the grounds, for example, that the negotiators had exceeded their mandate? In the case of UNICE, negotiations are undertaken only when there is a unanimous consensus among the member employer federations. Would the Commission allow an agreement to proceed to Council which UNICE (now BusinessEurope) purported to negotiate despite the opposition of one Member State confederation?

The examples multiply and the potential for Commission influence expands if the substance of agreements comes under scrutiny in light of Community law, itself not always predictable.

To justify its view as to the role of the Commission following the conclusion of an agreement under the social dialogue, the CFI asserted:[50]

> The Commission must act in conformity with the principles governing its action in the social policy field, more particularly expressed in Article 3(1) of the Agreement [now Article 138(1) EC], which states that 'the Commission shall have the task of promoting the consultation of management and labour at Community level and shall take any relevant measure to facilitate their dialogue by ensuring balanced support for the parties'.

Article 3(1) is indeed in the Social Policy Agreement. But this well-known provision has its origins in the Single European Act 1986, long before the Social Policy Agreement procedure was ever dreamed of. It clearly and unambiguously aimed to do no more than it stated, and was implemented through Commission support, mainly financial, for the social partners' dialogue. What is extraordinary is that the CFI sees words such as 'promoting the consultation' and 'to facilitate their dialogue' as justifying the conclusion which follows:[51]

> As the applicant and the Commission have rightly pointed out, on regaining the right to take part in the conduct of the procedure, the Commission must, in particular, examine the representativity of the signatories to the agreement in question …
>
> The Council, for its part, is required to verify whether the Commission has fulfilled its obligations under the Agreement, because, if that is not the case, the Council runs the risk of ratifying a procedural irregularity capable of vitiating the measure ultimately adopted by it.

The CFI interprets the provision of Article 3(1) (now Article 138(1) EC) as if it were a crucial procedural step engaging the EU institutions in obligations connected with the social dialogue, a step so essential that it can vitiate the social dialogue process as a whole. It is difficult to see how the provisions of Article 3(1), the substance of which was enacted in a context much earlier to and wholly outside the subsequent social dialogue procedure leading to

---

[50] Paragraph 84.     [51] Paragraphs 85 and 87.

directives, can be so interpreted. Provisions stipulating promotion and facilitation do not create obligations.[52]

In support of its conclusion that the Commission was under such obligations, the CFI cited the Commission's Communication of 1993 and quoted from paragraph 39 of that Communication.[53] The Communication, of course, does not constitute any legal authority for the Commission to assume the powers it asserts.

This assumption of power was hotly contested in the Opinion of ECOSOC on the Commission's Communication.[54] ECOSOC took the view that it is up to the social partners to decide whether their collective agreement should be put to the Council. The Commission has no discretion; if there is a joint request by the signatory parties, the Commission must propose it. Of course, the *Council* may reject the proposal. But the right to reject it is *not* given to the Commission. There is nothing in the Agreement which hints that the Commission can assess the agreement in terms of the criteria listed in the Communication: representativeness and mandate.[55] These go to the heart of the autonomy of the social partners.

It is suggested that the CFI read these obligations of the Commission and Council into the Social Policy Agreement without demonstrating any legal basis for such obligations.

The real basis for the CFI's interpretation emerges from principles which are not linked to the Social Policy Agreement, but to the orthodox procedure of EC legislation. Again, it was reliance on constitutional law reasoning which explains the CFI's approach to the EU social dialogue.

The autonomy of the social dialogue process is further compromised if the shadow of Commission scrutiny is enhanced further by the CFI's addition of the Council and, indeed, the Court's scrutiny. The constitutional sensitivity of such additional supervision was evident in the view expressed by the Legal Service of the Council shortly after the CFI's decision.[56]

The Legal Service was particularly concerned by the Court's rejection of the Council's argument that the Court not substitute its own assessment of the representativity of the social partners for that of the Council, having regard to the complexity of that assessment.[57] Considering the question of an appeal, the Legal Service noted that the Court had denied to the Council the degree of discretion normally recognised by the Court, particularly in the area of social

---

[52] If Article 3(1) was to be read as conferring such obligations on the Commission and Council, this might raise the question of its duty to take measures to override any obstruction of the social partners to development of the social dialogue (a duty to bargain?), and to implementation of agreements reached (*erga omnes* extension of agreements?).

[53] Paragraph 86.      [54] Opinion 94/C 397/17, OJ 397/40 of 31 December 1994.

[55] Contrast the Communication's rejection of the Council's power to alter any agreement reached through the social dialogue.

[56] *Note d'Information du Service Juridique: Affaire T-135/96, UEAPME contre Conseil*, Brussels, 7 July 1998.

[57] *Ibid.*, paragraphs 6, 7, 10, 21 and 26.

policy which involves complex considerations. The Legal Service asserted that the degree of control retained by the Court was excessive and its reasoning was damaging to the institutional prerogatives of the Council.[58]

This concern of the Council faced with the Court overriding its discretion is but a pale reflection of the concerns of the social partners faced with not one, but three levels of scrutiny: Commission, Council and Court. Such scrutiny might, and then only might, be justifiable if the process in question is indisputably of a legislative nature, raising issues of constitutional accountability. It is questionable at least whether it is compatible with the autonomy of the social dialogue which is arguably among the fundamental rights of labour and management recognised in the constitutional traditions of the Member States and embodied in ILO Conventions 87 and 98. Any such infringement of autonomy may be the source of future litigation.

## Conclusions

The *UEAPME* case marks a potential crossroads in the history of EC labour law.[59] This crossroads involves a choice of conceptual frameworks to define the legal nature of the EU social dialogue. The CFI makes a clear choice in the *UEAPME* decision. Unfortunately, though not surprisingly, the CFI does not canvass alternatives, but rather asserts a single vision of the EU social dialogue.

In the CFI's view, the EU social dialogue is equated with the EU legislative process; as such, it must attain the equivalent degree of democratic legitimacy. The constitutional implications of this vision are fundamental: it involves a role for the EU institutions in scrutinising the social partners (representativity), their dialogue (autonomy), and their agreements (legitimacy).

This perspective is historically linked to the origins of the EU social dialogue, which was developed as a consequence of the failure of the legislative process in developing EC labour law. The Social Policy Agreement was conceived under the pressure of the constitutional development of a social dimension in the Treaty on European Union. The dynamic of the EU social dialogue, as constructed in the Social Policy Agreement, links social dialogue with the EU legislative process: 'bargaining the shadow of the law'.

It is quite a different matter, however, to extrapolate from this historical evolution and functional dependence in the development of EC labour law to

---

[58] *Ibid.*, paragraph 25. The Legal Service of the Council quoted the CFI's statement of 'the fundamental democratic principle that the people must share in the exercise of power through a representative assembly' (*UEAPME*, paragraph 88). It added: 'the CFI states that the democratic legitimacy of the acts adopted by the Council by virtue of Article 2 of the Agreement results from the intervention of the European Parliament', but did not comment on whether this reflected on the power of the Council to confer democratic legitimacy.

[59] It remains a decision of the CFI and was not appealed. But, in itself, the decision by UEAPME not to appeal revealed the impact of EC law on the social dialogue in the form of the agreement by UNICE to involve UEAPME in the dialogue.

the assumption of political and legal equivalence of social dialogue and legislative processes, an assumption that the same or similar principles of political
legitimacy and legal institutional accountability should apply.[60]

This is to ignore the qualitative difference between the legislative machinery
of the EU institutions making EC labour law and the EU social dialogue law-
making machinery. The latter has its conceptual roots *not* exclusively in the
political legal traditions of constitutional arrangements, but *also*, indeed
mainly, in those of industrial relations. Specifically, the EU social dialogue is
perceived as akin to another level, transnational, of collective bargaining super-
imposed on national systems. This was the image reflected in the first path to
implementation of agreements laid out in Article 4(2) of the Social Policy
Agreement (Article 139(2) EC): articulation with national systems.[61]

*National labour laws* recognise the dual nature of labour law, based on law
and collective agreements, but do not confuse the political and legal analytical
tools used for each of them. At the same time, it would be a mistake simply to
extrapolate from national labour law experience to the EU and transpose the
national industrial relations model to EU level, to assume that *EC labour law*
should reflect the bifurcation of national labour laws into legislative and
collective bargaining trajectories. Instead, I have proposed that:[62]

> A structure of *European* labour law … should reflect the law and context of *both*
> the EC *and* of Member States' labour law traditions, both the various legal
> strategies adopted as a consequence of the political conjuncture of the EC at
> different moments of its history, and the interaction of these strategies with
> national labour laws.

In the *UEAPME* decision, the CFI opted for the EU constitutional law paradigm
of democratic legitimacy, institutional scrutiny and judicial review. I submit

---

[60] Cf. D. Obradovic, 'Accountability of interest groups in the Union lawmaking process', chapter 18
in P. Craig and C. Harlow (eds.), *Lawmaking in the European Union*, London: Kluwer, 1998,
p. 354, who concludes, at p. 384: 'The overlap between the spheres of responsibilities of the EU
institutions and the social partners is so great that it is practically impossible to determine exactly
where their respective responsibilities begin and end. As a result, the concept of accountability
under the [Social Policy] Agreement is blurred … the quest for accountability of the social
partners must be conceived, in many respects, as part of the quest for greater overall political
accountability in the European Union'.

[61] In a parallel enquiry into the legitimacy of the social dialogue process, Sandra Fredman similarly
outlines two models: 'the first relying on an industrial relations model, the second on a model of
participatory democracy'. The industrial relations model is said to be plausible, but to have
characteristics which make it fundamentally different from collective bargaining: the outcome is
more powerful in having legislative consequences; and the sanctions available to the parties are
weaker than in collective bargaining. Of the participatory democracy model, it is said that it
'makes more sense than a collective bargaining model of the strong influence of social dialogue
on legislation'. But it too is 'far from unproblematic'. She highlights a problem of the
participatory democracy model in 'the extent to which such corporatism appears to side-step
other important democratic institutions, particularly Parliament'. 'Social Law in the European
Union: The Impact of the Lawmaking Process', in Craig and Harlow (eds.), *Lawmaking in the
European Union*, p. 386, at pp. 408–11.

[62] See Chapter 1.

that this errs in looking exclusively to EC law for inspiration in developing a conceptual paradigm for the European social dialogue. European labour law cannot afford to abandon national labour law systems, traditionally rooted also in an industrial relations model.

The *UEAPME* decision may stimulate the social partners, the Member States and the other EU institutions more familiar with those traditions than judges in the European courts, to appreciate the advantages of the industrial relations paradigm. My view is, however, that both paradigms should be exploited to achieve the objective of a 'European' labour law.

The specific constitutional law concepts outlined by the CFI in *UEAPME* can be exploited to legitimise the evolution of the EU social dialogue. A pure constitutional-legislative paradigm based on a highly centralised EU constitutional structure is inappropriate. The *UEAPME* decision can be adapted to accommodate more traditional labour law concepts. This potential of the *UEAPME* decision to legitimise developments in the EU social dialogue will be outlined.

The *UEAPME* decision also serves to highlight the contribution of the constitutional paradigm to an EU social dialogue modelled on an industrial relations system. The final section outlines how the CFI's identification of Parliament as the source of democratic legitimacy can be developed in the current conjuncture.

## The potential of the CFI's constitutional paradigm for EU social dialogue

The implications of the concept of 'sufficient collective representativity' for the future development of the EU social dialogue are considerable. The EU social dialogue has had its most public successes to date at the intersectoral, or cross-industry level. Nonetheless, there has been considerable discussion of the potential for developing social dialogue at *other* levels, involving *other* social partners. The *UEAPME* decision opens the way for such developments by recognising as democratically legitimate agreements with a defined and specific scope between social partners who satisfy the conditions of 'sufficient collective representativity'. A number of such developments may be highlighted.

### Sectoral social dialogue

First, the sectoral level has been suggested as a candidate for EU social dialogue. An example is the public sector. The CFI specifically singled out the CEEP as an essential social partner in the context of the Agreement on Parental Leave:[63]

> So far as concerns CEEP ... that cross-industry organisation represents at Community level all undertakings in the public sector, regardless of their size ... it

---

[63]  *UEAPME*, paragraph 100.

is clear that if CEEP had not been one of the signatories to the framework agreement, this alone would have fundamentally affected the sufficiency of the collectively representational character of those signatories in view of the contents of that agreement, because then one particular category of undertakings, that of the public sector, would have been wholly without representation.

If this be so,[64] it opens the prospect of social dialogue between the CEEP and EU-level organisations representing labour in the public sector, for example, the European Public Services Union (EPSU), to reach social dialogue agreements deemed to be between social partners of 'sufficient collective representativity', and capable of being incorporated in directives as democratically legitimate.

## Employment policy agreements

The role of the social partners in the specific area of employment policy has been explicitly recognised. Following the Amsterdam Summit's agreement in June 1997 to include a new 'Employment' chapter, a special 'Jobs Summit' was convened under the Luxembourg Presidency in November 1997 which led to the adoption of the first 'Employment Policy Guidelines' for 1998 on 15 December 1997. These provided for the adoption of a common structure for National Action Plans, agreed at the end of January 1998, and the Member States agreed to submit their Plans by mid-April.

The Commission Communication for the Cardiff Summit of 15–16 June 1998, which evaluated the National Employment Plans drawn up by the Member States, included the rubric of 'Encourage the Social Partners to reinforce, implement and evaluate the impact of their contributions'.[65] The *UEAPME* decision would allow for the recognition of agreements limited in scope to specific areas of employment policy, provided the social partners negotiating them were organisations of labour and management of 'sufficient collective representativity' in the specific area affected by the agreement.

---

[64] The accuracy of the facts asserted by the CFI as regards CEEP may be questioned. For example, the CFI referred to UEAPME's assertion of 'the fact that CEEP represents solely the interests of undertakings governed by public law' (*UEAPME*, paragraph 97). But most Member State employers of civil servants (ministries and government departments) are not represented by CEEP. Yet the Parental Leave Directive may apply to them.

[65] 'Although some agreements have been already concluded, for instance regarding work opportunities for young people and other target groups, negotiations in areas such as flexibility of working life, work organisation and working time, are still to be developed. The Social Partners, at national and European levels, have a great responsibility, as called for in the Guidelines, and should intensify their efforts to contribute to the modernisation of the contractual and institutional framework for reconciling flexibility and security, establishment of systems for life-long learning, and the promotion of new forms of work organisation and employment patterns such as job rotation systems. Within such a comprehensive approach, the social partners need, therefore, to make an independent and proactive contribution to the employment strategy'. See *Agence Europe*, Documents No. 2090/2091, of 10 June 1998, page 9.

### Transnational collective agreements

The creation of a common currency allowing for transparent wage comparisons has increased the pressure towards coordination of bargaining agendas of the social partners in different Member States: 'Pay settlements in Belgium and the Netherlands already take account of developments in Germany.'[66] Collective agreements among social partners in a group of Member States could satisfy the requirement of 'sufficient collective representativity' if the geographical scope of the agreement was clearly circumscribed.

## 'European' labour law

The CFI in *UEAPME* highlighted the dual processes of creating EC labour law: the legislative process, involving the European Parliament, and the social dialogue process of the EU social partners. But the latter process is also of a dual nature, reflected in the alternative procedures of implementing social dialogue agreements prescribed in Article 4(2) of the Social Policy Agreement (Article 139(2) EC):

> Agreements concluded at Community level shall be implemented either in accordance with the procedures and practices specific to management and labour and the Member States or, in matters covered by Article 2 [now Article 137 EC], at the joint request of the signatory parties, by a Council decision on a proposal from the Commission.

This dual process of implementation signals emphatically the industrial relations origins of the EU social dialogue.[67]

The CFI did not attend to this alternative conceptual structure. It is important to note that the arguments presented to it by the parties were not so narrowly focused. Thus, the Council highlighted that:[68]

> The first procedure, being of a classically legislative nature, leads to the adoption of a Council measure on the basis of Article 2 of the Agreement ... The second procedure ... is essentially a contractual process conducted by and at the behest of parties representing economic and social interests.[69]

---

[66] 'Towards a Euro Wage?', IRS *Pay and Benefits Bulletin*, No. 457, October 1998, p. 5. On the prospects for European collective agreements on pay in multinational enterprises, see 'Pan-Europe Pay Deals Predicted', *Financial Times*, 30 June 1998, p. 3. This reported that 'Just over half of European multinationals believe economic and monetary union will lead to pan-European pay agreements and levels'. An initiative aimed at developing a wage bargaining strategy was the objective of a meeting in the Dutch town of Doorn on 4–5 September 1998.

[67] The Social Policy Agreement itself was, of course, based on an agreement of 31 October 1991 negotiated between the EU social partners and incorporated into the Treaty on European Union agreed at Maastricht in December 1991.

[68] *UEAPME*, paragraph 36.

[69] In *UEAPME*, paragraph 35, the Council states bluntly: '... the document which emerges is an agreement between private persons ...'.

UEAPME also emphasised:[70]

> the specific nature of Directive 96/34 ... Its sole purpose is to place Member States under an obligation to implement a framework agreement concluded by three general cross-industry organisations.

UEAPME argued:[71]

> First, the cross-industry organisations which negotiated the framework agreement chose to make it effective erga omnes, although they could have confined themselves to negotiating a simple agreement producing effects inter partes. Second, the Commission chose to submit to the Council a proposal for a Directive to make the framework agreement binding erga omnes whereas, under Article 4(2) of the Agreement, it could have opted for another of the legislative instruments provided for in Article 189 of the Treaty or – as the German Government maintains in its statement of position on the procedural issues raised by the Agreement – it could have proposed adoption merely of a decision sui generis.

This line of argumentation clarifies the unique amalgam in Article 4(2) of the Social Policy Agreement (Article 139(2) EC) of *EC* legislative processes and *Member State* labour law traditions of extension *erga omnes* of collective agreements reached between private organisations.

The extension *erga omnes* of collective agreements is a conceptual bridge between the pure *industrial relations paradigm* of articulation ('the procedures and practices specific to management and labour and the Member States') and the pure *constitutional law paradigm* of negotiated legislation ('at the joint request of the signatory parties, by a Council decision on a proposal from the Commission').

The first and second mechanisms of Article 4(2) (Article 139(2) EC) should be seen as functionally equivalent: the first uses industrial relations mechanisms of articulating the EU social dialogue with national collective bargaining systems to achieve *erga omnes* effects, and the second uses constitutional mechanisms of EU legislation to require Member States to implement the Directive/Agreement.

But both are essentially extension mechanisms for EU-level social dialogue agreements: that is their function. It is a mistake to impose radically different legal conceptual structures (of industrial relations or EU constitutional law) on to each mechanism. The genius of 'European' labour law is to find some way of combining these discourses, to see Article 4(2) (Article 139(2) EC) as creatively developing a synthesis appropriate to the evolving EU polity. The synthesis would combine the different conceptual apparatuses to accommodate their similar functions.

The CFI in *UEAPME* asserted that the EU social partners could achieve a degree of 'sufficient collective representativity' which would confer on them the

---

[70] *UEAPME*, paragraph 44.    [71] *UEAPME*, paragraph 45.

requisite *democratic legitimacy* to make an agreement forming the substance of a valid EC directive. The requirement of 'sufficient collective representativity' of the social partners negotiating the agreement/directive was deemed necessary since the Directive was not subject to scrutiny by the European Parliament, the indisputably democratically legitimate body.

From the point of view of the EU social partners, this confirmation by the CFI that they possess, in the case of the Parental Leave Directive, 'sufficient collective representativity', is welcome. But there were strings attached. As described above, the CFI warned that an assessment of 'sufficient collective representativity':

> was relative to the *specific* content of the agreement-directive in question;
>
> required the Council and Commission, when deciding to submit or approve the proposal for a directive based on the agreement, to adjudicate, on the basis of specified criteria, whether the EU social partners achieved 'sufficient collective representativity';
>
> allowed the Court itself to undertake its own assessment of 'sufficient collective representativity', based on its own criteria.

Taken together, therefore, any social partners' agreement which aims to achieve the status of an EC directive faces close scrutiny, not only of its substance, but of the democratic legitimacy of the social partners in terms of their 'sufficient collective representativity'.

This poses a potential threat to the autonomy of the social partners, both from the EU institutions (Commission, Council, Court) carrying out this scrutiny, and from the criteria they may choose to apply in their assessment.

It might, therefore, be a preferable option for the social partners to seek to achieve the necessary degree of democratic legitimacy from the EU institution which the Court has described without reserve as possessing that quality: the European Parliament.

The European Parliament may be willing to accept a process of social dialogue which respects the autonomy of the social partners. For example, the Committee on Employment and Social Affairs of the European Parliament tabled an Own-Initiative Report on Transnational Trade Union Rights on 20 March 1998.[72] This proposed that the Parliament:

---

[72] PE 223.118/Fin., Rapporteur: Mrs Ria Oomen-Ruijten. This Report originally aimed to convey to the Intergovernmental Conference the views of Parliament on amendments to the EC Treaty. A first draft of this Report, dated 14 January 1997, was discussed by the Committee in February 1997 (PE 220.024). This first draft Report proposed a series of amendments to the Treaty, including extending EU competence to cover fundamental trade union rights, and making it an EU objective to achieve them. Specifically, this draft Report proposed the inclusion of rights of association at EC level, and for this to be implemented through social dialogue (proposed Amendment 3, to Article 2, paragraph 4 of the Social Policy Agreement). This draft of February 1997 proposing Treaty amendments was overtaken by the Treaty of Amsterdam of June 1997.

4. Confirms its demand for enshrining in particular the fundamental transnational trade union rights (right of association including the right of collective bargaining and trade union action) in the Treaty on European Union;

5. Considers that the trade union organisations should be involved in establishing trade union rights at European level;

6. Calls on management and labour either themselves or as part of the social dialogue to draw up proposals for negotiating rules and principles.

This proposal carefully distinguishes the process of 'establishing trade union rights at European level' (paragraph 5), in which 'trade union organisations should be involved', from the social dialogue process 'to draw up proposals for negotiating rules and principles' (paragraph 6), in which 'management and labour' are engaged.

The Parliament thus recognises that negotiating rules and principles for the European social dialogue need to be established by the social partners. The need is for a social partners–EU institutional agreement which will:

i. establish a framework of negotiating rules and principles for the EU social dialogue; and

ii. provide the requisite democratic legitimacy required by the European Court.

Such an agreement could provide the basis for the formulation of a legal measure which establishes a legal framework of negotiating rules and principles for the EU social dialogue.

The decision of the CFI in *UEAPME* is a stunning reminder of how courts can shape the emerging European labour law. If the EU social dialogue plays a role in the future EC labour law, the issues of democratic legitimacy, representativity and autonomy cannot be avoided. The question is whether the courts are the best place for these questions to be decided. Rather, the European Parliament's Report 'calls on management and labour either themselves or as part of the social dialogue to draw up proposals for negotiating rules and principles'.

## Internal democratic legitimacy of the European social dialogue

Much literature, academic and official, exists on the formal legal and institutional dimensions of EU labour regulation through the social dialogue. However, this literature focuses on the EU-level social partners and the outcomes of their social dialogue in the form of framework agreements and directives. There is very little which attempts to describe the *process* of social dialogue as between the EU social partners.[73] And there is almost nothing on

---

[73] Rare exceptions are chapters by Kirsten Ahlberg in books resulting from research projects undertaken at the Swedish National Institute for Working Life. One outlines the social dialogue process which resulted in the framework agreement on fixed-term work and was published in 1999: K. Ahlberg, 'The Negotiations on Fixed-Term Work', in Christophe Vigneau, Kerstin

the EU social dialogue from the perspective of *the social partners in the Member States* which are affiliated to the EU social partners. The objective of this section of the chapter is to explore the extent to which the social partners in the Member States, affiliated with the EU social partners, are engaged in the EU social dialogue.[74] This provides a perspective into the democratic legitimacy of the EU social dialogue assessed in terms of the participation of those most affected by it.

The EU intersectoral social dialogue has produced framework agreements resulting in Directives on parental leave (1996), part-time work (1997) and fixed-term work (1999). These agreements provide some background experience for the social partners to develop the process of social dialogue.

An example from the trade union side is the case of the German trade union confederation, the DGB, which was not pleased with the Framework Agreement on Part-Time Work. The DGB voted against its ratification by the ETUC Executive Committee, but the Framework Agreement was nonetheless approved under the ETUC rules which allow for approval by a majority vote. As a result of this experience, the DGB took a more active role in the process of negotiating the framework agreement on fixed-term work. An example from the employer side was UEAPME's complaint to the European Court of First Instance concerning the parental leave agreement, which led UNICE to agree in future to include representatives of UEAPME in its negotiations team.

This section analyses in detail the process of EU social dialogue which produced the Framework Agreement on Fixed-Term Work, not so much in terms of the interactions between the EU social partners, but rather in terms of the engagement in the social dialogue process of representatives of the EU social partners' affiliates in the Member States. It analyses the procedures and practices through which social partners in the Member States are engaged in the EU social dialogue, and explores whether and how these can be developed or improved.

It thus constitutes a case study of the European social dialogue: the experience of negotiation of the Framework Agreement on Fixed-Term Work.[75]

---

Ahlberg, Brian Bercusson and Niklas Bruun, *Fixed-Term Work in the EU: A European Agreement against Discrimination and Abuse*, Stockholm: SALTSA, National Institute for Working Life, 1999, pp. 13–38. Another is a more detailed analysis of the unsuccessful social dialogue on temporary agency work, in Kerstin Ahlberg, Brian Bercusson, Niklas Bruun, Haris Kountouros, Christophe Vigneau and Loredana Zappalà, *Transnational Labour Regulation: A Case Study of Temporary Agency Work*, Brussels: Peter Lang, 2008.

[74] The following draws on a much more detailed report of a research project supported by the European Trade Union Institute; B. Bercusson, *The Role of the Social Partners in the Member States in Labour Regulation through the EU Social Dialogue*, Brussels, 2002. This analysed the experience of the social dialogue which produced the Agreement on Fixed-Term Work which was then incorporated into Council Directive 1999/70/EC of 28 June 1999 concerning the framework agreement on fixed-term work concluded by ETUC, UNICE and CEEP, OJ L175/43 of 10 July 1999.

[75] See Council Directive 1999/70/EC of 28 June 1999 concerning the Framework Agreement on fixed-term work concluded by ETUC, UNICE and CEEP; OJ 175/43 of 10 July 1999.

It aims to illuminate two issues: the democratic legitimacy of mechanisms of labour regulation, and the interaction of representative organisations of workers at various levels: EU, national and sectoral.[76]

The case study analyses the way in which the social partners, in particular, the European Trade Union Confederation (ETUC) and its affiliates have undertaken the EU social dialogue.[77] It is useful to begin by outlining certain features of the *actors*, the *processes* and the *outcomes* of the EU intersectoral social dialogue.

## Actors

The EU social dialogue engages the social partners in the Member States which are affiliated to the EU-level organisations: ETUC, UNICE (now BusinessEurope) and CEEP. The relationship between these EU intersectoral organisations and their national affiliates affects crucial aspects of the social dialogue. For example, the decisions:

- to undertake the social dialogue on a particular subject;
- to define the negotiating mandate;
- to decide whether to approve the agreement reached;
- to resolve disputes over interpretation of the agreement.

The account describes how the arrangements *within the national social partners*, and *between them and the central organisations at EU level*, operated in the EU-level social dialogue which produced the Framework Agreement on Fixed-Term Work.

## Processes

The involvement of the social partners in the Member States in the process of EU social dialogue is a function of their ability to participate in and monitor the activities of the negotiators. For example, the flow of information about the progress of negotiations downwards from the negotiators to the national social partners and outwards from them to their affiliates (regional, sectoral, local, etc.) and the communication of responses and reactions from the national social partners reflect the 'internal' dialogue within each of the social partners.

The nature and quality of this 'internal' dialogue has important consequences for the effectiveness of the social dialogue process, as well as its democratic legitimacy. The account investigates the processes and practices of communication

---

[76] 'The legitimacy of the EU system therefore relies greatly on the social partner organisations themselves'. T. Novitz and P. Syrpis, 'Assessing Legitimate Structures for the Making of Transnational Labour Law: The Durability of Corporatism', (2006) 35 *Industrial Law Journal* 367 at p. 394.

[77] The report focused mainly on the trade union side of the social dialogue simply because more material was available which illuminated that side of the social dialogue.

within the social partners during the process of social dialogue on the Framework Agreement on Fixed-Term Work, with a view to identifying problems highlighted by the social partners and indicating possible solutions.

## Outcomes

The framework agreements reached through the EU social dialogue have so far been implemented through Council decisions in the legal form of EC directives. The social partners in the Member States have been allocated a role in the transposition of the directives into national law.[78] However, the role of the social partners at national level has not been the same in all Member States. This is potentially important because framework agreements need not be implemented through a Council decision but may also be implemented through the alternative path of 'the procedures and practices specific to management and labour and the Member States'.[79] Thus, on 23 May 2002 the EU social partners at intersectoral level concluded a 'voluntary' framework agreement on telework which is intended to follow this second path.

The interaction between the social partners at national level and the EU social partners reflects some of the tensions resulting from the varying roles played by the social partners in different Member States in the transposition of the framework agreements reached through the EU social dialogue into national law.

## The operation of the social dialogue: 'normalisation'?

One starting point for analysis of the social dialogue is an initial presumption that social dialogue between the social partners, trade unions and employers, at EU level is analogous to collective bargaining at Member State level.[80]

In one sense, this captures a truth: that social dialogue is a manifestation of the 'normalisation' of EU labour law. As with national systems, EU labour law is to include norms created by the social partners.

However, there are great differences among the industrial relations and labour law systems of the Member States. In particular, legal regulation of the actors, processes and outcomes of the national systems of collective bargaining in Member States has undergone major transformations in each Member State over many decades. It is to be expected, therefore, that the evolution of the EU system of social dialogue will similarly undergo changes over time. Hence, the

---

[78] This is envisaged by the EC Treaty, Article 137(3). The General Considerations of both the Part-Time Work Agreement and the Fixed-Term Work Agreement include the paragraph: 'Whereas the social partners are best placed to find solutions that correspond to the needs of both employers and workers and must therefore be given a special role in the implementation and application of this agreement'.

[79] Article 139(2) EC.

[80] For an extended critical discussion and analysis, see Antonio Lo Faro, *Regulating Social Europe: Reality and Myth of Collective Bargaining in the EC Legal Order*, Oxford: Hart, 2000.

need to keep track of new developments and remain aware of the dynamics of the developing system.

One notable feature of the EU social dialogue is that it starts where many national systems of labour regulation end: the Treaty provisions (Articles 138–9 EC) which establish the EU social dialogue are aimed at an outcome in the form of binding EU legislation.

First, it is important to appreciate how much this was the result of a unique conjuncture. The overwhelming pressure of some Member States, in particular, France, for a social dimension to the Single European Market, met with adamant resistance to social legislation on the part, in particular, of the UK. This clash between irresistible force and immovable object was avoided in large part due to the neat footwork of the Delors Commission. The Commission was instrumental in persuading the EU social partners, in particular, the employers' organisation, UNICE, to agree to upgrade the social dialogue (in their Agreement of 31 October 1991) from what had been, up to then, at best, non-legally binding 'common understandings', to not merely 'agreements', but binding legislation. The Member States were persuaded to accept this Agreement in the Social Protocol to the Maastricht Treaty on European Union, while allowing the UK to save face by opting out.

But secondly, and more important, initially casting the EU social dialogue as a law-making process raises a question about its very nature in general, and its place in the EU legal and institutional order in particular. The legal status of the EU social dialogue raises, as with many other aspects of EU law, the question of the singular legal qualities of what the European Court characterised, in the seminal case of *Van Gend en Loos*,[81] as this 'new legal order of international law'. EU labour law as a new legal order of international labour law raises the question of the legal nature of the EU social dialogue.

This is not a purely academic or hypothetical exercise, as was vividly illustrated by the decision of the European Court of First Instance in *UEAPME*. In responding to a challenge to the Parental Leave Directive implementing the EU social partners' Framework Agreement on parental leave, the CFI was clearly torn between, on the one hand, confirming the autonomy of the social partners over their own negotiating process in the social dialogue, and, on other hand, allowing parties excluded from that process to challenge the outcome of the social dialogue process when that outcome took legislative form as a directive.

The question can be posed as follows: is the legal status of the EU social dialogue to follow a *constitutional* model or an *industrial relations* model? The answer to this question has fundamental implications for the legal status of the actors, processes and outcomes of the EU social dialogue. For example, as the *UEAPME* decision shows, if a constitutional model is adopted, there are questions of democratic legitimacy which warranted, in the view of the CFI, an

---

[81] *NV Algemene Transporten Expeditie Onderneming van Gend en Loos* v. *Nederlandse Administratie der Belastingen*, Case 26/62, [1963] ECR 1.

investigation into the representativity of the social partners. On the other hand, if an industrial relations model is adopted, then the issue of the legality of transnational strikes or other industrial action at EU level must be dealt with, an issue highlighted by the controversy over the conflict between free movement and transnational industrial action.[82]

There is clearly a great of deal of national experience to draw upon for concepts inspired by constitutional or industrial relations models. In the case of the original six Member States, there are the theories of the Italian *ordinamento intersindacale*, the French doctrine of extension of collective agreements, and the German concept of *tarifautonomie*. In the case of more recent adherents, there is the UK's reluctance to recognise collective agreements as legally binding, and, in the Nordic countries, a general policy to exclude legislative intervention.

Recent experience of social dialogue illustrates how these issues have developed, with particular implications for the actors involved in the social dialogue, the process itself and the outcomes in the form of agreements at EU level.

Two recent examples will serve as illustrations of the issues raised concerning the actors, employers' and trade union organisations at EU and national levels, which are engaged in the EU social dialogue.

First, the ETUC adopted in 1995 procedures for qualified majority voting in decisions on mandates and approval of agreements. The issue came to prominence in the case of the second Framework Agreement on Part-Time Work. As mentioned above, the German Confederation, the DGB, voted in the minority against the Agreement, which was approved. The DGB had been used to exercising an implicit veto within the ETUC in decisions of this magnitude.[83] The vote over the Part-Time Agreement led to much more active involvement of the DGB over the negotiations which followed over fixed-term work, which led to an agreement, and agency work, which did not.

Similarly, the launching of social dialogues over part-time work and fixed-term work highlighted the importance of institutional reforms at national level. These were necessary if voting on mandates and ratification of EU agreements by national confederations were adequately to reflect opinion in the national trade union movements and prevent a backlash over national control of events at EU level. The Nordic union confederations in particular have taken steps to try to promote the transparency of the process of EU social dialogue. As put by Dolvik:

> having virtually rejected the concept of European negotiations in 1992, they came to play a central role in establishing the ETUC 'bargaining order', and have subsequently served as active supporters of 'negotiated European legislation', partly motivated by the desire to prevent European legal intrusion into national systems of bargaining.

[82] See the discussion of the *Laval* and *Viking* cases in Chapter 21.
[83] J.E. Dolvik, 'Redrawing Boundaries of Solidarity? The ETUC, Social Dialogue and the Europeanisation of Trade Unions in the 1990s', in E. Gabaglio and R. Hoffmann (eds.), *The ETUC in the Mirror of Industrial Relations Research*, Brussels: ETUI, 1998, p. 317.

Secondly, steps towards reform and streamlining of a 'bargaining order' on the trade union side have not, so far, been matched by employers at EU level. They have preferred to continue along the path characterised by Wolfgang Streeck as the organisational weakness of European employers being exploited as a source of political strength in resisting the creation of an EU system of industrial relations. In contrast to the ETUC, Business Europe proceeds by way of consensus, which makes it possible for social dialogue agreements to be blocked by a few recalcitrant member employers' organisations.

This was particularly evident in the attempt to launch the social dialogue over proposals for a framework directive on information and consultation at national level, modelled on the European Works Councils Directive of 1994. When the initiative was first circulated by the Commission, the resistance of a small number of national employers' confederations led UNICE to declare that it would not engage in social dialogue with the ETUC. Under the UNICE constitution, affiliates representing three Member States affected by the decision can block a proposal to start negotiations. However, following discussion and further pressures, a special meeting of UNICE was called for 16 October 1998 to reconsider the decision. Despite this, an (even larger) minority again succeeded in blocking the path to social dialogue. This result led the Commission immediately to issue in November 1998 its proposal for a draft Directive. Despite the rearguard opposition of a number of Member States, political agreement on a draft Directive was reached under the Swedish Presidency during the first half of 2001, and was finally adopted by the Council on 23 March 2002.[84] This episode raised questions regarding UNICE's (now Business Europe's) internal constitutional arrangements, which many see as requiring reform if the EU social dialogue is to progress.

As these illustrations show, though not as legally visible as legislation or court decisions, the institutional arrangements *within* the national social partners, and the interactions *between* them and the central organisations at EU level, are vital elements in the operation of the EU-level social dialogue.

## The EU social dialogue on fixed-term work: an outline

### First proposals

The story begins in 1982, when the Commission proposal on temporary work was first put forward.[85] There followed vain efforts over eight years to reach agreement in the Council of Ministers. The proposal was finally withdrawn in

---

[84] Proposal for a Council Directive establishing a general framework for informing and consulting employees in the European Community, COM/98/612, 11 November 1998. Directive 2002/14/EC of the European Parliament and of the Council of 11 March 2002 establishing a general framework for informing and consulting employees in the European Community, OJ L80/29 of 23 March 2002.

[85] The next section is an introductory outline framework for the analysis in the following section of this chapter. It is based mainly on Kerstin Ahlberg's work, 'The Negotiations on Fixed-Term Work'.

1990. Instead, in place of the one draft directive, three separate proposals were put forward, tailored to different voting procedures. Only one was adopted, on a legal basis allowing for qualified majority voting, on the health and safety of temporary workers.[86] The other two remained stalled in the Council.

### First consultations lead to an agreement on part-time work

In the meantime, the Maastricht social dialogue procedure came into effect from 1 November 1993. The Commission initiated fresh consultations with the social partners in September 1995 on proposals on flexibility and security for 'atypical workers'. A second round of consultations took place during 1996 on an actual proposal, and in June 1996, the EU social partners announced that they were willing to negotiate and asked the Commission to interrupt the legislative process. The negotiating procedure was determined in the Social Dialogue Committee, a joint forum for representatives of both social partners at EU level and national affiliates to meet and discuss their positions and proposals. In June 1997, the social partners concluded a Framework Agreement on Part-Time Work.[87] At the same time, they expressed their intention to consider the need for other agreements and, at the end of 1997, the social partners decided to negotiate on fixed-term work.

### The Commission's role in negotiations on fixed-term work

The first step was to ask a neutral person to chair the negotiations. This is a common tradition in, for example, France and Belgium. Jo Walgrave, then President of the Belgian National Labour Council, had chaired the first two EU social dialogues leading to Framework Agreements on Parental Leave and Part-time Work. This time, the chair selected was Jean Degimbe, the former Director-General of D-G V of the Commission, assisted by Stefan Olsson, an administrator from D-G V.

It might appear that the Commission, through the presence of D-G V, was determined to play some role. However, the social partners insisted that the social dialogue is autonomous. They rejected the idea of tripartite negotiations and regarded both the individuals concerned as experts, not as Commission representatives. Their role was carefully circumscribed so the chair was not to be an active facilitator, but rather to play a more formal chairing role, sometimes answering questions directed to him or, at most, expressing views on the interpretation of provisions or concepts of EU law. However, the texts

---

[86] Council Directive 91/383 of 25 June 1991 supplementing the measures to encourage improvements in the safety and health of workers with a fixed-duration employment relationship or a temporary employment relationship, OJ 1991 L206/19.

[87] Council Directive 97/81/EC of 15 December 1997 concerning the framework agreement on part-time work concluded by UNICE, CEEP and the ETUC, OJ L14/9 of 20 January 1998.

were to be drafted exclusively by the parties. The Commission paid for the premises, language interpreters, the fees and expenses of the independent chair, and so on.

There is some evidence, however, that the Commission or its representatives may have been more active, ostensibly in the provision of technical advice, but also behind the scenes in informal meetings with spokespersons for each side. It seems probable that the Commission had some indirect influence on the social dialogue. It must be more than a coincidence that one of its former senior officials and present administrators were involved, however formally circumscribed their role. The Commission decides whether any resulting agreement is to be forwarded to the Council for approval. The CFI in its decision in the *UEAPME* case declared that the Commission must scrutinise the agreement for compliance with EU law, representativity of the parties, etc. Finally, if negotiations fail, the Commission may decide to proceed with legislative proposals and, for this reason alone, its influence would be felt in the course of the negotiations.

## Mandates

**CEEP**: The first organisation to decide its mandate for negotiations was CEEP. It was able to do so because its previous mandate on part-time work had included fixed-term work. This mandate was formulated in the CEEP's social affairs committee. This is a preparatory and consultative body. Members are appointed by national sections, with possible participation in meetings by associated members from non-EU countries. There are no voting rules, and an unrestricted number of participants. The proposal for the CEEP mandate was approved by its general assembly: 147 members from the fifteen Member States.

**UNICE**: The UNICE mandate emerged from a special social affairs committee meeting. This consultative body consists of persons nominated by UNICE's member organisations. It was then adopted by a consensus decision of UNICE's Council of Presidents on 5 December 1997. The Council of Presidents, the supreme decision-making body of UNICE, consists of one representative for each member organisation. The primary rule is decision by consensus. This does not require unanimity, but only if all reasonable attempts to reach common agreement fail is there a vote. The voting rules prescribe that affiliates representing three Member States affected by the decision can block a proposal to start negotiations. However, approval of a draft European agreement does require unanimity among the affected members. 'Affected' includes not only affiliates from EU Member States, but also from the EEA.

**ETUC**: The ETUC mandate was prepared in consultation with national trade union confederations and European Industry Federations (EIFs). The

Loan Receipt
Liverpool John Moores University
Library Services

**Borrower Name: Manjengwa, Charmaine LAWCMANJ**

**Borrower ID:** ********

European labour law /
31111012986301
**Due Date: 29/05/2018 23:59:00 BST**

Industrial relations law /
31111009693407
**Due Date: 29/05/2018 23:59:00 BST**

International and comparative labour law :
current challenges /
31111014223539
**Due Date: 29/05/2018 23:59:00 BST**

Total Items: 3
21/05/2018 17:14

Please keep your receipt in case of dispute.

procedure was laid down after conclusion of the Framework Agreement on Parental Leave in December 1995. This provided that ETUC member organisations are to receive all information and details of proposals concerning potential negotiations at least four weeks before a decision in the Executive Committee, the competent body. This information must allow for adequate consultations at national and federal level. From affiliates' responses to this information, the ETUC secretariat submits a draft decision to the Executive Committee.

The Executive Committee comprises representatives of the sixty-seven affiliated national confederations, the fourteen affiliated EIFs and the ETUC Women's Committee. The President, General Secretary and the Deputy General Secretaries are *ex officio* members. There are non-voting observers. A mandate for negotiations with European employers' organisations and the adoption of a draft agreement must have the support of at least two-thirds of the organisations directly concerned.

The mandate for the fixed-term work negotiations was decided on 5 March 1998. This mandate was subject to debate in the Executive Committee. Both the secretariat and some confederations questioned whether the mandate would bind the negotiators too tightly, especially through the precise limitations on the maximum duration of fixed-term contracts (the mandate specified three years) and the number of renewals of fixed-term contracts (the mandate specified two).

In conclusion: although mandates were the organisations' internal documents, they were soon leaked, and when negotiations started, all sides knew the mandates of the opposite parties.

## The political context of mandates and negotiations

The process of negotiations, including the formulation of demands in mandates, is affected by changes in the political context. In the case of the fixed-term negotiations, the ETUC mandate went beyond the earlier proposed draft directives which had failed to win the approval of the Council of Ministers. It is argued that the reason for going beyond those directives was the change in the voting rules in the Council since the beginning of the 1990s, with the Social Protocol allowing for qualified majority voting. There was also the change in the contemporary political scene, with twelve Member States governed by socialist or social democratic governments. Indeed, some former members of the ETUC Executive Committee were now in the cabinets of some Member State governments.

This provides an interesting point of comparison between the social dialogue process and the legislative process in regulating labour in the EU. In the legislative process, one key actor, the European Parliament (EP) may have its composition fixed at one election for a long period. This means that legislation processed through the EP does not reflect changes which may occur in national parliaments through national elections. On the one hand, this is a source of stability, in that shifts in national elections will be less disruptive of EU legislation through the EP. On the other hand, the EP may thereby become out of harmony with national parliaments and governments. Voting in the Council of Ministers reflects changes at national level much more quickly and closely. As a result, social dialogue negotiations (and mandates) will more quickly reflect politics in the Member States, as the representatives of the Member State governments will eventually vote on any agreement reached. The strength of demands in mandates, and concessions during negotiations may be affected by changes in anticipated voting in the Council of Ministers.

## The negotiating teams

**CEEP and UNICE** had a joint **negotiating group** consisting of thirty-one people. CEEP had eight representatives; UNICE had twenty-three: one from each country in the EEA, two from the UNICE social affairs committee, two from the UNICE secretariat and one spokesperson.

The employers' side also had a smaller **drafting group** of seven persons: Dan McAuley of the Irish employers' organisation (the spokesperson); the Secretary-General of CEEP (Jytte Fredensborg) and her assistant (Nunzia Gava), the UNICE social affairs director (Thérèse de Liedekerke), a representative of the Italian employers' organisation (*Confindustria*), the Danish employers' organisation, and the German employers' organisation, the BDA (Bundesvereinigung der Deutschen Arbeitsgeberverbande).

UNICE also invited three sectoral bodies to send experts to the negotiations: EuroCommerce, COPA (Committee of Agricultural Organisations in the EU) and the Confederation of the National Hotel and Restaurant Associations (HOTREC). Sectoral employers' bodies are not members of UNICE (unlike the ETUC, where sectoral organisations, the European Industry Federations (EIFs), are members of ETUC).

**ETUC**'s **negotiating group** comprised twenty-nine people: one from each country in the EEA, eight representing EIFs, one from the Women's Committee, one from Eurocadres (representing managerial and professional staff), and two from the secretariat.

The ETUC also had a smaller **drafting group**: Jean Lapeyre (the spokesperson) and Penny Clarke, both from the ETUC Secretariat, Jean-Paul Delcroix of the Belgian FGTB, Inge Kaufmann of the German DGB, Reinhard Kuhlmann of the European Metalworkers' Federation, Roger Sjostrand of LO-Sweden and Bernadette Tesch-Segol of Euro-FIET (International Federation of Commercial, Clerical, Professional and Technical Employees, now Uni-Europa).

## The negotiations

The Commission formally notified the three social partner organisations that it would interrupt the legislative process for nine months for negotiations beginning 23 March 1998. The first round began that day in Brussels. Two large delegations sat on either side of a long table, with more than sixty persons in the room. Although it was mostly the three spokespersons who spoke, all members were able to intervene. After this first meeting, the full delegations met once or twice a month.

There were a number of significant points reached during negotiations. One reflects the complex relationship between sectoral and intersectoral organisations. There was some debate at an early stage on whether temporary agency work should be covered. UNICE wanted it excluded, as their mandate dictated. ETUC was more ambivalent, as if only fixed-term work was regulated, employers might turn to agency work. On 22 April 1998, the International Confederation of Temporary Work Business (CIETT: the employers' organisation) and Euro-FIET (the trade union sectoral organisation representing workers in occupations where temporary agency work is frequent) sent a joint letter to the general secretaries of UNICE, CEEP and ETUC stating that it was inappropriate to include temporary agency work in the current negotiations. After long debate, the issue did not come up again in negotiations.

Towards summer, the negotiations began to encounter difficulties in reaching accommodation and these increased as autumn came and went. The biggest stumbling block concerned the trade union demand for some restriction on the use of fixed-term contracts and employers' resistance. Eventually, in November, the trade union side told the employers that they wanted to suspend negotiations and consult the ETUC Steering Committee (a body responsible for deciding on urgent and medium-term action and for overseeing negotiations with employers' organisations) on the question of whether it was worthwhile continuing or better to inform the Commission of a breakdown of negotiations and ask the legislator to take over. However, the result of the meeting of the ETUC Steering Committee on 19 November 1998, and of deliberations on the employers' side, was that negotiations were given another chance.

The next and penultimate bargaining round with full delegations was on 26–27 November 1998, but the parties were unable to reach agreement. As negotiations broke down, the ETUC delegation announced it would recommend to the ETUC Executive Committee of mid-December to stop negotiations and hand the initiative over to the Commission, unless the employers changed their position.

On 4 December 1998, there was a 'social dialogue mini-summit' on work organisation in Vienna, as this was during the Austrian Presidency of the Council. This gave the Presidents and General Secretaries of UNICE, CEEP and ETUC an opportunity to meet. They urged the spokespersons of the negotiating teams to try to reach a compromise. On 10 December 1998, Dan McAuley and Jean Lapeyre met and succeeded in working out a compromise. They went back to their organisations to ask if this compromise was a basis for further negotiations.

The ETUC Executive met on 14–15 December 1998 and, during their meeting, the employers sent a message saying they wanted to reopen negotiations.

The ETUC Executive was presented with the compromise clause, but was only asked to agree to continue negotiations for another month, to which it agreed. As the nine-month period allotted by the Commission was about to expire on 24 December, the parties had to ask the Commission for an additional three months.

The last negotiating round was scheduled for the week of 11–15 January 1999. After four days, on the evening of 14 January 1999, the delegations reached agreement, though not unanimously. Of nineteen ETUC delegates, one voted against and six abstained. The employers did not have to resort to voting.

The General Assembly of CEEP adopted the agreement unanimously on 25 January 1999; similarly, on 18 February 1999, by the Council of Presidents of UNICE. On 16 March 1999, the ETUC Executive Committee ratified the agreement by a large majority. The Framework Agreement was signed two days later.

### The outcomes: Agreement and Directive

The parties formally submitted the Agreement to the Commission, requesting that it be proposed to the Council to be made binding as a Directive. It became Council Directive 1999/70/EC when adopted on 28 June 1999.[88]

## The EU social dialogue on fixed-term work: analysis of the trade union side

Three distinct phases are analysed in this chapter on the EU social dialogue on fixed-term work: (i) formulation of the mandate, (ii) negotiations and (iii) ratification of the agreement.

In the **mandate** stage (between mid-November 1997 and mid-March 1998), the following three phases were identified:

(a) providing information on the national position: affiliates from ten Member States provided written information prior to a 'technical' meeting;

(b) participating in a 'technical' meeting aiming to elucidate issues (12 January 1998); confederations from eleven Member States participated in this meeting;

(c) providing further comments and views; correspondence indicates a number of national confederations taking an active and detailed interest in the content of the mandate, as well as expressing views as to the subsequent process of negotiations prior to its being initiated.

In the **negotiations** stage (mid-March 1998 to mid-January 1999), the following three phases were identified:

---

[88] Council Directive 1999/70/EC of 28 June 1999 concerning the Framework Agreement on fixed-term work concluded by ETUC, UNICE and CEEP. OJ L175/43 of 10 July 1999.

(a) the ten Negotiations Group meetings, in which all Member States had an affiliate represented, interspersed with the Drafting Group meetings, which included representatives of three national affiliates, two European Industry Federations (EIFs) and two representatives of the ETUC;

(b) the critical pre-final session vote on 8 January 1999;

(c) the vote on the final agreement on 14 January 1999, with the involvement of confederations from each of the fifteen Member States and six EIFs.

In the **ratification** stage (between mid-January 1999 and mid-March 1999), the following three phases were identified:

(a) reference back to affiliates for their consideration through their internal constitutional processes;

(b) meetings of ETUC bodies, the Industrial Relations Committee (26 February 1999) and the Women's Committee (2 March 1999);

(c) approval by the ETUC Executive Committee (15–16 March 1999).[89]

The experience of the EU social dialogue which produced the framework agreement on fixed-term work leads to the identification of a number of issues worthy of consideration. The following are ten such issues.

## 1. The EU 'bargaining order': internal constitutional arrangements of the EU social partners

The three successful EU social dialogues at intersectoral level which have produced directives provide some basis for establishing an EU 'bargaining order': the procedure to be followed by the social partners in conducting the social dialogue. Articles 138–9 of the EC Treaty, which provide the legal basis for the EU social dialogue, are notoriously inadequate as a framework. The absence of an established and structured bargaining order is a serious defect in terms of the legitimacy, transparency and efficacy of the EU social dialogue.

The aspect of the EU bargaining order of concern here is not so much that *between* the social partners, though this is of primary importance. The concern is rather with that part of the bargaining order which regulates the relationship between the EU social partners and their *affiliates* in the Member States.

In anticipation of the negotiations on fixed-term work, the meeting of the ETUC's Industrial Relations Committee held on 28 October 1997 prepared proposals to supplement the rules of procedure on the application of Article 13 of the ETUC Statutes by specifying the tasks allotted to, respectively, the (a) Secretariat; (b) the Executive Committee; (c) the Steering Committee; (d) the

---

[89] The vote at the ETUC Executive Committee meeting on 15 March 1999 indicates how different affiliates decided. In some cases, all we have is an indication as to how the affiliate voted. However, some insights are provided into the different types of responses of the ETUC affiliates between the approval of the Agreement by the Negotiating Committee on 14 January 1999 and the vote on ratification of the Agreement by the ETUC Executive Committee on 15 March 1999.

Industrial Relations Committee; (e) the Negotiations Group and (f) the Drafting Group. Four stages were envisaged: (1) preparing the mandate, (2) conducting the negotiations, (3) decision-making procedure on the results of the negotiations and (4) follow-up of the Framework Agreement in the legislative procedure.

The assumption appears to have been that the representatives of the affiliates on these various committees, bodies and delegations are responsible for ensuring that the information is channelled through to the affiliates in a timely and effective manner. This seems to be emphasised through the injunction calling for the commitment of representatives appointed to participate in the negotiating delegation to ensuring their availability throughout the negotiations and also calls to strengthen the logistical support for the negotiating delegation and the drafting group.

However, the extent to which representatives of the affiliates in the various bodies engaged in negotiations did in practice inform and consult their organisations was very uneven. It is questionable whether this situation, whereby some affiliates are continuously well informed and others much less so, is sustainable. It undermines both the effectiveness of negotiators, denied information, ideas and proposals coming up from the affiliates, and the legitimacy, and indeed the successful adoption of the outcome of negotiations, when affiliates are not regularly informed and consulted. It is true that the great diversity of organisations of workers in the different Member States and their different traditions of collective bargaining may make it difficult to find a common solution to this problem. But the EU social dialogue is unique, and requires a unique solution which can accommodate those traditions.

## 2. Adapting information and consultation mechanisms to negotiations

In the course of the EU social dialogue there are particular points in time which are of maximum concern to affiliates and which may require them to engage more actively.

The proposed ETUC bargaining order implied that certain moments in the bargaining process required particularly close attention on the part of affiliates. For example, the point of **determining the negotiating mandate**. An ETUC memo to affiliates on 4–5 December 1997 fixed a deadline of 24 February 1998. There was a flurry of activity and replies from some affiliates indicating consultation of their affiliates. The mandate was finally fixed by the ETUC Executive Committee meeting on 4–5 March 1998. A memorandum dated 27 February 1998 described the proposals for the mandate and included a Table (seven pages) with three columns indicating proposed text, amendments/comments from affiliates and the Secretariat's response. Each amendment in the second column has attached the national confederation or sectoral federation proposing it.

Some ETUC affiliates stated explicitly they had consulted their affiliates. Some had formally adopted a resolution approving the mandate and/or

commenting on it with amendments. But, for example, one EU sectoral federation stated this had been done only for the first time. And from some it was not
clear whether there had been any detailed consideration of the mandate.

It may not be feasible to have maximum engagement of all affiliates throughout the process. This will reflect the nature of internal procedures within
different national confederations and EU sectoral federations. It is a question
whether crucial points of the social dialogue process can always be identified in
advance, and whether the mechanisms can be put in place which will enable
affiliates to engage more closely without compromising the effectiveness of the
social dialogue process at these critical moments.

## 3. Negotiations Group and Drafting Group: composition and competences

The question is how to define the composition, and deal with the respective
roles of the Negotiations and Drafting Groups. The issue is primarily that of the
relative roles of each Group and their interaction. As to their respective roles,
the borderline between drafting and negotiating is not always clear.

It seems inevitable that there will be a need for a committee with restricted
numbers to undertake some negotiations, which will leave outside the representatives of many affiliates. This makes the reporting back procedure between
a restricted membership Drafting Group and a fully representative Negotiations
Group all the more essential.

In the case of the EU social dialogue on fixed-term work, the ETUC's
Negotiations Group comprised twenty-nine people, one from each country in
the European Economic Area (EEA), eight representing European industry
federations (EIFs), one from the Women's Committee, one from Eurocadres
and two from the ETUC Secretariat. The Drafting Group numbered seven: two
from the ETUC Secretariat, three from national affiliates (Belgium, Germany,
Sweden) and two from EIFs.

The Negotiations Group met prior to each meeting with the employers.
Apart from the unwieldy size of the Group, many representatives on the
Negotiating Group were usually not based in Brussels, and this reduced their
potential as a cohesive negotiating force. In contrast, the Drafting Group was
much smaller, and, whether by chance or design, six out of the seven members
were based in Brussels: the two from the ETUC Secretariat and the two from the
EIFs, and, of the three from national affiliates, the representative of the Belgian
trade unions and the representative of the Swedish trade unions, who was on
full-time secondment to the ETUC. In effect, the so-called Drafting Group
seemed to operate more as an 'Executive Committee' of the Negotiations
Group.

Certain factors may be relevant in constructing a relationship between
negotiating and drafting bodies, and between them and the organisations
represented on them.

First, as well as these bodies, there were other ETUC bodies which received regular reports on the negotiations: the ETUC Executive Committee and the ETUC Industrial Relations Committee. Affiliates could keep track of negotiations through these bodies as well as through their representatives on the Negotiations Group.

Secondly, of course, some affiliates were represented on the Drafting Group itself, and this gave them privileged access to developments. While reports went back from this Group to the Negotiations Committee, affiliates whose representatives were on the Drafting Group had some time advantage in consulting their own organisations.

Thirdly there may be scope for horizontal arrangements between groups of national affiliates, which may overcome some of the problems of lack of representatives on the smaller 'Executive Committee' of negotiators.

## 4. Vertical relationships and horizontal alliances among affiliates

The perception of negotiations in each of the social partners is one of purely bilateral and vertical relationships between individual affiliates and the EU level structures. In the case of the ETUC, this means relationships between the individual national confederations on the one hand, and the Drafting and Negotiating Groups and the ETUC Committees (Industrial Relations Committee, Executive Committee, and so on) on the other.

The problem of accommodating the large number of affiliates on negotiating bodies presents problems not only of the practical effectiveness of negotiations, but also of the legitimacy of their outcome. The issue is securing part of that required legitimacy by ensuring that affiliates are informed and consulted adequately about the progress of negotiations and are engaged in the decisions adopted in the course of negotiations.

There are at least two cases where horizontal relationships between affiliates may play a role in EU social dialogue: where individual affiliates communicate directly with each other; and where European Industry Federations are concerned.

The problem of engagement of numerous affiliates in negotiations may be ameliorated by formation of horizontal alliances among groups of affiliates, or, at least, facilitating direct communication among them. This could improve the speed with which information was disseminated and enhance the ability of individual affiliates to engage in the process of negotiations. The resulting sharing of information and, perhaps, expertise, could alleviate the position of affiliates with less resources and less direct access to and representation in Brussels. Increased horizontal communications might also lead to the adoption of common positions, which could improve the coherence of each side's negotiating stance. Forming such alliances might suffice to secure representation of the alliance on the 'Executive (Drafting Group) Committee', and offer guarantees of a flow of information and more effective consultation between that representative and the affiliates it represents. Purely hypothetically, it could be that arrangements among affiliates in the Benelux, Nordic or Anglo-Saxon countries would have some such potential, and could even overcome the ever-present problem of linguistic diversity.[90]

## 5. The sectoral dimension of the intersectoral social dialogue

The European Industry Federations (EIFs) representing national affiliates provide an alternative to purely national representation in the EU social dialogue. This provides a parallel path to the ETUC in bringing together at sectoral level the common interests of affiliates in different Member States. In sum, the EIFs provide a network of horizontal linkages among national affiliates which can be represented in the EU intersectoral social dialogue. They allow for cohesive presentation of sectoral demands common to affiliates across a range of Member States. The EIFs presence on the Drafting Group is thus particularly significant.

At the same time, EIFs replace national particularism with sectoral particularism. While overcoming national bias, the EIFs may further complicate negotiations as sectoral demands are added to national demands in an already complex set of issues to be negotiated.

The role of EIFs in intersectoral social dialogue raises in a different forum many of the fundamental questions underlying the EU social dialogue in general. Specifically, what is the relative weight to be attributed to the intersectoral and sectoral social dialogues, and the related question of the relative importance and roles of the actors in each: on the trade union side, the ETUC and the EIFs?

On the one hand, there has been no lack of argumentation and evidence as to the importance of the EU sectoral social dialogue, both in the past, and in the present and future.[91] However, the development of the EU sectoral social dialogue has suffered precisely due to the absence of EU sectoral employers' organisations and, where these exist, their reluctance to engage in EU sectoral social dialogue. Given the current absence of sectoral organisation and initiative on the side of employers, the engagement of EU sectoral organisations in the intersectoral dialogue could stimulate developments in the EU sectoral social dialogue.

A striking example of the interaction of intersectoral and sectoral social dialogues at EU level took place in the course of the negotiations over fixed-term work. The EIF sectoral federation, Euro-FIET (now UNI-Europa) agreed with the representative of the employers in the field of temporary agency work

---

[90] In the negotiations on fixed-term work, the Drafting Group did include representatives from Belgium (Benelux) and Sweden (Nordic affiliates), as well as from two EIFs.

[91] As in the creation of sectoral social dialogue committees under Commission Decision 98/500/EC of 20 May 1998 on the establishment of Sectoral Dialogue Committees promoting the Dialogue between the social partners at European level, OJ L225/27 of 12 August 1998.

(Confederation Internationale des Entreprises de Travail Temporaire, CIETT) to exclude this field from the scope of the negotiations in the intersectoral social dialogue on fixed-term work. A letter signed by the Director of Euro-FIET and the first vice-president of CIETT, dated 3 July 1998, and addressed to the UNICE, CEEP and ETUC, expressed their joint view that it was inappropriate to include temporary work businesses. Significantly, they concluded that it would undermine progress that they were trying to make at sectoral level.

It was stated, therefore, that any EU-level agreement on fixed-term contracts should exclude agency triangular relationships. However, this exclusion should be accompanied by a commitment to negotiate a specific agreement for this type of relationship, at the appropriate EU level. This request was acceded to by the EU intersectoral social partners and temporary agency work was excluded from the scope of the negotiations. The agreement eventually concluded did, however, include the commitment to undertake an EU intersectoral social dialogue on temporary agency work. These negotiations were unsuccessful and on 22 March 2001 the ETUC Executive Committee abandoned negotiations and called on the Commission to propose a directive regulating temporary agency work. The Commission finally adopted such a proposal one year later, on 20 March 2002.[92] In the meantime, however, on 11 October 2001, UNI-Europa (formerly Euro-FIET) and CIETT signed a joint declaration on temporary agency workers.[93]

## 6. Bilateral social dialogue at national level as an aid to successful EU social dialogue

Individual union confederations or employers' organisations at national level may pose problems specific to their national context which threaten to block progress in the EU social dialogue. Contacts between the social partners at national level may attempt to reach compromises where one or more of the national social partners are raising difficulties in the EU negotiations. A dispute could be resolved between the national social partners to avoid it contaminating the EU level negotiations.

In the social dialogue on fixed-term work, one such disputed issue concerned occupational pensions, which emerged as a problem for the national employers' confederation in one Member State. The ETUC stressed that it was not possible to make a general exclusion for occupational pensions, especially as part of pay. It was suggested that the trade union confederation and employers' organisation from that Member State should discuss the matter. This was undertaken and appears to have produced the desired interaction and a solution.

---

[92] Proposal for a Directive of the European Parliament and the Council on working conditions for temporary workers, Brussels, 20 March 2002, COM(2002) 149 final, 2002/0072(COD).

[93] The next day, 12 October 2001, the EU intersectoral social partners opened negotiations on telework, which were this time successful.

## 7. Breaking deadlocks in negotiations: the (temporary) role of mini-summits

It is not clear that the EU social dialogue has yet achieved the 'normalisation', the longer-term stability, which would ensure that the expectations of the parties are that obstacles encountered in negotiations will eventually be overcome. This apparent fragility may offer the temptation to some participants, national affiliates of the social partners, to perceive breakdowns in negotiations as more than the temporary and 'normal' checks to be encountered in a mature bargaining process, but rather an opportunity to wreck the process in its entirety. It may be necessary to develop mechanisms to avoid this temptation and break deadlocks. It seems that a change in the level of negotiations, in the form of 'mini-summits' between the leaders of the EU social partners, are used to achieve such breakthroughs.

At the penultimate (ninth) meeting of the Negotiations Group on 26–27 November 1998, the employers presented a text and their spokesperson reported on discussion among the employers' side following the blockage encountered in a meeting on 13 November 1998. In the plenary session which followed on 27 November 1998, the employers presented a further proposition making a strong plea in favour of maintaining flexibility. The ETUC side could not accept the employers' proposal and decided that there was therefore no point in continuing discussions. The negotiations were then suspended and it was agreed that reports would be made to each respective organisation describing the situation.

UNICE's Council of Presidents met on 3–4 December 1998 and reaffirmed its willingness to continue negotiations by trying to find a solution to the current blockages. The crucial event was a meeting of the presidents and general secretaries of ETUC, UNICE and CEEP at the mini-summit on 4 December 1998 in Vienna. On that occasion, the problem of the negotiations was discussed in an informal manner to see if a change in the employers' position was still possible. An informal contact took place with the employers' spokesperson on 10 December 1998, at which point a draft compromise was reached on one of the disputed clauses being negotiated. The employers' spokesman was advised that he must inform the ETUC definitively of the possibilities for the employers to change their position by midday on 15 December 1998, just before the ETUC's Executive Committee discussion. Two hours before the ETUC Executive was to consider whether to continue negotiations, UNICE accepted the compromise formula and informed the ETUC Executive. The Executive Committee agreed to continue negotiations by referring the matter to the Negotiations Group and the Drafting Group for them to deal with it.

In a mature process of EU social dialogue, there should be mechanisms of mediation and conciliation which may successfully break deadlocks and achieve the necessary agreement. Efforts should be made to develop such mechanisms at EU level, and reduce the reliance on interventions from the top level to achieve the necessary breakthrough.

## 8. Multiple social dialogues engaging different issues

The EU social dialogue undertaking the task of regulating employment and industrial relations, not to mention labour market and social policy issues in the EU, raises the prospect of multiple social dialogues. The implications for the process of negotiations, and, in particular, the relations between the EU level social partners and their affiliates, are onerous. Simultaneous negotiations over different issues can make the process complex and difficult. On the other hand, there can arise possibilities of trade-offs, both procedural (as progress on one issue is traded against delay in another) and substantive (as concessions in one set of negotiations are traded off for concessions in another).

When different issues have to be dealt with, the practical difficulties of ensuring adequate consultation by the EU level organisations with national organisations, and by national organisations with their affiliates, are multiplied. This may also lead to complicated trade-offs within national organisations as they too face issues of priorities, again leading to delays.

In sum, simultaneous social dialogues on a number of issues have to be carefully coordinated. The positive dimension of progress being due to possible trade-offs between negotiations on different issues may be outweighed by overload, complexity and resulting delay.

These issues were illustrated at the initiation of negotiations on fixed-term work, which was complicated by the simultaneous dispute over whether another issue, information and consultation at national level, would be the subject of social dialogue.

## 9. Resources and technical assistance for the EU social dialogue

The prospect of the EU social dialogue undertaking multiple regulatory tasks requires a level of material resources considerably beyond the current level of provision for the EU level social partners. The need of the social partners for technical and material assistance in their negotiations has long been acknowledged. An Opinion from the Economic and Social Committee in 1994 called for a secretariat for the EU social dialogue.[94] The lack of resources constitutes a serious obstacle to the social partners' engagement in regulating employment and industrial relations at EU level through their social dialogue.

Part of the requisite material resources consists of technical and expert assistance to the social partners to deal with the many complex issues, not least involving EC law, which arise in the course of negotiations. This assistance

---

[94] Opinion of the Economic and Social Committee (ECOSOC) on the Communication concerning the application of the Agreement on Social Policy, COM(93) 600 final, rapporteur: J.J. van Dijk, Brussels, 16 November 1994; OJ C397/40 of 31 December 1994.

could take different forms: it could be partisan, and available separately for each side; it could be 'neutral', perhaps provided by the Commission; or it could be provided as the result of a bilateral agreement to undertake research into a particular problem.

There are many issues which could be, and need to be addressed in the regulation of employment and industrial relations in the EU. Yet the current resources of the EU social partners preclude addressing more than one or two at a time. Given that negotiations often take many months, this means very few issues will ever be addressed. Whatever other obstacles may exist to the development of the EU social dialogue, it is absurd that the absence of the relatively minimal resources required should effectively constrain the capacity of the EU social partners and determine the pace at which they can undertake the EU social dialogue.[95]

## 10. The role of the Commission in the EU social dialogue

The position of the Commission in the EU social dialogue is extremely delicate. Formally, the person chairing the negotiations on fixed-term work, and his assistant, were paid by the Commission, which also provided logistical and financial support for the meetings of the social partners. But the social partners insisted on the bipartite nature of the social dialogue, autonomous from the Commission. Having said that, the record of documentation reveals something, if only partial, of the dynamic reality behind this formal position.[96]

The position of the social partners on this issue is ambivalent. Considerations, sometimes of a character derived from constitutional traditions in individual Member States, may dictate absolute autonomy of the social partners and their dialogue from any intervention by public authority, at EU level embodied in the Commission. On the other hand, the role of the Commission in the creation and maintenance of the EU social dialogue is undeniable and, perhaps, unavoidable. Its role in the development of the EU social dialogue, like its role in the process of European integration, is in continuous evolution. In this case, from the beginning, the consultations by the Commission of the social partners on the initiative to regulate forms of 'atypical work' affected the position of the social partners.

---

[95] For example, in past EU social dialogues there had been as many as thirty-seven different versions of the text under consideration, and the result had sometimes been confusion as to which version was under discussion, hindering the efficiency of the social dialogue.

[96] For example, Commission influence was felt early, when on 21–22 April 1998 a meeting of the Negotiations Group began with a technical legal seminar on the subject, with officials from the Commission's Legal Service and Directorate-General V, Employment and Social Affairs, as well as other Commission officials. In an account of the Negotiations Group meeting on 12–13 October 1998 and 23 October 1998, there is a reference to arguments and points of the employers' side of the Drafting Group. This includes a note that the President (Chair), Jean Degimbe, reminded the Drafting Group, not least the employers, that any agreement would be transposed into a directive, a regulatory measure aimed precisely to allow for harmonisation among Member States.

It is important to resolve, even if only for a determinate period, the precise responsibilities of the Commission in the EU social dialogue. These may or may not include providing for some or all of the objective requirements of the EU social dialogue: for resources, expertise,[97] an independent secretariat controlled by the social partners, an independent chair with specified powers of mediation or otherwise, and mechanisms for resolving deadlocks or obstacles to the success of negotiations.

[97] For example, after agreement was reached on 14 January 1999, there was a flurry of activity aimed at providing accurate translation of the agreement into all Community languages. The Commission played a role in this task, and in doing so was in communication with the social partners at EU and national levels. For example, a memorandum of 13 April 1999 from the Commission is addressed to the ETUC, UNICE and CEEP with comments on translations received to date from social partners in Italy, Spain, Germany, Finland and Portugal.

# Chapter 19

# Threats and challenges to and the future of the European social dialogue

## Threats and challenges to the European social dialogue

The constitutionalisation of the European social dialogue by the insertion of Articles 138 and 139 into the EC Treaty appeared to guarantee the social partners their position as *a*, if not *the* primary source of European labour law. The history of European labour law recounted in this book advises against complacency. Radical shifts in legal strategy have time and again reflected economic, political and social changes in Europe. The European social dialogue is not immune to these historical mutations.

This chapter examines challenges which have recently emerged. They reflect the institutional conjuncture of a weakened Commission and a Parliament keen to reassert itself in the area of social policy, a political conjuncture of a Council reflecting a conservative coalition of Member States with a deregulatory agenda, and an economic conjuncture of high unemployment, with weakened and defensive national trade unions, inevitably affecting their European organisation, the ETUC, and aggressive employer organisations at both national and European levels.

This conjuncture is not permanent. It was argued that social dialogue has deep roots in the social, economic and political structures of the Member States, making it an integral component of the European social model and the foundation for European labour law. That does not mean that the European social dialogue is beyond challenge. However, as some never tire of reminding us, challenges are also opportunities ...

## The Interinstitutional Agreement on Better Lawmaking 2003

An Interinstitutional Agreement on Better Lawmaking, dated 9 October 2003, was concluded between the European Parliament, the Council and the Commission.[1] It potentially threatens the achievement of the social partners

---

[1] The Interinstitutional Agreement was signed and ratified by the Council, Commission and the European Parliament on 16 December 1993. It was published in the Official Journal, OJ C321/ 2003 of 31 December 2003. Note also the Report from the Commission, *Better Lawmaking 2003*, pursuant to Article 9 of the Protocol on the application of the principles of subsidiarity and proportionality (11th Report), COM(2003)770, Brussels, 12 December 2003.

of a regulatory space for the European social dialogue in formulating EU policy in employment and industrial relations, and social policy in general. This text raises a number of important and disturbing issues as far as the social partners are concerned. Yet the social partners were not consulted in the preparation of this Agreement.

The Interinstitutional Agreement deals with two principal issues: (i) the normal EU legislative process, and (ii) 'alternative methods of regulation'. The normal EU legislative process is dealt with in the sections on 'Better coordination of the legislative process'[2] and 'Improving the quality of legislation'.[3] These sections ignore the special role of the social partners in the EU legislative process in the social policy field laid down in Articles 138–9 EC.

The special role of the social partners is referred to in the part on 'Use of alternative methods of regulation',[4] which deals generally with 'co-regulation' and 'self-regulation'. However, the social partners, the social dialogue process and the agreements which result are subjected to conditions which conflict with Articles 138–9 EC.[5]

## The normal EU legislative process as presented in the Interinstitutional Agreement

### The social partners

### The legislative timetable: accommodating social dialogue

The section on 'Better coordination of the legislative process' does not mention the social partners.[6] For example: 'The three Institutions will forward to each other their respective annual legislative timetables with a view to reaching agreement on joint annual programming.'[7]

The social partners' dialogue is not considered as a factor in this timetable.

### Social partners and others: the special role of the social partners in the social policy field

The statement on 'Pre-legislative consultation' provides:[8]

> During the period preceding the submission of legislative proposals, the Commission will, having informed the European Parliament and the Council, conduct the widest possible consultations, the results of which will be made public. In certain cases, where the Commission deems it appropriate, the Commission may submit a pre-legislative consultation document on which the European Parliament and the Council may choose to deliver an opinion.

---

[2] Paragraphs 3–15.    [3] Paragraphs 25–31.    [4] Paragraphs 16–23.

[5] For commentary, Christophe Vigneau, 'Partenaires sociaux européens et nouveaux modes communautaires de regulation: la fin des privilèges?', *Droit Social*, September–October 2004, 883–90.

[6] Paragraphs 3–9.    [7] Paragraph 4, second sub-paragraph.    [8] Paragraph 26.

In contrast, Article 138 EC requires that 'before submitting proposals in the social policy field, the Commission shall consult management and labour on the possible direction of Community action'.

## Social partners and EU institutions

Promises of better consultation in the Interinstitutional Agreement are not applied to the social partners. For example, on 'Choice of legislative instrument and legal basis':[9]

> The Commission will explain and justify to the European Parliament and to the Council its choice of legislative instrument ... It will consider any request in this connection from the legislative authority, and it will take account of the results of any consultations which it has undertaken before tabling its proposals ... In the event of a change being made to the legal basis after any Commission proposal has been presented, the European Parliament will be duly re-consulted by the Institution concerned, in full compliance with the case-law of the Court of Justice of the European Communities.

The Treaty requires that these same procedures must be followed with regard to the social partners with respect to Commission 'proposals in the social policy field'. For example, the choice of the relevant paragraph of Article 137 (e.g. qualified majority vote or unanimity).

## Conditioning the social dialogue process

As regards 'Use of alternative methods of regulation',[10] the 'alternative methods' of 'co-regulation' and 'self-regulation' appear intended to cover the European social dialogue and the agreements reached under it, as subsequent paragraphs refer to the social partners.[11]

Paragraph 17 stipulates conditions for the social dialogue process:

> The Commission will ensure that any use of co-regulation or self-regulation is always consistent with Community law and that it meets the criteria of transparency (in particular the publicising of agreements) and representativeness of the parties involved.

These conditions threaten the autonomy of both the process of social dialogue (transparency) and of the social partners (representativeness).

Paragraph 17 continues:

> These mechanisms will not be applicable where fundamental rights or important political options are at stake or in situations where the rules must be applied in a uniform fashion in all Member States.

The scope of matters excluded from the social dialogue by this sentence is potentially vast.

---

[9] Paragraphs 12 and 14.    [10] Paragraphs 16–17.    [11] Paragraphs 18, 19 and 22.

### Conditioning social dialogue agreements

Paragraph 17 stipulates conditions for social dialogue agreements: 'It must also represent added value for the general interest.' This subordinates the content of social dialogue agreements to a substantive condition nowhere evident in the Treaty. 'They must ensure swift and flexible regulation which does not affect the principles of competition or the unity of the internal market.' The European Court's exemption of social dialogue agreements from EU competition law is ignored.[12]

## Alternative methods of regulation

### Co-regulation

Co-regulation appears to be a form of delegation to the social partners:[13]

> Co-regulation means the mechanism whereby a Community legislative act entrusts the attainment of the objectives defined by the legislative authority to parties which are recognised in the field (such as … the social partners) … Agreements between the social partners must comply with the provisions laid down in Articles 138 and 139 of the EC Treaty.

The third sub-paragraph of paragraph 20 is the most alarming provision in the Interinstitutional Agreement:

> At the request of inter alia the European Parliament or of the Council, on a case-by-case basis and depending on the subject, the basic legislative act may include a provision for a two-month period of grace following notification of a draft agreement to the European Parliament and the Council. During that period, each Institution may either
>
> > suggest amendments, if it is considered that the draft agreement does not meet the objectives laid down by the legislative authority, or
> > object to the entry into force of that agreement and, possibly,
> > ask the Commission to submit a proposal for a legislative act.

As presently understood and applied, the position under Articles 138–9 EC is that:

1. The European Parliament has no formal power to suggest amendments to an agreement or object to its entry into force.
2. The Commission (a) has no power to refuse to propose the agreement for decision of the Council once there has been a 'joint request of the signatory parties'; (b) may not opt to submit an alternative 'proposal for a legislative act'; (c) or do so on the grounds that it does not 'meet the objectives laid down by the legislative authority'.

---

[12] *Albany International BV* v. *Stichting Bedrijfspensioenfonds Textielindustrie*, Case C-67/96; with joined Cases C-115/97, C-116/97 and C-117/97, [1999] ECR I-5751.

[13] Paragraphs 18–19.

3. The Council has no power to amend an agreement submitted by the Commission. It can only decide to adopt or reject it.

Instead, paragraph 20 of the Interinstitutional Agreement proposes that:

1. amendments may reopen social dialogue agreements concluded after extensive negotiations;
2. social dialogue agreements may be subordinated to the 'objectives laid down by the legislative authority';
3. social dialogue agreements concluded may be subject to the threat that the Commission will reject them and substitute a legislative act.

It is not easy to imagine a more serious threat to the European social dialogue.

## Self-regulation

The first part of paragraph 22 refers to:

> the possibility for ... the social partners ... to adopt common guidelines at European level (particularly codes of practice or sectoral agreements).

Sectoral agreements at European level may be concluded under the provisions of Articles 138–9 EC, and they 'shall be implemented' in accordance with Article 139(2). They are much more than 'common guidelines' or 'codes of practice'. This downgrading of sectoral agreements conflicts with the promotion of the sectoral social dialogue, ostensibly an important objective pursued by the Commission, which has established over thirty sectoral social dialogue committees. Paragraph 22 continues:

> where such initiatives are undertaken in areas which are not covered by the Treaties or in which the Union has not hitherto legislated ... the Commission will scrutinise self-regulation practices in order to verify that they comply with the provisions of the EC Treaty.

It is not easy to understand how the competence of the Commission can extend to initiatives *outside* the scope of the Treaties.

Paragraph 23 provides for the Commission to notify the Parliament and the Council, and to satisfy itself as to 'the representativeness of the parties concerned, sectoral and geographical cover and the added value of the commitments'. Even where these practices/agreements fall *within* the scope of the Treaties, the Interinstitutional Agreement assumes that the task of scrutinising these practices is appropriate for the Commission. It is highly questionable whether the autonomous activities of self-regulating social partners should come under such intensive scrutiny by the EU institutions. Many other more powerful, more intrusive, more dangerous regulatory actors are not subject to such scrutiny.

Finally, the Commission 'will, nonetheless, consider the possibility of putting forward a proposal for a legislative act, in particular at the request of the competent legislative authority or in the event of a failure to observe the above practices'. This is truly stunning: the Commission may intervene to replace the practice or agreement with a substitute legislative act not only when there are failures of representativeness, etc., but simply at the request of the competent legislative authority.

## Conclusion

The Interinstitutional Agreement aims to achieve 'Better Law-Making' – *without* the social partners. The contradicts the recognition of the EU social dialogue as the mandatory legislative procedure in Articles 138–9 EC. The Agreement's 'Alternative methods of regulation' include social dialogue, but the social dialogue is subject to the scrutiny and control of the other EU institutions. This goes against the guarantee of autonomy of the social partners provided for in the 'constitutional traditions and international obligations common to the Member States'.[14]

As stated earlier, the fundamental strategic issue is how to configure the role of the EU social partners and the EU social dialogue in the EU constitutional and legal order. Is it a role of autonomous regulation of social policy, and in particular, of the sphere of employment and industrial relations, by constitutionally recognised social partners? Or is the role of the social partners confined to an industrial relations sub-system subordinate to the internal market regulated by the EU institutions?

## The Commission's Report on 'Better Lawmaking 2003'

The General Secretary of the ETUC, John Monks, wrote to the President of the Commission, Romano Prodi, on 25 November 2003 expressing concern about the conflict between the Interinstitutional Agreement and the social dialogue, as well the Agreement's potential conflict with social dialogue agreements. The ETUC letter identified specific ways in which the social dialogue, as well as social dialogue agreements, are negatively affected by the Agreement. A response from Prodi dated 11 December 2003 sought to reassure the ETUC by asserting that Articles 138 and 139 'are not in any way affected' by the Agreement, which 'will therefore not impinge on the social dialogue'. The Commission did not respond to the specific points in the ETUC's letter. This may reflect a genuine view that the Agreement is not intended to, does not and will not affect the social dialogue and social dialogue agreements. Alternatively, and more dangerously, it reflects a Commission position on the social dialogue

---

[14] As stated in the Preamble to the EU Charter of Fundamental Rights. The last Recital of the Agreement emphasises that it 'is concluded without prejudice to the outcome of the IGC' which produced the proposed Constitutional Treaty. However, the active constitutional 'practice' proposed in the Agreement may have outweighed the passive text of a Constitutional Treaty, not least one not ratified.

and social dialogue agreements which allows more room for the Council and Parliament to challenge the social partners and the social dialogue, and limit the scope of, and amend, social dialogue agreements.

The latter view is reinforced by a Report from the Commission on the day following Prodi's letter, 12 December 2003.[15] Significantly, this Report includes a statement very similar to the language in Prodi's letter of 11 December 2003: 'The rules on the functioning of the social dialogue (Articles 138 and 139 TEC) and standardisation according to the "New Approach" are not affected by this agreement.'[16] The Report outlines the development of the Commission's position on 'Better Lawmaking'. There are a number of interesting points:

   i. frequency of Commission consultation of the social partners;
   ii. scope of the Commission's obligation to consult social partners;
   iii. minimum standards for Commission consultation of the social partners;
   iv. social dialogue and soft law;
   v. constraints on actors, processes and outcomes of social dialogue.

### i. Frequency of Commission consultation of the social partners

Annex 2, 'Public consultation in 2003', states:[17]

> The Commission is also engaged in various forms of institutionalised dialogue with interested parties in specific domains, the most developed being the *social dialogue*.

Public consultation is described by listing the numbers of Green Papers, Communications, reports and internet consultations in 2003, and for the last ten years. But *there is no information on social dialogue consultations*. Rather, it is claimed:[18]

> The sectoral pattern of consultation for 2003 is globally in line with previous years' patterns. The largest number of consultations concerned, in descending order, agriculture, *employment and social policy*, external relations, industry, justice and home affairs, transport and energy, environment, economic policy and information society.

This indicates that statistics exist. It may be possible to establish whether what the Commission calls consultations on 'employment and social policy' were with the social partners under Article 138, or were general public consultations; and whether the latter should have been within the Article 138 framework.

Unfortunately, no information is provided on how many times the Commission calculates that it consulted the social partners in compliance with Article 138. If the figures, and topics, were available for social dialogue

---

[15] Report from the Commission, *Better Lawmaking 2003*, pursuant to Article 9 of the Protocol on the application of the principles of subsidiarity and proportionality (11th Report), COM(2003) 770, Brussels, 12 December 2003.
[16] *Ibid.*, footnote 39 on page 11.   [17] *Ibid.*, page 32.   [18] *Ibid.*, page 33.

consultations by the Commission, they would indicate how alive the social dialogue process is from the Commission's point of view, and provide a basis to assess the implementation of the Interinstitutional Agreement.

### ii. Scope of the Commission's obligation to consult social partners

Frequency of consultation will depend on the scope of the obligation: which proposals fall within 'the social policy field' (Article 138(2)). This requires detailed consideration. A preliminary classification could include:

(a) substantive social policy issues concerning *industrial relations* in which the *social partners* have a direct interest (e.g. worker representation, work organisation);

(b) substantive social policy issues concerning *terms and conditions of employment* in which the *social partners* have a direct interest (e.g. working time, atypical work);

(c) substantive social policy issues in which *workers and employers* represented by the social partners have a direct interest (e.g. pensions, social security, employment policy);

(d) substantive social policy issues in which *workers and employers* represented by the social partners have an indirect interest (as consumers, citizens) (e.g. services of general interest);

(e) '*horizontal*' proposals concerning the procedure of formulating EU social policy, such as law-making procedures which determine the progress of social policy proposals;[19]

(f) '*institutional*' proposals whereby new agencies concerned with social policy are to be established.[20]

A classification of types of issues requiring consultation is necessary if the Commission is serious about securing adequate consultation of the social partners in the future.

### iii. Minimum standards for Commission consultation of the social partners

The Report of 12 December 2003, refers to a Communication of December 2002 on the adoption of minimum standards for public consultation and states:[21]

---

[19] If these did not come within the scope of Article 138, the process of social policy formation could marginalise the social partners. The Interinstitutional Agreement is a case in point. The social partners were not consulted although negotiations between the EU institutions were carried out over a considerable period.

[20] For example, the Report itself refers to new regulatory agencies, including one 'still under inter-institutional negotiation': the 'European railway agency'. Is it possible that this can proceed without involvement of social partners, or at least the railway trade unions? This is also an example of a 'horizontal' proposal with social policy implications (affecting employees/consumers) falling within Article 138 (especially as it may lead to a legal measure: a decision establishing the Agency).

[21] *Better Lawmaking*, page 33, footnote 96.

These new standards were adopted after wide consultation … Before adopting this Communication, the Commission indeed sought the opinion of citizens, interest groups, associations and operators … reported on the results and gave a feedback on the comments received.[22]

For example, one of the minimum standards for public consultation was a *minimum* public consultation period of at least eight weeks, and the Communication of December 2002 states: 'The time given to respondents was often above minimum standard.'[23] Yet this is the *maximum* period under the process used by the Commission for Article 138, and was only increased from six to eight weeks following the Commission's Communication on the social dialogue of 1998.[24]

Again, a set of minimum standards for the Commission's consultation of the social partners is necessary to secure adequate consultation of the social partners in the future.

### iv. Social dialogue and soft law

As regards the 'choice of instruments', the Commission states:[25]

the Commission suggested that, besides 'classical' instruments such as regulations and directives, the Union could consider using other instruments which may be more flexible and efficient under certain circumstances … the Commission proposed referring to them as '*alternative instruments*' … [In some cases, the Parliament and/or Council] have invited the Commission to abandon the idea of a directive in favour of 'soft-law' solutions such as recommendations. With the Interinstitutional Agreement on better lawmaking, the three institutions have for the first time established common definitions and agreed on conditions and procedures for use of co-regulation and self-regulation.

Co-regulation and self-regulation are where social dialogue appears. The equation is made between the outcomes of such co-regulation/self-regulation and 'soft law' (e.g. non-legally binding 'Recommendations'), as opposed to the 'hard law' of regulations/directives. This is despite the fact that social dialogue agreements may and have become directives under Article 138. The agreements themselves are not to be considered 'soft law', but have hard legal consequences.

The Report reinforces the association of 'soft law' with co-regulation and self-regulation, and then with social dialogue. It describes the 'main elements' of

---

[22] This highlights the inadequacy of the process followed in reaching the Interinstitutional Agreement on Better Lawmaking. Despite its importance, there was no consultation of the social partners. The Agreement covers law-making, including social policy proposals, and the social partners have an institutional position in this law-making process under Articles 138 and 139 EC which must be respected.

[23] *Better Lawmaking*, page 33.

[24] Commission Communication, *Adapting and Promoting the Social Dialogue at Community Level*, COM(98) 322 final, Brussels, 20 May 1998.

[25] *Better Lawmaking*, page 8, Section 2.2.e.

the Interinstitutional Agreement as including a '[S]table framework for "*soft law*" instruments that should facilitate their future use. The three institutions have for the first time established a common definition of co-regulation and self-regulation'.[26]

### v. Constraints on actors, processes and outcomes of social dialogue

The Report continues:[27]

> [The European Parliament, the Council and the Commission] also agreed on general limits and conditions to the use of those methods, defining the role of each institution in the process and ensuring that the prerogatives of the legislative authorities are respected. In particular, co-regulation and self-regulation 'will not be applicable where fundamental rights or important political options are at stake or in situations where the rules must be applied in a uniform fashion in all Member States'. Under co-regulation, following notification of a draft agreement prepared by interested parties, the Parliament and the Council will have the right to suggest amendments to the agreement, object to its entry into force and, possibly, ask the Commission to submit a proposal for a legislative act. As for self-regulation, the Commission will keep the legislators informed by reporting on the practices it regards as effective and satisfactory in terms of representativeness.

This paragraph reiterates the elements of paragraphs 17, 20 and 23 of the Interinstitutional Agreement to which the ETUC took particular exception in its letter of 25 November 2003.[28]

Prodi's letter of 11 December 2003 provides assurances which may appear to alleviate the threat, but the letter has no legal status, and could not alter the position of the other parties to the Interinstitutional Agreement, the Council and Parliament, who may insist that the Commission respects the Agreement.[29] Unless similar assurances to that in Prodi's letter could be obtained from the other EU institutions party to the Agreement, but especially if these were not

---

[26] Section 2.3 ('Action at the level of Community institutions'), page 11. Footnote 39 continues: 'The Inter-institutional Agreement on better lawmaking provides the following definitions: Co-regulation: "... the mechanism whereby a Community legislative act entrusts the attainment of the objectives defined by the legislative authority to parties which are recognised in the field (such as economic operators, *the social partners*, NGOS or associations to adopt amongst themselves and for themselves common *guidelines* at European level (particularly codes of practices or *sectoral agreements*)". The rules on the functioning of the social dialogue (Articles 138 and 139 TEC) and standardisation according to the "New Approach" are not affected by this agreement'.

[27] Section 2.3 ('Action at the level of Community institutions'), pages 11–12.

[28] It is difficult to understand the statement in footnote 39 on page 11 quoted in the preceding footnote, and the similar statement in Prodi's letter of 11 December 2003, that 'The rules on the functioning of the social dialogue (Articles 138 and 139 TEC) ... are not affected by this agreement'. Social dialogue and social dialogue agreements are both potentially dramatically affected.

[29] For example, it is not difficult to imagine Parliament, which has been very critical of the Framework Agreements on part-time work and fixed-term work, demanding that the Commission require amendments to agreements reached before they may be submitted to the Council.

forthcoming, it would reinforce the potential threat to the European social dialogue posed by the Interinstitutional Agreement.

## Two ominous challenges to the European social dialogue

### Revision of the Working Time Directive

On 30 December 2003, in fulfilment of the requirement to re-examine certain provisions of the Working Time Directive, the Commission issued a Communication which states that its aim is to consult the European Parliament and the Council, but also the ECOSOC, the Committee of the Regions and the *social partners* on a possible revision of the text:[30]

> this communication should be considered as the first phase of consultation pursuant to Article 138(2) of the Treaty. The Commission will of course subsequently consult the social partners on the content of all proposals envisaged (Article 138(3)).

This is repeated on the last page of the Communication, which adds: 'They are invited to give their *opinion* on the need to amend the Directive on the issues identified in Part Two. They will be consulted subsequently ...'.[31] However, Article 138(3) provides for an opinion to be forwarded *not* after the first, but subsequent to the second consultation.

The preparation of this Communication had been known for a long time. It is questionable whether beginning the social partner consultation required by Article 138 only when others are also being consulted is acceptable. For example, how does it compare with other first consultations? Had they advanced as far as a detailed Communication of this kind? Or were consultations initiated much earlier, allowing the social partners to act? The Commission's past practice has been that there is an eight-week period of consultation envisaged for the first consultation envisaged under Article 138(2). Yet the Communication stipulates: 'All interested organisations can send their comments and suggestions by e-mail only ... [to] reach us no later than 31 March 2004' (i.e. twelve and a half weeks after 5 January 2004).[32] If this is an Article 138 consultation, then it may be subject to the social partners' agreeing to engage in social dialogue. There is no mention of this possibility anywhere in the Communication, even though there have been numerous successful sectoral social dialogues on working time in various transport sectors.

In sum: the consultation over revision of the Working Time Directive envisages the social partners providing an opinion at the end of this first consultation, which is inconsistent with Article 138, begun long after it was known that the

---

[30] *Communication from the Commission to the Council, the European Parliament, the Economic and Social Committee and the Committee of the Regions concerning the re-exam of Directive 93/104/EC concerning certain aspects of the organization of working time.* COM(2003) 843 final, Brussels, 30 December 2003, page 4.

[31] *Ibid.*, page 24.     [32] *Ibid.*

Commission was considering revision of the Working Time Directive, engages all interested organisations, not only the social partners, exceeds the normal time period for social partner consultation, and makes no mention of social dialogue. These factors reinforce the case for the Communication not being the consultation required by Article 138(2), despite the Commission's claim. The Commission failed in its obligation under Article 138 EC.

Rather, it is further evidence (in addition to the Interinstitutional Agreement on Better Lawmaking) that the Commission is reducing the involvement of the social partners and the role of the social dialogue to the level of general public consultations on Commission initiatives. This contravenes Articles 138–9 EC.[33]

If the Communication *is* accepted as an Article 138 EC consultation, then, presumably, it is subject to the social partners' agreeing to social dialogue (Article 138(4) EC). If agreement could be reached, it could avoid legislative proposals by the Commission. However, this is now subject to all the threats posed by the Interinstitutional Agreement to 'co-regulation' or 'self-regulation', such as Parliament and Council suggesting amendments to the agreement, objecting to its entry into force and, possibly, asking the Commission to submit a proposal for a legislative act.[34]

The publication of the Commission's Communication of 30 December 2003 on re-examination of the Working Time Directive was considered at the ETUC Executive Committee meeting in Brussels on 17–18 March 2004 and the ETUC General Secretary wrote to the then Commissioner for Social Affairs, Stavros Dimas, on 24 March 2004 expressing the ETUC's position that this procedure was not in accordance with the Treaty because it did not recognise the special and unique position of the Social Partners under Article 138 of the Treaty. The

---

[33] The failure to engage social dialogue is particularly striking given the subject matter of the consultation which could lend itself to solutions reached through the social dialogue. For example, a large section of the Communication (Section 3, pages 16–20) is devoted to analysis of the *SIMAP* (*Sindicato de Médicos de Asistencia Pública (Simap)* v. *Conselleria de Sanidad y Consumo de la Generalidad Valenciana*, Case C-303/98, [2000] ECR I-7963) and *Jaeger* (*Landeshauptstadt Kiel* v. *Norbert Jaeger*, Case C-151/02, 9 September 2003) cases. *SIMAP* involved a trade union, and many medical staff concerned are represented by trade unions. This at least suggests there is considerable scope for EU sectoral social dialogue involving medical staff, hospitals and public sector authorities. For example, to define 'on-call' time in a way that will resolve problems in the health sector, and other sectors affected by these cases. Again, the Communication gives as one of the reasons for using individual opt-outs: 'the uncertainty as to the scope of the derogation in Article 17(1) of the Directive (workers whose working time is not measured and/or predetermined or may be determined by the workers themselves)' (page 14). Since many of these managerial employees are in trade unions, the social partners are well placed to negotiate solutions which would clarify application of this provision. Finally, the Communication concludes by expanding the scope of the consultation over working time to include 'Ensuring compatibility between work and family life': 'The Commission is firmly of the view that the revision of the Working Time Directive could be exploited in such a way as to encourage the Member States to take steps to improve the compatibility of work and family life' (Section 4, pages 20–1). There are obvious prospects for social dialogue, given the past record of Framework Agreements on parental leave and part-time work.

[34] Interinstitutional Agreement on Better Lawmaking, paragraph 20.

ETUC insisted that it was important to avoid confusing the provision of information and the gathering of relevant material on a current policy issue with the official and formal consultation procedures, which have an explicit legal base in the EC Treaty. The ETUC required the Commission, as guardian of the Treaties, to clarify its position on the current consultation process, and explicitly take measures to safeguard the specific and unique position of the social partners at European level.

These representations appeared to have led the Commission to reassess its position, at least formally, as can be illustrated by the contrast with the title of the Commission's second Communication on the subject, dated 19 May 2004: *Second Phase of Consultation of the Social Partners at Community Level concerning the revision of Directive 94/104/EC concerning certain aspects of the organization of working time.*[35]

However, in its Communication on restructuring and revision of the European Works Councils Directive, the Commission appeared to have regressed to its previous position.

### Proposals on restructuring and revision of the European Works Councils Directive[36]

On 31 March 2005, the Commission adopted a Communication on 'Restructuring and employment – Anticipating and accompanying restructuring in order to develop employment: the role of the European Union'.[37] Once again the Communication is not addressed explicitly to the social partners. Contrary to the objections made by the ETUC with regard to the re-examination of the Working Time Directive, the Commission seeks to involve interested organisations at national level by inviting them to comment, and these organisations necessarily must be others than the relevant social partners (as the European social partners represent their national affiliates). This fails once again to comply with Commission's obligations in not recognising the special and unique position of the social partners under Article 138 of the Treaty. This special and unique position aims to promote the European social dialogue, to promote the possibility of management and labour to influence the direction of proposals in the social policy field in an early stage, and to allow management and labour to contribute to the elaboration of social policies with their own specific instruments.

[35] Compare the first Communication, where the addressees in the title of the Communication are stated to be the Council, the Parliament, the Economic and Social Committee, and the Committee of the Regions. Only in some language versions were the social partners also mentioned explicitly (notably, not in the French, English and German web-versions, though they are mentioned, for instance, in the Danish, Dutch, Portuguese, Spanish and Swedish web-versions).

[36] The following section benefited from intense collaboration with Klaus Lörcher, formerly legal adviser to the ETUC.

[37] COM(2005) 120 final.

This repeated failure clearly to promote the European social dialogue is compounded in the case of the Communication of 31 March 2005 by further steps taken by the Commission.[38] Correspondence from the Directorate-General of Social Affairs in the week following publication of the Communication asserted the Commission's view that the first consultation of the social partners required by Article 138(2) EC was initiated as regards restructuring on 15 January 2002 and, as regards European Works Councils, the first stage consultation was launched on 19 April 2004. It confirmed that, as in the Communication of 31 March 2005, it 'constitutes at the same time the second phase of the consultation on corporate restructuring and European works councils under Article 138(3) of the Treaty'.[39]

The Commission is bringing together for a second stage consultation two subjects very different in substance as regards levels, regulatory measures and procedures. As regards levels, restructuring is mainly an issue on the national level; European works councils are a transnational issue. As regards regulatory measures, European works councils are already regulated by a Directive; restructuring is an issue without a coherent and comprehensive legislative instrument at Community level. As regards procedures, there have

[38] The key statements as regards the procedure of consultation of the social partners are the following (paragraph 2.4): 'The second phase of consultation [of the European social partners on company restructuring and European works councils] consists of calling on the social partners to become more involved in the ways and means of anticipating and managing restructuring. The fact is that they are the key players in terms of effective action on the restructuring front. This second-stage consultation should primarily consist of inviting the social partners to continue their ongoing work by encouraging the adoption of their best-practice guidelines on restructuring and European works councils. As early as January 2002, the Commission made the social partners aware of the restructuring issue, asking them to pinpoint and develop throughout Europe instances of good practice in terms of restructuring. They subsequently spelled out reference guidelines for managing change. The point of this new phase is to ensure that these guidelines are put into practice and developed further, and in particular to encourage the adoption of these guidelines. In April 2004, the Commission launched a first phase of consultation on revising the European works councils directive. European works councils have an essential role to play in anticipating and managing restructuring operations. Here again, the social partners have undertaken a Europe-wide review to establish principles or guidelines based on an examination of existing councils. In the light of this work and these contributions, the Commission takes the view that there is a need for more European social dialogue input on these two closely linked questions, as part of the partnership for growth and jobs which lies at the heart of the reinvigorated Lisbon strategy. The Commission is therefore encouraging the European social partners to intensify ongoing work and to start negotiations with a view to reaching an agreement among themselves'.

[39] 'As called for by the Communication on the Lisbon strategy, the European social partners at cross-sectoral and sectoral level have a specific role to play in the implementation of the various strands of the policies set out below. They are therefore invited to respond to the call made to them in point 2.4 of this Communication, which constitutes at the same time the second phase of the consultation on corporate restructuring and European works councils under Article 138(3) of the Treaty'. The justification for treating this Communication as the *second* consultation for *both* issues is stated in paragraph 2.4 of the Communication of 31 March 2005: 'the Commission takes the view that there is a need for more European social dialogue input on these two closely linked questions, as part of the partnership for growth and jobs which lies at the heart of the reinvigorated Lisbon strategy.'

been different procedures on consultation, the first on restructuring beginning in January 2002, the second on European works councils more than two years later, in April 2004. The two subjects are substantively and substantially divergent. While there may be some overlap (transnational restructuring), it is clear that European works councils engage many other issues in addition to restructuring, and restructuring may have no transnational dimension or not involve an enterprise with a European works council.

The Commission's Communication combining the consultation process on two such different topics constitutes a distortion of the social dialogue process. In principle, this constitutes a violation of Article 138 EC as, by forcing together two such potentially different social dialogues, the Commission is violating the autonomy of the social partners.

Apart from the principle of autonomy, there are more specific arguments that the Commission is violating Article 138 EC. The structure of Article 138 makes very clear the distinction between the legislative framework (Commission consultation: paragraphs 2 and 3), and the social dialogue framework (the social partners initiate: paragraph 4).

Article 138(3) EC (a second consultation) only applies *if two conditions are fulfilled*. First, 'the Commission considers *Community action* advisable'. Second, the Commission produces 'the envisaged *proposal*'. If these conditions are fulfilled, the Commission 'shall *consult* management and labour on the content of the envisaged proposal'. In fact, neither of the two essential preconditions for a second consultation is fulfilled by the Communication of 31 March 2005. No Community 'action' is envisaged; no 'proposal' is forthcoming.[40]

---

[40] As regards the first essential precondition, that 'the Commission considers Community action advisable', the 'Community action' which the Commission considers advisable in paragraph 2.4 of the Communication is 'encouraging the European social partners to intensify ongoing work and to start negotiations with a view to reaching an agreement among themselves.' The 'Community action' here could be (i) the Commission 'encouraging the European social partners'; (ii) the social partners 'intensifying ongoing work'; (iii) the social partners 'to start negotiations with a view to reaching an agreement'. However, it is questionable whether *any* of these constitute 'Community action' within the meaning of Article 138(3). As regards (i), the Commission 'encouraging' is too minimal to qualify as 'action'. As regards (ii), social partner action is not 'Community action' within the meaning of Article 138(3); it is autonomous of the Community. Further, to intensify 'ongoing work' is not 'action'. As regards (iii), according to Article 138(4), it is for the social partners, not the Commission, to decide whether to start negotiations with a view to reaching an agreement. In sum, read in its context, Article 138(3) EC requires much more concrete and specific 'Community action' by the Community, and, specifically, by the Commission. The second precondition is that the Commission produces 'the envisaged *proposal*'. Here, from the outset, the legislative framework should be borne in mind. The content of the proposal should be as precise as possible in order to give the social partners the possibility to comment effectively on a concrete proposal. It is to achieve such a proposal that the first stage of consultation aims at clarifying the possible direction of Community action. Contrary to this, the Commission's Communication is making a *formal* 'second' consultation (Article 138(3)), but in *substance*, only a 'first' consultation (Article 138(2)) on the possible direction of a possible proposal, not on the content of such a proposal. This is confirmed by the last of the 'Proposed measures' in the Annex of the Communication: 'Launch of the second phase

The clear distinction must be made and maintained both between the legislative and non-legislative frameworks and between the Commission and other actors. Article 138(3) refers to the Commission making a proposal for its *own* initiative; the Commission offers, in conformity with Article 138(4), the social partners the possibility to react and respond.[41]

The purpose of the Treaty provisions on the social dialogue is for the Commission actively to stimulate the European social dialogue with a concrete envisaged proposal, as explicitly required by the wording of Article 138(3). While it may be asked to what extent must the envisaged proposal be clear and explicit in its content, the Communication of 31 March 2005 unequivocally fails to provide any substantive content. It is a first phase consultation (if any) only on the possible direction of Community action, e.g. what form of legal instruments, etc. The subject-matter of the Communication includes no proposal with a concrete content.[42]

In sum: the 'Community action' which the Commission considers advisable in the Communication is so weak as not to satisfy the requirement of Article 138(3). The requirement of a *'proposal'* in Article 138(3) is not satisfied by a text 'encouraging the European social partners to intensify ongoing work and to start negotiations with a view to reaching an agreement among themselves'. The claim that this implements Article 138(3) is not consistent with the structure of the procedures envisaged in Article 138. If the Commission is 'promoting the consultation of management and labour', or proposing a 'measure to facilitate their dialogue', then it falls within Article 138(1). If the Commission is 'encouraging the European social partners … to start negotiations with a view to reaching an agreement among themselves', this is not a matter for the Commission in Article 138(3). It is the autonomous decision of the social partners under Article 138(4): 'management and labour may inform the Commission of their wish to initiate the process'. The claim that this implements the legislative procedure envisaged by Article 138 is not consistent with the specific requirements ('Community action', 'envisaged proposal') of Article 138(3).

of consultation of the social partners on restructuring and European works councils, in particular with a view to encouraging the adoption of their best-practice guidelines on restructuring and European works councils.' Where is the Commission's proposal required as an essential precondition for launching the second consultation under Article 138(3)?

[41] Article 138(3) is not to be interpreted as the Commission simply referring the matter to the social partners. This is hardly necessary, as the social partners can always act autonomously if they wish; such Commission initiatives would not require a Treaty framework.

[42] This becomes clearer by distinguishing the two subjects of the second consultation addressed in paragraph 2.4 of the Communication: (a) European works councils and (b) restructuring. As regards European works councils, only one point at the end of paragraph 2.4 of the Communication refers to European works councils: 'promoting best practice'. This can hardly be characterised as a 'proposal' for 'Community action'. As regards restructuring, two points at the end of paragraph 2.4 of the Communication refer to restructuring. These include 'encouraging adoption of the best practices' and a 'discussion on the way forward'. Again, these cannot be characterised as a 'proposal' for 'Community action'. The final point at the end of paragraph 2.4 appears to address both. It specifies 'devising a common approach'. Can this be characterised as a 'proposal' for 'Community action'?

In substance, the Commission is *not consulting* the social partners (on the content of a Community action) but referring the issues to the social partners. It expresses this in clear words:

> This second phase of consultation consists of calling on the social partners to become more involved ... This second-stage consultation should primarily consist of inviting the social partners to continue their ongoing work.

In principle, the social partners are not asked about their opinion on a proposal but rather called upon to react in the way the Commission wishes.[43] It is the task of the Commission to promote social dialogue through its own action in the form of a concrete proposal. As there is neither Community action nor an envisaged proposal, there is nothing for the Commission to consult about.

## Defending the European social dialogue

The problem of the Community institutions failing to comply with the obligations regarding the social dialogue laid down in Article 138 of the Treaty may be addressed in various ways. A legal response is one avenue of redress, and one such response, through judicial review, is considered below. However, the challenge to the European social dialogue is ultimately political, and should be addressed through political responses of the institutions and other actors, not least the social partners themselves.

### A legal response: judicial review

One response is to challenge the legal measures which result through judicial review. The measures emerging from the examples outlined above include the Interinstitutional Agreement on Better Lawmaking, a revised Working Time Directive or European Works Councils Directive, or a Community legal instrument on restructuring.

Such a challenge encounters formidable obstacles. This may be illustrated by perhaps the most difficult case of a possible challenge by the social partners to the legality of the Interinstitutional Agreement on Better Lawmaking before the European Court of First Instance under Article 230 EC.[44]

---

[43] The Commission might claim that, as stated in the Communication: 'They are therefore invited to respond to the call made to them in point 2.4 of this Communication, which constitutes at the same time the second phase of the consultation on corporate restructuring and European works councils under Article 138(3) of the Treaty.' But they always can do this independently: Article138 (4) EC.

[44] However, it is useful to bear in mind also possible challenges to legislative proposals or acts (e.g. a revised Working Time Directive) adopted without complying with social partner consultation procedures of Article 138 EC.

Article 230 EC provides for judicial review:

Any natural or legal person may ... institute proceedings against a decision addressed to that person or against a decision which, although in the form of a regulation or decision addressed to another person, is of direct and individual concern to the former.

An initial practical difficulty is speed: proceedings must be instituted within two months. The Interinstitutional Agreement was published in the Official Journal on 31 December 2003. The deadline for legal proceedings to be instituted was 29 February 2004. This gave little time for the European level organisations, complex structures with multitudes of affiliates, to consider and decide upon legal action.[45]

In terms of substance, is an Interinstitutional Agreement one of the 'acts' which can be challenged under Article 230? The Court can review acts other than recommendations and opinions. This covers regulations, decisions and directives. The Court has held this list is not exhaustive and other acts, *sui generis*, can also be reviewed provided they have binding force or produce legal effects.[46] Other Interinstitutional Agreements have ended up before the European Court when the parties have been in conflict.[47]

Further, is the Interinstitutional Agreement 'a decision addressed to that person' or 'a decision which, although in the form of a regulation or decision addressed to another person, is of direct and individual concern to the former'?[48] To whom is it addressed? Presumably, each EU institution's decision

---

[45] However, there is an exception to the general time limit rule in the case of acts tainted by particularly serious illegality, deemed to be 'non-existent'. Normal time limits for challenge do not apply, since such an act can never be legal. On the other hand, non-existent acts cannot be annulled, as there is no 'act'. But a judicial finding that the act is non-existent will have the same effect in practice.

[46] For example, Case 22/70, *Commission* v. *Council (ERTA)* [1971] ECR 263: a Council Resolution qualified as an act with legal consequences; Case 60/82, *IBM* v. *Commission*: a Commission letter initiating competition proceedings did not qualify as an act with legal consequences.

[47] For example, the Interinstitutional Agreement on Budgetary Discipline and Improvement of the Budgetary Procedure, 1999 OJ C172/1 (replacing an earlier agreement); see Case C-284/90, *Council* v. *European Parliament* [1992] ECR I-2277. The Interinstitutional Agreement on Better Lawmaking was adopted jointly by the Commission, the European Parliament and the Council, and it was ratified separately by each EU institution. In the case of the European Parliament, was it 'intended to produce legal effects vis-à-vis third parties'? Again, was the intention to create legal effects? What would be the consequences of violation of the Agreement by any of the parties to it? If so, what legal effects? If there were legal effects, how would these be enforced? Would the consequences be mainly political or legal? In Case 22/70, *Commission* v. *Council*, the Court said that the act in question, a Council Resolution 'could not have been simply the expression of the recognition of a voluntary coordination, but was designed to lay down a course of action binding on both the institutions and the Member States, and destined ultimately to be reflected in the tenor of the regulation'. [1971] ECR 263, paragraph 53. Is there anything in the Interinstitutional Agreement which affects third parties? For example, does the Agreement's provision for the Parliament to seek to amend social dialogue agreements amount to a 'legal effect'?

[48] In the leading cases, the decision in question is addressed by the Commission to a Member State. Case 25/61, *Plaumann & Co.* v. *Commission* [1963] ECR 95. A regulation has been accepted as a 'decision', though an act of general application, if it applies to a closed category of persons (a bundle of individual decisions), particularly one defined in the light of past events. Cases 41–44/70, *International Fruit Company BV* v. *Commission* [1971] ECR 411.

is addressed to the two others. Is the decision addressed to those other institutions 'of direct and individual concern to' the social partners?[49]

In the end, it may be argued in defence of the Agreement that it does not exclude consultation of the social partners. It only concerns closer consultation of the three EU institutions parties to the Agreement, with wider consultation of others.

## A political response: institutions and social partners

The Commission responded to the expressions of concern regarding the Interinstitutional Agreement by the ETUC with statements to the effect that the Agreement does not in any way affect Articles 138 and 139 EC; similarly, with the concerns regarding the consultations over the Working Time Directive and restructuring/European works councils. However, a clearer understanding needs to be achieved. This could be done, for example, by clarifying how the Interinstitutional Agreement and Articles 138 and 139 EC are to work together.

For example, how does the obligation to consult the social partners 'before submitting proposals in the social policy field … on the possible direction of Community action' (Article 138(2)) fit into the framework of information and consultation of the Council and Parliament set out in the Agreement? Negotiations with the Commission could achieve a clarification of the Agreement's

---

[49] The requirement of *direct concern* means a direct causal relationship between the Community act and its legal effects on the applicant. That act must directly affect the legal situation of the individual and leave no discretion to the addressees of that measure who are entrusted with the task of implementing it. The implementation must be automatic and result from Community rules without the application of other intermediate rules. This precludes measures where authorities have a certain margin of discretion. As regards *individual concern*, according to *Plaumann*, persons other than the person to whom the decision is addressed can claim to be individually concerned if an act 'affects them by reason of certain attributes which are peculiar to them or by reason of circumstances in which they are differentiated from all other persons and by virtue of these factors distinguishes them individually just as in the case of the person addressed'. A comment on the most recent cases (Case T-177/01, *Jégo-Quéré et Cie SA* v. *Commission*, judgment of the CFI of 3 May 2002, and Case C-50/00 P, *Unión de Pequeños Agricultores* v. *Council*, judgment of 25 July 2002) observes: 'The Court of Justice generally accepted that applicants who belonged to a "closed category", the membership of which was fixed at the time the act was taken, would be individually concerned by that act. However, this membership alone became insufficient and would be relevant only when the institution author of the act *was under an explicit and specific duty to take into account the consequences of the act on the members of that class*, or where an applicant possess specific rights (e.g. trade mark right). The courts nevertheless showed some flexibility and adopted a more liberal stance with regard to specific case law (e.g. competition, state aids or anti-dumping), due to the special role played by individuals in these policy fields and to the specific nature of the subject-matters concerned. In those cases, the courts have accepted that factors such as … *the involvement of an applicant in proceedings leading to the contested measure where the legislation grants the applicant procedural guarantees*, can help establishing that the applicant is individually concerned.' Marie-Pierre Granger, 'Towards a Liberalisation of Standing Conditions for Individuals Seeking Judicial Review of Community Acts', (2003) 66 *Modern Law Review* 124–38, at pp. 127–8.

operation and a set of minimum requirements for the procedures required under Articles 138 and 139 EC; for example, as to the frequency, scope, minimum standards, types of measures envisaged, etc. in the process of consultation.

It would be desirable to engage also the other EU institutions party to the Agreement on the practice of consultation over proposals, not least the Parliament. Resolving the problem of Parliament's extraneousness to the social dialogue process will not be easy. But if such agreement could be reached, it could be attached as a protocol to the Agreement.

An even better alternative would be for the social partners to negotiate an agreement dealing with the issues raised by the Interinstitutional Agreement. The implications of the Interinstitutional Agreement for marginalisation of the EU social dialogue in the process of making EU legislation on social policy could induce the ETUC, UNICE (BusinessEurope)/UEAPME and CEEP to undertake an updating of the 31 October 1991 Agreement on Social Policy. A joint agreement would carry much weight (as it did in Maastricht). The updating agreement could offset the impact of the Interinstitutional Agreement. The Commission, Council and Parliament could formally agree to incorporate such an agreement into the Interinstitutional Agreement; for example, a protocol to it which applies to the specific case of 'Better social policy law-making'. Or even become signatories to the updating agreement. This could be a separate 'protocol' to the Agreement related to social policy, a 'social chapter' of the Interinstitutional Agreement. The social partners could make a joint approach to the Commission for clarification of the Agreement, based on an agreement negotiated between the social partners as to the operation of Articles 138 and 139 EC.

In the longer term, this could act as a stimulus to the social dialogue in general. Clarification of consultation and social dialogue over Commission social policy initiatives would ensure Commission-inspired social dialogues are not in competition with social partner initiatives under the autonomous social dialogue.

## Conclusion

In conclusion, the Communication of 31 March 2005 was a shocking illustration of the degree to which the Commission has devalued the social dialogue process embodied in Articles 138–9 of the Treaty. While paying lip-service to the social dialogue, at least since 2003 the Commission has been instrumental in downgrading the social dialogue process which became part of the EC Treaty at Maastricht in 1992. Its actions strike a blow at the democratic life of the Union.

## The future of the European social dialogue

The state of the evolution of EU policies on labour regulation was indicated in the Commission's Communication of 9 February 2005 on the Social Agenda

2005–10.[50] What is striking is that there is not one single proposal for *new* legislation in the labour law field.[51] If labour legislation is not on the cards up to 2010, what is?

> While respecting the autonomy of the social partners, the Commission will continue to promote the European social dialogue at cross-industry and sectoral levels, especially by strengthening its logistic and technical support and by conducting consultations on the basis of Article 138 of the EC Treaty.

The focus on social dialogue is warranted because there is only one specific proposal in the Social Agenda which the Commission explicitly commits to adopting:

> The Commission plans to adopt a proposal designed to make it possible for the social partners to formalise the nature and results of transnational collective bargaining. The existence of this resource is essential but its use will remain optional and will depend entirely on the will of the social partners.

This commitment has to be seen in the context of the social dialogue as it has developed over twenty years, and particularly in the recent past.[52]

---

[50] Communication from the Commission on the Social Agenda, COM(2005) 33 final, Brussels, 9 February 2005.

[51] Bursting with slogans, it begins: "'A social Europe in the global economy: jobs and opportunities for all", this is the motto of the second phase of the Social Agenda covering the period up to 2010 … the vision that binds us together, confirmed in the Constitution, consists of ensuring …'. In the aftermath of the debacle of the French and Dutch referenda on the Constitutional Treaty, it seems, we are back to the drawing board. The new Social Agenda is packed with initiatives: 'a Green Paper on the intergenerational dimension', 'an annual meeting of all players concerned in a forum to evaluate the implementation of the agenda', 'an interdepartmental group to promote consideration of the external dimension of employment, social policy and decent work', and so on. There was also promised 'a Green Paper on the development of labour law': 'In this Green Paper, the Commission will analyse current trends in the new work patterns and the role of labour law in tackling these developments, by providing a more secure environment encouraging efficient transitions on the labour market. The discussion that this document will produce *could* [italics added] lead to proposals for a whole range of measures to modernise and simplify the current rules.' Or not. Duly produced almost two years later, on 22 November 2006: 'Modernising labour law to meet the challenges of the 21st century'. COM(2006) 798 final, Brussels, 22 November 2006. See Chapter 20.

[52] On 14 April 2005 the European Economic and Social Committee organised a conference in Brussels on the '20th Anniversary of the European Social Dialogue', bringing together many of those who played and are playing a central role in the social dialogue, beginning with Jacques Delors, and including past and present general secretaries of ETUC, UNICE, UEAPME and CEEP, and the Commissioner V. Spidla and Director-General O. Quintin of D-G V (Social Affairs). Part of what follows is derived from the Introduction and Conclusions I presented to the opening session of this conference. Other parts are a revised version of papers presented to a workshop of the project 'Citizenship and Democratic Legitimacy in Europe' (CIDEL) organised by ARENA, the Centre for European Studies of the University of Oslo, held in Stockholm on 10–11 June 2005 and at a joint seminar of King's College London Centre of European Law and the Max Planck Centre for Public and International Law in Heidelberg on 7 July 2005.

## An overview of the impact of the European social dialogue to date

Chou-en-Lai was said to have responded, when asked about the impact of the French revolution: 'it is too early to say'. One should be equally cautious in assessing the impact of the European social dialogue. Calculating the impact of major events is always risky.

To illustrate, many could justifiably claim to be the fathers of the EU social dialogue. But there is a mother, though she would doubtless be horrified to be given the honour. It was Mrs Thatcher, Prime Minister of the UK from 1979. She halted the programme of EU social legislation which was the result of the Social Action Programme of 1974. The then Treaty requirement of unanimous voting in the Council allowed her to veto the Commission's social policy proposals. It was this inability to launch a social dimension of the Single European Market through the legislative channel which stimulated the effort to find an alternative.

In the EU Member States, there was a well-known alternative: social dialogue. In a remarkable symbiosis of EU and Member State evolution, the initiative of 1985 by Jacques Delors launched the EU social dialogue. Mrs Thatcher can thus claim to have been among those, seeking deregulation, who are responsible for creating the EU social dialogue. The irony of history is that the most determined opponent of collective social dialogue at national level in the UK was the inspiration for collective social dialogue at EU level.

So when considering the balance sheet of the social dialogue twenty years later, it is best to be cautious. It may be that the failures of the social dialogue will be as important as its successes in producing a social dimension of the EU.

### How has the European social dialogue developed?

The dynamics of the social dialogue are illustrated by an early experience of failure, which nonetheless produced a success: the European Works Councils (EWC) Directive.[53] The EU social partners came close to agreement, but failed at the last moment.[54] The failure of social dialogue over European works councils led a then dynamic Commission to propose, and the eleven Member States (excluding the UK) to adopt, the EWCs Directive in 1994.

The catalyst for the European social dialogue which eventually led to the EWCs Directive was the Hoover affair of January 1993, the closure of a factory

---

[53] Council Directive 94/45/EC of 22 September 1994 on the establishment of a European Works Council or a procedure in Community-scale undertakings and Community-scale groups of undertakings for the purposes of informing and consulting employees. OJ L254/64 of 30 September 1994.

[54] The reasons for failure are disputed, though some point to the role of the British employers' organisation, the CBI. This reflected the odd position that, while the UK as a Member State had opted out of the Social Protocol, the UK social partners continued to participate in the social dialogue.

in Dijon and its transfer to the UK.[55] Similarly, the Renault affair, the closure of a factory employing some 3,000 workers in Vilvoorde, Belgium, in February 1997 led to a fresh Commission initiative on information and consultation of workers' representatives, following the refusal of the European employers' organisations to engage in social dialogue at all.[56] The eventual Framework Directive 2002/14 on information and consultation only emerged in March 2002 after long and painful negotiations among the institutions.[57]

This experience reveals two dynamics at work. First, in the short term, events can have a catalytic effect.[58] Secondly, the impact of catalysing events is subordinate to another, longer-term dynamic: 'bargaining in the shadow of the law'.

It has become clear that the willingness of the social partners to engage in social dialogue is dependent on the political balance of power in the EU institutions. If the Commission takes initiatives, if the Member States mobilise in Council and if Parliament is supportive, the social partners are confronted with the likelihood of regulation. A logical calculus of self-interest points to incentives to self-regulate via social dialogue.

This explains the 31 October 1991 agreement which led to the Maastricht Protocol and is now in Articles 138–9 EC.[59] Then, employers and unions at EU level, faced with the Dutch Presidency's draft of the Maastricht Treaty proposing expansion of social and labour competences exercised through qualified majority, agreed on the alternative of labour regulation through social dialogue.

But this dynamic is fragile. It is contingent on the political balance of power in the EU institutions. If the Commission does not push for social policy initiatives, if there are blocking minorities of Member States in the Council of Ministers, if the Parliament is not supportive, then the likelihood of legislative regulation recedes. In these circumstances, employers, in particular, are unlikely voluntarily to look to alternative forms of regulation, unless they can be offered incentives.

This is the major difference between European social dialogue and social dialogue in the Member States. Unlike trade unions in the Member States, the European Trade Union Confederation (ETUC) lacks the power to force employers to come to the bargaining table. This has become ever more evident. Employers will not agree to social dialogue, or, if they do, only on marginal

---

[55] 'The Hoover Affair and Social Dumping', *European Industrial Relations Review*, No. 230, March 1993, pp. 14–20.

[56] Marie-Ange Moreau, 'A propos de l'affaire Renault ...', (1997) *Droit Social*, No. 5, pp. 493–509. 'The Repercussions of the Vilvoorde Closure', *European Industrial Relations Review* No. 289, February 1998, pp. 22–5.

[57] Council Directive No. 2002/14 establishing a framework for informing and consulting employees in the European Community. OJ 2002 L80/29.

[58] However, this may not be the optimal dynamic of social dialogue, waiting on the next catalysing events.

[59] J.E. Dolvik, *An Emerging Island? ETUC, Social Dialogue and the Europeanisation of the Trade Unions in the 1990s*, Brussels: ETUI, 1999.

issues, and then only if the results do not take the form of binding obligations. They provide many justifications: the need to maintain competitiveness, flexibility, deregulation ... But the outcome is the impoverishment or worse of European social dialogue.

So the fundamental problem remains: how to engage employers in social dialogue. To address this problem, one should look at the achievements of the social dialogue to date, in order to understand its limitations.

## Characteristics of the main agreements achieved

These are well known: at intersectoral level, binding agreements on parental leave,[60] part-time work[61] and fixed term work,[62] 'voluntary' agreements on telework (2002) and work-related stress (2004) and harassment and violence at work (2007). But specific features of these achievements may be identified as significant.

First, the binding agreements tend to be linked to the European Employment Strategy: this is explicit in the Preambles of the Framework Agreements on part-time work and fixed-term work.[63] The question is whether the social dialogue agenda should be so limited to the EU's labour market agenda.

Secondly, there is a worrying link of the agreements to a dominant principle: non-discrimination. This characterises the agreements on both part-time and fixed-term workers, which proclaims the principle of non-discrimination as regards these categories of workers.[64] EU labour law, unlike *national* systems of

---

[60] Council Directive 96/34/EC of 3 June 1996 on the Framework Agreement on parental leave concluded by UNICE, CEEP and the ETUC. OJ L145/4 of 19 June 1996.

[61] Council Directive 97/81/EC of 15 December 1997 concerning the Framework Agreement on part-time work concluded by UNICE, CEEP and the ETUC. OJ L14/9 of 20 January 1998.

[62] Council Directive 1999/70/EC of 28 June 1999 concerning the Framework Agreement on fixed-term work concluded by ETUC, UNICE and CEEP. OJ L175/43 of 10 July 1999.

[63] There is divergence in the policies reflected in these agreements: part-time work is to be facilitated; fixed-term work is to be the exception, requiring justification. It may be asked: why this divergence? Does the agreement reflect a genuine trade-off between flexibility and security of employment? Or does it reflect a changing balance of power, evident in the subsequent failure to achieve a similar agreement on temporary agency work? Or was the weight of the gender factor in part-time work determining?

[64] Discrimination law has vastly expanded, at national level and in EC law. Apart from sex discrimination there are at least thirteen other grounds on which discrimination is prohibited (Directives (5): racial or ethnic origin, religion or belief, disability, age, sexual orientation; Council Directive 2000/43 of 29 June 2000 implementing the principle of equal treatment between persons irrespective of racial or ethnic origin, OJ 2000, L180/22; Council Directive 2000/78 of 27 November 2000 establishing a general framework for equal treatment in employment and occupation, OJ 2000, L303/16; EU Charter of Fundamental Rights (8): colour, social origin, genetic features, language, political or any other opinion, membership of a national minority, property and birth. The EU Charter of Fundamental Rights includes in Article 21(1) a general prohibition of 'any discrimination based on any ground such as sex, race, colour, ethnic or social origin, genetic features, language, religion or belief, political or any other opinion, membership of a national minority, property, birth, disability, age or sexual orientation'. Adding to this the established prohibition of discrimination on grounds of nationality and now the social dialogue directives' prohibition of discrimination against part-time and fixed-term workers, the total number of prohibited grounds comes to seventeen.

labour law and employment protection in Europe, still dominated by collective bargaining and employment protection legislation, risks being overwhelmed by ever more elaborate regulation of discrimination and its justifications. The risk is of social dialogue being distorted by the *acquis communautaire* on discrimination.

Thirdly, there is the critical difference between those outcomes of the social dialogue which have binding legal effects, the three framework agreements embodied in directives, and the other outcomes with uncertain legal effects. This raises the general question of implementation of the outcomes of the social dialogue.

### How were agreements implemented?

Article 139(2) EC provides two alternatives for implementation of the results of social dialogue:

> either in accordance with the procedures and practices specific to management and labour and the Member States or ... at the joint request of the signatory parties, by a Council decision on a proposal from the Commission.

The latter have in the past taken the form of legally binding directives. The former alternative of procedures and practices, however, is unclear as to its legally binding effect. This was highlighted in the differing views taken by the parties to the binding effect of the agreements on telework and on work-related stress, which were not transformed into directives.

The problem is twofold: not only are there fewer agreements, as most results of social dialogue take other forms: frameworks of action, orientations, joint opinion, guidelines, etc., but implementation of the latter, given their non-binding character, is judged ineffective.[65] On the question of the perceived lack of effectiveness, the Commission recommended that the social partners apply the methods of the open method of coordination: 'establishing goals or guidelines at European level, through regular national implementation reports and regular, systematic assessment of progress achieved'.[66]

---

[65] This is the considered opinion of the European Commission itself. In its Communication of 26 June 2002 on the role of social dialogue in European labour law, entitled 'The European social dialogue, a force for innovation and change' (COM(2002) 341 final, 26 June 2002), the Commission noted, under the heading 'Improving monitoring and implementation', that 'The European social partners have adopted joint opinions, statements and declarations on numerous occasions. More than 230 such joint sectoral texts have been issued and some 40 cross-industry texts ... However, in most cases, these texts did not include any provision for implementation and monitoring: they were responses to short-term concerns. They are not well known and their dissemination at national level has been limited. Their effectiveness can thus be called into question.'

[66] *Ibid.*, Section 2.4.1, p. 18. The inspiration of the open method of coordination is apparent. The OMC has been often criticised as to its effectiveness when implemented by Member States' administrations in the field of employment policy. Is it appropriate for the Work Programme of the Social Partners on Employment? If joint opinions and other non-regulatory instruments continue to be ineffective, their failure may imply other, more rigorous steps towards effectiveness may be necessary, including regulatory agreements and/or legislation.

The Commission's Communication on the social dialogue of August 2004, entitled 'Partnership for change in an enlarged Europe – Enhancing the contribution of European social dialogue', does not reveal any new dynamism.[67] Although 'the enlargement of the EU also presents a challenge for the European social dialogue', little is presented by way of a strategy to meet this challenge. Rather, with respect to all Member States, new and old, *laissez-faire* is the Commission's position on social dialogue.

The admission of a fatal lack of impact of the results of the social dialogue attributable to failures in the process of their implementation is only belatedly acknowledged and, even then, the tactics proposed are mishandled.[68] The only substantive initiative comes in the final section 4.5 of the Communication: 'Preparing further developments', where the Commission admits 'a need for a framework to help improve the consistency of the social dialogue outcomes and to improve transparency'. Confirming its passivity, the 'Commission's preferred approach would be for the social partners to negotiate their own framework'.[69]

## Options and outlook for the future of the social dialogue

### Some less obvious elements of a framework for European social dialogue

The temptation to proceed to 'formalise the nature and results' of the European social dialogue needs to take account of certain less obvious but equally critical exigencies.

First, the resources of the social partners are an important constraint. The social partners simply are not equipped to carry out social dialogues on more than one or two issues each year. Yet they are expected to contribute massively to development of the EU's social dimension.

Second, there are many important strategic and tactical lessons to be learned from the practical experience of previous social dialogues. Some of these were explored in an earlier chapter analysing the experience of the social dialogue on fixed-term work. This analysis identified important issues concerning not only the interactions between the EU social partners, but also the engagement of sectoral federations, and of representatives of the EU social partners' affiliates in the Member States. The relationship of the EU social partners and their

---

[67]    COM(2004) 557 final, Brussels, 12 August 2004.

[68]    *Better Lawmaking*, Section 4.4, 'Autonomous agreements', and see the critique in Chapter 17.

[69]    However, the Commission signals an interest in transnational collective bargaining, which appeared to be concretised in the new Social Agenda of 9 February 2005: 'The Commission plans to adopt a proposal designed to make it possible for the social partners *to formalise the nature and results of transnational collective bargaining*. The existence of this resource is essential but its use will remain optional and will depend entirely on the will of the social partners.' *Communication from the Commission on the Social Agenda*, COM(2005) 33 final, Brussels, 9 February 2005, Section 2: 'The Two Priority Areas'. Italics added. As noted in a previous chapter, however, the augurs for progress on this modest agenda are not good.

national affiliates affects the decisions to undertake the social dialogue on a particular subject, to define the negotiating mandate, to decide whether to approve the agreement reached and to resolve disputes over interpretation of the agreement.

Third, and more challenging, attention must be paid to the internal institutional dynamics of the social partners, UNICE (BusinessEurope) in particular. Experience has demonstrated the importance of the social partners' internal constitutional procedures. These can frustrate progress. For example, the ETUC adopted majority voting to prevent individual national affiliates imposing a veto on entering into social dialogue or adopting agreements reached. UNICE, however, has not.

More critical than any of these, however, is to acknowledge that the European social dialogue does not exist in a decision-making vacuum. The EU institutions continue to develop their law- and policy-making processes, and these interact with the law- and policy-making role of the social partners in the social dialogue.[70]

There is an unmistakable gap between the practice and the rhetoric of the Commission. The initial proposals for revision of the Working Time Directive in December 2003 and the proposals on restructuring and revision of the European Works Councils Directive in March 2005 seem to indicate that the Commission is sidelining a formal role for the EU social dialogue. In contrast to this practice, at a rhetorical level the Commission reiterates its commitment to the EU social dialogue.[71]

The present Commission's commitment to the social dialogue is questionable. As the political and economic conjuncture changes, there will be others to come. Their efforts will be assessed by how they deal with the fundamental problem of European social dialogue: how to engage employers and their European organisations.

## Options and outlook

What are the options and what is the outlook? Three options may be proposed, and their prospects assessed.

---

[70] Hence the discussion above of the potentially dangerous development in the form of the Interinstitutional Agreement on Better Lawmaking.

[71] As reflected in its 2004 Communication on the role of the social dialogue: 'The evolution of the social dialogue is consistent with the Commission's more general efforts to improve European governance. The social dialogue is indeed a pioneering example of improved consultation and the application of subsidiarity in practice and is widely recognised as making an essential contribution to better governance, as a result of the proximity of the social partners to the realities of the workplace. Indeed, the social partners are different in nature from other organisations, like pressure or interest groups, because of their ability to take part in collective bargaining.' *Partnership for Change in an Enlarged Europe – Enhancing the Contribution of European Social Dialogue*, Communication from the Commission, COM(2004) 557 final, Brussels, 12 August 2004, Section 3.1, page 6.

First, is a revival of the political dynamic feasible? If the EU institutions (Commission, Council, Parliament) combine to promote social initiatives aiming at legislative regulation, the social dialogue could take off again. The longer-term prospects are not predictable, but the political climate in the short and medium term makes this seem unlikely.

Second, can the ETUC achieve some measure of the power to force employers to the table? Again, this seems unlikely, perhaps not even in the longer term. However, catalytic events may allow for the mobilisation of political and perhaps even industrial power resources.

Third, will employers perceive advantages in engaging in social dialogue? Can they perceive the gains to be made in achieving flexibility through acceptance of new types of employment (fixed-term work, agency work), avoiding costly conflict over restructuring or even delocalisation, reaching consensus over corporate governance systems, or the financing of pension systems in crisis? It is not clear that European employers' organisations are able or willing to acknowledge these potential advantages, and, even less so, to carry their national affiliates with them.

### Longer-term stimuli

There are a number of longer-term stimuli to employers to engage in European social dialogue. Involvement in macro-economic policy could require employers to engage. ETUC attempts at transnational coordination of collective bargaining, if successful, could provide valuable support to coordination of Member States' economic policy and the monetary policy of the European Central Bank. Member States' and EU institutions' support for the ETUC's coordination efforts could persuade employers to engage in social dialogue at EU level, so as not to be left out. The Tripartite Social Summit for Growth and Employment established in 2002 offers a forum, but the task is formidable.

Again, major political failure could have catalytic effects. The debacle of the proposed Constitutional Treaty and the uncertain prospects for its successor could have dramatic consequences for EU political integration, let alone further enlargement. This could be accompanied by negative consequences for economic integration, even imperilling the future of the euro. Salvaging the political and economic momentum of European integration could require mobilising major actors in support, bringing pressure on employers to cooperate.

Other dynamic factors could impact on the evolution of the European social dialogue. Sectoral social dialogue is a potential element as yet to prove itself. The Commission's Communication of 2004 on the social dialogue raised the prospect of combining the sectoral social dialogue with European works councils in specific sectors.

Yet at the moment, there is great dissatisfaction from the side of the trade unions due to the minimal stimulus for social dialogue in the EU's latest Social Agenda of 9 February 2005. Prospective outcomes in the form of 'frameworks for action', 'joint opinions', 'declarations', etc. are insufficient. What is needed are binding undertakings by the social partners. Social partners' affiliates are not interested if whatever is done at EU level can be ignored. EU institutions will pay little attention to a social dialogue which cannot deliver what it promises.[72]

Social dialogue is one element in an emerging institutional architecture of a European social model. An essential element distinguishing the European social model from that of the USA is the engagement of the social partners in macro-level social dialogue, collective bargaining at sectoral and enterprise level, and participation at the level of the workplace. The initiative to create the EU social dialogue was of historic importance.

In historical perspective, the EU social dialogue owes its existence to the UK government's blocking legislation on the social dimension of the EU, leaving the path open to the alternative of the social dialogue. The UK did not succeed in blocking the revolutionary introduction of social dialogue as a mechanism for making EU social policy and law in the Maastricht Treaty. The new social dialogue mechanism produced the first social dialogue agreements. But since the three binding framework agreements were negotiated at intersectoral level between 1996 and 1999, the social dialogue has been in decline.

### What is to be done?

Specifically, three areas need desperately to be addressed if the European social dialogue is to develop and fulfil its potential.

First, there is a desperate need for bold initiatives which can stimulate the social partners to engage in social dialogue: to mobilise the dynamic of 'bargaining in the shadow of the law'.

Second, there is a desperate need for improving the capabilities of the social partners to undertake an effective social dialogue; both logistic and technical support[73] and their internal constitutional structures. Both will increase the potential of reaching agreements.

Third, there is a desperate need for action which will make effective in practice the results of the EU social dialogue, whatever form they take, but in particular, of agreements concluded.

### Conclusion

The Commission is responsible for ensuring respect for Treaty provisions. What the history and development of the social dialogue shows is that a dynamic, intelligent and subtle Commission, and social partners, led by

---

[72] Yet there is much which could be put on a social dialogue agenda. The ETUC has identified four areas of critical importance for the social dialogue agenda: (i) low growth, (ii) high unemployment, (iii) demographic change and (iv) restructuring. UNICE has yet to regard this agenda as one where binding undertakings can be entered into.

[73] To quote from the Commission's new Social Agenda, *Communication from the Commission on the Social Agenda*, COM(2005) 33 final, Brussels, 9 February 2005, page 8.

historically sensitive leaders, can achieve great things. Future generations will judge harshly those who allow the historic achievement of an EU social dialogue to wither and die.

The proposed Treaty Establishing a Constitution for Europe retained the legal framework for EU social dialogue, and, arguably, even strengthened it by providing for fundamental rights of association at all levels, collective bargaining at appropriate levels and collective action, including strike action. It remains to be seen whether the latter elements, which survive in the EU Charter of Fundamental Rights, become an active instrument for future developments in the EU's policies on labour regulation, or only a passive memorial to the achievements of the past.

**Section III**

# The futures of European labour law

**Part VI**

# Agendas and visions of European labour law

# Chapter 20

# The futures of European labour law: (1) the Commission's agenda – 'modernisation'

## Introduction: the futures of European labour law

The future of European labour law is part of the unfolding dynamic of European integration in which the political, economic and social context is critical. In particular, the institutional balance among the EU institutions and the Member States, an\d between them, is crucial. In this, European labour law is not so different from domestic labour laws, also contingent on national political, economic and social contexts and state and societal structures. But, as has been emphasised throughout this book, it is important to see EU law, and in particular European labour law, as not exclusively the province of states and EU institutions. Sub-national and supranational actors also play a role and the EU institutions and the Member States are all subject to the pressures of interest groups, not least trade unions and employers' organisations.

This is also the case of the European Court of Justice, where litigation strategy plays a role in determining which issues come to the fore. The consequences of litigation may also affect the future of European labour law. In two cases decided by the European Court of Justice at the end of 2007 – the *Viking* case, referred by the English Court of Appeal[1] and the *Laval* case, referred by the Swedish Labour Court[2] – the issue raised was whether EU law includes a fundamental right to take collective action, including strike action, as declared in Article 28 of the EU Charter of Fundamental Rights. The decision of the Court as to the fundamental right of workers and trade unions to take transnational collective action may have a catalytic effect on the future of European labour law.[3]

The evolution of European labour law impresses with the sheer variety of strategies adopted over the past half century. Its historical development confirms that the future of European labour law is unpredictable. Nonetheless, in concluding this book, the possible futures of European labour law will be outlined, looking to the contributions of different institutional actors.

---

[1] Case C-438/05, *International Transport Workers' Federation, Finnish Seamen's Union* v. *Viking Line ABP, OÜ Viking Line Eesti*, decided 11 December 2007.

[2] Case C-341/05, *Laval un Partneri Ltd* v. *Svenska Byggnadsarbetareförbundet, Svenska Byggnadsarbetareförbundet, avd. 1, Svenska Elektrikerförbundet*, decided 18 December 2007.

[3] See B. Bercusson, 'The Trade Union Movement and the European Union: Judgment Day', (2007) 13 *European Law Journal* (No. 3, May) 279–308.

First, a Green Paper, 'Modernising labour law to meet the challenges of the 21st century', launched by the present Commission, in November 2006, offers a radically different vision of the future of European labour law, one which downplays a collective framework engaging trade unions and rather adopts a neo-liberal programme of emphasis on structural 'reform' of labour markets to increase flexibility and enhance employment for unemployed labour market 'outsiders' at the expense of employed 'insiders'.

Second, this book has repeatedly highlighted the transformative potential of European Court decisions in shaping the evolution of European labour law. The Court's judgments in *Viking* and *Laval* highlight the potential consequences of judicial intervention in the future development of European labour law.[4] A vision of the future of European labour law will be offered looking to a concept of *ordre communautaire social*.[5]

Finally, the careful preparation by the EU Member States and the European Parliament of a constitutional framework in the form of the proposed Constitutional Treaty of 2004, incorporating an EU Charter with fundamental rights of labour, was derailed by the French and Dutch referenda of 2005. Subsequent attempts to recover something from the crash seem likely to produce a 'constitutional' outcome, if only in the shape of a 'Reform Treaty' agreed at the summit under the German Presidency of June 2007 and confirmed under the Portuguese Presidency at Lisbon in December 2007. The core of any such outcome includes the essential 'constitutional' element of the fundamental rights of labour in the EU Charter, which this book has argued are central to the future of European labour law. So one scenario looks to a 'constitutional' future for European labour law.[6]

## The Commission's agenda: 'modernisation'

A Green Paper,[7] 'Modernising labour law to meet the challenges of the 21st century',[8] launched by the Barroso Commission[9] in November 2006, offers a radical departure from traditional labour law. This chapter offers a framework for analysing the Barroso Commission's Green Paper, based on the historical context in which the Green Paper emerged, and a critical perspective[10] on the Green Paper which offers the prospect of future developments.

---

[4] See Chapter 21.    [5] A derivative of *ordre public communautaire*.    [6] See Chapter 22.

[7] This section draws substantially from the briefing prepared by the author for the Hearings of the Committee on Employment and Social Affairs of the European Parliament on the Commission's Green Paper, 21 March 2007.

[8] COM(2006) 798 final, Brussels, 22 November 2006.

[9] The Commission headed by President Barroso was appointed in 2004. The appointment lapses in 2009.

[10] Perhaps not as critical as some others; see the commentary in *Revue de Droit du Travail*, February 2007, pp. 72ff., including characterisation of its English style as 'Globish' and 'Oxymore' and its methodology as 'Une argumentation autoréférentielle' and 'L'histoire racontée aux enfants', Francois Gaudu, 'Un document qui ne tient pas le language de la verité', at p. 75.

### Historical context

The achievement of the Barroso Commission in the area of labour law has been virtually nil, and that of the preceding years of the twenty-first century was extremely modest.[11] The poverty of its ambition was evident in its Communication of 9 February 2005 on the Social Agenda 2006–10.[12] This included only one specific proposal which the Barroso Commission explicitly committed itself to adopting: on transnational collective bargaining.[13] The absence of achievement and lack of ambition are evident when compared with the European Commission's activity in the last decade of the twentieth century. This saw the vast expansion of the EU's labour law and employment policy competences by the Treaties of Maastricht (1991) and Amsterdam (1997). In that ten-year period, the Commission's initiatives produced Directives on health and safety for temporary and agency workers (1991), mandatory information on employment conditions for employees (1991), protection of pregnant and breastfeeding mothers (1992), working time (1993), European Works Councils (1994), parental leave (1996), part-time work (1997), the burden of proof in cases of sex discrimination (1997), fixed-term work (1999) and substantive amendments to the Directives on collective dismissals (1992) and transfers of undertakings (1998).

The achievement of the Maastricht Treaty of 1991 was to establish the EU social partners and the European social dialogue as constitutional elements in the making of European social and labour law and policy. After a fruitful initial

---

[11]  The last significant achievement was over five years ago, in March 2002 (Council Directive No. 2002/14 establishing a framework for informing and consulting employees in the European Community. OJ 2002 L80/29). Previous developments were directives on discrimination Directive 2000/78 of 27 November 2000 establishing a general framework for equal treatment in employment and occupation (OJ 2000 L303/16) aiming at 'combating discrimination on the ground of religion or belief, disability, age or sexual orientation as regards employment and occupation' (Article 1); Council Directive 2000/43 of 29 June 2000 implementing the principle of equal treatment between persons irrespective of racial or ethnic origin (OJ 2000 L180/22); Council Directive 2002/73/EC (OJ 2002 L269/15) amended Council Directive 76/207/EEC of 9 February 1976 on the implementation of the principle of equal treatment for men and women as regards access to employment, vocational training and promotion, and working conditions (OJ 1976 L39/40). There was also consolidation of directives, such as on working time (Directive 2003/88/EC of 4 November 2003 concerning certain aspects of the organisation of working time; OJ L299/9 of 18 November 2003 consolidated Council Directive 93/104/EC of 23 November 1993, OJ L307/18 of 13 December 1993, as amended by Directive 2000/34 of 22 June 2000, OJ L195/41).

[12]  Communication from the Commission on the Social Agenda, COM(2005) 33 final, Brussels, 9 February 2005.

[13]  'The Commission plans to adopt a proposal designed to make it possible for the social partners to formalise the nature and results of transnational collective bargaining. The existence of this resource is essential but its use will remain optional and will depend entirely on the will of the social partners.' And even this has been abandoned: in a conference organised by the Commission on 27 November 2006, the survey of transnational collective agreements conducted by D-G V was marginalised and the expert study proposing a directive was brusquely buried. Instead it was announced that no regulatory initiative was in prospect and the Commission planned at most another Communication in 2007.

period, however, the dynamic of the social dialogue has ceased to function. This is not least due to the resistance of European employers' organisations. But it is also due to the institutional passivity of the Commission in confronting the many problems facing workers and employers in the operation of the labour market.

It is surprising, therefore, and perhaps suspicious, when the Barroso Commission appears to have rediscovered ambition in a Green Paper entitled 'Modernising labour law to meet the challenges of the 21st century'. In light of its record, it seems highly unlikely that this Commission has any intention of regulating labour markets. To the contrary, its record suggests, if anything, that 'deregulation' is the driving force behind the 'modernising' initiative of the Barroso Commission.[14] The Green Paper projects a vision which seeks to transform the nature of labour law itself 'to meet the challenges of the 21st century'. The critical perspective offered here focuses on (I) the 'modernised' vision of labour law, (II) the role of collective labour law and (III) the role of EU labour law.

## I. The 'modernised' vision of labour law

The Green Paper begins Section 2: 'Labour Law in the EU – The Situation Today', under heading (a) 'Developments in the Member States', with the following statement:[15]

> The *original* purpose of labour law was to offset the inherent economic and social inequality within the *employment relationship*.

This is the generally accepted view. It continues:[16]

> From its origins labour law has been concerned to establish employment status as the main factor around which entitlements would be developed. *This traditional model reflects several key assumptions about employment status.*

So far, relatively uncontroversial. It then rehearses a number of factors which are asserted to 'have shown the need for increased flexibility' and to 'have

---

[14] This can be seen by comparing the Green Paper with an earlier draft of September 2006 (Communication from the Commission, Green Paper, 'Adapting labour law to ensure flexibility and security for all' (n.d.)). The draft was entitled 'Adapting labour law to ensure flexibility and security for all'. The title of the final Green Paper is 'Modernising labour law to meet the challenges of the 21st century'. The draft version echoed the Commission's focus on employment policy, one of the mantras of which had been balancing flexibility and security (given the branding spin of 'flexicurity'). Even this was too much for UNICE, however, which launched a ferocious attack on the draft, which led the General Secretary of the ETUC, John Monks, to write to Barroso on 12 October 2006 urging him not to draw back from the modest ambition of the Green Paper. In the final Green Paper, much of the content is similar to the earlier draft, though there are important changes. But the Barroso Commission does appear to have lifted its sights from labour market reforms of balancing flexibility and security to the modernising of labour law as a whole.

[15] Italics added.     [16] Italics added.

created a demand for a wider variety of employment contracts'. There follows the conclusion:[17]

> The *traditional model* of the employment relationship may *not prove well-suited* to all workers on regular permanent employment contracts facing the challenge of adapting to change … *Overly protective* terms and conditions can deter employers from hiring during economic upturns … Since the early 1990s, reform of national employment protection has focused on easing existing regulation to facilitate more contractual diversity. *Reforms* tended to increase flexibility 'on the margins', i.e. introducing *more flexible forms of employment with lesser protection against dismissal to promote the entry of newcomers* and disadvantaged job-seekers to the labour market.

In sum: the original purpose (to offset inequality between employer and employee) and traditional model (a secure employment status protected against dismissal) of labour law is no longer appropriate: it operates to the detriment of newcomers and jobseekers.

This is a breathtaking transformation. The *inequality and conflict* which labour law is to address is *no longer between employer and employee*. Rather, the new conflict is between workers with secure employment status and job-seekers. The 'modernised' purpose and model of labour law is to address this *conflict between workers*.[18] EU labour law is to intervene through legislative and political actions in the conflict between workers ('insiders') and the unemployed and 'atypical' workers ('outsiders') by promoting flexibility. Employers become neutral observers of this conflict.[19]

This modernised vision of labour law is the setting for the questions posed by the Green Paper. The answers indicated by the Commission's vision include

---

[17] Italics added.

[18] The opening paragraphs of the Introduction (section 1) of the Green Paper, seize upon an observation in the Kok Report, familiar in many other writings, that 'a two-tier labour market might emerge divided between permanently employed "insiders" and "outsiders", including those unemployed and detached from the labour market, as well as those precariously and informally employed'. From this it follows in the next section 2(b) on 'Action at the EU level' that the EU is to undertake 'a range of legislative and political actions … in the interest of establishing how new more flexible forms of work might be combined with minimum social rights for all workers.'

[19] The *draft* Green Paper's title was 'Adapting labour law to ensure flexibility and security', the familiar mantra. The reference to security has disappeared in the title of the final Green Paper. The mantra reappears at the opening paragraphs of the Green Paper and as 'flexicurity' at regular intervals thereafter. But the context is fundamentally different. The balance labour law seeks is no longer between flexibility for employers and security for workers. It is a balance between (increased) flexibility to promote outsiders' access to the labour market and (reduced) security for insiders (permanent workers). *'Modernised' labour law is to regulate a new balance: not unequal power between employers and workers, but between security (of employees) and inclusion (of the unemployed)*. Divide and rule … This is highlighted in the title of Section 3 'The key policy challenge – a flexible and *inclusive* labour market.' Statements in support abound in this section: 'the level of flexibility provided under standard contracts may need to be examined to enhance their capacity to facilitate recruitment, retention and the scope for progression within the labour market'; 'findings that stringent employment protection legislation tends to reduce the dynamism of the labour market, worsening the prospects of women, youths and older workers.'

that the 'priorities for meaningful labour law reform agenda' are to rebalance the conflict between insiders and outsiders in the labour market.

One of the Member States frequently cited as most successful in achieving flexible labour markets combined with a high level of social security for the unemployed and short transition periods between jobs is Denmark.[20] However, the Danish model (like that of Sweden and Finland) is also characterised by high trade union membership and the active engagement of trade unions in managing unemployment insurance.[21] EU labour law has encouraged trade union membership by promoting the role of collective representation in a number of directives. In light of declining trade union membership[22] and failures of these directives to secure collective representation, EU labour law needs to provide more effective protection for the fundamental rights of association, collective bargaining and collective action. EU labour law promoting trade unions could achieve better results in the form of flexible labour markets. In particular, it could influence Member States towards the engagement of trade unions in managing active labour market policies, including short transition periods between jobs.

'Modernising labour law' through EU intervention is possible, according to the Commission, only through promoting the emulation of active labour market policies. The Commission's Green Paper advocates 'more flexible employment protection' (which the EU has competence to regulate), to be eased through assistance to the unemployed (on which the EU lacks competence).[23] Measures to increase the security of workers while adapting to the need for flexibility of both employers and workers is to draw on experience in the EU. This is ostensibly the function of the European Employment Strategy implemented through the 'open method of coordination'. Yet its success is disputable.[24]

---

[20] However, the Danish model is characterised by relatively high expenditure on social security and active labour market policy as a proportion of GDP (3–5 per cent). This presents problems of a budgetary nature for Member States where expenditure is much lower. It poses particular difficulties for EU intervention, as social security is a jealously guarded Member State competence.

[21] 'Unemployment Insurance and Trade Union Membership', *European Industrial Relations Review* No. 392, September 2006, pp. 20–4.

[22] For the example of the UK, see B. Kersley, C. Alpin, J. Forth, A. Bryson, H. Bewley, G. Dix and S. Oxenbridge, *Inside the Workplace: First Findings from the 2004 Workplace Employment Relations Survey*, Department of Trade and Industry, 2005, pp. 35–6: 'Most striking of all, perhaps, was the continued decline of collective labour organisation. Employees were less likely to be union members than they were in 1998; workplaces were less likely to recognise unions for bargaining over pay and conditions; and collective bargaining was less prevalent'.

[23] Yet, in contrast to the Green Paper, flexible labour markets are not achieved by reducing job security (employment protection legislation). Rather, they are associated with high social security for the unemployed in systems characterised by high trade union membership. Modernisation of labour law could reinforce trade union membership and trade union engagement in unemployment insurance systems with a view to promoting flexible labour markets.

[24] See Chapter 6. There is an extensive literature on the operation of the European Employment Strategy and national labour market policies. In particular, the publications of the European

In November 2006 the European Commission published the 'Employment in Europe' report, a comprehensive and detailed analysis of labour market and employment policies in EU Member States covering five main topics on the employment situation in Member States: flexicurity, active labour market policies, human capital, technology and growth, and geographical mobility.[25] The Commission's Report, under the heading 'Flexibility and security in EU labour markets', refers to four key elements: (a) sufficiently flexible contractual arrangements; (b) effective active labour market policies; (c) credible lifelong learning systems; (d) modern social security systems.

The Report points to two different methods of evaluating the effectiveness of active labour market policies (ALMP), using either micro- or macro-econometric techniques. Most evaluations use *micro*-techniques, but the Report states that *macro*-techniques are preferable as capable of measuring indirect and long-run effects indicating *quite different policy conclusions* from those indicated by micro-techniques, and even reversing them.

For example, micro-studies are said to find that training has only modest impact on employment rates, compared with spending on employment incentives and public employment services. Job-search assistance and activation policies rank highly in helping the unemployed to find jobs, whereas direct job creation in the public sector shows even poorer outcomes than training programmes. Conversely, however, macro-econometric studies usually find that training is the only category of ALMP that seems to have a significant positive impact on labour market outcomes. By extending the post-participation effects of training, which may have a negative or only a slight positive effect during the first year or two, after that initial period, a growing number of studies have found evidence of a positive impact attributable to training. In sum, a key element in assessing the impact of ALMP may be whether a relatively short- or long-term impact is the objective.

The Green Paper proposes that EU labour law be 'modernised'. Its perspective is short-term, simplistic and narrowly focused on labour market policy. Unfortunately, it chooses labour law as its target. Its hasty conclusion is that unlike labour law in the Member States, EU labour law should depart from the original purpose and traditional model of employment.[26]

The original purpose and traditional model of labour law remain valid and should be reinforced, not dismantled.[27] Labour law and collective agreements

---

Employment Observatory (EEO). For example, the EEO's Autumn Review 2006 which reports on national actions on 'flexicurity', and its earlier Spring Review 2006 reviewing innovative labour market practices and policies across twenty-nine European countries. These are available on www.eu-employment-observatory.net.

[25] The report is available at ec.europa.eu/employment_social/employment_analysis/employ_2006_en.htm.

[26] The Commission nowhere embraces the longer-term implications of this for social protection and social security reflected in its reports on employment in Europe.

[27] Contrast other new thinking about labour law which, though critical, does not abandon the traditional role of labour law. See Nicola Countouris, review of G. Davidov and B. Langille (eds.),

should continue to support the original purpose and reinforce the traditional model. Nor is this a purely normative position. The economic and legal arguments for EU intervention are well known ('social policy as a productive factor'), if insufficiently acknowledged, or only rhetorically by the Barroso Commission. The EU should intervene to secure efficient functioning of the single European market, which depends on protection of employment security, decent labour standards and the active participation of workers through their collective organisations to ensure their interests are taken account of in economic decision-making at all levels.

## II. The role of collective labour law

The Green Paper proposes the challenge of 'modernising' labour law. The Commission states that it seeks:[28]

> To identify key challenges which have not yet yielded an adequate response and which reflect a clear deficit between the existing legal and contractual framework, on one hand, and the realities of the world of work on the other. *The focus is mainly on the personal scope of labour law rather than on issues of collective labour law.*

This is not a minor lapse. It speaks volumes that the Barroso Commission can consider embarking on a project to 'modernise labour law' with a focus on the personal scope of labour law affecting individual employment rather than on collective labour law.[29] It is nothing less than an attempt to transform (collective) *labour* law into (individual) *employment* law.

There are continual references to collective agreements throughout the Green Paper. But all are in the spirit of the question posed by the Commission's Green Paper: 'Can the adaptation of labour law *and collective agreements* contribute to improved flexibility and employment security and a reduction in labour market segmentation? If yes, then how?'[30] In other words, what role might collective

*Boundaries and Frontiers of Labour Law*, Oxford: Hart, 2006, in (2007) 36 *Industrial Law Journal* (June) 250–4 at p. 254: 'All contributors suggest, explicitly or implicitly, that the traditional "imbalance of power" rationale has to be assisted by new and more universalistic justifications – be they framed in terms of human freedom, market failures, "floor of rights" or equal treatment – capable of extending the benefits deriving from the application of labour law beyond employment and to the newly emerging personal work relationships.'

[28] In the first of four indents at the end of the first section ('Introduction – The purpose of this Green Paper'. Italics added).

[29] Jeremy Waddington speaks of 'the emergent contradiction in which unionists at European level support the principles of European integration based on some form of the European social model whereas in member states trade unionists mobilise against economic and welfare reforms introduced within the framework of EU economic strategies … Furthermore, it seems likely that this contradiction will become more visible if EC President Barroso continues to prioritise competitiveness within a neoliberal policy framework in preference to issues of social policy and employment growth': 'Trade Unions and the Defence of the European Social Model', (2005) 36 *Industrial Relations Journal* 518–40 at pp. 535–6.

[30] Question 2. Italics added.

agreements negotiated between the social partners play in promoting the flexible individual employment agenda?

It is not the adaptation of collective agreements, but their *promotion* which can contribute. The adaptation of labour law required is to promote collective agreements. The success of the Nordic model is built on this foundation. The adaptation of labour law to achieving labour market objectives requires a collective framework. Legislation can provide such a framework. But EU labour law has promoted flexibility through social dialogue, agreements between the social partners.

The purpose of labour law is to restore a balance of power in the individual employment relationship. Fragmentation of employment is only a threat if an individualised, segmented workforce is not protected and regulated within a collective framework. The potential for collective regulation is evident in the framework agreements on part-time work and fixed-term work reached through the European social dialogue. Similarly, protection may be secured by national collective agreements.[31]

There is widespread recognition of the role collective agreements can and do play in promoting this, as well as other agendas. What is shocking is the absence from a Green Paper on 'modernising labour law' of questions addressing the need for EU collective labour law to intervene to *support and reinforce* the role of trade unions, collective bargaining and collective agreements – so important to the individual employment agenda.

Rather, the assumption is that the status quo of EU collective labour law suffices. The position in a number of Member States (anti-union employers, reduced coverage of collective agreements, declining trade union membership) reveals the clear need for EU intervention to support collective bargaining if it wishes to promote its individual employment agenda.

It is universally acknowledged in the large majority of Member States that individual employment operates within a framework of collective bargaining. It is a distinctive characteristic of the European social model that it attributes a central role to social dialogue at EU and national levels in the form of social partnership. It would be a radical deviation from the European social model for the Commission to 'modernise labour law' by separating EU labour law on individual employment from EU collective labour law.

---

[31] For example, in the temporary work sector, in Germany, on 20 February 2003 a framework agreement was reached between trade unions grouped together by the central German trade union confederation, DGB, in a bargaining cartel and the employer's organisation in the temporary work sector, BZA. BZA (Bundesverband Zeitarbeit Personal-Dienstleistungen), the largest employers' organisation in the temporary work sector, with some 1,600 members. In 2002, an estimated 4,000 private sector temporary employment agencies were operating in Germany employing some 273,000 temporary workers. 'Collective Agreements in Place in Temporary Work Sector', *European Industrial Relations Review* No. 354, July 2003, at pp. 22–4. In Spain a national agreement was concluded in March 2005 for the telemarketing sector employing some 40,000 workers of whom some 90 per cent are temporary workers. 'National Accord Provides Security for Telemarketing Workers', *European Industrial Relations Review* No. 378, July 2005, at pp. 27–9.

Adaptation of labour law should reinforce this collective framework by intervening to support trade union membership and organisation and collective bargaining. Modernisation of labour law to meet the challenges of the twenty-first century starts with the collective dimension; not, as in the Green Paper, with individual employment law.

## III. The role of EU labour law

Though it is essential to challenge the Barroso Commission's reformulation of the traditional purpose and model of labour law, and to question the exclusion of collective labour law from a project of 'modernising labour law', it is also important not to respond wholly negatively to the Green Paper. Other questions posed by the Green Paper offer opportunities to suggest positive proposals.[32] A few examples will suffice.

The Commission raises the issue of whether clarity might be achieved in legal definitions of employment and self-employment if EU law were to propose such a definition, at least as regards employment rights regulated by EU law. National labour laws adopt a definition of 'employee', on which there is considerable convergence. It is at least arguable that a single European definition of 'employee' could and should be established for the purposes of *EU labour law*. The principle of equal treatment is fundamental to the *acquis communautaire social* and implies a common definition ensuring that this common category of workers enjoys the protection of EU labour law regardless of the Member State in which they work.

Major problems can arise if it is left to the Member States to define the concept of the employment relationship delimiting the scope of application of EU labour law.[33] Major discrepancies appear in the application of EU labour law in Member States. Further, opportunities are available for Member States to avoid it through manipulative definitions of their domestic legal concepts.[34] Clarity might be achieved in legal definitions of employment and self-employment if EU labour

---

[32] Questions 7–14. Though, given the Barroso Commission's passivity in the field of social policy, the prospect of initiatives, let alone legislative action, is minimal.

[33] For example, as proposed in the draft Directive on temporary agency work. Commission of the European Communities, Proposal for a Directive of the European Parliament and the Council on working conditions for temporary workers, COM(2002) 149 final, Brussels, 20 March 2002; Amended Proposal, COM(2002) 701 final, Brussels, 28 November 2002.

[34] One incongruity already revealed concerns the Part-Time Work Directive (Council Directive 97/81/EC of 15 December 1997 concerning the framework agreement on part-time work concluded by UNICE, CEEP and the ETUC, OJ L14/9 of 20 January 1998). In the UK, the relevant Regulations apply to all workers due to the impact of the EU definition of the scope of coverage of equality law (see the Part-time Worker (Prevention of Less Favourable Treatment) Regulations 2000, SI 2000, No. 1551, as amended). In contrast, the application in the UK of the Fixed-Term Work Directive (Council Directive 1999/70/EC of 28 June 1999 concerning the framework agreement on fixed-term work concluded by ETUC, UNICE and CEEP, OJ L175/43 of 10 July 1999) is limited to 'employees', not the wider category of 'workers'. See the Fixed-term Employees (Prevention of Less Favourable Treatment) Regulations 2002, SI 2002, No. 2034.

law were to propose a single European definition of 'employee', at least as regards employment rights regulated by EU law.[35]

The tenor of the Green Paper is that simplifications and/or reductions in existing labour laws contribute to making it easier for employers to take on new employees. However, what is required is not simplification or reduction of labour laws *per se*, but regulation assessed in terms of achieving its objectives. Reducing employment protection of 'atypical employees' leads to lower labour market participation and hence reduces the pool of employees available for hiring to employers. Providing rights to training increases the pool of capable employees, making it more attractive for employers to take on new employees. If the objective is to make it easier for employers to take on new employees, better regulation means more effective, not merely less or simpler labour laws.

Simplification and reduction may be achieved by eliminating the complexity attached to multiple labour law regimes attached to different types of workers (segmentation). Such diversity means employers are faced with choosing among different sets of labour and social costs, and, if they get it wrong, possible challenges by workers. A better solution might be a general legal framework applicable to all, or the vast majority of workers, or possibly, a sectoral approach. Again, the social partners may be best equipped to negotiate the legal framework appropriate to the needs of employers and workers.

Three examples will illustrate this approach: combating undeclared work, encouraging life-long learning and promoting a life-cycle approach to work.

The first example addresses the question of how labour law tackles undeclared work, encouraging employers and employees into the legitimate labour market. Undeclared work refers to forms of employment which evade the norms of employment regulations. The proliferation of such forms of employment and the consequences for workers in declared employment were highlighted by the Commission in an Explanatory Memorandum attached to a proposal for a Council Directive 'on a form of proof of an employment relationship'.[36] The Commission looked to the experience in the Member States to find formal requirements which made it easier for employment contracts and relationships to be identified. In the United Kingdom and Ireland, employers were required to inform employees in writing of the main conditions of their employment contract.[37] The result, Council Directive 91/533/EEC of 14 October 1991 on an

---

[35] As with equal pay in *Allonby* v. *Accrington & Rosendale College*, Case C-256/01, [2004] *Industrial Relations Law Reports* 224. The Report of EMPL on the application of Directive 96/71/EC on the posting of workers (2006/2038/INI; Final A6–0308/2006 of 28 September 2006; Rapporteur: Elisabeth Schroedter), included in its Motion for a European Parliament Resolution, paragraph 9: 'calls on the Commission to initiate negotiations with the Member States as a matter of urgency, with the aim of establishing transparent and consistent criteria for determining the status of "workers" and "self-employed persons" with regard to employment law'.

[36] COM(90) 563 final, Brussels, 8 January 1991, paragraphs 5–6.

[37] Tables on pages 6–7 of the Explanatory Memorandum.

employer's obligation to inform employees of the conditions applicable to the contract or employment relationship,[38] aimed to require proof of the existence of an employment relationship.

The objective, however, was more to provide information to the worker than to compel employers to acknowledge undeclared work and employees to engage in the legitimate labour market. The enforcement of requirements to provide information, and the sanctions available, have proved to be inadequate. The problem has been magnified by the increased mobility of workers with the accession of new Member States. In so far as such mobility is channelled through employment agencies, regulation of such businesses may achieve some degree of successful control over undeclared work. The correlation between undeclared work and problems linked to minimum wages and health and safety indicates that experience of enforcing such labour standards through labour inspectors is a potential mechanism to tackle undeclared work.[39] Trade unions could be valuable partners in combating undeclared work.

A second example addresses the question of how important it is for a successful active labour market policy to promote life-long learning/vocational training, and if so, what policy tools are best suited to this end. The Commission's Social Dialogue website includes a long list of social dialogue texts on the subject of training and lifelong learning.[40] In March 2002 the European social partners at intersectoral level (UNICE/UEAPME, CEEP and ETUC) adopted a framework of actions for the life-long development of competences and qualifications, as a contribution to the implementation of the Lisbon Strategy. The role of the social partners in life-long learning was acknowledged by the Kok Report of November 2004.[41] Particularly significant is a report by a group of eminent social scientists and senior civil servants, which concluded:[42]

> Empirically, a distinction between large enterprises and small and medium sized enterprises can be observed, with the latter clearly providing comparatively less training opportunities. However, it can also be observed that *social partnership*

---

[38] OJ L288/32 of 18 October 1991.

[39] The Commission's recent legal action against the UK, upheld by the European Court, condemning the UK government's advice to employers that they need not ensure that employees take the rest breaks guaranteed by the Working Time Directive is one instance of Commission action to enforce Community labour law. *Commission of the European Communities* v. *United Kingdom*, Case C-484/04, decided 7 September 2006. This needs to be expanded to compel employees to actively acknowledge undeclared work.

[40] Many in specific sectors: seafarers, mines, electricity, agriculture, railways, hairdressers, banking, insurance, maritime fishing, sugar, chemicals, and the hotel, restaurant and catering sector.

[41] One of its 'key recommendations' was (p. 33): 'Member States in close cooperation with social partners should adopt national strategies for lifelong learning by 2005, in order to address the rapid technological change, to raise labour market participation, to reduce unemployment and to enable people to work longer'.

[42] *Report of the High Level Group on the Future of Social Policy in an Enlarged European Union*, European Commission, Directorate-General for Employment and Social Affairs, May 2004, section 3.1.2, pp. 47–8. Italics added.

*does play an important role, as the small and medium sized enterprises which are covered by agreements tend to do much better and agreements at national level may implement lifelong learning* (as the recent national agreement in France).

The report considers how to foster the demand for lifelong learning, and concludes that:[43]

the increase of demand for lifelong learning depends on many conditions such as: ... *collective bargaining and individual labour contracts should incorporate more explicit rights and duties concerning lifelong learning in order to promote competitiveness and employability.*

The High Level Group's policy recommendation was categorical:[44]

The national strategies for lifelong learning should, at the level of working conditions: ... include *access to training activities as a standard ingredient of the employment contract and collective agreements.*[45]

A final example concerns what measures are needed to promote a life-cycle approach to work. A 1998 study of working time trends in the Member States of the EU over the previous twenty years emphasised the increasing importance of part-time work, interpreted as a concomitant of increasing female labour market participation.[46] The study revealed the diminishing role of general collectively agreed working time reductions while emphasising the key role played nonetheless by collective bargaining policy for working time reductions and providing a series of examples of the scope which the state has to demand and promote working time reductions. The study concludes by proposing coordinated action in three areas of policy:

firstly to encourage expansion of the system of institutions, with the aim of achieving equal status for women's work as a method of making an independent living; secondly, to make individual working time reductions easier so as to create a degree of individual choice during a person's working life (in contrast to a policy which for example, effectively allocates part-time working to women as a group); and thirdly, a return to collectively negotiated working time reductions.

The gender context of working life is central and implies a life-cycle approach to work.[47] However, it must be tackled through *collective*, not individual mechanisms.

---

[43] *Ibid.*, p. 48. Italics added.    [44] *Ibid.*, p. 49. Italics added.

[45] In this connection, it may be noted that the Charter of Fundamental Rights of the European Union includes Article 14(1): 'Everyone has the right to education and to have access to vocational and continuing training'.

[46] S. Lehndorff, 'From "Collective" to "Individual" Reductions in Working Time? Trends and Experience with Working Time in the European Union', *Transfer: European Review of Labour and Research*, No. 4/98, Winter 1998, pp. 598–620.

[47] See Jean-Yves Boulin and Reiner Hoffmann, 'The Conceptualisation of Working Time Over the Whole Life Cycle', in J.-Y. Boulin and R. Hoffmann (eds.), *New Paths in Working Time Policy*, Brussels: European Trade Union Institute, 1999, pp. 11–48.

## Conclusion

The vision presented by the Green Paper confronts the cold light of the reality of what can be expected of the Barroso Commission. This Commission's congenital passivity in the social field means that any measures which emerge are likely to reflect its deregulatory vision. As to the future, the Green Paper offers some basis for proposals which a future Commission could usefully prepare to continue the development of the EU labour law required by the European social model. But given what it wants to do to European labour law, and its record, it is likely the Barroso Commission will do nothing. Perhaps this is for the best.

# Chapter 21

# The futures of European labour law: (2) the European Court's agenda and *ordre communautaire social*

Interventions by the European Court of Justice may have a critical impact on the future of European labour law. Thus, the decisions of the European Court of Justice in *Viking* and *Laval* were widely expected to be significant.[1] In the event, they may precipitate a crisis for the European social model and for the EU itself.[2]

The institutional architecture of the European social model looks to the autonomous trade union movement as the backbone of Social Europe.[3] As elaborated in this book, European labour law's fundamental principles and rights at both collective and individual level look to collective bargaining and

Parts of this chapter draw on B. Bercusson, 'The Trade Union Movement and the European Union: Judgment Day', (2007) 13 *European Law Journal* (No. 3, May) 279–308; and B. Bercusson, *Collective Action and Economic Freedoms: Assessment of the Opinions of the Advocates-General in Laval and Viking and Six Alternative Solutions*, Brussels: European Trade Union Institute (ETUI-REHS), 2007 (57 pp.), available, together with an Executive Summary in French, at www.etui-rehs.org/research/publications. I owe much to discussions during 2004–6 in the Task Force, led by Catelene Passchier, Confederal Secretary, established by the European Trade Union Confederation (ETUC) to coordinate the legal teams in the *Viking* and *Laval* cases, in the legal team of the International Transport Workers' Federation (ITF), headed by Deirdre Fitzpatrick, Legal Officer, and in the European Trade Union Institute's (ETUI) Research Group on Transnational Trade Union Rights, which I coordinated (Thomas Blanke (Oldenburg), Niklas Bruun (Helsinki), Filip Dorssemont (Utrecht), Antoine Jacobs (Tilburg), Yota Kravaritou (Thessaloniki), Klaus Lörcher (Berlin), Isabelle Schömann (ETUI), Bruno Veneziani (Bari) and Christophe Vigneau (Paris)).

[1] Case C-438/05 *Viking Line Abp OU Viking Line Eesti* v. *The International Transport Workers' Federation, The Finnish Seamen's Union*; decided 11 December 2007; Case C-341/05, *Laval un Partneri Ltd.* v. *Svenska Byggnadsarbetareforbundet, Svenska Byggnadsarbetareforbundet, Avdelning 1, Svenska Elektrikerforbundet*, decided 18 December 2007. At least in that respect, they did not disappoint.

[2] The EU social model's industrial relations system was similarly at the heart of recent EU legislative conflicts over the exercise of economic freedoms, with disastrous consequences for ratification of the proposed Constitutional Treaty. See proposal for a Directive on Services in the Internal Market, COM (2004) 2/3 final, adopted 13 January 2004. Now Directive 2006/123/EC of the European Parliament and of the Council of 12 December 2006 on services in the internal market, OJ L376/26 of 27 December 2006. The Deputy General Secretary of the Swedish trade union confederation, LO, Erland Olausson, warned that a negative outcome in the *Laval* case could result in Sweden's leaving the EU. See the document on Item 5 of the Agenda of the Executive Committee of the European Trade Union Confederation (ETUC) meeting on 4–5 March 2008, 'ETUC response to ECJ judgements Viking and *Laval*', and the Resolution adopted by the Executive Committee at that meeting.

[3] See Chapter 8.

collective action by trade unions and employers' organisations as the collective framework for individual employment protection.

The European Union, a transnational European economy, like the national economies of the Member States, requires an economic balance of power between employers and workers. In the Member States, this balance is achieved, in part, through the collective action of trade unions and organisations of employers. The social partners at EU level have not achieved this balance of power.

EU law on free movement transforms the balance of economic power in the EU. The freedom of enterprises to move throughout the single European market has shifted the balance of economic power towards employers. This is particularly evident in the overwhelming economic power of multinational enterprises, the magnitude of transnational capital movements, the social dumping effects of global trade, delocalisation, unemployment and deskilling.

The danger of the changing balance of economic power is exacerbated by competition over labour standards. The threat of 'social dumping' within the EU, the result of disparities in wages and working conditions among the Member States, exacerbated by the accession of new Member States, has led to challenges which have yet to be accommodated in EU law.

Together, the changing balance of power and competition over labour standards has weakened European economic integration and undermined support for the European political project. There are ominous signs of strain, such as rejection of the proposed Constitutional Treaty, the disputes over the Services Directive, and resistance to further enlargement for fear of migration of labour from new Member States. Trade unions are not opposed to EU economic integration. But labour is not a commodity.

One response to the shift in the economic balance of power resulting from the growth of the transnational economy is trade unions' traditional defence of collective bargaining and collective action. A crucial element in maintaining a balance of economic power *within* Member States is the legal right to collective bargaining and to take collective action. National labour laws include the right to collective action. Though legal systems differ, no Member State outlaws collective action.

Constrained by membership of the EU, Member States adapted their law to the EU's guarantee of free movement in the single market. The EU law of the common market transformed national rules governing the free movement of goods, services, capital or workers. However, national laws have not yet adapted to trade unions' response in the form of collective action which impacts on the transnational economy.

Globalisation means that collective action frequently has an impact beyond national borders.[4] National rules on collective action are inadequate to regulate

---

[4] For a analysis of three sectors, motor manufacturing, maritime shipping and clothing and textile manufacturing, where 'unions have engaged in transnational activities in an effort to reassert control over labour markets and competition', see Mark Anner, Ian Greer, Marco Hauptmeier,

transnational collective action having an impact on free movement in the EU. The legal problem arises where *national* laws on *collective action* encounter *EU law* (and adapted national law) on the *economic freedoms of movement* of goods, services, capital or workers.

The references to the European Court of Justice (ECJ) by the Swedish Labour Court in *Laval* and by the English Court of Appeal in *Viking* highlighted this issue of the limits to economic freedoms of employers.[5] Specifically: may EC Treaty provisions on free movement be limited by collective action which is lawful under national law.[6]

## The *Viking* and *Laval* cases

### *Viking*

Not surprisingly, it was an organisation of workers operating in the globalised market of international transport, the International Transport Workers' Federation (ITF), which has been in the forefront of these developments. The campaign by the ITF against flags of convenience (FOC) involves ITF affiliates

---

Nathan Lillie and Nik Winchester, 'The Industrial Determinants of Transnational Solidarity: Global Interunion Politics in Three Sectors', (2006) 12 *European Journal of Industrial Relations* 7–27. The authors conclude: 'Only in maritime shipping have [unions] built industry-level structures to [reassert control]. These structures enjoy solid support within the ITF union coalition' (p. 23). It is perhaps not surprising, therefore, that the first major challenge to such transnational solidarity using EU law was aimed at the ITF. See below, Case C-438/05 *Viking Line Abp OU Viking Line Eesti* v. *The International Transport Workers' Federation, The Finnish Seamen's Union*; decided 11 December 2007.

[5]  The substance of this issue was translated tortuously into ten questions of law put to European Court of Justice by the English Court of Appeal in the *Viking* case. In the *Viking* case, there were written and oral submissions to the ECJ by fourteen Member States (Austria, Belgium, Czech Republic, Denmark, Estonia, Finland, France, Germany, Ireland, Italy, Latvia, Poland, Sweden and the UK) and Norway, as well as the parties and the Commission. In *Laval*, submissions were made by fourteen Member States and Iceland and Norway, as well as the parties and the Commission. Twelve of the fourteen Member States making submissions in *Viking* also made them in *Laval*, but not Italy or the UK, though the UK did appear at the oral hearing in *Laval*. Spain and Lithuania made submissions in *Laval*, but not in *Viking*. In a significant innovation, for the first time in its history, the European Trade Union Confederation (ETUC) intervened by submitting a letter attached to the written submission of the International Transport Workers' Federation (ITF). The submissions addressed some or all of the questions posed by the English Court of Appeal, but often, given their perceived significance, more directly the underlying issues of substance. The account of the submissions which follows draws on the written submissions of the parties, the Member States and the Commission, and the notes made by the author at the oral hearing before the ECJ in Luxembourg on 10 January 2007.

[6]  For earlier commentary on the *Laval* case, see K. Ahlberg, N. Bruun and J. Malmberg, 'The *Vaxholm* Case from a Swedish and European Perspective', (2006) 12 *Transfer: European Review of Labour and Research* (No. 2, Summer 2006) 155–66; Ronnie Eklund, 'The *Laval* Case', (2006) 35 *Industrial Law Journal* (No. 2, June) 202–8; on *Viking*, T. Blanke, 'The *Viking* Case', (2006) 12 *Transfer: European Review of Labour and Research* (No. 2, Summer 2006) 251–66; A.C.L. Davies, 'One Step Forward, Two Steps Back? The *Viking* and *Laval* Cases in the ECJ', (2006) 35 *Industrial Law Journal* (No. 1, March) 75–86.

taking industrial action in support of other affiliated unions in dispute, often in other countries.[7]

The *Viking* case concerned industrial action by the Finnish Seamen's Union (FSU) in Helsinki against Viking Line Abp (Viking). Viking, a Finnish shipping company, owns and operates the ferry, *Rosella*, registered under the Finnish flag and with a predominantly Finnish crew covered by a collective agreement negotiated by the FSU. The *Rosella* operates between Helsinki in Finland, a member of the EU since 1995, and Tallinn in Estonia, which became a member of the EU in May 2004. During 2003, Viking decided to re-flag the *Rosella* to Estonia, which would allow the company to replace the predominantly Finnish crew with Estonian seafarers, and to negotiate cheaper terms and conditions of employment with an Estonian trade union. In late 2003, Viking began negotiating with the FSU about the possible re-flagging.

Negotiations between Viking and the FSU for a new collective agreement for the *Rosella* were unsuccessful and the FSU gave notice of industrial action beginning 2 December 2003. The right to strike is protected in Finnish law by Article 13 of the Finnish Constitution as a fundamental right in Finnish law. It is accepted that the FSU had a right to take strike action to protect its members' jobs and the terms and conditions of the crew.

The FSU, an ITF affiliate, requested that the ITF assist by informing its affiliates of the situation and by asking those affiliates to refrain from negotiating with Viking pursuant to the ITF Flags of Convenience policy. Under the FOC policy, affiliates have agreed that the wages and conditions of employment of seafarers should be negotiated with the affiliate in the country where the ship is ultimately beneficially owned. In this case, the *Rosella* would remain owned by Viking, a Finnish company, even if re-flagged to Estonia. According to the FOC policy, therefore, the FSU would keep the negotiation rights for the *Rosella* after the re-flagging. To support the FSU, on 6 November 2003, the ITF sent a letter to all affiliates in the terms requested. Further meetings took place and on 2 December 2003, a settlement agreement was reached. Viking claimed they were forced to capitulate because of the threat of strike action.

On 18 August 2004, shortly after Estonia became an EU Member State, Viking commenced an application in the Commercial Court of England and Wales for an order to stop the ITF and the FSU from taking any action to prevent the re-flagging of the *Rosella*. Viking was able to start proceedings in England because the ITF has its headquarters in London. On 16 June 2005, the English Commercial Court granted an order requiring the ITF and the FSU to refrain from taking any action to prevent the re-flagging, and further requiring the ITF to publish a notice withdrawing its letter to its affiliated trade unions. The judge considered that the actions of the ITF and the FSU were contrary

---

[7] The FOC campaign provides examples of industrial action which risk falling outside the immunities of British law. As such it has been the subject of some of the leading cases in the UK courts over the past twenty years.

to European law. The ITF and the FSU appealed against this decision to the Court of Appeal.

In a judgment given on 3 November 2005, the Court of Appeal decided that the case raised important and difficult questions of European law and referred a series of questions to the European Court of Justice. It also set aside the order granted by the Commercial Court against the ITF and the FSU. Proceedings in London were on hold until the ECJ provided answers to the questions that the Court of Appeal has requested. Once the ECJ answers the questions referred to it, the case will be returned to the Court of Appeal for a final decision. However, the judgment of the ECJ will become part of European law and will apply throughout the EU.

### Laval

Baltic Bygg AB, a fully owned Swedish subsidiary of Laval un Partneri Ltd. (Laval), a Latvian company, was awarded a public works contract in June 2004 by the City of Vaxholm in Sweden for construction works on a school.[8] Negotiations on a collective agreement between the Swedish Building Workers' Union (Svenska Byggnadsarbetareförbundet ('Byggnads') and Laval began in June 2004, but Laval refused to sign a collective agreement on terms acceptable to Byggnads. Instead, Laval entered into a collective agreement with the Latvian Trade Union of Construction Workers. Byggnads gave notice of industrial action and industrial action was taken by Bygnadds and the Swedish Electricians' Union (Svenska Elektrikerförbundet) in late 2004, including a peaceful boycott of the building and construction work. The right to strike is protected as a fundamental right by the Swedish Constitution. Laval commenced proceedings before the Swedish Labour Court claiming, *inter alia*, violation of its freedom of movement under the EC Treaty. The industrial action continued and Baltic Bygg AB went bankrupt. The Swedish Labour Court referred questions to the ECJ.

## The issues at stake

Due to the ITF being based in London, Viking was able to initiate proceedings before the British High Court. As in the *Laval* case, the employer's claim was based on EU law: that the industrial action had violated the employer's freedom of establishment and to provide services, as provided in the EC Treaty, Articles 43 and 49. As the unions did in the Swedish Labour Court in the *Laval* case with the Swedish Constitution, the FSU in the *Viking* case invoked the Finnish Constitution which protects the fundamental right to strike. At first instance in the English High Court in June 2005, the judge upheld the employer's complaint: EU law overrode any national law, even the national constitution of a Member State.

[8] Latvia became an EU Member State in May 2004. Sweden has been an EU Member State since 1995.

However, the EC Treaty provisions on free movement are not absolute. Free movement is limited by public policy considerations, both in the Treaty[9] and as developed by the European Court of Justice through its extensive case-law. The reference to the ECJ by the English Court of Appeal in *Viking* highlights this issue of the limits to free movement: whether EC Treaty provisions on free movement may be limited by collective action which is lawful under national law. One specific issue raised is whether EU law includes a fundamental right to take collective action, including strike action, as declared in Article 28 of the EU Charter of Fundamental Rights.

This chapter analyses the responses to the questions referred to the ECJ as they reflect the substantive issues, first, in submissions to the Court, then in the Opinions of the Advocates-General, and finally by the Court in its judgments in the two cases.[10] The purpose is to highlight the different positions adopted as regards the underlying substantive issues, and the consequent options available to the ECJ.

The questions confronting the ECJ required it take a definitive position on the future of European labour law. The choices before the Court may be characterised as either 'opting-out' or 'opting-in'.

For the Court could have 'opted-out' of a role in shaping the future of European labour law. By (i) following its own precedent in *Albany*[11] and excluding collective action from the scope of Treaty provisions on economic freedom; (ii) invoking the concept of 'subsidiarity', leaving it to Member States to develop solutions to the clash between national laws and EU laws as regards trade union rights of collective action and employers' economic freedoms; or (iii) by rejecting the application to trade unions of Treaty provisions on economic freedom (no horizontal direct effect).

Instead, in both *Viking* and *Laval*, the ECJ chose to 'opt-in' and present a doctrinal approach towards the Treaty's economic freedoms in relation to European labour law. In *Laval*, it projected a specific regulatory vision for a system of collective bargaining which it regarded as consistent with transnational economic freedoms. In so doing, the Court rejected the submissions, mainly from the 'old' Member States, that the Treaty did not preclude collective action by trade unions to defend the interests of workers threatened by 'social dumping'.

---

[9]  Articles 30 (goods), 39(3) (workers), 46(1) (establishment), 55 (services), 58(1) (capital).

[10]  The *grande chambre* of the ECJ making the decisions comprised thirteen judges. The Court in both cases was composed of V. Skouris (Greece), P. Jann (Austria), A Rosas (Finland), K. Lenaerts (Belgium), U. Lohmus (Estonia), L. Bay Larsen (Denmark), R. Schintgen (Luxembourg), R. Silva de Lapuerta (Spain), K. Schiemann (United Kingdom), J. Makarczyk (Poland), P. Kuris (Lithuania), E. Levits (Latvia) and A. O Caoimh (Ireland). In sum: nine from the 'old' Member States and four from the 'new' Member States. There were judges from the three Baltic states (Estonia, Latvia and Lithuania), but none from France, Germany or Italy.

[11]  *Albany International BV* v. *Stichting Bedrijfspensioenfonds Textielindustrie*, Case C-67/96; with joined Cases C-115/97, C-116/97 and C-117/97, [1999] ECR I-5751.

The Court's approach appears to be based on an outdated European Community law doctrine of the primacy of the single market. It is reminiscent of, if not actually harking back to, a nineteenth-century ideology of the illegitimacy of collective action by workers and their organisations which interferes with the trade and commerce of employers in the market. It is thus at odds with the wider aims of the European Union promoted by the EU's legislative institutions and vital to the European trade union movement. This chapter will critically assess the Court's intervention in light of the *acquis communautaire social* of European labour law described in this book.

The chapter suggests that if the Court wishes to contribute to the future of European labour law, it must adopt a different agenda, from a doctrinal point of view, and proposes a concept embodying the *acquis* of European labour law: *ordre communautaire social*.

### 'Opting-out' (1): *Albany*: tempering economic freedoms

In *Albany*, the ECJ had acknowledged that the interpretation of EC Treaty provisions on competition policy must be conditioned by other Treaty provisions on social policy; specifically, on collective action in the form of collective bargaining and social dialogue. The Court refused to apply the Treaty's provisions on competition to condemn collective agreements.[12]

Both Advocates-General Mengozzi in *Laval* and Maduro in *Viking* in their Opinions reject the parallel[13] that economic freedoms must similarly be conditioned by the fundamental right to collective action.[14] Both Advocates-General reject the solution excluding collective action from the scope of the Treaty provisions on economic freedoms.[15] Instead, they seek to reconcile

---

[12] 'It is beyond question that certain restrictions of competition are inherent in collective agreements between organisations representing employers and workers. However, the social policy objectives pursued by such agreements would be seriously undermined if management and labour were *subject to* Article [81(1)] of the Treaty when seeking jointly to adopt measures to improve conditions of work and employment. It therefore follows from an interpretation of the provisions of the Treaty as a whole which is both effective and consistent that agreements concluded in the context of collective negotiations between management and labour in pursuit of such objectives must, by virtue of their nature and purpose, be regarded as *falling outside* the scope of Article [81(1) EC].' *Albany International BV* v. *Stichting Bedrijfspensioenfonds Textielindustrie*, Case C-67/96; with joined Cases C-115/97, C-116/97 and C-117/97, [1999] ECR I-5751, paras. 59–60 (italics added).

[13] That the free movement provisions of the Treaty, including Articles 43 and 49, cannot be interpreted as negating the social policy objectives pursued by collective agreements by outlawing collective action, which falls outside or is not subject to Treaty provisions and is, rather, a matter for Member State regulation.

[14] Although upholding the existence of a fundamental right to strike protected by Community law, they refused this 'opt-out' and addressed the substantive issues. However, in most other respects, the solutions they proposed to the fundamental problems were very different.

[15] The ETUC provided an historical perspective in its letter attached to the ITF's written submission: 'The evolution of the legal rules in Europe may be characterised as a progression

workers' collective industrial action with employers' economic freedom of movement.[16]

As for the ECJ, the parallel with *Albany* – the proposition that just as collective agreements fall outside the Treaty's competition provisions, so collective action falls outside the Treaty's free movement provisions – was rejected.[17] The reasoning is unconvincing. The Court accepts that *Albany* 'held that the social policy objectives pursued by such agreements would be seriously undermined if management and labour were subject to [the Treaty's competition provisions] when seeking jointly to adopt measures to improve conditions of work and employment'.[18] It might seem obvious that collective action aims to achieve the same social policy objectives. But the Court concludes: 'those two

---

from repression, via toleration, to recognition … The *Viking* case is an attempt to turn the clock back, not merely to the period of toleration, but to that of repression. Viking's arguments, reminiscent of ancient doctrines of restraint of trade and collective conspiracy invoked before national courts in historic labour law cases of the nineteenth century, interpret the language of the Treaty of Rome as reflecting long-abandoned doctrines condemning collective action by workers.' See A. Jacobs, 'Collective Self-Regulation', Chapter 5 in B.A. Hepple (ed.), *The Making of Labour Law in Europe: A Comparative Study of Nine Countries up to 1945*, London: Mansell, 1986, pp. 193–241.

[16] But their reasoning is different. Advocate-General Mengozzi in *Laval* acknowledges the issue raised by *Albany* as to the compatibility of collective action and free movement (para. 61). He concludes that there is a fundamental right to take collective action protected by the EU legal order (paras. 62–78). However, he decided that Member States may restrict the *exercise* of this fundamental right (para. 80), including in order to comply with their EU obligation to ensure freedom of movement (paras. 81–3). The outcome is the need to reconcile the fundamental right with economic freedoms (para. 85). Advocate-General Maduro in *Viking* also upholds a general principle of Community law protecting the fundamental right to strike (para. 60). But he asserts that fundamental rights can be reconciled with economic freedoms (paras. 23–4). The fundamental right to strike as a public interest, like other public interests, can be assessed together with the rules on free movement (para. 25). He acknowledges that *Albany* held that collective agreements fall outside competition provisions of the Treaty in light of the contradiction between them (para. 26). However, he distinguishes competition provisions from free movement provisions, and rejects the analogy with *Albany*, simply asserting there is no risk of contradiction (para. 27).

[17] The Court states, first (para. 35) 'that the organisation of collective action by trade unions must be regarded as covered by the legal autonomy which those organisations, which are not public law entities, enjoy pursuant to the trade union rights accorded to them, inter alia, by national law.' The principle of trade union autonomy is protected not only by 'trade union rights accorded … by national law' but also by ILO Conventions. Here it is sacrificed. This could be challenged. Secondly (para. 36): 'collective action such as that at issue in the main proceedings, which may be the trade unions' last resort to ensure the success of their claim to regulate the work of Viking's employees collectively, must be considered to be inextricably linked to the collective agreement the conclusion of which FSU is seeking.' The inextricable link of collective action with collective agreements is proclaimed, but with the strange result that although collective agreements are outside the Treaty's competition provisions, the collective action which produced the agreement may breach the Treaty's free movement provisions. It is not clear how the conclusion follows that trade union collective action therefore falls within Article 43, except by virtue of the strange proposition which precedes these statements in para. 34: 'Since working conditions in the different Member States are governed sometimes by provisions laid down by law or regulation and sometimes by collective agreements and other acts concluded or adopted by private persons, limiting application of the prohibitions laid down by these articles to acts of a public authority would risk creating inequality in its application'.

[18] Para. 49.

sets of provisions [competition and free movement] are to be applied in different circumstances',[19] and states:[20]

> it cannot be considered that it is inherent in the very exercise of trade union rights and the right to take collective action that those fundamental [economic] freedoms will be prejudiced to a certain degree.[21]

It is submitted that *Viking* and *Laval* involve collective industrial action with consequent inevitable effects on free movement. The ECJ in *Albany* offers a clear and unambiguous solution: Community law on free movement does not apply to collective action by workers and trade unions, protected as a fundamental right by the Community legal order.[22]

## 'Opting-out' (2): subsidiarity

Similar to the reasoning in *Albany*, one argument before the Court[23] in *Viking* and *Laval* was that the principle of subsidiarity precludes EC law intervening to regulate collective action by workers and their organisations, an area of law jealously guarded by Member States from EU intervention.[24] In *Viking*, the Commission stated that it was preferable that collective action be governed by national law and disputes left to Member States to resolve.[25]

---

[19] Para. 53.   [20] Para. 52.

[21] It is not clear what the point would be of collective action that did not somehow prejudice the economic freedom of employers to a certain degree.

[22] To paraphrase the Court's judgment in *Albany*, para. 60: 'It is beyond question that certain restrictions on free movement of goods, services and workers are inherent when collective action is taken by workers or their organisations. However, the fundamental rights to freedom of association and to take collective action would be seriously undermined if workers and their organisations were subject to Article 28 [43, 49] of the Treaty when seeking to take collective action to defend their interests, including strike action. It therefore follows from an interpretation of the provisions of the EU Charter and the Treaty which is both effective and consistent that collective action by workers or their organisations to defend their interests, including strike action, must, by virtue of its nature and purpose, be regarded as falling outside the scope of Article 28 [43, 49] of the Treaty'. A qualified solution following *Albany* would be to allow national courts to look to the 'nature and purpose' of the collective action. If the collective action by workers or their organisations is of the nature reflected in the fundamental right, and its purpose is to defend their interests and promote the objectives of improving living and working conditions, it should be regarded as falling outside the scope of the free movement provisions of the Treaty.

[23] The submissions pursuing this line of argument in *Viking* took different positions. Member States taking the view that the collective action of trade unions fell within the regulatory competence of the EC included the Czech Republic, Estonia, Latvia and the UK. Those denying EC competence asserted Member State competence: France, Ireland, Italy and Sweden.

[24] Article 137(5) EC. See also the 'Monti Regulation', Council Regulation (EC) No. 2679/98 of 7 December 1998 on the functioning of the internal market in relation to the free movement of goods among the Member States. OJ L337/8 of 12 December 1998, Article 2. The Finnish social model establishes a specific balance between economic freedoms and fundamental rights. Transnational collective action potentially engages courts in different Member States. Viking was attempting to use EU law to require an English court to assess the Finnish social model. This presents grave risks.

[25] Providing an overarching historical perspective, the ETUC stated in its letter attached to the ITF written submission (paras. 4 and 6): 'The precise contours of the rules governing collective action

This argument cut no ice with the Advocates General or the Court, wedded to economic freedoms in a transnational internal market. In *Viking* the Court declared:[26]

> in principle, collective action initiated by a trade union or a group of trade unions against an undertaking in order to induce that undertaking to enter into a collective agreement, the terms of which are liable to deter it from exercising freedom of establishment, is not excluded from the scope of [Article 43 EC].

The Court thereby threw down a gauntlet to the legislative institutions of the Community whose policy priorities were clearly different.[27]

Further, the Court did not address the inevitable problems of private international law. Transnational collective action potentially engages courts in different Member States. Cross-border collective action raises difficult questions in private international law: which national court has jurisdiction and the law of which Member State applies? Different laws and different courts take different views regarding the legality of cross-border collective action. The question is whether, and if so, the extent to which Community law should attempt to intervene. In the case of cross-border collective action, problems arise as to which country's court has jurisdiction and which country's law

---

in each Member State are the outcome of different national historical experience … In the Member States of the EU the rules governing collective industrial action reflect an established equilibrium in the balance of forces between the social partners. It would produce a shock of incalculable magnitude if this equilibrium, carefully constructed over time in different Member States, were to be destabilised by an intervention reflecting Viking's interpretation of Community law'.

[26] *Viking*, para. 55.

[27] There was a clear signal from the EU legislative institutions in the recent adoption on 12 December 2006 of the Services Directive (Directive 2006/123/EC of the European Parliament and of the Council of 12 December 2006 on services in the internal market, L376/36 of 27 December 2006). This is explicitly concerned to protect *national* social models, in particular, as regards collective bargaining, collective agreements and collective action. Article 1(6) states that the Directive on services in the internal market is not to affect 'the relationship between employers and workers, *which Member States apply in accordance with national law which respects Community law*'. Similarly, Recital 14, that it does not affect labour law, that is 'the right to strike and to take industrial action *in accordance with national law and practices which respect Community law*', reaffirms the autonomy of national social models (italics added). The phrase 'which respects Community law' qualifies national labour law. But these provisions of Article 1(6) and Recital 14 (and Article 1(7)) make clear that Community law on the internal market freedoms of employers does not limit national labour laws in general or fundamental rights to take collective action in particular. The ITF and FSU, in their oral submission of 10 January 2007, highlighted the adoption on 12 December 2006 of the Services Directive, arguing that certain of its provisions (e.g. Article 1(6)) would be absurd if Articles 43 or 49 EC on free movement were interpreted as Viking proposed: not only to affect but to override the Services Directive's respect for 'the right to negotiate and conclude collective agreements, the right to strike and to take industrial action …' (Recital 14). The provisions of the Directive on services in the internal market are powerful indications that Articles 43 or 49 EC on free movement are not to be interpreted so as to override the Services Directive's respect for 'the exercise of fundamental rights as recognised in the Member States and by Community law …the right to negotiate, conclude and enforce collective agreements and to take industrial action in accordance with national law and practices …' (Directive 2006/123/EC, Article 1(7)).

applies[28] and whether judgments of one national court are to be applied in another Member State.[29]

## 'Opting-out' (3): horizontal direct effect

The question was whether employers can use the EC Treaty Articles 43 (freedom of establishment) and 49 (freedom of services) to stop trade unions taking collective action which interferes with their economic freedom of movement (horizontal direct effect). In the Court's doctrine, these Treaty provisions were aimed at action by public authorities (vertical direct effect). The only exceptions were actions classified as regulatory or quasi-regulatory[30] in cases involving professional associations.[31]

---

[28] Determining which court has jurisdiction in cross-border collective action has potentially profound consequences in industrial disputes. There is *no uniform approach* in the Member States on this subject. The decision on jurisdiction in the case of cross-border transfers is left to *national* laws, with the ensuing risk of conflicting solutions. To illustrate: there are potentially serious consequences if the collective action is taken by trade unions in Member State A, but the court with jurisdiction to decide the dispute is in Member State B. The potential confusion is compounded if the court in Member State B is required to apply the law of Member State A. As the *Viking* case shows, this is far from hypothetical: a British court is to apply Finnish law to collective action taken by a Finnish trade union in Finland.

[29] Again, if the Court in Member State A makes a decision in a dispute involving cross-border collective action, it may be necessary to enforce that decision against workers or a trade union in Member State B. For example, employers in Member State A have won their case and wish to enforce the decision against the workers or a trade union in Member State B. The workers or trade union may object, arguing that the rules of Member State B are so different that enforcement of that judgment by courts in Member State B is not required by Regulation 44/2001 on jurisdiction and the recognition and enforcement of judgments in civil and commercial matters (depending on whether disputes over collective rights are considered to be civil or commercial matters). The employers may seek to enforce the judgment of the court of Member State A in Member State B. The potential for litigation is impressive. Public policy rules may apply to preclude enforcement (as was possible in Finland had Viking sought to enforce the judgment of the English court).

[30] In its written observations, Viking argued that collective bargaining agreements entered into by the FSU do regulate employment in a collective manner, that in Finland it is collective agreements rather than legislation that set minimum wages and this highlights the quasi-public role of the trade unions under Finnish law.

[31] Such associations were caught as having the primary aim of regulating access to the labour market, conflicting with the Treaty's provisions on free movement. Case C-415/93 *Union Royale des Sociétés de Football Association ASBL & others* v. *Jean-Marc Bosman* [1995] ECR I-4921; Case C-309/99 *Wouters, Savelbergh, Price Waterhouse Belastingadviseurs BV* v. *Algemene Raad van de Nederlandse Orde van Advocaten* [2002] ECR I-1577. As to the alleged parallel with professional associations regulating access to the labour market, the FSU argued that this was not the case with trade unions engaging in collective action in pursuance of a collective agreement which regulates substantive terms and conditions of employment, not free movement. The general consensus in the submissions to the Court was that these Treaty provisions do not have full horizontal direct effect. The submissions were concerned, rather, with whether the specific actions of the FSU or the ITF could be classified as regulatory or quasi-regulatory. The Member States were divided. The view that Article 43 is directly applicable also to trade unions was upheld straightforwardly by the governments of the Czech Republic, Estonia, Latvia and Poland. Ireland was circumspect. Other Member States took the opposing view: Austria, Belgium, Finland, France, Italy, Germany, Norway and Sweden.

Both Advocates-General Mengozzi and Maduro took the view that there is horizontal direct effect of the free movement provisions of the Treaty as regards establishment and services.[32] Advocate-General Mengozzi was cautious in holding that in the specific case before him, in the context of the wide powers of trade unions in the specific Swedish model of collective employment relations, Article 49 is capable of direct effect.[33] Advocate-General Maduro was much more ambitious. He asserts the general proposition that Treaty provisions apply to private action capable of effectively restricting the exercise of free movement by obstacles that cannot reasonably be circumvented.[34] He acknowledges that it is not simple to 'determine whether that is the situation',[35] and is anxious to protect the autonomous action of private actors.[36] But he concludes that 'the actions of the FSU and the ITF are capable of effectively restricting the exercise of the right to freedom of establishment of an undertaking such as Viking'.[37]

The ECJ in *Viking* was even more robust. Trade unions are singled out by the Court as subject to complaints that their collective action violates the economic freedoms of others. The formulation is extremely wide: the economic freedoms may be invoked by 'any individual who has an interest in compliance with the obligations laid down and ... applies in particular to all agreements intended to regulate paid labour collectively'.[38] Moreover, the Court focuses such complaints on trade unions:[39]

> in exercising their autonomous power, pursuant to their trade union rights, to negotiate with employers or professional organisations the conditions of employment and pay of workers, trade unions participate in the drawing up of agreements to regulate paid work collectively.

However, rather than these 'trade union rights' providing protection for the established economic function of collective bargaining, the Court concludes

---

[32] There is an apparent contradiction between the position of the Advocates-General on *Albany* and on horizontal direct effect. On the one hand, in refusing to apply *Albany*, they reject the parallel between competition and free movement so as to exempt collective action from both sets of provisions. On the other hand, their argument on horizontal direct effect implies a parallel between competition provisions (which have horizontal direct effect) and free movement provisions. This is particularly evident in the Opinion of Advocate-General Maduro.

[33] Paras. 160–1.

[34] Paras. 43 and 48. There are substantial preliminary problems to do with his criteria of when these Treaty provisions have horizontal direct effect. When is the private actor/defendant 'capable' of 'effectively' restricting free movement and what action does so 'unreasonably'?

[35] Para. 43.    [36] Para. 49.    [37] Para. 55.

[38] Para. 58. This cites the parallel of a complaint of violation of the principle of equal pay between men and women (Case 43/75, *Defrenne*). Economic freedoms are regarded as equivalent to human rights to equal treatment, a questionable analogy. The Court cites the case-law on free movement of goods (para. 62), but does not mention the EU legislative provisions expressly shielding collective action in the case of free movement of goods (the 'Monti Regulation') and the similar protection of collective action and collective agreements recently provided in the Directive on free movement of services.

[39] Para. 65.

that Article 43 'is capable of conferring rights on a private undertaking which may be relied on against a trade union or association of trade unions'.[40]

The Court reaffirms that 'freedom of establishment constitutes one of the fundamental principles of the Community'[41] which 'would be rendered meaningless if the Member State of origin could prohibit undertakings from leaving in order to establish themselves in another Member State'.[42] From this, however, the Court makes the unconvincing analogy with collective action by trade unions:[43]

> it cannot be disputed that collective action such as that envisaged by FSU has the effect of making less attractive or even pointless, as the national court has pointed out, Viking's exercise of its right to freedom of establishment.

And:[44]

> collective action taken in order to implement the ITF's policy of combating flags of convenience … must be considered to be at least liable to restrict Viking's exercise of its right to freedom of establishment.

The conclusion 'follows that collective action such as that at issue in the main proceedings constitutes a restriction on freedom of establishment within the meaning of Article 43'.[45] The Court's conclusion is subject to many objections, both doctrinal and practical.

## Doctrinal objections to horizontal direct effect

### Collective agreements are not restrictions on freedom to provide services

The European Parliament and Council have declared unequivocally that collective agreements are *not* restrictions on free movement of services. In the Services Directive the target is those requirements which are deemed to violate the rules on free movement.[46] Article 4(7) ('Definitions') stipulates that collective agreements are not such requirements:[47]

> '*requirement*' means any obligation, prohibition, condition or limit provided for in the laws, regulations or administrative provisions of the Member States or in consequence of case-law, administrative practice, the rules of *professional* bodies, or the collective rules of *professional* associations or other *professional* organisations, adopted in the exercise of their legal autonomy. *Rules laid down in collective agreements negotiated by the social partners shall not as such be seen as requirements within the meaning of this Directive.*

The Directive's rules on free movement do not apply to collective agreements. Collective agreements are distinguished not only from state measures, but

---

[40] Para. 66. The compatibility of this general proposition with ILO Conventions is questionable.
[41] Para. 68.    [42] Para. 69.    [43] Para. 72.    [44] Para. 73.    [45] Para. 74.
[46] Directive 2006/123/EC of the European Parliament and of the Council of 12 December 2006 on services in the internal market, OJ L376/26 of 27 December 2006.
[47] Italics added.

also from those of professional bodies or associations. As they lack the regulatory effect to be deemed *requirements* subject to the Services Directive's rules on free movement, the same argument should apply to Articles 43 and 49 EC.[48]

## Collective action is not a regulatory measure

The Commission in *Viking* took the view that Article 43 EC does not have horizontal direct effect so as to confer rights on a private undertaking which may be relied on against a trade union or an association of trade unions in respect of collective action by that union or association of unions. In contrast, Articles 39 and 49 catch provisions adopted in a collective manner as if they were state measures. It follows that Articles 43 and 49 apply to regulatory measures adopted by quasi-public bodies. But that is not the situation in this case. The ITF and FSU are not regulatory bodies. The threat to strike and the sending of the circular are not regulatory measures.

## Trade unions are not regulatory bodies as 'emanations of the state' [49]

Directives do not have horizontal direct effect. They apply only vertically, to the state, However, they apply also to 'emanations of the state'. Criteria of 'emanations' were laid down in *Foster* v. *British Gas*: bodies established/controlled by the state, endowed by the state with regulatory powers and providing a public service.[50] If the same criteria were to apply to determine the horizontal direct effect of Articles 43 and 49, trade unions would not be such bodies. There is no delegation of state authority.

## Horizontal direct effect violates freedom of association

Trade unions represent the interests of workers and, like other private actors, are free to pursue their private interests without the constraint of direct effect. To subject them to horizontal direct effect would affect their freedom of association.[51]

## Horizontal direct effect harmonises EC law on collective action

Article 137(5) EC excludes harmonising directives on pay, the right of association, the right to strike and lockout. Applying Articles 43 and 49 horizontally to trade unions and collective action would be effective harmonisation of laws of Member States – by outlawing collective action – thereby circumventing the policy of exclusion exemplified by Article 137(5).[52]

---

[48] The link is made through the legal basis of the Services Directive: the first and third sentence of Article 47(2) and Article 55 EC. See further, Recitals 5 and 6.
[49] Submission made by the French government in *Viking*.
[50] Case C-188/89 [1990] ECR I-3313.
[51] Submission made by the German government in *Viking*.
[52] *Ibid.*

### Practical objections to horizontal direct effect

### A flood of complaints against collective agreements

To apply horizontal direct effect to collective agreements as having regulatory effect would open the floodgates. The immense diversity of national industrial relations and collective bargaining systems means it is scarcely conceivable that each and every collective agreement could be characterised as having the regulatory effect required to fall within the scope of the free movement provisions.[53] National courts would be flooded with complaints that particular collective agreements fall within the scope of Article 43 or 49. Ultimately, the ECJ would be confronted with endless references from national courts asking whether a specific collective agreement in a particular Member State's collective bargaining system possessed the requisite regulatory effect.[54]

### Can criteria distinguish agreements having regulatory effect?

Nor is it practical to refer the question of whether collective agreements have regulatory effect to national courts. First, criteria would be needed to distinguish regulatory agreements. The major differences *between* Member States' national industrial relations systems, reflecting different social models, and *within* national models, among an extraordinary variety of forms and legal effects of collective agreement, would make it impossible to devise and then sensibly apply such criteria. Secondly, these criteria would be applied to continual challenges to collective agreements and action, many of which would inevitably be referred to the European Court.

### Conclusion on horizontal direct effect

On balance, it appears clearer and more consistent with the EU social policy protecting the autonomy of social partners and the social function of collective agreements to regard them as not subject to the horizontal direct effect of the free movement provisions of the Treaty.[55] The analogy between state action and collective action can and should be contested. Not least because it has been explicitly rejected both with regard to free movement of goods (the 'Monti Regulation') and free movement of services (the Services Directive).

---

[53] For example, in the UK, collective agreements lack legal effect and are relatively sparse in their coverage of the workforce and it would then seem absurd to treat them the same as *erga omnes* collective agreements

[54] The English Court of Appeal referred the question to the ECJ on the grounds that it was difficult to contemplate such an outcome.

[55] There are risks for others in the application of horizontal direct effect. For example, powerful private actors, such as multinational enterprises, are potentially vulnerable to horizontal direct effect. See T. Novitz, 'Navigating Between Economic and Social Rights in Europe: The Practical Problems Ahead', *Competition Law Insight* (October 2007) who points to the consequences of horizontal direct effect on distribution agreements concluded by private actors and suggests that it 'could undermine established European competition law'.

Either the freedom of establishment at stake in *Viking* is unique in regarding collective action as a restriction, or else those EU legislative measures may now be regarded as subject to the Court's interpretation that the Treaty overrides them. The result would be that fundamental rights to collective action in national law are subject to free movement of goods (despite 'Monti') and collective action and collective agreements are restrictions subject to free movement of services in Article 49 (despite being explicitly declared not to be such restrictions for the purposes of the Services Directive). The Court's ruling is a direct challenge to the choices of the EU's legislative institutions.

## 'Opting-in' (1): balancing workers' right to take collective action with employers' economic freedom

The Court of Appeal's reference to the ECJ in *Viking* included a number of questions which raised the issue of whether, and if so, how a balance might be struck between the economic freedoms of undertakings and the social rights of trade unions and workers.[56] The issues were addressed through the lens of established precedent: (i) what exceptions/derogations to free movement are available, for example, under Article 46 EC allowing for justifications on grounds of public policy,[57] and whether in *Viking* they included protection of workers and fundamental rights; and, (ii) in light of principles such as proportionality, how are such justifications to be balanced against the free movement of goods.[58]

### Justifications

### (i) A fundamental right to take collective action

In *Viking*, the ITF and FSU submission was unequivocal: as a matter of principle, collective action can be justified on the basis that it constitutes

---

[56] The approach to these questions was signalled by the Court of Appeal's invoking a number of phrases which duly attracted the attention of most of the submissions: justification of restrictions on free movement on the basis of public policy, including fundamental rights and protection of workers; striking a fair balance between fundamental social rights and economic freedom; and assessment of 'proportionality'.

[57] Article 46 EC: 'The provisions of this Chapter and measures taken in pursuance thereof shall not prejudice the applicability of provisions laid down by law, regulation or administrative action providing for special treatment for foreign nationals on grounds of public policy, public security or public health.'

[58] As in *Schmidberger* (Case C-112/00 *Eugen Schmidberger, Internationale Transporte und Planzuge* v. *Republic of Austria* [2003] ECR I-5659): where EU law recognises a number of fundamental rights, and these conflict, a balance has to be sought in light of principles such as proportionality. In *Schmidberger*, the fundamental right to freedom of expression, had to be balanced against the free movement of goods. A demonstration by environmental protesters in the Brenner Pass was not contrary to EU law although it prevented the free movement of goods, because it was proportionate (e.g. limited in time, properly authorised, etc.). The argument in *Viking* was whether there was a fundamental right to take collective action to be balanced against freedom of establishment, and, if so, what was the correct balance.

a fundamental right protected *by Community law*.[59] The submissions reflected a broad consensus (except for the UK) as to the existence of a fundamental right to take collective action.[60] This was echoed by Advocates-General Mengozzi in *Laval* and Maduro in *Viking*, both of whom acknowledged the existence of a fundamental right to collective action protected by the Community legal order.[61] In its judgment in *Viking*, the Court unequivocally declares that:[62]

> the right to take collective action, including the right to strike, must therefore be recognised as a fundamental right which forms an integral part of the general principles of Community law the observance of which the Court ensures.[63]

Protection of this fundamental right:[64]

---

[59] To this proposition there were varying degrees of assent in the submissions of the Member States. Some were explicit: Austria, Belgium, Finland, France, Germany, Ireland, Italy, Norway and Sweden. Others were implicit: although they denied the protection afforded by the right in this case, there was confirmation that such a fundamental social right did exist: the Czech Republic, Denmark, Estonia, Latvia, Poland and even Viking. The only unequivocal assertion that there was no fundamental right to take collective action in Community law came from the UK. The representative of the Commission, in his oral submission cited the ECHR, Article 11, ILO Conventions, the European Social Charter and the EU Charter, Article 28. He concluded: the right to collective action seems in principle to be part of the general principle of EU law that protects fundamental rights. Member States have a wide margin of appreciation. But EU law precludes measures which deny the essence of the fundamental rights protected.

[60] Cf. the Services Directive which provides strong evidence of the EU legislative bodies' evaluation of fundamental rights. Article 1(7) of the Services Directive provides (italics added): 'This Directive does not affect the exercise of fundamental rights as recognised in the Member States *and by Community law*. Nor does it affect the right to negotiate, conclude and enforce collective agreements and to take industrial action in accordance with national law and practices which respect Community law.' Recital 15 provides (italics added): 'This Directive respects the exercise of fundamental rights applicable in the Member States and as recognised in the Charter of Fundamental Rights of the European Union and the accompanying explanations, *reconciling them* with the fundamental freedoms laid down in Articles 43 and 49 of the Treaty. Those fundamental rights include the right to take industrial action in accordance with national law and practices which respect Community law'. Recital 15's explicit reference to the EU Charter is significant. The reference to reconciliation with fundamental freedoms in Articles 43 and 49 may be read as confirming that, in particular, the right to take industrial action *can be reconciled* with Articles 43 and 49 – the point at stake in *Viking*. The position is further elaborated, if not clarified, by Recital 83, concerned with derogations from the freedom to provide services and exceptional measures against a given provider: 'In addition, any restriction of the free movement of services should be permitted, by way of exception, only if it is consistent with fundamental rights which form an integral part of the general principles of law enshrined in the Community legal order'.

[61] Opinion of Advocate-General Mengozzi, 23 May 2007, paras. 78, 142; Opinion of Advocate-General Maduro, 23 May 2007, para. 60.

[62] Para. 44. See also in *Laval*, paras. 90–1.

[63] The Court continues: 'the exercise of that right may none the less be subject to certain restrictions. As is reaffirmed by Article 28 of the Charter of Fundamental Rights of the European Union, those rights are to be protected in accordance with Community law and national law and practices'.

[64] *Ibid.*, para. 45.

is a legitimate interest which, in principle, justifies a restriction … even under a fundamental freedom guaranteed by the Treaty, such as the free movement of goods [*Schmidberger*] or freedom to provide services [*Omega*].[65]

An important point arises regarding restrictions on the right to strike in national law. In reply to the Danish government's argument that the Community does not have competence to regulate the right to strike,[66] the Court states:[67]

> even if, in the areas which fall outside the scope of the Community's competence, the Member States are still free, in principle, to lay down the conditions governing the existence and exercise of the rights in question, the fact remains that, when exercising that competence, the Member States must nevertheless comply with Community law.

Although the Court intends by this to assert the Treaty's economic freedoms (Article 43) in the face of national, even constitutional rights to strike,[68] the Court immediately proceeds to declare that the right to take collective action is a fundamental right protected by Community law.[69] The logical conclusion is that, while *unrestricted* national laws on strikes are subject to the Treaty's protection of economic freedoms, *more restrictive* national laws are equally subject to the Treaty's protection of the right to strike. National laws are open to challenge where they limit the right to strike protected by Community law.[70]

### (ii) The public interest in protection of workers: 'social dumping'

Viking took the view that protection of workers is not within the scope of public policy for the purposes of Article 46. The trade unions took the opposite view.[71] Advocates-General Mengozzi and Maduro both took the view that collective industrial action which restricts free movement may be legitimate on the basis of the risks to workers of social dumping:[72]

---

[65] *Omega*, Case C-36/02 [2004] ECR I-9609. Though its 'exercise must be reconciled with the requirements relating to rights protected under the Treaty and in accordance with the principle of proportionality'. See further below as to this significant qualification.

[66] Para. 39.    [67] Para. 40.    [68] Para. 41.    [69] Paras. 43–4.

[70] In other words, harmonisation cuts both ways.

[71] Some Member States supported Viking: Estonia. Others, while supporting Viking, were more nuanced: Poland, Latvia and the UK. Some Member States were unequivocally supportive of the trade unions on the point of principle: Finland, Germany and Italy.

[72] Mengozzi, in *Laval*, para. 249. Again in para. 251: '… the right to take collective action is allowed not only in order to defend the interests of trade union members but also to enable them to pursue legitimate objectives recognised by Community law, such as the protection of workers in general and the fight against social dumping in the Member State concerned'. Also Maduro, in *Viking*, paras. 58–60. 'Yet, while the right to freedom of establishment generates overall benefits, it also often has painful consequences, in particular for the workers of companies that have decided to relocate. Inevitably the realisation of economic progress through intra-community trade involves the risk for workers throughout the Community of having to undergo changes of working circumstances or even suffer the loss of their jobs. This risk, when it materialised for the crew of the *Rosella*, is exactly what prompted the actions of the FSU and the ITF.' The background in both cases was enlargement to new Member States with lower labour costs and the consequent risk of social dumping.

However, as we know, the Court has accepted that the overriding reasons relating to the public interest that are capable of justifying a restriction on the freedom to provide services include both the protection of workers and the fight against social dumping.

Similarly, the Court in *Viking* declares clearly the proposition derived from its case-law that:[73]

a restriction on freedom of establishment can be accepted only if it pursues a legitimate aim compatible with the Treaty and is justified by overriding reasons of public interest [and is] suitable for securing the attainment of the objective pursued and must not go beyond what is necessary in order to attain it.

It then continues by stating:[74]

that the right to take collective action for the protection of workers is a legitimate interest which, in principle justifies a restriction of one of the fundamental freedoms guaranteed by the Treaty … and that the protection of workers is one of the overriding reasons of public interest recognised by the Court.

This is followed by even more positive statements as to the Community's endorsement of social policy[75], and:[76]

Since the Community has thus not only an economic but also a social purpose, the rights under the provisions of the Treaty on the free movement of goods, persons, services and capital must be balanced against the objectives pursued by social policy, which include, as is clear from the first paragraph of Article 136 EC, inter alia, improved living and working conditions, so as to make possible their harmonisation while improvement is being maintained, proper social protection and dialogue between management and labour.

The conclusion is[77]

In the present case, it is for the national court to ascertain whether the objectives pursued by FSU and ITF by means of the collective action which they initiated concerned the protection of workers.[78]

Left at that, the vast majority of collective actions would be justifiable.

However, there is a major problem. It is not simply that the Advocates-General, and then the Court, pose a number of additional conditions for collective action to be justifiable. Significantly, and perhaps fatal to certainty in the law, each of the Advocates-General, and then the Court, provides a *different* formulation of these conditions.[79]

---

[73] Para. 75.    [74] Para. 77.    [75] Para. 78.    [76] Para. 79.    [77] Para. 80.

[78] On the face of it, the FSU and the ITF would need only to convince the English Court of Appeal that their action concerned the protection of workers.

[79] Even when using the familiar terminology of 'proportionality', the criteria invoked differ. The often widely different conclusions do not inspire confidence as to the accuracy of their assessment of the correct balance between fundamental rights and economic freedoms in Community law, let alone provide certainty to the social partners or national courts in a most sensitive area of European labour law.

### Advocate-General Mengozzi in Laval: 'proportionality'[80]

Advocate-General Mengozzi's assessment of the legitimacy of collective action is based on the criterion of 'proportionality'. This is applied, with very different results, to (i) the *primary* collective action taken by the Swedish Building Workers Union[81] relating to (a) the *pay* claim, (b) *other* terms and conditions, and (ii) the *solidarity* action by the Swedish Electricians' Trade Union.[82]

### (i) The 'proportionality' of primary action

(a) *'The proportionality of collective action' to impose a rate of **pay** in accord-*
    *ance with a collective agreement*[83]

Advocate General Mengozzi's position can be summarised as follows: (i) collective action to support a pay claim generally satisfies the criterion of proportionality,[84] (ii) even where the wage claim might be excessive,[85] (iii) unless, in the case of a service provider from another Member State, the workers already have equivalent or essentially similar entitlement.[86]

---

[80] For Advocate-General Mengozzi in *Laval*, 'proportionality' is the central concept in the assessment of the balance in EU law between economic freedom and collective action. 'Proportionality' is a superficially easy solution to the problem. The concept has the apparent advantage of being familiar in EC law. It appears also to allow for the exercise by national courts of a degree of discretion enabling them to take into account their national context, enabling them to apply EU law as far as possible consistently with national conceptions of what is or is not proportionate collective action. But application of a criterion of proportionality requires further guidance to national courts. A close look at the Opinion of Advocate-General Mengozzi reveals the difficulties encountered.

[81] *Svenska Byggnadsarbetareforbundet.*    [82] *Svenska Elektrikerforbundet.*    [83] Paras. 254ff.

[84] Paras. 254–5: '… the taking of collective action in order to compel a service provider of a Member State to agree to pay the remuneration determined in accordance with a collective agreement … is in general appropriate to attaining the objectives pursued, since the mere threat of collective action by trade unions will encourage employers to enter into the collective agreement which they are under pressure to sign'. Para. 258: '… exercise of the right to take collective action in order to compel a service provider to subscribe to the rate of pay applied in the sector in question in the host Member State is, in principle, a less restrictive measure than automatic subjection to a similar rate of pay which, without being a minimum rate of pay, is set by national legislation …'.

[85] Paras. 259–60: 'Admittedly, such a system is liable to produce unforeseeable results or indeed, in certain circumstances, to allow wage claims that might be excessive. However, those circumstances are inherent in a system of collective employment relations which is based on and favour negotiation between both sides of industry, and, therefore, contractual freedom, rather than intervention by the national legislature. I do not think that, at its present stage of development, Community law can encroach upon that approach to employment relationships through the application of one of the fundamental freedoms of movement provided for in the Treaty'.

[86] Paras. 263–4: 'proportionality of restrictions … is possible where it is established that the protection conferred by those restrictions is not guaranteed by *identical or essentially similar* obligations by which the undertaking is already bound in the Member State where it is established … [This] requires host Member States, and in particular their courts, to assess the equivalence or essential similarity of the protection already available to posted workers under legislation and/or collective agreements in the Member State where the service provider is established, in particular as regards the pay such workers receive'. On the facts of the case (para. 273): 'If the gross wage paid by Laval was not the same as or essentially similar to that determined in accordance with the Byggnadsarbetareforbundet agreement fall-back clause, which I believe to

This appears broadly to reflect the position in the Posting of Workers Directive 96/71.[87] Advocate-General Mengozzi states that collective action to enforce a collective agreement is less restrictive than the requirement laid down in Directive 96/71: 'automatic subjection to a similar rate of pay which, without being a minimum rate of pay, is set by national legislation ...'.[88]

be the case but cannot be certain, it could in my view be concluded that the collective action, in so far as it sought to impose the rate of pay provided for by the Byggnadsarbetareforbundet collective agreement, would not be disproportionate to the objectives of protecting workers and combating social dumping'.

[87] Directive 96/71/EC concerning the posting of workers in the framework of the provision of services. OJ 1996 L18/1.

[88] On the one hand, Advocate-General Mengozzi goes *beyond* the Posting Directive. His endorsement of collective action to enforce pay provisions of collective agreements is apparently *not limited* to the construction sector (though that is the sector in question in *Laval*). On the other hand, Advocate-General Mengozzi appears to continue the ECJ's case-law on the Posting Directive by subjecting approval of collective action to secure application of a collective agreement to an important condition: the collective agreement must not replicate 'equivalent or essentially similar entitlement' already guaranteed to the workers concerned. *Arblade* v. *Leloup and Sofrage SARL*, Cases C-369/96 and C-276/96, [1999] ECR I-8453; judgment of 23 November 1999. This is a gloss imposed by the ECJ on the Posting Directive, which includes no such condition. It can be criticised on grounds of *practical reality*: it fails to take account of the sectoral context and of the transnational dimension. As regards *the sectoral context*, national courts are obliged to make an assessment of whether provisions on pay in another Member State are 'equivalent or essentially similar' to those in the collective agreement in question. This is an extraordinarily difficult task in practice. It is rendered even more difficult due to the potential of provisions on 'pay' to include a range of benefits of great variety and complexity, such as holiday entitlements and social insurance payments. Comparison of benefits across such a wide range available in different Member States is extremely difficult. Such a exercise was required by the ECJ in *Mazzoleni*, Case C-165/98, [2001] ECR I-2189, where the Court insisted that national authorities determine whether French and Belgian workers 'enjoy an equivalent position overall in relation to remuneration, taxation and social security contributions' (para. 35). As regards *the transnational dimension*, even where equivalent entitlements may be identified, prescribing compliance with the national collective agreement is important as surveillance by the trade union party to the agreement is essential to its effective application. See *Finalarte Sociedad de Construcao Civil Lda and others* v. *Urlaiubs- und Lobnausgleichskasse der Bauwirthschaft*, Cases C-49–50/98, C-52/98, C-54/98, C-68/98 and C-71/98, [2001] ECR I-7831. *Wolff & Müller* v. *Pereira*. Case C-60/03, judgment of 12 October 2004. The Community legislator in the Services Directive did not require such a condition for the application of labour standards in the context of cross-border provision of services. Rather, it excluded labour law in general as a factor to be considered in free movement and explicitly provided that collective agreements were not to be considered obstacles to free movement (Articles 4(7) and 16(3)). This made unnecessary any assessment of their proportionality regarding free movement. Instead, Advocate-General Mengozzi has both (i) adopted the condition (i.e. 'absence of equivalent protection') posited by the ECJ – as to when collective agreements within the Posting Directive may be enforced by Member States to apply – similarly as a condition for collective action by trade unions to enforce collective agreements; and (ii) extended this jurisprudence to cover collective action aimed at enforcing collective agreements in *other* sectors, beyond the construction sector covered by the Posting Directive. Both these propositions raise doctrinal and practical problems. In *doctrinal* terms, they deviate from the legislative policy agreed in the Services Directive (wholesale exclusion of labour law as a factor in free movement (the (amended) Services Directive provides that the rules on freedom of establishment and free movement of services are not to affect labour law and employment conditions. This is spelled out in Article 1 ('Subject matter'), para 6. See also Recital 14), stipulating that collective agreements are not obstacles to free movement, and guaranteeing fundamental rights to collective action). While extending the policy of the Posting

## (b) 'The proportionality of the collective action' to impose **other terms and conditions** of a collective agreement[89]

However, Advocate General Mengozzi departs from the framework indicated by the Posting Directive and its jurisprudence by the assertion that to make it a condition of the pay claim that the employer agree to *all* the terms of a collective agreement may be disproportionate.[90] The proposition can be summarised as follows. In the context of posting of workers, the conditions for which collective action is taken must entail, for the workers concerned, a *real advantage* which contributes *significantly* to their social protection and is not already guaranteed by obligations that are the same or essentially similar to those by which the service provider is already bound in the Member State in which it is established.[91] All the more so if the action is against an employer bound by a collective agreement in another Member State providing the same or essentially similar conditions.[92] In this specific case, collective action to require Laval to agree to *all* terms and conditions of a collective agreement as a condition of application of a particular pay agreement was disproportionate.[93]

Directive regarding collective agreements on pay to other sectors, they retain the doctrinal gloss of subjecting application of such collective agreements to the condition that equivalent protection is not available in the country of origin. In *practical* terms, the 'equivalent protection' test is extremely difficult to apply even when comparing an *existing* collective agreement with what is prescribed in the country of origin. It is virtually impossible if the test is applied to collective action seeking a collective agreement where *none has yet been agreed.*

[89] Paras. 279ff.

[90] Para. 280: '… the fact of making the very possibility of applying a given rate of pay conditional upon prior signing up to all the conditions of a collective agreement that apply in practice to undertakings established in Sweden in the same sector and in a similar situation goes beyond what is necessary to ensure the protection of workers and to prevent social dumping'.

[91] Para. 282: 'That approach is, in my view, consonant with the case-law which requires, first, that the conditions laid down by the rules of the host Member State for the provision of services in the context of the posting of workers entail, for the workers concerned, a real advantage which contributes significantly to their social protection and, second, as stated earlier, that the protection offered by such conditions is not already guaranteed by obligations that are the same or essentially similar to those by which the service provider is already bound in the Member State in which it is established'.

[92] Para. 281: 'That assessment extends *a fortiori* to a situation in which, as in this case, the undertaking which temporarily posts workers to the host Member State is bound by a collective agreement legally entered into in another Member State. In such a situation, it would in my view be contrary to the principle of proportionality to seek, even following collective action taken in accordance with domestic law, to make a service provider of another Member State comply either with conditions which are not designed to attain the objects for which the taking of collective action is justified or with conditions that duplicate those to which that provider is subject in the Member State in which it is established, in particular under the collective agreement concluded in that Member State'.

[93] Para. 280, see footnote 90 above. Advocate-General Mengozzi's proposition may be criticised on a number of practical grounds. First, he was wise not to enter the minefield of assessing the value of a trade union demand and consequent collective action regarding pay (paras. 259–60, see footnote 85 above). The same caution should be exercised regarding other terms and conditions of employment. Secondly, to insist on the trade union not linking pay demands to demands on other terms and conditions of employment is to ignore the reality of bargaining practice. Bargaining frequently links pay demands not only to other benefits (e.g. pensions, holidays), but

### (ii) The proportionality of *solidarity* action

Advocate-General Mengozzi concludes that the proportionality of solidarity action, even where it is the main contributor to the effectiveness of the collective action, is dependent on that of the primary action. If the primary action is proportionate, the solidarity action is not to be assessed differently.[94] The obvious criticism here is that the legality of solidarity action is dependent on determining whether the primary action is proportionate, and therefore lawful. This is an impossibly complex assessment for the national judge to make. It depends on whether the primary action is about pay, the action is not linked to other terms and conditions,[95] and there is no equivalent protection. Or, if the primary action is not about pay, then whether there is a significant/real advantage to the workers which is also not already guaranteed by equivalent provision.

### Conclusion: 'proportionality' in the Opinion of Advocate-General Mengozzi

The criterion of proportionality as proposed by Advocate-General Mengozzi has major disadvantages. Without further specification, it is too vague to be applied to the many forms which collective action takes (ranging from normal collective bargaining to workplace occupations). It will give rise to great divergences in the practice of national courts, both probably *within* national systems and certainly *between* national systems. Collective action in one Member State

---

to working time, working practices and other provisions of collective agreements related to productivity. Contrary to much public policy on macro-economic management, the proposition is an inducement for unions to place all their demands under the heading of pay increases. Finally, the Posting Directive, Article 3, requires compliance with terms relating not only to pay, but also to working time, holidays, health, safety and hygiene, maternity and pregnancy and equal treatment between men and women and other non-discrimination provisions. Compliance is not subject to the condition that the terms constitute 'a real advantage which contributes significantly to their social protection'. Further, the Directive allows Member States to extend mandatory application of collective agreements to other terms and conditions of employment (Article 3(10)), without any condition as to proportionality or equivalence. To be consistent with this, the inference of Advocate-General Mengozzi's proposition would be that collective action should be lawful at least where one Member State has done this. But the result would be uneven application of the EC law on free movement and collective action depending on whether a Member State had exercised that option. In sum: Advocate-General Mengozzi's application of the principle of 'proportionality' to assessing the balance between workers' collective action in support of a bargaining demand and resulting obstruction of an employer's economic freedom is fraught with doctrinal and practical difficulties.

[94] Paras. 305–6: 'Finally, for the sake of completeness with regard to the problem of the proportionality of restrictions deriving from the collective action in question in this case, I do not think that, in the context of the review that the national court should carry out in that connection – including its assessment of the wellfoundedness of the action for damages brought by Laval against the trade unions in this case – it need treat the defendants in the main proceedings differently by drawing a distinction between, first, Byggnadsarbetareforbundet and its local branch, which initiated the blockade, and, second, the SEF [the Swedish electricians' trade union Svenska Elektrikerforbundet (SEF)], which carried out the solidarity action. Although it was the latter action that caused the stoppage of work on the Vaxholm building site and mainly contributed to Laval's terminating the posting of Latvian workers to that site, the fact nevertheless remains that, in law, that action was necessarily dependent upon the setting up of the blockade.'

[95] One need only contemplate the problem of solidarity action which differs from the primary action in being taken not ostensibly about pay, or ostensibly linked to other terms and conditions.

may be deemed an unacceptably disproportionate restriction on Community economic freedoms while identical collective action in another Member State is considered a wholly acceptable restriction. Not least, such divergences will inevitably give rise to references to the ECJ questioning national courts' application of the criteria.[96]

Advocate-General Mengozzi's Opinion illustrates the risks entailed in laying down general propositions of proportionality to be applied to collective action in the very diverse systems of industrial relations and collective bargaining operating in different sectors across twenty-seven Member States.[97]

### Advocate-General Maduro in *Viking*: timing and voluntary solidarity

On the one hand, Advocate-General Maduro in *Viking*[98] categorically declares, in principle, the protection in the EU legal order of fundamental rights to take

[96] The lessons of the Acquired Rights Directive 77/187 and the definition of 'transfer of an undertaking' are all too plain to see.

[97] The *Laval* case itself illustrates this. The distinction between collective action in support of pay claims, as contrasted with action in support of (all?) other terms of a collective agreement, is perhaps explicable only by the specific facts of the dispute in *Laval*. This concerned posted workers in Sweden and the Posting of Workers Directive 96/71, which highlights the mandatory nature of minimum pay standards in collective agreements in the construction sector. A summary of the task facing the national court is provided in para. 284: 'In order to assess the proportionality of the collective action taken by the defendants in the main proceedings, the national court, when considering the conditions of the Byggnadsarbetareforbundet collective agreement that the collective action was intended to induce Laval to sign, even before starting any negotiation as to the applicable rate of pay or applying the rate of pay determined in accordance with the fallback clause in that agreement, should: – first, with regard to possible terms and conditions of employment provided for in the Byggnadsarbetareforbundet collective agreement – which, as we have seen in the part of this opinion concerning Directive 96/71, relate to matters other than those listed in the first subparagraph of Article 3(1) – verify whether, in so far as those conditions are governed by public policy conditions in Sweden within the meaning of Article 3(10) of that directive, the subjection of Laval to those conditions did not go further than was necessary to attain the objectives pursued by the collective action concerned; second, with regard to the other conditions of the Byggnadsarbetareforbundet collective agreement, verify whether those conditions involved a real advantage that made a significant contribution to the social protection of posted workers and did not duplicate any identical or essentially similar protection offered to them by the legislation and/or collective agreement applicable to Laval in the Member State in which it is established.'

[98] Advocate-General Maduro's Opinion in *Viking* includes a number of general statements of policy and principle. Some are more questionable than others. The assertion that the Treaty's economic order is based on a 'social contract' between workers and society is a claim requiring more argumentation than is provided in the Opinion. Paragraphs 59–60: 'Although the Treaty establishes the common market, it does not turn a blind eye to the workers who are adversely affected by its negative traits. On the contrary, the European economic order is firmly anchored in a social contract: workers throughout Europe must accept the recurring negative consequences that are inherent in the common market's creation of increasing prosperity, in exchange for which society must commit itself to the general improvement of their living and working conditions, and to the provision of economic support to those workers who, as a consequence of market forces, come into difficulties. As its preamble demonstrates, that contract is embodied in the Treaty … This touches upon a major challenge for the Community and its Member States: to look after those workers who are harmed as a consequence of the operation of the common market, while at the same time securing the overall benefits from intra-Community

collective action.[99] On the other hand, however, his Opinion outlines specific conditions for lawful collective action. Instead of Mengozzi's criterion of 'proportionality', Maduro proposes to assess the lawfulness of collective action using two criteria: (i) collective action: *timing* is everything; (ii) solidarity action must be *voluntary*.[100] These criteria aimed to address the different positions in the *Viking* case of the Finnish Seamen's Union (collective action) and the International Transport Workers' Federation (solidarity action).[101]

### Collective action: timing is everything

According to Advocate-General Maduro, workers may take collective action to protect their jobs and working conditions against relocation by employers of their economic activities to other Member States provided this collective action is taken *before* the relocation.[102] This appears to derive from a broader statement of the principle of equivalence: that collective action in cases of intra-Community relocation is not treated less favourably than in cases of

trade'. This is admirable sentiment but it is both legally questionable under present Treaty provisions (the imbalance between the Community's competence to promote market forces and its competence to provide social protection raises questions as to the existence of this 'social contract') and wholly unrealistic in the present political climate.

[99] Paragraph 60: 'The right to associate and the right to collective action are essential instruments for workers to express their voice and to make governments and employers live up to their part of the social contract. They provide the means to emphasise that relocation, while ultimately gainful for society, entails costs for the workers who will become displaced, and that those costs should not be borne by those workers alone. Accordingly, the rights to associate and to collective action are of a fundamental character within the Community legal order, as the Charter of Fundamental Rights of the European Union reaffirms. The key question, however, that lies behind the present case, is to what ends collective action may be used and how far it may go'.

[100] Whereas 'proportionality' is the central concept in Advocate-General Mengozzi's assessment of the balance in EU law between economic freedom and collective action, Maduro's Opinion never even uses the word 'proportionality', though para. 25 contains an indirect reference to proportionality: '... the Court has consistently recognised that public interests relating to social policy may justify certain restrictions on freedom of movement, as long as these restrictions do not go beyond what is necessary'. Both Mengozzi and Maduro cite the consequences for workers of the free movement of employers which allows for relocation of their economic activities to areas of lower labour costs: social dumping. Mengozzi invokes 'proportionality' to allow for some collective action by workers to protect their interests. Instead, Advocate-General Maduro invokes formal criteria which are completely novel, having no foundation in existing doctrine. Close examination reveals substantial problems in their practical application.

[101] This is my reading of the somewhat enigmatic para. 63: 'In order to establish whether the policy of coordinated collective action currently under consideration has the effect of partitioning the labour market in breach of the principle of non-discrimination, it is useful to distinguish between two types of collective action that may be at issue in the present case: collective action to persuade Viking Line to maintain the jobs and working conditions of the current crew and collective action to improve the terms of employment of seafarers throughout the Community'.

[102] Para. 66: 'Thus, in principle, Community law does not preclude trade unions from taking collective action which has the effect of restricting the right of establishment of an undertaking that intends to relocate to another Member State, in order to protect the workers of that undertaking'. Para. 67: '... collective action to persuade an undertaking to maintain its current jobs and working conditions ... represents a legitimate way for workers to preserve their rights and corresponds to what would usually happen if relocation were to take place within a Member State'.

relocation within national borders.[103] However, collective action *after* the relocation amounts to discrimination against the jobs and working conditions of workers in the other Member State.[104] This is deemed to be partitioning the labour market, a form of discrimination on grounds of nationality prohibited by EU law.[105]

Making the lawfulness of collective action conditional on timing offers every incentive to employers not to disclose their decision to relocate. This conflicts with their obligations under Community directives to inform and

[103]  Para. 65: 'In view of the margin of discretion which Community law leaves to the Member States, it is for the national court to determine, in the light of the applicable domestic rules regarding the exercise of the right to collective action, whether the action under consideration goes beyond what domestic law considers lawful for the purpose of protecting the interests of the current crew. However, when making this determination, national courts have a duty under Community law to guarantee that cases of intra-Community relocation are not treated less favourably than relocations within national borders'.

[104]  Para. 67: 'However, collective action to persuade an undertaking to maintain its current jobs and working conditions must not be confused with collective action to prevent an undertaking from providing its services once it has relocated abroad. The first type of collective action represents a legitimate way for workers to preserve their rights and corresponds to what would usually happen if relocation were to take place within a Member State. Yet, that cannot be said of collective action that merely seeks to prevent an undertaking that has moved elsewhere from lawfully providing its services in the Member State in which it was previously established'. The last sentence seems directly to contradict the policy of both the Posting Directive and the Services Directive. Both allow the host Member State to enforce domestic labour standards in law and collective agreements. If so, it seems trade unions should be allowed to take collective action in their own Member State to enforce collective agreements against undertakings which have relocated and now seek to provide services in the host Member State.

[105]  Para. 62: 'A coordinated policy of collective action among unions normally constitutes a legitimate means to protect the wages and working conditions of seafarers. Yet, collective action that has the effect of partitioning the labour market and that impedes the hiring of seafarers from certain Member States in order to protect the jobs of seafarers in other Member States would strike at the heart of the principle of non-discrimination on which the common market is founded'. The objection to collective action after relocation is that it is a form of discrimination on grounds of nationality prohibited by EU law. This will presumably not be the case where collective action is directed against relocation to a *non-EU* Member State. Nor does collective action partition the EU labour market where the workers employed by the relocating employer are *non-EU* nationals. Paragraph 68: 'Blocking or threatening to block, through collective action, an undertaking established in one Member State from lawfully providing its services in another Member State is essentially the type of trade barrier that the Court held to be incompatible with the Treaty in *Commission* v. *France*, since it entirely negates the rationale of the common market. Furthermore, to allow those kinds of action would carry the risk of creating an atmosphere of constant retaliation between social groups in different Member States, which could gravely threaten the common market and the spirit of solidarity embedded in it'. This invokes a strange notion of 'solidarity': the spirit of solidarity is that of the common market, said to be threatened by collective action, but not by relocation! There is another, quite different, non-market spirit of solidarity: social solidarity. If anything, that is threatened by relocation, and strengthened by collective action. So like Michelle Everson's 'market citizenship' (M. Everson, 'The Legacy of the Market Citizen', in J. Shaw and G. More (eds.), *New Legal Dynamics of European Union*, Oxford: Oxford University Press, 1995), we have the concept of 'market solidarity' – an oxymoron, as markets consist of individualised atomised actors, the converse to collective (social) solidarity manifest in trade unions' collective action.

consult employees' representatives about such decisions.[106] There would be considerable irony in a situation where an employer violating the obligation to inform and consult before relocating was thereby protected from collective action. Conversely, it offers incentives to workers and their trade unions to commence collective action as soon as possible.[107]

### Solidarity action must be voluntary

The criterion of lawfulness is whether affiliates called upon to take collective solidarity action do so voluntarily, or are obliged to do so.[108] This presents both

[106] The Collective Dismissals Directive 98/59/EC, the Acquired Rights Directive 2001/23; the European Works Councils Directive 94/45/EC, the framework Directive 2002/14 on information and consultation.

[107] Again, practical issues arise of when collective action can be deemed to have begun. If the collective action is taken *before* the undertaking relocates outside the Member State, the action is lawful. If the undertaking has relocated and seeks to provide services *back* to the Member State of origin, it is unlawful. The question of timing is difficult: when can relocation be said to have occurred? No guidance is offered. There are severe difficulties in making legality dependent on contingencies of fact. The maritime transport sector in *Viking* illustrates the practical difficulty of determining when relocation has taken place. Is it when the company has formally registered in another Member State, when the registration of the ship itself has changed, when the ship begins its voyages under the new flag, when the crew is replaced …? The lawfulness of collective action depends on the arbitrary selection of a date. Again, there are incentives to employer secrecy and hasty trade union collective action. These lend themselves to manipulation. Advocate-General Maduro appears to distinguish between services and other sectors. This is especially difficult if 'establishment' is the issue: are services established by simply registering an office? Is manufacturing different? Is transfer of substantial assets required before relocation is deemed to occur? There is an uncanny parallel with the concept of transfer of an undertaking (when does the transfer occur, what constitutes a transfer …?). Council Directive 77/187 of 14 February 1977 on the approximation of the laws of the Member States relating to the safeguarding of employees' rights in the event of transfers of undertakings, businesses or parts of businesses, OJ L61/26, as amended by Directive 98/50/EC of 29 June 1998, OJ L201/88; consolidated in Directive 2001/23 of 12 March 2001, OJ L/82/16. This appears to distinguish collective action against relocation of manufacturing (more easily protected) from collective action against services (less easily protected). Or will this provide the same protection to manufacturing relocations that is now offered to cross border relocation of services by the Posting Directive and more recently the Services Directive? Both the Posting Directive and the Services Directive aim precisely at the solidarity achieved by requiring equal treatment – between workers in the host state and workers from other Member States providing services in the host state – including terms of employment in collective agreements.

[108] Paras. 70–2: 'Naturally, the FSU may, together with the ITF and other unions, use coordinated collective action as a means to improve the terms of employment of seafarers throughout the Community. A policy aimed at coordinating the national unions so as to promote a certain level of rights for seafarers is consistent with their right to collective action. In principle, it constitutes a reasonable method of counter-balancing the actions of undertakings who seek to lower their labour costs by exercising their rights to freedom of movement. One must not ignore, in that regard, the fact that workers have a lower degree of mobility than capital or undertakings. When they cannot vote with their feet, workers must act through coalition. The recognition of their right to act collectively on a European level thus simply transposes the logic of national collective action to the European stage. However, in the same way as there are limits to the right of collective action when exercised at the national level, there are limits to that right when exercised on a European level. A policy of coordinated collective action could easily be abused in a discriminatory manner if it operated on the basis of an obligation imposed on all national

conceptual and practical problems. There is some artificiality in the distinction of voluntary v. compulsory compliance. There is a distinction between being under an obligation as a member of the federation, and being obliged to act as result of the federation's power.[109] The former may be correct, the latter not. The analogy with other international organisations, not least the ILO, is instructive. Which power, if any, of the federation (for example, the ITF or the ETUC) over affiliates failing to comply suffices to render the action compulsory: reprimand, financial penalty, suspension, expulsion? Are any of these sufficiently compelling to oblige the affiliate to comply? Once more there are difficulties in making legality depend on conditions which may be manipulated. Would a formal amendment to the statutes of the organisation suffice to render compliance 'voluntary'?

### Conclusion on the Opinion of Advocate-General Maduro

In the Opinion of Advocate-General Maduro, collective action is a fundamental right protected in EU law. However, this protection is contingent on collective action not partitioning labour markets. This means that it should not impede the hiring of workers from some Member States in order to protect jobs of workers in other Member States. Collective action aims to improve labour standards in general and EU law protects such collective action if it is undertaken *before* relocation has occurred, or, in case of solidarity action, if it is *voluntary* for all unions involved. If these conditions are satisfied, then coordinated collective action is legitimate.[110]

> unions to support collective action by any of their fellow unions. It would enable any national union to summon the assistance of other unions in order to make relocation to another Member State conditional on the application of its own preferred standards of worker protection,
> even after relocation has taken place. In effect, therefore, such a policy would be liable to protect the collective bargaining power of some national unions at the expense of the interests of others, and to partition the labour market in breach of the rules on freedom of movement. By contrast, if other unions were in effect free to choose, in a given situation, whether or not to participate in collective action, then the danger of discriminatory abuse of a coordinated policy would be prevented. Whether this is the situation in the circumstances of the present case must be left to the referring court.'

[109] See H.L.A. Hart, *The Concept of Law*, Oxford: Oxford University Press, 1961.

[110] In *Viking*, therefore, the ITF and FSU would have to demonstrate to the English Court of Appeal that these conditions were satisfied. The answers offered by Advocate-General Maduro to the questions posed by the Court of Appeal would indicate the following. As regards the ITF: UK domestic rules make *all* solidarity action unlawful, whether it engages intra-Community relocation or not. Yet the Opinion states that *voluntary* solidarity action, taken *before* the service is relocated, is protected as reflecting a fundamental right protected by the EU legal order. Arguably, this overrides any conflicting domestic law. The ITF would have to show that (i) the collective action preceded the relocation; (ii) affiliates were not compelled to take solidarity action. For the future, the ITF's Flag-of-Convenience policy (FOC) could be formulated to secure this. Specifically, as regards solidarity action affecting relocation (re-flagging) to non-EU Member States not protected by EU law on non-discrimination on grounds of nationality. As regards the FSU: Finnish law protects solidarity action against relocation *within* Finland. *Equivalent* protection must be available for solidarity action which is intra-EU. This is the case here. The EU right to collective action is said to be contingent on it being (i) before relocation and (ii) voluntary, not compulsory. As these conditions do not apply to domestic relocations,

### The ECJ in *Viking*: 'proportionality', predictability and arbitrating the merits of social dumping

The Court in *Viking* affirms the proposition that restrictions on economic freedom are acceptable if in pursuit of a legitimate aim, justified by the public interest, suitable for its attainment and not going beyond what is necessary.[111] Further, the right to take collective action to protect workers is a legitimate interest and protection of workers is itself a public interest.[112] However, qualifications soon follow.

### 'Proportionality' and fundamental rights

The most striking of these concerns the qualification of the fundamental right to take collective action. The Court confirmed that protection of this fundamental right:[113]

> is a legitimate interest which, in principle, justifies a restriction ... even under a fundamental freedom guaranteed by the Treaty, such as the free movement of goods [*Schmidberger*] or freedom to provide services [*Omega*].

However, the Court continues:[114]

> However, in *Schmidberger* and *Omega*, the Court held that the exercise of the fundamental rights at issue, that is, freedom of expression and freedom of assembly and respect for human dignity, respectively, does not fall outside the scope of the provisions of the Treaty and considered that such exercise must be reconciled with the requirements relating to rights protected under the Treaty and in accordance with the principle of proportionality.

The submissions in *Viking* achieved a consensus (except for the UK) as to the existence of a fundamental right to take collective action. Where the submissions differed was in their approach to the questions posed by the English Court of Appeal as to the 'fair balance between the fundamental social right to take collective action and the freedom to establish and provide services, and is it ... proportionate'.[115]

In their oral submission, the ITF and FSU made two specific points as regards balancing fundamental rights and economic freedoms. First, the *presumption*

---

can they be imposed on the FSU in this case? Or, dangerously, could they be deemed now to override domestic law so as to impose them as conditions for *domestic* solidarity action? If so, the FSU also would have to demonstrate that it took action preceding the relocation (would this be re-flagging (establishment) or the actual provision of services?).

[111] Para. 75.   [112] Para. 77.   [113] Para. 45.   [114] Para. 46.

[115] Questions 8 and 9. As regards the contentions as to whether and when there is a fair balance, some Member States struck a note of neutrality (Belgium), others were categorically negative as regards the fundamental right concerning the balance in the present case (the Czech Republic, Estonia and Latvia), while others were categorical in the opposite direction: Sweden. Similarly, as regards the principle of proportionality, Member States tended to follow their assessment of the balance, fair or unfair, in their assessment of whether the collective action was proportionate. In the negative: the Czech Republic, Estonia, Latvia and Poland. More positive: Belgium, Ireland and Finland. Other Member States insisted the assessment was not for the ECJ, but for national courts to determine: Germany.

should be that economic freedoms *are* consistent with the exercise of funda-mental rights. Both economic freedoms and the rights of workers to take collective action and to engage in collective bargaining are consistent with and necessary for the functioning of an efficient market. Secondly, fundamental social rights are not derogations from the economic freedoms but are protected by EU law. Accordingly, in balancing the rights in this case the question is not whether fundamental rights justify restrictions on free movement; rather free movement must be interpreted to respect fundamental rights.[116]

These considerations reflect important differences between the *Viking* case and *Schmidberger*. Four in particular: the first two apply to both the FSU and the ITF, the third is specific to the FSU, and the fourth to the ITF.

First, Viking is seeking to restrain the FSU and the ITF from taking *any* collective action *in the future*. The consequence of this is that the workers in Finland represented by the FSU will be entirely powerless in negotiations to try and save jobs lost following any re-flagging to Estonia.[117]

Secondly this case is different to *Schmidberger* in that one private party, an employer (Viking) is seeking to prevent other private parties, the trade unions, both FSU and ITF, from exercising fundamental rights. There is the difficulty of applying to private parties the 'margin of appreciation' afforded to Member States under *Schmidberger*. But of even greater importance is the risk in attempt-ing to balance what are essentially opposing *economic* interests of trade unions and employers.[118]

---

[116] This is exemplified by the approach taken by Advocate-General Stix-Hackl in the *Omega* case: 'The need to reconcile the requirements of the protection of fundamental rights cannot therefore mean weighing up fundamental freedoms against fundamental rights per se, which would imply that the protection of fundamental rights is negotiable. It is also necessary to examine the extent to which the fundamental rights concerned admit of restrictions. The provisions on the fundamental freedom concerned and particularly the circumstances in which the exceptions are permissible must then be construed as far as possible in such a way as to preclude measures that exceed allowable impingement on the fundamental rights concerned and hence preclude those measures that are not reconcilable with fundamental rights.' Case C-36/02 *Omega Spielhallen- und Automatenaufstellungs-GmbH* v. *Oberbrgermeisterin der Bundesstadt Bonn* [2004] ECR I-9609, para 53.

[117] The Finnish social model will also be seriously undermined. This would be calamitous not only for the workers concerned and for the Finnish social model, but also for workers and the social models of the other Member States where the right to collective action by trade unions and their international organisations is protected. The ITF and all its EU affiliates would be similarly crippled.

[118] Workers only have negotiating power because of their ability collectively to withdraw their labour. Courts in the Member States, very sensibly, have been extremely cautious in invoking any test of proportionality as regards the right to strike. It is a right inextricably linked to the collective bargaining process and must be assessed in the context of that process. It is difficult sensibly in practice to apply any test of proportionality to the demands made by the trade unions in that process. It is in the very nature of negotiations that both parties set demands at their highest and through negotiation over time seek a compromise, if necessary, with the assistance of mediation and conciliation. At what stage of this process and against what criteria is the test of proportionality to be applied? Any test based on proportionality in assessing the legitimacy of collective action is generally avoided in the industrial relations models of Member States for the very reason that it is essential to maintain the impartiality of the state in economic conflicts.

The third difference specifically concerns the FSU and the Finnish social model. As the court explained in *Schmidberger*, the competent authorities enjoy a 'wide margin of discretion' when striking a fair balance between the protection accorded to environmental demonstrators as a result of the fundamental right of freedom of expression and free movement of goods. The protection afforded by the Finnish social model and Finnish law to the FSU in the exercise of its right to strike meets the test in *Schmidberger*.

The fourth and final difference specifically concerns the ITF. The question of the referring court considers the justification of the ITF's FOC policy itself rather than any action taken under it by its affiliates. Yet the ITF as such takes no collective action. The FOC policy is agreed by and implemented though its affiliates. It would be logical to adopt a consistent approach as regards the ITF, an international trade union acting in a transnational context, to that applied to the FSU's actions in a national context.[119] In fact, the action taken by the ITF which is to be balanced against Viking's economic freedom is much less than the action taken by national affiliates, like the FSU, whose action is protected by virtue of compliance with their Member State social models. The difference is that the ITF, unlike the FSU, operates in an integrated single European market. EU internal market law has conferred transnational economic freedoms on employers. These should be balanced with transnational fundamental social rights of workers and their organisations.[120]

The right to take collective action is a fundamental right protected by Community law, and in the EU context protects *transnational* collective action.[121] It would be wholly disproportionate, and inconsistent with the fundamental rights to collective action protected in Member States' constitutions, in international instruments and in the EU Charter, for a transnational trade union organisation to be denied the right to issue a request to its affiliates to take collective action which is lawful within their national social models. The

---

[119] The ITF does not have workers as members. The ITF's action consists of sending a circular to affiliated trade unions. Collective action, if any, by an ITF affiliate on receipt of the circular, to show solidarity with the FSU would be action identical to that of the FSU were it to have received such a circular – action consistent with the social model of the Member State concerned. The nature of the ITF action is modest indeed: issuing a circular. The ITF affiliates would be expected to act lawfully within their national social models. Furthermore, the ITF affiliates are autonomous and can choose not to show solidarity even if legally able to do so. To adopt this approach would jeopardise their membership of the ITF but it is a choice they can make. Accordingly it cannot be presumed that collective action would necessarily be taken.

[120] Like *national* collective action, *transnational* collective action is a vital element in achieving economic efficiency in the Single European Market by requiring enterprises to consider the interests of workers. Economic efficiency demands that transnational free movement of enterprises be balanced with rights of workers and trade unions to take transnational collective action and engage in transnational collective bargaining.

[121] This does not rely on the Finnish model, but on EU law, reflecting the protection of this fundamental right as the majoritarian position in the national laws and constitutions of Member States, and by the EU Charter of Fundamental Rights, ILO Conventions, the Community Charter and the European Social Charter.

ECJ, instead, subjects this fundamental right to a test of 'proportionality' weighted in favour of the protection of the transnational economic freedoms of employers.

### 'Proportionality' and protection of workers

Further on the negative side, the Court declares, first, that the public interest of protection of workers 'would no longer be tenable if it were established that the jobs or conditions of employment at issue were not jeopardised or under serious threat'.[122] Secondly, even if so 'it would have to ascertain whether the collective action ... is suitable for ensuring the achievement of the objective pursued and does not go beyond what is necessary to attain that objective'.[123] The language, particularly of the second condition, is familiar from the Court's case law stipulating the criterion of 'proportionality', and 'it is ultimately for the national court, which has sole jurisdiction to assess the facts and interpret the national legislation, to determine whether and to what extent such collective action meets those requirements'.[124] The Court goes on to 'provide guidance'.[125]

Significantly, however, this 'guidance' differs for the FSU (primary collective action) and the ITF (secondary or solidarity action). As regards the FSU, there are positive and negative signals. Positive is the following proposition:[126]

> As regards the appropriateness of the action taken by FSU for attaining the objectives pursued in the case in the main proceedings, it should be borne in mind that it is common ground that collective action, like collective negotiations and collective agreements, may, in the particular circumstances of a case, be one of the main ways in which trade unions protect the interests of their members.

Negative is the next proposition:[127]

> As regards the question of whether or not the collective action at issue in the main proceedings goes beyond what is necessary to achieve the objective pursued, it is for the national court to examine, in particular, on the one hand, whether, under the national rules and collective agreement law applicable to that action, FSU did not have *other means at its disposal which were less restrictive of freedom of establishment* in order to bring to a successful conclusion the collective negotiations entered into with Viking, and, on the other, whether that trade union had *exhausted those means* before initiating such action.[128]

Similarly, as regards the ITF, there are positive and negative signals. Negative is the blanket statement that, as regards the FOC policy which 'results in shipowners being prevented from registering their vessels in a State other

---

[122] Para. 81.    [123] Para. 82.    [124] Para. 85.

[125] Para. 85: '... the Court of Justice, which is called on to provide answers of use to the national court, may provide guidance ... in order to enable to national court to give judgment in the particular case before it'.

[126] Para. 86.    [127] Para. 87, italics added.

[128] Again, the principle of trade union autonomy is threatened as courts are called upon to judge what action unions should take to protect their members.

than that of which the beneficial owners of those vessels are nationals, the restrictions on freedom of establishment resulting from such action cannot be objectively justified'.[129] This is offset by the positive statement that immediately follows: 'the objective of that policy is also to protect and improve seafarers' terms and conditions of employment'.[130] Taken together, the positive and negative signals in this 'guidance', both as regards the FSU and the ITF, make the national court's task highly unpredictable.[131]

### An 'anti-social dumping principle' of proportionality?

There were some additional, and potentially significant, indications from the Court regarding the legitimacy of collective action in the face of the threat of social dumping. This is not formulated explicitly as an 'anti-social dumping principle', but its substance is indicative of such a principle.

### Primary action (the FSU)

As regards the FSU's primary action, the question concerns the public interest test of protection of workers which 'would no longer be tenable if it were established that the jobs or conditions of employment at issue were not jeopardised or under serious threat'.[132] The Court then proceeds to provide indicators (but only by way of example: 'in particular') of what would establish 'that the jobs or conditions of employment at issue were not jeopardised or under serious threat'. This would require an 'undertaking' by the employer that was:[133]

> from a *legal* point of view, as *binding* as the terms of a collective agreement[134] and if it was of such a nature as to provide a *guarantee* to the workers that the *statutory* provisions would be complied with and the terms of the *collective agreement* governing their working relationship *maintained*.[135]

On the one hand, the substance of this appears to be that the only way an employer can show there is no jeopardy or threat is to guarantee jobs and

---

[129] Para. 88. This is either a misunderstanding or a misrepresentation of the FOC policy which was previously clearly stated to concern negotiating rights and not registration (para. 8).

[130] Para. 88.

[131] For example, as regards the FSU, the litigation in *Viking* revealed the complexities lying beneath the requirement that other means less restrictive than collective action had been exhausted. Following the ECJ's decision, and prior to the anticipated hearing before the English Court of Appeal, expert evidence was prepared as to the precise steps taken by the FSU (including compulsory intervention by a state mediator consistent with Finnish law) prior to preparing collective action. It remained highly uncertain whether this would satisfy the test of exhausting other means less restrictive than collective action. As regards the ITF, it was completely unpredictable how the national court would weigh the FOC policy's restricting freedom of establishment against its objective of protecting seafarers.

[132] Para. 81.      [133] Para. 82, italics added.

[134] Here the perennial problem that, in the UK, collective agreements (where they exist) are not usually legally binding.

[135] Note the parallel with the protection of workers under the Transfer of Undertakings Directive. The parallel is reinforced if 'working relationship' includes the collective relationship with the union, as presumably it does as it is in a collective agreement.

conditions of employment. Otherwise, collective action is justifiable. In practice, this is normally a trade union's negotiating position.[136] Failure to give the guarantee, to reach a collective agreement, so that jobs or conditions or employment are 'not jeopardised or under serious threat', *ipso facto* justifies collective action. Collective action will not be taken in practice if collective agreements are reached guaranteeing no jeopardy or threat to jobs and conditions.

On the other hand, the requirement of an undertaking 'from a *legal* point of view, as *binding* as the terms of a collective agreement and [...] of such a nature as to provide a *guarantee* to the workers that the *statutory* provisions would be complied with and the terms of the *collective agreement* governing their working relationship *maintained*' raises considerable problems. First, the legal nature of a collective agreement varies in different Member States, as does its enforceability. Secondly, questions will arise as to the precise legal nature, substantive content and enforceability of a given 'undertaking'.[137] To apply the ECJ's test, the national court would be in the position of assessing the employer's undertaking as compared with the union's demands. The proceedings are transformed into a substantive arbitration on the merits, not a legal dispute. The collective labour laws of the Member States have aimed precisely to avoid placing national courts in the position which the ECJ postulates is required by EU law.

### Secondary or solidarity action (the ITF)

As regards the ITF, the Court states:[138]

ITF is required, when asked by one of its members, to initiate solidarity action ... irrespective of whether or not that owner's exercise of its right of freedom of

---

[136] An important caveat is that the collective action envisaged here is defensive. The guidance is not directed towards collective action which aims to support demands for improvement of working conditions. The Court's subjecting defensive collective action to conditions opens the prospect of challenges to the lawfulness of such 'offensive' collective action, but provides no guidance whatever. Contrast the statement by Advocate-General Mengozzi in *Laval*, paras. 259–60: 'Admittedly, such a system is liable to produce unforeseeable results or indeed, in certain circumstances, to allow wage claims that might be excessive. However, those circumstances are inherent in a system of collective employment relations which is based on and favour negotiation between both sides of industry, and, therefore, contractual freedom, rather than intervention by the national legislature. I do not think that, at its present stage of development, Community law can encroach upon that approach to employment relationships through the application of one of the fundamental freedoms of movement provided for in the Treaty'.

[137] Again, the litigation in *Viking* revealed the complexities lying beneath the surface of the bland requirement of an 'undertaking'. The employer in *Viking* had given its undertaking to the English court, not to the trade union. Following the ECJ's decision, and prior to the anticipated hearing before the English Court of Appeal, expert evidence was prepared questioning the legal nature of that undertaking and its enforceability, in Finland and the UK. Similarly, its content (for example, promises of redeployment rather than redundancy, exclusion of fixed-term employees) was challenged as not acceptable to the FSU. *Viking* was settled following the ECJ's decision only days before it was due to heard in the Court of Appeal; consequently, these issues did not need to be resolved in court.

[138] Para. 89, italics added.

establishment is liable to have a harmful effect on the work or conditions of employment of its employees. Therefore, as Viking argued during the hearing without being contradicted by ITF in that regard, the policy of reserving the right of collective negotiations to trade unions of the State of which the beneficial owner of a vessel is a national is also applicable where the vessel is registered in a State which guarantees workers a *higher* level of social protection than they would enjoy in the first State.

The implication is that solidarity action is only unlawful if higher (or equivalent) conditions are available in the state of re-flagging. If not, collective action is justifiable to protect workers' conditions. However, if the state of re-flagging guarantees a higher level, collective action is unlikely to be taken to insist on lower conditions! It may be argued that, as a matter of practice, conjecture about future conditions in the state of re-flagging cannot be foreseen. The answer is: as in the case of the FSU, they should be guaranteed by legally binding agreements.[139]

### Conclusion: bad for trade unions (as employers exploit unpredictability) and bad for the courts (arbitrating on the merits of social dumping)

The substance of the ECJ's propositions regarding the FSU and ITF may be characterised as justifying collective action where employers do not guarantee equivalent jobs and conditions, in the form of legally binding collective agreements. The FSU's collective action is justifiable as, in the absence of such binding agreements, jobs or conditions or employment may be presumed to be 'jeopardised or under serious threat'. The ITF's action is justified where higher or equivalent conditions cannot be guaranteed. In substance, this is a principle that collective action is justifiable to counter 'social dumping' – where existing jobs and conditions are threatened and no guarantees are forthcoming of equivalent protection.[140]

However, the conditions and requirements postulated by the ECJ remain highly uncertain and the result of their application by national courts is highly

---

[139] The next paragraph of the Court's judgment does not clearly state this, but it may be read in by implication (para. 90): '… collective action such as that at issue in the main proceedings, which seeks to induce an undertaking whose registered office is in a given Member State to enter into a collective work agreement with a trade union established in that State and to apply the terms set out in that agreement to the employees of a subsidiary of that undertaking established in another Member State, constitutes a restriction within the meaning of that Article [43]. That restriction may, in principle, be justified by an overriding reason of public interest, such as the protection of workers, provided that it is established that the restriction is suitable for the attainment of the legitimate objective pursued and does not go beyond what is necessary to achieve that objective'.

[140] The principle is reminiscent of case law on the Posting Directive: *Arblade, et al.*, which allows the host Member State to impose mandatory employment conditions unless equivalent protection is provided by the home Member State. This element is found in Advocate-General Mengozzi's Opinion in *Laval*. At a more fundamental level, it translates as an application of the equal treatment principle: the exercise of freedom of establishment to another Member State is conditional on equal treatment of workers before and after the relocation.

unpredictable. This is particularly problematic for trade unions. Employers are able to exploit the uncertainty to threaten legal action seeking compensation, often for substantial amounts, placing unions in a position of extreme risk of potentially unlimited damages claims.[141] It is also problematic for national courts. They are placed in the invidious position of arbitrating as between the demands by trade unions for protection of jobs and conditions, and the undertakings offered by employers in response.

### The ECJ's model of transnational collective bargaining in *Laval*: 'proportionality', predictability and maximum standards

In both *Viking* and *Laval*, the ECJ addressed the issue of how the Treaty's economic freedoms are to be interpreted in relation to European labour law. The Advocates-General and the ECJ confronted issues of fundamental rights, social dumping and the lawfulness of primary and secondary action. However, in its judgment in *Laval*, the ECJ's ambitions extended even further. The ECJ chose to project a specific industrial relations model of collective bargaining which it considered to be consistent with transnational economic freedoms, an undertaking which would make even seasoned experts in comparative and transnational industrial relations pause. The outcome reveals perhaps that

---

[141] It did not take long for this risk to materialise. The *Financial Times* (12 March 2008, page 2) contains the following report (Kevin Done, 'BA Uses EU Law to Prevent Strike by Pilots'): 'British Airways is looking to use competition law [*sic*] and a threat to seek "unlimited damages" against the UK pilots' union in order to stop them going on strike. An overwhelming majority of BA's 3,200 pilots voted last month in favour of taking strike action over BA's plans to set up OpenSkies, a new airline subsidiary, with a pilot workforce separate to its mainline operations, which fly to and from Heathrow and Gatwick airports. Conciliation talks aimed at resolving the bitter dispute over future pilot staffing at BA subsidiary airlines in Europe collapsed on Friday. BALPA, the pilots' union, had planned to issue dates for its first strikes, which would ground the airline, but was forced to postpone the move when BA warned the union it had "a valid legal claim" against it, if it "took the disproportionate step of calling a strike". The union said yesterday that BA was claiming its pilots could not legally pursue their concerns over job security because of European legislation. BALPA said BA was claiming it had a fundamental right under article 43 of the EC Treaty to establish operations in another European Union member state. The right included both establishing new airline services in other EU states, as well as acquiring existing operations from other airlines. BA was claiming that BALPA was seeking to limit that right by insisting that there should be a single pilot workforce with a shared seniority list to determine pilot employment. BA has already begun to recruit pilots for OpenSkies. Jim McAuslan, BALPA general-secretary, said BA "should be at the negotiating table" and not using European legislation, designed to ensure free competition between companies, in order to restrict the freedoms of trades unions in industrial disputes. He said that BALPA was seeking a High Court hearing to clarify whether the European legislation could be used in an industrial dispute and whether the union could rely on the strike ballot to avoid a claim for unlimited damages. The union has won court backing for the strike vote to remain valid beyond the normal 28-day limit until applicability of European law is clarified. It rules out taking any strike action during the Easter holiday period. BA said yesterday it was "pleased" BALPA had recognised it had "a strong legal case". It said that "any strike action would be unlawful", and the union had therefore decided not to issue strike dates. OpenSkies is BA's most ambitious attempt to take advantage of the US/European Union "open skies" treaty liberalising transatlantic aviation'. This illustrates the magnitude of the threat confronting European trade unions when aggressive employers try to use (abuse) the Treaty's economic freedoms.

creating a model of European industrial relations is too important a matter to be left to judges.

## The Court adopts a model dictated by its controversial view of the Posting Directive

In *Laval*, the ECJ offers a specific vision of (i) the labour standards which are protected by Community law, (ii) Community law's regulation of the nature and role of collective bargaining, and (iii) the legality of collective action in the EU single market.[142] Through the prism of the Posting Directive, the Court proposes a model of a collective bargaining system consistent with the economic freedoms protected by the Treaty.[143]

In brief, the ECJ in *Laval* regards the Posting Directive as determining the 'maximum' labour standards applicable to transnational service providers in the European single market.[144] A 'maximum' vision has implications for collective action: collective action aiming to impose higher standards is unlawful. This may be disputed as inconsistent with the decision in *Viking*. Moreover,

---

[142] The questions referred by the Swedish Labour Court focused on the transposition of the Posting Directive by Sweden. Consequently, the judgment focused on an assessment of the specific Swedish collective bargaining system and its relation to the Posting Directive's requirements. Directive 96/71/EC concerning the posting of workers in the framework of the provision of services. OJ 1996 L18/1. The Posting Directive became the crucial element in the ECJ's vision. Sweden did not attempt to reconcile the Directive with the Swedish decentralised and flexible Swedish collective bargaining system. Or, indeed, with Community law on free movement in general. See para. 110 of the judgment: '... lack of provisions, of any kind, which are sufficiently precise and accessible that they do not render it impossible or excessively difficult in practice for such an undertaking [foreign service provider] to determine the obligations with which it is required to comply as regards minimum pay ...'. One consequence of the decision in *Laval* appears to be that it requires a dramatic transformation of the Swedish system. But, as will be argued, accommodation may be possible through a more subtle interpretation (which the ECJ appears to overlook) of how the Posting Directive can operate in the Swedish system. This interpretation reconciles the Directive with the collective bargaining systems of Sweden and of other EU Member States by accepting collective agreements which *explicitly* allow for flexibility as envisaged by Advocate-General Bot in his Opinion in Case C-346/06, *Rechtsanwalt Dr. Dirk Rüffert* v. *Land Niedersachsen*, ECJ decision of 3 April 2008. Opinion of Advocate-General Bot, 20 September 2007. This could become a model for an EU-wide collective bargaining policy: EU transnational collective agreements establishing minimum standards with flexibility allowed for national variations.

[143] The Court's model can be characterised as a return to a (neo-) corporatist structure of industrial relations in which the social partners are primary actors through collective bargaining, but the state (or the EU) exercises overall control through regulation of the legal effects of the outcomes of the action of the social partners (collective agreements). Consciously or not, it may be that this vision reflects the neo-corporatist (1970s and 1980s) experience and memories both of the ECJ judges from some pre-enlargement Member States and, perhaps also, the experience of judges from some of the newer ex-Soviet bloc Member States. This model presented problems for some Member States' collective bargaining systems, notably Sweden. Alternatively, it may be see as dictated by a policy aiming at geopolitical stability through economic integration of enterprises in the new Member States – enabling them to exploit their labour cost advantage – at the expense of workers and their organisations in the 'old' Member States.

[144] Reaffirmed in Case C-346/06, *Rechtsanwalt Dr. Dirk Rüffert* v. *Land Niedersachsen*, ECJ decision of 3 April 2008.

the ECJ's model, based on its interpretation of the Posting Directive, is inconsistent with the EU legislator's intention behind the Posting Directive, which was to stipulate 'minimum' labour standards.

This requires attention to be paid to the model of collective bargaining reflected in the Posting Directive.[145] What is the Posting Directive's model and how does it relate to the vision of labour standards, collective bargaining and collective action projected by the ECJ?

### The Posting Directive's model of labour regulation in the EU

The Posting Directive begins with a vision of mandatory labour standards established by *legislation* as regards certain terms and conditions of employment.[146] Labour standards established by *collective agreements* are also mandatory, but must (i) 'have been declared universally applicable within the meaning of paragraph 8';[147] and (ii) apply to specified activities in the construction sector.[148]

The model of mandatory labour standards is thereby narrowly defined. Crucially, however, the Directive goes on to allow for further mandatory labour standards as regards (i) other types of collective agreement;[149] and (ii) the scope of application of the Directive with respect both to other terms and conditions of employment and other sectors.[150] The initial rigid[151] and

---

[145] There are fascinating antecedents in its formulations reflecting labour standards in public procurement (ILO Convention 94 of 1949 Labour Standards (Public Contracts) and, before, in the UK, Fair Wages Resolutions). See B. Bercusson, *Fair Wages Resolutions*, London: Mansell, London, 1978.

[146] Article 3(1) reads: 'Member States shall ensure that, whatever the law applicable to the employment relationship, the undertakings referred to in Article 1(1) guarantee workers posted to their territory the terms and conditions of employment covering the following matters which, in the Member State where the work is carried out, are laid down: – by law, regulation or administrative provisions, and/or – by collective agreements or arbitration awards which have been declared universally applicable within the meaning of paragraph 8, insofar as they concern the activities referred to in the Annex: (a) maximum work periods and minimum rest periods; (b) minimum paid annual holidays; (c) the minimum rates of pay, including overtime rates'.

[147] Article 3(8): '"Collective agreements or arbitration awards which have been declared universally applicable" means collective agreements or arbitration awards which must be observed by all undertakings in the geographical area and in the profession or industry concerned'. Cf. ILO Convention No. 94 of 1949.

[148] Article 3(1): '... insofar as they concern the activities referred to in the Annex.'

[149] Article 3(8): 'In the absence of a system for declaring collective agreements or arbitration awards to be of universal application within the meaning of the first subparagraph, Member States may, if they so decide, base themselves on: collective agreements or arbitration awards which are generally applicable to all similar undertakings in the geographical area and in the profession or industry concerned; and/or collective agreements which have been concluded by the most representative employers' and labour organizations at national level and which are applied throughout national territory'.

[150] Article 3(10): 'This Directive shall not preclude the application by Member States, in compliance with the Treaty, to national undertakings and to the undertakings of other States, on a basis of equality of treatment, of: terms and conditions of employment on matters other than those referred to in the first subparagraph of paragraph 1 in the case of public policy provisions; terms and conditions of employment laid down in the collective agreements or arbitration awards within the meaning of paragraph 8 and concerning activities other than those referred to in the Annex'.

[151] Exclusively legislation and universally applicable collective agreements.

narrow[152] vision of mandatory labour standards is therefore made flexible and potentially expanded by allowing a wider role for collective bargaining.[153]

### Sweden's failure to adopt the Posting Directive's model

The ECJ's view was that Sweden had failed to use the options available under the Posting Directive's vision of mandatory labour standards: 'Sweden does not have a system for declaring collective agreements universally applicable.'[154] Later in the judgment, under the heading: *'The possibilities available to the Member States for determining the terms and conditions of employment applicable to posted workers, including minimum rates of pay'*, after reciting the provisions in the two indents of the second sub-paragraph of Article 3(8), the ECJ states that 'recourse to the latter possibility requires, first, that the Member State must so decide …'.[155] The ECJ continues:[156]

> It is common ground that, in Sweden, the terms and conditions of employment covering the matters listed in Article 3(1), first subparagraph, (a) to (g) of Directive 96/71, save for minimum rates of pay, have been laid down by law. It is also not disputed that the collective agreements have not been declared universally applicable, and that that Member State has not made use of the possibility provided for in the second subparagraph of Article 3(8) of that Directive.[157]

---

[152] Limited scope of terms and conditions of employment; construction sector activities only.

[153] Further, Article 3(7) allows for more favourable conditions.

[154] Para. 7. At that point, the ECJ does not refer to the alternative possibilities for collective agreements to apply in the second sub-paragraph of Article 3(8). Rather, the ECJ expressly states that 'not all Swedish employers are bound by a collective agreement'. It is not clear if this is intended to exclude those other possibilities. It may be argued that it does not. The first indent of the second subparagraph of Article 3(8) refers to: 'collective agreements or arbitration awards which are generally applicable to all similar undertakings in the geographical area and in the profession or industry concerned'. The phrase *'generally* applicable' might allow for some leeway in requiring that the agreement apply to *all* undertakings. The definition of the relevant collective agreements in the second sub-paragraph of Article 3(8), second indent, includes: 'collective agreements which have been concluded by the most representative employers' and labour organizations at national level and which are applied throughout national territory'. This would include the Swedish national collective agreements ('applied throughout national territory') which explicitly leave it to local bargaining to fix the minimum rates of pay. The requirement that the agreement be 'applied throughout national territory' arguably leaves scope for the agreement not to apply to all Swedish employers. In both cases, the collective agreements under the Swedish collective bargaining system are not excluded from the second sub-paragraph of Article 3(8). See Torgeir Aarvaag Stokke, 'The Anatomy of Two-tier Bargaining Models', (2008) 14 *European Journal of Industrial Relations* (No. 1) 7–24.

[155] Para. 66.    [156] Para. 67.

[157] Again, in para. 70: '… the first subparagraph of Article 3(1) of Directive 96/71 relates only to minimum rates of pay. Therefore, that provision cannot be relied on to justify an obligation on such service providers to comply with rates of pay such as those which the trade unions seek in this case to impose in the framework of the Swedish system, which do not constitute minimum wages and are not, moreover, laid down in accordance with the means set out in that regard in Article 3(1) and (8) of the directive'. One question is whether Sweden did 'decide' to make use of the second sub-paragraph of Article 3(8): collective agreements setting standards. Need an explicit decision be made? Article 3(8) provides that 'Member States may, if they so decide'. The Swedish system arguably has so 'decided' by virtue of its well-known non-legislative, but regulated and orderly, industrial relations system. The decision in *Laval* is revealed as an

In other words, the ECJ decided that the labour standards negotiated in Sweden's flexible and decentralised system of collective wage bargaining fall outside the Posting Directive. As such, collective action to secure or enforce those collectively negotiated standards is unlawful (italics added):[158]

> It must therefore be concluded at this stage that *a Member State* in which the minimum rates of pay are not determined in accordance with one of the means provided for in Article 3(1) and (8) of Directive 96/71 *is not entitled*, pursuant to that directive, *to impose on undertakings* established in other Member States, in the framework of the transnational provision of services, *negotiation at the place of work*, on a case-by-case basis, having regard to the qualifications and tasks of the employees, so that the undertakings concerned may ascertain the wages which they are to pay their posted workers.[159]

### Collective bargaining violates Article 49 EC

Crucially, the ECJ appears to consider that it is the *Treaty provisions* on free movement of services which dictate this result, not the Posting Directive. Following its finding that the Posting Directive has not been implemented in the Swedish context, the ECJ invokes Article 49 EC to support its conclusion: 'It is necessary to assess further, the obligations on undertakings established in another Member State which stem from such a system for determining wages with regard to Article 49 EC.'[160] Collective bargaining as a method for achieving labour standards, 'negotiation at the place of work', is deemed to violate Article 49.

The ECJ's decision in *Laval* is contestable, to say the least. Its interpretation of Article 49 declaring collective bargaining to be a restriction on free movement of service providers conflicts with the Services Directive's explicit provision that collective bargaining is not a restriction.[161] It is inconsistent with the Posting Directive's mechanism providing for cooperation on information about terms and conditions of employment which aims to ensure sufficient certainty and transparency.[162] At the most fundamental level, the ECJ's vision is in conflict with the EU's policy in support of social dialogue: 'The social

---

impractical and unnecessary interpretation of the Directive that undermines the Swedish collective bargaining system.

[158] Para. 71, italics added.

[159] This is to condemn precisely the flexible and decentralised system of collective bargaining in Sweden, which is advocated by the Commission, among others. The judgment reveals the ECJ's lack of industrial relations experience or expertise. One question is whether the ECJ would insist on this even if Sweden did explicitly decide to use the possibilities in the indents under Article 3(8).

[160] Para. 72.

[161] The target of the Services Directive is those *requirements* which are deemed to violate the rules on free movement. Article 4 ('Definitions'), in Article 4(7) stipulates that collective agreements are *not* such requirements.

[162] For example, the ECJ (para. 6) quotes Article 4 of the Posting Directive concerning cooperation among Member States regarding information about terms and conditions of employment. Article 4(4): 'Each Member State shall take the appropriate measures to make the information on the terms and conditions of employment referred to in Article 3 generally available'. Para. 9 of the judgment refers to the Swedish authorities ensuring transparency. Para. 35 refers to the

dialogue is rooted in the history of the European continent, and this distinguishes the Union from most other regions of the world.'[163] The ECJ's decision raises fundamental questions as to the Court's interpretation of Article 49 and other Treaty provisions on economic freedoms in relation to the systems of industrial relations at national and European level, and to the European social model in general.

### The Posting Directive as a 'maximum standard' model of collective bargaining acceptable to EC law

This interpretation of Article 49 in effect condemns established collective bargaining systems of Member States which interfere with transnational economic freedoms provided for in the EC Treaty. It was driven by the finding of the ECJ in *Laval* that Sweden had failed to transpose the Posting Directive, to implement it 'in accordance with one of the means provided for in Article 3(1) and (8) of Directive 96/71'.

The Court's decision in *Laval* imposes a regulatory model of collective bargaining on Member States based on the Posting Directive. Article 49 is interpreted as meaning that collective agreements and collective action to enforce agreements are obstacles to free movement of services. In effect, the ECJ imposes the constraints of the Posting Directive on Member States' systems. Only the model prescribed by the Posting Directive can protect their national collective bargaining systems from the impact of the Treaty provisions on economic freedoms. And the Posting Directive is interpreted as stipulating a maximum level of labour standards: those established in legislation and universally applicable collective agreements covering a narrow range of terms and conditions in construction activities. Member States and trade unions can do no more to protect themselves against 'social dumping'.

The ECJ's finding that Sweden failed to use the means available had the consequence that the Swedish system of collective bargaining produces labour

request by Laval to the Swedish authorities for information and their reply: it was for social partners to agree wages. Para. 36 states that Laval refused to sign a collective agreement on other terms as it did not know the wages in advance. By definition, wages will not be known until negotiations are concluded. The ECJ appears to argue that collective bargaining is a restriction on free movement of service providers due to uncertainty and lack of transparency. Para. 100: '[A restriction on the freedom to provide services within the meaning of Article 49] is all the more true of the fact that, in order to ascertain the minimum wage rates to be paid to their posted workers, those undertakings may be forced, by way of collective action, into negotiations with the trade unions of unspecified duration at the place at which the services in question are to be provided'. The lack of transparency as to what negotiations might produce produces uncertainty for enterprises seeking to enter the market. There is a contradiction in so far as the ECJ states that collective action is disproportionate where there are other means of achieving the objective which are less restrictive. Negotiation is precisely such a method and in this case there had been negotiations preceding the collective action. The Court seems to be saying that negotiation is a disproportionate method of protecting workers' interests because of the lack of certainty affecting foreign service providers. Of course, (i) uncertainty is inherent in negotiations, and (ii) equally affects domestic service providers; i.e. no discrimination.

[163]  The introduction to the Commission's Communication on *The European Social Dialogue – A Force for Innovation and Change*, COM(2002) 341 final, Brussels, 26 June 2002, p. 6.

standards that (i) fall outside the Posting Directive's permitted standards; and (ii) thereby violate Article 49 EC as constituting obstacles to free movement of service providers by virtue of the uncertainty as to their obligations.[164]

### The Posting Directive's other models of collective bargaining acceptable to EC law

The next section of the ECJ's answer to the first question posed by the Swedish Labour Court[165] concerned '*matters which may be covered by the terms and conditions of work applicable to posted workers*'. The question was what obligations may be imposed on service providers by virtue of the Posting Directive's specific transposition in the Swedish context. The substantive conclusion is: *maximum* standards only. Arguably, however, this *maximum* standard of obligations does *not* apply in a context where a Member State takes advantage, as Sweden did not,[166] of the means provided for in the Posting Directive, and specifically, the options provided in the two indents of the second sub-paragraph of Article 3(8).[167]

The implication is that Member States using the options available in the second sub-paragraph of Article 3(8) (and Article 3(10)) of the Posting Directive have nothing to fear from Article 49 EC. In particular, Member States have the option to go beyond universally applicable collective agreements covering a narrow range of terms and conditions in the construction sector. If Member States use this option to combat social dumping, collective action to protect these labour standards is permitted. Failure to do so, however, leaves Member

---

[164] However, as elaborated below, this gives rise to the implication that a Member State implementing the Directive in accordance with the means provided by the Posting Directive *can* protect its collective bargaining system.

[165] Paras. 73ff.

[166] In my view, the decision in *Laval* is specific to the Swedish context of a failure to use the options available under the Posting Directive. I suggest that had Sweden done so, its collective bargaining system, and the labour standards prescribed under it, could be accommodated by the Directive. The ECJ could have achieved this result by referring to Sweden's use of the indents in the second sub-paragraph of Article 3(8); specifically, national agreements allowing for flexible negotiations at local level. But not having done so, Sweden was condemned. The ECJ held that the Swedish collective bargaining system violates Article 49 due to its effects on service providers, in particular, the absence of precise and certain labour standards. Consequently, collective action to enforce labour standards in Swedish collective agreements was unlawful. Conversely, however, if Sweden had used the options available in the indents of the second sub-paragraph of Article 3(8), service providers would be obliged to respect those collective agreements. This would achieve the requisite certainty needed for compliance with Article 49, and collective action to enforce these labour standards would be lawful.

[167] To adapt the ECJ's conclusion in paragraph 71: 'It must therefore be concluded at this stage that a Member State in which the minimum rates of pay *are* [not] determined in accordance with one of the means provided for in Article 3(1) and (8) of Directive 96/71 *is* [not] entitled, pursuant to that directive, to impose on undertakings established in other Member States, in the framework of the transnational provision of services, negotiation at the place of work, on a case-by-case basis, having regard to the qualifications and tasks of the employees, so that the undertakings concerned may ascertain the wages which they are to pay their posted workers'. The means provided by the Posting Directive to determine labour standards arguably allow for a flexible collective bargaining system.

States only with the maximum standard of universally applicable agreements covering a narrow range of terms and conditions in construction activities.

The outcome of the decision in *Laval* remains, however, that the ECJ has used the Posting Directive to impose on Member States what it considers to be a model of collective bargaining compatible with the economic freedoms of the EC Treaty. This is indeed an enterprise of ambition, perhaps beyond the competence, in every sense, of the ECJ.

### Interim conclusion

The conditions and requirements postulated by the ECJ for collective action to be lawful create great uncertainty. Their application by national courts is highly unpredictable. This is particularly problematic for trade unions, as employers are able to exploit the uncertainty to threaten legal action seeking substantial monetary compensation, putting unions at risk of potentially unlimited damages claims.[168] It is also problematic for national courts placed in the invidious position of arbitrating as between demands by trade unions for protection of jobs and conditions, and undertakings offered by employers in response.

Any advantage of the ECJ's apparent formulation of a general 'anti-social dumping principle' in *Viking*, already questionable due to the unpredictability of applying 'proportionality' in practice, appears to be undermined by the quite different criterion applied by the Court to determine the lawfulness of collective action in *Laval*.

The doctrinal basis of the interpretation of the economic freedoms in the Treaty in *Laval* is the Posting Directive. The interpretation is driven by a policy (i) promoting wage competition in the internal market, the opposite of an anti-social dumping principle, and (ii) stipulating a maximum standard of protection, prohibiting collective action to achieve higher standards, thereby violating fundamental rights of collective bargaining and collective action by the social partners.[169]

Which of these principles: for (*Laval*) or against (*Viking*) social dumping is to prevail? The struggle is unlikely to conclude with these two decisions of the ECJ, for at least three reasons. First, due to political pressures, the other EU institutions are unlikely to stand by, not least with the prospect of elections to

---

[168] See the threat by British Airways reported in the *Financial Times* (12 March 2008, page 2), Note 141 above.

[169] In *Laval*, the Court's approach was influenced by the questions referred by the Swedish Labour Court concerning Swedish transposition of the Posting Directive and Sweden's *Lex Britannia*. The reference by the Swedish Court concerning the Posting Directive had an impact on the more general question of the Community law on collective action. In *Laval*, the ECJ transforms what appears in the *Viking* judgment to be a general 'anti-social dumping principle' protecting jobs and working conditions. Instead, the Posting Directive is invoked to establish the maximum objective of collective action. Collective action to achieve labour standards higher than those postulated in the Posting Directive is unlawful. The Posting Directive is interpreted as stipulating a maximum standard. Social dumping to drive higher standards down to that level is deemed to be the exercise of economic freedom protected by the Treaty and cannot be restrained through collective action.

the European Parliament and a new Commission in 2009.[170] Secondly, other cases are likely to be referred to the ECJ from national courts seeking clarification or reconciliation of the principles in *Viking* and *Laval*. Thirdly, there is the prospect of disobedience by national courts. Swedish courts are unlikely to reverse a century of disengagement from collective disputes and become active interveners adjudicating on the proportionality of collective action. Constitutional courts in Member States where the right to strike is protected by the national constitution (Sweden, Finland, Germany, France, Italy, among others) are likely to question the competence of both the ECJ and of EU law to override established constitutional practice regarding collective action.

The role of the ECJ in the future of European labour law depends on whether it can recover from the self-inflicted blows of its decisions in *Viking* and *Laval*. One lesson of *Viking* and *Laval* is that creating European labour law is too serious a matter to be left to judges. But the unsatisfactory result produced by the ECJ in these cases was not inevitable. Other solutions were available for an ECJ choosing to 'opt-in' and regulate collective action.[171]

## 'Opting-in' (2): interpretation of Treaty provisions on economic freedoms and social policy

In the submissions of a number of Member States in the *Viking* proceedings, it was proposed that the provisions on the economic freedoms in Title III of the Treaty should be *interpreted* so as to be consistent with the social policy provisions of Title XI of the Treaty.[172] Adopting a historical

---

[170] See Chapter 22.

[171] See the proposals in Bercusson, 'The Trade Union Movement and the European Union: Judgment Day'; *Collective Action and Economic Freedoms*; *The European Court of Justice, Labour Law and ILO Standards*, proceedings of the Colloquium, 50 Years of EU – 50 Years of Jurisdiction of the European Court of Justice Concerning Labour and Social Law, organised by the Federal Ministry of Labour and Social Affairs, Federal Republic of Germany, EU Council Presidency, Berlin, 25 June 2007 (forthcoming); 'Fostering Social Europe in the Single Market', in *The Future of Legal Europe*, proceedings of a conference to mark fifteen years of the Academy of European Law Trier, 27–29 September 2007 (forthcoming).

[172] The Belgian government submitted that Community law cannot be interpreted in such a way that it would automatically impair exercise of the fundamental rights as recognised by the Union and the Member States. The French government, that Article 43 EC is to be interpreted as meaning that collective action taken by trade unions does not fall within their scope. The Swedish government, that Article 43 is not to be interpreted in such a way as to prevent a trade union or a federation of trade unions from taking collective measures to protect their members' interests. The German government noted that the ECJ had formulated a concept of restriction of fundamental freedoms in broad terms, but in this case there should be strict interpretation, to take into account principles of freedom of contract and freedom of association. The Irish government similarly argued that the right of establishment should not be interpreted so broadly as to call into question competence reserved to Member States under Title XI, and that core industrial relations activities fall within Title XI and should be regulated by national law. The Finnish government, citing *Albany*, argued that the social objectives of collective agreements may not be undermined by Community law. That would be the consequence if trade unions were unable to take industrial action to achieve a collective agreement. In its oral submission, the Commission was succinct: Articles 43 and 49 are to be interpreted so that social policy falls outside them.

perspective, the ETUC's letter attached to the ITF submission shared this approach:[173]

> The ETUC considers that the relationship between economic freedoms of movement and fundamental social rights to collective action should be consistent with the evolution of the EU from a purely economic Community establishing a common market to a European Union with a social policy aimed at protecting workers employed in the common market who are also citizens of the Union ...
>
> Economic provisions of the Treaty have to be interpreted in light of changes in the scope of activities of the EU.[174]

The rationale for this interpretive approach lies in the view that collective action by trade unions, like the free movement of undertakings, is consistent with the effective functioning of the internal market.

## Reconciling collective action by trade unions with the economic freedoms of employers

Prior to becoming Advocate-General, Miguel Poiares Maduro developed a complex argument regarding the constitutional development of the EU through the ECJ,[175] concluding:[176]

---

[173] Paras. 14, 16, 18.

[174] The submission continued: 'The ETUC considers that the correct analogy with *Albany* is that the free movement provisions of the Treaty must be interpreted consistently with the fundamental right to collective action, as a general principle of EC law, in accordance with *ordre communautaire social*, i.e. principles which reflect the general *acquis communautaire* of social policy of the EU and, in particular, the regulation of employment and industrial relations in the Treaty and relevant secondary legislation'.

[175] The argument looks to the balance between negative and positive integration, the former favouring economic freedoms and the latter social rights. Factors advancing the former include qualified majority voting rules in the legislative process and frequent access by powerful economic actors to the judicial process, while the latter are constrained by unanimity rules in the legislative process and less frequent access to the judicial process by those in need of social protection. Indeed Maduro hints at the need for trade union intervention when he says 'Moreover, the fact that the European Constitution is mainly a result of the judicial development of the Treaty rules supported by litigation means that the European Constitution will be a result of representation and participation in such a judicial process'. Miguel Poiares Maduro, 'Striking the Elusive Balance Between Economic Freedom and Social Rights in the EU', Chapter 13 in Philip Alston (ed.), *The EU and Human Rights*, Oxford: Oxford University Press, 1999, pp. 449–472, at p. 455. He points out the argument that 'the European Union is an attempt to answer to those current global market competition trends by creating a new forum in which protective social rights and policies can be agreed and enforced', and highlights that 'labour lawyers try to reinstate the primacy of social rights over the market through common regulations at the European level' (p. 465).

[176] Drawing on concepts developed by Albert Hirschman, *Exit, Voice and Loyalty: Responses to Decline in Firms, Organizations and States*, Cambridge, MA: Harvard University Press, 1970. Maduro, 'Striking the Elusive Balance', pp. 469, 470. As Maduro stated in his earlier book, *We The Court: The European Court of Justice and the European Economic Constitution* (Oxford: Hart, 1998), at pp. 138–9: 'From a representative point of view, a market operating at its best will be a market where decisions are the result of voluntary transactions in which all the people affected participate, and in which all costs and benefits and alternative transactions are taken into account. Such a market would be an ideal decision-maker from the point of view of resource

In this respect, the system requires a set of social rights that can be said to guarantee participation and representation in market decisions and, by internalizing costs which tend to be ignored in those decisions, increase efficiency. Those social rights are related to forms of voice and exit in the market ... rights of participation and representation such as the freedom of association, the right to collective bargaining, and the right to collective action should be considered as instrumental to a fully functioning integrated market which can increase efficiency and wealth maximization.

On this basis, he advances a specific proposal: 'fundamental social rights should be used as criteria for accepting national measures which restrict trade on social and economic grounds'.[177] Maduro advocates the position of social rights:[178]

allocation efficiency. Of course this ideal market will rarely, if ever, exist. But for our purposes what is important is not determining when the market is the "best" or even when it is "at its best", but rather when it is "better" than the alternative available institutions.' See generally, Chapter 4: 'The Alternative Models of the European Economic Constitution', pp. 103–9.

[177] Maduro, 'Striking the Elusive Balance', p. 471. Specific to the concerns in the *Viking* case is the view Maduro has taken in other writings of what he calls 'majoritarian activism', which he sums up in this chapter as follows: 'Moreover, the Court has limited the effects of negative integration on national regulation whenever national regulations corresponded to a European majoritarian policy. If a certain social regulation is shared by a majority of Member States it has normally been upheld by the Court even if restricting trade.' *Ibid.*, p. 451. This suggests the value of arguments stressing the recognition of a fundamental right to strike in the national legal orders of Member States. See Chapter 13.

[178] *Ibid.*, p. 459. On a number of occasions he refers to 'a hard core of social rights' which includes 'the rights to collective action and collective bargaining'. He states (pp. 461–2): 'The right to collective bargaining, the freedom of association, the right to collective action ["rights immediately effective and judicially enforceable"] ... are either expressly protected by other Treaty provisions [than Article 117, now Article 136] or should be considered as part of the "constitutional traditions common to the Member States". Though certainty and coherence could have been gained by the introduction of a catalogue of fundamental rights into the Treaties the difficulty of reaching an agreement on a specific catalogue has always prevented that from happening. This should not exclude from the concept of fundamental rights which has been developed by the Court a hard core of fundamental social rights which are either part of the common constitutional traditions of the Member States and/or referred to in other EU or international sources.' There follows a footnote 51 in which Maduro refers to the Community Charter of the Fundamental Social Rights of Workers of 1989, and 'for a recent international example, including some of the rights which it has been argued constitute fundamental social rights: the ILO Declaration on Fundamental Principles and Rights at Work, approved at the 86th Session, Geneva, June 1998'. Maduro also develops other interesting arguments: 'As we have seen, in the field of the free movement of goods (and, to a more limited extent, services), the Court has for long considered as restrictions to trade national regulations that do not discriminate against imports, but may, nevertheless, affect trade by affecting market access in general. In this way, many national regulations limiting economic freedom (including regulations protecting social rights) have been challenged under Community rules since the limits to economic freedom are also conceived as limits to free trade and market access. The same broad scope has not been given to the free movement of workers, which could be used to challenge national regulations restricting certain social rights. In fact, in the same way that it is possible to argue that regulation of the market creates barriers to trade, it would be possible to argue that workers will need a minimal degree of protection effectively to exercise free movement. For example, it could be argued that a prohibition, in a Member State, on striking or becoming a Union member could deter workers from other Member States where those rights existed from moving to that Member State'. *Ibid.*, pp. 457–8.

It will be important for social rights to be inserted into the discourse of market integration and the European Economic Constitution. An important step will be the inclusion of social rights in the jurisprudential catalogue of social rights developed by the Court to be applied to Community legislation and, in some cases, national legislation (notably, whenever a national rule restricts one of the free movement rules).[179]

The rationale for free movement is market integration. Market integration is premised on market efficiency. Market efficiency requires collective action by workers and trade unions to ensure their voice is heard and their interests are taken account of. As stated in the ETUC's letter attached to the ITF's written submission:[180]

> Developments in EC law since 1957 support the view that EC law, like national legal and constitutional orders and international labour law, recognises and promotes collective self-regulation, including the legality of collective action …
>
> More detailed regulation of labour standards and working conditions is normally to be left to social dialogue, negotiations between the social partners. EU law highly values this process of improvement of living and working conditions and therefore protects it in various ways.

The Commission constantly cites the role of social dialogue as central to the EU economic model. Market integration, economic free movement and trade union collective action are to be reconciled in interpretations of the Treaty's provisions on free movement.[181]

---

[179] The question is whether the restrictions on free movement envisaged by the Treaty, even as later expansively interpreted by the ECJ, can be interpreted to apply so as to prohibit collective action or proscribe collective agreements. This argument failed with respect to the competition provisions of the Treaty in *Albany*, but has now been resurrected under the free movement provisions.

[180] Paras. 9, 11.

[181] Economic provisions of the Treaty have come to be reinterpreted in light of changes in the scope of activities of the EU. For example, the Commission must now take employment into account due to Article 127(2) EC inserted by the Treaty of Amsterdam, which requires that: 'The objective of a high level of employment shall be taken into consideration in the formulation and implementation of Community policies and activities.' Even before, in interpreting the Treaty provisions on competition, the ECJ has explained that an agreement's beneficial effect on employment 'since it improved the general conditions of production, especially when market objectives are unfavourable, comes within the framework of the objectives to which reference may be had pursuant to Article [81(3)]'. Case 26/76 *Metro-SB-Grobmarkte GmbH & Co LG* v. *Commission & SABA* [1977] ECR 1875, para 43. See the discussion in K. Mortelmans, 'Towards Convergence in the Application of the Rules on Free Movement and on Competition', (2001) 38 *Common Market Law Review* 613–49. By way of analogy to social policy, a survey suggests that: 'The most recent decisions in the field of environmental agreements come close to making environmental policy a "core" factor in competition cases. I have suggested that this is so because the Commission is transforming the definition of economic efficiency to include the concept of sustainable development. Another possible argument in support of the approach in these cases is that the duty imposed by Article 6 EC to integrate environmental protection in the Community policies and activities referred to in Article 3 EC means that environmental protection is normatively superior to the core values of EC competition law, and may thereby act as a "trump" to justify even anticompetitive environmental agreements if these are necessary to safeguard the environment.' G. Monti, 'Article 81 EC and Public Policy', (2002) 39 *Common Market Law Review* 1057 at p. 1078. The ECJ's decision in *Albany* is a crucial illustration where

The ITF and FSU, in their oral submission in *Viking*, were able once more to invoke the recently adopted Services Directive in support. The (amended) Services Directive provides that the rules on freedom of establishment and free movement of services are not to affect labour law and employment conditions.[182]

This is not merely a limitation on the scope (subject matter) of the directive. It is recognition that employment conditions, including those laid down in collective agreements, are not considered to be restrictions on free movement[183] within the meaning attributed to that phrase in Community law.[184]

the Court acknowledged that the EC Treaty provisions on competition policy must be conditioned by other Treaty provisions on social policy; specifically, collective action in the form of collective bargaining/social dialogue. Of these cases it is said: 'The vital point, however, is that, as in *Wouters* ... the Court in *Albany International* did not deny that the rules restricted competition. But it placed its investigation into the scope of Article 81(1) in a wider context. The Treaty competition rules are porous: the very scope of Article 81(1) is influenced by policy objectives located elsewhere in the framework of EC law and policy. It is worth recalling that both Articles 28 and 49 on the free movement of goods and services respectively offer similar insight into the way in which the Court interprets EC trade law in a manner that seeks to avoid trampling other regulatory objectives underfoot. In fact an apparent convergence between the assumptions of EC law of free movement and EC competition law emerges from the ruling in *Wouters*. The Dutch rules prohibiting multi-disciplinary partnerships between members of the Bar and accountants were not only attacked as violations of Article 81 but also as violations of Articles 49 (ex 59) EC concerning the free movement of services'. Stephen Weatherill, *Cases and Materials on EU Law*, 6th edn, Oxford: Oxford University Press, 2003), p. 526. Weatherill concludes (p. 527): 'The key to this case seems to be a refusal explicitly to accommodate a "rule of reason" within EC competition law but a readiness to use the interpretative rule that restrictions on competition be seen in their full legal and economic context as a basis for permitting Article 81(1)'s scope to be affected by a range of (loosely stated) public interest considerations'.

[182] This is spelled out in Article 1 ('Subject matter'), para. 6. See also Recital 14: that employment conditions, etc. are not affected by, and, conversely, do not affect, free movement is further supported by the provision in Article 16(3) (italics added): 'The Member State to which the provider moves shall not be prevented from imposing requirements with regard to the provision of a service activity, where they are justified for reasons of public policy, public security, public health or the protection of the environment and in accordance with paragraph 1. *Nor shall that Member State be prevented from applying, in accordance with Community law, its rules on employment conditions, including those laid down in collective agreements*'. See also Recital 86.

[183] In its written submission, Viking had referred to two factual developments since the Court of Appeal hearing. Viking had agreed a new collective bargaining agreement with the FSU, though still above Estonian levels. It had also ordered a new vessel suitable for use on the route, but argued that in order for it to be profitable, it would have to be flagged to Estonia and subject to an Estonian collective agreement. It argued that the Treaty precluded collective action restricting its economic freedom to do so. In its oral submission, Viking reiterated that as the ship was running at a loss and Viking would have to sell it, the collective action and agreement was damaging its economic freedom. In contrast, the absence of any restriction on Viking's rights was highlighted by events subsequent to the Court of Appeal's judgment. Viking and the FSU concluded a collective agreement which was to remain in force until 2008. This did not dissuade Viking from carrying out its plans to set up a place of establishment in Estonia. In fact it set up an Estonian subsidiary – Viking Eesti. Also, it appeared the financial position of Viking is buoyant and passenger traffic is on the increase. Other recent events in the maritime sector in the Baltic also served to illustrate how in accordance with the well-functioning Finnish social model, the market operates effectively to balance the economic interests of management and labour. For example, the FSU concluded a collective agreement covering three Estonian vessels, Estonian flag and Estonian crew, which serve the route between Helsinki and Tallinn and Helsinki and Rostock (in Germany).

[184] Again, the submissions of the Member States revealed divisions. Some were convinced of the restrictive effect of collective action on economic freedom: the Czech Republic, Estonia, Latvia and Poland. The UK's position reflected its view that *Albany* was not applicable by way of

The challenge posed in the *Viking* litigation aimed precisely at the cross-border element in the collective action by the ITF and FSU.[185] The implications for transnational collective bargaining and collective action in the European Single Market were clearly understood by the ETUC, the organisation representing trade union confederations in all the EU Member States. Transnational collective action by trade unions in an integrated European economy, like most economic decision-making by enterprises, invariably affects undertakings in more than one Member State.[186] The claim that the consequences reflect discrimination on grounds of nationality is pervasive.[187] The ETUC perceived the threat that allowing claims based on alleged nationality discrimination

analogy to this case as it was attributable to a specific tension between Treaty Articles on competition and social policy. Other Member States were adamant that collective action and collective agreements do not constitute restrictions on economic freedom: Belgium, Germany, Italy, Finland, Ireland, Norway and Sweden.

[185] Transnational collective action is alleged to inherently entail discrimination on grounds of nationality. The FSU was alleged to be concerned with protecting Finnish workers or Finnish collective agreements, and hence discriminating against Estonian workers and Estonian collective agreements. The ITF's FOC was inherently discriminatory as requiring Viking to negotiate exclusively with a trade union in the Member State where the beneficial owners were established, and not in the Member State where the ship was to be registered.

[186] 'The role of the EU social partners, including the ETUC, in transnational industrial relations at EU level inevitably may entail engagement in disputes with cross-border effects. As part of its role as an association of trade unions, the ETUC, and its affiliates, have been involved in supporting various forms of collective action by trade unions in other Member States. The ETUC, like the ITF, may potentially be engaged when one of its affiliates undertakes collective industrial action and the ETUC would call for solidarity from other ETUC affiliates. The implications of the *Viking* case for the ETUC could be that, by calling for solidarity, the ETUC could face a claim in a Belgian court, like the ITF in the UK court, that its appeal for solidarity action violates EC law on free movement. The European trade union movement as a whole thus has a major, direct and practical interest in the outcome of this case'. ETUC letter attached to the ITF's written submission, paras. 20–1.

[187] The submission by Viking stated bluntly that application of the FOC is dependent solely upon the country in which the owner of the vessel is established. This is direct discrimination. It reiterated the trial judge's finding of fact that the main objective of the FSU action was to protect Finnish jobs. Subjective intention is relevant, albeit not conclusive. The submissions by a number of Member States agreed with Viking that the collective action at issue was discriminatory on grounds of nationality: the Czech Republic, Estonia, Latvia and Poland took an unequivocal position. Ireland was more measured. Consistent with the trade unions' position were the submissions of a number of other Member States: Austria, Belgium, Finland, Germany and Italy. The trade unions, however, noted that the recently adopted Directive on services in the internal market does not contain a specific provision declaring collective agreements to be non-discriminatory *per se*. However, it follows from the wholesale exclusion from the subject matter of this Directive on free movement of services of 'rules laid down in collective agreements negotiated by the social partners' (these not being deemed 'requirements' (Article 4(7)) that an interpretation of the provisions of the Directive as a whole which is both effective and consistent is that agreements concluded in the context of collective negotiations between management and labour must be regarded as falling outside the scope of the Directive (as put by the ECJ in *Albany*, paras. 59–60). This can only be interpreted to mean that collective agreements are not discriminatory *as far as rules on free movement are concerned*. Not being 'requirements', rules laid down in collective agreements are not prohibited as 'discriminatory requirements' (Article 14(1)), they need not satisfy the principle of non-discrimination (Article 16(1)(a)), and they are justifiable under the provision in Article 16(3). The same principle applies to Articles 43 and 49 EC.

would have for the prospects of an integrated European industrial relations system:[188]

> An interpretation of the free movement provisions of the Treaty outlawing collective action with cross-border effects would fatally undermine the development of an EU industrial relations system as a fundamental element in European integration.

## Conclusion

The argument over whether collective bargaining, collective agreements and collective action are essential to the effective and equitable functioning of the labour market goes to the heart of the debates over European labour regulation. Is European labour law to include a collective dimension, or is it confined to an EU law of individual employment? Are the social models of the Member States, historically rooted in the social dialogue, sustainable unless the EU supports the collective dimension of labour relations? The discrepancy between the growing power of employers benefiting from European transnational economic integration and the relative weakness of a declining labour movement, which remains largely confined to national boundaries in its collective bargaining and collective action, has profound implications for the future of the European social model.

In *Viking* and *Laval*, attempts by trade unions taking collective action to re-establish the balance of economic power in an integrated European market were challenged by employers invoking EC law. They were defended by the European trade union movement:[189]

> Although the case concerns the specific collective actions of the FSU and the ITF, it is of the greatest importance to acknowledge that their actions are in no way unusual or exceptional. The FSU and the ITF have taken exactly the same type of collective industrial action as is taken on a regular, normal and systematic basis by organisations of workers everywhere in the European Union. Collective industrial action is part of the ordinary conduct of industrial relations involving the social partners engaged in collective bargaining …
>
> The restrictions on employers' activities inherent in collective industrial action by workers may – and with the coming about of the internal market this may more frequently be the case – affect cross-border production and transport activities of the employer. However, this was also the case long before the economic integration of the European single market …
>
> It cannot seriously be contended that the 1957 Treaty is to be interpreted, almost half a century later, to produce a violent overthrow of the norms established in national industrial relations systems.

The ECJ was confronted with this challenge. The EU legislative institutions were placed in a virtually identical position when confronted with the Commission's

---

[188]  ETUC letter attached to the ITF's written submission, para. 22.
[189]  As put by the ETUC in its letter attached to the ITF's written submission, *ibid.*, paras. 2, 7, 8.

proposed Directive on Services. The outcome of the intensive debate over the Services Directive proclaimed that collective bargaining, collective agreements and collective action were not restrictions on free movement of services. The ECJ's failure to meet the same challenge threatens not only the European trade union movement, but also the ECJ and even the future of European integration.

## Conclusions on the ECJ decisions in *Viking* and *Laval*

The decisions of the ECJ in *Laval* and *Viking* have provoked deep concern across the trade union and labour movements of the Member States of the EU. European labour law requires lawyers knowledgeable and experienced in labour matters and industrial relations. For the ECJ to intervene in an area where, over a century of struggle and with great sacrifices in many national contexts, a framework of fundamental rights and protection has been constructed governing industrial relations, and in a few short pages of judgment to reshape it along contours dictated by internal market law, is not acceptable. Such intervention at national level would require extensive, lengthy and delicate consultation with the social partners. Even then, it has produced tumultuous outcomes. All the more likely if done without such consultation, in a court room in Luxembourg by judges ambitious to reshape EU industrial relations.

The European Court spectacularly failed to establish clear rules of European labour law governing collective action. The Opinions of each of the Advocates-General and each of the judgments of the ECJ in *Viking* and *Laval* prescribe very different principles for determining the legality of collective action. This does not produce certainty, nor inspire confidence in a judicial role in the regulation of collective action. The widely different propositions may be summarised very succinctly as follows.

For Advocate-General Mengozzi in *Laval*, the lawfulness of primary collective action is subject to the criterion of 'proportionality', which requires a *real advantage* which contributes *significantly* to workers' protection. The lawfulness of solidarity action depends on the lawfulness of primary action. In complete contrast, for Advocate-General Maduro in *Viking*, to be lawful, primary collective action must be taken *before* relocation. Solidarity action depends on whether it is *voluntary*.

The ECJ in *Viking* disregards Maduro's Opinion and, like Mengozzi, invokes the criterion of 'proportionality'. This requires a *serious threat* to jobs and conditions (not present where there is a legally binding guarantee of statutory provisions and collective agreements). But also, collective action must be *suitable* to achieve the objective, not go beyond what is *necessary* and any other less restrictive means have been exhausted. Solidarity action cannot be objectively justified, though it is to be balanced with workers' protection.

In contrast, the same ECJ in *Laval* looks to the Posting Directive for the criterion of lawful collective action. Collective action is lawful only to secure standards stipulated in the Posting Directive: legislation and collective agreements declared universally applicable in the construction sector. These are maximum standards. Transnational collective action to impose higher standards is unlawful as violating the Treaty's economic freedoms. Member States may extend this to include other collective agreements, other terms of employment and other sectors. But not negotiation at the workplace, which prevents transnational undertakings from ascertaining labour standards with certainty.

A superficially common criterion of 'proportionality' masks real differences. Advocate-General Mengozzi in *Laval* explicitly invokes 'proportionality', but this is not to be applied to primary collective action in support of pay claims, even if 'excessive', though such action may be unlawful if linked to other terms of collective agreement. Similarly for solidarity action. This is contradicted by the ECJ in *Laval*, for whom the criterion of 'proportionality' is implicit: collective action is lawful only up to the maximum standards allowed by the Posting Directive. But not if standards are uncertain, as in negotiation at the workplace. For Advocate-General Maduro in *Viking*, the criterion of 'proportionality' is, at best, implicit: primary action is lawful if before relocation; solidarity action is lawful if voluntary. These concepts disappear in the ECJ's judgment in *Viking*, which evokes the criterion of 'proportionality' explicitly. Primary action is lawful if suitable to meet a serious threat, is not more than necessary and less restrictive means available are exhausted. Solidarity action is not proportionate, though it may protect workers.

In sum, there are two broadly opposing principles in the judgments of *Laval* and *Viking*, positing two different legal outcomes for the legality of collective action. In *Viking*, legality depends on whether the action satisfies a general anti-social dumping principle (but subject to 'proportionality'). In *Laval*, legality is subject to the maximum standards principle of the Posting Directive (which may be extended, but subject to 'certainty'). So much for predictability.

The outcome is deeply unsatisfactory. Fundamental rights are given lip service, but then trampled on in the name of archaic market fundamentalism. Hobbled by the historical baggage of the internal market, the court falls into ahistorical application of market concepts to a Europe which is not that of the common market of 1957, nor the Single European Market of 1985, but, post-Maastricht, a Europe with a social dimension even larger in its ambitions.

The studiously ignored elephant lurking in the European social model lumbered onto the stage before the ECJ in *Viking* and *Laval*: the consequences of the disparity in wage costs and labour standards between the old Member States and the new accession states. It is a bracing reminder to EU lawyers of the power of political and economic context to influence legal doctrine that the new Member States making submissions were unanimous on one side of the arguments on issues of fundamental legal doctrine (horizontal direct effect, discrimination, proportionality) and the old Member States virtually unanimous on the other.

The interesting and heartening exception was the consensus over the existence of a fundamental right to collective action – the legacy perhaps of international labour law,[190] but also the recognition of this fundamental right in Article 28 of the EU Charter and the ferment surrounding its incorporation into the proposed Constitutional Treaty. This consensus takes as its point of departure the recognition in international labour law that certain fundamental rights of trade unions, to collective bargaining, collective agreements and collective action, are to be maintained for the long term.[191]

The fundamental long-term significance of the EU legal order recognising the fundamental rights of trade unions was brought out by the ETUC's letter attached to the submission of the ITF:[192]

---

[190] ILO Conventions Nos. 87 and 98, the European Social Charter, the European Convention on Human Rights.

[191] Regardless of what is claimed to be the short-term benefit of lower labour costs to some Member States. There is a tendency towards a somewhat one-sided debate emphasising the benefits to new EU Member States (or rather the often multinational enterprises taking advantage) of their low labour costs. What about the workers? As revealed in the debates over the Services Directive, workers moving to provide the services have to live in the old Member States. There are notorious examples of the desperation of workers from the new Member States forced to survive on lower wages. It is also not in the short- or long-term interest of new Member States if skilled workers emigrate to take even unskilled jobs undercutting the labour standards of workers in old Member States. As stated in one analysis of the dispute in *Laval*: 'It will be tempting for new member states such as Latvia to use their "comparative advantage" in low wages and inferior working conditions to reach some parity within the liberalized EU. However, any gains would be short-lived if they depress the wages and working conditions of their wealthier neighbours'. Harsher: 'This dispute reflects the difference between advanced democratic societies with strong labour movements and what, despite the sustained efforts of many in the Baltic States, are still often electoral oligarchies in which labour rights are routinely sacrificed in the search for economic prosperity. The current imbalance of power in post-communist states such as Latvia, in which organized labour is largely silent (or indeed silenced), makes for potentially insurmountable obstacles to the achievement of modern European-style industrial relations. The notion of labour as a legitimized "social partner" with the right to engage freely in collective bargaining is daily contradicted in both law and practice.' Charles Woolfson and Jeff Summers, 'Labour Mobility in Construction: European Implications of the Laval un Partneri Dispute with Swedish Labour', (2006) 12 *European Journal of Industrial Relations* 49–68, pp. 62, 63. There is evident inconsistency with the established principle of free movement of workers. In the older manufacturing economy, workers moving to old Member States are entitled to equal treatment. However, if they move to provide services from service providers, they are not entitled to equal treatment. The disparity in principle did not survive the European Parliament's scrutiny of the Services Directive. The right to take collective action to demand equal treatment does not aim to discriminate against free movement of workers. There is no demand to take collective action to stop workers coming in if they are paid the *same* conditions, only to stop unequal conditions. There are undertakings in the old Member States who also do not adhere to collectively determined labour standards. This raises a spectre of a complaint by domestic employers of discrimination. They cannot invoke EU law when collective action is taken against them. However, if the collective action is taken because the workers subject to unequal treatment come from another Member State, according to *Viking*, the employer would be able to do so. Finally, in the longer term, and even the short term in some sectors, as labour standards converge, the competition which currently operates as between new and old Member States will engage states outside Europe, able to offer labour cost advantages which exceed even those of the new Member States. Denial of rights to take collective action may be much harder to justify when enterprises move productive and profitable undertakings in order to exploit even lower paid workers. The consequences of unrestrained social dumping are not confined to 'old' Europe.

[192] Paras. 23–7.

Trade unions in the Member States, affiliated to the ETUC, support the single European market. However, there are increasingly concerns as to the balance of economic power in the transnational EU market.

Free movement of enterprise is transforming the balance of economic power in the EU. The freedom of enterprises to move throughout the single European market has shifted the balance of economic power towards employers. National and transnational collective action by workers and their organisations is one response, with a view to restore the balance.

A crucial element in maintaining a balance of economic power in Member States is the legal right to take collective action. The employers' parties to the Viking case seek to use Community law to override national and international guarantees of the right to collective action.

To the contrary, the ETUC considers that Community law on free movement is to be interpreted consistently with national and international protection of the right to collective action, thereby providing for a balance of economic power in the single European market.

Trade unions are in favour of European economic integration. But labour is not a commodity. Competition over labour standards threatens economic integration and undermines support for the European project. Collective industrial action is not protectionism. Community law on free movement, if interpreted consistently with the legal recognition of collective action in national law, Member States' constitutions, and international law, will encourage support for European integration by trade unions and their representative at EU level, the ETUC.

Before the ECJ decisions in *Viking* and *Laval*, I wrote that the future of the trade union movement, but also of the European Union, might depend on whether on judgment day the ECJ decides that the EU legal order upholds the right of trade unions to take transnational collective action.[193]

---

[193] It remained to be seen whether the ECJ could develop doctrinal solutions to the particular set of problems arising in those cases. To summarise one possible approach: national laws regulate collective action with purely internal national implications. EU law has no role. Where collective action has transnational implications involving movement between Member States, there are at least four possible options. (1) National systems determine whether transnational collective action is lawful. EU law does not intervene. This is highly problematic: many national laws have not addressed the problem. Different national rules distort the market as transnational operations of employers in some countries are protected while others are exposed to collective action. EU law would abandon an area vital to the operation of the transnational economy. There are already EU interventions. Examples are the Council Regulation (EC) No. 2679/98 of 7 December 1998 on the functioning of the internal market in relation to the free movement of goods among the Member States (OJ L337/8 of 12 December 1998), Article 2. The Preamble to the Posted Workers' Directive 96/71/EC includes a similar provision (Recital 22). (2) Minimal EU law intervention: the EU Charter of Fundamental Rights establishes a fundamental right to take collective action (Article 28). National limitations are acceptable provided they respect the essence of the right (Article 52(1) of the EU Charter). This EU fundamental right overrides EU *economic* freedoms, notably free movement. However, it may not prevail, and should be balanced against *non-economic* fundamental rights (e.g. discrimination, environmental protection). (3) EU law regulates transnational collective action. Collective action may have a restrictive effect on the exercise of free movement (e.g. of capital or establishment). The argument is that exercise of free movement is balanced by the *ordre communautaire social* (see below). There is now a substantial body of EU law

The judgments in *Viking* and *Laval* reveal both an excess of ambition and a poverty of imagination. Resort to familiar legal concepts, such as 'proportionality', is not adequate. The problems of labour regulation in a European industrial relations system are more complex, and the solutions available from national experience are more sophisticated. The Court's rhetorical flourishes of a Social Europe and fundamental rights are flattened by the juggernaut of an ideology postulating economic freedoms. The Opinions and judgments produced uncertain, impractical concepts and, perhaps worst of all worlds,

(ranging from labour law Directives to Employment Guidelines) and policy (including e.g. soft law on restructuring) regulating decision-making by enterprises which affects workers. These impose both substantive obligations and procedural constraints (e.g. information and consultation). Taken together, these comprise the *acquis communautaire social*. One premise behind procedural constraints is that they obviate the need for autonomous collective action. The corollary is that failure to comply with procedural requirements allows for collective action. Further, that following exhaustion of procedures, the *ultima ratio* of collective action is permitted. There may be decisions affecting workers which escape the procedural constraints; e.g. they fall outside the scope, however widely defined, of decision-making; the undertakings concerned fall below the threshold specified for application; or for some other reason. In such cases, the lack of constraints on the part of the undertaking is balanced by the absence of constraint on collective action by workers and their organisations. The prospect of lawful collective action may act as an incentive on these undertakings to voluntarily adopt the norms of the *acquis communautaire social*. A calibrated approach may be adopted with respect to different aspects of free movement. Free movement involving *workers* (which may also overlap with provision of services) is particularly sensitive. Collective action is legitimate where procedural constraints are not followed and/or the substantive outcomes may be characterised as social dumping. Free movement involving *services or goods* (without the element of workers crossing borders) may also be restricted by collective action, whether or not aimed specifically at curtailing cross-border provision of goods or services. Collective action is to be regarded not as a restriction, but as a cost or risk incurred by undertakings exercising free movement. The *Cassis de Dijon* 'rule of reason' test allows mandatory requirements of public policy to justify restrictions on free movement. Collective action by the state to protect the environment or consumers may be invoked to justify restrictions on free movement. Collective action by trade unions to protect workers' interests may be invoked as public policy according to *ordre communautaire social*. The 'rule of reason' also engages the proportionality principle. National experience provides some guidance in the application of the proportionality principle. The right to collective action as a fundamental right may be weighed against other fundamental rights. Where other fundamental rights (social, human, not economic freedoms) are involved, the solution often adopted is not restricting the right to collective action through a proportionality test, but through provision for a minimum level of services to be maintained. Other constitutional rights, however, may include economic freedoms of employers. However, courts are reluctant to apply a proportionality test in cases of such conflicts, as this involves interfering with the constitutionally protected autonomy of the social partners. One limitation may be where the collective action is aimed at the economic existence of the employer. Finally, free movement of *capital* is in a class of its own. In an era of economic globalisation, unrestricted movement of capital and consequent massive flows of capital across borders have perhaps the greatest impact on workers. Yet it is perhaps the least amenable to protection through the *acquis communautaire social*. The imbalance of economic power consequent on global capital mobility makes collective action much less able to redress the balance. It can scarcely offer resistance. Real constraints will come through a qualitative improvement in the *acquis communautaire social*. However, in its absence, collective action should not be limited by EU law. (4) Finally, as a general rule, there is a *prima facie* presumption that transnational collective action is lawful where linked with or related to transnational and national collective bargaining/social dialogue. In sum: transnational collective action is lawful where it promotes the *ordre communautaire social*: social dialogue, improved working conditions, equal treatment, fundamental rights.

solutions open to exploitation by employers abusing economic freedoms. This may provoke a negative reaction from the trade union and labour movements of Europe which could be damaging, if not fatal, to European integration. The judgments reveal more than ever the need for political intervention with deep engagement of the social partners. Is there any scope for the European Court to contribute?

## *Ordre communautaire social*

The future of European labour law depends on principles which reflect the general *acquis communautaire* of social policy of the EU and, in particular, the regulation of employment and industrial relations in the Treaty and relevant secondary legislation. Title III of the original Treaty of Rome, 'Social Policy', contained only two Chapters with only 12 Articles.[194]

The vast expansion of the competences of the EU in the area of employment and industrial relations came with the creation of the European Union by the Maastricht Treaty. The embrace by the EU of extensive competences in the area of employment and industrial relations has radical consequences for the law of the common market.

The ECJ recognised the implications of this transformation for the nature of the EU in a decision of 10 February 2000.[195] The case concerned the exclusion of part-time workers from supplementary occupational pension schemes. As formulated by the national court posing the question for the ECJ, the claim for a retrospective application of the principle of equal pay would risk distortion

---

[194] In the first Chapter on Social Provisions, the first of the six Articles comprising the Chapter, Article 117, stated (italics added): 'Member States agree upon the need to *promote improved working conditions and an improved standard of living for workers, so as to make possible their harmonization while the improvement is being maintained.* They believe that such a development will ensue not only from the functioning of the common market, which will favour the harmonization of social systems, but also from the procedures provided for in this Treaty [including judicial procedures] and from the approximation of provisions laid down by law, regulation or administrative action.' Now Article 136 EC, para. 1: 'The Community and the Member States, having in mind fundamental social rights such as those set out in the European Social Charter signed at Turin on 19 October 1961 and in the 1989 Community Charter of the Fundamental Social Rights of Workers, shall have as their objectives the promotion of employment, improved living and working conditions, so as to make possible their harmonisation while the improvement is being maintained, proper social protection, dialogue between management and labour, the development of human resources with a view to lasting high employment and the combating of exclusion.' The social competences of the European Economic Community (EEC) under the Treaty of Rome were very limited. Article 119 (now Article 141 EC) on equal pay for equal work was the notable exception to the Rome Treaty's concentration on free movement in a common market. There was a specific extension of Community competences to health and safety in the working environment in the Single European Act 1986.

[195] Case C-50/96, *Deutsche Telekom AG* v. *Schroder* [2000] ECR I-743. There is similar reasoning in the Opinion of Advocate-General Tesauro and the judgment of the ECJ in *P.* v. *S. and Cornwall County Council*, Case C-13/94, [1996] ECR I-2143.

of competition and have a detrimental economic impact on employers. Nonetheless the Court concluded:[196]

> it must be concluded that the *economic aim* pursued by Article 119 of the Treaty, namely the elimination of distortions of competition between undertakings established in different Member States, *is secondary to the social aim* pursued by the same provision, which constitutes the expression of a *fundamental human right*.

### What is the *ordre communautaire social*?

The ECJ's jurisdiction in labour law points to the need to identify and promote the common traditions and legal and constitutional practices protecting fundamental social, labour and trade union rights in the laws of the Member States.[197] Some such fundamental trade union rights are recognised in all (or most) Member States. In a Member State, a claim to rights in the EU Charter, as a question of EU law, could be referred by a national court to the ECJ under Article 234 of the EC Treaty. In interpreting the right at EU level, the ECJ could draw upon a range of sources, including international law, in particular, ILO Conventions, Council of Europe measures and existing EC law.

The ECJ's labour law jurisdiction cannot rely on the European Convention for the Protection of Human Rights (ECHR) of 1950. The ECHR is not focused on protection of the rights of workers.[198] Social and labour rights are the focus

---

[196] *Ibid.*, para. 57. Italics added.

[197] As elaborated in Chapter 9, for example, freedom of association in trade unions has acquired constitutional status in some Member States. Sometimes this is a part of a constitutional guarantee of a general right of association, sometimes, the guarantee is granted by ordinary legislation or 'basic agreements' between the social partners. Does a trade union's 'right to freedom of association' also include other collective trade union rights, such as the right to collective bargaining and collective agreements, the right to strike or take other industrial action? On 8 June 2007, in *Health Services and Support – Facilities Subsector Bargaining Assn.* v. *British Columbia*, 2007 SCC 27, the Supreme Court of Canada, reversing both the trial court and the British Columbia Court of Appeal, decided by a six to one majority that earlier decisions of the Supreme Court for the exclusion of collective bargaining from the protection of the freedom of association guaranteed by section 2(d) of the Canadian Charter of Rights and Freedoms ('Everyone has the following fundamental freedoms: … (d) freedom of association [liberté d'association]') did not withstand principled scrutiny and should be rejected. The Supreme Court declared that freedom of association guaranteed by section 2(d) of the Charter includes a procedural right to collective bargaining (paragraph 20): 'Our conclusion that s. 2(d) of the Charter protects a process of collective bargaining rests on four propositions. First, a review of the s. 2(d) jurisprudence of this Court reveals that the reasons evoked in the past for holding that the guarantee of freedom of association does not extend to collective bargaining can no longer stand. Second, an interpretation of s. 2(d) that precludes collective bargaining from its ambit is inconsistent with Canada's historic recognition of the importance of collective bargaining to freedom of association. Third, collective bargaining is an integral component of freedom of association in international law, which may inform the interpretation of Charter guarantees. Finally, interpreting s. 2(d) as including a right to collective bargaining is consistent with, and indeed, promotes, other Charter rights, freedoms and values'. Different Member State concepts of 'freedom of association' include some, many or even all of these elements.

[198] In Case C-112/00, *Eugen Schmidberger, Internationale Transporte und Planzuge* v. *Republic of Austria*, [2003] ECR I-5659, the Court seemed willing to contemplate restrictions on freedom of expression or assembly, as allowed by the ECHR. In Case C-499/04, *Hans Werhof* v. *Freeway*

of the European Social Charter (ESC) 1961 (revised in 1996).[199] These rights have acquired constitutional status in some Member States. Though the ESC is within the category of the international treaties referred to in *Nold*, and, indeed, is explicitly referred to in Article 136 of the EC Treaty, the Court has not yet been willing to invoke the ESC as it does the ECHR. Moreover, ratification by all Member States (including the twelve recent accession states) of ILO Conventions No. 87 of 1948 (Freedom of Association and Protection of the Right to Organise) and No. 98 of 1949 (Application of the Principles of the Right to Organise and to Bargain Collectively) has produced a common foundation of trade union rights in all Member States.

The ECJ could play a role in constitutionalising the EU social model by adopting a specific interpretive framework for relevant provisions of the Treaties and secondary legislation. This overriding interpretive framework comprises the accumulated body of EU social and labour law, the *acquis communautaire social*, including five principles of what may be called *ordre communautaire social*:

(a)  a universal premise of international labour law based on the Constitution of the ILO to which all Member States belong: 'labour is not a commodity';

(b)  the activities of the Community shall include 'a policy in the social sphere' (Article 3(1)(j) EC) and the Community and the Member States 'shall have as their objectives ... improved living and working conditions' (Article 136 EC);

(c)  respect for fundamental rights of workers reflected in the Community Charter of the Fundamental Social Rights of Workers 1989, the European Social Charter signed at Turin on 19 October 1961 (both cited in Article 136 EC), and the EU Charter of Fundamental Rights solemnly proclaimed by the European Parliament, the European Council and the Commission at Nice on 7 December 2000;

---

*Traffic Systems GmbH & Co. KG*, decided 9 March 2006, the ECJ cited the ECHR as protecting the negative right of association of employers not to be bound by collective agreements, but did not refer to the decision of the European Court of Human Rights in *Wilson, National Union of Journalists and Others* v. *United Kingdom*, judgment of 2 July 2002, Reports of Judgments and decisions 2002-V; [2002] *Industrial Relations Law Reports* 128 upholding the right of workers to freedom of association as protecting their adhesion to collective agreements. See the critique in the Opinion of Advocate-General Mengozzi in *Laval*, paras. 71–4. But see now the decision of European Court of Human Rights in *Evaldsson and others* v. *Sweden*, 13 February 2007. The Court found a violation of the ECHR's protection of property where a collective agreement requiring an employer to deduct amounts from a worker's salary and pay them to the union to reimburse the union for the costs of monitoring salary payments, where the workers concerned were not union members and objected to the deductions. The Court held there was insufficient accountability and the deductions were disproportionate: '... given that the Swedish authorities organised its labour market by delegating the regulation and legislation of important labour issues to independent organisations through a system of collective agreements, the Court found that the State was under the obligation to protect the applicants' interests by holding those organisations accountable for their activities'.

[199]  All Member States (including the twelve recent accession states) have ratified either the 1961 or the 1996 Social Charters of the Council of Europe.

(d)  the distinctive characteristic of the European social model which attributes a central role to social dialogue at EU and national levels in the form of social partnership;[200]

(e)  the common market principle of equal treatment of all workers without discrimination based on nationality.

In brief, the ECJ is to interpret and apply EU law in the light of *ordre comunautaire social*: labour is not a commodity like others (goods, capital), free movement is subject to the objective of improved working conditions, respecting the fundamental rights of workers as human beings, acknowledging the central role of social dialogue and social partnership at EU and national levels, and adhering to the strict principle of equal treatment without regard to nationality.

The submission here is that the interpretive framework for European law should be based on the *acquis communautaire social* which can be summarised in the above five principles of what may be called *ordre communautaire social*. The EU social constitution is to reflect the *ordre communautaire social*.[201]

### Why *ordre communautaire social*?

The prevailing model of national labour regulation coupled with collective bargaining has come under increasing pressure as globalisation of the economy tends both to undermine national labour standards and to weaken the control that democratic institutions exercise over market activity.[202] Similarly, international

---

[200]  See the 'Overview' in B. Bercusson and N. Bruun, *European Industrial Relations Dictionary*, European Foundation for the Improvement of Living and Working Conditions, Luxembourg: Office for Official Publications of the European Communities, 2005, pp. 2–50, especially pp. 4–11.

[201]  The elaboration of the *ordre communautaire social* is a major task for the future. Its subtle intricacies are illustrated by a recent case in the French Cour de Cassation which denied that the failure to give a hearing to employee representatives in case of initiating an insolvency procedure constituted a serious violation of the fundamental right to be heard (Cass. Com., 27 June 2006, pouvoi no. 0-3-19.863). The case arose in the context of a decision by an English court in insolvency proceedings concerning an English company which affected an establishment in France. The plaintiffs sought to prevent recognition of the English court's decision by the French courts due to the failure with respect to the hearing of employee representatives, arguing, *inter alia*, that the English court's decision was thereby contrary to fundamental principles of French law and hence was manifestly contrary to *ordre public*. The Cour de Cassation rejected the argument, looking to the strict interpretation of *ordre public* required by the Brussels Convention of 1968 (and the Brussels Regulation of 22 December 2000 replacing it) on mutual recognition of judgments. A perceptive comment on the case, however, observes that insolvency proceedings have different stages and that failure to hear the employees' representatives at a later stage might be considered to violate 'ordre public procédural' in light of the ECJ's recognition of Article 6 ECHR. Further, it is suggested that total failure to engage employees may be construed as contrary to 'ordre public substantiel' sufficient to refuse recognition of a foreign judgment ignoring such a fundamental right, which outweighs the policy of mutual recognition. The author of the comment adds that such developments would be part of the construction of 'a social Europe whose contours are as yet largely indeterminate ('la construction d'une Europe sociale aux contours encore largement indéfinis'). Etienne Pataut, *Revue de Droit du Travail*, November 2006, 344–6 at p. 346.

[202]  B. Bercusson and C. Estlund, 'Introduction', in B. Bercusson and C. Estlund (eds.), *Regulating Labour in the Wake of Globalization: New Challenges, New Institutions*, Oxford: Hart, 2008, vol. II of the Columbia-London Series, pp. 1–18.

labour regulation is challenged by the organisation of production in different countries and global markets dominated by multinational corporations and global financial integration. The combined result of these developments has been intense international competition and an erosion of the ability of individual states to enforce their own labour standards. Globalisation and cross-border mobility of trade and capital also threaten traditional collective bargaining strategies organised geographically without the capacity to challenge transnationally organised employers.

While globalisation erodes national-level controls, it also potentially extends the reach of the advanced economies, and potentially of their social norms, beyond national boundaries. The role of regional integration in the process of economic globalisation is well known. The European Union is the most advanced modern example of regional economic integration providing a transnational legal framework including a growing body of regulations governing employment standards and industrial relations.

As both national labour law and collective bargaining institutions are being undercut and weakened by globalisation, the question is how to overcome the limitations of national and international labour regulation. European labour law offers the prospect of achieving regulatory institutions and techniques capable of formulating and implementing labour standards in an effective and legitimate system of transnational labour regulation in the global economy.

The experience of a European labour law based on the *ordre communautaire social* can be used to develop a system of transnational labour regulation. European labour law illustrates the potential of formulation of transnational labour standards linked with effective methods of implementation and enforcement at national level (e.g. EU directives and enforcement through national judicial mechanisms). Lessons from European labour may be usefully extrapolated to transnational labour regulation beyond Europe.

The ECJ's jurisdiction in labour law offers the prospect of consolidating the EU as a major player in the emerging legal order of globalisation. It becomes a leader, not a follower in the wake of the ILO and the WTO. EC labour law, by virtue of its character as a supranational law with supremacy over national labour laws, already partakes of the character of a higher norm. The EU Charter's fundamental rights of labour, if the ECJ is up to this challenge, could yet become a model for international labour law.[203]

---

[203] Bercusson, *The European Court of Justice, Labour Law and ILO Standards.*

# Chapter 22

# The futures of European labour law: (3) the agenda of the Member States and of the European Parliament – the Lisbon Treaty and after

## A 'constitutional' future for European labour law

On 25 March 2007, the fiftieth anniversary of the Treaty of Rome,[1] the twenty-seven Member States of the European Union meeting in Berlin acknowledged the need to 'always renew the political shape of Europe in keeping with the times'.[2] They declared their united objective of 'placing the European Union on a renewed common basis[3] before the European Parliament elections in 2009'. Following the debacle of the rejection by France and the Netherlands in 2005 of the proposed Treaty Establishing a Constitution for Europe,[4] a final effort was being launched. At the press conference concluding the fiftieth anniversary celebrations, the German Chancellor, Angela Merkel, declared her intention that the June 2007 summit under the German Presidency should agree a road map. A new draft Treaty/Constitution was to be elaborated during the coming Portuguese Presidency of the Council so as to be ready by the end of 2007, to be ratified thereafter by the Member States during the period up to the European Parliament elections in June 2009.

---

[1] This section draws on B. Bercusson (ed.), *Manifesto for a Social Constitution: 8 Options for the European Union*, Brussels: European Trade Union Institute (ETUI-REHS), 2007 (133 pp.). also available in French and German.

[2] 'adapter la construction politique de l'Europe aux realités nouvelles'.

[3] 'bases communes rénovées'. The *Financial Times* reported a senior aide to the German Chancellor, Angela Merkel, to the effect that: 'The [German] chancellery crafted this diplomatic formulation to avoid mentioning the planned European constitution by name, something to which the Czech Republic, but also Poland and the UK had objected. "We decided very early on that we did not want to have a hefty controversy this weekend", said another Merkel aide. "Now is not the time. We will talk about it in June, when we have a new partner in Paris," he added, alluding to the imminent French presidential election.' 'Merkel Heals Rift with Prague on EU Celebration', *Financial Times*, 24–25 March 2007, p. 8.

[4] The Convention on the Future of Europe submitted the proposal for a Constitutional Treaty in July 2003. Draft Constitution proposed by the Convention on the Future of Europe, Draft Treaty Establishing a Constitution for Europe, CONV 850/03, Brussels, 18 July 2003. This was adopted, with some amendments, by the Member States at a summit in June 2004. Treaty Establishing a Constitution for Europe adopted by the Member States in the Intergovernmental Conference meeting in Brussels 17–18 June 2004, OJ C310/1 of 16 December 2004. Although ratified by most Member States, the rejection of the proposed Constitution by referenda in France and the Netherlands in May 2005 led to a so-called 'period of reflection'.

The Berlin Declaration asserted that the European model 'combines economic success and social responsibility'.[5] The concerns over 'Social Europe' during the preparation of the Constitutional Treaty led to the inclusion of explicit social values,[6] social and employment objectives,[7] fundamental social rights,[8] recognition of the role of the social partners,[9] a strengthened 'mainstreaming' anti-discrimination clause[10] and a 'mainstreaming' social clause.[11] Nonetheless, anxieties about the adequacy of the social dimension of the Constitutional Treaty were highlighted in the referendum in France which rejected it in May 2005.

In the 'period of reflection' which followed the constitutional debacle, a number of proposals emerged. In mid-December 2005, Angela Merkel,

[5] 'solidarité sociale'.

[6] Part I, Article I-2: 'The Union is founded on the values of respect for human dignity, freedom, democracy, equality, the rule of law and respect for human rights, including the rights of persons belonging to minorities. These values are common to the Member States in a society in which pluralism, non-discrimination, tolerance, justice, solidarity and equality between women and men prevail'. Proposed to be added as new Article 1a EC by the Treaty of Lisbon.

[7] Part I, Article I-3(3): 'The Union shall work for the sustainable development of Europe based on balanced economic growth and price stability, a highly competitive social market economy, aiming at full employment and social progress, and a high level of protection and improvement of the quality of the environment. It shall promote scientific and technological advance. It shall combat social exclusion and discrimination, and shall promote social justice and protection, equality between women and men, solidarity between generations and protection of the rights of the child'. Proposed to be added in new Article 2(3) EC by the Treaty of Lisbon.

[8] Part II, EU Charter, and Article I-9(1): 'The Union shall recognise the rights, freedoms and principles set out in the Charter of Fundamental Rights which constitutes Part II'. Part II amended the initial Charter; see Charter of Fundamental Rights of the European Union, proclaimed at the meeting of the European Council held in Nice from 7 to 9 December 2000, and adopted by the Commission, the Council and the Member States, OJ C364/01 of 18 December 2000. As new Article 6 EC TEU proposed by the Treaty of Lisbon this reads: 'The Union recognises the rights, freedoms and principles set out in the Charter of Fundamental Rights of the European Union of 7 December 2000, as adapted at Strasbourg, on 12 December 2007, which shall have the same legal value as the Treaties'.

[9] Part I, Article I-48: 'The Union recognises and promotes the role of the social partners at its level, taking into account the diversity of national systems. It shall facilitate dialogue between the social partners, respecting their autonomy. The Tripartite Social Summit for Growth and Employment shall contribute to social dialogue'. Proposed to be added as new Article 136a EC by the Treaty of Lisbon.

[10] Part III, Article III-118: 'In defining and implementing the policies and activities referred to in this Part, the Union shall aim to combat discrimination based on sex, racial or ethnic origin, religion or belief, disability, age or sexual orientation'. Proposed to be added as new Article 5b EC by the Treaty of Lisbon. The Constitution retained the 'mainstreaming' clause on equality between men and women: Part II, Article III-116: 'In all the activities referred to in this Part, the Union shall aim to eliminate inequalities, and to promote equality, between women and men'. Proposed to be retained also in the Lisbon Treaty.

[11] Part III, Article III-117: 'In defining and implementing the policies and actions referred to in this Part, the Union shall take into account requirements linked to the promotion of a high level of employment, the guarantee of adequate social protection, the fight against social exclusion, and a high level of education, training and protection of human health'. Proposed to be added as new Article 5a EC by the Treaty of Lisbon, except beginning: 'In defining and implementing its policies and activities, the Union shall take into account …'.

proposed adding a 'social protocol' to the Constitution, though she declared this would not be legally binding. The European Parliament's Plenary debate (16–19 January 2006) on the Duff/Voggenhuber Report[12] referred to the suggestion that 'declarations or extra protocols ... be added to the constitutional Treaty'.[13] The German Presidency proposal of a 'Protocol on the Social Dimension of Europe' was intended as a vehicle for enhanced cooperation by a 'core group'.[14]

A number of options were available to the Member States wishing to make progress[15] towards a Constitution for the EU which recognised the importance of the social dimension.[16] The purpose of the formulation of these options was, generally, to illustrate the alternatives available to those who wish to proceed to develop a constitutional framework for the EU; and specifically, to demonstrate how the social dimension could be strengthened under the various options.

## The summit of 21–22 June 2007

The summit of 21–22 June 2007 under the German Presidency determined to tackle the constitutional impasse, and with the newly elected President of France, Nicolas Sarkozy and the imminent departure of the Prime Minister of the United Kingdom, Tony Blair, was preceded by more than the usual feverish negotiations. As regards one core issue, the EU Charter, the Member States proposed a 'Mandate' for an Intergovernmental Conference (IGC) to prepare a

---

[12] European Parliament, Committee on Constitutional Affairs, *Report on the Period of Reflection: The Structure, Subjects and Context for an Assessment of the Debate on the European Union*, Co-rapporteurs, Andrew Duff and Johannes Voggenhuber, Final, A6–0414/2005, 16 December 2005.

[13] The text of the Parliament's Resolution adopted on 19 January 2006 refers to a number of options including 'seeking to clarify or add to the present text' (paragraph 28).

[14] A proposal along these lines was the basis of a discussion at an ETUC workshop in Berlin on 28 March 2006. Draft prepared by Andreas Maurer of the WSZ-Berlin proposing a text entailing a substantial broadening of competences in the social field to which Member States, who 'wish to go jointly further in the social field' can subscribe (or not).

[15] On 14 February 2007, nine Member States (Belgium, Bulgaria, Cyprus, France, Greece, Hungary, Italy, Luxembourg and Spain) met in Luxembourg and issued a proclamation directed to all the other Member States calling for the relaunching of Social Europe, including the development of a European labour law. 'Neuf pays européens veulent relancer l'Europe sociale', *Liaisons Sociales Europe*, No. 170, 22 February–7 March 2007, p. 1.

[16] A number of these options were presented and discussed at a second ETUC workshop in Brussels on 27 February 2007. The ETUI Research Group on Transnational Trade Union Rights prepared eight options: (1) Parts I and II of the proposed Constitutional Treaty, separated from Part III; (2) a 'Social Protocol'; (3) 'enhanced cooperation'; (4) the 'Schengen' model; (5) constitutionalisation through the European Court of Justice, in particular, using the EU Charter; (6) a non-binding 'Social Declaration'; (7) an 'interpretive' instrument; (8) inserting a reference to a legally binding EU Charter in Part I. The last of these was eventually a solution adopted by the Lisbon Treaty. Bercusson (ed.), *Manifesto for a Social Constitution*.

'Reform Treaty'. This led to what is now the Lisbon Treaty's proposal to replace Article 6 of the Treaty on European Union (TEU)[17] with the following text:

1. The Union recognises the rights, freedoms and principles set out in the Charter of Fundamental Rights of 7 December 2000, as adapted at Strasbourg, on 12 December 2007,[18] which shall have the same legal value as the Treaties.

   The provisions of the Charter shall not extend in any way the competences of the Union as defined in the Treaties.
   The rights, freedoms and principles in the Charter shall be interpreted in accordance with the general provisions in Title VII of the Charter governing its interpretation and application and with due regard to the explanations referred to in the Charter, that set out the sources of those provisions.[19]

2. The Union shall accede to the European Convention for the Protection of Human Rights and Fundamental Freedoms. Such accession shall not affect the Union's competences as defined in the Treaties.

3. Fundamental rights, as guaranteed by the European Convention for the Protection of Human Rights and Fundamental Freedoms and as they result from the constitutional traditions common to the Member States, shall constitute general principles of the Union's law.

This text duly adopted at the Lisbon Summit in December 2007 is proposed to be ratified by the Member States. As it stands, this wording presents a number of problems.

---

[17] Article 6 TEU currently reads:

  1. The Union is founded on the principles of liberty, democracy, respect for human rights and fundamental freedoms, and the rule of law, principles which are common to the Member States.
  2. The Union shall respect fundamental rights, as guaranteed by the European Convention for the Protection of Human Rights and Fundamental Freedoms signed in Rome on 4 November 1950 and as they result from the constitutional traditions common to the Member States, as general principles of Community law.
  3. The Union shall respect the national identities of its Member States.
  4. The Union shall provide itself with the means necessary to attain its objectives and carry through its policies.

[18] The EU Charter, initially proclaimed at Nice in December 2000, as 'adjusted' (with respect its Preamble and 'horizontal' Articles 51–4) to the form it eventually took in EU Constitutional Treaty, was reproclaimed at Strasbourg on 12 December 2007.

[19] This last paragraph is an amalgam of (i) the provision added to the Preamble to the Charter by the Convention on the Future of Europe: 'In this context the Charter will be interpreted by the courts of the Union and the Member States with due regard to the explanations prepared under the authority of the Praesidium of the Convention which drafted the Charter and updated under the responsibility of the Praesidium of the European Convention'; and (ii) the new paragraph (7) added to Article 52 of the Charter by the Member States meeting to adopt the Constitutional Treaty incorporating the Charter in June 2004: 'The explanations drawn up as a way of providing guidance in the interpretation of the Charter of Fundamental Rights shall be given due regard by the courts of the Union and of the Member States'. Both additions were instigated by the representatives of the UK government. This paragraph was not in the draft IGC Mandate circulated by the German Presidency of the Council on 19 June, just prior to the summit of 21–22 June 2007. It may be supposed that its insertion was due once again to pressure exerted by the UK government, which later opted-out of the Charter!

## European labour law in the proposed 'Reform' Treaty of Lisbon

The starting point is the legal position of the EU Charter in the Lisbon Treaty compared to Article I-9 of the then proposed, now defunct, Constitutional Treaty. Article I-9 stated:

1. The Union shall recognise the rights, freedoms and principles set out in the Charter of Fundamental Rights which constitutes Part II.
2. The Union shall accede to the European Convention for the Protection of Human Rights and Fundamental Freedoms. Such accession shall not affect the Union's competences as defined in the Constitution.
3. Fundamental rights, as guaranteed by the European Convention for the Protection of Human Rights and Fundamental Freedoms and as they result from the constitutional traditions common to the Member States, shall constitute general principles of the Union's law.

The present text of Articles 6(1) and 6(2) TEU provides:

1. The Union is founded on the principles of liberty, democracy, respect for human rights and fundamental freedoms, and the rule of law, principles which are common to the Member States.[20]
2. The Union shall respect fundamental rights, as guaranteed by the European Convention for the Protection of Human Rights and Fundamental Freedoms signed in Rome on 4 November 1950 and as they result from the constitutional traditions common to the Member States, as general principles of Community law.

The Lisbon Treaty's proposed replacement Article 6 replicates paragraphs 2 and 3 of Article I-9 of the Constitutional Treaty. The main difference is in paragraph 1:

1. The Union recognises[21] the rights, freedoms and principles set out in the Charter of Fundamental Rights of 7 December 2000, *as adapted* at Strasbourg, on 12 December 2007, which shall have *the same legal value* as the Treaties.

   The provisions of the Charter *shall not extend in any way the competences* of the Union as defined in the Treaties.

   The rights, freedoms and principles in the Charter shall be interpreted in accordance with the general provisions in Title VII of the Charter governing its interpretation and application *and with due regard to the explanations referred to in the Charter, that set out the sources of those provisions.*

---

[20] Cf. the Constitutional Treaty, Part I, Article I-2, now replicated in the proposed new Article 1a EC, to be inserted by the Lisbon Treaty.

[21] Article I-9 of the Constitutional Treaty used the wording '*shall recognise*'. Though the wording of the Constitutional Treaty is preferable, there is probably not much difference in the wording of proposed first subparagraph of Article 6(1) TEU: '*recognises*'. The problems arise with the remaining language of Article 6(1).

### 'Adapted'

There were two 'adaptations' of the Charter of 7 December 2000. The first 'adaptation' was by the Convention on the Future of Europe. This explicitly declared that it did not in any way change, but merely clarified the meaning of the Charter.[22] The word 'adapted' used here implies there has been substantive change.[23]

### 'Explanations'

The second 'adaptation' was made by the Member States at the summit on 18 June 2004. These changes were not accompanied by statements limiting their effect to clarification. They were promoted by the UK. They include the new Article 52(7), referring to the 'explanations'. These 'explanations' were also 'updated' on the initiative of the UK. The Protocol to the Lisbon Treaty purporting to enable the UK to opt-out of the Charter[24] highlights the irony of it having forced these changes on to the other Member States.

### 'Which shall have the same legal value as the Treaties'

This puts fundamental rights on a par with other provisions of the Treaties;[25] not least, the economic freedoms. Article I-9 of the Constitutional Treaty referred to the Charter in Part II. The economic freedoms were in Part III. There was an inherent hierarchy: the Charter comes first, and may be presumed

---

[22] The 'adjustments' to the EU Charter adopted by the Convention were proposed by its Working Group II on the Charter and described as follows in its Final Report Section A.II.1: 'It is important to note that these adjustments proposed by the Group do not reflect modifications of substance. On the contrary, they would serve to confirm, and render absolutely clear and legally watertight, certain key elements of the overall consensus on the Charter on which the previous Convention had already agreed ... all drafting adjustments proposed herein fully respect the basic premise of the Group's work, i.e. to leave intact the substance agreed by consensus within the previous Convention'. See B. Bercusson (ed.), *European Labour Law and the EU Charter of Fundamental Rights*, Baden-Baden: Nomos, 2006, p. 469.

[23] By way of illustration, alternative formulations, in order of preference (from good to bad): are (1) '... set out in the Charter of Fundamental Rights of 7 December 2000, which shall have ...'; (2) '... set out in the Charter of Fundamental Rights of 7 December 2000, *adopted at Strasbourg*, on 12 December 2007, which shall have ...; (3) '... set out in the Charter of Fundamental Rights of 7 December 2000, *as* adopted in Strasbourg, on 12 December 2007, which shall have ...'. The present proposal, 'as adapted', is the worst.

[24] Lisbon Treaty, Protocol on the application of the Charter of Fundamental Rights of the European Union to Poland and to the United Kingdom.

[25] The proposed Lisbon Treaty amended the TEU and the EC Treaties. It proposes to amend Article 1 TEU to read: 'The Union shall be founded on the present Treaty and on the Treaty on the Functioning of the European Union (hereinafter referred to as "the Treaties"). Those two Treaties shall have the same legal value. The Union shall replace and succeed the European Community'. A similar provision providing for 'the same legal value' of the Treaties is inserted into the new Article 1a of the EC Treaty, renamed the Treaty on the Functioning of the European Union.

to be on a different, higher, level. The Charter should have this higher status. If the intention is simply to make the Charter legally binding, there are many other possible formulations.[26]

It is not clear what the nature of this legally binding value should be. The Constitutional Treaty arguably attributed to the Charter a special legal value by placing it in Part II, separate from Part III. The wording proposed tries to *foreclose* other options by limiting it to the *same* legal value as the Treaties.[27]

This appears to be an attempt to downgrade the Charter. There are many other formulations which can give the Charter the binding legal value appropriate to its status as protecting fundamental rights, recognised by the eighteen Member States ratifying the Constitutional Treaty. The proposed wording appears to downgrade the Charter to having no more value than other parts of the Treaty. The stated intention is 'giving it legally binding force'.[28]

## 'Shall not extend in any way the competences as defined in the Treaties'

This reflects the repeated concerns of the UK, already evident in amendments to the Charter made by the Convention on the Future of Europe (called 'adjustments' or 'clarifications'). The Convention added to:

---

[26] For example: 'The Union and the Member States shall recognise and respect fundamental rights, freedoms and principles as guaranteed by the EU Charter of Fundamental Rights (OJ C364/01 of 18 December 2000), hereby confirmed as a legally binding part of this Treaty, which shall constitute an integral part of the general principles of the Union's law inspired by the constitutional traditions common to the Member States, the protection of which is ensured by the European Court of Justice.' However, it might be simplest to use the language of the Charter itself (Article 51(1)): 'The provisions of this Charter *shall be legally binding on* [instead of "are addressed to"] the institutions, bodies, offices and agencies of the Union, with due regard for the principle of subsidiarity and on the Member States only when they are implementing Union law.' Section II of the 'IGC Mandate' (Amendments to the EU Treaty) of June 2007 stated that there would be a cross-reference to the Charter (paragraph 9): 'giving it legally binding value and setting out the scope of its application'. At a minimum, the proposed provision could have adopted this language of the IGC Mandate: 'The Union recognises the rights, freedoms and principles set out in the Charter of Fundamental Rights of 7 December 2000, which shall have legally binding value'.

[27] In this sense, the proposed revision of Article 6 TEU goes *beyond* the Mandate by giving the Charter *only* the same legal value as the Treaties.

[28] See the Declaration at the IGC of June 2004, below. At a minimum, this could be achieved simply by attaching it as a Protocol to the EC Treaty. The wording would be: '… set out in the Charter of Fundamental Rights of 7 December 2000. The Charter is annexed as a Protocol to the EC Treaty'. This leaves open the possibility that, though legally binding as an integral part of the Treaty, it has a value over and above other Treaty provisions. However, it would be preferable for the wording unambiguously to identify the Charter as *superior* to other Treaty provisions. This is the effect achieved with respect to fundamental rights in the ECHR and common constitutional traditions in the proposed paragraph 3 of the replaced Article 6 TEU. The Charter should be given equal recognition and status to these sources of fundamental rights, as general principles of the Union's law.

*Article 51(1)* the words: 'and respecting the limits of the powers of the Union as conferred on it in the other Parts of the Constitution'.

*Article 51(2)*: '[does not] extend the field of application of Union law beyond the powers of the Union or establish any new power or task for the Union, or modify powers and tasks defined in the other parts of the Constitution'.[29]

The proposed wording simply adds new and further confusing language.[30]

Arguably, the equivalent of 'not extend' is 'to maintain' the present position. Existing competences are preserved, and fundamental rights are protected by the Community legal order. The EU Charter does not (need to) extend competences of the Union.[31] Moreover, as the Charter has the same legal value as the Treaties, the provision implies a mutual engagement: the Treaties shall not be invoked to limit competences defined in the Charter.[32]

## The Charter and general principles of the Union's law

As proposed, the Charter's fundamental rights have the same legal value as the economic freedoms in the Treaties. However, they are segregated from the 'fundamental rights' referred to in the Lisbon Treaty's proposed Article 6(3) TEU: those 'guaranteed by the ECHR and as they result from the constitutional traditions common to the Member States'. These fundamental rights are not postulated as having the same value as the Treaties. Is this because they are seen

---

[29] This was substituted for the wording used by the Convention which drafted the Charter: '[does not] establish any new power or task for the Community or the Union, or modify powers and tasks defined by the Treaties'.

[30] If necessary, it would be better, rather than introduce new language, to reflect the wording of the Charter itself (Article 51(1) and (2)): 'The provisions of the Charter shall respect the limits of the powers of the Union as conferred on it in the Treaties and do not extend the field of application of Union law beyond the powers of the Union or establish any new power or task for the Union, or modify powers and tasks defined in the Treaties'. An alternative would be to use the same wording as proposed in the Lisbon Treaty's proposed revision of Article 6 TEU, paragraph 2: the provisions of the Charter *'shall not affect the Union's competences as defined in the Treaties'*. The words proposed in the Lisbon Treaty's proposed revision of Article 6 TEU, paragraph 1, 'shall not extend', might be read as implying a limit to the scope of the Union's competences, and further, that the fundamental rights in the Charter shall not extend these competences. The words in paragraph 2, that accession to the ECHR 'shall not affect the Union's competences' do not purport to limit the scope of the Union's competences. They accept the existing scope of competences, which *includes* protection of fundamental rights, especially after accession to the ECHR, and consequently, accession 'does not affect the Union's competences as defined in the Treaties'. Given the European Court's respect for the ECHR, it is important the Treaty should be seen to grant equal respect to the EU Charter.

[31] Cf. Article 51(2) of the Charter, as 'adjusted' by the Convention on the Future of Europe and the Member States' summit of June 2004 ('adjusted' provision in italics): 'This Charter does not *extend the field of application of Union law beyond the powers of the Union or* establish any new power or task for the Union, or modify powers and tasks defined in the other Parts of the Constitution'.

[32] Contrast wording which might stipulate that that the Charter shall not 'not create' new competences. Rather, the wording aims to preserve existing competences, and if existing competences allow for the protection of fundamental right, the wording has no limiting effect on competences.

as superior to the Treaties, so that the Treaties cannot violate these fundamental rights? They 'constitute general principles of the Union's law'. The Treaties must be interpreted consistently with these general principles: the ECHR and the common constitutional traditions.

The EU Charter is not explicitly included as guaranteeing fundamental rights which 'constitute general principles of the Union's law'. This omission is controversial because the European Court has repeatedly referred to the Charter as reflecting precisely the fundamental rights protected as a general principle of the Union's law. The proposed provision appears to separate the Charter from this fundamental principle.

It is true that the proposed Article 6(3) is identical to Article I-9(3) of the Constitutional Treaty. But that provision did not affect the Charter the same way this provision does. The Charter was given separate constitutional status in Part II of the Constitutional Treaty, as recognised in the first paragraph of Article I-9. It was arguably superior to the economic freedoms in Part III of the Constitutional Treaty. Here it appears to be reduced to just a reference in the Treaty, with no greater legal value.[33]

At the summit in June 2007, the Member States agreed to mandate the proposed Intergovernmental Conference as follows:

> The IGC will agree the following *Declaration:*[34]
> The Conference declares that:
>
> 1. The Charter of Fundamental Rights, which has legally binding force, confirms the fundamental rights guaranteed by the ECHR and as they result from the constitutional traditions common to the Member States.
> 2. The Charter does not extend the field of application of Union law beyond powers of the Union or establish any new power or task for the Union, or modify powers and tasks as defined by the Treaties.[35]

The substance of the proposed Lisbon Treaty is to amend the EC Treaty and the TEU. It does not purport to be a constitutional treaty. From the political perspective, of course, that is the whole point – to avoid the need for referenda.

From a legal perspective, it tends to reduce the legal weight of the revisions proposed. In particular, the legal weight of the Charter is apparently reduced

---

[33] It would have been better to reassert the special status of the Charter (as a constitutional, fundamental and/or general principle of Union law). The simple solution would have been to add the Charter to the list in the proposed Article 6(3): 'Fundamental rights, as guaranteed by the EU Charter of Fundamental Rights, the European Convention ...'

[34] It is not clear whether this was intended as a 'Declaration' or a 'Protocol'.

[35] There follows: 'Two delegations reserved their right to consider whether they would join in this Protocol.' It was not then known whether the two delegations (the UK and Poland) were reserving: the legally binding force part or the no extension of powers part, and, if these two delegations reserved their position, whether this meant the Protocol (and Treaty) could not be adopted, as unanimity was required. There is a footnote 20 referring to the UK opt-out: 'The following *Protocol* will be annexed to the Treaties'. The proposed replacement of Article 6 TEU provides in paragraph 1 that the Charter 'shall have the same legal value as the Treaties'. Does the reference here to 'legally binding force' do more than repeat this? If so, why a different formula?

from being of constitutional significance to being apparently equated to other Treaty provisions.[36]

## Conclusion

The incorporation of fundamental economic and social rights of individual workers by the EU Charter of Fundamental Rights proclaimed on 7 December 2000 was an epochal step in promotion of a European social model. Ironically, however, the Treaty of Lisbon will enhance the legal status of the Charter, but may actually diminish the legal status of the fundamental rights it includes.

This is because the European Court has now repeatedly declared that the fundamental rights in the Charter are protected as a general principle of EC law. In Case C-540/03, *European Parliament* v. *Council*, decided 27 June 2006, the Court stated that, while not legally binding itself, the Charter reaffirms rights which are legally binding due to their provenance from other sources which are recognised by Community law as legally binding sources. Thus, in the cases of *Laval* (Case C-341/05) and *Viking* (Case C-438/05), the Court cites Article 28 of the Charter in confirming that the right to take collective action 'must therefore be recognised as a fundamental right which forms an integral part of the general principles of Community law the observance of which the Court ensures'.[37]

The fundamental rights in the Charter are heavily qualified by 'horizontal' provisions (Articles 51–4). These provisions in the Charter of December 2000 were repeatedly 'adjusted', first by the Convention on the Future of Europe, and again at the summit in June 2004 which accepted the Charter as Part II of the

---

[36] In order to counter this apparent equivalence of the Charter to mere additional Treaty provisions, it would have been desirable to give the Charter a special and higher profile in the Treaties. As described above, this could be achieved by removing the reference to the Charter having 'the same legal value as the Treaties'. Instead, there are suggested above other methods of making the Charter legally binding: (i) by a specific formulation; (ii) using wording from the Charter itself; (iii) using wording from the IGC Mandate; (iv) attaching the Charter as a Protocol to the EC Treaty (Article 311 EC), binding but not explicitly of 'the same legal value' as other Treaty provisions; and (v) finally, by adding the Charter to the list in the proposed Article 6(3) TEU of sources of fundamental rights constituting general principles of the Union's law. A revised proposal would read (changes in italics):

1. The Union recognises the rights, freedoms and principles set out in the Charter of Fundamental Rights of 7 December 2000. *The Charter is annexed as a Protocol to the EC Treaty.*
2. The Union shall accede to the European Convention for the Protection of Human Rights and Fundamental Freedoms. Such accession shall not affect the Union's competences as defined in the Treaties.
3. Fundamental rights, as guaranteed by *the EU Charter of Fundamental Rights*, the European Convention for the Protection of Human Rights and Fundamental Freedoms and as they result from the constitutional traditions common to the Member States shall constitute general principles of the Union's law.

[37] *Viking*, paragraph 44; *Laval*, paragraph 91.

Constitutional Treaty. The Charter of the Treaty of Lisbon is that last version in which considerable 'adjustments' were made to the 'horizontal' provisions with the intention of limiting the scope and legal effects of the Charter. The Lisbon Treaty may dilute the legal status of the Charter's fundamental rights as general principles of EC law.

## Is there an opt-out by the UK and Poland?

The UK government, and then Poland, insisted upon an opt-out from a legally binding EU Charter of Fundamental Rights, which the UK had solemnly proclaimed together with the other EU Member States in December 2000.[38] The other Member States acceded to this demand. A Protocol to the Lisbon Treaty provides:[39]

The HIGH CONTRACTING PARTIES,

Whereas in Article 6 of the Treaty on European Union, the Union recognises the rights, freedoms and principles set out in the Charter of Fundamental Rights of the European Union;

Whereas the Charter is to be applied in strict accordance with the provisions of the aforementioned Article 6 and Title VII of the Charter itself;

Whereas the aforementioned Article 6 requires the Charter to be applied and interpreted by the courts of Poland and of the United Kingdom strictly in accordance with the explanations referred to in that Article;

Whereas the Charter contains both rights and principles;

Whereas the Charter contains both provisions which are civil and political in character and those which are economic and social in character;

Whereas the Charter reaffirms the rights, freedoms and principles recognised in the Union and makes those rights more visible, but does not create new rights or principles;

Recalling the obligations devolving upon Poland and the United Kingdom under the Treaty on European Union, the Treaty on the Functioning of the European Union, and Union law generally;

Noting the wish of Poland and the United Kingdom to clarify certain aspects of the application of the Charter;

Desirous therefore of clarifying the application of the Charter in relation to the laws and administrative actions of Poland and of the United Kingdom and of its justiciability within Poland and within the United Kingdom;

Reaffirming that references in this Protocol to the operation of specific provisions of the Charter are strictly without prejudice to the operation of other provisions of the Charter;

---

[38] Thus fulfilling Bob Hepple's prescience in greeting the Charter: 'Not for the first time in EU negotiations, the UK secured a number of important modifications in the interests of consensus, only at the end to resile from the legal consequences.' 'The EU Charter of Fundamental Rights', (2001) 30 *Industrial Law Journal* 225–31, at p. 225.

[39] Protocol on the application of the Charter of Fundamental Rights of the European Union to Poland and to the United Kingdom.

Reaffirming that this Protocol is without prejudice to the application of the Charter to other Member States;

Reaffirming that this Protocol is without prejudice to other obligations devolving upon Poland and the United Kingdom under the Treaty on European Union, the Treaty on the Functioning of the European Union, and Union law generally;

Have agreed upon the following provisions which shall be annexed to the Treaty on European Union and to the Treaty on the Functioning of the European Union:

Article 1

1.  The Charter does not extend the ability of the Court of Justice of the European Union, or any court or tribunal of Poland or of the United Kingdom, to find that the laws, regulations nor administrative provisions, practices or action of Poland or of the United Kingdom are inconsistent with the fundamental rights, freedoms and principles that it reaffirms.

2.  In particular, and for the avoidance of doubt, nothing in Title IV[40] of the Charter creates justiciable rights applicable to Poland or the United Kingdom except in so far as Poland or the United Kingdom has provided for such rights in its national law.

Article 2

To the extent that a provision of the Charter refers to national laws and practices, it shall only apply to Poland or the United Kingdom to the extent that the rights or principles that it contains are recognised in the law or practices of Poland or of the United Kingdom.

The Recitals to the Protocol purport to bind the other Member States to the UK's interpretation of the Charter in an instrument aimed precisely to exempt the UK from application of the Charter – an exercise breathtaking in its audacity![41]

---

[40]  The 'Solidarity' Title including Article 27: 'Workers' right to information and consultation within the undertaking'; Article 28: 'Right of collective bargaining and action'; Article 30: 'Protection in the event of unjustified dismissal'; Article 31: 'Fair and just working conditions'.

[41]  This Protocol is rumoured to have been drafted by the then UK Attorney-General, Lord Goldsmith, on the day prior to his resignation from the UK government, anticipating that of his political master, Tony Blair, days later. It is at least questionable whether this text will achieve its purpose. The *Financial Times* editorial on 25 June 2007, following the summit, observed: 'Mr Blair tried to prevent the charter on fundamental rights from being made legally binding. He failed. But he has won a lengthy protocol insisting that it cannot be used to challenge UK laws: in effect, it is another opt-out. It may not be legally enforceable, for it discriminates in the application of fundamental rights'. The aftermath of the summit produced a subtly structured confusion orchestrated by the UK government leaving the field clear for media speculation. Along the lines of: 'What we have done is made the wording clearer to show that the European Court should not make changes which alter or make the charter worse ... We need this because of the way the British common law system works, which is entirely different from continental Europe.' Gary Titley at http://news.bbc.co.uk/1/hi/uk_politics/6962092.stm. I am grateful to Owen Tudor, Head of the European Union and International Relations Department of the British Trades Union Congress, for this reference. The government accepted that the UK is still a signatory to the Charter, so they do support it; they just don't want to give it constitutional force.

One view is that the Protocol does not even amount to an opt-out of the application of the Charter.[42] Indeed, the Recitals to the Protocol refer to clarifying the Charter rather than opting-out.[43] Article 1(1) of the Protocol purposes not to 'extend the ability of the Court of Justice' as regards fundamental rights, but as the Court's present ability in this respect is not challenged, no extension is required.

Similarly, Article 1(2) of the Protocol asserts that for the avoidance of doubt Title IV may not create justiciable rights applicable to Poland and the United Kingdom.[44] The implication is that Title IV rights might well be justiciable in the other Member States. However, this may be so in so far as such rights are already protected in the Community legal order, and their justiciability is not affected by the Charter. To declare that Title IV of the Charter does not created justiciable rights applicable to Poland and the United Kingdom, therefore, does not affect the position.

The outcome can be summarised as follows. The UK has opted-out of the Charter. This is supposed to mean that the European Court cannot use the Charter to override UK laws. However, this will not prevent a litigant asking a UK court to override a particular UK law which arguably brutally violates the Charter's guaranteed right. Nor will it prevent a UK court deciding that there is enough uncertainty to refer the matter to the ECJ in Luxembourg.

The ECJ will likely follow its established jurisprudence, that protection of fundamental rights is a general principle of Community law which the ECJ is pledged to uphold. Further, that the EU Charter merely reflects these fundamental rights protected by EC law. Hence the opt-out does not matter: UK laws which violate the rights guaranteed by this general principle of EC law (as reflected in the Charter) cannot stand. One awaits the UK labour law case which follows this trajectory.

## The Treaty of Lisbon and Social Europe

The reference to the EU Charter, including fundamental rights of labour, is the most significant feature of the Treaty of Lisbon in terms of its potential consequences for European labour law. However, there are a number of other 'social' provisions in the Lisbon Treaty. These provisions were taken over from the failed Constitutional Treaty, and perhaps because of that loss of momentum, appear, at least in the short term, to be more cosmetic than substantial.

---

[42] See, for example, the evidence of Sir David Edwards, a former judge of the ECJ, and of Professor Damian Chalmers to the House of Lord European Select Committee.

[43] 'Noting the wish of Poland and the United Kingdom to clarify certain aspects of the application of the Charter; Desirous therefore of clarifying the application of the Charter in relation to the laws and administrative actions of Poland and of the United Kingdom and of its justiciability within Poland and within the United Kingdom'.

[44] 'In particular, and for the avoidance of doubt, nothing in Title IV of the Charter creates justiciable rights applicable to Poland or the United Kingdom except in so far as Poland or the United Kingdom has provided for such rights in its national law'.

## Social values

The Lisbon Treaty proposes to insert into the Treaty on European Union a new Article 1a:[45]

> The Union is founded on the values of respect for human dignity, freedom, democracy, equality, the rule of law and respect for human rights, including the rights of persons belonging to minorities. These values are common to the Member States in a society in which pluralism, non-discrimination, tolerance, justice, solidarity and equality between women and men prevail.

## Mainstreaming social policy

The Lisbon Treaty proposes to insert into the former EC Treaty, to be denominated the Treaty on the Functioning of the European Union, a new Article 5a on 'mainstreaming' social policy:[46]

> In defining and implementing its policies and activities, the Union shall take into account requirements linked to the promotion of a high level of employment, the guarantee of adequate social protection, the fight against social exclusion, and a high level of education, training and protection of human health.

The former Article 3(2) EC 'mainstreaming' equality between women and men is retained[47] and supplemented by a new Article 5a EC:

> In defining and implementing its policies and activities, the Union shall aim to combat discrimination based on sex, racial or ethnic origin, religion or belief, disability, age or sexual orientation.

## The role of the 'social partners'

The Lisbon Treaty proposes to insert into the former EC Treaty, to be denominated the Treaty on the Functioning of the European Union, a new Article 136a:[48]

> The Union recognises and promotes the role of the social partners at its level, taking into account the diversity of national systems. It shall facilitate dialogue between the social partners, respecting their autonomy.
>     The Tripartite Social Summit for Growth and Employment shall contribute to social dialogue.

This provision raises a number of issues.

The reference in the first part of the first sentence is to the 'the social partners at [Union] level'; so not apparently at other levels, especially, Member State

---

[45] Formerly in the Constitutional Treaty, Part I, Article I-2.

[46] Formerly in the Constitutional Treaty, Part III, Article III-117.

[47] Though reworded: 'In all its activities, the Community shall aim to eliminate inequalities, and to promote equality, between men and women'.

[48] Formerly in the Constitutional Treaty, Part I, Article I-48.

level. However, the reference to 'taking into account the diversity of national systems' raises a question about the apparently exclusive reference to 'recognises and promotes the role of the social partners *at [Union] level*'. To 'recognise and promote the social partners at Union level', it might be necessary to intervene ('recognise and promote' the social partners) at national level. Weak (low union density) or non-existent (e.g. sectoral employers' organisations) national social partners would affect recognition and promotion of the social partners at Union level.

However, the phrase 'recognises and promotes' does not specify what action the Union may take. Compare Article 137(1) EC whereby 'the Community shall support and complement', but which does not itself require or authorise specific action until Article 137(2) EC states 'To this end, the Council may adopt, by means of directives …'.[49] The Lisbon Treaty does not indicate specific action.

The second sentence promises to 'facilitate dialogue between the social partners, respecting their autonomy'. The reference is to 'the social partners', *not only* at Union level. If the EU is to facilitate dialogue also at other levels, does this include Member State level? The autonomy of social partners at all levels is to be respected. Or is the reference to 'respecting their autonomy' intended exclusively for the social partners at Union level? Arguably not. However, if it refers to securing the autonomy of social partners in the Member States, this could create difficulties. A European industrial relations system inevitably engages social partners also at national level (e.g. majority votes on framework agreements), and may interfere with their autonomy. Is the autonomy of social partners at Union level protected by the reference in the previous part to 'taking into account the diversity of national systems'?

If specific actions are not indicated, at least one specific forum, time and place is the focus for such action: 'The Tripartite Social Summit for Growth and Employment'. An important institutional link is thereby established between the social partners, the social dialogue and the broad economic policies of the EU.

Heretofore, the EU institutions have regularly called upon the social partners and the social dialogue to contribute to the European Employment Strategy (EES). This contribution, however, has been severely handicapped by the limited resources available to the social partners to carry out the responsibilities allocated to them in the EES. This provision reflects a welcome recognition of the need for reciprocity: 'The Tripartite Social Summit for Growth and Employment shall contribute to social dialogue'.

## Social Europe beyond the Treaty of Lisbon: operationalising the horizontal social clause

The Treaty of Lisbon is the product of the febrile political context of the European Union following the debacle of the Constitutional Treaty. The

---

[49] Cf. Article III-104 of the proposed Constitutional Treaty.

Treaty is in the process of being ratified in the aftermath of the ECJ decisions in *Viking* and *Laval*, an increasingly controversial legal context,[50] and in an economic context of instability in global financial markets and its consequences for economic growth, if not economic recession. This context is critical for the evolution of European labour law and for the future of the Lisbon Treaty.[51]

The Lisbon Treaty proposes to replace the present Article 2 of the Treaty on European Union with a new Article 2, including in sub-paragraph 3:[52]

> The Union shall establish an internal market. It shall work for the sustainable development of Europe based on balanced economic growth and price stability, a highly competitive social market economy, *aiming at full employment and social progress*, and a high level of protection and improvement of the quality of the environment. It shall promote scientific and technological advance. It shall combat social exclusion and discrimination, and shall *promote social justice* and protection, equality between women and men, solidarity between generations and protection of the rights of the child.

The Lisbon Treaty's proposed new horizontal social clause, new Article 5a EC, provides:

> In defining and implementing its policies and activities, the Union shall take into account requirements linked to the promotion of a high level of employment, the guarantee of adequate social protection, the fight against social exclusion, and a high level of education, training and protection of human health.

The question is how the Lisbon Treaty can achieve its objective of social progress and work to promote social justice. The new horizontal social clause needs to be made effectively operational by acquiring more precise meaning.

## Rethinking Treaty provisions on economic freedoms

In *Laval* and *Viking*, the ECJ focused on the Treaty's provisions guaranteeing economic freedoms. These were characterised as equivalent, and indeed potentially superior to fundamental rights. What is needed is a different interpretive framework for economic freedoms. The market economy is not limited to the

---

[50] As mentioned in Chapter 21, British Airways invoked these decisions of the ECJ to threaten BALPA, the pilots' union, which was organising collective action over plans to use non-BA pilots in a new subsidiary. Reported in the *Financial Times*, 12 March 2008, page 2. On 15 March 2008, more than 1,000 British Airways pilots marched on BA's Heathrow headquarters. A spokesman said given that roughly 2,000 of BA's 3,000 pilots are usually either on duty or resting before or after flights, the turnout was very high. 'Every pilot who could be there was there, which was quite remarkable,' the spokesman said. BALPA challenged BA before the High Court on 19–22 May 2008, but withdrew due to the exorbitant legal costs involved and the prospect of enormous damages should BA succeed.

[51] For example, the European Trade Union Confederation at its Executive Meeting of 4–5 March 2008 considered its response to the *Viking* and *Laval* decisions in the context of the ratification of the Lisbon Treaty.

[52] Italics added.

economic freedoms of enterprises only. Market freedom includes the freedom of action of collective actors both of capital (enterprises) and labour (trade unions).[53] The economic freedom of movement of one side should not be invoked to restrain the economic freedom of action of the other side, as the ECJ has done in *Viking* and *Laval*. In a parallel case of alleged conflict between the Treaty's provisions on competition and collective agreements, the ECJ had refused to outlaw collective agreements in order to preserve competition.[54] Unfortunately, the ECJ rejected this approach in *Laval* and *Viking*, distinguishing the Treaty's competition provisions from free movement provisions. This could be remedied by provisions requiring a more even-handed interpretive framework for economic freedoms.[55]

The attack could be on the *substance* of the ECJ's approach to EC law (market primacy), or on the exercise by the EU of its *competences* (subsidiarity), and hence the scope of the ECJ's jurisdiction; or indeed both.[56] The task is to redraft

---

[53] As stated by Miguel Maduro: 'the system requires a set of social rights that can be said to guarantee participation and representation in market decisions and, by internalizing costs which tend to be ignored in those decisions, increase efficiency … rights of participation and representation such as the freedom of association, the right to collective bargaining, and the right to collective action should be considered as instrumental to a fully functioning integrated market which can increase efficiency and wealth maximization'. 'Striking the Elusive Balance Between Economic Freedom and Social Rights in the EU', in P. Alston (ed.), *The EU and Human Rights*, Oxford: Oxford University Press, 1999, pp. 449–72, at p. 470.

[54] *Albany International BV* v. *Stichting Bedrijfspensioenfonds Textielindustrie*, Case C-67/96; with joined Cases C-115/97, C-116/97 and C-117/97; [1999] ECR I-5751.

[55] For example, a rebuttable presumption in favour of collective action. There should be a rebuttable presumption that collective action is presumed to be in response to a serious threat to jobs and working conditions. This may be rebutted when challenged by the employer. As stated in *Viking*, the presumption may be rebutted if the employer gives a legally binding undertaking providing guarantees in the form of a collective agreement. In the absence of such a collective agreement, judges should not intervene to restrain collective action in the course of collective bargaining. Or interpreting 'proportionality' in light of the *acquis communautaire social*. The lawfulness of collective action is conditional on 'proportionality' (*Viking*) and is explicitly linked to the Posting Directive (*Laval*). Why the Posting Directive? Collective action is proportionate where the employer fails to comply with obligations under the general *acquis communautaire social* protecting the rights of workers as an objective of general interest recognised by the Union. In doctrinal terms, this is a specifically EU criterion based on the *acquis communautaire social* reflected in Articles 27 and 28 of the EU Charter: protection by EU law of the transnational economic freedom of employers is balanced with protection of transnational collective action by workers who should be properly informed and consulted before decisions affecting them are made. The common element is the prevention of 'social dumping'.

[56] Or a combination, focusing on the limitation to transnational matters. The ECJ may determine rules on transnational collective action, but not on matters purely internal to Member States not affected by EC law. What is the consequence if there are radically different rules on transnational and national collective action, and between the national rules in different Member States? Do such differences inherently impede free movement, deterring employers, and hence violate the Treaty? Miguel Maduro has suggested that such differences might impede free movement of workers, as some might avoid moving to Member States where their rights to take collective action are more restricted. What are the criteria of 'transnationality'? Is national action caught only if there is actual obstruction of a transnational market relationship, or is it sufficient if it merely (potentially) impedes market access?

the provision on economic freedoms in such a way as to reduce or eliminate their negative impact on fundamental rights; specifically, on collective action, and so as to protect workers.

For example, the primacy of economic freedoms could be attacked by reformulating the provisions to include the statement that economic freedoms may not be interpreted as affecting in any way the exercise of fundamental rights based on the 'common constitutional traditions' of the Member States; specifically, as regards protection of the right to collective action.[57] This also removes the primary obligation of Member States (and national law) to comply with the EU internal market objective.[58]

### An 'anti-social dumping principle' against abuse of the exercise of economic freedoms

*Laval* and *Viking* both contain expressions by the Advocates-General and the ECJ of concern about 'social dumping'. The unrestrained exercise of economic freedom of movement may threaten existing jobs and working conditions. This may be characterised as an 'abuse' of the exercise of economic freedoms. A condition of the exercise of economic freedom is that there is a guarantee of

---

[57]   Cf. the 'Monti Regulation'. Council Regulation (EC) No. 2679/98 of 7 December 1998 on the functioning of the internal market in relation to the free movement of goods among the Member States. OJ L337/8 of 12 December 1998; Article 2: 'This Regulation may not be interpreted as affecting in any way the exercise of fundamental rights as recognised in Member States, including the right or freedom to strike. These rights may also include the right or freedom to take other actions covered by the specific industrial relations systems in Member States.' Article 1(7) of the Services Directive provides: 'This Directive does not affect the exercise of fundamental rights as recognised in the Member States and by Community law. Nor does it affect the right to negotiate, conclude and enforce collective agreements and to take industrial action in accordance with national law and practices which respect Community law'. Article 1(7) of the Services Directive provides: 'This Directive does not affect the exercise of fundamental rights as recognised in the Member States and by Community law. Nor does it affect the right to negotiate, conclude and enforce collective agreements and to take industrial action in accordance with national law and practices which respect Community law'. Recital 15 provides: 'This Directive respects the exercise of fundamental rights applicable in the Member States and as recognised in the Charter of fundamental Rights of the European Union and the accompanying explanations, reconciling them with the fundamental freedoms laid down in Articles 43 and 49 of the Treaty. Those fundamental rights include the right to take industrial action in accordance with national law and practices which respect Community law.' Directive 2006/123/EC of the European Parliament and of the Council of 12 December 2006 on services in the internal market, OJ L376/26 of 27 December 2006.

[58]   Thus reinforcing the ECJ's jurisprudence establishing a general principle of substance that EC law protects fundamental rights. One approach would be to add a fifth fundamental economic freedom for collective labour. The fundamental economic freedoms of employers are usually exercised through the collective organisational form of corporate capital. The Treaty's economic freedom of workers applies only to individual workers. The task is to draft a fifth fundamental economic freedom of collective organisations of workers. This could build on the precedent of the recognition of management and labour as institutional actors in the Maastricht Agreement's provisions on social dialogue.

existing jobs and working conditions. Failure to provide such a guarantee justifies collective action against such an abuse.[59]

## A non-regression clause

The references in the social policy objectives listed in Article 136 EC to 'improved living and working conditions' and 'harmonisation while the improvement is being maintained' argue for a general principle of 'non-regression' in Community social policy. This could be made more explicit and elaborate as a principle of Community law.

## A more favourable treatment clause

The ECJ adopted a bizarre interpretation in *Laval* of Article 3(7) of the Posting Directive restricting the freedom of Member States to require more favourable treatment of workers. This was in order to support its view of the Directive as a stipulating a 'maximum standard'.[60] This could be addressed by amending the Posting Directive. But this principle is found in many other legislative provisions and the ECJ's interpretation may be dangerous more generally. An attempt should be made to clarify and extend the principle in a specific EU legal measure, or even in the Treaty.

## A standard social safeguard clause in directives

Directives already contain standard clauses; for example, regarding obligations of Member States as regards effective enforcement. A standard social safeguard clause could be formulated in the Treaty for inclusion in directives.[61] This could include the following provisions:

- explicitly protecting national standards (e.g. as in the 'Monti Regulation');
- substantive provisions protecting fundamental rights and collective agreements per se (as in the Services Directive);

---

[59] The Note by the Legal Service of the Commission on *Laval* states (paras. 10–11): 'The Court acknowledges that such a restriction [on freedom to provide services] may be justified in order to protect workers on the basis of an overriding reason of public interest, such as combating social dumping (paragraph 103). It seems the Court does not leave any room for the imposition of terms and conditions going beyond the nucleus of mandatory rules, unless they can be justified as public policy provisions'. This may imply that the Commission might be willing to address what is perceived to be a serious limitation. And the acknowledgment, by the ECJ, of social dumping provides a policy reason for undertaking to amend what is perceived as the obstacle: the Posting Directive, as so narrowly interpreted by the ECJ. This could be done by amending Directive 96/71 (Directive 96/71/EC concerning the posting of workers in the framework of the provision of services. OJ 1996 L18/1) to explicitly stipulate wider set of standards, collective agreements that acknowledge different industrial relations systems. The Legal Commission states this was intended (paragraph 3): 'The Court would therefore seem to agree with the proposition advanced by the Commission in its written observations to the effect that the Community legislator must have intended Directive 96/71 to encompass all existing systems in the Member States governing labour relations'.

[60] Reaffirmed in Case C-346/06, *Rechtsanwalt Dr. Dirk Rüffert* v. *Land Niedersachsen*, ECJ decision of 3 April 2008.

[61] Consistent with the Lisbon Treaty's proposed new horizontal social clause, new Article 5a EC.

- a non-regression principle, following Article 136 EC, made more explicit and elaborate; or
- allowing national provisions more favourable to workers;[62]
- specifying obligations on Member States to provide information to employers on labour standards.[63]

## Conclusion: 'social progress' and 'social justice'

The Lisbon Treaty proposes to replace the present Article 2 of the Treaty on European Union with a new Article 2, including in sub-paragraph 3 including references to 'social progress' and 'social justice'.[64] Mainstream European Community law specialists took it for granted, and even labour lawyers were not entirely surprised by the decisions of the European Court of Justice (ECJ) in *Viking* and *Laval*. The ECJ did not abandon decades of decisions dominated by the promotion of economic freedoms in the common market. In *Laval* and *Viking*, the ECJ regarded collective action by workers and their organisations primarily in terms of its impact on the economic freedoms of the common market.[65]

What was shocking, if not surprising, is how little weight was given by the ECJ to other, arguably equal if not more prominent, EU policies. These include fundamental rights (the EU Charter's freedom of association, collective bargaining and collective action), improvement of working conditions (Article 136 EC), the public policy of protection of workers against unfair competition (social dumping), and so on. Each of these was mentioned in the judgments in *Laval* and *Viking*, but ultimately subordinated to the economic freedoms of employers in the common market.

This is a threat to the entire *acquis communautaire social*. If economic freedoms override collective action, why not the rest of the *acquis communautaire social*? For example, economic freedoms may be invoked against the many directives requiring information and consultation of workers and their representatives. Such requirements restrict the economic freedoms of management to make speedy decisions in restructuring undertakings.[66] The economic

---

[62] Overriding the ECJ's bizarre interpretation of Article 3(7) of the Posting Directive.

[63] A requirement in the public procurement directives, said to promote the transparency of the single market.

[64] 'The Union shall establish an internal market. It shall work for the sustainable development of Europe based on balanced economic growth and price stability, a highly competitive social market economy, aiming at full employment and social progress, and a high level of protection and improvement of the quality of the environment. It shall promote scientific and technological advance. It shall combat social exclusion and discrimination, and shall promote social justice and protection, equality between women and men, solidarity between generations and protection of the rights of the child'. Formerly in the Constitutional Treaty, Part I, Article I-3(3).

[65] Sophie Robin-Olivier, 'Son raisonnement est, dans les grandes lignes, empreint du plus grand classicisme' (roughly: Its overall reasoning reflects its most classic traditions). 'Liberté de l'action syndicale *vs* liberté d'établissement', *Revue de Droit du Travail*, January 2008, p. 8.

[66] An item in the *Financial Times* of 28 February 2008 (page 24) reported: 'A new power struggle has broken out between Gaz de France and Suez, this time between the two companies' European

freedoms in the Treaty could be invoked to circumscribe the entire *acquis communautaire social*.

The Lisbon Treaty affirms that 'The Union shall establish an internal market', but a 'social market economy, aiming at full employment and *social progress*' and 'shall promote *social justice* and protection'. It may be necessary to redress the imbalance in Community law as presently interpreted by the ECJ (and also the present Commission) by challenging the primacy given to the internal market over all other Community policies.

Not least, human rights are not mere derogations from economic freedoms; rather the reverse. The ECJ regards the fundamental right to collective action as only a potentially exceptional derogation from the Treaty's guarantee of economic freedoms. As such, collective action must be justified.[67] At the same time, the ECJ also declares the fundamental right to collective action to be protected as a general principle of Community law. The Lisbon Treaty provides that the EU Charter is to have the same legal status as the Treaties and proposes that the EU ratifies the European Convention on Human Rights. At least, the ECJ's approach should be reversed: economic freedoms may exceptionally derogate from fundamental rights guaranteed by Community law, but this has to be justified, and any derogation from fundamental rights is only permitted if 'proportionate' (necessary and no alternative is available).[68]

There remains considerable dissatisfaction with the meagre social content of the Lisbon Treaty. Though it may not be practical to improve the social content of the Lisbon Treaty itself, it may be possible to improve the social dimension of the EU in the course of the ratification process of the Lisbon Treaty. The Member States have to decide whether to ratify the text of the Lisbon Treaty. Some of the Member States would have preferred a stronger social dimension. They cannot alter the text of the Lisbon Treaty. However, they may, in the course of ratifying the Lisbon Treaty, undertake commitments to a stronger social dimension including some of the substantive changes

---

works councils, which are crucial to breaking the union impasse that has repeatedly delayed the creation of the E 75bn ($113bn) energy giant. GdF's European unions are demanding that they represent the enlarged group when the merger is complete before they will give the non-binding opinion that is required under French law before the companies' board can approve the deal. Suez is resisting the demand and both sides are seeking agreement ahead of the next works council meeting on March 11. Failure to find a compromise could throw the merger timetable off track, further delaying a deal that has already been two years in the making. GdF's French unions also have yet to give their opinion and have been using efficient delaying tactics against the merger. Jean-François Cirelli, GdF chief executive, said he remained "reasonably confident" that the deadline of June 30 could still be met, and that the European unions would give their opinion at the March meeting. Discussions with unions had entered a more positive phase, he said.'

[67] This approach, also applied by the ECJ to freedom of assembly and association in *Schmidberger*, is offensive to fundamental human rights. Case C-112/00, *Eugen Schmidberger, Internationale Transporte und Planzuge* v. *Republic of Austria*, [2003] ECR I-5659.

[68] This is the approach proposed by Advocate-General Stix-Hackl in her Opinion in *Omega*. Case C-36/02, *Omega Spielhallen- und Automatenaufstellungs-GmbH* v. *Oberburgermeisterin der Bundesstadt Bonn*, [2004] ECR I-9609.

outlined earlier in this chapter. As to the *legal form* of such a commitment, a number of alternatives may be envisaged.[69]

A number of Member States could, while ratifying the Lisbon Treaty, adopt a *Protocol* on a stronger social dimension.[70] After ratification, these Member States would undertake to persuade all Member States to agree to attach this Protocol to the Treaties, though it would only bind those Member States which adopted it. Alternatively, Article 43 TEU allows for *enhanced cooperation* by a majority of the Member States.[71] If at least fourteen Member States agreed in the course of ratifying the Lisbon Treaty that they wished to adopt provisions for a stronger social dimension, the mechanism of enhanced cooperation could allow this, leaving it open to other Member States to join later. A stronger social dimension could follow the road of the *Schengen model*.[72] The Schengen Agreement harmonising border controls was made initially by only five Member States in 1985. More Member States gradually joined, so that it now includes twenty-five Member States (except Ireland and the UK, but including also Iceland, Norway and Switzerland). In 1997, a Protocol attached to the Treaty of Amsterdam incorporated these advances into the legal framework of the EU. A 'Social Schengen Agreement' could be adopted as part of a common ratification of the Lisbon Treaty. Member States desiring a stronger social dimension could attach to their ratification of the Lisbon Treaty a commonly agreed '*social declaration*'.[73] Though not legally binding, this could have a future impact on the political agenda of the EU institutions, including the Commission's Action Programme and the Court's interpretation of the EU Charter's social provisions.[74] The UK and Poland attached an 'opt-out' to the Lisbon Treaty excluding application of the EU Charter to their laws. An inverse

---

[69] The following draws on some of the ideas prepared for the ETUC Congress in Seville in May 2007 by a group of European labour law professors, the Research Group on Transnational Trade Union Rights of the ETUI-REHS. Bercusson (ed.), *Manifesto for a Social Constitution*. The eight options were: (1) Parts I and II separated from Part III of the Constitutional Treaty; (2) A 'Social Protocol' to the Constitutional Treaty; (3) Enhanced cooperation; (4) The Schengen Model: 'Variable Geometry'; (5) A Social Constitution through the European Court of Justice; (6) A Non-Binding Social Declaration; (7) An Interpretive Instrument; (8) Inserting a reference to a legally binding EU Charter into Part I of the Constitutional Treaty. Most options focused on a potential role for the EU Charter of Fundamental Rights. After the French and Dutch referenda rejecting the Constitutional Treaty, there were fears that, despite ratification by eighteen Member States, the EU Charter might be abandoned. Certainly some Member States, not least the United Kingdom, were suggesting the Charter was an obstacle to future progress. Other Member States, however, were equally adamant that the Charter be retained. Our proposals explored a spectrum of methods to retain it. In the event, it was the last of the options proposed which emerged in the Treaty of Lisbon adopted in December 2007.

[70] See B. Bercusson, Option 2: A 'Social Protocol' to the Constitutional Treaty', *ibid.*, pp. 30–1 and 63–73.

[71] See Antoine Jacobs, Option 3: Enhanced cooperation, *ibid.*, pp. 32–3 and 63–75.

[72] See Isabelle Schömann, Option 4: The Schengen Model: 'Variable Geometry', *ibid.*, pp. 33–4 and 85–94.

[73] See Yota Kravaritou, Option 6: A Non-Binding Social Declaration, *ibid.*, pp. 36–7 and 105–10.

[74] See B. Bercusson, Option 7: An Interpretive Instrument, *ibid.*, pp. 37–8 and 111–23.

'social opt-out' could be modelled on Article 1 of this opt-out: 'The Treaties do not extend the ability of the Court of Justice or any court or tribunal to find that the laws or practices of the Member States regulating collective bargaining and collective action are inconsistent with the economic freedoms that they affirm.'[75] Member States desiring a stronger social dimension could attach this formula to their ratification of the Lisbon Treaty as an *interpretive guide*.

In the aftermath of the Lisbon Treaty and the decisions in *Laval* and *Viking*, one future of European labour law depends on whether the Member States and the European Parliament explore new paths to a stronger social dimension of the European Union. One future for European labour law requires the democratically legitimised institutions of the EU, the Member States in Council and the European Parliament, to act to secure the Lisbon Treaty's promises of social progress and social justice in the European Union.

[75] Cf. the 'Monti Regulation', Article 2, and Article 1(7) and Recital 15 of the Services Directive, cited above.

# Index